PHILIP'S NAVIGATOR

TRUCKERS Britain

www.philips-maps.co.uk
First published in 2009 by Philip's
a division of Octopus Publishing Group Ltd
www.octopusbooks.co.uk
Endeavour House, 189 Shaftesbury Avenue,
London WC2H 8JY
An Hachette UK Company
www.hachette.co.uk
Third edition 2012
First impression 2012
ISBN 978-1-84907-233-5
Cartography by Philip's
Copyright © 2012 Philip's

Ordnance Survey®

This product includes mapping data licensed from Ordnance Survey®, with the permission of the Controller of Her Majesty's Stationery Office.
© Crown copyright 2012. All rights reserved. Licence number 100011710

Data for the speed cameras provided by PocketGPSWorld.com Ltd.

Information for National Parks, Areas of Outstanding Natural Beauty, National Trails and Country Parks in Wales supplied by the Countryside Council for Wales.

Information for National Parks, Areas of Outstanding Natural Beauty, National Trails and Country Parks in England supplied by Natural England. Data for Regional Parks, Long Distance Footpaths and Country Parks in Scotland provided by Scottish Natural Heritage.

Information for Forest Parks supplied by the Forestry Commission

Information for the RSPB reserves provided by the RSPB

Gaelic name forms used in the Western Isles provided by Comhairle nan Eilean.

Data for the National Nature Reserves in England provided by Natural England. Data for the National Nature Reserves in Wales provided by Countryside Council for Wales. Darparwyd data'n ymwneud â Gwarchodfeydd Natur Cenedlaethol Cymru gan Gyngor Cefn Gwlad Cymru.

Information on the location of National Nature Reserves in Scotland was provided by Scottish Natural Heritage.

Data for National Scenic Areas in Scotland provided by the Scottish Executive Office. Crown copyright material is reproduced with the permission of the Controller of HMSO and the Queen's Printer for Scotland. Licence number C02W0003960.

Printed in China

Contents

Road map symbols

M25	Motorway
16 — 17	Motorway junctions – full access, restricted access
	Toll motorway
Pease Pottage Services	Motorway service area
	Motorway under construction
S	Primary route – dual, single carriageway, services – under construction, narrow
Cardiff	Primary destination
25 — 26	Numbered junctions – full, restricted access
	A road – dual, single carriageway – under construction, narrow
	B road – dual, single carriageway – under construction, narrow
	Minor road – dual, single carriageway
	Drive or track
	Urban side roads (height, weight and width restrictions not shown)
12'9" 13'0"	Height restriction, width restriction – feet and inches
12.5	Tunnel, weight restriction – tonnes
2	Distance in miles
Toll	Roundabout, multi-level junction, Toll, steep gradient – points downhill
40 — 40	Speed camera – single, multiple
CLEVELAND WAY	National trail – England and Wales
GREAT GLEN WAY	Long distance footpath – Scotland
YATTON ROPLEY	Railway with station, level crossing, tunnel Preserved railway with level crossing, station, tunnel Tramway
	National boundary
	County or unitary authority boundary
CALAIS 1:30	Car ferry, catamaran Passenger ferry, catamaran Ferry destination, journey time – hours: minutes Hovercraft
V P	Internal ferry – car, passenger
	Principal airport, other airport or airfield
MENDIP HILLS	Area of outstanding natural beauty, National Forest – England and Wales, Forest park, National park, National scenic area – Scotland, Regional park
	Woodland
	Beach – sand, shingle
KENNET AND AVON CANAL	Navigable river or canal
6	Lock, flight of locks, canal bridge number
965	Viewpoint, spot height – in metres Linear antiquity
P&R	Park and ride
29	Adjoining page number
SY 80 70	Ordnance Survey National Grid reference – see page 402

Road map scale 1: 100 000 or 1.58 miles to 1 inch

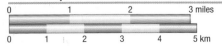

Road map scale (Isle of Man and parts of Scotland) 1: 200 000 or 3.15 miles to 1 inch

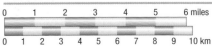

Tourist information

BYLAND ABBEY	Abbey or priory	HOLTON HEATH	National nature reserve
WOODHENGE	Ancient monument		Marina
SEALIFE CENTRE	Aquarium or dolphinarium	NAT MARITIME MUSEUM	Maritime or military museum
CITY MUSEUM AND ART GALLERY	Art collection or museum	SILVERSTONE	Motor racing circuit
TATE ST IVES	Art gallery	CUMBERLAND PENCIL MUSEUM	Museum
1644	Battle site and date		Picnic area
ABBOTSBURY SWANNERY	Bird sanctuary or aviary	WEST SOMERSET RAILWAY	Preserved railway
	Camping site	THIRSK	Racecourse
	Caravan site	LEAHILL TURRET	Roman antiquity
BAMBURGH CASTLE	Castle	BOYTON MARSHES	RSPB reserve
YORK MINSTER	Cathedral	THRIGBY HALL	Safari park
SANDHAM MEMORIAL CHAPEL	Church of interest	FREEPORT BRAINTREE	Shopping village
	Country park	MILLENNIUM STADIUM	Sports venue
SEVEN SISTERS	– England and Wales	ALTON TOWERS	Theme park
LOCHORE MEADOWS	– Scotland		Tourist information centre
ROYAL BATH & WEST SHOWGROUND	County show ground		– open all year – open seasonally
MONK PARK FARM	Farm park	NATIONAL RAILWAY MUSEUM	Transport collection
HILLIER GARDENS AND ARBORETUM	Garden, arboretum	LEVANT MINE	World heritage site
ST ANDREWS	Golf course – 18-hole	HELMSLEY	Youth hostel
TYNTESFIELD	Historic house	MARWELL	Zoo
SS GREAT BRITAIN	Historic ship	SUTTON BANK VISITOR CENTRE	Other place of interest
HATFIELD HOUSE	House and garden	GLENFIDDICH DISTILLERY	
MUSEUM OF DARTMOOR LIFE	Local museum		

Approach map symbols

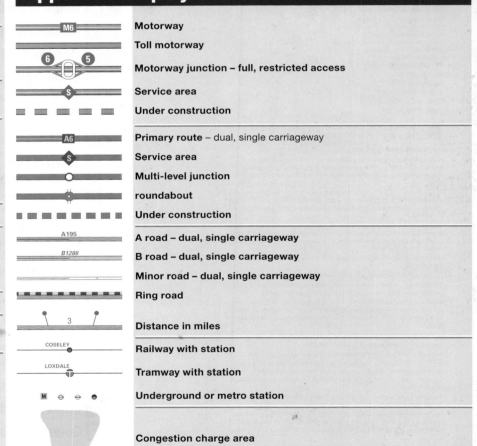

M6	Motorway
	Toll motorway
6 — 5	Motorway junction – full, restricted access
S	Service area
	Under construction
A6	Primary route – dual, single carriageway
S	Service area
	Multi-level junction
	roundabout
	Under construction
A195	A road – dual, single carriageway
B1288	B road – dual, single carriageway
	Minor road – dual, single carriageway
	Ring road
3	Distance in miles
COSELEY	Railway with station
LOXDALE	Tramway with station
M	Underground or metro station
	Congestion charge area

Speed Cameras

Fixed camera locations are shown using the 40 symbol. In congested areas the 40 symbol is used to show that there are two or more cameras on the road indicated.

Due to the restrictions of scale the camera locations are only approximate and cannot indicate the operating direction of the camera. Mobile camera sites, and cameras located on roads not included on the mapping are not shown. Where two or more cameras are shown on the same road, drivers are warned that this may indicate that a SPEC system is in operation. These cameras use the time taken to drive between the two camera positions to calculate the speed of the vehicle. At the time of going to press, some local authorities were considering decommissioning their speed cameras.

Load and vehicle restrictions

Any information on height, width and weight restrictions in the UK as noted on pages 1–314 of this atlas have been derived from the relevant OS material used to compile this atlas. Any information on height, width and weight restrictions on the Isle of Man has been derived from the relevant information as supplied by the Isle of Man Highways Department. Where a warning sign is displayed, any height obstructions, including but not limited to low bridges and overhead cables, are shown in the atlas where such obstructions cross navigable roads selected for inclusion. Height restrictions lower than 16'6" and width restrictions narrower than 13 feet, are all shown in 3 inch multiples and have been rounded down where necessary. Weight restrictions indicate weak bridges and the maximum gross weight which could be supported is shown in tonnes. While every effort has been made to include all relevant and accurate information, due to limitations of scale a single symbol may be used to indicate more than one feature and it is not possible to show restrictions on urban side roads.

England

A1 Truckstop Colsterworth

200 A1

Bourne Road, Colsterworth, Grantham, Lincolnshire NG33 5JN
01478 860916 · SK93842371 155 E8
At Colsterworth take A151 Bourne. Site is 200 yards on right.

Mon 24hr **Tue** 24hr **Wed** 24hr **Thu** 24hr **Fri** 24hr **Sat** By appointment **Sun** Closed

Mon 0600–2200 **Tue** 0600–2200 **Wed** 0600–2200 **Thu** 0600–2200 **Fri** 0600–2200 **Sat** 0700–1400 **Sun** Closed

A19 Services North

16 A19

Ron Perry & Son Ltd, Elwick, Hartlepool, Teesside TS27 3HH
+44 (0)1740 644223
sales@ronperry.co.uk
www.ronperry.co.uk
NZ45022902 234 F5
2 miles north of junction with A689

Mon 0600–2100 **Tue** 0600–2100 **Wed** 0600–2100 **Thu** 0600–2100 **Fri** 0600–2100 **Sat** 0600–2100 **Sun** 0600–2100

Mon 0630–1730 **Tue** 0630–1730 **Wed** 0630–1730 **Thu** 0630–1730 **Fri** 0630–1730 **Sat** 0630–1600 **Sun** 0603–1600

A19 Services South

20 A19

Ron Perry & Son Ltd, Elwick, Hartlepool, Teesside TS27 3HH
+44 (0)1740 644223
sales@ronperry.co.uk
www.ronperry.co.uk
NZ45072914 234 F5
3 miles south of junction with A179

Mon 24hr **Tue** 24hr **Wed** 24hr **Thu** 24hr **Fri** 24hr **Sat** 24hr **Sun** 24hr

Mon 0630–1730 **Tue** 0630–1730 **Wed** 0630–1730 **Thu** 0630–1730 **Fri** 0630–1730 **Sat** 0630–1600 **Sun** 0630–1600

Adderstone Services

30 A1

Belford, Northumberland NE70 7JU
+44 (0)1668 213000
james@purdylodge.co.uk
www.purdylodge.co.uk
NU13213020 264 C4
About 13 miles north of A1068 Alnwick turnoff.

Mon 24hr **Tue** 24hr **Wed** 24hr **Thu** 24hr **Fri** 24hr **Sat** 24hr **Sun** 24hr

Mon 24hr **Tue** 24hr **Wed** 24hr **Thu** 24hr **Fri** 24hr **Sat** 24hr **Sun** 24hr

Airport Café

20–40 M20 J11 (5 miles)

A20 Main Road, Sellindge, Ashford, Kent TN25 6DA
+44 (0)1303 813185
TR11253669 54 F6 · From M20 J11, take A20 Sellindge for 5 miles.

Mon 0700–1600 **Tue** 0700–1600 **Wed** 0700–1600 **Thu** 0700–1600 **Fri** 0700–1600 **Sat** 0700–1430 **Sun** 0800–1430

Mon 0700–1600 **Tue** 0700–1600 **Wed** 0700–1600 **Thu** 0700–1600 **Fri** 0700–1600 **Sat** 0700–1430 **Sun** 0800–1430

Albion Inn and Truckstop

16 M5 J23 (8 miles)

14 Bath Road, Ashcott, Somerset TA7 9QT
+44 (0)1458 210281
www.thealbionashcott.co.uk
ST42373722 44 F2
From M5 J23 take A39 Glastonbury. Site is on right after 8 miles.

Mon 24hr **Tue** 24hr **Wed** 24hr **Thu** 24hr **Fri** 24hr **Sat** 24hr **Sun** 24hr

Mon 0800–2100 **Tue** 0800–2100 **Wed** 0800–2100 **Thu** 0800–2100 **Fri** 0800–2100 **Sat** 0800–2100 **Sun** 0800–1500

Ardleigh Truckstop

40 A12 J29 (2 miles)

Ardleigh, Colchester, Essex CO7 7SL
+44 (0)1543 469183
d.brosnan@virgin.net
www.truckstop.co.uk
TM04842682 107 F10
From A12 J29 take A120 Harwich/ Clacton for 2 miles.

Mon 0630–1945 **Tue** 0630–1945 **Wed** 0630–1945 **Thu** 0630–1945 **Fri** 0630–1645 **Sat** 0800–1345 **Sun** 0900–1345

Mon 0630–1700 **Tue** 0630–1700 **Wed** 0630–1700 **Thu** 0630–1700 **Fri** 0630–1700 **Sat** 0800–1400 **Sun** 0800–1400

Ashford International Truckstop

-euros 335 M20 J10 (1 mile)

Waterbrook Avenue, Sevington, Ashford, Kent TN24 0LH
+44 (0)1233 502919
www.ashfordtruckstop.co.uk
TR03273974 54 F4 · From M20 J10 take A2070 Sevington. Follow signs.

Mon 24hr **Tue** 24hr **Wed** 24hr **Thu** 24hr **Fri** 24hr **Sat** 24hr **Sun** 24hr

Mon 24hr **Tue** 24hr **Wed** 24hr **Thu** 24hr **Fri** 24hr **Sat** 24hr **Sun** 24hr

AWJ Penrith Truckstop

200 M6 J40 (1 mile)

Penrith Industrial Estate, Penrith, Cumbria CA11 9EH
+44 (0)1768 866995
info@awjtruckstop.co.uk
www.awjtruckstop.co.uk
NY50682954 230 F6 · From M6 J40, follow the signs for the truckstop.

Mon 0600–2400 **Tue** 24hr **Wed** 24hr **Thu** 24hr **Fri** 24hr **Sat** 2400–1200 **Sun** Closed

Mon 0600–2400 **Tue** 24hr **Wed** 24hr **Thu** 24hr **Fri** 24hr **Sat** 2400–1100 **Sun** Closed

Barney's Café

30–45 M180 J5

Melton Ross Road (A18), Barnetby, North Lincolnshire DN38 6LB +44 (0)1652 680966
TA05521065 200 E5
From M180/A180 J5 head for Humberside Airport. The site is 300 yards along on the right.

Mon 0600–2100 **Tue** 0600–2100 **Wed** 0600–2100 **Thu** 0600–2100 **Fri** 0600–2000 **Sat** 0600–1400 **Sun** Closed

Mon 0600–2100 **Tue** 0600–2100 **Wed** 0600–2100 **Thu** 0600–2100 **Fri** 0600–2000 **Sat** 0600–1400 **Sun** Closed

Barton Lorry Park

40 A1(M) J56

Barton, Richmond, North Yorkshire DL10 6NF
+44 (0)1325 377777
NZ21920799 224 D4
From A1(M) J56 head for Barton. The site is on the right after 100 yards.

Mon 24hr **Tue** 24hr **Wed** 24hr **Thu** 24hr **Fri** 24hr **Sat** 24hr **Sun** 24hr

Mon 0600–2200 **Tue** 0600–2200 **Wed** 0600–2200 **Thu** 0600–2200 **Fri** 0600–2100 **Sat** 0700–1500 **Sun** 0600–2100

Birmingham Truckstop

100 M42 J6 (5m) M6 J5 (6¾m)

The Wharf, Wharf Road, Tyseley, Birmingham B11 2EB
0121 628 2339 · SP11598441
134 G2 From M42 J6, take A45 west-bound 4½ miles to A4040. After ½ mile right into Wharfdale Road, then 1st right. From M42 J5, take A41 west-bound 5 miles to A4040. After 1¼ miles, left into Wharfdale Road, then 1st right.

Mon 24hr **Tue** 24hr **Wed** 24hr **Thu** 24hr **Fri** 24hr **Sat** 24hr **Sun** 24hr

Mon 0600–2100 **Tue** 0600–2100 **Wed** 0600–2100 **Thu** 0600–2100 **Fri** 0600–2100 **Sat** Closed **Sun** Closed

Bistro Café

15 A1 (3 miles)

Barrowby View, Nottingham Road, Sedgebrook, Lincolnshire NG32 2EP 01949 842164
frankish687@btinternet.com
SK85503766 155 B7
From A1 A52 junction take A52 Nottingham for 3 miles

Mon 0630–1500 **Tue** 0630–1500 **Wed** 0630–1500 **Thu** 0630–1500 **Fri** 0630–1500 **Sat** 0630–1500 **Sun** 0700–1400

Mon 0630–1500 **Tue** 0630–1500 **Wed** 0630–1500 **Thu** 0630–1500 **Fri** 0630–1500 **Sat** 0630–1500 **Sun** 0700–1400

Boss Hoggs Café

40 A12 J33/A14 J55

London Road, Copdock, Ipswich, Suffolk IP8 3JW
+44 (0)1473 730797
TM10793982 108 D2 · From A12 J33/ A14 J55, take A12 Colchester. Take 1st exit on right, site is 100 yards on.

Mon 0700–1500 **Tue** 0700–1500 **Wed** 0700–1500 **Thu** 0700–1500 **Fri** 0700–1500 **Sat** Closed **Sun** Closed

Mon 0700–1500 **Tue** 0700–1500 **Wed** 0700–1500 **Thu** 0700–1500 **Fri** 0700–1500 **Sat** Closed **Sun** Closed

Caenby Corner Transport Café

30 M180 J4 (10 miles)

Caenby Corner, Glentham, Lincolnshire LN8 2AR
+44 (0)1673 878388
abacuswecan@btinternet.com
SK96718939 189 D7
From M180 J4 take A15 Lincoln. After 10 miles, take A361 Market Rasen. Site is immediately on right.

Mon 0700–2100 **Tue** 0700–2100 **Wed** 0700–2100 **Thu** 0700–2100 **Fri** 0700–1800 **Sat** 0700–1600 **Sun** 0700–1600

Mon 0700–2100 **Tue** 0700–2100 **Wed** 0700–2100 **Thu** 0700–2100 **Fri** 0700–1800 **Sat** 0700–1600 **Sun** 0700–1600

Symbols

- Accommodation
- Advanced booking
- Cafe
- Cash machine
- CCTV
- Fuel
- Truckwash
- Nearest main road. This may be a few miles away
- Security
- Shop
- Showers
- Parking spaces
- Toilets
- TV
- Opening hours

Truckstops near motorways are shown in blue, those near primary routes are green and those on other routes are shown in black.

SK93842371 Ordnance Survey National Grid reference
155 E8 Page and grid reference in this atlas

Café Royal

A35

Tannery Road, Off West Street, Bridport, Dorset DT6 3QX
SY46309293 16 C5
The café is in the centre of Bridport at the bus station on the B3162. Parking is in local authority's West Street Coach Park opposite

Mon 0600–1900 **Tue** 0600–1900 **Wed** 0600–1900 **Thu** 0600–1900 **Fri** 0600–1900 **Sat** 0600–1900 **Sun** 0600–1900

Mon 0600–1900 **Tue** 0600–1900 **Wed** 0600–1900 **Thu** 0600–1900 **Fri** 0600–1900 **Sat** 0600–1900 **Sun** 0600–1900

Chippenham PitStop

70 M4 J17

Oakley Acres, Dreycott Cerne, Chippenham, Wiltshire SN15 5LH
+44 (0)1249 750645
69094@compass-group.co.uk
ST92507938 62 D2
From M4 J17 follow 'Services' sign on B4122 Sutton Benger. The site is on the right after ½ miles.

Mon 24hr **Tue** 24hr **Wed** 24hr **Thu** 24hr **Fri** 24hr **Sat** 24hr **Sun** 24hr

Mon 0600–2130 **Tue** 0600–2130 **Wed** 0600–2130 **Thu** 0600–2130 **Fri** 0600–2130 **Sat** 0800–1230 **Sun** Closed

Chris's Café

30 M40 J5 (5 miles)

Wycombe Road, Studley Green, Stokenchurch, Buckinghamshire HP14 3XB
+44 (0)1494 482121
www.chrisscafe.co.uk
SU79069513 84 F3
From M40 J5 take the A40 High Wycombe for 5 miles. Site is on right.

Mon 0630–1900 **Tue** 0600–1900 **Wed** 0600–1900 **Thu** 0600–1900 **Fri** 0600–1400 **Sat** 0630–1200 **Sun** Closed

Mon 0630–1900 **Tue** 0600–1900 **Wed** 0600–1900 **Thu** 0600–1900 **Fri** 0600–1400 **Sat** 0600–1200 **Sun** Closed

Cleveland Truckstop

250 A19/A66 (5¾ miles)

1–5 Puddlers Road, Southbank, Middlesbrough, Cleveland TS6 6TX
+44 (0)1642 465055
cnetex@btinternet.com
NZ53672109 234 G6
From A19/A66 junction take A66 (Middlesbrough bypass) Redcar 5¾ miles, exit left onto Normanby Road, 1st right. Site is third left.

Mon 24hr **Tue** 24hr **Wed** 24hr **Thu** 24hr **Fri** 24hr **Sat** 24hr **Sun** 24hr

Mon 0600–2130 **Tue** 0600–2130 **Wed** 0600–2130 **Thu** 0600–2130 **Fri** 0600–1600 **Sat** Closed **Sun** Closed

Crewe Truck Stop

120 M6 J16 (4 miles) M6 J17 (5½ miles)

Cowley Way, (off Weston Road), Crewe, Cheshire CW1 6DD
+44 (0)7894 622250
SJ71365432 168 E2
From M16 J16 take A500 Crewe. At roundabout take A5020. Cross next roundabout and traffic lights. Take 2nd left. From M6 J17 take A534 5 miles. At roundabout take first exit (A5020). After 400 yards turn right into Cowley Way.

Mon 24hr **Tue** 24hr **Wed** 24hr **Thu** 24hr **Fri** 24hr **Sat** 24hr **Sun** 24hr

Mon 0600–1400 and 1700–2100 **Tue** 0600–1400 and 1700–2100 **Wed** 0600–1400 and 1700–2100 **Thu** 0600–1400 and 1700–2100 **Fri** 0600–1400 and 1700–2100 **Sat** 0600–1400 **Sun** Closed

Crown Road Vehicle Park

35 M25 J25 (3 miles)

Crown Road Vehicle Park, Enfield EN1 1TH +44 (0)208 443 0602
TQ34769640 86 F4
From M25 J25 take A10 London 2¾ miles, then A110 Chingford ½ miles, turn left into Crown Road. Site is on right after 100 yards.

Mon 24hr **Tue** 24hr **Wed** 24hr **Thu** 24hr **Fri** 24hr **Sat** 24hr **Sun** 24hr

Mon 24hr **Tue** 24hr **Wed** 24hr **Thu** 24hr **Fri** 24hr **Sat** 24hr **Sun** 24hr
Tea / coffee area only

Dinkys Dinahs

12 A5

Welshpool Road, Ford, Shrewsbury, Shropshire SY5 9LG
+44 (0)1743 850070
SJ41231323 149 G8
From the A5 west of Shrewsbury take the A458 Welshpool for 2 miles. The site is in a layby on the right.

Mon 24hr **Tue** 24hr **Wed** 24hr **Thu** 24hr **Fri** 24hr **Sat** 24hr **Sun** 24hr

Mon 24hr **Tue** 24hr **Wed** 24hr **Thu** 24hr **Fri** 24hr **Sat** 24hr **Sun** 24hr

Docklands Diner and Truckwash

45 M62 J36

Anderson Road, Goole, E Yorkshire DN14 6UD
+44 (0)1405 766349
docklandsdinertruckwash@google.com www.docklands-diner-and-truckwash-goole.co.uk
SE73412361 199 C8
From J36 take A614 Goole at first set of traffic lights (½ miles) turn right into Anderson Road. Site visible on left within 150 yards. Entrance is in A.W. Nielson Road.

Mon 0615–2200 **Tue** 0615–2200 **Wed** 0615–2200 **Thu** 0615–2200 **Fri** 0615–1400 **Sat** Closed **Sun** Closed

Mon 0615–2200 **Tue** 0615–2200 **Wed** 0615–2200 **Thu** 0615–2200 **Fri** 0615–1400 **Sat** Closed **Sun** Closed

Ellesmere Port Truckstop

48 M53 J8

Portside North, Merseyton Road, Ellesmere Port, Cheshire CH65 2HQ
+44 (0)151 355 5241
moroils@live.co.uk
SJ39987769 182 F5
At M53 J8 take A5032 towards the Docks. Take 1st left, go over level crossing and almost immediately take a hard left.

Mon 0600–2200 **Tue** 0600–2200 **Wed** 0600–2200 **Thu** 0600–2200 **Fri** 0600–2200 **Sat** 0600–1300 **Sun** Closed

Mon 0800–1900 **Tue** 0800–1900 **Wed** 0800–1900 **Thu** 0800–1900 **Fri** 0800–1400 **Sat** 0900–1200 **Sun** Closed

Heywood Distribution Park

200 M66 J3 (1½ miles)

Pilsworth Road, Heywood, Manchester, Greater Manchester OL10 2TT +44 (0)1706 368645
david.driver@fsmail.net
www.heywooddistributionpark.com · SD84310948 195 F10
From M62, M60 and M66 follow 'Heywood Distribution Park' signs leave M66 J3 (Pilsworth) and follow signs for truck stop.

Mon 24hr **Tue** 24hr **Wed** 24hr **Thu** 24hr **Fri** 24hr **Sat** 24hr **Sun** 24hr

Mon 0700–2200 **Tue** 0700–2200 **Wed** 0700–2200 **Thu** 0700–2200 **Fri** 0700–2200 **Sat** 0700–2200 **Sun** 0700–2200

HF Veale & Sons

10 A37 (1½ miles)

Broadway Garage, Chilcompton, Radstock, Bath, Somerset BA3 4JW
+44 (0)1761 232298
nfo@hfveale.co.uk
www.hfveale.co.uk
ST64355134 44 C6
Take the B3139 off the A 37 at Shepton Mallet.

Mon 0530–2100 **Tue** 0530–2100 **Wed** 0530–2100 **Thu** 0530–2100 **Fri** 0530–2100 **Sat** 0700–2100 **Sun** 0700–2100

Hillside Café

10–20 A36

A36 Codford, Warminster, Wiltshire BA12 0JZ
+44 (0)1985 850712
admin@hillsidecafe.co.uk
www.hillsidecafe.co.uk
ST95624058 46 E3
The site is on the A36 between Codford St Peter and Upton Lovell

Mon 0600–1700 **Tue** 0600–1700 **Wed** 0600–1700 **Thu** 0600–1700 **Fri** 0600–1700 **Sat** Closed **Sun** Closed

Mon 0600–1700 **Tue** 0600–1700 **Wed** 0600–1700 **Thu** 0600–1700 **Fri** 0600–1700 **Sat** Closed **Sun** Closed

Thurso Overnight Lorry Park
A9

Skiach Services
A9

A90

The Newtonmore Grill

Stracathro Services
A9

Motorgrill Ballinluig
A90

Horse Shoe Café

Moto Kinross

Moto Stirling
M9
Muirpark Truckstop
Westway Lorry Park
M8
Roadchef Bothwell (southbound)
M8
Roadchef Hamilton (northbound)
M74
Cedar Café
A1

Redmoss Truckstop   Welcome Break Abington

Adderstone Services

Roadchef Annandale Water
M74
Lockerbie Truckstop
A74(M)
Eardley International
Welcome Break Gretna
Nightowl Truckstop Carlisle
Kingstown Truck Park
M6
Moto Washington

A1(M)
A19 Services
Cleveland Truckstop
AWJ Penrith Truckstop
A19
Barton Lorry Park
Junction 38 Services
A1
Londonderry Lodge
Quernhow A1 Café and Truckstop
Truckhaven Carnforth
A1(M)   A64
York Lorry Park
M6
Moto Wetherby
Sue's Pitstop Café
M65
M62
Docklands Diner and Truckwash
Whitley Bridge Pallets and Truckstop
Heywood Distribution Park   Redbeck Motel
M62
M180   Ulceby Truckstop
M1
Moto Doncaster North   Barney's Café
M18
A15
Poplar 2000 Services – Lymm Truckstop   The Stockyard Truckstop   Caenby Corner Transport Café
Ellesmere Port Truckstop   Lets Eat Café
Junction 29 Truckstop
Crewe Truck Stop   M6   Ranch Café and Cattle Market Lorry Park
M1   Langrick Station Café
Midway Truckstop   Moto Stafford   A1
Northbound   Bistro Café
The Salt Box Café
A5   PJ's Transport Café   A1 Truckstop Colsterworth
Dinkys Dinahs   M54   Truckers Rest   Junction 23 Lorry Park   Necton Diner
Standeford Farm Café   M1
Stibbington Diner
Harry Tuffins   Birmingham Truckstop   A1(M)
Transport Café   M6
Lincoln Farm Café   Nightowl Truckstop Rugby   Hilltop Café
M40   A14
Red Lion Café & Truckstop   M11
M5   Jack's Hill Café   Super Sausage Café   Boss Hoggs Café   Orwell Crossing Lorry Park
Moto Cherwell Valley   M1   The Truckstop Café   A12
(Crawley Crossing Bunker Stop)   Ardleigh Truckstop
M40   Watling Street Truckstop
Roadchef Pont Abraham   South Mimms   J26 Truckstop
M4   Swindon   Chris's Café   Truckstop   Crown Road Vehicle Park
Moto Swansea   Truckstop   M25
Cardiff Gate Services   M4   Roadchef Magor   Square Deal Café   Merry Chest Café
Cardiff West Services   The Avon Lodge   M4   M2
Chippenham   Moto Reading   Oakdene Café   Moto Medway
PitStop
HF Veale and Sons   M25   Ashford International Truckstop
Albion Inn and Truckstop   A39   Nunney Catch Café   Airport Café
M5   Hillside Café   M3
The Old Willoughby Hedge Café
A303   M27
Morgan's Café   Portsmouth Truckstop
A30   A35
Café Royal
Pie Stop Café

Smokey Joe's Café
A30

IV

Hilltop Café

52 A14 J44

Lorry Park, Rougham Hill, Bury St Edmunds, Suffolk IP33 2RU
+44 (0)7860 170112
TL86926335 125 E7
Follow signs from the A14 near to Bury St Edmunds. The site is 200 yards from A14 J44.

Mon 24hr **Tue** 24hr **Wed** 24hr **Thu** 24hr **Fri** 24hr **Sat** 24hr **Sun** 24hr

Mon 0630–2000 **Tue** 0630–2000 **Wed** 0630–2000 **Thu** 0630–2000 **Fri** 0630–1600 **Sat** Closed **Sun** Closed

J26 Truckstop

50 J26 M25

Skilletts Hill Farm, Honey Lane, Waltham Abbey, Essex EN9 3QU
01992 801900
www.junction26.org
TQ40489978 86 E5
M25 J26 westbound take 4th exit go under M25 and entrance is on left; eastbound take 3rd exit, go right round next roundabout, back under M25 and entrance is on left.

Mon 0600–2200 **Tue** 0600–2200 **Wed** 0600–2200 **Thu** 0600–2200 **Fri** 0600–2000 **Sat** 0600–1400 **Sun** Closed

Mon 0600–2100 **Tue** 0600–2100 **Wed** 0600–2100 **Thu** 0600–2100 **Fri** 0600–2000 **Sat** 0600–1400 **Sun** Closed
Last order for hot food 1 hour before closing

Jacks Hill Café

48 M1 J15A (6 miles)

Watling Street, Towcester, Northamptonshire NN12 8ET
+44 (0)1327 351350
SP68475007 120 G3
From M1 J15A, take A43 Oxford, after 6 miles turn right onto A5. Site is 300yds on left.

Mon 24hr **Tue** 24hr **Wed** 24hr **Thu** 24hr **Fri** 24hr **Sat** 24hr **Sun** 24hr

Mon 0600–2130 **Tue** 0600–2130 **Wed** 0600–2130 **Thu** 0600–2130 **Fri** 0600–2030 **Sat** 0600–1430 **Sun** 0730–1400

Junction 23 Lorry Park

180 M1 J23

Ashby Road East, Shepshed, Loughborough, Leicestershire LE12 9BS
+44 (0)1509 507480
www.j23truckstop.co.uk
SK48631832 153 F9
From M1 J23 take A512 Ashby-de-la-Zouch. Site is ¼ miles on right.

Mon 24hr **Tue** 24hr **Wed** 24hr **Thu** 24hr **Fri** 24hr **Sat** 24hr **Sun** 24hr

Mon 0600–2100 **Tue** 0600–2100 **Wed** 0600–2100 **Thu** 0600–2100 **Fri** 0600–2100 **Sat** 0600–1130 **Sun** Closed

Junction 29 Truckstop

100 M1 J29

Hardwick View Road, Holmewood Ind Est, Chesterfield, Derbyshire S42 5SA
+44 (0)1246 856536
www.junction29.co.uk
SK43716583 170 B6
From M1 J29 take A6175 Clay Cross. Follow 'Lorry Park' signs.

Mon 24hr **Tue** 24hr **Wed** 24hr **Thu** 24hr **Fri** 24hr **Sat** 24hr **Sun** 24hr

Mon 0500–2300 **Tue** 0500–2300 **Wed** 0500–2300 **Thu** 0500–2300 **Fri** 0500–2300 **Sat** 0600–1100 **Sun** Closed

Junction 38 Services

90 M6 J38

Old Tebay, Penrith, Cumbria CA10 3SS +44 (0)1539 624505
feedback@westmorland.com
www.westmoreland.com
NY61550488 222 E2
From M6 J38 take A685, at 1st roundabout take 1st exit. Site is on left after 100 yards.

Mon 24hr **Tue** 24hr **Wed** 24hr **Thu** 24hr **Fri** 24hr **Sat** 24hr **Sun** 24hr

Mon 0715–2100 **Tue** 0715–2100 **Wed** 0715–2100 **Thu** 0715–2100 **Fri** 0715–2100 **Sat** 0715–2100 **Sun** 0715–2100

Kingstown Truck Park

30–40 M6 J44

Millbrook Road, Kingstown Ind Est, Carlisle, Cumbria CA3 0EU
+44 (0)777 577 0973
neikor@aol.com
NY39335920 239 F9
M6 J44 take A7 Carlisle, right at 2nd lights, 2nd right, 200 yards on right

Mon 24hr **Tue** 24hr **Wed** 24hr **Thu** 24hr **Fri** 24hr **Sat** 24hr **Sun** 24hr

Mon 0700–2000 **Tue** 0700–2000 **Wed** 0700–2000 **Thu** 0700–2000 **Fri** 0700–2000 **Sat** 0700–1700 **Sun** Closed

Langrick Station Café

25 A16/A17 (6 miles)

B1192 Main Road, Langrick, Boston, Lincolnshire PE22 7AH
+44 (0)1205 280023
TF26454786 174 F3
From A16 take A1121 Boston 3½ miles, then B1192 Brothertoft 2½ miles. From A17 take A1121 Sleaford 3½ miles, then B1192 Brothertoft 2½ miles.

Mon 24hr **Tue** 24hr **Wed** 24hr **Thu** 24hr **Fri** 24hr **Sat** 24hr **Sun** 24hr

Mon 0630–0200 **Tue** 0630–0200 **Wed** 0630–0200 **Thu** 0630–0200 **Fri** 0630–0200 **Sat** 0700–1300 **Sun** 0900–1500

Lets Eat Café

10 Jct 10 M56 (3 miles)

A49 Tarporley Road, Lower Whitley, Warrington, Cheshire WA4 4EZ
+44 (0)1928 717322
SJ60607745 183 F10
M56 J10 take the A49 Whitchurch. Cafe is on right after 3 miles.

Mon 0900–1700 **Tue** 0900–1700 **Wed** 0900–1700 **Thu** 0900–1700 **Fri** 0900–1700 **Sat** 0900–1700 **Sun** 1000–1600

Mon 0900–1700 **Tue** 0900–1700 **Wed** 0900–1700 **Thu** 0900–1700 **Fri** 0900–1700 **Sat** 0900–1700 **Sun** 1000–1600

Lincoln Farm Café

200 M42 J6 (3 miles)

A452 Kenilworth Road, Hampton in Arden, Solihull, Warwickshire B92 0LS
+44 (0)1675 442301
SP21928014 134 G4
From M42 J6, take A45 B'ham (E) 1 mile, then A452 Leamington 2 miles. Site is on right.

Mon 0400–2400 **Tue** 0400–2400 **Wed** 0400–2400 **Thu** 0400–2400 **Fri** 0400–2300 **Sat** Closed **Sun** Closed

Mon 0600–2400 **Tue** 0600–2400 **Wed** 0600–2400 **Thu** 0600–2400 **Fri** 0400–2300 **Sat** Closed **Sun** Closed

Londonderry Lodge

24 A1

Londonderry, Northallerton, North Yorkshire DL7 9ND
+44 (0)1677 422143
claredalton@btconnect.com
SE30248779 214 B6
On the old A1 about 12 miles south of Scotch Corner. Leave the A1(M) at J50 (northbound) or J51 (southbound).

Mon 24hr **Tue** 24hr **Wed** 24hr **Thu** 24hr **Fri** 24hr **Sat** Closed **Sun** Closed

Mon 0500–2300 **Tue** 0500–2300 **Wed** 0500–2300 **Thu** 0500–2300 **Fri** 0500–2300 **Sat** Closed **Sun** Closed

Merry Chest Café

30 M25 J1b (3 miles)

Watling Street, Bean, Dartford, Kent DA2 8AH
+44 (0)1474 832371
TQ59297277 68 E5
From M25 J1b (via A225 Dartford slip) take A296 Bean 3 miles.

Mon 0900–1700 **Tue** 0900–1700 **Wed** 0900–1700 **Thu** 0900–1700 **Fri** 0900–1700 **Sat** 0900–1700 **Sun** 1000–1600

Mon 0900–1700 **Tue** 0900–1700 **Wed** 0900–1700 **Thu** 0900–1700 **Fri** 0900–1700 **Sat** 0900–1700 **Sun** 1000–1600

Midway Truckstop

35 M54

Prees Heath, Whitchurch, Shropshire SY13 4JT
+44 (0)1948 663160
SJ55663804 149 B11
The site is off the roundabout at the the southern intersection of the A41 the A49 at Whitchurch.

Mon 24hr **Tue** 24hr **Wed** 24hr **Thu** 24hr **Fri** 24hr **Sat** 24hr **Sun** 24hr

Mon 0545–2000 **Tue** 0545–2000 **Wed** 0545–2000 **Thu** 0545–2000 **Fri** 0545–2000 **Sat** Closed **Sun** Closed

Morgan's Transport Café

15–20 M5 J27 (2½ miles)

Burlescombe, Nr Tiverton, Devon EX16 7JX
+44 (0)1823 672273
ST07891563 27 D9
From M5 J27 take the A38 Wellington. Cafe is 2½ miles on left.

Mon 0700–1400 **Tue** 0700–1400 **Wed** 0700–1400 **Thu** 0700–1400 **Fri** 0700–1400 **Sat** 0700–1030 **Sun** Closed

Mon 0700–1400 **Tue** 0700–1400 **Wed** 0700–1400 **Thu** 0700–1400 **Fri** 0700–1400 **Sat** 0700–1030 **Sun** Closed

Moto Cherwell Valley

747 M40 J10

M40 J10, Northampton Road, Ardley, Bicester, Oxfordshire OX27 7RD
+44 (0)1869 346060
www.moto-way.co.uk
SP55272817 101 F11
At M40 J10, signposted from M40 and A43

Mon 24hr **Tue** 24hr **Wed** 24hr **Thu** 24hr **Fri** 24hr **Sat** 24hr **Sun** 24hr

Mon 24hr **Tue** 24hr **Wed** 24hr **Thu** 24hr **Fri** 24hr **Sat** 24hr **Sun** 24hr

Moto Doncaster North

30 J5 M18/M180

J5 M18/M180, Doncaster, South Yorkshire DN8 5GS
+44 (0)1302 847700
www.moto-way.co.uk
SE66921112 199 E7
Site is at M18 J5, signposted from M18 and M180.

Mon 24hr **Tue** 24hr **Wed** 24hr **Thu** 24hr **Fri** 24hr **Sat** 24hr **Sun** 24hr

Mon 24hr **Tue** 24hr **Wed** 24hr **Thu** 24hr **Fri** 24hr **Sat** 24hr **Sun** 24hr

Moto Medway

137 M2 J4/5

M2 J4/5, Rainhorn, Gillingham, Kent ME8 8PQ
+44 (0)1634 236900
www.moto-way.co.uk
TQ81746347 69 G10
On the M2 just east of J4.

Mon 24hr **Tue** 24hr **Wed** 24hr **Thu** 24hr **Fri** 24hr **Sat** 24hr **Sun** 24hr

Mon 24hr **Tue** 24hr **Wed** 24hr **Thu** 24hr **Fri** 24hr **Sat** 24hr **Sun** 24hr

Moto Reading

55 M4 J12

M4 Junction 11/12, Burghfield, Reading, Berkshire RG30 3UQ
+44 (0)1189 566966
www.moto-way.co.uk
SU67166976 65 F7
Between M4 J11 and J12

Mon 24hr **Tue** 24hr **Wed** 24hr **Thu** 24hr **Fri** 24hr **Sat** 24hr **Sun** 24hr

Mon 24hr **Tue** 24hr **Wed** 24hr **Thu** 24hr **Fri** 24hr **Sat** 24hr **Sun** 24hr

Moto Stafford Northbound

80 M6 J14 (4 miles)

M6 Junction 14/15, Stone, Staffordshire ST15 0EU
+44 (0)1785 810504
www.moto-way.co.uk
SJ88593184 151 C7
About 4 miles north of M6 J14

Mon 24hr **Tue** 24hr **Wed** 24hr **Thu** 24hr **Fri** 24hr **Sat** 24hr **Sun** 24hr

Mon 24hr **Tue** 24hr **Wed** 24hr **Thu** 24hr **Fri** 24hr **Sat** 24hr **Sun** 24hr

Moto Washington

56 A1(M) J64

A1(M), Portobello, Birtley, County Durham DH3 2SJ
+44 (0)191 4103436
www.moto-way.co.uk
NZ28375506 243 F7
A1(M) North of J64

Mon 24hr **Tue** 24hr **Wed** 24hr **Thu** 24hr **Fri** 24hr **Sat** 24hr **Sun** 24hr

Mon 24hr **Tue** 24hr **Wed** 24hr **Thu** 24hr **Fri** 24hr **Sat** 24hr **Sun** 24hr

Moto Wetherby

60 J46 A1(M)

J46 A1(M), Kirk Deighton, Wetherby, West Yorkshire LS22 5GT
+44 (0)1937 545 080
www.moto-way.co.uk
SE41425013 206 C4
A1(M) J46, signposted from A1 and A1(M),

Mon 24hr **Tue** 24hr **Wed** 24hr **Thu** 24hr **Fri** 24hr **Sat** 24hr **Sun** 24hr

Mon 24hr **Tue** 24hr **Wed** 24hr **Thu** 24hr **Fri** 24hr **Sat** 24hr **Sun** 24hr

Necton Diner

100 A47

Norwich Road, Necton, Norfolk PE37 8DQ +44 (0)1760 724180
TF87701010 159 G7 · On the A47 at the northern edge of Necton.

Mon 0800–1830 **Tue** 0800–1830 **Wed** 0800–1830 **Thu** 0800–1830 **Fri** 0800–1500 **Sat** 0800–1400 **Sun** Closed

Nightowl Truckstop Carlisle

200 M6 J44 (300 yds)

Parkhouse Road, Kingstown Industrial Estate, Carlisle, Cumbria CA3 0JR +44 (0)1288 534192
www.nightowltruckstops.co.uk/carlisle.aspx · NY39155969 239 F9
M6 J44 take A75 Carlisle. After 150 yards, turn right at traffic lights, cross over the mini-roundabout. The site is 100 yards on the left.

Mon 24hr **Tue** 24hr **Wed** 24hr **Thu** 24hr **Fri** 24hr **Sat** 2400–1300 **Sun** 1800–2400

Mon 0600–2300 **Tue** 0500–2300 **Wed** 0500–2300 **Thu** 0500–2300 **Fri** 0500–2300 **Sat** 0600–1200 **Sun** 1800–2200

Nightowl Truckstop Rugby

240 M1 J18 (2½ miles) or M6 J1 (3½ miles)

(A5) Watling Street, Clifton upon Dunsmore, Rugby, Warwickshire CV23 0AE +44 (0)1788 535115
www.nightowltruckstops.co.uk/rugby.aspx · SP55317628 119 B11
From M1 J18, take A5 northbound. The site is on the right after 2½ miles. From M6 J1, take A426 Rugby. After 1 mile take the A5 London. Site is on left after 2½ miles.

Mon 24hr **Tue** 24hr **Wed** 24hr **Thu** 24hr **Fri** 24hr **Sat** 0000–1200 **Sun** 1500–2400

Mon 0600–2230 **Tue** 0600–2230 **Wed** 0600–2230 **Thu** 0600–2230 **Fri** 0600–2130 **Sat** Closed **Sun** Closed

Nunney Catch Café

30 A361

A361, Nunney Catch, Nr Frome, Somerset BA11 4NZ
+44 (0)1373 836331
ST73704476 45 E8
From junction of A361 and A359, follow sign for Green Pits Lane directly off roundabout.

Mon 0700–1500 **Tue** 0700–1500 **Wed** 0700–1500 **Thu** 0700–1500 **Fri** 0700–1500 **Sat** 0700–1300 **Sun** Closed

Mon 0700–1500 **Tue** 0700–1500 **Wed** 0700–1500 **Thu** 0700–1500 **Fri** 0700–1500 **Sat** 0700–1300 **Sun** Closed

Oakdene Café

10 M26 J2a, M20 J2 (¾ mile)

London Road, Wrotham, Sevenoaks, Kent TN15 7RR
+44 (0)1732 884873
janetjevons@yahoo.co.uk
www.oakdenecafe.co.uk
TQ62725869 52 B6
The site is on the A20. From M20 J2 take A20 Wrotham; site is on left after ¾ miles. From M26 J2a take A20 Wrotham. Site is signposted from slip road and is on right after 300 yards.

Mon 0900–1700 **Tue** 0900–1700 **Wed** 0900–1700 **Thu** 0900–1700 **Fri** 0900–1700 **Sat** 0900–1700 **Sun** 1000–1400

Mon 0900–1700 **Tue** 0900–1700 **Wed** 0900–1700 **Thu** 0900–1700 **Fri** 0900–1700 **Sat** 0900–1700 **Sun** 1000–1400

Orwell Crossing Lorry Park

229 A14

A14 Eastbound, Nacton, Ipswich, Suffolk IP10 0DD
+44 (0)1473 659140
reception@orwellcrossing.com
www.orwellcrossing.com
TM21484120 108 C4
Eastbound on A14, cross Orwell Bridge and take 2nd slip road, site is on the left. Westbound, turn round at J27 and take 1st slip.

Mon 24hr **Tue** 24hr **Wed** 24hr **Thu** 24hr **Fri** 24hr **Sat** 24hr **Sun** 24hr

Mon 24hr **Tue** 24hr **Wed** 24hr **Thu** 24hr **Fri** 24hr **Sat** 24hr **Sun** 24hr

Pie Stop Café

15 A30

Pennygillam Industrial Estate, Pennygillam Way, Launceston, Cornwall PL15 7ED
+44 (0)7593 579789
SX32138365 12 E2
From A30 to Bodmin, take A388 (B3254) Launceston, take a sharp right into Western Road. Pennygillam Way is the 4th left. Site is in cash & carry car park.

Mon 0730–1500 **Tue** 0730–1500 **Wed** 0730–1500 **Thu** 0730–1500 **Fri** 0730–1500 **Sat** 0730–1400 **Sun** Closed

Mon 0730–1500 **Tue** 0730–1500 **Wed** 0730–1500 **Thu** 0730–1500 **Fri** 0730–1500 **Sat** 0730–1400 **Sun** Closed

PJ's Transport Café

25 A50 (1 mile)

Sudbury Services, Litchfield Road, Sudbury, Derbyshire DE6 5GX
+44 (0)1283 820669
SK16183025 152 C3
From A5, about 5 miles east of Uttoxeter take A515 Lichfield. Site is on left after 1 mile.

Mon 0700–2200 **Tue** 0700–2200 **Wed** 0700–2200 **Thu** 0700–2200 **Fri** 0700–1800 **Sat** Closed **Sun** Closed

Mon 0700–2200 **Tue** 0700–2200 **Wed** 0700–2200 **Thu** 0700–2200 **Fri** 0700–1800 **Sat** Closed **Sun** Closed

Poplar 2000 Services – Lymm Truckstop

600 M6 J20 or M56 J9

Cliffe Lane, Lymm, Cheshire WA13 0SP
+44 (0)1925 757777
www.moto-way.co.uk
SJ66578481 183 E11
From M6 J20 or M56 J9, follow signs for services.

Mon 24hr **Tue** 24hr **Wed** 24hr **Thu** 24hr **Fri** 24hr **Sat** 24hr **Sun** 24hr

Mon 24hr **Tue** 24hr **Wed** 24hr **Thu** 24hr **Fri** 24hr **Sat** 24hr **Sun** 24hr

Portsmouth truckstop

80 A27

Railway Triangle, Walton Road, Farlington, Portsmouth PO6 1UJ
+44 (0)23 9237 6000
info@portsmouthtruckstop.co.uk
www.portsmouthtruckstop.co.uk
SU67070451 33 G11
From A27 follow signs for Farlington Services.1st left into Walton Road. Bear left, take first right. Site is just before the next bend.

Mon 24hr **Tue** 24hr **Wed** 24hr **Thu** 24hr **Fri** 24hr **Sat** 24hr **Sun** 24hr

Mon 0700–2000 **Tue** 0700–2000 **Wed** 0700–2000 **Thu** 0700–2000 **Fri** 0700–1500 **Sat** 0730–1300 **Sun** Closed

Quernhow A1 Café and Truckstop

P 45 A1

Great North Road, Nr Sinderby, Thirsk, North Yorkshire YO7 4LG
+44 (0)7795 814360
SE33798054 214 C6
On the old A1, about 15 miles south of Scotch Corner. Leave the A1(M) at J50 (northbound) or J51 (southbound).

Mon 0700–1900 Tue 0700–1900 Wed 0700–1900 Thu 0700–1900 Fri 0700–1900 Sat 0700–1300 Sun Closed

Mon 0700–1900 Tue 0700–1900 Wed 0700–1900 Thu 0700–1900 Fri 0700–1900 Sat 0700–1300 Sun Closed
Northbound only

Ranch Café & Cattle Market Lorry Park

P 150 A46

Cattle Market, Old Great North Rd, Newark, Nottinghamshire NG24 1BL +44 (0)1636 611198
SK79525457 172 E3 ·From A1 Carlton-on-Trent, take B1164 east, 1st left Great North Rd 1½ m on right.

Mon 24hr Tue 24hr Wed 24hr Thu 24hr Fri 24hr Sat 24hr Sun 24hr

Mon 0800–2100 Tue 0600–2100 Wed 0600–2100 Thu 0600–2100 Fri 0600–2000 Sat Closed Sun Closed

Red Lion Café & Truckstop

P 150 J16 M1

Weedon Road (A45), Upper Heyford, Northampton, Northamptonshire NN7 4DE
+44 (0)1604 831914
www.redliontruckstop.com
SP68075976 120 F3
From M1 J16, take A45 Northampton. Café in layby of westbound carriageway after 500 yards.

Mon 24hr Tue 24hr Wed 24hr Thu 24hr Fri 24hr Sat 24hr Sun 24hr

Mon 0630–2300 Tue 0630–2300 Wed 0630–2300 Thu 0630–2300 Fri 0630–2300 Sat 0630–2300 Sun 0630–2300

Redbeck Motel

P 40 M62 J31

Doncaster Road, Crofton, Wakefield, West Yorkshire WF4 1RR
+44 (0)1924862730
www.redbecksite11.com
SE36611882 197 D11
The site is on the A638, 2 miles east of Wakefield city centre.

Mon 24hr Tue 24hr Wed 24hr Thu 24hr Fri 24hr Sat 24hr Sun 24hr

Mon 24hr Tue 24hr Wed 24hr Thu 24hr Fri 24hr Sat 24hr Sun 24hr

Smokey Joe's Café

P 20 A30 (½/1 mile)

Blackwater, Nr Redruth, Cornwall TR16 5BJ +44 (0)1209 821810
SW72584486 4 G4
From A30 eastbound take A3047 Scorrier. At roundabout take unmarked road parallel to A30 for ½ miles. Westbound, take A3047 (also marked A307, B397, B398). At first junction turn right and cross over the A30. Bear round to right and at roundabout take unmarked road parallel to A30 for ½ miles.

Mon 0700–2200 Tue 0700–2200 Wed 0700–2200 Thu 0700–2200 Fri 0700–2200 Sat 0700–2200 Sun 0700–2200

Mon 0700–2200 Tue 0700–2200 Wed 0700–2200 Thu 0700–2200 Fri 0700–2200 Sat 0700–2200 Sun 0700–2200

South Mimms Truckstop

P 120 M25 J23

St Albans Road, South Mimms, Potters Bar, Hertfordshire EN6 6NE
+44 (0)1707 649998
mimms.truckstop@welcome-break.co.uk
www.welcomebreak.co.uk
TL22810045 86 E2
Leave the M25 at Junction 23 and follow signs for 'lorry services'

Mon 24hr Tue 24hr Wed 24hr Thu 24hr Fri 24hr Sat 24hr Sun 24hr

Mon 24hr Tue 24hr Wed 24hr Thu 24hr Fri 24hr Sat 24hr Sun 24hr

Square Deal Café

P 20 A4

Bath Road, Knowl Hill, Nr Reading, Berkshire RG10 9UR
+44 (0)1628 822426
info@squaredealcafe.com
www.squaredealcafe.com
SU82287948 65 D10
2½ miles east of Twyford on the A4.

Mon 0630–1430 Tue 0630–1430 Wed 0630–1430 Thu 0630–1430 Fri 0630–1430 Sat Closed Sun Closed

Mon 0630–1430 Tue 0630–1430 Wed 0630–1430 Thu 0630–1430 Fri 0630–1430 Sat Closed Sun Closed

Standeford Farm Café

P 60 M54 J2 (2½ miles)

Streamway Hooks, Stafford Road, Standeford, West Midlands WV10 7BN
+44 (0)1902 790389
SJ91160797 133 B8
M54 J2, take A449 Stafford for 2½ miles

Mon 0545–1930 Tue 0545–1930 Wed 0545–1930 Thu 0545–1930 Fri 0545–1930 Sat 0545–1400 Sun Closed

Mon 0545–1930 Tue 0545–1930 Wed 0545–1930 Thu 0545–1930 Fri 0545–1930 Sat 0545–1400 Sun Closed

Stibbington Diner

P 52 A1

2 Old North Road, Stibbington, Peterborough PE8 6LR
+44 (0)1780 782891
stibbycafe@btconnect.com
TL08769829 137 D11
The site is adjacent to the A1 south-bound south of Wansford. Follow Nene Valley Railway then services signs from A1.

Mon 0600–2400 Tue 24hr Wed 24hr Thu 24hr Fri 24hr Sat 2400–1400 Sun Closed

Mon 0600–2400 Tue 24hr Wed 24hr Thu 24hr Fri 24hr Sat 2400–1400 Sun Closed

Sue's Pitstop Café

P 40 M1 J46 (4 miles) A1M J42 (2 miles)

Unit 4 Ledston Luck Enterprise Park, Ridge Road, Kippax, Leeds, West Yorkshire LS25 7BF
+44 (0)113 2863307
SE42953073 206 G4
From M1 J4,6 take A63 Selby. After 3½ miles, take the A656 Castleford. Turn left after ½ miles. From A1(M) J42 or A1, take A63 Leeds. After 1½ miles turn left onto A656 Castleford. Turn left after ½ miles.

Mon 0700–1500 Tue 0700–1500 Wed 0700–1500 Thu 0700–1500 Fri 0700–1500 Sat 0700–1100 Sun Closed

Mon 0700–1500 Tue 0700–1500 Wed 0700–1500 Thu 0700–1500 Fri 0700–1500 Sat 0700–1100 Sun Closed

Super Sausage Café

P 20 A5 J15–15A

A5 Watling Street, Potterspury, Towcester, Northamptonshire NN12 7QD
+44 (0)1908 542964
gail@supersausagecafe.co.uk
www.supersaugecafe.co.uk
SP74944376 102 C4
On A5 between Stony Stratford and Towcester, 1km north of Potterspury

Mon 0700–1445 Tue 0700–1445 Wed 0700–1445 Thu 0700–1445 Fri 0700–1445 Sat 0700–1445 Sun 0700–1445

Mon 0700–1445 Tue 0700–1445 Wed 0700–1445 Thu 0700–1445 Fri 0700–1445 Sat 0700–1445 Sun 0700–1445
Hours may vary during events at Silverstone.

Swindon Truckstop

P 80 M4 J15 and A419

A420, Oxford Road, Swindon, Wiltshire SN3 4ER
+44 (0)1793 824812
enquiries@swindontruckstop.co.uk
www.swindontruckstop.co.uk
SU18808642 63 B7
From M4 J15 take A419 north then the A420. Use the Sainsbury service road to enter site.

Mon 0600–2100 Tue 0600–2100 Wed 0600–2100 Thu 0600–2100 Fri 0600–2100 Sat 0600–2100 Sun 0600–2100

Mon 0600–2000 Tue 0600–2000 Wed 0600–2000 Thu 0600–2000 Fri 0600–2000 Sat 0600–2000 Sun 0600–2000

The Avon Lodge

P 60 M5 J18

Third Way, Avonmouth, Bristol, Avon BS11 9YP
+44 (0)117 9827706
avonlodge@btconnect.com
ST52227868 60 D4
From M5 J18, head towards Avonmouth. Third Way is reached via Avonmouth Way.

Mon 0700–2300 Tue 0600–2300 Wed 0600–2300 Thu 0600–2300 Fri 0600–2300 Sat 0600–1100 Sun Closed

Mon 0700–2300 Tue 0700–2300 Wed 0700–2300 Thu 0700–2300 Fri 0700–2300 Sat 0600–1100 Sun Closed

The Old Willoughby Hedge Café

P 15 A303

A303 Layby, West Knoyle, Salisbury, Wiltshire BA12 6AQ
+44 (0)1963 371099 or 01747 830803 (café)
lcvreg@aol.com
ST86313350 45 G11
The site is on the westbound side of the A303, 3 miles to the east of Mere.

Mon 0800–1800 Tue 0800–1800 Wed 0800–1800 Thu 0800–1800 Fri 0800–1800 Sat 0800–1800 Sun 1000–1700

Mon 0800–1800 Tue 0800–1800 Wed 0800–1800 Thu 0800–1800 Fri 0800–1800 Sat 0800–1800 Sun 1000–1700

The Salt Box Café

P 30 A50 (1 mile)

No.2, Derby Road, Hatton, Derbyshire DE65 5PT
+44 (0)1283 813189
SK21733080 152 C4
From A50, take A511 for Burton-on-Trent. Site is on right after 1 mile. HGVs should access from A511, not main entrance.

Mon 0500–2000 Tue 0800–2200 Wed 0600–2400 Thu 0600–2400 Fri 0800–1400 Sat 0700–1700 Sun Closed

Mon 0500–2000 Tue 0800–2200 Wed 0600–2400 Thu 0600–2400 Fri 0800–1400 Sat 0700–1700 Sun Closed
Toilets 24hr

The Stockyard Truckstop

P 250 M18 J1 (1 mile)

Hellaby Lane, Hellaby, Rotherham, South Yorkshire S66 8HN
+44 (0)1709 700200/730083
www.thestockyard.co.uk
SK50549331 187 C8 From M18 J1 take A631 Maltby. Left at roundabout, follow for 1 mile site on left.

Mon 0600–2400 Tue 0500–2400 Wed 0500–2400 Thu 0500–2400 Fri 0500–2400 Sat 0600–1000, 1600–2400 Sun 0700–1030, 1200–1600

Mon 0600–2400 Tue 0500–2400 Wed 0500–2400 Thu 0500–2400 Fri 0500–2400 Sat 0600–1000, 1600–2400 Sun 0700–1030, 1200–1600
Food limited Saturday evenings

The Truckstop Café (Crawley Crossing Bunker Stop)

P 40 M1 J13

Bedford Road, Husborne Crawley, Bedfordshire MK43 0UT
+44 (0)1908 281086
SP95823696 103 D9
From M1 J13 take A4012 Woburn. Site is 300 yards on left.

Mon 24 hours Tue 24 hours Wed 24 hours Thu 24 hours Fri 24 hours Sat 24 hours Sun 24 hours

Mon 0700–2200 Tue 0600–2200 Wed 0600–2200 Thu 0600–2200 Fri 0600–2000 Sat 0700–1200 Sun Closed

Truckers Rest

P 75 M6 J12/11A

A5 Watling Street, Four Crosses, Cannock, Staffordshire WS11 1SF
+44 (0)1543 469183
SJ95740933 133 B9
From M6 J12 take A5 Cannock for 1½ miles, site is on the right.

Mon 0700–2300 Tue 0700–2300 Wed 0700–2300 Thu 0700–2300 Fri 0700–2300 Sat 0600–1600 Sun 0800–1800

Mon 0700–2300 Tue 0700–2300 Wed 0700–2300 Thu 0700–2300 Fri 0700–2300 Sat 0600–1600 Sun 0800–1800

Truckhaven Carnforth

P 250 M6 J35

Scotland Road, Warton, Carnforth, Lancashire LA5 9RQ
+44 (0)1524 736699
www.truckhavencarnforth.co.uk
SD50777171 211 E10
M6 J35 take A601(M), then A6 Carnforth. Site is 600 yards on left.

Mon 24hr Tue 24hr Wed 24hr Thu 24hr Fri 24hr Sat 24hr Sun 24hr

Mon 24hr Tue 24hr Wed 24hr Thu 24hr Fri 24hr Sat 24hr Sun 24hr

Ulceby Truckstop

P 52 A160

Ulceby Road, Ulceby, Immingham, Lincolnshire DN40 3JB
+44 (0)1469 540606
www.truck-stop.co.uk
TA13711546 200 D6 · At junction of A160 and A1077 Ulceby Road

Mon 24hr Tue 24hr Wed 24hr Thu 24hr Fri 24hr Sat 24hr Sun 24hr

Mon 24hr Tue 24hr Wed 24hr Thu 24hr Fri 24hr Sat 24hr Sun 24hr

Watling Street Truckstop

P 60 M1 J9

London Road, Flamstead, St Albans, Hertfordshire AL3 8HA
01582 840215
TL08531508 85 B9
From M1 J9, take A5 Dunstable. The site on the right after 200yds.

Mon 0600–2200 Tue 0600–2200 Wed 0600–2200 Thu 0600–2200 Fri 0600–1930 Sat 0700–1900 Sun 0700–1900

Mon 0600–2200 Tue 0600–2200 Wed 0600–2200 Thu 0600–2200 Fri 0600–1930 Sat 0700–1900 Sun 0700–1900

Whitley Bridge Pallets & Truckstop

P 40 M62 J34

Unit 6 The Malting Industrial Estate, Whitley Bridge, Goole, East Yorkshire DN14 0HH
+44 (0)1977 662881
www.anvsjpallets.co.uk
SE55442285 198 C5
At M62 J34, follow sign for 'local traffic', turn left to ind est before level crossing

Mon 24hr Tue 24hr Wed 24hr Thu 24hr Fri 24hr Sat 24hr Sun 24hr

York Lorry Park

P 30 (night) A64

York Auction Centre, Murton, York, North Yorkshire YO19 5GF
+44 (0)1904 489731
www.york.gov.uk/transport/Parking/lorry_parks
SE65175219 207 C9
At Junction of A64, A1070 and A166, take latter, then take first left (Murton Lane) and follow signs to lorry park. HGVs should not try direct approach from A64 southbound; weight limit.

Mon 1600–0900 Tue 1600–0900 Wed 1600–0900 Thu 1600–0900 Fri 1600–0900 Sat Closed Sun Closed
Last arrivals 2300. Must leave by 0900

Mon 0700–0900 then 1600–2100 Tue 0700–0900 then 1600–2100 Wed 0700–0900 then 1600–2100 Thu 0700–0900 then 1600–2100 Fri 0700–0900 then 1600–2100 Sat Closed Sun Closed

Scotland

Cedar Cafe

A1

Granthouse, Berwickshire TD11 3RP
01361 850371
NT81746571 272 B6
In a layby off the southbound carriageway of the A1 about ½ miles south of Grantshouse.

Mon 0800–2000 Tue 0800–2000 Wed 0800–2000 Thu 0800–2000 Fri 0800–2000 Sat 0800–1700 Sun 0800–2000
Parking is in the adjacent layby.

Eardley International

P 25 A74(M) J19

Old Burnswark Station, Ecclefechan, Lockerbie, Dumfriesshire DG11 3JD
01576 300500
www.eardleyinternational.com
NY18477526 238 B5
From A74(M) J19, take the B7076 Ecclefechan, then follow the signs.

Mon 24hr Tue 24hr Wed 24hr Thu 24hr Fri 24hr Sat 24hr Sun 24hr

Mon 0600–2100 Tue 0600–2100 Wed 0600–2100 Thu 0600–2100 Fri 0600–2100 Sat 0730–1300 Sun Closed
Last food orders taken 2030. To order food in advance, call 07841 996 607.

Horse Shoe Cafe

P 20 A90 Inchture Junction (1 mile)

Abernyte Road, Inchture, Perthshire PH14 9RS
01828 686283
NO27952910 286 E6
From the Inchture Junction of the A90 between Perth and Dundee, take B983 Abernyte for 1 mile. Take 1st exit at roundabout; site is on left.

Mon 0800–2100 Tue 0800–2100 Wed 0800–2100 Thu 0800–2100 Fri 0800–2100 Sat 0800–1500 Sun 0800–1900

Lockerbie Lorry Park / Truck Stop

P 400 A74(M) /J17 (3½ miles)

nr Dinwoodie Mains, Johnstonebridge, Lockerbie, Dumfriesshire DG11 2SL
7768654663
www.lockerbielorrypark.co.uk
NY10468956 248 F4
Northbound A74(M) J17 take B7068 Lockerbie. Cross over the motorway. At the roundabout, take the 1st exit and follow the signs. Southbound, take the B7068 Lockerbie, turn left. At the roundabout take the 1st exit and follow the signs.

Mon 24hr Tue 24hr Wed 24hr Thu 24hr Fri 24hr Sat 24hr Sun 24hr

Mon 0600–2300 Tue 0600–2300 Wed 0600–2300 Thu 0600–2300 Fri 0600–2200 Sat 0800–1500 Sun 0800–1500

Moto Kinross

P 20 M90 J6

Turfhills Tourist Centre, Kinross, Perth and Kinross KY13 7NQ
01577 863123
www.moto-way.com
NO10770276 286 G5 Junction 6 M90

Mon 24hr Tue 24hr Wed 24hr Thu 24hr Fri 24hr Sat 24hr Sun 24hr

Mon 24hr Tue 24hr Wed 24hr Thu 24hr Fri 24hr Sat 24hr Sun 24hr

Moto Stirling

P 10 M9 J9/M80 J9

Pirnhall, Stirling FK7 8EU
01786 813614
www.moto-way.com
NS80388866 278 D6
From M9/M80 J9 follow signs to services.

Mon 24hr Tue 24hr Wed 24hr Thu 24hr Fri 24hr Sat 24hr Sun 24hr

Mon 24hr Tue 24hr Wed 24hr Thu 24hr Fri 24hr Sat 24hr Sun 24hr

Motorgrill Ballinluig

P 25 A827

Ballinluig Services, Pitlochry, Perthshire PH9 0LG
01796 482212
www.ballinluigservices.co.uk
NN97715266 286 B3
Off A9 at the A827 junction - 20 miles north of Perth

Mon 0700–2200 Tue 0700–2200 Wed 0700–2200 Thu 0700–2200 Fri 0700–2200 Sat 0700–2200 Sun 0700–2200

Mon 0800–2030 Tue 0800–2030 Wed 0800–2030 Thu 0800–2030 Fri 0800–2030 Sat 0800–2030 Sun 0800–2030

Muirpark Truckstop

✕ 🛏 ♿ ♨ 📺 ⛽ 🅿 25
🅰 M9 J9/M80 J9 (2¼ miles)

✉ Falkirk Road, Bannockburn, Stirling FK7 8AL
☎ 01786 818866
NS82038916 278 D6
From M9 J9/M80 J9, take the A91 Stirling. After 1½ miles, take 3rd exit at roundabout (Falkirk Road). Site is ¾ miles on left.

🕐 Mon 24hr Tue 24hr Wed 24hr Thu 24hr Fri 24hr Sat 24hr Sun 24hr

✕ Mon 0600–2000 Tue 0600–2000 Wed 0600–2000 Thu 0600–2000 Fri 0630–1400 Sat Closed Sun Closed

Red Moss Truck Stop

✕ ♿ ♨ 📺 ⛽ 🚩 🅿 35
🅰 M74 J11 (5 miles; A74(M) J13 (4 miles)

✉ Carlisle Road (Old A74) by Crawfordjohn, S Lanarkshire ML12 6SX ☎ 07831 571856
🖥 www.redmoss.wordpress.com/truck-stop · NS87412704 259 D9
Southbound, from M74 J11 take the B7078 (A70) Edinburgh. After 1½ miles, take the A70 Douglas, pass under the M74, cross over the roundabout and take the 1st left onto the B7078 for 3½ miles. Northbound, from M74 J13 take the A702 Edinburgh, B7078 Douglas for 4 miles.

🕐 Mon 0500–2300 Tue 0500–2300 Wed 0500–2300 Thu 0500–2300 Fri 0500–2300 Sat 1300–2300 Sun 1300–2300

✕ Mon 0500–2300 Tue 0500–2300 Wed 0500–2300 Thu 0500–2300 Fri 0500–2300 Sat 1300–2300 Sun 1300–2300

Roadchef Annandale Water

✕ 🛏 ♿ ♨ ⛽ ♨ 📺
🅿 35 🅰 A74(M) J16

✉ Johnstonebridge Lockerbie, Dumfriesshire DG11 1HD
☎ 01576 470870
🖥 www.roadchef.com
NY10349257 248 E4
Follow signs from A74M J16.

🕐 Mon 24hr Tue 24hr Wed 24hr Thu 24hr Fri 24hr Sat 24hr Sun 24hr

✕ Mon 24hr Tue 24hr Wed 24hr Thu 24hr Fri 24hr Sat 24hr Sun 24hr

Roadchef Bothwell (southbound)

✕ 🛏 ♿ ♨ 📺
🅿 35 🅰 M74 J4/J5

✉ M74 Southbound, Bothwell, S Lanarkshire G71 8BG
☎ 01698 854123
🖥 www.roadchef.com
NS70915978 268 D4
On M74 between M74 J4 and J5.

🕐 Mon 24hr Tue 24hr Wed 24hr Thu 24hr Fri 24hr Sat 24hr Sun 24hr

✕ Mon 24hr Tue 24hr Wed 24hr Thu 24hr Fri 24hr Sat 24hr Sun 24hr

Roadchef Hamilton (northbound)

✕ 🛏 ♿ ♨ ⛽ ♨ 💷 ♨ 📺
🅿 25 🅰 M74 J6

✉ M74 Northbound, Hamilton, South Lanarkshire ML3 6JW
☎ 01698 282176
🖥 www.roadchef.com
NS72495675 268 D4
Signposted from M74, 1 mile north of J6

🕐 Mon 24hr Tue 24hr Wed 24hr Thu 24hr Fri 24hr Sat 24hr Sun 24hr

✕ Mon 24hr Tue 24hr Wed 24hr Thu 24hr Fri 24hr Sat 24hr Sun 24hr

Skiach Services

✕ 🛏 ♿ ♨ ⛽ 💷 ♨ 📺 🅿 15
🅰 A9 (2 miles)

✉ 4D Industrial Est, Evanton, Dingwall, Highland IV16 9XJ
☎ 0800 833534
🖥 www.gleaner.co.uk/skiach.html
NH62946773 300 C6
From the A9 north of Inverness, take the B9716 Ardross 2 miles east of the Cromarty Firth Bridge. Take the first left.

🕐 Mon 24hr Tue 24hr Wed 24hr Thu 24hr Fri 24hr Sat 24hr Sun 24hr

✕ Mon 0700–2100 Tue 0700–2100 Wed 0700–2100 Thu 0700–2100 Fri 0700–2100 Sat 0700–2100 Sun 0800–2100

Stracathro Services

✕ 🛏 ♿ ♨ ⛽ ♨ 🅿 80 🅰 A90

✉ Near Brechin, Angus DD9 7PX
☎ 01674 840234
NO62746476 293 G8 · On the A90 between Stonehaven and Dundee.

🕐 Mon 24hr Tue 24hr Wed 24hr Thu 24hr Fri 24hr Sat 24hr Sun 24hr

✕ Mon 0600–2100 Tue 0600–2100 Wed 0600–2100 Thu 0600–2100 Fri 0600–2100 Sat 0600–2000 Sun 0700–2100
Showers are available during the cafe's opening hours.

The Newtonmore Grill

✕ ♿ 📺 🅿 20 🅰 A9

✉ Perth Road, Newtonmore, Inverness-shire PH20 1BB
☎ 01540 673702
NN70999853 291 D9
From the A9 16 miles west of Aviemore, take the B9150 Newtonmore (Perth Road). Site is on the left just before you reach the village.

✕ Mon 1200–1500, 1800–2300
Tue 1200–1500, 1800–2300
Wed 1200–1500, 1800–2300
Thu 1200–1500, 1800–2300
Fri 1200–1500, 1800–2300
Sat 1200–1500, 1800–2300
Sun 1200–1500, 1800–2300

Thurso Overnight Lorry Park

♿ 🔒 🚩 🅿 24 🅰 A9

✉ Riverside Road, Thurso, Highland
ND12006841 310 C5
From A9 northbound, cross the traffic lights, go over the bridge and take the first right. No facilities on-site but the town centre shops, cafés and takaways are only a short walk away.

🕐 Mon 24hr Tue 24hr Wed 24hr Thu 24hr Fri 24hr Sat 24hr Sun 24hr

---

Welcome Break Abington

✕ 🛏 ♿ ♨ ⛽ B 💷 ♨ 📺
🅿 15 🅰 M74 J13

✉ M74. Abington, Biggar, South Lanarkshire ML12 6RG
☎ 01864 502637
🖥 www.welcomebreak.co.uk
NS93052482 259 E10
Signposted from M74/A74(M) J13

🕐 Mon 24hr Tue 24hr Wed 24hr Thu 24hr Fri 24hr Sat 24hr Sun 24hr

✕ Mon 24hr Tue 24hr Wed 24hr Thu 24hr Fri 24hr Sat 24hr Sun 24hr
Restaurant

Welcome Break Gretna

✕ 🛏 ♿ ♨ ⛽ B 💷 ♨ 📺
🅿 40 🅰 A74(M) J22

✉ A74(M) Trunk Road, Gretna Green, Dumfries DG16 5HQ
☎ 01461 337567
🖥 www.welcomebreak.co.uk/motorway-service/gretna-green
NY30576877 239 D8
Signposted from A74(M) J22

🕐 Mon 24hr Tue 24hr Wed 24hr Thu 24hr Fri 24hr Sat 24hr Sun 24hr

✕ Mon 24hr Tue 24hr Wed 24hr Thu 24hr Fri 24hr Sat 24hr Sun 24hr
Restaurant

Westway Lorry Park

♿ 🔒 🚩 🅿 24
🅰 M8 J26 (3 miles) M8 J27 (1 mile)

✉ Westway, Porterfield Road, Paisley, Renfrewshire PA4 8DJ
☎ 0141 8866373
🖥 www.westway-park.com
NS49656704 267 B9
From M8 J26 (westbound), take A8 Renfrew. At 1st roundabout take 3rd exit; at second roundabout take 2nd exit (Glasgow Road); at 3rd roundabout take second exit (Glebe St); after 1 mile, turn left into Paisley Road; after 1 mile, turn right into Porterfield Road. From M8 J27 (eastbound), take A741 Paisley. Take second exit at roundabout. After 1 mile, turn left into Porterfield Road. Site is on left.

🕐 Mon 24hr Tue 24hr Wed 24hr Thu 24hr Fri 24hr Sat 24hr Sun 24hr

---

Wales

Cardiff Gate Services

✕ 🛏 ♿ ♨ ⛽ B 💷 ♨ 📺
🅿 20 🅰 M4 J30

✉ Cardiff Cardiff Gate Business Park, Pontprenau, Cardiff CF23 8RA
☎ 02920 541122
🖥 www.welcomebreak.co.uk
ST21668290 59 C8
Signposted from M4 J30

🕐 Mon 24hr Tue 24hr Wed 24hr Thu 24hr Fri 24hr Sat 24hr Sun 24hr

✕ Mon 24hr Tue 24hr Wed 24hr Thu 24hr Fri 24hr Sat 24hr Sun 24hr

Cardiff West Services

✕ 🛏 ♿ ♨ ⛽ 💷 ♨ 📺
🅿 30 🅰 M4, J33

✉ Pontyclun,, Rhondda CF72 8SA
☎ 02920 891141
🖥 www.moto-way.com
ST09337964 58 D5
M4, J33

🕐 Mon 24hr Tue 24hr Wed 24hr Thu 24hr Fri 24hr Sat 24hr Sun 24hr

✕ Mon 24hr Tue 24hr Wed 24hr Thu 24hr Fri 24hr Sat 24hr Sun 24hr

Harry Tuffins Transport Café

✕ 🛏 ♿ ♨ ⛽ 💷 🅿 🅰 A483

✉ Crosslike Supermarket, Churchstoke, Montgomery, Powys SY15 6AR
☎ 01588 620226
🖥 www.harrytuffin.co.uk
SO27949381 130 E5
From A483 1 mile south of Welshpool take A490 Fron 8½ miles, then take A489 Craven Arms. Site is on right after ¾ miles.

🕐 Mon 0700–1900 Tue 0700–1900 Wed 0700–1900 Thu 0700–2000 Fri 0700–2000 Sat 0700–1930 Sun 0700–1800

🕐 Mon 0800–1600 Tue 0800–1600 Wed 0800–1600 Thu 0800–1600 Fri 0800–1600 Sat 0800–1600 Sun 0800–1600
No hot meals after 14.30; there are no dedicated truck bays, but the car park is large.

Moto Swansea

✕ ♿ ♨ ⛽ B 💷 🅿 35
🅰 M4

✉ Penllergaer, Swansea. SA4 1GT
☎ 01792 896222
🖥 www.moto-way.com
SS62099958 75 F10
Signposted from M4 J47.

🕐 Mon 24hr Tue 24hr Wed 24hr Thu 24hr Fri 24hr Sat 24hr Sun 24hr

✕ Mon 24hr Tue 24hr Wed 24hr Thu 24hr Fri 24hr Sat 24hr Sun 24hr

Roadchef Magor

✕ 🛏 ♿ ♨ ⛽ B ♨ 🅿 25
🅰 M4 J23a

✉ Magor, Caldicot, Monmouthshire NP26 3YL
☎ 01633 881515
🖥 www.roadchef.com
ST42118805 60 B2
Signposted off the M4 J23a

🕐 Mon 24hr Tue 24hr Wed 24hr Thu 24hr Fri 24hr Sat 24hr Sun 24hr

✕ Mon 24hr Tue 24hr Wed 24hr Thu 24hr Fri 24hr Sat 24hr Sun 24hr

Roadchef Pont Abraham

✕ 🛏 ♿ ♨ ⛽ 💷 🅿 20
🅰 M4 J49

✉ Llanedi, Pontarddulais, Carmarthenshire SA4 0FU
☎ 01792 884663
🖥 www.roadchef.com
SN57500734 75 D9
M4 J49

🕐 Mon 24hr Tue 24hr Wed 24hr Thu 24hr Fri 24hr Sat 24hr Sun 24hr

✕ Mon 24hr Tue 24hr Wed 24hr Thu 24hr Fri 24hr Sat 24hr Sun 24hr

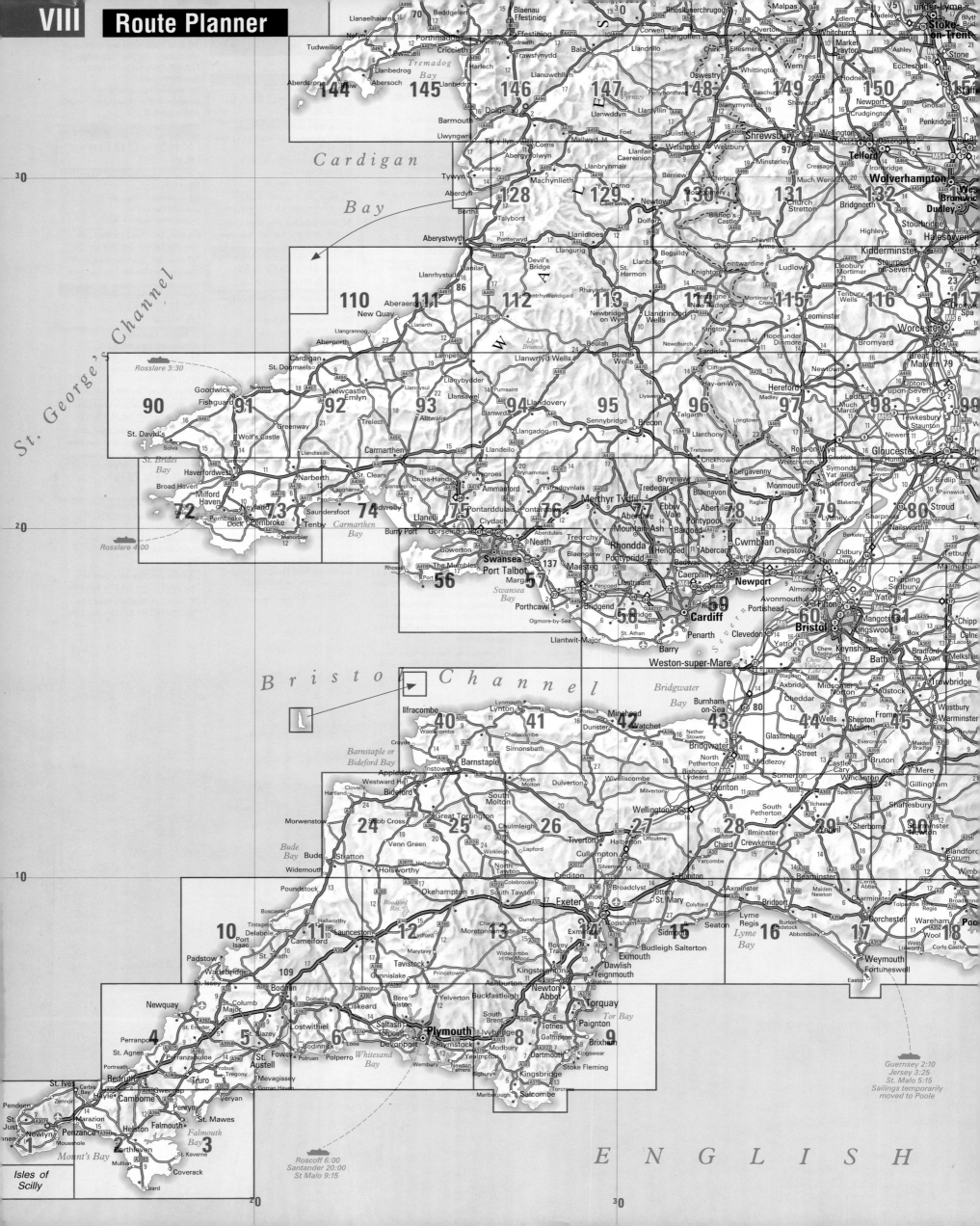

Scale 1:1000000   1cm = 10km   1 inch = 15.78 miles

C H A N N E L

NORTH SEA

Amsterdam 15:30

Rotterdam 10:15
Zeebrugge 12:15

Bridlington Bay

The Wash

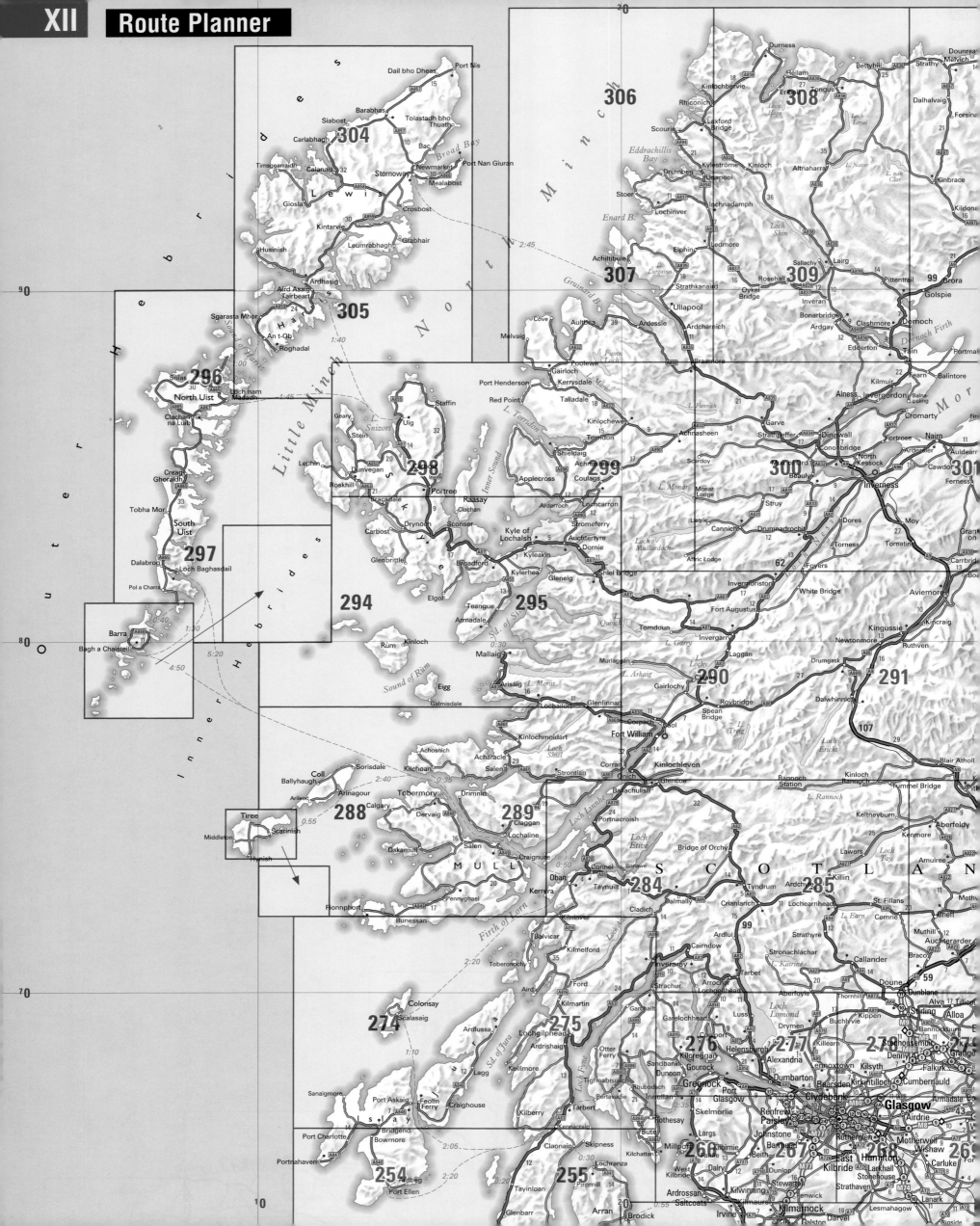

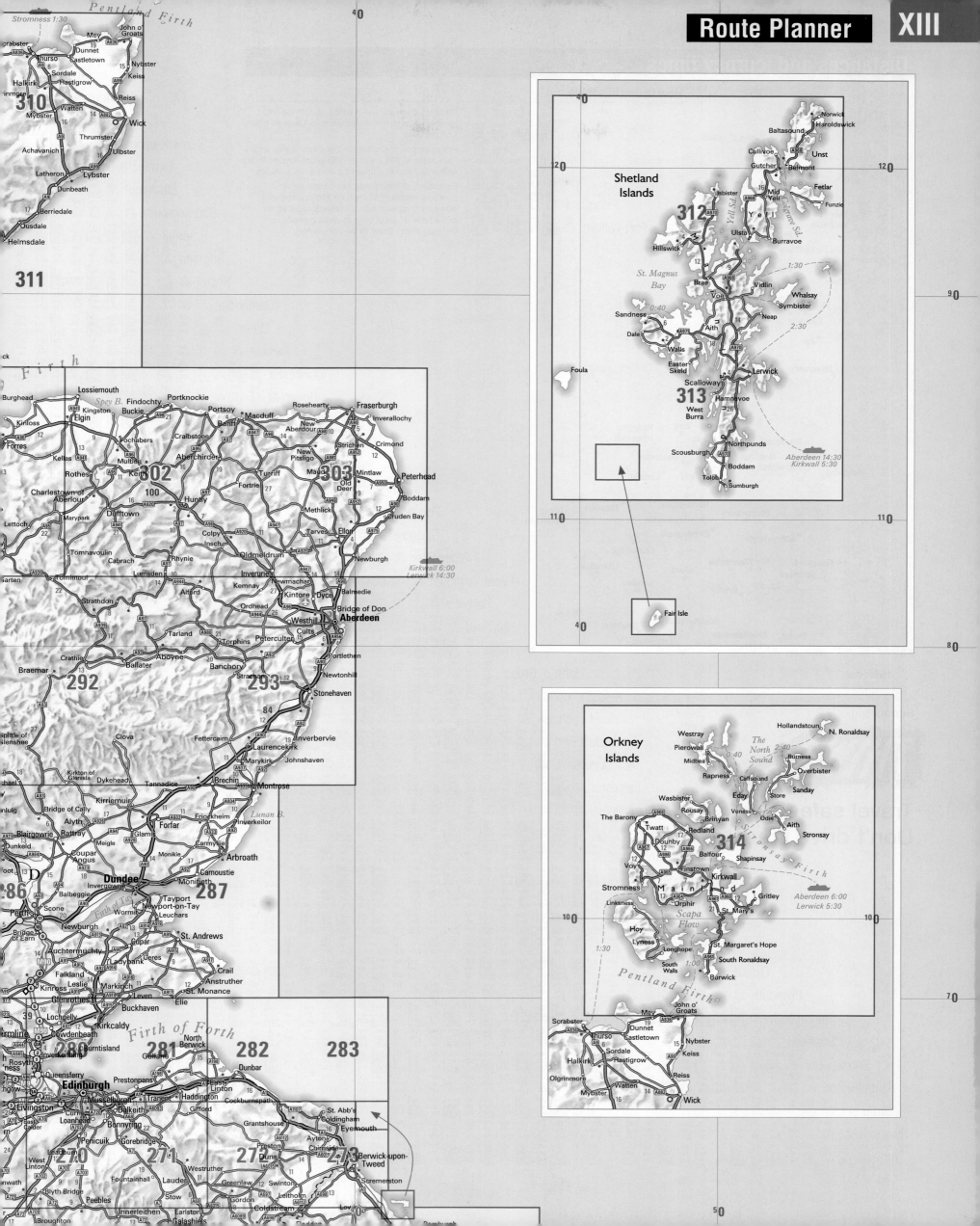

Pentland Firth

Stromness 1:30
Mey
John o'Groats
Crabster
Thurso Castletown Nybster
Sordale Keiss
Halkirk Hastigrow Reiss
Olrigmore
310 Watten Wick
Mybster
Thrumster Ulbster
Achavanich
Latheron Lybster
Dunbeath
Berriedale
Ousdale
Helmsdale

311

Burghead Lossiemouth Portknockie
Kinloss Findochty Portsoy Rosehearty Fraserburgh
Elgin Kingston Buckie Macduff Inverallochy
Forres Fochabers Banff New Aberdour Crimond
Kellas Mulben Craibstone New Pitsligo Maud
Rothes Keith Aberchirder Turriff Mintlaw Peterhead
Charlestown of 302 100 Huntly Fortrie Old Deer A950 Boddam
Aberlour Dufftown 303 Methlick Cruden Bay
Marypark Colpy Tarves Ellon Newburgh
Tomnavoulin Rhynie Insch Oldmeldrum
Cabrach Lumsden Inverurie Newmachar
Tomintoul Alford Kemnay Kintore Dyce Balmedie
Strathdon Ordhead Bridge of Don
Westhill Aberdeen
292 Tarland Torphins Petercultr Cults
Braemar Crathie Aboyne Portlethen
Ballater Banchory 293 Newtonhill
Strachan Stonehaven
84
spittle of
Glenshee Clova Fettercairn Inverbervie
Laurencekirk Johnshaven
Kirkton of Marykirk
Glenisla Dykehead Tannadice Brechin Montrose
Bridge of Cally Kirriemuir Friockheim
Alyth Meigle Glamis Inverkeilor
Blairgowrie Rattray Forfar Lunan B.
Dunkeld Coupar Monikie Carmyllie
Angus Arbroath
286 Scone Invergowrie Dundee 287 Carnoustie
Perth Balbeggie Monifieth
Newburgh Tayport Newport-on-Tay
Bridge of Earn Wormit Leuchars
Auchtermuchty Cupar St. Andrews
M90 Ladybank Ceres
Falkland Crail
Kinross Leslie Markinch Anstruther
Glenrothes Leven St. Monance
Lochgelly Elie
280 Cowdenbeath Kirkcaldy
Dunfermline Burntisland Firth of Forth
280 Inverkeithing 281 282 283
Rosyth Gullane North Berwick
Queensferry Prestonpans Dunbar
Edinburgh Musselburgh East Linton
Livingston Dalkeith Haddington
Currie Tranent Gifford Cockburnspath
Loanhead St. Abb's
270 Penicuik Coldingham
Gorebridge Grantshouse Eyemouth
West Bonnyrigg Ayton
Linton 271 272 Chirnside 273 Berwick-upon-
Leadburn Duns Tweed
Blyth Bridge Fountainhall Lauder Swinton Scremerston
Peebles Greenlaw Leitholm
Broughton Innerleithen Stow Gordon Coldstream
Earlston
Galashiels

Shetland Islands

Norwick
Haroldswick
Baltasound
Cullivoe Unst
Gutcher Belmont
312 Fetlar
Isbister Mid Yell Funzie
Hillswick Ye Burravoe
Ulsta
St. Magnus Brae Vidlin
Bay Voe Whalsay
Sandness Aith Symbister
Dale Neap
Walls A970 Lerwick
Easter 313
Skeld Scalloway
Foula Hamnavoe
West 26
Burra
Scousburgh Northpunds
Boddam Aberdeen 14:30
Toloba Kirkwall 5:30
Sumburgh

Kirkwall 6:00
Lerwick 14:30

Orkney Islands

Westray Hollandstoun
Pierowall The N. Ronaldsay
Midbea North Burness
Rapness Sound Overbister
Wasbister Calfsound Sanday
Eday Store
The Barony Rousay Veness Odie
Twatt Brinyan Aith
Dounby Redland 314 Stronsay
Voy A967 Balfour Shapinsay
Finstown Stronsay
Stromness Mainland Kirkwall Firth
Linksness Orphir Gritley
Hoy St. Mary's Aberdeen 6:00
Scapa St. Margaret's Hope Lerwick 5:30
Lyness Flow
Longhope South Ronaldsay
South Burwick
Walls
Pentland Firth

Scrabster Mey
John o'
Groats
Thurso Dunnet
Castletown
Sordale Nybster
Halkirk Hastigrow Keiss
Olrigmore Reiss
Watten Wick
Mybster

Distances and journey times

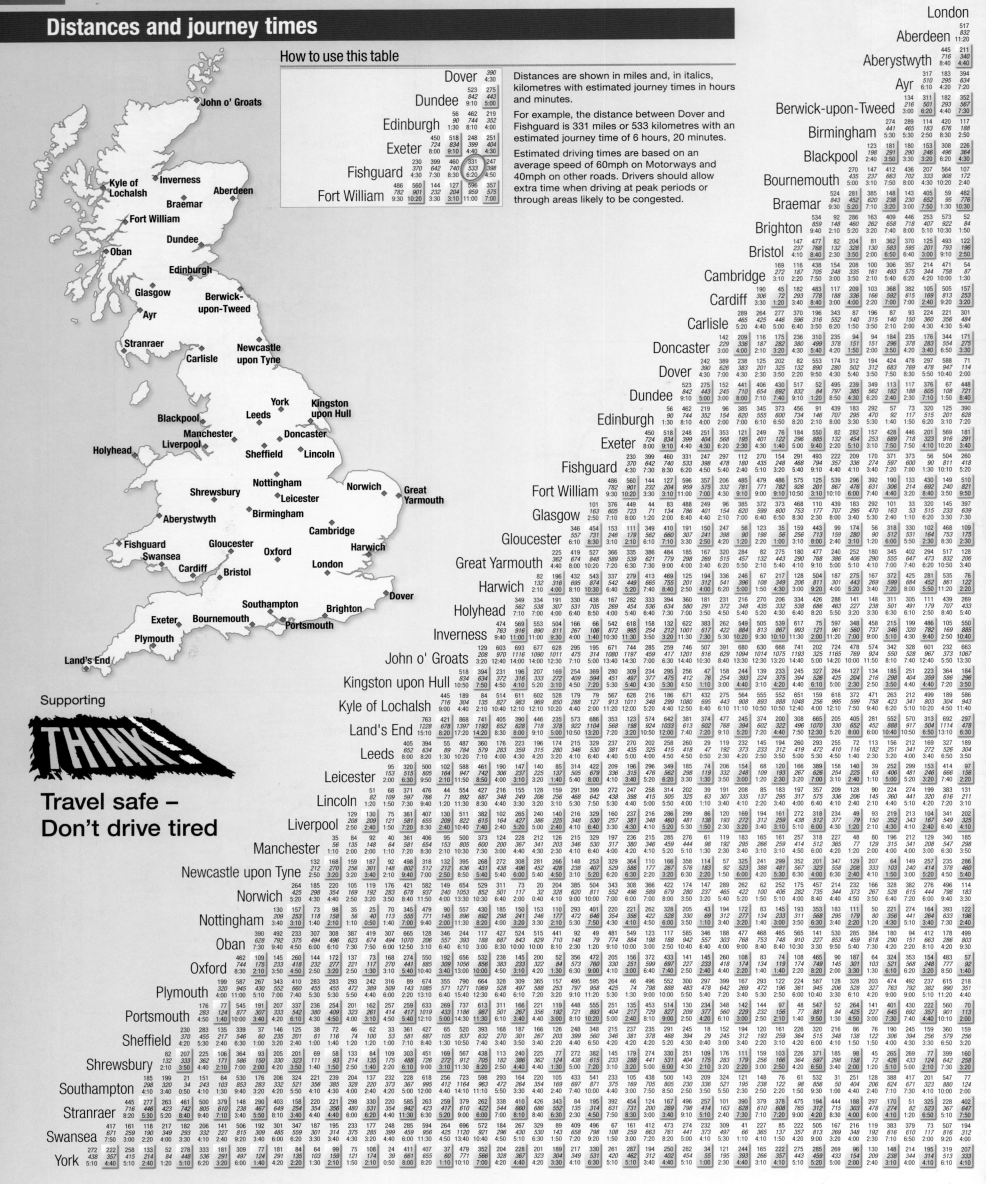

How to use this table

Distances are shown in miles and, in italics, kilometres with estimated journey times in hours and minutes.

For example, the distance between Dover and Fishguard is 331 miles or 533 kilometres with an estimated journey time of 6 hours, 20 minutes.

Estimated driving times are based on an average speed of 60mph on Motorways and 40mph on other roads. Drivers should allow extra time when driving at peak periods or through areas likely to be congested.

Supporting

THINK!

Travel safe –
Don't drive tired

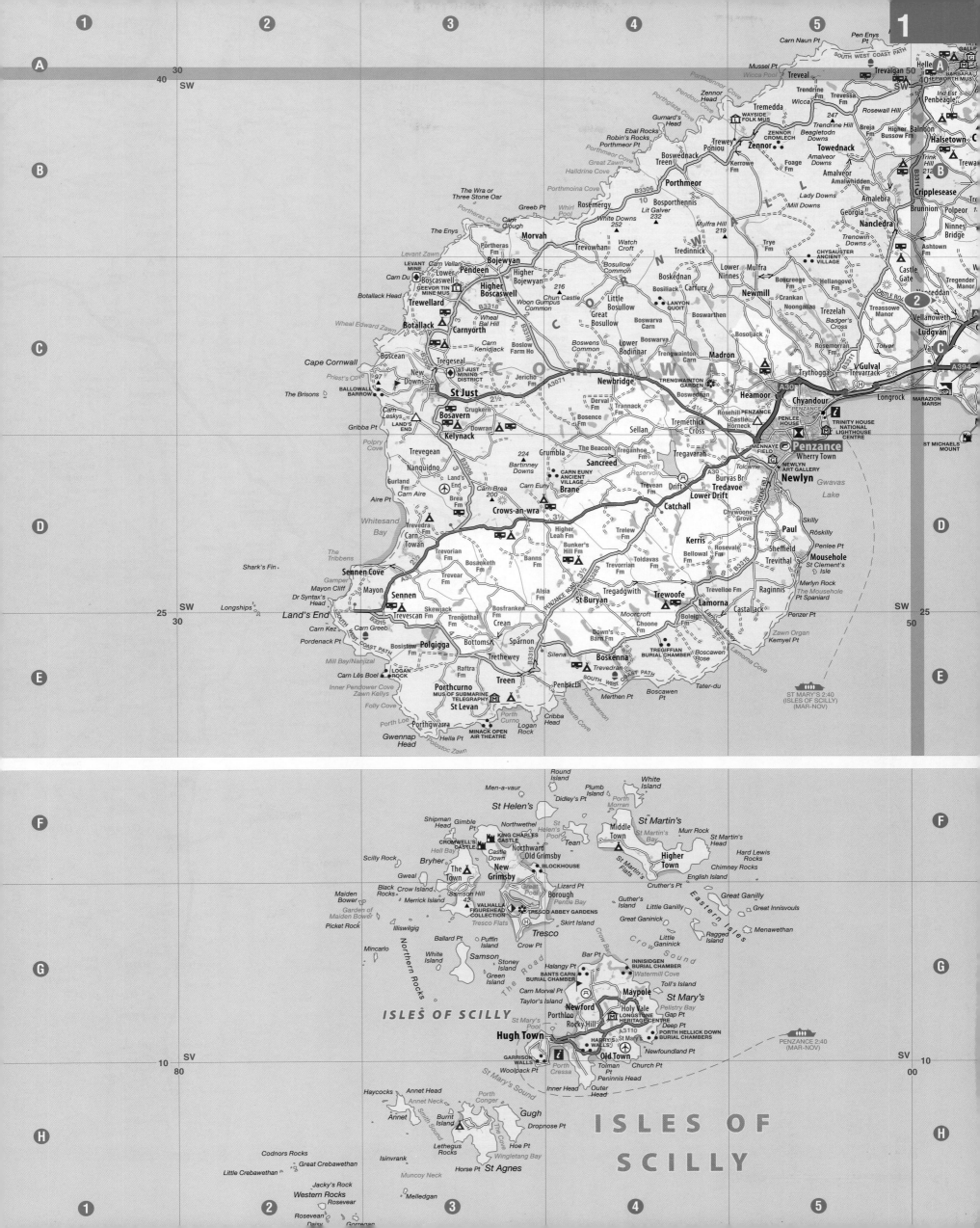

80
00
SW

80

70
SW
80

The Island
Tintagel Head
Gle
Dunderhole Pt
TINTAGEL
Penhallic Pt

Treba
Gull Rock
Port William
Dennis Pt
Backways Cove
Start Pt

Trerubles Cove
Tregardock Cliff
Jacket's Pt
Crookmoyle Rock
Delabole Pt
Dannonchapel
We
Port Isaac Bay
Barrett's Zawn
Ranie Pt
Tresungers Pt
SOUTH WEST COAST PATH

Newland
Rumps Pt
The Mouls
Com Head
Varley Head
Scarnor Pt
Reedy Cliff
Lobber Pt
Port Isaac
Port Gaverne
Trewetha
Treore Fm
Pendoggett

Pentire Pt
83
Pentire Fm
Port Quin Bay
Doyden Pt
Carnweather Pt
Trevan Pt
Port Quin
Kellan Head
Pine Haven
Scarrabine Fm
LONG CROSS VICTORIAN GDNS
Trelights
B3267
Poltreworgey
153

Padstow Bay
Pentireglaze Haven
New Polzeath
Trenant
Porteath
Plain Street
Carruan
St Endellion
Pennytinney
Lanow Fm
139
Trelill

Gulland Rock
Pepper Hole
Stepper Pt
The Narrows
Polzeath
Shilla Mill
Gunvenna
Trewiston Fm
Trevanger
Treglyn Down
Tregellist
Trevine
Trequite
Trelill

Butter Hole
Gunver Head
Daymer Bay
Trebetherick
Trebetherick Pt
Pityme
St Minver
Tredrizzick
Treglyn
B3314
Rooke Fm
Trewethern
St Kew
Greater Brighter Fm

Trevose Head
Stinking Cove
Dinas Head
Merope Rocks
Round Hole
Mother Ivey's or Polventon Bay
Harlyn Bay
Porthmissen Bridge
Round Hole
Crugmeer
Tregirls Fm
Harbour Cove
Gun Pt
PRIDEAUX PLACE
Rock
Splatt
Penmayne
Tresfrisa
Blakes Keiro
Carclaze Fm
Chapel Amble
Penpont Fm
Hendra
St Kew Highway
Trevisu Manor
Trewhan

Quies
Toll
Trevone
Trethillick
Treator
Stoptide
Porthilly
Trevelver
Cant Cove
River Camel
Gutt Bridge
Lower Amble
Tregorden
Kelly
Rocksea Fm
Dinham's Br
Trebel

Booby's Bay
Constantine Bay
Constantine Bay
Harlyn
Windmill
7.0
Ind Est
B3276
Padstow
MUSEUM
Town Bar
Porthilly Cove
7.5
Trewornan
A39
A389

Treyarnon Pt
Trethias Island
Warren Cove
Pepper Cove
Fox Cove
Dinas
Dennis Hill
Oldtown
Oldtown Cove
Bodellick
Tregunna
Perlees Fm
Burniere
Bodieve
Ball
Three Holes Cross
St Mabyn
Trethic

Minnows Islands
Will's Rock
Trescore Islands
Trevorrick
Trehemborne
Carnevas
Shop
St Merryn
Trewithen Fm
Treravel Fm
Sea Mills
Tregonce
Trevorrick
Trevigus
Trevanson
Edmonton
Dunveth
Ind Est
10
Hingham Mill
Trevilder

Porth Mear
Porthcothan
Trevethan
Trevean
Highlanes
Burgois
Tregonna
CORNWALL
Penhale
Whitecross
Wadebridge
St Breock
Egloshayle
Clapper
Sladesbridge
Lower Croan
Cranford
PENCARFOW HOUSE

High Cove
Park Head
Trevemedar
Trevio
Lewidden Fm
St Merryn Airfield (disused)
Treleigh Fm
Little Petherick
Mellingey
St Issey
Trevance
A389
ROYAL CORNWALL SHOWGROUND
17
Trelyll Fm
Polmorla
Tredinnick
Treraven
River
Costislost
Bozion Fm
Costislost
Plantn
Trescowe Brake
Park

Diggory's Island
Queen Bess Rock
BEDRUTHEN STEPS
Tregona
Gollan
Trerair Fm
Treburrick
Penrose
Treglinnick
Pentruse
St Ervan
Rumford
Tredinnick
Blable Ho
Pawton Manor Fm
Hay
Pengelly Fm
Bishop's Wood
Polgeel Wood
Burlorne Tregoose
Polbrock
Washaway
Lane-end

4
wnhill
St Eval Airfield (disused)
Trevisker Fm
Bogee Fm
St Jidgey
Cannalidgey
Scotland Corner
208
Costislost
LON NE
5
urlawn
Mount Charles

0 1 2 3miles
0 1 2 3 4 5 km

High Cove
Trenance Pt
Bear's Downs
Long Stone
St Eval
Trelow Downs
GREATLY GREAT ADVENTURE PARK
LON NE
5
Higher Cransworth
Brocton
Penaligon Downs

2
3
4
5
6
Trenance
Bogee Common
A39
Great Grogley
3

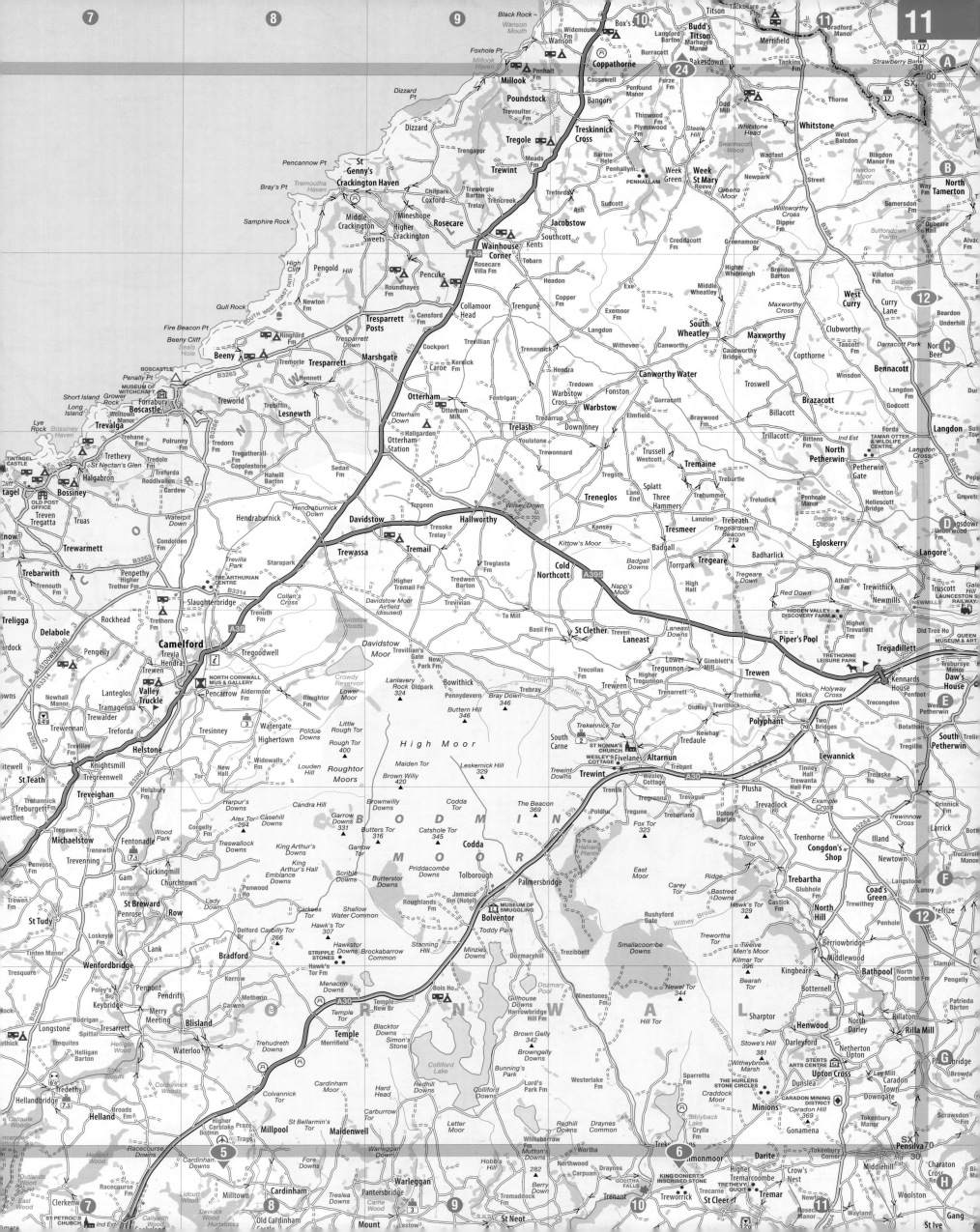

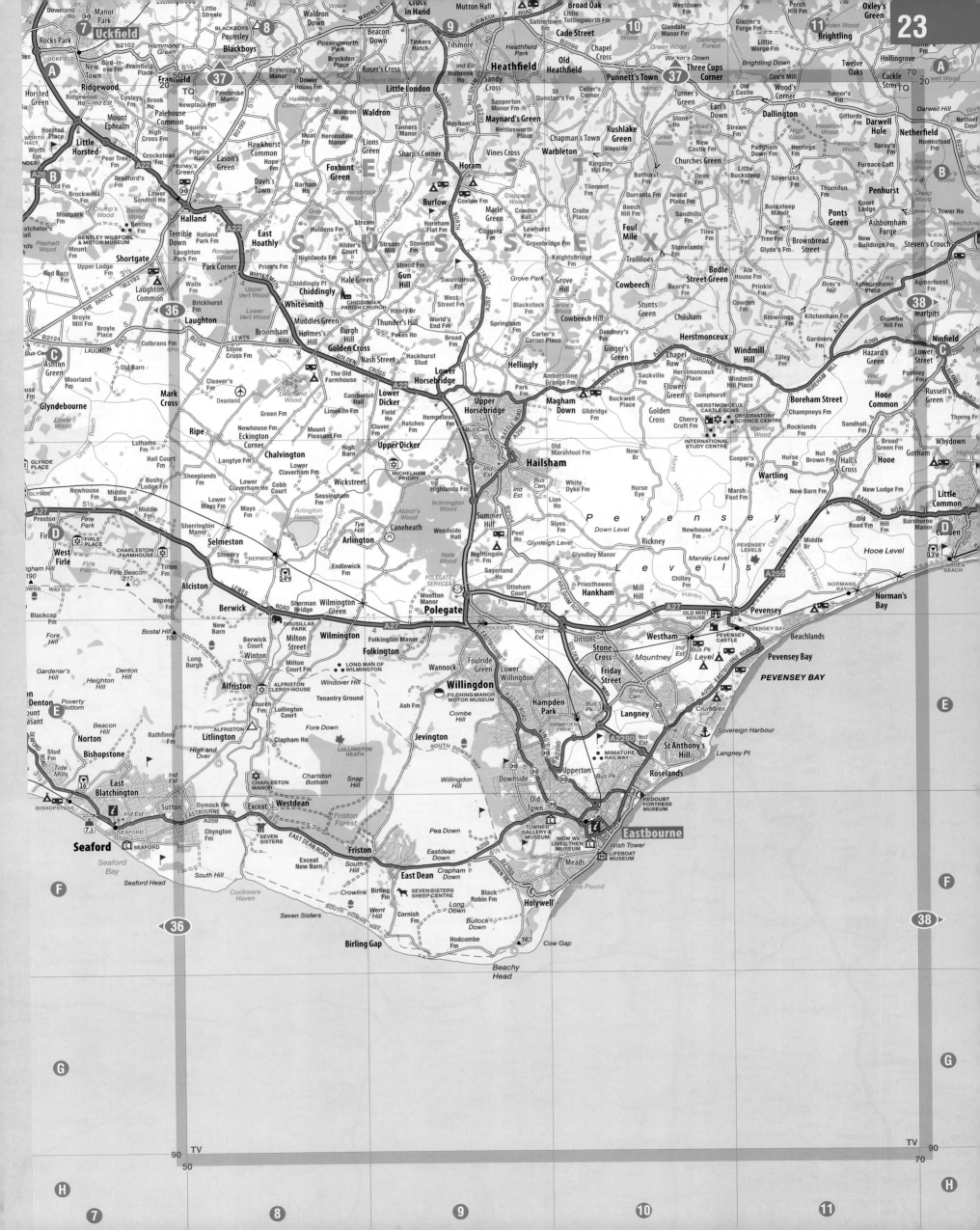

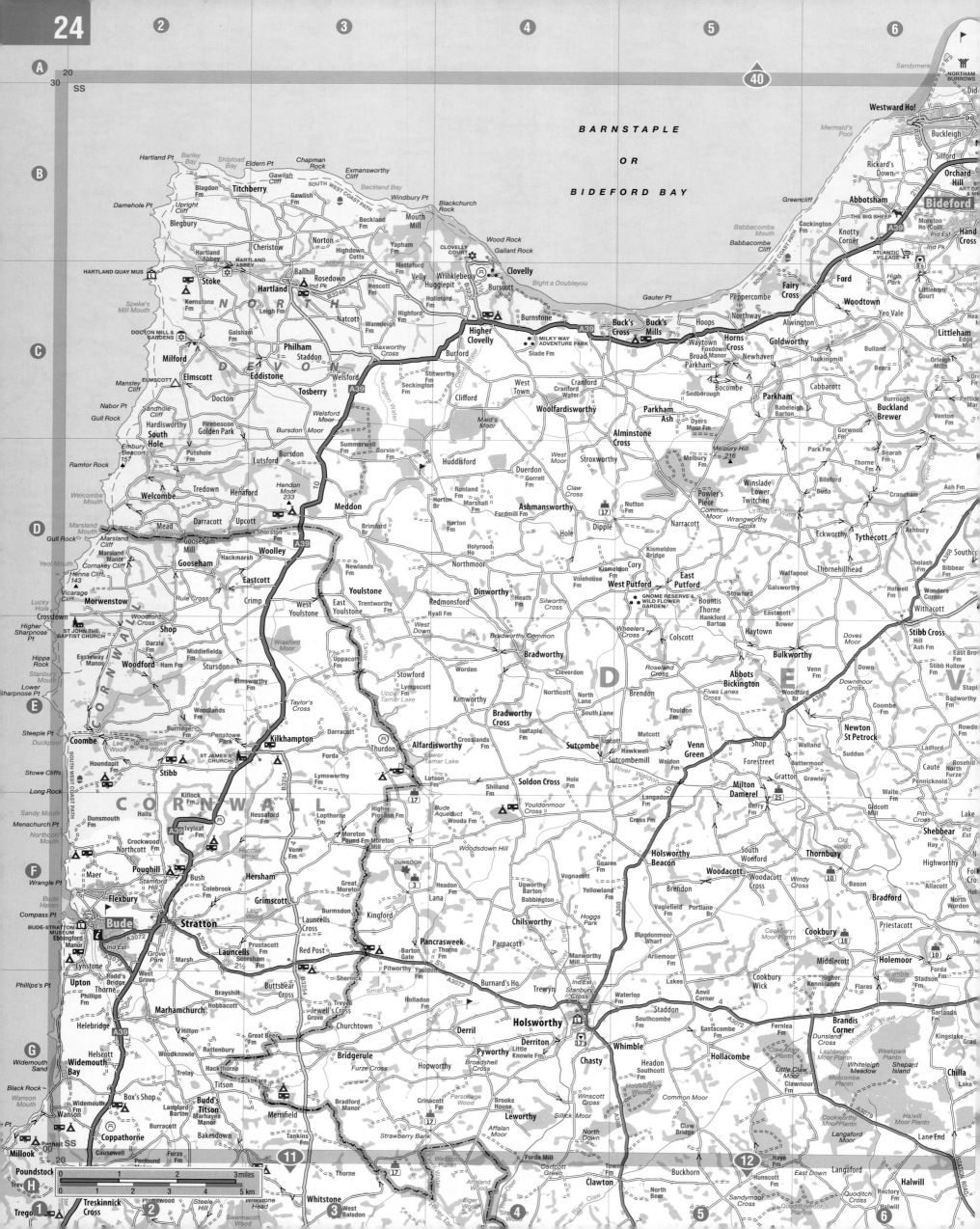

A
40
60
SS

B

C

Hen & Chickens
North West Pt
Seals' Rock
North East Pt
Gannets' Rock
Gannets' Bay
St James's Stone
LUNDY MARINE NATURE RESERVE
Jenny's Cove
Tibbetts Hill 138▲
Tibbett's Pt
Lundy
Dead Cow Pt
Ackland's Moor 142▲
Lundy Roads
45
BIDEFORD 2:00 (MAR-OCT)
ILFRACOMBE 2:00 (MAR-OCT)
45
Halftide Rock
Beacon Hill
Castle Hill
Rat Island
Surf Pt
South West Pt
15   SS
15

D
LUNDY 2:00 (MAR-OCT)
Capstone Pt
Samson's Bay
Water Mouth
WATERMOUTH CASTLE
Rawn's Rocks
Blackstone Pt
Trentishoe
SOUTH WEST COAST PATH
South Dean Pt
Elwill Bay
Highv
Hele Bay
Little Hangman 218
Gt Hangman 318
Holdstone Down 349
Trentishoe Down
Ilfracombe
MUSEUM
Hele
Hole Fm
Hangman Pt
Holdstone Fm
Trentishoe Manor
Walner
Hea
Bull Pt
Pensport Rock
Shag Pt
Flat Pt
Chambercombe
OLD CORN MILL
Goosewell
Lester Cliff
Girt Fm
Girt Down
Holdstone
Knap Down
Verwill
Tattiscombe
Lee Bay
Lincombe
CHAMBERCOMBE MANOR
Kitstone Hill
Berrynarbor
Lee
NORTH DEVON
Nutcombe Fm Westleigh
Truckham
Dean
Cowley Wood
Rockham Bay
Lee
Higher Slade
Warmscombe
Sterridge
Ruggaton Fm
Stoneditch Hill
LON
FM LANE

D (cont)
Morte Pt
North Morte Fm
Higher Warcombe
Whitestone
Higher Slade
Lower Slade
Slade Resrs
Oakridge Fm
Bowden Fm
Smythen Fm
Henstridge
WILDLIFE & DINOSAUR PARK
South Ley
Kentisbury
Higher Kentisbury Fm
Mortehoe
Shaftsboro Fm
Campscott Fm
Two Pots
Hempster Fm
A3123
Kentisbury Down
Preston Ho
Bridwick
Borough Cross
Little Shelfin Fm
Ind Est
2 A3123
Hore Down
Stapleton Fm
Berry Down Cross
River Yeo
Cleave Fm
Bugford Stonecombe
A39
Grunta Pool
Borough Fm
Manor Fm
Trimstone
Outer Narracott
Berry Down
Highlands
Patchole
Northcote Fm
Kentisbury Ford
Halls Cross
Wistlandpound Reservoir

E
Woolacombe
Mill Rock
Ossaborough
Ivycott
Willingcott
Cheglinch
Hillcrest Fm
Centery Fm
Collacott
Wigmore Fm
Dingles Fm
Clifton
East Down
Arlington Beccott
Huckham
Besshill
Exmo
Morte Bay
Roadway
Dean
Dean Cross
Higher Aylescott
Bittadon
Fullabrook
Burland Fm
Little Silver
Hewish Down
Bowden Corner
Churchill
Churchill Down
Arlington
White Cawsey
Tidicombe
Black Rock
Pickwell Down
Spreacombe Manor
North Downs
West Down
Fullabrook Down
Metcombe Down
ARLINGTON COURT
Garman's Down
Deerpark Wood
Rye Park
Putsborough Sand
Castle Street Fm
Buckland Fm
Stoneyard Wood
Okewill Cross
Loxhore Cott

F
Baggy Pt
SOUTH WEST COAST PATH
Vention
Pickwell
Buckland Cross
Winsham Down Ho
Halsinger Down
Beara Down
Patsford
Swindon Down
Viveham Fm
Plaistow Barton
Milltown
Whitefield Down
South Woolley
Loxhore
Croyde Bay
Putsborough
Georgeham
North Buckland
Gipsy Corner
Whiddon
Muddiford
The Warren
Chilbridge
Lower Loxhore
Ora Hill
Croyde
Forda
Darracott
Nethercott
Upcott
Halsinger
Winsham
Beara
Middle Marwood
Crockers
Higher Muddiford
Plaistow Mill
South Hill
Waytown Fm
Sepscott Fm
Shirwell
Brightlycott
Chelfham
Horridge
Stoke Rivers
Croyde Bay
South Hole Fm
Buckland Manor
Knowle
Boode
Marwood
Whitehall
MARWOOD HILL
Kingsheanton
Shirwell Cross
Bratton Flemi
CROYDE ROAD   SAUNTON   ROAD 4½
Lobb
Pippacott
Luscott Barton
Waterlake
Prixford
BROOMHILL SCULPTURE GARDENS
Varley Fm
Youlston Wood
Bratton Cross
B5231
Saunton
Sandy Lane Fm
Braunton
Shop Cent
Braunton Down
Mainstone
West Ashford
Springfield Cross
Guineaford
Burridge
Kingdon's Gardens
Northleigh
Birch

G
Saunton Sands
ELLIOT GALLERY
Heanton Punchardon
Velator
Wrafton
Chivenor
A361 5
Ashford
Upcott Ho
Bradiford
Pilton
Pottington Ind Est
Derby
Waytown
Goodleigh
Middle Dean Fm
Hutcherton Down
Braunton Burrows
Braunton Marsh
Penhill Pt
SOUTH WEST COAST PATH
Youlden Ho
Coombe Willeshigh
Dean Head
Gunn
Stone Cross
Airy Pt
Horsey Island
Allen's Rock
Saltpill Duck Pond
BARNSTAPLE
MUSEUM OF BARNSTAPLE & NORTH DEVON
Bus Stn
Westacott
Birch
Accott
Danger area
ST ANNE'S CHAPEL & MUSEUM
P&R
Newport
Portmor
East Acland
Sandick
Sandick Cross
LUNDY 2:00 (MAR-OCT)
River Taw
Muddlebridge
BICKINGTON ROAD
A3125
Lake 1½
Rumsam
Landkey
Harford
Hurscott

H
Crow Rock
Broad Sands
Instow Sands
Yelland
Lower Yelland
Fremington
Combrew
Bickington
Ind Est
Sticklepath
Bishops Tawton
Landkey Newland
Swimbridge Newland
Yeoland Ho
Riverton
Bywood Fm
Sandymere
Appledore
N DEVON MARITIME MUSEUM
Instow
The Quay
Worlington
Collacott Fm
Brynsworthy
Upcott Fm
Roundswell
Hollamoor Clump
NORTH DEVON FARM PARK
Lane End Fm
NORTHAM BURROWS
Diddywell
24
River Torridge
Fullingcott
Huish
Eastacombe
Tawstock
25
Swimbridge
Kerscott
High Fm

0   1   2   3 miles
0   1   2   3   4   5 km

Northam
Silford
Rickard's
Westleigh
Holmacott
A39
Horwood
Prospect Corner
St John's Chapel
Rushcott Fm
Stonyland
Uppacott
Halmpstone Manor
Summer Moor
TAPELEY PARK GARDENS
Coombe Fm Trayhill
Huish Moor
A377
Downrew Ho
Horswell Fm
Hannaford
Hangman's Hill

1   2   3   4   5   6

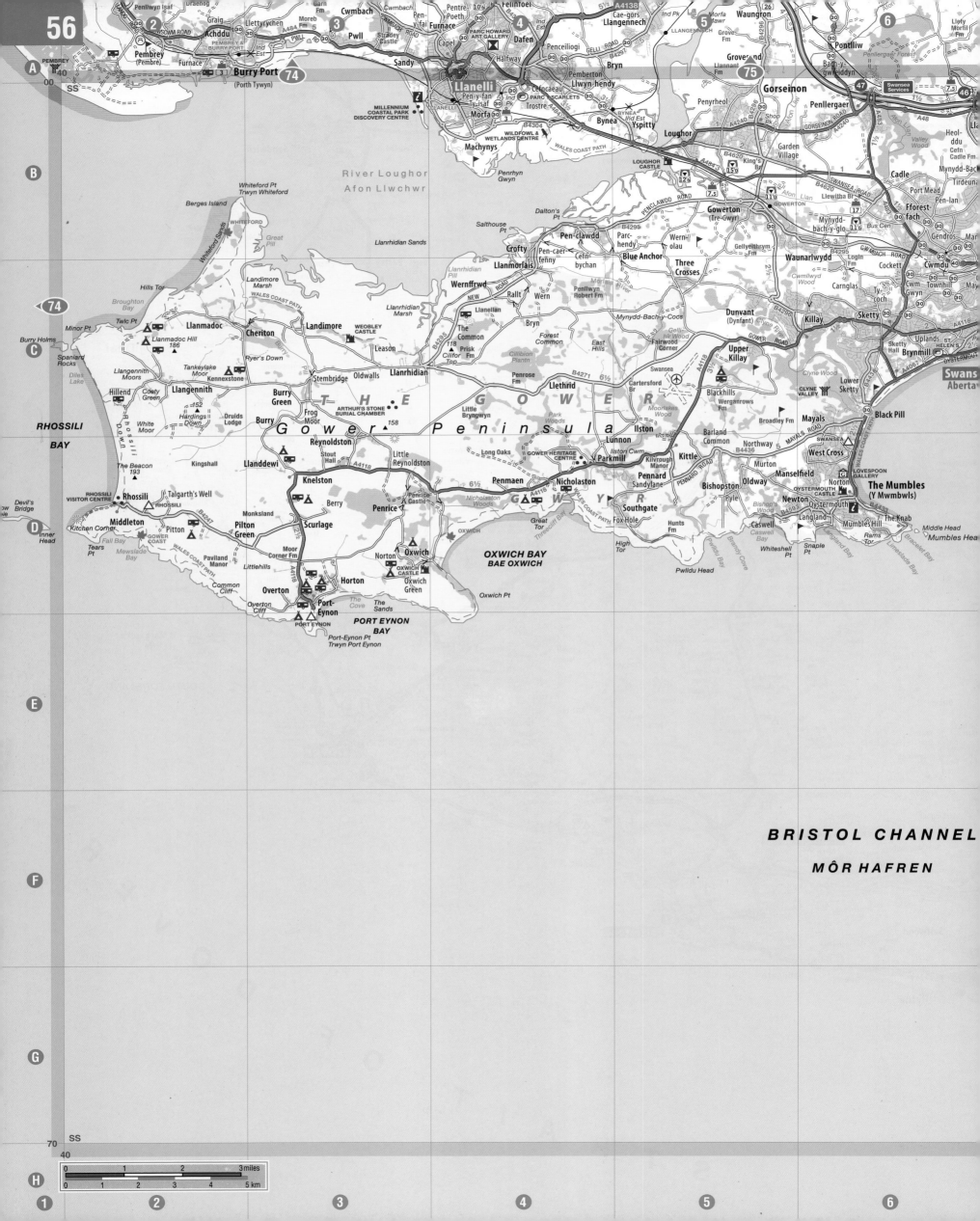

A

00

SS

B

River Loughor
Afon Llwchwr

74

C

RHOSSILI
BAY

D

Inner
Head

THE GOWER

Gower Peninsula

GOWER

E

F

BRISTOL CHANNEL

MÔR HAFREN

G

70

SS

40

H

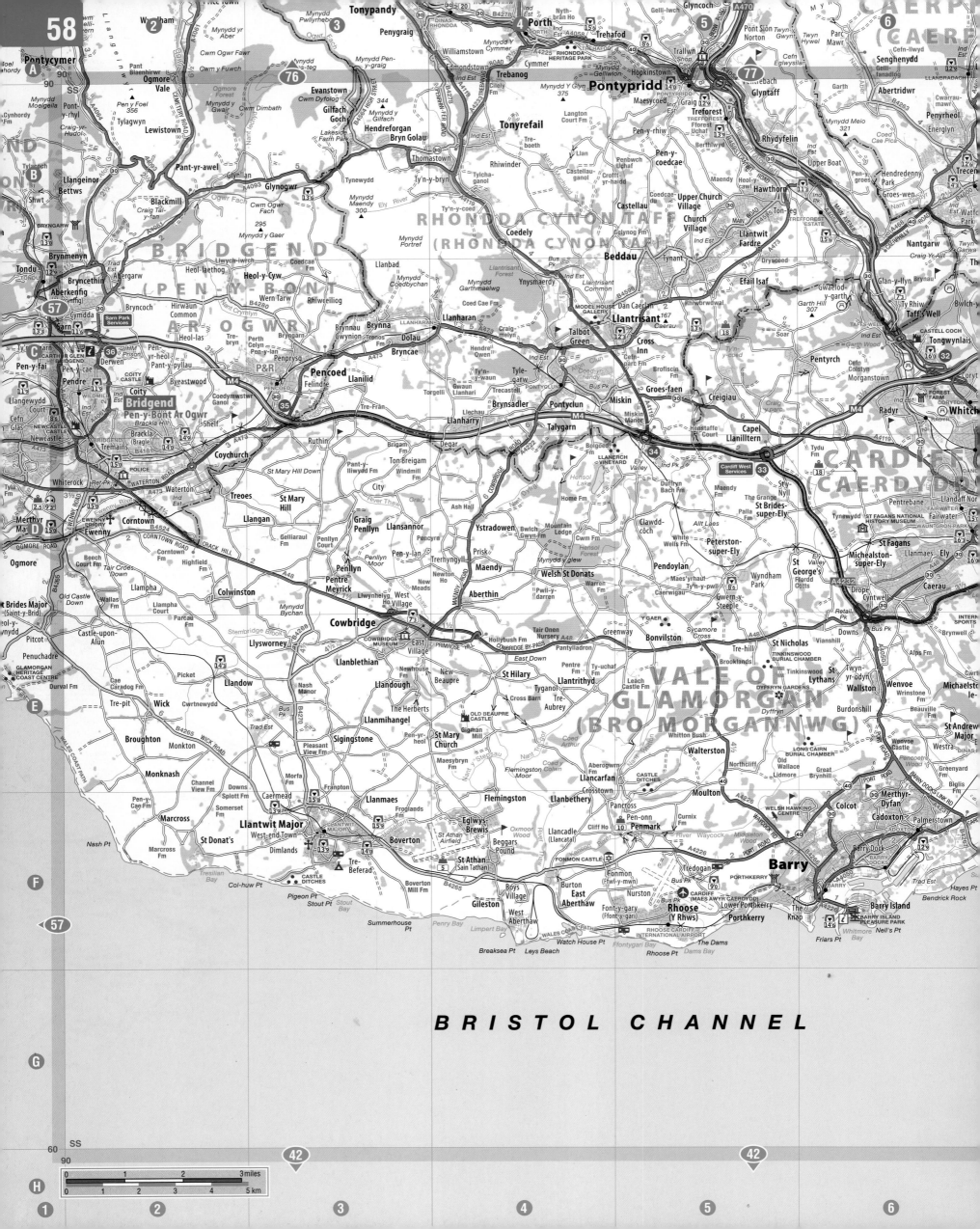

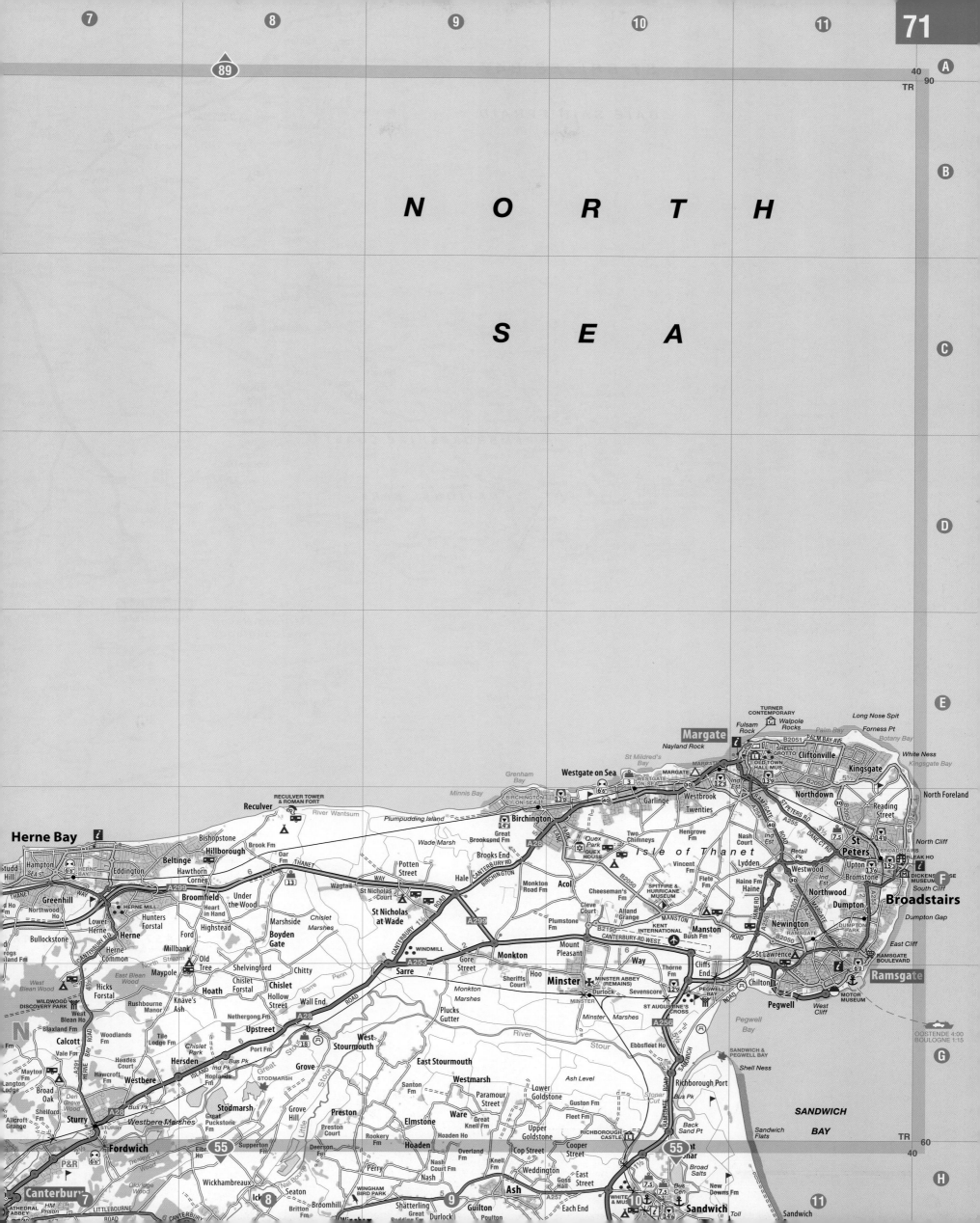

A
40
90
TR

B

N O R T H

S E A

C

D

E

TURNER
CONTEMPORARY
Long Nose Spit
Fulsam Rock
Walpole Rocks
Palm Bay
Forness Pt
Margate
Botany Bay
Nayland Rock
St Mildred's Bay
Cliftonville
White Ness
Kingsgate Bay
Westgate on Sea
MARGATE
OLD TOWN
HALL MUS
Kingsgate
Grenham Bay
WESTGATE ON SEA
Northdown
Birchington Bay
Westbrook
North Foreland
Minnis Bay
Garlinge
BIRCHINGTON ON SEA
Twenties
Reading Street
Reculver
RECULVER TOWER & ROMAN FORT
Birchington
North Cliff
River Wantsum
Plumpudding Island
Two Chimneys
Hengrove Fm
Nash Court
St Peters
Herne Bay
Bishopstone
Wade Marsh
Brooksend Fm
Quex Park QUEX HOUSE
Isle of Thanet
Lydden
Bleak Ho
Hillborough
Brook Fm
Brooks End
Vincent Fm
Retail Pk
DICKENS MUSEUM
Beltinge
Hawthorn
Oar Fm
THANET WAY
Potten Street
Hale
CANTERBURY RD
Acol
B2050
Flete Fm
Westwood
South Cliff
Eddington
Corner
Under the Wood
St Nicholas Court
SPITFIRE & HURRICANE MUSEUM
Haine Fm Haine
Northwood
Broadstairs
Greenhill
Broomfield
Monkton Road Fm
Cleve Court
Alland Grange
MANSTON
Manston
Newington
Dumpton
Dumpton Gap
Northwood Ho
Hunters Forstal
Heart in Hand
Marshside
Chislet Park
Plumstone Fm
Bush Fm
RAMSGATE
East Cliff
Lower Herne
Ford
Highstead
St Nicholas at Wade
WINDMILL
KENT INTERNATIONAL
St Lawrence
RAMSGATE BOULEVARD
Bullockstone
Herne
Millbank
Gore Street
Mount Pleasant
CANTERBURY-RD-WEST
Way
Thorne Fm
Cliffs End
Chilton
MOTOR MUSEUM
Ramsgate
Herne Common
Old Tree
Shelvingford
Chitty
Sarre
Monkton
Sheriffs Court
Hoo Fm
Minster
MINSTER ABBEY (REMAINS)
Sevenscore
PEGWELL BAY
West Cliff
West Blean Wood
Maypole
Hoath
Chislet Forstal
Wall End
Durlock
MINSTER
Pegwell
WILDWOOD DISCOVERY PARK
Hicks Forstal
Rushbourne Manor
Knave's Ash
Chislet Hollow Street
Penn
Monkton Marshes
ST AUGUSTINE'S CROSS
Pegwell Bay
West Blean Ho
Plucks Gutter
Minster Marshes
A256
OOSTENDE 4:00
BOULOGNE 1:15
N
Blaxland Fm
Woodlands Fm
Tile Lodge Fm
Upstreet
Port Fm
River
Stour
G
Calcott
Vale Fm
Hoades Court
Bus Pk
Grove
East Stourmouth
Ebbsfleet Ho
SANDWICH & PEGWELL BAY
Mayton Fm
Hawcroft Fm
Hersden
STODMARSH
Lower Goldstone
Shell Ness
Langton Lodge
Westbere
Hoplands
West Stourmouth
Santon Fm
Ash Level
SANDWICH
Broad Oak
Den Grove Wood
ISLAND
Westmarsh
Paramour Street
Upper Goldstone
Guston Fm
Richborough Port
Sheldwich Grange
Westbere Marshes
Stodmarsh
Grove Hill
Ware
Great Knell Fm
Fleet Fm
Stonar Cut
Back Sand Pt
SANDWICH BAY
Allcroft Grange
Great Puckstone Fm
Preston
Elmstone
Sandwich Flats
TR
60
40
Sturry
Supperton Fm
Preston Court
Rookery Fm
Upper Goldstone
RICHBOROUGH CASTLE
Cooper Street
Broad Salts
H
HM Prison
Fordwich
55
Elbr Ho
Hoaden
Deerson Fm
Nash Court Fm
Overland Fm
Knell Fm
55
New Downs Fm
Sandwich
Canterbury
CATHEDRAL ABBEY
Wickhambreaux
Ick
Seaton
Perry
Hoaden Ho
Weddington
East Street
Toll
7
8
Broomhill
9
Shatterling
Guilton
Poulton
10
WHITE & MUS
Sandwich
11
WINGHAM BIRD PARK
Ash
Each End
A257
Sandwich
Nash
Great
Durlock
Littlebourne
Road

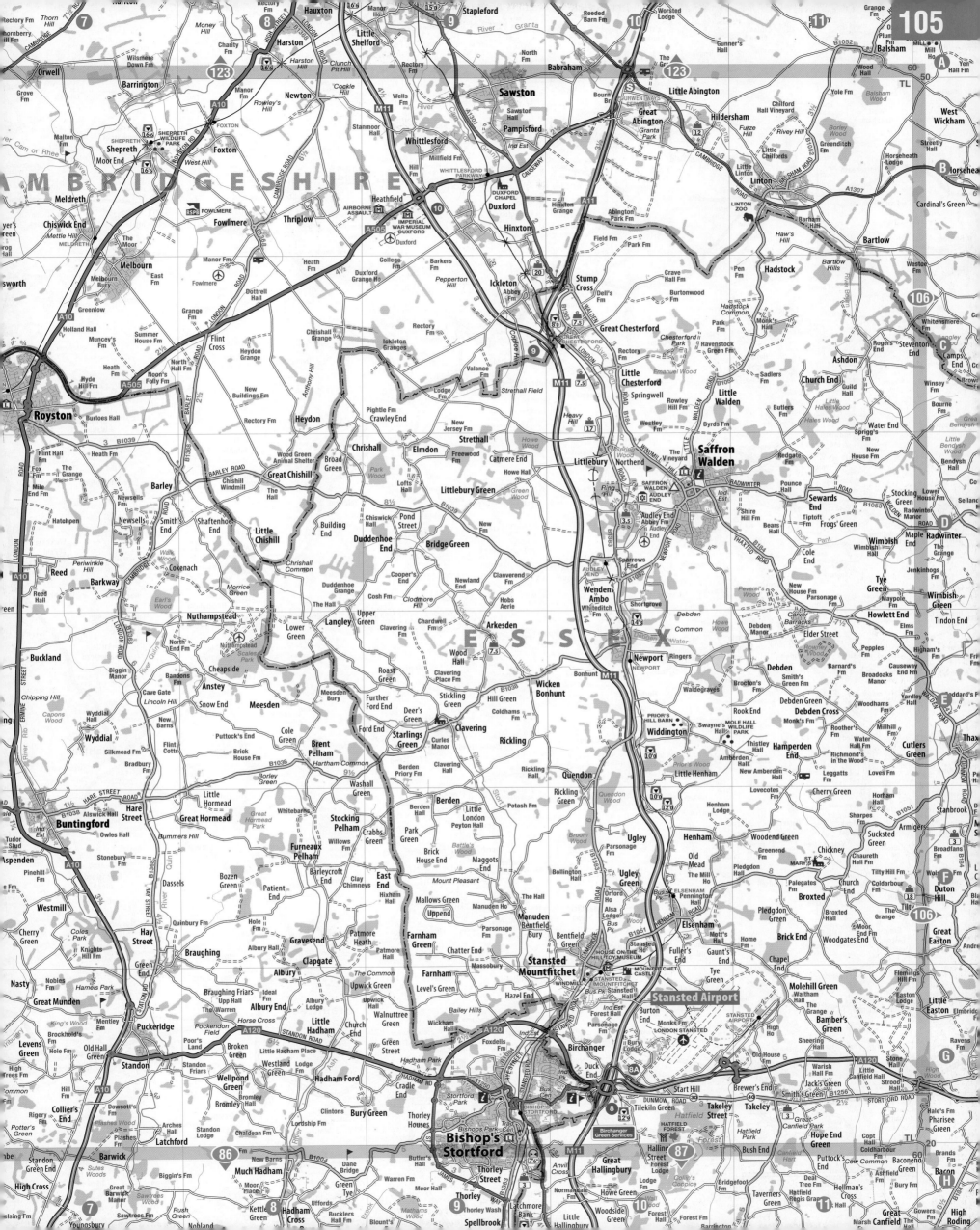

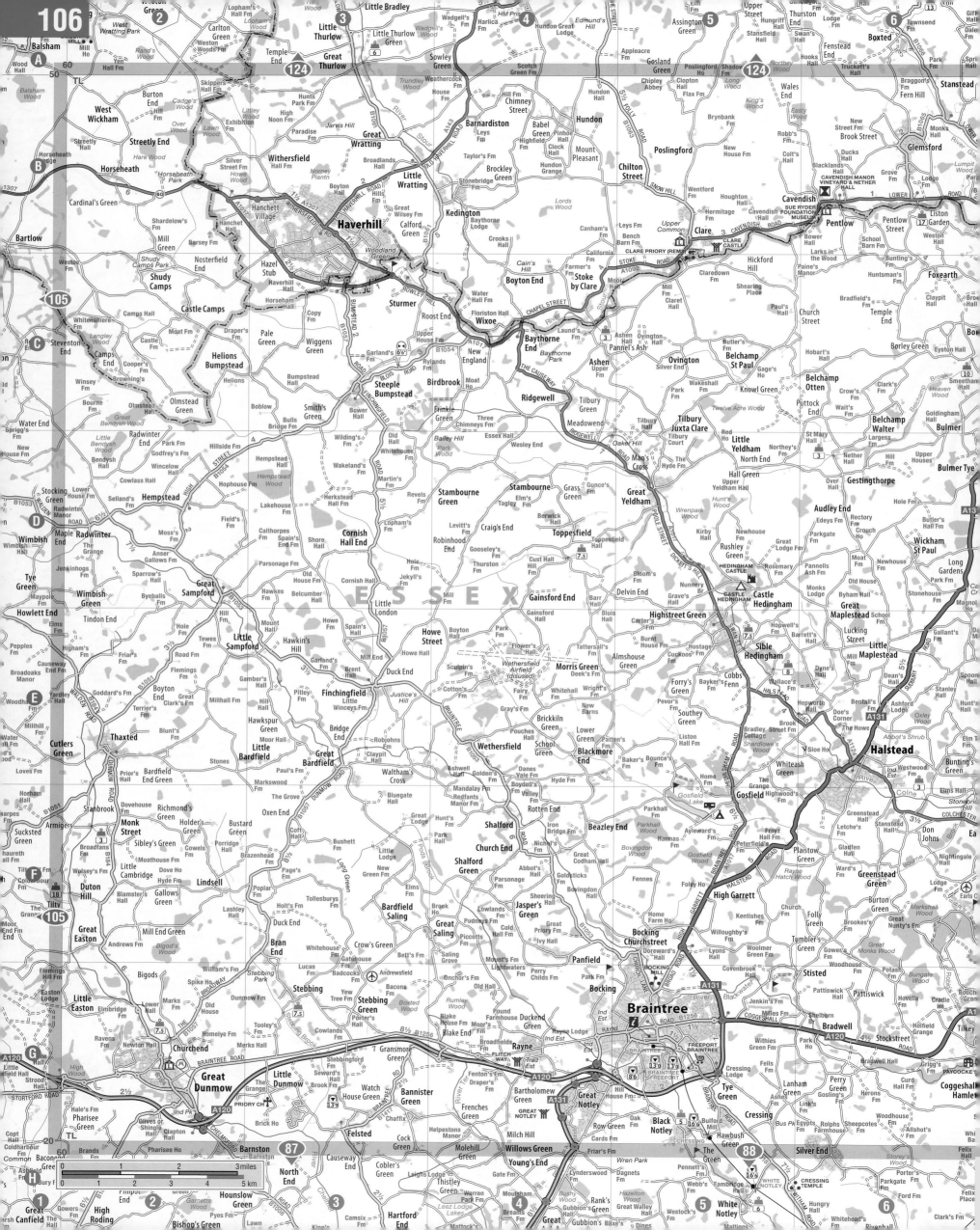

N O R T H

S E A

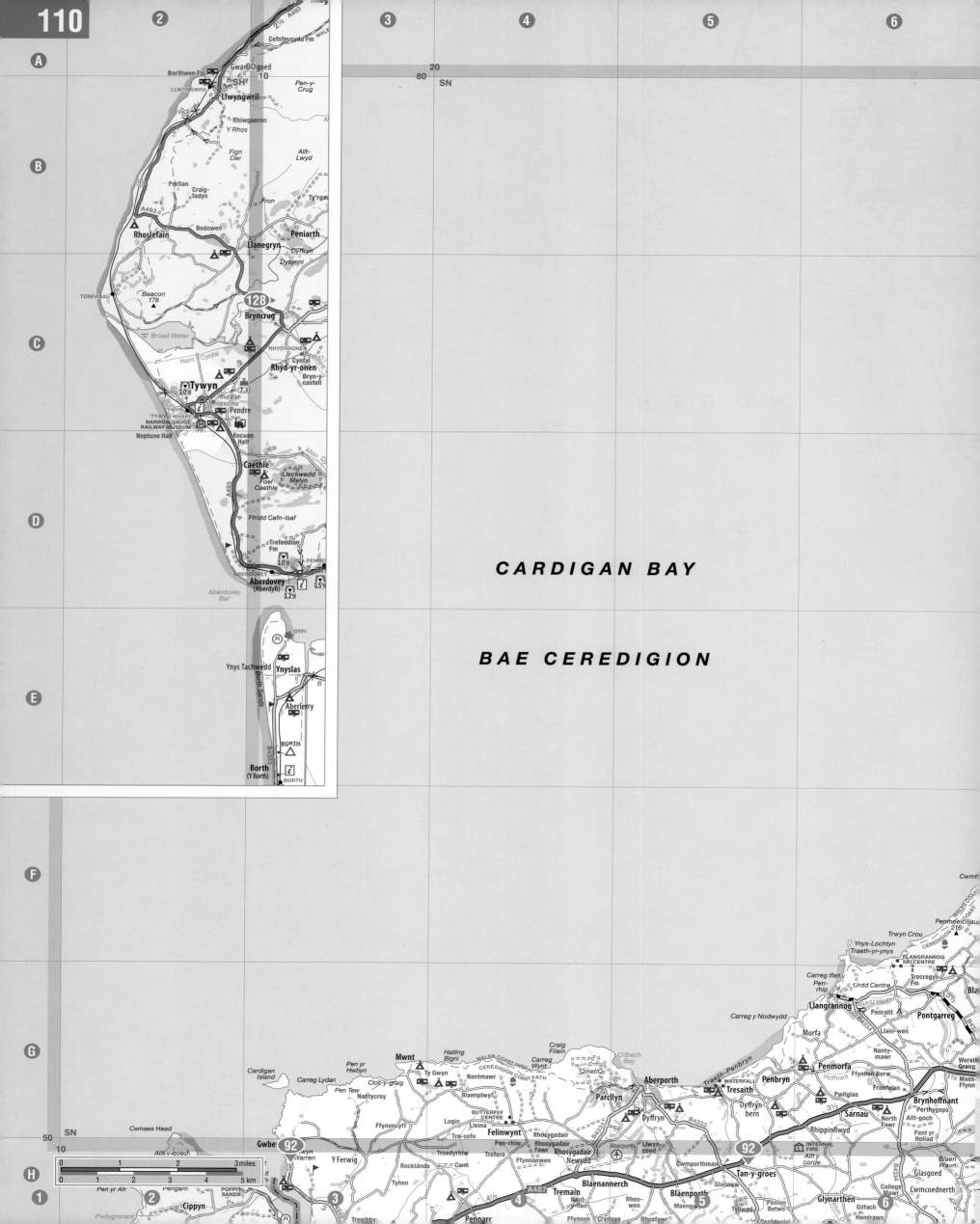

CARDIGAN BAY

BAE CEREDIGION

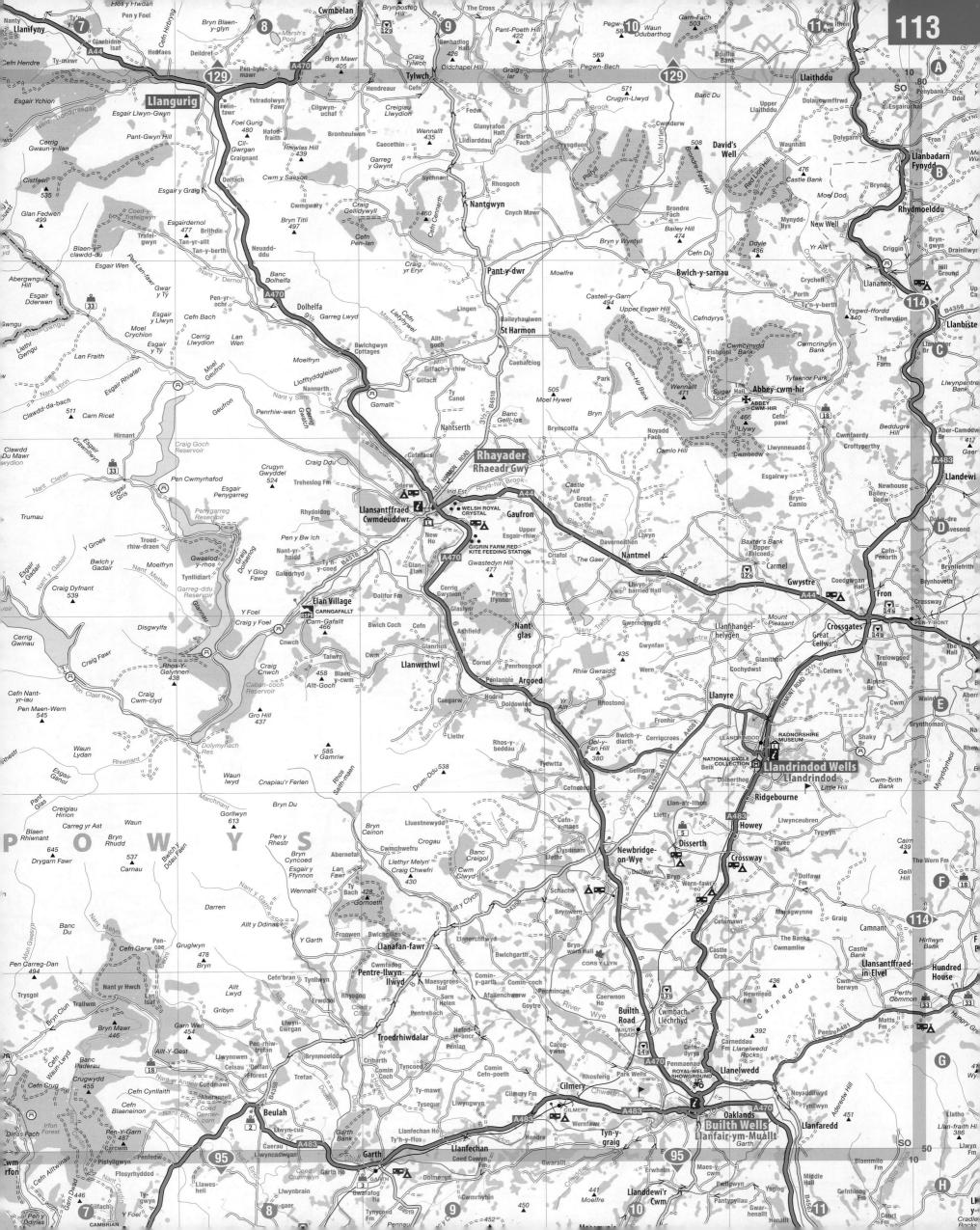

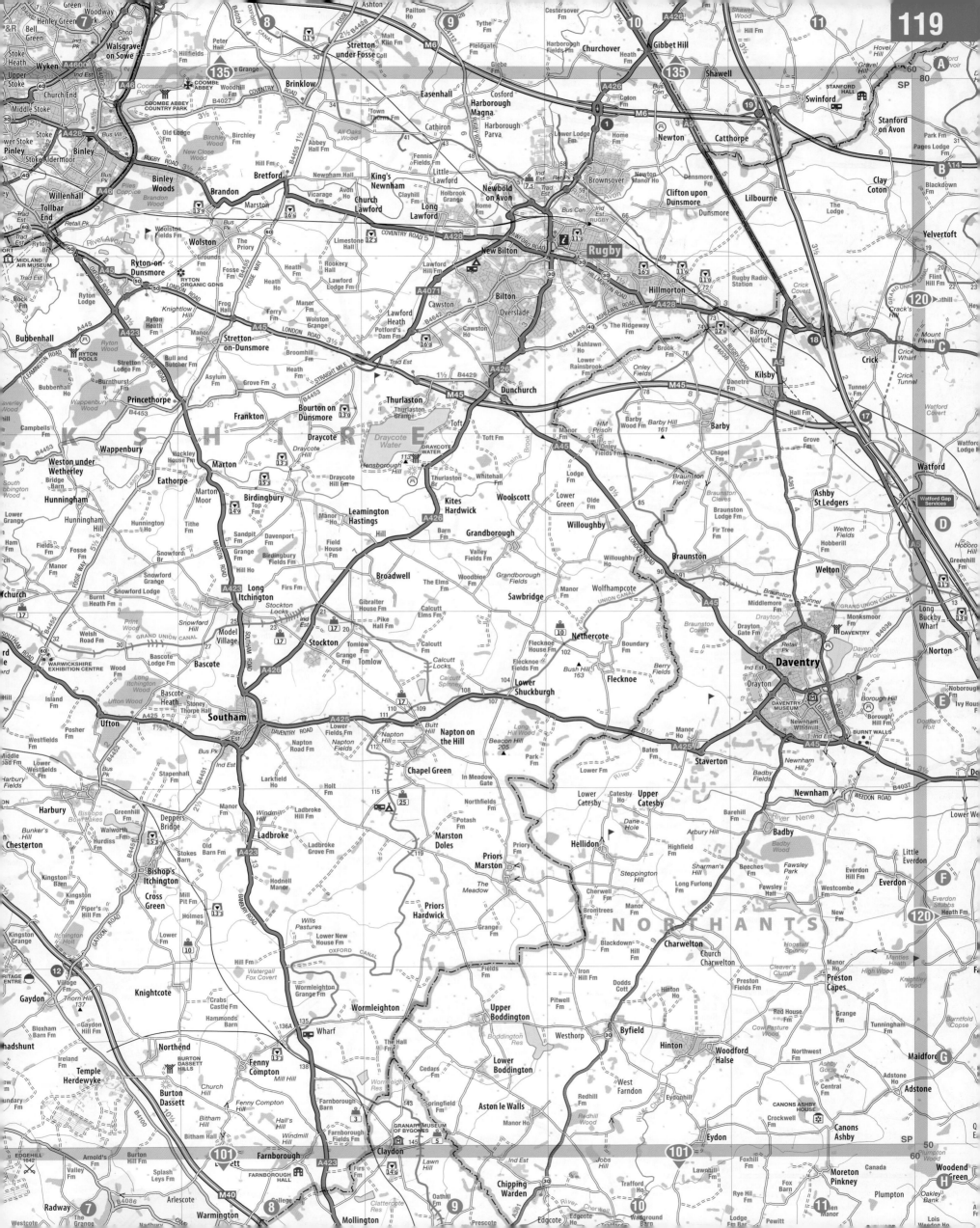

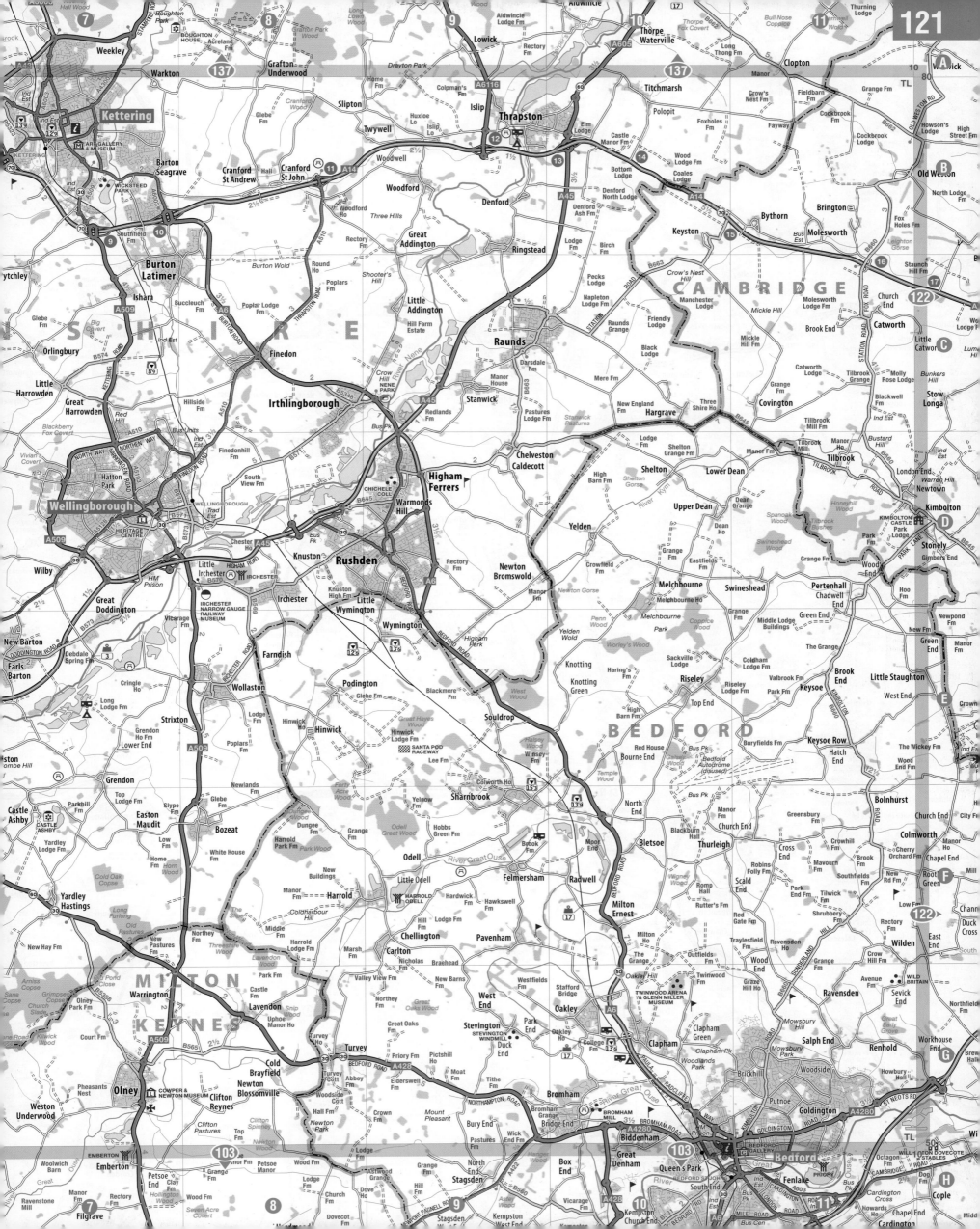

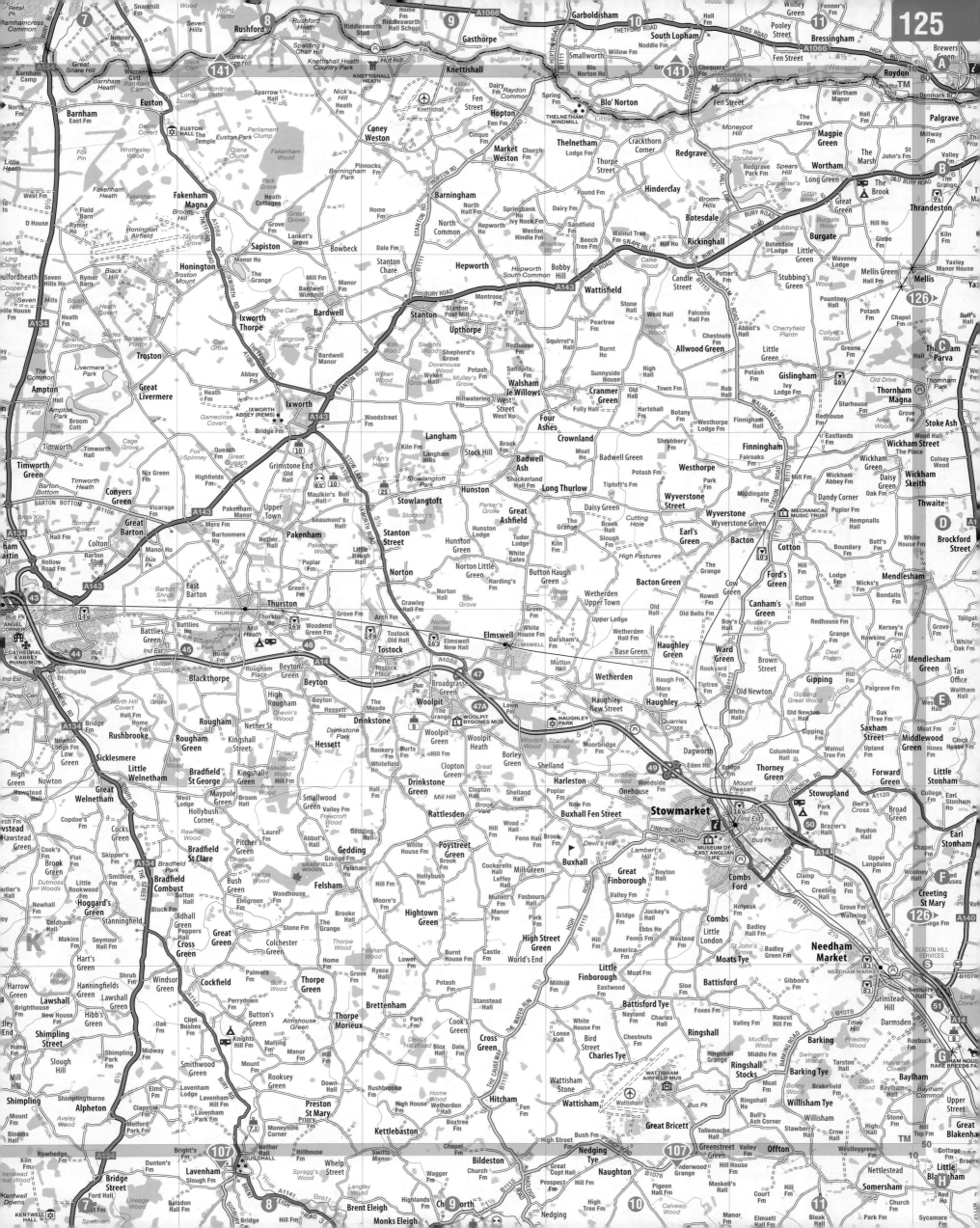

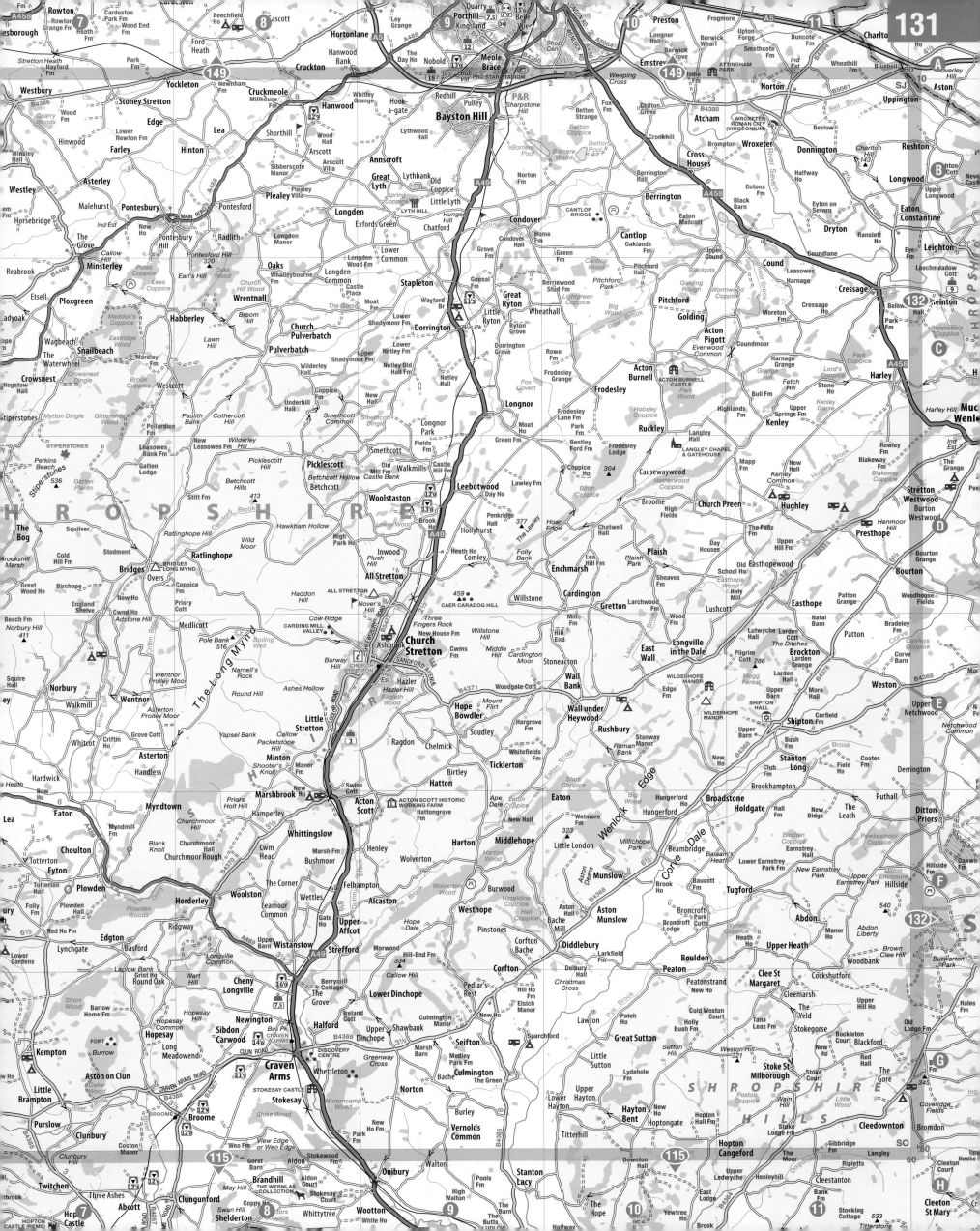

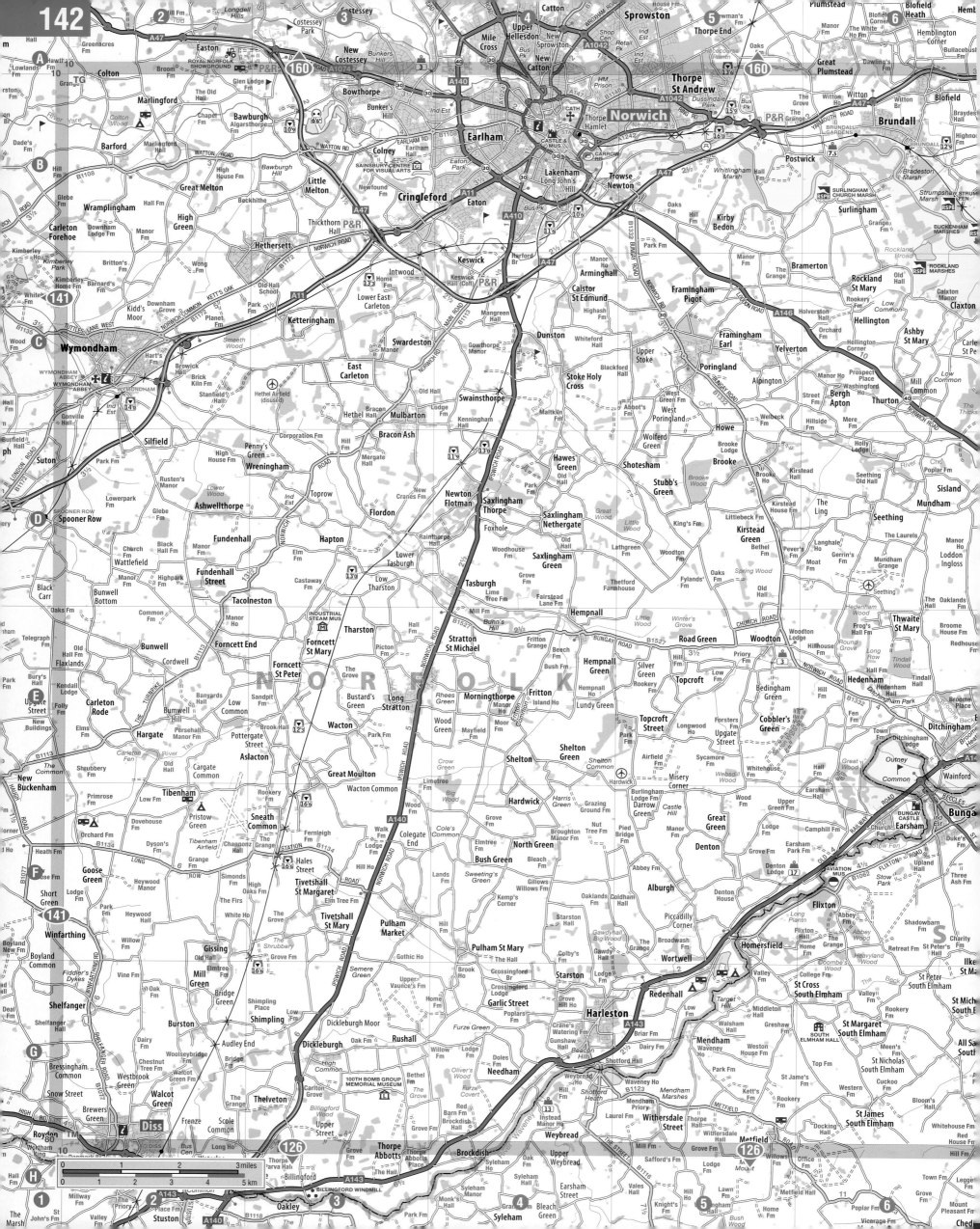

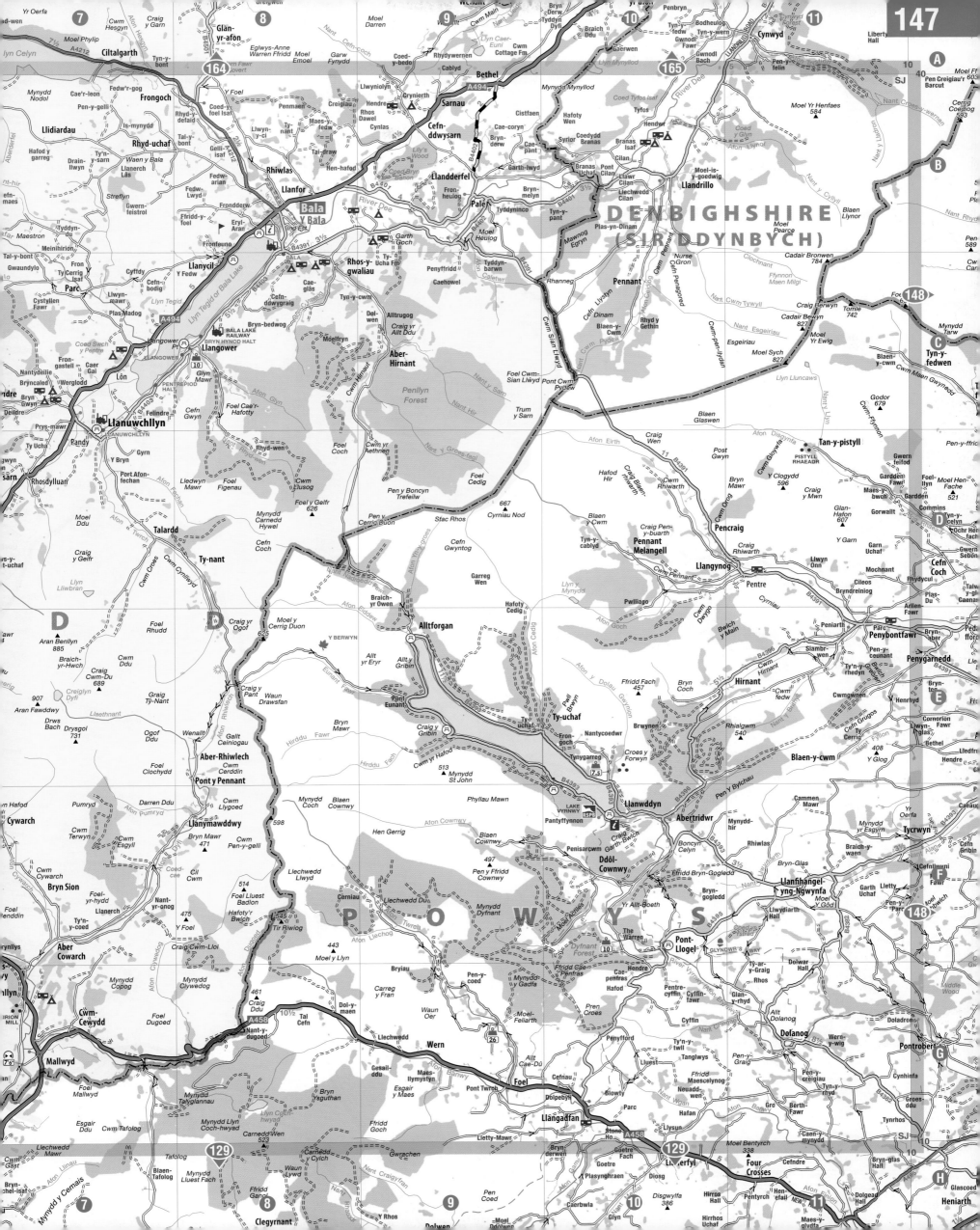

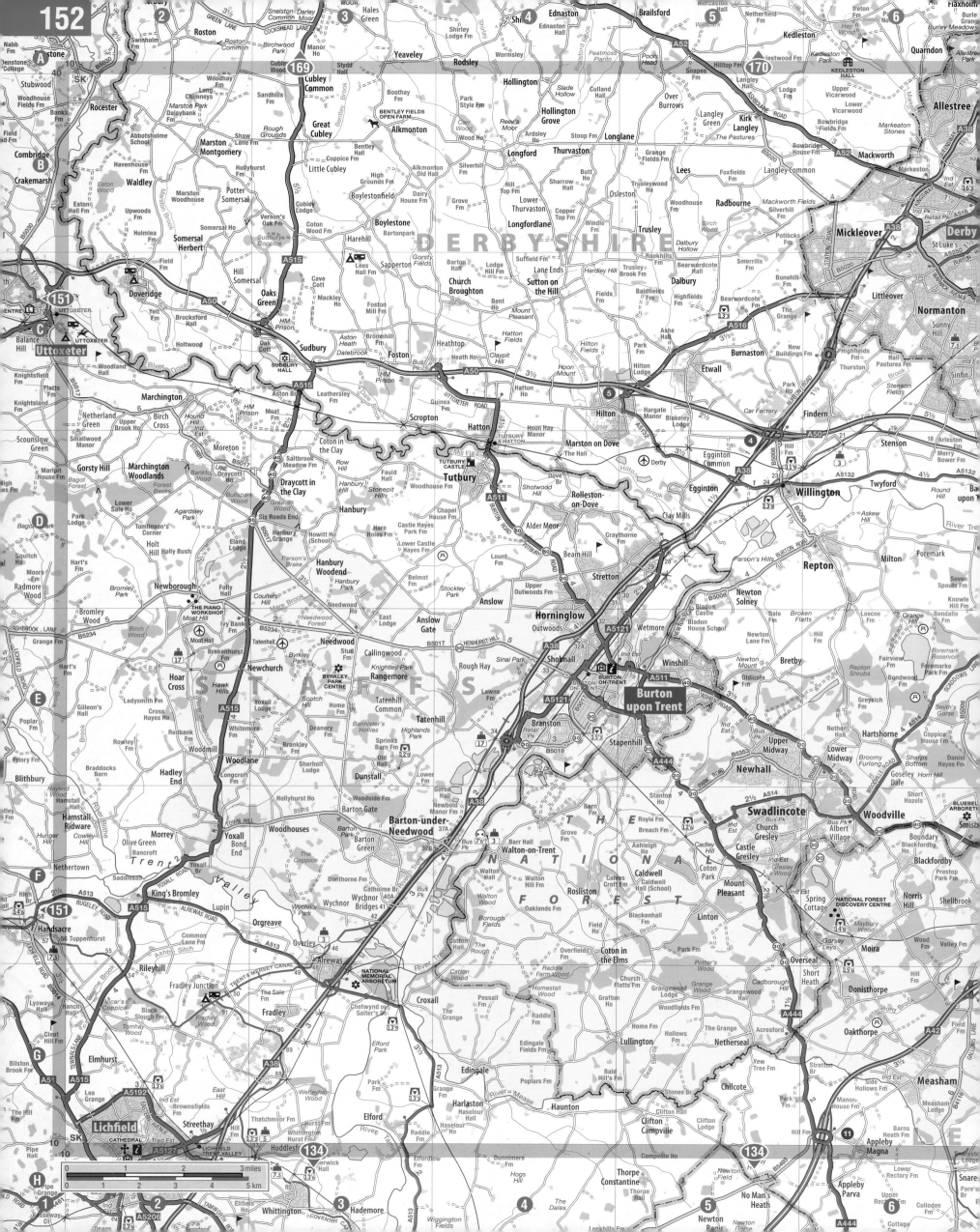

NORTH

SEA

NORFOLK COAST

THE BROADS

Great Yarmouth

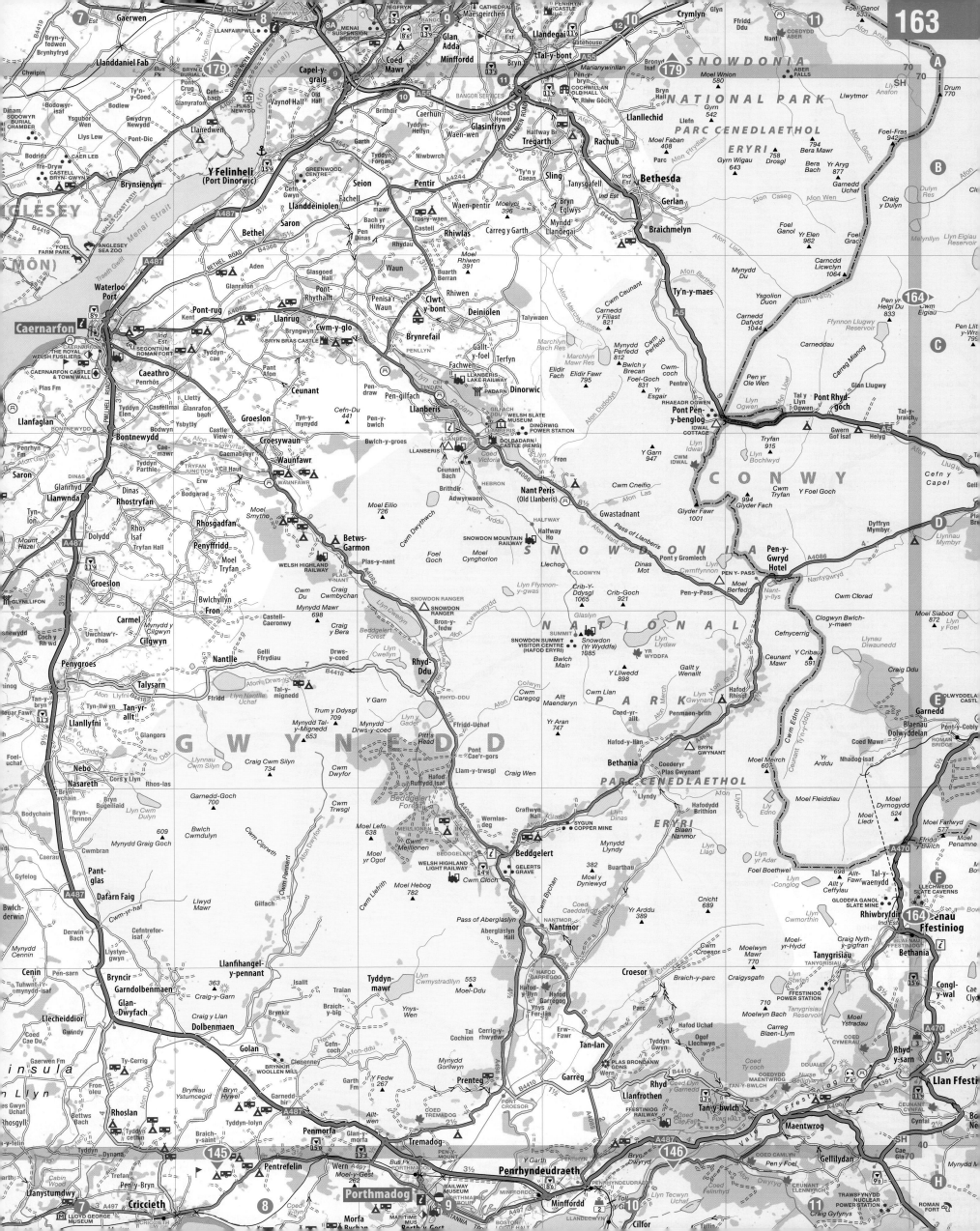

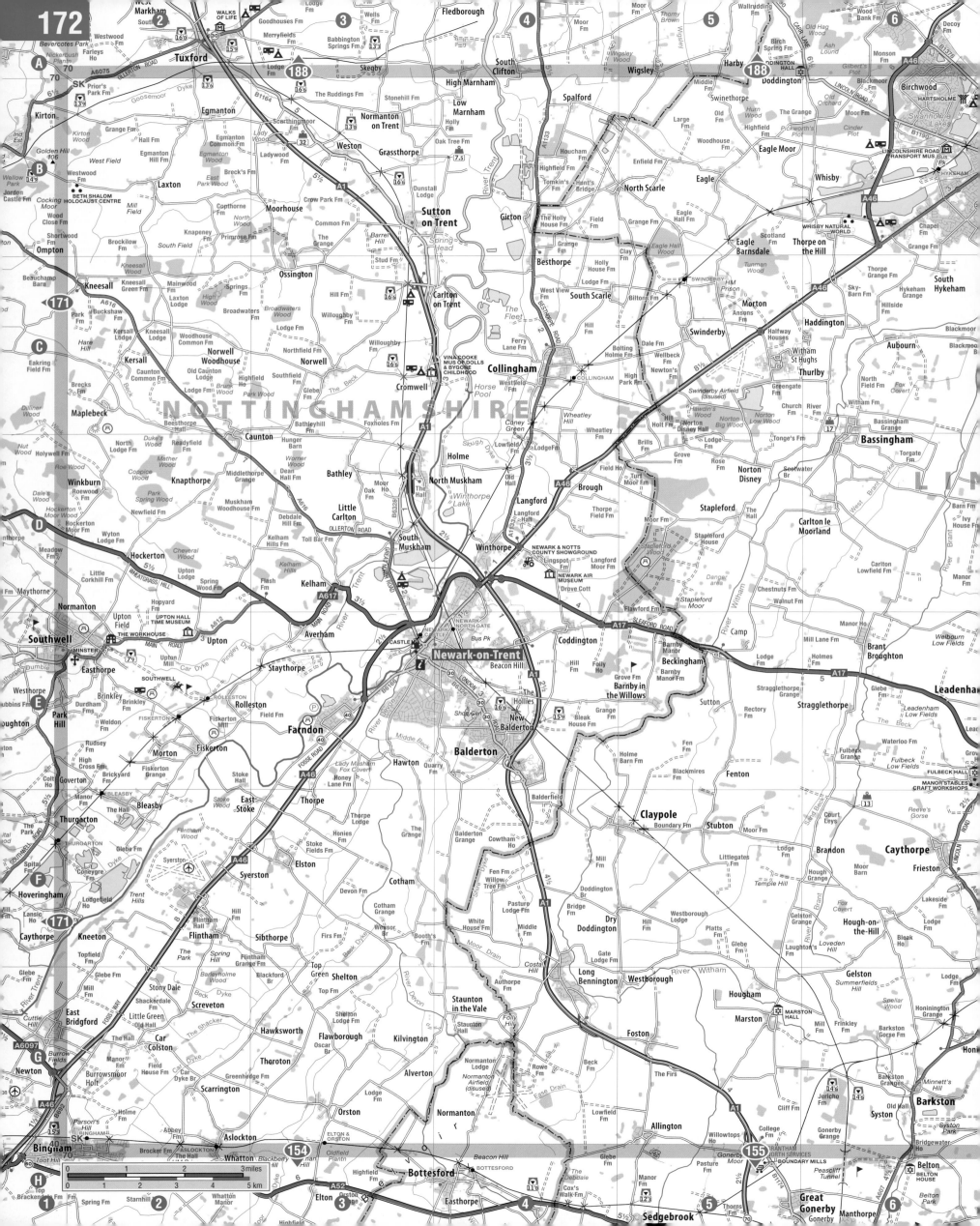

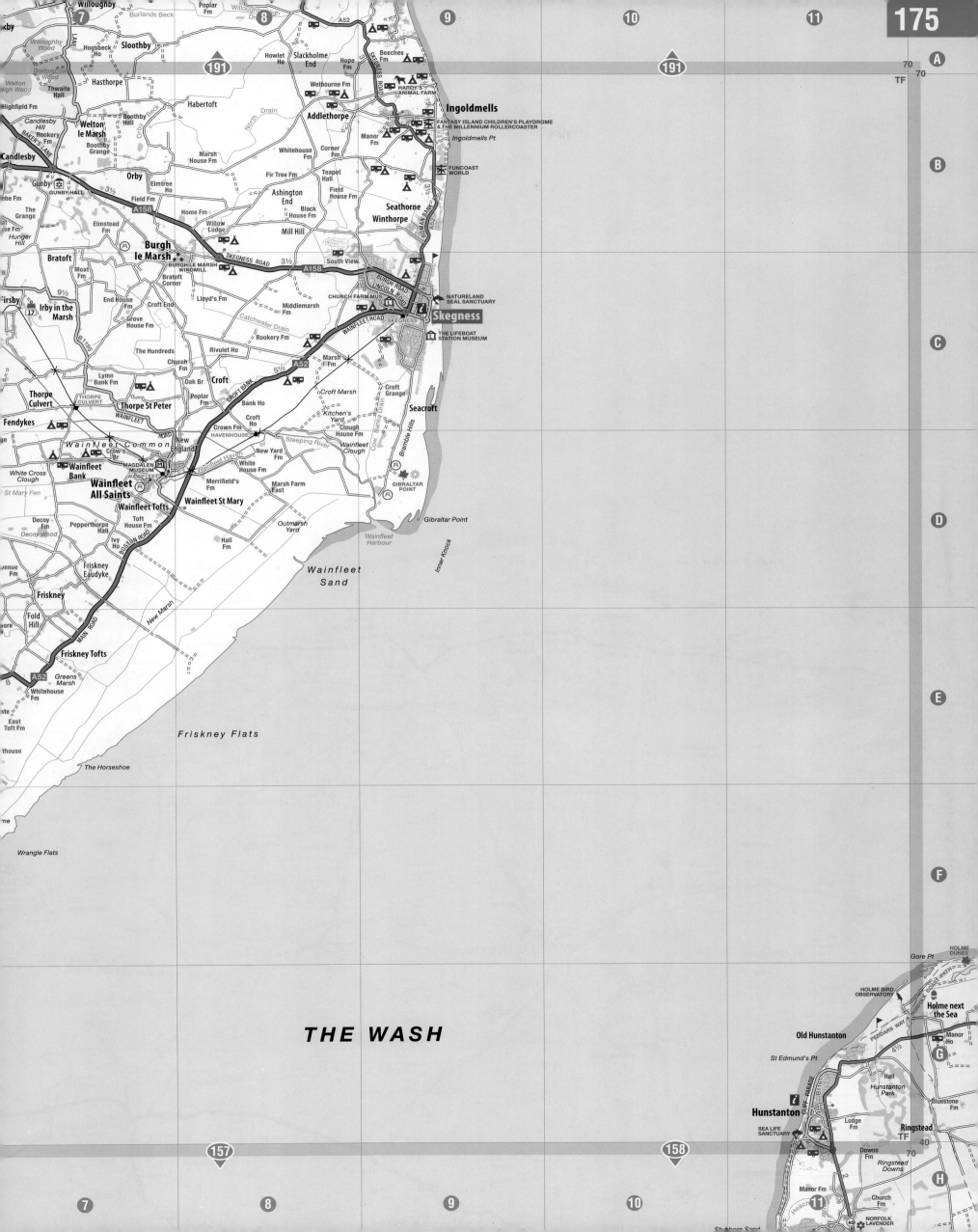

THE WASH

N O R T H

S E A

Saltfleet

Sea View Fm

Rimac

SALTFLEETBY THEDDLETHORPE

Saltfleetby All Saints

Lodge Fm

Theddlethorpe St Helen

Manor Ho

Hall Fm

Theddlethorpe All Saints

High Gate

Will Row

Gas Terminal

North End

THE SEAL SANCTUARY & NATURE CENTRE

Westfield Fm

Stain Hill

Meers Bank

Mablethorpe Hall

FUN FAIR

Mablethorpe

Strubby Grange

Poplar Fm

Grange Fm

Trusthorpe

Earl's Br

Willow Fm

Bamber's Br

Strubby

Thorpe

Trusthorpe Hall

Maltby le Marsh

Sutton on Sea

Manor Ho

Poplar Lodge Fm

Sandilands

Mill Hill

Beesby

Abbey Fm

Beesby Grange

Manor Fm

Hagnaby

Washdyke Br

Hannah

Sea Bank Fm

Saleby

America Fm

Glebe Fm

Markby

Priory Fm

Saleby Manor

Cob Hill

College Fm

Asserby

The Grange

Thoresthorpe

Asserby Turn

Willow Fm

Black House Fm

Bilsby

Dryby Fm

Moat Ho

Wold Sea Fm

Anderby Creek

Alford

The Grange

Huttoft

The Manor

Manor Fm

Bilsby Field

Thurlby

Anderby

Farlesthorpe Fen

Wolla Bank

Mumby

Langham Fm

Chapel Six Marshes

Farlesthorpe

Manor Ho

Manor Fm

School Fm

Mill Hill

Cumberworth

Cherry Fm

Mickleberry Hill

Authorpe Row

Chapel Pt

Chapman's Fm

Mawthorpe

Elsom Fm

Helsey

Croft Fm

Bonthorpe

Manor Fm

Listoft

Hogsthorpe

Chapel St Leonards

Willoughby

Poplar Fm

Burlands Beck

Willoughby High Drain

Willoughby Wood

Sloothby

Hogsbeck Fm

Hasthorpe

Howlet Ho

Slackholme End

Hope Fm

Beeches Fm

Highfield Fm

Welton High Wood

Thwaite Hall

Welbourne Fm

HARDY'S ANIMAL FARM

Candlesby Hill

Welton le Marsh

Boothby Hall

Habertoft

Ingoldmells

Boothby Grange

Addlethorpe

FANTASY ISLAND CHILDREN'S PLAYDROME & THE MILLENNIUM ROLLERCOASTER

Manor Fm

Ingoldmells Pt

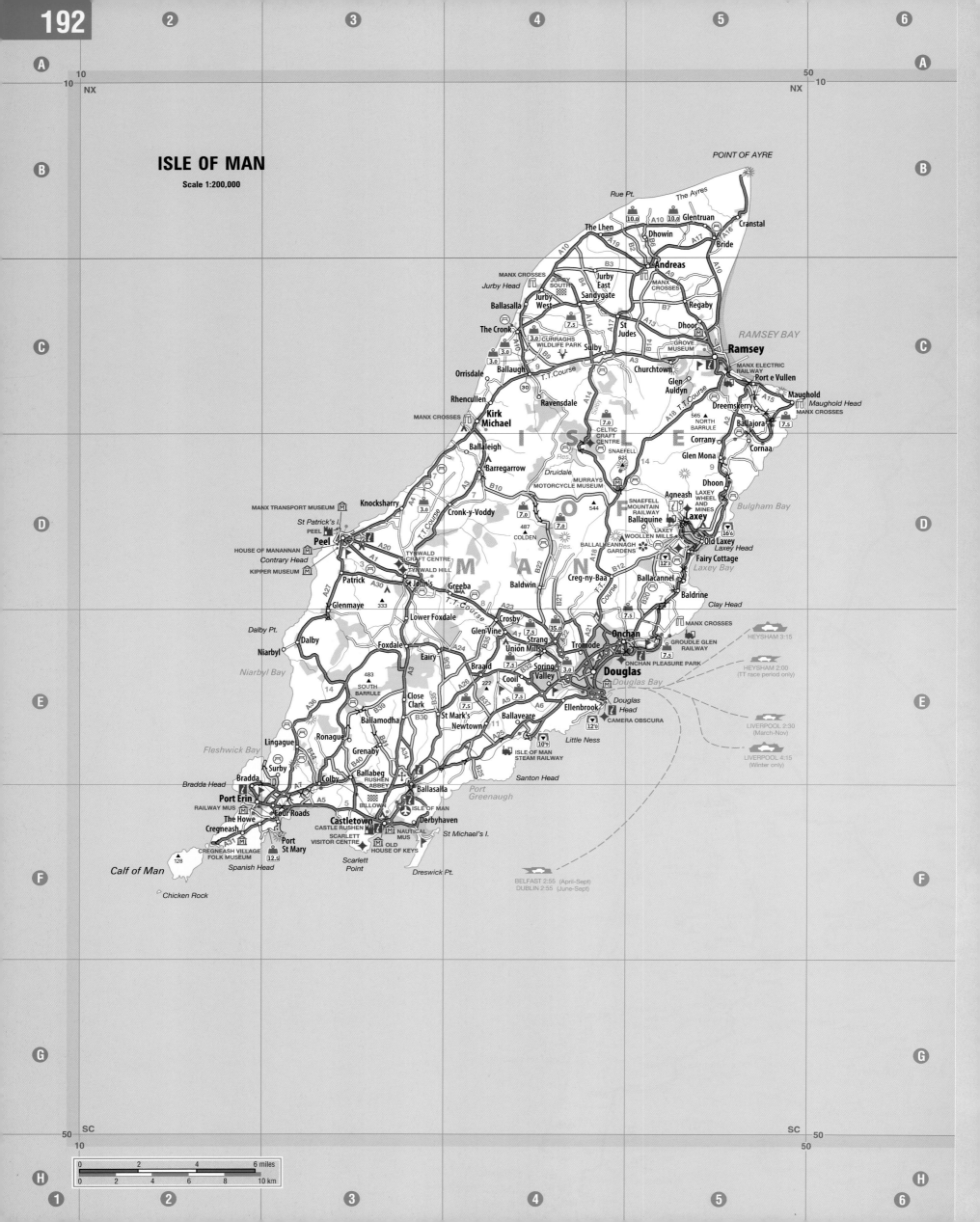

ISLE OF MAN

Scale 1:200,000

POINT OF AYRE

Rue Pt.   The Ayres

The Lhen   Glentruan   Cranstal
Dhowin   Bride

MANX CROSSES   Jurby East
Jurby Head   Jurby SOUTH   Andreas
Jurby West   Sandygate   MANX CROSSES
Ballasalla   Regaby
The Cronk   St Judes   Dhoor
CURRAGHS WILDLIFE PARK   RAMSEY BAY
Orrisdale   Sulby   GROVE MUSEUM   Ramsey
Ballaugh   Churchtown   MANX ELECTRIC RAILWAY
Glen Auldyn   Port e Vullen
Rhencullen   Maughold
Ravensdale   Dreemskerry   Maughold Head
Kirk Michael   565 NORTH BARRULE   Ballajora   MANX CROSSES
MANX CROSSES   Ballaleigh   CELTIC CRAFT CENTRE   Corrany   Cornaa
Barregarrow   SNAEFELL 621   Glen Mona
Druidale   9   Dhoon
MURRAYS MOTORCYCLE MUSEUM   Agneash   LAXEY WHEEL AND MINES   Bulgham Bay
Knocksharry   MANX TRANSPORT MUSEUM   Cronk-y-Voddy   SNAEFELL MOUNTAIN RAILWAY   544   Ballaquine   Laxey
St Patrick's I.   487 COLDEN   LAXEY WOOLLEN MILLS   Old Laxey
PEEL   BALLALHEANNAGH GARDENS   Laxey Head
HOUSE OF MANANNAN   Peel   Fairy Cottage
Contrary Head   TYNWALD CRAFT CENTRE   Laxey Bay
KIPPER MUSEUM   Patrick   TYNWALD HILL   Baldwin   Creg-ny-Baa   Ballacannel
St John's   Greeba   Baldrine
Glenmaye   333   Clay Head
Dalby Pt.   Lower Foxdale   Crosby   MANX CROSSES
Dalby   Glen Vine   35.0   Onchan   GROUDLE GLEN RAILWAY
Niarbyl   Foxdale   Strang   Tromode   ONCHAN PLEASURE PARK
Fairy   Union Mills   Spring Valley   Douglas
Niarbyl Bay   Braaid   Cooil   Douglas Bay
483 SOUTH BARRULE   Ballaveare   Douglas Head
Lingague   Close Clark   St Mark's Newtown   Ellenbrook   CAMERA OBSCURA
Fleshwick Bay   Ronague   Ballamodha   A6   Little Ness
Surby   Grenaby   ISLE OF MAN STEAM RAILWAY
Bradda   Ballabeg   RUSHEN ABBEY   Santon Head
Bradda Head   Colby   BILLOWN   Port Greenaugh
Port Erin   Four Roads   Ballasalla   HEYSHAM 3:15
RAILWAY MUS   ISLE OF MAN   HEYSHAM 2:00 (TT race period only)
The Howe   Castletown   Derbyhaven   LIVERPOOL 2:30 (March-Nov)
Cregneash   CASTLE RUSHEN   St Michael's I.   LIVERPOOL 4:15 (Winter only)
CREGNEASH VILLAGE FOLK MUSEUM   SCARLETT VISITOR CENTRE   NAUTICAL MUS
128   Port St Mary   OLD HOUSE OF KEYS
Calf of Man   Spanish Head   Scarlett Point   Dreswick Pt.   BELFAST 2:55 (April-Sept) DUBLIN 2:55 (June-Sept)
Chicken Rock

0   2   4   6 miles
0 2 4 6 8 10 km

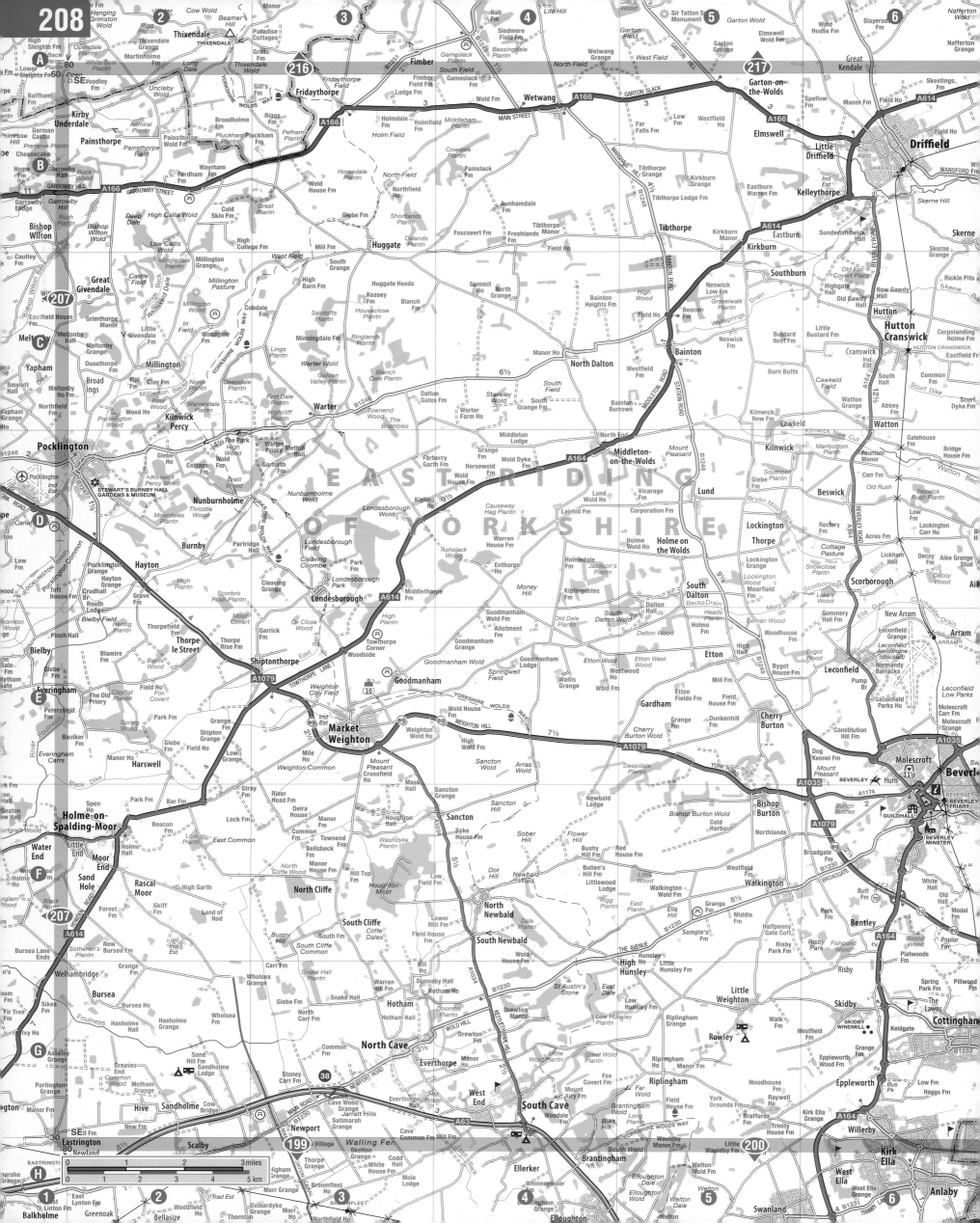

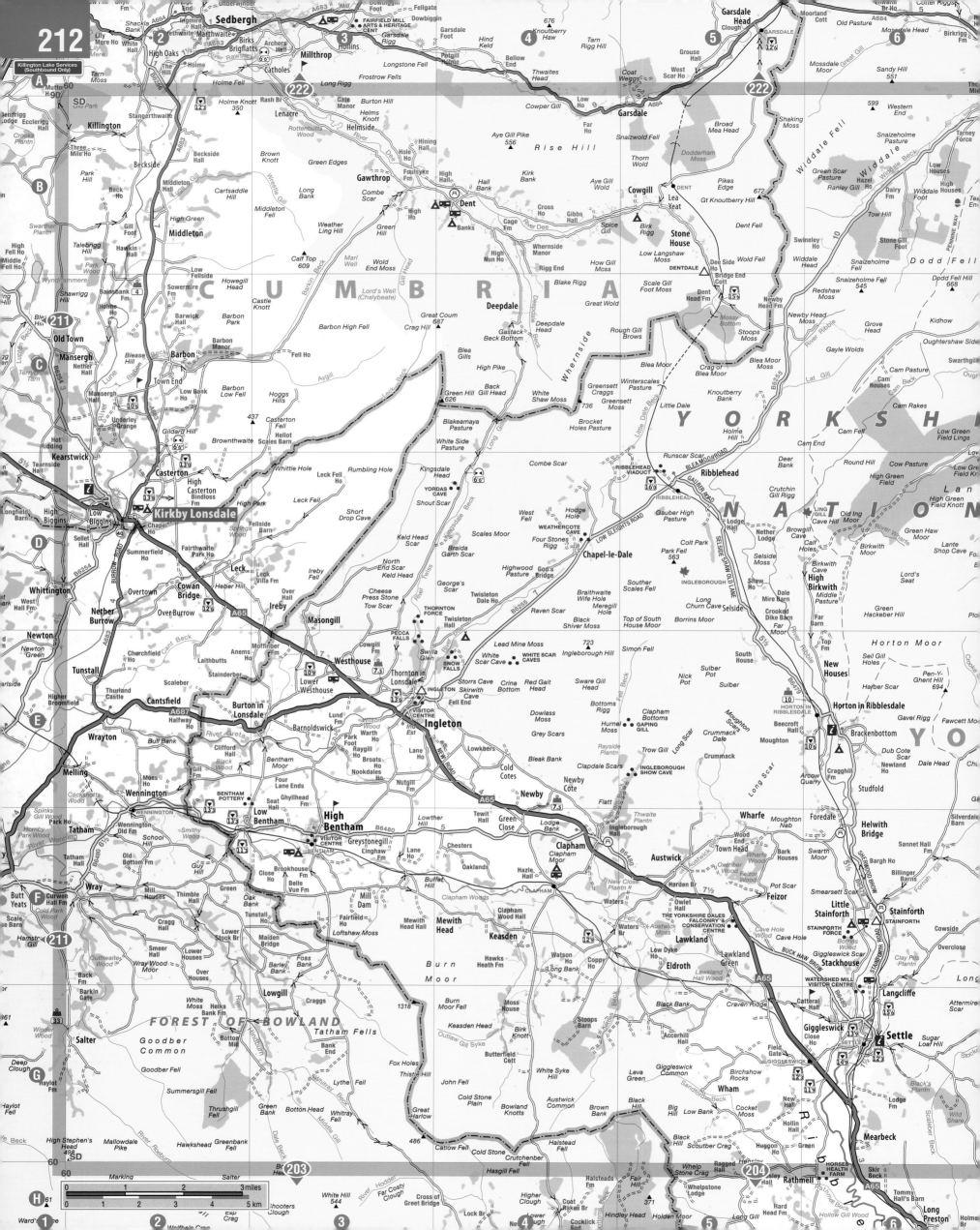

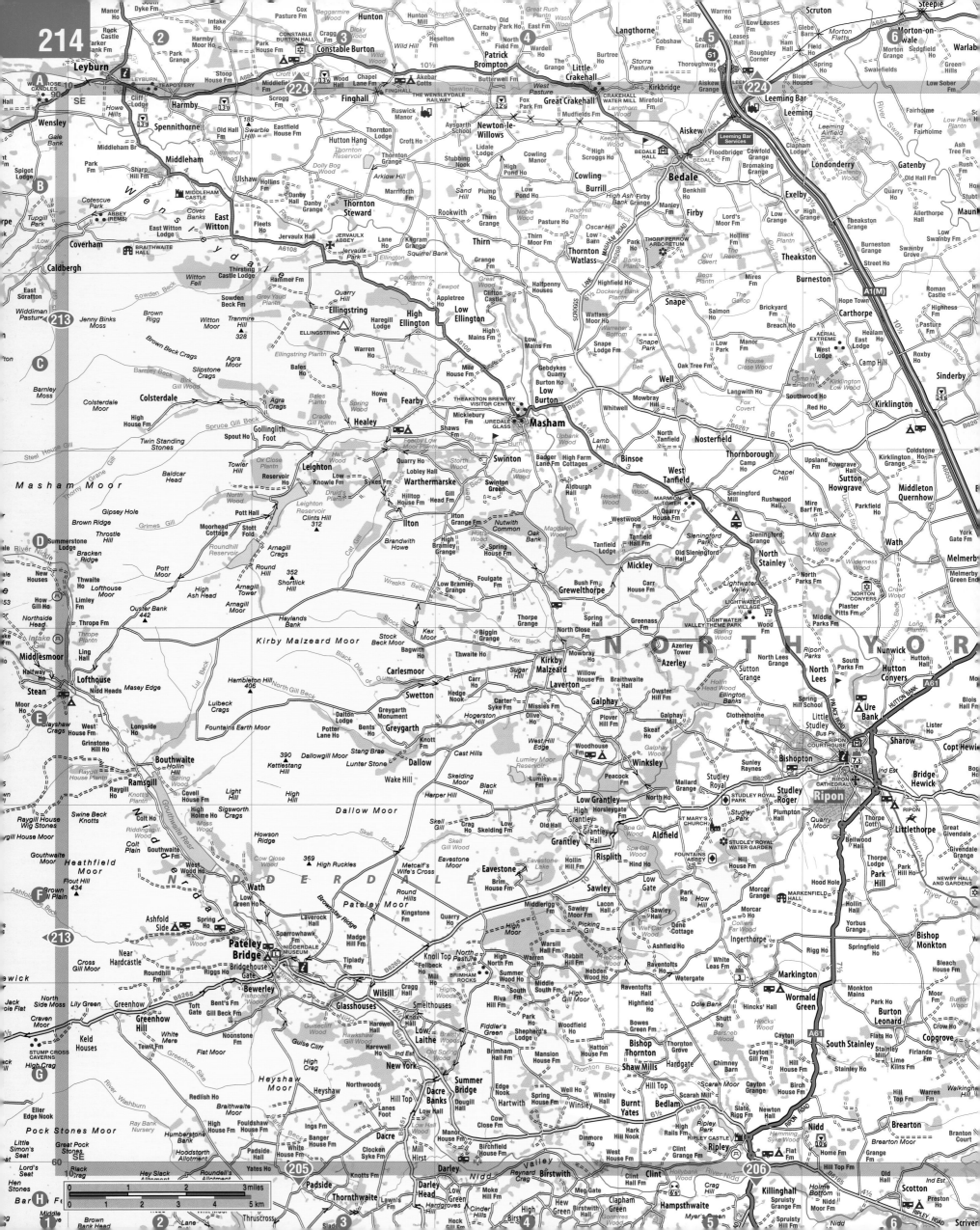

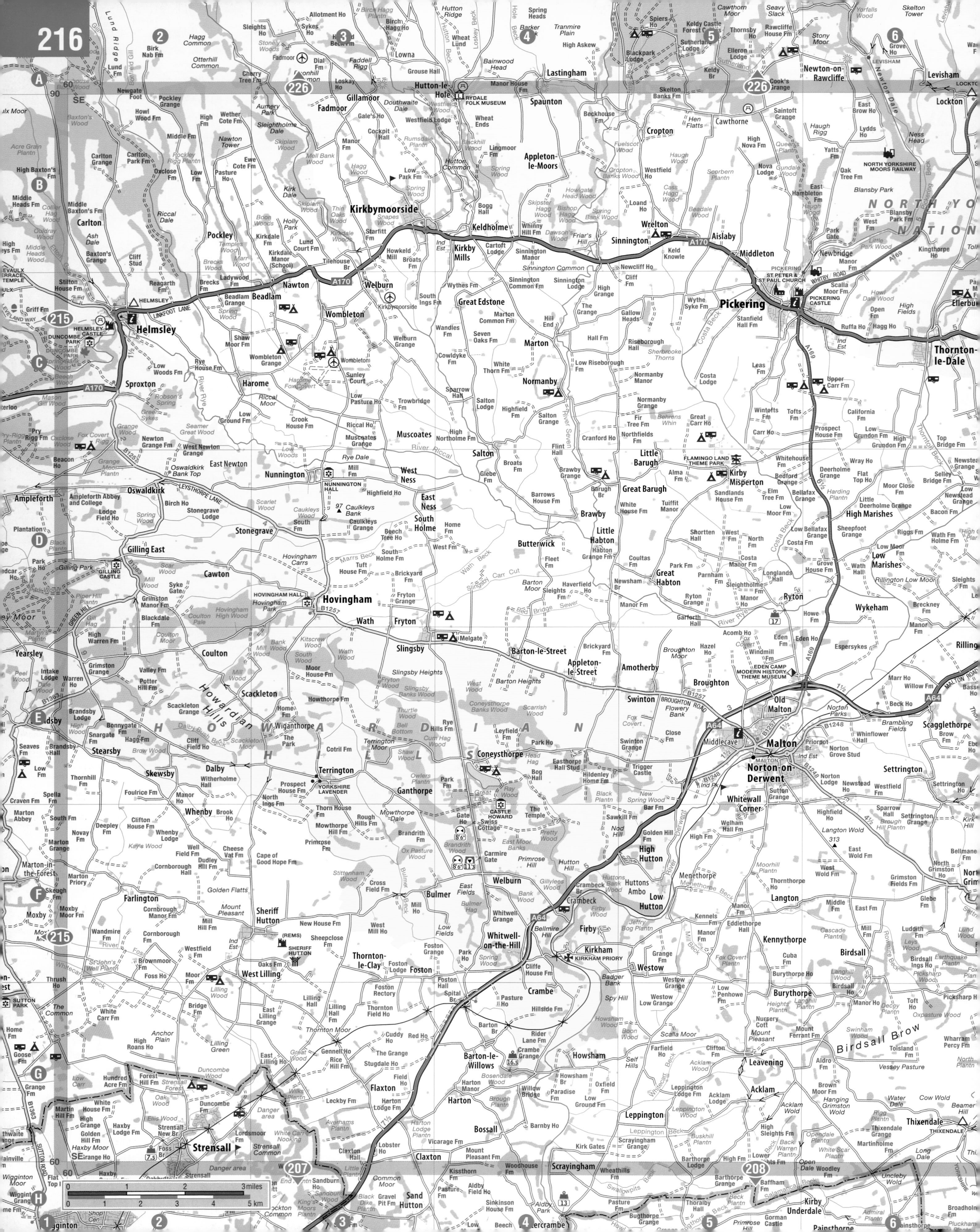

Helmsley
Kirkbymoorside
Pickering
Malton
Norton-on-Derwent
Old Malton
Thornton-le-Dale
Hovingham
Sheriff Hutton
Strensall
Hutton-le-Hole
RYDALE FOLK MUSEUM
Lastingham
Spaunton
Appleton-le-Moors
Cropton
Cawthorne
Newton-on-Rawcliffe
Levisham
Lockton
NORTH YORKSHIRE MOORS RAILWAY
NORTH YORK MOORS NATIONAL PARK
Gillamoor
Fadmoor
Keldholme
Kirkby Mills
Sinnington
Wrelton
Aislaby
Middleton
PICKERING CASTLE
ST PETER & ST PAUL CHURCH
Nawton
Beadlam
Wombleton
Welburn
Great Edstone
Marton
Normanby
Salton
Harome
Sproxton
Pockley
Carlton
DUNCOMBE PARK
HELMSLEY CASTLE
Oswaldkirk
Ampleforth
Ampleforth Abbey and College
Nunnington
NUNNINGTON HALL
Stonegrave
West Ness
East Ness
South Holme
Muscoates
Gilling East
GILLING CASTLE
Cawton
Coulton
Scackleton
Yearsley
HOVINGHAM HALL
Wath
Fryton
Slingsby
Barton-le-Street
Appleton-le-Street
Amotherby
Swinton
Broughton
Little Barugh
Great Barugh
Kirby Misperton
FLAMINGO LAND THEME PARK
Brawby
Little Habton
Great Habton
Butterwick
Ryton
Wykeham
Low Marishes
High Marishes
EDEN CAMP MODERN HISTORY THEME MUSEUM
Howardian Hills
HOWARDIAN HILLS
Coneysthorpe
CASTLE HOWARD
Terrington
YORKSHIRE LAVENDER
Ganthorpe
Dalby
Skewsby
Stearsby
Brandsby
Whenby
Farlington
Bulmer
Welburn
Whitwell-on-the-Hill
Crambeck
Firby
Kirkham
KIRKHAM PRIORY
Westow
Crambe
Foston
Thornton-le-Clay
West Lilling
SHERIFF HUTTON
Flaxton
Harton
Barton-le-Willows
Howsham
Bossall
Claxton
Sand Hutton
Scrayingham
Leppington
Acklam
Leavening
Burythorpe
Birdsall
Kennythorpe
Langton
Settrington
Scagglethorpe
Thixendale
Birdsall Brow
Huttons Ambo
High Hutton
Low Hutton
Menethorpe
Whitewall Corner
Middlecave
Kirby Underdale
SUTTON PARK
A170
A169
A64
B1257
B1363
B1248
226
215
207
208
0 1 2 3 miles
0 1 2 3 4 5 km

NORTH

SEA

FILEY

BAY

BRIDLINGTON

BAY

EAST RIDING

OF YORKSHIRE

Yons Nab
Lebberston Cliff
Gristhorpe Cliff
Cunstone Nab
The Wyke
Cliff Fm
Newbiggin
North Cliff
Club Pt
WOLDS WAY
Filey Field
Filey Brigg
Brigg End
Gristhorpe
Carr Ho
Filey
Filey Sands
Beacon Hill
Muston
Muston Grange
Muston Sands
Lowfield Fm
Royal Oak
Primrose Valley
Hunmanby Sands
Pilmoor Fm
Foxhill Fm
Hunmanby Moor
Hunmanby Gap
Airy Hill Fm
Ind Est
Moor Fm
Rosedale Fm
Graffitoe Fm
Moor Ho
Reighton Sands
Reighton Gap
Barf Fm
Vicarage Fm
Moor Fm
Speeton Sands
Reighton
Speeton Hills
Speeton Cliffs
Dale Fm
Reighton Field
Speeton Moor
Buckton Cliffs
Speeton Grange
Speeton
Hill Fm
Bartindale Fm
Speeton Gate
Standard Hill
Bempton Cliffs
Scale Nab
Cat Nab
Gull Nook
Bartindale Fm
Field Greenlands Fm
Bempton Hall
Bempton Grange
Wandale Fm
Wasters Plantn
Grindale Field
North Dale
High Huntow Fm
Buckton
North Cliff
Thornwick Bay
Burton Fleming
Maidensgrave Fm
Finley Hill
Grindale
Fox Covert Plantn
East Leys Fm
North Mount
Newsham Field
Bempton
Dykes Plantn
Dane's Dyke
North Landing
North Moor
Cradle Head
Stottle Bank Nook
Flamborough Head
FLAMBOROUGH HEAD LIGHTHOUSE
High Stacks
Butterwicks Fm
Lynhams
The Crofts
Flatmere Plantn
Selwicks Bay
Charlestone Fm
North Wood
East Crags Wood
High Easton Fm
Field Ho
High Barn
Flamborough Road
Flamborough
Beacon Fm
Highcliffe Manor
Old Fall Plantn
Springdale Fm
Binsdale Fm
Boynton
Eastfield Fm
Ind Est
Marton Road
Sewerby
Sewerby Hall & Garden
Sewerby Rocks
South Landing
Ruds
Thorpe Hall
West Low Wood
Fish Ponds Wood
Wandale Fm
Priory
Bayle Museum
Old Town
Bondsville Model Village
North Sands
Temple Fm
Carnaby Temple
Hallowkiln Wood
High Wood
Bridlington
The Spa
Old Penny Memories
West Hill
Ind Est
Bessingby
Hilderthorpe
South Side Mount
Carnaby
Kingsgate
P&R
Tufthill Fm
Haisthorpe Field
Thornholme Field
Haisthorpe
Wilstrorpe
South Sands
Burton Agnes Field
Thornholme
Park Rose Birds of Prey Centre
Ind Est
Carnaby Moor
Brackendale Fm
Auburn Fm
Fraisthorpe
Fraisthorpe Sands
Harpham Grange
Burton Agnes Hall
Burton Agnes Manor House
Burton Agnes
Oak Wood Fm
Burton Agnes Stud Fm
Demming Fm
Burtoncarr Ho
Hords Covert
Harpham
Little Kelk Fm
Turtle Hill Fm
Woodside Fm
Thornholme Moor
Gransmoor Wood
Low Stonehills
High Stonehills
Hamiltonhill Fm
Gransmoor Low Ho
Gransmoor Lodge
Barmston Sands
Barmston
Great Kelk
Park Ho
Lissett
Allison Lane End
Barmston Main Drain

CUMBRIA

Bewcastle Fell · Kielder Forest · Forest Park · Paddaburn · Wark · Northumberland · National Park · Black Fell · Spadeadam Forest · Thirlwall Common (North Side) · Whiteside

Cuddy's Hall · Strubbins Hill · Blacklyne Ho · Black Knors 248 · Sighty Crag 518 · Horse Head · Black Knowe 492 · Rushy Knowe · Allerybank · Crookburn Hill · Arthur Seat · Baileyhead · Bailey Head · Black Knors · Long Bar · Long Crags · Hopehouse · Great Tongue Rigg · West Cleugh · Clintburn

Blackpool Gate · Oakshaw Ford · Shawhead · Brownhill · Bankhead · Rawney · New Ho · Park Head · Grey Hill · Bullcleugh Gate · Blackrigg Foot · Danger area · Churnside Lodge · Shank End · Spy Rigg · Long Rigg · Great Watch Hill · Haining · Round Top 325 · Felcia Crags · Round Hill 310

Crossings · Sleetbeck · The Flatt · Holmehead · Crew Crag · Whiteside End · Greyfell Common · Gaylock Hill · Cammock Rigg · White Brae · Breakshaw Hill · Butterburn Flow · Gowany Knowe · Butterburn · Lampert · Black Fell · Blue Hemmel

Roughsike · Roadhead · Bewcastle · Shopford · Borderrigg · Barron's Pike · Gilbert's Hill · Jock's Hill · Whipper Slack · Butterburn · Cheeseburn Hill · Deer Hill · Gavelock Hill · Great Buckster · Hopealone · Robinrock Flothers

Stapleton · Allergarth · The Show · White Rigg · Gillalees Beacon 310 · Spadeadam Fm · Low King Hill · Jerrycalf Rigg · Berry Hill · Tip Hill · Bell's Braes · Burn Divot · Hugh's Hill · Rushey Hill · Wall Shield · Benkshill · Swallow Crags

Kirkcambeck · West Hall · Kingbridge Ford Br · Tweedy Hill · Palmer Hill · Highstead Ash · Waterhead Common · Popping Stone · Gilsland Spa · War Carr · Cairny Croft · Hadrian's Wall · Cawfields Milecastle · Whiteside · Benks Hills · Ventners Hall · Edges Green · Cowburn Hall · Sook Hill

Banks · Lanercost · Burtholme · Walton · Garthside · Low Wall · Howgill · Banks Ho · Low Broom Hill · Low Row · Trywell Lodge · Hill Head · Gilsland · Willowford · Birdoswald (Camboglanna) Roman Fort · Harrow's Scar Milecastle · Poltross Burn Milecastle · Greenhead · Walltown · Haltwhistle Common · Milestone Ho · Stanegate

Newtown · Kirby Moor · Brampton · Quarrybeck · Naworth Castle · Naworth Park · Denton Foot · Denton Ho · Low Houses · Birch Craig · Cleugh Head · Denton Fell · Black Rigg · Whamoss Rigg · Hartleyburn Common (North Side) · Cross Rigg · Blenkinsopp Hall · Haltwhistle · Melkridge · Blenkinsopp Common · Featherstone Common · Wydon Eals · Broomhouse · Warren Ho · Plenmeller · Blackcleugh Rigg · Bridle Rd

Irthington · Red Hills · Old Church Fm · Middle Park · Aaron's Town · Milton Hall · Milton · Kirkhouse · Moss Hill · Scarrow Hill · Greenside Rigg · Greentarn Rigg · Back Dike · Cocklit Hill · Byers Hall · Bridge End · Park Village · Rowfoot · Ramshaw Fell · Cairn End · Plenmeller Common

Low Geltbridge · Gelt Ho · Edmond Castle · Park Barns · Wood's Hill · Hallbankgate · Tindale · Tarnhouse Rigg · Follysyke Cotts · Haining Ho · Haining Burn · Hill Ho · Clover Fm · Lambley · Coanwood · Hargill Ho · Todhillwood · Peat Ho

Hayton · Talkin · Farlam · Boon Hill · Highfell Clesketts · Geltsdale · Talkin Tarn · Midgeholme · Halton Lea Gate · Byers Fell · Hag Wood · Lambley Common · Stonehouse · Burn Ho · Garbutt Hill · Wolf Hills

How · Greenwell · Chapel Ho · Hill Fm · Talkin Head Fm · Whinney Fell · Forest Head · Tindale Fells · Haltonlea (South Side) · Byers Pike 458 · Hartleyburn Common (South Side) · Lambley Common · Tows Bank · Quarry Ho · Coanwood Common · Laws Fell · Brown Rigg · Parkhead

Castle Carrock · Greenwell · Ring Gate · Garth Head · River Gelt · Brown Fell · Kelky Fell · Simmerson Hill · Cold Fell 621 · Blackburn Head · Larchet Fell · Butt of Blackburn · Whittwham · Eals · Wallace's Crags · Ashholme Common · Dun Hill

Cumwhitton · Faugh · Oaktree Lodge · Long Dyke · Castle Carrock Fell · Tarnmonath Fell · Knotts Wood · King's Forest of Geltsdale · Great Blacklaw Hill 595 · Faugh Cleugh · Thinhope Burn · Side Ho · Glendue Fell · Knarsdale Hall · The Bog · Knarsdale · Snope Common · Pike Rigg · Whitfield Moor

Albyfield · Cardunneth Pike · Turnberry · Geltsdale Ho · Cumrew Fell · Middle Top · Geltsdale Middle · West Dun Hill · Three Pikes 585 · Hartchyside · Knarsdale Forest · Aules Ho · Far Ho · Town Green · Slaggyford · Black Hill · Williamston Common · Low Bradshaw Hill · Barhaugh Common · Dewley Fell

Cumrew · Moorthwaite Moss · Chapel Well · Gateshaw Mill · Newbiggin · Croglin Fell · The Combs · Blotting Raise 591 · Newbiggin Fell · Butt Ho · Gelt Burn · Three Pikes · Hartchyside · Far Town · Ayle · Ayle Common · Barhaugh Common · Dewley Fell · Whitfield Law · Morleyhill · Willyshaw Rigg 497

NY · Eden Banks · Hornsby · Lawson Hill · Cairnhead Fm · Sumburgh Ho · Fieldhead · Broad Mea · Dyer's Cross 4 · High Shield · Grey Nag · Knar Burn · Kirkhaugh · South Tynedale Railway · Lintley · Castle Nook · Kirkside Wood · Clarghyll Hall · Whitely Castle · White Ho · Newshield Moss · Ayle · Long Cross

Scale:
0 — 1 — 2 — 3 miles
0 — 1 — 2 — 3 — 4 — 5 km

2 **3** **4** **5** **6**

A

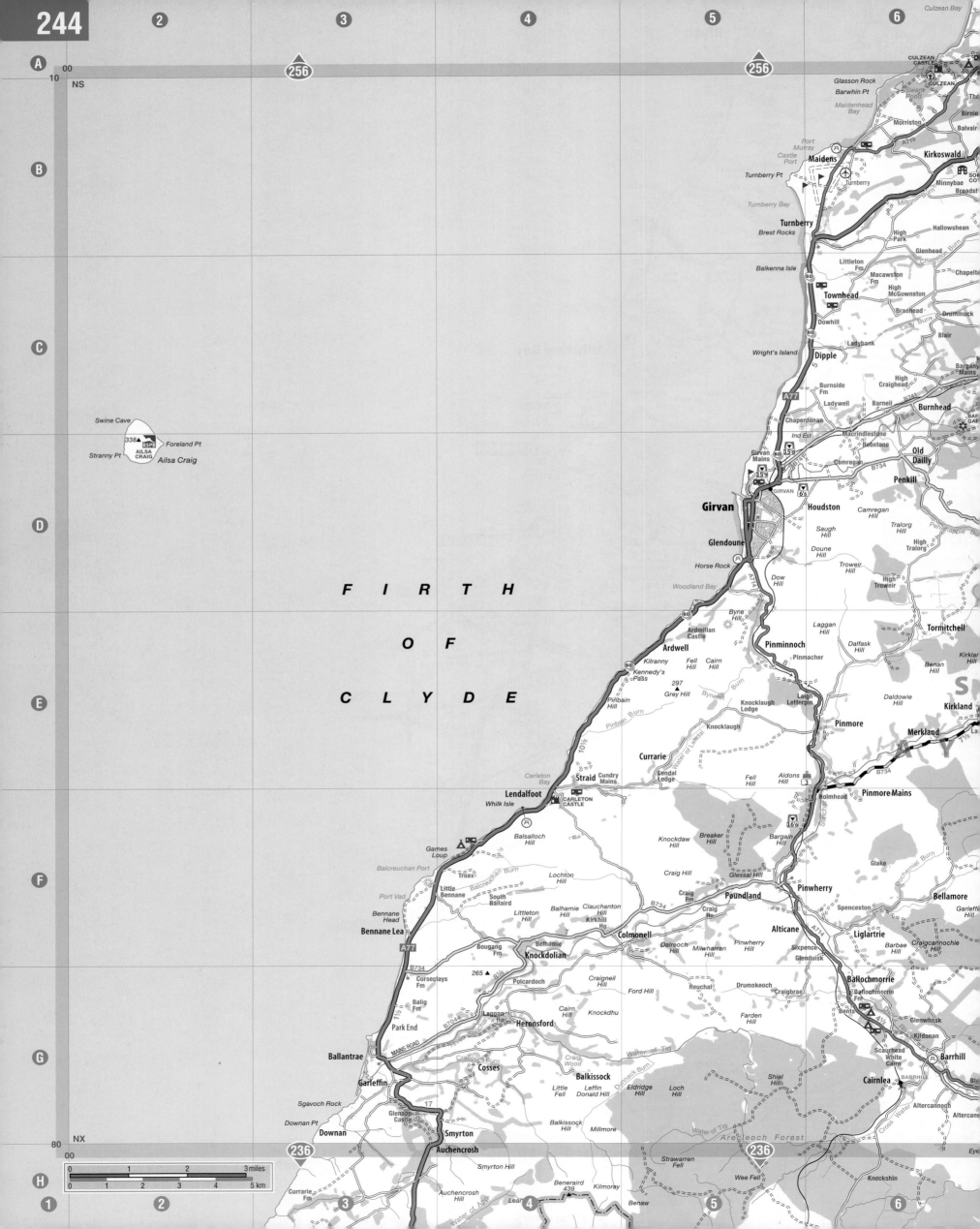

NS

Culzean Bay

CULZEAN CASTLE

CULZEAN

Glasson Rock
Barwhin Pt
Maidenhead Bay

Port Murray
Castle Port

Birnie
Balvair

Morriston

B

Maidens

Turnberry Pt

Turnberry

KIRKOSWALD

Minnybae
Broadsh

Turnberry Bay

Brest Rocks

Turnberry

High Park

Hallowshean

Glenhead

Balkenna Isle

Littleton Fm

Macawston Fm

High McGownston

Chapelle

Townhead

Braehead

Drummuck

Dowhill

C

Wright's Island

Ladybank

Blair

Dipple

Ladybank

High Craighead

Bargany Mains

Burnside Fm

Chaperdonan

Ladywell

Barneil

Burnhead

Swine Cave

Foreland Pt

338

AILSA CRAIG

RSPB

Stranny Pt

Ailsa Craig

A77

Ind Est

Macrindlestone

Robstone

Old Dailly

Girvan Mains

Camregan

Penkill

15.0

Camregan Hill

Tralorg Hill

D

Girvan

Houdston

Saugh Hill

High Tralorg

Glendoune

Doune Hill

Troweir Hill

High Troweir

Horse Rock

Woodland Bay

A714

Dow Hill

Byne Hill

Laggan Hill

Dalfask Hill

Benan Hill

Kirklar Hill

Ardmillan Castle

Pinminnoch

Pinmacher

F I R T H

Ardwell

Kilranny

Fell Hill

Cairn Hill

O F

Kennedy's Pass

297

Grey Hill

Knocklaugh Lodge

Laigh Letterpin

Daldowie Hill

Kirkland

Pinbain Hill

E

C L Y D E

Knocklaugh

Pinmore

Merkland

La

Currarie

Lendal Lodge

Fell Hill

Aldons Hill

Carleton Bay

Straid

Cundry Mains

Holmhead

Pinmore Mains

Lendalfoot

CARLETON CASTLE

16.6

Whilk Isle

Knockdaw Hill

Breaker Hill

Bargain Hill

Balsalloch Hill

Games Loup

Glake

Craig Hill

Glessal Hill

F

Balcreuchan Port

Troax

Lochton Hill

Pinwherry

Bellamore

Port Vad

Little Bennane

South Ballaird

Littleton Hill

Balhamie Hill

Clauchanton Hill

B734

Craig Fm

Poundland

Spenceston

Garleffi Hill

Bennane Head

Kirkhill Ho

Craig Ho

Liglartrie

Bennane Lea

Belhamie Fm

Colmonell

Dalreoch Hill

Pinwherry Hill

Barbae Hill

Craigcannochie

Bougang Fm

Knockdolian

A714

Alticane

Sixpence

A77

Glenduisk

Ballochmorrie

B734

Corseclays Fm

265

Craigneil Hill

Ballochmorrie Fm

Polcardoch

Ford Hill

Reuchal

Drumskeoch

Craigbrae

Glenwhask

Balig Fm

Cairn Hill

Knockdhu

Farden Hill

Bents

Kildonan

G

Park End

Laggan Ho

Heronsford

Scaurhead White Cairn

Barrhill

Ballantrae

MAINS ROAD

B7044

Craig Wood

Water of Tig

Shiel Hills

BARRHI

Garleffin

Crailloch Burn

Cosses

Cairnlea

Altercannoch

Sgavoch Rock

Balkissock

Little Fell

Loch Hill

Altercanr

Downan Pt

Glenapp Castle

17

Eldridge Hill

Downan

Smyrton

Balkissock Hill

Millmore

Water of Tig

Eye

NS

NX

Auchencrosh

Smyrton Hill

Arecleoch Forest

H

0   1   2   3 miles
0 1 2 3 4 5 km

Currarie Fm

Auchencrosh Hill

Beneraird
439

Kilmoray

Benaw

Strawarren Fell

Wee Fell

Knockshin

1 **2** **3** **4** **5** **6**

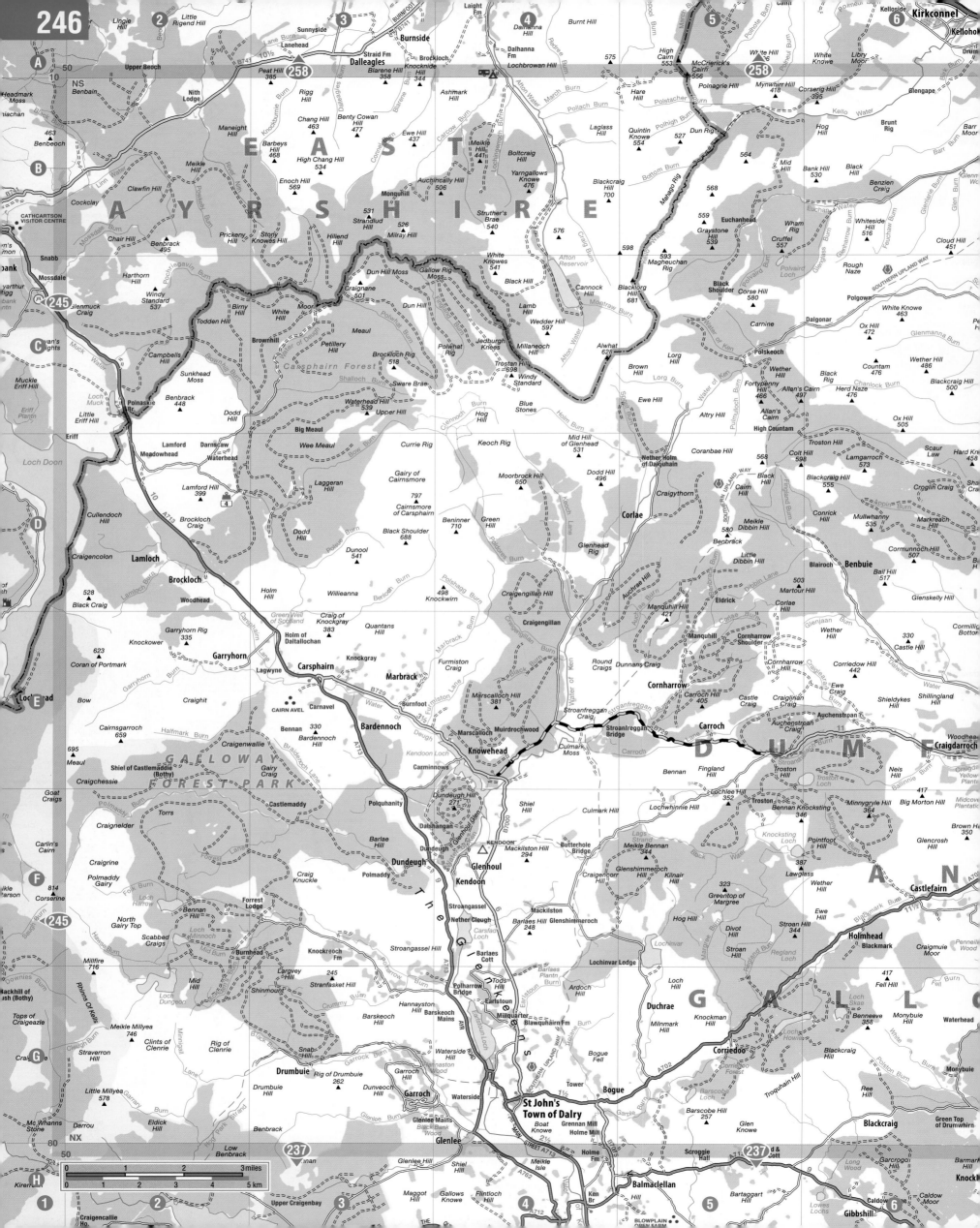

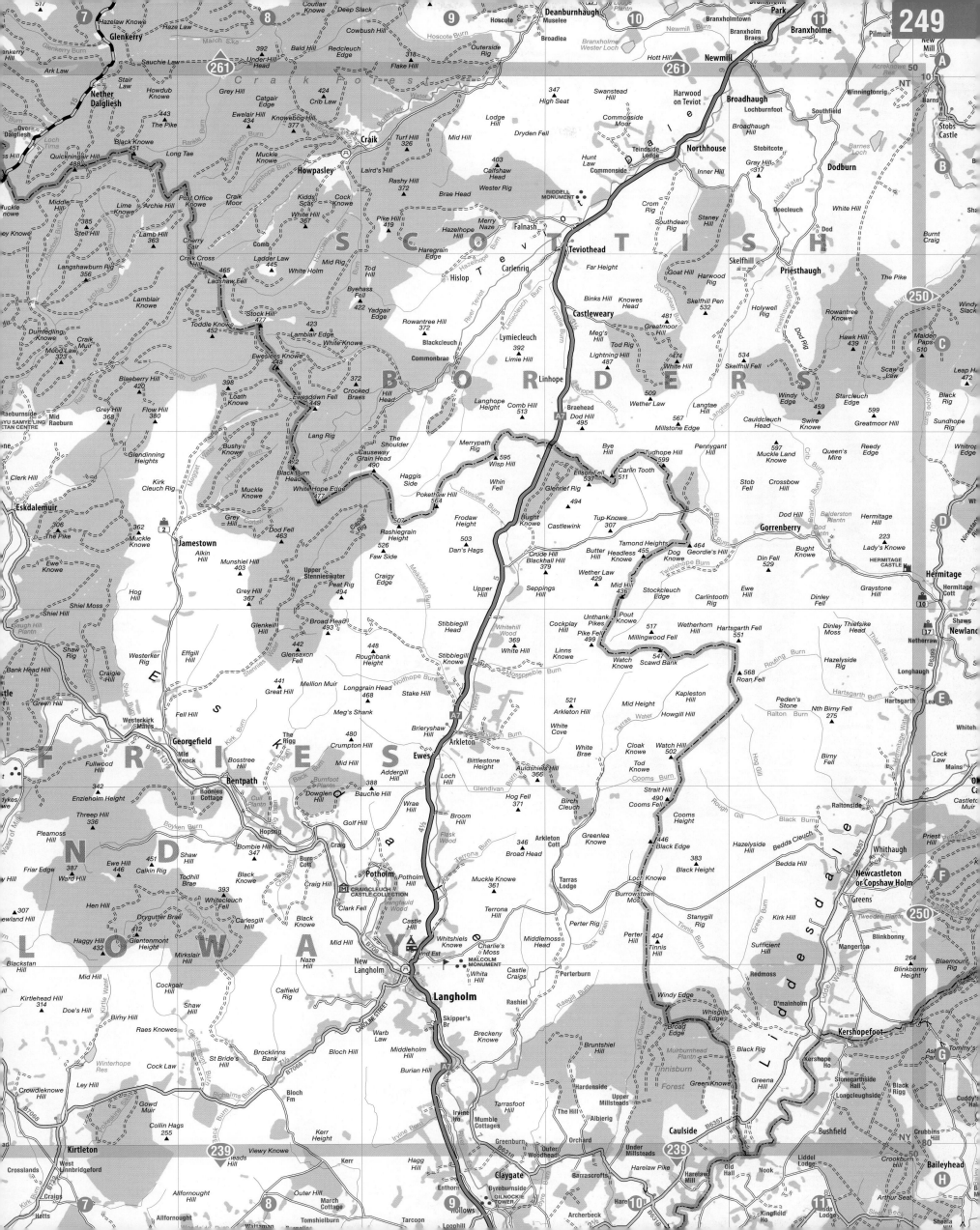

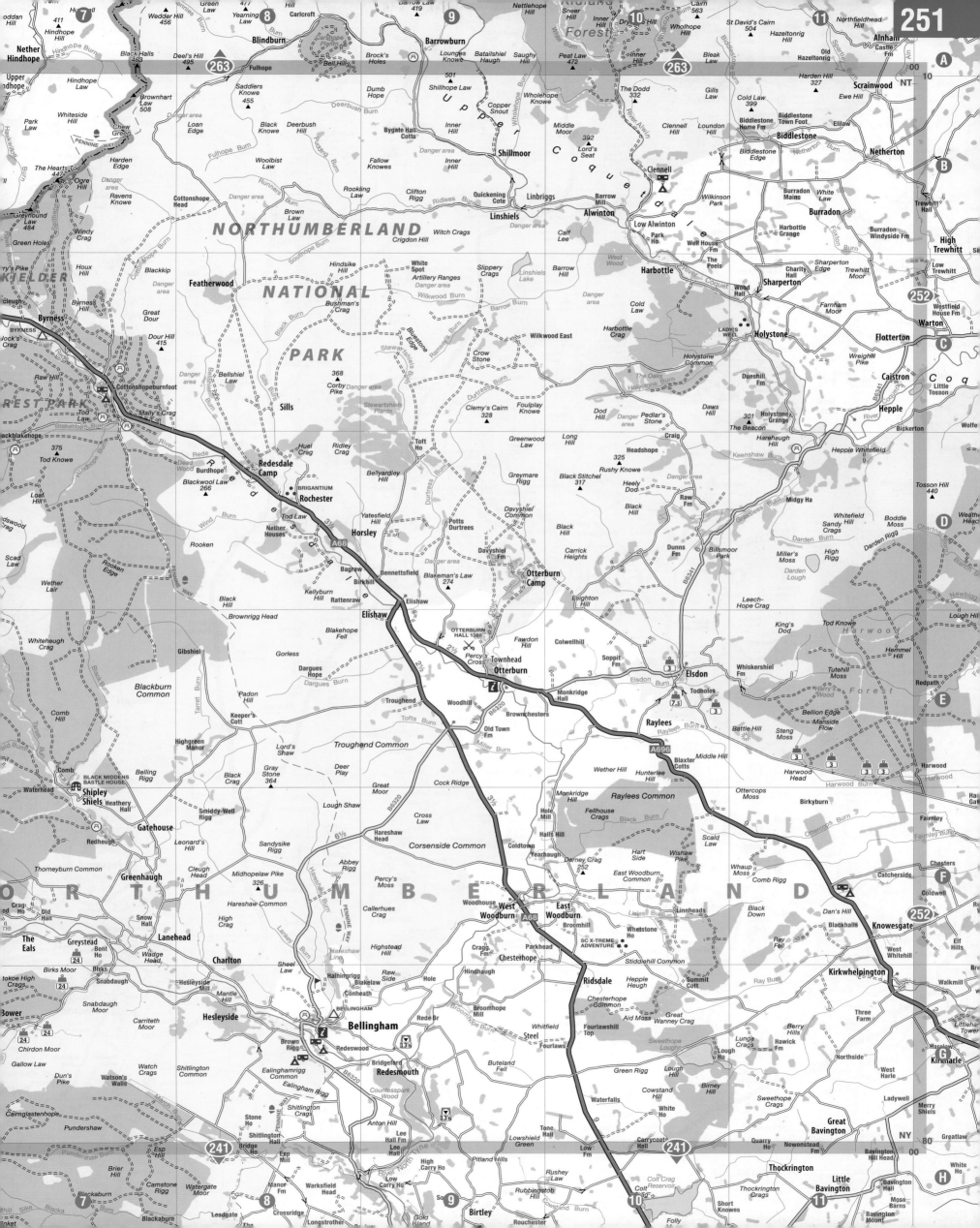

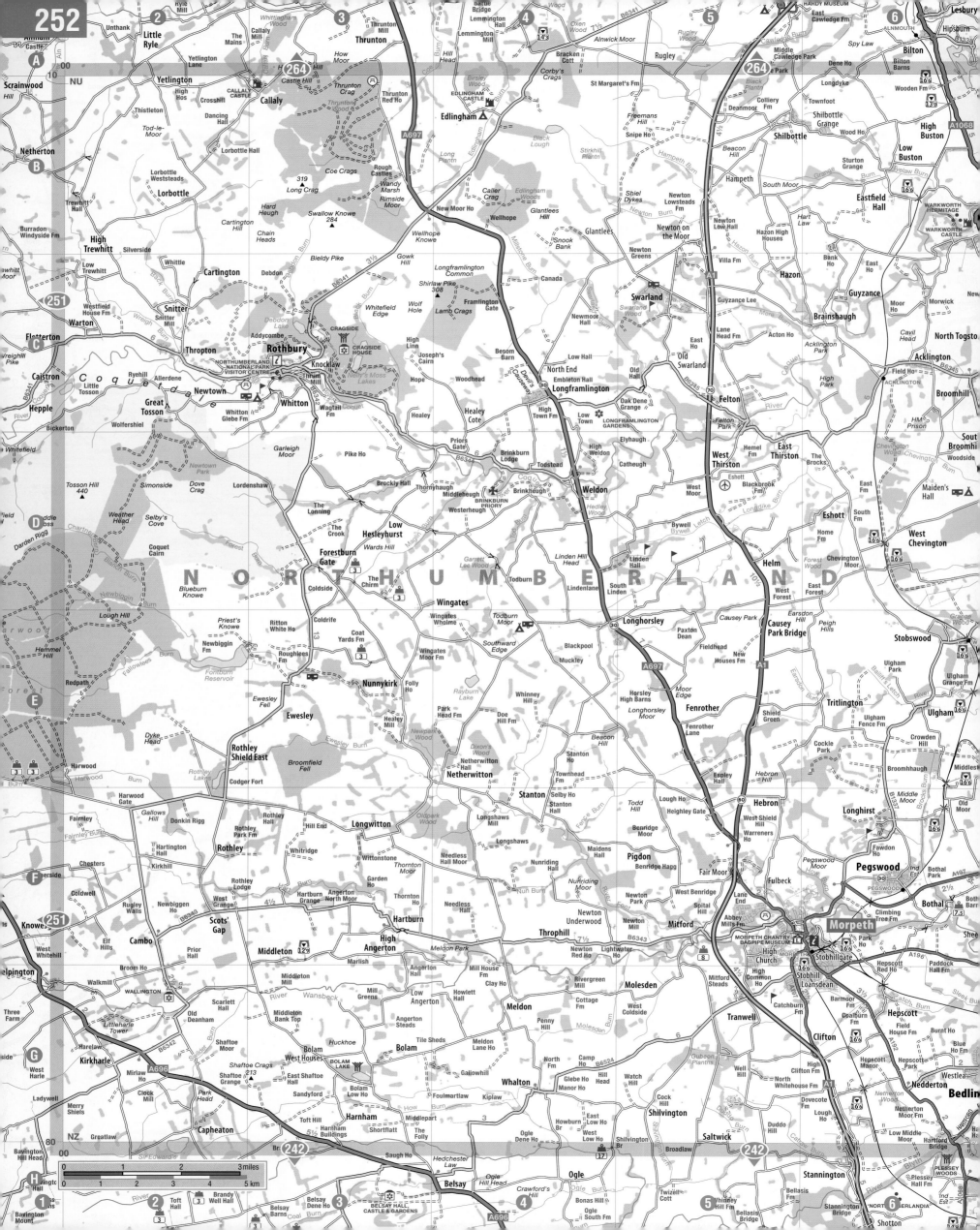

N O R T H

S E A

Marden Rocks
Birling
arkworth
Gloster Hill
Amble
Moorhouse Fm
High Hauxley
Togston Hall
Radcliffe
Low Hauxley
Togston East Fm
A1068
Danger area
Ladyburn Lake
Hadston
DRURIDGE BAY
Druridge Bay
Whitefield Ho
Chibburn Fm
High Chibburn
Widdrington
Hemscott Hill
A1068
GTON
Highthorn
Cresswell
Warkworthlane Cott
Hagg House
Ellington
Cresswell Home Fm
Linton
Lynemouth
East Moor Fm
Potland Fm
Works
QUEEN ELIZABETH II
Woodhorn
WOODHORN COLLIERY MUS
WOODHORN CHURCH MUS
A189
Bus Cen
Woodbridge
Ashington
Newbiggin-by-the-Sea
Hirst
North Seaton
Newbiggin Bay
WANSBECK
North Seaton Colliery
Stakeford
West Sleekburn
Guide Post
Scotland Gate
Bomarsund
Bus Cen
Cambois
Choppington
East Sleekburn
Bedlington Station
Mount Pleasant Fm
North Blyth
Bebside
Cowpen
Cowpen Road
Blyth
Humford Mill
A189
Isabella Pit
South Beach
East Hartford
Low Horton Fm
New Delaval
Newsham
South Newsham
Gloucester Lodge Fm
Shankhouse
Laverock Hall
Stickley Fm
Lysdon Fm

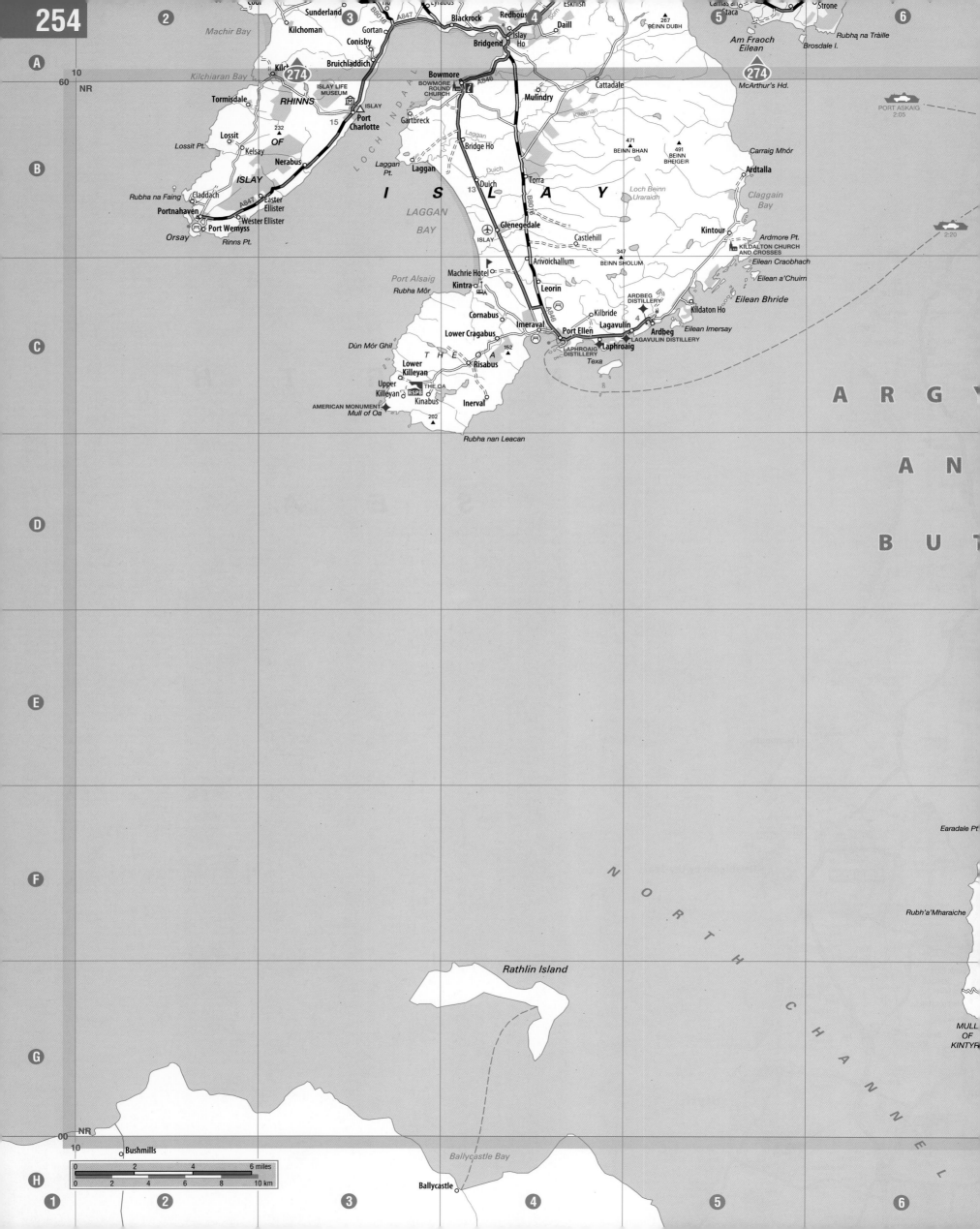

① ② ③ ④ ⑤ ⑥

A

Machir Bay
Sunderland
Kilchoman
Gortan
Conisby
A847
Blackrock
Redhous
Daill
Islay Ho
Bridgend
Eskrilish
Camas an
Staca
BEINN DUBH
267
Am Fraoch
Eilean
Brosdale I.
Rubha na Tràille
Strone

Kilchiaran Bay
Kilr
274
Bowmore
BOWMORE
ROUND
CHURCH
A846
Cattadale
Mulindry
McArthur's Hd.
274
PORT ASKAIG
2:05

B

10
60
NR
ISLAY LIFE
MUSEUM
RHINNS
Tormisdale
ISLAY
Lossit
Lossit Pt.
Kelsay
Nerabus
232
Port
Charlotte
15
Port Charlotte
OF
Gartbreck
Laggan
Pt.
Bridge Ho
Laggan
Duich
Torra
13 Duich
Laggan
471
BEINN BHAN
491
BEINN
BHEIGEIR
Carraig Mhòr
Ardtalla
Loch Beinn
Uraraidh
Claggain
Bay

ISLAY
Rubha na Faing
Claddach
Portnahaven
Easter
Ellister
Wester Ellister
Port Wemyss
Orsay
Rinns Pt.
A847
ISLAY
LAGGAN
BAY
ISLAY
Glenegedale
Castlehill
BEINN SHOLUM
347
Kintour
Ardmore Pt.
KILDALTON CHURCH
AND CROSSES
Eilean Craobhach
Eilean a'Chuirn

C

Port Alsaig
Rubha Mòr
Machrie Hotel
Kintra
Arivoichallum
Leorin
ARDBEG
DISTILLERY
Eilean Bhride
Kildaton Ho
Eilean Imersay

Dùn Mòr Ghil
Cornabus
Lower Cragabus
Imeraval
Kilbride
Port Ellen
Lagavulin
Ardbeg
Laphroaig
LAGAVULIN DISTILLERY
THE O A
152
Risabus
LAPHROAIG
DISTILLERY
Texa
Lower
Killeyan
Upper
Killeyan
THE OA
RSPB
Kinabus
Inerval
AMERICAN MONUMENT
Mull of Oa
202
Rubha nan Leacan

A R G Y

D

A N

B U T

E

F

NORTH
Earadale Pt
Rubh'a'Mharaiche

G

Rathlin Island
C H A N N E L
MULL
OF
KINTYRE

H

60 NR
10
Bushmills

0   2   4   6 miles
0 2 4 6 8 10 km

Ballycastle Bay
Ballycastle

① ② ③ ④ ⑤ ⑥

Saltcoats

South Bay
TOWN
NORTH AYRSHIRE
MUSEUM
Outer
Nebbock

BRODICK 0:55

A
00
40
NS
Merkland

Glenshant
Hill

Glen Rosa

Creag
Rosa

Torr
Breac

Glenrosa

B
Maol Donn
368

Merkland
Wood

Merkland Pt
Wine Port

BRODICK
CASTLE
Cladach
Old Quay

ARRAN AROMATICS
VISITOR CENTRE

ARDROSSAN 0:55

Glen Shurig

ISLE OF ARRAN
HERITAGE MUSEUM

THE STRING

B880

Brodick

Glen Cloy

A841

Strathwhillan

Corriegills Pt

North
Corriegills

n Gaoithe

Glen Ormidale

Fairy
Glen

South
Corriegills

Dun
Dubh

Sgiath
Bhán

255

Clauchland
Hills

Clauchlands
Fm

Clauchlands Pt

Kerr's
Port

Hamilton Isle

Cnoc
Breac

Cnoc
Dubh

Meall
Buidhe

Clauchlands

C
Isle
Margnaheglish

Blairbeg

Benlister Glen

Benlister Burn

of
Lamlash

Mullach
Beag

Holy Island

The Ross
311

Monamore
Br

Cordon

White Pt

314
Mullach Mor

F I R T H

O F

C L Y D E

Cnoc
Dubh

Monamore
Glen

A841

Gortonallister

Pillar Rock Pt

Arran

The Knowe
Fm

Urie
Loch

Kingscross
Pt

Cnoc
Dubh

Auchencairn

Kingscross

D
Dvein

Knockenkelly

Sandbraes

Glas
Choirein

NORTH

Borrach

North Kiscadale

Cnoc
Donn

Cnoc an
Fheidh

Cnoc Mòr

South Kiscadale

Whiting Bay

GLENASHDALE
FALLS

Glenashdale Burn

Largymore

Auchareoch

AYRSHIRE

Kilmory Water

Torr
dubh Mòr

Cnoc
Craobhach

Cnoc na
Garbad

Largymeanoch

Cnoc na
Comhairle

Largybeg

Largybeg Pt

Port na
Gaillin

E
Torr a'
Chrannain

Margenaish
Fm

Levencorroch
Hill

Dippin Head

Southbank

Levencorroch

Dippin

East
Bennan

Auchenhew

Drumla

Porta
Leacach

West
Bennan

Port a'Ghillie
Ghlais

Porta Buidhe

Kildonan

Port
Dearg

STRUEY
ROCKS

Bennan Head

Sound of Pladda

Pladda

F

255

Broad Craig

G

Culzean Bay

H
10
NS

244

244

CULZEAN
CASTLE

CULZEAN

Glasson Rock

Barwhin Pt

Swan

Maidens

The

0   1   2   3miles

0   1   2   3   4   5 km

Maidenhead
Bay

Port
Murray

A719

Morriston

Balvair

Castle

Kirkoswald

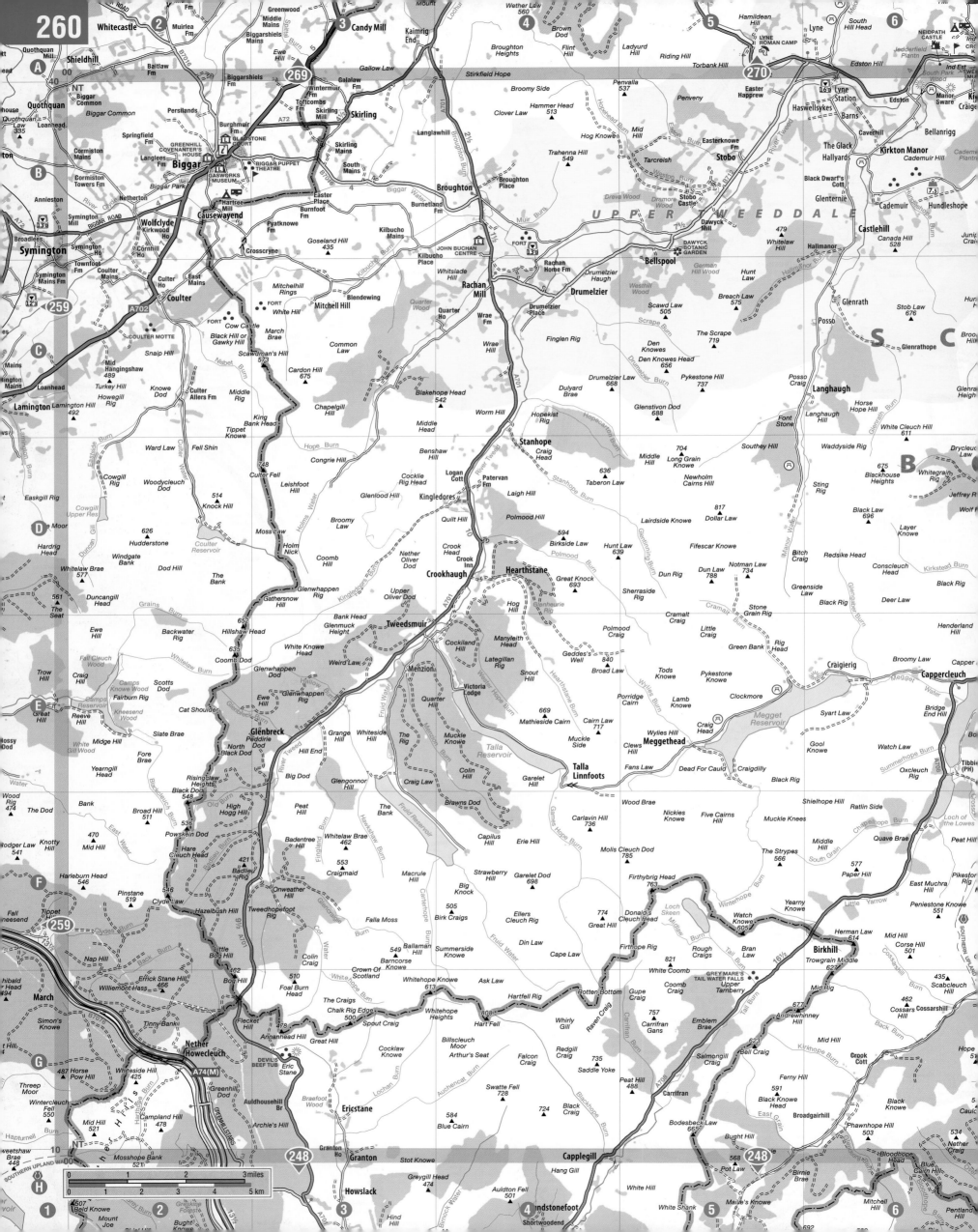

N O R T H

S E A

Castle Pt
DUNSTANBURGH
CASTLE
Queen
Margaret's Cove

Craster
96

Cullernose Pt

Howick

Rumbling Kern
Red
Stead
129
Howick
Haven

Sugar Sands
Low
Stead
Howdiemont Sands

houghton

Red Ends

Boulmer

Boulmer
Haven
field

Seaton Pt

Marden Rocks

mouth
Alnmouth
Bay

gstone

mbleton
Bay

on Pt

253

253

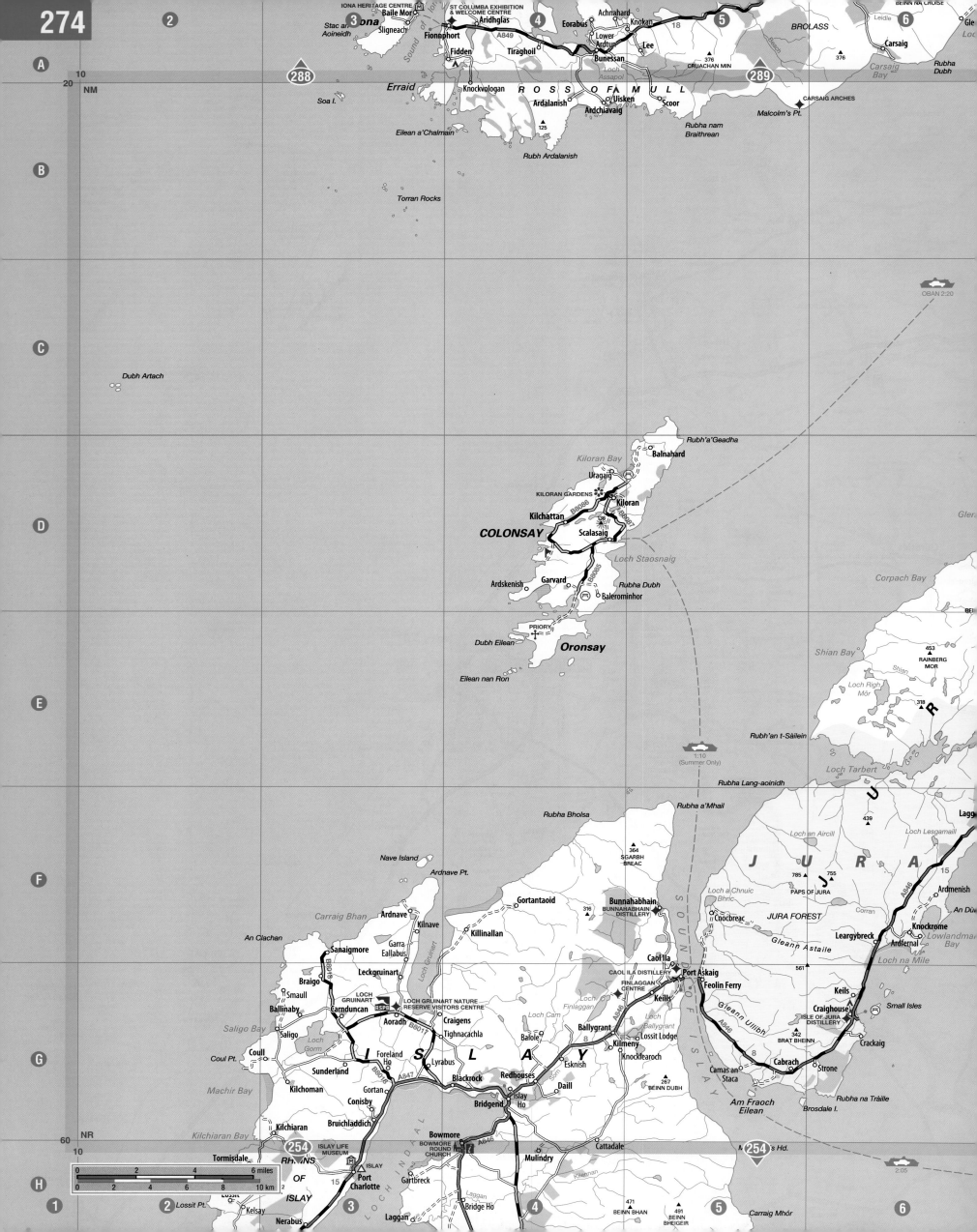

A
B
C
D
E
F
G
H

60
00
NT

2
3
4
5
6

287
North Ness
ISLE OF MAY
Isle of May
South Ness

◄281

NORTH

SEA

Bass Rock

Gin Head
TANTALLON CASTLE
Auldhame
Car Rocks

Scoughall
Scoughall Rocks
New Mains
Whitekirk Covert
Peffer Sands

Pilmuir Burn
Whitekirk
Whitekirk Br
Ravensheugh Sands
Frances Craig
Tyninghame Links
Tyne Sands

Oak Wood
Tyninghame
Salt Greens Plantn
Firth Plantn
Hedderwick Hill
Heckies Hole
JOHN MUIR
Belhaven Bay
Long Craigs
Scart Rock
Meikle Spiker

Smeaton
Preston Ho
Hedderwick
Belhaven
BELHAVEN ROAD
Dunbar
Mill Stone Neuk

Preston Mains
Preston
JOHN MUIR BIRTHPLACE
Ind Est
White Sands
Knowes
West Barns
EDINBURGH RD
A1087
A199
Broxburn
PRESTON MILL & PHANTASSIE DOVECOT
Phantassie
Barns Ness

281
Traprain
Howmuir
Hedderwick
South Belton
Old Belton
Spott Burn
Dunbar Cement Works
East Barns

Grangemuir
Bielhill
Bielmill
Wester Broomhouse
Little Pinkerton
Chapel Pt
Skateraw Harbour
Torness Pt
Long Craig
Pitcox
Meiklerig Wood
Spott
Spott Fm
Doon Hill
Meikle Pinkerton
Skateraw
Thorntonloch Power Sta
Thorntonloch

Luggate Burn
Ruchlaw Mains
Spott West Mains
Spott Mill
Pinkerton Hill
Thurston Manor
Crowhill
Whittingehame Mains
Stenton
Bennet's Burn
THE CHESTERS (FORT)
Brunt Hill
The Brunt
Innerwick
Thurston Mains

Whittingehame Ho
Ruchlaw West Mains
Pressmennan Wood
Highside Hill
Thurston Mains Burn

Deuchrie Dod
Rammer Wood
EAST
Halls
Blaik Law
Ogle Burn
Old Branxton
Bilsdean Creek
Reed Pt

Garvald Grange
Birks Plantn
Deuchrie Wood
High Wood
Berry Hill
Needle Hill
Blackcastle Hill
Oldhamstocks Mains
DUNGLASS COLLEGIATE CHURCH
Belvidera Wood
Cove Harbour
Cove
Cove Fm
Pease Bay
Red Rock

Stoneypath Tower
Lothian Edge
Oldhamstocks
Cockburnspath
Dovecot Hall
Greenheugh Pt
Siccar Pt
Garvald
Robin Tup's Plantn
Common Plantn
Moorcock Hall
Sheeppath Glen
Stottencleugh
Neuk Fm
Meikle Poo Craig
Hirst Rocks

NRAW ABBEY
Garvald Mains
LOTHIAN
Deuchrie Edge
Watch Law
Bransly Hill
Dunglass Burn
272
Stockbridge
Tower Fm
Old Cambus Townhead
Old Cambus

NT
60
Dunbar Common
272
Birny Knowe
Old Townhead
A1107
Penmanshiel Wood

BLACK WOOD
0   1   2   3 miles
0   1   2   3   4   5 km
WHITE CASTLE (FORT)
Clints Dod
Bachil Rig
Friardykes Dod
Mony's Burn
Saddle Hill
Wightman Hill
Ecclaw
Greenside Wood
Meikle Black Law
Cambus Wood

Lumsdaine

St Abb's Head
ST ABB'S HEAD
Horsecastle Bay

Bell
Hill

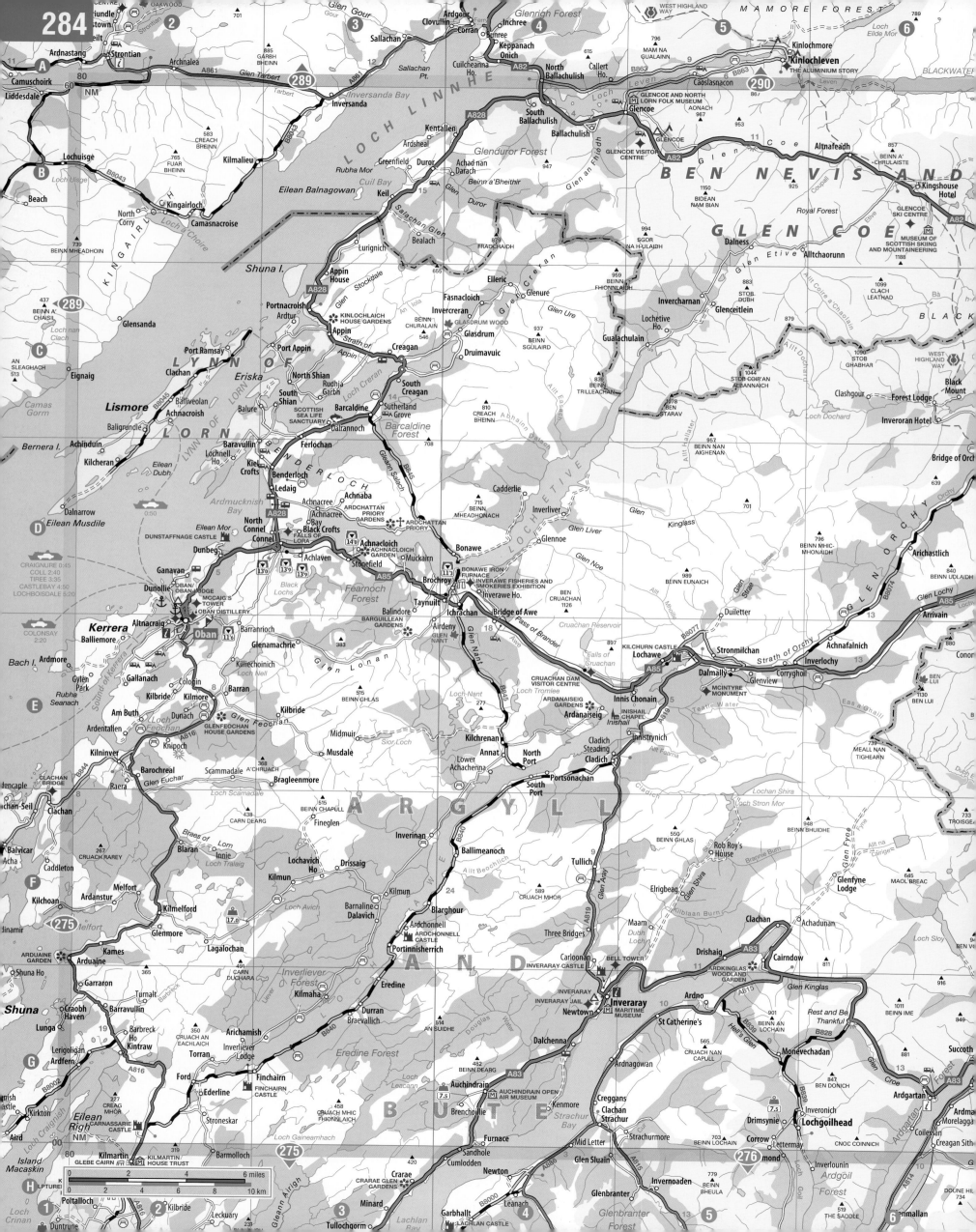

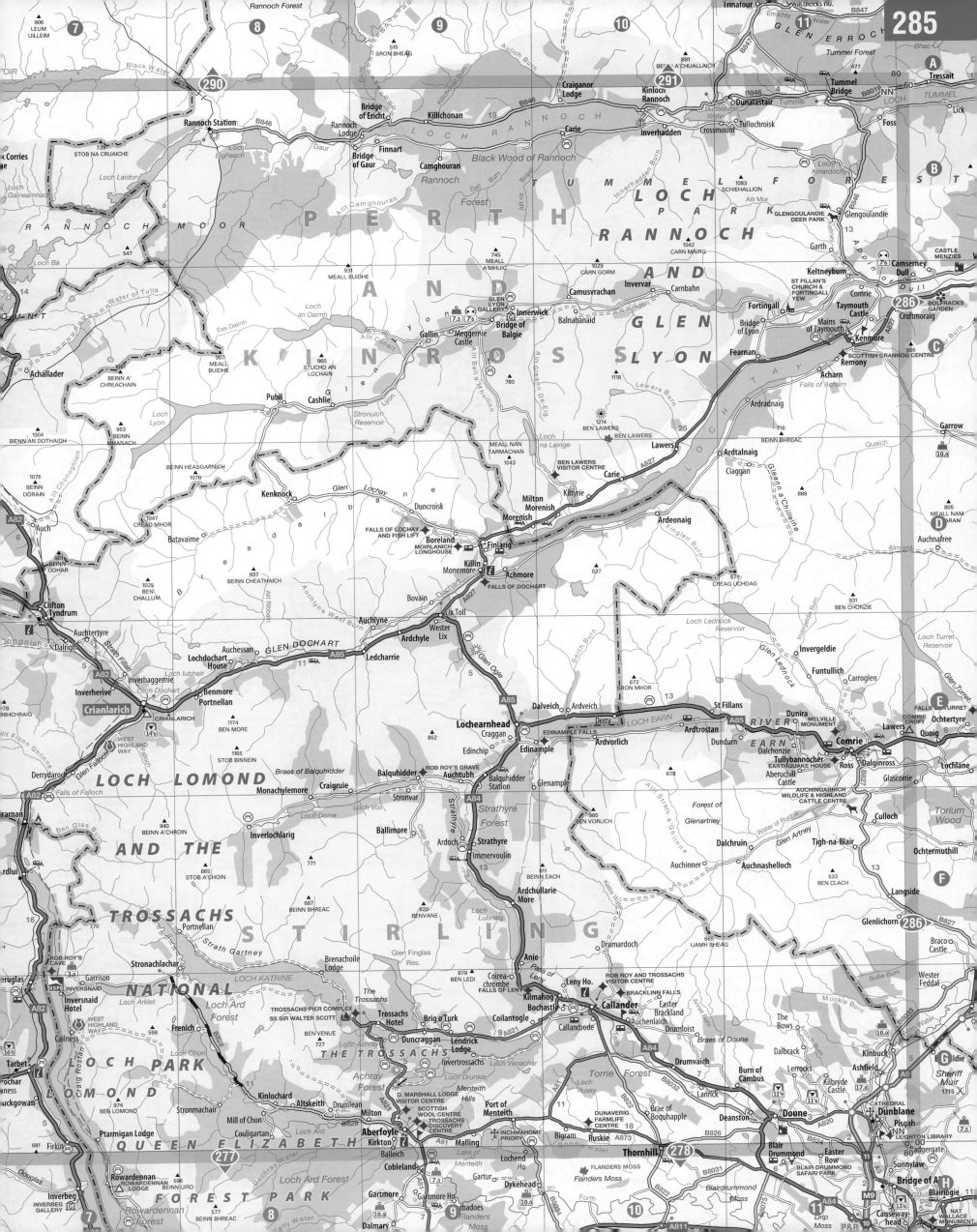

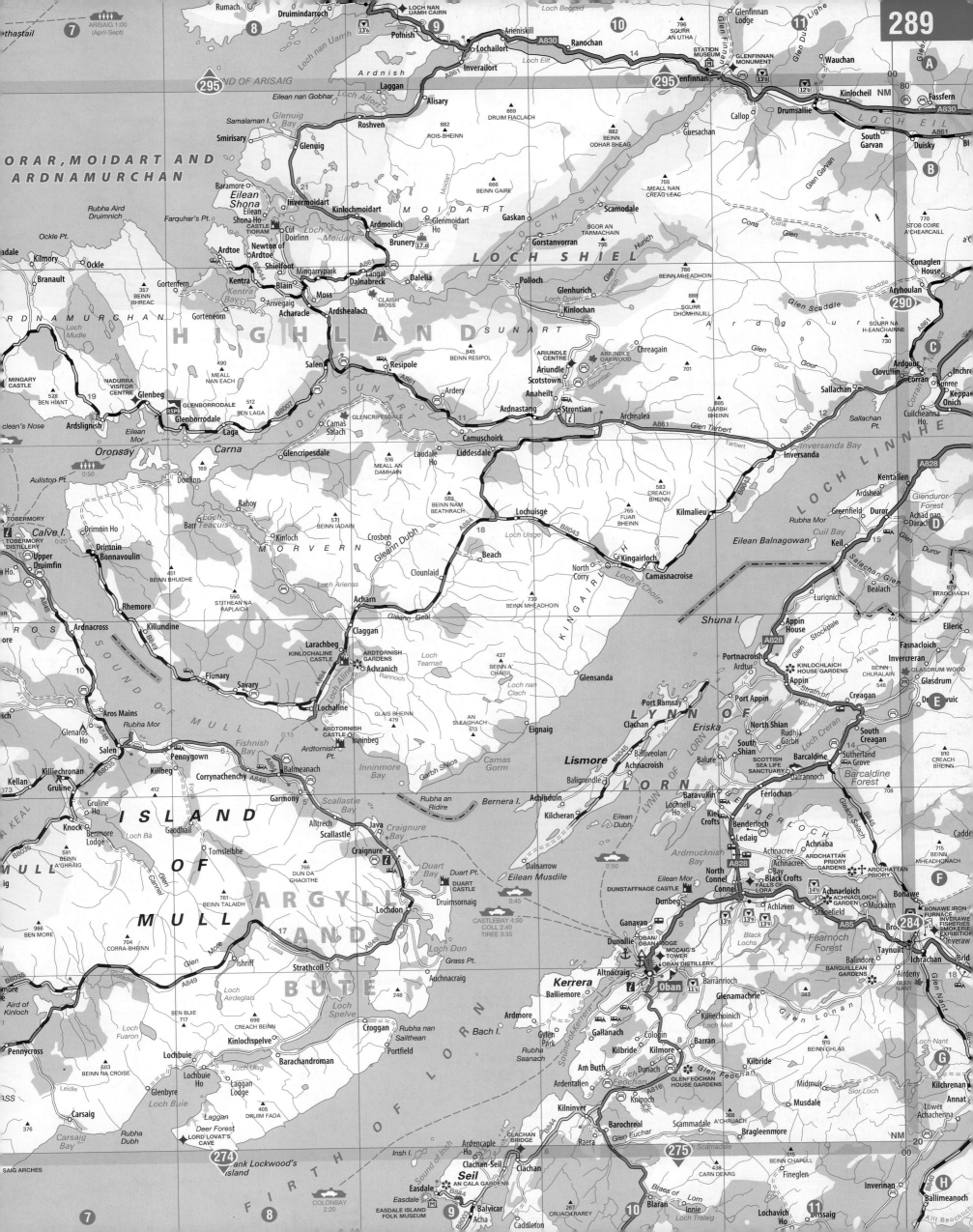

2   **3**   **4** Roag Vatten   Baimeanach   **5** Loch Connan   **6** ermor Shuli   **7**
Ramasaig   THE AROS
Hoe Rape   **4** Orbost   EXPERIENCE
                   Macleod's   Greep   Harlosh   Heatherfield
                   Tables   Balmore   417
              488   B885
              HEALABHAL BHEAG   10   Glenmore
A   Eabost   A87
00   Hoe Point   Loch   West   Ose
40   Varkasaig Eabost   Bracadale Totardor   Loch   Mugeary
NG   Ullinish   Duagrich
                         Geodha Mor   Harlosh I.   Tarner I. Struan Coillore
                                     Loch Bracadale   Gesto   ROINEVAL
B   Wiay   Oronsay   Ho Portnalong   439
                                                    Ardtreck   Loch
                   MACLEOD'S MAIDENS   Idrigill Point   Fiskavaig   Harport   Drynoch   Crossal
                                                    Rubha   Fernilea
                                                    nan Clach ARNAVAL TALISKER   A863
                                                              369 DISTILLERY Satran
                                                            Gleann Oraid Carbost Merkadale   Drynoch
                                                    Talisker Bay   Sligachan
                                                         Talisker   Hotel
C   Glen Brittle
                                                              Eynort Forest   SGURR NAN
                                                         445 Grula   GILLEAN
                                                         BEINN BHREAC   459   964
                                                                                SGURR
                                                                              A'GHREADAIDH
              297   Loch Eynort   973
                                                    Kraiknish   MINGINIS
                                                                  GLENBRITTLE   CUILLIN HILLS
D   Glenbrittle House
                                                              Bualintur   992
                                                              Culnaneam SGURR
                                                                   ALASDAIR Loch
                                                    Rubh an Dunain   924 Coruisk
                                                                        SGURR
                                                                        NAN EAG
                                                         Soay Sound   **Soay**
                                                              Mol-chlach
                                                                        PRINC

E   **Canna**
                        Garrisdale Pt.   A'Chill   Rubha Shamhnan Insir
                                          Canna Harbour
                                   Sanday   Sound of Canna Kilmory
                                                 Guirdil   0:55   MALLAIG 2:30
                                                 Bay   388 Kilmory Glen   (Sat only)
                                                       Kinloch Glen   Rubha na Roinne
                                          A'Bhrideanach   Kinloch
F   Oigh-sgeir   Schooner Pt. 571 R Ù M KINLOCH Rubha Port
                                                 ORVAL   RÙM CASTLE na Caranean
                                          Harris Glen Harris 812
                                                       ASKIVAL
                                          Rubha Sgorr an t-Snidhe 781
                                                       AINSHVAL   1:00
                                                                  1:10 SOUND OF RÙM
                                          Rubha nam
                                          Meirleach
                                                         Bay of Laig   Cleada
G   Rubha an   Laig
00   Fhasaidh
NM   **Eigg**
                                                         Sandavore
              393
              AN SGURR Galm
                                          Eilean nan Each   SOUND OF EIGG
80   Gallanach   Port Mor   0:35
00 NM   **288**   **288** 137
              288

H 0   2   4   6 miles
       0   2   4   6   8   10 km

1   **2**   **3**   **4**   **5**   **6**

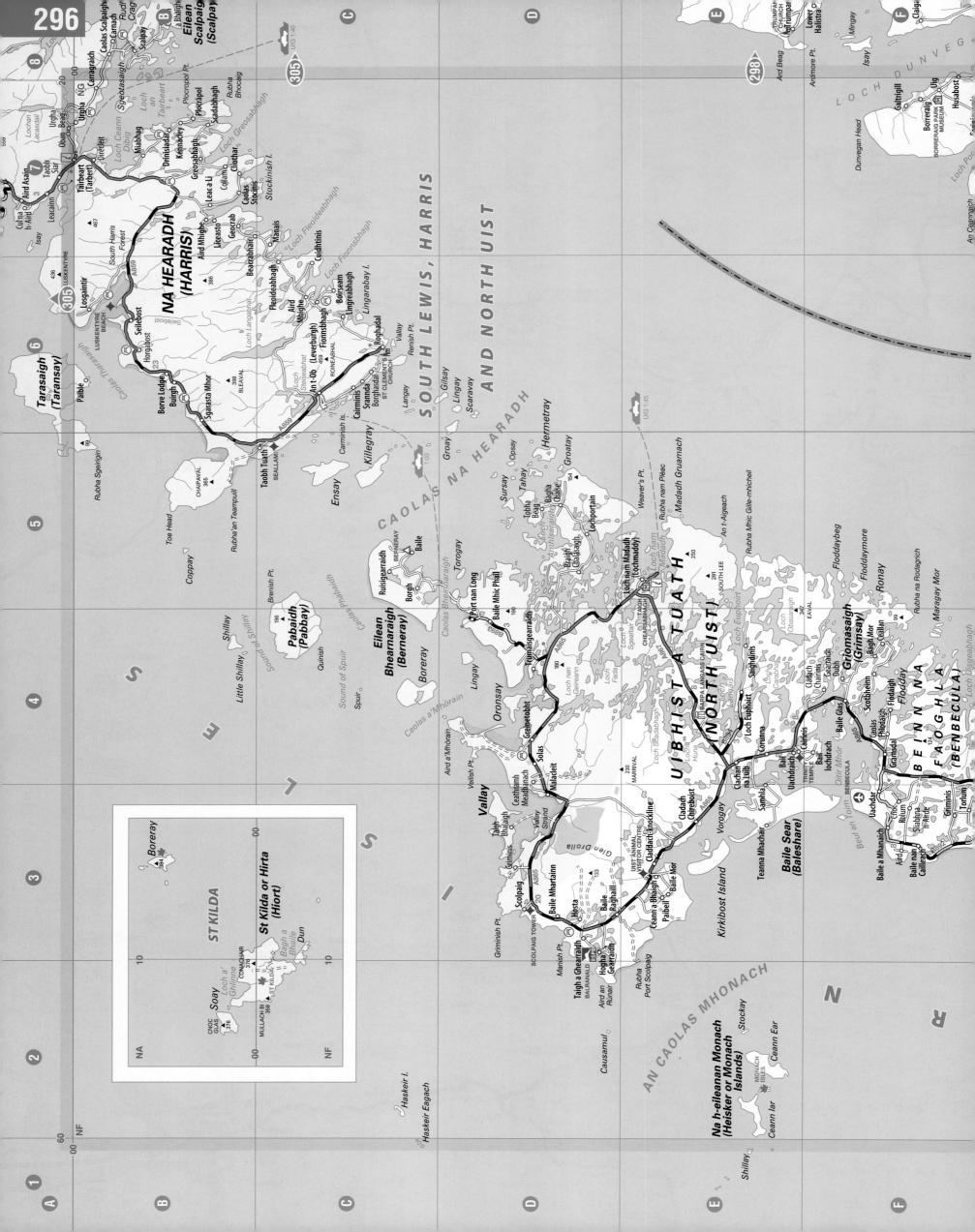

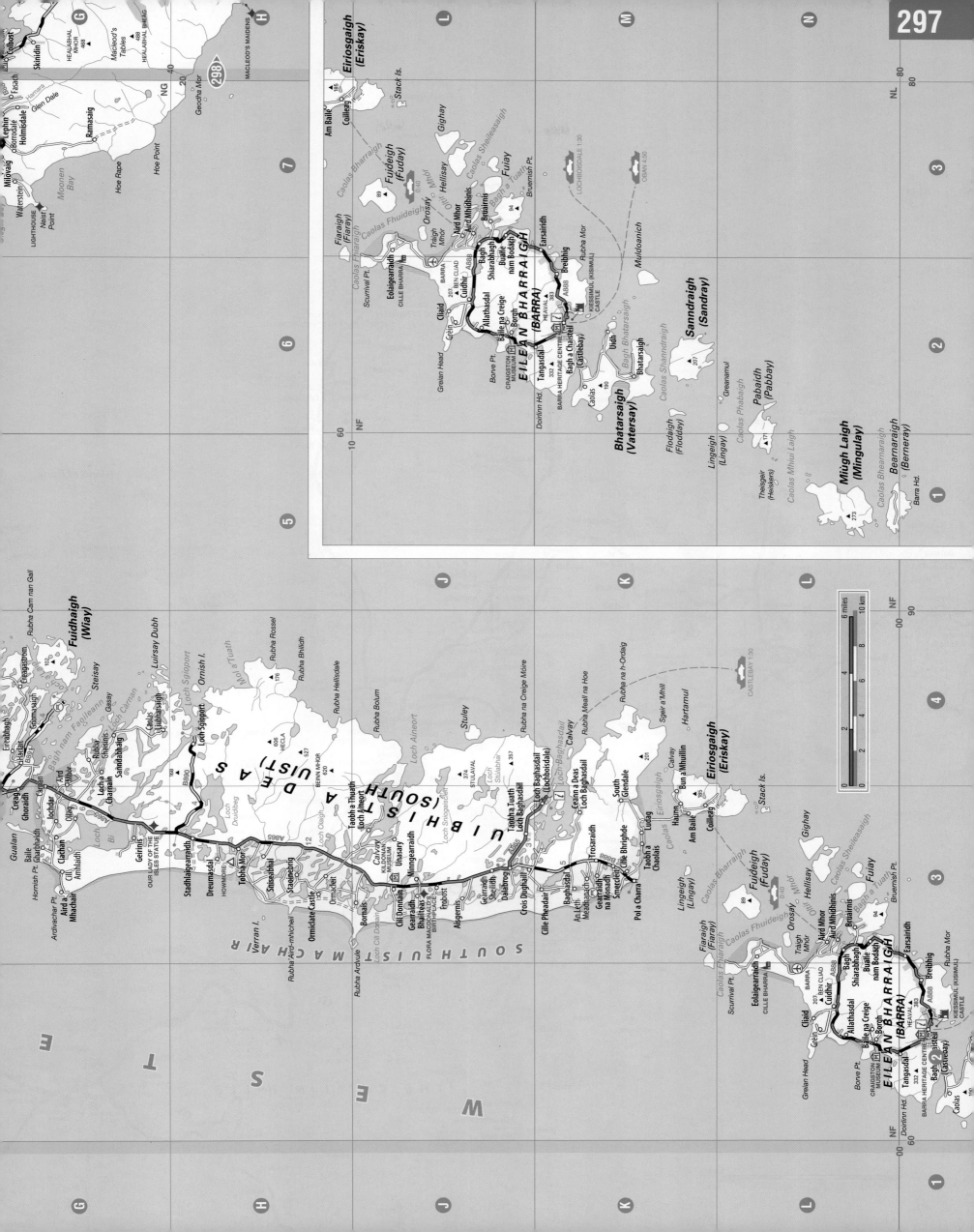

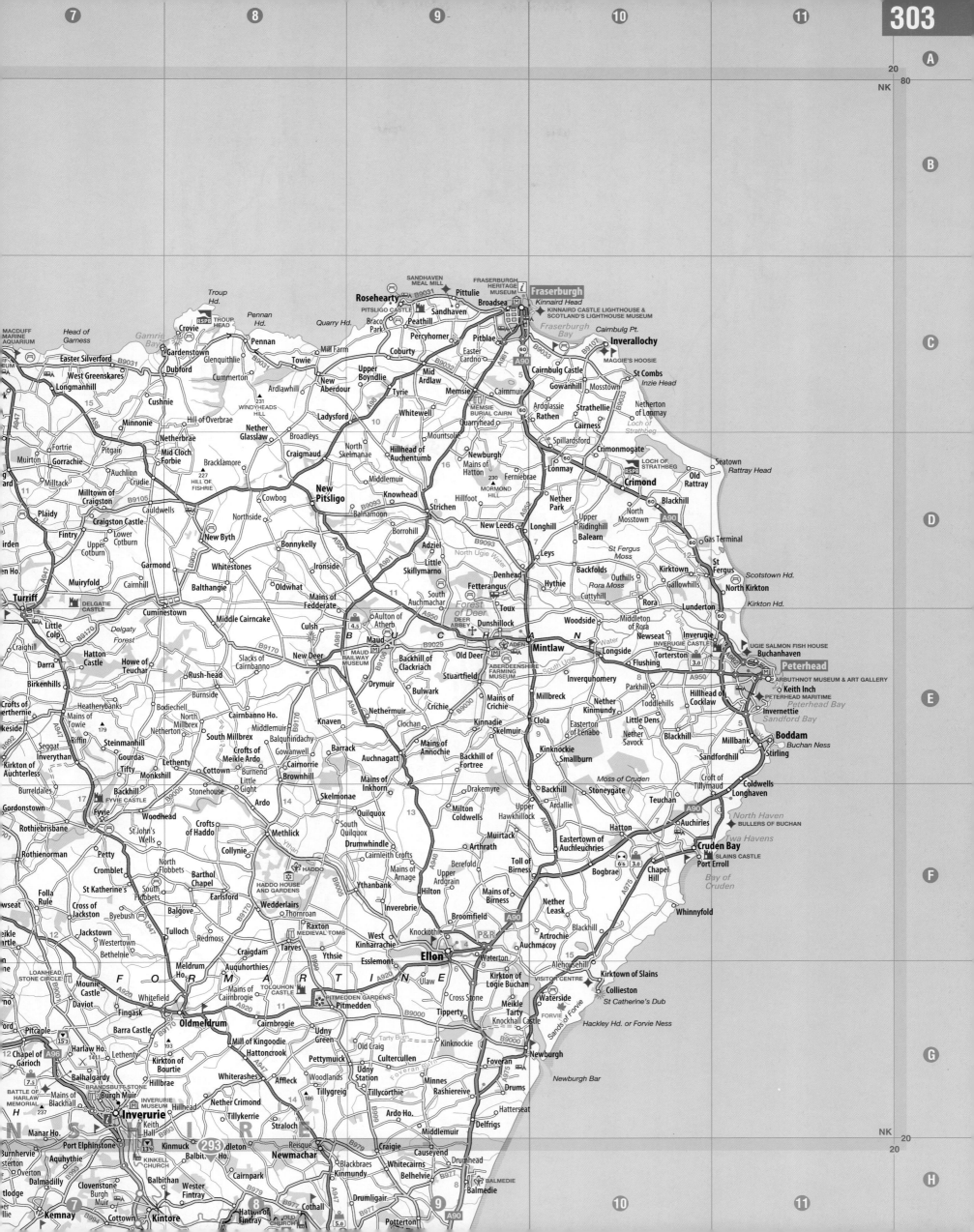

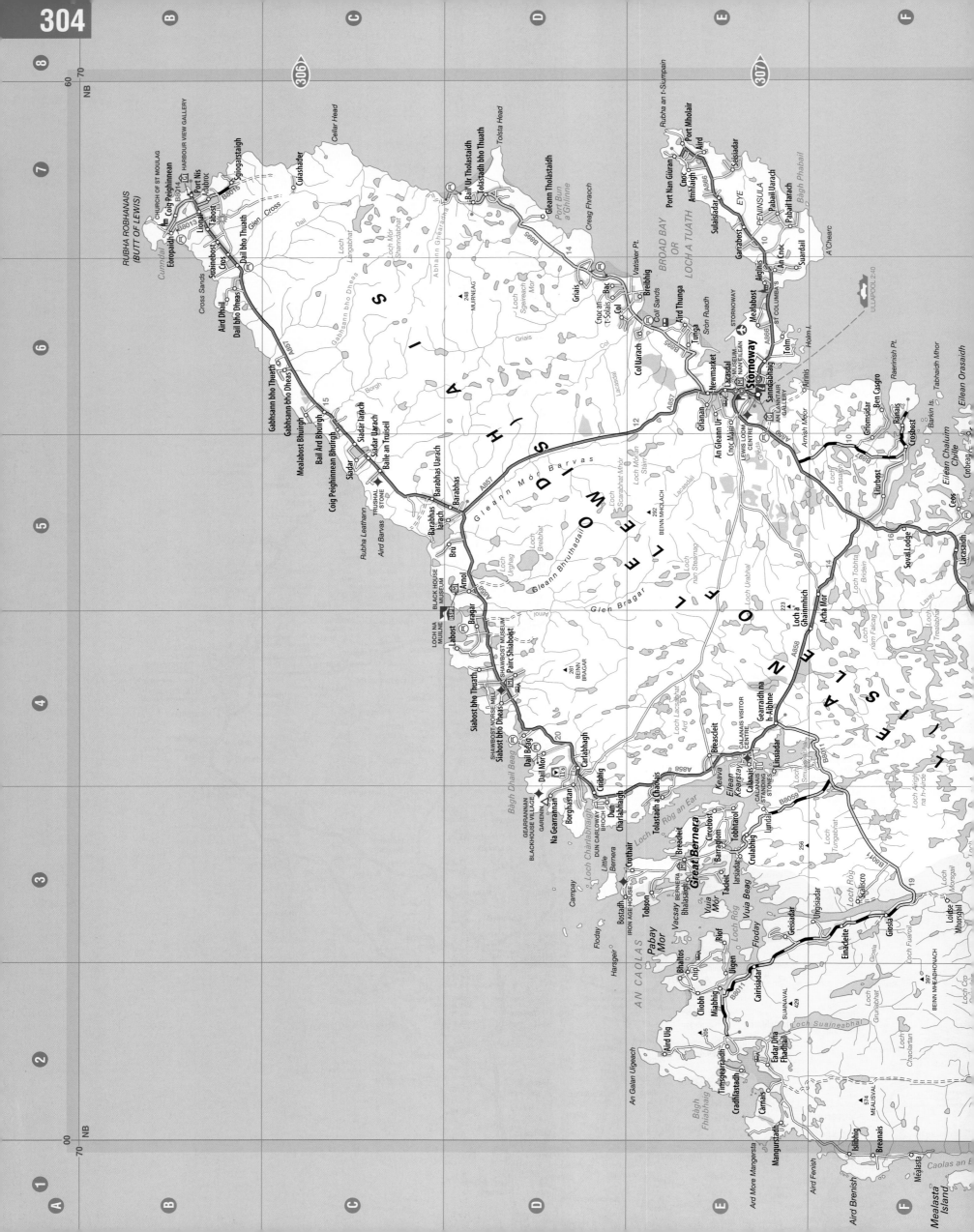

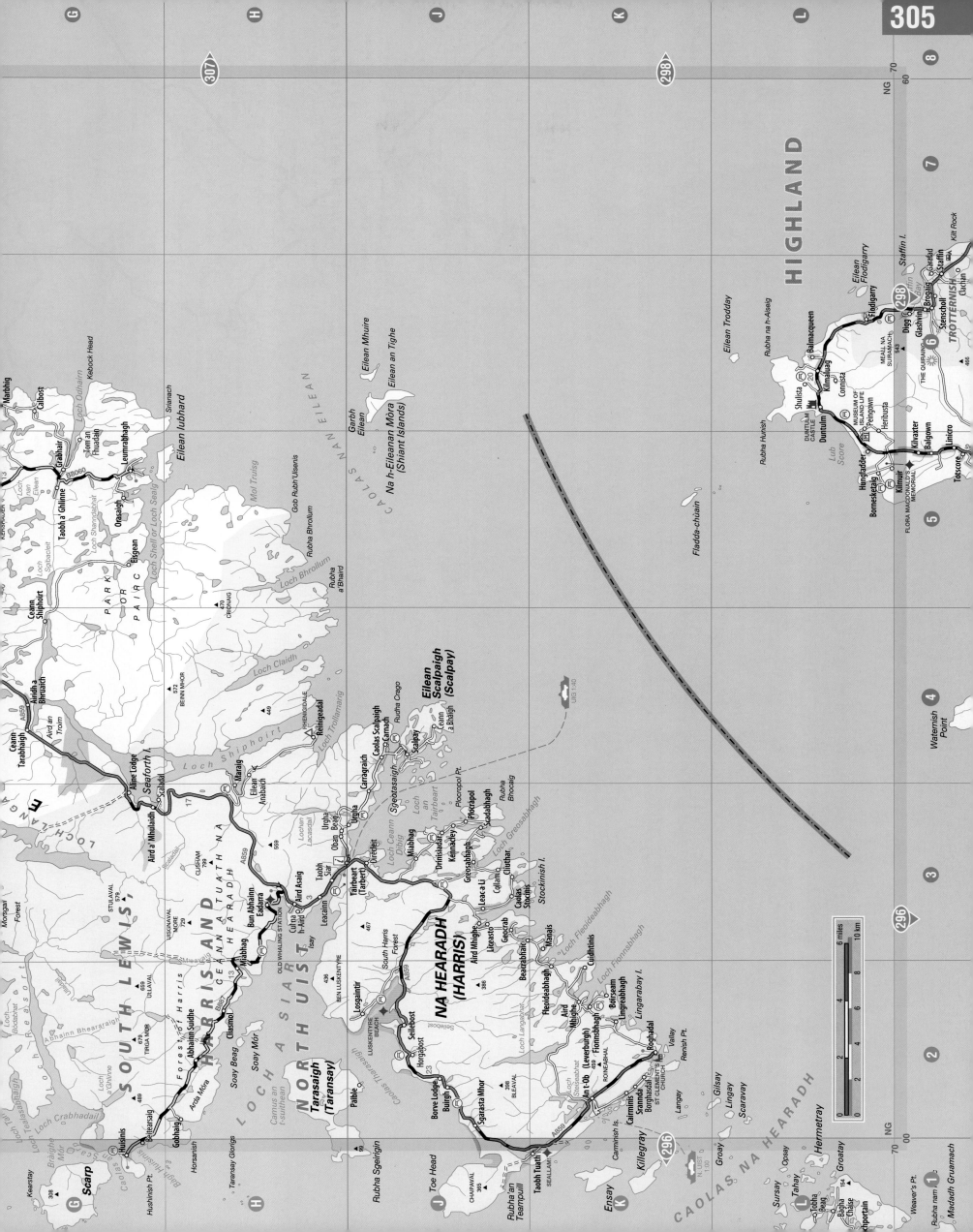

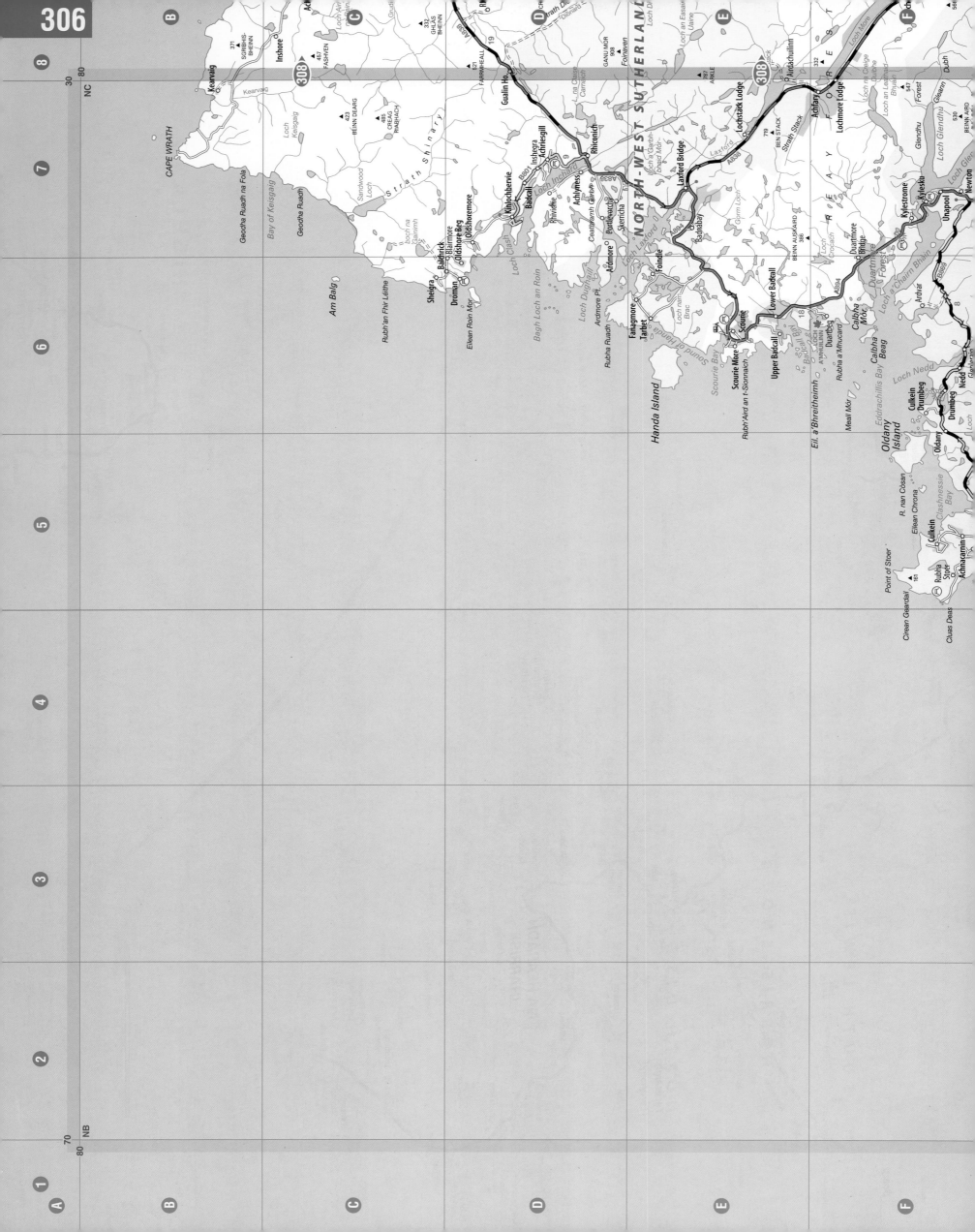

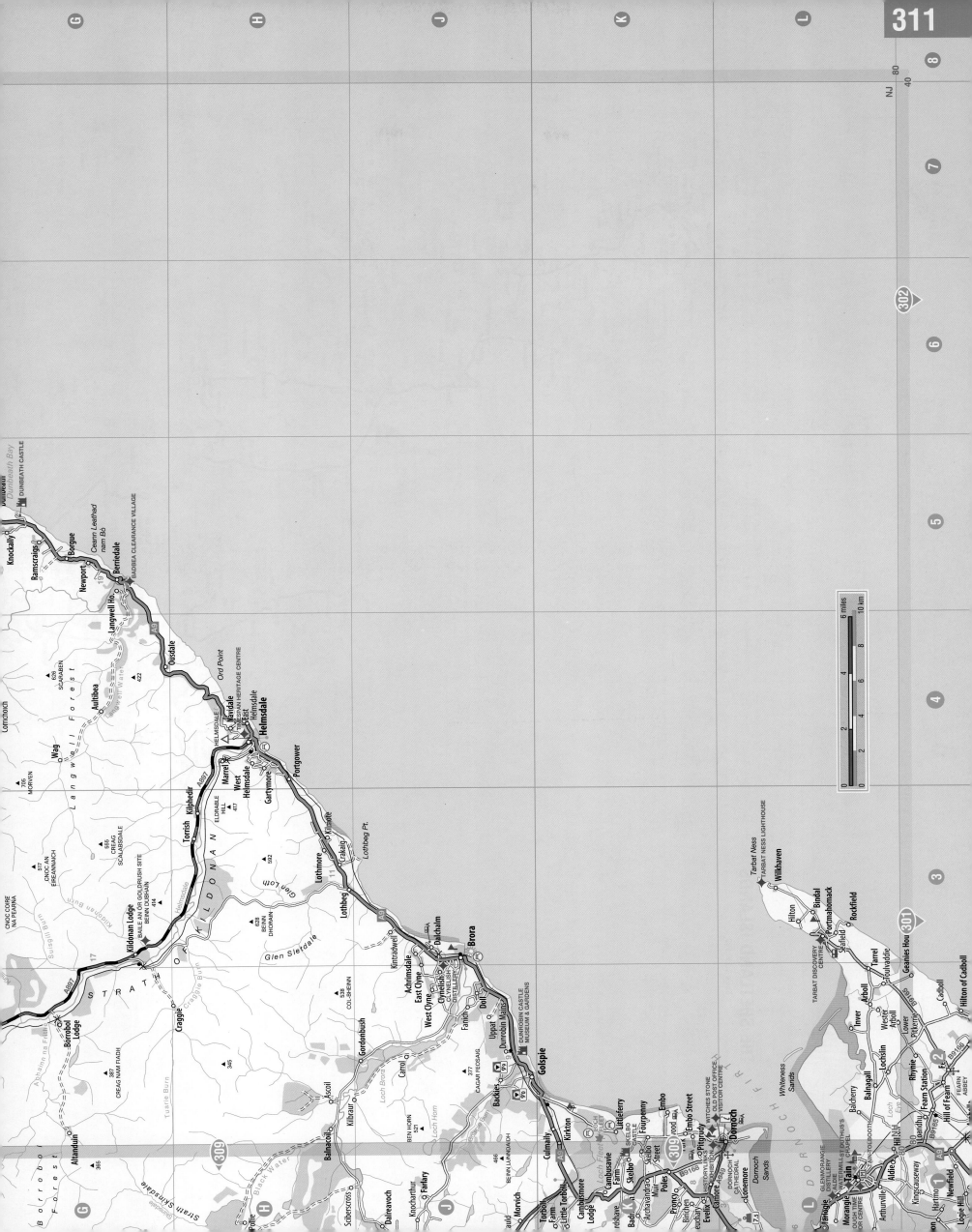

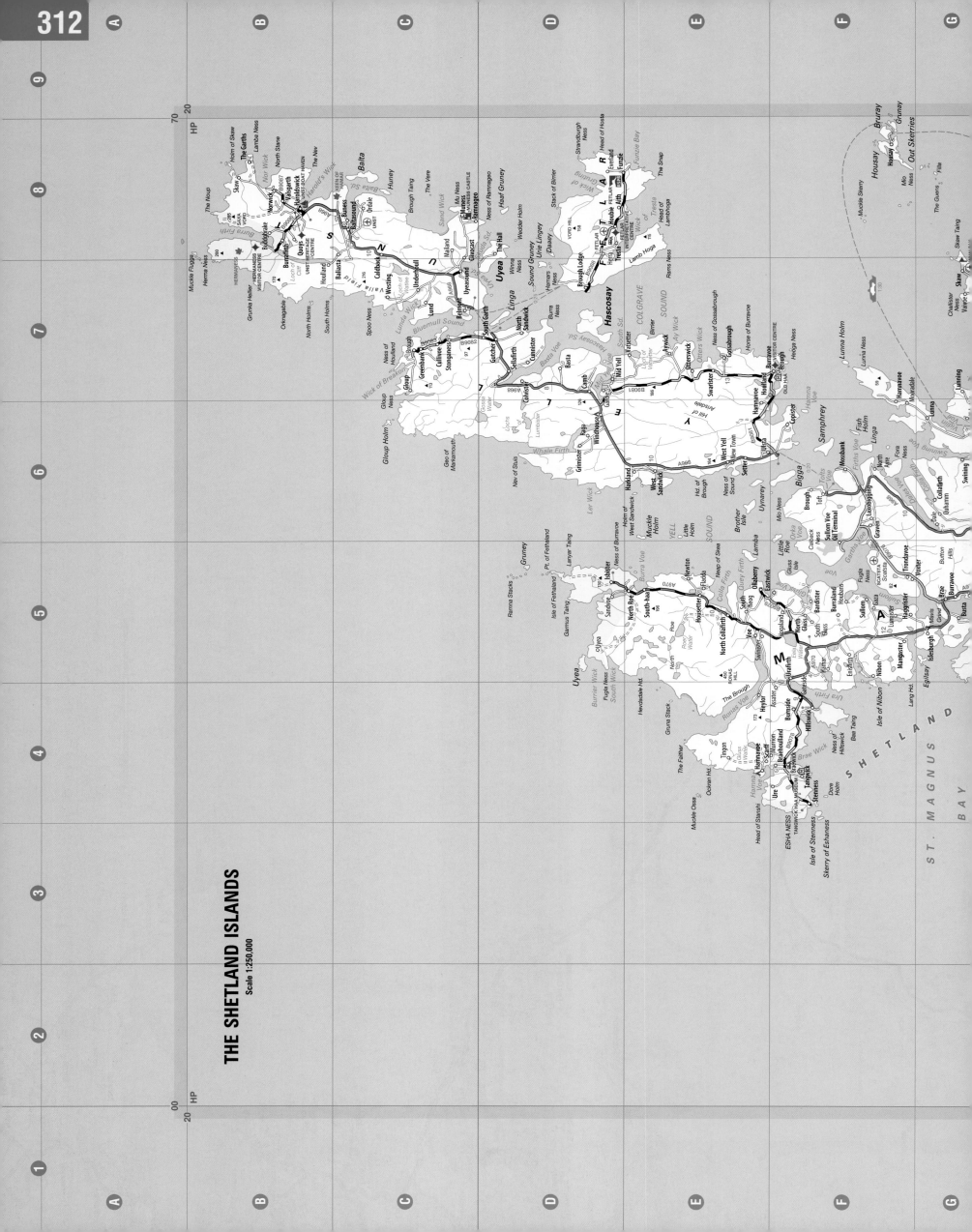

THE SHETLAND ISLANDS

Scale 1:250,000

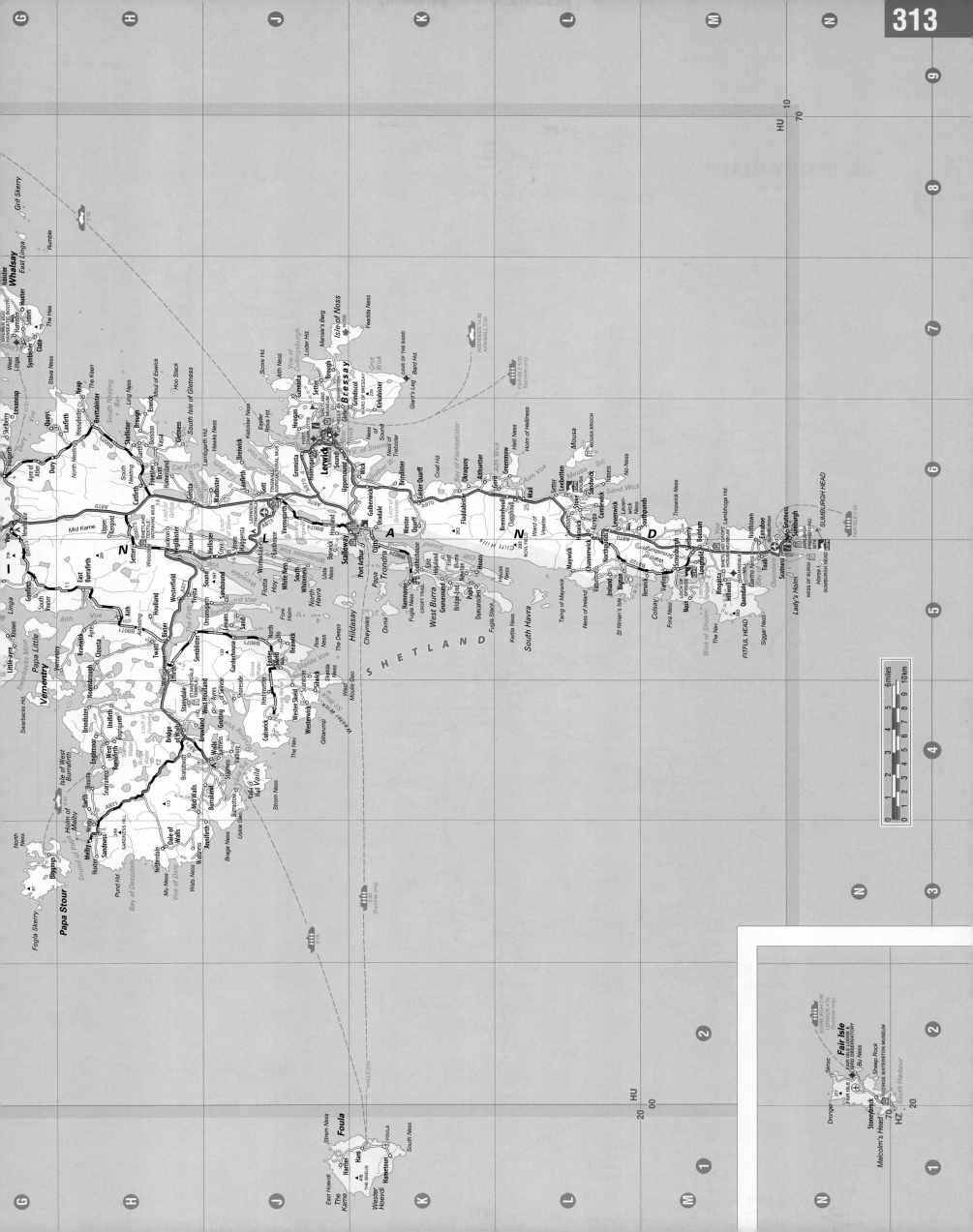

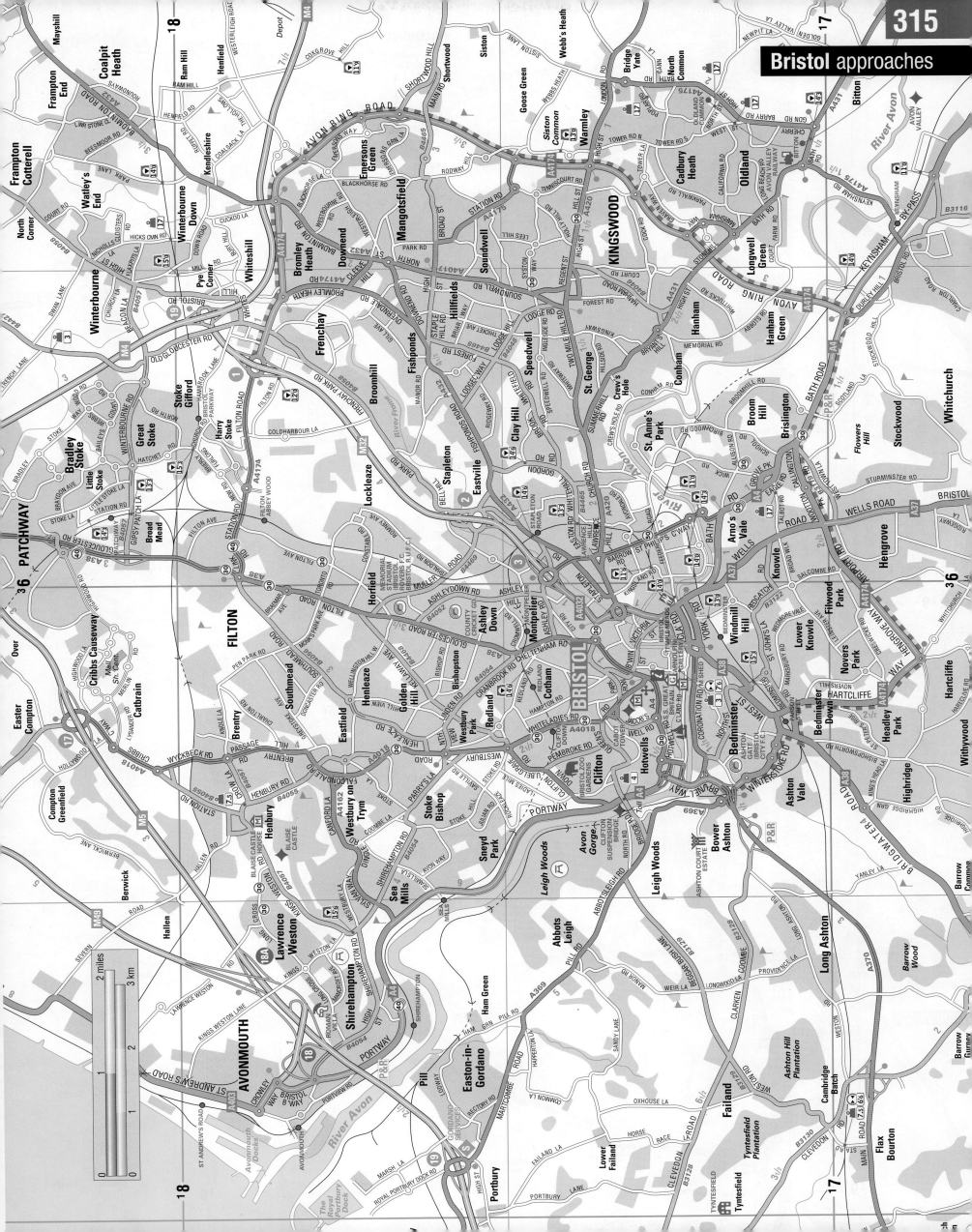

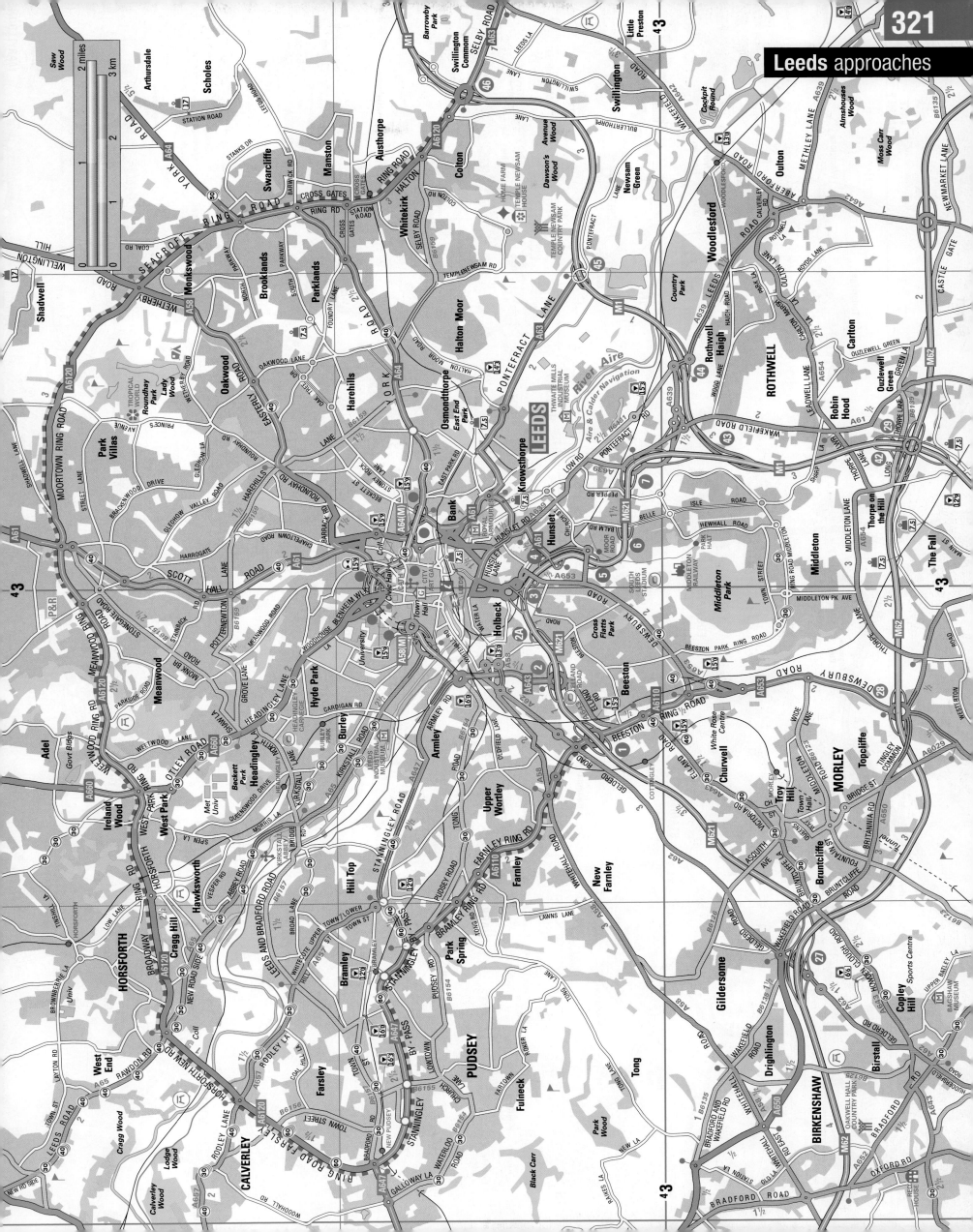

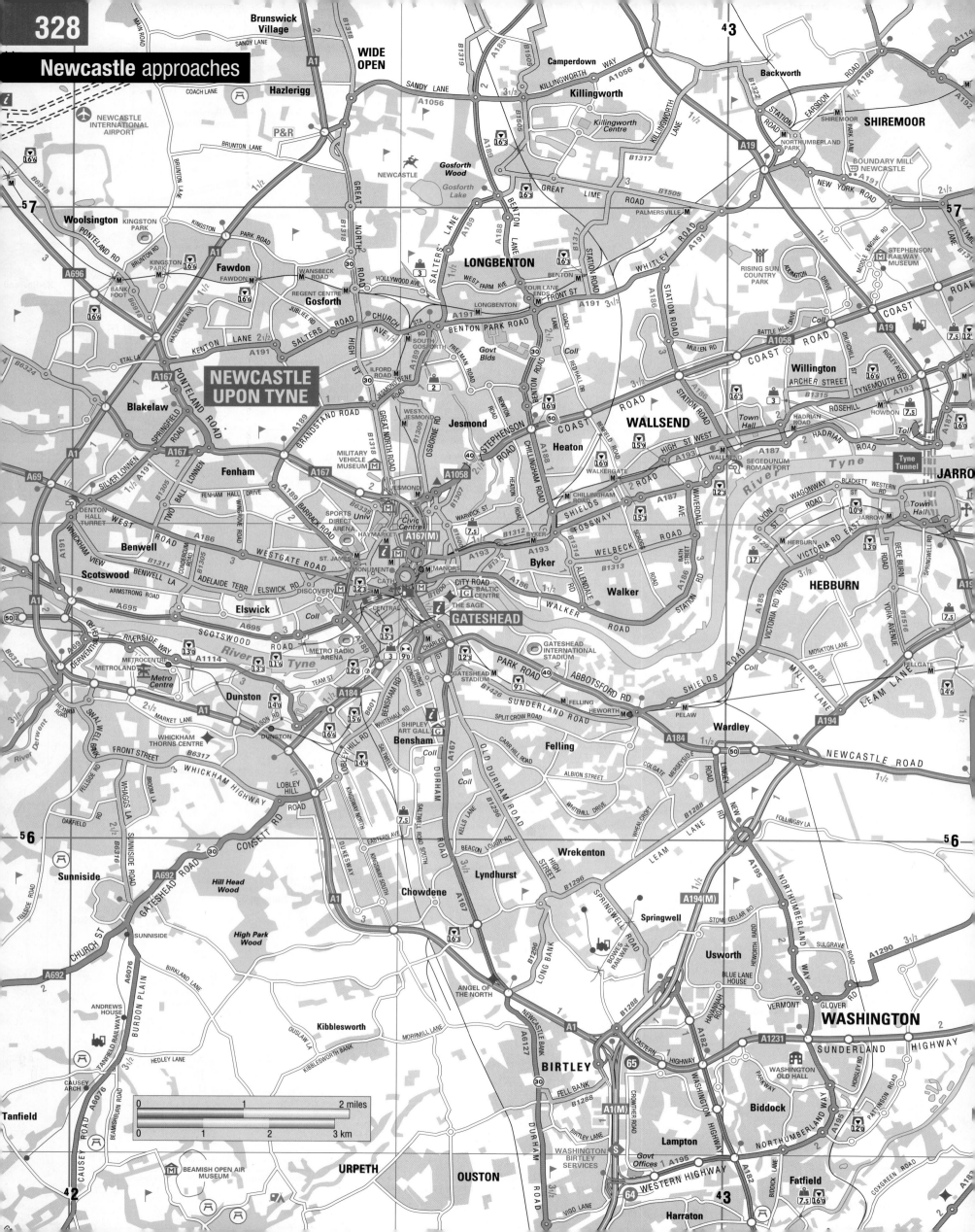

Nottingham approaches

Aberdeen page 293 • Aberystwyth page 128 • Ashford page 54 • Ayr page 257 • Bangor page 179 • Barrow-in-Furness page 210 • Bath page 61 • Berwick-upon-Tweed page 273

331

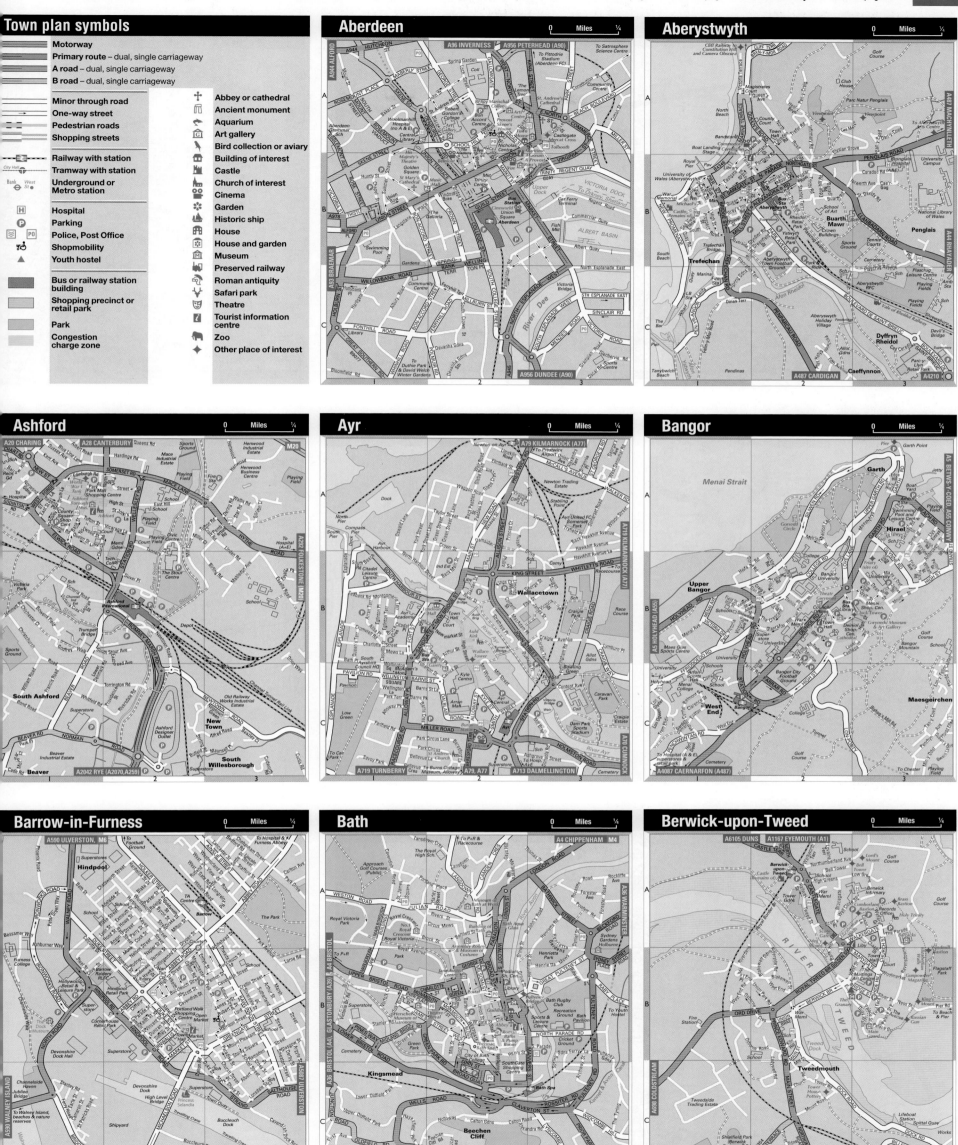

Town plan symbols

- Motorway
- Primary route – dual, single carriageway
- A road – dual, single carriageway
- B road – dual, single carriageway

- Minor through road
- One-way street
- Pedestrian roads
- Shopping streets

- Railway with station
- Tramway with station
- Underground or Metro station

- **H** Hospital
- **P** Parking
- Police, Post Office
- Shopmobility
- Youth hostel

- Bus or railway station building
- Shopping precinct or retail park
- Park
- Congestion charge zone

- Abbey or cathedral
- Ancient monument
- Aquarium
- Art gallery
- Bird collection or aviary
- Building of interest
- Castle
- Church of interest
- Cinema
- Garden
- Historic ship
- House
- House and garden
- Museum
- Preserved railway
- Roman antiquity
- Safari park
- Theatre
- Tourist information centre
- Zoo
- Other place of interest

Aberdeen

Aberystwyth

Ashford

Ayr

Bangor

Barrow-in-Furness

Bath

Berwick-upon-Tweed

Birmingham
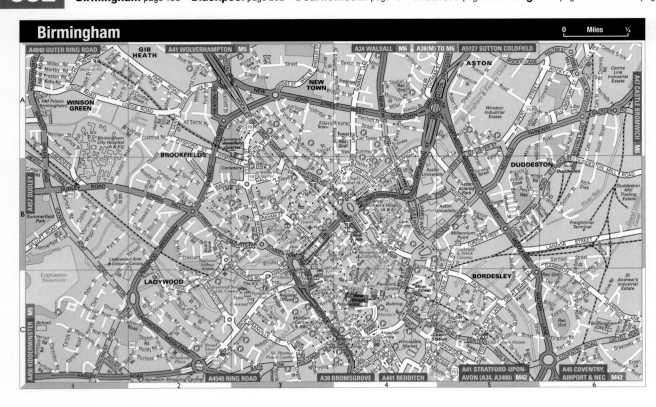

Blackpool

Bournemouth
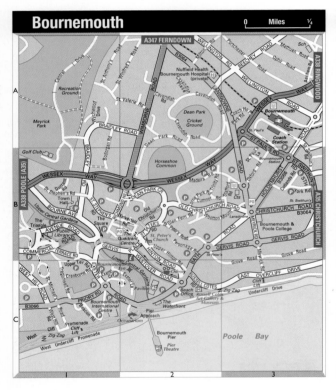

Bradford
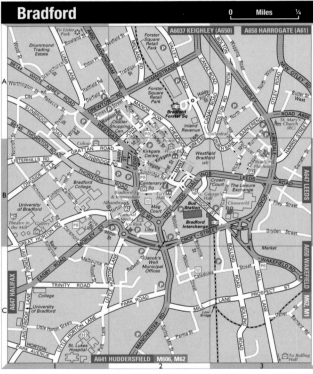

Brighton
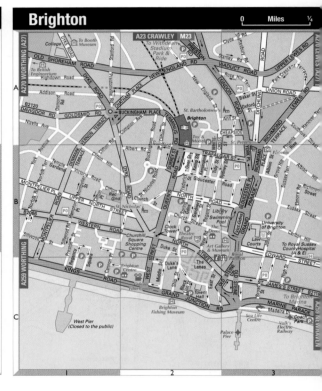

Bristol
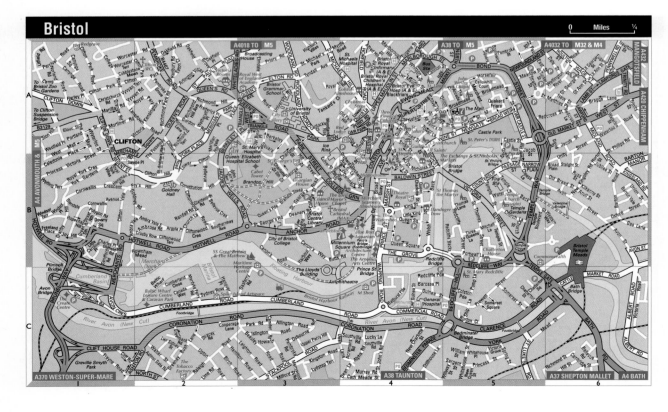

Bury St Edmunds
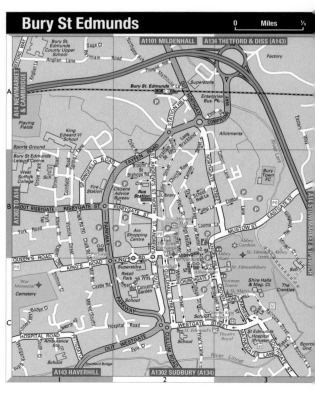

Cambridge page 123 ● **Canterbury** page 54 ● **Cardiff** page 59 ● **Carlisle** page 239 ● **Chelmsford** page 88 ● **Cheltenham** page 99 ● **Chester** page 166 ● **Chichester** page 22 ● **Colchester** page 107

333

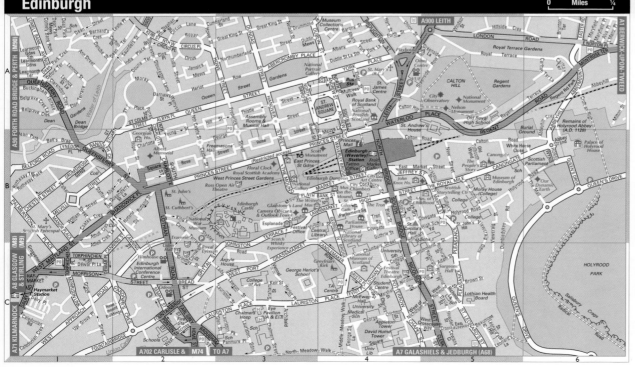

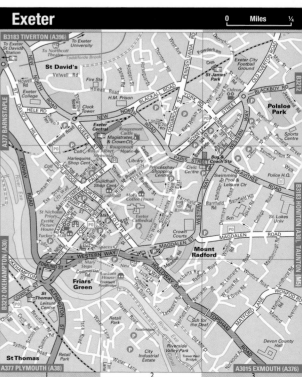

Fort William page 290 ● **Glasgow** page 267 ● **Gloucester** page 80 ● **Grimsby** page 201 ● **Hanley (Stoke-on-Tent)** page 168 ● **Harrogate** page 206 ● **Holyhead** page 178 ● **Hull** page 200

335

Fort William

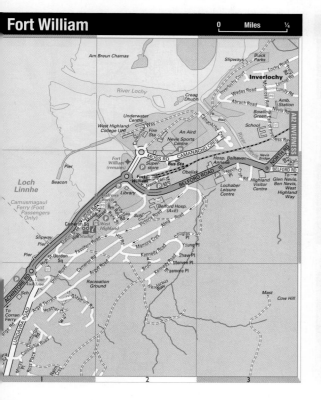

Glasgow

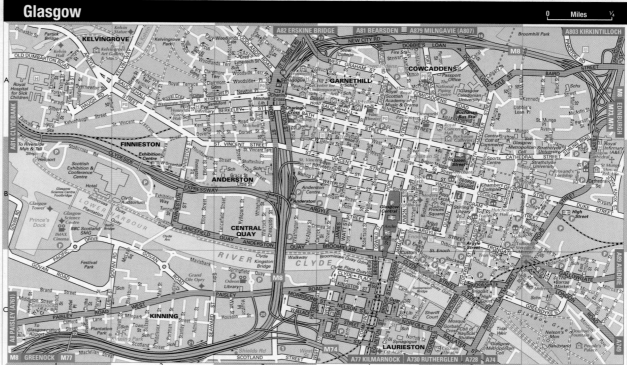

Gloucester

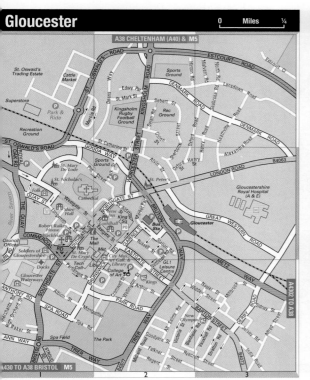

Grimsby

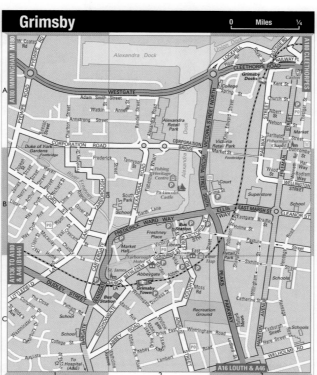

Hanley (Stoke-on-Trent)

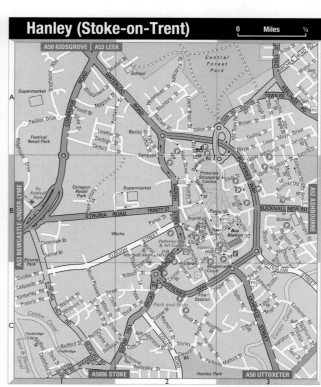

Harrogate

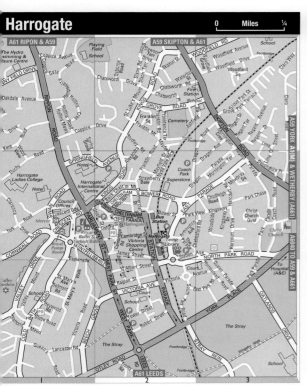

Holyhead / Caergybi

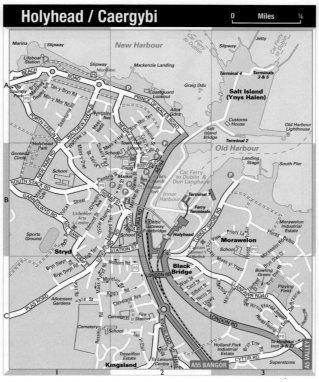

Hull

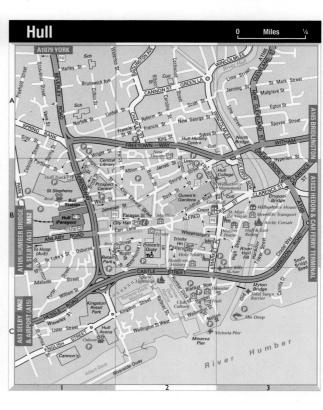

Inverness

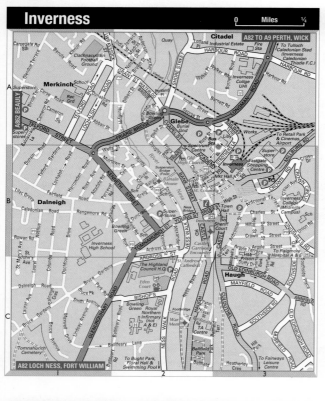

Ipswich

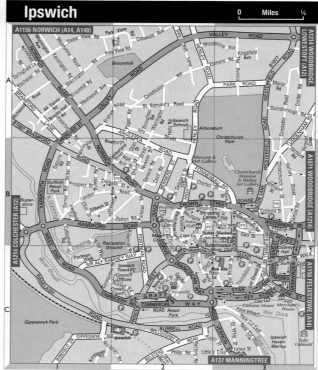

Kendal

King's Lynn

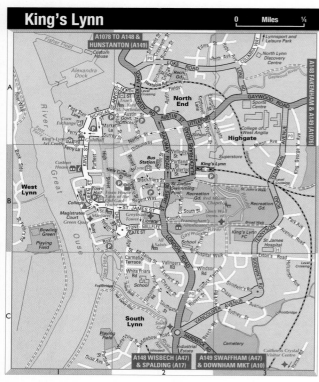

Leeds

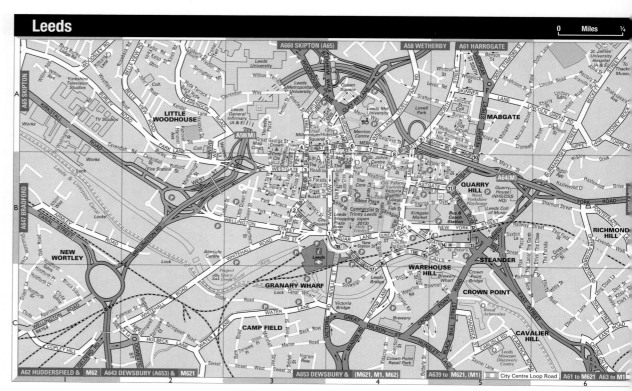

Lancaster

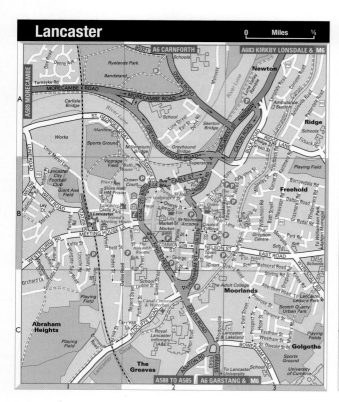

Leicester

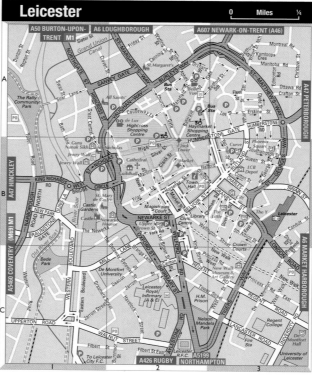

Lewes

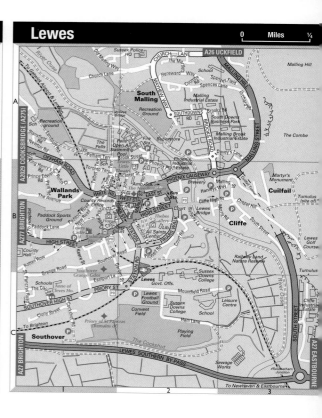

Lincoln page 189 • Liverpool page 182 • Llandudno page 180 • Llanelli page 56 • Luton page 103 • Macclesfield page 184 • Manchester page 184

337

Lincoln

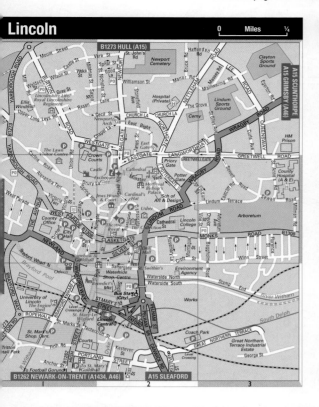

Liverpool

Llandudno

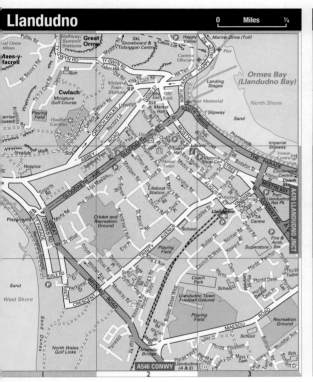

Llanelli

Luton

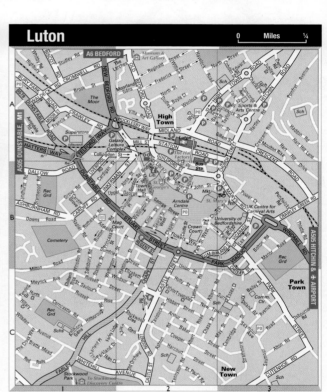

Macclesfield

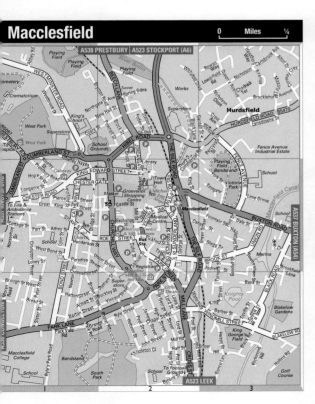

Manchester

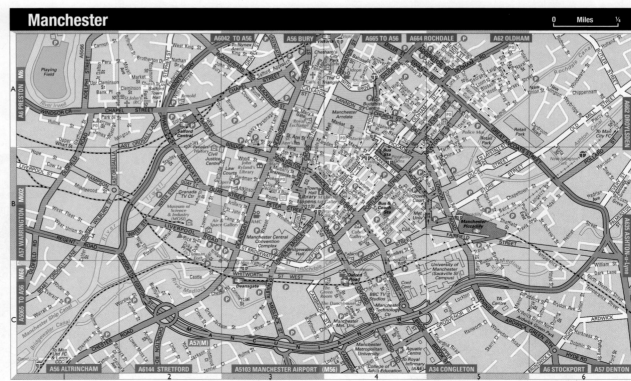

Maidstone

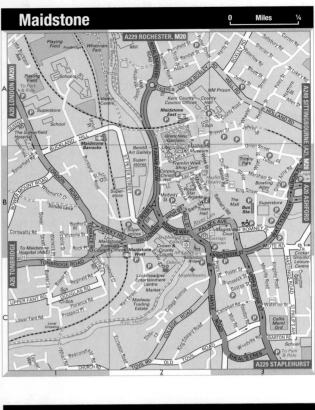

Merthyr Tydfil / Merthyr Tudful

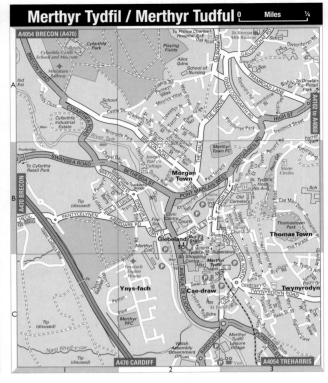

Middlesbrough

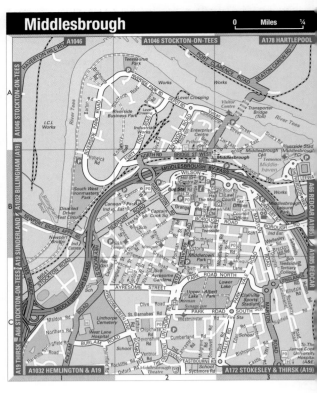

Milton Keynes

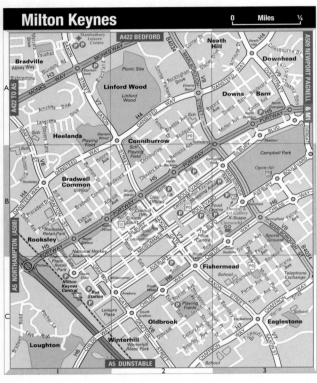

Newcastle upon Tyne

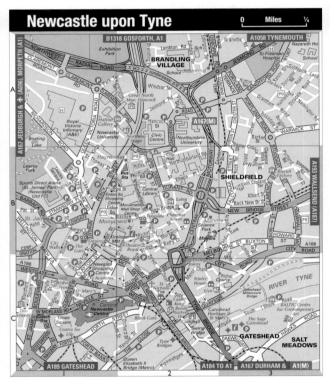

Newport / Casnewydd

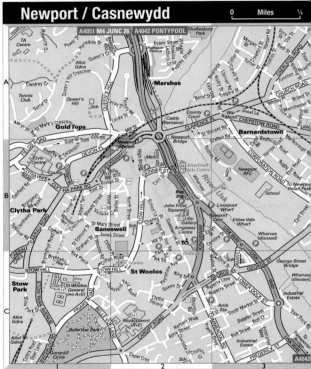

Newquay

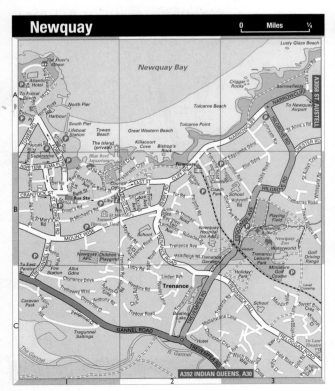

Newtown / Y Drenewydd

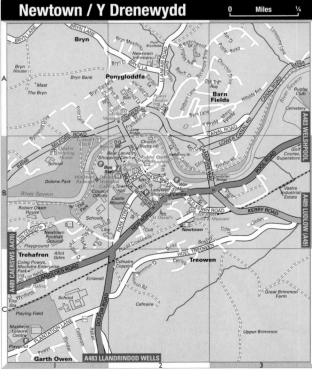

Northampton

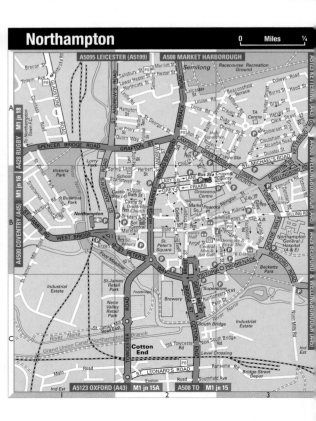

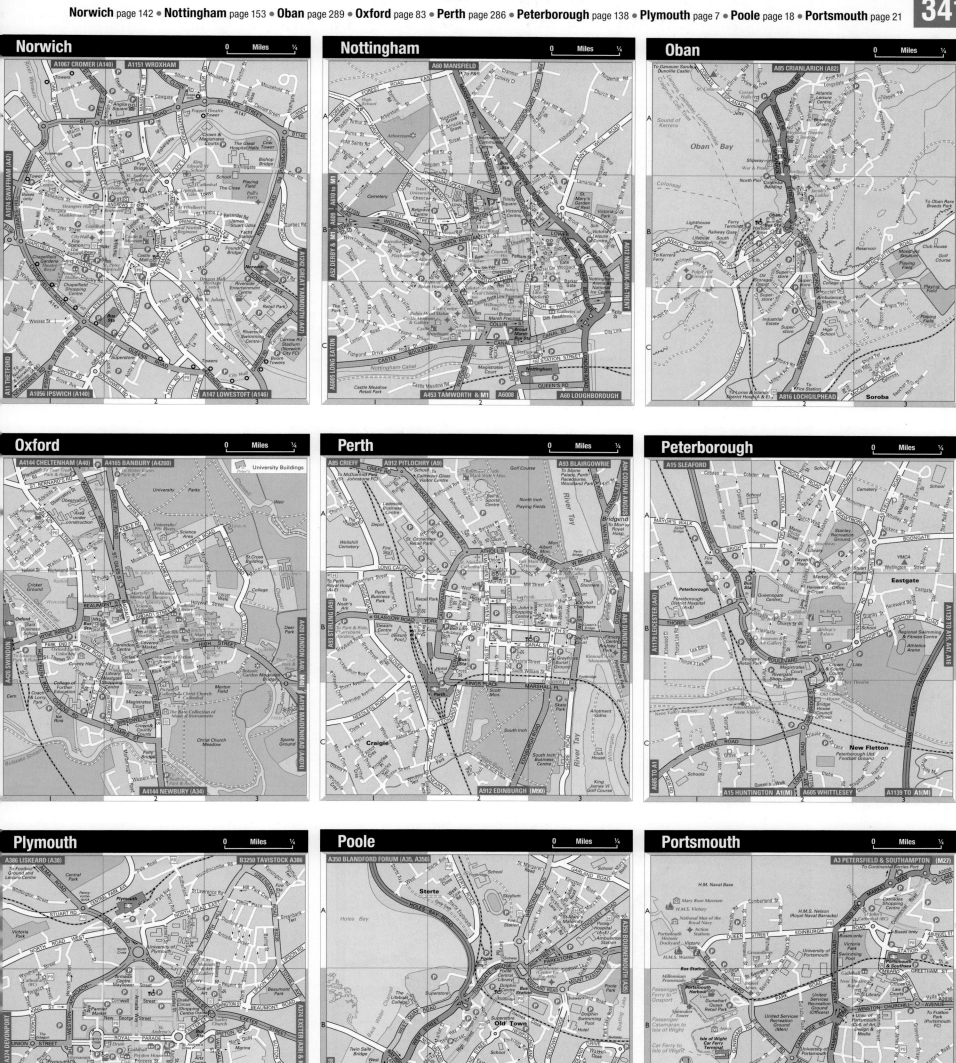

Preston
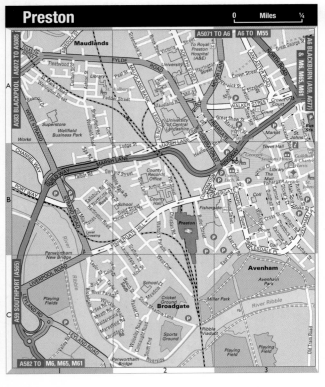

Reading
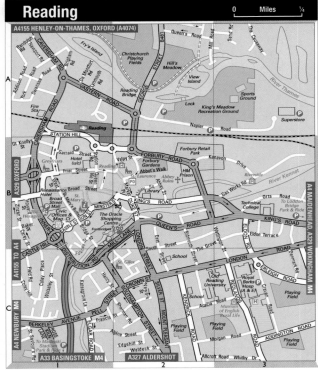

St Andrews
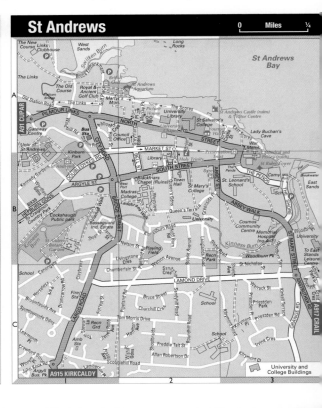

Salisbury
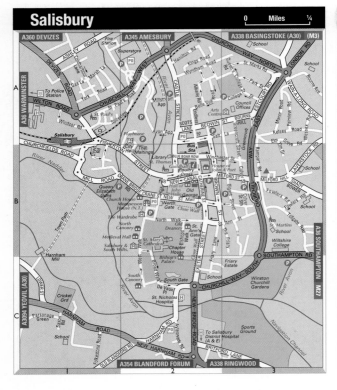

Scarborough
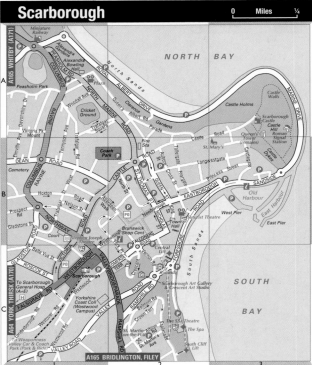

Shrewsbury
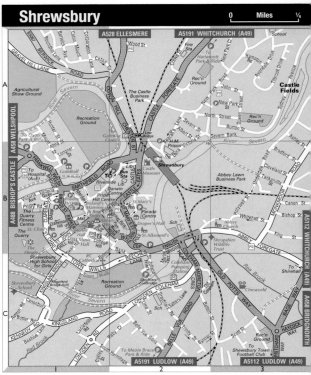

Sheffield
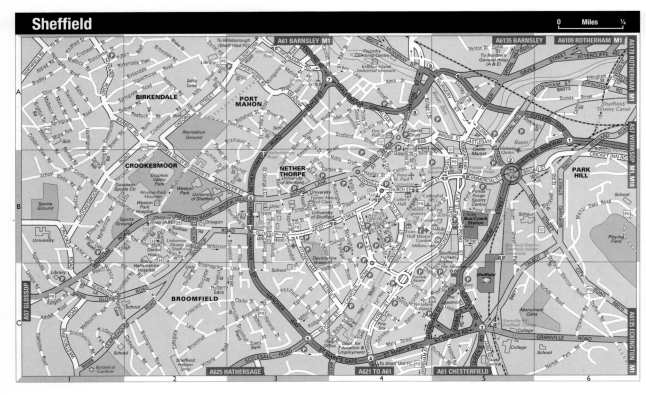

Southampton
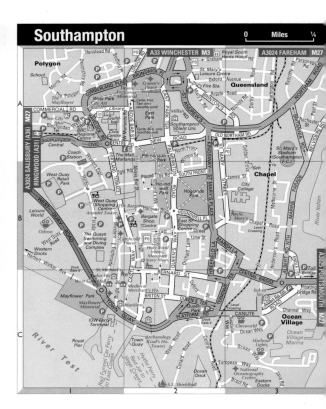

Southend page 69 • Stirling page 278 • Stoke page 168 • Stratford-upon-Avon page 118 • Sunderland page 243 • Swansea page 56 • Swindon page 63 • Taunton page 28 • Telford page 132

343

Southend-on-Sea

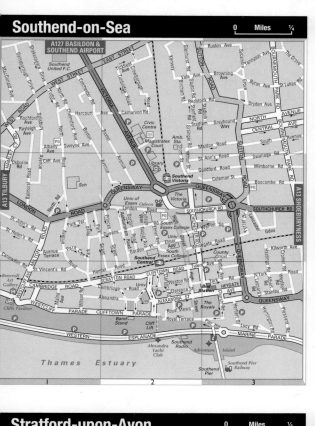

Stirling

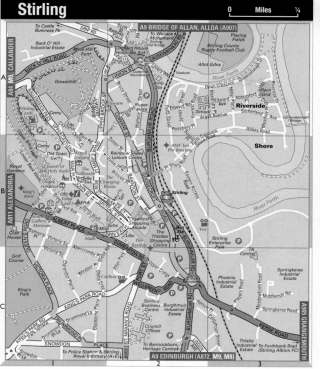

Stoke

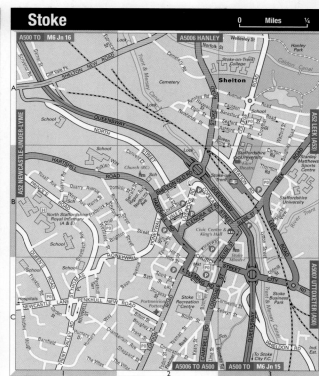

Stratford-upon-Avon

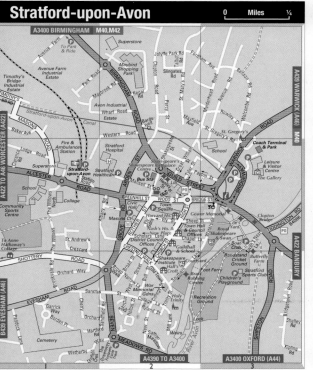

Sunderland

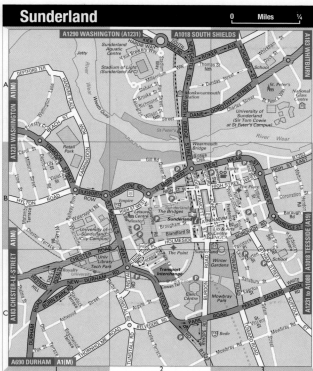

Swansea / Abertawe

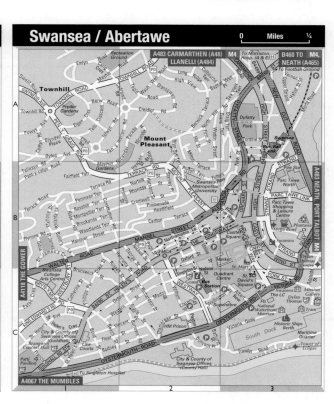

Swindon

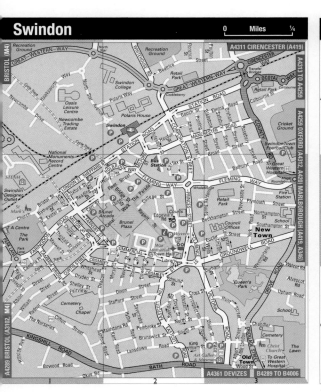

Taunton

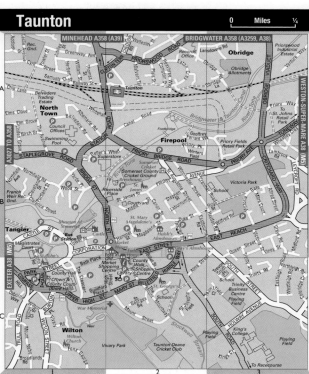

Telford

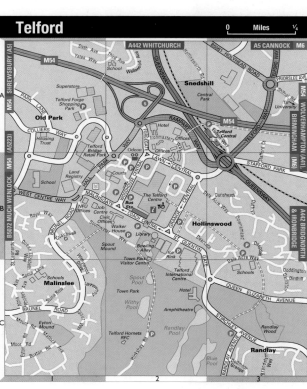

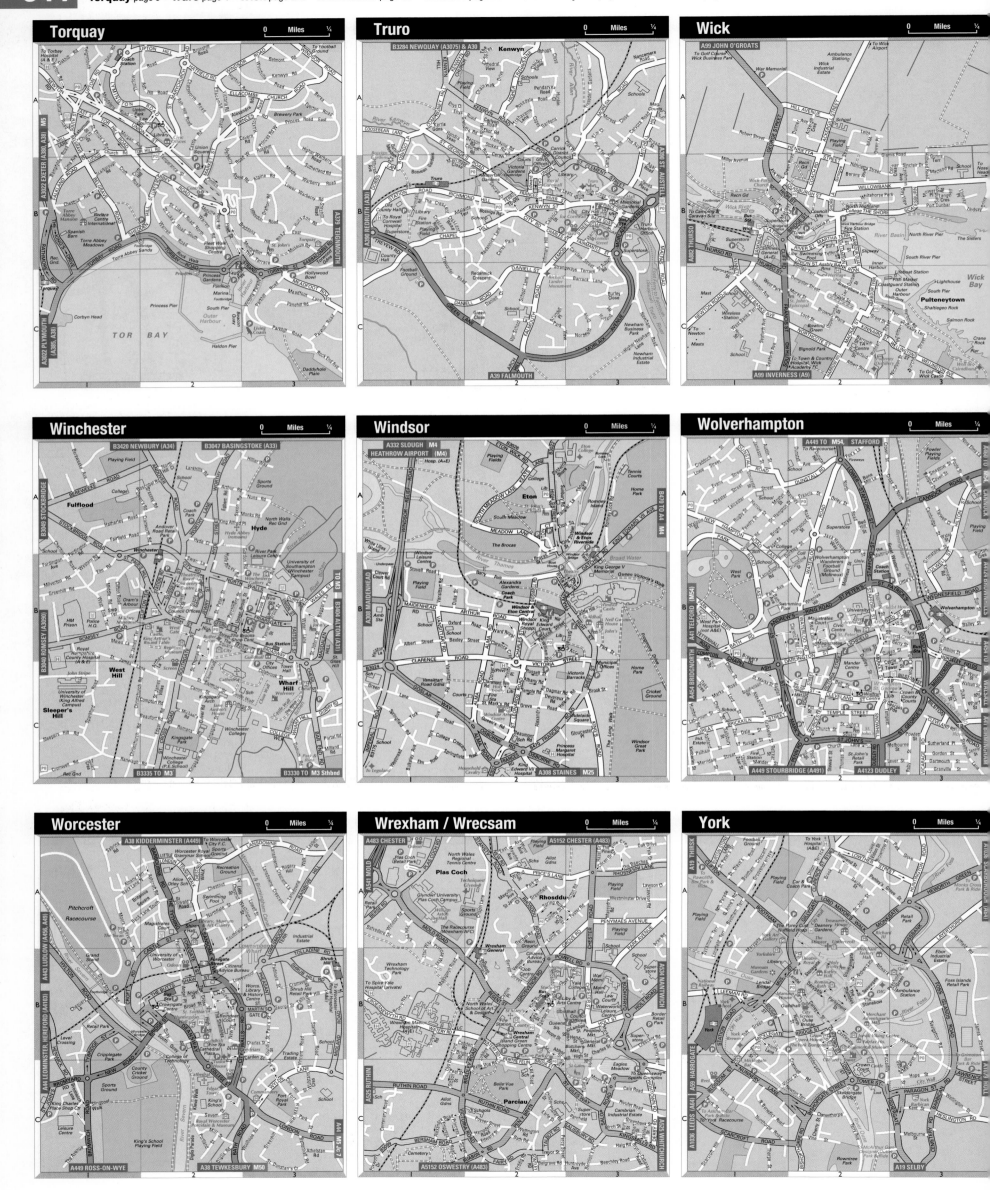

Aberdeen • Aberystwyth • Ashford • Ayr • Bangor • Barrow-in-Furness • Bath • Berwick-upon-Tweed • Birmingham 345

Town plan indexes

Aberdeen 331

Aberdeen B2
Aberdeen Grammar School A1
Academy, The B2
Albert Basin B3
Albert Quay B3
Albury Rd C1
Alford Pl B1
Art Gallery A2
Arts Ctr A2
Back Wynd A2
Baker St A1
Beach Blvd A3
Belmont B2
Belmont St B2
Berry St A2
Blackfriars St A2
Bloomfield Rd C1
Bon Accord Ctr A2
Bon-Accord St B1/C1
Bridge St B2
Broad St A2
Bus Station B2
Car Ferry Terminal B3
Castlegate A3
Central Library A1
Chapel St B1
Cineworld B2
College A2
College St B2
Commerce St A3
Commercial Quay B3
Community Ctr A3/C1
Constitution St A3
Cotton St A3
Crown St B2
Denburn Rd A2
Devanha Gdns C2
Devanha Gdns South C2
East North St A3
Esslemont Ave A1
Ferryhill Rd C2
Ferryhill Terr C2
Fish Market B3
Fonthill Rd C1
Galleria, The B1
Gallowgate A2
George St A2
Glenbervie Rd C3
Golden Sq B1
Grampian Rd C3
Great Southern Rd C1
Guild St B2
Hardgate B1/C1
His Majesty's Theatre A1
Holburn St C1
Hollybank Pl C1
Huntly St B1
Hutcheon St A1
Information Ctr B2
John St A2
Justice St A3
King St A2
Langstane Pl B1
Lemon Tree, The A2
Library C1
Loch St A2
Maberly St A1
Marischal College A2
Maritime Mus & Provost Ross's Ho B2
Market St B2/B3
Menzies Rd C3
Mercat Cross A3
Millburn St C2
Miller St A3
Market B2
Mount St A1
Music Hall B1
North Esp East C3
North Esp West C2
Oscar Rd C3
Palmerston Rd C2
Park St A3
Police Station A2
Polmuir Rd C2
Post Office A1/A2/A3/B1/C3
Provost Skene's Ho A2
Queen St A2
Regent Quay B3
Regent Road B3
Robert Gordon's Coll. A2
Rose St B1
Rosemount Pl A1
Rosemount Viaduct A1
St Andrew St A2
St Andrew's Cath A3
St Mary's Cathedral B1
St Nicholas Ctr A2
St Nicholas St A2
School Hill A2
Sinclair Rd C3
Skene Sq A1
Skene St B1
South College St C2
South Crown St C2
South Esp East C3
South Esp West C3
South Mount St A1
Sports Ctr C3
Spring Garden A2
Springbank Terr C2
Summer St B1
Swimming Pool B1
Thistle St B1
Tolbooth A3
Town House A2
Trinity Ctr B2
Trinity Quay B3
Union Row B1
Union Square B2
Union St B1/B2
Upper Dock B3
Upper Kirkgate A2
Victoria Bridge C3
Victoria Dock B3
Victoria Rd C3
Victoria St B2
Virginia St A3
Vue B2
Wellington Pl B2
West North St A2
Whinhill Rd C1
Willowbank Rd C1
Windmill Brae B2
Woolmanhill Hospl A1

Aberystwyth 331

Aberystwyth Holiday Village C2
Aberystwyth RFC C3
Aberystwyth Sta B2
Aberystwyth Town Football Ground B2
Alexandra Rd B2
Ambulance Station C3
Baker St B1
Banadl Rd B2
Bandstand A1
Bath St A2
Boat Landing Stage A1
Bvd de Saint-Brieuc C3
Bridge St B1
Bronglais Hospital B3
Bryn-y-Mor Rd A2
Buarth Rd B2
Bus Station B2
Cae Ceredig C3
Cae Melyn A2
Cae'r-Gog B3
Cambrian St B2
Caradoc Rd B3
Caravan Site C2
Castle (Remains of) B1
Castle St B1
Cemetery B3
Ceredigion Mus A1
Chalybeate St B1
Cliff Terr A2
Club House A2
Commodore A1
County Court A2
Crown Buildings B2
Dan-y-Coed A3
Dinas Terr C1
Eastgate B1
Edge-hill Rd B2
Elm Tree Ave B2
Elysian Gr A2
Felin-y-Mor Rd C1
Fifth Ave C2
Fire Station C1
Glanrafon Terr B1
Glyndŵr Rd B2
Golf Course A3
Gray's Inn Rd B1
Great Darkgate St B1
Greenfield St B2
Heol-y-Bryn A2
High St B1
Infirmary Rd A2
Information Ctr B1
Iorwerth Ave B3
King St B1
Lauraplace B1
Library B1
Lifeboat Station C1
Llanbadarn Rd B3
Loveden Rd A2
Magistrates Court A1
Marina C1
Marine Terr A1
Market B1
Mill St B1
Moor La B2
National Liby of Wales B3
New Promenade B1
New St B1
North Beach A1
North Parade B2
North Rd A2
Northgate St B2
Parc Natur Penglais A3
Parc-y-Llyn Retail Pk C3
Park & Ride B2
Park Ave B2
Pavillion B1
Pendinas C1
Penglais Rd B3
Penrheidol C2
Pen-y-Craig A2
Pen-yr-angor C1
Pier St B1
Plas Ave B3
Plas Helyg C2
Plascrug Ave B2/C3
Plascrug Leisure Ctr C3
Police Station C2
Poplar Row B2
Portland Rd B2
Portland St A2
Post Office B1/B3
Powell St B1
Prospect St B1
Quay Rd B1
Queen St B1
Queen's Ave A2
Queen's Rd A2
Rheidol Retail Park B2
Riverside Terr B1
St Davids Rd B3
St Michael's B1
School of Art B2
Seaview Pl B1
South Beach B1
South Rd B1
Sports Ground B2
Spring Gdns C1
Stanley Terr B2
Swimming Pool & L Ctr C3
Superstore B2/C3
Tanybwlch Beach C1
Tennis Courts B3
Terrace Rd B1
The Bar C1
Town Hall A2
Trefechan Bridge B1
Trefechan Rd C2
Trefor Rd A2
Trinity Rd B2
University Campus B3
University of Wales (Aberystwyth) B1
Vale of Rheidol Railway C3
Vaynor St B2
Victoria Terr A1
Viewpoint A2
Viewpoint A3
War Memorial B1
Wharf Quay C1
Y Lanfa C1
Ystwyth Retail Park B2

Ashford 331

Albert Rd A1
Alfred Rd C3
Apsley St A1
Ashford A1
Ashford Borough Museum A1
Ashford Int Station B2
Bank St A1
Barrowhill Gdns A1
Beaver Industrial Est. C1
Beaver Rd C1
Beazley Ct C1
Birling Rd B3
Blue Line La A1
Bond Rd C1
Bowens Field B1
Bulleid Pl C2
Cade Rd C1
Chart Rd A1
Chichester Cl B1
Christchurch Rd B1
Chunnel Industrial Est. B1
Church Rd A1
Civic Ctr A2
County Square Sh Ctr A1
Court A1
Court A1
Croft Rd A3
Cudworth Rd C3
Curtis Rd C3
Dering Rd A3
Dover Pl B2
Drum La A1
East Hill A2
East St A1
Eastmead Ave B2
Edinburgh Rd A1
Elwick Rd A1
Essella Pk B3
Essella Rd B3
Fire Sta A3
Forge La A1
Francis Rd C1
George St B1
Godfrey Walk B1
Godinton Rd A1
Gordon Cl A3
Hardinge Rd A2
Henwood A3
Henwood Business Ctr A3
Henwood Ind Est A3
High St A2
Hythe Rd A3
Information Ctr A1
Jemmett Rd B1
Kent Ave A1
Library A1
Linden Rd B3
Lower Denmark Rd C1
Mabledon Ave B3
Mace Industrial Estate A2
Mace La A2
Maunsell Pl C3
McArthur Glen Designer Outlet C2
Memorial Gdns A2
Mill Ct A2
Miller Cl A2
Mortimer Cl C1
New St A1
Newtown Green C3
Newtown Rd B2/C3
Norman Rd C1
North St A2
Norwood Gdns A1
Norwood St A1
Old Railway Works Industrial Estate C3
Orion Way C3
Pk Mall Shopping Ctr A1
Park Pl A1
Park St A1/A2
Pemberton Rd A3
Police Station A1
Post Office A1/A3
Providence St C2
Queen St A1
Queens Rd A2
Regents Pl A1
Riversdale Rd C2
Romney Marsh Rd B2
St John's La A2
Somerset Rd A2
South Stour Ave B2
Star Rd A3
Station Rd B2
Stirling Rd C2
Stour Ctr, The B2
Sussex Ave A1
Tannery La A2
Technical College B2
Torrington Rd C2
Trumper Bridge B1
Tufton Rd A3
Tufton St A1
Vicarage La A2
Victoria Cres B1
Victoria Park B1
Victoria Rd B1
Wallis Rd A3
Wellesley Rd A2
West St A1
Whitfeld Rd C1
William Rd C1
World War I Tank A1

Ayr 331

Ailsa Pl B1
Alexandra Terr A3
Allison St B2
Alloway Pk C1
Alloway Pl C1
Alloway St C2
Arran Mall C2
Arran Terr B1
Arthur St B2
Ashgrove St C2
Auld Brig B2
Auld Kirk B2
Ayr B2
Ayr Academy B1
Ayr Central Sh Ctr C2
Ayr Harbour A1
Ayr United FC A3
Back Hawkhill Ave A3
Back Main St B2
Back Peebles St A2
Barns Cres C1
Barns Pk C1
Barns St C1
Barns Street La C1
Bath Pl B1
Bellevue Cres C1
Bellevue La C1
Beresford La C2
Beresford Terr C2
Boswell Pk B2
Britannia Pl A3
Bruce Cres B1
Burns Statue C2
Bus Sta B1
Carrick St C2
Cassillis St B1
Cathcart St B1
Charlotte St B1
Citadel Leisure Ctr B1
Citadel Pl B1
Compass Pier A1
Content Ave C3
Content St B2
Craigie Ave B3
Craigie Rd B3
Craigie Way B3
Cromwell Rd B1
Crown St A2
Dalblair Rd C2
Dam Park Sports Stadium C3
Damside A2
Dongola Rd C3
Eglinton Pl B1
Eglinton Terr B1
Elba St B2
Elmbank St A2
Esplanade B1
Farifield Rd C1
Fort St B1
Fothringham Rd C3
Fullarton St C1
Gaiety C2
Garden St B2
George St B2
George's Ave A3
Glebe Cres A2
Glebe Rd A2
Gorden Terr B3
Green St A2
Green Street La A2
Hawkhill Ave A3
Hawkhill Avenue La B3
High St B2
Holmston Rd C3
Information Ctr B1
James St B3
John St B2
King St B2
Kings Ct B2
Kyle Ctr C2
Kyle St C2
Library B2
Limekiln Rd A2
Limonds Wynd B2
Loudoun Hall B2
Lymburn Pl B3
Macadam Pl B2
Main St B2
Mcadam's Monument C1
Mccall's Ave A3
Mews La B1
Mill Brae C3
Mill St C2
Mill Wynd C2
Miller Rd C1
Montgomerie Terr B1
New Bridge B2
New Bridge St B2
New Rd A2
Newmarket St B2
Newton-on-Ayr Sta A2
North Harbour St B1
North Pier A1
Odeon C2
Oswald La A1
Park Circus C1
Park Circus La C1
Park Terr C1
Pavilion Rd C1
Peebles St A2
Philip Sq B2
Police Station B2
Post Office A2/B2
Prestwick Rd B1
Princes Ct A2
Queen St B3
Queen's Terr B1
Racecourse Rd C1
River St B2
Riverside Pl B2
Russell Dr A2
St Andrews Church C2
St George's Rd A3
Sandgate B1
Savoy Park C1
Seabank Rd B2
Smith St C2
Somerset Rd A3
South Beach Rd B1
South Harbour St B1
South Pier A1
Station Rd C2
Strathaye Pl B2
Taylor St A2
Town Hall B2
Tryfield Pl A3
Turner's Bridge B2
Union Ave A3
Victoria Bridge C3
Victoria St B3
Viewfield Rd A3
Virginia Gdns A2
Waggon Rd A2
Walker Rd A3
Wallace Tower B2
Weaver St A2
Weir Rd A2
Wellington La C1
Wellington Sq C1
West Sanouhar Rd A3
Whitletts Rd B3
Wilson St A3
York St A1
York Street La B1

Bangor 331

Abbey Rd C2
Albert St B1
Ambrose St A3
Ambulance Station A3
Arfon Sports Hall C1
Ashley Rd B3
Bangor City Football Ground C2
Bangor Mountain B3
Bangor Station C1
Bangor University B2
Beach Rd A3
Belmont St C1
Bishop's Mill Rd C3
Boat Yard A3
Brick St B3
Buckley Rd B2
Bus Station B2
Caellepa B2
Caernarfon Rd C1
Cathedral B2
Cemetery C1
Clarence St C1
Clock Tower B3
College B2/C2
College La B2
College Rd B2
Convent La C1
Council Offices B2
Craig y Don Rd B2
Dean St B3
Deiniol Rd B2
Deiniol Shopping Ctr B2
Deiniol St B2
Edge Hill A3
Euston Rd C1
Fairview Rd A3
Farrar Rd C2
Ffordd Cynfal C1
Ffordd Elfed C3
Ffordd Islwyn A3
Ffordd y Castell C3
Ffriddoedd Rd B1
Field St B3
Fountain St A3
Friars Ave B3
Friars Rd B3
Friary (Site of) B3
Gardd Deman C1
Garth Hill A3
Garth Point A3
Garth Rd A3
Glanrafon B2
Glanrafon Hill B2
Glynne Rd B3
Golf Course B3
Golf Course C2
Gorad Rd B1
Gorsedd Circle A2
Gwern Las C3
Gwynedd Museum & Art Gallery B2
Heol Dewi C1
High St B3/C2
Hill St B1
Holyhead Rd B1
Hwfa Rd B1
Information Ctr B2
James St B3
Library B2
Llys Emrys A3
Lon Ogwen C1
Lon-Pobty C2
Lon-y-Felin C3
Lon-y-Glyder C1
Love La B2
Lower Penrallt Rd B2
Lower St B2
Maes Glas Sports Ctr B1
Maes-y-Dref B3
Maeshyfryd A3
Meirion La A2
Meirion Rd A2
Menai Ave B1
Menai College C1
Menai Shopping Ctr B3
Min-y-Ddol C3
Minafon B2
Mount St B3
Orme Rd A3
Parc Victoria B1
Penchwintan Rd C1
Penlon Gr B3
Penrhyn Ave C3
Pier A3
Police Station B2
Post Office B2/B3/C1/C3
Prince's Rd B2
Queen's Ave C3
Sackville Rd B2
St Paul's St B2
Seion Rd A3
Seiriol Rd A3
Siliwen Rd A2
Snowdon View B1
Station Rd C1
Strand St B3
Swimming Pool and Leisure Ctr A3
Tan-y-Coed C3
Tegid Rd B3
Temple Rd B2
The Crescent B2
Theatr Gwynedd B2
Totton Rd A3
Town Hall B2
Treflan B2
Trem Elidir C1
Upper Garth Rd A3
Victoria Ave B1
Victoria Dr B1
Victoria St B1
Vron St B2
Well St B3
West End C1
William St B3
York Pl B3

Barrow-in-Furness 331

Abbey Rd A3/B2
Adelaide St A2
Ainslie St A3
Albert St C3
Allison St B3
Anson St A2
Argyle St B3
Arthur St B3
Ashburner Way A1
Barrow Raiders RLFC B1
Barrow Station A2
Bath St A1/B2
Bedford Rd A3
Bessamer Way A1
Blake St A1/A2
Bridge Rd C1
Buccleuch Dock C3
Buccleuch Dock Rd C2/C3
Buccleuch St B2/B3
Byron St A2
Calcutta St A1
Cameron St C1
Carlton Ave A3
Cavendish Dock Rd C3
Cavendish St B2/B3
Channelside Walk B1
Channelside Haven C1
Chatsworth St A2
Cheltenham St A3
Church St C3
Clifford St B2
Clive St B1
Collingwood St B2
Cook St A2
Cornerhouse Retail Pk B2
Cornwallis St B2
Courts B2
Crellin St B3
Cross St C3
Dalkeith St B2
Dalton Rd B2/C2
Derby St B3
Devonshire Dock C2
Devonshire Dock Hall B2
Dock Museum, The B1
Drake St A2
Dryden St A2
Duke St A1/B2/C3
Duncan St B2
Dundee St C2
Dundonald St B2
Earle St C1
Emlyn St B2
Exmouth St A2
Farm St C2
Fell St B3
Fenton St B3
Ferry Rd C1
Forum 28 B2
Furness College B1
Glasgow St B3
Goldsmith St A2
Greengate St B3
Hardwick St A2
Harrison St B3
Hartington St A2
Hawke St B2
Hibbert Rd A2
High Level Bridge C2
High St B2
Hindpool Retail Park B2
Hindpool Rd B2
Holker St A2
Hollywood Ret & L Pk B1
Hood St A2
Howard St A2
Howe St A2
Information Ctr B2
Ironworks Rd A1/B1
James St B3
Jubliee Bridge C1
Keith St B2
Keyes St A2
Lancaster St A3
Lawson St B2
Library B2
Lincoln St A3
Longreins Rd A3
Lonsdale St C3
Lord St B3
Lorne Rd B3
Lyon St A2
Manchester St B2
Market B2
Market St B2
Marsh St B3
Michaelson Rd C2
Milton St A2
Monk St B2
Mount Pleasant B3
Nan Tait Ctr B2
Napier St B2
Nelson St B2
North Rd B1
Open Market B2
Parade St B2
Paradise St B3
Park Ave A3
Park Dr A3
Parker St A2
Parry St A2
Peter Green Way A1
Phoenix Rd A1
Police Station B2
Portland Walk Sh Ctr B2
Post Office A3/B2
Princess Selandia C2
Raleigh St A2
Ramsden St B3
Rawlinson St B3
Robert St B3
Rodney St B2
Rutland St A2
St Patricks Rd C1
Salthouse Rd C3
School St B2
Scott St B2
Settle St A3
Shore St C3
Sidney St B2
Silverdale St B3
Slater St B2
Smeaton St B3
Stafford St A3
Stanley Rd C1
Stark St C3
Steel St B1
Storey Sq B3
Strand C3
Superstore A1/B1/C3
Sutherland St B3
TA Ctr A2
The Park A3
Thwaite St B3
Town Hall B2
Town Quay C3
Vernon St B2
Vincent St B2
Walney Rd A1
West Gate Rd A2
West View Rd A3
Westmorland St A3
Whitehead St A3
Wordsworth St A2

Bath 331

Alexandra Park C2
Alexandra Rd C2
Approach Golf Courses (Public) A1
Bath Aqua Glass A2
Archway St C3
Assembly Rooms & Mus of Costume A2
Avon St B2
Barton St B2
Bath Abbey B2
Bath City College B2
Bath Pavilion B3
Bath Rugby Club B3
Bath Spa Station C3
Bathwick St A3
Beckford Road A3
Beechen Cliff Rd C2
Bennett St A2
Bloomfield Ave C1
Broad Quay C2
Broad St B2
Brock St A1
Building of Bath Museum A2
Bus Station C2
Calton Gdns C2
Calton Rd C2
Camden Cr A2
Cavendish Rd A1
Cemetery B1
Charlotte St B2
Chaucer Rd C2
Cheap St B2
Circus Mews A2
Claverton St C2
Corn St C2
Cricket Ground B3
Daniel St A3
Edward St B3
Ferry La B3
First Ave C1
Forester Ave A3
Forester Rd A3
Gays Hill A2
George St B2
Great Pulteney St B3
Green Park B1
Green Park Rd B2
Grove St B2
Guildhall B2
Harley St A2
Hayesfield Park C1
Henrietta Gdns A3
Henrietta Mews B3
Henrietta Park B3
Henrietta Rd A3
Henrietta St B3
Henry St B2
Herschel Museum of Astronomy B1
Holburne Museum B3
Holloway C2
Information Ctr B2
James St West B1/B2
Jane Austen Ctr B2
Julian Rd A1
Junction Rd C1
Kipling Ave C2
Lansdown Ctr A1
Lansdown Gr A2
Lansdown Rd A2
Library B2
London Rd A3
London St A3
Lower Bristol Rd B1
Lower Oldfield Park C1
Lyncombe Hill C3
Manvers St B3
Maple Gr C1
Margaret's Hill A2
Marlborough Bldgs A1
Marlborough La B1
Midland Bridge Rd B1
Milk St B2
Milsom St B2
Monmouth St B2
Morford St A2
Museum of Bath at Work A2
New King St B1
No 1 Royal Cres A1
Norfolk Bldgs B1
Norfolk Cr B1
North Parade Rd B3
Oldfield Rd C1
Paragon A2
Pines Way B1
Podium Shopping Ctr B2
Police Station B3
Portland Pl A2
Post Office A1/A3/B2/C1/C2
Postal Museum B2
Powlett Rd A3
Prior Park Rd C3
Pulteney Bridge B2
Pulteney Gdns B3
Pulteney Rd B3/C3
Queen Sq B2
Raby Pl B3
Recreation Ground B3
Rivers St A2
Rockliffe Ave A3
Rockliffe Rd A3
Roman Baths & Pump Room B2
Rossiter Rd C3
Royal Ave A1
Royal Cr A1
Royal High School, The A2
Royal Victoria Park A1
St James Sq A1
St John's Rd A3
Shakespeare Ave C2
Southgate C2
South Pde B3
Sports & Leisure Ctr B3
Spring Gdns C3
Stall St B2
Stanier Rd B1
Superstore B1
Sydney Gdns A3
Sydney Pl B3
Sydney Rd B3
Theatre Royal B2
Thermae Bath Spa B2
The Tyning C3
Thomas St A3
Union St B2
Upper Bristol Rd B1
Upper Oldfield Park C1
Victoria Art Gallery B2
Victoria Bridge Rd B1
Walcot St B2
Wells Rd C1
Westgate Buildings B2
Westgate St B2
Weston Rd A1
Widcombe Hill C3

Berwick-upon-Tweed 331

Bank Hill B2
Barracks A3
Bell Tower A3
Bell Tower Pl A2
Berwick Br A2
Berwick Infirmary H A3
Berwick-upon-Tweed A2
Billendean Rd C3
Blakewell Gdns B2
Blakewell St B2
Brass Bastion A3
Bridge St B3
Brucegate St A2
Castle (Remains of) A2
Castle Terr A2
Castlegate A2
Chapel St A3
Church Rd C2
Church St B3
Court B3
Coxon's La A3
Cumberland Bastion A3
Dean Dr C2
Dock Rd C2/C3
Elizabethan Walls A2/B3
Fire Station B1
Flagstaff Park B3
Football Ground C3
Foul Ford B3
Golden Sq B2
Golf Course A3
Greenwood C1
Gunpowder Magazine B3
Hide Hill B3
High Greens A2
Holy Trinity A3
Information Ctr A2
Kiln Hill B2
King's Mount B3
Ladywell Rd C2
Library A3
Lifeboat Station C3
Lord's Mount A3
Lovaine Terr A2
Low Greens A3
Main Guard B3
Main St B2/C2
Maltings Art Ctr, The B3
Marygate B3
Meg's Mount A2
Middle St C3
Mill St C2
Mount Rd C2
Museum B3
Ness St B3
North Rd A2
Northumberland Ave A2
Northumberland Rd C2
Ord Dr B1
Osborne Cr B2
Osborne Rd B1
Palace Gr B3
Palace St B3
Palace St East B3
Pier Rd B3
Playing Field C1
Police Station B3
Post Office A2/B2/B2
Prince Edward Rd B2
Prior Rd C2
Quay Walls B3
Railway St A2
Ravensdowne B3
Records Office A3
Riverdene B1
Riverside Rd B2
Royal Border Br A2
Royal Tweed Br B2
Russian Gun B3
Scots Gate A2
Scott's Pl A2
Shielfield Park (Berwick Rangers FC) C1
Shielfield Terr C2
Silver St B3
Spittal Quay C3
Superstores C2
The Avenue B3
The Granary B3
The Parade A3
Tower Gdns A2
Tower Ho Pottery C2
Tower Rd C2
Town Hall B3
Turret Gdns C2
Tweed Dock B2
Tweed St A2
Tweedside Trading Est C1
Union Brae B2
Union Park Rd B2
Walkergate A3
Wallace Gr A3
War Memorial A2
War Memorial B2
Warkworth Terr A2
Well Close Sq A2
West End B2
West End Pl B1
West End Rd B1
West St B3
West St C3
Windmill Bastion B3
Woolmarket B3
Works C3

Birmingham 332

Abbey St A2
Aberdeen St A1
Acorn Gr B2
Adams St A5
Adderley St C5
Albert St B4/B5
Albion St B2
Alcester St C5
Aldgate Gr A3
Alexandra Theatre C3
All Saint's St A2
All Saints Rd A2
Allcock St C5
Allesley St A4
Allison St C4
Alma Cr B6
Alston Rd C1
Arcadian Ctr C4
Arthur St C6
Assay Office B3
Aston Expressway A5
Aston Science Park B5
Aston St B4
Aston University B4/B5
Avenue Rd A5
BT Tower B3
Bacchus Rd A1
Bagot St B4
Banbury St B5
Barford Rd B1
Barford St C4
Barn St C5
Barnwell Rd C6
Barr St A3
Barrack St B5
Bartholomew St C4
Barwick St B4
Bath Row C3

Beaufort Rd C1
Belmont Row B5
Benson Rd A1
Berkley St C3
Bexhill Gr C3
Birchall St C5
Birmingham City FC C6
Birmingham City Hospital (A&E) A1
Bishopsgate St C3
Blews St A4
Bloomsbury St A6
Blucher St C3
Bordesley St C4
Bowyer St C5
Bradburne Way A5
Bradford St C5
Branston St A3
Brearley St A4
Brewery St A4
Bridge St A3
Bridge St C3
Bridge St West A4
Brindley Dr B3
Broad St C3
Broad St UGC C2
Broadway Plaza C2
Bromley St C5
Bromsgrove St C4
Brookfield Rd A2
Browning St C2
Bryant St A1
Buckingham St A3
Bullring C4
Bull St B4
Cambridge St C3
Camden Dr B3
Camden St B2
Cannon St C4
Cardigan St B5
Carlisle St A1
Carlyle Rd C1
Caroline St B3
Carver St B2
Cato St A6
Cattell Rd C6
Cattells Gr A6
Cawdor Cr C1
Cecil St B4
Cemetery A2/B2
Cemetery La A2
Ctr Link Industrial Est A6
Charlotte St B3
Cheapside C4
Chester St A5
Children's Hospital (A&E) B4
Church St B4
Claremont Rd A2
Clarendon Rd C1
Clark St C1
Clement St B3
Clissold St B2
Cliveland St B4
Coach Station C5
College St B2
Colmore Circus B4
Colmore Row B4
Commercial St C3
Constitution Hill B3
Convention Ctr, The C3
Cope St B2
Coplow St B1
Corporation St B4
Council House B3
County Court B4
Coveley Gr A2
Coventry Rd C6
Coventry St C5
Cox St B3
Crabtree Rd A2
Cregoe St C3
Crescent Ave A2
Crescent Theatre C3
Cromwell St A6
Cromwell St B3
Curzon St B5
Cuthbert Rd B1
Dale End B4
Dart St C6
Dartmouth Circus A4
Dartmouth Middleway A5
Dental Hospital B4
Deritend C5
Devon St A6
Devonshire St A1
Digbeth Civic Hall C5
Digbeth High St C4
Dolman St B6
Dover St A1
Duchess Rd C2
Duddeston B6
Duddeston Manor Rd B5
Duddeston Mill Rd B6
Duddeston Mill Trading Estate B6
Dudley Rd B1
Edgbaston Sh Ctr C2
Edmund St B3
Edward St B3
Elkington St A4
Ellen St B2
Ellis St C3
Erskine St B6
Essex St C4
Eyre St B2
Farm Croft A3
Farm St A3
Fazeley St B4/C5
Felstead Way B5
Finstall Cl B5
Five Ways C2
Fleet St B3
Floodgate St C5
Ford St A2
Fore St C4
Forster St B5
Francis Rd C2
Francis St B5
Frankfort St A4
Frederick St B3
Freeth St C1
Freightliner Terminal B6
Garrison La C6
Garrison St B6
Gas St C3
Geach St A4
George St B3
George St West B2
Gibb St C5
Gillott Rd B1
Gilby Rd C2
Glover St C5
Goode Ave A2
Goodrick Way A6
Gordon St B6
Graham St B3
Granville St C3
Gray St C6
Great Barr St C5
Great Charles St B3
Great Francis St B6
Great Hampton Row A3
Great Hampton St A3
Great King St A3
Great Lister St A5
Great Tindal St C2
Green La C6
Green St C5
Greenway St C6
Grosvenor St West C2
Guest Gr A3
Guild Cl C2
Guildford Dr A4
Guthrie Cl A3
Hagley Rd C1
Hall St B3
Hampton St A3
Handsworth New Rd A1
Hanley St B4
Harford St A3
Harmer Rd A2
Harold Rd C1
Hatchett St A4
Heath Mill La C5
Heath St B1
Heath St South B1
Heaton St A2
Heneage St B5
Henrietta St B4
Herbert Rd C6
High St C4
High St C5
Hilden Rd B5
Hill St C3/C4
Hindlow Cl B6
Hingeston St B2
Hippodrome Theatre C4
HM Prison A1
Hockley Circus A2
Hockley Hill A3
Hockley St A3
Holliday St C3
Holloway Circus C4
Holloway Head C3
Holt St B5
Hooper St B1
Horse Fair C4
Hospital St A4
Howard St B3
Howe St B5
Hubert St A5
Hunters Rd A2
Hunters Vale A3
Huntly Rd C2
Hurst St C4
Icknield Port Rd B1
Icknield Sq B2
Icknield St A2/B2
Ikon Gallery C3
Information Ctr C4
Inge St C4
Irving St C3
Ivy La C5
James Watt Queensway B4
Jennens Rd B5
Jewellery Quarter A3
Jewellery Quarter Museum B3
John Bright St C4
Keeley St C6
Kellett Rd B5
Kent St C4
Kenyon St B3
Key Hill A3
Kilby Ave C2
King Edwards Rd B2
King Edwards Rd C3
Kingston Rd C6
Kirby Rd A1
Ladywood Arts & L Ctr B1
Ladywood Middleway C2/C3
Ladywood Rd C1
Lancaster St B4
Landor St B6
Law Courts B4
Lawford Cl B5
Lawley Middleway B5
Ledbury Cl C2
Ledsam St B2
Lees St A1
Legge La B3
Lennox St A3
Library A6/C3
Library Walk B2
Lighthorne Ave B2
Link Rd B1
Lionel St B3
Lister St B5
Little Ann St C5
Little Hall Rd A6
Liverpool St C5
Livery St B3/B4
Lodge Rd A1
Lord St A5
Love La A5
Loveday St B4
Lower Dartmouth St C6
Lower Loveday St B4
Lower Tower St A4
Lower Trinty St C5
Ludgate Hill B3
Mailbox Ctr & BBC C3
Margaret St B3
Markby Rd A1
Marroway St B1
Maxstoke St C6
Melvina Rd A6
Meriden St C4
Metropolitan (RC) B4
Midland St B6
Milk St C5
Mill St A5
Millennium Point B5
Miller St A4
Milton St A4
Moat La C4
Montague Rd C1
Montague St C5
Monument Rd C1
Moor Street C4
Moor St Queensway C4
Moorsom St A4
Morville St C2
Mosborough Cr A3
Moseley St C4
Mott St B3
Mus & Art Gallery B3
Musgrave Rd A1
National Indoor Arena C2
National Sea Life Centre C3
Navigation St C3
Nechell's Park Rd A6
Nechells Parkway B5
Nechells Pl A6
New Bartholomew St C4
New Canal St C5
New John St West A3
New Spring St B2
New St C4
New Street C4
New Summer St A4
New Town Row A4
Newhall Hill B3
Newhall St B3
Newton St B4
Newtown A4
Noel Rd C1
Norman St A1
Northbrook St B1
Northwood St B3
Norton St A2
Old Crown House C5
Old Rep Theatre, The C4
Old Snow Hill B4
Oliver Rd C1
Oliver St A5
Osler St C1
Oxford St C5
Pallasades Ctr C4
Palmer St C5
Paradise Circus C3
Paradise St C3
Park Rd A2
Park St C4
Pavilions Ctr C4
Paxton Rd A2
Peel St A1
Penn St B5
Pershore St C4
Phillips St A4
Pickford St C5
Pinfold St C4
Pitsford St A2
Plough & Harrow Rd C1
Police Station A4/B1/B4/C2/C4
Pope St B2
Portland Rd C1
Post Office A3/A5/B1/B3/B4/B5/C2/C3/C5
Preston Rd A1
Price St B4
Princip St B4
Printing House St B4
Priory Queensway B4
Pritchett St A4
Proctor St A5
Queensway B3
Radnor St A2
Rea St C4
Regent Pl B3
Register Office C3
Repertory Theatre C3
Reservoir Rd C1
Richard St A5
River St C5
Rocky La A5/A6
Rodney Cl C2
Roseberry St B2
Rotton Park St B1
Rupert St A5
Ruston St C2
Ryland St C2
St Andrew's Ind Est C6
St Andrew's Rd C6
St Andrew's St C6
St Bolton St C6
St Chads Queensway B4
St Clements Rd A6
St George's St A3
St James Pl B5
St Marks Cr B2
St Martin's C4
St Paul's B3
St Paul's B3
St Paul's Sq B3
St Philip's B4
St Stephen's St A4
St Thomas' Peace Garden C3
St Vincent St C2
Saltley Rd A6
Sand Pits Pde B3
Severn St C3
Shadwell St B4
Sheepcote St C2
Shefford Rd A4
Sherborne St C2
Shylton's Croft C2
Skipton Rd C2
Smallbrook Queensway C4
Smith St A3
Snow Hill B4
Snow Hill Queensway B4
Soho, Benson Rd A1
South Rd A2
Spencer St B3
Spring Hill B2
Staniforth St B4
Station St C4
Steelhouse La B4
Stephenson St C4
Steward St B2
Stirling Rd C1
Stour St B2
Suffolk St C3
Summer Hill Rd B2
Summer Hill St B2
Summer Hill Terr B2
Summer La A4
Summer Row B3
Summerfield Cr B1
Summerfield Park B1
Sutton St C3
Swallow St C3
Sydney Rd C6
Symphony Hall C3
Talbot St A1
Temple Row C4
Temple St C4
Templefield St C6
Tenby St B3
Tenby St North B2
Tennant St C2/C3
The Crescent A2
Thimble Mill La A6
Thinktank (Science & Discovery) B5
Thomas St A4
Thorpe St C4
Tilton Rd C6
Tower St A4
Town Hall C3
Trent St C5
Turner's Buildings A1
Unett St A3
Union Terr B5
Upper Trinity St C5
Uxbridge St A3
Vauxhall Gr B5
Vauxhall Rd B5
Vernon Rd C1
Vesey St B4
Viaduct St B5
Victoria Sq C3
Villa St A3
Vittoria St B3
Vyse St B3
Walter St A6
Wardlow Rd A5
Warstone La B2
Washington St C3
Water St B3
Waterworks Rd C1
Watery La C5
Well St A3
Western Rd B1
Wharf St A2
Wheeler St A3
Whitehouse St A5
Whitmore St A2
Whittall St B4
Wholesale Market C4
Wiggin St B1
Willes Rd A1
Windsor Industrial Est A5
Windsor St A5
Windsor St B5
Winson Green Rd A1
Witton St C6
Wolseley St C6
Woodcock St B5

Blackpool 332

Abingdon St A1
Addison Cr A3
Adelaide St B1
Albert Rd B2
Alfred St B2
Ascot Rd A3
Ashton Rd C2
Auburn Gr C3
Bank Hey St B1
Banks St A1
Beech Ave A3
Bela Gr C2
Belmont Ave B2
Birley St A1
Blackpool & Fleetwood Tram B1
Blackpool & The Fylde College B2
Blackpool FC C2
Blackpool North A2
Blackpool Tower B1
Blundell St C1
Bonny St B1
Breck Rd B3
Bryan Rd A3
Buchanan St A2
Cambridge Rd A3
Caunce St A2/A3
Central Dr B1/C2
Central Pier C1
Central Pier C1
Central Pier Theatre C1
Chapel St C1
Charles St A2
Charnley Rd B2
Church St A1/A2
Clinton Ave B2
Coach Station A2/C1
Cocker St A1
Cocker St A1
Coleridge Rd A3
Collingwood Ave A3
Condor Gr C3
Cookson St A2
Coronation St B1
Corporation St A1
Courts B1
Cumberland Ave B3
Cunliffe Rd C3
Dale St C1
Devonshire Rd A3
Devonshire Sq A3
Dickson Rd A1
Elizabeth St A2
Ferguson Rd C3
Forest Gate B3
Foxhall Rd C1
Foxhall Sq C1
Freckleton St C2
George St A2
Gloucester Ave B3
Golden Mile, The C1
Gorse Rd B3
Gorton St A2
Grand Theatre, The B1
Granville Rd A2
Grasmere Rd C2
Grosvenor St A2
Grundy Art Gallery A1
Harvey Rd B3
Hornby Rd B2
Hounds Hill Sh Ctr B1
Hull Rd B1
Ibbison Ct C2
Information Ctr A1
Kent Rd C2
Keswick Rd C2
King St A2
Knox Gr C3
Laycock Gate A3
Layton Rd A3
Leamington Rd B2
Leeds Rd B3
Leicester Rd B2
Levens Gr C2
Library A1
Lifeboat Station B1
Lincoln Rd B2
Liverpool Rd B3
Livingstone Rd B2
London Rd A3
Louis Tussaud's Waxworks B1
Lune Gr C2
Lytham Rd C1
Manchester Sq C1
Manor Rd B3
Maple Ave B3
Market St A1
Marlboro Rd B3
Mere Rd B3
Milbourne St A2
Newcastle Ave B3
Newton Dr A3
North Pier A1
North Pier A1
North Pier Theatre A1
Odeon C2
Olive Gr B3
Palatine Rd B2
Park Rd B2/C3
Peter St A2
Police Station B1
Post Office A1/A3B1/B2/B3
Princess Pde A1
Princess St C1/C2
Promenade A1/C1
Queen St A1
Queen Victoria Rd C2
Raikes Pde B2
Reads Ave B2
Regent Rd B2
Register Office B2
Ribble Rd B2
Rigby Rd C1/C2
Ripon Rd B3
St Albans Rd B3
St Ives Ave C3
St Vincent Ave C3
Salisbury Rd B3
Salthouse Ave C2
Salvation Army Ctr A2
Sands Way C2
Sealife Ctr B1
Seasiders Way C1
Selbourne Rd A2
Sharrow Gr C3
Somerset Ave C3
Springfield Rd A1
South King St B2
Sutton Pl B2
Talbot Rd A1/A2
Thornber Gr C2
Topping St A1
Tower B1
Town Hall A1
Tram Depot C1
Tyldesley Rd C1
Vance Rd B1
Victoria St B1
Victory Rd A2
Wayman Rd A3
Westmorland Ave C2/C3
Whitegate Dr B3
Winter Gardens Theatre B1
Woodland Gr B3
Woolman Rd B2

Bournemouth 332

Ascham Rd A3
Avenue Rd B1
Bath Rd C2
Beacon Rd C1
Beach Office C2
Beechey Rd A3
Bodorgan Rd B1
Bourne Ave B1
Bournemouth & Poole College B3
Bournemouth Eye C2
Bournemouth Int Ctr C1
Bournemouth Pier C2
Bournemouth Sta A3
Bournemouth Sta B3
Braidley Rd A1
Cavendish Place A2
Cavendish Rd A2
Central Drive A1
Christchurch Rd B3
Cliff Lift C1/C3
Coach House Pl A3
Coach Station A3
Commercial Rd B1
Cotlands Rd B3
Courts B3
Cranborne Rd C1
Cricket Ground A2
Cumnor Rd B2
Dean Park A2
Dean Park Cr B2
Dean Park Rd A2
Durrant Rd B1
East Overcliff Dr C3
Exeter Cr C1
Exeter La C2
Exeter Rd C1
Gervis Place B1
Gervis Rd B3
Glen Fern Rd B2
Golf Club B1
Grove Rd B3
Hinton Rd C2
Holdenhurst Rd B3
Horseshoe Common B2
Nuffield Health Bournemouth Hospital (private) A2
Information Ctr B2
Lansdowne B3
Lansdowne Rd A2
Lorne Park Rd B2
Lower Central Gdns B1/C2
Madeira Rd B2
Methuen Rd A3
Meyrick Park A1
Meyrick Rd B3
Milton Rd A2
Oceanarium C2
Odeon Cinema C2
Old Christchurch Rd B2
Ophir Rd A3
Oxford Rd B3
Park Rd A3
Parsonage Rd B2
Pavilion C2
Pier Approach C2
Pier Theatre C2
Police Station A3/B3
Portchester Rd A3
Post Office B1/B3
Priory Rd C1
Quadrant, The B2
Recreation Ground A1
Richmond Hill Rd B1
Russell Cotes Art Gallery & Museum C2
Russell Cotes Rd C2
St Anthony's Rd A1
St Michael's Rd C1
St Paul's A3
St Paul's La B3
St Paul's Rd A3
St Peter's B2
St Peter's B2
St Peter's Rd B2
St Stephen's Rd B1/B2
St Swithun's B3
St Swithun's Rd B3
St Swithun's Rd South B3
St Valerie Rd A2
St Winifred's Rd A2
Stafford Rd B3
Terrace Rd B1
The Square B1
The Triangle B1
Town Hall B1
Tregonwell Rd C1
Trinity Rd B2
Undercliff Drive C3
Upper Central Gdns B1
Upper Hinton Rd B2
Upper Terr Rd C1
Waterfront, The C2
Wellington Rd A2/A3
Wessex Way A3/B1/B2
West Cliff Promenade C1
West Hill Rd C1
West Undercliff Prom C1
Westover Rd B2
Wimborne Rd A2
Wootton Mount B2
Wychwood Dr A1
Yelverton Rd B2
York Rd B3
Zig-Zag Walks C1/C3

Bradford 332

Alhambra B2
Back Ashgrove B1
Barkerend Rd A3
Barnard Rd C3
Barry St B2
Bolling Rd C3
Bolton Rd A3
Bowland St A1
Bradford 1 B2
Bradford College B1
Bradford Forster Sq A2
Bradford Interchange B3
Bradford Playhouse B3
Bridge St B2
Britannia St B2
Burnett St B3
Bus Station B2
Butler St West A3
Caledonia St C2
Canal Rd A2
Carlton St B1
Cathedral A3
Centenary Sq B2
Chapel St B3
Cheapside A2
Church Bank B3
Cineworld B3
City Hall B2
City Rd A1
Claremont B1
Colour Museum B1
Croft St B2
Crown Court B3
Darfield St A1
Darley St A2
Drewton Rd A1
Drummond Trading Estate A1
Dryden St B3
Dyson St A1
Easby Rd C1
East Parade B3
Eldon Pl A1
Filey St B3
Forster Square Ret Pk A2
Gallery II B1
Garnett St B3
Godwin St B2
Gracechurch St A1
Grattan Rd B1
Great Horton Rd B1/B2
Grove Terr B1
Hall Ings B2
Hall La C3
Hallfield Rd A1
Hammstrasse A2
Harris St B3
Holdsworth St A2
Ice Rink B2
Impressions B2
Information Ctr B2
Ivegate B2
Inland Revenue A2
Jacob's Well Municipal Offices B2
James St A2
John St A2
Kirkgate B2
Kirkgate Ctr B2
Laisteridge La C1
Leeds Rd B3
Library B1/B2
Listerhills Rd B1
Little Horton La C1
Little Horton Gn C1
Longside La B1
Lower Kirkgate B2
Lumb La A1
Magistrates Court B2
Manchester Rd C2
Manningham La A1
Manor Row A2
Market C3
Market St B2
Melbourne Place C1
Midland Rd A2
Mill La C2
Morley St B1
National Media B2
Nelson St B2/C2
Nesfield St A2
New Otley Rd A3
Norcroft St B1
North Parade A2
North St A3
North Wing A3
Oastler Shopping Ctr A2
Otley Rd A3
Park Ave C1
Park La C1
Park Rd C2
Parma St C2
Peace Museum B2
Peckover St B3
Piccadilly A2
Police Station B2/C2
Post Office A2/B1/B2/C3
Princes Way B2
Prospect St C3
Radwell Drive C2
Rawson Rd A1
Rebecca St A1
Richmond Rd B1
Russell St C1
St George's Hall B2
St Lukes Hospital C1
St Mary's A3
Shipley Airedale Rd A3/B3
Simes St A1
Smith St B1
Spring Mill St C2
Stott Hill A3
Sunbridge Rd A1/B1/B2
The Leisure Exchange B3
Theatre in the Mill B1
Thornton Rd A1/B1
Trafalgar St A2
Trinity Rd C1
Tumbling Hill St B1
Tyrrel St B2
Univ of Bradford B1/C1
Usher St C3
Valley Rd A2
Vicar La B3
Wakefield Rd C3
Wapping Rd A3
Westgate A1
White Abbey Rd A1
Wigan Rd A1
Wilton St B1
Wood St A1
Wool Exchange B2
Worthington St A1

Brighton 332

Addison Rd A1
Albert Rd B2
Albion Hill B3
Albion St B3
Ann St A3
Art Gallery & Mus B3
Baker St A3
Black Lion St C2
Brighton A2
Brighton Ctr C2
Brighton Fishing Museum C2
Broad St C3
Buckingham Pl A2
Buckingham Rd B2
Cannon Pl C1
Carlton Hill B3
Chatham Pl A1
Cheapside A3
Church St B2
Churchill Sq Sh Ctr B2
Clifton Hill B1
Clifton Pl B1
Clifton Rd B1
Clifton St A2
Clifton Terr B1
Clock Tower B2
Clyde Rd A3
Coach Park C3
Compton Ave A2
Davigdor Rd A1
Denmark Terr B1
Ditchling Rd A3
Dome, The B2
Duke St B2
Duke's La C2
Dyke Rd A1/B2
East St C2
Edward St B3
Elmore Rd B3
Frederick St B2
Gardner St B2
Gloucester Pl B3
Gloucester Rd B2
Goldsmid Rd A1
Grand Junction Rd C2
Grand Pde B3
Grove Hill B3
Guildford St A2
Hampton Pl B1
Hanover Terr A3
High St C3
Highdown Rd A1
Information Ctr C2
John St B3
Kemp St B2
Kensington Pl B2
Kings Rd C1
Law Courts B3
Lewes Rd A3
Library B2
London Rd A3
Madeira Dr C3
Marine Pde C3
Middle St C2
Montpelier Pl B1
Montpelier Rd B1
Montpelier St B1
New England Rd A2
New England St A2
New Rd B2
Nizells Ave A1
Norfolk Rd B1
Norfolk Terr B1
North Rd B2
North St B2
Odeon Cinema C2
Old Shoreham Rd A1
Old Steine C3
Osmond Rd A1
Over St B2
Oxford St A3
Palace Pier C3
Park Crescent Terr A3
Phoenix Art Gallery B3
Phoenix Rise A3
Police Station B3
Post Office A1/A2/A3/B1/B2/B3/C3
Preston Rd A2
Preston St B1
Prestonville Rd A1
Queen's Rd B2
Regency Sq C1
Regent St B2
Richmond Pl B3
Richmond St B3
Richmond Terr A3
Rose Hill Terr A3
Royal Alexandra Hospital B1
Royal Pavilion B2
St Bartholomew's A3
St James's St C3
St Nicholas Rd B2
St Nicholas' B2
St Peter's A3
Sea Life Ctr C3
Shaftesbury Rd A3
Ship St C2
Sillwood Rd B1
Sillwood St B1
Southover St A3
Spring Gdns B2
Stanford Rd A1
Stanley Rd A3
Surrey St B2
Sussex St B3
Sussex Terr B3
Swimming Pool B3
Sydney St B3
Temple Gdns B1
Terminus Rd A2
The Lanes C2
Theatre Royal B2
Tidy St B2
Town Hall C2
Toy & Model Mus A2
Trafalgar St B2
Union Rd A3
University of Brighton B3
Upper Lewes Rd A3
Upper North St B1
Viaduct Rd A3
Victoria Gdns B3
Victoria Rd B1
Volk's Electric Railway C3
West Pier (Closed to the Public) C1
West St C2
Western Rd B1
Whitecross St B2
York Ave B1
York Pl B3

Bristol 332

Acramans Rd C4
Albert Rd C6
Alfred Hill A4
All Saint's St A4
All Saints' A4
Allington Rd C3
Alpha Rd C4
Ambra Vale B1
Ambra Vale East B2
Ambrose Rd B2
Amphitheatre C3
Anchor Rd B3
Anvil St B6
Architecture Ctr B4
Argyle Pl B2
Arlington Villas A2
Arnolfini Arts Ctr, The B4
Art Gallery A3
Ashton Gate Rd C2
Ashton Rd C1
at-Bristol B3
Avon Bridge C1
Avon Cr C1
Avon St B6
Baldwin St B4
Baltic Wharf C2
Baltic Wharf Leisure Ctr & Caravan Park C2
Barossa Pl C4
Barton Manor B6
Barton Rd B6
Barton Vale B6
Bath Rd C6
Bathurst Basin C4
Bathurst Parade C4
Beauley Rd C3
Bedminster Bridge C5
Bedminster Parade C4
Bellevue B2
Bellevue Cr B2
Bellevue Rd C6
Berkeley Pl A2
Berkeley Sq A3
Birch Rd C2
Blackfriars A4
Bond St A5
Braggs La A6
Brandon Hill B3
Brandon Steep B3
Bristol Bridge B5
Bristol Cath (CE) B3
Bristol Central Library B3
Bristol Eye Hospital (A&E) A4
Bristol Grammar School A3
Bristol Harbour Railway C3
Bristol Marina C2
Bristol Royal Children's Hospital A4
Bristol Royal Infirmary (A&E) A4
Bristol Temple Meads Station B6
Broad Plain B6
Broad Quay B4
Broad St A4
Broad Weir A5
Broadcasting House A3
Broadmead A5
Brunel Way C1
Brunswick Sq A5
Burton Cl C5
Bus Station A4
Butts Rd B3
Cabot Tower B3
Caledonia Pl B1
Callowhill Ct A5
Cambridge St C6
Camden Rd C3
Camp Rd A1
Canada Way C2
Cannon St A4
Canon's Rd B3/B4
Canon's Way B3
Cantock's Cl A3
Canynge Rd A1
Canynge Sq A1
Castle Park A5
Castle St A5
Catherine Meade St C4
Cattle Market Rd C6
Charles Pl B1
Charlotte St B3
Charlotte St South B3
Chatterton House B5
Chatterton Sq C5
Chatterton St C5
Cheese La B5
Christchurch A4
Christchurch Rd A1
Christmas Steps A4
Church La B2/B5
Church St B5

Bury St Edmunds • Cambridge • Canterbury • Cardiff • Carlisle 347

City Museum A3
City of Bristol College B3
Clare St B4
Clarence Rd C5
Cliff Rd C1
Clift House Rd C1
Clifton Cath (RC) A2
Clifton Down A1
Clifton Down Rd A1
Clifton Hill B2
Clifton Park A1/A2
Clifton Park Rd A1
Clifton Rd A2
Cliftonwood Cr B2
Cliftonwood Rd B2
Cliftonwood Terr B2
Clifton Vale B1
Cobblestone Mews A1
College Green B3
College Rd A1
College St B3
Colston Almshouses A4
Colston Ave B4
Colston Hall B4
Colston Parade C5
Colston St A4
Commercial Rd C4
Constitution Hill B2
Cooperage La C2
Corn St B4
Cornwallis Ave B1
Cornwallis Cr B1
Coronation Rd C2/C4
Council House B3
Counterslip B5
Courts A4
Create Ctr, The C1
Crosby Row B2
Culver St B3
Cumberland Basin C1
Cumberland Cl C2
Cumberland Rd C2/C3
Dale St A6
David St A6
Dean La C4
Deanery Rd B3
Denmark St B4
Dowry Sq B1
East St A5
Eaton Cr A2
Elmdale Rd A3
Elton Rd A3
Eugene St A4/A6
Exchange, The and St Nicholas' Mkts B4
Fairfax St A4
Fire Station B5
Floating Harbour C3
Foster Almshouses A4
Frayne Rd C1
Frederick Pl A2
Freeland Pl B1
Frogmore St B3
Fry's Hill B2
Gas La B6
Gasferry Rd C3
General Hospital C4
Georgian House B3
Glendale B1
Glentworth Rd B2
Gloucester St A1
Goldney Hall B2
Goldney Rd B1
Gordon Rd A2
Granby Hill B1
Grange Rd A1
Great Ann St A6
Great George St A6/B3
Great George Rd B3
Great Western Way B6
Green St North B1
Green St South B1
Greenay Bush La C2
Greenbank Rd C2
Greville Smyth Park C1
Guildhall A4
Guinea St C4
Hamilton Rd C3
Hanbury Rd A2
Hanover Pl C2
Harbour Way B3
Harley Pl A1
Haymarket A5
Hensman's Hill B1
High St B4
Highbury Villas A3
Hill St B3
Hill St C6
Hippodrome B4
Hopechapel Hill B1
Horfield Rd A4
Horton St B6
Host St A4
Hotwell Rd B1/B2
Houlton St A6
Howard Rd C3
Ice Rink B3
IMAX Cinema B4
Information Ctr B4
Islington Rd C3
Jacob St A5/A6
Jacob's Wells Rd B2
John Carr's Terr B2
John Wesley's Chapel A5
Joy Hill B1
Jubilee St B6
Kensington Pl A2
Kilkenny St B6
King St B4
Kingsland Rd B6
Kingston Rd C3
Lamb St A6
Lansdown Rd A2
Lawford St A6
Lawfords Gate A6
Leighton Rd C3
Lewins Mead A4
Lime Rd C2
Little Ann St A6
Little Caroline Pl B1
Little George St A6
Little King St B4
Litfield Rd A1
Llandoger Trow B4
Lloyds' Building, The C3
Lodge St A4
Lord Mayor's Chapel, The B4
Lower Castle St A5
Lower Church La A4
Lower Clifton Hill B2
Lower Guinea St C4
Lower Lamb St B3
Lower Maudlin St A4
Lower Park Rd A4
Lower Sidney St C2
Lucky La C4
Lydstep Terr C3
Mall (Galleries Shopping Ctr), The A5
Manilla Rd A1
Mardyke Ferry Rd C2
Maritime Heritage Ctr B3
Marlborough Hill A4
Marlborough St A4
Marsh St B4
Mead St C5
Meadow St A5
Merchant Dock B2
Merchant Seamen's Almshouses B4
Merchant St A5
Merchants Rd A1
Merchants Rd C1
Meridian Pl A2
Meridian Vale A2
Merrywood Rd C3
Midland Rd A6
Milford St C3
Millennium Sq B3
Mitchell La B5
Mortimer Rd A1
M Shed C4
Murray Rd C4
Myrtle Rd A3
Narrow Plain B5
Narrow Quay B4
Nelson St A4
New Charlotte St C4
New Kingsley Rd B6
New Queen St C5
New St A6
Newfoundland St A5
Newgate A5
Newton St A6
Norland Rd A1
North St C2
Oakfield Gr A2
Oakfield Pl A2
Oakfield Rd A2
Old Bread St B6
Old Market St A6
Old Park Hill A4
Oldfield Rd B1
Orchard Ave B4
Orchard La B4
Orchard St B4
Osbourne Rd C3
Oxford St B6
Park Pl A2
Park Rd C3
Park Row A3
Park St A3
Passage St B5
Pembroke Gr A2
Pembroke Rd A2
Pembroke Rd C3
Pembroke St A5
Penn St A5
Pennywell Rd A6
Percival Rd A1
Pero's Bridge B4
Perry Rd A4
Pip & Jay A5
Plimsoll Bridge B1
Police Sta A4/A6
Polygon Rd B1
Portland St A1
Portwall La B5
Post Office A1/A3/A4/A5/A6/B1/B4/C4/C5
Prewett St C5
Prince St B4
Prince St Bridge C4
Princess St C5
Princess Victoria St B1
Priory Rd A3
Pump La C5
QEH Theatre A2
Queen Charlotte St B4
Quakers Friars A5
Quay St A4
Queen Elizabeth Hospital School B2
Queen Sq B4
Queen St A5
Queen's Ave A3
Queen's Parade B3
Queen's Rd A2/A3
Raleigh Rd C2
Randall Rd B2
Redcliffe Backs B5
Redcliffe Bridge B4
Redcliffe Hill C5
Redcliffe Parade C4
Redcliffe St B5
Redcliffe Way B5
Redcross La A6
Redcross St A6
Redgrave Theatre A1
Red Lodge A4
Regent St B1
Richmond Hill A2
Richmond Hill Ave A2
Richmond La A2
Richmond Park Rd A2
Richmond St C6
Richmond Terr A2
River St A6
Rownham Mead B2
Royal Fort Rd A3
Royal Park A2
Royal West of England Academy A3
Royal York Cr B1
Royal York Villas B1
Rupert St A4
Russ St B6
St Andrew's Walk B2
St George's B3
St George's Rd B3
St James A4
St John's A4
St John's Rd C4
St Luke's Rd C5
St Mary Redcliffe C5
St Mary's Hospital A3
St Matthias Park A6
St Michael's Hill A3
St Michael's Hospl A4
St Michael's Park A3
St Nicholas St B4
St Paul St A5
St Paul's Rd A2
St Peter's (ruin) A5
St Philip's Bridge B5
St Philips Rd A6
St Stephen's B4
St Stephen's St B4
St Thomas St B5
St Thomas the Martyr B5
Sandford Rd B1
Sargent St C5
Saville Pl B1
Ship La C5
Silver St A4
Sion Hill A1
Small St A4
Smeaton Rd C1
Somerset Sq C5
Somerset St C5
Southernhay Ave B2
Southville Rd C4
Spike Island Artspace C2
Spring St C5
SS Great Britain and The Matthew B2
Stackpool Rd C3
Staight St B6
Stillhouse La C4
Stracey Rd C2
Stratton St A5
Sydney Row C2
Tankard's Cl A3
Temple Back B5
Temple Boulevard B5
Temple Bridge B5
Temple Church B5
Temple Circus B5
Temple Gate C5
Temple St B5
Temple Way B5
Terrell St A4
The Arcade A5
The Fosseway A2
The Grove B4
The Horsefair A5
The Mall A1
Theatre Royal B4
Thomas La B5
Three Kings of Cologne A4
Three Queens La B5
Tobacco Factory, The C2
Tower Hill B5
Tower La A4
Trenchard St A4
Triangle South A3
Triangle West A3
Trinity Rd A6
Trinity St A6
Tucker St A5
Tyndall Ave A3
Union St A5
Union St B6
Unity St A6
Unity St B3
University of Bristol A3
University Rd A3
Upper Maudlin St A4
Upper Perry Hill C3
Upper Byron Pl A3
Upton Rd C2
Valentine Bridge B6
Victoria Gr C5
Victoria Rd C6
Victoria Rooms A2
Victoria Sq A2
Victoria St B5
Vyvyan Rd A1
Vyvyan Terr A1
Wade St A6
Walter St C2
Wapping Rd C4
Water La B5
Waterloo Rd A6
Waterloo St A1
Waterloo St A6
Watershed, The B4
Welling Terr B1
Wellington Rd A6
Welsh Back B4
West Mall A1
West St A6
Westfield Pl A1
Wetherell Pl A2
Whitehouse Pl C5
Whitehouse St C5
Whiteladies Rd A2
Whitson St A4
William St C5
Willway St C5
Windsor Pl B1
Windsor Terr B1
Wine St A4
Woodland Rise A3
Woodland Rd A3
Worcester Rd A1
Worcester Terr A1
YHA B4
York Gdns B1
York Pl A2
York Rd C5

Bury St Edmunds 332

Abbey Gardens B3
Abbey Gate B3
Abbeygate St B2
Albert Cr B1
Albert St B1
Ambulance Sta C1
Angel Hill B2
Angel La B2
Anglian Lane A1
Arc Shopping Ctr B2
Athenaeum C2
Baker's La C3
Beetons Way A1
Bishops Rd B2
Bloomfield St B2
Bridewell La C2
Bullen Cl C1
Bury St Edmunds ≥ A2
Bury St Edmunds County Upper School A1
Bury St Edmunds L Ctr B1
Bury Town FC B3
Bus Station B2
Butter Mkt B2
Cannon St B2
Castle Rd C1
Cemetery C1
Chalk Rd (N) B1
Chalk Rd (S) B1
Church Row B2
Churchgate St C2
Citizens Advice Bureau B2
College St C2
Compiegne Way A3
Corn Exchange, The B2
Cornfield Rd B1
Cotton Lane B3
Courts B2
Covent Garden C2
Crown St C3
Cullum Rd C2
Eastern Way A3
Eastgate St B3
Enterprise Bsns Park A2
Etna Rd A2
Eyre Cl C2
Fire Station B1
Friar's Lane C2
Gage Cl A1
Garland St B2
Greene King Brewery C3
Grove Park B1
Grove Rd B1
Guildhall C2
Guildhall St C2
Hatter St C2
High Baxter St B2
Honey Hill C3
Hospital Rd C1/C2
Ickworth Dr C1
Information Ctr B2
Ipswich St A2
King Edward VI School A1
King's Rd C1/B2
Library B2
Long Brackland A2
Looms La B2
Lwr Baxter St B2
Malthouse La A2
Maynewater La C3
Mill Rd C1
Mill Rd (South) C1
Minden Close B3
Moyses Hall B2
Mustow St B3
Norman Tower C3
Northgate Ave A2
Northgate St B2
Nutshell, The B2
Osier Rd A2
Out Northgate A2
Out Risbygate B1
Out Westgate C2
Parkway B1/C2
Parkway B1
Peckham St B2
Petticoat La C1
Phoenix Day Hospl C1
Pinners Way C1
Police Station C3
Post Office B2/B3
Pump La B2
Queen's Rd B1
Raingate St C3
Raynham Rd A1
Retail Park C2
Risbygate St B1/B2
Robert Boby Way C2
St Andrew's St North B2
St Andrew's St South B2
St Botolph's La C3
St Edmunds Hospital (private) C3
St Edmund's C2
St Edmund's Abbey (Remains) B3
St Edmundsbury C3
St John's St B2
St Marys C3
School Hall La B2
Shillitoe Cl C1
Shire Halls & Magistrates Ct C3
South Cl C1
Southgate St C3
Sparhawk St C3
Spring Lane B1
Springfield Rd B1
Station Hill A2
Swan La C3
Tayfen Rd B2
The Vinefields B3
Theatre Royal C3
Thingoe Hill A2
Victoria St B1
War Memorial C1
Well St B2
West Suffolk College B1
Westgarth Gdns C1
Westgate St C2
Whiting St C2
York Rd B1
York Terr B1

Cambridge 333

Abbey Rd A3
ADC A2
Anglia Ruskin Univ B3
Archaeology & Anthropology B2
Art Gallery A1
Arts Picture House B2
Arts Theatre B1
Auckland Rd A3
Bateman St C2
BBC C3
Benet St B1
Bradmore St B3
Bridge St A1
Broad St B3
Brookside C2
Brunswick Terr A3
Burleigh St B3
Bus Station B2
Butt Green A2
Cambridge Contemporary Art Gallery B1
Castle Mound A1
Castle St A1
Chesterton La A1
Christ's (Coll) B2
Christ's Pieces B2
City Rd B3
Clare (Coll) B1
Clarendon St B2
Coe Fen C2
Coronation St C2
Corpus Christi (Coll) B1
Council Offices C3
Cross St C3
Crusoe Bridge C1
Darwin (Coll) C1
Devonshire Rd C3
Downing (Coll) C2
Downing St B2
Earl St B2
East Rd B3
Eden St B3
Elizabeth Way A3
Elm St B2
Emery St B3
Emmanuel (Coll) B2
Emmanuel Rd B2
Emmanuel St B2
Fair St A3
Fenners Physical Education Ctr C3
Fire Station B3
Fitzroy St A3
Fitzwilliam Mus C2
Fitzwilliam St C2
Folk Museum A1
Glisson Rd C3
Gonville & Caius (Coll) B1
Gonville Place C2
Grafton Ctr A3
Grand Arcade B2
Gresham Rd C3
Green St B1
Guest Rd B3
Guildhall B2
Harvey Rd C3
Hills Rd C3
Hobson St B2
Hughes Hall (Coll) B3
Information Ctr B2
James St A3
Jesus (Coll) A2
Jesus Green A2
Jesus La A2
Jesus Terr B3
John St B3
Kelsey Kerridge Sports Ctr B3
King St A2
King's (Coll) B1
King's Coll Chapel B1
King's Parade B1
Lammas Land Rec Gd C1
Lensfield Rd C2
Little St Mary's La B1
Lyndewod Rd C3
Magdalene (Coll) A1
Magdalene St A1
Maid's Causeway A3
Malcolm St A2
Market Hill B1
Market St B1
Mathematical Bridge B1
Mawson Rd C3
Midsummer Common A3
Mill La B1
Mill Rd B3
Mill St C3
Napier St A3
New Square A2
Newmarket Rd A3
Newnham Rd C1
Norfolk St B3
Northampton St A1
Norwich St C2
Orchard St B2
Panton St C2
Paradise Nature Reserve C1
Paradise St B3
Park Parade A1
Park St A2
Park Terr B2
Parker St B2
Parker's Piece B2
Parkside B3
Parkside Pools B3
Parsonage St A3
Pemberton Terr C2
Pembroke (Coll) B2
Pembroke St B1
Perowne St B3
Peterhouse (Coll) C1
Petty Cury B2
Police Station B3
Post Office A1/A3/B2/B3/C1/C2/C3
Queens' (Coll) B1
Queen's La B1
Queen's Rd B1
Regent St B2
Regent Terr B2
Ridley Hall (Coll) C1
Riverside A3
Round Church, The A1
Russell St C2
St Andrew's St B2
St Benet's B1
St Catharine's (Coll) B1
St Eligius St C2
St John's (Coll) A1
St Mary's B1
St Paul's Rd C3
Saxon St C2
Scott Polar Institute & Museum C2
Sedgwick Museum B2
Sheep's Green C1
Shire Hall A1
Sidgwick Ave C1
Sidney St A2
Sidney Sussex (Coll) A2
Silver St B1
Station Rd C3
Tenison Ave C3
Tenison Rd C3
Tennis Court Rd B2
The Backs B1
The Fen Causeway C1
Thompson's La A1
Trinity (Coll) A1
Trinity Hall (Coll) B1
Trinity St B1
Trumpington Rd C2
Trumpington St B1
Union Rd C2
University Botanic Gardens C2
Victoria Ave A2
Victoria St B2
Warkworth St B3
Warkworth Terr B3
Wesley House (Coll) A2
West Rd B1
Westcott House (Coll) A2
Westminster (Coll) A1
Whipple B2
Willis Rd B3
Willow Walk A2
Zoology B2

Canterbury 333

Artillery St B2
Barton Mill Rd A3
Beaconsfield Rd A1
Beverley Rd A1
Bingley's Island B1
Black Griffin La B1
Broad Oak Rd A2
Broad St B2
Brymore Rd A3
Burgate B2
Bus Station C2
Canterbury College C3
Canterbury East ≥ C1
Canterbury Tales, The B2
Canterbury West ≥ A1
Castle C1
Castle Row C1
Castle St C1
Cathedral B2
Chaucer Rd A3
Christ Church Univ B3
Christchurch Gate B2
City Council Offices A3
City Wall B2
Coach Park A2
College Rd B3
Cossington Rd C2
Court B2
Craddock Rd A3
Crown & County Courts B3
Dane John Gdns C2
Dane John Mound C1
Deanery B2
Dover St C2
Duck La B2
Eastbridge Hospl B1
Edgar Rd B3
Ersham Rd C3
Ethelbert Rd C3
Fire Station C2
Forty Acres Rd A1
Gordon Rd C1
Greyfriars B1
Guildford Rd C1
Havelock St B2
Heaton Rd C1
High St B2
HM Prison B3
Information Ctr A2/B2
Ivy La B2
Ivy Pl C1
King St B2
King's School B2/B3
King's School Leisure Facilities A2
Kingsmead Leisure Ctr A2
Kingsmead Rd A2
Kirby's La B1
Lansdown Rd C2
Lime Kiln Rd C1
Longport B3
Lower Chantry La C3
Mandeville Rd A1
Market Way A2
Marlowe Arcade B2
Marlowe Ave C2
Marlowe Theatre B2
Martyrs Field Rd C1
Mead Way B1
Military Rd B2
Monastery St B2
Mus of Canterbury (Rupert Bear Mus) B1
New Dover Rd C3
Norman Rd C2
North Holmes Rd B3
North La B1
Northgate A2
Nunnery Fields C2
Nunnery Rd C2
Oaten Hill C2
Odeon Cinema C2
Old Dover Rd C2
Old Palace B2
Old Ruttington La B2
Old Weavers B2
Orchard St B1
Oxford Rd C1
Palace St B2
Pilgrims Way C3
Pin Hill C1
Pine Tree Ave A1
Police Station C2
Post Office B2/C1/C2
Pound La B1
Puckle La C2
Raymond Ave C2
Registry Office A2
Rheims Way B1
Rhodaus Cl C2
Rhodaus Town C2
Roman Museum B2
Roper Gateway A1
Roper Rd A1
Rose La B2
Royal Museum B2
St Augustine's Abbey (remains) B3
St Augustine's Rd C3
St Dunstan's A1
St Dunstan's St A1
St George's Pl C2
St George's St B2
St George's Tower B2
St Gregory's Rd B3
St John's Hospital A2
St Margaret's St B2
St Martin's B3
St Martin's Ave B3
St Martin's Rd B3
St Michael's Rd A1
St Mildred's C1
St Peter's Gr B1
St Peter's La B2
St Peter's Pl B1
St Peter's St B1
St Radigunds St B2
St Stephen's Ct A1
St Stephen's Path A1
St Stephen's Rd A2
Salisbury Rd A1
Simmonds Rd C1
Spring La C3
Station Rd West B1
Stour St B1
Sturry Rd A3
The Causeway A2
The Friars B2
Tourtel Rd A3
Tudor Rd C1
Union St B2
University for the Creative Arts C3
Vernon Pl C2
Victoria Rd C1
Watling St B2
Westgate Gdns B1
Westgate Towers B1
Whitefriars B2
Whitehall Gdns B1
Whitehall Rd B1
Wincheap C1
York Rd C1
Zealand Rd C2

Cardiff *Caerdydd* **333**

Adam St B3
Alexandra Gdns A2
Allerton St C1
Arran St A3
ATRiuM (Univ of Glamorgan) C3
Beauchamp St C1
Bedford St A3
Blackfriars Priory (rems) B1
Boulevard De Nantes B2
Brains Brewery C2
Brook St B1
Bus Station C2
Bute Park B1
Bute St C2
Bute Terr C3
Callaghan Sq C2/C3
Capitol Sh Ctr, The B3
Cardiff Arms Park (Cardiff RFC) B1
Cardiff Bridge B1
Cardiff Castle B2
Cardiff Central Sta ≥ C2
Cardiff Ctr Trading Est C3
Cardiff Univ A1/A2/B3
Cardiff University Student's Union A2
Caroline St C2
Castle Green B2
Castle Mews A1
Castle St (Heol y Castell) B1
Cathays Station ≥ A2
Celerity Drive C3
Central Library C2
Central Sq C2
Charles St (Heol Siarl) B3
Churchill Way B3
City Hall A2
City Rd A3
Clare Rd C1
Clare St C1
Coburn St A3
Coldstream Terr B1
College Rd A1
Colum Rd A1
Court C2
Court Rd C1
Craiglee Drive C3
Cranbrook St A3
Customhouse St C2
Cyfartha St A3
Despenser Place C1
Despenser St C1
Dinas St C1
Duke St (Heol y Dug) B2
Dumfries Place B3
East Grove A3
Ellen St C3
Fire Station B3
Fitzalan Place B3
Fitzhamon Emb C1
Fitzhamon La C1
g39 B2
Gloucester St C1
Glynrhondda St A2
Gordon Rd A3
Gorsedd Gdns B2
Green St B1
Greyfriars Rd B2
HM Prison B3
Hafod St C1
Herbert St C3
High St B2
Industrial Estate C3
John St C3
Jubilee St C1
King Edward VII Ave A1
Kingsway (Ffordd y Brenin) B2
Knox Rd B3
Law Courts B2
Llanbleddian Gdns A2
Llantwit St A2
Lloyd George Ave C3
Lower Cathedral Rd B1
Lowther Rd A3
Magistrates Court B3
Mansion House A3
Mardy St C1
Mark St B1
Market B2
Mary Ann St C3
Merches Gdns C1
Mill La C2
Millennium Bridge B1
Millennium Plaza Leisure Complex C1
Millennium Stadium C1
Millennium Stadium Tours (Gate 3) B2
Miskin St A2
Monmouth St C1
Motorpoint Arena Cardiff C3
Museum Ave A2
Museum Place A2
National Museum of Wales A2
National War Meml A2
Neville Place C1
New Theatre B2
Newport Rd B3
Northcote La A3
Northcote St A3
Park Grove A4
Park Place A2
Park St C2
Penarth Rd C2
Pendyris St C1
Plantaganet St C1
Quay St B2
Queen Anne Sq A1
Queen St (Heol y Frenhines) B2
Queen St Station ≥ B3
Regimental Museums B2
Rhymney St A3
Richmond Rd A3
Royal Welsh College of Music and Drama A1
Russell St A3
Ruthin Gdns A2
St Andrews Place A2
St David's B2
St David's 2 C2
St David's Ctr B2
St David's Hall B2
St John The Baptist B2
St Mary St (Heol Eglwys Fair) B2
St Peter's St A3
Salisbury Rd A3
Sandon St B3
Schooner Way C3
Scott Rd C2
Scott St C2
Senghennydd Rd A2
Sherman Theatre A2
Sophia Gardens A1
South Wales Baptist College A3
Stafford Rd C1
Station Terr B3
Stuttgarter Strasse B2
Sussex St C1
Taffs Mead Emb C1
Talworth St A3
Temple of Peace & Health A1
The Cardiff Story B2
The Friary B2
The Hayes B2
The Parade A3
The Walk A3
Treharris St A3
Trinity St B2
Tudor La C1
Tudor St C1
Welsh Assembly Offices A1
Welsh Inst of Sport A1
West Grove A3
Westgate St (Heol y Porth) B2
Windsor Place B3
Womanby St B2
Wood St C2
Working St B2
Wyeverne Rd A2

Carlisle 333

Abbey St A1
Aglionby St B3
Albion St C3
Alexander St C3
AMF Bowl C2
Annetwell St A1
Bank St B2
Bitts Park A1
Blackfriars St B2
Blencome St C1
Blunt St C1
Botchergate B2
Boustead's Grassing C2
Bowman St B3
Broad St B3
Bridge St A1
Brook St C3
Brunswick St B2
Bus Station B2
Caldew Bridge A1
Caldew St C1
Carlisle (Citadel) Station B2
Carlisle College A2
Castle A1
Castle St A1
Castle Way A1
Cathedral A1
Cecil St B2
Chapel St A2
Charles St B3
Charlotte St B1
Chatsworth Square A2
Chiswick St B2
Citadel, The B2
City Walls A1
Civic Ctr A2
Clifton St C1
Close St B3
Collingwood St C1
Colville St C1
Colville Terr C1
Court B2
Court St B2
Crosby St B2
Crown St C2
Currock Rd C2
Dacre Rd A1
Dale St C1
Denton St C1
Devonshire Walk A1
Duke's Rd A2
East Dale St C1
East Norfolk St C1
Eden Bridge A2
Edward St B3
Elm St B1
English St B2
Fire Station A2
Fisher St A1
Flower St B3
Freer St C1
Fusehill St B3
Georgian Way A2
Gloucester Rd C3
Golf Course A2
Graham St C1
Grey St B3
Guildhall Museum A2
Halfey's La B3
Hardwicke Circus A2
Hart St B3
Hewson St C2
Howard Pl A3
Howe St B3
Information Ctr A2
James St B2
Junction St B1
King St B2
Lancaster St B2
Lanes Shopping Ctr B2
Laserquest B2
Library A2/B1
Lime St B1
Lindisfarne St C3
Linton St B3
Lismore Pl A3
Lismore St B3
London Rd C3
Lonsdale Rd B2
Lord St C3
Lorne Cres B1
Lorne St B1
Lowther St B2
Market Hall A2
Mary St B2
Memorial Bridge A3
Metcalfe St C1
Milbourne St B1
Myddleton St B3

348 Chelmsford • Cheltenham • Chester • Chichester • Colchester • Coventry • Derby • Dorchester

Nelson St C1
Norfolk St C1
Old Town Hall A2
Oswald St C3
Peter St A2
Petteril St B3
Police Station ≋ A2
Portland Pl B2
Portland Sq B2
Post Office A2/B2/B3/C1/C3
Princess St C2
Pugin St B1
Red Bank Terr C2
Regent St C3
Richardson St C1
Rickerby Park A3
Rickergate A2
River St B3
Rome St C2
Rydal St B3
St Cuthbert's B2
St Cuthbert's La B2
St James' Park C1
St James' Rd C1
St Nicholas St C3
Sands Ctr A2
Scotch St A2
Shaddongate B1
Sheffield St B1
South Henry St B3
South John St C2
South St B3
Spencer St B2
Sports Ctr A2
Strand Rd A2
Swimming Baths B2
Sybil St B3
Tait St B2
Thomas St B1
Thomson St C3
Trafalgar St C1
Tullie Ho Museum A1
Tyne St C3
University of Cumbria B3
Viaduct Estate Rd B1
Victoria Pl A2
Victoria Viaduct B2
Vue B2
Warwick Rd B2
Warwick Sq B3
Water St B2
West Walls B1
Westmorland St C1

Chelmsford 333

Ambulance Station B1
Anchor St C1
Anglia Ruskin Univ A2
Arbour La A3
Baddow Rd B2/C3
Baker St C1
Barrack Sq B2
Bellmead B2
Bishop Hall La A2
Bishop Rd A2
Bond St B2
Boswells Dr B3
Boudicca Mews C2
Bouverie Rd C2
Bradford St C1
Braemar Ave C1
Brook St A2
Broomfield Rd A1
Burns Cres C2
Bus Station B1
Can Bridge Way B2
Cedar Ave A1
Cedar Ave West A1
Cemetery A1
Cemetery A2
Cemetery C1
Central Park B1
Chelmsford ✝ B2
Chelmsford ≋ A1
Chichester Dr A3
Chinery Cl A3
Cinema B2
Civic Ctr A1
Civic Theatre B1
College C1
Cottage Pl A2
County Cricket Ground B2
County Hall B2
Coval Ave B1
Coval La B1
Coval Wells B1
Crown Court B2
Duke St B2
Elm Rd C1
Elms Dr A1
Essex Record Office, The B3
Fairfield Rd B1
Falcons Mead B1
George St C2
Glebe Rd A1
Godfrey's Mews C2
Goldlay Ave C3
Goldlay Rd C2
Grove Rd C2
HM Prison A3
Hall St C2
Hamlet Rd C2
Hart St C1
Henry Rd A2
High Bridge Rd B2
High Chelmer Sh Ctr B2
High St B2
Hill Cres B3
Hill Rd Sth B3
Hill Rd B3
Hillview Rd A3
Hoffmans Way A2
Hospital H B2
Lady La C2
Langdale Gdns C3
Legg St B2
Library B2
Library C2
Lionfield Terr A3
Lower Anchor St C1
Lynmouth Ave C2
Lynmouth Gdns C3
Magistrates Court B2
Maltese Rd A1
Manor Rd C2
Marconi Rd A2
Market B2
Market Rd B2
Marlborough Rd C1
Meadows Sh Ctr, The B2
Meadowside A3
Mews Ct C2
Mildmay Rd C2
Moulsham Dr C2
Moulsham Mill ✦ C3
Moulsham St C1/C2
Navigation Rd B3
New London Rd B2/C1
New St A2/B2
New Writtle St C1
Nursery Rd C2
Orchard St C2
Park Rd B1
Parker Rd C2
Parklands Dr A3
Parkway A1/B1/B2
Police Station A2
Post Office A3/B2/C2
Primrose Hill A1
Prykes Dr B1
Queen St C1
Queen's Rd B3
Railway St A1
Rainsford Rd A1
Ransomes Way A2
Rectory La A2
Regina Rd A2
Riverside Ice & L Ctr B2
Riverside Retail Park A3
Rosebery Rd C2
Rothesay Ave C1
St John's Rd C2
Sandringham Pl B3
Seymour St B1
Shrublands Cl B3
Southborough Rd C1
Springfield Basin B3
Springfield Rd A3/B2/B3
Stapleford Cl C1
Swiss Ave A1
Telford Pl A3
The Meades B1
Tindal St B2
Townfield St A1
Trinity Rd B3
University B1
Upper Bridge Rd C1
Upper Roman Rd C2
Van Dieman's Rd C3
Viaduct Rd B1
Vicarage Rd C1
Victoria Rd A2
Victoria Rd South B2
Vincents Rd C2
Waterloo La B2
Weight Rd B3
Westfield Ave A1
Wharf Rd B3
Writtle Rd C1
YMCA A2
York Rd C1

Cheltenham 333

Albert Rd A3
Albion St B3
All Saints Rd B3
Ambrose St B2
Andover Rd C1
Art Gallery & Mus B2
Axiom Ctr B3
Back Montpellier Terr C2
Bandstand ✦ C2
Bath Pde B2
Bath Rd C2
Bays Hill Rd C1
Beechwood Pl Sh Ctr B3
Bennington St B2
Berkeley St B3
Brewery A2
Brunswick St South A2
Bus Station B2
CAB B2
Carlton St B3
Central Cross Road A3
Cheltenham College C2
Cheltenham FC A3
Cheltenham General (A&E) H C3
Christchurch Rd B1
Cineworld A2
Clarence Rd A2
Clarence Sq A2
Clarence St B2
Cleeveland St A1
Coach Park A2
College Baths Road C3
College Rd C2
Colletts Dr A1
Corpus St C3
Devonshire St A2
Douro Rd B1
Duke St B3
Dunalley Pde A2
Dunalley St A2
Everyman B2
Evesham Rd A3
Fairview Rd B3
Fairview St B3
Fire Station C3
Folly La A2
Gloucester Rd A1
Grosvenor St B3
Grove St A1
Gustav Holst A3
Hanover St A2
Hatherley St C1
Henrietta St A2
Hewlett Rd B3
High St B2/B3
Hudson St A2
Imperial Gdns C2
Imperial La B2
Imperial Sq C2
Information Ctr B2
Keynsham Rd C3
King St A2
Knapp Rd B2
Ladies College B2
Lansdown Cr C1
Lansdown Rd C1
Leighton Rd B3
London Rd C3
Lypiatt Rd C1
Malvern Rd B1
Manser St A2
Market St A1
Marle Hill Pde A2
Marle Hill Rd A2
Millbrook St A1
Milsom St A2
Montpellier Gdns C2
Montpellier Gr C2
Montpellier Pde C2
Montpellier Spa Rd C2
Montpellier St C1
Montpellier Terr C2
Montpellier Walk C2
New St B2
North Pl B2
Old Bath Rd C3
Oriel Rd B2
Overton Park Rd B1
Overton Rd B1
Oxford St C3
Parabola Rd B1
Park Pl C1
Park St A1
Pittville Circus A3
Pittville Cr A3
Pittville Lawn A3
Playhouse B2
Police Station B1/C1
Portland St B3
Post Office B2/C2
Prestbury Rd A3
Prince's Rd C1
Priory St B3
Promenade B2
Queen St A1
Recreation Ground A2
Regent Arcade B2
Regent St B2
Rodney Rd B2
Royal Cr B2
Royal Wells Rd B2
St George's Pl B2
St Georges Rd B1
St Gregory's B2
St James St B3
St John's Ave B3
St Luke's Rd C2
St Margarets Rd A2
St Mary's B2
St Matthew's B2
St Paul's La A2
St Paul's Rd A2
St Paul's St A2
St Stephen's Rd C1
Sandford Lido C3
Sandford Mill Road C3
Sandford Park C3
Sandford Rd C2
Selkirk St A3
Sherborne Pl B3
Sherborne St B3
Suffolk Pde C2
Suffolk Rd C1
Suffolk Sq C1
Sun St A1
Swindon Rd B2
Sydenham Villas Rd C3
Tewkesbury Rd A1
The Courtyard B1
Thirlstaine Rd C2
Tivoli Rd C1
Tivoli St C1
Town Hall & Theatre B2
Townsend St A1
Trafalgar St C2
Union St B3
Univ of Gloucestershire (Francis Cl Hall) A2
Univ of Gloucestershire (Hardwick) A1
Victoria Pl B3
Victoria St A2
Victoria Walk C2
Wel Pl B2
Wellesley Rd A2
Wellington Rd A3
Wellington Sq A3
Wellington St B2
West Drive A3
Western Rd B1
Winchcombe St B3

Chester 333

Abbey Gateway A2
Appleyards La C3
Bedward Row B1
Beeston View C3
Bishop Lloyd's Pal B2
Black Diamond St A2
Bottoms La C3
Boughton B3
Bouverie St A1
Bridge St B2
Bridgegate C2
British Heritage Ctr B2
Brook St A3
Brown's La C2
Bus Station A2
Cambrian Rd A1
Canal St A2
Carrick Rd C1
Castle C2
Castle Dr C2
Cathedral ✝ B2
Catherine St A1
Chester ≋ A3
Cheyney Rd A1
Chichester St A1
City Rd A3
City Walls B1/B2
City Walls Rd B1
Cornwall St A2
County Hall C2
Cross Hey C3
Cuppin St B2
Curzon Park North C1
Curzon Park South C1
Dee Basin A1
Dee La B3
Delamere St A2
Dewa Roman Experience B2
Duke St B2
Eastgate B2
Eastgate St B2
Eaton Rd C2
Edinburgh Way C3
Elizabeth Cr B3
Fire Station A2
Foregate St B2
Frodsham St B2
Gamul House B2
Garden La A1
Gateway Theatre B2
George St A2
Gladstone Ave A1
God's Providence House B2
Gorse Stacks A2
Greenway St C2
Grosvenor Bridge C1
Grosvenor Museum B2
Grosvenor Park B3
Grosvenor Precinct B2
Grosvenor Rd C1
Grosvenor St B2
Groves Rd B3
Guildhall Museum B1
Handbridge C2
Hartington St C3
Hoole Way A2
Hunter St B2
Information Ctr B2
King Charles' Tower ✦ A2
King St A2
Leisure Ctr B2
Library B2
Lightfoot St A3
Little Roodee C2
Liverpool Rd A2
Love St B3
Lower Bridge St B2
Lower Park Rd B3
Lyon St A2
Magistrates Court B2
Meadows La C3
Military Museum C2
Milton St A3
New Crane St B1
Nicholas St B2
Northgate A2
Northgate St A2
Nun's Rd B1
Old Dee Bridge ✦ C2
Overleigh Rd C2
Park St B2
Police Station B2
Post Office A2/A3/B2/C2
Princess St B2
Queen St B2
Queen's Park Rd C3
Queen's Rd A3
Race Course B1
Raymond St A1
River La C2
Roman Amphitheatre & Gardens B2
Roodee, The (Chester Racecourse) B1
Russell St A3
St Anne St A2
St George's Cr C3
St Martin's Gate A1
St Martin's Way B1
St Oswalds Way A2
Saughall Rd A1
Sealand Rd A1
South View Rd A1
Stanley Palace B1
Station Rd A3
Steven St A3
The Bars B3
The Cross B2
The Groves B3
The Meadows B3
Tower Rd B1
Town Hall B2
Union St B3
Vicar's La B2
Victoria Cr C3
Victoria Rd A2
Walpole St A1
Water Tower St A1
Watergate B1
Watergate St B2
Whipcord La A1
White Friars B2
York St B3

Chichester 333

Adelaide Rd A3
Alexandra Rd A3
Arts Ctr B2
Ave de Chartres B1/B2
Barlow Rd A1
Basin Rd C2
Beech Ave B1
Bishops Pal Gardens B2
Bishopsgate Walk A3
Bramber Rd C3
Broyle Rd A2
Bus Station B2
Caledonian Rd B3
Cambrai Ave B3
Canal Wharf C2
Canon La B2
Cathedral ✝ B2
Cavendish St A1
Cawley Rd B2
Cedar Dr A1
Chapel St A2
Cherry Orchard Rd C3
Chichester By-Pass C2/C3
Chichester Cinema B3
Chichester Festival Theatre A2
Chichester ≋ B2
Churchside A2
Cineworld C1
City Walls B2
Cleveland Rd B3
College La A2
College of Science & Technology B1
Cory Close C2
Council Offices B2
County Hall B2
Courts B2
District B2
Duncan Rd A1
Durnford Cl A1
East Pallant B2
East Row B2
East St B2
East Walls B3
Eastland Rd C3
Ettrick Cl B3
Ettrick Rd B3
Exton Rd C3
Fire Station A2
Football Ground A2
Franklin Pl A2
Friary (Remains of) A2
Garland Cl C3
Green La A3
Grove Rd C3
Guilden Rd B3
Guildhall A2
Hawthorn Cl A1
Hay Rd C3
Henty Gdns B1
Herald Dr C3
Information Ctr B2
John's St B2
Joys Croft A3
Jubilee Pk A3
Jubilee Rd A3
Juxon Cl B1
Kent Rd A3
King George Gdns A2
King's Ave C2
Kingsham Ave C3
Kingsham Rd C2
Laburnum Gr B2
Leigh Rd C1
Lennox Rd A3
Lewis Rd A3
Library B2
Lion St B2
Litten Terr A3
Little London B2
Lyndhurst Rd B3
Market B3
Market Ave B2
Market Cross B2
Market Rd B3
Martlet Cl C2
Melbourne Rd A3
Mount La B1
New Park Rd A3
Newlands La A1
North Pallant B2
North St A2
North Walls A2
Northgate A2
Oak Ave A1
Oak Cl A1
Oaklands Park A2
Oaklands Way A2
Orchard Ave A1
Orchard St A1
Ormonde Ave B3
Pallant House B2
Parchment St A1
Parklands Rd A1/B1
Peter Weston Pl B3
Police Station C2
Post Office A1/B2/B3
Priory La A2
Priory Park A2
Priory Rd A2
Queen's Ave C1
Riverside A3
Roman Amphitheatre B3
St Cyriacs A2
St Pancras A3
St Paul's Rd A2
St Richard's Hospital (A+E) H A3
Shamrock Cl A3
Sherbourne Rd A1
Somerstown A2
South Bank C2
South Downs Planetarium ✦ C2
South Pallant B2
South St B2
Southgate B2
Spitalfield La A3
Stirling Rd B3
Stockbridge Rd C1/C2
Swanfield Dr A3
Terminus Ind Est C1
Terminus Rd C1
The Hornet B3
The Litten A3
Tower St A2
Tozer Way A3
Turnbull Rd A3
Upton Rd C1
Velyn Ave B3
Via Ravenna B1
Walnut Ave A1
West St B2
Westgate B1
Westgate Fields B1
Westgate Leisure Ctr B1
Weston Ave C1
Whyke Cl C3
Whyke La B3
Whyke Rd C3
Winden Ave B3

Colchester 333

Abbey Gateway ✝ C2
Albert St A1
Albion Grove C2
Alexandra Rd C1
Artillery St C3
Arts Ctr B1
Balkerne Hill B1
Barrack St C3
Beaconsfield Rd C1
Beche Rd C3
Bergholt Rd A1
Bourne Rd C3
Brick Kiln Rd A1
Bristol Rd B2
Broadlands Way A3
Brook St B3
Bury Cl B2
Bus Sta B2
Butt Rd C1
Camp Folley North C2
Camp Folley South C2
Campion Rd C2
Cannon St C3
Canterbury Rd C2
Castle B2
Castle Park B2
Castle Rd B2
Catchpool Rd A1
Causton Rd B1
Cavalry Barracks C1
Chandlers Row C3
Circular Rd East C2
Circular Rd North C1
Circular Rd West C1
Clarendon Way A1
Claudius Rd C2
Colchester Camp Abbey Field C1
Colchester Institute B1
Colchester ≋ A1
Colchester Town ≋ C2
Colne Bank Ave A1
Colne View Retail Park A2
Compton Rd A3
Cowdray Ave A1/A2
Cowdray Ctr, The A2
Crouch St B1
Crowhurst Rd B1
Culver Square Sh Ctr B1
Culver St East B2
Culver St West B1
Dilbridge Rd A3
East Hill B2
East St B3
East Stockwell St B1
Eld La B1
Essex Hall Rd A1
Exeter Dr B2
Fairfax Rd C2
Fire Station A2
Flagstaff Rd C1
George St B2
Gladstone Rd C2
Golden Noble Hill C2
Goring Rd A3
Granville Rd C3
Greenstead Rd B3
Guildford Rd B2
Harsnett Rd C3
Harwich Rd B3
Head St B1
High St B1/B2
High Woods Ctry Park A2
Hollytrees B2
Hythe Hill C3
Information Ctr B2
Ipswich Rd A3
Jarmin Rd A2
Kendall Rd C2
Kimberley Rd C3
King Stephen Rd C3
Le Cateau Barracks C1
Leisure World A2
Library B1
Lincoln Way B2
Lion Walk Sh Ctr B1
Lisle Rd C2
Lucas Rd C2
Magdalen Green C3
Magdalen St C2
Maidenburgh St B2
Maldon Rd C1
Manor Rd B1
Margaret Rd A1
Mason Rd A2
Mercers Way A1
Mercury B1
Mersea Rd C2
Meyrick Cr C2
Mile End Rd A1
Military Rd C2
Mill St C2
Minories B2
Moorside B3
Morant Rd C3
Napier Rd C2
Natural History B2
New Town Rd C2
Norfolk Cr A3
North Hill B1
North Station Rd A1
Northgate St B1
Nunns Rd B1
Odeon B1
Old Coach Rd B3
Old Heath Rd C3
Osborne St B2
Petrolea Cl A1
Police Station C1
Popes La B1
Port La C3
Post Office B1/B2/C2
Priory St B2
Queen St B2
Rawstorn Rd B1
Rebon St C3
Recreation Rd C3
Ripple Way A3
Roman Rd B2
Roman Wall B2
Romford Cl A3
Rosebery Ave B2
St Andrews Ave B3
St Andrews Gdns B3
St Botolph St B2
St Botolphs C2
St John's Abbey (site of) ✝ C2
St John's St B1
St Johns Walk Sh Ctr B1
St Leonards Rd C3
St Marys Fields B1
St Peters B1
St Peter's St B1
Salisbury Ave C1
Serpentine Walk A1
Sheepen Pl B1
Sheepen Rd B1
Sir Isaac's Walk B1
Smythies Ave B2
South St C1
South Way C1
Sports Way A2
Suffolk Cl A3
Town Hall B1
Valentine Dr A3
Victor Rd C3
Wakefield Cl B2
Wellesley Rd C1
Wells Rd B2/B3
West St C1
West Stockwell St B1
Weston Rd C3
Westway A1
Wickham Rd C1
Wimpole Rd C3
Winchester Rd C2
Winnock Rd C2
Wolfe Ave C2
Worcester Rd B2

Coventry 334

Abbots La A1
Albany Rd B1
Alma St B3
Art Faculty B3
Asthill Grove C2
Bablake School A1
Barras La A1/B1
Barrs Hill School A1
Belgrade B2
Bishop Burges St A2
Bond's Hospital B1
Broad Gate B2
Broadway C1
Bus Station A3
Butts Radial B1
Canal Basin ✦ A2
Canterbury St A3
Cathedral ✝ B3
Chester St A1
Cheylesmore Manor House B2
Christ Church Spire ✦ B2
City Walls & Gates ✦ A2
Corporation St B2
Council House B2
Coundon Rd A1
Coventry Station ≋ C2
Coventry Transport Museum A2
Cox St A3
Croft Rd B1
Dalton Rd C1
Deasy Rd C3
Earl St B2
Eaton Rd C2
Fairfax St B2
Foleshill Rd A2
Ford's Hospital B2
Fowler Rd A1
Friars Rd C2
Gordon St C1
Gosford St B3
Greyfriars Green ✦ B2
Greyfriars Rd B2
Gulson Rd B3
Hales St A2
Harnall Lane East A3
Harnall Lane West A2
Herbert Art Gallery & Museum B3
Hertford St B2
Hewitt Ave A1
High St B2
Hill St B1
Holy Trinity B2
Holyhead Rd A1
Howard St A3
Huntingdon Rd C1
Information Ctr B2
Jordan Well B3
King Henry VIII School C1
Lady Godiva Statue ✦ B2
Lamb St A2
Leicester Row A2
Library B2
Little Park St B2
London Rd C3
Lower Ford St B3
Magistrates & Crown Courts B2
Manor House Drive B2
Manor Rd C2
Market B2
Martyr's Memorial ✦ C2
Meadow St B1
Meriden St A1
Michaelmas Rd C2
Middleborough Rd A1
Mile La C3
Millennium Place ✦ A2
Much Park St B3
Naul's Mill Park A1
New Union B2
Park Rd C2
Parkside C3
Post Office B2
Primrose Hill St A3
Priory Gardens & Visitor Ctr B2
Priory St B3
Puma Way C3
Quarryfield La C3
Queen's Rd B1
Quinton Rd C2
Radford Rd A2
Raglan St B3
Retail Park C1
Ringway (Hill Cross) A1
Ringway (Queens) B1
Ringway (Rudge) B1
Ringway (St Johns) B3
Ringway (St Nicholas) A2
Ringway (St Patricks) C2
Ringway (Swanswell) A2
Ringway (Whitefriars) B3
St John St B2
St John The Baptist B2
St Nicholas St A2
Skydome B1
Spencer Ave C1
Spencer Park C1
Spon St B1
Sports Ctr B3
Stoney Rd C2
Stoney Stanton Rd A3
Swanswell Pool A3
Sydney Stringer Acad A3
Technical College B1
Technology Park C3
The Precinct B2
Theatre B1
Thomas Landsdail St C2
Tomson Ave A1
Top Green C1
Trinity St B2
University B3
University Sports Ctr B3
Upper Hill St A1
Upper Well St A2
Victoria St A3
Vine St A3
Warwick Rd C2
Waveley Rd B1
Westminster Rd C1
White St A3
Windsor St B1

Derby 334

Abbey St C1
Agard St B1
Albert St B2
Albion St B2
Ambulance Station B1
Arthur St A1
Ashlyn Rd B3
Assembly Rooms B2
Babington La C2
Becket St B1
Belper Rd A1
Bold La B1
Bradshaw Way C2
Bradshaw Way Ret Pk C2
Bridge St B1
Brook St B1
Burrows Walk C2
Burton Rd C1
Bus Station B2
Caesar St A2
Canal St C3
Carrington St C3
Cathedral ✝ B2
Cathedral Rd B1
Charnwood St C2
Chester Green Rd A2
City Rd A2
Clarke St A3
Cock Pitt B3
Council House B2
Courts B1
Cranmer Rd B3
Crompton St C1
Crown & County Courts B2
Crown Walk C2
Curzon St B1
Darley Grove A1
Derby ≋ C3
Derbyshire County Cricket Ground B3
Derwent Business Ctr A2
Derwent St B2
Devonshire Walk C2
Drewry La C1
Duffield Rd A1
Duke St A2
Dunton Cl B3
Eagle Market C2
Eastgate B3
East St B2
Exeter St B2
Farm St C1
Ford St B1
Forester St C1
Fox St A2
Friar Gate B1
Friary St B1
Full St B2
Gerard St C1
Gower St C2
Green La C2
Grey St C1
Guildhall B2
Harcourt St C1
Highfield Rd A1
Hill La C2
Information Ctr B2
Iron Gate B2
John St C3
Joseph Wright Ctr B1
Kedleston Rd A1
Key St B2
King Alfred St C1
King St A1
Kingston St A1
Lara Croft Way C2
Leopold St C2
Library B1
Liversage St C3
Lodge La B1
London Rd C2
London Rd Community Hospital H C2
Macklin St C1
Mansfield Rd A2
Market B2
Market Pl B2
May St C1
Meadow La B3
Melbourne St C2
Mercian Way C1
Midland Rd C3
Monk St C1
Morledge B2
Mount St C1
Mus & Art Gallery B1
Noble St C3
North Parade A1
North St A1
Nottingham Rd B3
Osmaston Rd C2
Otter St A1
Park St C3
Parker St A1
Pickfords House B1
Playhouse C2
Police HQ A2
Police Station B2
Post Office A1/A2/B1/B2/C2/C3
Prime Enterprise Park A2
Pride Parkway C3
Prime Parkway A2
Queens Leisure Ctr B1
Racecourse A3
Railway Terr C3
Register Office B2
Sacheverel St C2
Sadler Gate B1
St Alkmund's Way B1/B2
St Helens House ✦ A1
St Mary's A1
St Mary's Bridge A2
St Mary's Bridge Chapel A2
St Mary's Gate B1
St Paul's Rd A2
St Peter's C2
St Peter's St C2
Siddals Rd C3
Silk Mill B2
Sir Frank Whittle Rd A3
Spa La C1
Spring St C1
Stafford St B1
Station Approach C3
Stockbrook St C1
Stores Rd A3
Traffic St C2
Wardwick B1
Werburgh St C1
West Ave A1
Westfield Ctr C2
West Meadows Ind Est B3
Wharf Rd A2
Wilmot St C2
Wilson St C1
Wood's La C1

Dorchester 334

Ackerman Rd B3
Acland Rd A2
Albert Rd A1
Alexandra Rd B1
Alfred Place B3
Alfred Rd B2
Alington Ave C3
Alington Rd B3
Ambulance Station B3
Ashley Rd B1
Balmoral Cres C3
Barnes Way B2/C2
Borough Gdns A1
Bridport Rd A1
Buckingham Way C3
Caters Place A1
Cemetery A3/C1
Charles St A2
Coburg Rd B1
Colliton St A1
Cornwall Rd A1
Cromwell Rd B1
Culliford Rd B2
Culliford Rd North B2
Dagmar Rd B1
Damer's Rd B1
Diggory Cres C2
Dinosaur Museum A2
Dorchester Bypass C2
Dorchester South Station ≋ B1
Dorchester West Station ≋ B1
Dorset County Council Offices A1
Dorset County (A+E) H B1

Dumfries • Dundee • Durham • Edinburgh • Exeter • Fort William 349

Dorset County Mus A1
Duchy Close C3
Duke's Ave B2
Durngate St A2
Durnover Court A3
Eddison Ave B3
Edward Rd B1
Egdon Rd C2
Elizabeth Frink Statue B2
Farfrae Cres B2
Forum Ctr, The B1
Friary Hill A2
Friary Lane A2
Frome Terr A2
Garland Cres C3
Glyde Path Rd A1
Government Offices B3
Gt Western Rd B1
Grosvenor Cres C1
Grosvenor Rd C1
HM Prison A1
Herringston Rd C1
High St East A2
High St Fordington A2
High Street West A1
Holloway Rd A2
Icen Way A2
Keep Military Museum, The A1
Kings Rd A3/B3
Kingsbere Cres C2
Lancaster Rd B2
Library A1
Lime Cl C1
Linden Ave B2
London Cl A3
London Rd A2/A3
Lubbecke Way A3
Lucetta La B2
Maiden Castle Rd C1
Manor Rd C2
Maumbury Rd B1
Maumbury Rings B1
Mellstock Ave C2
Mill St A3
Miller's Cl A1
Mistover Cl C1
Monmouth Rd B1/B2
Nature Reserve A2
North Sq A2
Northernhay A1
Old Crown Court & Cells A1
Olga Rd B1
Orchard St A2
Police Station B1
Post Office A1/B1
Pound Lane A2
Poundbury Rd A1
Prince of Wales Rd B2
Prince's St A1
Queen's Ave B1
Roman Town House A1
Roman Wall A1
Rothesay Rd C2
St George's Rd B3
Salisbury Field A2
Sandringham Sports Ctr B3
Shaston Cres C2
Smokey Hole La B3
South Court Ave C1
South St B1
South Walks Rd B2
Superstore C3
Teddy Bear House A1
Temple Cl C1
Terracotta Warriors & Teddy Bear Mus A2
The Grove A1
Town Hall A2
Town Pump A2
Trinity St A1
Tutankhamun Ex A1
Victoria Rd B1
Weatherbury Way C2
Wellbridge Cl C1
West Mills Rd A1
West Walks Rd A1
Weymouth Ave C1
Williams Ave B1
Winterbourne (BMI) C1
Wollaston Rd A2
York Rd B2

Dumfries 334

Academy St A2
Aldermanhill Rd B3
Ambulance Station C3
Annan Rd A3
Ardwall Rd A3
Ashfield Dr A1
Atkinson Rd C1
Averill Cres C1
Balliol Ave C1
Bank St B2
Bankend Rd C3
Barn Slaps B3
Barrie Ave B3
Beech Ave A1
Bowling Green A3
Brewery St B1
Brodie Ave C2
Brooke St B2
Broomlands Dr C1
Brooms Rd B3
Buccleuch St A2
Burns House B2
Burns Mausoleum B3
Burns St B2
Burns Statue A2
Bus Station B1
Cardoness St A3
Castle St A2
Catherine St A2
Cattle Market A3
Cemetery B3
Cemetery C2
Church Cres A2
Church St B2
College Rd A1
College St A1
Corbelly Hill B1
Convent, The B1
Corberry Park B1
Cornwall Mt A3
County Offices A2
Court A2
Craigs Rd C3
Cresswell Ave B3
Cresswell Hill B3
Cumberland St B3
David Keswick Athletic Ctr A3
David St B1
Dock Park C3
Dockhead B2
Dumfries A3
Dumfries Academy A2
Dumfries Museum & Camera Obscura B2
Dumfries Royal Infirmary (A&E) C3
East Riverside Dr C3
Edinburgh Rd A2
English St B2
Fire Station B3
Friar's Vennel A2
Galloway St B1
George Douglas Dr C1
George St A2
Gladstone Rd C2
Glasgow St A1
Glebe St B3
Glencaple Rd C3
Goldie Ave A1
Goldie Cres A1
Golf Course C3
Greyfriars A2
Grierson Ave B3
HM Prison B1
Hamilton Ave C1
Hamilton Starke Park C2
Hazelrigg Ave C1
Henry St B3
Hermitage Dr C1
High Cemetery C3
High St A2
Hill Ave C2
Hill St B1
Holm Ave C2
Hoods Loaning A3
Howgate St B1
Huntingdon Rd A3
Information Ctr B2
Irish St B2
Irving St A2
King St A1
Kingholm Rd C3
Kirkpatrick Ct C2
Laurieknowe B1
Leafield Rd B3
Library A2
Lochfield Rd A1
Loreburn Pk A3
Loreburn St A2
Loreburne Sh Ctr B2
Lover's Walk A2
Martin Ave B3
Maryholm Dr A1
Mausoleum B3
Maxwell St B1
McKie Ave B3
Mews La A2
Mid Steeple B2
Mill Green B2
Mill Rd B1
Moat Rd C2
Moffat Rd A3
Mountainhall Pk C3
Nelson St B1
New Abbey Rd B1/C1
New Bridge B1
Newall Terr A2
Nith Ave A2
Nith Bank C3
Nithbank Hospital C3
Nithside Ave A1
Odeon B2
Old Bridge B1
Old Bridge House B1
Palmerston Park (Queen of the South FC) A1
Park Rd C1
Pleasance Ave C1
Police HQ A3
Police Station A2
Portland Dr A1
Post Office A2/B1/B2/B3/B3
Priestlands Dr C1
Primrose St B1
Queen St B3
Queensberry St A2
Rae St A2
Richmond Ave C2
Robert Burns Ctr B2
Roberts Cres C1
Robertson Ave C3
Robinson Dr C1
Rosefield Rd C2
Rosemount St B1
Rotchell Park C1
Rotchell Rd B1
Rugby Football Gd C1
Ryedale Rd C2
St Andrews B2
St John the Evangelist A2
St Josephs College B3
St Mary's Ind Est A3
St Mary's St A3
St Michael St B2
St Michael's B2
St Michael's Bridge B2
St Michael's Bridge Rd B2
St Michael's Cemetery B3
Shakespeare St B2
Solway Dr C2
Stakeford St A1
Stark Cres C2
Station Rd A3
Steel Ave A1
Sunderries Ave A1
Sunderries Rd A1
Suspension Brae B2
Swimming Pool A1
Terregles St B1
Theatre Royal B2
Troqueer Rd C2
Union St A1
Wallace St B3
Welldale B2
West Riverside Dr C2
White Sands B2

Dundee 334

Adelaide Pl A1
Airlie Pl C1
Albany Terr A1
Albert St A3
Alexander St A2
Ann St A2
Arthurstone Terr A3
Bank St B2
Barrack Rd A1
Barrack St B2
Bell St B2
Blackscroft A3
Blinshall St B1
Brown St B1
Bus Station B3
Caird Hall B2
Camperdown St B3
Candle La B3
Carmichael St A1
City Churches B2
City Quay B3
City Sq B2
Commercial St B2
Constable St A3
Constitution Ct A1
Constitution Cres A1
Constitution St A1/B2
Cotton Rd A3
Courthouse Sq B1
Cowgate A3
Crescent St A3
Crichton St B2
Dens Brae A3
Dens Rd A3
Discovery Point C2
Douglas St B1
Drummond St A1
Dudhope Castle A1
Dudhope St A2
Dudhope Terr A1
Dundee C2
Dundee College A1
Dundee Contemporary Arts C2
Dundee High School B2
Dundee Repertory C2
Dura St A3
East Dock St B3
East Whale La B3
East Marketgait B3
Erskine St A3
Euclid Cr B2
Forebank Rd A2
Foundry La A3
Frigate Unicorn B3
Gallagher Retail Park B3
Gellatly St B3
Government Offices C2
Guthrie St B1
Hawkhill B1
Hilltown A2
Howff Cemetery, The B2
Information Ctr B2
King St A3
Kinghorne Rd A1
Ladywell Ave A3
Laurel Bank A2
Law Hill, The A1
Law Rd A1
Law St A1
Library A2
Little Theatre A2
Lochee Rd B1
Lower Princes St A3
Lyon St A3
McManus Museum & Art Gallery B2
Meadow Side B2
Meadowside St Pauls B2
Mercat Cross B2
Murraygate B2
Nelson St A2
Nethergate B2/C1
North Marketgait B2
North Lindsay St B2
Old Hawkhill B1
Olympia Leisure Ctr B3
Overgate Shopping Ctr B2
Park Pl B1
Perth Rd C1
Police Station A2/B1
Post Office B2
Princes St A3
Prospect Pl A2
Reform St B2
Riverside Dr C2
Roseangle C1
Rosebank St A2
RRS Discovery C2
St Andrew's C2
St Pauls Episcopal B3
Science Ctr C2
Seagate B2
Sheriffs Court B1
South George St A2
South Marketgait B3
South Tay St B2
South Ward Rd B2
Steps A2
Tay Road Bridge C3
Tayside House B2
Trades La B3
Union St B2
Union Terr A1
University Library B2
University of Abertay B2
University of Dundee B1
Upper Constitution St A1
Verdant Works B1
Victoria Dock B3
Victoria Rd A2
Victoria St A3
West Marketgait B1/B2
Ward Rd B1
Wellgate B2
West Bell St B1
Westfield Pl C1
William St A3
Wishart Arch A3

Durham 334

Alexander Cr B2
Allergate B2
Archery Rise C1
Assize Courts B3
Back Western Hill A1
Bakehouse La A3
Baths B3
Baths Bridge B3
Boat House B3
Bowling A2
Boyd St C3
Bus Station B2
Castle B2
Castle Chare B2
Cathedral B2
Church St C3
Clay La C1
Claypath B3
College of St Hild & St Bede B3
County Hall A1
County Hospital B1
Crook Hall & Gardens A3
Crossgate B2
Crossgate Peth C1
Darlington Rd C1
Durham A2
Durham Light Infantry Mus & Arts Ctr A2
Durham School C2
Ellam Ave C1
Elvet Bridge B3
Elvet Court B3
Farnley Hey B1
Ferens Cl A3
Fieldhouse La A1
Flass St B1
Framwelgate A2
Framwelgate Bridge B2
Framwelgate Peth A2
Framwelgate Waterside A2
Frankland La A3
Freeman's Pl A3
Gala & Sacred Journey B3
Gate Sh Ctr, The B2
Geoffrey Ave C1
Gilesgate B3
Grey College C3
Hallgarth St C3
Hatfield College B3
Hawthorn Terr B1
Heritage Ctr B3
HM Prison B3
Information Ctr B3
John St B1
Kingsgate Bridge B3
Laburnum Terr B1
Lawson Terr B1
Leazes Rd B2/B3
Library B2
Margery La B2
Mavin St C3
Millburngate B2
Millburngate Bridge B2
Millennium Bridge (foot/cycle) A2
Mountjoy Research Ctr C3
Mus of Archaeology B2
Nevilledale Terr B1
New Elvet B3
New Elvet Bridge B3
North Bailey B3
North End A1
North Rd A1/B2
Observatory C1
Old Elvet B3
Oriental Museum C2
Oswald Court C3
Parkside B2
Passport Office A2
Percy Terr B1
Pimlico C2
Police Station B3
Post Office A1/B2
Potters Bank C1/C2
Prebends Bridge C2
Prebends Walk C2
Prince Bishops Sh Ctr B3
Princes St A1
Providence Row A3
Quarryheads La C2
Redhills La B1
Redhills Terr B1
Saddler St B3
St Chad's College C3
St Cuthbert's Society C2
St John's College C2
St Margaret's B2
St Mary The Less C2
St Mary's College C2
St Monica Grove B1
St Nicholas' B3
St Oswald's C3
Sidegate A2
Silver St B2
Add Sixth Form Ctr (Durham Gilesgate) A3
South Bailey C2
South Rd C3
South St B2
Springwell Ave A1
Stockton Rd C3
Students' Rec Ctr B3
Sutton St B2
The Avenue B1
The Crescent A1
The Grove A1
The Sands A3
Town Hall B2
Treasury Museum B2
University B2
University Arts Block B3
University Library C3
Univ Science Site C3
Walkergate Ctr A3
Wearside Dr A3
Western Hill A1
Wharton Park A2
Whinney Hill C3

Edinburgh 334

Abbey Strand B6
Abbeyhill B6
Abbeyhill Cr B6
Abbeymount A6
Abercromby Pl A3
Adam St C5
Albany La A4
Albany St A4
Albert Memorial B2
Albyn Pl A2
Alva Pl A6
Alva St B1
Ann St A1
Appleton Tower C4
Archibald Pl C3
Argyle House C3
Assembly Rooms & Musical Hall A3
Atholl Cr B1
Atholl Crescent La C1
Bank St B4
Barony St A4
Beaumont Pl C5
Belford Rd B1
Belgrave Cr A1
Belgrave Crescent La A1
Bell's Brae B1
Blackfriars St B4
Blair St B4
Bread St C2
Bristo Pl C4
Bristo St C4
Brougham St C2
Broughton St A4
Brown St C5
Brunton Terr A6
Buckingham Terr A1
Burial Ground A6
Bus Station A4
Caledonian Cr C1
Caledonian Rd C1
Calton Hill A4
Calton Hill A5
Calton Rd B4
Camera Obscura & Outlook Tower B3
Candlemaker Row C4
Canning St B2
Canongate B5
Canongate B5
Carlton St A1
Carlton Terr A6
Carlton Terrace La A6
Castle St B2
Castle Terr B2
Castlehill B3
Central Library B4
Chalmers Hospital C3
Chalmers St C3
Chambers St C4
Chapel St C4
Charles St C4
Charlotte Sq B2
Chester St B1
Circus La A2
Circus Pl A2
City Art Ctr B4
City Chambers B4
City Observatory A5
Clarendon Cr A1
Clerk St C5
Coates Cr B1
Cockburn St B4
College of Art C3
Comely Bank Ave A1
Comely Bank Row A1
Cornwall St C2
Cowans Cl C5
Cowgate B4
Cranston St B5
Crichton St C4
Croft-An-Righ A6
Cumberland St A2
Dalry Pl C1
Dalry Rd C1
Danube St A1
Darnawy St A2
David Hume Tower C4
Davie St C5
Dean Bridge A1
Dean Gdns A1
Dean Park Cr A1
Dean Park Mews A1
Dean Park St A1
Dean Path B1
Dean St A1
Dean Terr A1
Dewar Pl C1
Dewar Place La C1
Doune Terr A2
Drummond Pl A3
Drummond St C5
Drumsheugh Gdns B1
Dublin Mews A3
Dublin St A4
Dublin Street La South A4
Dumbiedykes Rd B5
Dundas St A3
Earl Grey St C2
East Crosscauseway C5
East Market St B4
East Norton Pl A6
East Princes St Gdns B3
Easter Rd A6
Edinburgh (Waverley) B4
Edinburgh Castle B3
Edinburgh Dungeon B4
Edinburgh International Conference Ctr C2
Elder St A4
Esplanade B3
Eton Terr A1
Eye Pavilion C3
Festival Office B3
Festival Theatre Edinburgh C4
Filmhouse C2
Fire Station C2
Floral Clock B3
Forres St A2
Forth St A4
Fountainbridge C2
Frederick St A3
Freemasons' Hall B3
Fruit Market B4
Gardner's Cr C2
George Heriot's School C3
George IV Bridge B4
George Sq C4
George Sq La C4
George St B3
Georgian House B2
Gladstone's Land B3
Glen St C3
Gloucester La A2
Gloucester Pl A2
Gloucester St A2
Graham St C3
Grassmarket C3
Great King St A3
Great Stuart B1
Greenside La A5
Greenside Row A5
Greyfriars Kirk C4
Grindlay St C2
Grosvenor St C1
Grove St C1
Gullan's Cl B5
Guthrie St B4
Hanover St A3
Hart St A4
Haymarket C1
Haymarket Station C1
Heriot Pl C3
Heriot Row A2
High School Yard B5
High St B4
Hill Pl C5
Hill St A2
Hillside Cr A5
Holyrood Park C6
Holyrood Rd B5
Home St C2
Hope St B2
Horse Wynd B6
Howden St C5
Howe St A2
India Pl A2
India St A2
Infirmary St B4
Information Ctr B4
Jamaica Mews A2
Jeffrey St B4
John Knox House B4
Johnston Terr C3
Keir St C3
Kerr St A2
King's Stables Rd B2
Lady Lawson St C3
Lauriston Gdns C3
Lauriston Park C3
Lauriston Pl C3
Lauriston St C3
Lawnmarket B3
Learmonth Gdns A1
Learmonth Terr A1
Leith St A4
Lennox St A1
Lennox St La A1
Leslie Pl A2
London Rd A5
Lothian Health Board C5
Lothian Rd B2
Lothian St C4
Lower Menz Pl A6
Lynedoch Pl B1
Manor Pl B1
Market St B4
Marshall St C4
Maryfield A6
Maryfield Pl A6
McEwan Hall C4
Medical School C4
Melville St B1
Meuse La B4
Middle Meadow Walk C4
Milton St A6
Montrose Terr A6
Moray House (college) B5
Moray Place A2
Morrison Link C1
Morrison St C1
Mound Pl B3
Multrees Walk A4
Mus Collections Ctr A4
Mus of Childhood B5
Mus of Edinburgh B5
Mus on the Mound B4
National Gallery B3
National Library of Scotland B4
National Monument A5
National Museum of Scotland C4
National Portrait Gallery B4
National Records Scotland A4
Nelson Monument A5
Nelson St A3
New St B5
Nicolson Sq C4
Nicolson St C4
Niddry St B4
North Bridge B4
North Meadow Walk C3
North Bank St B3
North Castle St A2
North Charlotte St A2
North St Andrew St A4
North St David St A3
North West Circus Pl A2
Northumberland St A3
Odeon C2
Old Royal High School A5
Old Tolbooth Wynd B5
Omni Ctr A4
Our Dynamic Earth B6
Oxford Terr A1
Pal of Holyrood Ho B6
Palmerston Pl B1
Panmure Pl C3
Parliament House B4
Parliament Sq B4
People's Story, The B5
Playhouse Theatre A4
Pleasance C5
Police Station A4
Ponton St C2
Post Office A3/A4/B5/C1/C2/C4/C5
Potterrow C4
Princes Mall B4
Princes St B3
Queen St A2
Queen Street Gdns A3
Queen's Dr B6/C6
Queensferry Rd A1
Queensferry St B1
Queensferry Street La B2
Radical Rd C6
Randolph Cr B1
Regent Gdns A5
Regent Rd B5
Regent Rd Park A6
Regent Terr A5
Remains of Holyrood Abbey (AD 1128) A6
Richmond La C5
Richmond Pl C5
Rose St B2
Rosemount Bldgs C1
Ross Open Air Theatre B3
Rothesay Pl B1
Rothesay Terr B1
Roxburgh Pl C5
Roxburgh St C5
Royal Bank of Scotland A4
Royal Circus A2
Royal Lyceum C2
Royal Scottish Acad B3
Royal Terr A5
Royal Terrace Gdns A5
Rutland Sq B2
Rutland St B2
St Andrew Sq A4
St Andrew's House A4
St Bernard's Cr A1
St Cecilia's Hall B4
St Colme St A2
St Cuthbert's B2
St Giles' B4
St James Ctr A4
St John St B5
St John's B2
St John's Hill B5
St Leonard's Hill C5
St Leonard's La C5
St Leonard's St C5
St Mary's (RC) A4
St Mary's Scottish Episcopal B1
St Mary's St B5
St Stephen St A2
Salisbury Crags C6
Saunders St A2
Scotch Whisky Experience B3
Scott Monument B4
Scottish Parliament B6
Scottish Storytelling Ctr B5
Semple St C2
Shandwick Pl B2
South Bridge B4
South Charlotte St B2
South College St C4
South Learmonth Gdns A1
South St Andrew St A4
South St David St A3
Spittal St C2
Stafford St B1
Student Ctr C4
Surgeons' Hall C5
TA Ctr C4
Tattoo Office B4
Teviot Pl C4
The Mall B6
The Mound B3
The Royal Mile B5
The Writer's Mus B4
Thistle St A3
Torphichen Pl C1
Torphichen St C1
Traverse Theatre B2
Tron Sq B4
Tron, The B4
Union St A4
University C4
University Library C4
Upper Grove Pl C1
Usher Hall C2
Vennel C3
Victoria St B3
Viewcraig Gdns B5
Viewcraig St B5
VUE A4
Walker St B1
Waterloo Pl A4
Waverley Bridge B4
Wemyss Pl A2
West Approach Rd C1
West Crosscauseway C5
West Maitland St C1
West of Nicholson St C4
West Port C3
West Princes St Gdns B3
West Richmond St C5
West Tollcross C2
White Horse Cl B5
William St B1
Windsor St A5
York La A4
York Pl A4
Young St B2

Exeter 334

Alphington St C1
Athelstan Rd B3
Bampfylde St B2
Barnardo Rd C3
Barnfield Hill B3
Barnfield Rd B2/B3
Barnfield Theatre B2
Bartholomew St East B1
Bartholomew St West B1
Bear St B2
Beaufort Rd C1
Bedford St B2
Belgrave Rd A3
Belmont Rd A3
Blackall Rd A2
Blackboy Rd A3
Bonhay Rd B1
Bull Meadow Rd C2
Bus & Coach Sta B3
Castle St B2
Cecil Rd C1
Cheeke St A3
Church Rd C1
Chute St A3
City Industrial Estate C2
City Wall B1/B2
Civic Ctr B2
Clifton Rd B3
Clifton St B3
Clock Tower A1
College Rd B3
Colleton Cr C2
Commercial Rd C1
Coombe St B2
Cowick St C1
Crown Courts B2
Custom House C2
Danes' Rd A2
Denmark Rd B3
Devon County Hall C3
Devonshire Pl A3
Dinham Rd B1
East Grove Rd C3
Edmund St C1
Elmgrove Rd A1
Exe St B1
Exeter Cathedral B2
Exeter Central Sta A1
Exeter City Football Ground A3
Exeter College A1
Exeter Picture Ho B1
Fire Station A1
Fore St B1
Friars Walk C2
Guildhall B2
Guildhall Shopping Ctr B2
Harlequins Sh Ctr B1
Haven Rd C2
Heavitree Rd B3
Hele Rd A1
High St B2
HM Prison A2
Holloway St C2
Hoopern St A2
Horseguards A2
Howell Rd A1
Information Ctr B3
Iron Bridge B1
Isca Rd C1
Jesmond Rd A3
King William St A2
King St B1
Larkbeare Rd C2
Leisure Ctr C1
Library B2
Longbrook St A2
Longbrook Terr A2
Lower North St B1
Lucky La C2
Lyndhurst Rd C3
Magdalen Rd B3
Magdalen St B2
Magistrates & Crown Courts A2
Market B2
Market St B2
Marlborough Rd C3
Mary Arches St B1
Matford Ave C3
Matford La C3
Matford Rd C3
May St A3
Mol's Coffee House B2
New Theatre C2
New Bridge St B1
New North Rd A1/A2
North St B1
Northernhay St B1
Norwood Ave C3
Odeon A3
Okehampton St C1
Old Mill Cl C2
Old Tiverton Rd A3
Oxford Rd A3
Paris St B2
Parr St A3
Paul St B1
Pennsylvania Rd A2
Police HQ B3
Portland Street A3
Post Office A3/B1/B3/C1
Powderham Cr A3
Preston St B1
Princesshay Sh Ctr B2
Queen St A1
Queens Rd C1
Queen's Terr A1
Radford Rd C2
Richmond Rd A1
Roberts Rd C2
Rougemont Castle A2
Rougemont House B2
Royal Albert Memorial Museum B2
St David's Hill A1
St James' Pk Sta A3
St James' Rd A3
St Leonard's Rd C3
St Lukes University B3
St Mary Steps C1
St Nicholas Priory B1
St Thomas Station C1
Sandford Walk B3
School for the Deaf C2
School Rd C1
Sidwell St A2
Smythen St B1
South St B2
Southernhay East B2
Southernhay West B2
Spacex Gallery B1
Spicer Rd B3
Sports Ctr A3
Summerland St A3
Swimming Pool & L Ctr B3
Sydney Rd C1
Tan La C2
The Quay C2
Thornton Hill A2
Topsham Rd C3
Tucker's Hall B1
Tudor St B1
Velwell Rd A1
Verney St A3
Water La C1/C2
Weirfield Rd C2
Well St A3
West Ave A2
West Grove Rd C3
Western Way A3/B1/B2
Wonford Rd B3/C3
York Rd A2

Fort William 335

Abrach Rd A3
Achintore Rd C1
Alma Rd B2
Am Breun Chamas A2
Ambulance Station A3
An Aird A2
Argyll Rd C1
Argyll Terr C1
Bank St B2
Belford Hospital B2
Belford Rd B2/B3
Black Parks A3
Braemore Pl C2
Bruce Pl C2
Bus Station B2
Camanachd Cr A3/B2
Cameron Rd C1
Cameron Sq B1
Carmichael Way A2
Claggan Rd B3
Connochie Rd C1
Cow Hill C3
Creag Dhubh A2
Croft Rd B3
Douglas Pl B2
Dudley Rd B2
Dumbarton Rd C1
Earl of Inverness Rd A3
Fassifern Rd B1
Fire Station A2
Fort William B2
Fort William (Remains) B2
Glasdrum Rd C1
Glen Nevis Pl B3
Gordon Sq B1
Grange Rd C1
Heather Croft Rd C1
Henderson Row C2
High St B1
Highland Visitor Ctr B3
Hill Rd B2
Hospital Belhaven Annexe B3
Information Ctr A3
Inverlochy Ct A3
Kennedy Rd B2/C2
Library B2
Lime Tree Gallery C1
Linnhe Rd B1
Lochaber Leisure Ctr B3
Lochiel Rd A3
Lochy Rd A3
Lundavra Cres C1
Lundavra Rd C1
Lundy Rd A3
Mamore Cr B2
Mary St B2
Middle St B1
Montrose Ave A3

Moray Pl C1
Morven Pl C2
Moss Rd B2
Nairn Cres C1
Nevis Bridge B3
Nevis Rd A3
Nevis Sports Ctr A2
Nevis Terr B2
North Rd B3
Obelisk B2
Parade Rd B2
Police Station A3/C1
Post Office A3/B2
Ross Pl C1
St Andrews B2
Shaw Pl B2
Station Brae B1
Studio B1
Treig Rd A3
Underwater Ctr A2
Union Rd C1
Victoria Rd B2
Wades Rd A3
West Highland B2
West Highland College UHI A2
Young Pl B2

Glasgow 335

Admiral St C2
Albert Bridge C5
Albion St B5
Anderston B3
Anderston Ctr B3
Anderston Quay B3
Arches B4
Argyle St A1/A2/B3/B4/B5
Argyle Street B5
Argyll Arcade B5
Arlington St A3
Arts Ctr B3
Ashley St A3
Bain St C6
Baird St A6
Baliol St A3
Ballater St C5
Barras, The (Market) C6
Bath St A3
BBC Scotland/SMG B1
Bell St C6
Bell's Bridge B1
Bentinck St A2
Berkeley St A3
Bishop La B3
Black St A6
Blackburn St C2
Blackfriars St B6
Blantyre St A1
Blythswood Sq A4
Blythswood St B4
Bothwell St B4
Brand St C1
Breadalbane St A2
Bridge St C4
Bridge St C4
Bridgegate C5
Briggait C5
Broomhill Park A6
Broomielaw B4
Broomielaw Quay Gdns B3
Brown St B4
Brunswick St B5
Buccleuch St A3
Buchanan Bus Station A5
Buchanan Galleries A5
Buchanan St B5
Buchanan St B5
Cadogan St B4
Caledonian University A5
Calgary St A5
Cambridge St A4
Canal St A5
Candleriggs B5
Carlton Pl C4
Carnarvon St A3
Carrick St B4
Castle St B6
Cathedral Sq B6
Cathedral St B5
Central College of Commerce B5
Ctr for Contemporary Arts A4
Centre St C4
Cessnock C1
Cessnock St C1
Charing Cross A3
Charlotte St C6
Cheapside St B3
Cineworld A5
Citizens' Theatre C5
City Chambers Complex B5
City Halls B5
Clairmont Gdns A2
Claremont St A2
Claremont Terr A2
Claythorne St C6
Cleveland St A3
Clifford La C1
Clifford St C1
Clifton Pl A2
Clifton St A2
Clutha St C1
Clyde Arc B2
Clyde Auditorium B2
Clyde Pl C4
Clyde Place Quay C4
Clyde St C5
Clyde Walkway C3
Clydeside Expressway B2
Coburg St C4
Cochrane St B5
College of Nautical Studies C5
College St B6
Collins St B6
Commerce St C4
Cook St C4
Cornwall St C2
Couper St A5
Cowcaddens A4
Cowcaddens Rd A4
Crimea St B3
Custom House C4
Custom Ho Quay Gdns C4
Dalhousie St A4
Dental Hospital A4
Derby St A2
Dobbie's Loan A4/A5
Dobbie's Loan Pl A5
Dorset St A3
Douglas St B4
Doulton Fountain C6
Dover St A2
Drury St B4
Drygate B6
Duke St B6
Dunaskin St A1
Dunblane St A4
Dundas St B5
Dunlop St C5
East Campbell St C6
Eastvale Pl A1
Eglinton St C4
Elderslie St A3
Elliot St B2
Elmbank St A3
Esmond St A1
Exhibition Ctr B2
Exhibition Way B2
Eye Infirmary A2
Festival Park C1
Film Theatre A4
Finnieston Quay B2
Finnieston Sq B2
Finnieston St B2
Fitzroy Pl A2
Florence St C5
Fox St C5
Gallowgate C6
Garnet St A3
Garnethill St A4
Garscube Rd A4
George Sq B5
George St B5
George V Bridge C4
Gilbert St A1
Glasgow Bridge C4
Glasgow Cathedral B6
Glasgow Central B4
Glasgow Green C6
Glasgow Metropolitan College B5/C5
Glasgow Tower B1
Glasgow Science Ctr B1
Glasgow Science Ctr Footbridge B1
Glassford St B5
Glebe St A6
Gorbals Cross C5
Gorbals St C5
Gordon St B4
Govan Rd B1/C1/C2
Grace St B3
Grand Ole Opry C2
Grafton Pl A5
Grant St A3
Granville St A3
Gray St A2
Greendyke St C6
Harley St C1
Harvie St C1
Haugh Rd A1
Heliport B1
Henry Wood Hall A2
High Court C5
High St B6
High Street B6
Hill St A3
Holland St A3
Holm St B4
Hope St A5
Houldsworth St B2
Houston Pl C3
Houston St C3
Howard St C5
Hunter St C6
Hutcheson St B5
Hutchesons Hall B5
Hydepark St B3
Imax Cinema B1
India St A3
Information Ctr B5
Ingram St B5
Jamaica St B4
James Watt St B4
John Knox St B6
John St B5
Kelvin Hall A1
Kelvin Statue A2
Kelvin Way A2
Kelvingrove Art Gallery & Museum A1
Kelvingrove Park A2
Kelvingrove St A2
Kelvinhaugh St A1
Kennedy St A6
Kent Rd A2
Killermont St A5
King St B5
King's A3
Kingston Bridge C3
Kingston St C4
Kinning Park C2
Kyle St A5
Lancefield Quay B2
Lancefield St B3
Langshot St C1
Lendel Pl C1
Lighthouse B4
Lister St A6
Little St B3
London Rd C6
Lorne St C1
Lower Harbour B1
Lumsden St A1
Lymburn St A1
Lyndoch Cr A3
Lynedoch Pl A3
Lynedoch St A3
Maclellan St C1
Mair St C2
Maitland St A4
Mavisbank Gdns C2
Mcalpine St B3
Mcaslin St A6
McLean Sq C2
McLellan Gallery A4
McPhater St A4
Merchants' House B5
Middlesex St C2
Middleton St C1
Midland St B4
Miller St B5
Millroad St C6
Milnpark St C2
Milton St A4
Minerva St B2
Mitchell Library A3
Mitchell St West B4
Mitchell Theatre A3
Modern Art Gallery B5
Moir St C6
Molendinar St C6
Moncur St C6
Montieth Row C6
Montrose St B5
Morrison St C3
Mosque C5
Nairn St A1
Nelson Mandela Sq B5
Nelson St C4
Nelson's Monument C6
New City Rd A4
Newton St A3
Newton Pl A3
Nicholson St C4
Nile St B5
Norfolk Court C4
Norfolk St C4
North Frederick St B5
North Hanover St B5
North Portland St B6
North St A3
North Wallace St A5
O2 Academy C4
Odeon C3
Old Dumbarton Rd A1
Osborne St B5/C5
Oswald St B4
Overnewton St A1
Oxford St C4
Pacific Dr B1
Paisley Rd C3
Paisley Rd West C1
Park Circus A2
Park Gdns A2
Park St South A2
Park Terr A2
Parkgrove Terr A2
Parnie St C5
Parson St A6
Partick Bridge A1
Passport Office A5
Pavilion Theatre A4
Pembroke St A3
People's Palace C6
Pinkston Rd A6
Piping Ctr, The National A5
Pitt St A4/B4
Plantation Park C1
Plantation Quay B1
Police Sta A4/A6/B5
Port Dundas Rd A5
Port St B2
Portman St C2
Prince's Dock B1
Princes Sq B5
Provand's Lordship B6
Queen St B5
Queen Street B5
Renfrew St A3/A4
Renton St A5
Richmond St B5
Robertson St B4
Rose St A4
Rottenrow B5
Royal Concert Hall A5
Royal Cr A2
Royal Exchange Sq B5
Royal Highland Fusiliers Museum A3
Royal Hospital For Sick Children A1
Royal Infirmary B6
Royal Scottish Academy of Music & Drama A4
Royal Terr A2
Rutland Cr C2
St Kent St C6
St Andrew's (RC) C5
St Andrew's C6
St Andrew's St C5
St Enoch B5
St Enoch Shopping Ctr B5
St Enoch Sq B4
St George's Rd A3
St James Rd B6
St Mungo Ave A5/A6
St Mungo Museum of Religious Life B6
St Mungo Pl A6
St Vincent Cr A2
St Vincent Pl B5
St Vincent St B3/B4
St Vincent Street Church B4
St Vincent Terr B3
Saltmarket C5
Sandyford Pl A3
Sauchiehall St A2/A4
School of Art A4
Scotland St C2
Scott St A4
Scottish Exhibition & Conference Ctr B1
Seaward St C2
Shaftesbury St B3
Sheriff Court C5
Shields Rd C3
Shuttle St B6
Somerset Pl A2
South Portland St C4
Springburn Rd A6
Springfield Quay C3
Stanley St C2
Stevenson St C6
Stewart St A4
Stirling Rd B6
Stirling's Library B5
Stobcross Quay B1
Stobcross Rd B1
Stock Exchange B5
Stockwell Pl C5
Stockwell St B5
Stow College A4
Strathclyde University B6
Sussex St C2
Synagogues A3/C4
Taylor Pl A6
Tenement House A3
Teviot St A1
Theatre Royal A4
Tolbooth Steeple & Mercat Cross C6
Tower St C2
Trades House B5
Tradeston St C4
Transport Museum A1
Tron C5
Trongate B5
Tunnel St B2
Turnbull St C5
Union St B4
Victoria Bridge C5
Virginia St B5
West Greenhill Pl B2
West Regent St A4
Wallace St C3
Walls St B6
Walmer Cr C1
Warrock St B3
Washington St B3
Waterloo St B4
Watson St B6
Watt St C3
Wellington St B4
West Campbell St B4
West George St B4
West Graham St A4
West Regent St B4
West St C4
West St C4
Westminster Terr A2
Whitehall St B3
Wilson St B5
Woodlands Gate A3
Woodlands Rd A3
Woodlands Terr A2
Woodside Cr A3
Woodside Pl A3
Woodside Terr A3
York St B4
Yorkhill Pde A1
Yorkhill St A1

Gloucester 335

Albion St C1
Alexandra Rd B3
Alfred St C3
All Saints Rd C2
Alvin St B2
Arthur St C2
Baker St C1
Barton St C2
Blackfriars B1
Blenheim Rd C2
Bristol Rd C1
Brunswick Rd C2
Bruton Way B2
Bus Station B2
Cattle Market A1
City Council Offices B1
City Mus, Art Gall & Library B2
Clarence St B2
College of Art C2
Commercial Rd B1
Cromwell St C2
Deans Way A2
Denmark Rd A3
Derby Rd C3
Docks C1
Eastgate St B2
Edwy Pde A2
Estcourt Cl A3
Estcourt Rd A3
Falkner St C2
Folk Museum B1
GL1 Leisure Ctr C2
Gloucester Cath B1
Gloucester Station B2
Gloucestershire Royal Hospital (A&E) B3
Gloucester Waterways C1
Goodyere St C2
Gouda Way A1
Great Western Rd B3
Guildhall B2
Heathville Rd A3
Henry Rd B3
Henry St B2
High Orchard St C1
Hinton Rd A2
India Rd C3
Information Ctr B1
Jersey Rd C3
King's C2
King's Sq B2
Kingsholm Rd A2
Kingsholm Rugby Football Ground A2
Lansdown Rd A3
Library C2
Llanthony Rd C1
London Rd B3
Longsmith St B1
Malvern Rd A3
Market Pde B2
Merchants Rd C1
Mercia Rd A1
Metz Way C3
Midland Rd C2
Millbrook St C3
Market B2
Montpellier C1
Napier St C3
Nettleton Rd C2
New Inn B2
New Olympus C3
North Rd A3
Northgate St B2
Oxford Rd A2
Oxford St B2
Pk & Ride Gloucester A1
Park Rd C2
Park St B2
Parliament St C1
Pitt St B1
Police Station B1
Post Office B2
Quay St B1
Recreation Gd A1/A2
Regent St C2
Robert Raikes Ho B1
Royal Oak Rd B1
Russell St B2
Ryecroft St C2
St Aldate St B2
St Ann Way C1
St Catherine St A2
St Mark St A2
St Mary De Crypt B1
St Mary De Lode B1
St Nicholas's B1
St Oswald's Rd A1
St Oswald's Trading Estate A1
St Peter's B2
Seabroke Rd A3
Sebert St A2
Severn Rd C1
Sherborne St B2
Shire Hall B1
Sidney St C3
Soldiers of Gloucestershire B1
Southgate St B1/C1
Spa Field C1
Spa Rd C1
Sports Ground A2/B2
Station Rd B2
Stratton Rd C3
Stroud Rd C1
Superstore A1
Swan Rd A2
Technical College C1
The Mall B2
The Park C2
The Quay B1
Trier Way C1/C2
Union St A2
Vauxhall Rd C3
Victoria St C2
Wellington St C2
Westgate St B1
Widden St C2
Worcester St B2

Grimsby 335

Abbey Drive East C2
Abbey Drive West C2
Abbey Park Rd C2
Abbey Rd C2
Abbey Walk C2
Abbeygate Sh Ctr C2
Abbotsway C2
Adam Smith St A1/A2
Ainslie St C2
Albert St A3
Alexandra Dock A2/B2
Alexandra Retail Park A2
Alexandra Rd A2/B2
Annesley St A2
Armstrong St A1
Arthur St B1
Augusta St C1
Bargate C1
Beeson St A1
Bethlehem St C2
Bodiam Way B3
Bradley St B3
Brighowgate C1/C2
Bus Station B2/C2
Canterbury Dr C1
Cartergate B1/C1
Catherine St C3
Caxton A3
Chantry La B1
Charlton St A1
Church La C2
Church St A3
Cleethorpe Rd A3
College C2
College St C1
Compton Dr C1
Corporation Bridge A2
Corporation Rd A1
Court B3
Crescent St B1
Deansgate C1
Doughty Rd C2
Dover St B1
Duchess St C2
Dudley St C1
Duke of York Gardens B1
Duncombe St B3
Earl La B1
East Marsh St B3
East St B2
Eastgate B3
Eastside Rd A3
Eaton Ct C1
Eleanor St B3
Ellis Way B3
Fisherman's Chapel A3
Fisherman's Wharf B2
Fishing Heritage Ctr B2
Flour Sq A3
Frederick St B3
Frederick Ward Way B2
Freeman St A3/B3
Freshney Dr B1
Freshney Pl B2
Garden St C2
Garibaldi St A3
Garth La B2
Grime St B3
Grimsby Docks Sta A3
Grimsby Town Sta C2
Hainton Ave C3
Har Way B3
Hare St C3
Harrison St B1
Haven Ave B1
Hay Croft Ave B1
Hay Croft St B1
Heneage Rd B3/C3
Henry St B1
Holme St B3
Hume St C1
James St B1
Joseph St B1
Kent St A3
King Edward St A3
Lambert Rd C2
Library B2
Lime St B1
Lister St B1
Littlefield La C1
Lockhill A3
Lord St B1
Ludford St C3
Macaulay St B1
Mallard Mews C3
Manor Ave C2
Market A3
Market Hall B2
Market St B3
Moss Rd C2
Nelson St A3
New St B2
Osbourne St B2
Pasture St B3
Peaks Parkway C3
Pelham Rd C1
Police Station A3
Post Office B1/B2/C2
PS Lincoln Castle B2
Pyewipe Rd A1
Railway Pl A3
Railway St A3
Recreation Ground C2
Rendel St A2
Retail Park B3
Richard St B1
Ripon St B1
Robinson St East B3
Royal St A3
St Hilda's Ave C1
St James B2
Sheepfold St B3/C3
Sixhills St C3
South Park B2
Spring St A3
Superstore B3
Tasburgh St C3
Tennyson St B2
The Close C1
Thesiger St A3
Time Trap C2
Town Hall B2
Veal St B1
Victoria Retail Park A3
Victoria St North A2
Victoria St South B2
Victoria St West B2
Watkin St A1
Welholme Ave C2
Welholme Rd C3
Wellington St B3
Wellowgate C2
Werneth Rd B3
West Coates Rd A1
Westgate A2
Westminster Dr C1
Willingham St C3
Wintringham Rd C2
Wood St B3
Yarborough Dr B1
Yarborough Hotel C2

Hanley 335

Acton St A3
Albion St B2
Argyle St C1
Ashbourne Gr A2
Avoca St A3
Baskerville Rd B3
Bedford Rd C1
Bedford St C1
Bethesda St B2
Bexley St A2
Birches Head Rd A3
Botteslow St C3
Boundary St A2
Broad St C2
Broom St A3
Bryan St A2
Bucknall New Rd B3
Bucknall Old Rd B3
Bus Station B3
Cannon St C2
Castlefield St C1
Cavendish St B1
Central Forest Pk A2
Charles St B3
Cheapside B2
Chell St A3
Clarke St C1
Cleveland Rd C2
Clifford St C3
Clough St B2
Clyde St C1
College Rd C2
Cooper St C2
Corbridge Rd A1
Cutts St C2
Davis St C1
Denbigh St A1
Derby St C3
Dilke St A3
Dundas St A3
Dundee Rd C1
Dyke St B3
Eastwood Rd C3
Eaton St A3
Etruria Park B1
Etruria Rd B1
Etruria Vale Rd C1
Festing St A3
Festival Retail Park A1
Fire Station C2
Foundry St B2
Franklyn St C3
Garnet St B1
Garth St B3
George St A3
Gilman St B3
Glass St B3
Goodson St B3
Greyhound Way A1
Grove Pl C1
Hampton St C3
Hanley Park C2
Harding Rd C2
Hassall St B3
Havelock Pl C1
Hazlehurst St C3
Hinde St C2
Hope St B2
Houghton St C2
Hulton St A3
Information Ctr B3
Jasper St C2
Jervis St A3
John Bright St A3
John St B2
Keelings Rd A3
Kimberley Rd C1
Ladysmith Rd C1
Lawrence St C2
Leek Rd C3
Library C2
Lichfield St C3
Linfield Rd B3
Loftus St A2
Lower Bedford St C1
Lower Bryan St A2
Lower Mayer St A3
Lowther St A1
Magistrates Court C2
Malham St A2
Marsh St B2
Matlock St C3
Mayer St A3
Milton St C1
Mitchell Memorial Theatre B2
Morley St B2
Moston St A3
Mount Pleasant C1
Mulgrave St A1
Mynors St B3
Nelson Pl B3
New Century St B1
Octagon Retail Park B1
Ogden Rd C3
Old Hall St B3
Old Town Rd A3
Pall Mall B2
Palmerston St C3
Park and Ride C2
Parker St B2
Pavilion Dr A1
Pelham St C3
Percy St B2
Piccadilly B2
Picton St B3
Plough St A3
Police Station C2
Portland St A1
Post Office A3/B3/C3
Potteries Museum & Art Gallery B2
Potteries Sh Ctr B2
Potteries Way C2
Powell St A1
Pretoria Rd C1
Quadrant Rd B2
Ranelagh St C2
Raymond St C2
Rectory Rd C1
Regent Rd C2
Regent Theatre B2
Richmond Terr C2
Ridgehouse Dr A1
Robson St C2
St Ann St B3
St Luke St B3
Sampson St B2
Shaw St A1
Sheaf St C2
Shearer St C1
Shelton New Rd C1
Shirley Rd C2
Slippery La B2
Snow Hill C2
Spur St C3
Stafford St B2
Statham St B2
Stubbs La C3
Sun St C1
Supermarket A1/B2
Talbot St C3
The Parkway C2
Town Hall B2
Town Rd A3
Trinity St B2
Union St A2
Upper Hillchurch St A3
Upper Huntbach St B3
Victoria Hall Theatre B3
Warner St C2
Warwick St C1
Waterloo Rd A1
Waterloo St B3
Well St B3
Wellesley St C2
Wellington Rd B3
Wellington St B3
Whitehaven Dr A2
Whitmore St C1
Windermere St A1
Woodall St A1
Yates St C2
York St A2

Harrogate 335

Albert St C2
Alexandra Rd B2
Arthington Ave B2
Ashfield Rd A2
Back Cheltenham Mount B2
Beech Grove C1
Belmont Rd C1
Bilton Dr A2
Bower Rd B2
Bower St B2
Bus Station B2
Cambridge Rd B2
Cambridge St B2
Cemetery A2
Chatsworth Pl A2
Chatsworth Grove A2
Chatsworth Rd A2
Chelmsford Rd B3
Cheltenham Cr B2
Cheltenham Mt B2
Cheltenham Pde B2
Christ Church B3
Christ Church Oval B3
Chudleigh Rd B3
Clarence Dr B1
Claro Rd A3
Claro Way A3
Coach Park B2
Coach Rd B3
Cold Bath Rd C1
Commercial St B2
Coppice Ave A1
Coppice Dr A1
Coppice Gate A1
Cornwall Rd B1
Council Offices B1
Court C3
Crescent Gdns B1
Crescent Rd B1
Dawson Terr A2
Devonshire Pl B3
Diamond Mews C1
Dixon Rd A2
Dixon Terr A2
Dragon Ave B3
Dragon Parade B2
Dragon Rd B2
Duchy Rd B1
East Parade B2
East Park Rd C3
Esplanade B1
Fire Station A2
Franklin Mount A2
Franklin Rd B2
Franklin Square A2
Glebe Rd C1
Grove Park Ct A3
Grove Park Terr A3
Grove Rd A2
Hampswaite Rd A1
Harcourt Dr B3
Harcourt Rd B3
Harrogate B2
Harrogate Int Ctr B1
Harrogate Ladies Coll B1
Harrogate Theatre B2
Heywood Rd C1
Hollins Cr A1
Hollins Mews A1
Hollins Rd A1
Homestead Rd C3
Hydro Leisure Ctr, The A1
Information Ctr B1
James St B2
Jenny Field Dr A1
John St B2
Kent Dr A1
Kent Rd A1
Kings Rd A2
Kingsway B3
Kingsway Dr B3
Lancaster Rd C1
Leeds Rd C2
Lime Grove B3
Lime St A3
Mayfield Grove B2
Mayfield Pl A2
Mercer B1
Montpellier Hill B1
Mornington Cr A3
Mornington Terr B3
Mowbray Sq B3
North Park Rd B3
Nydd Vale Rd B2
Oakdale Ave A1
Oatlands Dr C3
Odeon B2
Osborne Rd A2
Otley Rd C2
Oxford St B2
Park Chase B3
Park Parade B3
Park View B2
Parliament St B1
Police Station B3
Post Office B2/C1
Providence Terr A2
Queen Parade C3
Queen's Rd C1
Raglan St C2
Regent Ave A3
Regent Grove A3
Regent Parade A3
Regent St A3
Regent Terr A3
Rippon Rd A1
Robert St C2
Royal Baths & Turkish Baths B1
Royal Pump Room B1
St Luke's Mount A2
St Mary's Ave C1
St Mary's Walk C1
Scargill Rd A1
Skipton Rd A3
Skipton St A2
Slingsby Walk C3
South Park Rd C2
Spring Grove A1
Springfield Ave B1
Station Ave B2
Station Parade B2
Strawberry Dale B2
Stray Rein C3
Studley Rd A2
Superstore B2
Swan Rd B1
The Parade B2
The Stray C2/C3
Tower St C2
Trinity Rd C2
Union St B2
Valley Dr C1
Valley Gardens C1
Valley Mount C1
Victoria Ave C2
Victoria Rd C1
Victoria Shopping Ctr B2
Waterloo St A2
West Park C2
West Park St C2
Wood View A1
Woodfield Ave A3
Woodfield Dr A3
Woodfield Grove A3
Woodfield Rd A3
Woodfield Square A3
Woodside B3
York Pl C3
York Rd B1

Holyhead *Caergybi* 335

Armenia St A2
Arthur St C2
Beach Rd A1
Boston St B2
Bowling Green C3
Bryn Erw Rd C3
Bryn Glas Cl C3
Bryn Glas Rd C3
Bryn Gwyn Rd C1
Bryn Marchog A1
Bryn Mor Terr A2
Bryngoleu Ave A1
Cae Braenar C3
Cambria St B1
Captain Skinner's Obelisk B2
Cecil St C2
Celtic Gateway Footbridge C2
Cemetery C1/C2
Cleveland Ave C2
Coastguard Lookout A2
Court B2
Customs House A3
Cybi Pl A2
Cyttir Rd C3
Edmund St B1
Empire B2
Ferry Terminals B2
Ffordd Beibio B3
Ffordd Feurig C3
Ffordd Hirnos C3
Ffordd Jasper C3
Ffordd Tudur B3
Fire Station C2
Garreglwyd Rd B1
Gilbert St C2
Gorsedd Circle B1
Gwelfor Ave A1
Harbour View B3
Henry St C2
High Terr C1
Hill St B2
Holborn Rd C2
Holland Park Ind Est C3
Holyhead Park B1
Holyhead Station B2
Information Ctr B2
King's Rd C2
Kingsland Rd C2
Lewascote C3
Library B2
Lifeboat Station A1
Llanfawr Cl C3
Llanfawr Rd C3
Lligwy St C2
Lon Deg C3
London Rd C3
Longford Rd B1
Longford Terr B1
Maes Cybi B1
Maes Hedd A1
Maes-Hyfryd Rd C1
Maes-y-Dref B1
Maes-yr-Haf A2/B1
Maes-yr-Ysgol C3
Marchog C3
Marina A1
Maritime Museum A1
Market B2
Market St B2
Mill Bank B1
Min-y-Mor Rd A1
Morawelon Ind Est B3

Hull • Inverness • Ipswich • Kendal • King's Lynn • Lancaster • Leeds 351

Morawelon Rd B3
Moreton Rd C1
New Park Rd B1
Newry St A2
Old Harbour Lighthouse A3
Plas Rd C1
Police Station B2
Porth-y-Felin Rd A1
Post Office A1/B1/B2/B3/C2/C3
Prince of Wales Rd A2
Priory La B3
Pump St C1
Queens Park B1
Reseifion Rd C1
Rock St B1
Roman Fort B2
St Cybi St B2
St Cybi's Church B2
St Seiriol's Cl B1
Salt Island Bridge A2
Seabourne Rd A1
South Stack Rd B1
Sports Ground B1
Stanley St B2
Station St B2
Tan-y-Bryn Rd A1
Tan-yr-Efail C2
Tara St C1
Thomas St B1
Town Hall A2
Treseifion Estate C2
Turkey Shore Rd B2
Ucheldre Arts Ctr ✦ B1
Ucheldre Ave B1
Upper Baptist St B1
Victoria Rd B2
Victoria Terr B2
Vulcan St B1
Walthew Ave A1
Walthew La A1
Wian St C2

Hull 335

Adelaide St C1
Albert Dock C1
Albion St B2
Alfred Gelder St B2
Anlaby Rd B1
Arctic Corsair ✦ B3
Beverley Rd A1
Blanket Row C2
Bond St B2
Bridlington Ave A2
Brook St B1
Brunswick Ave A1
Bus Station B1
Camilla Cl C3
Cannon St A2
Cannon's C1
Caroline St A2
Carr La B2
Castle St C2
Central Library B1
Charles St A2
Citadel Way B3
City Hall B2
City Hall Theatre B2
Clarence St B3
Cleveland St A3
Clifton St A1
Club Culture C2
Colonial St B1
Court B2
Deep, The C3
Dock Office Row B3
Dock St B2
Dinostar C2
Drypool Bridge B3
Egton St A3
English St C1
Ferens Gallery B2
Ferensway B1
Francis St A2
Francis St West A2
Freehold St A1
Freetown Way A2
Fruit Theatre C2
Garrison Rd B3
George St B2
Gibson St A2
Great Thornton St B1
Great Union St A3
Green La A2
Grey St A1
Grimston St B2
Grosvenor St A1
Guildhall B2
Guildhall Rd B2
Hands-on History B2
Harley St A1
Hessle Rd C1
High St B3
Holy Trinity B2
Hull & East Riding Museum B3
Hull Arena C1
Hull College B3
Hull History Ctr A2
Hull (Paragon) Sta B1
Hull Truck Theatre B1
Humber Dock Marina C2
Humber Dock St C2
Humber St C2
Hyperion St A3
Information Ctr B2
Jameson St B1
Jarratt St B2
Jenning St A3
King Billy Statue ✦ C2
King Edward St B2
King St A2
Kingston Retail Park C1
Kingston St C2
Liddell St A1
Lime St A3
Lister St C1
Lockwood St A2
Maister House B3
Maritime Museum B2
Market B2
Market Place B2
Minerva Pier C2
Mulgrave St A3
Myton Bridge C3
Myton St B1
NAPA (Northern Acad of Performing Arts) B1
Nelson St C2
New Cleveland St A3
New George St A2
New Theatre A2
Norfolk St A1
North Bridge A3
North St B1
Odeon C1
Old Harbour C3
Osborne St B1
Paragon St B2
Park St B1
Percy St A2
Pier St C2
Police Station B1
Post Office A1/B1/B2
Porter St C1
Portland St B1
Posterngate B2
Prince's Quay B2
Prospect Ctr B1
Prospect St B1
Queen's Gdns B2
Railway Dock Marina C2
Railway St C2
Real B1
Red Gallery B1
Reform St A2
Retail Park B1
River Hull Footbridge B3
Riverside Quay C2
Roper St B2
St James St C1
St Luke's St B1
St Mark St A3
St Mary the Virgin B3
St Stephens Sh Ctr B1
Scott St A2
South Bridge Rd B3
Spring Bank A1
Spring St B1
Spurn Lightship C2
Spyvee St A3
Streetlife Transport Museum B3
Sykes St A2
Tidal Surge Barrier ✦ C3
Tower St B3
Trinity House B2
University B2
Vane St A1
Victoria Pier ✦ C2
Waterhouse La B2
Waterloo St A1
Waverley St C1
Wellington St C2
Wellington St West C2
West St B1
Whitefriargate B2
Wilberforce Dr B2
Wilberforce House B3
Wilberforce Monument ✦ B3
William St C1
Wincolmlee A3
Witham A3
Wright St A1

Inverness 336

Abban St A1
Academy St B2
Alexander Pl B2
Anderson St A2
Annfield Rd C3
Ardconnel St B3
Ardconnel Terr B3
Ardross Pl B2
Ardross St B2
Argyle St B3
Argyle Terr B3
Attadale Rd B1
Ballifeary La C2
Ballifeary Rd C1/C2
Balnacraig La A1
Balnain House ✦ B2
Balnain St B2
Bank St B2
Bellfield Park C2
Bellfield Terr C3
Benula Rd A1
Birnie Terr A1
Bishop's Rd C2
Bowling Green A2
Bowling Green B2
Bowling Green C2
Bridge St B2
Brown St A2
Bruce Ave C1
Bruce Gdns C1
Bruce Pk C1
Burial Ground A2
Burnett Rd A3
Bus Station B3
Caledonian Rd B1
Cameron Rd A1
Cameron Sq A1
Carse Rd A1
Carsegate Rd Sth A1
Castle Garrison Encounter ✦ B2
Castle Rd B2
Castle St B3
Celt St B2
Chapel St A2
Charles St B3
Church St B2
Clachnacuddin Football Ground A1
Columba Rd B1/C1
Crown Ave B3
Crown Circus B3
Crown Dr B3
Crown Rd B3
Crown St B3
Culduthel Rd C3
Dalneigh Cres C1
Dalneigh Rd C1
Denny St B3
Dochfour Dr B1/C1
Douglas Row B2
Duffy Dr C3
Dunabban Rd A1
Dunain Rd B1
Duncraig St B2
Eastgate Shopping Ctr B3
Eden Court C2
Fairfield Rd B1
Falcon Sq B3
Fire Station A3
Fraser St B2
Fraser St C2
Friars' Bridge A2
Friars' La B2
Friars' St A2
George St A2
Gilbert St A2
Glebe St A2
Glendoe Terr A1
Glenurquhart Rd C1
Gordon Terr B3
Gordonville Rd C2
Grant St A2
Greig St B2
HM Prison B3
Harbour Rd A3
Harrowden Rd B1
Haugh Rd C2
Heatherley Cres C3
High St B3
Highland Council HQ, The C2
Hill Park C3
Hill St B3
Huntly Pl A2
Huntly St B2
India St A2
Industrial Estate A3
Information Ctr B2
Innes St A2
Inverness B3
Inverness College (Midmills Campus) B3
Inverness College UHI A3
Inverness High School B1
Inverness Museum B2
Jamaica St A2
Kenneth St B2
Kilmuir Rd A1
King St B2
Kingsmills Rd B3
Laurel Ave B1/C1
Library A3
Lilac Gr B1
Lindsay Ave C1
Lochalsh Rd A1/B1
Longman Rd A3
Lotland Pl A2
Lower Kessock St A1
Madras St A2
Market Hall B3
Maxwell Dr C1
Mayfield Rd C3
Millburn Rd B3
Mitchell's La C3
Montague Row B2
Muirfield Rd C3
Muirtown St B1
Nelson St A2
Ness Bank C2
Ness Bridge B2
Ness Walk B2/C2
Old Edinburgh Rd C3
Old High Church B2
Park Rd C1
Paton St C2
Perceval Rd B1
Planefield Rd B2
Police Station A3
Porterfield Bank C3
Porterfield Rd C3
Portland Pl A2
Post Office A2/B1/B2/B3
Queen St B2
Queensgate B2
Railway Terr A3
Rangemore Rd B1
Reay St B3
Riverside St A2
Rose St A2
Ross Ave B1
Rowan Rd B1
Royal Northern Infirmary C2
St Andrew's Cath C2
St Columba B2
St John's Ave C1
St Mary's Ave C1
Sheriff Court B3
Shore St A2
Smith Ave C1
Southside Pl C3
Southside Rd C3
Spectrum Ctr B3
Strothers La B3
Superstore B2
TA Ctr C2
Telford Gdns B1
Telford Rd A1
Telford St A1
Tomnahurich Cemetery C1
Tomnahurich St B2
Town Hall B3
Union Rd B3
Union St B3
Walker Pl A2
Walker Rd A3
War Memorial ✦ C2
Waterloo Bridge A2
Wells St B1
Young St B2

Ipswich 336

Alderman Rd B2
All Saints' Rd A1
Alpe St B2
Ancaster Rd C1
Ancient House B3
Anglesea Rd B2
Ann St B2
Arboretum A2
Austin St C2
Belstead Rd C2
Berners St B2
Bibb Way B1
Birkfield Dr C1
Black Horse La B2
Bolton La B3
Bond St C3
Bowthorpe Cl B2
Bramford La A1
Bramford Rd A1
Bridge St C2
Brookfield Rd A1
Brooks Hall Rd A1
Broomhill A2
Broomhill Rd A1
Broughton Rd A2
Bulwer Rd B1
Burrell Rd C2
Butter Market B2
Butter Market Ctr B3
Carr St B3
Cecil Rd B2
Cecilia St C2
Chancery Rd C2
Charles St B2
Chevallier St A1
Christchurch Mansion & Wolsey Art Gallery B3
Christchurch Park A3
Christchurch St B3
Cineworld C2
Civic Ctr B2
Civic Dr B2
Clarkson St B1
Cobbold St B3
Commercial Rd C2
Constable Rd A3
Constantine Rd C1
Constitution Hill A2
Corder Rd A3
Corn Exchange B2
Cotswold Ave A2
Council Offices C2
County Hall B3
Crown Court C2
Crown St B2
Cullingham Rd B1
Cumberland St B2
Curriers La B2
Dale Hall La A2
Dales View Rd A1
Dalton Rd B2
Dillwyn St B1
Elliot St B1
Elm St B2
Elsmere Rd A3
Falcon St C2
Felaw St C3
Flint Wharf C3
Fonnereau Rd B2
Fore St C3
Foundation St C3
Franciscan Way C2
Friars St C2
Gainsborough Rd A3
Gatacre Rd B1
Geneva Rd B2
Gippeswyk Ave C1
Gippeswyk Park C1
Grafton Way C2
Graham Rd A1
Grimwade St C3
Great Whip St C3
Handford Cut B1
Handford Rd B1
Henley Rd A2
Hervey St B3
High St B2
Holly Rd A2
Information Ctr B3
Ipswich Haven Marina ✦ C3
Ipswich School A2
Ipswich Station C2
Ipswich Town FC (Portman Road) C2
Ivry St A2
Kensington Rd A1
Kesteven Rd C1
Key St C3
Kingsfield Ave A3
Kitchener Rd A1
Magistrates Court B2
Little's Cr C2
London Rd B1
Low Brook St C3
Lower Orwell St C3
Luther Rd C2
Manor Rd A3
Mornington Ave A1
Mus & Art Gallery B2
Museum St B2
Neale St B3
New Cardinal St C2
New Cut East C3
New Cut West C3
New Wolsey B2
Newson St B2
Norwich Rd A1/B1
Oban St B2
Old Customs House C3
Old Foundry Rd B3
Old Merchant's Ho C3
Orford St B2
Paget Rd A2
Park Rd A3
Park View Rd A2
Peter's St C2
Philip Rd C2
Pine Ave A2
Pine View Rd A2
Police Station B2
Portman Rd B2
Portman Walk C1
Post Office B2/B3
Princes St C2
Prospect St B1
Queen St B2
Ranelagh Rd C1
Recreation Ground B1
Rectory Rd C2
Regent Theatre B3
Retail Park C2
Richmond Rd A1
Rope Walk C3
Rose La C2
Russell Rd C2
St Edmund's Rd A2
St George's St B2
St Helen's St B3
Samuel Rd B3
Sherrington Rd A1
Silent St C2
Sir Alf Ramsey Way C1
Sirdar Rd B1
Soane St B3
Springfield La A1
Star La C3
Stevenson Rd B1
Suffolk College C3
Suffolk Retail Park B1
Superstore B1
Surrey Rd B1
Tacket St C3
Tavern St B3
The Avenue A3
Tolly Cobbold Mus C3
Tower Ramparts B2
Tower Ramparts Shopping Ctr B2
Tower St B3
Town Hall B2
Tuddenham Rd A3
Upper Brook St B3
Upper Orwell St B3
Valley Rd A2
Vermont Cr B3
Vermont Rd B3
Vernon St C3
Warrington Rd A2
Waterloo Rd A1
Waterworks St C3
Wellington St B1
West End Rd B1
Westerfield Rd A3
Westgate St B2
Westholme Rd A1
Westwood Ave A1
Willoughby Rd C2
Withipoll St B3
Woodbridge Rd B3
Woodstone Ave A3
Yarmouth Rd B1

Kendal 336

Abbot Hall Art Gallery & Museum of Lakeland Life C2
Ambulance Station A2
Anchorite Fields C2
Anchorite Rd C2
Ann St A3
Appleby Rd A3
Archers Meadow C3
Ashleigh Rd A2
Aynam Rd B2
Bankfield Rd B1
Beast Banks B2
Beezon Fields A2
Beezon Rd A2
Beezon Trad Est A3
Belmont B2
Birchwood Cl C1
Blackhall Rd B2
Brewery Arts Ctr B2
Bridge St B2
Brigsteer Rd C1
Burneside Rd A2
Bus Station B2
Buttery Well La C2
Canal Head North B3
Captain French La C2
Caroline St A2
Castle Hill B3
Castle Howe B2
Castle Rd B3
Castle St A3/B3
Cedar Gr C1
Council Offices B2
County Council Offices A2
Cricket Ground A3
Cricket Ground C3
Cross La C2
Dockray Hall Ind Est A2
Dowker's La B2
Dry Ski Slope ✦ B3
East View B1
Echo Barn Hill C1
Elephant Yard Sh Ctr B2
Fairfield La A1
Finkle St B2
Fire Station A2
Fletcher Square C3
Football Ground C3
Fowling La A3
Gillinggate C2
Glebe Rd C2
Golf Course B1
Goose Holme B3
Gooseholme Bridge B3
Green St A1
Greengate C2
Greengate La C1/C2
Greenside B1
Greenwood C1
Gulfs Rd B2
High Tenterfell B1
Highgate B2
Hillswood Ave C1
Horncop La A2
Information Ctr B2
K Village and Heritage Ctr ✦ C2
Kendal Business Park A3
Kendal Castle (Remains) ✦ B3
Kendal Fell B1
Kendal Green A1
Kendal A3
Kendal Station A3
Kent Pl B2
Kirkbarrow C2
Kirkland C2
Library B2
Library Rd B2
Little Aynam B3
Little Wood B1
Long Cl C1
Longpool A3
Lound Rd C3
Lound St C3
Low Fellside B2
Lowther St B2
Maple Dr C1
Market Pl B2
Maude St B2
Miller Bridge B2
Milnthorpe Rd C2
Mint St A3
Mintsfeet Rd A3
Mintsfeet Rd South A2
New Rd B2
Noble's Rest B2
Parish Church C2
Park Side Rd C3
Parkside Bsns Park C3
Parr St B3
Police Station A2
Post Office A3/B2/C2
Quaker Tapestry ✦ B2
Queen's Rd B1
Riverside Walk C2
Rydal Mount A2
Sandes Ave A2
Sandgate A3
Sandylands Rd A3
Serpentine Rd B1
Serpentine Wood B1
Shap Rd A3
South Rd C2
Stainbank Rd C1
Station Rd A3
Stramongate B2
Stramongate Bridge B2
Stricklandgate A2/B2
Sunnyside C3
Thorny Hills B3
Town Hall B2
Undercliff Rd B1
Underwood C1
Union St A2
Vicar's Fields C2
Vicarage Dr C1/C2
Wainwright Yd Sh Ctr B2
Wasdale Cl C3
Well Ings C2
Westmorland Shopping Ctr & Market Hall B2
Westwood Ave C1
Wildman St A3
Windermere Rd A1
YHA B2
YWCA B2

King's Lynn 336

Albert St A2
Albion St B2
All Saints B2
All Saints St B2
Austin Fields A2
Austin St A2
Avenue Rd B3
Bank Side B1
Beech Rd C2
Birch Tree Cl B2
Birchwood St A2
Blackfriars Rd B2
Blackfriars St B2
Boal St B1
Bridge St B2
Broad St B2
Broad Walk B3
Burkitt St A2
Bus Station A2
Carmelite Terr C2
Chapel St A2
Chase Ave C3
Checker St C2
Church St B2
Clough La B2
Coburg St B2
College of West Anglia A3
Columbia Way A3
Corn Exchange A1
County Court Rd B2
Cresswell St A2
Custom House A1
Eastgate St A2
Edma St A2
Exton's Rd C3
Ferry La B1
Ferry St A1
Framingham's Almshouses B2
Friars St C2
Friars Walk C2
Gaywood Rd A3
George St A2
Gladstone Rd C2
Goodwin's Rd C3
Green Quay ✦ B1
Greyfriars' Tower ✦ B2
Guanock Terr C2
Guildhall A1
Hansa Rd C3
Hardwick Rd C2
Hextable Rd A2
High St B1
Holcombe Ave C3
Hospital Walk C2
Information Ctr B1
John Kennedy Rd A2
Kettlewell Lane A2
King George V Ave B3
King's Lynn Art Ctr A1
King's Lynn FC B3
King's Lynn Station B2
King St B1
Library B2
Littleport St A2
Loke Rd A2
London Rd B2
Lynn Museum B2
Majestic B2
Magistrates Court B1
Market La A1
Millfleet B2
Milton Ave A3
Nar Valley Walk C2
Nelson St B1
New Conduit St B2
Norfolk St A2
North Lynn Discovery Ctr ✦ A3
North St A2
Oldsunway B2
Ouse Ave C1
Page Stair Lane A1
Park Ave B3
Police Station B2
Portland Pl C1
Portland St B2
Post Office A3/C2
Purfleet B1
Queen St B1
Raby Ave A3
Railway Rd A2
Red Mount Chapel B3
Regent Way B2
River Walk A1
Robert St C2
Saddlebow Rd C2
St Ann's St A1
St James' Rd B2
St James' Swimming Pool B2
St James St B2
St John's Walk B3
St Margaret's B1
St Nicholas A2
St Nicholas St A2
St Peter's Rd B1
Sir Lewis St A2
Smith Ave A3
South Everard St C2
South Gate ✦ C2
South Quay B1
South St B2
Southgate St C2
Stonegate St B2
Surrey St A1
Sydney St C3
Tennyson Ave B3
Tennyson Rd B3
Tower St B2
Town Hall B1
Town Ho & Tales of The Old Gaol Ho B1
Town Wall (Remains) ✦ B3
True's Yard Mus A2
Valingers Rd C2
Vancouver Ave C2
Waterloo St B2
Wellesley St B2
White Friars Rd C2
Windsor Rd C2
Winfarthing St C2
Wyatt St A2
York Rd C3

Lancaster 336

Aberdeen Rd C3
Adult College, The C3
Aldcliffe Rd C2
Alfred St B3
Ambleside Rd A3
Ambulance Sta A3
Ashfield Ave B1
Ashton Rd C2
Assembly Rooms B2
Balmoral Rd B3
Bath House B2
Bath Mill La B3
Bath St B3
Blades St B1
Borrowdale Rd B3
Bowerham Rd C3
Brewery La B2
Bridge La B2
Brook St C1
Bulk Rd A3
Bulk St B2
Bus Station B2
Cable St B2
Canal Cruises & Waterbus ✦ C2
Carlisle Bridge A1
Carr House La C2
Castle B1
Castle Park B1
Caton Rd A3
China St B2
Church St B2
City Museum B2
Clarence St C3
Common Gdn St B2
Coniston Rd A3
Cottage Museum B2
Council Offices B2
Court B2
Cromwell Rd C1
Crown Court B2
Dale St C3
Dallas Rd B1/C1
Dalton Rd B3
Dalton Sq B2
Damside St B2
De Vitre St B3
Dee Rd A1
Denny Ave A1
Derby Rd A2
Dukes B2
Earl St A2
East Rd B3
Eastham St C3
Edward St B3
Fairfield Rd B1
Fenton St B2
Firbank Rd A3
Fire Station B2
Friend's Meeting Ho B1
Garnet St B3
George St B2
Giant Axe Field B1
Grand, The B2
Grasmere Rd B3
Greaves Rd C2
Green St A3
Gregson Ctr, The B3
Gregson Rd C3
Greyhound Bridge A2
Greyhound Bridge Rd A2
High St B2
Hill Side B1
Hope St C3
Hubert Pl B1
Information Ctr B2
Judges Lodgings B2
Kelsy St B1
Kentmere Rd B3
King St B2
Kingsway A3
Kirkes Rd C3
Lancaster & Lakeland C3
Lancaster City Football Club B1
Lancaster Station B1
Langdale Rd A3
Ley Ct B1
Library B2
Lincoln Rd B1
Lindow St C2
Lodge St B2
Long Marsh La B1
Lune Rd A1
Lune St A2
Lune Valley Ramble A3
Mainway A2
Maritime Museum A1
Market St B2
Marketgate Sh Ctr B2
Meadowside C2
Meeting House La B1
Millennium Bridge A2
Moor La B2
Moorgate B3
Morecambe Rd A1/A2
Nelson St B2
North Rd B2
Orchard La C1
Owen Rd A2
Park Rd B3
Parliament St A3
Patterdale Rd A3
Penny St B2
Police Station B2
Portland St C2
Post Office A3/B1/B2/B3/C3
Primrose St C3
Priory B1
Prospect St C3
Quarry Rd B3
Queen St C2
Regent St C2
Ridge La A3
Ridge St A3
Royal Lancaster Infirmary (A&E) C2
Rydal Rd B3
Ryelands Park A1
St Georges Quay A1
St John's B2
St Leonard's Gate B2
St Martin's Rd C3
St Nicholas Arcades Shopping Ctr B2
St Oswald St C3
St Peter's B3
St Peter's Rd B3
Salisbury Rd B1
Scotch Quarry Urban Park C3
Shire Hall/HM Prison B1
Sibsey St B1
Skerton Bridge A2
South Rd C2
Station Rd B1
Stirling Rd C3
Storey Ave B1
Sunnyside La C1
Sylvester St C1
Tarnsyke Rd A1
Thurnham St C2
Town Hall B2
Troutbeck Rd B3
Ulleswater Rd B3
University of Cumbria C3
Vicarage Field B1
Vue B2
West Rd B1
Westbourne Dr C1
Westbourne Rd B1
Westham St C3
Wheatfield St B1
Williamson Rd B3
Willow La B1
Windermere Rd B3
Wingate-Saul Rd B1
Wolseley St B3
Woodville St B3
Wyresdale Rd C3

Leeds 336

Aire St B3
Aireside Ctr B2
Albion Pl B4
Albion St B4
Albion Way B1
Alma St A6
Arcades B4
Armley Rd B1
Back Burley Lodge Rd A1
Back Hyde Terr A2
Back Row C3
Bath Rd C3
Beckett St A6
Bedford St B3
Belgrave St A4
Belle View Rd A2
Benson St A5
Black Bull St C5
Blenheim Walk A3
Boar La B4
Bond St B4
Bow St C5
Bowman La C4
Brewery ✦ C4
Bridge St A5/B5
Briggate B4
Bruce Gdns C1
Burley Rd A1
Burley St B1
Burmantofs St B6
Bus & Coach Station B5
Butterly St C4
Butts Cr B4
Brewery Wharf C5
Byron St A5
Call La B4
Calverley St A3/B3
Canal St B1
Canal Wharf C3
Carlisle Rd C5
Cavendish Rd A1
Cavendish St A2
Chadwick St C5
Cherry Pl A6
Cherry Row A5
City Museum A4
City Pal of Varieties B4
City Sq B3
Civic Hall A3
Clarence Road C5
Clarendon Rd A2
Clarendon Way A3
Clark La C6
Clay Pit La A4
Cloberry St A2
Clyde Approach C1
Clyde Gdns C1
Coleman St C2
Commercial St B4
Concord St A5
Cookridge St A4
Copley Hill C1
Corn Exchange B4
Cromer Terr A2
Cromwell St A5
Cross Catherine St B6
Cross Green La C6
Cross Stamford St A5
Crown & County Courts A3
Crown Point Bridge C5
Crown Point Retail Pk C4
Crown Point Rd C4
David St C3
Dent St C6
Derwent Pl C3
Dial St C6
Dock St C4
Dolly La A6
Domestic St C2
Duke St B5
Duncan St B4
Dyer St B5
East Field St B6
East Pde B3
East St C5
Eastgate B5
Easy Rd C6
Edward St B4
Ellerby La C6
Ellerby Rd C6
Fenton St A3
Fire Station B2
Fish St B4
Flax Pl B5
Gelderd Rd C1
George St B4
Globe Rd C2
Gloucester Cr B1
Gower St A5
Grafton St A4
Grand Theatre B4
Granville Rd A6
Great George St A3
Great Wilson St C4
Greek St B3
Green La C1
Hanover Ave A2
Hanover La A2
Hanover Sq A2
Hanover Way A2
Harewood St B4
Harrison St B4
Haslewood Cl B6
Haslewood Drive B6
High Court B5
Holbeck La C2
Holdforth Cl C1
Holdforth Gdns B1
Holdforth Gr C1
Holdforth Pl C1
Holy Trinity B4

Hope Rd A5
Hunslet La C4
Hunslet Rd C4
Hyde Terr A2
Infirmary St B3
Information Ctr B3
Ingram Row C3
Junction St C4
Kelso Gdns A2
Kelso Rd A2
Kelso St A2
Kendal La A2
Kendell St C4
Kidacre St C4
King Edward St B4
King St B3
Kippax Pl C6
Kirkgate B4
Kirkgate Market B4
Kirkstall Rd A1
Kitson St C6
Lady La B4
Lands La B4
Lavender Walk B6
Leeds Art Gallery B3
Leeds Bridge C4
Leeds Coll of Music B5
Leeds General Infirmary (A&E) A3
Leeds Metropolitan University A3/A4
Leeds Museum Discovery Ctr C5
Leeds Shopping Plaza B4
Leeds Station B3
Leeds University A3
Library B3
Lincoln Green Rd A6
Lincoln Rd A6
Lindsey Gdns A6
Lindsey Rd A6
Lisbon St B3
Little Queen St B3
Long Close La C6
Lord St C2
Lovell Park A4
Lovell Park Rd A4
Lovell Rd A5
Lower Brunswick St A5
Mabgate A5
Macauly St A5
Magistrates Court A3
Manor Rd C3
Mark La B4
Marlborough St B2
Marsh La B5
Marshall St C3
Meadow La C4
Meadow Rd C4
Melbourne St A5
Merrion Ctr A4
Merrion St A4
Merrion Way A4
Mill St B5
Millennium Sq A3
Mount Preston St A2
Mushroom St A5
Neville St C4
New Briggate A4/B4
New Market St B4
New Station St B4
New York Rd A5
New York St B5
Nile St A5
Nippet La A6
North St A4
Northern St B3
Oak Rd B1
Oxford Pl B3
Oxford Row A3
Park Cross St B3
Park La A2
Park Pl B3
Park Row B4
Park Sq B3
Park Sq East B3
Park Sq West B3
Park St B3
Police Station B5
Pontefract La B6
Portland Cr A3
Portland Way A3
Post Office B4/B5
Project Space Leeds C2
Quarry House (NHS/DSS Headquarters) B5
Quebec St B3
Queen St B3
Railway St B5
Rectory St A6
Regent St A5
Richmond St C5
Rigton Approach B6
Rigton Dr B6
Rillbank La A1
Rosebank Rd A1
Royal Armouries C5
Russell St B3
Rutland St B2
St Anne's Cath (RC) ✝ A4
St Anne's St B4
St James' Hospital A6
St Johns Ctr B4
St John's Rd A2
St Mary's St B5
St Pauls St B3
St Peter's B5
Saxton La B5
Sayner La C5
Shakespeare Ave A6
Shannon St B6
Sheepscar St South A5
Siddall St C3
Skinner La A5
South Pde B3
Sovereign St C4
Spence La C2
Springfield Mount A2
Springwell Ct C2
Springwell Rd C2
Springwell St C2
Stoney Rock La A6
Studio Rd A1
Sutton St C2
Sweet St C3
Sweet St West C3
Swinegate B4
Templar St B5
The Calls B5
The Close B6
The Core B4
The Drive B6
The Garth B5
The Headrow B3/B4
The Lane B5
The Light B4
The Parade B6
Thoresby Pl A3
Torre Rd A6
Town Hall A3
Union Pl C3
Union St B5
Upper Accomodation Rd B6
Upper Basinghall St B4
Vicar La B4
Victoria Bridge C4
Victoria Quarter B4
Victoria Rd C4
Vue B4
Wade La A4
Washington St A1
Water La C3
Waterloo Rd C4
Wellington Rd B2/C1
Wellington St B3
West St B2
West Yorkshire Playhouse B5
Westfield Rd A1
Westgate B3
Whitehall Rd B3/C2
Whitelock St A5
Willis St C6
Willow Approach A1
Willow Ave A1
Willow Terrace Rd A3
Wintoun St A5
Woodhouse La A3/A4
Woodsley Rd A1
York Pl B3
York Rd B6
Yorkshire TV Studios A1

Leicester 336

Abbey St A2
All Saints' A1
Aylestone Rd C2
Bath La A1
Bede Park C1
Bedford St A3
Bedford St South A3
Belgrave Gate A2
Belle Vue A2
Belvoir St B2
Braunstone Gate B1
Burleys Way A2
Burnmoor St C2
Bus Station A2
Canning St A2
Carlton St C2
Castle B1
Castle Gardens B1
Cathedral ✝ B2
Causeway La A2
Charles St B3
Chatham St B2
Christow St A3
Church Gate A2
City Gallery B3
Civic Ctr B2
Clank St B2
Clock Tower ✦ B2
Clyde St A3
Colton St B3
Conduit St B3
Crafton St A3
Craven St A1
Crown Courts B3
Curve B3
De Lux A2
De Montfort Hall C3
De Montfort St C3
De Montfort Univ C1
Deacon St C2
Dover St B3
Duns La B1
Dunton St A1
East St B3
Eastern Boulevard C1
Edmonton Rd A3
Erskine St A3
Filbert St C1
Filbert St East C2
Fire Station C3
Fleet St A3
Friar La B2
Friday St A2
Gateway St C2
Glebe St B3
Granby St B3
Grange La C2
Grasmere St C1
Great Central St A1
Guildhall B2
Guru Nanak Sikh Museum B1
Halford St B2
Havelock St C2
Haymarket Sh Ctr A2
High St A2
Highcross St A1
Highcross Sh Ctr A2
HM Prison C2
Horsefair St B2
Humberstone Gate B2
Humberstone Rd A3
Infirmary St C2
Information Ctr B2
Jarrom St C2
Jewry Wall B1
Kamloops Cr A3
King Richards Rd B1
King St B2
Lancaster Rd C3
LCB Depot B3
Lee St A3
Leicester RFC C2
Leicester Royal Infirmary (A&E) C2
Leicester Station B3
Library B2
Little Theatre, The B3
London Rd C3
Lower Brown St B2
Magistrates Court B2
Manitoba Rd A3
Mansfield St A2
Market ✦ A2
Market St B2
Mill La C2
Montreal Rd A3
Narborough Rd North B1
Nelson Mandela Park C2
New Park St B1
New St B2
New Walk C3
New Walk Museum & Art Gallery C3
Newarke Houses B2
Newarke St B2
Northgate St A1
Orchard St A2
Ottawa Rd A3
Oxford St C2
Upper Brown St B2
Phoenix Square B3
Police Station A3
Post Office A1/B2/C2/C3
Prebend St C3
Princess Rd East C3
Princess Rd West C3
Queen St B3
Regent College C3
Regent Rd C2/C3
Repton St A1
Rutland St B3
St George St B3
St Georges Way B3
St John St A2
St Margaret's A2
St Margaret's Way A2
St Martins B2
St Mary de Castro B1
St Matthew's Way A3
St Nicholas B1
St Nicholas Circle B1
Sanvey Gate A2
Silver St B2
Slater St A1
Soar La A1
South Albion St B3
Southampton St B3
Swain St B3
Swan St A1
The Gateway C2
The Newarke B1
The Rally Com Park A2
Tigers Way C3
Tower St C3
Town Hall B2
Tudor Rd B1
University of Leicester C3
University Rd C3
Upperton Rd C1
Vaughan Way A2
Walnut St C2
Watling St A2
Welford Rd B2
Wellington St B2
West Bridge B1
West St C3
West Walk C3
Western Boulevard C1
Western Rd C1
Wharf St North A3
Wharf St South A3
Y' Theatre, The B3
Yeoman St B3
York Rd B2

Lewes 336

Abinger Pl B1
All Saints Ctr B2
Ambulance Station B2
Anne of Cleves Ho C1
Barbican Ho Mus B1
Brewery B2
Brook St A2
Brooks Rd A2
Bus Station B2
Castle Ditch La B1
Castle Precincts B1
Chapel Hill B3
Church La A1/A2
Cliffe High St B2
Cliffe Industrial Estate C3
Cluny St C1
Cockshut Rd C1
Convent Field C1
Coombe Rd A2
County Hall B1
County Records Office B1
Court B2
Court Rd B2
Crown Court B2
Cuilfail Tunnel B3
Davey's La A3
East St B2
Eastport La C1
Fire Station A2
Fisher St B2
Friars Walk B2
Garden St B1
Government Offices C2
Grange Rd B1
Ham La C2
Harveys Way B2
Hereward Way A2
High St B1/B2
Hop Gallery B2
Information Ctr B2
Keere St B1
King Henry's Rd B1
Lancaster St B2
Landport Rd A1
Leisure Ctr C3
Lewes Bridge B2
Lewes Castle B1
Lewes Football Gd C2
Lewes Golf Course B3
Lewes Southern By-Pass C2
Lewes Station B2
Library B2
Malling Ind Est A2
Malling Brook Ind Est A3
Malling Hill A3
Malling St A3/B3
Market St B2
Martyr's Monument B3
Mayhew Way A2
Morris Rd B3
Mountfield Rd C2
New Rd B1
Newton Rd A1
North St A2/B2
Offham Rd B1
Old Malling Way A1
Orchard Rd A3
Paddock La B1
Paddock Rd B1
Paddock Sports Gd B1
Park Rd B1
Pelham Terr A1
Pells Open Air Swimming Pool A1
Phoenix Causeway B2
Phoenix Ind Est B2
Phoenix Pl B2
Pinwell Rd B2
Police Station B1
Post Office A2/B1/B2/C1
Prince Edward's Rd B1
Priory St C1
Priory of St Pancras (remains of) ✦ C1
Railway La B2
Railway Land Nature Reserve B3
Rotten Row B1
Rufus Cl B1
St Pancras Rd C1
St John St B2
St John's Terr B1
St Nicholas La B2
Sewage Works C3
South Downs Bsns Pk A3
South St B3/C3
Southdowns Rd A2
Southerham Junction C3
Southover Grange Gdns ✦ B1
Southover High St C1
Southover Rd B1
Spences Field A3
Spences La A2
Stansfield Rd A1
Station Rd B2
Station St B2
Sun St B1
Sussex Downs College C2
Sussex Police HQ A2
Talbot Terr B1
The Avenue B1
The Course C1
The Martlets A2
The Needlemakers ✦ B2
The Pells A1
Thebes Gallery B2
Toronto Terr B1
Town Hall B2
West St B2
White Hill B1
Willeys Bridge A1

Lincoln 337

Alexandra Terr B1
Anchor St C1
Arboretum B3
Arboretum Ave B3
Baggholme Rd B3
Bailgate A2
Beaumont Fee B1
Brayford Way C1
Brayford Wharf East C1
Brayford Wharf North B1
Bruce Rd A2
Burton Rd A1
Bus Station (City) C2
Canwick Rd C2
Cardinal's Hat ✦ B2
Carline Rd B1
Castle B1
Castle St A1
Cathedral ✝ B2
Cathedral St B2
Cecil St A2
Chapel La A2
Cheviot St B3
Church La A2
City Hall B1
Clasketgate B2
Clayton Sports Gd A3
Coach Park C2
Collection, The B2
County Hospl (A&E) B3
County Office B1
Courts C1
Croft St B2
Cross St C2
Crown Courts B1
Curle Ave A3
Danesgate B2
Drill Hall B2
Drury La B1
East Bight A2
East Gate A2
Eastcliff Rd B3
Eastgate B2
Egerton Rd A3
Ellis Windmill A1
Engine Shed, The C1
Environment Agency C2
Exchequer Gate ✦ B2
Firth Rd C1
Flaxengate B2
Florence St B3
George St C3
Good La A2
Gray St A1
Great Northern Terr C3
Great Northern Terrace Industrial Estate C3
Greetwell Rd B3
Greetwellgate B3
Haffenden Rd A2
High St B2/C1
HM Prison A3
Hospital (Private) A2
Hungate B2
James St A2
Jews House & Ct B2
Kesteven St C2
Langworthgate A2
Lawn Visitor Ctr, The B1
Lee Rd A3
Library B2
Lincoln College B2
Lincoln Central Sta C2
Lincolnshire Life/Royal Lincolnshire Regiment Museum A1
Lindum Rd B2
Lindum Sports Ground A3
Lindum Terr B3
Mainwaring Rd A3
Manor Rd A2
Market C2
Massey Rd A3
Medieval Bishop's Palace B2
Mildmay St A1
Mill Rd A1
Millman Rd B3
Minster Yard B2
Monks Rd B3
Montague St B2
Mount St A1
Nettleham Rd A2
Newland B1
Newport A2
Newport Arch A2
Newport Cemetery A2
Northgate A2
Odeon C1
Orchard St B1
Oxford St C2
Park St B1
Pelham Bridge C2
Pelham St C2
Police Station B1
Portland St C2
Post Office A1/A2/B1/B3/C2
Potter Gate B2
Priory Gate B2
Queensway A3
Rasen La A1
Ropewalk C1
Rosemary La B2
St Anne's Rd B3
St Benedict's C1
St Giles Ave A3
St John's Rd A2
St Marks St C1
St Mark's Sh Ctr C1
St Mary-Le-Wigford C1
St Mary's St C2
St Nicholas St A2
St Swithin's B2
Saltergate C1
Saxon St A1
Sch of Art & Design B2
Sewell Rd B3
Silver St B2
Sincil St C2
Spital St A2
Spring Hill B1
Stamp End C3
Steep Hill B2
Stonebow & Guildhall C2
Stonefield Ave A2
Tentercroft St C1
The Avenue B1
The Grove A3
Theatre Royal B2
Tritton Retail Park C1
Tritton Rd C1
Union Rd B1
University of Lincoln C1
Upper Lindum St B3
Upper Long Leys Rd A1
Usher B2
Vere St A2
Victoria St B1
Victoria Terr B1
Vine St B3
Wake St A1
Waldeck St A1
Waterside Sh Ctr C2
Waterside North C2
Waterside South C2
West Pde B1
Westgate A2
Wigford Way C1
Williamson St A2
Wilson St A1
Winn St B3
Wragby Rd A3
Yarborough Rd A1

Liverpool 337

Abercromby Sq C5
Acc Liverpool ✦ C2
Addison St A3
Adelaide Rd B6
Ainsworth St B4
Albany Rd B6
Albert Dock C2
Albert Edward Rd B6
Angela St C6
Anson St B4
Archbishop Blanche High School B6
Argyle St C3
Arrad St C4
Ashton St B5
Audley St A4
Back Leeds St A2
Basnett St B3
Bath St A1
Beatles Story C2
Beckwith St C3
Bedford Close C5
Bedford St North C5
Bedford St South C5
Benson St C4
Berry St C4
Birkett St A4
Bixteth St B2
Blackburne Place C4
Bluecoat B3
Bold Place C4
Bold St C4
Bolton St B3
Bridport St B4
Bronte St B4
Brook St A1
Brownlow Hill B4/B5
Brownlow St B5
Brunswick Rd A5
Brunswick St B1
Bus Station C2
Butler Cr A6
Byrom St A3
Caledonia St C4
Cambridge St C5
Camden St A4
Canada Blvd B1
Canning Dock C2
Canterbury St A4
Cardwell St C6
Carver St A4
Cases St B3
Castle St B2
Catherine St C5
Cavern Club B3
Central Library A3
Central Station B3
Chapel St B2
Charlotte St B3
Chatham Place C6
Chatham St C5
Cheapside B2
Chestnut St C5
Christian St A3
Church St B3
Churchill Way North A3
Churchill Way South B3
Clarence St B4
Coach Station A4
Cobden St A5
Cockspur St A2
College St C3
College St North A5
College St South A5
Colquitt St C4
Comus St A3
Concert St C3
Connaught Rd B6
Cook St B2
Copperas Hill B4
Cornwallis St C3
Covent Garden B2
Craven St A4
Cropper St B3
Crown St B5/C6
Cumberland St B2
Cunard Building B1
Dale St B2
Dansie St B4
Daulby St B5
Dawson St B3
Derby Sq B2
Drury La B2
Duckinfield St B4
Duke St C3
Earle St A2
East St A2
Eaton St A2
Edgar St A3
Edge La B6
Edinburgh Rd A6
Edmund St B2
Elizabeth St B5
Elliot St B3
Empire Theatre B4
Empress Rd B6
Epworth St A5
Erskine St A5
Everyman Theatre C5
Exchange St East B2
Fact Ctr, The ✦ C4
Falkland St A5
Falkner St C5/C6
Farnworth St A6
Fenwick St B2
Fielding St A6
Fleet St C3
Fraser St A4
Freemasons Row A2
Gardner Row A3
Gascoyne St A2
George Pier Head C1
George St B2
Gibraltar Road A1
Gilbert St C3
Gildart St A4
Gill St B4
Goree B2
Gower St C2
Gradwell St C3
Great Crosshall St A3
Great George St C4
Great Howard St A1
Great Newton St B4
Greek St B4
Green La B4
Greenside A5
Greetham St C3
Gregson St A5
Grenville St C3
Grinfield St C6
Grove St C5
Guelph St A6
Hackins Hey B2
Haigh St A4
Hall La B6
Hanover St B3
Harbord St C6
Hardman St C4
Harker St A4
Hart St B4
Hatton Garden A2
Hawke St B4
Helsby St B6
Henry St C3
HM Customs & Excise National Museum C2
Highfield St A2
Highgate St B6
Hilbre St B4
Hope Place C4
Hope St C4
Houghton St B3
Hunter St A3
Hutchinson St A6
Information Ctr C2
Institute For The Performing Arts C4
Irvine St B6
Irwell St B2
Islington A4
James St B2
James St Station B2
Jenkinson St A4
Johnson St A3
Jubilee Drive B6
Kempston St A4
Kensington A6
Kensington Gdns B6
Kensington St A6
Kent St C3
King Edward St A1
Kinglake St B6
Knight St C4
Lace St A3
Langsdale St A4
Law Courts C2
Leece St C4
Leeds St A2
Leopold Rd B6
Lime St B3
Lime St Station B4
Little Woolton St B5
Liver St C2
Liverpool John Moores University A3/B4/C4
Liverpool Landing Stage B1
Liverpool One C2
London Rd A4/B4
Lord Nelson St B4
Lord St B2
Lovat St C6
Low Hill A5
Low Wood St A6
Lydia Ann St C3
Mansfield St A4
Marmaduke St B6
Marsden St A6
Martensen St B6
Marybone A3
Maryland St C4
Mason St B6
Mathew St B2
May St B4
Melville Place C6
Merseyside Maritime Museum C2
Metquarter B3
Metropolitan Cathedral (RC) ✝ B5
Midghall St A2
Molyneux Rd A6
Moor Place B4
Moorfields B2
Moorfields Station B2
Moss St A5
Mount Pleasant B4/B5
Mount St C4
Mount Vernon B6
Mulberry St C5
Municipal Buildings B2
Mus of Liverpool C2
Myrtle Gdns C6
Myrtle St C5
Naylor St A2
Nelson St C4
Neptune Theatre B3
New Islington A4
New Quay B1
Newington St C3
North John St B2
North St A3
North View B6
Norton St A4
Oakes St B5
O2 Academy
Odeon B4
Old Hall St A1
Old Leeds St A2
Oldham Place C4
Oldham St C4
Olive St C6
Open Eye Gallery C3
Oriel St A2
Ormond St B2
Orphan St C6
Overbury St C6
Overton St B6
Oxford St C5
Paisley St A1
Pall Mall A2
Paradise St C3
Park La C3
Parker St B3
Parr St C3
Peach St B5
Pembroke Place B4
Pembroke St B5
Philharmonic Hall C5
Pickop St A2
Pilgrim St C4
Pitt St C3
Playhouse Theatre B3
Pleasant St B4
Police HQ C2
Police Station A4/B4
Pomona St B4
Port of Liverpool Building B2
Post Office A2/A4/A5/A6/B2/B3/B4/C4
Pownall St C2
Prescot St A5
Preston St B3
Princes Dock A1
Princes Gdns A2
Princes Jetty A1
Princes Pde B1
Princes St B2
Pythian St A6
Queen Sq Bus Station B3
Queensland St C6
Queensway Tunnel (Docks exit) B1
Queensway Tunnel (Entrance) B3
Radio City B2
Ranelagh St B3
Redcross St B2
Renfrew St B6
Renshaw St B4
Richmond Row A4
Richmond St B3
Rigby St A2
Roberts St A1
Rock St B4
Rodney St C4
Rokeby St A4
Romily St A6
Roscoe La C4
Roscoe St C4
Rose Hill A3
Royal Court Theatre B3
Royal Liver Building B1
Royal Liverpool Hospital (A&E) B5
Royal Mail St B4
Rumford Place B2
Rumford St B2
Russell St B4
St Andrew St B4
St Anne St A4
St Georges Hall B3
St John's Ctr B3
St John's Gdns B3
St John's La B3
St Joseph's Cr A4
St Minishull St B5
St Nicholas Place B1
St Paul's Sq A2
St Vincent Way B4
Salisbury St A4
Salthouse Dock C2
Salthouse Quay C2
Sandon St C5
Saxony Rd B6
Schomberg St A6
School La B2
Seel St C3
Seymour St B4
Shaw St A5
Sidney Place C6
Sir Thomas St B3
Skelhorne St B4
Slater St C3
Slavery Museum C2
Smithdown La B6
Soho Sq A4
Soho St A4
South John St B2
Springfield A4
Stafford St A4
Standish St A3
Stanley St B2
Strand St C2
Suffolk St C3
Tabley St C3
Tarleton St B3
Tate Gallery C2
Teck St B6
Temple St B2
The Beacon ✦ B3
The Strand B2
Tithebarn St B2
Town Hall B2
Traffic Police HQ C6
Trowbridge St B4
Trueman St A3
Union St B2
Unity Theatre C4
University C5
University of Liverpool B5
Upper Duke St C4
Upper Frederick St C3
Upper Baker St A6
Vauxhall Rd A2
Vernon St B2
Victoria Gallery & Museum B5
Victoria St B2
Vine St C5
Wakefield St A4
Walker Art Gallery A3
Walker St A6
Wapping C2
Water St B1/B2
Waterloo Rd A1
Wavertree Rd B6
West Derby Rd A6
West Derby St B5
Whitechapel B3
Western Approaches War Museum B2
Whitley Gdns A5
William Brown St B3
William Henry St A4
Williamson Sq B3
Williamson St B3
Williamson's Tunnels Heritage Ctr ✦ C6
Women's Hospital C6
Wood St B3
World Museum, Liverpool A3
York St C3

Llandudno 337

Abbey Pl B1
Abbey Rd B1
Adelphi St B3
Alexandra Rd C2
Anglesey Rd A1
Argyll Rd B3
Arvon Ave A2
Atlee Cl C3
Augusta St B3
Back Madoc St B2
Bodafon St B3
Bodhyfryd Rd A2
Bodnant Cr C3
Bodnant Rd C3
Bridge Rd C2
Bryniau Rd C1
Builder St B3
Builder St West C2
Cabin Lift A2
Camera Obscura ✦ A3
Caroline Rd B2
Chapel St A2
Charlton St B3
Church Cr C1
Church Walks A2
Claremont Rd B2
Clement Ave A2
Clifton Rd B2
Clonmel St B3
Coach Station B3
Conway Rd B3
Council St West C3
Cricket and Rec Gd B2
Cwlach Rd A2
Cwlach St A1
Cwm Howard La C3
Cwm Pl C3
Cwm Rd C3
Dale Rd C1
Deganwy Ave B2
Denness Pl C2
Dinas Rd C2
Dolydd B1
Erol Pl B2
Ewloe Dr C3
Fairways C2
Ffordd Dewi C3
Ffordd Dulyn C2
Ffordd Dwyfor C3
Ffordd Elisabeth C3
Ffordd Gwynedd C3
Ffordd Las C3
Ffordd Morfa C3
Ffordd Penrhyn C3
Ffordd Tudno C3
Ffordd yr Orsedd C3
Ffordd Ysbyty C2
Fire & Ambulance Sta B3
Garage St B3
George St A2
Gloddaeth Ave B1
Gloddaeth St B2
Gogarth Rd B1
Great Orme Mines ✦ A1
Great Ormes Rd B1
Happy Valley A2
Happy Valley Rd A3
Haulfre Gardens A1
Herkomer Cr C1
Hill Terr A2
Home Front Mus B2
Hospice B1
Howard Rd B3
Information Ctr B2
Invalids' Walk B1
James St B2
Jubilee St B3
King's Ave C2
King's Rd C2
Knowles Rd C2
Lees Rd C2
Library B2
Lifeboat Station B2
Llandudno A2
Llandudno (A&E) C3
Llandudno Station B3
Llandudno Town Football Ground C2
Llewelyn Ave A2
Lloyd St West B1
Lloyd St B2
Llwynon Rd A1
Llys Maelgwn B1
Madoc St B2
Maelgwn Rd B2
Maesdu Bridge C2
Maesdu Rd C2/C3
Maes-y-Cwm C3
Maes-y-Orsedd C3
Marian Pl C2
Marian Rd C2
Marine Drive (Toll) A3
Market Hall A2
Market St A2
Miniature Golf Course A1
Morfa Rd B1
Mostyn B3
Mostyn Broadway B3

Mostyn St B3
Mowbray Rd C2
New St B2
Norman Rd B3
North Parade A2
North Wales Golf Links C1
Old Bank Gallery A2
Old Rd A2
Oxford Rd B3
Parc Llandudno Ret Pk B3
Pier ✦ A3
Plas Rd A2
Police Station B3
Post Office B3/C2
Promenade A3
Pyllau Rd A1
Rectory La A2
Rhuddlan Ave C3
St Andrew's Ave B2
St Andrew's Pl B2
St Beuno's Rd A1
St David's Pl B2
St David's Rd B2
St George's Pl A3
St Mary's Rd B2
St Seriol's Rd B2
Salisbury Pass B1
Salisbury Rd B2
Somerset St B3
South Parade A2
Stephen St B3
TA Ctr B3
Tabor Hill A2
The Oval B1
The Parade B3
Town Hall A2
Trinity Ave B1
Trinity Cres C1
Trinity Sq B3
Tudno St A2
Ty-Coch Rd A2
Ty-Gwyn Rd A1/A2
Ty'n-y-Coed Rd A1
Vaughan St B3
Victoria Shopping Ctr B3
Victoria Tram Station A2
War Memorial ✦ A2
Werny Wylan C3
West Parade B1
Whiston Pass A2
Winllan Ave C2
Wyddfyd Rd A2
York Rd A2

Llanelli 337

Alban Rd B3
Albert St B1
Als St B3
Amos St C1
Andrew St A3
Ann St C2
Annesley St B2
Arfryn Ave A3
Arthur St B2
Belvedere Rd A1
Bigyn La B3
Bigyn Park Terr C3
Bigyn Rd C3
Bond Ave C3
Brettenham St A1
Bridge St B2
Bryn Pl C1
Bryn Rd C1
Bryn Terr C1
Brynhyfryd Rd A2
Brynmelyn Ave A3
Brynmor Rd B1
Bryn-More Rd C1
Burry St C1
Bus Station B2
Caersalem Terr C2
Cambrian St C1
Caswell St C3
Cedric St B3
Cemetery A2
Chapman St A1
Charles Terr C2
Church St B2
Clos Caer Elms A1
Clos Sant Paul C2
Coastal Link Rd B1/C1
Coldstream St B2
Coleshill Terr B1
College Hill B3
College Sq B3
Copperworks Rd C2
Coronation Rd C3
Corporation Ave A3
Council Offices B2
Court B2
Cowell St B2
Cradock St C2
Craig Ave C3
Cricket Ground A1
Derwent St A1
Dillwyn St C2
Druce St C1
Elizabeth St B2
Emma St C2
Erw Rd B1
Felinfoel Rd A2
Fire Station A3
Firth Rd C3
Fron Terr C3
Furnace Rugby Football Ground A1
Gelli-On B2
George St C2
Gilbert Cres A2
Gilbert Rd A2
Glanmor Rd C2
Glanmor Terr C2
Glasfryn Terr A3
Glenalla Rd B3
Glevering St B3
Goring Rd A2
Gorsedd Circle A2
Grant St C3
Graveyard C2
Great Western Cl C2
Greenway St B1
Hall St B2
Harries Ave A2
Hedley Terr A2
Heol Elli B3
Heol Goffa A3
Heol Nant-y-Felin A3
Heol Siloh B2
Hick St C2
High St C1
Indoor Bowls Ctr B1
Inkerman St B2
Island Pl B2
James St B2
John St B2
King George Ave B3
Lake View Cl A2
Lakefield Pl C1
Lakefield Rd C1
Langland Rd C3
Leisure Ctr B1
Library B2
Llanelli House B2
Llanelli Parish Church B2
Llanelli RUFC (Stradey Park) A1
Llanelli Station C2
Llewellyn St C2
Lliedi Cres A3
Lloyd St B2
Llys Alys B3
Llys Fran A3
Llysnewedd C1
Long Row A3
Maes Gors C2
Maesyrhaf A3
Mansel St C3
Marblehall Rd B3
Marborough Rd A2
Margam St C3
Marged St C2
Marine St C1
Market B2
Market St B2
Marsh St C2
Martin Rd C3
Miles St A1
Mill La A3/B2
Mincing La B2
Murray St B2
Myn y Mor B1
Nathan St C1
Nelson Terr C1
Nevill St C2
New Dock Rd C2
New Rd A1
New Zealand St A1
Old Lodge C2
Old Rd A2
Paddock St C2
Palace Ave B3
Parc Howard A2
Parc Howard Museum & Art Gallery A2
Park Cres B1
Park St B2
Parkview Terr B1
Pemberton St C2
Pembrey Rd A1
Peoples Park B1
Police Station B2
Post Office A1/A2/B2/C1/C2
Pottery Pl B3
Pottery St B3
Princess St B1
Prospect Pl A2
Pryce St A1
Queen Mary's Walk C3
Queen Victoria Rd C1
Raby St B1
Railway Terr C2
Ralph St B2
Ralph Terr C1
Regalia Terr B3
Rhydyrafon A3
Richard St B2
Robinson St B2
Roland Ave A1
Russell St C3
St David's Cl C1
St Elli Shopping Ctr B2
St Margaret's Dr A1
Spowart Ave A1
Station Rd B2/C2
Stepney Pl B2
Stepney St B2
Stewart St A1
Stradey Park Ave A1
Sunny Hill A2
Swansea Rd A3
TA Ctr B2
Talbot St C3
Temple St B3
The Avenue Cilfig A2
The Mariners C1
Theatr Elli B2
Thomas St A2
Toft Pl A3
Town Hall B2
Traeth Ffordd C1
Trinity Rd C3
Trinity Terr C2
Tunnel Rd B3
Tyisha Rd C3
Union Blgs A2
Upper Robinson St B2
Vauxhall Rd B2
Walter's Rd B3
Waun Lanyrafon B2
Waun Rd A3
Wern Rd B3
West End A2
Y Bwthyn C3
Zion Row B3

London 338

Abbey Orchard St E4
Abbey St E8
Abchurch La D7
Abingdon St E5
Achilles Way D3
Acton St B5
Addington St E5
Air St D4
Albany St B3
Albemarle St D4
Albert Embankment F5
Alberta St F6
Aldenham St A4
Alderney St F3
Aldersgate St C7
Aldford St D3
Aldgate ⊖ C8
Aldgate High St C8
Aldwych C5
Allsop Pl B2
Alscot Rd E8
Amwell St B6
Andrew Borde St C4
Angel ⊖ A6
Appold St C8
Argyle Sq B5
Argyle St B5
Argyll St C4
Arnold Circus B8
Artillery La C8
Artillery Row E4
Ashbridge St B2
Association of Photographers Gallery B7
Baker St ⊖ B2
Baker St B2
Balaclava Rd F8
Balcombe St B2
Baldwin's Gdns C6
Balfour St F7
Baltic St B7
Bank ⊖ C7
Bank Museum C7
Bank of England C7
Bankside D7
Bankside Gallery D7
Banner St B7
Barbican ⊖ C7
Barbican Gallery C7
Basil St E2
Bastwick St B7
Bateman's Row B8
Bath St B7
Bath Terr E7
Bayley St C4
Baylis Rd E6
Bayswater Rd D2
Beak St D4
Beauchamp Pl E2
Bedford Row C5
Bedford Sq C4
Bedford St D5
Bedford Way B4
Beech St C7
Belgrave Pl E3
Belgrave Rd F4
Belgrave Sq E3
Bell La C8
Belvedere Rd E5
Berkeley Sq D3
Berkeley St D3
Bermondsey St E8
Bernard St B5
Berners Pl C4
Berners St C4
Berwick St C4
Bessborough St F4
Bethnal Green Rd B8
Bevenden St B7
Bevis Marks C8
BFI London IMAX Cinema D6
Bidborough St B5
Binney St C3
Birdcage Walk E4
Bishopsgate C8
Black Prince Rd F5
Blackfriars ⊖ D6
Blackfriars Bridge D6
Blackfriars Rd E6
Blandford St C2
Blomfield St C7
Bloomsbury St C4
Bloomsbury Way C5
Bolton St D3
Bond St ⊖ C3
Borough ⊖ E7
Borough High St E6
Borough Rd E6
Boswell St C5
Bourne St F3
Bow St C5
Bowling Green La B6
Brad St D6
Brandon St F7
Bressenden Pl E4
Brewer St D4
Brick St D3
Bridge St E5
Britain at War D8
Britannia Walk B7
British Library B4
British Museum C5
Britton St B6
Broad Sanctuary E4
Broadley St C2
Broadway E4
Brompton Rd E2
Brompton Sq E2
Brook Dr F6
Brook St D3
Brown St C2
Brunswick Pl B7
Brunswick Sq B5
Brushfield St C8
Bruton St D3
Bryanston St C2
Buckingham Gate E4
Buckingham Palace E4
Buckingham Palace Rd F3
Bunhill Row B7
Byward St D8
Cabinet War Rooms & Churchill Museum E4
Cadogan La E3
Cadogan Pl E3
Cadogan Sq F2
Cadogan St F2
Cale St F2
Caledonian Rd A5
Calshot St A5
Calthorpe St B5
Calvert Ave B8
Cambridge Circus C4
Cambridge Sq C2
Cambridge St F3
Camomile St C8
Cannon St D7
Cannon St ⊖ D7
Capland St B1
Carey St C5
Carlisle La E5
Carlisle Pl E4
Carlton House Terr D4
Carmelite St D6
Carnaby St C4
Carter La C6
Carthusian St C7
Cartwright Gdns B5
Castle Baynard St D6
Cavendish Pl C3
Cavendish Sq C3
Caxton Hall E4
Caxton St E4
Central St B7
Chalton St B4
Chancery Lane ⊖ C6
Chapel St C2
Chapel St E3
Charing Cross ⊖ D5
Charing Cross Rd C4
Charles II St D4
Charles Sq B7
Charles St D3
Charlotte Rd B8
Charlotte St C4
Chart St B7
Charterhouse Sq C6
Charterhouse St C6
Chatham St F7
Cheapside C7
Chenies St C4
Chesham St E3
Chester Sq F3
Chester Way F6
Chesterfield Hill D3
Cheval Pl E2
Chiltern St C3
Chiswell St C7
Church St C2
City Garden Row A6
City Rd B7
City Thameslink C6
City University, The B6
Claremont Sq A6
Clarendon St F3
Clarges St D3
Clerkenwell Cl B6
Clerkenwell Green B6
Clerkenwell Rd B6
Cleveland St C4
Clifford St D4
Clink Prison Mus D7
Cliveden Pl F3
Clock Museum C7
Club Row B8
Cockspur St D4
Coleman St C7
Columbia Rd B8
Commercial Rd C9
Commercial St C8
Compton St B6
Conduit St D3
Congreve St F8
Connaught Sq C2
Connaught St C2
Constitution Hill E3
Copperfield St E6
Coptic St C5
Cornhill C7
Cornwall Rd D6
Coronet St B8
County St E7
Courtauld Gallery D5
Courtenay St F6
Covent Garden ⊖ D5
Covent Garden ✦ D5
Cowcross St C6
Cowper St B7
Crampton St F7
Cranbourn St D4
Craven St D5
Crawford Pl C2
Crawford St C2
Creechurch La C8
Cricket Museum B1
Cromer St B5
Cromwell Rd F1
Crosby Row E7
Crucifix La E8
Cumberland Gate D2
Cumberland St F3
Cumberland Terr A3
Cuming Mus F7
Curtain Rd B8
Curzon St D3
Dante Rd F6
D'arblay St C4
Davies St C3
Dean St C4
Deluxe Gallery B8
Denbigh Pl F4
Denmark St C4
Dering St C3
Devonshire St C3
Diana, Princess of Wales Memorial Garden ✦ D1
Diana, Princess of Wales Memorial Walk E4
Dingley Rd B7
Dorset St C2
Doughty St B5
Douglas St F4
Dover St D3
Downing St E5
Draycott Avenue F2
Draycott Pl F2
Druid St E8
Drummond St B4
Drury La C5
Drysdale St B8
Duchess St C3
Dufferin St B7
Duke of Wellington Pl E3
Duke St C3/D3
Duke St Hill D7
Duke's Pl C8
Duncannon St D5
Dunton Rd F8
East Rd B7
East St F7
Eastcastle St C4
Eastcheap D8
Eastman Dental Hospital B5
Eaton Gate F3
Eaton Pl E3
Eaton Sq E3
Eaton Terr F3
Ebury Bridge F3
Ebury Bridge Rd F3
Eccleston Bridge F3
Eccleston Sq F3
Eccleston St E3
Edgware Rd C2
Edgware Rd ⊖ C2
Egerton Gdns E2
Eldon St C7
Elephant & Castle F7
Elephant and Castle ⊖ E6
Elephant Rd F7
Elizabeth Bridge F3
Elizabeth St F3
Elm Tree Rd B1
Elystan Pl F2
Elystan St F2
Embankment ⊖ D5
Endell St C5
Endsleigh Pl B4
Enid St E8
Ennismore Gdns E2
Erasmus St F4
Euston ⊖ B4
Euston Rd B4
Euston Square ⊖ B4
Evelina Children's Hospital E5
Eversholt St A4
Exhibition Rd E1
Exmouth Market B6
Fair St E8
Falmouth Rd E7
Fann St B7
Farringdon ⊖ C6
Farringdon Rd C6
Farringdon St C6
Featherstone St B7
Fenchurch St D8
Fenchurch St D8
Fetter La C6
Finsbury Circus C7
Finsbury Pavement C7
Finsbury Sq B7
Fitzalan St F6
Fitzmaurice Pl D3
Fleet St C6
Fleming Lab. Mus C1
Floral St D5
Florence Nightingale Museum E5
Folgate St C8
Fore St C7
Foster La C7
Francis St F4
Frazier St E6
Freemason's Hall C5
Friday St C7
Fulham Rd F1
Gainsford St E8
Garden Row E6
Gee St B7
Geological Mus E1
George Row E9
George St C2
Gerrard St D4
Gibson Rd F5
Giltspur St C6
Glasshouse St D4
Glasshouse Walk F5
Gloucester Pl C2
Gloucester Sq C1
Gloucester St F4
Golden Hinde D7
Golden La B7
Golden Sq D4
Goodge St ⊖ C4
Goodge St C4
Gordon Hospital F4
Gordon Sq B4
Goswell Rd B6
Gough St B5
Goulston St C8
Gower St B4
Gracechurch St D7
Grafton Way B4
Graham Terr F3
Grange Rd E8
Grange Walk E8
Gray's Inn Rd B5
Great College St E5
Great Cumberland Pl C2
Great Dover St E7
Great Eastern St B8
Great Guildford St D7
Great Marlborough St C4
Great Ormond St B5
Great Ormond Street Children's Hospital B5
Great Percy St B5
Great Peter St E4
Great Portland St ⊖ B3
Great Portland St C3
Great Queen St C5
Great Russell St C4
Great Scotland Yd D5
Great Smith St E4
Great Suffolk St D6/E6
Great Titchfield St C4
Great Tower St D8
Great Windmill St D4
Greek St C4
Green Park ⊖ D4
Green St D3
Greencoat Pl F4
Gresham St C7
Greville St B5/C6
Greycoat Hosp Sch E4
Greycoat Pl E4
Grosvenor Cres E3
Grosvenor Gdns E3
Grosvenor Pl E3
Grosvenor Sq D3
Grosvenor St D3
Grove End Rd B1
Guards Museum and Chapel E4
Guildhall Art Gallery C7
Guilford St B5
Guy's Hospital D7
Haberdasher St B7
Hackney Rd B8
Half Moon St D3
Halkin St E3
Hall PL B1
Hall St B6
Hallam St C3
Hamilton CL B1
Hampstead Rd B4
Hanover Sq C3
Hans Cres E2
Hans Rd E2
Hanway St C4
Hardwick St B6
Harewood Ave B2
Harley St C3
Harper Rd E7
Harrington Rd F1
Harrison St B5
Harrowby St C2
Hasker St F2
Hastings St B5
Hatfields D6
Hayles St F6
Haymarket D4
Hayne St C6
Hay's Galleria D8
Hay's Mews D3
Hayward Gallery D5
Helmet Row B7
Herbrand St B5
Hercules Rd E5
Hertford St D3
Heygate St F7
High Holborn C5
Hill St D3
HMS Belfast D8
Hobart Pl E3
Holborn ⊖ C5
Holborn C6
Holborn Viaduct C6
Holland St D6
Holmes Mus B2
Holywell La B8
Horse Guards' Rd D4
Horseferry Rd F4
Houndsditch C8
Houses of Parliament E5
Howland St C4
Hoxton Sq B8
Hoxton St B8
Hugh St F3
Hunter St B5
Hunterian Mus C5
Hyde Park D2
Hyde Park Cnr ⊖ E3
Hyde Park Cres C2
Hyde Park St C2
Imperial Coll London E1
Imperial College Rd E1
Imperial War Mus E6
Inner Circle B3
Institute of Archaeology (London Univ) B4
Ironmonger Row B7
Jacob St E9
Jamaica Rd E8
James St C3
James St D5
Jermyn St D4
Jockey's Fields C5
John Carpenter St D6
John Fisher St D9
John Islip St F5
John St B5
Johnathan St F5
Judd St B5
Kennings Way F6
Kennington ⊖ F6
Kennington La F6
Kennington Park Rd F6
Kennington Rd E6/F6
Kensington Gardens D1
Kensington Gore E1
Kensington Rd E1
Keyworth St E6
King Charles St E5
King St D4
King William St C7
Kingley St C4
King's Cross A5
King's Cross Rd B5
King's Cross St Pancras ⊖ A5
King's Rd F2
Kingsland Rd B8
Kingsway C5
Kinnerton St E3
Kipling St E7
Knightsbridge ⊖ E2
Lamb St C8
Lambeth Bridge F5
Lambeth High St F5
Lambeth North ⊖ E6
Lambeth Palace E5
Lambeth Palace Rd E5
Lambeth Rd E6
Lambeth Walk F5
Lamb's Conduit St C5
Lancaster Gate ⊖ D1
Lancaster Pl D5
Lancaster St E6
Lancaster Terr D1
Langham Pl C3
Lant St E7
Leadenhall St C8
Leake St E5
Leather La C6
Leathermarket St E8
Leicester Sq ⊖ D4
Leicester St D4
Leonard St B7
Leroy St E8
Lever St B7
Lexington St D4
Lidlington Pl A4
Lime St D8
Lincoln's Inn Fields C5
Lindsey St C6
Lisle St D4
Lisson Gr B1
Lisson St C2
Liverpool St C8
Liverpool St ⊖ C8
Lloyd Baker St B6
Lloyd Sq B6
Lodge Rd B2
Lollard St F6
Lombard St C7
London Aquarium E5
London Bridge ⊖ D7
London Bridge Hospital D7
London City Hall D8
London Dungeon D7
London Film Mus E5
London Guildhall Univ C7
London Rd E6
London St C1
London Transport Museum D5
London Wall C7
London-Eye ✦ E5
Long Acre D5
Long La C6
Long La E7
Longford St B3
Lord's Cricket Gd (MCC & Middlesex CCC) B1
Lower Belgrave St E3
Lower Grosvenor Pl E3
Lower Marsh E6
Lower Sloane St F3
Lower Thames St D7
Lowndes St E3
Ludgate Circus C6
Ludgate Hill C6
Luxborough St C3
Lyall St E3
Macclesfield Rd B7
Madame Tussaud's ✦ B3
Maddox St D3
Malet St C4
Maltby St E8
Manchester Sq C3
Manchester St C3
Manciple St E7
Mandela Way F8
Mandeville Pl C3
Mansell St D8
Mansion House C7
Mansion House ⊖ D7
Maple St C4
Marble Arch ⊖ C2
Marble Arch D2
Marchmont St B5
Margaret St C4
Margery St B6
Mark La D8
Marlborough Rd D4
Marshall St C4
Marshalsea Rd E7
Marsham St E4
Marylebone ⊖ B2
Marylebone High St C3
Marylebone La C3
Marylebone Rd B3/C2
Marylebone St C3
Mecklenburgh Sq B5
Middle Temple La C6
Middlesex St (Petticoat La) C8
Midland Rd A4
Millbank F5
Milner St F2
Minories C8
Monck St E4
Monkton St F6
Monmouth St C5
Montagu Pl C2
Montagu Sq C2
Montagu St C5
Montague Pl C4
Montpelier St E2
Montpelier Walk E2
Monument ⊖ D7
Monument St D7
Monument, The ✦ D7
Moor La C7
Moorfields C7
Moorfields Eye Hospital B7
Moorgate C7
Moorgate ⊖ C7
Moreland St B6
Morley St E6
Mortimer St C4
Mossop St F2
Mount Pleasant B6
Mount St D3
Murray Gr A7
Mus of Gdn History E5
Museum of London C7
Museum St C5
Myddelton Sq B6
Myddelton St B6
National Film Theatre D5
National Gallery D4
National Hospital B5
National Portrait Gallery D4
Natural History Museum E1
Neal St C5
Nelson's Column ✦ D5
Neville St F1
New Bond St C3/D3
New Bridge St C6
New Cavendish St C3
New Change C7
New Fetter La C6
New Inn Yard B8
New Kent Rd F7
New North Rd A7
New Oxford St C4
New Scotland Yard E4
New Sq C5
Newburn St F5
Newgate St C6
Newington Butts F6
Newington Cswy E7
Newton St C5
Nile St B7
Noble St C7
Noel St C4
Norfolk Cres C2
Norfolk Sq C1
North Audley St D3
North Carriage Dr D2
North Cres C4
North Ride D2
North Row D3
North Wharf Rd C1
Northampton Sq B6
Northington St B5
Northumberland Ave D5
Norton Folgate C8
Nottingham Pl C3
Old Bailey C6
Old Broad St C7
Old Brompton Rd F1
Old Compton St C4
Old County Hall E5
Old Gloucester St C5
Old Jamaica Rd E9
Old Kent Rd F8
Old King Edward St C7
Old Marylebone Rd C2
Old Montague St C9
Old Nichol St B8
Old Paradise St F5
Old Spitalfields Mkt C8
Old St B7
Old St ⊖ B7
Old Vic E6
Onslow Gdns F1
Onslow Sq F1
Ontario St E6
Open Air Theatre B3
Operating Theatre Museum D7
Orange St D4
Orchard St C3
Ossulston St A4
Outer Circle B2
Ovington Sq E2
Oxford Circus ⊖ C4
Oxford St C3/C4
Paddington Green Hospital C1
Paddington St C3
Page's Walk E8
Palace St E4
Pall Mall D4
Pall Mall East D4
Pancras Rd A5
Panton St D4
Paris Gdn D6
Park Cres B3
Park La D3
Park Rd B2
Park St D3
Park St D7
Parker St C5
Parliament Sq E5
Parliament St E5
Paternoster Sq C6
Paul St B7
Pear Tree St B6
Pelham Cres F2
Pelham St F1
Penfold St C2
Penton Pl F6
Penton Rise B5
Penton St A6
Pentonville Rd A5/A6
Percival St B6
Petticoat La (Middlesex St) C8
Petty France E4
Phoenix Pl B5
Phoenix Rd A4
Photo Gallery D4
Piccadilly D3
Piccadilly Circus ⊖ D4
Pilgrimage St E7
Pimlico ⊖ F4
Pimlico Rd F3
Pitfield St B8
Pollock's Toy Mus C4
Polygon Rd A4
Pont St E2
Porchester Pl C2
Portland Pl C3
Portman Mews C3
Portman Sq C3
Portman St C2
Portugal St C5
Poultry C7
Praed St C1
Primrose St C8
Prince Consort Rd E1
Prince's Gdns E1
Princes St C7
Procter St C5
Provost St B7
Quaker St B8
Queen Anne St C3
Queen Elizabeth Hall D5
Queen Elizabeth St E8
Queen Sq B5
Queen St D7
Queen Street Pl D7
Queen Victoria St D6
Queens Gallery E4
Queensberry Pl F1
Quilter St B9
Radnor St B7
Rathbone Pl C4
Rawlings St F2
Rawstorne St B6
Red Lion Sq C5
Red Lion St C5
Redchurch St B8
Redcross Way D7
Reedworth St F6
Regency St F4
Regent Sq B5
Regent St C4
Regent's Park B3
Richmond Terr E5
Ridgmount St C4
Riley Rd E8
Rivington St B8
Robert St B3
Rochester Row F4
Rockingham St E7
Rodney Rd F7
Rolls Rd F8
Ropemaker St C7
Rosebery Ave B6
Rossmore Rd B2
Rothsay St E8
Rotten Row E2
Roupell St D6
Royal Acad of Arts D4
Royal Academy of Dramatic Art B4
Royal Acad of Music B3
Royal Albert Hall E1
Royal Brompton Hospital F1, F2
Royal Coll of Nursing C3
Royal Coll of Surgeons C5
Royal Festival Hall D5
Royal London Hosital for Integrated Medicine C5
Royal Marsden Hospital F1
Royal National Theatre D6
Royal National Throat, Nose and Ear Hospital B5
Royal Opera House D5
Rushworth St E6
Russell Sq B4
Russell Square ⊖ B5
Rutland Gate E2
Sackville St D4
Sadlers Wells B6
Saffron Hill C6
St Alban's St D4
St Andrew St C6
St Barnabas St F3
St Bartholomew's Hospital C6
St Botolph St C8
St Bride St C6
St George's Dr F4
St George's Rd E6
St George's Sq F4
St Giles High St C4
St James's Palace D4
St James's Park ⊖ E4
St James's St D4
St John St B6
St John's Wood Rd B1
St Margaret St E5
St Mark's Hosp B6
St Martin's La D5
St Martin's Le Grand C7
St Mary Axe C8
St Mary's Hosp C1
St Pancras Int A5
St Paul's ⊖ C7
St Paul's Cath ✝ C7
St Paul's Churchyard C6
St Thomas' Hosp E5
St Thomas St D7
Sale Pl C2
Sancroft St F5
Savile Row D4
Savoy Pl D5
Savoy St D5
School of Hygiene & Tropical Medicine C4
Science Mus E1
Scrutton St B8
Sekforde St B6
Serpentine Gallery E1
Serpentine Rd D2
Seven Dials C5
Seward St B6
Seymour Pl C2
Seymour St C2
Shad Thames D8/E8
Shaftesbury Ave D4
Shakespeare's Globe Theatre D7
Shepherd Market D3

Sherwood St D4
Shoe La C6
Shoreditch High St B8
Shoreditch High St ⊖ B8
Shorts Gdns C5
Shouldham St C2
Sidmouth St B5
Silk St C7
Sir John Soane's Museum C5
Skinner St B6
Sloane Ave F2
Sloane Sq F2
Sloane Square ⊖ F3
Sloane St E2
Snow Hill C6
Soho Sq C4
Somerset House D5
South Audley St D3
South Carriage Dr E2
South Eaton Pl F3
South Kensington ⊖ F1
South Molton St C3
South Parade F1
South Pl C7
South St D3
South Terr F2
South Wharf Rd C1
Southampton Row C5
Southampton St D5
Southwark ⊖ D6
Southwark Bridge D7
Southwark Bridge Rd D7
Southwark Cath ✝ D7
Southwark Park Rd F8
Southwark St D7
Spa Rd E8
Speakers' Corner D2
Spencer St B6
Spital Sq C8
Spring St C1
Stamford St D6
Stanhope St B4
Stanhope Terr D1
Stephenson Way B4
Stock Exchange C6
Stoney St D7
Strand C6
Strathearn Pl D2
Stratton St D3
Sumner St D6
Sussex Gdns C1
Sussex Pl C1
Sussex Sq D1
Sussex St F3
Sutton's Way B7
Swan St E7
Swanfield St B8
Swinton St B5
Sydney Pl F1
Sydney St F2
Tabard St E7
Tabernacle St B7
Tachbrook St F4
Tanner St E8
Tate Britain F5
Tate Modern D7
Tavistock Pl B5
Tavistock Sq B4
Tea & Coffee Mus D7
Temple ⊖ D6
Temple Ave D6
Temple Pl D5
Terminus Pl E3
Thayer St C3
The Barbican Centre for Arts C7
The Cut E6
The Mall E4
Theobald's Rd C5
Thorney St F5
Threadneedle St C7
Throgmorton St C7
Thurloe Pl F1
Thurloe Sq F2
Tonbridge St B5
Tooley St D8
Torrington Pl B4
Tothill St E4
Tottenham Court Rd B4
Tottenham Ct Rd ⊖ C4
Tottenham St C4
Tower Bridge ✦ D8
Tower Bridge App D8
Tower Bridge Rd E8
Tower Hill D8
Tower Hill ⊖ D8
Tower of London, The D8
Toynbee St C8
Trafalgar Square D4
Trinity Sq D8
Trinity St E7
Trocadero Centre D4
Tudor St D6
Turin St B9
Turnmill St C6
Tyers St F5
Ufford St E6
Union St D6
Univ Coll Hospl B4
University of London C4
Univ of Westminster C3
University St B4
Upper Belgrave St E3
Upper Berkeley St C2
Upper Brook St D3
Upper Grosvenor St D3
Upper Ground D6
Upper Montague St C2
Upper St Martin's La D5
Upper Thames St D7
Upper Wimpole St C3
Upper Woburn Pl B4
Vauxhall Bridge Rd F4
Vauxhall St F5
Vere St C3
Vernon Pl C5
Vestry St B7
Victoria ≥⊖ E3
Victoria and Albert Mus E1
Victoria Coach Station F3
Victoria Embankment D5
Victoria Pl Sh Ctr F3
Victoria St E4
Villiers St D5
Vincent Sq F4
Vinopolis City of Wine D7
Virginia Rd B8
Wakley St B6
Walbrook C7
Walcot Sq F6
Wallace Collection C3
Walnut Tree Walk F6
Walton St F2
Walworth Rd F7
Wardour St C4/D4
Warner St B6
Warren St ⊖ B4
Warren St B4
Warwick Sq F4
Warwick Way F3
Waterloo ≥⊖ E6
Waterloo Bridge D5
Waterloo East ≥ D6
Waterloo Rd E6
Watling St C7
Webber St E6
Welbeck St C3
Wellington Arch ✦ E3
Wellington Mus E3
Wellington Rd B2
Wellington Row B9
Wells St C4
Wenlock St A7
Wentworth St C8
West Carriage Dr D2
West Smithfield C6
West Sq E6
Westbourne St D1
Westbourne Terr C1
Westminster ⊖ E5
Westminster Abbey ✝ E5
Westminster Bridge E5
Westminster Bridge Rd E6
Westminster Cathedral (RC) ✝ E4
Westminster City Hall E4
Westminster Hall E5
Weston St E7
Weymouth St C3
Wharf Rd A7
Wharton St B5
Whitcomb St D4
White Cube B8
White Lion Hill D6
White Lion St A6
Whitechapel Rd C9
Whitecross St B7
Whitefriars St C6
Whitehall D5
Whitehall Pl D5
Wigmore Hall C3
Wigmore St C3
William IV St D5
Willow Walk F8
Wilmington Sq B6
Wilson St C7
Wilton Cres E3
Wilton Rd F4
Wimpole St C3
Winchester St F3
Wincott St F6
Windmill Walk D6
Woburn Pl B5
Woburn Sq B4
Wood St C7
Woodbridge St B6
Wootton St D6
Wormwood St C8
Worship St B7
Wren St B5
Wynyatt St B6
York Rd E5
York St C2
York Terrace East B3
York Terrace West B3
York Way A5

Luton 337

Adelaide St B1
Albert Rd C2
Alma St B2
Alton Rd C3
Anthony Gdns C1
Arndale Ctr B2
Arthur St C2
Ashburnham Rd B1
Ashton Rd C2
Avondale Rd A1
Back St A2
Bailey St C3
Baker St C2
Biscot Rd A1
Bolton Rd B3
Boyle Cl A2
Brantwood Rd B1
Bretts Mead C1
Bridge St B2
Brook St A1
Brunswick St A3
Burr St A3
Bury Park Rd A1
Bus Station B2
Bute St B2
Buxton Rd B2
Cambridge St C3
Cardiff Grove B1
Cardiff Rd B1
Cardigan St A2
Castle St B2/C2
Chapel St C2
Charles St A3
Chase St C2
Cheapside B2
Chequer St C3
Chiltern Rise C1
Church St B2/B3
Cinema A2
Cobden St A3
Collingdon St A1
Community Ctr C3
Concorde Ave A3
Corncastle Rd C1
Cowper St C2
Crawley Green Rd B3
Crawley Rd A1
Crescent Rise A3
Crescent Rd A3
Cromwell Rd A1
Cross St A2
Crown Court B2
Cumberland St B2
Cutenhoe Rd C3
Dallow Rd B1
Downs Rd B1
Dudley St A2
Duke St A2
Dumfries St B1
Dunstable Place B2
Dunstable Rd A1/B1
Edward St A3
Elizabeth St C2
Essex Cl C3
Farley Hill C1
Farley Lodge C1
Flowers Way B2
Francis St A1
Frederick St A2
Galaxy L Complex A2
George St B2
George St West B2
Gillam St A3
Gordon St B2
Grove Rd B1
Guildford St A2
Haddon Rd A3
Harcourt St C2
Hart Hill Drive A3
Hart Hill Lane A3
Hartley Rd A3
Hastings St B2
Hat Factory, The B2
Hatters Way A1
Havelock Rd A2
Hibbert St C2
High Town Rd A3
Highbury Rd A1
Hightown Community Sports & Arts Ctr A3
Hillary Cres C1
Hillborough Rd C1
Hitchin Rd A3
Holly St C2
Holm C1
Hucklesby Way A2
Hunts Cl C1
Information Ctr B2
Inkerman St A2
John St B2
Jubilee St A3
Kelvin Cl C2
King St B2
Kingsland Rd C3
Latimer Rd C2
Lawn Gdns C2
Lea Rd B3
Library B2
Library Rd B2
Liverpool Rd B1
London Rd C2
Luton Station ≥ A2
Lyndhurst Rd B1
Magistrates Court B2
Manchester St B2
Manor Rd B3
May St C3
Meyrick Ave C1
Midland Rd A2
Mill St A2
Milton Rd B1
Moor St A1
Moor, The A1
Moorland Gdns A2
Moulton Rise A3
Museum & Art Gallery A2
Napier Rd B1
New Bedford Rd A1
New Town St C2
North St A3
Old Bedford Rd A2
Old Orchard C2
Osbourne Rd C3
Oxen Rd A3
Park Sq B2
Park St B3/C3
Park St West B2
Park Viaduct B3
Parkland Drive C1
Police Station B1
Pomfret Ave A3
Pondwicks Rd B3
Post Office A1/A2/B2/C3
Power Court B3
Princess St B1
Red Rails C1
Regent St B2
Reginald St A2
Rothesay Rd B1
Russell Rise C1
Russell St C1
St Ann's Rd B3
St George's B2
St Mary's B3
St Marys Rd B3
St Paul's Rd C2
St Saviour's Cres C1
Salisbury Rd B1
Seymour Ave C3
Seymour Rd C3
Silver St B2
South Rd C2
Stanley St B1
Station Rd A2
Stockwood Cres C2
Stockwood Park C1
Strathmore Ave C2
Stuart St B2
Studley Rd A1
Surrey St C3
Sutherland Place C1
Tavistock St C2
Taylor St A3
Telford Way A1
Tennyson Rd C2
Tenzing Grove C1
The Cross Way C1
The Larches A2
Thistle Rd B3
Town Hall B2
Townsley Cl C2
UK Ctr for Carnival Arts ✦ B3
Union St B2
Univ of Bedfordshire B3
Upper George St B2
Vicarage St B3
Villa Rd A2
Waldeck Rd A1
Wellington St B1/B2
Wenlock St A2
Whitby Rd A1
Whitehill Ave C1
William St A2
Wilsden Ave C1
Windmill Rd B3
Windsor St C2
Winsdon Rd B1
York St A3

Macclesfield 337

108 Steps B2
Abbey Rd A1
Alton Dr A3
Armett St C1
Athey St B1
Bank St C3
Barber St C3
Barton St C1
Beech La A2
Beswick St B1
Black La A2
Black Rd C3
Blakelow Gardens C3
Blakelow Rd C3
Bond St B1/C1
Bread St C1
Bridge St B1
Brock St A2
Brocklehurst Ave A3
Brook St B3
Brookfield La B3
Brough St West C1
Brown St C1
Brynton Rd A2
Buckley St C2
Bus Station B2
Buxton Rd B3
Byrons St C2
Canal St B3
Carlsbrook Ave A3
Castle St B2
Catherine St B1
Cemetery A1
Chadwick Terr A3
Chapel St C2
Charlotte St B2
Chester Rd B1
Chestergate B1
Christ Church B1
Churchill Way B2
Coare St A1
Commercial Rd B2
Conway Cres A3
Copper St C3
Cottage St B1
Court A2
Court B2
Crematorium A1
Crew Ave A3
Crompton Rd B1/C1
Cross St C2
Crossall St C1
Cumberland St A1/B1
Dale St B3
Duke St B2
Eastgate B3
Exchange St B2
Fence Ave B3
Fence Ave Ind Est A3
Flint St B3
Foden St A2
Fountain St B3
Gateway Gallery ✦ B1
Garden St A3
Gas Rd B2
George St B2
Glegg St B3
Golf Course C3
Goodall St B3
Grange Rd C1
Great King St B1
Green St B3
Grosvenor Sh Ctr B2
Gunco La C3
Half St C2
Hallefield Rd B3
Hatton St C1
Hawthorn Way A3
Heapy St C3
Henderson St B1
Heritage Ctr & Silk Museum B2
Hibel Rd A2
High St C2
Hobson St C2
Hollins Rd C3
Hope St West B1
Horseshoe Dr B1
Hurdsfield Rd A3
Information Ctr B2
James St C2
Jodrell St B3
John St C2
Jordangate A2
King Edward St B2
King George's Field C3
King St B2
King's School A1
Knight Pool C3
Knight St C3
Lansdowne St A3
Library B2
Lime Gr B3
Little Theatre C2
Loney St B1
Longacre St B1
Lord St C2
Lowe St C2
Lowerfield Rd A3
Lyon St B1
Macclesfield College C1
Macclesfield Sta ≥ B2
Marina B3
Market B2
Market Pl B2
Masons La A3
Mill La C2
Mill Rd C2
Mill St B2
Moran Rd C1
New Hall St A2
Newton St C1
Nicholson Ave A3
Nicholson Cl A3
Northgate Ave A2
Old Mill La C2
Paradise Mill C2
Paradise St B1
Park Green B2
Park La C1
Park Rd C1
Park St C2
Park Vale Rd C1
Parr St B1
Peel St C2
Percyvale St A3
Peter St C1
Pickford St B2
Pierce St B1
Pinfold St B1
Pitt St C2
Police Station B2
Pool St C2
Poplar Rd C2
Post Office B1/B2/B3
Pownall St A2
Prestbury Rd A1/B1
Queen Victoria St B2
Queen's Ave A3
Registrar B2
Richmond Hill C3
Riseley St B1
Roan Ct B3
Roe St B2
Rowan Way A3
Ryle St C2
Ryle's Park Rd C1
St George's St C2
St Michael's B2
Samuel St B2
Saville St C3
Shaw St B1
Slater St C1
Snow Hill C3
South Park C1
Spring Gdns A2
Statham St C2
Station St A2
Steeple St A3
Sunderland St B2
Superstore A1/A2/C2
Swettenham St B3
The Silk Rd A2/B2
Thistleton Cl C2
Thorp St B2
Town Hall B2
Townley St B2
Turnock St C3
Union Rd B3
Union St B2
Victoria Park B3
Vincent St C2
Waters Green B2
Waterside C2
West Bond St B1
West Park A1
West Park Museum A1
Westbrook Dr A1
Westminster Rd A1
Whalley Hayes B1
Windmill St C3
Withyfold Dr A2
York St B3

Maidstone 340

Albion Pl B3
All Saints B2
Allen St A3
Amphitheatre ✦ C2
Archbishop's Pal B2
Bank St B2
Barker Rd C2
Barton Rd C3
Beaconsfield Rd C1
Bedford Pl B1
Bentlif Art Gallery B2
Bishops Way B2
Bluett St A3
Bower La C1
Bower Mount Rd B1
Bower Pl C1
Bower St B1
Bowling Alley B3
Boxley Rd A3
Brenchley Gardens A2
Brewer St A3
Broadway B2
Brunswick St C3
Buckland Hill A1
Buckland Rd B1
Bus Station B3
Campbell Rd C3
Carriage Museum B2
Church Rd C1
Church St B3
Cinema C2
College Ave C2
College Rd C2
Collis Memorial Gdn C3
Cornwallis Rd B1
Corpus Christi Hall B2
County Hall A2
County Rd A3
Crompton Gdns C3
Crown & County Courts B2
Curzon Rd A3
Dixon Cl C2
Douglas Rd C1
Earl St B2
Eccleston Rd C2
Fairmeadow B2
Fisher St A2
Florence Rd C1
Foley St A3
Foster St C3
Fremlin Walk Sh Ctr B2
Gabriel's Hill B3
George St C3
Grecian St A3
Hardy St A3
Hart St C2
Hastings Rd C3
Hayle Rd C3
Hazlitt Theatre B2
Heathorn St A3
Hedley St A3
High St B2
HM Prison A3
Holland Rd A3
Hope St A2
Information Ctr B2
James St A3
James Whatman Way A2
Jeffrey St A3
Kent County Council Offices A2
King Edward Rd C2
King St B3
Kingsley Rd C3
Knightrider St B3
Launder Way C1
Lesley Pl A1
Library B2
Little Buckland Ave A1
Lockmeadow Leisure Complex C2
London Rd B1
Lower Boxley Rd A2
Lower Fant Rd C1
Magistrates Court B3
Maidstone Barracks Station A1
Maidstone Borough Council Offices B1
Maidstone East Sta ≥ A2
Maidstone Museum B2
Maidstone West Sta ≥ B2
Market C2
Market Buildings B2
Marsham St B3
Medway St B2
Medway Trading Est C2
Melville Rd C3
Mill St B2
Millennium Bridge C2
Mote Rd B3
Muir Rd C3
Old Tovil Rd C2
Palace Ave B3
Perryfield St A2
Police Station B3
Post Office A2/B2/B3/C3
Priory Rd C3
Prospect Pl C1
Pudding La B2
Queen Anne Rd B3
Queens Rd A1
Randall St A2
Rawdon Rd C3
Reginald Rd C1
Rock Pl B1
Rocky Hill B1
Romney Pl B3
Rose Yard B2
Rowland Cl C1
Royal Engineers' Rd A2
Royal Star Arcade B2
St Annes Ct B1
St Faith's St B2
St Luke's Rd A3
St Peter's Br B2
St Peter St B2
St Philip's Ave C3
Salisbury Rd A3
Sandling Rd A2
Scott St A2
Scrubs La B1
Sheal's Cres C3
Somerfield La B1
Somerfield Rd B1
Staceys St A2
Station Rd A2
Superstore A1/B2/B3
Terrace Rd B1
The Mall C3
The Somerfield Hospital A1
Tonbridge Rd C1
Tovil Rd C2
Town Hall B2
Trinity Park B3
Tufton St B3
Union St B3
Upper Fant Rd C1
Upper Stone St C3
Victoria St B1
Visitor Ctr A1
Warwick Pl B1
Wat Tyler Way B3
Waterloo St C3
Waterlow Rd A3
Week St B2
Well Rd A3
Westree Rd C1
Wharf Rd C1
Whatman Park A1
Wheeler St A3
Whitchurch Cl B1
Woodville Rd C3
Wyatt St B3
Wyke Manor Rd B3

Manchester 337

Adair St B6
Addington St A5
Adelphi St A1
Air & Space Gallery B2
Albert Sq B3
Albion St C3
AMC Great Northern B3
Ancoats Gr B6
Ancoats Gr North B6
Angela St C2
Aquatic Ctr C4
Ardwick Green Park C5
Ardwick Green North C5
Ardwick Green South C5
Arlington St A2
Artillery St B3
Arundel St C2
Atherton St B2
Atkinson St B3
Aytoun St B4
Back Piccadilly A4
Baird St B5
Balloon St A4
Bank Pl A1
Baring St B5
Barrack St C1
Barrow St A1
BBC TV Studios C4
Bendix St A5
Bengal St A5
Berry St C5
Blackfriars Rd A3
Blackfriars St A3
Blantyre St C2
Bloom St B4
Blossom St A5
Boad St B5
Bombay St B4
Booth St A3
Booth St B4
Bootle St B3
Brazennose St B3
Brewer St A5
Bridge St A3
Bridgewater Hall B3
Bridgewater Pl A4
Bridgewater St B2
Brook St C4
Brotherton Dr A2
Brown St A3
Brown St B4
Brunswick St C6
Brydon Ave C6
Buddhist Ctr C4
Bury St A2
Bus & Coach Station B4
Bus Station B4
Butler St A6
Buxton St C5
Byrom St B3
Cable St A5
Calder St B1
Cambridge St C3/C4
Camp St B3
Canal St B4
Cannon St A1
Cannon St A4
Cardroom Rd A6
Carruthers St A6
Castle St C2
Cateaton St A3
Cathedral ✝ A3
Cathedral St A3
Cavendish St C4
Chapel St A1/A3
Chapeltown St B5
Charles St C4
Charlotte St B4
Chatham St B4
Cheapside A3
Chepstow St B3
Chester Rd C1/C2
Chester St C4
Chetham's (Dept Store) A3
China La B5
Chippenham Rd A6
Chorlton Rd C2
Chorlton St B4
Church St A2
Church St A4
City Park A4
City Rd C3
Civil Justice Ctr B2
Cleminson St A2
Clowes St A3
College Land A3
Coll of Adult Ed C4
Collier St B2
Commercial St C3
Conference Ctr C4
Cooper St B4
Copperas St A4
Cornbrook C1
Cornell St A5
Cornerhouse C4
Corporation St A4
Cotter St C6
Cotton St A5
Cow La B1
Cross St B3
Crown Court B4
Crown St C2
Cube Gallery B4
Dalberg St C6
Dale St A4/B5
Dancehouse, The C4
Dantzic St A4
Dark La C6
Dawson St C2
Dean St A5
Deansgate A3/B3
Deansgate Station ≥ C3
Dolphin St C6
Downing St C5
Ducie St B5
Duke Pl B2
Duke St B2
Durling St C6
East Ordsall La A2/B1
Edge St A4
Egerton St C2
Ellesmere St C1
Everard St C1
Every St B6
Fairfield St B5
Faulkner St B4
Fennel St A3
Ford St A2
Ford St C6
Fountain St B4
Frederick St A2
Gartside St B2
Gaythorne St A1
George Leigh St A5
George St A1
George St B4
G-Mex C3
Goadsby St A4
Gore St A2
Goulden St A5
Granada TV Ctr B2
Granby Row B4
Gravel St A3
Great Ancoats St A5
Great Bridgewater St B3
Great George St A1
Great Jackson St C2
Great Marlborough St C4
Greengate A3
Green Room, The C4
Grosvenor St C5
Gun St A5
Hadrian Ave B6
Hall St B3
Hampson St B1
Hanover St A4
Hanworth Cl C5
Hardman St B3
Harkness St C6
Harrison St B6
Hart St B4
Helmet St B6
Henry St A5
Heyrod St B6
High St A4
Higher Ardwick C6
Hilton St A4/A5
Holland St A6
Hood St A5
Hope St B1
Hope St B4
Houldsworth St A5
Hoyle St C6
Hulme Hall Rd C1
Hulme St A1
Hulme St C3
Hyde Rd C6
Information Ctr B3
Irwell St A2
Islington St A2
Jackson Cr C2
Jackson's Row B3
James St A1
Jenner Cl C2
Jersey St A5
John Dalton St A1
John Dalton St B3
John Ryland's Library B3
John St A2
Kennedy St B3
Kincardine Rd C5
King St A3
King St West A3
Law Courts B3
Laystall St B5
Lever St A5
Library B3
Linby St C2
Little Lever St A4
Liverpool Rd B2
Liverpool St B1
Lloyd St B3
Lockton Cl C5
London Rd B5
Long Millgate A3
Longacre St B6
Loom St A5
Lower Byrom St B2
Lower Mosley St B3
Lower Moss La C2
Lower Ormond St C4
Loxford La C4
Luna St A5
Major St B4
Manchester Arndale A4
Manchester Art Gallery B4
Manchester Central Convension Complex B3
Manchester Metropolitan University B4/C4
Manchester Piccadilly Station ≥ B5
Manchester Technology Ctr C4
Mancunian Way C3
Manor St C5
Marble St A4
Market St A2
Market St A4
Market St A4
Marsden St A3
Marshall St A5
Mayan Ave A2
Medlock St C3
Middlewood St B1
Miller St A4
Minshull St B4
Mosley St A4
Mosley St B4
Mount St B3
Mulberry St B3
Murray St A5
Museum of Science & Industry (MOSI) B2
Nathan Dr A2
Naval St A5
New Bailey St A2
New Elm Rd B2
New Islington A6
New Quay St B2
New Union St A6
Newgate St A4
Newton St A5
Nicholas St B4
North Western St C6
Oak St A4
Odeon A4
Old Mill St A6
Oldfield Rd A1/C1
Oldham Rd A5
Oldham St A4
Opera House B3
Ordsall La C1
Oxford Rd C4
Oxford Rd ≥ C4
Oxford St B4
Paddock St C6
Palace Theatre B4
Pall Mall A3
Palmerston St B6
Park St A1
Parker St B4
Peak St B5
Penfield Cl C5
Peoples' History Museum B2
Peru St A1
Peter St B3
Piccadilly A4
Piccadilly B5
Piccadilly Gdns B4
Piercy St A6
Poland St A5
Police Museum A5
Police Station B3/B5
Pollard St B6
Port St A5
Portland St B4
Portugal St East B5
Post Office A1/A4/A5/B3
Potato Wharf B2
Princess St B3/C4
Pritchard St C4
Quay St A2
Quay St B2
Queen St B3
Radium St A5
Redhill St A5
Regent Rd B1
Renold Theatre A2
Retail Park A5
Rice St B2
Richmond St B4
River St C3
Roby St B5
Rodney St A6
Roman Fort B2
Rosamond St A2
Royal Exchange A3
Sackville St B4
St Andrew's St B6
St Ann St A3
St Ann's A3
St George's Ave C1
St James St B4
St John St B3
St John's Cath (RC) ✝ A2
St Mary's B3
St Mary's Gate A3
St Mary's Parsonage A3
St Peter's Sq B3
St Stephen St A2
Salford Approach A3
Salford Central ≥ A2
Sheffield St B5
Shepley St B5
Sherratt St A5
Shudehill A4
Shudehill A4
Sidney St C4
Silk St A5
Silver St B4
Skerry Cl C5
Snell St B6
South King St B3
Sparkle St B5
Spear St A4
Spring Gdns A4
Stanley St A2/B2
Station Approach B5
Store St B5
Swan St A4
Tariff St B5
Tatton St C1
Temperance St B6/C6
The Triangle A4
Thirsk St C6
Thomas St A4
Thompson St A5
Tib La B3
Tib St A4
Town Hall (Manchester) B3
Town Hall (Salford) A2
Trafford St C3
Travis St B5
Trinity Way A2
Turner St A4
Union St C6

University of Manchester (Sackville Street Campus) C5
Upper Brook St C5
Upper Cleminson St A1
Upper Wharf St A1
Urbis Museum A4
Vesta St B6
Victoria A4
Victoria Station A4
Victoria St A3
Wadesdon Rd C5
Water St B2
Watson St B3
West Fleet St B1
West King St A2
West Mosley St B4
West Union St B1
Weybridge Rd A6
Whitworth St B4
Whitworth St West C3
Wilburn St B1
William St A2
William St C6
Wilmott St C3
Windmill St B3
Windsor Cr A1
Withy Gr A4
Woden St C1
Wood St B3
Woodward St A6
Worrall St C1
Worsley St C2
York St B4
York St C2
York St C4

Merthyr Tydfil
Merthyr Tudful 340

Aberdare Rd B2
Abermorlais Terr B2
Alexandra Rd A3
Alma St C3
Arfryn Pl C3
Argyle St C3
Avenue De Clichy C2
Bethesda St B2
Bishops Gr A3
Brecon Rd A1/B2
Briarmead A3
Bryn St C3
Bryntirion Rd B3/C3
Bus Station B2
Caedraw Rd C2
Cae Mari Dwn B3
Castle Sq A1
Castle St B2
Chapel C2
Chapel Bank B1
Church St B3
Civic Ctr B2
Coedcae'r Ct C3
Court B3
Courts B2
Court St C3
Cromwell St B2
Cyfarthfa Castle School and Museum A1
Cyfarthfa Ind Est A1
Cyfarthfa Park A1
Cyfarthfa Rd A1
Dane St A2
Dane Terr A2
Danyparc B3
Darren View A3
Dixon St B2
Dyke St C3
Dynevor St B2
Elwyn Dr C3
Fire Station B2
Fothergill St B3
Galonuchaf Rd A3
Garth St B2
Georgetown B2
Grawen Terr A2
Grove Pk A2
Gurnos Rd A2
Gwaelodygarth Rd A2/A3
Gwaunfarren Gr A3
Gwaunfarren Rd A3
Gwendoline St A3
Hampton St C3
Hanover St A2
Heol S O Davies B1
Heol-Gerrig B1
Highland View C3
High St A3/B2/B3/C2
Howell Cl B1
Information Ctr B2
Jackson's Bridge B2
James St C3
John St B3
Joseph Parry's Cott B2
Lancaster St A2
Library B2
Llewellyn St A2
Llwyfen St B2
Llwyn Berry B1
Llwyn Dic Penderyn B1
Llwyn-y-Gelynen C1
Lower Thomas St B3
Market C2
Mary St C3
Masonic St C2
Merthyr RFC C2
Merthyr College B2
Merthyr Town FC B3
Merthyr Tydfil Leisure Village C3
Merthyr Tydfil Sta C3
Meyrick Villas A2
Miniature Railway A1
Mount St A2
Nantygwenith St B1
Norman Terr B2
Oak Rd A2
Old Cemetery B3
Pandy Cl A1
Pantycelynen B1
Park Terr B2
Penlan View C2
Penry St B2
Pentwyn Villas A2
Penyard Rd B3
Penydarren Park A3
Penydarren Rd B3
Plymouth St C3
Police Station C2
Pont Marlais West B2
Post Office A3/B2/C3
Quarry Row B2
Queen's Rd B3
Rees St C3
Rhydycar Link C2
Riverside Park A1
St David's B3
St Tydfil's C2
St Tydfil's Ave C3
St Tydfil's Hospital (No A+E) B3
St Tydfil's Sq Sh Ctr C2
Saxon St A2
School of Nursing A2
Seward St A3
Shiloh La B3
Stone Circles B3
Stuart St A2
Summerhill Pl B3
Superstore B3
Swan St C2
Swansea Rd B1
Taff Glen View C3
Taff Vale Ct B3
Theatre Soar B2
The Grove A2
The Parade B3
The Walk B2
Thomastown Park B3
Tramroad La A3
Tramroad Side B2
Tramroad Side North B3
Tramroad Side South C3
Trevithick Gdns C3
Trevithick St A3
Tudor Terr B2
Twynyrodyn Rd C3
Union St B3
Upper Colliers Row B1
Upper Thomas St B3
Victoria St B2
Vue C3
Vulcan Rd B2
Warlow St C3
Well St A2
Welsh Assembly Government Offices C2
Wern La C3
West Gr A2
William St C3
Yew St C3
Ynysfach Engine Ho C2
Ynysfach Rd C2

Middlesbrough 340

Abingdon Rd C3
Acklam Rd C1
Albert Park C3
Albert Rd B2
Albert Terr C2
Aubrey St C3
Ayresome Gdns C2
Ayresome Green La C1
Ayresome St C2
Barton Rd A1
Bilsdale Rd C3
Bishopton Rd C3
Borough Rd B2/B3
Bowes Rd A2
Breckon Hill Rd B3
Bridge St East B3
Bridge St West B2
Brighouse Rd A1
Burlam Rd C1
Bus Station B2
Cannon Park B1
Cannon Park Way B2
Cannon St B1
Captain Cook Sq B2
Carlow St C1
Castle Way C3
Chipchase Rd C2
Cineworld B3
Clairville Sports Stadium C3
Cleveland Ctr B2
Clive Rd C2
Commercial St A2
Corporation Rd B2
Costa St C2
Council Offices B3
Crescent Rd C2
Cumberland Rd C2
Depot Rd A2
Derwent St B2
Devonshire Rd C2
Diamond Rd B2
Disabled Driver Test Circuit B1
Dorman Museum C2
Douglas St B3
Eastbourne Rd C2
Eden Rd C3
Enterprise Ctr A2
Forty Foot Rd A2
Gilkes St B2
Gosford St A2
Grange Rd B2
Gresham Rd B2
Harehills Rd C1
Harford St C2
Hartington Rd B2
Haverton Hill Rd A1
Hey Wood St B1
Highfield Rd C3
Hill St Ctr B2
Holwick Rd B1
Hutton Rd C3
ICI Works A1
Information Ctr B2
Lambton Rd C3
Lancaster Rd C2
Lansdowne Rd C3
Latham Rd C2
Law Courts B2/B3
Lees Rd B2
Leeway B3
Linthorpe Cemetery C1
Linthorpe Rd B2
Lloyd St B2
Longford St C2
Longlands Rd C3
Lower East St A3
Lower Lake C3
Maldon Rd C1
Manor St B2
Marsh St B2
Marton Rd B3
Middlehaven B3
Middlesbrough By-Pass B2/C1
Middlesbrough Coll B3
Middlesbrough L Park B3
Middlesbrough Sta B2
Middlesbrough Theatre C2
Middletown Park C2
MIMA B3
Mosque B2
Mosque C3
Mulgrave Rd A2
North Ormesby Rd B3
Newport Bridge B1
Newport Bridge Approach Rd B1
Newport Rd B2
North Rd B2
Northern Rd C1
Outram St B2
Oxford Rd C2
Park La C2
Park Rd North C2
Park Rd South C2
Park Vale Rd C3
Parliament Rd B1
Police Station A2
Port Clarence Rd A3
Portman St B2
Post Office B2/B3/C1/C2/C3
Princes Rd B2
Python A2
Riverside Bsns Park A2
Riverside Park Rd A1
Riverside Stadium (Middlesbrough FC) B3
Rockliffe Rd C2
Romaldkirk Rd B1
Roman Rd C2
Roseberry Rd C3
St Barnabas' Rd C2
St Paul's Rd B2
Saltwells Rd B3
Scott's Rd A3
Seaton Carew Rd A3
Shepherdson Way B3
Sikh Temple B2
Snowdon Rd A2
South West Ironmasters Park B1
Southfield Rd B2
Southwell Rd C2
Springfield Rd C1
Startforth Rd A2
Stockton Rd C1
Stockton St A2
Surrey St C2
Sycamore Rd C2
Synagogue C2
Tax Offices B3
Tees Viaduct C1
Teessaurus Park A2
Teesside Tertiary Coll C3
Temenos B3
The Avenue C2
The Crescent C2
Thornfield Rd C1
Town Hall B2
Transporter Bridge (Toll) A3
Union St B2
University of Teesside B2
Upper Lake C2
Valley Rd C3
Ventnor Rd C2
Victoria Rd B2
Visitor Ctr A3
Vulcan St A2
Warwick St C2
Wellesley Rd B3
West Lane Hospital C1
Westminster Rd C2
Wilson St B2
Windward Way B3
Woodlands Rd B2
York Rd C3

Milton Keynes 340

Abbey Way A1
Arbrook Ave B1
Armourer Dr A3
Arncliffe Dr A1
Avebury C2
Avebury Blvd C2
Bankfield B3
Bayard Ave A2
Belvedere A2
Bishopstone A1
Blundells Rd A1
Boycott Ave C2
Bradwell Comm Blvd B1
Bradwell Rd C1
Bramble Ave A2
Brearley Ave C2
Breckland A1
Brill Place B1
Burnham Dr B1
Bus Station C1
Campbell Park B3
Cantle Ave A3
Central Milton Keynes Shopping Area B2
Century Ave C2
Chaffron Way C3
Childs Way C1
Christ the Cornerstone B2
Cineworld B2
Civic Offices B2
Cleavers Ave B2
Colesbourne Dr A3
Conniburrow Blvd B2
County Court B2
Currier Dr A2
Dansteed Way A2/A3/B1
Deltic Ave B1
Downs Barn A2
Downs Barn Blvd A3
Eaglestone C3
Eelbrook Ave B1
Elder Gate B1
Evans Gate C2
Fairford Cr A3
Falcon Ave B3
Fennel Dr A2
Fishermead Blvd C3
Food Ctr B3
Fulwoods Dr C3
Glazier Dr A2
Glovers La A1
Grafton Gate C1
Grafton St A1/C2
Gurnards Ave B3
Harrier Dr C3
Ibstone Ave B1
Langcliffe Dr A1
Leisure Plaza C1
Leys Rd C1
Library B2
Linford Wood A2
Marlborough Gate B3
Marlborough St A2/B3
Mercers Dr A1
Midsummer C2
Midsummer Blvd B2
Milton Keynes Central C1
Monks Way A1
Mullen Ave A3
Mullion Pl C3
National Hockey Stadium B1
Neath Hill A3
North Elder C1
North Grafton B1
North Overgate A3
North Row B2
North Saxon B2
North Secklow B2
North Skeldon A3
North Witan B1
Oakley Gdns A3
Oldbrook Blvd C2
Open-Air Theatre B3
Overgate A3
Overstreet A3
Patriot Dr B1
Pencarrow Pl B3
Penryn Ave B3
Perran Ave C3
Pitcher La C1
Place Retail Park, The C1
Point Ctr, The B2
Police Station B2
Portway B2
Post Office A2/B2/C3
Precedent Dr B1
Quinton Dr B1
Ramsons Ave B2
Rockingham Dr A2
Rooksley B1
Rooksley Retail Park C1
Saxon Gate B2
Saxon St A1/C3
Secklow Gate B2
Shackleton Pl C2
Silbury Blvd B2
Skeldon A3
South Grafton C2
South Row C2
South Saxon C2
South Secklow B3
South Witan C2
Springfield B3
Stanton Wood A1
Stantonbury A1
Stantonbury L Ctr A1
Strudwick Dr C2
Sunrise Parkway A2
Telephone Exchange C3
The Boundary C3
Theatre & Art Gallery B3
Tolcarne Ave C3
Towan Ave C3
Trueman Pl C2
Vauxhall A1
Winterhill Retail Park C2
Witan Gate B2
X-Scape B3

Newcastle upon Tyne 340

Albert St B3
Argyle St B3
Back New Bridge St B3
BALTIC Ctr for Contemporary Art C3
Barker St A3
Barrack Rd B1
Bath La B1
Bell's Court B2
Bessie Surtees Ho C2
Bigg Market C2
Biscuit Factory B3
Black Gate C2
Blackett St B2
Blandford Sq C1
Boating Lake A1
Boyd St B3
Brandling Park A2
Bus Station B2
Buxton St B3
Byron St A3
Camden St B2
Castle Keep C2
Central C1
Central Library B2
Central Motorway B2
Chester St A3
City Hall B2
City Rd B3/C3
City Walls C1
Civic Ctr A2
Claremont Rd A1
Clarence St B3
Clarence Walk B3
Clayton St C1/B1
Clayton St West C1
Coach Station C1
College St B2
Collingwood St C2
Copland Terr B3
Coppice Way B3
Corporation St B1
Courts C3
Crawhall Rd B3
Dean St C2
Discovery C1
Dinsdale Pl A3
Dinsdale Rd A3
Doncaster Rd A3
Durant Rd B2
Eldon Sq B1
Eldon Sq Shopping Ctr B2
Ellison Pl B2
Empire B1
Eskdale Terr A2
Eslington Terr A2
Exhibition Park A1
Falconar St B3
Fenkle St C1
Forth Banks C1
Forth St C1
Gallowgate B1
Gateshead Heritage @ St Mary's C3
Gateshead Millennium Bridge C3
Gibson St B3
Goldspink La A3
Grainger Market B2
Grainger St B2
Grantham Rd A3
Granville Rd A3
Great North Mus:Hancock A2
Grey St B2
Groat Market C2
Guildhall C2
Hancock St A2
Hanover St C2
Hatton Gallery A1
Hawks Rd C3
Haymarket B2
Heber St B1
Helmsley Rd A3
High Bridge B2
High Level Bridge C2
Hillgate C3
Howard St B3
Hutton Terr A3
Information Ctr C3
Jesmond A2
Jesmond Rd A2/A3
John Dobson St B2
John George Joicey Museum C2
Jubilee Rd B3
Kelvin Gr A3
Kensington Terr A2
Laing Gallery B2
Lambton Rd A2
Leazes Cr B1
Leazes La B1
Leazes Park B1
Leazes Park Rd B1
Leazes Terr B1
Live C2
Low Friar St C1
Manor Chare C2
Manors B2
Manors Station B2
Market St B2
Melbourne St B2
Mill Rd C3
Mill Volvo Tyne C1
Monument B2
Monument Mall Sh Ctr B2
Morpeth St A2
Mosley St C2
Napier St A3
Nazareth House A3
New Bridge St B2/B3
Newcastle Central Station C1
Newcastle University A1
Newgate Shopping Ctr C1
Newgate St B1
Newington Rd A3
Northern Stage Theatre A2
Northumberland Rd B2
Northumberland St B2
Northumbria Univ A2
Northwest Radial Rd A1
O2 Academy C1
Oakwellgate C3
Orchard St C1
Osborne Rd A2
Osborne Terr A3
Pandon C3
Pandon Bank B3
Park Terr A1
Percy St B1
Pilgrim St B2
Pipewellgate C2
Pitt St B1
Plummer Tower A2
Police Station B2
Portland Rd A3/B3
Portland Terr A3
Post Office A3/B1/B2/B3
Pottery La C1
Prudhoe Pl B1
Prudhoe St B1
Quayside C2
Queen Elizabeth II Bridge C2
Queen Victoria Rd A1
Richardson Rd A1
Ridley Pl B2
Rock Terr B3
Rosedale Terr A3
Royal Victoria Infirmary A1
Sage Gateshead, The C3
St Andrew's St B1
St James B1
St James' Blvd C1
Sports Direct Arena (St James' Park) (Newcastle Utd FC) B1
St Mary's (RC) C1
St Mary's Place B2
St Nicholas C2
St Nicholas St C2
St Thomas' St B1
Sandyford Rd A2/A3
Science Park B2
Shield St B3
Shieldfield B3
Simpson Terr B3
South Shore Rd C3
South St C1
Starbeck Ave A3
Stepney Rd B3
Stoddart St B3
Stowell St B1
Strawberry Pl B1
Swing Bridge C2
Temple St C1
Terrace Pl B1
The Close C2
The Gate B1
The Side C2
Theatre Royal B2
Times Sq C1
Tower St B3
Trinity House C2
Tyne Bridge C2
Tyne Bridges C2
Tyneside B2
Victoria Sq A2
Warwick St A3
Waterloo St C1
Wellington St B1
Westgate Rd C1/C2
Windsor Terr A2
Worswick St B2
Wretham Pl B3

Newport
Casnewydd 340

Albert Terr B1
Allt-yr-Yn Ave A1
Alma St C2
Ambulance Station C3
Bailey St B2
Barrack Hill A2
Bath St A3
Bedford Rd B3
Belle Vue La C1
Belle Vue Park C1
Bishop St A3
Blewitt St B1
Bolt Cl C3
Bolt St C3
Bond St A2
Bosworth Dr A1
Bridge St B1
Bristol St A3
Bryngwyn Rd B1
Brynhyfryd Ave C1
Brynhyfryd Rd C1
Bus Station B2
Caerau Cres C1
Caerau Rd B1
Caerleon Rd A3
Capel Cres C2
Cardiff Rd C2
Caroline St B3
Castle (Remains) A2
Cedar Rd B3
Charles St B2
Charlotte Dr C2
Chepstow Rd A3
Church Rd A3
City Cinema B1
Civic Ctr B1
Clarence Pl A2
Clifton Pl B1
Clifton Rd C1
Clyffard Cres B1
Clytha Park Rd B1
Clytha Sq C2
Coldra Rd C1
Collier St A3
Colne St B3
Comfrey Cl A1
Commercial Rd C3
Commercial St B2
Corelli St A3
Corn St B2
Corporation Rd B3
Coulson Cl C2
County Court A2
Courts A1
Courts B1
Crawford St A3
Cyril St B3
Dean St A3
Devon Pl B1
Dewsland Park Rd C2
Dolman B2
Dolphin St C3
East Dock Rd C3
East St B1
East Usk Rd A3
Ebbw Vale Wharf B3
Emlyn St B2
Enterprise Way C3
Eton Rd B3
Evans St A2
Factory Rd A2
Fields Rd B1
Francis Dr C2
Frederick St C3
Friars Rd C1
Gaer La C1
George St C3
George Street Bridge C3
Godfrey Rd B1
Gold Tops B1
Gore St A3
Gorsedd Circle C1
Grafton Rd A3
Graham St B1
Granville St C3
Harlequin Dr A1
Harrow Rd B3
Herbert Rd A3
Herbert Walk C2
Hereford St A3
High St B2
Hill St B2
Hoskins St A2
Information Ctr B2
Ivor Sq B2
John Frost Sq B2
Jones St B1
Junction Rd A3
Keynshaw Ave C2
King St C2
Kingsway B2
Kingsway Ctr B2
Ledbury Dr A2
Library A3
Library, Museum & Art Gallery B2
Liverpool Wharf B3
Llanthewy Rd B1
Llanvair Rd A3
Locke St A2
Lower Dock St C3
Lucas St A2
Manchester St A3
Market B2
Marlborough Rd B3
Mellon St C3
Mill St A2
Morgan St A3
Mountjoy Rd C2
Newport Bridge A2
Newport Ctr B2
Newport RFC B3
Newport Station B2
North St B2
Oakfield Rd B1
Park Sq C2
Police Station A3/C2
Post Office B1/B2/C1/C3
Power St A1
Prince St A3
Pugsley St A2
Queen St C2
Queen's Cl A1
Queen's Hill A1
Queen's Hill Cres A1
Queensway B2
Railway St B2
Riverfront Arts Ctr B2
Riverside A3
Rodney Rd B2
Royal Gwent (A+E) C2
Rudry St A3
Rugby Rd B3
Ruperra La C3
Ruperra St C3
St Edmund St B1
St Mark's Cres A1
St Mary St B1
St Vincent Rd A3
St Woolos C2
St Woolos General (no A+E) C1
St Woolos Rd B1
School La B2
Serpentine Rd B1
Shaftesbury Park A2
Sheaf La A3
Skinner St B2
Sorrel Dr A1
South Market St C3
Spencer Rd B1
Stow Hill B2/C1/C2
Stow Park Ave C1
Stow Park Dr C1
TA Ctr A1
Talbot St B2
Tennis Club A1
Tregare St A3
Trostrey St A3
Tunnel Terr B1
Turner St A3
Upper Dock St B2
Usk St A3
Usk Way B3/C3
Victoria Cr B1
War Memorial A3
Waterloo Rd C1
West St B1
Wharves B2
Wheeler St A2
Whitby Pl A3
Windsor Terr B1
York Pl C1

Newquay 340

Agar Rd B2
Alma Pl B1
Ambulance Station B2
Anthony Rd C1
Atlantic Hotel A1
Bank St B1
Barrowfields A3
Bay View Terr B2
Beachfield Ave B1
Beach Rd B1
Beacon Rd A1
Belmont Pl A1
Berry Rd B2
Blue Reef Aquarium B1
Boating Lake C2
Bus Station B1
Chapel Hill B1
Chester Rd A3
Cheviot Rd C1/C2
Chichester Cres C2
Chynance Dr C1
Chyverton Cl C1
Cliff Rd B2
Coach Park B2
Colvreath Rd A3
Council Offices B1
Crantock St B1
Criggar Rocks A3
Dale Cl C3
Dale Rd C3
Dane Rd A1
East St B2
Edgcumbe Ave B3
Edgcumbe Gdns B3
Eliot Gdns B3
Elm Cl C3
Ennor's Rd B1
Fernhill Rd B1
Fire Station B1
Fore St B1
Gannel Rd C2
Golf Driving Range B3
Gover La B1
Great Western Beach A2
Grosvenor Ave B2
Harbour A1
Hawkins Rd C2
Headleigh Rd B2
Hilgrove Rd A3/B3
Holywell Rd B3
Hope Terr B1
Huer's House, The A1
Information Ctr B1
Island Cres B2
Jubilee St B1
Kew Cl C3
Killacourt Cove A2
King Edward Cres A1
Lanhenvor Ave B2
Library B1
Lifeboat Station A1
Linden Ave C2
Listry Rd C2
Lusty Glaze Beach A3
Lusty Glaze Rd A3
Manor Rd B1
Marcus Hill B2
Mayfield Rd B2
Meadowside C3
Mellanvrane La C2
Michell Ave B2
Miniature Golf Course C3
Miniature Railway B3
Mount Wise B1
Mowhay Cl C3
Narrowcliff A3
Newquay B2
Newquay Hospital (no A&E) B2
Newquay Town Football Ground B1
Newquay Zoo B3
North Pier A1
North Quay Hill A1
Oakleigh Terr B2
Pargolla Rd B2
Pendragon Cres C3
Pengannel Cl C1
Penina Ave C3
Police Sta & Courts B2
Post Office B1/B2
Quarry Park Rd B3
Rawley La C2
Reeds Way B1
Robartes Rd B2
St Anne's Rd A3
St Aubyn Cres B3
St George's Rd B1
St John's Rd B1
St Mary's Rd B1
St Michael's B1
St Michael's Rd B1
St Thomas' Rd B2
Seymour Ave B2
South Pier A1
South Quay Hill A1
Sweet Briar Cres C3
Sydney Rd A1
The Crescent B1
Tolcarne Beach A2
Tolcarne Point A2
Tolcarne Rd B2
Tor Rd B2
Towan Beach A1
Towan Blystra Rd B3
Tower Rd A1
Trebarwith Cres B2
Tredour Rd C2
Treforda Rd C3
Tregoss Rd B3
Tregunnel Hill B1/C1
Tregunnel Saltings C1
Trelawney Rd B2
Treloggan La C3
Treloggan Rd C3
Trembath Cres C1
Trenance Ave B2
Trenance Gardens B2
Trenance La C2
Trenance Leisure Park B3
Trenance Rd B2
Trenarth Rd B2
Treninnick Hill C3
Tretherras Rd B3
Trethewey Way C1
Trevemper Rd C2
Tunnels Through Time B1
Ulalia Rd B3
Vivian Cl B2
Waterworld B3
Whitegate Rd B3
Wych Hazel Way C3

Newtown
Y Drenewydd 340

Ash Cl A3
Back La B2
Baptist Chapel B2
Barn La A2
Bear Lanes Sh Ctr B2
Beech Cl A2
Beechwood Dr A2
Brimmon Cl C2
Brimmon Rd C2
Broad St B2
Bryn Bank A1
Bryn Cl A2
Bryn Gdns A1
Bryn House A1
Bryn La A1/A2
Bryn Meadows A2
Bryn St A2
Brynglais Ave A2
Brynglais Cl A2
Bus Station B2
Byrnwood Dr A1
Cambrian Bridge B3
Cambrian Gdns B2
Cambrian Way B2
Canal Rd A3
Castle Mound B2
Cedewain C1
Cefnaire C2
Cefnaire Coppice C2
Ceiriog C2
Cemetery A3
Church (Remains of) B2
Churchill Dr A3
Cledan B3
Colwyn B3
Commercial St A2
Council Offices B1
Crescent St A1
Cwm Llanfair A2
Davies Memorial Gallery B2
Dinas C2
Dolafon Rd B3
Dolerw Park B1
Dolfor Rd C1
Eirianell C1
Fairfield Dr A2
Ffordd Croesawdy B2
Fire Station C1
Frankwell St A2
Frolic St B2
Fron La A1
Garden La A2
Gas St B2
Glyndŵr C1
Golwgydre La B2
Gorsedd Circle B1
Great Brimmon Farm C3
Hafren C1
Halfpenny Bridge B2
High St B2
Hillside Ave A3
Hoel Treowen C2
Information Ctr B2
Kerry Rd B3
Ladywell Shopping Ctr B2
Library B1
Llanfair Rd A2
Llanidloes Rd C1
Llys Ifor A2
Lon Cerddyn B1
Lonesome La A3
Long Bridge A2
Lon Helyg C1
Lower Canal Rd B3
Maldwyn Leisure Ctr C1
Market B2
Market St B2
Milford Rd B1
Mill Cl B2
Miniature Railway B1
Mwyn Fynydd A3
New Church St B2
New Rd B2
Newtown Football Gd B1
Newtown Infirmary A2
Newtown Station B2
Oak Tree Ave A3
Old Kerry Rd B2
Oldbarn La A2
Park Cl B1
Parklands B1
Park La B1
Park St B2
Pavillion Ct C1
Plantation La C1
Police Station B1
Pont Brynfedw A2
Pool Rd B3
Poplar Rd A3
Post Office B2/C1
Powys C1
Powys Theatre A2
Pryce Jones Stores & Museum B2
Quaker Meeting Ho B1
Regent B2
Robert Owen House B1
Robert Owen Mus B2
Rugby Club A3
St David's B2
School La A2
Sheaf St B3
Short Bridge St B2

356 Northampton • Norwich • Nottingham • Oban • Oxford • Perth • Peterborough • Plymouth

Stone St B2
Sycamore Dr A2
Textile Museum B2
The Bryn A1
The Park B1
Town Hall B2
Union St A2
Upper Brimmon C3
Vastre Industrial Est B3
War Memorial B2
WHSmith Museum B2
Wynfields C1
Y Ffrydd A3

Northampton 340

78 Derngate B3
Abington Sq B3
Abington St B3
Alcombe St A3
All Saints' B2
Ambush St B1
Angel St B2
Arundel St A2
Ash St A2
Auctioneers Way C2
Bailiff St A2
Barrack Rd A2
Beaconsfield Terr A3
Becketts Park C3
Bedford Rd B3
Billing Rd B3
Brecon St A1
Brewery C2
Bridge St C2
Bridge St Depot C3
Broad St B2
Burns St A3
Bus Station B2
Campbell St A2
Castle (Site of) B2
Castle St B2
Cattle Market Rd C2
Central Museum & Art Gallery B2
Charles St A3
Cheyne Walk B3
Church La A2
Clare St A3
Cloutsham St A3
College St B2
Colwyn Rd A3
Cotton End C2
Countess Rd A1
County Hall B2
Court A2
Craven St A3
Crown & County Courts B3
Denmark Rd B3
Derngate B3
Derngate & Royal Theatres B3
Doddridge Church B2
Duke St A3
Dunster St A3
Earl St A3
Euston Rd C2
Fire Station A3
Foot Meadow B2
Gladstone Rd A1
Gold St B2
Grafton St A2
Gray St A3
Green St B1
Greenwood Rd B1
Greyfriars B2
Grosvenor Ctr B2
Grove Rd A3
Guildhall B2
Hampton St A2
Harding Terr A2
Hazelwood Rd B3
Herbert St B2
Hervey St A3
Hester St A2
Holy Sepulchre A2
Hood St A3
Horse Market B2
Hunter St A3
Information Ctr B1
Kettering Rd A3
Kingswell St B2
Lady's La B2
Leicester St A2
Leslie Rd A2
Library B3
Lorne Rd A2
Lorry Park A1
Louise Rd A2
Lower Harding St A2
Lower Hester St A2
Lower Mounts B3
Lower Priory St A2
Main Rd C1
Marefair B2
Market Sq B2
Marlboro Rd B1
Marriott St A2
Military Rd A3
Nene Valley Retail Pk C1
New South Bridge Rd C2
Northampton General Hospital (A&E) B3
Northampton Sta B1
Northcote St A2
Nunn Mills Rd C3
Old Towcester Rd C2
Overstone Rd A3
Peacock Pl B2
Pembroke Rd A1
Penn Court C2
Police Station B3
Post Office A1/A2/B3/C2
Quorn Way A2
Ransome Rd C3
Regent Sq A2
Robert St A2
St Andrew's Rd B1
St Andrew's St A2
St Edmund's Rd B3
St George's St A2
St Giles B3
St Giles St B3
St Giles' Terr B3
St James' Mill Rd B1
St James' Mill Rd East C1
St James Park Rd B1
St James Retail Park C1
St James Rd B1
St Leonard's Rd C2
St Mary's St B2
St Michael's Rd A3
St Peter's B2
St Peter's Sq Sh Prec. B2
St Peter's Way B2
Salisbury St A2
Scarletwell St B2
Semilong Rd A2
Sheep St B2
Sol Central (L Ctr) B2
Somerset St A3
South Bridge C2
Southfield Ave C2
Spencer Bridge Rd A1
Spencer Rd A3
Spring Gdns B3
Spring La B2
Swan St B3
TA Ctr A3
Tanner St B2
The Drapery B2
The Ridings B3
Tintern Ave A1
Towcester Rd C2
Upper Bath St B2
Upper Mounts A2
Victoria Park A1
Victoria Promenade B2
Victoria Rd B3
Victoria St A2
Wellingborough Rd B3
West Bridge B1
York Rd B3

Norwich 341

Albion Way C3
All Saints Green C2
Anchor Cl A3
Anchor St A3
Anglia Sq A2
Argyle St C3
Arts Ctr B1
Ashby St C2
Assembly House B1
Bank Plain B2
Barker St A1
Barn Rd A1
Barrack St A3
Ber St C2
Bethel St B1
Bishop Bridge A3
Bishopbridge Rd A3
Bishopgate A3
Blackfriars St A2
Botolph St A2
Bracondale C3
Brazen Gate C2
Bridewell B2
Brunswick Rd C1
Bull Close Rd A2
Bus Station C2
Calvert St A2
Cannell Green A3
Carrow Rd C3
Castle Mall B2
Castle Meadow B2
Castle & Museum B2
Cathedral B2
Cattlemarket St B2
Chantry Rd C1
Chapel Loke C2
Chapelfield East B1
Chapelfield Gdns B1
Chapelfield North B1
Chapelfield Rd B1
Chapelfield Sh Ctr C1
City Hall B1
City Rd C2
City Wall C1/C3
Colegate A2
Coslany St B1
Cow Hill B1
Cow Tower A3
Cowgate A2
Crown & Magistrates Courts A2
Dragon Hall Heritage Ctr C3
Duke St A1
Edward St A2
Elm Hill B2
Erpingham Gate B2
Fire Station B1
Fishergate A2
Foundry Bridge B3
Fye Bridge A2
Garden St C2
Gas Hill B3
Grapes Hill B1
Great Hospl Halls, The A3
Grove Ave C1
Grove Rd C1
Guildhall B1
Gurney Rd A3
Hall Rd C2
Heathgate A3
Heigham St A1
Horn's La C2
Information Ctr B1
Ipswich Rd C1
James Stuart Gdns B3
King Edward VI School B2
King St B2
King St C3
Koblenz Ave C3
Library B1
London St B2
Lower Clarence Rd B3
Lower Cl B3
Maddermarket B1
Magdalen St A2
Mariners La C2
Market B2
Market Ave B2
Mountergate B3
Mousehold St A3
Newmarket Rd C1
Norfolk Gallery B2
Norfolk St C1
Norwich City FC C3
Norwich Station B3
Oak St A1
Palace St A2
Pitt St A1
Playhouse B2
Post Office A2/B2/C2
Pottergate B1
Prince of Wales Rd B2
Princes St B2
Pull's Ferry B3
Puppet Theatre A2
Quebec Rd B3
Queen St B2
Queens Rd C2
Recorder Rd B3
Retail Park C3
Riverside Entertainment Ctr C3
Riverside Swimming Ctr C3
Riverside Rd B3
Rosary Rd B3
Rose La B3
Rouen Rd C2
Royal Norfolk Regiment Museum B2
St Andrew's & Blackfriars Hall B2
St Andrews St B2
St Augustines St A1
St Benedicts St B1
St Ethelbert's Gate B2
St Faiths La B3
St Georges St A2
St Giles St B1
St James Cl A3
St Julians C2
St Martin's La A1
St Peter Mancroft B2
St Peters St B1
St Stephens Rd C1
St Stephens St C1
Silver Rd A2
Silver St A2
Southwell Rd C2
Strangers Hall B1
Superstore C2
Surrey St C2
Sussex St A1
The Close B3
The Forum B1
The Walk B2
Theatre Royal B1
Theatre St B1
Thorn La C2
Thorpe Rd B3
Tombland B2
Union St C1
Vauxhall St B1
Victoria St C1
Walpole St B1
Wensum St A2
Wessex St C1
Westwick St A1
Wherry Rd C3
Whitefriars A2
Willow La B1
Yacht Station B3

Nottingham 341

Abbotsford Dr A3
Addison St A1
Albert Hall B1
Alfred St South A3
Alfreton Rd B1
All Saints Rd A1
Annesley Gr A2
Arboretum A1
Arboretum St A1
Arthur St A1
Arts Theatre B3
Ashforth St A3
Balmoral Rd A1
Barker Gate B3
Bath St B3
Belgrave Ctr B1
Bellar Gate B3
Belward St B3
Blue Bell Hill Rd B3
Brewhouse Yard C2
Broad Marsh Bus Sta C2
Broad Marsh Precinct C2
Broad St B3
Brook St B3
Burns St A1
Burton St B2
Bus Station A2
Canal St C2
Carlton St B3
Carrington St C2
Castle Blvd C1
Castle C2
Castle Gate C2
Castle Mdw Retail Pk C1
Castle Meadow Rd C1
Castle Museum & Gallery C2
Castle Rd C2
Castle Wharf C2
Cavendish Rd East C1
Cemetery B1
Chaucer St B1
Cheapside B2
Church Rd A3
City Link C3
City of Caves C2
Clarendon St B1
Cliff Rd C3
Clumber Rd East C1
Clumber St B2
College St B1
Collin St C2
Conway Cl A2
Council House B2
Court B2
Cranbrook St B3
Cranmer St A2
Cromwell St B1
Curzon St B3
Derby Rd B1
Dryden St A2
Fishpond Dr C1
Fletcher Gate B3
Forest Rd East A1
Forest Rd West A1
Friar La C2
Galleries of Justice C3
Gedling Gr A1
Gedling St B3
George St B3
Gill St A2
Glasshouse St B2
Goldsmith St B2
Goose Gate B3
Great Freeman St A2
Guildhall B2
Hamilton Dr C1
Hampden St A1
Heathcote St B3
High Pavement C3
High School A1
Holles Cr C1
Hope Dr C1
Hungerhill Rd A3
Huntingdon Dr C1
Huntingdon St A2
Information Ctr B2
Instow Rise A3
International Com Ctr A2
Kent St B3
King St B2
Lace Ctr, The C2
Lace Market B3
Lace Mkt Theatre C3
Lamartine St B3
Lenton Rd C1
Lewis Cl A3
Lincoln St B2
London Rd C3
Long Row B2
Low Pavement C2
Lower Parliament St B3
Magistrates Court C2
Maid Marian Way B2
Mansfield Rd A2/B2
Middle Hill C2
Milton St B2
Mount St B2
National Ice Ctr C3
Newcastle Dr B1
Newstead Gr A2
North Sherwood St A2
Nottingham Arena C3
Nottingham Station C3
Old Market Square B2
Oliver St A1
Park Dr C1
Park Row C1
Park Terr B1
Park Valley C1
Peas Hill Rd A3
Peel St A1
Pelham St B2
Peveril Dr C1
Plantagenet St A3
Playhouse Theatre B1
Plumptre St C3
Police Station B2
Poplar St C3
Portland Rd B1
Post Office B2
Queen's Rd C3
Raleigh St A1
Regent St B1
Rick St B3
Robin Hood Statue C2
Robin Hood St B3
Royal Ctr B2
Royal Children Inn C2
Royal Concert Hall B2
St Ann's Hill Rd A2
St Ann's Way A2
St Ann's Well Rd A3
St Barnabas B1
St James' St B2
St Mark's St B3
St Mary's Gdn of Rest B3
St Mary's Gate B3
St Nicholas C2
St Peter's C2
St Peter's Gate B2
Salutation Inn C2
Shakespeare St B2
Shelton St A2
South Pde B2
South Rd C1
South Sherwood St B2
Station St C3
Station Street C3
Stoney St B3
Talbot St B1
Tales of Robin Hood C2
Tattershall Dr C1
Tennis Dr B1
Tennyson St A1
The Park C1
The Ropewalk B1
Theatre Royal B2
Trent St C3
Trent University A2/B2
Trent University B2
Trinity Square Sh Ctr B2
Trip To Jerusalem Inn C2
Union Rd B3
Upper Parliament St B2
Victoria Ctr B2
Victoria Leisure Ctr B3
Victoria Park B3
Victoria St B2
Walter St A1
Warser Gate B3
Watkin St A2
Waverley St A1
Wheeler Gate B2
Wilford Rd C2
Wilford St C2
Willoughby House C2
Wollaton St B1
Woodborough Rd A2
Woolpack La B3
York St A2

Oban 341

Aird's Cres B2
Albany St B2
Albert La A2
Albert Rd A2
Alma Cres B1
Ambulance Station C2
Angus Terr C3
Ardconnel Rd A2
Ardconnel Terr B2
Argyll Sq B2
Argyll St B2
Atlantis Leisure Ctr A2
Bayview Rd A1
Benvoulin Rd A2
Bowling Green A2
Breadalbane St A2
Bus Station B2
Campbell St B2
College B2
Colonsay Terr C3
Columba Building B2
Combie St B2
Corran Brae A1
Corran Esplanade A1/A2
Corran Halls A2
Court B2
Crannaig-a-Mhinisteir B1
Crannog La C2
Croft Ave A2
Dalintart Dr C3
Dalriach Rd A2
Distillery B2
Drummore Rd C2
Duncraggan Rd A2
Dunollie Rd A2
Dunuaran Rd B1
Feochan Gr C3
Ferry Terminal B1
Gallanach Rd B1
George St A2
Glencruitten Dr C3
Glencruitten Rd B3
Glenmore Rd C1
Glenshellach Rd C1
Glenshellach Terr B2
Harbour Bowl B2
Hazeldean Cres A3
High St B2
Highland Theatre Cinema A2
Hill St B2
Industrial Estate C2
Information Ctr B2
Islay Rd C3
Jacob's Ladder B2
Jura Rd C3
Knipoch Pl C3
Laurel Cres A2
Laurel Rd A2/A3
Library B1
Lifeboat Station B1
Lighthouse Pier B1
Lismore Cres A2
Lochavullin Dr B2
Lochavullin Rd C2
Lochside St B2
Longsdale Cres A3
Longsdale Rd A2/A3
Longsdale Terr A3
Lunga Rd C3
Lynn Rd C2
Market St B2
McCaig Rd C3
McCaig's Tower A2
Mill La C2
Miller Rd C2
Millpark Ave C2
Millpark Rd C2
Mossfield Ave B3
Mossfield Dr B3
Mossfield Stadium B3
Nant Dr C3
Nelson Rd C2
North Pier B2
Nursery La A2
Oban B2
Police Station B2
Polvinister Rd B3
Post Office A2/B2
Pulpit Dr C1
Pulpit Hill C1
Pulpit Hill Viewpoint B1
Quarry Rd C2
Queen's Park Pl B2
Railway Quay B1
Rockfield Rd B2
St Columba's A1
St John's A2
Scalpay Terr C3
Shore St B1
Shuna Terr C3
Sinclair Dr C2
Soroba Rd B2/C2
South Pier B2
Stevenson St B2
Tweedale St B2
Ulva Rd C2
Villa Rd B1
War & Peace A2

Oxford 341

Adelaide St A1
Albert St A1
All Souls (Coll) B2
Ashmolean Mus B2
Balliol (Coll) B2
Banbury Rd A2
Bate Collection of Musical Instruments C2
Beaumont St B1
Becket St B1
Blackhall Rd A2
Blue Boar St B2
Bodleian Library B2
Botanic Garden B3
Brasenose (Coll) B2
Brewer St C2
Broad St B2
Burton-Taylor Theatre B2
Bus Station B1
Canal St A1
Cardigan St A1
Carfax Tower B2
Castle B1
Castle St B1
Catte St B2
Cemetery C1
Christ Church (Coll) B2
Christ Church Cath C2
Christ Church Mdw C2
Clarendon Ctr B2
Coach & Lorry Park C1
College B3
Coll of Further Ed C1
Cornmarket St B2
Corpus Christi (Coll) B2
County Hall B1
Covered Market B2
Cowley Pl C3
Cranham St A1
Cranham Terr A1
Cricket Ground B1
Crown & County Courts C2
Deer Park B3
Exeter (Coll) B2
Folly Bridge C2
George St B1
Great Clarendon St A1
Hart St A1
Hertford (Coll) B2
High St B3
Hollybush Row B1
Holywell St B2
Hythe Bridge St B1
Ice Rink C1
Information Ctr B2
Jericho St A1
Jesus (Coll) B2
Jowett Walk B3
Juxon St A1
Keble (Coll) A2
Keble Rd A2
Library B2
Linacre (Coll) A3
Lincoln (Coll) B2
Little Clarendon St A1
Longwall St B3
Magdalen (Coll) B3
Magdalen Bridge B2
Magdalen St B2
Magistrate's Court C2
Manchester (Coll) B2
Manor Rd B2
Mansfield (Coll) A2
Mansfield Rd A3
Market B1
Marlborough Rd C2
Martyrs' Memorial B2
Merton Field B3
Merton (Coll) B3
Merton St B2
Mus of Modern Art B2
Museum of Oxford B2
Museum Rd A2
New College (Coll) B3
New Inn Hall St B2
New Rd B1
New Theatre B2
Norfolk St C1
Nuffield (Coll) B1
Observatory A1
Observatory St A1
Odeon B1/B2
Old Fire Station B1
Old Greyfriars St C2
Oriel (Coll) B2
Oxford Station B1
Oxford Story, The B2
Oxford University Research Ctrs A1
Oxpens Rd C1
Paradise Sq C1
Paradise St B1
Park End St B1
Parks Rd A2/B2
Pembroke (Coll) C2
Phoenix A1
Picture Gallery C2
Plantation Rd A1
Playhouse B2
Police Station C2
Post Office A1/B2
Pusey St B1
Queen's La B3
Queen's (Coll) B3
Radcliffe Camera B2
Rewley Rd B1
Richmond Rd A1
Rose La B3
Ruskin (Coll) B1
Saïd Business School B1
St Aldates C2
St Anne's (Coll) A1
St Antony's (Coll) A1
St Bernard's Rd A1
St Catherine's (Coll) B3
St Cross Building A3
St Cross Rd A3
St Edmund Hall (Coll) B3
St Giles St A2
St Hilda's (Coll) C3
St John St B2
St John's (Coll) B2
St Mary the Virgin B2
St Michael at the Northgate B2
St Peter's (Coll) B1
St Thomas St B1
Science Area A2
Science Museum B2
Sheldonian Theatre B2
Somerville (Coll) A1
South Parks Rd A2
Speedwell St C2
Sports Ground C3
Thames St C2
Town Hall B2
Trinity (Coll) B2
Turl St B2
University Coll (Coll) B3
Univ Mus & Pitt Rivers Mus A2
University Parks A2
Wadham (Coll) B2
Walton Cr A1
Walton St A1
Western Rd C2
Westgate Sh Ctr B2
Woodstock Rd A1
Worcester (Coll) B1

Perth 341

A K Bell Library B2
Abbot Cres C1
Abbot St C1
Albany Terr A1
Albert Monument A3
Alexandra St B2
Atholl St A2
Balhousie Ave A2
Balhousie Castle Black Watch Museum A2
Balhousie St A2
Ballantine Pl A1
Barossa Pl A2
Barossa St A2
Barrack St A2
Bell's Sports Ctr A2
Bellwood B3
Blair St B1
Burn Park C1
Bus Station B2
Caledonian Rd B2
Canal Cres B2
Canal St B3
Cavendish Ave C1
Charles St B2
Charlotte Pl A2
Charlotte St A3
Church St A1
City Hall B3
Club House C3
Clyde Pl C1
Commercial St A3
Concert Hall B3
Council Chambers B3
County Pl B2
Court B3
Craigie Pl C2
Crieff Rd A1
Croft Park C2
Cross St B2
Darnhall Cres C1
Darnhall Dr C1
Dewars Ctr B1
Dundee Rd B3
Dunkeld Rd A1
Earl's Dykes B1
Edinburgh Rd C3
Elibank St B1
Fair Maid's House A3
Fergusson B3
Feus Rd A1
Fire Station A1
Fitness Ctr B3
Foundary La A2
Friar St C2
George St B3
Glamis Pl C1
Glasgow Rd B1
Glenearn Rd C2
Glover St B1/C1
Golf Course A2
Gowrie St A3
Gray St B1
Graybank Rd B1
Greyfriars Burial Grnd B3
Hay St A2
High St B2/B3
Hotel B2
Inchaffray St A1
Industrial/Retail Park B1
Information Ctr B2
Isla Rd A3
James St B2
Keir St A3
King Edward St B3
King James VI Golf Course C3
King St B2
Kings Pl C2
Kinnoull Causeway B2
Kinnoull Aisle 'Monument' B3
Kinnoull St B2
Knowelea Pl C1
Knowelea Terr C1
Ladeside Business Ctr A1
Leisure Pool B1
Leonard St B2
Lickley St B2
Lochie Brae A3
Long Causeway A1
Low St A2
Main St A3
Marshall Pl C3
Melville St A2
Mill St B3
Milne St B2
Murray Cres C1
Murray St B2
Needless Rd C1
New Rd B2
North Inch A3
North Methven St A2
Park Pl C1
Perth B2
Perth Bridge A3
Perth Business Park B1
Perth Museum & Art Gallery B3
Perth Station C2
Pickletulllum Rd B1
Pitheavlis Cres C1
Playhouse B2
Police Station B2
Pomarium St B2
Post Office A3/B2/C2
Princes St B3
Priory Pl C2
Queen St C1
Queen's Bridge B3
Riggs Rd B1
Riverside B3
Riverside Park B3
Rodney Park B3
Rose Terr A2
St Catherines Ret Pk A1
St Catherine's Rd A1/A2
St John St B3
St John's Kirk B3
St John's Shopping Ctr B2
St Leonards Bridge C2
St Ninians Cathedral A2
Scott Monument C2
Scott St B2
Sheriff Court B3
Shore Rd C3
Skate Park C3
South Inch C2
South Inch Bsns Ctr C3
South Inch Park C2
South Inch View C2
South Methven St B2
South St B3
South William St B2
Stormont St A2
Strathmore St A3
Stuart Ave C1
Tay St B3
The Stables A1
The Stanners B3
Union La A2
Victoria St B2
Watergate B3
Wellshill Cemetery A1
West Bridge St A3
West Mill St B2
Whitefriers Cres B1
Whitefriers St B1
Wilson St C1
Windsor Terr C1
Woodside Cres C1
York Pl B2
Young St C1

Peterborough 341

Athletics Arena B3
Bishop's Palace B2
Bishop's Rd B2/B3
Boongate A3
Bourges Boulevard A1
Bourges Retail Pk B1/B2
Bridge House (Council Offices) C2
Bridge St B2
Bright St A1
Broadway A2
Broadway A2
Brook St A2
Burghley Rd A2
Bus Station B2
Cavendish St A3
Charles St A3
Church St B2
Church Walk A2
Cobden Ave A1
Cobden St A1
Cowgate B2
Craig St A2
Crawthorne Rd A2
Cripple Sidings La C2
Cromwell Rd A1
Dickens St A3
Eastfield Rd A3
Eastgate B3
Fire Station A1
Fletton Ave C2
Frank Perkins Parkway C3
Geneva St A2
George St C1
Gladstone St A1
Glebe Rd C2
Gloucester Rd C3
Granby St B3
Grove St C1
Guildhall B2
Hadrians Ct C3
Henry St A2
Hereward Cross (Sh) B2
Hereward Rd B3
Information Ctr B2
Jubilee St C1
Key Theatre C2
Kent Rd B1
Kirkwood Cl B1
Lea Gdns B1
Library A2
Lincoln Rd A2
London Rd C2
Long Causeway B2
Lower Bridge St C2
Magistrates Court B2
Manor House St A2
Mayor's Walk A1
Midland Rd A1
Monument St A2
Morris St A3
Mus & Art Gallery B2
Nene Valley Railway C1
New Rd A2
New Rd C1
Northminster A2
Old Customs House C2
Oundle Rd C1
Padholme Rd A3
Palmerston Rd C1
Park Rd A2
Passport Office B2
Peterborough District Hospital (A+E) B1
Peterborough Sta B1
Peterborough Nene Valley C1
Peterborough United FC C2
Police Station B2
Post Office A3/B1/B2/B3/C1
Priestgate B2
Queen's Walk C2
Queensgate Ctr B2
Railworld C1
Regional Swimming & Fitness Ctr B3
River La B1
Rivergate Sh Ctr B2
Riverside Mead C3
Russell St A1
St John's B2
St John's St A3
St Marks St A2
St Peter's B2
St Peter's Rd B2
Saxon Rd A3
Spital Bridge A1
Stagshaw Dr C3
Star Rd B3
Thorpe Lea Rd B1
Thorpe Rd B1
Thorpe's Lea Rd B1
Tower St A2
Town Hall B2
Viersen Platz B2
Vineyard Rd B3
Wake Rd B3
Wellington St A3
Wentworth St B2
Westgate B2
Whalley St A3
Wharf Rd C1
Whitsed St A3
YMCA A3

Plymouth 341

Alma Rd A1
Anstis St B1
Armada Ctr B2
Armada St A3
Armada Way B2
Arts Ctr B2
Athenaeum B1
Athenaeum St C1
Barbican C3
Barbican C3
Baring St A3
Bath St B1
Beaumont Park B3
Beaumont Rd B3
Black Friars Gin Distillery C2
Breton Side B3
Bus Station B2
Castle St C3
Cathedral (RC) B1
Cecil St B1
Central Park A1
Central Park Ave A2
Charles Church B3
Charles Cross B3
Charles St B2
City Museum & Art Gallery B2
Citadel Rd C2
Citadel Rd East C2
Civic Ctr B2
Cliff Rd C1
Clifton Pl A3
Cobourg St A2
College of Art B2
Continental Ferry Port B1
Cornwall St B2
Dale Rd A2
Deptford Pl A3
Derry Ave A2
Derry's Cross B1
Drake Circus B2
Drake Cir Sh Ctr B2
Drake's Memorial C2
Drum B2
Eastlake St B2
Ebrington St B3
Elizabethan House C3
Elliot St C1
Endsleigh Pl A2
Exeter St B3
Fire Station A3
Fish Quay C3
Gibbons St A3
Glen Park Ave A2
Grand Pde C1
Great Western Rd C1
Greenbank Rd A3
Greenbank Terr A3
Guildhall B2

Flat St B5
Foley St A6
Foundry Climbing Ctr A4
Fulton Rd A1
Furnace Hill A4
Furnival Rd A5
Furnival Sq C4
Furnival St C4
Garden St B3
Gell St B3
Gibraltar St A4
Glebe Rd B1
Glencoe Rd C6
Glossop Rd B2/B3/C1
Gloucester St C2
Granville Rd C6
Granville Rd/ Sheffield College 🚊 C5
Graves Gallery 🏛 B5
Greave Rd B3
Greene La A4
Hadfield St A1
Hanover St C3
Hanover Way C3
Harcourt Rd B1
Harmer La B5
Havelock St C2
Hawley St B4
Haymarket B5
Headford St C3
Heavygate Rd A1
Henry St A3
High St B4
Hodgson St C3
Holberry Gdns C2
Hollis Croft B4
Holly St B4
Hounsfield Rd B3
Howard Rd A1
Hoyle St A3
Hyde Park 🚊 A6
Infirmary Rd A3
Infirmary Rd 🚊 A3
Information Ctr ℹ B4
Jericho St A3
Johnson St A5
Kelham Island Industrial Museum 🏛 A4
Lawson Rd C1
Leadmill Rd C5
Leadmill St C5
Leadmill, The C5
Leamington St A1
Leavy Rd B3
Lee Croft B4
Leopold St B4
Leveson St A6
Library A2
Library B5
Library C1
Lyceum Theatre 🎭 B5
Malinda St A3
Maltravers St A5
Manor Oaks Rd B6
Mappin St B3
Marlborough Rd B1
Mary St C4
Matilda St C4
Matlock Rd A1
Meadow St A3
Melbourn Rd A1
Melbourne Ave C1
Millennium Galleries 🏛 B5
Milton St C3
Mitchell St B3
Mona Ave A1
Mona Rd A1
Montgomery Terr Rd A3
Montgomery Theatre 🎭 B4
Monument Gdns C6
Moor Oaks Rd B1
Moore St C3
Mowbray St A4
Mushroom La B2
Netherthorpe Rd B3
Netherthorpe Rd 🚊 B3
Newbould La C1
Nile St C1
Norfolk Park Rd C6
Norfolk Rd C6
Norfolk St B4
North Church St B4
Northfield Rd A1
Northumberland Rd B1
Nursery St A5
O2 Academy 🎭 B5
Oakholme Rd C1
Octagon B2
Odeon 🎥 B5
Old St B6
Oxford St A2
Paradise St B4
Park La C2
Park Sq B5
Parker's Rd B1
Pearson Building (Univ) C2
Penistone Rd A3
Pinstone St B4
Pitt St B3
Police Station 🚓 A4/B5
Pond Hill B5
Pond St B5
Ponds Forge Sports Ctr B5
Portobello St B3
Post Office 📮 A1/A2/B3/B4/B5/B6/C1/C3/C4/C6
Powell St A2
Queen St B4
Queen's Rd C5
Ramsey Rd B1
Red Hill B3
Redcar Rd B1
Regent St B3
Rockingham St B4
Roebuck Rd A2
Royal Hallamshire Hospital Ⓗ C2
Russell St A4
Rutland Park C1
St George's Cl B3
St Mary's Gate C3
St Mary's Rd C4/C5
St Peter & St Paul Cathedral ✝ B4
St Philip's Rd A3
Savile St A5
School Rd B1
Scotland St A4
Severn Rd B1
Shalesmoor A4
Shalesmoor 🚊 A3
Sheaf St B5
Sheffield Hallam Univ B5
Sheffield Ice Sports Ctr – Skate Central C5
Sheffield Parkway A6
Sheffield Station ⇌ C5
Sheffield Sta/ Sheffield Hallam University 🚊 B5
Sheffield University B2
Shepherd St A3
Shipton St A2
Shoreham St C4
Showroom, The 🎥 C5
Shrewsbury Rd C5
Sidney St C4
Site Gallery 🏛 C5
Slinn St A1
Smithfield A4
Snig Hill A5
Snow La A4
Solly St B3
Southbourne Rd C1
South La C4
South Street Park B5
Spital Hill A5
Spital St A5
Spring Hill B1
Spring Hill Rd B1
Springvale Rd A1
Stafford Rd C6
Stafford St B6
Stanley St A5
Suffolk Rd C5
Summer St B2
Sunny Bank C3
Surrey St B4
Sussex St A6
Sutton St B3
Sydney Rd A2
Sylvester St C4
Talbot St B5
Taptonville Rd B1
Tax Office C4
Tenter St B4
The Moor C4
Town Hall 🏢 B4
Townend St A1
Townhead St B4
Trafalgar St B4
Tree Root Walk B2
Trinity St A4
Trippet La B4
Turner Mus of Glass 🏛 B3
Union St B4
Univ Drama Studio 🎭 B2
Univ of Sheffield 🚊 B3
Upper Allen St A3
Upper Hanover St B3
Upperthorpe Rd A2/A3
Verdon St A5
Victoria Quays ✦ B5
Victoria Rd C2
Victoria St B3
Waingate B5
Watery St A3
Watson Rd C1
Wellesley Rd B2
Wellington St C3
West Bar A4
West Bar Green A4
West One B3
West St B3
West St 🚊 B4
Westbourne Rd C1
Western Bank B2
Western Rd A1
Weston Park B2
Weston Park Hospl Ⓗ B2
Weston Park Mus 🏛 B2
Weston St B2
Wharncliffe Rd C3
Whitham Rd B1
Wicker A5
Wilkinson St B2
William St C3
Winter Garden ✦ B4
Winter St B2
York St B4
Yorkshire Artspace C5
Young St C4

Shrewsbury 342

Abbey Church ⛪ B3
Abbey Foregate B3
Abbey Lawn Bsns Park B3
Abbots House 🏠 B2
Agricultural Show Gd A1
Albert St A2
Alma St B1
Ashley St A3
Ashton Rd C1
Avondale Dr A3
Bage Way C3
Barker St B1
Beacall's La A2
Beeches La C2
Beehive La C1
Belle Vue Gdns C2
Belle Vue Rd C2
Belmont Bank C1
Berwick Ave A1
Berwick Rd A1
Betton St C2
Bishop St B3
Bradford St B3
Bridge St B1
Bus Station B2
Butcher Row B2
Burton St A3
Butler Rd C1
Bynner St C2
Canon St B3
Canonbury C1
Castle Bsns Park, The A2
Castle Foregate A2
Castle Gates B2
Castle Museum ♜ B2
Castle St B2
Cathedral (RC) ✝ C1
Chester St A2
Cineworld 🎥 C3
Claremont Bank B1
Claremont Hill B1
Cleveland St B3
Coleham Head B2
Coleham Pumping Station 🏛 C2
College Hill B1
Corporation La A1
Coton Cres A1
Coton Hill A2
Coton Mount A1
Crescent La C1
Crewe St A2
Cross Hill B1
Darwin Ctr B2
Dingle, The ❀ B1
Dogpole B2
Draper's Hall 🏠 B2
English Bridge B2
Fish St B2
Frankwell B1
Gateway Ctr, The 🏛 A2
Gravel Hill La A1
Greyfriars Rd C2
Guildhall 🏢 B1
Hampton Rd A3
Haycock Way C3
HM Prison B2
High St B1
Hills La B1
Holywell St B3
Hunter St A1
Information Ctr ℹ B1
Ireland's Mansion & Bear Steps 🏠 B1
John St A3
Kennedy Rd C1
King St B3
Kingsland Bridge C1
Kingsland Bridge (toll) C1
Kingsland Rd C1
Library B2
Lime St C2
Longden Coleham C2
Longden Rd C1
Longner St B1
Luciefelde Rd C1
Mardol B1
Market B1
Marine Terr C2
Monkmoor Rd B3
Moreton Cr C2
Mount St A1
Music Hall 🎭 B1
New Park Cl A3
New Park Rd A2
New Park St A3
North St A2
Oakley St C1
Old Coleham C2
Old Market Hall 🎥 B1
Old Potts Way C3
Parade Ctr B2
Police Station 🚓 B1
Post Office 📮 A2/B1/B2/B3
Pride Hill B1
Pride Hill Ctr B1
Priory Rd B1
Pritchard Way C3
Queen St A3
Raby Cr C2
Rad Brook C1
Rea Brook C3
Riverside B1
Roundhill La A1
Rowley's House 🏛 B1
St Alkmund's ⛪ B2
St Chad's ⛪ B1
St Chad's Terr B1
St John's Hill B1
St Julians Friars C2
St Mary's ⛪ B2
St Mary's St B2
Salters La C2
Scott St C3
Severn Bank A3
Severn St A2
Shrewsbury ⇌ B2
Shrewsbury High School for Girls C1
Shrewsbury School ✦ C1
Shropshire Wildlife Trust ✦ B3
Smithfield Rd B1
South Hermitage C1
Swan Hill B1
Sydney Ave A3
Tankerville St B3
The Dana B2
The Quarry B1
The Square B1
Tilbrook Dr A3
Town Walls C1
Trinity St C2
Underdale Rd B3
Victoria Ave B1
Victoria Quay B1
Victoria St B2
Welsh Bridge B1
Whitehall St B3
Wood St A2
Wyle Cop B2

Southampton 342

Above Bar St A2
Albert Rd North B3
Albert Rd South C3
Anderson's Rd B3
Archaeology Mus (God's Ho Tower) 🏛 C2
Argyle Rd A2
Arundel Tower ✦ B1
Bargate, The ✦ B2
Bargate Shopping Ctr B2
BBC Regional Ctr A1
Bedford Pl A1
Belvidere Rd A3
Bernard St C2
Blechynden Terr A1
Brazil Rd C3
Brinton's Rd A2
Britannia Rd A3
Briton St C2
Brunswick Pl A2
Bugle St C1
Canute Rd C3
Castle Way C2
Catchcold Tower ✦ B1
Central Bridge C3
Central Rd C2
Channel Way C3
Chapel Rd B3
Cineworld 🎥 C3
City Art Gallery 🏛 A1
City College B3
Civic Ctr A1
Civic Ctr Rd A1
Coach Station B1
Commercial Rd A1
Cumberland Pl A1
Cunard Rd C2
Derby Rd A3
Devonshire Rd A1
Dock Gate 4 C2
Dock Gate 8 B1
East Park A2
East Park Terr A2
East St B2
East St Shopping Ctr B2
Endle St B3
European Way C2
Fire Station A2
Floating Bridge Rd C3
Golden Gr A3
Graham Rd A2
Guildhall A1
Hanover Bldgs B2
Harbour Lights 🎥 C3
Harbour Pde B1
Hartington Rd A3
Havelock Rd A1
Henstead Rd A1
Herbert Walker Ave B1
High St B2
Hoglands Park B2
Holy Rood (Rems), Merchant Navy Memorial ⛪ B2
Houndwell Park B2
Houndwell Pl B2
Hythe Ferry C2
Information Ctr ℹ A1
Isle of Wight Ferry Terminal C1
James St B3
Java Rd C2
Kingsway A2
Leisure World B1
Library A1
Lime St B2
London Rd A2
Marine Pde B3
Maritime 🏛 C1
Marsh La B2
Mayflower Meml ✦ C1
Mayflower Park C1
Mayflower Theatre, The 🎭 A1
Medieval Merchant's House 🏠 C1
Melbourne St B3
Millais 🏛 A2
Morris Rd A1
National Oceanography Ctr ✦ C3
Neptune Way C3
New Rd A2
Nichols Rd A3
North Front A2
Northam Rd A3
Ocean Dock C2
Ocean Village Marina C3
Ocean Way C3
Odeon 🎥 B1
Ogle Rd B1
Old Northam Rd A2
Orchard La B2
Oxford Ave A2
Oxford St C2
Palmerston Park A2
Palmerston Rd A2
Parsonage Rd A3
Peel St A3
Platform Rd C2
Police Station 🚓 A1
Portland Terr B1
Post Office 📮 A2/A3/B2
Pound Tree Rd B2
Quays Swimming & Diving Complex, The B1
Queen's Park C2
Queen's Peace Fountain ✦ A2
Queen's Terr C2
Queen's Way B2
Radcliffe Rd A3
Rochester St A3
Royal Pier C1
Royal South Hants Hospital Ⓗ A2
St Andrew's Rd A2
St Mary St A2
St Mary's ⛪ B3
St Mary's Leisure Ctr A2
St Mary's Pl B2
St Mary's Rd A2
St Mary's Stadium (Southampton FC) A3
St Michael's ⛪ C1
Solent Sky 🏛 C3
South Front B2
Southampton Central Station ⇌ A1
Southampton Solent University A2
SS Shieldhall ⛴ C2
Terminus Terr C2
The Mall, Marlands A1
The Polygon A1
Threefield La B2
Titanic Engineers' Memorial ✦ A2
Town Quay C1
Town Walls B2
Tudor House 🏠 C1
Vincent's Walk B2
West Gate Hall 🏠 C1
West Marlands Rd A1
West Park A1
West Park Rd A1
West Quay Rd B1
West Quay Retail Park B1
West Quay Sh Ctr B1
West Rd C2
Western Esplanade B1
Winton St A2

Southend-on-Sea 343

Adventure Island ✦ C3
Albany Ave A1
Albert Rd C3
Alexandra Rd C2
Alexandra St C2
Alexandra Yacht Club ✦ C2
Ashburnham Rd B2
Ave Rd B1
Avenue Terr B1
Balmoral Rd B1
Baltic Ave B3
Baxter Ave A2/B2
Beecroft Art Gallery 🏛 C1
Bircham Rd A2
Boscombe Rd B3
Boston Ave A1/B2
Bournemouth Park Rd A3
Browning Ave A3
Bus Station C3
Byron Ave A3
Cambridge Rd C1/C2
Canewdon Rd B1
Carnarvon Rd A2
Central Ave A3
Chelmsford Ave A1
Chichester Rd B2
Church Rd C3
Civic Ctr A2
Clarence Rd C2
Clarence St C2
Cliff Ave B1
Cliffs Pavilion 🎭 C1
Clifftown Parade C2
Clifftown Rd C2
Colchester Rd A1
College Way B2
Coleman St B3
County Court B3
Cromer Rd B3
Crowborough Rd A2
Dryden Ave A3
East St A2
Elmer App B2
Elmer Ave B2
Gainsborough Dr A1
Gayton Rd A2
Glenhurst Rd A2
Gordon Pl B2
Gordon Rd B2
Grainger Rd A2
Greyhound Way A3
Guildford Rd B3
Hamlet Ct Rd B1
Hamlet Rd C1
Harcourt Ave A1
Hartington Rd C3
Hastings Rd B3
Herbert Gr C3
Heygate Ave C3
High St B2/C2
Information Ctr ℹ C3
Kenway A2
Kilworth Ave B3
Lancaster Gdns B3
Library B2
London Rd B1
Lucy Rd C3
MacDonald Ave A1
Magistrates Court A2
Maldon Rd A2
Maine Ave C1
Marine Rd C1
Marine Parade C3
Milton Rd B1
Milton St B2
Napier Ave B2
North Ave A3
North Rd A1/B1
Odeon 🎥 B2
Osborne Rd B1
Park Cres B1
Park Rd B1
Park St B1
Park Terr B1
Pier Hill C3
Pleasant Rd C3
Police Station 🚓 A2
Post Office 📮 B2/B3
Princes St B2
Queens Rd B2
Queensway B2/B3/C3
Rayleigh Ave A1
Redstock Rd A2
Rochford Ave A1
Royal Mews C2
Royal Terr C2
Royals Sh Ctr, The C3
Ruskin Ave A3
St Ann's Rd B3
St Helen's Rd B1
St John's Rd B1
St Leonard's Rd C3
St Lukes Rd A3
St Vincent's Rd C1
Salisbury Ave A1/B1
Scratton Rd C2
Shakespeare Dr A1
Short St A2
South Ave A3
Southchurch Rd B3
South Essex College B2
Southend Central ⇌ B2
Southend Pier Railway 🚂 C3
Southend Radio C2
Southend United FC A1
Southend Victoria ⇌ B2
Stadium Rd A2
Stanfield Rd A2
Stanley Rd C3
Sutton Rd A3/B3
Swanage Rd B3
Sweyne Ave A1
Sycamore Gr A3
Tennyson Ave A3
The Grove A3
Tickfield Ave A2
Tudor Rd A1
Tunbridge Rd A2
Tylers Ave B3
Tyrrel Dr B3
Univ of Essex B2/C2
Vale Ave A2
Victoria Ave A2
Victoria Sh Ctr, The B2
Warrior Sq B3
Wesley Rd C3
West Rd A1
West St A1
Westcliff Ave C1
Westcliff Parade C1
Western Esplanade C1
Weston Rd C2
Whitegate Rd B3
Wilson Rd C1
Wimborne Rd B3
York Rd C3

Stirling 343

Abbey Rd A3
Abbotsford Pl A3
Abercromby Pl C1
Albert Halls 🎭 B1
Albert Pl B1
Alexandra Pl A3
Allan Park C2
Ambulance Station A2
AMF Ten Pin Bowling ✦ B2
Argyll Ave A3
Argyll's Lodging ✦ B1
Back O' Hill Ind Est A1
Back O' Hill Rd A1
Baker St B2
Ballengeich Pass A1
Balmoral Pl B1
Barn Rd B1
Barnton St B2
Bow St B1
Bruce St A2
Burghmuir Ind Est C2
Burghmuir Rd A2/B2/C2
Bus Station B2
Cambuskenneth Bridge A3
Carlton 🎥 C2
Castle Ct B1
Causewayhead Rd A2
Cemetery A1
Church of the Holy Rude ⛪ B1
Clarendon Pl C1
Club House B1
Colquhoun St C3
Corn Exchange B2
Council Offices C2
Court B2
Cowane 🎭 A2
Cowane St A2
Cowane's Hospital 🏠 B1
Crawford Sh Arc B2
Crofthead Rd A1
Dean Cres A3
Douglas St A2
Drip Rd A1
Drummond La C1
Drummond Pl C1
Drummond Pl La C1
Dumbarton Rd C2
Eastern Access Rd B2
Edward Ave A3
Edward Rd A2
Forrest Rd A2
Fort A1
Forth Cres B2
Forth St A2
Gladstone Pl C1
Glebe Ave C1
Glebe Cres C1
Golf Course C1
Goosecroft Rd B2
Gowanhill A1
Greenwood Ave B1
Harvey Wynd A1
Information Ctr ℹ B1
Irvine Pl B2
James St A2
John St B1
Kerse Rd C3
King's Knot ✦ B1
King's Park C1
King's Park Rd C1
Laurencecroft Rd A2
Leisure Pool B2
Library B2
Linden Ave C2
Lovers Wk A2
Lower Back Walk B1
Lower Bridge St A2
Lower Castlehill A1
Mar Pl B1
Meadow Pl A3
Meadowforth Rd C3
Middlemuir Rd C3
Millar Pl A3
Morris Terr B2
Mote Hill A1
Murray Pl B2
Nelson Pl C2
Old Town Cemetery B1
Old Town Jail ✦ B1
Orchard House Hospital (No A+E) Ⓗ A2
Park Terr C1
Phoenix Industrial Est C3
Players Rd C3
Port St C2
Princes St B2
Queen St B2
Queen's Rd B1
Queenshaugh Dr A3
Rainbow Slides B2
Ramsay Pl A2
Riverside Dr A3
Ronald Pl A1
Rosebery Pl A2
Royal Gardens B1
Royal Gdns B1
St Mary's Wynd B1
St Ninian's Rd C2
Scott St A2
Seaforth Pl B2
Shore Rd B2
Smith Art Gallery & Museum 🏛 B1
Snowdon Pl C1
Snowdon Pl La C1
Spittal St B2
Springkerse Ind Est C3
Springkerse Rd C3
Stirling Business Ctr C2
Stirling Castle ♜ A1
Stirling County Rugby Football Club A3
Stirling Enterprise Pk B3
Stirling Old Bridge A2
Stirling Station ⇌ B2
Superstore A2
Sutherland Ave A3
TA Ctr C3
Tannery La A2
The Bastion ✦ C2
The Changing Room 🏛 B1
Thistle Industrial Est C3
Thistles Sh Ctr, The B2
Tollbooth, The ✦ B1
Town Wall B1
Union St A2
Upper Back Walk B1
Upper Bridge St A1
Upper Castlehill B1
Upper Craigs C2
Victoria Pl C1
Victoria Rd B1
Victoria Sq B1/C1
Vue 🎥 B2
Wallace St A2
Waverley Cres A3
Wellgreen Rd C2
Windsor Pl C1
YHA ▲ B1

Stoke 343

Ashford St A3
Avenue Rd A3
Aynsley Rd A2
Barnfield C1
Bath St C2
Beresford St A3
Bilton St C2
Boon Ave C2
Booth St C2
Boothen Rd C2/C3
Boughey St C2
Boughley Rd B3
Brighton St B1
Campbell Rd C2
Carlton Rd B3
Cauldon Rd A3
Cemetery A2
Cemetery Rd A2
Chamberlain Ave C1
Church (RC) ⛪ B2
Church St C2
City Rd C3
Civic Ctr & King's Hall 🏢 B3
Cliff Vale Pk A1
College Rd A3
Convent Cl B2
Copeland St B2
Cornwallis St C3
Corporation St C2
Crowther St A3
Dominic St B1
Elenora St B2
Elgin St B2
Epworth St A3
Etruscan St A1
Film Theatre 🎥 B3
Fleming Rd C2
Fletcher Rd C2
Floyd St B2
Foden St C2
Frank St C2
Franklin Rd C1
Frederick Ave B1
Garden St C1
Garner St A1
Gerrard St B2
Glebe St B3
Greatbach Ave B1
Hanley Park A3
Harris St B1
Hartshill Rd B1
Hayward St A2
Hide St B2
Higson Ave B2
Hill St B2
Honeywall B2
Hunters Dr C1
Hunters Way C2
Keary St C2
Kingsway B2
Leek Rd B3
Library C2
Lime St C2
Liverpool Rd B2
London Rd C2
Lonsdale St C2
Lovatt St B2
Lytton St B3
Market C2
Newcastle La C1
Newlands St A2
Norfolk St A2
North St A1/B2
North Staffordshire Royal Infirmary (A&E) Ⓗ B1
Northcote Ave B2
Oldmill St C3
Oriel St B1
Oxford St B1
Penkhull New Rd C1
Penkhull St C1
Police Station 🚓 C2
Portmeirion Pottery ✦ C2
Post Office 📮 A3/B1/B3/C1/C2
Prince's Rd B1
Pump St B2
Quarry Ave B1
Quarry Rd B1
Queen Anne St A3
Queen's Rd C1
Queensway A1/B2/C3
Richmond St B1
Rothwell St C1
St Peter's ⛪ B3
St Thomas Pl C1
Scrivenor Rd A1
Seaford St A3
Selwyn St C3
Shelton New Rd A1
Shelton Old Rd B2
Sheppard St C2
Spark St C2
Spencer Rd B3
Spode St C2
Squires View B3
Staffordshire Univ B3
Stanley Matthews Sports Ctr B3
Station Rd B3
Stoke Business Park C3
Stoke Recreation Ctr C2
Stoke Rd A2
Stoke-on-Trent Coll A3
Stoke-on-Trent Sta ⇌ B3
Sturgess St C2
The Villas C1
Thistley Hough C1
Thornton Rd B3
Tolkien Way B1
Trent Valley Rd C1
Vale St B2
Watford St A3
Wellesley St A3
West Ave B1
Westland St B1
Yeaman St C2
Yoxall Ave B1

Stratford-upon-Avon 343

Albany Rd B1
Alcester Rd B1
Ambulance Station B1
Arden St B2
Avenue Farm A1
Ave Farm Ind Est A1
Avenue Rd A3
Avon Industrial Estate A2
Baker Ave A1
Bandstand C3
Benson Rd A3
Birmingham Rd A2
Boat Club B3
Borden Pl C1
Brass Rubbing Ctr ✦ C2
Bridge St B2
Bridgetown Rd C3
Bridgeway B3
Broad St C2
Broad Walk C2
Brookvale Rd C1
Bull St C2
Bus Station B2
Butterfly Farm ✦ C3
Cemetery C1
Chapel La B2
Cherry Orchard C1
Chestnut Walk B2
Children's Playground C3
Church St C2
Civic Hall B2
Clarence Rd B1
Clopton Bridge ✦ B3
Clopton Rd A2
Coach Terminal & Park B3
College B1
College La C2
College St C2
Community Sports Ctr B1
Council Offices (District) B2
Courtyard 🎭 C2
Cox's Yard ✦ B3
Cricket Ground C3
Ely Gdns B2
Ely St B2
Evesham Rd C1
Fire Station B1
Foot Ferry C3
Fordham Ave A2
Gallery, The 🏛 B3
Garrick Way C1
Gower Memorial ✦ B3
Great William St B2
Greenhill St B2
Grove Rd B2
Guild St B2
Guildhall & School 🏠 B2
Hall's Croft 🏠 C2
Hartford Rd C1
Harvard House 🏠 B2
Henley St B2
High St B2
Holton St C2
Holy Trinity ⛪ C2
Information Ctr ℹ B3
Jolyffe Park Rd A2
Kipling Rd C3
Leisure & Visitor Ctr B3
Library B2
Lodge Rd B1
Maidenhead Rd A3
Mansell St B2
Masons Court B2
Masons Rd A1
Maybird Shopping Pk A2
Maybrook Rd A1
Mayfield Ave A2
Meer St B2
Mill La C2
Moat House Hotel B3
Narrow La C2
Nash's Ho & New Pl 🏠 B2
New St C2
Old Town C2
Orchard Way C1
Paddock La C1
Park Rd A1
Payton St B2
Percy St A2
Police Station 🚓 B2
Post Office 📮 B2/B3
Recreation Ground C2
Regal Road A2
Rother St B2
Rowley Cr A3
Royal Shakespeare & Swan Theatres 🎭 B3
Ryland St C2
Saffron Meadow C2
St Andrew's Cr B1
St Gregory's ⛪ A3
St Gregory's Rd A3
St Mary's Rd A2
Sanctus Dr C2
Sanctus St C1
Sandfield Rd C2
Scholars La B2
Seven Meadows Rd C2
Shakespeare Ctr ✦ B2
Shakespeare Institute C2
Shakespeare St B2
Shakespeare's Birthplace ✦ B2
Sheep St B2
Shelley Rd C3
Shipston Rd C3
Shottery Rd C1
Slingates Rd A2
Southern La C2
Station Rd B1
Stratford Healthcare Ⓗ B2
Stratford Hospital Ⓗ B2
Stratford Sports Club B1
Stratford-upon-Avon Station ⇌ B1
Swan's Nest La B3
Talbot Rd A2
The Greenway C2
The Willows B1
The Willows North B1
Tiddington Rd B3
Timothy's Bridge Industrial Estate A1
Timothy's Bridge Rd A1
Town Hall & Council Offices B2
Town Sq B2
Trinity St C2
Tyler St B2
War Memorial Gdns B3
Warwick Rd B3
Waterside B3
Welcombe Rd A3
West St C2
Western Rd A2
Wharf Rd A2
Wood St B2

Sunderland 343

Albion Pl C2
Alliance Pl B1
Argyle St C2
Ashwood St C1
Athenaeum St B2
Azalea Terr C2
Beach St A1
Bede Theatre 🎭 C3
Bedford St B2
Beechwood Terr C1
Belvedere Rd C2
Blandford St B2
Borough Rd B3

Bridge Cr B2
Bridge St B2
Brooke St A2
Brougham St B2
Burdon Rd C2
Burn Park C1
Burn Park Rd C1
Burn Park Tech Park C1
Carol St B1
Charles St A3
Chester Rd C1
Chester Terr B1
Church St A3
Civic Ctr C2
Cork St B3
Coronation St B3
Cowan Terr C2
Crowtree Rd B2
Dame Dorothy St A2
Deptford Rd B1
Deptford Terr A1
Derby St C2
Derwent St C2
Dock St A3
Dundas St A2
Durham Rd C1
Easington St A2
Egerton St C3
Empire B2
Empire Theatre B2
Farringdon Row B1
Fawcett St B2
Fox St C1
Foyle St B3
Frederick St B3
Gill Rd B2
Hanover Pl A1
Havelock Terr C1
Hay St A2
Headworth Sq B3
Hendon Rd B3
High St East B3
High St West B2/B3
Holmeside B2
Hylton Rd B1
Information Ctr B2
John St B3
Kier Hardie Way A2
Lambton St B3
Laura St C3
Lawrence St B3
Leisure Ctr B2
Library & Arts Ctr B3
Lily St B1
Lime St B1
Livingstone Rd B2
Low Row B2
Matamba Terr B1
Millburn St B1
Millennium Way A2
Minster B2
Monkwearmouth Station Museum A2
Mowbray Park C3
Mowbray Rd C3
Murton St C3
National Glass Ctr A3
New Durham Rd C1
Newcastle Rd A2
Nile St B3
Norfolk St B3
North Bridge St A2
Northern Gallery for Contemporary Art B3
Otto Terr C1
Park La C2
Park Lane C2
Park Rd C2
Paul's Rd B3
Peel St C3
Police Station B2
Post Office B2
Priestly Cr A1
Queen St B2
Railway Row B1
Retail Park B1
Richmond St A2
Roker Ave A2
Royalty Theatre C1
Ryhope Rd C2
St Mary's Way B2
St Michael's Way B2
St Peter's A3
St Peter's A2
St Peter's Way A3
St Vincent St C3
Salem Rd C3
Salem St C3
Salisbury St C3
Sans St B3
Silkworth Row B1
Southwick Rd A2
Stadium of Light (Sunderland AFC) A2
Stadium Way A2
Stobart St A2
Stockton Rd C2
Suffolk St C3
Sunderland Aquatic Ctr A2
Sunderland B2
Sunderland Mus B3
Sunderland Station B2
Sunderland St B3
Tatham St C3
Tavistock Pl B3
The Bridges B2
The Place B3
The Royalty C1
Thelma St C1
Thomas St North A2
Thornholme Rd C1
Toward Rd C3
Transport Interchange C2
Trimdon St Way B1
Tunstall Rd C2
University C1
University Library C1
University of Sunderland (City Campus) B1
University of Sunderland (Sir Tom Cowie at St Peter's Campus) A3
Vaux Brewery Way A2
Villiers St B3
Villiers St South B3
Vine Pl C2
Violet St B1
Walton La B3
Waterworks Rd B1
Wearmouth Bridge B2
Wellington La A1
West Sunniside B3
West Wear St B3
Westbourne Rd B1
Western Hill C1
Wharncliffe B1
Whickham St A3
White House Rd C3
Wilson St North A2
Winter Gdns C3
Wreath Quay A1

Swansea
Abertawe 343

Adelaide St C3
Albert Row C3
Alexandra Rd B3
Argyle St C1
Baptist Well Pl A2
Beach St C1
Belle Vue Way B3
Berw Rd A1
Berwick Terr A2
Bond St C1
Brangwyn Concert Hall C1
Bridge St A3
Brookands Terr B1
Brunswick St C1
Bryn-Syfi Terr A2
Bryn-y-Mor Rd C1
Bullins La B1
Burrows Rd C1
Bus/Rail link A3
Bus Station C2
Cadfan Rd A1
Cadrawd Rd A1
Caer St B3
Carig Cr A1
Carlton Terr B2
Carmarthen Rd A3
Castle Square B3
Castle St B3
Catherine St C1
City & County of Swansea Offices (County Hall) C2
City & County of Swansea Offices (Guildhall) C1
Clarence St C2
Colbourne Terr A2
Constitution Hill B1
Court B3
Creidiol Rd A2
Cromwell St B2
Duke St B1
Dunvant Pl C2
Dyfatty Park A3
Dyfatty St A3
Dyfed Ave A1
Dylan Thomas Ctr B3
Dylan Thomas Theatre C3
Eaton Cr C1
Eigen Cr A1
Elfed Rd A1
Emlyn Rd A1
Evans Terr A3
Fairfield Terr B1
Ffynone Dr B1
Ffynone Rd B1
Fire Station B3
Firm St A2
Fleet St C1
Francis St C1
Fullers Row B2
George St B2
Glamorgan St C2
Glyndŵr Pl C1
Graig Terr A3
Grand Theatre C2
Granogwen Rd A2
Guildhall Rd South C1
Gwent Rd A1
Gwynedd Ave A1
Hafod St A3
Hanover St B1
Harcourt St B2
Harries St A2
Heathfield B2
Henrietta St B1
Hewson St B2
High St A3/B3
High View A2
Hill St A2
Historic Ships Berth C3
HM Prison C2
Information Ctr C2
Islwyn Rd A1
King Edward's Rd C1
Law Courts C1
Library B3
Long Ridge A2
Madoc St C2
Mansel St B2
Maritime Quarter C3
Market B3
Mayhill Gdns B1
Mayhill Rd A1
Mega Bowl B3
Milton Terr A2
Mission Gallery C3
Montpellier Terr B1
Morfa Rd A3
Mount Pleasant B2
National Waterfront Museum C3
Nelson St C2
New Cut Rd A3
New St A3
Nicander Pde A2
Nicander Pl A2
Nicholl St B2
Norfolk St B2
North Hill Rd A2
Northampton La B2
Orchard St B3
Oxford St B2
Oystermouth Rd C1
Page St B2
Pant-y-Celyn Rd B1
Parc Tawe Link B3
Parc Tawe North B3
Parc Tawe Sh & L Ctr B3
Patti Pavilion C1
Paxton St C2
Penmaen Terr B1
Pen-y-Graig Rd A1
Phillips Pde C1
Picton Terr B2
Plantasia B3
Police Station B2
Post Office A1/A2/B2/C1
Powys Ave A1
Primrose St B2
Princess Way B3
Promenade B2
Pryder Gdns A1
Quadrant Ctr C2
Quay Park B3
Rhianfa La B1
Rhondda St B2
Richardson St C2
Rodney St C1
Rose Hill B1
Rosehill Terr B1
Russell St B1
St David's Sq C3
St Helen's Ave C1
St Helen's Cr C1
St Helen's Rd C1
St James Gdns B1
St James's Cr B1
St Mary's B3
Sea View Terr A3
Singleton St C2
South Dock C3
Stanley Pl B2
Strand B3
Swansea Castle B3
Swansea Coll Arts Ctr C1
Swansea Metropolitan University B2
Swansea Museum C3
Swansea Station A3
Taliesyn Rd B1
Tan y Marian Rd A1
Tegid Rd A2
Teilo Cr A1
Terrace Rd B1/B2
The Kingsway B2
The LC C3
Tontine St A3
Tower of Eclipse C3
Townhill Rd A1
Tram Museum C3
Trawler Rd C3
Union St B2
Upper Strand A3
Vernon St A3
Victoria Quay C3
Victoria Rd B3
Vincent St C1
Walter Rd B1
Watkin St A2
Waun-Wen Rd A2
Wellington St C2
Westbury St C1
Western St C1
Westway C2
William St C2
Wind St B3
Woodlands Terr B1
YMCA B2
York St C3

Swindon 343

Albert St C3
Albion St C1
Alfred St A2
Alvescot Rd C3
Art Gallery & Mus C3
Ashford Rd C1
Aylesbury St A2
Bath Rd C2
Bathampton St B1
Bathurst Rd B3
Beatrice St A2
Beckhampton St B3
Bowood Rd C1
Bristol St B1
Broad St A3
Brunel Arcade B2
Brunel Plaza B2
Brunswick St C2
Bus Station B2
Cambria Bridge Rd B1
Cambria Place B1
Canal Walk B2
Carfax St B2
Carr St B1
Cemetery C1/C3
Chandler Cl C3
Chapel C1
Chester St B1
Christ Church C3
Church Place B1
Cirencester Way A3
Clarence St B2
Clifton St C1
Cockleberry A2
Colbourne A3
Colbourne St A3
College St B2
Commercial Rd B2
Corporation St A2
Council Offices B3
County Rd A3
Courts B2
Cricket Ground A3
Cricklade Street C3
Crombey St B1/C2
Cross St C2
Curtis St B1
Deacon St C1
Designer Outlet (Great Western) B1
Dixon St C2
Dover St C2
Dowling St C2
Drove Rd C3
Dryden St C1
Durham St C3
East St B1
Eastcott Hill C2
Eastcott Rd C2
Edgeware Rd B2
Edmund St C2
Elmina Rd A3
Emlyn Square B1
Euclid St B3
Exeter St B1
Fairview C1
Faringdon Rd B1
Farnsby St B1
Fire Station B3
Fleet St B2
Fleming Way B2/B3
Florence St A2
Gladstone St A3
Gooch St A2
Graham St A3
Great Western Way A1/A2
Groundwell Rd B3
Hawksworth Way A1
Haydon St A2
Henry St B2
Hillside Ave C1
Holbrook Way B2
Hunt St C3
Hydro B1
Hythe Rd C2
Information Ctr B2
Joseph St C1
Kent Rd C2
King William St C2
Kingshill Rd C1
Lansdown Rd C2
Leicester St B3
Library B2
Lincoln St B3
Little London C3
London St B1
Magic Roundabout B3
Maidstone Rd C2
Manchester Rd A3
Maxwell St B1
Milford St B2
Milton Rd B1
Morse St C2
National Monuments Record Ctr B1
Newcastle St B3
Newcombe Drive A1
Newcombe Trading Estate A1
Newhall St C2
North St C2
North Star Ave A1
North Star A1
Northampton St B3
Oasis Leisure Ctr A1
Ocotal Way A3
Okus Rd C1
Old Town C3
Oxford St B1
Park Lane B1
Park Lane B1
Pembroke St C2
Plymouth St B3
Polaris House A2
Polaris Way A2
Police Station B2
Ponting St A2
Post Office B1/B2/C1/C3
Poulton St A3
Princes St B2
Prospect Hill C2
Prospect Place C2
Queen St B2
Queen's Park C3
Radnor St C1
Read St C1
Reading St B1
Regent St B2
Retail Park A2/A3/B3
Rosebery St A3
St Mark's B1
Salisbury St A3
Savernake St C2
Shelley St C1
Sheppard St B1
South St C2
Southampton St B3
Spring Gardens B3
Stafford Street C2
Stanier St C2
Station Road A2
STEAM B1
Swindon College A2
Swindon Rd C2
Swindon Station A2
Swindon Town Football Club A3
T A Ctr B1
Tennyson St B1
The Lawn C3
The Nurseries C1
The Parade B2
The Park B1
Theobald St B1
Town Hall B2
Transfer Bridges A3
Union St C2
Upham Rd C3
Victoria Rd C3
Walcot Rd B3
War Memorial B2
Wells St B3
Western St C2
Westmorland Rd B3
Whalebridge B2
Whitehead St C1
Whitehouse Rd A2
William St C1
Wood St C3
Wyvern Theatre & Arts Ctr B2
York Rd B3

Taunton 343

Addison Gr A1
Albemarle Rd A1
Alfred St B3
Alma St C2
Bath Pl C1
Belvedere Rd A1
Billet St B2
Billetfield C2
Birch Gr A1
Brewhouse Theatre B2
Bridge St B1
Bridgwater & Taunton Canal A2
Broadlands Rd C1
Burton Pl C1
Bus Station B1
Canal Rd A2
Cann St C1
Canon St B2
Castle B1
Castle St B1
Cheddon Rd A2
Chip Lane A1
Clarence St B1
Cleveland St B1
Clifton Terr A2
Coleridge Cres C3
Compass Hill C1
Compton Cl A2
Corporation St B1
Council Offices A1
County Walk Sh Ctr C2
Courtyard B2
Cranmer Rd B2
Critchard Way B3
Cyril St A1
Deller's Wharf B1
Duke St B2
East Reach B3
East St B3
Eastbourne Rd B2
Eastleigh Rd C3
Eaton Cres A2
Elm Gr A1
Elms Cl A1
Fons George C1
Fore St B2
Fowler St A1
French Weir Rec Grd B1
Geoffrey Farrant Wk A2
Gray's Almshouses B2
Grays Rd B3
Greenway Ave A1
Guildford Pl C1
Hammet St B2
Haydon Rd B3
Heavitree Way A2
Herbert St A1
High St C2
Holway Ave C3
Hugo St B3
Huish's Almshouses B2
Hurdle Way C2
Information Ctr C2
Jubilee St A1
King's College C3
Kings Cl C3
Laburnum St B2
Lambrook Rd B3
Lansdowne Rd A3
Leslie Ave A1
Leycroft Rd B3
Library C2
Linden Gr A1
Magdalene St B2
Magistrates Court B1
Malvern Terr A2
Market House B2
Mary St C2
Middle St B2
Midford Rd B3
Mitre Court B3
Mount Nebo C1
Mount St C2
Mountway C2
Mus of Somerset B1
North St B2
Northfield Ave B1
Northfield Rd B1
Northleigh Rd C3
Obridge Allotments A3
Obridge Lane A3
Obridge Rd A3
Obridge Viaduct A3
Old Mkt Shopping Ctr C2
Osborne Way C1
Park St C1
Paul St C2
Plais St A2
Playing Field C3
Police Station C1
Portland St B1
Post Office B1/B2/C1
Priorswood Ind Est A3
Priorswood Rd A2
Priory Ave B2
Priory Bridge Rd B2
Priory Fields Retail Pk A3
Priory Park A2
Priory Way A3
Queen St B3
Railway St A1
Records Office A2
Recreation Grd A1
Riverside Place B2
St Augustine St B2
St George's C2
St Georges Sq C2
St James B2
St James St B2
St John's C1
St John's Rd B1
St Josephs Field C2
St Mary Magdalene's B2
Samuels Ct A1
Shire Hall & Law Courts C1
Somerset County Cricket Ground B2
Somerset County Hall C1
Somerset Cricket B2
South Rd C3
South St C3
Staplegrove Rd B1
Station Rd A1
Stephen St B2
Swimming Pool A1
Tancred St B2
Tauntfield Cl C3
Taunton Dean Cricket Club C2
Taunton Station A2
The Avenue A1
The Crescent C1
The Mount C2
Thomas St A1
Toneway A3
Tower St B1
Trevor Smith Pl C3
Trinity Business Ctr C3
Trinity Rd C3
Trinity St B3
Trull Rd C1
Tudor House B2
Upper High St C1
Venture Way A3
Victoria Gate B3
Victoria Park B3
Victoria St B3
Viney St B3
Vivary Park C2
Vivary Rd C1
War Memorial C1
Wellesley St A2
Wheatley Cres A3
Whitehall A1
Wilfred Rd B3
William St A1
Wilton Church C1
Wilton Cl C1
Wilton Gr C1
Wilton St C1
Winchester St B2
Winters Field B2
Wood St B1
Yarde Pl B1

Telford 343

Alma Ave C1
Amphitheatre C2
Bowling Alley B2
Brandsfarm Way C3
Brunel Rd B1
Bus Station B2
Buxton Rd C1
Central Park A2
Civic Offices B2
Coach Central B2
Coachwell Cl B1
Colliers Way A1
Courts B2
Dale Acre Way B3
Darliston C3
Deepdale B3
Deercote B2
Dinthill C3
Doddington C3
Dodmoor Grange C3
Downemead B3
Duffryn B3
Dunsheath B3
Euston Way A3
Eyton Mound C1
Eyton Rd C1
Forgegate A2
Grange Central B2
Hall Park Way B1
Hinkshay Rd C2
Hollinsworth Rd A2
Holyhead Rd A3
Housing Trust A1
Ice Rink B2
Information Ctr B2
Ironmasters Way A2
Job Ctr B1
Land Registry B1
Lawn Central B2
Lawnswood C1
Library B2
Malinsgate B1
Matlock Ave C1
Moor Rd C1
Mount Rd C1
NFU Offices B1
Odeon B2
Park Lane A1
Police Station B1
Priorslee Ave A3
Queen Elizabeth Ave C3
Queen Elizabeth Way B1
Queensway A2/B3
Rampart Way A2
Randlay Ave C3
Randlay Wood C3
Rhodes Ave C1
Royal Way B1
St Leonards Rd B1
St Quentin Gate B2
Shifnal Rd A3
Sixth Ave A1
Southwater Way B1
Spout Lane C1
Spout Mound B1
Spout Way C1
Stafford Court B3
Stafford Park B3
Stirchley Ave C3
Stone Row C1
Telford Bridge Ret Pk A1
Telford Central Sta A3
Telford Ctr, The B2
Telford Forge Ret Pk A1
Telford Hornets RFC C2
Telford Int Ctr C2
Telford Way A3
Third Ave A2
Town Park C2
Town Park Visitor Ctr B2
Walker House B2
Wellswood Ave A2
West Ctr Way B1
Withywood Drive C1
Woodhouse Central B2
Yates Way A1

Torquay 344

Abbey Rd B2
Alexandra Rd A2
Alpine Rd B3
Ash Hill Rd A2
Babbacombe Rd B3
Bampfylde Rd B1
Barton Rd A1
Beacon Quay C2
Belgrave Rd A1/B1
Belmont Rd A3
Berea Rd A3
Braddons Hill Rd East B3
Brewery Park A3
Bronshill Rd A2
Castle Rd A2
Cavern Rd A3
Central B2
Chatsworth Rd A2
Chestnut Ave B1
Church St A1
Civic Offices A2
Coach Station A1
Corbyn Head C1
Croft Hill B1
Croft Rd B1
Daddyhole Plain C3
East St A1
Egerton Rd A3
Ellacombe Church Rd A3
Ellacombe Rd A2
Falkland Rd B1
Fleet St B2
Fleet Walk Sh Ctr B2
Grafton Rd B3
Haldon Pier C2
Hatfield Rd A2
Highbury Rd A2
Higher Warberry Rd A3
Hillesdon Rd B3
Hollywood Bowl C3
Hoxton Rd A3
Hunsdon Rd B3
Information Ctr B2
Inner Harbour C3
Kenwyn Rd A3
Laburnum St A1
Law Courts A2
Library A2
Lime Ave B1
Living Coasts C3
Lower Warberry Rd B3
Lucius St B1
Lymington Rd A1
Magdalene Rd A1
Marina C2
Market St B2
Meadfoot Lane C3
Meadfoot Rd C3
Melville St B2
Middle Warberry Rd B3
Mill Lane A1
Montpellier Rd B3
Morgan Ave A1
Museum Rd B3
Newton Rd A1
Oakhill Rd A1
Outer Harbour C2
Parkhill Rd C3
Pavilion C2
Pimlico B2
Police Station A1
Post Office A1/B2
Princes Rd A3
Princes Rd East A3
Princes Rd West A3
Princess Gdns C2
Princess Pier C2
Princess Theatre C2
Rathmore Rd B1
Recreation Grd B1
Riviera Ctr Int B1
Rock End Ave C3
Rock Rd B2
Rock Walk B2
Rosehill Rd A3
St Efride's Rd A1
St John's B3
St Luke's Rd B2
St Luke's Rd North B2
St Luke's Rd South B2
St Marychurch Rd A2
Scarborough Rd B1
Shedden Hill B2
South Pier C2
South St A1
Spanish Barn B1
Stitchill Rd B3
Strand B3
Sutherland Rd B3
Teignmouth Rd A1
Temperance St B2
The King's Drive B1
The Terrace B3
Thurlow Rd A1
Tor Bay B1
Tor Church Rd A1
Tor Hill Rd A1
Torbay Rd B2
Torquay Museum B3
Torquay Station C1
Torre Abbey Mansion B1
Torre Abbey Meadows B1
Torre Abbey Sands B1
Torwood Gdns B3
Torwood St C3
Union Square A2
Union St A1
Upton Hill A2
Upton Park A1
Upton Rd A1
Vanehill Rd C3
Vansittart Rd A1
Vaughan Parade C2
Victoria Parade C3
Victoria Rd A2
Warberry Rd West B2
Warren Rd B2
Windsor Rd A2/A3
Woodville Rd A3

Truro 344

Adelaide Ter B1
Agar Rd B3
Arch Hill C2
Arundell Pl C2
Avondale Rd B1
Back Quay B3
Barrack La C3
Barton Meadow A1
Benson Rd A2
Bishops Cl A2
Bosvean Gdns B1
Bosvigo Gardens B1
Bosvigo La A1
Bosvigo Rd B2
Broad St A3
Burley Cl C3
Bus Station B3
Calenick St C2
Campfield Hill B3
Carclew St B3
Carew Rd A2
Carey Park B2
Carlyon Rd A2
Carvoza Rd A3
Castle St B2
Cathedral View A2
Chainwalk Dr A2
Chapel Hill B1
Charles St B2
City Hall B3
City Rd B2
Coinage Hall B3
Comprigney Hill A1
Coosebean La A1
Copes Gdns A2
County Hall B1
Courtney Rd A2
Crescent Rd B1
Crescent Rise B1
Daniell Court C2
Daniell Rd C2
Daniell St C2
Daubuz Cl A2
Dobbs La B1
Edward St B2
Eliot Rd A2
Elm Court A3
Enys Cl A1
Enys Rd A1
Fairmantle St B3
Falmouth Rd C2
Ferris Town B2
Fire Station B1
Frances St B2
George St B2
Green Cl C2
Green La C1
Grenville Rd A2
Hall For Cornwall B3
Hendra Rd A2
Hendra Vean A1
High Cross B3
Higher Newham La C3
Higher Trehaverne A2
Hillcrest Ave B1
Hospital B2
Hunkin Cl A2
Hurland Rd C3
Infirmary Hill B2
James Pl B3
Kenwyn Church Rd A1
Kenwyn Hill A1
Kenwyn Rd A2
Kenwyn St B2
Kerris Gdns A1
King St B3
Lemon Quay B3
Lemon St Gallery B3
Library B1/B3
Malpas Rd B3
Market B3
Memorial Gdns B3
Merrifield Close B1
Mitchell Hill A3
Moresk Cl A3
Moresk Rd A3
Morlaix Ave C3
Nancemere Rd A3
Newham Bsns Park C3
Newham Industrial Est C3
Newham Rd C3
Northfield Dr C3
Oak Way A3
Old County Hall B1
Pal's Terr A3
Park View C2
Pendarves Rd A2
Plaza Cinema B3
Police Station B3
Post Office B2/B3
Prince's St B3
Pydar St A2
Quay St B3
Redannick Cres C2
Redannick La B2
Richard Lander Monument C2
Richmond Hill B1
River St B2
Rosedale Rd A2
Royal Cornwall Mus B2
St Aubyn Rd C3
St Clement St B3
St George's Rd A1
School La C2
Station Rd B1
Stokes Rd A2
Strangways Terr C3
Tabernacle St B3
The Avenue A3
The Crescent B1
The Leats B2
The Spires A2
Trehaverne La A2
Tremayne Rd A2
Treseder's Gdns A3
Treworder Rd B1
Treyew Rd B1
Truro Cathedral B3
Truro Harbour Office B3
Truro Station B3
Union St B2
Upper School La C2
Victoria Gdns B2
Waterfall Gdns B2

Wick 344

Ackergill Cres A2
Ackergill St A2
Albert St C2
Ambulance Station A2
Argyle Sq C2
Assembly Rooms C2
Bank Row C2
Bankhead B1
Barons Well B2
Barrogill St C2
Bay View B3
Bexley Terr C3
Bignold Park C2
Bowling Green C2
Breadalbane Terr C2
Bridge of Wick B1
Bridge St B2
Brown Pl C2
Burn St B2
Bus Station B1
Caithness General Hospital (A+E) B1
Cliff Rd B1
Coach Rd B2
Coastguard Station C3
Corner Cres B3
Coronation St C1
Council Offices B2
Court B2
Crane Rock C3
Dempster St C2
Dunnet Ave A2
Fire Station B2
Fish Market C3
Francis St C1
George St A1
Girnigoe St B2
Glamis Rd B2
Gowrie Pl B1
Grant St C2
Green Rd B2
Gunns Terr B3
Harbour Quay B2
Harbour Rd C3
Harbour Terr C2
Harrow Hill C2
Henrietta St A2/B2
Heritage Museum C2
High St B2
Hill Ave A2
Hillhead Rd B3
Hood St C1
Huddart St C2
Information Ctr B2
Kenneth St C1
Kinnaird St C2
Kirk Hill B1
Langwell Cres B3
Leishman Ave B3
Leith Walk A2
Library B2
Lifeboat Station C3
Lighthouse C3
Lindsay Dr B3
Lindsay Pl B3
Loch St C2
Louisburgh St B2
Lower Dunbar St C2
Macleay La B1
Macleod Rd B3
MacRae St C2
Martha Terr B2
Miller Ave B1
Miller La B1
Moray St C2
Mowat Pl B3
Murchison St C3
Newton Ave C1
Newton Rd C1
Nicolson St C3
North Highland Coll B2
North River Pier B3
Northcote St C2
Owen Pl A2
Police Station B1
Port Dunbar B3
Post Office B2/C2

Pulteney Distillery ✦ C2
River St B2
Robert St A1
Rutherford St C2
St John's Episcopal ⛪ C2
Sandigoe Rd B3
Scalesburn B3
Seaforth Ave C1
Shore La B2
Sinclair Dr B3
Sinclair Terr C2
Smith Terr C3
South Pier C3
South Quay C3
South Rd C1
South River Pier B3
Station Rd B1
Swimming Pool B2
TA Ctr C2
Telford St B2
The Shore B2
Thurso Rd B1
Thurso St B1
Town Hall B2
Union St B2
Upper Dunbar St C2
Vansittart St C3
Victoria Pl B2
War Memorial A1
Well of Cairndhuna ✦ C3
Wellington Ave C3
Wellington St C3
West Banks Ave C1
West Banks Terr C1
West Park C1
Whitehorse Park B2
Wick Harbour Bridge B2
Wick Industrial Estate A2
Wick Parish Church ⛪ B1
Wick Station ⇌ B1
Williamson St B2
Willowbank B2

Winchester 344

Andover Rd A2
Andover Rd Retail Pk A2
Archery La C2
Arthur Rd A2
Bar End Rd C3
Beaufort Rd C2
Beggar's La B3
Bereweeke Ave A1
Bereweeke Rd A1
Boscobel Rd A2
Brassey Rd A2
Broadway B3
Brooks Sh Ctr, The B3
Bus Station B3
Butter Cross ✦ B2
Canon St C2
Castle Wall C2/C3
Castle, King Arthur's Round Table B2
Cathedral ✝ C2
Cheriton Rd A1
Chesil St C3
Chesil Theatre C3
Christchurch Rd C1
City Museum B2
City Offices C3
City Rd B2
Clifton Rd B1
Clifton Terr B2
Close Wall C2/C3
Coach Park A2
Colebrook St C3
College St C2
College Walk C3
Compton Rd C2
County Council Offices B2
Cranworth Rd A2
Cromwell Rd C1
Culver Rd C2
Domum Rd C3
Durngate Pl B3
Eastgate St B3
Edgar Rd C2
Egbert Rd A2
Elm Rd B1
Fairfield Rd A1
Fire Station B3
Fordington Ave B1
Fordington Rd A1
Friarsgate B3
Gordon Rd B3
Greenhill Rd B1
Guildhall B3
HM Prison B1
Hatherley Rd A1
High St B2
Hillier Way A3
Hyde Abbey (Remains) ✝ A2
Hyde Abbey Rd B2
Hyde Cl A2
Hyde St A2
Information Ctr ℹ B3
Jane Austen's Ho C2
Jewry St B2
John Stripe Theatre C1
King Alfred Pl A2
Kingsgate Arch C2
Kingsgate Park C2
Kingsgate Rd C2
Kingsgate St C2
Lankhills Rd A2
Library B2
Lower Brook St B3
Magdalen Hill B3
Market La B2
Mews La B1
Middle Brook St B3
Middle Rd B1
Military Museums B2
Milland Rd C3
Milverton Rd B1
Monks Rd A3
North Hill Cl A2
North Walls B2
North Walls Rec Gnd A3
Nuns Rd A3
Oram's Arbour B1
Owen's Rd A2
Parchment St B2
Park & Ride C3
Park Ave B3
Playing Field A1
Police HQ B1
Police Station B3
Portal Rd C3
Post Office B2/C1
Quarry Rd C3
Ranelagh Rd C1
Regiment Museum B2
River Park Leisure Ctr B3
Romans' Rd C2
Romsey Rd B1
Royal Hampshire County Hospital (A&E) B1
St Cross Rd C2
St George's St B2
St Giles Hill C3
St James' La B1
St James' Terr B1
St James Villas C2
St John's ⛪ B3
St John's St B3
St Michael's Rd C2
St Paul's Hill B1
St Peter St B2
St Swithun St C2
St Thomas St C2
Saxon Rd A2
School of Art B3
Screen C2
Sleepers Hill Rd C1
Southgate St B2
Sparkford Rd C1
Staple Gdns B2
Station Rd B2
Step Terr B1
Stockbridge Rd A1
Stuart Cres C1
Sussex St B2
Swan Lane B2
Tanner St B3
The Square B2
The Weirs C3
The Winchester Gallery B3
Theatre Royal B2
Tower St B2
Town Hall C3
Union St B3
Univ of Winchester (King Alfred Campus) C1
Upper Brook St B2
Wales St B3
Water Lane B3
West End Terr B1
West Gate B2
Western Rd B1
Wharf Hill C3
Winchester College C2
Winchester Station ⇌ A2
Wolvesey Castle C3
Worthy Lane A2
Worthy Rd A2

Windsor 344

Adelaide Sq C3
Albany Rd C2
Albert St B1
Alexandra Gdns B2
Alexandra Rd C2
Alma Rd B2
Ambulance Station B1
Arthur Rd B2
Bachelors Acre B3
Barry Ave B2
Beaumont Rd C2
Bexley St B1
Boat House B2
Brocas St B2
Brook St C3
Bulkeley Ave C1
Castle Hill B3
Charles St B2
Claremont Rd C2
Clarence Cr B2
Clarence Rd B1
Clewer Court Rd B1
Coach Park B2
College Cr C1
Courts C2
Cricket Ground C3
Dagmar Rd C2
Datchet Rd B3
Devereux Rd C2
Dorset Rd C2
Duke St B1
Elm Rd C1
Eton College ✦ A3
Eton Ct A2
Eton Sq A2
Eton Wick Rd A2
Fire Station C2
Farm Yard B3
Frances Rd C2
Frogmore Dr B3
Gloucester Pl C3
Goslar Way C1
Goswell Hill B2
Goswell Rd B2
Green La C1
Grove Rd C2
Guildhall B3
Helena Rd C2
Helston La B1
High St A2/B3
Holy Trinity ⛪ C2
Hospital (Private) C2
Household Cavalry C2
Imperial Rd C1
Information Ctr ℹ B2/B3
Keats La A2
King Edward Ct B2
King Edward VII Ave A3
King Edward VII Hospital C2
King George V Meml B3
King's Rd C3
King Stable St A2
Library C2
Maidenhead Rd B1
Meadow La A2
Municipal Offices C3
Nell Gwynne's Ho B3
Osborne Rd C2
Oxford Rd B1
Park St B3
Peascod St B2
Police Station C2
Post Office A2
Princess Margaret Hospital C2
Queen Victoria's Walk B3
Queen's Rd C2
River St B2
Romney Island A3
Romney Lock A3
Romney Lock Rd A3
Russell St C2
St John's ⛪ B3
St John's Chapel ⛪ A2
St Leonards Rd C2
St Mark's Rd C2
Sheet St C3
South Meadow A2
South Meadow La A2
Springfield Rd C1
Stovell Rd B1
Sunbury Rd A2
Tangier La A2
Tangier St A3
Temple Rd C2
Thames St B3
The Brocas A2
The Home Park A3/C3
The Long Walk C3
Theatre Royal B3
Trinity Pl C2
Vansittart Rd B1/C1
Vansittart Rd Gdns C1
Victoria Barracks C2
Victoria St C2
Ward Royal B2
Westmead C1
White Lilies Island A1
William St B2
Windsor Arts Ctr C2
Windsor Castle B3
Windsor & Eton Central ⇌ B2
Windsor & Eton Riverside ⇌ A3
Windsor Bridge B3
Windsor Great Park C3
Windsor Leisure Ctr B1
Windsor Relief Rd A1
Windsor Royal Sh B2
York Ave C1
York Rd C1

Wolverhampton 344

Albion St B3
Alexandra St C1
Arena B2
Arts Gallery B2
Ashland St C1
Austin St A1
Badger Dr A3
Bailey St B3
Bath Ave B1
Bath Rd B1
Bell St C2
Berry St B3
Bilston Rd C3
Bilston St C3
Birmingham Canal A3
Bone Mill La A2
Brewery Rd B1
Bright St A1
Burton Cres B3
Bus Station B3
Cambridge St A3
Camp St B2
Cannock Rd A3
Castle St C2
Chapel Ash C1
Cherry St C1
Chester St A1
Church La C2
Church St C2
Civic Ctr B2
Clarence Rd B2
Cleveland St C2
Clifton St C1
Coach Station B2
Compton Rd B1
Corn Hill B3
Coven St A3
Craddock St A1
Cross St North A2
Crown & County Courts C3
Crown St A2
Culwell St B3
Dale St C1
Darlington St C1
Dartmouth St C3
Devon Rd A1
Drummond St B2
Dudley Rd C2
Dudley St B2
Duke St C3
Dunkley St B1
Dunstall Ave A2
Dunstall Hill A2
Dunstall Rd A1/A2
Evans St A1
Fawdry St A1
Field St B3
Fire Station C1
Fiveways A2
Fowler Playing Fields A3
Fox's La A2
Francis St A2
Fryer St B3
Gloucester St A1
Gordon St C3
Graiseley St C1
Grand B3
Granville St C3
Great Brickkiln St C1
Great Hampton St A1
Great Western St A2
Grimstone St B3
Harrow St A1
Hilton St A3
Horseley Fields C3
Humber Rd C1
Jack Hayward Way A2
Jameson St A1
Jenner St C3
Kennedy Rd B3
Kimberley St C1
King St B2
Laburnum St C1
Lansdowne Rd B1
Leicester St A1
Lever St C3
Library C3
Lichfield St B2
Light House B3
Little's La B3
Lock St B3
Lord St C1
Lowe St A1
Lower Stafford St A2
Magistrates Court B2
Mander Ctr C2
Mander St C1
Market St B2
Market C3
Melbourne St C3
Merridale St C1
Middlecross C3
Molineux St B2
Mostyn St A1
New Hampton Rd East A1
Nine Elms La A3
North Rd A2
Oaks Cres C1
Oxley St A2
Paget St A1
Park Ave B1
Park Road East A1
Park Road West B1
Paul St C2
Pelham St C1
Penn Rd C2
Piper's Row B3
Pitt St C2
Police Station C3
Pool St C2
Poole St A3
Post Office A1/A2/B2/B2
Powlett St C3
Queen St B2
Raby St C3
Raglan St C1
Railway Dr B3
Red Hill St A2
Red Lion St B2
Retreat St C1
Ring Rd B2
Rugby St A1
Russell St C1
St Andrew's B1
St David's B3
St George's C3
St George's Pde C2
St James St C3
St John's C2
St John's ⛪ C2
St John's Retail Park C2
St John's Square C2
St Mark's C1
St Marks Rd C1
St Marks St C1
St Patrick's B2
St Peter's B2
St Peter's ⛪ B2
Salisbury St C1
Salop St C2
School St C2
Sherwood St A2
Smestow St A3
Snowhill C2
Springfield Rd A3
Stafford St B2
Staveley Rd A1
Steelhouse La C3
Stephenson St C1
Stewart St C2
Sun St B3
Sutherland Pl C3
Tempest St C2
Temple St C2
Tettenhall Rd B1
The Maltings B2
The Royal (Metro) C3
Thomas St C2
Thornley St B2
Tower St C2
University B2
Upper Zoar St C1
Vicarage Rd C3
Victoria St C2
Walpole St A1
Walsall St C3
Ward St C3
Warwick St C3
Water St A3
Waterloo Rd B2
Wednesfield Rd B3
West Pk (not A&E) B1
West Park Swimming Pool B1
Wharf St C3
Whitmore Hill B2
Wolverhampton ⇌ B3
Wolverhampton St George's (Metro) C2
Wolverhampton Wanderers Football Ground (Molineux) B2
Worcester St C2
Wulfrun Ctr C2
Yarwell Cl A3
York St C3
Zoar St C1

Worcester 344

Albany Terr A1
Alice Otley School A2
Angel Pl B2
Angel St B2
Ashcroft Rd A2
Athelstan Rd C3
Back Lane North A1
Back Lane South A1
Barbourne Rd A2
Bath Rd C2
Battenhall Rd C3
Bridge St B2
Britannia Sq A1
Broad St B2
Bromwich La C1
Bromwich Rd C1
Bromyard Rd C1
Bus Station B2
Carden St B3
Castle St A2
Cathedral ✝ C2
Cathedral Plaza B2
Charles St B3
Chequers La B1
Chestnut St A2
Chestnut Walk A2
Citizens' Advice Bureau B2
City Walls Rd B2
Cole Hill C3
College of Technology B2
College St C2
Commandery C3
County Cricket Gd C1
Cripplegate Park B1
Croft Rd B1
Cromwell St B3
Crowngate Ctr B2
Deansway B2
Diglis Pde C2
Diglis Rd C2
Edgar Tower ✦ C2
Farrier St A2
Fire Station B2
Foregate St B2
Foregate Street ⇌ B2
Fort Royal Hill C3
Fort Royal Park C3
Foundry St B3
Friar St C2
George St B3
Grand Stand Rd B1
Greenhill C3
Greyfriars B2
Guildhall B2
Henwick Rd B1
High St B2
Hill St B3
Huntingdon Hall B2
Hylton Rd B1
Information Ctr ℹ B2
King Charles Place Shopping Centre C1
King's School C2
King's School Playing Field C2
Kleve Walk C2
Lansdowne Cr A3
Lansdowne Rd A3
Lansdowne Walk A3
Laslett St A3
Leisure Ctr A3
Library, Museum & Art Gallery A2
Little Chestnut St A2
Little London A2
London Rd C3
Lowell St A3
Lowesmoor B2
Lowesmoor Terr A3
Lowesmoor Wharf A3
Magistrates Court A2
Midland Rd B3
Mill St C2
Moors Severn Terr A1
New Rd C1
New St B2
Northfield St A2
Odeon B2
Padmore St B3
Park St C3
Pheasant St B3
Pitchcroft Racecourse A1
Police Station A2
Portland St C2
Post Office B2
Quay St B2
Queen St B2
Rainbow Hill A3
Recreation Ground A2
Reindeer Court B2
Rogers Hill A3
Sabrina Rd A1
St Dunstan's Cr C3
St John's C1
St Martin's Gate B3
St Oswald's Rd A2
St Paul's St B3
St Swithin's Church B2
St Wulstans Cr C3
Sansome Walk A2
Severn St C2
Shaw St B2
Shire Hall A2
Shrub Hill ⇌ B3
Shrub Hill Retail Park B3
Shrub Hill Rd B3
Slingpool Walk C1
South Quay B2
Southfield St A2
Sports Ground A2/C1
Stanley Rd B3
Swan, The A1
Swimming Pool A2
Tallow Hill B3
Tennis Walk A2
The Avenue C1
The Butts B2
The Cross B2
The Shambles B2
The Tything A2
Tolladine Rd B3
Tudor House ✦ B2
Tybridge St B1
Univ of Worcester B2
Vincent Rd B3
Vue C2
Washington St A3
Woolhope Rd C3
Worcester Bridge B2
Worcester Library & History Ctr B3
Worcester Porcelain Museum C2
Worcester Royal Grammar School A2
Wylds La C3

Wrexham *Wrecsam* 344

Abbot St B2
Acton Rd A3
Albert St C3
Alexandra Rd C1
Aran Rd A3
Barnfield C3
Bath Rd C2
Beechley Rd C3
Belgrave Rd C2
Belle Vue Park C2
Belle Vue Rd C2
Belvedere Dr A1
Bennion's Rd C3
Berse Rd A1
Bersham Rd C1
Birch St C3
Bodhyfryd B3
Border Retail Park B3
Bradley Rd C2
Bright St B1
Bron-y-Nant B1
Brook St C2
Bryn-y-Cabanau Rd C3
Bury St C3
Bus Station B2
Butchers Market B3
Caia Rd C3
Cambrian Ind Est C3
Caxton Pl B2
Cemetery C1
Centenary Rd C1
Chapel St C2
Charles St B3
Chester Rd A3
Chester St B3
Cilcen Gr A3
Citizens Advice Bureau B2
Cobden Rd B1
Council Offices B3
County B2
Crescent Rd B3
Crispin La A2
Croesnewyth Rd B1
Cross St A2
Cunliffe St A2
Derby Rd C3
Dolydd Rd B1
Duke St B2
Eagles Meadow C3
Earle St C2
East Ave A2
Edward St C2
Egerton St B2
Empress Rd C1
Erddig Rd C2
Fairy Rd C2
Fire Station B2
Foster Rd A3
Foxwood Dr C1
Garden Rd A2
General Market B3
Gerald St B2
Gibson St C1
Glyndŵr University Plas Coch Campus A1
Greenbank St C3
Greenfield A2
Grosvenor Rd B2
Grove Park B2
Grove Park Rd B3
Grove Rd A3
Guildhall B2
Haig Rd C3
Hampden Rd C2
Hazel Gr A3
Henblas St B3
High St B3
Hightown Rd C3
Hill St B2
Holt Rd B3
Holt St B3
Hope St B2
Huntroyde Ave C3
Information Ctr ℹ B3
Island Gn Sh Ctr B2
Job Ctr B2
Jubilee Rd B2
King St B2
Kingsmills Rd C3
Lambpit St B3
Law Courts B3
Lawson Cl A3
Lawson Rd A3
Lea Rd C2
Library & Arts Ctr B2
Lilac Way B1
Llys David Lord B1
Lorne St A2
Maesgwyn Rd B1
Maesydre Rd A3
Manley Rd B3
Market St B3
Mawddy Ave A2
Mayville Ave A2
Memorial Gallery B2
Memorial Hall B3
Mold Rd A1
Mount St C3
Neville Cres A3
New Rd A2
North Wales Regional Tennis Ctr A1
North Wales School of Art & Design B2
Oak Dr A3
Park Ave A3
Park St A2
Peel St C1
Pentre Felin C2
Pen y Bryn C2
Penymaes Ave A3
Peoples Market B3
Percy St C2
Plas Coch Retail Park A1
Plas Coch Rd A1
Police Station B3
Poplar Rd C2
Post Office A2/B2/C2/C3
Powell Rd B3
Poyser St C2
Price's La A2
Primose Way B1
Princess St C1
Queen St B3
Queens Sq B2
Regent St B2
Rhosddu Rd A2/B2
Rhosnesni La A3
Rivulet Rd C3
Ruabon Rd C2
Ruthin Rd C1/C2
St Giles ⛪ C3
St Giles Way C3
St James Ct A2
St Mary's ✝ B2
Salisbury Rd C3
Salop Rd C3
Sontley Rd C2
Spring Rd A2
Stanley St C3
Stansty Rd A2
Station Approach B2
Studio B2
Talbot Rd C2
Techniquest Glyndŵr ✦ A2
The Beeches A3
The Pines A3
Town Hill C2
Trevor St C2
Trinity St B2
Tuttle St C3
Vale Park A1
Vernon St B2
Vicarage Hill B2
Victoria Rd A2
Walnut St A2
War Memorial B3
Waterworld L Ctr ✦ B3
Watery Rd B1/B2
Wellington Rd C2
Westminster Dr A3
William Aston Hall A1
Windsor Rd A1
Wrexham AFC A1
Wrexham Central ⇌ B2
Wrexham General ⇌ B2
Wrexham Maelor Hospital (A+E) A1
Wrexham Technology Park B1
Wynn Ave A2
Yale College B3
Yale Gr A3
Yorke St C3

York 344

Aldwark B2
Ambulance Station B3
Barbican Rd C3
Barley Hall B2
Bishopgate St C2
Bishopthorpe Rd C2
Blossom St C1
Bootham A1
Bootham Cr A1
Bootham Terr A1
Bridge St B2
Brook St A2
Brownlow St A2
Burton Stone La A1
Castle Museum C2
Castlegate B2
Cemetery Rd C3
Cherry St C2
City Screen B2
City Wall A2/B1/C3
Clarence St A2
Clementhorpe C2
Clifford St B2
Clifford's Tower B2
Clifton A1
Coach park A2
Coney St B2
Cromwell Rd C2
Crown Court C2
Davygate B2
Deanery Gdns A2
DIG ✦ B2
Ebor Industrial Estate B3
Fairfax House B2
Fishergate C3
Foss Islands Retail Pk B3
Foss Islands Rd B3
Fossbank A3
Garden St A2
George St C3
Gillygate A2
Goodramgate B2
Grand Opera House B2
Grosvenor Terr A1
Guildhall B2
Hallfield Rd A3
Heslington Rd C3
Heworth Green A3
Holy Trinity ⛪ B2
Hope St C3
Huntington Rd A3
Information Ctr ℹ B2
James St B3
Jorvik Viking Ctr B2
Kent St C3
Lawrence St C3
Layerthorpe A3
Leeman Rd B1
Lendal B2
Lendal Bridge B1
Library B1
Longfield Terr A1
Lord Mayor's Walk A2
Lower Eldon St A2
Lowther St A2
Mansion House B2
Margaret St C3
Marygate A1
Melbourne St C3
Merchant Adventurer's Hall B2
Merchant Taylors' Hall B2
Micklegate B1
Micklegate Bar C1
Minster, The ✝ A2
Monkgate A2
Moss St C1
Museum Gdns B1
Museum St B1
National Railway Museum B1
Navigation Rd B3
Newton Terr C2
North Pde A1
North St B2
Nunnery La C1
Nunthorpe Rd C1
Ouse Bridge B2
Paragon St C3
Park Gr A3
Park St C1
Parliament St B2
Peasholme Green B3
Penley's Grove St A2
Piccadilly B2
Police Station B2
Post Office B1/B2/C3
Priory St B1
Purey Cust Nuffield Hospital, The A2
Queen Anne's Rd A1
Quilt Museum A2
Reel C1
Regimental Mus B2
Richard III Museum A2
Roman Bath B2
Rowntree Park C2
St Andrewgate B2
St Benedict Rd C1
St John St A2
St Olave's Rd A1
St Peter's Gr A1
St Saviourgate B2
Scarcroft Hill C1
Scarcroft Rd C1
Skeldergate C2
Skeldergate Bridge C2
Station Rd B1
Stonegate B2
Sycamore Terr A1
Terry Ave C2
The Shambles B2
The Stonebow B2
Theatre Royal B2
Thorpe St C1
Toft Green B1
Tower St C2
Townend St A2
Treasurer's House A2
Trinity La B1
Undercroft Mus A2
Union Terr A2
Victor St C2
Vine St C2
Walmgate B3
Wellington St C3
York Art Gallery A1
York Barbican C3
York Brewery ✦ B1
York Dungeon, The B2
York Station ⇌ B1

W Isles
Highland
Moray
Aberds
Aberdeen
Perth and Kinross
Angus
Dundee
Argyll and Bute
Stirling
Fife
Glasgow
Edin
E Loth
N Ayrs
S Lanark
Midloth
E Ayrs
Borders
S Ayrs
Dumfries and Galloway
Northumberland
Tyne and Wear
Hartlepool
Redcar and Cleveland
Middlesbrough
Darlington
Stockton-on-Tees
Cumbria
Durham
IoM
North Yorkshire
York
E Yorks
Blackpool
Lancs
W Yorks
N Lincs
NE Lincs
Anglesey
Mers
Gtr Man
S Yorks
Conwy
Flint
Denb
Ches
Derbys
Notts
Lincolnshire
Gwyn
Wrex
Staffs
Telford
Leics
Rutland
Norfolk
Shrops
W Mid
Cambs
Ceredigion
Powys
Worcs
Warks
Northants
Suffolk
Hereford
Bedford
C Beds
Pembs
Carms
Glos
Bucks
Herts
Essex
Mon
Oxon
Swansea
Southend
Medway
Cardiff
Bristol
London
Wilts
W Berks
Hants
Surrey
Kent
Somerset
Soton
W Sus
E Sus
Devon
Dorset
IoW
Cornwall
Bmouth
Poole
Ptsmouth
Brighton
Torbay
Plymouth
Scilly

Abbreviations used in the index

Aberdeen Aberdeen City
Aberds Aberdeenshire
Ald Alderney
Anglesey Isle of Anglesey
Angus Angus
Argyll Argyll and Bute
Bath Bath and North East Somerset
Bedford Bedford
Bl Gwent Blaenau Gwent
Blackburn Blackburn with Darwen
Blackpool Blackpool
Bmouth Bournemouth
Borders Scottish Borders
Brack Bracknell
Bridgend Bridgend
Brighton City of Brighton and Hove
Bristol City and County of Bristol
Bucks Buckinghamshire
C Beds Central Bedfordshire
Caerph Caerphilly
Cambs Cambridgeshire
Cardiff Cardiff
Carms Carmarthenshire
Ceredig Ceredigion
Ches E Cheshire East
Ches W Cheshire West and Chester
Clack Clackmannanshire
Conwy Conwy
Corn Cornwall
Cumb Cumbria
Darl Darlington
Denb Denbighshire
Derby City of Derby
Derbys Derbyshire
Devon Devon
Dorset Dorset
Dumfries Dumfries and Galloway
Dundee Dundee City
Durham Durham
E Ayrs East Ayrshire
E Dunb East Dunbartonshire
E Loth East Lothian
E Renf East Renfrewshire
E Sus East Sussex
E Yorks East Riding of Yorkshire
Edin City of Edinburgh
Essex Essex
Falk Falkirk
Fife Fife
Flint Flintshire
Glasgow City of Glasgow
Glos Gloucestershire
Gtr Man Greater Manchester
Guern Guernsey
Gwyn Gwynedd
Halton Halton
Hants Hampshire
Hereford Herefordshire
Herts Hertfordshire
Highld Highland
Hrtlpl Hartlepool
Hull Hull
IoM Isle of Man
IoW Isle of Wight
Invclyd Inverclyde
Jersey Jersey
Kent Kent
Lancs Lancashire
Leicester City of Leicester
Leics Leicestershire
Lincs Lincolnshire
London Greater London
Luton Luton
M Keynes Milton Keynes
M Tydf Merthyr Tydfil
Mbro Middlesbrough
Medway Medway
Mers Merseyside
Midloth Midlothian
Mon Monmouthshire
Moray Moray
N Ayrs North Ayrshire
N Lincs North Lincolnshire
N Lanark North Lanarkshire
N Som North Somerset
N Yorks North Yorkshire
NE Lincs North East Lincolnshire
Neath Neath Port Talbot
Newport City and County of Newport
Norf Norfolk
Northants Northamptonshire
Northumb Northumberland
Nottingham City of Nottingham
Notts Nottinghamshire
Orkney Orkney
Oxon Oxfordshire
Pboro Peterborough
Pembs Pembrokeshire
Perth Perth and Kinross
Plym Plymouth
Poole Poole
Powys Powys
Ptsmth Portsmouth
Reading Reading
Redcar Redcar and Cleveland
Renfs Renfrewshire
Rhondda Rhondda Cynon Taff
Rutland Rutland
S Ayrs South Ayrshire
S Glos South Gloucestershire
S Lanark South Lanarkshire
S Yorks South Yorkshire
Scilly Scilly
Shetland Shetland
Shrops Shropshire
Slough Slough
Som Somerset
Soton Southampton
Staffs Staffordshire
Southend Southend-on-Sea
Stirling Stirling
Stockton Stockton-on-Tees
Stoke Stoke-on-Trent
Suff Suffolk
Sur Surrey
Swansea Swansea
Swindon Swindon
T&W Tyne and Wear
Telford Telford & Wrekin
Thurrock Thurrock
Torbay Torbay
Torf Torfaen
V Glam The Vale of Glamorgan
W Berks West Berkshire
W Dunb West Dunbartonshire
W Isles Western Isles
W Loth West Lothian
W Mid West Midlands
W Sus West Sussex
W Yorks West Yorkshire
Warks Warwickshire
Warr Warrington
Wilts Wiltshire
Windsor Windsor and Maidenhead
Wokingham Wokingham
Worcs Worcestershire
Wrex Wrexham
York City of York

Index to road maps of Britain

How to use the index

Example **Blatherwycke** Northants **137** D9

grid square
page number
county or unitary authority

on's Hill Sur 50 E3
on's Town Cumb 240 E2
Kettleby Leics 154 E4
Lench Worcs 117 G10
as Combe Som 30 C2
erley Worcs 116 D5
erton Essex 89 B8
erton Worcs 117 G9
erwick Northumb 264 G4
ess End Essex 87 C9
ess Roding Essex 87 C9
ey Devon 27 E10
ey-cwm-hir Powys 113 C11
ey Dore Hereford 97 E7
ey Field Essex 107 G9
ey Gate Kent 53 B9
ey Green Shrops 149 C10
ey Green Staffs 169 D7
ey Hey Gtr Man 184 B5
ey Hulton Stoke 168 F6
ey Mead Sur 66 F4
ey St Bathans
ders 272 C5
ey Town Cumb 238 G5
ey Village Lancs 194 C6
ey Wood London 68 D3
eycwmhir Powys 113 C11
eydale Glos 80 B5
eydale S Yorks 186 E4
eydale Park
rks 186 E4
eyhill Edin 280 G5
eystead Lancs 203 C7
ots Bickington
on 24 E5
ots Bromley Staffs 151 E11
ots Langley Herts 85 E9
ots Leigh N Som 60 E4
ot's Meads W Ches 166 B5
ots Morton Worcs 117 F10
ots Ripton Cambs 122 B4
ots Salford Warks 117 G11
ots Worthy Hants 48 G3
otsbury Dorset 17 D7
otsford W Sus 36 C4
otsham Devon 24 B6
otskerswell Devon 9 B7
otsleigh Devon 8 F6
otsley Cambs 122 F4
otstone Hants 48 G5
otswood Hants 32 C5
otswood Sur 50 C4
otts Ann Hants 47 E10
ott Shrops 115 B7
on Shrops 131 F11
y S Yorks 186 B6
r Ceredig 93 B9
r-Arad Carms 92 D6
r-banc Ceredig 93 C7
r Cowarch Gwyn 147 F7
r-Giâr Carms 93 C10
r-gwynfi Neath 57 B11
r-Hirnant Gwyn 147 C9
r miwl =
ermule Powys 130 E3
r-nant Rhondda 77 E8
r-oer Wrex 166 F3
r-Rhiwlech Gwyn 147 E8
r-Village Powys 96 G2
raeron Ceredig 111 E9
raman Rhondda 77 E8
rangell Gwyn 146 G6
rarder Highld 290 E6
rarder House
hld 300 G6
rarder Lodge
hld 291 E7
rargie Perth 286 F5
rarth Ceredig 111 E9
ravon Neath 57 C8
rbargoed Caerph 77 E11
rbechan Powys 130 E2
rbeeg Bl Gwent 78 E2
rbran Powys 95 F9
rcanaid M Tydf 77 E9
rcarn Caerph 78 G2
rcastle Pembs 91 E7
rcegir Powys 128 C6
rchalder Highld 290 C5
rchirder Aberds 302 D6

Abercorn W Loth 279 F11
Abercraf Powys 76 C4
Abercregan Neath 57 B11
Abercrombie Fife 287 G9
Abercwmboi Rhondda 77 F8
Abercych Pembs 92 C4
Abercynafon Powys 77 B9
Abercynffig =
Aberkenfig Bridgend 57 E11
Abercynon Rhondda 77 F9
Aberdâr = Aberdare
Rhondda 77 E7
Aberdalgie Perth 286 E4
Aberdare = Aberdâr
Rhondda 77 E7
Aberdaron Gwyn 144 D3
Aberdeen Aberdeen 293 C11
Aberdesach Gwyn 162 E6
Aberdour Fife 280 D3
Aberdovey =
Aberdyfi Gwyn 128 D2
Aberdulais Neath 76 E3
Aberdyfi =
Aberdovey Gwyn 128 D2
Aberedw Powys 95 B11
Abereiddy Pembs 90 E5
Abererch Gwyn 145 B7
Aberfan M Tydf 77 E9
Aberfeldy Perth 286 C2
Aberffraw Anglesey 162 B5
Aberffrwd Ceredig 112 B3
Aberffrwd Mon 78 D5
Aberford W Yorks 206 F4
Aberfoyle Stirl 285 G9
Abergarw Bridgend 58 C2
Abergarwed Neath 76 E4
Abergavenny Mon 78 C3
Abergele Conwy 180 F6
Abergorlech Carms 93 E11
Abergwaun =
Fishguard Pembs 91 D9
Abergwesyn Powys 113 G7
Abergwili Carms 93 G8
Abergwynant Gwyn 146 F3
Abergwynfi Neath 57 B11
Abergwyngregyn
Gwyn 179 G11
Abergynolwyn Gwyn 128 B3
Aberhosan Powys 128 D6
Aberkenfig =
Abercynffig Bridgend 57 E11
Aberlady E Loth 281 E9
Aberlemno Angus 287 B9
Aberlerry Ceredig 128 E2
Aberllefenni Gwyn 128 B5
Aberllydan =
Broad Haven Pembs 72 C5
Aberllynfi =
Three Cocks Powys 96 D3
Abermagwr Ceredig 112 C3
Abermaw =
Barmouth Gwyn 146 F2
Abermeurig Ceredig 111 F11
Abermorddu Flint 166 D4
Abermule =
Aber-miwl Powys 130 E3
Abernaint Powys 148 E2
Abernant Carms 92 G6
Abernant Powys 130 D3
Abernethy Perth 286 F5
Abernyte Perth 286 D6
Aberogwr =
Ogmore by Sea V Glam 57 F11
Aberpennar =
Mountain Ash Rhondda 77 F8
Aberporth Ceredig 110 G5
Aberriw = Berriew
Powys 130 C3
Abersoch Gwyn 144 D6
Abersychan Torf 78 E3
Abertawe = Swansea
Swansea 56 C6
Aberteifi = Cardigan
Ceredig 92 B3
Aberthin V Glam 58 D4
Abertillery Bl Gwent 78 E2
Abertridwr Caerph 58 B6
Abertridwr Powys 147 F10
Abertrinant Gwyn 128 B2
Abertysswg Caerph 77 D10
Aberuchill Castle
Perth 285 E11
Aberuthven Perth 286 F3
Aberyscir Powys 95 F9
Aberystwyth Ceredig 111 A11
Abhainn Suidhe
W Isles 305 H2
Abingdon Oxon 83 F7
Abinger Common Sur 50 D6
Abinger Hammer Sur 50 D5
Abington Northants 120 E5
Abington S Lnrk 259 E10
Abington Pigotts
Cambs 104 C6
Abington Vale Northants 120 E5
Abingworth W Sus 35 D10
Ablington Glos 81 D10
Ablington Wilts 47 D7
Abney Derbys 185 F11
Aboyne Aberds 293 D7
Abraham Heights
Lancs 211 G9
Abram Gtr Man 194 G6
Abriachan Highld 300 F5
Abridge Essex 87 F7
Abronhill N Lnrk 278 F5
Abshot Hants 33 F8
Abson S Glos 61 E8
Abthorpe Northants 102 B2
Abune-the-Hill Orkney 314 D2
Aby Lincs 190 F6
Acaster Malbis York 207 D7
Acaster Selby N Yorks 207 E7
Accrington Lancs 195 B9
Acha Argyll 275 B8
Acha Argyll 288 D3
Acha Mor W Isles 304 F5
Achabraid Argyll 275 E9
Achachork Highld 298 E4
Achadh nan Darach
Highld 284 B4
Achadh an Eas Highld 308 F6
Achadunan Argyll 284 F5
Achafolla Argyll 275 B8
Achagary Highld 308 D7
Achaglass Argyll 255 C8
Achahoish Argyll 275 F8
Achalader Perth 286 C5
Achallader Argyll 285 C7
Achalone Highld 310 D5
Ach'an Todhair Highld 290 F2
Achanalt Highld 300 C2
Achanamara Argyll 275 E8
Achandunie Highld 300 B6
Achanelid Argyll 275 E11
Achany Highld 309 J5
Achaphubuil Highld 290 F2
Acharacle Highld 289 C8
Acharn Highld 289 D9
Acharn Perth 285 C11
Acharole Highld 310 D6
Acharossan Argyll 275 F10
Acharry Muir Highld 309 K6
Achath Aberds 293 B9
Achavanich Highld 310 E5
Achavelgin Highld 301 D9
Achavraat Highld 301 E9
Achddu Carms 74 E6
Achdregnie Moray 302 G2
Achduart Highld 307 J5
Achentoul Highld 310 F2
Achfary Highld 306 F7
Achfrish Highld 309 H5
Achgarve Highld 307 K3
Achiemore Highld 308 C3
Achiemore Highld 310 D2
A'Chill Highld 294 E4
Achiltibuie Highld 307 J5
Achina Highld 308 C7
Achinahuagh Highld 308 C6
Achindaul Highld 290 E3
Achindown Highld 301 E8
Achinduich Highld 309 J5
Achinduin Argyll 289 F10
Achingills Highld 310 C5
Achininver Highld 308 C5
Achintee Highld 290 F3
Achintee Highld 299 E9
Achintraid Highld 295 B10
Achlaven Argyll 289 F11
Achlean Highld 291 D10
Achleck Argyll 288 E6
Achlorachan Highld 300 D3
Achluachrach Highld 290 E4
Achlyness Highld 306 D7
Achmelvich Highld 307 G5
Achmore Highld 295 B10
Achmore Stirl 285 D9
Achnaba Argyll 275 E10
Achnaba Argyll 289 F11
Achnabat Highld 300 F5
Achnabreck Argyll 275 D9
Achnacarnin Highld 306 F5
Achnacarry Highld 290 E3
Achnacloich Argyll 289 F11
Achnacloich Highld 295 E7
Achnaconeran Highld 290 B6
Achnacraig Argyll 288 E6
Achnacree Argyll 289 F11
Achnacree Bay Argyll 289 F11
Achnacroish Argyll 289 E10
Achnadrish Argyll 288 D6
Achnafalnich Argyll 284 E6
Achnagarron Highld 300 C6
Achnaha Highld 288 C6
Achnahanat Highld 309 K5
Achnahannet Highld 301 G9
Achnahard Argyll 288 G5
Achnairn Highld 309 H5
Achnaluachrach
Highld 309 J6
Achnandarach Highld 295 B10
Achnanellan Highld 290 E2
Achnasaul Highld 290 E3
Achnasheen Highld 299 D11
Achnashelloch Argyll 275 D9
Achnavast Highld 310 C4
Achneigie Highld 299 B10
Achormlarie Highld 309 K6
Achorn Highld 310 F5
Achosnich Highld 288 C6
Achranich Highld 289 E9
Achreamie Highld 310 C4
Achriabhach Highld 290 G3
Achriesgill Highld 306 D7
Achrimsdale Highld 311 J3
Achtoty Highld 308 C6
Achurch Northants 137 G10
Achuvoldrach Highld 308 D5
Achvaich Highld 309 K7
Achvarasdal Highld 310 C3
Ackenthwaite Cumb 211 C10
Ackergill Highld 310 D7
Acklam M'bro 225 B9
Acklam N Yorks 216 G5
Ackleton Shrops 132 D5
Acklington Northumb 252 C6
Ackton W Yorks 198 C2
Ackworth Moor Top
W Yorks 198 D2
Acle Norf 161 G8
Acock's Green W Mid 134 G2
Acol Kent 71 F10
Acomb Northumb 241 D10
Acomb York 207 C7
Acre Gtr Man 196 F2
Acre Lancs 195 C9
Acre Street W Sus 21 B11
Acrefair Wrex 166 G3
Acres Nook Staffs 168 E4
Acton Dorset 18 F5
Acton E Ches 167 E10
Acton London 67 C8
Acton Shrops 130 G6
Acton Staffs 168 G4
Acton Suff 107 C7
Acton Worcs 116 D6
Acton Wrex 166 E4
Acton Beauchamp
Hereford 116 G3
Acton Bridge W Ches 183 F9
Acton Burnell Shrops 131 C10
Acton Green Hereford 116 G3
Acton Green London 67 D8
Acton Pigott Shrops 131 C10
Acton Place Suff 107 B7
Acton Reynald Shrops 149 E10
Acton Round Shrops 132 D2
Acton Scott Shrops 131 F9
Acton Trussell Staffs 151 F8
Acton Turville S Glos 61 C10
Adabroc W Isles 304 B7
Adambrae W Loth 269 A10
Adam's Green Dorset 29 F8
Adbaston Staffs 150 D5
Adber Dorset 29 C9
Adbolton Notts 154 B2
Adderbury Oxon 101 D9
Adderley Shrops 150 B3
Adderley Green Stoke 168 G6
Adderstone Northumb 264 C4
Addiewell W Loth 269 C9
Addingham W Yorks 205 D7
Addingham Moorside
W Yorks 205 D7
Addington Bucks 102 F4
Addington Corn 6 B5
Addington Kent 53 B7
Addington London 67 G11
Addinston Borders 271 E10
Addiscombe London 67 F10
Addlestone Sur 66 G5
Addlestonemoor Sur 66 F4
Addlethorpe Lincs 175 B8
Adel W Yorks 205 F11
Adeney Telford 150 F4
Adeyfield Herts 85 D9
Adfa Powys 129 C11
Adforton Hereford 115 C8
Adgestone I o W 21 D7
Adisham Kent 55 C8
Adlestrop Glos 100 F4
Adlingfleet E Yorks 199 C10
Adlington E Ches 184 E6
Adlington Lancs 194 E6
Adlington Park Lancs 194 E5
Admaston Staffs 151 E10
Admaston Telford 150 G2
Admington Warks 100 B4
Adpar Ceredig 92 C6
Adsborough Som 28 B3
Adscombe Som 43 F7
Adstock Bucks 102 E4
Adstone Northants 119 G11
Adswood Gtr Man 184 D5
Adversane W Sus 35 C9
Advie Highld 301 F11
Adwalton W Yorks 197 B8
Adwell Oxon 83 F11
Adwick le Street
S Yorks 198 F4
Adwick upon Dearne
S Yorks 198 G3
Adziel Aberds 303 D9
Ae Dumfries 247 F11
Ae Village Dumfries 247 F11
Affetside Gtr Man 195 E9
Affleck Aberds 303 G8
Affpuddle Dorset 18 C2
Affric Lodge Highld 299 G11
Afon Eitha Wrex 166 F3
Afon-wen Flint 181 G10
Afon Wen Gwyn 145 B8
Afton I o W 20 D2
Agar Nook Leics 153 G9
Agbrigg W Yorks 197 D10
Aggborough Worcs 116 B6
Agglethorpe N Yorks 213 B11
Aglionby Cumb 239 F10
Agneash I o M 192 D5
Aifft Denb 165 B10
Aigburth Mers 182 D5
Aiginis W Isles 304 E6
Aike E Yorks 209 D7
Aikenway Moray 302 E2
Aikerness Orkney 314 A4
Aikers Orkney 314 G4
Aiketgate Cumb 230 B5
Aikton Cumb 239 G7
Ailby Lincs 190 F6
Ailey Hereford 96 B6
Ailstone Warks 118 G4
Ailsworth P'boro 138 D2
Aimes Green Essex 86 E5
Ainderby Quernhow
N Yorks 215 C7
Ainderby Steeple
N Yorks 224 G6
Aingers Green Essex 108 G2
Ainley Top W Yorks 196 D6
Ainsdale Mers 193 E10
Ainsdale-on-Sea
Mers 193 E9
Ainstable Cumb 230 B6
Ainsworth Gtr Man 195 E9
Ainthorpe N Yorks 226 D4
Aintree Mers 182 B5
Aird Argyll 275 C8
Aird Dumfries 236 C2
Aird Highld 299 B7
Aird Highld 296 F3
Aird W Isles 304 E7
Aird a Mhachair
W Isles 297 G3
Aird a' Mhulaidh
W Isles 305 G3
Aird Asaig W Isles 305 H3
Aird Dhail W Isles 304 B6
Aird Mhòr W Isles 297 G4
Aird Mhidhinis W Isles 297 L3
Aird Mhighe W Isles 296 C6
Aird Mhighe W Isles 305 J3
Aird Mhor W Isles 297 L3
Aird of Sleat Highld 295 E7
Aird Thunga W Isles 304 E6
Aird Uig W Isles 304 E2
Airdachuilinn Highld 306 E7
Airdens Highld 309 K6
Airdeny Argyll 289 G11
Airdrie N Lnrk 268 B5
Airds of Kells Dumfries 237 B8
Airdtorrisdale Highld 308 C6
Aire View N Yorks 204 D5
Airedale W Yorks 198 B3
Airidh a Bhruaich
W Isles 305 G4
Airieland Dumfries 237 D9
Airinis W Isles 304 E6
Airlie Angus 287 B7
Airlies Dumfries 236 D5
Airmyn E Yorks 199 B8
Airntully Perth 286 D4
Airor Highld 295 E9
Airth Falk 279 D7
Airthrey Castle Stirl 278 B6
Airton N Yorks 204 B4
Airy Hill N Yorks 227 D7
Airyhassen Dumfries 236 E5
Airyligg Dumfries 236 C4
Aisby Lincs 155 B10
Aisby Lincs 188 C5
Aisgernis W Isles 297 J3
Aish Devon 8 C3
Aish Devon 8 D6
Aisholt Som 43 F7
Aiskew N Yorks 214 B5
Aislaby N Yorks 216 B5
Aislaby N Yorks 227 D7
Aislaby Stockton 225 C8
Aisthorpe Lincs 188 E6
Aith Orkney 314 E2
Aith Shetland 312 D8
Aith Shetland 313 H5
Aithnen Powys 148 E4
Aithsetter Shetland 313 K6
Aitkenhead S Ayrs 245 B8
Aitnoch Highld 301 F9
Akeld Northumb 263 D11
Akeley Bucks 102 D4
Akenham Suff 108 B2
Albany T & W 243 F7
Albaston Corn 12 G4
Alberbury Shrops 149 G7
Albert Town Pembs 72 B6
Albert Village Leics 152 F6
Albourne W Sus 36 D3
Albourne Green W Sus 36 D3
Albrighton Shrops 132 C6
Albrighton Shrops 149 F9
Albro Castle Ceredig 92 B3
Alburgh Norf 142 F5
Albury Herts 105 G8
Albury Sur 50 D5
Albury End Herts 105 G8
Albury Heath Sur 50 D5
Alby Hill Norf 160 C3
Albyfield Cumb 240 G2
Alcaig Highld 300 D5
Alcaston Shrops 131 F9
Alcester Dorset 30 C5
Alcester Warks 117 F11
Alcester Lane's End
W Mid 133 G11
Alciston E Sus 23 D8
Alcombe Som 42 D3
Alcombe Wilts 61 F10
Alconbury Cambs 122 B3
Alconbury Weston
Cambs 122 B3
Aldbar Castle Angus 287 B9
Aldborough N Yorks 215 F8
Aldborough Norf 160 C3
Aldborough Hatch
London 68 B3
Aldbourne Wilts 63 D9
Aldbrough E Yorks 209 F10
Aldbrough St John
N Yorks 224 C4
Aldbury Herts 85 C7
Aldcliffe Lancs 211 G9
Aldclune Perth 291 G11
Aldeburgh Suff 127 F9
Aldeby Norf 143 E8
Aldenham Herts 85 F10
Alder Forest Gtr Man 184 B3
Alder Moor Staffs 152 D4
Alder Row Som 45 E9
Alderbrook E Sus 37 B8
Alderbury Wilts 31 B11
Aldercar Derbys 170 F6
Alderford Norf 160 F2
Alderholt Dorset 31 E10
Alderley Glos 80 G3
Alderley Edge E Ches 184 F4
Alderman's Green
W Mid 135 G7
Aldermaston W Berks 64 F5
Aldermaston Soke
W Berks 64 G6
Aldermaston Wharf
W Berks 64 F6
Alderminster Warks 100 B4
Aldermoor Soton 32 D5
Alderney Poole 18 C6
Alder's End Hereford 98 C2
Aldersbrook London 68 B2
Aldersey Green
W Ches 167 D7
Aldershawe Staffs 134 B2
Aldershot Hants 49 C11
Alderton Glos 99 E10
Alderton Northants 102 B4
Alderton Shrops 149 E9
Alderton Suff 108 C6
Alderton Wilts 61 C10
Alderton Fields Glos 99 E10
Alderwasley Derbys 170 E4
Aldfield N Yorks 214 F5
Aldford W Ches 166 D6
Aldgate Rutland 137 C9
Aldham Essex 107 F8
Aldham Suff 107 B10
Aldie Highld 309 L7
Aldingbourne W Sus 22 B6
Aldingham Cumb 210 E5
Aldington Kent 54 F5
Aldington Worcs 99 C11
Aldington Frith Kent 54 F4
Aldivalloch Moray 302 G3
Aldochlay Argyll 277 C7
Aldon Shrops 115 B8
Aldoth Cumb 229 B8
Aldourie Castle Highld 300 F6
Aldreth Cambs 123 C8
Aldridge W Mid 133 C11
Aldringham Suff 127 E8
Aldrington Brighton 36 F3
Aldsworth Glos 81 C11
Aldunie Moray 302 G3
Aldwark Derbys 170 D2
Aldwark N Yorks 215 G9
Aldwarke S Yorks 186 C6
Aldwick W Sus 22 D6
Aldwincle Northants 137 G10
Aldworth W Berks 64 D5
Ale Oak Shrops 130 G4
Alehouseburn Aberds 302 C6
Alehousehill Aberds 303 G10
Alexandria W Dunb 277 F7
Aley Som 43 F7
Aley Green C Beds 85 B9
Alfardisworthy Devon 24 E3
Alfington Devon 15 B8
Alfold Sur 50 G4
Alfold Bars W Sus 50 G4
Alfold Crossways Sur 50 F4
Alford Aberds 293 B7
Alford Lincs 191 F7
Alford Som 44 G6
Alfred's Well Worcs 117 C8
Alfreton Derbys 170 D6
Alfrick Worcs 116 G4
Alfrick Pound Worcs 116 G4
Alfriston E Sus 23 E8
Algakirk Lincs 156 B5
Algaltraig Argyll 275 F11
Algarkirk Lincs 156 B5
Alhampton Som 44 G6
Aline Lodge W Isles 305 G3
Alisary Highld 289 B9
Alkborough N Lincs 199 C11
Alkerton Glos 80 D3
Alkerton Oxon 101 C7
Alkham Kent 55 E9
Alkington Shrops 149 B10
Alkmonton Derbys 152 B3
Alkrington Garden
Village Gtr Man 195 G11
All Cannings Wilts 62 G5
All Saints Devon 28 G4
All Saints South
Elmham Suff 142 G6
All Stretton Shrops 131 D9
Alladale Lodge Highld 309 L4
Allaleigh Devon 8 E6
Allanaquoich Aberds 292 D3
Allanbank Borders 271 F10
Allanbank N Lnrk 268 D6
Allangrange Mains
Highld 300 D6
Allanshaugh Borders 271 F8
Allanshaws Borders 271 G9
Allanton Borders 273 E7
Allanton N Lnrk 269 D7
Allanton S Lnrk 268 E4
Allaston Glos 79 E10
Allathasdal W Isles 297 L2
Allbrook Hants 33 C7
Allen End Warks 134 D3
Allendale Town
Northumb 241 F8
Allenheads Northumb 232 B3
Allens Green Herts 87 B7
Allensford Durham 242 G3
Allensmore Hereford 97 D9
Allenton Derby 153 C7
Allenwood Cumb 239 F11
Aller Devon 9 B7
Aller Devon 27 F9
Aller Dorset 30 G3
Aller Som 28 B6
Aller Park Devon 9 B7
Allerby Cumb 229 D7
Allerford Som 27 B11
Allerford Som 42 D2
Allerston N Yorks 217 C7
Allerthorpe E Yorks 207 D11
Allerton Mers 182 D6
Allerton W Yorks 205 G8
Allerton Bywater
W Yorks 198 B2
Allerton Mauleverer
N Yorks 206 B4
Allesley W Mid 134 G6
Allestree Derby 152 B6
Allet Corn 4 F5
Allexton Leics 136 C6
Allgreave E Ches 169 B7
Allhallows Medway 69 D10
Allhallows-on-Sea
Medway 69 D10
Alligin Shuas Highld 299 D8
Allimore Green Staffs 151 F7
Allington Kent 53 B8
Allington Lincs 172 G5
Allington Wilts 47 F8
Allington Wilts 61 D11
Allington Wilts 62 G5
Allington Bar Wilts 61 E11
Allithwaite Cumb 211 D7
Alloa Clack 279 C7
Allonby Cumb 229 C7
Allostock W Ches 184 G2
Alloway S Ayrs 257 F8
Allowenshay Som 28 E5
Allscot Shrops 132 D4
Allscott Telford 150 G2
Allt Carms 75 E9
Allt-na-giubhsaich
Aberds 292 E4
Allt na h-Airbhe Highld 307 K6
Allt-nan-sùgh Highld 295 C11
Allt-yr-yn Newport 59 B9
Alltami Flint 166 B3
Alltbeithe Highld 290 C2
Alltchaorunn Highld 284 B5
Alltforgan Powys 147 E9
Alltmawr Powys 95 B11
Alltnacaillich Highld 308 E4
Alltrech Argyll 289 F8
Alltsigh Highld 290 B6
Alltwalis Carms 93 E8
Alltwen Neath 76 E2
Alltyblaca Ceredig 93 B10
Allwood Green Suff 125 C10
Alma Notts 171 E7
Almagill Dumfries 238 B3
Almeley Hereford 114 G6

Almeley Wooton Hereford 114 G6
Almer Dorset 18 B4
Almholme S Yorks 198 F5
Almington Staffs 150 C4
Alminstone Cross Devon 24 C4
Almondbank Perth 286 E4
Almondbury W Yorks 197 D7
Almondsbury S Glos 60 C6
Almondvale W Loth 269 B11
Almshouse Green Essex 106 E5
Alne N Yorks 215 F9
Alne End Warks 118 F2
Alne Hills Warks 118 E2
Alne Station N Yorks 215 F10
Alness Highld 300 C6
Alnessferry Highld 300 C6
Alnham Northumb 263 G11
Alnmouth Northumb 264 G6
Alnwick Northumb 264 G5
Alperton London 67 C7
Alphamstone Essex 107 D7
Alpheton Suff 125 G7
Alphington Devon 14 C4
Alpington Norf 142 C5
Alport Derbys 170 C2
Alport Powys 130 D5
Alpraham E Ches 167 D9
Alresford Essex 107 G11
Alrewas Staffs 152 F3
Alsager E Ches 168 D3
Alsagers Bank Staffs 168 F4
Alscot Bucks 84 E4
Alsop en le Dale Derbys 169 D11
Alston Cumb 231 B10
Alston Devon 28 G4
Alston Sutton Som 44 C2
Alstone Glos 99 E9
Alstone Glos 99 G8
Alstone Som 43 D10
Alstonefield Staffs 169 D10
Alswear Devon 26 C2
Alt Gtr Man 196 G2
Alt Hill Gtr Man 196 G2
Altandhu Highld 307 H4
Altanduin Highld 311 G2
Altarnun Corn 11 E10
Altass Highld 309 J4
Altbough Hereford 97 E10
Altdargue Aberds 293 C7
Alterwall Highld 310 C6
Altham Lancs 203 G11
Althorne Essex 88 F6
Althorpe N Lincs 199 F10
Alticane S Ayrs 244 F6
Alticry Dumfries 236 D4
Altmore Windsor 65 D11
Altnabreac Station Highld 310 E4
Altnacealgach Hotel Highld 307 H7
Altnacraig Argyll 289 G10
Altnafeadh Highld 284 B6
Altnaharra Highld 308 F5
Altofts W Yorks 197 C11
Alton Derbys 170 C5
Alton Hants 49 F8
Alton Staffs 169 G9
Alton Wilts 47 D7
Alton Barnes Wilts 62 G6
Alton Pancras Dorset 30 G2
Alton Priors Wilts 62 G6
Altonhill E Ayrs 257 B10
Altonside Moray 302 D2
Altour Highld 290 E4
Altrincham Gtr Man 184 D3
Altrua Highld 290 E4
Altskeith Stirl 285 G8
Altyre Ho Moray 301 D10
Alum Rock W Mid 134 F2
Alva Clack 279 B7
Alvanley W Ches 183 G7
Alvaston Derby 153 C7
Alvechurch Worcs 117 C10
Alvecote Warks 134 C4
Alvediston Wilts 31 C7
Alveley Shrops 132 G5
Alverdiscott Devon 25 B8
Alverstoke Hants 21 B8
Alverstone I o W 21 D7
Alverthorpe W Yorks 197 C10
Alverton Notts 172 G3
Alves Moray 301 C11
Alvescot Oxon 82 E3
Alveston S Glos 60 B6
Alveston Warks 118 F4
Alveston Down S Glos 60 B6
Alveston Hill Warks 118 G4
Alvie Highld 291 C10
Alvingham Lincs 190 C5
Alvington Glos 79 E10
Alvington Som 29 D8
Alwalton Cambs 138 D2
Alway Newport 59 B10
Alweston Dorset 29 E11
Alwington Devon 24 C6
Alwinton Northumb 251 B10
Alwoodley W Yorks 205 E11
Alwoodley Gates W Yorks 206 E2
Alwoodley Park W Yorks 205 E11
Alyth Perth 286 C6
Am Baile W Isles 297 K3
Am Buth Argyll 289 G10
Amalebra Corn 1 B5
Amalveor Corn 1 B5
Amatnatua Highld 309 K4
Ambaston Derbys 153 C8
Amber Hill Lincs 174 F2
Ambergate Derbys 170 E4
Amberley Glos 80 E5
Amberley Hereford 97 B10
Amberley W Sus 35 E8
Amble Northumb 253 C7
Amblecote W Mid 133 F7
Ambler Thorn W Yorks 196 B5
Ambleside Cumb 221 E7
Ambleston Pembs 91 F10
Ambrosden Oxon 83 B10
Amcotts N Lincs 199 E11
Amen Corner Brack 65 F10
Amersham Bucks 85 F7
Amersham Common Bucks 85 F7
Amersham Old Town Bucks 85 F7
Amersham on the Hill Bucks 85 F7
Amerton Staffs 151 D9
Amesbury Bath 45 B7
Amesbury Wilts 47 E7
Ameysford Dorset 31 G9
Amington Staffs 134 C4
Amisfield Dumfries 247 G11
Amlwch Anglesey 178 C6
Amlwch Port Anglesey 179 C7
Ammanford = Rhydaman Carms 75 C10
Ammerham Som 28 F5
Amod Argyll 255 D8
Amotherby N Yorks 216 E4
Ampfield Hants 32 C6
Ampleforth N Yorks 215 D11
Ampney Crucis Glos 81 E9
Ampney St Mary Glos 81 E9
Ampney St Peter Glos 81 E9
Amport Hants 47 E9
Ampthill C Beds 103 D10
Ampton Suff 125 C7
Amroth Pembs 73 D11
Amulree Perth 286 D2
Amwell Herts 85 C11
An Caol Highld 298 D6
An Cnoc W Isles 304 E6
An Gleann Ur W Isles 304 E6
An Leth Meadhanach W Isles 297 K3
An t-Ob W Isles 296 C6
Anagach Highld 301 G10
Anaheilt Highld 289 C10
Anancaun Highld 299 C10
Ancarraig Highld 300 G4
Ancaster Lincs 173 G7
Anchor Shrops 130 G3
Anchor Corner Norf 141 D10
Anchor Street Norf 160 E6
Anchorage Park Ptsmth 33 G11
Anchorsholme Blkpool 202 E2
Ancoats Gtr Man 184 B5
Ancroft Northumb 273 F9
Ancroft Northmoor Northumb 273 F9
Ancrum Borders 262 E4
Ancton W Sus 35 G7
Ancumtoun Orkney 314 A7
Anderby Lincs 191 F8
Anderby Creek Lincs 191 F8
Andersea Som 43 G10
Andersfield Som 43 G8
Anderson Dorset 18 B3
Anderton Corn 7 E8
Anderton Lancs 194 E6
Anderton W Ches 183 F10
Andertons Mill Lancs 194 E4
Andover Hants 47 D11
Andover Down Hants 47 D11
Andoversford Glos 81 B8
Andreas I o M 192 C5
Andwell Hants 49 C7
Anelog Gwyn 144 D3
Anerley London 67 F10
Anfield Mers 182 C5
Angarrack Corn 2 B3
Angarrick Corn 3 B7
Angelbank Shrops 115 B11
Angersleigh Som 27 D11
Angerton Cumb 238 F6
Angle Pembs 72 E5
Angmering W Sus 35 G9
Angram N Yorks 206 D6
Angram N Yorks 223 F7
Anick Northumb 241 D11
Anie Stirl 285 F9
Ankerdine Hill Worcs 116 F4
Ankerville Highld 301 B8
Anlaby E Yorks 200 B4
Anlaby Park Hull 200 B5
Anmer Norf 158 D4
Anmore Hants 33 E11
Anna Valley Hants 47 E10
Annan Dumfries 238 D5
Annaside Cumb 210 B1
Annat Argyll 284 E4
Annat Highld 290 D5
Annat Highld 299 D8
Annbank S Ayrs 257 E10
Annesley Notts 171 E8
Annesley Woodhouse Notts 171 E7
Annfield Plain Durham 242 G5
Anniesland Glasgow 267 B10
Annifirth Shetland 313 J3
Annis Hill Suff 143 F7
Annishader Highld 298 D4
Annitsford T & W 243 C7
Ann's Hill Hants 33 G9
Annscroft Shrops 131 B9
Annwell Place Derbys 152 F6
Ansdell Lancs 193 B10
Ansells End Herts 85 B11
Ansford Som 44 G6
Ansley Warks 134 E5
Ansley Common Warks 134 E6
Anslow Staffs 152 D4
Anslow Gate Staffs 152 D3
Ansteadbrook Sur 50 G2
Anstey Herts 105 E8
Anstey Leics 135 B10
Anstruther Easter Fife 287 G9
Anstruther Wester Fife 287 G9
Ansty Hants 49 E8
Ansty W Sus 36 C3
Ansty Warks 135 G7
Ansty Wilts 31 B7
Ansty Coombe Wilts 31 B7
Ansty Cross Dorset 30 G3
Anthill Common Hants 33 E10
Anthony Corn 7 E7
Anthony's Cross Glos 98 G4
Anthorn Cumb 238 F5
Antingham Norf 160 C5
Anton's Gowt Lincs 174 F3
Antonshill Falk 279 E7
Antony Corn 7 E7
Antony Passage Corn 7 D8
Antrobus W Ches 183 F10
Anvil Green Kent 54 D6
Anvilles W Berks 63 F10
Anwick Lincs 173 E10
Anwoth Dumfries 237 D7
Aonachan Highld 290 E4
Aoradh Argyll 274 G3
Apedale Staffs 168 F4
Aperfield London 52 B2
Apes Dale Worcs 117 C9
Apes Hall Cambs 139 E11
Apethorpe Northants 137 D10
Apeton Staffs 151 F7
Apley Lincs 189 F10
Apley Forge Shrops 132 D4
Apperknowle Derbys 186 F5
Apperley Glos 99 F7
Apperley Bridge W Yorks 205 F9
Apperley Dene Northumb 242 F3
Appersett N Yorks 223 G7
Appin Argyll 289 E11
Appin House Argyll 289 E11
Appleby N Lincs 200 E3
Appleby-in-Westmorland Cumb 231 G9
Appleby Magna Leics 134 B6
Appleby Parva Leics 134 B6
Applecross Highld 299 E7
Applecross Ho Highld 299 E7
Appledore Devon 27 E9
Appledore Devon 40 G3
Appledore Kent 39 B7
Appledore Heath Kent 54 G3
Appleford Oxon 83 G8
Applegarthtown Dumfries 248 G4
Applehouse Hill Windsor 65 C10
Applemore Hants 32 F5
Appleshaw Hants 47 D10
Applethwaite Cumb 229 F11
Appleton Halton 183 D8
Appleton Oxon 82 E6
Appleton-le-Moors N Yorks 216 B4
Appleton-le-Street N Yorks 216 E4
Appleton Park Warr 183 E10
Appleton Roebuck N Yorks 207 E7
Appleton Thorn Warr 183 E10
Appleton Wiske N Yorks 225 E7
Appletreehall Borders 262 F2
Appletreewick N Yorks 213 G11
Appley I o W 21 C8
Appley Som 27 C9
Appley Bridge Lancs 194 F4
Apse Heath I o W 21 E7
Apsey Green Suff 126 E5
Apsley Herts 85 D9
Apsley End C Beds 104 E2
Apuldram W Sus 22 C4
Aqueduct Telford 132 B3
Aquhythie Aberds 293 B9
Arabella Highld 301 B8
Arbeadie Aberds 293 D8
Arberth = Narberth Pembs 73 C10
Arbirlot Angus 287 C10
Arboll Highld 311 L2
Arborfield Wokingham 65 F9
Arborfield Cross Wokingham 65 F9
Arborfield Garrison Wokingham 65 F9
Arbourthorne S Yorks 186 D5
Arbroath Angus 287 C10
Arbury Cambs 123 E8
Arbuthnott Aberds 293 F9
Archavandra Muir Highld 309 K7
Archdeacon Newton Darl 224 B5
Archenfield Hereford 96 C5
Archiestown Moray 302 E2
Archnalea Highld 289 C10
Arclid E Ches 168 C3
Arclid Green E Ches 168 C3
Ard-dhubh Highld 299 E7
Ardachu Highld 309 J6
Ardailly Argyll 255 B7
Ardalanish Argyll 274 B4
Ardallie Aberds 303 F10
Ardalum Ho Argyll 288 F6
Ardamaleish Argyll 275 G11
Ardanaiseig Argyll 284 E4
Ardaneaskan Highld 295 B10
Ardanstur Argyll 275 B9
Ardargie House Hotel Perth 286 F4
Ardarroch Highld 295 B10
Ardban Highld 295 B9
Ardbeg Argyll 254 C5
Ardbeg Argyll 276 E3
Ardcharnich Highld 307 L6
Ardchiavaig Argyll 274 B4
Ardchonnell Argyll 275 B10
Ardchronie Highld 309 L6
Ardchuilk Highld 300 F2
Ardchullarie More Stirl 285 F9
Ardchyle Stirl 285 E9
Ardclach Highld 301 E9
Arddleen Powys 148 F5
Ardechvie Highld 290 D3
Ardeley Herts 104 F6
Ardelve Highld 295 C10
Arden Argyll 277 E7
Arden E Renf 267 D10
Arden Park Gtr Man 184 C6
Ardencaple Ho Argyll 275 B8
Ardendrain Highld 300 F5
Ardens Grafton Warks 118 G2
Ardentallen Argyll 289 G10
Ardentinny Argyll 276 D3
Ardentraive Argyll 275 F11
Ardeonaig Stirl 285 D10
Ardersier Highld 301 D7
Ardery Highld 289 C9
Ardessie Highld 307 L5
Ardfern Argyll 275 C9
Ardfernal Argyll 274 F6
Ardgartan Argyll 284 G6
Ardgay Highld 309 K5
Ardglassie Aberds 303 C10
Ardgour Highld 290 G2
Ardgye Moray 301 C11
Ardheslaig Highld 299 D7
Ardiecow Moray 302 C5
Ardinamir Argyll 275 B8
Ardindrean Highld 307 L6
Ardingly W Sus 36 B4
Ardington Oxon 64 B2
Ardington Wick Oxon 64 B2
Ardintoul Highld 295 C10
Ardlair Aberds 302 G5
Ardlair Highld 299 B9
Ardlamey Argyll 255 C7
Ardlamont Ho Argyll 275 G10
Ardlawhill Aberds 303 C8
Ardleigh Essex 107 F11
Ardleigh Green London 68 B4
Ardleigh Heath Essex 107 E10
Ardler Perth 286 C6
Ardley Oxon 101 F10
Ardley End Essex 87 C8
Ardlui Argyll 285 F7
Ardlussa Argyll 275 E7
Ardmair Highld 307 K6
Ardmay Argyll 284 G6
Ardmenish Argyll 274 F6
Ardminish Argyll 255 C7
Ardmolich Highld 289 B9
Ardmore Argyll 289 G9
Ardmore Highld 306 D7
Ardmore Highld 309 L7
Ardnacross Argyll 289 E7
Ardnadam Argyll 276 E3
Ardnagowan Argyll 284 G4
Ardnagrask Highld 300 E5
Ardnarff Highld 295 B10
Ardnastang Highld 289 C10
Ardnave Argyll 274 F3
Ardneil N Ayrs 266 F3
Ardno Argyll 284 G5
Ardo Aberds 303 F8
Ardo Ho Aberds 303 G9
Ardoch Argyll 277 F7
Ardoch Perth 286 D4
Ardoch Stirl 285 F9
Ardochy House Highld 290 C4
Ardoyne Aberds 302 G6
Ardpatrick Argyll 275 G8
Ardpatrick Ho Argyll 255 B8
Ardpeaton Argyll 276 D4
Ardradnaig Perth 285 C11
Ardrishaig Argyll 275 E9
Ardross Fife 287 G9
Ardross Highld 300 B6
Ardross Castle Highld 300 B6
Ardrossan N Ayrs 266 G4
Ardshave Highld 309 K7
Ardsheal Highld 289 D11
Ardshealach Highld 289 C8
Ardskenish Argyll 274 D4
Ardsley S Yorks 197 F11
Ardslignish Highld 289 C7
Ardtalla Argyll 254 B5
Ardtalnaig Perth 285 D11
Ardtaraig Argyll 275 E11
Ardtoe Highld 289 B8
Ardtreck Highld 294 B5
Ardtrostan Perth 285 E10
Ardtur Argyll 289 E11
Arduaine Argyll 275 B8
Ardullie Highld 300 C5
Ardvannie Highld 309 L6
Ardvar Highld 306 F6
Ardvasar Highld 295 E8
Ardveich Stirl 285 E10
Ardverikie Highld 291 E7
Ardvorlich Perth 285 E10
Ardwell Dumfries 236 E3
Ardwell Moray 302 F3
Ardwell S Ayrs 244 E5
Ardwell Mains Dumfries 236 E3
Ardwick Gtr Man 184 B5
Areley Kings Worcs 116 C6
Arford Hants 49 F10
Argoed Caerph 77 F11
Argoed Powys 113 E9
Argoed Powys 130 E5
Argoed Shrops 130 G6
Argoed Shrops 148 E6
Argoed Mill Powys 113 E9
Argos Hill E Sus 37 B9
Arichamish Argyll 275 C10
Arichastlich Argyll 284 D6
Aridhglas Argyll 288 G5
Arieniskill Highld 295 G9
Arileod Argyll 288 D3
Arinacrinachd Highld 299 D7
Arinagour Argyll 288 D4
Arineckaig Highld 299 E9
Arion Orkney 314 E2
Arisaig Highld 295 G8
Ariundle Highld 289 C10
Arivegaig Highld 289 C8
Arivoichallum Argyll 254 C4
Arkendale N Yorks 215 G7
Arkesden Essex 105 E9
Arkholme Lancs 211 E11
Arkle Town N Yorks 223 E10
Arkleby Cumb 229 D8
Arkleton Dumfries 249 E9
Arkley London 86 F2
Arksey S Yorks 198 F5
Arkwright Town Derbys 186 G6
Arle Glos 99 G8
Arlebrook Glos 80 D4
Arlecdon Cumb 219 B10
Arlescote Warks 101 B7
Arlesey C Beds 104 D3
Arleston Telford 150 G3
Arley E Ches 183 E11
Arley Green E Ches 183 E11
Arlingham Glos 80 C2
Arlington Devon 40 E6
Arlington E Sus 23 D8
Arlington Glos 81 D10
Arlington Beccott Devon 40 E6
Armadale Highld 308 C7
Armadale W Loth 269 B8
Armadale Castle Highld 295 E8
Armathwaite Cumb 230 B6
Armigers Essex 105 F11
Arminghall Norf 142 C5
Armitage Staffs 151 F11
Armitage Bridge W Yorks 196 E6
Armley W Yorks 205 G11
Armscote Warks 100 C4
Armsdale Staffs 150 C5
Armshead Staffs 168 F6
Armston Northants 137 F11
Armthorpe S Yorks 198 F6
Arnabost Argyll 288 D4
Arnaby Cumb 210 C3
Arncliffe N Yorks 213 E8
Arncroach Fife 287 G9
Arndilly Ho Moray 302 E2
Arne Dorset 18 D5
Arnesby Leics 136 E2
Arngask Perth 286 F5
Arnisdale Highld 295 D10
Arnish Highld 298 E5
Arniston Midloth 270 C6
Arnol W Isles 304 D5
Arnold E Yorks 209 E8
Arnold Notts 171 F9
Arno's Vale Bristol 60 E6
Arnprior Stirl 278 C2
Arnside Cumb 211 D9
Aros Mains Argyll 289 E7
Arowry Wrex 149 B9
Arpafeelie Highld 300 D6
Arpinge Kent 55 F7
Arrad Foot Cumb 210 C6
Arram E Yorks 208 E6
Arrathorne N Yorks 224 G4
Arreton I o W 20 D6
Arrington Cambs 122 G6
Arrivain Argyll 284 D6
Arrochar Argyll 284 G6
Arrow Warks 117 F11
Arrow Green Hereford 115 F8
Arrowe Hill Mers 182 D3
Arrowfield Top Worcs 117 C10
Arrunden W Yorks 196 F6
Arscaig Highld 309 H5
Arscott Shrops 131 B8
Arthill E Ches 184 D2
Arthington W Yorks 205 E11
Arthingworth Northants 136 G5
Arthog Gwyn 146 G2
Arthrath Aberds 303 F9
Arthursdale W Yorks 206 F3
Arthurstone Perth 286 C6
Arthurville Highld 309 L7
Artington Sur 50 D3
Artrochie Aberds 303 F10
Arundel W Sus 35 F8
Aryhoulan Highld 290 G2
Asby Cumb 229 G7
Ascog Argyll 266 C2
Ascoil Highld 311 H2
Ascot Windsor 66 F2
Ascott Warks 100 E6
Ascott d'Oyley Oxon 82 B4
Ascott Earl Oxon 82 B3
Ascott-under-Wychwood Oxon 82 B4
Asenby N Yorks 215 D7
Asfordby Leics 154 F4
Asfordby Hill Leics 154 F4
Asgarby Lincs 173 F10
Asgarby Lincs 174 B4
Ash Devon 8 F6
Ash Dorset 30 E5
Ash Kent 55 B9
Ash Kent 68 G5
Ash Som 28 C3
Ash Som 29 C7
Ash Sur 49 C11
Ash Bank Staffs 168 F6
Ash Bullayne Devon 26 G3
Ash Green Sur 50 D2
Ash Green Warks 134 F6
Ash Grove Wrex 166 G5
Ash Hill Devon 14 G4
Ash Magna Shrops 149 B11
Ash Mill Devon 26 C3
Ash Moor Devon 26 D3
Ash Parva Shrops 149 B11
Ash Priors Som 27 B11
Ash Street Suff 107 B10
Ash Thomas Devon 27 E8
Ash Vale Sur 49 C11
Ashaig Highld 295 C8
Ashampstead W Berks 64 D5
Ashampstead Green W Berks 64 D5
Ashansworth Hants 48 B2
Ashbank Kent 53 C10
Ashbeer Som 42 F5
Ashbocking Suff 126 G3
Ashbourne Derbys 169 F11
Ashbrittle Som 27 C9
Ashbrook Shrops 131 E9
Ashburnham Forge E Sus 23 B11
Ashburton Devon 8 B5
Ashbury Devon 12 B6
Ashbury Oxon 63 C9
Ashby N Lincs 200 F2
Ashby by Partney Lincs 174 B6
Ashby cum Fenby NE Lincs 201 G9
Ashby de la Launde Lincs 173 D9
Ashby-de-la-Zouch Leics 153 F7
Ashby Folville Leics 154 G4
Ashby Hill NE Lincs 201 G8
Ashby Magna Leics 135 E11
Ashby Parva Leics 135 F10
Ashby Puerorum Lincs 190 G4
Ashby St Ledgers Northants 119 D11
Ashby St Mary Norf 142 C6
Ashchurch Glos 99 E8
Ashcombe Devon 14 F4
Ashcombe Park N Som 59 G10
Ashcott Som 44 F2
Ashcott Corner Som 44 F2
Ashculme Devon 27 E10
Ashdon Essex 105 C11
Ashe Hants 48 D4
Asheldham Essex 89 E7
Ashen Essex 106 C4
Ashendon Bucks 84 C2
Asheridge Bucks 84 E6
Ashey I o W 21 D7
Ashfield Argyll 275 E8
Ashfield Carms 94 F3
Ashfield Hants 32 D5
Ashfield Hereford 97 G11
Ashfield Shrops 148 D6
Ashfield Stirl 285 G11
Ashfield Suff 126 E4
Ashfield Cum Thorpe Suff 126 E4
Ashfield Green Suff 124 F5
Ashfield Green Suff 126 C5
Ashfields Shrops 150 D4
Ashfold Crossways W Sus 36 B2
Ashfold Side N Yorks 214 F2
Ashford Devon 8 F3
Ashford Devon 40 F4
Ashford Hants 31 E10
Ashford Kent 54 E4
Ashford Sur 66 E5
Ashford Bowdler Shrops 115 C10
Ashford Carbonell Shrops 115 C10
Ashford Common Sur 66 E5
Ashford Hill Hants 64 G5
Ashford in the Water Derbys 185 G11
Ashgate Derbys 186 G5
Ashgill S Lnrk 268 F5
Ashgrove Bath 45 B8
Ashiestiel Borders 261 B10
Ashill Devon 27 E9
Ashill Norf 141 C7
Ashill Som 28 D4
Ashingdon Essex 88 G5
Ashington Northumb 253 F7
Ashington Poole 18 B6
Ashington Som 29 C9
Ashington W Sus 35 D10
Ashington End Lincs 175 B8
Ashintully Castle Perth 292 G3
Ashkirk Borders 261 E11
Ashlett Hants 33 G7
Ashleworth Glos 98 F6
Ashley Cambs 124 E3
Ashley Devon 25 E10
Ashley Dorset 31 G10
Ashley E Ches 184 E3
Ashley Glos 80 G6
Ashley Hants 19 B11
Ashley Hants 47 G11
Ashley Kent 55 D10
Ashley Northants 136 E5
Ashley Staffs 150 B5
Ashley Wilts 61 F10
Ashley Dale Staffs 150 B5
Ashley Down Bristol 60 D5
Ashley Green Bucks 85 D7
Ashley Heath Ches 184 D3
Ashley Heath Dorset 31 G10
Ashley Heath Staffs 150 B4
Ashley Moor Hereford 115 D9
Ashley Park Sur 66 F6
Ashleyhay Derbys 170 E3
Ashmanhaugh Norf 160 E6
Ashmansworth Hants 48 B2
Ashmansworthy Devon 24 D4
Ashmead Green Glos 80 F3
Ashmill Devon 12 B3
Ashmore Dorset 30 D6
Ashmore Green W Berks 64 F4
Ashmore Lake W Mid 133 D9
Ashmore Park W Mid 133 C9
Ashnashellach Lodge Highld 299 E10
Ashopton Derbys 185 D11
Ashorne Warks 118 F6
Ashover Derbys 170 C4
Ashover Hay Derbys 170 C5
Ashow Warks 118 C6
Ashperton Hereford 98 C2
Ashprington Devon 8 D6
Ashreigney Devon 25 E10
Ashridge Court Devon 25 G11
Ashtead Sur 51 B7
Ashton Corn 2 D4
Ashton Hants 33 D9
Ashton Hereford 115 E10
Ashton Invclyd 276 F4
Ashton Northants 102 B5
Ashton Northants 137 F11
Ashton P'boro 138 B2
Ashton Som 44 D2
Ashton Common Wilts 45 B11
Ashton Gate Bristol 60 E5
Ashton Green E Sus 23 C7
Ashton Hayes W Ches 167 B8
Ashton Heath Halton 183 F9
Ashton-in-Makerfield Gtr Man 183 B9
Ashton Keynes Wilts 81 G8
Ashton under Hill Worcs 99 D9
Ashton-under-Lyne Gtr Man 184 B6
Ashton upon Mersey Gtr Man 184 C3
Ashton Vale Bristol 60 E5
Ashurst Hants 32 E4
Ashurst Kent 52 F4
Ashurst Lancs 194 F3
Ashurst W Sus 35 D11
Ashurst Bridge Hants 32 E4
Ashurst Wood W Sus 52 F2
Ashvale Bl Gwent 77 C10
Ashwater Devon 12 B3
Ashwell Devon 14 G3
Ashwell Herts 104 D5
Ashwell Rutland 155 G7
Ashwell Som 28 D5
Ashwell End Herts 104 C5
Ashwellthorpe Norf 142 D2
Ashwick Som 44 D6
Ashwicken Norf 158 F4
Ashwood Staffs 133 F7
Ashybank Borders 262 F2
Askam in Furness Cumb 210 D4
Askern S Yorks 198 E5
Askerswell Dorset 16 C6
Askerton Hill Lincs 172 F4
Askett Bucks 84 D4
Askham Cumb 230 G6
Askham Notts 188 G2
Askham Bryan York 207 D7
Askham Richard York 206 D6
Asknish Argyll 275 D10
Askrigg N Yorks 223 G8
Askwith N Yorks 205 D9
Aslackby Lincs 155 C11
Aslacton Norf 142 E3
Aslockton Notts 154 B4
Asloun Aberds 293 B7
Asney Som 44 F3
Aspall Suff 126 D3
Aspatria Cumb 229 C8
Aspenden Herts 105 F7
Asperton Lincs 156 B5
Aspley Nottingham 171 G8
Aspley Staffs 150 C6
Aspley Guise C Beds 103 D8
Aspley Heath C Beds 103 D8
Aspley Heath Warks 117 C11
Aspull Gtr Man 194 F6
Aspull Common Gtr Man 183 B10
Assater Shetland 312 F4
Asselby E Yorks 199 B8
Asserby Lincs 191 F7
Asserby Turn Lincs 191 F7
Assington Suff 107 D8
Assington Green Suff 124 G5
Assynt Ho Highld 300 C5
Astbury E Ches 168 C4
Astcote Northants 120 G3
Asterby Lincs 190 F3
Asterley Shrops 131 B7
Asterton Shrops 131 E7
Asthall Oxon 82 C3
Asthall Leigh Oxon 82 C4
Astle E Ches 184 G4
Astle Highld 309 K7
Astley Gtr Man 195 G8
Astley Shrops 149 F10
Astley Warks 134 F6
Astley Worcs 116 D5
Astley Abbotts Shrops 132 D4
Astley Bridge Gtr Man 195 E8
Astley Cross Worcs 116 D6
Astley Green Gtr Man 184 B2
Astmoor Halton 183 E8
Aston Derbys 185 E11
Aston Derbys 152 C3
Aston E Ches 167 F10
Aston Flint 166 B4
Aston Hereford 115 C9
Aston Hereford 115 E9
Aston Herts 104 G5
Aston Oxon 82 E4
Aston Powys 130 E5
Aston S Yorks 187 D7
Aston Shrops 132 E6
Aston Shrops 149 D10
Aston Staffs 151 E7
Aston Staffs 168 G3
Aston Telford 132 B2
Aston W Ches 183 F9
Aston W Mid 133 F11
Aston Wokingham 65 C9
Aston Abbotts Bucks 102 G6
Aston Bank Worcs 116 C2
Aston Botterell Shrops 132 G2
Aston-by-Stone Staffs 151 C8
Aston Cantlow Warks 118 F2
Aston Clinton Bucks 84 C5
Aston Crews Hereford 98 G3
Aston Cross Glos 99 E8
Aston End Herts 104 G5
Aston Eyre Shrops 132 E3
Aston Fields Worcs 117 D9
Aston Flamville Leics 135 E9
Aston Ingham Hereford 98 G3
Aston juxta Mondrum E Ches 167 D11
Aston le Walls Northants 119 G9
Aston Magna Glos 100 D3
Aston Munslow Shrops 131 F10
Aston on Carrant Glos 99 E8
Aston on Clun Shrops 131 G7
Aston-on-Trent Derbys 153 D8
Aston Pigott Shrops 130 B6
Aston Rogers Shrops 130 B6
Aston Rowant Oxon 84 F2
Aston Sandford Bucks 84 D3
Aston Somerville Worcs 99 D10
Aston Square Shrops 148 D6
Aston Subedge Glos 100 C2
Aston Tirrold Oxon 64 B5
Aston Upthorpe Oxon 64 B5
Astrop Northants 101 D10
Astrope Herts 84 C5
Astwick C Beds 104 D4
Astwith Derbys 170 C6
Astwood M Keynes 103 B9
Astwood Worcs 117 D8
Astwood Worcs 117 F7
Astwood Bank Worcs 117 E10
Aswarby Lincs 173 G9
Aswardby Lincs 190 G5
Atch Lench Worcs 117 G10
Atcham Shrops 131 B10
Athelhampton Dorset 17 C11
Athelington Suff 126 C4
Athelney Som 28 B4
Athelstaneford E Loth 281 F10
Atherfield Green I o W 20 F5
Atherington Devon 25 C9
Atherington W Sus 35 G8
Athersley North S Yorks 197 F11
Athersley South S Yorks 197 F11
Atherstone Som 28 D5
Atherstone Warks 134 D6
Atherstone on Stour Warks 118 G4
Atherton Gtr Man 195 G7
Athnamulloch Highld 299 G11
Athron Hall Perth 286 G4
Atley Hill N Yorks 224 E5
Atlow Derbys 170 F2
Attadale Highld 295 B11
Attadale Ho Highld 295 B11
Attenborough Notts 153 B10
Atterbury M Keynes 103 D7
Atterby Lincs 189 C7
Attercliffe S Yorks 186 D5
Atterley Shrops 132 D2
Atterton Leics 135 D7
Attleborough Norf 141 D10
Attleborough Warks 135 E7
Attlebridge Norf 160 F2
Attleton Green Suff 124 G4
Atwick E Yorks 209 C9
Atworth Wilts 61 F11
Auberrow Hereford 97 B9
Aubourn Lincs 172 C6
Auch Argyll 285 D7
Auchagallon N Ayrs 255 D9
Auchallater Aberds 292 E3
Auchareoch N Ayrs 255 E10
Aucharnie Aberds 302 E6
Auchattie Aberds 293 D8
Auchavan Angus 292 G3
Auchbreck Moray 302 G2
Auchenback E Renf 267 D10
Auchenbainzie Dumfries 247 D8
Auchenblae Aberds 293 F9
Auchenbrack Dumfries 247 D7
Auchenbreck Argyll 255 C8
Auchenbreck Argyll 275 E11
Auchencairn Dumfries 237 D9
Auchencairn Dumfries 247 G11
Auchencairn N Ayrs 256 D2
Auchencairn Ho Dumfries 237 D10
Auchencar N Ayrs 255 D9
Auchencarroch W Dunb 277 E8
Auchencrosh S Ayrs 236 B3
Auchencrow Borders 273 C7
Auchendinny Midloth 270 C5
Auchengray S Lnrk 269 E9
Auchenhalrig Moray 302 C3
Auchenharvie N Ayrs 266 G5
Auchenheath S Lnrk 268 G6
Auchenhew N Ayrs 256 E2
Auchenlaich Stirl 285 G10
Auchenleck Dumfries 237 D9
Auchenlochan Argyll 275 F10
Auchenmalg Dumfries 236 D4
Auchenreoch E Dunb 278 F3
Auchensoul S Ayrs 245 E7
Auchentibber S Lnrk 268 E3
Auchentiber N Ayrs 267 F7
Auchertyre Highld 295 C10
Auchessan Stirl 285 E8
Auchgourish Highld 291 B11
Auchinairn E Dunb 268 B2
Auchindrain Argyll 284 G4
Auchindrean Highld 307 L6
Auchininna Aberds 302 E6
Auchinleck Dumfries 236 B6
Auchinleck E Ayrs 258 E3
Auchinloch N Lnrk 278 G3
Auchinner Perth 285 F10
Auchinraith S Lnrk 268 D3
Auchinroath Moray 302 D2
Auchinstarry N Lnrk 278 F4
Auchintoul Aberds 293 B7
Auchintoul Highld 309 K5
Auchiries Aberds 303 F10
Auchlee Aberds 293 D10
Auchleeks Ho Perth 291 G9
Auchleven Aberds 302 G6
Auchlinn Aberds 303 D7
Auchlochan S Lnrk 259 B8
Auchlossan Aberds 293 C7
Auchlunachan Highld 307 L6
Auchlunies Aberds 293 D10
Auchlyne Stirl 285 E9
Auchmacoy Aberds 303 F9
Auchmair Moray 302 G3
Auchmantle Dumfries 236 C3
Auchmenzie Aberds 302 G5
Auchmillan E Ayrs 258 D2
Auchmithie Angus 287 C10
Auchmore Highld 300 D4
Auchmuirbridge Fife 286 G6
Auchmull Angus 293 F7
Auchnacraig Argyll 289 G9
Auchnacree Angus 292 G6
Auchnafree Perth 286 D2
Auchnagallin Highld 301 F10
Auchnagarron Argyll 275 E11
Auchnagatt Aberds 303 E9
Auchnaha Argyll 275 E10
Auchnahillin Highld 301 F7
Auchnarrow Moray 302 G2
Auchnashelloch Perth 285 F11
Auchnotteroch Dumfries 236 C1
Aucholzie Aberds 292 D5
Auchrannie Angus 286 B6
Auchroisk Highld 301 G10
Auchronie Angus 292 E6
Auchterarder Perth 286 F3
Auchteraw Highld 290 C5
Auchterderran Fife 280 B4
Auchterhouse Angus 287 D7
Auchtermuchty Fife 286 F6
Auchterneed Highld 300 D4
Auchtertool Fife 280 C4
Auchtertyre Moray 301 D11
Auchtertyre Stirl 285
Auchtubh Stirl 285
Auckengill Highld 310
Auckley S Yorks 199
Audenshaw Gtr Man 184
Audlem E Ches 167
Audley Staffs 168
Audley End Essex 105
Audley End Essex 106
Audley End Norf 142
Audley End Suff 125
Auds Aberds 302
Aughertree Cumb 229
Aughton E Yorks 207
Aughton Lancs 193
Aughton Lancs 211
Aughton S Yorks 187
Aughton Wilts 47
Aughton Park Lancs 194
Aukside Durham 232
Auldearn Highld 301
Aulden Hereford 115
Auldgirth Dumfries 247
Auldhame E Loth 281
Auldhouse S Lnrk 268
Auldtown of Carnoustie Aberds 302
Ault a'chruinn Highld 295
Ault Hucknall Derbys 171
Aultanrynie Highld 308
Aultbea Highld 307
Aultdearg Highld 300
Aultgrishan Highld 307
Aultguish Inn Highld 300
Aultibea Highld 311
Aultiphurst Highld 310
Aultivullin Highld 310
Aultmore Highld 301
Aultmore Moray 302
Aultnagoire Highld 300
Aultnamain Inn Highld 309
Aultnaslat Highld 290
Aulton Aberds 302
Aulton of Atherb Aberds 303
Aultvaich Highld 300
Aunby Lincs 155
Aundorach Highld 291
Aunk Devon 27
Aunsby Lincs 155
Auquhorthies Aberds 303
Aust S Glos 60
Austen Fen Lincs 190
Austendike Lincs 156
Austenwood Bucks 66
Austerfield S Yorks 187
Austerlands Gtr Man 196
Austhorpe W Yorks 206
Austrey Warks 134
Austwick N Yorks 212
Authorpe Lincs 190
Authorpe Row Lincs 191
Avebury Wilts 62
Avebury Trusloe Wilts 62
Aveley Thurrock 68
Avening Glos 80
Avening Green S Glos 80
Averham Notts 172
Avernish Highld 295
Avery Hill London 68
Aveton Gifford Devon 8
Avielochan Highld 291
Aviemore Highld 291
Avington Hants 48
Avington W Berks 63
Avoch Highld 301
Avon Hants 19
Avon Wilts 62
Avon Dassett Warks 101
Avonbridge Falk 279
Avoncliff Wilts 45
Avonmouth Bristol 60
Avonwick Devon 8
Awbridge Hants 32
Awhirk Dumfries 236
Awkley S Glos 60
Awliscombe Devon 27
Awre Glos 80
Awsworth Notts 171
Axbridge Som 44
Axford Hants 48
Axford Wilts 63
Axmansford Hants 64
Axminster Devon 15
Axmouth Devon 15
Axton Flint 181
Axtown Devon 7
Axwell Park T & W 242
Aycliff Kent 55
Aycliffe Durham 233
Aydon Northumb 242
Aykley Heads Durham 233
Aylburton Glos 79
Aylburton Common Glos 79
Ayle Northumb 231
Aylesbeare Devon 14
Aylesbury Bucks 84
Aylesby NE Lincs 201
Aylesford Kent 53
Aylesham Kent 55
Aylestone Leicester 135
Aylestone Hill Hereford 97
Aylestone Park Leicester 135
Aylmerton Norf 160
Aylsham Norf 160
Aylton Hereford 98
Aylworth Glos 100
Aymestrey Hereford 115
Aynho Northants 101
Ayot Green Herts 86
Ayot St Lawrence Herts 85
Ayot St Peter Herts 86
Ayr S Ayrs 257
Ayre of Atler Shetland 313
Ayres Shetland 313
Ayres End Herts 85
Ayres of Selivoe Shetland 313
Ayres Quay T & W 243
Aysgarth N Yorks 213
Ayshford Devon 27
Ayside Cumb 211
Ayston Rutland 137
Aythorpe Roding Essex 87
Ayton Borders 273
Ayton T & W 243
Ayton Castle Borders 273
Aywick Shetland 312
Azerley N Yorks 214

B

Babbacombe Torbay 9
Babbington Notts 171
Babbinswood Shrops 148
Babbs Green Herts 86
Babcary Som 29
Babel Carms 94

Beckingham Notts 188 D3
Beckington Som 45 C10
Beckjay Shrops 115 B7
Beckley E Sus 38 C5
Beckley Hants 19 B10
Beckley Oxon 83 C9
Beckley Furnace E Sus 38 C4
Beckside Cumb 212 B2
Beckton London 68 C2
Beckwith N Yorks 205 C11
Beckwithshaw N Yorks 205 C11
Becontree London 68 B3
Bed-y-coedwr Gwyn 146 D4
Bedale N Yorks 214 B5
Bedburn Durham 233 E8
Bedchester Dorset 30 D5
Beddau Rhondda 58 B5
Beddgelert Gwyn 163 F9
Beddingham E Sus 36 F6
Beddington London 67 G10
Beddington Corner London 67 F9
Bedfield Suff 126 D4
Bedford Beds 121 G11
Bedford Gtr Man 183 B11
Bedford Park London 67 D8
Bedgebury Cross Kent 53 G8
Bedgrove Bucks 84 C4
Bedham W Sus 35 C8
Bedhampton Hants 22 B2
Bedingfield Suff 126 D3
Bedingham Green Norf 142 E5
Bedlam N Yorks 214 G5
Bedlam Som 45 D9
Bedlam Street W Sus 36 D3
Bedlar's Green Essex 105 G10
Bedlington Northumb 253 G7
Bedlington Station Northumb 253 G7
Bedlinog M Tydf 77 E9
Bedminster Bristol 60 E5
Bedminster Down Bristol 60 F5
Bedmond Herts 85 E9
Bednall Staffs 151 F9
Bednall Head Staffs 151 F9
Bedrule Borders 262 F4
Bedstone Shrops 115 B7
Bedwas Caerph 59 B7
Bedwell Herts 104 G4
Bedwell Wrex 166 F5
Bedwellty Caerph 77 E11
Bedwellty Pits Bl Gwent 77 D11
Bedwlwyn Wrex 148 B4
Bedworth Warks 135 F7
Bedworth Heath Warks 134 F6
Bedworth Woodlands Warks 134 F6
Beeby Leics 136 B3
Beech Hants 49 F7
Beech Staffs 151 B7
Beech Hill Gtr Man 194 F5
Beech Hill W Berks 65 G7
Beech Lanes W Mid 133 F10
Beechcliff Staffs 151 B7
Beechcliffe W Yorks 205 E7
Beechen Cliff Bath 61 G9
Beechingstoke Wilts 46 B5
Beechwood Halton 183 E8
Beechwood Newport 59 B10
Beechwood W Mid 118 B5
Beechwood W Yorks 206 F2
Beecroft C Beds 103 G10
Beedon W Berks 64 D3
Beedon Hill W Berks 64 D3
Beeford E Yorks 209 C8
Beeley Derbys 170 B3
Beelsby NE Lincs 201 G8
Beenham W Berks 64 F5
Beenham Stocks W Berks 64 F5
Beenham's Heath Windsor 65 D10
Beeny Corn 11 C8
Beer Devon 15 D10
Beer Som 44 G2
Beer Hackett Dorset 29 E9
Beercrocombe Som 28 C4
Beesands Devon 8 G6
Beesby Lincs 191 E7
Beeslack Midloth 270 C4
Beeson Devon 8 G6
Beeston C Beds 104 B3
Beeston Norf 159 F8
Beeston Notts 153 B10
Beeston W Ches 167 D8
Beeston W Yorks 205 G11
Beeston Hill W Yorks 205 G11
Beeston Park Side W Yorks 197 B9
Beeston Regis Norf 177 E11
Beeston Royds W Yorks 205 G11
Beeston St Lawrence Norf 160 E6
Beeswing Dumfries 237 C10
Beetham Cumb 211 D9
Beetham Som 28 E3
Beetley Norf 159 F9
Beffcote Staffs 150 F6
Began Cardiff 59 C8
Begbroke Oxon 83 C7
Begdale Cambs 139 B9
Begelly Pembs 73 D10
Beggar Hill Essex 87 E10
Beggarington Hill W Yorks 197 C9
Beggars Ash Hereford 98 D4
Beggar's Bush Powys 114 E5
Beggars Bush W Sus 35 F11
Beggars Pound V Glam 58 F4
Beggearn Huish Som 42 F4
Beguildy Powys 114 B3
Beighton Norf 143 B7
Beighton S Yorks 186 E6
Beighton Hill Derbys 170 E3
Beili-glas Mon 78 C4
Beitearsaig W Isles 305 G1
Beith N Ayrs 266 E6
Bekesbourne Kent 55 B7
Bekesbourne Hill Kent 55 B7
Belah Cumb 239 F9
Belan Powys 130 C4
Belaugh Norf 160 F5
Belbins Hants 32 C5
Belbroughton Worcs 117 B8
Belchalwell Dorset 30 F3
Belchalwell Street Dorset 30 F3
Belchamp Otten Essex 106 C6
Belchamp St Paul Essex 106 C5
Belchamp Walter Essex 106 C6
Belcher's Bar Leics 135 B8
Belchford Lincs 190 F3
Beleybridge Fife 287 F9
Belfield Gtr Man 196 E2
Belford Northumb 264 C4
Belgrano Conwy 181 F7
Belgrave Leicester 135 B11
Belgrave Staffs 134 C4
Belgrave W Ches 166 C5
Belgravia London 67 D9
Belhaven E Loth 282 F3
Belhelvie Aberds 293 B11
Belhinnie Aberds 302 G4
Bell Bar Herts 86 D3
Bell Busk N Yorks 204 B4
Bell Common Essex 86 E6
Bell End Worcs 117 B8
Bell Green London 67 E11
Bell Green W Mid 135 G7
Bell Heath Worcs 117 B9
Bell Hill Hants 34 C2
Bell o' th' Hill W Ches 167 F8
Bellabeg Aberds 292 B5
Bellamore S Ayrs 244 F6
Bellanoch Argyll 275 D8
Bellanrigg Borders 260 B6
Bellasize E Yorks 199 B10
Bellaty Angus 286 B6
Belle Eau Park Notts 171 D11
Belle Green S Yorks 197 F11
Belle Isle W Yorks 197 B10
Belle Vale Mers 182 D6
Belle Vale W Mid 133 G9
Belle Vue Cumb 228 E8
Belle Vue Cumb 239 F9
Belle Vue Gtr Man 184 B5
Belle Vue S Yorks 198 G5
Belle Vue Shrops 149 G9
Belle Vue W Yorks 197 D10
Belleau Lincs 190 F6
Bellehiglash Moray 301 F11
Bellerby N Yorks 224 G2
Bellever Devon 13 F9
Bellevue Worcs 117 C9
Bellfield E Ayrs 257 B10
Bellfields Sur 50 C3
Bellehill Angus 293 G7
Bellingdon Bucks 84 D6
Bellingham London 67 E11
Bellingham Northumb 251 G8
Bellmount Norf 157 E10
Belloch Argyll 255 D7
Bellochantuy Argyll 255 D7
Bell's Close T & W 242 E5
Bell's Corner Suff 107 D9
Bells Yew Green E Sus 52 F6
Bellsbank E Ayrs 245 C11
Bellshill N Lnrk 268 C4
Bellshill Northumb 264 C4
Bellside N Lnrk 268 D6
Bellsmyre W Dunb 277 F8
Bellspool Borders 260 B5
Bellsquarry W Loth 269 C10
Belluton Bath 60 G6
Bellyeoman Fife 280 D2
Belmaduthy Highld 300 D6
Belmesthorpe Rutland 155 G10
Belmont Blkburn 195 D7
Belmont Durham 234 C2
Belmont E Sus 38 E4
Belmont Harrow 67 G9
Belmont Oxon 63 B11
Belmont S Ayrs 257 E8
Belmont Shetland 312 C7
Belmont Sutton 85 G11
Belnacraig Aberds 292 B5
Belnagarrow Moray 302 E3
Belnie Lincs 156 C5
Belowda Corn 5 C9
Belper Derbys 170 F4
Belper Lane End Derbys 170 F4
Belph Derbys 187 F8
Belsay Northumb 242 B4
Belses Borders 262 D3
Belsford Devon 8 D5
Belsize Herts 85 E8
Belstead Suff 108 C2
Belston S Ayrs 257 E9
Belstone Devon 13 C8
Belstone Corner Devon 13 B8
Belthorn Blkburn 195 C8
Beltinge Kent 71 F7
Beltingham Northumb 241 E7
Beltoft N Lincs 199 F10
Belton Leics 153 E8
Belton Lincs 155 B8
Belton N Lincs 199 F9
Belton Norf 143 C9
Belton in Rutland Rutland 136 C6
Beltring Kent 53 D7
Belts of Collonach Aberds 293 D8
Belvedere London 68 D3
Belvedere W Loth 269 B9
Belvoir Leics 154 C6
Bembridge I o W 21 D8
Bemersyde Borders 262 C3
Bemerton Wilts 46 G6
Bemerton Heath Wilts 46 G6
Bempton E Yorks 218 E3
Ben Alder Lodge Highld 291 F7
Ben Armine Lodge Highld 309 H7
Ben Casgro W Isles 304 F6
Ben Rhydding W Yorks 205 D8
Benacre Suff 143 G10
Benbuie Dumfries 246 D6
Benchill Gtr Man 184 D4
Bencombe Glos 80 F3
Benderloch Argyll 289 F11
Bendish Herts 104 G3
Bendronaig Lodge Highld 299 F10
Benenden Kent 53 G10
Benfield Dumfries 236 C5
Benfieldside Durham 242 G3
Bengal Pembs 91 E9
Bengate Norf 160 D6
Bengeo Herts 86 C4
Bengeworth Worcs 99 C10
Bengrove Glos 99 E9
Benhall Glos 99 G8
Benhall Green Suff 127 E7
Benhall Street Suff 127 E7
Benhilton London 67 F9
Benholm Aberds 293 G10
Beningbrough N Yorks 206 B6
Benington Herts 104 G5
Benington Lincs 174 F5
Benington Sea End Lincs 174 F6
Benllech Anglesey 179 E8
Benmore Argyll 276 E2
Benmore Stirl 285 E8
Benmore Lodge Argyll 289 F7
Benmore Lodge Highld 309 H3
Bennacott Corn 11 C11
Bennah Devon 14 E2
Bennan N Ayrs 255 E10
Bennane Lea S Ayrs 244 F3
Bennetland E Yorks 199 B10
Bennetsfield Highld 300 D6
Bennett End Bucks 84 F3
Bennetts End Herts 85 D9
Benniworth Lincs 190 E2
Benover Kent 53 D8
Bensham T & W 242 E6
Benslie N Ayrs 266 G6
Benson Oxon 83 G10
Benston Shetland 313 H6
Bent Aberds 293 F8
Bent Gate Lancs 195 C9
Benter Som 44 D6
Bentfield Bury Essex 105 F9
Bentfield Green Essex 105 F10
Bentgate Gtr Man 196 E2
Benthall Northumb 264 D6
Benthall Shrops 132 C3
Bentham Glos 80 B6
Benthoul Aberdeen 293 C10
Bentilee Stoke 168 F6
Bentlass Pembs 73 E7
Bentlawnt Shrops 130 C6
Bentley E Yorks 208 F6
Bentley Essex 87 F9
Bentley Hants 49 E9
Bentley S Yorks 198 F5
Bentley Suff 108 D2
Bentley W Mid 133 D9
Bentley Warks 134 D5
Bentley Worcs 117 D9
Bentley Common Warks 134 D5
Bentley Heath Herts 86 F2
Bentley Heath W Mid 118 B3
Bentley Rise S Yorks 198 G5
Benton Devon 41 F7
Benton Green W Mid 118 B5
Bentpath Dumfries 249 E8
Bents W Loth 269 C9
Bents Head W Yorks 205 F7
Bentwichen Devon 41 G8
Bentworth Hants 49 E7
Benvie Dundee 287 D7
Benville Dorset 29 G8
Benwell T & W 242 E6
Benwick Cambs 138 E6
Beobridge Shrops 132 E5
Beoley Worcs 117 D11
Beoraidbeg Highld 295 F8
Bepton W Sus 34 D5
Berden Essex 105 F9
Bere Alston Devon 7 B8
Bere Ferrers Devon 7 C9
Bere Regis Dorset 18 C2
Berechurch Essex 107 G9
Berefold Aberds 303 F9
Berepper Corn 2 E5
Bergh Apton Norf 142 C6
Berghers Hill Bucks 66 B2
Berhill Som 44 F2
Berinsfield Oxon 83 F9
Berkeley Glos 79 F11
Berkeley Heath Glos 79 F11
Berkeley Road Glos 80 E2
Berkeley Towers E Ches 167 E11
Berkhamsted Herts 85 D7
Berkley Som 45 D10
Berkley Down Som 45 D9
Berkley Marsh Som 45 D10
Berkswell W Mid 118 B4
Bermondsey London 67 D10
Bermuda Warks 135 F7
Bernards Heath Herts 85 D11
Bernera Highld 295 C10
Berner's Cross Devon 25 F10
Berner's Hill E Sus 53 G8
Berners Roding Essex 87 D10
Bernice Argyll 276 C2
Bernisdale Highld 298 D4
Berrick Salome Oxon 83 G10
Berriedale Highld 311 G5
Berrier Cumb 230 F3
Berriew = Aberriw Powys 130 C3
Berrington Northumb 273 G10
Berrington Shrops 131 B10
Berrington Worcs 115 D11
Berrington Green Worcs 115 D11
Berriowbridge Corn 11 F11
Berrow Som 43 C10
Berrow Worcs 98 E5
Berrow Green Worcs 116 F4
Berry Swansea 56 D3
Berry Brow W Yorks 196 E6
Berry Cross Devon 25 E7
Berry Down Cross Devon 40 E5
Berry Hill Glos 79 C9
Berry Hill Pembs 91 C11
Berry Hill Stoke 168 F6
Berry Hill Worcs 117 E7
Berry Moor S Yorks 197 G9
Berry Pomeroy Devon 8 C6
Berryfield Wilts 61 G11
Berrygate Hill E Yorks 201 C8
Berryhillock Moray 302 C5
Berrylands London 67 F7
Berrynarbor Devon 40 D5
Berry's Green London 52 B2
Berrysbridge Devon 26 G6
Bersham Wrex 166 F4
Berstane Orkney 314 E4
Berth-ddu Flint 166 B2
Berthengam Flint 181 F10
Berwick E Sus 23 D8
Berwick Kent 54 F6
Berwick S Glos 60 C5
Berwick Bassett Wilts 62 E5
Berwick Hill Northumb 242 B5
Berwick St James Wilts 46 F5
Berwick St John Wilts 30 C6
Berwick St Leonard Wilts 46 G2
Berwick-upon-Tweed Northumb 273 E9
Berwick Wharf Shrops 149 G10
Berwyn Denb 165 G11
Bescaby Leics 154 D6
Bescar Lancs 193 E11
Bescot W Mid 133 D10
Besford Shrops 149 E11
Besford Worcs 99 C8
Bessacarr S Yorks 198 G6
Bessels Green Kent 52 B4
Bessels Leigh Oxon 83 E7
Besses o' th' Barn Gtr Man 195 F10
Bessingby E Yorks 218 F3
Bessingham Norf 160 B3
Best Beech Hill E Sus 52 G6
Besthorpe Norf 141 D11
Besthorpe Notts 172 C4
Bestwood Nottingham 171 G9
Bestwood Village Notts 171 F9
Beswick E Yorks 208 D6
Beswick Gtr Man 184 B5
Betchcott Shrops 131 D8
Betchton Heath E Ches 168 C3
Betchworth Sur 51 D8
Bethania Ceredig 111 E11
Bethania Gwyn 163 E10
Bethania Gwyn 164 F2
Bethany Corn 6 D6
Bethel Anglesey 178 G5
Bethel Corn 5 E10
Bethel Gwyn 147 B9
Bethel Gwyn 163 B8
Bethelnie Aberds 303 F7
Bethersden Kent 54 E2
Bethesda Gwyn 163 B10
Bethesda Pembs 73 B9
Bethlehem Carms 94 F3
Bethnal Green London 67 C10
Betley Staffs 168 F3
Betley Common Staffs 168 F2
Betsham Kent 68 E6
Betteshanger Kent 55 C10
Bettiscombe Dorset 16 B3
Bettisfield Wrex 149 B9
Betton Shrops 130 C6
Betton Shrops 150 B3
Betton Strange Shrops 131 B10
Bettws Bridgend 58 B2
Bettws Mon 78 B3
Bettws Newport 78 G3
Bettws Cedewain Powys 130 D2
Bettws Gwerfil Goch Denb 165 F8
Bettws Ifan Ceredig 92 B6
Bettws Newydd Mon 78 D5
Bettws-y-crwyn Shrops 130 G4
Bettyhill Highld 308 C7
Betws Bridgend 57 D11
Betws Carms 75 C10
Betws Bledrws Ceredig 111 G11
Betws-Garmon Gwyn 163 D8
Betws Ifan Ceredig 92 B6
Betws-y-Coed Conwy 164 D4
Betws-yn-Rhos Conwy 180 G6
Beulah Ceredig 92 B5
Beulah Powys 113 G8
Bevendean Brighton 36 F4
Bevercotes Notts 187 G11
Bevere Worcs 116 F6
Beverley E Yorks 208 F6
Beverston Glos 80 G5
Bevington Glos 79 F11
Bewaldeth Cumb 229 E10
Bewbush W Sus 51 F8
Bewcastle Cumb 240 C3
Bewdley Worcs 116 B5
Bewerley N Yorks 214 G3
Bewholme E Yorks 209 C9
Bewley Common Wilts 62 F2
Bewlie Borders 262 D3
Bewlie Mains Borders 262 D3
Bewsey Warr 183 D9
Bexfield Norf 159 D10
Bexhill E Sus 38 F2
Bexley London 68 E3
Bexleyheath London 68 D3
Bexleyhill W Sus 34 B6
Bexon Kent 53 B11
Bexwell Norf 140 C2
Beyton Suff 125 E8
Beyton Green Suff 125 E8
Bhalasaigh W Isles 304 E3
Bhaltos W Isles 304 E2
Bhatarsaigh W Isles 297 M2
Bhlàraidh Highld 290 B5
Bibstone S Glos 79 G11
Bibury Glos 81 D10
Bicester Oxon 101 G11
Bickenhall Som 28 D3
Bickenhill W Mid 134 G3
Bicker Lincs 156 B4
Bicker Bar Lincs 156 B4
Bicker Gauntlet Lincs 156 B4
Bickershaw Gtr Man 194 G6
Bickerstaffe Lancs 194 G2
Bickerton Devon 9 G11
Bickerton E Ches 167 E8
Bickerton N Yorks 206 C5
Bickford Staffs 151 G7
Bickham Som 42 E3
Bickington Devon 26 B3
Bickington Devon 13 G11
Bickington Devon 40 G4
Bickleigh Devon 7 C10
Bickleigh Devon 26 F6
Bickleton Devon 40 G4
Bickley London 68 F2
Bickley W Ches 167 F8
Bickley Worcs 116 C2
Bickley Moss W Ches 167 F8
Bickley Town W Ches 167 F8
Bickleywood W Ches 167 F8
Bickmarsh Warks 100 B2
Bicknacre Essex 88 E3
Bicknoller Som 42 F6
Bicknor Kent 53 B11
Bickton Hants 31 E11
Bicton Hereford 115 E9
Bicton Pembs 72 D4
Bicton Shrops 130 G5
Bicton Shrops 149 F8
Bicton Heath Shrops 149 G9
Bidborough Kent 52 E5
Bidden Hants 49 D8
Biddenden Kent 53 F11
Biddenden Green Kent 53 E11
Biddenham Beds 103 B10
Biddestone Wilts 61 E11
Biddick T & W 243 F8
Biddick Hall T & W 243 E9
Biddisham Som 43 C11
Biddlesden Bucks 102 C2
Biddlestone Northumb 251 B11
Biddulph Staffs 168 D5
Biddulph Moor Staffs 168 D6
Bideford Devon 25 B7
Bidford-on-Avon Warks 118 G2
Bidlake Devon 12 D5
Bidston Mers 182 C3
Bidston Hill Mers 182 D3
Bidwell C Beds 103 G10
Bielby E Yorks 207 E11
Bieldside Aberdeen 293 C10
Bierley I o W 20 F6
Bierley W Yorks 205 G9
Bierton Bucks 84 B4
Big Mancot Flint 166 B4
Big Sand Highld 299 B7
Bigbury Devon 8 F3
Bigbury-on-Sea Devon 8 G3
Bigby Lincs 200 F5
Bigfrith Windsor 65 C11
Biggar Cumb 210 F3
Biggar S Lnrk 260 B2
Biggar Road N Lnrk 268 C5
Biggin Derbys 169 D11
Biggin Derbys 170 F3
Biggin N Yorks 206 F6
Biggin Thurrock 69 D7
Biggin Hill London 52 B2
Biggings Shetland 313 G3
Biggleswade C Beds 104 C3
Bighouse Highld 310 C2
Bighton Hants 48 G6
Biglands Cumb 239 G7
Bignall End Staffs 168 E4
Bignor W Sus 35 E7
Bigods Essex 106 G2
Bigram Stirl 285 G10
Bigrigg Cumb 219 C10
Bigswell Orkney 314 E3
Bigton Shetland 313 L5
Bilberry Corn 5 C10
Bilborough Nottingham 171 G8
Bilbrook Som 42 E4
Bilbrook Staffs 133 C7
Bilbrough N Yorks 206 D6
Bilbster Highld 310 D6
Bilby Notts 187 E10
Bildershaw Durham 233 G10
Bildeston Suff 107 B9
Bill Quay T & W 243 E7
Billacombe Plym 7 E10
Billacott Corn 11 C11
Billericay Essex 87 G11
Billesdon Leics 136 C4
Billesley W Mid 133 G11
Billesley Warks 118 F2
Billesley Common W Mid 133 G11
Billingborough Lincs 156 C2
Billinge Mers 194 G4
Billingford Norf 126 B3
Billingford Norf 159 E10
Billingham Stockton 234 G5
Billinghay Lincs 173 E11
Billingley S Yorks 198 G2
Billingshurst W Sus 35 B9
Billingsley Shrops 132 F4
Billington C Beds 103 G8
Billington Lancs 203 F10
Billington Staffs 151 E7
Billockby Norf 161 G8
Billy Mill T & W 243 D8
Billy Row Durham 233 D9
Bilmarsh Shrops 149 D9
Bilsborrow Lancs 202 F6
Bilsby Lincs 191 F7
Bilsby Field Lincs 191 F7
Bilsdon Devon 14 C2
Bilsham W Sus 35 G7
Bilsington Kent 54 G4
Bilson Green Glos 79 C11
Bilsthorpe Notts 171 C10
Bilsthorpe Moor Notts 171 D11
Bilston Midloth 270 C5
Bilston W Mid 133 D9
Bilstone Leics 135 B7
Bilting Kent 54 D5
Bilton E Yorks 209 G9
Bilton N Yorks 206 B2
Bilton Northumb 264 G6
Bilton Warks 119 C9
Bilton Haggs N Yorks 206 D5
Bilton in Ainsty N Yorks 206 D5
Bimbister Orkney 314 E3
Binbrook Lincs 190 C2
Binchester Blocks Durham 233 E10
Bincombe Dorset 17 E9
Bincombe Som 43 F7
Bindal Highld 311 L3
Bindon Som 27 C10
Binegar Som 44 D6
Bines Green W Sus 35 D11
Binfield Brack 65 E10
Binfield Heath Oxon 65 D8
Bingfield Northumb 241 C11
Bingham Edin 280 G6
Bingham Notts 154 B4
Bingley W Yorks 205 F8
Bings Heath Shrops 149 F10
Binham Norf 159 B9
Binley Hants 48 C2
Binley W Mid 119 B7
Binley Woods Warks 119 B7
Binnegar Dorset 18 D3
Binniehill Falk 279 G7
Binscombe Sur 50 D3
Binsey Oxon 83 D7
Binsoe N Yorks 214 D4
Binstead Hants 49 E9
Binstead I o W 21 C7
Binsted Hants 49 E9
Binsted W Sus 35 F7
Binton Warks 118 G2
Bintree Norf 159 E10
Binweston Shrops 130 C6
Birch Essex 88 B6
Birch Gtr Man 195 F11
Birch Acre Worcs 117 C11
Birch Berrow Worcs 116 E4
Birch Cross Staffs 152 C2
Birch Green Essex 88 B6
Birch Green Herts 86 C3
Birch Green Lancs 194 F3
Birch Green Worcs 99 B7
Birch Heath W Ches 167 C8
Birch Hill Brack 65 F11
Birch Hill W Ches 183 G8
Birch Vale Derbys 185 D8
Birch Wood Som 28 E2
Bircham Newton Norf 158 C5
Bircham Tofts Norf 158 C5
Birchall Hereford 98 D3
Birchall Staffs 169 E7
Birchan Coppice Worcs 116 C6
Birchanger Essex 105 G10
Birchburn N Ayrs 255 E10
Birchden E Sus 52 F4
Birchencliffe W Yorks 196 D6
Birchend Hereford 98 C3
Birchendale Staffs 151 B11
Bircher Hereford 115 D9
Birches Green W Mid 134 E2
Birches Head Stoke 168 F5
Birchett's Green E Sus 53 G7
Birchfield Highld 301 G9
Birchfield W Mid 133 E11
Birchgrove Cardiff 59 D7
Birchgrove E Sus 36 B6
Birchgrove Swansea 57 B8
Birchhall Corner Essex 107 E10
Birchill Devon 28 G4
Birchills W Mid 133 D10
Birchington Kent 71 F9
Birchley Heath Warks 134 E5
Birchmoor Warks 134 C5
Birchmoor Green C Beds 103 E8
Bircholt Forstal Kent 54 E5
Birchover Derbys 170 C2
Birchwood Herts 86 D2
Birchwood Lincs 172 B6
Birchwood Som 28 E2
Birchwood Warr 183 C10
Birchy Hill Hants 19 B11
Bircotes Notts 187 C10
Bird Street Suff 125 G10
Birdbrook Essex 106 C4
Birdbush Wilts 30 C6
Birdfield Argyll 275 D10
Birdforth N Yorks 215 D9
Birdham W Sus 22 D4
Birdholme Derbys 170 B5
Birdingbury Warks 119 D8
Birdlip Glos 80 C6
Birds Edge W Yorks 197 F8
Birds End Suff 124 E5
Birds Green Essex 87 D9
Birdsall N Yorks 216 F6
Birdsgreen Shrops 132 F5
Birdsmoorgate Dorset 28 G5
Birdston E Dunb 278 F3
Birdwell S Yorks 197 G10
Birdwood Glos 80 B2
Birgham Borders 263 B7
Birichen Highld 309 K7
Birkacre Lancs 194 D5
Birkby Cumb 229 D7
Birkby N Yorks 224 E6
Birkby W Yorks 196 D6
Birkdale Mers 193 D10
Birkenbog Aberds 302 C5
Birkenhead Mers 182 D4
Birkenhills Aberds 303 E7
Birkenshaw N Lnrk 268 C3
Birkenshaw S Lnrk 268 F5
Birkenshaw W Yorks 197 B8
Birkenshaw Bottoms W Yorks 197 B8
Birkenside Borders 271 G11
Birkett Mire Cumb 230 G2
Birkhall Aberds 292 D5
Birkhill Angus 287 D7
Birkhill Borders 260 F6
Birkhill Borders 271 G11
Birkholme Lincs 155 E9
Birkhouse W Yorks 197 C7
Birkin N Yorks 198 B4
Birks Cumb 222 G3
Birks W Yorks 197 B9
Birkshaw Northumb 241 D7
Birley Hereford 115 G9
Birley Carr S Yorks 186 C4
Birley Edge S Yorks 186 C4
Birleyhay Derbys 186 E5
Birling Kent 69 G7
Birling Northumb 252 B6
Birling Gap E Sus 23 F9
Birlingham Worcs 99 C8
Birmingham W Mid 133 F11
Birnam Perth 286 C4
Birniehill S Lnrk 268 E2
Birse Aberds 293 D7
Birsemore Aberds 293 D7
Birstall Leics 135 B11
Birstall W Yorks 197 B8
Birstall Smithies W Yorks 197 B8
Birstwith N Yorks 205 B10
Birthorpe Lincs 156 C2
Birtle Gtr Man 195 E10
Birtley Hereford 115 D7
Birtley Northumb 241 B9
Birtley Shrops 131 E9
Birtley T & W 243 F7
Birtley Green Sur 50 E4
Birts Street Worcs 98 D5
Birtsmorton Worcs 98 D6
Bisbrooke Rutland 137 D7
Biscathorpe Lincs 190 D2
Biscombe Som 27 E11
Biscot Luton 103 G11
Biscovey Corn 5 E11
Bish Mill Devon 26 B2
Bisham Windsor 65 C10
Bishampton Worcs 117 G9
Bishon Common Hereford 97 C8
Bishop Auckland Durham 233 F10
Bishop Burton E Yorks 208 F5
Bishop Kinkell Highld 300 D5
Bishop Middleham Durham 234 E2
Bishop Monkton N Yorks 214 F6
Bishop Norton Lincs 189 C7
Bishop Sutton Bath 44 B5
Bishop Thornton N Yorks 214 G5
Bishop Wilton E Yorks 207 B11
Bishopbridge Lincs 189 C8
Bishopbriggs E Dunb 278 G2
Bishopdown Wilts 47 G7
Bishopmill Moray 302 C2
Bishops Cannings Wilts 62 G4
Bishop's Castle Shrops 130 F6
Bishop's Caundle Dorset 29 E11
Bishop's Cleeve Glos 99 F9
Bishop's Down Dorset 29 E11
Bishops Frome Hereford 98 B3
Bishops Green Essex 87 B10
Bishop's Green W Berks 64 G4
Bishop's Hull Som 28 C2
Bishop's Itchington Warks 119 F7
Bishops Lydeard Som 27 B11
Bishops Norton Glos 98 G6
Bishops Nympton Devon 26 C3
Bishop's Offley Staffs 150 D5
Bishop's Quay Corn 2 D6
Bishop's Stortford Herts 105 G9
Bishop's Sutton Hants 48 G6
Bishop's Tachbrook Warks 118 E6
Bishops Tawton Devon 40 G5
Bishop's Wood Staffs 132 B6
Bishopsbourne Kent 55 C7
Bishopsgarth Stockton 234 G4
Bishopsgate Sur 66 E3
Bishopsteignton Devon 14 G4
Bishopstoke Hants 33 D7
Bishopston Bristol 60 D5
Bishopston Swansea 56 D5
Bishopstone Bucks 84 C4
Bishopstone E Sus 23 E7
Bishopstone Hereford 97 C8
Bishopstone Kent 71 F8
Bishopstone Swindon 63 C8
Bishopstone Wilts 31 B9
Bishopstrow Wilts 45 E11
Bishopswood Som 28 E3
Bishopsworth Bristol 60 F5
Bishopthorpe York 207 D7
Bishopton Darl 234 G3
Bishopton Dumfries 236 E6
Bishopton N Yorks 214 E6
Bishopton Renfs 277 G8
Bishopton Warks 118 F3
Bishopwearmouth T & W 243 F9
Bishpool Newport 59 B10
Bishton Newport 59 B11
Bishton Staffs 151 E10
Bisley Glos 80 D6
Bisley Sur 50 B3
Bisley Camp Sur 50 B2
Bispham Blkpool 202 E2
Bispham Green Lancs 194 E3
Bissoe Corn 4 G5
Bissom Corn 3 C7
Bisterne Hants 31 G10
Bisterne Close Hants 32 G2
Bitchet Green Kent 52 C5
Bitchfield Lincs 155 D9
Bittadon Devon 40 E4
Bittaford Devon 8 D3
Bittering Norf 159 F8
Bitterley Shrops 115 B11
Bitterne Soton 33 E7
Bitterne Park Soton 32 E6
Bitterscote Staffs 134 C4
Bitteswell Leics 135 F10
Bittles Green Dorset 30 C5
Bitton S Glos 61 F7
Bix Oxon 65 B8
Bixter Shetland 313 H5
Blaby Leics 135 D11
Black Bank Cambs 139 F10
Black Bank Warks 135 F7
Black Banks Darl 224 C5
Black Barn Lincs 157 D8
Black Bourton Oxon 82 E3
Black Callerton T & W 242 D5
Black Carr Norf 141 D11
Black Clauchrie S Ayrs 245 G7
Black Corner W Sus 51 F9
Black Corries Lodge Highld 284 B6
Black Crofts Argyll 289 F11
Black Cross Corn 5 C8
Black Dam Hants 48 C6
Black Dog Devon 26 F4
Black Heddon Northumb 242 B3
Black Hill W Yorks 204 E6
Black Horse Drove Cambs 139 E11
Black Lake W Mid 133 E9
Black Lane Gtr Man 195 F9
Black Marsh Shrops 130 D6
Black Moor Lancs 194 E3
Black Moor W Yorks 205 F11
Black Mount Argyll 284 C6
Black Notley Essex 106 G5
Black Park Wrex 166 G4
Black Pill Swansea 56 C6
Black Pole Lancs 202 F5
Black Rock Brighton 36 G4
Black Rock Corn 2 C5
Black Street Suff 143 F10
Black Tar Pembs 73 D7
Black Torrington Devon 25 F7
Black Vein Caerph 78 G2
Blackacre Dumfries 248 E2
Blackadder West Borders 272 E6
Blackawton Devon 8 E6
Blackbeck Cumb 219 D10
Blackbird Leys Oxon 83 E9
Blackborough Devon 27 F9
Blackborough Norf 158 G3
Blackborough End Norf 158 G3
Blackboys E Sus 37 C8
Blackbraes Aberds 293 B10
Blackbrook Derbys 170 F4
Blackbrook Derbys 185 E9
Blackbrook Mers 183 B8
Blackbrook Staffs 150 B5
Blackbrook Sur 51 D7
Blackburn Aberds 293 B10
Blackburn Aberds 302 F5
Blackburn Blkburn 195 B7
Blackburn S Yorks 186 C5
Blackburn W Loth 269 B9
Blackcastle Midloth 271 D8
Blackchambers Aberds 293 B9
Blackcraig Dumfries 246 G6
Blackcraigs Angus 293 E7
Blackden Heath E Ches 184 G3
Blackditch Oxon 82 D6
Blackdog Aberds 293 B11
Blackdown Dorset 28 G5
Blackdown Hants 33 C8
Blackdown Warks 118 D6
Blackdyke Cumb 238 G4
Blackdykes E Loth 281 E11
Blacker Hill S Yorks 197 G11
Blacketts Kent 70 F2
Blackfell T & W 243 F7
Blackfen London 68 E3
Blackfield Hants 32 G6
Blackford Cumb 239 E9
Blackford Dumfries 248 G4
Blackford Perth 286 G2
Blackford Shrops 131 G11
Blackford Som 29 B11
Blackford Som 42 D2
Blackford Som 44 D2
Blackford Bridge Gtr Man 195 F10
Blackfordby Leics 152 F6
Blackfords Staffs 151 G9
Blackgang I o W 20 F5
Blackgate Angus 287 B8
Blackhall Aberds 293 D8
Blackhall Edin 280 G4
Blackhall Renfs 267 C9
Blackhall Colliery Durham 234 D5
Blackhall Mill T & W 242 F4
Blackhall Rocks Durham 234 D5
Blackham E Sus 52 F3
Blackhaugh Borders 261 B10
Blackheath Essex 107 G10
Blackheath London 67 D11
Blackheath Suff 127 C8
Blackheath Sur 50 D4
Blackheath W Mid 133 F9
Blackheath Park London 68 D2
Blackhill Aberds 303 D10
Blackhill Aberds 303 E10
Blackhill Aberds 303 F10
Blackhill Durham 242 G3
Blackhill Hants 32 D4
Blackhill Highld 298 D3
Blackhillock Moray 302 E4
Blackhills Highld 301 D9
Blackhills Moray 302 D2
Blackhills Swansea 56 C5
Blackhorse Devon 14 C5
Blackhorse S Glos 61 D7
Blackjack Lincs 156 B5
Blackland Wilts 62 F4
Blacklands E Sus 38 E4
Blacklands Hereford 98 C2
Blacklaw Aberds 302 D6
Blackleach Lancs 202 G5
Blackley Gtr Man 195 G11
Blackley W Yorks 196 D6
Blacklunans Perth 292 G3
Blackmarstone Hereford 97 D10
Blackmill Bridgend 58 B2
Blackminster Worcs 99 C11
Blackmoor Bath 60 G5
Blackmoor Gtr Man 195 G7
Blackmoor Hants 49 G9
Blackmoor N Som 60 G3
Blackmoor Som 27 D11
Blackmoor Gate Devon 41 E7
Blackmoorfoot W Yorks 196 E5
Blackmore Essex 87
Blackmore Shrops 130
Blackmore End Essex 106
Blackmore End Herts 85 E
Blackmore End Worcs 98
Blackness Aberds 293
Blackness E Sus 52
Blackness Falk 279 F
Blacknest Hants 49
Blacknest Windsor 66
Blacknoll Dorset 18
Blacko Lancs 204
Blackoe Shrops 149 E
Blackpark Dumfries 236
Blackpole Worcs 117
Blackpool Blkpool 202
Blackpool Devon 7 E
Blackpool Devon 9
Blackpool Devon 14
Blackpool Pembs 73
Blackpool Gate Cumb 240
Blackridge W Loth 269
Blackrock Argyll 274
Blackrock Bath 60
Blackrock Mon 78
Blackrod Gtr Man 194
Blackshaw Dumfries 238
Blackshaw Head W Yorks 196
Blackshaw Moor Staffs 169
Blacksmith's Corner Suff 108
Blacksmith's Green Suff 126
Blacksnape Blkburn 195
Blackstone W Sus 36
Blackstone Worcs 116
Blackthorn Oxon 83
Blackthorpe Suff 125
Blacktoft E Yorks 199
Blacktop Aberdeen 293
Blacktown Newport 59
Blackwall Derbys 170
Blackwall London 67
Blackwall Tunnel London 67
Blackwater Corn 4
Blackwater Dorset 19
Blackwater Hants 49
Blackwater I o W 20
Blackwater Norf 159
Blackwater Som 28
Blackwater Lodge Moray 302
Blackwaterfoot N Ayrs 255
Blackweir Cardiff 59
Blackwell Cumb 239
Blackwell Darl 224
Blackwell Derbys 170
Blackwell Derbys 185
Blackwell Devon 27
Blackwell W Sus 51
Blackwell Warks 100
Blackwell Worcs 117
Blackwood Caerph 77
Blackwood S Lnrk 268
Blackwood Warr 183
Blackwood Hill Staffs 168
Blacon W Ches 166
Bladbean Kent 55
Blades N Yorks 223
Bladnoch Dumfries 236
Bladon Oxon 82
Blaen-Cil-Llech Ceredig 92
Blaen Clydach Rhondda 77
Blaen-gwynfi Neath 57
Blaen-pant Ceredig 92
Blaen-waun Carms 92
Blaen-waun Ceredig 111
Blaen-y-coed Carms 92
Blaen-y-cwm Bl Gwent 77
Blaen-y-Cwm Denb 147
Blaen-y-cwm Gwyn 146
Blaen-y-cwm Powys 147
Blaenannerch Ceredig 92
Blaenau Carms 75
Blaenau Flint 166
Blaenau Dolwyddelan Conwy 164
Blaenau Ffestiniog Gwyn 164
Blaenau-Gwent Bl Gwent 78
Blaenavon Torf 78
Blaenbedw Fawr Ceredig 111
Blaencaerau Bridgend 57
Blaencelyn Ceredig 111
Blaencwm Rhondda 76
Blaendulais = Seven Sisters Neath 76
Blaendyryn Powys 95
Blaenffos Pembs 92
Blaengarw Bridgend 76
Blaengwrach Neath 76
Blaengwynfi Neath 57
Blaenllechau Rhondda 77
Blaenpennal Ceredig 112
Blaenplwyf Ceredig 111
Blaenporth Ceredig 92
Blaenrhondda Rhondda 76
Blaenwaun Carms 92
Blaenycwm Ceredig 112
Blagdon N Som 44
Blagdon Torbay 9
Blagdon Hill Som 28
Blagill Cumb 231
Blaguegate Lancs 194
Blaich Highld 290
Blain Highld 289
Blaina Bl Gwent 78
Blainacraig Ho Aberds 293
Blair Fife 280
Blair Atholl Perth 291
Blair Drummond Stirl 278
Blairbeg N Ayrs 256
Blairburn Fife 279
Blairdaff Aberds 293
Blairdryne Aberds 293
Blairglas Argyll 276
Blairgorm Highld 301
Blairgowrie Perth 286
Blairhall Fife 279
Blairhill N Lnrk 268
Blairingone Perth 279
Blairland N Ayrs 266
Blairlinn N Lnrk 278
Blairlogie Stirl 278
Blairlomond Argyll 276
Blairmore Argyll 276
Blairmore Highld 306
Blairnamarrow Moray 292
Blairquhosh Stirl 277
Blair's Ferry Argyll 275
Blairskaith E Dunb 277
Blaisdon Glos 80
Blaise Hamlet Bristol 60
Blake End Essex 106
Blakebrook Worcs 116
Blakedown Worcs 117
Blakelands M Keynes 103
Blakelaw Borders 263

kelaw T & W 242 D6
keley Staffs 133 E7
keley Lane Staffs 169 F7
kelow E Ches 167 E11
kemere Hereford 97 C7
kenall Heath W Mid 133 C10
keney Glos 79 D11
keney Norf 177 E8
kenhall E Sus 168 F2
kenhall W Mid 133 D8
keshall Worcs 132 G6
kesley Northants 120 G2
nchland Northumb 241 G11
nd Hill N Yorks 205 C10
ndford Camp Dorset 30 F6
ndford Forum Dorset 30 F5
ndford St Mary
orset 30 F5
ndy Highld 308 D6
nefield Stirl 277 F11
nerne Borders 272 D6
nk Bank Staffs 168 F4
nkney Lincs 173 C9
ntyre S Lnrk 268 D3
r a'Chaorainn
ghld 290 G3
ran Argyll 275 B9
rghour Argyll 275 B10
rmachfoldach
ghld 290 G2
rnalearoch Highld 307 K6
rnat Hill Essex 88 C2
shford Hants 31 F11
ston Leics 136 D6
tchbridge Som 45 D9
therwycke Northants 137 D9
with Cumb 210 B5
xhall Suff 127 F7
xton S Yorks 199 G7
ydon T & W 242 E5
ydon Burn T & W 242 E5
ydon Haughs T & W 242 E5
ach Green Cumb 219 B9
ach Green Suff 126 B4
adney Som 44 D3
adon N Som 43 B10
ak Acre Hereford 98 B2
ak Hall M Keynes 103 D7
ak Hey Nook Gtr Man 196 F4
ak Hill Hants 31 E10
an Kent 70 G6
asby Lincs 189 E10
asby Notts 172 F2
asby Moor Lincs 189 E10
asdale Lincs 173 F7
atarn Cumb 222 C4
bocraigs Fife 287 F8
ddfa Powys 114 D4
dington Glos 100 G4
dlow Bucks 84 E3
dlow Ridge Bucks 84 F3
et Wilts 45 B11
gbie E Loth 271 C9
gbury Devon 24 B2
ncarn Cumb 231 E8
ncogo Cumb 229 B9
ndworth Hants 34 E2
nheim Oxon 83 D9
nheim Oxon 83 E9
nheim Park Norf 158 C6
nkinsopp Hall
rthumb 240 E5
nnerhasset Cumb 229 C9
rvie Castle Moray 301 D10
tchingdon Oxon 83 B8
tchingley Sur 51 C10
tchley M Keynes 103 E7
tchley Shrops 150 C2
therston Pembs 91 G11
tsoe Beds 121 F10
wbury Oxon 64 B4
by Kent 54 F4
ckling Norf 160 D3
dworth Notts 171 D9
dworth Bottoms
tts 171 E9
dworth Dale Notts 171 E9
dburn Northumb 263 G8
dcrake Cumb 229 E8
ndley Heath Sur 51 D11
ndmoor Som 28 E3
ngery Highld 310 E7
sland Corn 11 G8
s Gate Worcs 116 C4
ssford Hants 31 E11
sworth Northants 120 G4
hbury Staffs 151 E11
terlees Cumb 238 G4
' Norton Norf 125 B10
ckley Glos 100 D3
field Norf 142 B6
field Heath Norf 160 G6
odman's Corner
f 143 D10
omfield Bath 45 B7
omfield Bath 61 G8
omfield Borders 262 E3
omfield W Mid 133 E9
omsbury London 67 C10
re Staffs 150 C4
re Staffs 169 F10
reheath Staffs 150 B4
ssomfield W Mid 118 B2
unt's Green Staffs 151 C11
wick Mers 193 D11
winghouse Corn 4 E4
xham Oxon 101 D8
xholm Lincs 173 E9
xwich W Mid 133 C9
xworth Dorset 18 C3
berhouses N Yorks 205 B9
e Anchor Corn 5 D8
e Anchor Som 42 E4
e Anchor Swansea 56 B4
e Bell Hill Kent 69 G8
e Hill Herts 104 G5
e Row Essex 89 C8
e Town Kent 70 D2
e Vein Wilts 61 F10
ebell Telford 149 G11
ecairn Borders 271 G10
etown Kent 54 B2
ewater Kent 68 E5
ghasary Highld 307 J6
ndellsands Mers 182 B4
ndeston Suff 143 D10
ndies Staffs 132 F6
nham C Beds 122 G3
nsdon St Andrew
indon 62 B6
ntington Worcs 117 C7
ntisham Cambs 123 C7
nts Corn 6 C6
nt's Green Warks 118 D2
rton Stoke 168 G5
oorough Lincs 188 C6
ford Suff 127 B8
mhill Staffs 150 G6
mhill Lawns Staffs 150 G6
th Borders 270 F2
th Northumb 253 G8
th Notts 187 D10
Blyth Bridge Borders 270 F2
Blyth End Warks 134 E4
Blythburgh Suff 127 B9
Blythe Borders 271 F11
Blythe Bridge Staffs 169 G7
Blythe Marsh Staffs 169 G7
Blythswood Renfs 267 B10
Blyton Lincs 188 C5
Boarhills Fife 287 F9
Boarhunt Hants 33 F10
Boars Hill Oxon 83 E7
Boarsgreave Lancs 195 C10
Boarshead E Sus 52 G4
Boarstall Bucks 83 C10
Boasley Cross Devon 12 C5
Boat of Garten
Highld 291 B11
Boath Highld 300 B5
Bobbing Kent 69 F11
Bobbington Staffs 132 E6
Bobbingworth Essex 87 D8
Bobby Hill Suff 125 C10
Boblainy Highld 300 F4
Bocaddon Corn 6 D3
Bochastle Stirl 285 G10
Bockhanger Kent 54 E4
Bocking Essex 106 G5
Bocking Churchstreet
Essex 106 F5
Bocking's Elm Essex 89 B11
Bockleton Worcs 115 E11
Bockmer End Bucks 65 B10
Bocombe Devon 24 C5
Bodantionail Highld 299 B7
Boddam Aberds 303 E11
Boddam Shetland 313 M5
Bodden Som 44 E6
Boddington Glos 99 F7
Bodedern Anglesey 178 E4
Bodellick Corn 10 G5
Bodelva Corn 5 E11
Bodelwyddan Denb 181 F8
Bodenham Hereford 115 G10
Bodenham Wilts 31 B11
Bodenham Bank
Hereford 98 E2
Bodenham Moor
Hereford 115 G10
Bodermid Gwyn 144 D3
Bodewryd Anglesey 178 C5
Bodfari Denb 181 G9
Bodffordd Anglesey 178 F6
Bodham Norf 177 E10
Bodiam E Sus 38 B3
Bodicote Oxon 101 D9
Bodiechell Aberds 303 E7
Bodieve Corn 10 G5
Bodiggo Corn 5 D10
Bodilly Corn 2 C5
Bodinnick Corn 6 E2
Bodle Street Green
E Sus 23 C11
Bodley Devon 41 D7
Bodmin Corn 5 B11
Bodmiscombe Devon 27 F10
Bodney Norf 140 D6
Bodorgan Anglesey 162 B5
Bodsham Kent 54 D6
Boduan Gwyn 144 B6
Boduel Corn 6 C4
Bodwen Corn 5 C10
Bodymoor Heath
Warks 134 D4
Bofarnel Corn 6 C2
Bogallan Highld 300 D6
Bogbrae Aberds 303 F10
Bogend Borders 272 F5
Bogend Notts 171 F7
Bogend S Ayrs 257 C9
Bogentory Aberds 293 C9
Boghall Midloth 270 B4
Boghall W Loth 269 B9
Boghead Aberds 293 D8
Boghead S Lnrk 268 G5
Bogmoor Moray 302 C3
Bogniebrae Aberds 302 E5
Bogniebrae Aberds 302 E6
Bognor Regis W Sus 22 D6
Bograxie Aberds 293 B9
Bogs Aberds 302 G5
Bogs Bank Borders 270 E3
Bogside N Lnrk 268 E6
Bogthorn W Yorks 204 F6
Bogton Aberds 302 D6
Bogtown Aberds 302 C5
Bogue Dumfries 246 G4
Bohemia E Sus 38 E4
Bohemia Wilts 32 D2
Bohenie Highld 290 E4
Bohetherick Corn 7 B8
Bohortha Corn 3 C9
Bohuntine Highld 290 E4
Bohuntinville Highld 290 E4
Boirseam W Isles 296 C6
Bojewyan Corn 1 C3
Bokiddick Corn 5 C11
Bolahaul Fm Carms 74 B6
Bolam Durham 233 G9
Bolam Northumb 252 G3
Bolam West Houses
Northumb 252 G3
Bolas Heath Telford 150 E3
Bolberry Devon 9 G8
Bold Heath Mers 183 D8
Boldmere W Mid 134 E2
Boldon T & W 243 E9
Boldon Colliery T & W 243 E8
Boldre Hants 20 B2
Boldron Durham 223 C10
Bole Notts 188 D3
Bole Hill Derbys 186 G4
Bolehall Staffs 134 C4
Bolehill Derbys 170 E3
Bolehill Derbys 186 F5
Bolehill S Yorks 186 E5
Bolenowe Corn 2 B5
Boleside Borders 261 C11
Boley Park Staffs 134 B2
Bolham Devon 27 E7
Bolham Notts 188 E2
Bolham Water Devon 27 E11
Bolholt Gtr Man 195 E9
Bolingey Corn 4 E5
Bolitho Corn 2 C5
Bollihope Durham 232 E6
Bollington E Ches 184 F6
Bollington Cross
E Ches 184 F6
Bolney W Sus 36 C3
Bolnhurst Beds 121 F11
Bolnore W Sus 36 C4
Bolshan Angus 287 B10
Bolsover Derbys 187 G7
Bolsterstone S Yorks 186 B3
Bolstone Hereford 97 E11
Boltby N Yorks 215 B9
Bolter End Bucks 84 G3
Bolton Cumb 231 G8
Bolton E Loth 281 G10
Bolton E Yorks 207 C11
Bolton Gtr Man 195 F8
Bolton Northumb 264 G4
Bolton W Yorks 205 F9
Bolton Abbey N Yorks 205 C7
Bolton Bridge N Yorks 205 C7
Bolton-by-Bowland
Lancs 203 D11
Bolton Green Lancs 194 D5
Bolton Houses Lancs 202 G4
Bolton-le-Sands Lancs 211 F9
Bolton Low Houses
Cumb 229 C10
Bolton New Houses
Cumb 229 C10
Bolton-on-Swale
N Yorks 224 F5
Bolton Percy N Yorks 206 E6
Bolton Town End Lancs 211 F9
Bolton upon Dearne
S Yorks 198 G3
Bolton Wood Lane
Cumb 229 C11
Bolton Woods W Yorks 205 F9
Boltonfellend Cumb 239 D11
Boltongate Cumb 229 C10
Boltshope Park Durham 232 B4
Bolventor Corn 11 F9
Bomarsund Northumb 253 G7
Bombie Dumfries 237 D9
Bomby Cumb 221 B10
Bomere Heath Shrops 149 F9
Bon-y-maen Swansea 57 B7
Bonaly Edin 270 B4
Bonar Bridge Highld 309 K6
Bonawe Argyll 284 D4
Bonby N Lincs 200 D4
Boncath Pembs 92 D4
Bonchester Bridge
Borders 262 G3
Bonchurch I o W 21 F7
Bond End Staffs 152 F2
Bondend Glos 80 B5
Bondleigh Devon 25 G11
Bondman Hays Leics 135 B9
Bonds Lancs 202 E5
Bondstones Devon 25 F9
Bonehill Devon 13 F10
Bonehill Staffs 134 C3
Bo'ness Falk 279 E9
Bonhill W Dunb 277 F7
Boningale Shrops 132 C6
Bonjedward Borders 262 E5
Bonkle N Lnrk 268 D6
Bonnavoulin Highld 289 D7
Bonning Gate Cumb 221 F9
Bonnington Borders 261 B7
Bonnington Edin 270 B2
Bonnington Kent 54 F5
Bonnybank Fife 287 G7
Bonnybridge Falk 278 E6
Bonnykelly Aberds 303 D8
Bonnyrigg and
Lasswade Midloth 270 B6
Bonnyton Aberds 302 F6
Bonnyton Angus 287 B10
Bonnyton Angus 287 D7
Bonnyton E Ayrs 257 B10
Bonsall Derbys 170 D3
Bonskeid House Perth 291 G10
Bonson Som 43 E8
Bont Mon 78 B5
Bont-Dolgadfan Powys 129 C7
Bont Fawr Carms 94 F4
Bont goch = Elerch
Ceredig 128 F3
Bont-newydd Conwy 181 G8
Bont Newydd Gwyn 146 E5
Bont Newydd Gwyn 164 G2
Bontddu Gwyn 146 F3
Bonthorpe Lincs 191 G7
Bontnewydd Ceredig 112 D2
Bontnewydd Gwyn 163 D7
Bontuchel Denb 165 D9
Bonvilston =
Tresimwn V Glam 58 E5
Boode Devon 40 F4
Booker Bucks 84 G4
Bookham Dorset 30 G2
Booleybank Shrops 149 D11
Boon Borders 271 F11
Boon Hill Staffs 168 E4
Boorley Green Hants 33 E8
Boosbeck Redcar 226 B3
Boose's Green Essex 106 E6
Boot Cumb 220 E3
Boot Street Suff 108 B4
Booth Staffs 151 D10
Booth W Yorks 196 B4
Booth Bank E Ches 184 D2
Booth Bridge Lancs 204 D4
Booth Green E Ches 184 E6
Booth Wood W Yorks 196 D4
Boothby Graffoe Lincs 173 D7
Boothby Pagnell Lincs 155 C9
Boothen Stoke 168 G5
Boothferry E Yorks 199 B8
Boothgate Derbys 170 F5
Boothroyd W Yorks 197 C8
Boothsdale W Ches 167 B8
Boothstown Gtr Man 195 G8
Boothtown W Yorks 196 B5
Boothville Northants 120 E5
Bootle Cumb 210 B2
Bootle Mers 182 B4
Booton Norf 160 E2
Boots Green W Ches 184 G3
Booze N Yorks 223 E10
Boquhan Stirl 277 D10
Boquio Corn 2 C5
Boraston Shrops 116 D2
Boraston Dale Shrops 116 C2
Borden Kent 69 G11
Borden W Sus 34 C4
Border Cumb 238 G5
Bordesley W Mid 133 F11
Bordesley Green W Mid 134 F2
Bordlands Borders 270 F3
Bordley N Yorks 213 G8
Bordon Hants 49 F10
Bordon Camp Hants 49 F9
Boreham Essex 88 D3
Boreham Wilts 45 E11
Boreham Street E Sus 23 C11
Borehamwood Herts 85 F11
Boreland Dumfries 236 C5
Boreland Dumfries 248 E5
Boreland Fife 280 C6
Boreland Stirl 285 D9
Boreland of Southwick
Dumfries 237 C11
Boreley Worcs 116 D6
Borestone Stirl 278 C5
Borgh W Isles 296 C5
Borgh W Isles 297 L2
Borghasdal W Isles 296 C6
Borghastan W Isles 304 D4
Borgie Highld 308 D6
Borgue Dumfries 237 E8
Borgue Highld 311 G5
Borley Essex 106 C6
Borley Green Essex 106 C6
Borley Green Suff 125 E9
Bornais W Isles 297 J3
Bornesketaig Highld 298 B3
Borness Dumfries 237 E8
Borough Scilly 1 G3
Borough Green Kent 52 B6
Borough Marsh
Wokingham 65 D9
Borough Park Staffs 134 B4
Borough Post Som 28 C4
Boroughbridge
N Yorks 215 F7
Borras Wrex 166 E4
Borras Head Wrex 166 E5
Borreraig Highld 296 F7
Borrobol Lodge Highld 311 G2
Borrodale Highld 297 G7
Borrohill Aberds 303 D9
Borrowash Derbys 153 C8
Borrowby N Yorks 215 B8
Borrowby N Yorks 226 B5
Borrowdale Cumb 220 C5
Borrowfield Aberds 293 D10
Borrowston Highld 310 E7
Borrowston Mains
Falk 279 E9
Borstal Medway 69 F8
Borth = Y Borth
Ceredig 128 E2
Borth-y-Gest Gwyn 145 B11
Borthwick Midloth 271 D7
Borthwickbrae
Borders 261 G10
Borthwickshiels
Borders 261 F10
Borve Highld 298 E4
Borve Lodge W Isles 305 J2
Borwick Lancs 211 E10
Borwick Rails Cumb 210 D3
Bosavern Corn 1 C3
Bosbury Hereford 98 C3
Boscadjack Corn 2 C5
Boscastle Corn 11 C8
Boscean Corn 1 C3
Boscombe Bmouth 19 C8
Boscombe Wilts 47 F8
Boscomoor Staffs 151 G8
Boscoppa Corn 5 E10
Boscreege Corn 2 C3
Bosham W Sus 22 C4
Bosham Hoe W Sus 22 C4
Bosherston Pembs 73 G7
Boskednan Corn 1 C4
Boskenna Corn 1 E4
Bosleake Corn 4 G3
Bosley E Ches 168 B6
Boslowick Corn 3 C7
Boslymon Corn 5 C11
Bosoughan Corn 5 C7
Bosporthennis Corn 1 B4
Bossall N Yorks 216 G4
Bossiney Corn 11 D7
Bossingham Kent 54 D6
Bossington Hants 47 G10
Bossington Kent 55 B8
Bossington Som 41 D11
Bostadh W Isles 304 D3
Bostock Green W Ches 167 B11
Boston Lincs 174 G4
Boston Long Hedges
Lincs 174 F5
Boston Spa W Yorks 206 D4
Boston West Lincs 174 F3
Boswednack Corn 1 B4
Boswin Corn 2 C5
Boswinger Corn 5 G9
Boswyn Corn 2 B5
Botallack Corn 1 C3
Botany Bay London 86 F3
Botany Bay Mon 79 E8
Botcherby Cumb 239 F10
Botcheston Leics 135 B9
Botesdale Suff 125 B10
Bothal Northumb 252 F6
Bothampstead W Berks 64 D4
Bothamsall Notts 187 G11
Bothel Cumb 229 D9
Bothenhampton Dorset 16 C5
Bothwell S Lnrk 268 D4
Bothy Highld 290 F4
Botley Bucks 85 E7
Botley Hants 33 E8
Botley Oxon 83 D7
Botloe's Green Glos 98 F4
Botolph Claydon Bucks 102 G4
Botolphs W Sus 35 F11
Bottacks Highld 300 C4
Botternell Corn 11 G11
Bottesford Leics 154 B6
Bottesford N Lincs 199 F11
Bottisham Cambs 123 E10
Bottlesford Wilts 46 B6
Bottom Boat W Yorks 197 C11
Bottom House Staffs 169 E8
Bottom o' th' Moor
Gtr Man 195 E7
Bottom of Hutton Lancs 194 B3
Bottom Pond Kent 53 B11
Bottomcraig Fife 287 E7
Bottomley W Yorks 196 D5
Bottoms Corn 1 E3
Bottreaux Mill Devon 26 B4
Bottrells Close Bucks 85 G7
Botts Green Warks 134 E4
Botusfleming Corn 7 C8
Botwnnog Gwyn 144 C5
Bough Beech Kent 52 D3
Boughrood Powys 96 D2
Boughrood Brest Powys 96 D2
Boughspring Glos 79 F9
Boughton Lincs 173 F10
Boughton Norf 140 C3
Boughton Northants 120 D5
Boughton Notts 171 B11
Boughton W Ches 166 B6
Boughton Aluph Kent 54 D4
Boughton Corner Kent 54 D4
Boughton Green Kent 53 C9
Boughton Heath
W Ches 166 B6
Boughton Lees Kent 54 D4
Boughton Malherbe
Kent 53 D11
Boughton Monchelsea
Kent 53 C9
Boughton Street Kent 54 B5
Bougton End C Beds 103 D9
Boulby Redcar 226 B5
Bould Oxon 100 G4
Boulden Shrops 131 F10
Boulder Clough W Yorks 196 C4
Bouldnor I o W 20 D3
Bouldon Shrops 131 F10
Boulmer Northumb 265 G7
Boulsdon Glos 98 G4
Boulston Pembs 73 C7
Boultenstone Aberds 292 B6
Boultham Lincs 173 B7
Boultham Moor Lincs 173 B7
Boulton Derbys 153 C7
Boulton Moor Derbys 153 C7
Boundary Leics 152 F6
Boundary Staffs 169 G7
Boundstone Sur 49 E10
Bountis Thorne Devon 24 D5
Bourn Cambs 122 F6
Bournbrook W Mid 133 G10
Bourne Lincs 155 E11
Bourne N Som 59 G11
Bourne End Beds 121 E10
Bourne End Bucks 65 B11
Bourne End C Beds 103 C9
Bourne End Herts 85 D8
Bourne Vale W Mid 133 D11
Bourne Valley Poole 19 C7
Bournemouth Bmouth 19 C7
Bournes Green Glos 80 E6
Bournes Green Sthend 70 B2
Bournes Green Worcs 117 C8
Bournheath Worcs 117 C9
Bournmoor Durham 243 G8
Bournside Glos 99 G8
Bournstream Glos 80 G2
Bournville W Mid 133 G10
Bourton Bucks 102 E4
Bourton Dorset 45 G9
Bourton N Som 59 G11
Bourton Oxon 63 B8
Bourton Shrops 131 D11
Bourton Wilts 62 G4
Bourton on Dunsmore
Warks 119 C8
Bourton-on-the-Hill
Glos 100 E3
Bourton-on-the-Water
Glos 100 G3
Bourtreehill N Ayrs 257 B8
Bousd Argyll 288 C4
Bousta Shetland 313 H4
Boustead Hill Cumb 239 F7
Bouth Cumb 210 B6
Bouthwaite N Yorks 214 E2
Bouts Worcs 117 F10
Bovain Stirl 285 D9
Boveney Bucks 66 D2
Boveridge Dorset 31 E9
Boverton V Glam 58 F3
Bovey Tracey Devon 14 F2
Bovingdon Herts 85 E8
Bovingdon Green Bucks 65 B10
Bovingdon Green Herts 85 E8
Bovinger Essex 87 D8
Bovington Camp Dorset 18 D2
Bow Borders 271 G9
Bow Devon 8 D6
Bow Devon 26 G2
Bow Orkney 314 G3
Bow Oxon 82 G4
Bow Brickhill M Keynes 103 E8
Bow Broom S Yorks 187 B7
Bow Common London 67 C11
Bow of Fife Fife 287 F7
Bow Street Ceredig 128 G2
Bow Street Norf 141 D10
Bowbank Durham 232 G4
Bowbeck Suff 125 B8
Bowbridge Glos 80 E5
Bowbrook Shrops 149 G9
Bowburn Durham 234 D2
Bowcombe I o W 20 D5
Bowd Devon 15 C8
Bowden Borders 262 C3
Bowden Devon 8 F6
Bowden Dorset 30 C3
Bowden Hill Wilts 62 F2
Bowdens Som 28 B6
Bowderdale Cumb 222 E3
Bowdon Gtr Man 184 D3
Bower Highld 310 C6
Bower Northumb 251 G7
Bower Ashton Bristol 60 E5
Bower Heath Herts 85 B10
Bower Hinton Som 29 D7
Bower House Tye Suff 107 C9
Bowerchalke Wilts 31 C8
Bowerhill Wilts 62 G2
Bowerhope Borders 261 E7
Bowermadden Highld 310 C6
Bowers Staffs 150 B6
Bowers Gifford Essex 69 B9
Bowershall Fife 279 C11
Bowertower Highld 310 C6
Bowes Durham 223 C9
Bowes Park London 86 G4
Bowgreave Lancs 202 E5
Bowgreen Gtr Man 184 D3
Bowhill Borders 261 D10
Bowhill Fife 280 B4
Bowhouse Dumfries 238 D2
Bowhousebog or Liquo
N Lnrk 269 D7
Bowing Park Mers 182 D6
Bowismiln Borders 262 E2
Bowithick Corn 11 E9
Bowker's Green Lancs 194 G2
Bowland Bridge Cumb 211 B8
Bowldown Wilts 62 F4
Bowlee Gtr Man 195 F10
Bowlees Durham 232 F4
Bowler's Town E Sus 38 C6
Bowley Hereford 115 G10
Bowley Lane Hereford 98 B3
Bowley Town Hereford 115 G10
Bowlhead Green Sur 50 F2
Bowling W Dunb 277 G9
Bowling W Yorks 205 G9
Bowling Alley Hants 49 D9
Bowling Bank Wrex 166 F5
Bowling Green Corn 5 D10
Bowling Green Corn 12 G3
Bowling Green Glos 81 E8
Bowling Green Hants 19 B11
Bowling Green Shrops 150 D2
Bowling Green W Mid 133 F8
Bowling Green Worcs 116 G6
Bowlish Som 44 E6
Bowmans Kent 68 E4
Bowmanstead Cumb 220 F6
Bowmore Argyll 254 B4
Bowness-on-Solway
Cumb 238 E6
Bowness-on-
Windermere Cumb 221 F8
Bowridge Hill Dorset 30 B4
Bowrie-fauld Angus 287 C9
Bowsden Northumb 273 G9
Bowsey Hill Windsor 65 C10
Bowshank Borders 271 G9
Bowside Lodge Highld 310 C2
Bowston Cumb 221 F9
Bowthorpe Norf 142 B3
Bowyer's Common Hants 34 B3
Box Glos 80 E5
Box Wilts 61 F10
Box End Beds 103 B10
Box Hill Sur 51 C7
Box Hill Wilts 61 F10
Box Trees W Mid 118 C2
Boxbush Glos 80 C2
Boxbush Glos 98 G3
Boxford Suff 107 C9
Boxford W Berks 64 E2
Boxgrove W Sus 22 B6
Boxley Kent 53 B9
Boxmoor Herts 85 D9
Box's Shop Corn 24 G2
Boxted Essex 107 E9
Boxted Suff 124 G6
Boxted Cross Essex 107 E10
Boxted Heath Essex 107 E10
Boxwell Glos 80 G4
Boxworth Cambs 122 E6
Boxworth End Cambs 123 D7
Boyatt Wood Hants 32 C6
Boyden End Suff 124 F4
Boyden Gate Kent 71 F8
Boyland Common Norf 141 G11
Boylestone Derbys 152 B3
Boylestonfield Derbys 152 B3
Boyn Hill Windsor 65 C11
Boyndie Aberds 302 C6
Boynton E Yorks 218 F2
Boys Hill Dorset 29 E11
Boys Village V Glam 58 F4
Boysack Angus 287 C10
Boysack Angus 287 C9
Boythorpe Derbys 186 G5
Boyton Corn 12 C2
Boyton Suff 109 B7
Boyton Wilts 46 F3
Boyton Cross Essex 87 D10
Boyton End Essex 106 E2
Boyton End Suff 106 C4
Bozeat Northants 121 F8
Bozen Green Herts 105 F8
Brù W Isles 304 D5
Braaid I o M 192 E4
Braal Castle Highld 310 C5
Brabling Green Suff 126 E5
Brabourne Kent 54 E5
Brabourne Lees Kent 54 E5
Brabster Highld 310 C7
Bracadale Highld 294 B5
Bracara Highld 295 F9
Braceborough Lincs 155 G11
Bracebridge Lincs 173 B7
Bracebridge Heath
Lincs 173 B7
Bracebridge Low Fields
Lincs 173 B7
Braceby Lincs 155 B10
Bracewell Lancs 204 D3
Bracken Bank W Yorks 204 F6
Bracken Hill W Yorks 197 C7
Bracken Park W Yorks 206 E3
Brackenber Cumb 222 B4
Brackenbottom N Yorks 212 E6
Brackenfield Derbys 170 D5
Brackenhall W Yorks 197 D7
Brackenlands Cumb 229 B11
Brackenthwaite Cumb 229 B11
Brackenthwaite Cumb 229 G9
Brackenthwaite
N Yorks 205 C11
Brackla = Bragle
Bridgend 58 D2
Bracklamore Aberds 303 D8
Bracklesham W Sus 22 D4
Brackletter Highld 290 E3
Brackley Argyll 255 C8
Brackley Northants 101 D11
Brackloch Highld 307 G6
Bracknell Brack 65 F11
Braco Perth 286 G2
Braco Castle Perth 286 F2
Braco Park Aberds 303 C9
Bracobrae Moray 302 D5
Bracon N Lincs 199 F9
Bracon Ash Norf 142 D3
Bracorina Highld 295 F9
Bradaford Devon 12 C3
Bradbourne Derbys 170 E2
Bradbury Durham 234 F2
Bradda I o M 192 F2
Bradden Northants 102 B2
Braddock Corn 6 C3
Braddocks Hay Staffs 168 D5
Bradeley Stoke 168 E5
Bradeley Green E Ches 167 G8
Bradenham Bucks 84 F4
Bradenham Norf 141 B8
Bradenstoke Wilts 62 D4
Brades Village W Mid 133 E9
Bradfield Devon 27 F9
Bradfield Essex 108 E2
Bradfield Norf 160 C5
Bradfield W Berks 64 E6
Bradfield Combust Suff 125 F7
Bradfield Green
E Ches 167 D11
Bradfield Heath Essex 108 F2
Bradfield St Clare Suff 125 F8
Bradfield St George
Suff 125 E8
Bradford Corn 11 F8
Bradford Derbys 170 C2
Bradford Devon 24 F6
Bradford Gtr Man 184 B5
Bradford Northumb 264 C5
Bradford W Yorks 205 G9
Bradford Abbas Dorset 29 E9
Bradford Leigh Wilts 61 G10
Bradford-on-Avon
Wilts 61 G10
Bradford-on-Tone Som 27 C11
Bradford Peverell Dorset 17 C9
Bradgate S Yorks 186 C6
Bradiford Devon 40 G5
Brading I o W 21 D8
Bradley Derbys 170 F2
Bradley Glos 80 G3
Bradley Hants 48 E6
Bradley NE Lincs 201 F8
Bradley Staffs 151 F7
Bradley W Mid 133 D8
Bradley W Yorks 197 C7
Bradley Wrex 166 E4
Bradley Cross Som 44 C3
Bradley Fold Gtr Man 195 F9
Bradley Green Glos 80 G2
Bradley Green Som 43 F9
Bradley Green W Ches 167 F8
Bradley Green Warks 134 C5
Bradley Green Worcs 117 E9
Bradley in the Moors
Staffs 169 G9
Bradley Mills W Yorks 197 D7
Bradley Mount E Ches 184 F6
Bradley Stoke S Glos 60 C6
Bradlow Hereford 98 D4
Bradmore Notts 153 C11
Bradmore W Mid 133 D7
Bradney Shrops 132 D5
Bradney Som 43 F10
Bradninch Devon 27 G8
Bradnock's Marsh
W Mid 118 B4
Bradnop Staffs 169 D8
Bradnor Green Hereford 114 F5
Bradpole Dorset 16 C5
Bradshaw Gtr Man 195 E8
Bradshaw Staffs 168 D6
Bradshaw W Yorks 196 E5
Bradshaw W Yorks 205 G7
Bradstone Devon 12 E3
Bradville M Keynes 102 C6
Bradwall Green E Ches 168 C3
Bradway S Yorks 186 E4
Bradwell Derbys 185 E11
Bradwell Devon 40 E3
Bradwell Essex 106 G6
Bradwell M Keynes 102 D6
Bradwell Norf 143 C10
Bradwell Staffs 168 F4
Bradwell Common
M Keynes 102 D6
Bradwell Grove Oxon 82 D2
Bradwell Hills Derbys 185 E11
Bradwell on Sea Essex 89 D8
Bradwell Waterside
Essex 89 D7
Bradworthy Devon 24 E4
Bradworthy Cross Devon 24 E4
Brae Dumfries 237 B10
Brae Highld 307 L3
Brae Highld 309 J4
Brae Shetland 312 G5
Brae of Achnahaird
Highld 307 H5
Brae of Boquhapple
Stirl 285 G10
Brae Roy Lodge Highld 290 D5
Braeantra Highld 300 B5
Braebuster Orkney 314 F5
Braedownie Angus 292 F4
Braeface Falk 278 E5
Braefield Highld 300 F4
Braefindon Highld 300 D6
Braegrum Perth 286 E4
Braehead Dumfries 236 D6
Braehead Orkney 314 B4
Braehead Orkney 314 F5
Braehead S Ayrs 257 E8
Braehead S Lnrk 259 C8
Braehead S Lnrk 267 D11
Braehead S Lnrk 269 E9
Braehead Stirl 278 C6
Braehead of Lunan
Angus 287 B10
Braehoulland Shetland 312 F4
Braehour Highld 310 D4
Braehungie Highld 310 F5
Braeintra Highld 295 B10
Braelangwell Lodge
Highld 309 K5
Braemar Aberds 292 D3
Braemore Highld 299 B11
Braemore Highld 310 F4
Braepark Edin 280 F3
Braes of Enzie Moray 302 D3
Braes of Ullapool
Highld 307 K6
Braeside Invclyd 276 F4
Braeswick Orkney 314 C6
Braevallich Argyll 275 C10
Braewick Shetland 312 H4
Braewick Shetland 313 H5
Brafferton Darl 233 G11
Brafferton N Yorks 215 E8
Brafield-on-the-Green
Northants 120 F6
Bragar W Isles 304 D4
Bragbury End Herts 104 G5
Bragenham Bucks 103 F8
Bragle = Brackla
Bridgend 58 D2
Bragleenmore Argyll 289 G11
Braichmelyn Gwyn 163 B10
Braichyfedw Powys 129 E7
Braid Edin 280 G4
Braides Lancs 202 C4
Braidfauld Glasgow 268 C2
Braidley N Yorks 213 C10
Braids Argyll 255 C8
Braidwood S Lnrk 268 F6
Braigh Chalasaigh
W Isles 296 D5
Braigo Argyll 274 G3
Brailsford Derbys 170 G3
Brailsford Green
Derbys 170 G3
Braingortan Argyll 275 F11
Brain's Green Glos 79 D11
Brainshaugh Northumb 252 C6
Braintree Essex 106 G5
Braiseworth Suff 126 C2
Braishfield Hants 32 B5
Braiswick Essex 107 F9
Braithwaite Cumb 229 G10
Braithwaite S Yorks 198 E6
Braithwaite W Yorks 204 E6
Braithwell S Yorks 187 C8
Brakefield Green Norf 141 B10
Brakenhill W Yorks 198 D2
Bramber W Sus 35 E11
Bramblecombe Dorset 30 G3
Brambridge Hants 33 C7
Bramcote Notts 153 B10
Bramcote Warks 135 F8
Bramcote Hills Notts 153 B10
Bramcote Mains Warks 135 F8
Bramdean Hants 33 B10
Bramerton Norf 142 C5
Bramfield Herts 86 B3
Bramfield Suff 127 C7
Bramford Suff 108 B2
Bramford W Mid 133 E8
Bramhall Gtr Man 184 D5
Bramhall Moor Gtr Man 184 D6
Bramhall Park Gtr Man 184 D5
Bramham W Yorks 206 E4
Bramhope W Yorks 205 E11
Bramley Derbys 186 F6
Bramley Hants 48 B6
Bramley S Yorks 187 C7
Bramley Sur 50 E4
Bramley W Yorks 205 F10
Bramley Corner Hants 48 B6
Bramley Green Hants 49 B7
Bramley Head N Yorks 205 B8
Bramley Vale Derbys 171 B7
Bramling Kent 55 B8
Brampford Speke Devon 14 B4
Brampton Cambs 122 C4
Brampton Cumb 231 G9
Brampton Cumb 240 E2
Brampton Derbys 186 G5
Brampton Hereford 97 D8
Brampton Lincs 188 F4
Brampton Norf 160 E4
Brampton S Yorks 198 G2
Brampton Suff 143 G8
Brampton Abbotts
Hereford 98 F2
Brampton Ash Northants 136 F5
Brampton Bryan
Hereford 115 C7
Brampton en le
Morthen S Yorks 187 D7
Brampton Park Cambs 122 C4
Brampton Street Suff 143 G8
Bramshall Staffs 151 C11
Bramshaw Hants 32 D3
Bramshill Hants 65 G8
Bramshott Hants 49 G10
Bramwell Som 28 B6
Bran End Essex 106 F3
Branatwatt Shetland 313 H4
Branault Highld 289 C7
Branbridges Kent 53 D7
Brancaster Norf 176 E3
Brancaster Staithe Norf 176 E3
Brancepeth Durham 233 D10
Branch End Northumb 242 E3
Branchill Moray 301 D10
Branchton Invclyd 276 F4
Brand End Lincs 174 F5
Brand Green Glos 98 F4
Brand Green Hereford 98 C5
Branderburgh Moray 302 B2
Brandesburton E Yorks 209 D8
Brandeston Suff 126 E4
Brandhill Shrops 115 B8
Brandis Corner Devon 24 G6
Brandish Street Som 42 D2
Brandiston Norf 160 E2
Brandlingill Cumb 229 F8
Brandon Durham 233 D10
Brandon Lincs 172 F6
Brandon Northumb 264 F2
Brandon Suff 140 F5
Brandon Warks 119 B8
Brandon Bank Cambs 140 F2
Brandon Creek Norf 140 E2
Brandon Parva Norf 141 B11
Brands Hill Windsor 66 D4
Brandsby N Yorks 215 E11
Brandwood Shrops 149 D9
Brandwood End W Mid 117 B11
Brandy Carr W Yorks 197 C10
Brandy Hole Essex 88 F4
Brandy Wharf Lincs 189 B8
Brandyquoy Orkney 314 G4
Brane Corn 1 D4
Branksome Darl 224 B5
Branksome Poole 18 C6
Branksome Park Poole 19 C7
Bransbury Hants 48 E2
Bransby Lincs 188 F5
Branscombe Devon 15 D9
Bransford Worcs 116 G5
Bransgore Hants 19 B9
Branshill Clack 279 C7
Bransholme Hull 209 G8
Branson's Cross Worcs 117 C11
Branston Leics 154 D6
Branston Lincs 173 B8
Branston Staffs 152 E4
Branston Booths Lincs 173 B9
Branstone I o W 21 E7
Bransty Cumb 219 B9
Brant Broughton Lincs 172 E6
Brantham Suff 108 E2
Branthwaite Cumb 229 D11
Branthwaite Cumb 229 G7
Branthwaite Edge
Cumb 229 G7
Brantingham E Yorks 200 B2
Branton Northumb 264 F2
Branton S Yorks 198 G6
Branton Green N Yorks 215 G8
Branxholm Park
Borders 261 G11
Branxholme Borders 261 G11
Branxton Northumb 263 B9
Brascote Leics 135 C8
Brassey Green W Ches 167 C8
Brassington Derbys 170 E2
Brasted Kent 52 C3
Brasted Chart Kent 52 C3
Brathens Aberds 293 D8
Bratoft Lincs 175 B7
Brattle Kent 54 G2
Brattleby Lincs 188 E6
Bratton Som 42 D2
Bratton Telford 150 G2
Bratton Wilts 46 C2
Bratton Clovelly Devon 12 C5
Bratton Fleming Devon 40 F6
Bratton Seymour Som 29 B11
Braughing Herts 105 F7
Braughing Friars Herts 105 G8
Braulen Lodge Highld 300 F2
Braunston Northants 119 D10
Braunston-in-Rutland
Rutland 136 B6
Braunstone Leics 135 C11
Braunstone Town
Leicester 135 C11
Braunton Devon 40 F3
Brawby N Yorks 216 D4
Brawith N Yorks 225 D10
Brawl Highld 310 C2
Brawlbin Highld 310 D4
Bray Windsor 66 D2
Bray Shop Corn 12 G2
Bray Wick Windsor 65 D11
Braybrooke Northants 136 G5
Braydon Side Wilts 62 B4
Brayford Devon 41 G7
Brayfordhill Devon 41 G7
Brays Grove Essex 87 D7
Braystones Cumb 219 D10
Brayswick Worcs 98 B6
Braythorn N Yorks 205 D10
Brayton N Yorks 207 G8
Braytown Dorset 18 D2
Braywoodside Windsor 65 D11
Brazacott Corn 11 C11
Brazenhill Staffs 151 E7
Brea Corn 4 G3
Breach Bath 60 G6
Breach Kent 69 F10
Breach W Sus 22 B3
Breachacha Castle
Argyll 288 D3
Breachwood Green
Herts 104 G2
Breacleit W Isles 304 E3
Bread Street Glos 80 D4
Breaden Heath Shrops 149 B8
Breadsall Derbys 153 B7
Breadsall Hilltop Derby 153 B7
Breadstone Glos 80 E2
Breage Corn 2 D4
Breakachy Highld 300 E4
Brealeys Devon 25 D8
Bream Glos 79 D10
Breamore Hants 31 D11
Bream's Meend Glos 79 D9
Brean Som 43 B9
Breanais W Isles 304 F1
Brearley W Yorks 196 B4
Brearton N Yorks 214 G6
Breascleit W Isles 304 E4
Breaston Derbys 153 C9
Brechfa Carms 93 E10
Brechin Angus 293 G7
Breck of Cruan Orkney 314 E3
Breckan Orkney 314 F2
Breckles Norf 141 E9
Breckrey Highld 298 C5
Brecks S Yorks 187 C7
Brecon Powys 95 F10
Bredbury Gtr Man 184 C6
Bredbury Green Gtr Man 184 C6
Brede E Sus 38 D4
Bredenbury Hereford 116 F2
Bredfield Suff 126 G5
Bredgar Kent 69 G11

Bredhurst Kent 69 G9
Bredicot Worcs 117 G8
Bredon Worcs 99 D8
Bredon's Hardwick Worcs 99 D8
Bredon's Norton Worcs 99 D8
Bredwardine Hereford 96 C6
Breedon on the Hill Leics 153 E8
Breeds Essex 87 C11
Breedy Butts Lancs 202 E2
Breibhig W Isles 297 M2
Breibhig W Isles 304 E6
Breich W Loth 269 C9
Breightmet Gtr Man 195 F8
Breighton E Yorks 207 G10
Breinton Hereford 97 D9
Breinton Common Hereford 97 C9
Breiwick Shetland 313 J6
Brelston Green Hereford 97 G11
Bremhill Wilts 62 E3
Bremhill Wick Wilts 62 E3
Bremirehoull Shetland 313 L6
Brenachoile Lodge Stirl 285 G8
Brenchley Kent 53 E7
Brenchoillie Argyll 284 G4
Brendon Devon 24 E5
Brendon Devon 24 F5
Brendon Devon 41 D9
Brenkley T & W 242 B6
Brent Corn 6 E4
Brent Eleigh Suff 107 B8
Brent Knoll Som 43 C10
Brent Mill Devon 8 D3
Brent Pelham Herts 105 E8
Brentford London 67 D7
Brentford End London 67 D7
Brentingby Leics 154 F5
Brentry Bristol 60 D5
Brentwood Essex 87 G9
Brenzett Kent 39 B8
Brenzett Green Kent 39 B8
Brereton Staffs 151 F11
Brereton Cross Staffs 151 F11
Brereton Green E Ches 168 C3
Brereton Heath E Ches 168 C4
Breretonhill Staffs 151 F11
Bressingham Norf 141 G11
Bressingham Common Norf 141 G11
Bretby Derbys 152 E5
Bretford Warks 119 B8
Bretforton Worcs 99 C11
Bretherdale Head Cumb 221 E11
Bretherton Lancs 194 C3
Brettabister Shetland 313 H6
Brettenham Norf 141 G8
Brettenham Suff 125 G9
Bretton Derbys 186 F2
Bretton Flint 166 C5
Bretton P'boro 138 C3
Brewer Street Sur 51 C10
Brewer's End Essex 105 G11
Brewers Green Norf 142 G2
Brewlands Bridge Angus 292 G3
Brewood Staffs 133 B7
Briach Moray 301 D10
Briants Puddle Dorset 18 C2
Briar Hill Northants 120 F4
Brick End Essex 105 F11
Brick Hill Sur 66 G3
Brick House End Essex 105 F9
Brick Houses S Yorks 186 E4
Brick-kiln End Notts 171 D9
Brickendon Herts 86 D4
Bricket Wood Herts 85 E10
Brickfields Worcs 117 F7
Brickhill Beds 121 G11
Brickhouses E Ches 168 C3
Brickkiln Green Essex 106 E4
Bricklehampton Worcs 99 C9
Bride I o M 192 B5
Bridekirk Cumb 229 E8
Bridell Pembs 92 C3
Bridestowe Devon 12 D6
Brideswell Aberds 302 F5
Bridford Devon 14 D2
Bridfordmills Devon 14 D2
Bridge Corn 2 D6
Bridge Corn 4 G3
Bridge Kent 55 C7
Bridge Som 28 F5
Bridge Ball Devon 41 D8
Bridge End Beds 121 G10
Bridge End Cumb 230 B3
Bridge End Devon 8 F3
Bridge End Durham 232 D6
Bridge End Essex 106 E3
Bridge End Flint 166 D4
Bridge End Hereford 98 B2
Bridge End Lincs 156 B2
Bridge End Northumb 241 D10
Bridge End Northumb 241 E10
Bridge End Oxon 83 G9
Bridge-End Shetland 313 K5
Bridge End Sur 50 B5
Bridge End Warks 118 E5
Bridge End Worcs 98 E6
Bridge Green Essex 105 D9
Bridge Green Norf 142 G2
Bridge Hewick N Yorks 214 E6
Bridge Ho Argyll 254 B4
Bridge of Alford Aberds 293 B7
Bridge of Allan Stirl 278 B5
Bridge of Avon Moray 301 F11
Bridge of Avon Moray 301 G11
Bridge of Awe Argyll 284 E4
Bridge of Balgie Perth 285 C9
Bridge of Cally Perth 286 B5
Bridge of Canny Aberds 293 D8
Bridge of Craigisla Angus 286 B6
Bridge of Dee Dumfries 237 D9
Bridge of Don Aberdeen 293 B11
Bridge of Dun Angus 287 B10
Bridge of Dye Aberds 293 E8
Bridge of Earn Perth 286 F5
Bridge of Ericht Perth 285 B9
Bridge of Feugh Aberds 293 D9
Bridge of Forss Highld 310 C4
Bridge of Gairn Aberds 292 D5
Bridge of Gaur Perth 285 B9
Bridge of Lyon Perth 285 C11
Bridge of Muchalls Aberds 293 D10
Bridge of Muick Aberds 292 D5
Bridge of Oich Highld 290 C5
Bridge of Orchy Argyll 284 D6
Bridge of Waith Orkney 314 E2
Bridge of Walls Shetland 313 H4
Bridge of Weir Renfs 267 B7
Bridge Reeve Devon 25 E11
Bridge Sollers Hereford 97 C8
Bridge Street Suff 107 B7
Bridge Town Warks 118 G4
Bridge Trafford W Ches 183 G7
Bridge Yate S Glos 61 E7
Bridgefoot Aberds 292 C6
Bridgefoot Angus 287 D7
Bridgefoot Cumb 229 F7
Bridgehampton Som 29 C9
Bridgehill Durham 242 G3
Bridgeholm Green Derbys 185 E8
Bridgehouse Gate N Yorks 214 F3
Bridgelands Borders 261 C11
Bridgemary Hants 33 G9
Bridgemere E Ches 168 F2
Bridgemont Derbys 185 E8
Bridgend Aberds 293 B7
Bridgend Aberds 302 F5
Bridgend Angus 293 G7
Bridgend Argyll 255 D8
Bridgend Argyll 274 G4
Bridgend Argyll 275 D9
Bridgend Corn 6 D2
Bridgend Cumb 221 C7
Bridgend Devon 7 F11
Bridgend Fife 287 F7
Bridgend Glos 80 E4
Bridgend Highld 300 D3
Bridgend Invclyd 276 F5
Bridgend Moray 302 F3
Bridgend N Lnrk 278 G3
Bridgend Pembs 92 B3
Bridgend W Loth 279 F10
Bridgend = Pen-y-Bont ar-ogwr Bridgend 58 C2
Bridgend of Lintrathen Angus 286 B6
Bridgeness Falk 279 E10
Bridgerule Devon 24 G3
Bridges Corn 5 D10
Bridges Shrops 131 D7
Bridgeton Glasgow 268 C2
Bridgetown Corn 12 D2
Bridgetown Devon 8 C6
Bridgetown Som 42 G2
Bridgetown Staffs 133 B9
Bridgham Norf 141 F9
Bridgnorth Shrops 132 E4
Bridgtown Staffs 133 B9
Bridgwater Som 43 F10
Bridlington E Yorks 218 F3
Bridport Dorset 16 C5
Bridstow Hereford 97 G11
Brierfield Lancs 204 F2
Brierholme Carr S Yorks 199 E7
Brierley Glos 79 B10
Brierley Hereford 115 F9
Brierley S Yorks 198 E2
Brierley Hill W Mid 133 F8
Brierton Hrtlpl 234 E5
Briery Cumb 229 G11
Briery Hill Bl Gwent 77 D11
Briestfield W Yorks 197 D8
Brig o'Turk Stirl 285 G9
Brigflatts Cumb 222 G2
Brigg N Lincs 200 F3
Brigg N Lincs 200 F4
Briggate Norf 160 D6
Briggswath N Yorks 227 D7
Brigham Cumb 229 E7
Brigham Cumb 229 G11
Brigham E Yorks 209 C7
Brighouse W Yorks 196 C6
Brighstone I o W 20 E4
Brightgate Derbys 170 D3
Brighthampton Oxon 82 E5
Brightholmlee S Yorks 186 B3
Brightley Devon 13 B7
Brightling E Sus 37 C11
Brightlingsea Essex 89 B9
Brighton Brighton 36 G4
Brighton Corn 5 E8
Brighton Hill Hants 48 D6
Brighton le Sands Mers 182 B4
Brightons Falk 279 F8
Brightside S Yorks 186 D5
Brightwalton W Berks 64 D2
Brightwalton Green W Berks 64 D2
Brightwalton Holt W Berks 64 D2
Brightwell Suff 108 C4
Brightwell Baldwin Oxon 83 F11
Brightwell cum Sotwell Oxon 83 G9
Brigmerston Wilts 47 D7
Brignall Durham 223 C11
Brigsley NE Lincs 201 G9
Brigsteer Cumb 211 B9
Brigstock Northants 137 F8
Brill Bucks 83 C11
Brill Corn 2 D6
Brilley Hereford 96 B5
Brilley Mountain Powys 114 G5
Brimaston Pembs 91 G8
Brimfield Hereford 115 D10
Brimington Derbys 186 G6
Brimington Common Derbys 186 G6
Brimley Devon 13 F11
Brimley Devon 28 G4
Brimps Hill Glos 79 B11
Brimpsfield Glos 80 C6
Brimpton W Berks 64 G5
Brimpton Common W Berks 64 G5
Brims Orkney 314 H2
Brims Castle Highld 310 B4
Brimscombe Glos 80 E5
Brimsdown London 86 F5
Brimstage Mers 182 E4
Brinacory Highld 295 F9
Brincliffe S Yorks 186 D4
Brind E Yorks 207 G10
Brindham Som 44 E4
Brindister Shetland 313 H4
Brindister Shetland 313 K6
Brindle Lancs 194 C6
Brindle Heath Gtr Man 195 G10
Brindley E Ches 167 E9
Brindley Ford Stoke 168 E5
Brindwoodgate Derbys 186 F4
Brineton Staffs 150 G6
Bringewood Forge Hereford 115 C9
Bringhurst Leics 136 E6
Bringsty Common Hereford 116 F4
Brington Cambs 121 B11
Brinian Orkney 314 D4
Briningham Norf 159 C10
Brinkhill Lincs 190 G5
Brinkley Cambs 124 G2
Brinkley Notts 172 E2
Brinkley Hill Hereford 97 E11
Brinklow M Keynes 103 D8
Brinklow Warks 119 B8
Brinkworth Wilts 62 C4
Brinmore Highld 300 G6
Brinnington Gtr Man 184 C6
Brinscall Lancs 194 C6
Brinsea N Som 60 G2
Brinsford Staffs 133 B8
Brinsley Notts 171 F7
Brinsop Hereford 97 C8
Brinsop Common Hereford 97 C8
Brinsworth S Yorks 186 D6
Brinsworthy Devon 41 G9
Brinton Norf 159 B10
Brisco Cumb 239 G10
Briscoe Cumb 219 C10
Briscoerigg N Yorks 205 C11
Brisley Norf 159 E8
Brislington Bristol 60 E6
Brissenden Green Kent 54 F2
Bristnall Fields W Mid 133 F9
Bristol Bristol 60 E5
Briston Norf 159 C11
Britain Bottom S Glos 61 B9
Britannia Lancs 195 C11
Britford Wilts 31 B11
Brithdir Caerph 77 E11
Brithdir Ceredig 92 B6
Brithdir Gwyn 146 F5
Brithem Bottom Devon 27 E8
British Torf 78 E3
Briton Ferry = Llansawel Neath 57 C8
Britten's Bath 45 B7
Britwell Slough 66 C3
Britwell Salome Oxon 83 G11
Brixham Torbay 9 D8
Brixton Devon 7 E11
Brixton London 67 D10
Brixton Deverill Wilts 45 F11
Brixworth Northants 120 C4
Brize Norton Oxon 82 D4
Broad Alley Worcs 117 D7
Broad Blunsdon Swindon 81 G11
Broad Campden Glos 100 D3
Broad Carr W Yorks 196 D5
Broad Chalke Wilts 31 B8
Broad Clough Lancs 195 C11
Broad Colney Herts 85 E11
Broad Common Worcs 117 D7
Broad Ford Kent 53 F8
Broad Green C Beds 103 C9
Broad Green Cambs 124 F3
Broad Green Essex 105 D8
Broad Green Essex 107 G7
Broad Green London 67 F10
Broad Green Mers 182 C6
Broad Green Suff 124 F5
Broad Green Suff 125 F11
Broad Green Worcs 116 F5
Broad Green Worcs 117 C9
Broad Haven = Aberllydan Pembs 72 C5
Broad Heath Powys 114 E6
Broad Heath Staffs 151 D7
Broad Heath Worcs 116 D3
Broad Hill Cambs 123 B11
Broad Hinton Wilts 62 D6
Broad Ings E Yorks 208 C2
Broad Lane Corn 4 G3
Broad Lanes Shrops 132 F5
Broad Laying Hants 64 G2
Broad Layings Hants 64 G2
Broad Marston Worcs 100 B2
Broad Meadow Staffs 168 F4
Broad Oak Carms 93 G11
Broad Oak Cumb 220 G2
Broad Oak Dorset 30 E3
Broad Oak E Sus 37 C10
Broad Oak E Sus 38 D4
Broad Oak Hants 49 C9
Broad Oak Hereford 97 G9
Broad Oak Kent 54 F4
Broad Oak Kent 71 G7
Broad Oak Mers 183 B8
Broad Oak Shrops 132 F5
Broad Parkham Devon 24 C5
Broad Street E Sus 38 D5
Broad Street Kent 53 B10
Broad Street Kent 54 E6
Broad Street Kent 55 E7
Broad Street Medway 69 E9
Broad Street Suff 107 C9
Broad Street Wilts 46 B6
Broad Street Green Essex 88 D5
Broad Tenterden Kent 53 G11
Broad Town Wilts 62 D5
Broadbottom Gtr Man 185 C7
Broadbridge W Sus 22 B4
Broadbridge Heath W Sus 50 G6
Broadbury Devon 12 B5
Broadbush Swindon 81 G11
Broadclyst Devon 14 B5
Broadfield Gtr Man 195 E10
Broadfield Invclyd 276 G6
Broadfield Lancs 194 C4
Broadfield Lancs 195 B8
Broadfield Pembs 73 E10
Broadfield W Sus 51 G9
Broadford Highld 295 C8
Broadford Sur 50 D3
Broadford Bridge W Sus 35 C9
Broadgate Hants 32 C6
Broadgrass Green Suff 125 E9
Broadgreen Wood Herts 86 D4
Broadhalgh Gtr Man 195 E11
Broadham Green Sur 51 C11
Broadhaugh Borders 249 B10
Broadhaven Highld 310 D7
Broadheath Gtr Man 184 D3
Broadhembury Devon 27 G10
Broadhempston Devon 8 B6
Broadholm Derbys 170 F4
Broadholme Derbys 170 F5
Broadholme Lincs 188 G5
Broadland Row E Sus 38 D4
Broadlands Devon 14 G3
Broadlane Corn 2 C4
Broadlay Carms 74 D5
Broadley Lancs 195 D11
Broadley Moray 302 C3
Broadley Common Essex 86 D6
Broadleys Aberds 303 C8
Broadmayne Dorset 17 D10
Broadmeadows Borders 261 C10
Broadmere Hants 48 D6
Broadmoor Pembs 73 D9
Broadmoor Sur 50 D6
Broadmoor Common Hereford 98 D2
Broadmore Green Worcs 116 G6
Broadoak Dorset 16 B4
Broadoak Glos 80 C2
Broadoak Hants 33 E8
Broadoak Shrops 149 F9
Broadoak Wrex 166 D5
Broadoak End Herts 86 C4
Broadoak Park Gtr Man 195 G9
Broadplat Oxon 65 C8
Broadrashes Moray 302 D4
Broadrock Glos 79 F8
Broad's Green Essex 87 C11
Broad's Green Wilts 62 F3
Broadsands Torbay 9 D7
Broadsea Aberds 303 C9
Broadshard Som 28 E6
Broadstairs Kent 71 F11
Broadstone Kent 53 D11
Broadstone Mon 79 E8
Broadstone Poole 18 B6
Broadstone Shrops 131 F10
Broadstreet Common Newport 59 C11
Broadwas Worcs 116 F5
Broadwater Herts 104 G4
Broadwater W Sus 35 G11
Broadwater Down Kent 52 F5
Broadwaters Worcs 116 B6
Broadwath Cumb 239 F11
Broadway Carms 74 D3
Broadway Carms 74 D5
Broadway Pembs 72 C5
Broadway Som 28 D4
Broadway Suff 127 B7
Broadway Worcs 99 D11
Broadway Lands Hereford 97 E11
Broadwell Glos 79 C9
Broadwell Glos 100 F4
Broadwell Oxon 82 E3
Broadwell Warks 119 D9
Broadwey Dorset 17 E9
Broadwindsor Dorset 28 G6
Broadwood Kelly Devon 25 F10
Broadwoodwidger Devon 12 D4
Brobury Hereford 96 C6
Brochel Highld 298 E5
Brochroy Argyll 284 D4
Brock Lancs 202 E6
Brock Hill Essex 88 F2
Brockamin Worcs 116 G5
Brockbridge Hants 33 D10
Brockdish Norf 126 B4
Brockencote Worcs 117 C7
Brockenhurst Hants 32 G4
Brocketsbrae S Lnrk 259 B8
Brockfield Devon 28 F4
Brockford Green Suff 126 D2
Brockford Street Suff 126 D2
Brockhall Northants 120 E2
Brockhall Village Lancs 203 F10
Brockham Sur 51 D7
Brockham End Bath 61 F8
Brockham Park Sur 51 D8
Brockhampton Glos 99 F8
Brockhampton Glos 99 G10
Brockhampton Hants 22 B2
Brockhampton Hereford 97 E11
Brockhampton Green Dorset 30 F2
Brockhill Borders 261 E9
Brockholes W Yorks 197 E7
Brockhollands Glos 79 D10
Brockhurst Derbys 170 C4
Brockhurst Hants 33 G10
Brockhurst Warks 135 G9
Brocklebank Cumb 230 C2
Brocklehirst Dumfries 238 C3
Brocklesby Lincs 200 E6
Brockley London 67 E11
Brockley N Som 60 F3
Brockley Corner Suff 124 C6
Brockley Green Suff 106 B4
Brockley Green Suff 124 G6
Brockleymoor Cumb 230 D5
Brockloch Dumfries 246 D2
Brockmanton Hereford 115 F10
Brockmoor W Mid 133 F8
Brock's Green Hants 64 G4
Brock's Watering Norf 142 E2
Brockscombe Devon 12 C5
Brockton Shrops 130 C6
Brockton Shrops 130 F6
Brockton Shrops 131 E11
Brockton Shrops 132 C4
Brockton Staffs 150 C6
Brockton Telford 150 F4
Brockweir Glos 79 E8
Brockwell Som 42 E2
Brockwood Hants 33 B10
Brockworth Glos 80 B5
Brocton Corn 5 B10
Brocton Staffs 151 F9
Brodick N Ayrs 256 B2
Brodie Moray 301 D9
Brodiesord Aberds 302 C5
Brodsworth S Yorks 198 F4
Brogaig Highld 298 C4
Brogborough C Beds 103 D9
Broke Hall Suff 108 C3
Broken Cross E Ches 184 G5
Broken Cross W Ches 183 G11
Broken Green Herts 105 G8
Brokenborough Wilts 62 B2
Brokerswood Wilts 45 C10
Brokes N Yorks 224 F3
Brombil Neath 57 D9
Bromborough Mers 182 E4
Bromborough Pool Mers 182 E4
Bromdon Shrops 132 G2
Brome Suff 126 B2
Brome Street Suff 126 B3
Bromesberrow Glos 98 E4
Bromesberrow Heath Glos 98 E4
Bromeswell Suff 126 G6
Bromfield Cumb 229 B9
Bromfield Shrops 115 B9
Bromford W Mid 134 E2
Bromham Beds 121 G10
Bromham Wilts 62 F3
Bromley Herts 105 G8
Bromley London 67 C11
Bromley S Yorks 186 B4
Bromley Shrops 132 D4
Bromley Shrops 149 D8
Bromley Tower Hamlets 68 F2
Bromley W Mid 133 F8
Bromley Common London 68 F2
Bromley Cross Essex 107 F11
Bromley Cross Gtr Man 195 E8
Bromley Green Kent 54 F3
Bromley Hall Staffs 150 C5
Bromley Heath S Glos 61 D7
Bromley Park London 67 F11
Bromley Wood Staffs 152 E2
Bromlow Shrops 130 C6
Brompton London 67 D9
Brompton Medway 69 F9
Brompton N Yorks 217 C8
Brompton N Yorks 225 F7
Brompton Shrops 131 B10
Brompton-by-Sawdon N Yorks 217 C8
Brompton-on-Swale N Yorks 224 F4
Brompton Ralph Som 42 G5
Brompton Regis Som 42 G3
Bromsash Hereford 98 G2
Bromsberrow Heath Glos 98 E4
Bromsgrove Worcs 117 C9
Bromstead Common Staffs 150 F6
Bromstead Heath Staffs 150 F6
Bromstone Kent 71 F11
Bromyard Hereford 116 G3
Bromyard Downs Hereford 116 F3
Bronaber Gwyn 146 C4
Broncroft Shrops 131 F10
Brondesbury London 67 C8
Brondesbury Park London 67 C8
Broneirion Powys 129 F10
Brongest Ceredig 92 B6
Brongwyn Ceredig 92 C5
Bronington Wrex 149 B9
Bronllys Powys 96 D2
Bronnant Ceredig 112 D2
Bronwydd Ceredig 93 C7
Bronwydd Arms Carms 93 G8
Bronydd Powys 96 B4
Bronygarth Shrops 148 B5
Brook Carms 74 D3
Brook Devon 12 G5
Brook Devon 14 C2
Brook Hants 32 B4
Brook Hants 32 E3
Brook I o W 20 E3
Brook Kent 54 E5
Brook Sur 50 D5
Brook Sur 50 F2
Brook Bottom Gtr Man 185 D7
Brook Bottom Gtr Man 196 G3
Brook Bottom Lancs 202 E6
Brook End Beds 121 E11
Brook End C Beds 104 B3
Brook End Cambs 121 C11
Brook End Herts 104 F6
Brook End M Keynes 103 C8
Brook End Wilts 61 C10
Brook End Worcs 99 B7
Brook Green London 67 D8
Brook Green Suff 125 F7
Brook Hill Hants 32 E3
Brook Hill Notts 153 C11
Brook Place Sur 66 G3
Brook Street Essex 87 G9
Brook Street Kent 52 D5
Brook Street Kent 54 G2
Brook Street Suff 106 B6
Brook Street W Sus 36 B4
Brook Waters Wilts 30 C6
Brooke Norf 142 D5
Brooke Rutland 136 B6
Brookenby Lincs 190 B2
Brookend Glos 79 E11
Brookend Glos 79 F9
Brookend Oxon 100 G6
Brookfield Derbys 185 B8
Brookfield Lancs 203 G7
Brookfield M'bro 225 B9
Brookfield Renfs 267 C8
Brookfoot W Yorks 196 C6
Brookgreen I o W 20 E3
Brookhampton Oxon 83 F10
Brookhampton Shrops 131 E11
Brookhampton Som 29 B10
Brookhouse Blkburn 195 B7
Brookhouse Denb 165 B9
Brookhouse E Ches 184 F6
Brookhouse Lancs 211 G10
Brookhouse S Yorks 187 D8
Brookhouse W Yorks 196 B5
Brookhouse Green E Ches 168 C4
Brookhouses Derbys 185 D8
Brookhouses Staffs 169 G7
Brookhurst Mers 182 E4
Brookland Kent 39 B7
Brooklands Dumfries 237 B10
Brooklands Gtr Man 184 C3
Brooklands Shrops 167 G8
Brooklands Sur 66 G5
Brooklands W Yorks 206 F2
Brookleigh Devon 14 B5
Brookmans Park Herts 86 E2
Brookpits W Sus 35 G8
Brookrow Shrops 116 C2
Brooks Corn 6 C3
Brooks Powys 130 D2
Brooks End Kent 71 F9
Brooks Green W Sus 35 C10
Brooksbottoms Gtr Man 195 D9
Brooksby Leics 154 F3
Brookside Brack 66 E2
Brookside Derbys 186 G5
Brookside Telford 132 B3
Brookthorpe Glos 80 C4
Brookvale Halton 183 E8
Brookville Norf 140 D4
Brookwood Sur 50 B2
Broom C Beds 104 C3
Broom Cumb 231 G9
Broom Devon 28 G4
Broom E Renf 267 D10
Broom Pembs 73 D10
Broom S Yorks 186 C6
Broom Warks 117 G11
Broom Green Norf 159 E9
Broom Hill Bristol 60 E6
Broom Hill Dorset 31 G8
Broom Hill Durham 242 G4
Broom Hill London 68 F3
Broom Hill Suff 108 B5
Broom Hill Worcs 117 B8
Broom Street Kent 70 G4
Broombank Worcs 116 C3
Broome Norf 143 E7
Broome Shrops 131 D10
Broome Shrops 131 G8
Broome Worcs 117 B8
Broome Park Northumb 264 G4
Broomedge Warr 184 D2
Broomer's Corner W Sus 35 C10
Broomershill W Sus 35 D9
Broomfield Aberds 303 F9
Broomfield Cumb 230 B2
Broomfield Essex 88 D2
Broomfield Kent 53 C10
Broomfield Kent 71 F7
Broomfield Som 43 G8
Broomfield Wilts 61 D11
Broomfields Shrops 149 F8
Broomfleet E Yorks 199 B11
Broomhall E Ches 167 F10
Broomhall Windsor 66 F3
Broomhall Green E Ches 167 F10
Broomham E Sus 23 C8
Broomhaugh Northumb 242 E2
Broomhill Borders 261 D11
Broomhill Bristol 60 D6
Broomhill Highld 301 G9
Broomhill Kent 55 B8
Broomhill Norf 140 C2
Broomhill Northumb 252 C6
Broomhill Notts 171 F8
Broomhill S Yorks 198 G2
Broomhill W Ches 167 B7
Broomhill Bank Kent 52 E5
Broomholm Norf 160 C6
Broomhouse Glasgow 268 C3
Broomlands N Ayrs 257 B8
Broomley Northumb 242 E2
Broompark Durham 233 C10
Broomridge Stirl 278 C6
Broom's Barn Suff 124 D5
Broom's Green Glos 98 E4
Broomsgrove E Sus 38 E4
Broomsthorpe Norf 158 D6
Broomton Highld 301 B8
Broomy Hill Hereford 97 D9
Broomy Lodge Hants 32 E2
Broomyshaw Staffs 169 F9
Brora Highld 311 J3
Broseley Shrops 132 C3
Brotherhouse Bar Lincs 156 G5
Brotheridge Green Worcs 98 C6
Brotherlee Durham 232 D4
Brotherstone Borders 262 B4
Brothertoft Lincs 174 F3
Brotherton N Yorks 198 B3
Brothybeck Cumb 230 C2
Brotton Redcar 226 B3
Broubster Highld 310 C4
Brough Cumb 222 C5
Brough Derbys 185 E11
Brough E Yorks 200 B2
Brough Highld 310 B6
Brough Notts 172 D4
Brough Orkney 314 H4
Brough Orkney 314 E3
Brough Shetland 312 C7
Brough Shetland 312 F6
Brough Shetland 312 F7
Brough Shetland 313 G7
Brough Shetland 313 H6
Brough Shetland 313 J7
Brough Lodge Shetland 312 D7
Brough Sowerby Cumb 222 C5
Broughall Shrops 167 G9
Broughton Borders 260 B4
Broughton Bucks 84 C4
Broughton Cambs 122 B5
Broughton Edin 280 F5
Broughton Flint 166 C4
Broughton Hants 47 G10
Broughton Lancs 202 F6
Broughton M Keynes 103 C7
Broughton N Lincs 200 F3
Broughton N Yorks 204 C4
Broughton N Yorks 216 E5
Broughton Northants 120 B6
Broughton Orkney 314 B4
Broughton Oxon 101 D8
Broughton Shrops 132 E6
Broughton Staffs 150 C5
Broughton V Glam 58 E2
Broughton Astley Leics 135 E10
Broughton Beck Cumb 210 C5
Broughton Common N Lincs 200 E3
Broughton Common Wilts 61 G11
Broughton Cross Cumb 229 E7
Broughton Gifford Wilts 61 G11
Broughton Green Worcs 117 E9
Broughton Hackett Worcs 117 G8
Broughton in Furness Cumb 210 B4
Broughton Lodges Leics 154 E4
Broughton Mills Cumb 220 G4
Broughton Moor Cumb 228 E6
Broughton Park Gtr Man 195 G10
Broughton Poggs Oxon 82 E2
Broughtown Orkney 314 B6
Broughty Ferry Dundee 287 D8
Brow Edge Cumb 211 C7
Browhouses Dumfries 239 D7
Browland Shetland 313 H4
Brown Bank N Yorks 205 C10
Brown Candover Hants 48 F5
Brown Edge Lancs 193 E11
Brown Edge Mers 183 C8
Brown Edge Staffs 168 E6
Brown Heath Hants 33 D8
Brown Heath W Ches 167 B7
Brown Knowl W Ches 167 E7
Brown Lees Staffs 168 D5
Brown Moor W Yorks 206 G3
Brown Street Suff 125 E11
Brownber Cumb 222 D4
Brownbread Street E Sus 23 B11
Brownedge E Ches 168 C3
Brownheath Devon 27 D10
Brownheath Shrops 149 D9
Brownheath Common Worcs 117 E7
Brownhill Aberds 302 E6
Brownhill Aberds 303 E8
Brownhill Blkburn 203 G9
Brownhill Shrops 149 E8
Brownhills Fife 287 F9
Brownhills Shrops 150 B3
Brownhills W Mid 133 B10
Brownieside Northumb 264 E5
Browninghill Green Hants 48 B5
Brownlow E Ches 168 C4
Brownlow Mers 194 G4
Brownlow Fold Gtr Man 195 E8
Brownlow Heath E Ches 168 C4
Brownmuir Aberds 293 F9
Brown's Bank E Ches 167 G10
Brown's End Glos 98 E4
Brown's Green W Mid 133 E10
Browns Wood M Keynes 103 D8
Brownshill Glos 80 E5
Brownshill Green W Mid 134 G6
Brownside Lancs 204 G3
Brownsover Warks 119 B10
Brownston Devon 8 E3
Brownsburn N Lnrk 268 C5
Browston Green Norf 143 C9
Browtop Cumb 229 G7
Broxa N Yorks 227 G8
Broxbourne Herts 86 D5
Broxburn E Loth 282 F3
Broxburn W Loth 279 G11
Broxfield Northumb 264 F6
Broxholme Lincs 188 F6
Broxted Essex 105 F11
Broxton W Ches 167 E7
Broxtowe Nottingham 171 G8
Broxwood Hereford 115 G7
Broyle Side E Sus 23 C7
Bruairnis W Isles 297 L3
Bruan Highld 310 F7
Bruar Lodge Perth 291 F10
Brucefield Fife 280 D2
Brucehill W Dunb 277 F7
Bruche Warr 183 D10
Brucklebog Aberds 293 D9
Bruera W Ches 166 C6
Bruern Abbey Oxon 100 G5
Bruichladdich Argyll 274 G3
Bruisyard Suff 126 D6
Bruisyard Street Suff 126 D6
Brumby N Lincs 199 F11
Brunant Powys 130 B5
Brund Staffs 169 C10
Brundall Norf 142 B6
Brundish Norf 143 D7
Brundish Suff 126 D5
Brundish Street Suff 126 C5
Brundon Suff 107 C7
Brunery Highld 289 B9
Brunnion Corn 2 B2
Brunshaw Lancs 204 G3
Brunstane Edin 280 G6
Brunstock Cumb 239 F10
Brunswick Gtr Man 184 B4
Brunswick Park London 86 G3
Brunswick Village T & W 242 C6
Brunt Hamersland Shetland 313 H6
Bruntcliffe W Yorks 197 B9
Brunthwaite W Yorks 205 D7
Bruntingthorpe Leics 136 F2
Brunton Fife 287 E7
Brunton Northumb 264 E6
Brunton Wilts 47 B8
Brushes Gtr Man 185 B7
Brushfield Derbys 185 G11
Brushford Devon 25 F11
Brushford Som 26 B6
Bruton Som 45 G7
Bryans Midloth 270 C6
Bryan's Green Worcs 117 D7
Bryanston Dorset 30 F5
Bryant's Bottom Bucks 84 F5
Brydekirk Dumfries 238 C5
Bryher Scilly 1 G3
Brymbo Conwy 180 G4
Brymbo Wrex 166 E3
Brympton Som 29 D8
Brympton D'Evercy Som 29 D8
Bryn Caerph 77 F11
Bryn Carms 75 E8
Bryn Gtr Man 194 G5
Bryn Gwyn 179 G9
Bryn Neath 57 C10
Bryn Powys 130 C3
Bryn Rhondda 76 D6
Bryn Shrops 130 F5
Bryn Swansea 56 C4
Bryn W Ches 183 G10
Bryn Bwbach Gwyn 146 B2
Bryn-coch Neath 57 B8
Bryn Celyn Anglesey 179 F10
Bryn Celyn Flint 181 F11
Bryn Common Flint 166 D3
Bryn Du Anglesey 178 G4
Bryn Dulas Conwy 180 F6
Bryn Eglwys Gwyn 163 B10
Bryn Gates Gtr Man 194 G5
Bryn-glas Conwy 164 B4
Bryn Golau Rhondda 58 B3
Bryn-henllan Pembs 91 D10
Bryn-Iwan Carms 92 E6
Bryn-mawr Gwyn 144 C4
Bryn Mawr Powys 148 F5
Bryn Myrddin Carms 93 G8
Bryn-nantllech Conwy 164 B6
Bryn-newydd Denb 165 G11
Bryn Offa Wrex 166 F4
Bryn Pen-y-lan Wrex 166 G4
Bryn-penarth Powys 130 C2
Bryn Pydew Conwy 180 F4
Bryn Rhyd-yr-Arian Conwy 165 B7
Bryn-rhys Conwy 180 F4
Bryn Saith Marchog Denb 165 E9
Bryn Sion Gwyn 147 F7
Bryn Tanat Powys 148 E4
Bryn-y-cochin Shrops 149 B7
Bryn-y-gwenin Mon 78 B4
Bryn-y-maen Conwy 180 F4
Bryn-yr-Eos Wrex 166 G3
Bryn-yr-eryr Gwyn 162 F5
Bryn-yr-ogof Denb 165 D11
Brynafan Ceredig 112 C4
Brynamman Carms 76 C2
Brynawel Caerph 77 G11
Brynberian Pembs 92 D2
Brynbryddan Neath 57 C9
Bryncae Rhondda 58 C3
Bryncethin Bridgend 58 C2
Brynbryddan Neath 57 C9
Bryncae Rhondda 58 C3
Bryncethin Bridgend 58 C2
Bryncir Gwyn 163 G7
Bryncoch Bridgend 58 C2
Bryncroes Gwyn 144 C4
Bryncrug Gwyn 128 C2
Brynderwen Powys 130 D3
Bryndu Carms 75 D8
Bryneglwys Denb 165 F10
Brynford Flint 181 G11
Brynglas Newport 59 B10
Brynglas Sta Gwyn 128 C2
Bryngwran Anglesey 178 F4
Bryngwyn Ceredig 92 B5
Bryngwyn Mon 78 D5
Bryngwyn Powys 96 B3
Brynhenllan Pembs 91 D10
Brynheulog Bridgend 57 C11
Brynhoffnant Ceredig 110 G6
Bryniau Denb 181 E9
Bryning Lancs 194 B2
Brynithel Bl Gwent 78 E2
Brynllywarch Powys 130 F3
Brynmawr Bl Gwent 77 C11
Brynmenyn Bridgend 58 B2
Brynmill Swansea 56 C6
Brynmorfudd Conwy 164 C4
Brynna Rhondda 58 C3
Brynnau Gwynion Rhondda 58 C3
Brynore Shrops 149 B7
Brynrefail Anglesey 179 D7
Brynrefail Gwyn 163 C9
Brynsadler Rhondda 58 C4
Brynsiencyn Anglesey 163 B7
Brynsworthy Devon 40 G4
Brynteg Anglesey 179 E7
Brynteg Ceredig 93 C9
Brynteg Wrex 166 E4
Bryntirion Bridgend 57 E11
Buaile nam Bodach W Isles 297 L3
Bualintur Highld 294 C6
Bualnaluib Highld 307 K3
Buarthmeini Gwyn 146 C6
Bubbenhall Warks 119 C7
Bubblewell Glos 80 E5
Bubnell Derbys 186 G2
Bubwith E Yorks 207 F10
Buccleuch Borders 261 G8
Buchan Hill W Sus 51
Buchanan Smithy Stirl 277
Buchanhaven Aberds 303
Buchanty Perth 286
Buchley E Dunb 277
Buchlyvie Stirl 277
Buck Hill Wilts 62
Buckabank Cumb 230
Buckbury Worcs 98
Buckden Cambs 122
Buckden N Yorks 213
Buckenham Norf 143
Buckerell Devon 27
Bucket Corner Hants 32
Buckfast Devon 8
Buckfastleigh Devon 8
Buckham Dorset 29
Buckhaven Fife 281
Buckholm Borders 261
Buckholt Mon 79
Buckhorn Devon 12
Buckhorn Weston Dorset 30
Buckhurst Kent 53
Buckhurst Hill Essex 86
Buckie Moray 302
Buckies Highld 310
Buckingham Bucks 102
Buckland Bucks 84
Buckland Devon 8
Buckland Devon 14
Buckland Glos 99
Buckland Hants 20
Buckland Herts 105
Buckland Kent 55
Buckland Oxon 82
Buckland Sur 51
Buckland Brewer Devon 24
Buckland Common Bucks 84
Buckland Dinham Som 45
Buckland Down Som 45
Buckland End W Mid 134
Buckland Filleigh Devon 25
Buckland in the Moor Devon 13
Buckland Marsh Oxon 82
Buckland Monachorum Devon 7
Buckland Newton Dorset 29
Buckland Ripers Dorset 17
Buckland St Mary Som 28
Buckland Valley Kent 55
Bucklands Borders 262
Bucklandwharf Bucks 84
Bucklebury W Berks 64
Bucklebury Alley W Berks 64
Bucklegate Lincs 156
Buckleigh Devon 24
Bucklerheads Angus 287
Bucklers Hard Hants 20
Bucklesham Suff 108
Buckley = Bwcle Flint 166
Buckley Green Warks 118
Buckley Hill Mers 182
Bucklow Hill E Ches 184
Buckminster Leics 155
Buckmoorend Bucks 84
Bucknall Lincs 173
Bucknall Stoke 168
Bucknell Oxon 101
Bucknell Shrops 115
Buckoak W Ches 183
Buckover S Glos 79
Buckpool Moray 302
Buckpool W Mid 133
Buckridge Worcs 116
Buck's Cross Devon 24
Bucks Green W Sus 50
Bucks Hill Herts 85
Bucks Horn Oak Hants 49
Buck's Mills Devon 24
Bucksburn Aberdeen 293
Buckshaw Village Lancs 194
Buckskin Hants 48
Buckton E Yorks 218
Buckton Hereford 115
Buckton Northumb 264
Buckton Vale Gtr Man 196
Buckworth Cambs 122
Budbrooke Warks 118
Budby Notts 171
Buddgbrake Shetland 312
Buddileigh Staffs 168
Budd's Titson Corn 24
Bude Corn 24
Budge's Shop Corn 6
Budlake Devon 14
Budle Northumb 264
Budleigh Som 27
Budleigh Salterton Devon 15
Budlett's Common E Sus 37
Budock Water Corn 3
Budworth Heath W Ches 183
Buersil Head Gtr Man 196
Buerton E Ches 167
Buffler's Holt Bucks 102
Bufton Leics 135
Bugbrooke Northants 120
Bugford Devon 40
Bughtlin Edin 280
Buglawton E Ches 168
Bugle Corn 5
Bugle Gate Worcs 116
Bugley Dorset 30
Bugley Wilts 45
Bugthorpe E Yorks 207
Building End Essex 105
Buildwas Shrops 132
Builth Road Powys 113
Builth Wells Powys 113
Buirgh W Isles 305
Bulbourne Herts 84
Bulbridge Wilts 46
Bulby Lincs 155
Bulcote Notts 171
Buldoo Highld 310
Bulford Wilts 47
Bulford Camp Wilts 47
Bulkeley E Ches 167
Bulkeley Hall Shrops 168
Bulkington Warks 135
Bulkington Wilts 46
Bulkworthy Devon 24
Bull Bay = Porthllechog Anglesey 178
Bull Hill Hants 20
Bullamoor N Yorks 225
Bullbridge Derbys 170
Bullbrook Brack 65
Bulleign Kent 53
Bullenhill Wilts 45
Bullen's Green Herts 86
Bulley Glos 80
Bullgill Cumb 229
Bullhurst Hill Derbys 170
Bullinghope Hereford 97
Bullington Hants 48
Bullington Lincs 189

o Glos 79 D11
ock's Horn Wilts 81 G7
ockstone Kent 71 F7
s Cross London 86 F4
s Green Herts 86 B3
s Green Norf 143 E8
s Green Som 45 D8
's Hill Hereford 97 G11
ood Argyll 276 G3
whole Bottom Mon 79 F7
ner Essex 106 C6
ner N Yorks 216 F3
ner Tye Essex 106 D6
han Thurrock 68 B6
trode Herts 85 E8
hy Shrops 148 G6
erhythe E Sus 38 F3
vark Aberds 303 E9
vark Mon 79 G8
vell Nottingham 171 F8
vell Forest
ingham 171 F8
vick Leics 136 E3
vick Northants 137 E9
ble's Green Essex 86 D6
vell Hill Norf 142 E2
Abhainn Eadarra
sles 305 H3
a'Mhuillin W Isles 297 K3
Loyne Highld 290 C4
acaimb Highld 295 G8
arkaig Highld 295 E8
oury E Ches 167 D9
oury Heath E Ches 167 D9
ce Common Sur 51 D8
chrew Highld 300 E6
dalloch Highld 295 C10
ess Shetland 312 C8
essan Argyll 288 G5
gay Suff 142 F6
ker's Hill Cambs 139 B8
kers Hill Gtr Man 184 D6
kers Hill Lincs 174 E3
ker's Hill Lincs 189 G7
ker's Hill Norf 142 B3
ker's Hill Oxon 83 B7
ker's Hill Suff 143 C10
oit Highld 300 G5
nahabhain Argyll 274 F5
ny Notts 153 D11
ny Hill Notts 153 D11
ree Highld 290 G2
roy Highld 290 E4
sley Bank E Ches 167 G11
stead Hants 32 C6
tait Highld 300 F3
tingford Herts 105 F7
ting's Green
ex 106 E6
well Norf 142 E2
well Bottom Norf 142 D2
tach Highld 310 F5
age Derbys 185 G8
age Leics 135 E8
age Wilts 63 G8
cher Hereford 114 E6
chett's Green
dsor 65 C10
combe Wilts 46 G5
cot Oxon 83 F9
cot Worcs 117 C9
cote Shrops 132 D4
cott Bucks 84 B4
cott Bucks 103 G7
cott Som 44 D4
liehouse Edin 270 B5
lon T & W 243 E9
lonshill V Glam 58 E6
drop Oxon 101 D7
es Suff 107 E8
es Green Suff 107 D8
ord Devon 24 C4
ord E Ches 167 E10
ord Oxon 82 C3
ord Shrops 115 D11
ord Som 44 E5
g Argyll 288 E5
g Argyll 288 G6
gar Orkney 314 D3
gate Hants 31 D11
gate Suff 125 B11
gates Hants 34 B3
gh End Herts 104 E2
gedin Powys 148 G4
gess Hill W Sus 36 D4
gh Suff 126 G4
gh by Sands Cumb 239 F8
gh Castle Norf 143 B9
gh Common Norf 141 E11
gh Heath Sur 51 B8
gh Hill E Sus 23 C8
gh Hill E Sus 38 B2
gh le Marsh Lincs 175 B8
gh Muir Aberds 293 B9
gh Muir Aberds 303 G7
gh next Aylsham
f 160 D4
gh on Bain Lincs 190 D2
gh St Margaret =
ggburgh Norf 161 G8
gh St Peter Norf 143 E9
gh Stubbs Norf 159 C10
ghclere Hants 64 G3
ghclere Common
ts 64 G3
ghead Moray 301 C11
ghfield W Berks 65 F7
ghfield Common
Berks 64 F6
ghfield Hill W Berks 65 F7
ghill Hereford 97 C9
ghwallis S Yorks 198 E4
gois Corn 10 G4
gham Kent 69 G8
gham Court Kent 69 G8
nton Hants 34 C2
wand E Ches 167 E10
awn Corn 10 G5
leigh Brack 65 E11
eigh Glos 80 E5
lescombe Devon 27 D9
lestone Dorset 17 C11
estone Devon 8 F6
ley Hants 32 G2
ley Rutland 155 G7
ley Shrops 131 G9
ley W Yorks 205 G11
ley Beacon Hants 32 G2
ley Gate Hereford 97 B11
Yorks 205 D9
ley Lawn Hants 32 G2
ley Lodge Hants 32 F2
ley Street Hants 32 G2
ley Woodhead
Yorks 205 E9
eydam E Ches 167 G10
inch Som 28 B3
ingham Green
f 161 G7
lingjobb Powys 114 F5
lish Park Worcs 116 C6
Burlorne Tregoose
Corn 5 B10
Burlow E Sus 23 B9
Burlton Shrops 149 D9
Burmantofts W Yorks 206 G2
Burmarsh Hereford 97 B10
Burmarsh Kent 54 G5
Burmington Warks 100 D5
Burn N Yorks 198 B5
Burn Bridge N Yorks 206 C2
Burn Naze Lancs 202 E2
Burn of Cambus Stirl 285 G11
Burnage Gtr Man 184 C5
Burnard's Ho Devon 24 G4
Burnaston Derbys 152 C5
Burnbank S Lnrk 268 D4
Burnby E Yorks 208 D2
Burncross S Yorks 186 B4
Burndell W Sus 35 G7
Burnden Gtr Man 195 F8
Burnedge Gtr Man 196 E2
Burnend Aberds 303 E8
Burneside Cumb 221 F10
Burness Orkney 314 B6
Burneston N Yorks 214 B6
Burnett Bath 61 F7
Burnfoot Borders 261 G10
Burnfoot Borders 262 F2
Burnfoot Dumfries 239 C7
Burnfoot Dumfries 247 E11
Burnfoot E Ayrs 245 B10
Burnfoot N Lnrk 268 B5
Burnfoot Perth 286 G3
Burngreave S Yorks 186 D5
Burnham Bucks 66 C2
Burnham N Lincs 200 D5
Burnham Deepdale
Norf 176 E4
Burnham Green Herts 86 B3
Burnham Market Norf 176 E4
Burnham Norton Norf 176 E4
Burnham-on-Crouch
Essex 88 F6
Burnham-on-Sea Som 43 D10
Burnham Overy
Staithe Norf 176 E4
Burnham Overy Town
Norf 176 E4
Burnham Thorpe Norf 176 E5
Burnhead Aberds 293 D10
Burnhead Borders 262 F2
Burnhead Dumfries 247 D9
Burnhead Dumfries 247 G10
Burnhead S Ayrs 244 C6
Burnhervie Aberds 293 B9
Burnhill Green Staffs 132 C5
Burnhope Durham 233 B9
Burnhouse N Ayrs 267 E7
Burnhouse Mains
Borders 271 F8
Burniere Corn 10 G5
Burniestrype Moray 302 C3
Burniston N Yorks 227 G10
Burnlee W Yorks 196 F6
Burnley Lancs 204 G2
Burnley Lane Lancs 204 G2
Burnley Wood Lancs 204 G2
Burnmouth Borders 273 C9
Burnopfield Durham 242 F5
Burnrigg Cumb 239 F11
Burn's Green Herts 104 G6
Burnsall N Yorks 213 G10
Burnside Aberds 303 E8
Burnside Angus 287 B9
Burnside E Ayrs 258 G3
Burnside Fife 286 G5
Burnside Perth 286 E4
Burnside S Lnrk 268 C2
Burnside Shetland 312 F4
Burnside T & W 243 G8
Burnside W Loth 279 G11
Burnside of Duntrune
Angus 287 D8
Burnstone Devon 24 C4
Burnswark Dumfries 238 B5
Burnt Ash Glos 80 E5
Burnt Heath Derbys 186 F2
Burnt Heath Essex 107 F11
Burnt Hill W Berks 64 E5
Burnt Houses Durham 233 G8
Burnt Mills Essex 88 G2
Burnt Oak E Sus 37 B8
Burnt Oak London 86 G2
Burnt Tree W Mid 133 E9
Burnt Yates N Yorks 214 G5
Burntcommon Sur 50 C4
Burntheath Derbys 152 C4
Burnthouse Corn 3 B7
Burntisland Fife 280 D4
Burnton E Ayrs 245 B11
Burnturk Fife 287 G7
Burntwood Staffs 133 B11
Burntwood Green
Staffs 133 B11
Burntwood Pentre
Flint 166 C3
Burnworthy Som 27 D11
Burnwynd Edin 270 B2
Burpham Sur 50 C4
Burpham W Sus 35 F8
Burradon Northumb 251 B11
Burradon T & W 243 C7
Burrafirth Shetland 312 B8
Burraland Shetland 312 F5
Burraland Shetland 313 J4
Burras Corn 2 C5
Burrastow Shetland 313 J4
Burraton Corn 7 D8
Burraton Coombe Corn 7 D8
Burravoe Shetland 312 F7
Burravoe Shetland 312 G5
Burray Village Orkney 314 G4
Burreldales Aberds 303 F7
Burrells Cumb 222 B3
Burrelton Perth 286 D6
Burridge Devon 28 F4
Burridge Devon 40 F5
Burridge Hants 33 E8
Burrigill Highld 310 F6
Burrill N Yorks 214 B4
Burringham N Lincs 199 F10
Burrington Devon 25 D10
Burrington Hereford 115 C8
Burrington N Som 44 B3
Burrough End Cambs 124 F2
Burrough Green Cambs 124 F2
Burrough on the Hill
Leics 154 G5
Burroughs Grove Bucks 65 B11
Burroughston Orkney 314 D5
Burrow Devon 14 B5
Burrow Som 28 C6
Burrow Som 42 E2
Burrow-bridge Som 28 B5
Burrowbridge Som 43 G11
Burrowhill Sur 66 G3
Burrows Cross Sur 50 D5
Burrowsmoor Holt
Notts 172 G2
Burrsville Park Essex 89 B11
Burrswood Kent 52 F4
Burry Swansea 56 C3
Burry Green Swansea 56 C3
Burry Port =
Porth Tywyn Carms 74 E6
Burscott Devon 24 C4
Burscough Lancs 194 E2
Burscough Bridge
Lancs 194 E2
Bursdon Devon 24 D3
Bursea E Yorks 208 G2
Burshill E Yorks 209 D7
Bursledon Hants 33 F7
Burslem Stoke 168 F5
Burstall Suff 107 C11
Burstallhill Suff 107 B11
Burstock Dorset 28 G6
Burston Devon 26 G2
Burston Norf 142 G2
Burston Staffs 151 C8
Burstow Sur 51 E10
Burstwick E Yorks 201 B8
Burtersett N Yorks 213 B7
Burtholme Cumb 240 E2
Burthorpe Suff 124 E5
Burthwaite Cumb 230 B4
Burtle Som 43 E11
Burtle Hill Som 43 E11
Burtoft Lincs 156 B5
Burton Dorset 17 C9
Burton Dorset 19 C9
Burton Lincs 189 G7
Burton Northumb 264 C5
Burton Pembs 73 D7
Burton Som 29 E8
Burton Som 43 E7
Burton V Glam 58 F4
Burton W Ches 167 C8
Burton W Ches 182 G4
Burton Wilts 45 G10
Burton Wilts 61 D10
Burton Wrex 166 D5
Burton Agnes E Yorks 218 G2
Burton Bradstock
Dorset 16 D5
Burton Corner Lincs 174 F4
Burton Dassett Warks 119 G7
Burton End Cambs 106 B2
Burton End Essex 105 G10
Burton Ferry Pembs 73 D7
Burton Fleming
E Yorks 217 E11
Burton Green Essex 106 F6
Burton Green W Mid 118 B5
Burton Green Wrex 166 D4
Burton Hastings Warks 135 F8
Burton-in-Kendal
Cumb 211 D10
Burton in Lonsdale
N Yorks 212 E3
Burton Joyce Notts 171 G10
Burton Latimer
Northants 121 C8
Burton Lazars Leics 154 F5
Burton-le-Coggles
Lincs 155 D9
Burton Leonard
N Yorks 214 G6
Burton Manor Staffs 151 E8
Burton on the Wolds
Leics 153 E11
Burton Overy Leics 136 D3
Burton Pedwardine
Lincs 173 G10
Burton Pidsea E Yorks 209 G10
Burton Salmon N Yorks 198 B3
Burton Stather N Lincs 199 D11
Burton upon Stather
N Lincs 199 D11
Burton upon Trent
Staffs 152 E5
Burton Westwood
Shrops 132 D2
Burtonwood Warr 183 C9
Burwardsley W Ches 167 D8
Burwarton Shrops 132 F2
Burwash E Sus 37 C11
Burwash Common
E Sus 37 C10
Burwash Weald E Sus 37 C10
Burwell Cambs 123 D11
Burwell Lincs 190 F5
Burwen Anglesey 178 C6
Burwick Orkney 314 H4
Burwick Shetland 313 J5
Burwood Shrops 131 F9
Burwood Park Sur 66 G6
Bury Cambs 138 G5
Bury Gtr Man 195 E10
Bury Som 26 B6
Bury W Sus 35 E8
Bury End Beds 121 G9
Bury End C Beds 104 E2
Bury End Worcs 99 D11
Bury Green Herts 86 E4
Bury Green Herts 105 G8
Bury Hollow W Sus 35 E8
Bury Park Luton 103 G11
Bury St Edmunds Suff 125 E7
Buryas Br Corn 1 D4
Burybank Staffs 151 B7
Bury's Bank W Berks 64 F3
Burythorpe N Yorks 216 G5
Busbiehill N Ayrs 257 B9
Busbridge Sur 50 E3
Busby E Renf 267 D11
Buscot Oxon 82 F2
Buscott Som 44 F2
Bush Aberds 293 G9
Bush Corn 24 F2
Bush Bank Hereford 115 G9
Bush Crathie Aberds 292 D4
Bush End Essex 87 B9
Bush Estate Norf 161 D8
Bush Green Norf 141 D10
Bush Green Norf 142 F4
Bush Green Suff 125 F8
Bush Hill Park London 86 F4
Bushbury Sur 51 D7
Bushbury W Mid 133 C8
Bushby Leics 136 C3
Bushey Dorset 18 E5
Bushey Herts 85 G10
Bushey Ground Oxon 82 D4
Bushey Heath Herts 85 G11
Bushey Mead London 67 F8
Bushfield Cumb 249 G11
Bushley Worcs 99 E7
Bushley Green Worcs 99 E7
Bushmead Beds 122 E2
Bushmoor Shrops 131 F8
Bushton Wilts 62 D5
Bushy Common Norf 159 G9
Bushy Hill Sur 50 C4
Busk Cumb 231 C8
Busk Gtr Man 196 F2
Buslingthorpe Lincs 189 D9
Bussage Glos 80 E5
Bussex Som 43 F11
Busta Shetland 312 G5
Bustard Green Essex 106 F2
Bustard's Green Norf 142 E3
Bustatoun Orkney 314 A7
Busveal Corn 4 G4
Butcher's Common
Norf 160 E6
Butcher's Cross E Sus 37 B9
Butcombe N Som 60 G4
Bute Town Caerph 77 D10
Butetown Cardiff 59 D7
Butlane Head Shrops 149 G8
Butleigh Som 44 G4
Butleigh Wootton Som 44 G4
Butler's Cross Bucks 84 D4
Butlers Cross Bucks 85 G7
Butler's End Warks 134 G4
Butler's Hill Notts 171 F8
Butlers Marston
Warks 118 G6
Butlersbank Shrops 149 E11
Butley Suff 127 G7
Butley High Corner
Suff 109 B7
Butley Low Corner
Suff 109 B7
Butley Town E Ches 184 F6
Butlocks Heath Hants 33 F7
Butt Green E Ches 167 E11
Butt Lane Staffs 168 E4
Butt Yeats Lancs 211 F11
Butter Bank Staffs 151 E7
Butterburn Cumb 240 C5
Buttercrambe N Yorks 207 B10
Butteriss Gate Corn 2 C6
Butterknowle Durham 233 F8
Butterleigh Devon 27 F7
Butterley Derbys 170 C4
Butterley Derbys 170 E6
Buttermere Cumb 220 B3
Buttermere Wilts 63 G10
Butterrow Glos 80 E5
Butters Green Staffs 168 E4
Buttershaw W Yorks 196 B6
Butterstone Perth 286 C4
Butterton Staffs 168 G4
Butterton Staffs 169 D9
Butterwick Cumb 221 B10
Butterwick Durham 234 F3
Butterwick Lincs 174 G5
Butterwick N Yorks 216 D4
Butterwick N Yorks 217 E9
Butteryhaugh
Northumb 250 E4
Buttington Powys 130 B5
Button Haugh Green
Suff 125 D9
Buttonbridge Shrops 116 B4
Buttonoak Worcs 116 B5
Button's Green Suff 125 G8
Butts Devon 14 D2
Butt's Green Essex 88 E3
Butts Green Essex 105 E9
Butt's Green Hants 32 B4
Buttsash Hants 32 F6
Buttsbear Cross Corn 24 G3
Buttsbury Essex 87 F11
Buttsole Kent 55 C10
Buxhall Suff 125 F10
Buxhall Fen Street
Suff 125 F10
Buxley Borders 272 E6
Buxted E Sus 37 C7
Buxton Derbys 185 G9
Buxton Norf 160 E4
Buxworth Derbys 185 E8
Bwcle = Buckley Flint 166 C3
Bwlch Flint 181 G11
Bwlch Powys 96 G2
Bwlch-derwin Gwyn 163 F7
Bwlch-Llan Ceredig 111 F11
Bwlch-newydd Carms 93 G7
Bwlch-y-cibau Powys 148 F3
Bwlch-y-cwm Cardiff 58 C6
Bwlch-y-fadfa Ceredig 93 B8
Bwlch-y-ffridd Powys 129 D11
Bwlch-y-Plain Powys 114 B4
Bwlch-y-sarnau
Powys 113 C10
Bwlchgwyn Wrex 166 E3
Bwlchnewydd Carms 93 G7
Bwlchtocyn Gwyn 144 D6
Bwlchyddar Powys 148 E3
Bwlchygroes Pembs 92 D4
Bwlchyllyn Gwyn 163 D8
Bybrook Kent 54 E4
Bycross Hereford 97 C7
Bye Green Bucks 84 C5
Byeastwood Bridgend 58 C2
Byebush Aberds 303 F7
Byerhope Northumb 232 B3
Byermoor T & W 242 F5
Byers Green Durham 233 E10
Byfield Northants 119 G10
Byfleet Sur 66 G5
Byford Hereford 97 C7
Byford Common
Hereford 97 C7
Bygrave Herts 104 D5
Byker T & W 243 E7
Byland Abbey N Yorks 215 D10
Bylchau Conwy 165 C7
Byley W Ches 168 B2
Bynea Carms 56 B4
Byram N Yorks 198 B3
Byrness Northumb 251 C7
Bythorn Cambs 121 B11
Byton Hereford 115 E7
Byton Hand Hereford 115 E7
Bywell Northumb 242 E2
Byworth W Sus 35 C7

C

Cabbacott Devon 24 C6
Cabbage Hill Brack 65 E11
Cabharstadh W Isles 304 F5
Cabin Shrops 130 F6
Cablea Perth 286 D3
Cabourne Lincs 200 G6
Cabrach Argyll 274 G5
Cabrach Moray 302 G3
Cabrich Highld 300 E5
Cabus Lancs 202 D5
Cackle Hill Lincs 157 D7
Cackle Street E Sus 23 B11
Cackle Street E Sus 37 B7
Cackle Street E Sus 38 D4
Cackleshaw W Yorks 204 F6
Cad Green Som 28 D4
Cadboll Highld 301 B8
Cadbury Devon 26 G6
Cadbury Barton Devon 25 D11
Cadbury Heath S Glos 61 E7
Cadder E Dunb 278 G2
Cadderlie Argyll 284 D4
Caddington C Beds 85 B9
Caddleton Argyll 275 B8
Caddonfoot Borders 261 C10
Caddonlee Borders 261 B10
Cade Street E Sus 37 C10
Cadeby Leics 135 C8
Cadeby S Yorks 198 G4
Cadeleigh Devon 26 F6
Cademuir Borders 260 B6
Cader Denb 165 C8
Cadger Path Angus 287 B8
Cadgwith Corn 2 G6
Cadham Fife 286 G6
Cadishead Gtr Man 184 C2
Cadle Swansea 56 B6
Cadley Lancs 202 G6
Cadley Wilts 47 C8
Cadley Wilts 63 F8
Cadmore End Bucks 84 G3
Cadnam Hants 32 E3
Cadney N Lincs 200 G4
Cadney Bank Wrex 149 C9
Cadole Flint 166 C2
Cadoxton V Glam 58 F6
Cadoxton-Juxta-Neath
Neath 57 B9
Cadshaw Blkburn 195 D8
Cadwell Herts 104 E3
Cadzow S Lnrk 268 E4
Cae Clyd Gwyn 164 G2
Cae-gors Carms 75 E9
Caeathro Gwyn 163 C7
Caehopkin Powys 76 C4
Caemorgan Ceredig 92 B3
Caenby Lincs 189 D8
Caenby Corner Lincs 189 D7
Cae'r-bont Powys 76 C4
Cae'r-bryn Carms 75 C9
Caer-Estyn Wrex 166 D4
Caer-Farchell Pembs 90 F5
Cae'r-Lan Powys 76 C4
Caer Llan Mon 79 D7
Caerau Bridgend 57 C11
Caerau Cardiff 58 D6
Caerau Park Newport 59 B9
Caerdeon Gwyn 146 F2
Caerfarchell Pembs 90 F5
Caerffili = Caerphilly
Caerph 59 B7
Caerfyrddin =
Carmarthen Carms 93 G8
Caergeiliog Anglesey 178 F4
Caergwrle Flint 166 D4
Caergybi = Holyhead
Anglesey 178 E2
Caerhendy Neath 57 C9
Caerhun Gwyn 163 B9
Caerleon Newport 78 G4
Caermead V Glam 58 F3
Caermeini Pembs 92 E2
Caernarfon Gwyn 163 C7
Caerphilly = Caerffili
Caerph 59 B7
Caersws Powys 129 E10
Caerwedros Ceredig 111 F7
Caerwent Mon 79 G7
Caerwent Brook Mon 60 B3
Caerwych Gwyn 146 B2
Caerwys Flint 181 G10
Caethle Gwyn 128 D2
Cage Green Kent 52 D5
Caggan Highld 291 B10
Caggle Street Mon 78 B5
Cailness Stirl 285 G7
Caim Anglesey 179 E10
Cainscross Glos 80 D4
Caio Carms 94 D3
Cairinis W Isles 296 E4
Cairisiadar W Isles 304 E2
Cairminis W Isles 296 C6
Cairnbaan Argyll 275 D9
Cairnbanno Ho Aberds 303 E8
Cairnborrow Aberds 302 E4
Cairnbrogie Aberds 303 G8
Cairnbulg Castle
Aberds 303 C10
Cairncross Angus 292 F6
Cairncross Borders 273 C7
Cairnderry Dumfries 236 B5
Cairndow Argyll 284 F5
Cairness Aberds 303 C10
Cairneyhill Fife 279 D10
Cairnfield Ho Moray 302 C4
Cairngaan Dumfries 236 F3
Cairngarroch Dumfries 236 E2
Cairnhill Aberds 302 F6
Cairnhill Aberds 303 D7
Cairnhill N Lnrk 268 C5
Cairnie Aberds 293 C10
Cairnie Aberds 302 E4
Cairnlea S Ayrs 244 G6
Cairnleith Crofts
Aberds 303 F9
Cairnmuir Aberds 303 C9
Cairnorrie Aberds 303 E8
Cairnpark Aberds 293 B10
Cairnpark Dumfries 247 D9
Cairnryan Dumfries 236 C2
Cairnton Orkney 314 F3
Cairston Orkney 314 E2
Caister-on-Sea Norf 161 G10
Caistor Lincs 200 G6
Caistor St Edmund
Norf 142 C4
Caistron Northumb 251 C11
Caitha Bowland
Borders 271 G9
Cakebole Worcs 117 C7
Calais Street Suff 107 D9
Calanais W Isles 304 E4
Calbost W Isles 305 G6
Calbourne I o W 20 D4
Calceby Lincs 190 F5
Calcoed Flint 181 G11
Calcot Glos 81 C9
Calcot W Berks 65 E7
Calcot Row W Berks 65 E7
Calcott Kent 71 G7
Calcott Shrops 149 G8
Calcott's Green Glos 80 B3
Calcutt N Yorks 206 B2
Calcutt Wilts 81 G10
Caldback Shetland 312 C8
Caldbeck Cumb 230 D2
Caldbergh N Yorks 213 B11
Caldecote Cambs 122 F6
Caldecote Cambs 138 F2
Caldecote Herts 104 D4
Caldecote Northants 120 G3
Caldecote Warks 135 E7
Caldecote Hill Herts 85 G11
Caldecott Northants 121 D9
Caldecott Oxon 83 F7
Caldecott Rutland 137 E7
Caldecotte M Keynes 103 D7
Calder Cumb 219 E10
Calder Bridge Cumb 219 D10
Calder Grove W Yorks 197 D10
Calder Hall Cumb 219 E10
Calder Mains Highld 310 D4
Calder Vale Lancs 202 D6
Calderbank N Lnrk 268 C5
Calderbrook Gtr Man 196 D2
Caldercruix N Lnrk 268 B6
Caldermill S Lnrk 268 G3
Caldermoor Gtr Man 196 D2
Calderstones Mers 182 D6
Calderwood S Lnrk 268 D2
Caldhame Angus 287 C8
Caldicot =
Cil-y-coed Mon 60 B3
Caldmore W Mid 133 D10
Caldwell Derbys 152 F5
Caldwell N Yorks 224 C3
Caldy Mers 182 D2
Cale Green Gtr Man 184 D5
Caledrhydiau Ceredig 111 G9
Calenick Corn 4 G6
Caleys Fields Worcs 100 C4
Calf Heath Staffs 133 B8
Calford Green Suff 106 B3
Calfsound Orkney 314 C5
Calgary Argyll 288 D5
Caliach Argyll 288 D5
Califer Moray 301 D10
California Cambs 139 G10
California Falk 279 F8
California Norf 161 G10
California Suff 108 C3
California W Mid 133 G10
Calke Derbys 153 E7
Callakille Highld 298 D6
Callaly Northumb 252 B3
Callander Stirl 285 G10
Callandrode Stirl 285 G10
Callands Warr 183 C9
Callaughton Shrops 132 D2
Callendar Park Falk 279 F7
Callerton T & W 242 D5
Callerton Lane End
T & W 242 D5
Callestick Corn 4 E5
Calligarry Highld 295 E8
Callington Corn 7 B7
Callingwood Staffs 152 E3
Calloose Corn 2 B3
Callop Highld 289 B11
Callow Derbys 170 E3
Callow Hereford 97 E9
Callow End Worcs 98 B6
Callow Hill Mon 79 B8
Callow Hill Som 44 E4
Callow Hill Wilts 62 C4
Callow Hill Worcs 116 C4
Callow Marsh Hereford 98 B3
Callows Grave Worcs 115 D11
Calmore Hants 32 E4
Calmsden Glos 81 D8
Calne Wilts 62 E4
Calne Marsh Wilts 62 E4
Calow Derbys 186 G6
Calow Green Derbys 170 B6
Calrofold E Ches 184 G6
Calshot Hants 33 G7
Calstock Corn 7 B8
Calstone Wellington
Wilts 62 F4
Calthorpe Norf 160 C3
Calthorpe Oxon 101 D9
Calthwaite Cumb 230 C5
Calton Glasgow 268 C2
Calton N Yorks 204 B4
Calton Staffs 169 E10
Calton Lees Derbys 170 B3
Calvadnack Corn 2 B5
Calveley E Ches 167 D9
Calver Derbys 186 G2
Calver Hill Hereford 97 B7
Calver Sough Derbys 186 F2
Calverhall Shrops 150 B2
Calverleigh Devon 26 E6
Calverley W Yorks 205 F10
Calvert Bucks 102 G3
Calverton M Keynes 102 D5
Calverton Notts 171 F10
Calvine Perth 291 G10
Calvo Cumb 238 G4
Cam Glos 80 F3
Camaghael Highld 290 F3
Camas an Staca Argyll 274 G5
Camas-luinie Highld 295 C11
Camas Salach Highld 289 C8
Camasnacroise Highld 289 D10
Camastianavaig Highld 295 B7
Camasunary Highld 295 D7
Camault Muir Highld 300 E5
Camb Shetland 312 D7
Camber E Sus 39 D7
Camberley Sur 65 G11
Camberwell London 67 D10
Camblesforth N Yorks 199 B7
Cambo Northumb 252 F2
Cambois Northumb 253 G8
Camborne Corn 4 G3
Cambourne Cambs 122 F6
Cambridge Borders 271 F11
Cambridge Cambs 123 F9
Cambridge Glos 80 E3
Cambridge W Yorks 205 D10
Cambridge Batch N Som 60 F4
Cambridge Town Sthend 70 C2
Cambrose Corn 4 F3
Cambus Clack 279 C7
Cambusavie Farm
Highld 309 K7
Cambusbarron Stirl 278 C5
Cambusdrenny Stirl 278 C5
Cambuskenneth Stirl 278 C6
Cambuslang S Lnrk 268 D2
Cambusmore Lodge
Highld 309 K7
Cambusnethan N Lnrk 268 D6
Camden London 67 C9
Camden Hill Kent 53 F9
Camden Park Kent 52 F5
Camel Green Dorset 31 E10
Cameley Bath 44 B6
Camelford Corn 11 E8
Camelon Falk 279 E7
Camelsdale Sur 49 G11
Camer Kent 69 F7
Cameron Fife 280 B6
Cameron Bridge Fife 280 B6
Camerory Highld 301 F10
Camer's Green Worcs 98 D5
Camerton Bath 45 B7
Camerton Cumb 228 E6
Camerton E Yorks 201 B8
Camghouran Perth 285 B9
Cammachmore
Aberds 293 D11
Cammeringham Lincs 188 E6
Camnant Powys 113 F11
Camoquhill Stirl 277 D10
Camore Highld 309 K7
Camp Lincs 172 E5
Camp Corner Oxon 83 E10
Camp Hill N Yorks 214 C6
Camp Hill Pembs 73 C10
Camp Hill W Yorks 196 D5
Camp Hill Warks 134 E6
Camp Town W Yorks 206 F2
Campbeltown Argyll 255 E8
Camperdown T & W 243 C7
Camphill Derbys 185 F11
Campion Hills Warks 118 D6
Campions Essex 87 C7
Cample Dumfries 247 E9
Campmuir Perth 286 D6
Camps End Cambs 106 C2
Camps Heath Suff 143 E10
Campsall S Yorks 198 E4
Campsea Ashe Suff 126 F6
Campsey Ash Suff 126 F6
Campsfield Oxon 83 B7
Campton C Beds 104 D2
Camptoun E Loth 281 F10
Camptown Borders 262 G5
Camquhart Argyll 275 E10
Camrose Pembs 91 G8
Camserney Perth 286 C2
Camster Highld 310 E6
Camuschoirk Highld 289 C9
Camuscross Highld 295 D8
Camusnagaul Highld 290 F2
Camusnagaul Highld 307 L5
Camusrory Highld 295 F10
Camusteel Highld 299 E7
Camusterrach Highld 299 E7
Camusvrachan Perth 285 C10
Canada Hants 32 D3
Canada Lincs 200 G6
Canadia E Sus 38 D2
Canal Foot Cumb 210 D6
Canal Side S Yorks 199 E7
Canbus Clack 279 C7
Candacraig Ho Aberds 292 B5
Candle Street Suff 125 C10
Candlesby Lincs 175 B7
Candy Mill S Lnrk 269 G11
Cane End Oxon 65 D7
Caneheath E Sus 23 D9
Canewdon Essex 88 G5
Canford Bottom Dorset 31 G8
Canford Cliffs Poole 19 D7
Canford Heath Poole 18 C6
Canford Magna Poole 18 B6
Cangate Norf 160 F6
Canham's Green Suff 125 D11
Canholes Derbys 185 G8
Canisbay Highld 310 B7
Canklow S Yorks 186 C6
Canley W Mid 118 B6
Cann Dorset 30 C5
Cann Common Dorset 30 C5
Cannalidgey Corn 5 B8
Cannard's Grave Som 44 E6
Cannich Highld 300 F3
Canning Town London 68 C2
Cannington Som 43 F9
Cannock Staffs 133 B9
Cannock Wood Staffs 151 G10
Cannon's Green Essex 87 D9
Cannop Glos 79 C10
Canon Bridge Hereford 97 C8
Canon Frome Hereford 98 C3
Canon Pyon Hereford 97 B9
Canonbie Dumfries 239 B9
Canonbury London 67 C10
Canons Ashby
Northants 119 G11
Canons Park London 85 G11
Canon's Town Corn 2 B2
Canonsgrove Som 28 C2
Canterbury Kent 54 B6
Cantley Norf 143 C7
Cantley S Yorks 198 G6
Cantlop Shrops 131 B10
Canton Cardiff 59 D7
Cantraybruich Highld 301 E7
Cantraydoune Highld 301 E7
Cantraywood Highld 301 E7
Cantsfield Lancs 212 E2
Canvey Island Essex 69 C9
Canwick Lincs 173 B7
Canworthy Water Corn 11 C10
Caol Highld 290 F3
Caol Ila Argyll 274 F5
Caolas Argyll 288 E2
Caolas W Isles 297 M2
Caolas Fhlodaigh
W Isles 296 F4
Caolas Liubharsaigh
W Isles 297 G4
Caolas Scalpaigh
W Isles 305 J4
Caolas Stocinis W Isles 305 J3
Caoslasnacon Highld 290 G3
Capel Carms 75 E8
Capel Kent 52 E6
Capel Sur 51 E7
Capel Bangor Ceredig 128 G3
Capel Betws Lleucu
Ceredig 112 F2
Capel Carmel Gwyn 144 D3
Capel Coch Anglesey 179 E7
Capel Cross Kent 53 E8
Capel Curig Conwy 164 D2
Capel Cynon Ceredig 93 B7
Capel Dewi Carms 93 G9
Capel Dewi Ceredig 93 C9
Capel Dewi Ceredig 128 G2
Capel Garmon Conwy 164 D4
Capel Green Suff 109 B7
Capel-gwyn Anglesey 178 F4
Capel Gwyn Carms 93 G9
Capel Gwynfe Carms 94 G4
Capel Hendre Carms 75 C9
Capel Hermon Gwyn 146 D4
Capel Isaac Carms 93 F11
Capel Iwan Carms 92 D5
Capel-le-Ferne Kent 55 F8
Capel Llanilltern Cardiff 58 C5
Capel Mawr Anglesey 178 G6
Capel Newydd =
Newchapel Pembs 92 D4
Capel Parc Anglesey 178 D6
Capel St Andrew Suff 109 B7
Capel St Mary Suff 107 D11
Capel Seion Carms 75 C8
Capel Seion Ceredig 112 B2
Capel Siloam Conwy 164 E4
Capel Tygwydd Ceredig 92 C5
Capel Uchaf Gwyn 162 F6
Capel-y-ffin Powys 96 E5
Capel-y-graig Gwyn 163 B8
Capelulo Conwy 180 F2
Capenhurst W Ches 182 G5
Capernwray Lancs 211 E10
Capheaton Northumb 252 G2
Capland Som 28 D4
Cappercleuch Borders 260 E6
Cappegill Dumfries 248 B4
Capstone Medway 69 F9
Captain Fold Gtr Man 195 E11
Capton Devon 8 E6
Capton Som 42 F5
Caputh Perth 286 D4
Car Colston Notts 172 G2
Caradon Town Corn 11 G11
Carbis Corn 5 D10
Carbis Bay Corn 2 B2
Carbost Highld 294 B5
Carbost Highld 298 E4
Carbrain N Lnrk 278 G5
Carbrooke Norf 141 C9
Carburton Notts 187 G10
Carcant Borders 271 E7
Carcary Angus 287 B10
Carclaze Corn 5 E10
Carclew Corn 3 B7
Carcroft S Yorks 198 E4
Cardenden Fife 280 C4
Cardeston Shrops 149 G7
Cardew Cumb 230 B2
Cardewlees Cumb 239 G8
Cardiff Cardiff 59 D7
Cardigan = Aberteifi
Ceredig 92 B3
Cardinal's Green
Cambs 106 B2
Cardington Beds 103 B11
Cardington Shrops 131 D10
Cardinham Corn 6 B2
Cardonald Glasgow 267 C10
Cardow Moray 301 E11
Cardrona Borders 261 B8
Cardross Argyll 276 F6
Cardurnock Cumb 238 F5
Care Village Leics 136 D4
Careby Lincs 155 F10
Careston Angus 293 G7
Careston Castle Angus 287 B9
Carew Pembs 73 E8
Carew Cheriton Pembs 73 E8
Carew Newton Pembs 73 E8
Carey Hereford 97 E11
Carey Park Corn 6 E4
Carfin N Lnrk 268 D5
Carfrae E Loth 271 B11
Carfury Corn 1 C4
Cargate Common
Norf 142 E2
Cargenbridge
Dumfries 237 B11
Cargill Perth 286 D5
Cargo Cumb 239 F9
Cargo Fleet M'bro 234 G6
Cargreen Corn 7 C8
Carham Northumb 263 B8
Carhampton Som 42 E4
Carharrack Corn 4 G4
Carie Perth 285 B10
Carie Perth 285 D10
Carines Corn 4 D5
Carisbrooke I o W 20 D5
Cark Cumb 211 D7
Carkeel Corn 7 C8
Carlabhagh W Isles 304 D4
Carland Cross Corn 5 E7
Carlbury N Yorks 224 B4
Carlby Lincs 155 G11
Carlecotes S Yorks 197 G7
Carleen Corn 2 C4
Carlenrig Borders 249 C9
Carlesmoor N Yorks 214 E3
Carleton Cumb 219 D10
Carleton Cumb 230 F6
Carleton Cumb 239 G10
Carleton Lancs 202 F2
Carleton N Yorks 204 D5
Carleton W Yorks 198 C3
Carleton Forehoe
Norf 141 B11
Carleton Hall Cumb 219 F11
Carleton-in-Craven
N Yorks 204 D5
Carleton Rode Norf 142 E2
Carleton St Peter Norf 142 C6
Carley Hill T & W 243 F9
Carlidnack Corn 3 D7
Carlin How Redcar 226 B4
Carlincraig Aberds 302 E6
Carlingcott Bath 45 B7
Carlinghow W Yorks 197 C8
Carlingwark Devon 27 E11
Carlisle Cumb 239 F10
Carloggas Corn 5 B7
Carloggas Corn 5 E9
Carloonan Argyll 284 F4
Carlops Borders 270 D3
Carlton Beds 121 F9
Carlton Cambs 124 G2
Carlton Leics 135 C7
Carlton N Yorks 198 C6
Carlton N Yorks 213 C11
Carlton N Yorks 216 B2
Carlton N Yorks 224 C3
Carlton Notts 171 G10
Carlton S Yorks 197 E11
Carlton Stockton 234 G3
Carlton Suff 127 E7
Carlton W Yorks 197 B10
Carlton Colville Suff 143 F10
Carlton Curlieu Leics 136 D3
Carlton Green Cambs 124 G2
Carlton Husthwaite
N Yorks 215 D9
Carlton in Cleveland
N Yorks 225 E10
Carlton in Lindrick
Notts 187 E9
Carlton le Moorland
Lincs 172 D6
Carlton Miniott N Yorks 215 C7
Carlton on Trent Notts 172 C3
Carlton Purlieus
Northants 136 F6
Carlton Scroop Lincs 172 G6
Carluddon Corn 5 D10
Carluke S Lnrk 268 E6
Carlyon Bay Corn 5 E11
Carmarthen =
Caerfyrddin Carms 93 G8
Carmel Anglesey 178 E5
Carmel Carms 75 B9
Carmel Flint 181 F11
Carmel Gwyn 163 E7
Carmel Powys 113 D11
Carmichael S Lnrk 259 B10
Carminow Cross Corn 5 B11
Carmont Aberds 293 E10
Carmunnock Glasgow 268 D2
Carmyle Glasgow 268 C2
Carmyllie Angus 287 C9
Carn Arthen Corn 2 B5
Carn Brea Village Corn 4 G3
Carn-gorm Highld 295 C11
Carn Towan Corn 1 D3
Carnaby E Yorks 218 F2
Carnach Highld 299 G10
Carnach Highld 307 K5
Carnach W Isles 305 J4
Carnachy Highld 308 D7
Càrnais W Isles 304 E2
Càrnan W Isles 297 G3
Carnbahn Perth 285 C10
Carnbee Fife 287 G9
Carnbo Perth 286 G4
Carnbrea Corn 4 G3
Carnbroe N Lnrk 268 C4
Carndu Highld 295 C10
Carnduff S Lnrk 268 F3
Carnduncan Argyll 274 G3
Carne Corn 3 B10
Carne Corn 3 E7
Carne Corn 5 D9
Carnebone Corn 2 C6
Carnedd Powys 129 E10
Carnetown Rhondda 77 G9
Carnforth Lancs 211 E10
Carnforth Lancs 211 E9
Carnglas Swansea 56 C6

Carnhedryn Pembs 90 F6
Carnhedryn Uchaf Pembs 90 F5
Carnhell Green Corn 2 B4
Carnhot Corn 4 F4
Carnkie Corn 2 B5
Carnkie Corn 2 C6
Carnkief Corn 4 E5
Carno Powys 129 D9
Carnoch Highld 300 D2
Carnoch Highld 300 F3
Carnock Fife 279 D10
Carnon Downs Corn 4 G5
Carnousie Aberds 302 D6
Carnoustie Angus 287 D9
Carnsmerry Corn 5 D10
Carntyne Glasgow 268 B2
Carnwadric E Renf 267 D10
Carnwath S Lnrk 269 F9
Carnyorth Corn 1 C3
Caroe Corn 11 C9
Carol Green W Mid 118 B5
Carpalla Corn 5 E9
Carpenders Park Herts 85 G10
Carpenter's Hill Worcs 117 C11
Carperby N Yorks 213 B10
Carpley Green N Yorks 213 B8
Carr Gtr Man 195 D9
Carr S Yorks 187 C8
Carr Bank Cumb 211 D9
Carr Cross Lancs 193 E11
Carr Gate W Yorks 197 C10
Carr Green Gtr Man 184 D2
Carr Hill T & W 243 E7
Carr Houses Mers 193 G10
Carr Vale Derbys 171 B7
Carradale Argyll 255 D9
Carragraich W Isles 305 J3
Carrbridge Highld 301 G9
Carrbrook Gtr Man 196 G3
Carreg-wen Pembs 92 C4
Carreg y Garth Gwyn 163 B9
Carreglefn Anglesey 178 D5
Carrhouse Devon 26 F3
Carrick Argyll 275 E10
Carrick Dumfries 237 D7
Carrick Fife 287 E8
Carrick Castle Argyll 276 C3
Carrick Ho Orkney 314 C5
Carriden Falk 279 E10
Carrington Gtr Man 184 C2
Carrington Lincs 174 E4
Carrington Midloth 270 C6
Carrington Nottingham 171 G9
Carroch Dumfries 246 E5
Carrog Conwy 164 F3
Carrog Denb 165 G10
Carroglen Perth 285 E11
Carrol Highld 311 J2
Carron Falk 279 E7
Carron Moray 302 E2
Carron Bridge Stirl 278 E4
Carronbridge Dumfries 247 D9
Carronshore Falk 279 E7
Carrot Angus 287 C8
Carrow Hill Mon 78 G6
Carroway Head Staffs 134 D3
Carrshield Northumb 232 B2
Carrutherstown Dumfries 238 C4
Carrville Durham 234 C2
Carry Argyll 275 G10
Carsaig Argyll 275 E8
Carsaig Argyll 289 G7
Carscreugh Dumfries 236 D4
Carse Gray Angus 287 B8
Carse Ho Argyll 275 G8
Carsegowan Dumfries 236 D6
Carseriggan Dumfries 236 C5
Carsethorn Dumfries 237 D11
Carshalton London 67 G9
Carshalton Beeches London 67 G9
Carshalton on the Hill London 67 G9
Carsington Derbys 170 E3
Carskiey Argyll 255 G7
Carsluith Dumfries 236 D6
Carsphairn Dumfries 246 E3
Carstairs S Lnrk 269 F8
Carstairs Junction S Lnrk 269 F9
Carswell Marsh Oxon 82 F4
Cartbridge Sur 50 B4
Carter Knowle S Yorks 186 E4
Carterhaugh Borders 261 D10
Carter's Clay Hants 32 C4
Carter's Green Essex 87 C8
Carter's Hill Wokingham 65 F9
Carterspiece Glos 79 C9
Carterton Oxon 82 D3
Carterway Heads Northumb 242 G2
Carthamartha Corn 12 F3
Carthew Corn 2 B5
Carthew Corn 5 D10
Carthorpe N Yorks 214 C6
Cartington Northumb 252 C2
Cartland S Lnrk 269 F7
Cartledge Derbys 186 F4
Cartmel Cumb 211 D7
Cartmel Fell Cumb 211 B8
Cartsdyke Invclyd 276 F5
Cartworth W Yorks 196 F6
Carty Port Dumfries 236 C6
Carway Carms 75 D7
Carwinley Cumb 239 C10
Carwynnen Corn 2 B5
Cary Fitzpaine Som 29 B9
Carzantic Corn 12 E3
Carzield Dumfries 247 G11
Carzise Corn 2 C3
Cas Mael = Puncheston Pembs 91 F10
Cascob Powys 114 D4
Cashes Green Glos 80 D4
Cashlie Perth 285 C8
Cashmoor Dorset 31 E7
Cassey Compton Glos 81 C9
Cassington Oxon 83 C7
Cassop Durham 234 D2
Castallack Corn 1 D5
Castell Conwy 164 B3
Castell Denb 165 B10
Castell-Howell Ceredig 93 B8
Castell nedd = Neath Neath 57 B8
Castell Newydd Emlyn = Newcastle Emlyn Carms 92 C6
Castell-y-bwch Torf 78 G3
Castell-y-rhingyll Carms 75 C9
Castellau Rhondda 58 B5
Casterton Cumb 212 D2
Castle Devon 28 G4
Castle Som 27 B9
Castle Acre Norf 158 F6
Castle Ashby Northants 121 F7
Castle Bolton N Yorks 223 G10
Castle Bromwich W Mid 134 F2
Castle Bytham Lincs 155 F9
Castle Caereinion Powys 130 B3
Castle Camps Cambs 106 C2
Castle Carlton Lincs 190 E5
Castle Carrock Cumb 240 F2
Castle Cary Som 44 G6
Castle Combe Wilts 61 D10
Castle Donington Leics 153 D8
Castle Douglas Dumfries 237 C9
Castle Eaton Swindon 81 F10
Castle Eden Durham 234 D4
Castle End P'boro 138 B2
Castle Fields Shrops 149 G10
Castle Forbes Aberds 293 B8
Castle Frome Hereford 98 B3
Castle Gate Corn 1 C5
Castle Green London 68 C3
Castle Green S Yorks 197 G9
Castle Green Sur 66 G3
Castle Gresley Derbys 152 F5
Castle Heaton Northumb 273 G8
Castle Hedingham Essex 106 D5
Castle Hill E Sus 37 B9
Castle Hill Gtr Man 184 C6
Castle Hill Kent 53 E7
Castle Hill Suff 108 B3
Castle Hill Worcs 116 F5
Castle Huntly Perth 287 E7
Castle Kennedy Dumfries 236 D3
Castle O'er Dumfries 248 E6
Castle Rising Norf 158 E3
Castle Street W Yorks 196 C3
Castle Stuart Highld 301 E7
Castle Toward Argyll 266 B2
Castle Town W Sus 36 E2
Castle-upon-Alun V Glam 58 E2
Castle Vale W Mid 134 E2
Castlebythe Pembs 91 F10
Castlecary N Lnrk 278 F5
Castlecraig Borders 270 G2
Castlecraig Highld 301 C8
Castlecroft Staffs 133 D7
Castlefairn Dumfries 246 F6
Castlefields Halton 183 E8
Castleford W Yorks 198 B2
Castlegreen Shrops 130 F6
Castlehead Renfs 267 C9
Castlehill Argyll 254 B4
Castlehill Borders 260 B6
Castlehill Highld 310 C5
Castlehill S Ayrs 257 E9
Castlehill W Dunb 277 F7
Castlemaddy Dumfries 246 F3
Castlemartin Pembs 72 F6
Castlemilk Dumfries 238 B5
Castlemilk Glasgow 268 D2
Castlemorris Pembs 91 E8
Castlemorton Worcs 98 D5
Castlerigg Cumb 229 G11
Castleside Durham 233 B7
Castlethorpe M Keynes 102 C6
Castlethorpe N Lincs 200 F3
Castleton Angus 287 C7
Castleton Argyll 275 E9
Castleton Derbys 185 E11
Castleton Gtr Man 195 E11
Castleton Moray 301 G11
Castleton N Yorks 226 D3
Castleton Newport 59 C9
Castleton Village Highld 300 E6
Castletown Cumb 230 E6
Castletown Dorset 17 G9
Castletown Highld 301 E7
Castletown Highld 310 C5
Castletown I o M 192 F3
Castletown Staffs 151 E8
Castletown T & W 243 F9
Castletown W Ches 166 E6
Castletump Glos 98 F4
Castleweary Borders 249 C10
Castlewigg Dumfries 236 E6
Castley N Yorks 205 D11
Castling's Heath Suff 107 C9
Caston Norf 141 D9
Castor P'boro 138 D2
Caswell Swansea 56 D5
Cat Bank Cumb 220 F6
Cat Hill S Yorks 197 F8
Catacol N Ayrs 255 C10
Catbrain S Glos 60 C5
Catbrook Mon 79 E8
Catchall Corn 1 D4
Catchems Corner W Mid 118 B4
Catchems End Worcs 116 B5
Catchgate Durham 242 G5
Catchory Highld 310 D6
Catcleugh Northumb 250 C6
Catcliffe S Yorks 186 D6
Catcomb Wilts 62 D4
Catcott Som 43 F11
Caterham Sur 51 B10
Catfield Norf 161 E7
Catfirth Shetland 313 H6
Catford London 67 E11
Catforth Lancs 202 F5
Cathays Cardiff 59 D7
Cathays Park Cardiff 59 D7
Cathcart Glasgow 267 C11
Cathedine Powys 96 F2
Catherine-de-Barnes W Mid 134 G3
Catherine Slack W Yorks 196 B5
Catherington Hants 33 E11
Catherton Shrops 116 B3
Cathiron Warks 119 B9
Catholes Cumb 222 G3
Cathpair Borders 271 F9
Catisfield Hants 33 F8
Catley Lane Head Gtr Man 195 D11
Catley Southfield Hereford 98 C3
Catlodge Highld 291 D8
Catlowdy Cumb 239 B11
Catmere End Essex 105 D9
Catmore W Berks 64 C3
Caton Devon 13 G11
Caton Lancs 211 G10
Caton Green Lancs 211 F10
Catrine E Ayrs 258 D2
Cat's Ash Newport 78 G5
Cat's Common Norf 160 E6
Cats Edge Staffs 169 E7
Cat's Hill Cross Staffs 150 C6
Catsfield E Sus 38 E2
Catsfield Stream E Sus 38 E2
Catsgore Som 29 B8
Catsham Som 44 G5
Catshaw S Yorks 197 G8
Catshill W Mid 133 B11
Catshill Worcs 117 C9
Castlackburn Borders 261 D8
Catslip Oxon 65 B8
Catstree Shrops 132 D4
Cattadale Argyll 274 G4
Cattal N Yorks 206 C4
Cattawade Suff 108 E2
Cattedown Plym 7 E9
Catterall Lancs 202 E5
Catterick N Yorks 224 F4
Catterick Bridge N Yorks 224 F4
Catterick Garrison N Yorks 224 F3
Catterlen Cumb 230 E5
Catterline Aberds 293 F10
Catterton N Yorks 206 D6
Catteshall Sur 50 E3
Catthorpe Leics 119 B11
Cattistock Dorset 17 B7
Cattle End Northants 102 C3
Catton N Yorks 215 D7
Catton Northumb 241 F8
Catwick E Yorks 209 D8
Catworth Cambs 121 C11
Caudle Green Glos 80 C6
Caudlesprings Norf 141 C8
Caulcott C Beds 103 C9
Caulcott Oxon 101 G10
Cauld Borders 261 G11
Cauldcoats Holdings Falk 279 F10
Cauldcots Angus 287 C10
Cauldhame Stirl 278 C2
Cauldmill Borders 262 G2
Cauldon Staffs 169 F9
Cauldon Lowe Staffs 169 F9
Cauldwells Aberds 303 D7
Caulkerbush Dumfries 237 D11
Caulside Dumfries 249 G10
Caundle Marsh Dorset 29 E11
Caunsall Worcs 132 G6
Caunton Notts 172 D2
Causeway Hants 33 E11
Causeway Hants 34 C2
Causeway Mon 60 B2
Causeway End Cumb 210 C6
Causeway End Cumb 211 B9
Causeway End Dumfries 236 C6
Causeway End Essex 87 B11
Causeway End Wilts 62 C4
Causeway Foot W Yorks 197 E7
Causeway Foot W Yorks 205 G7
Causeway Green W Mid 133 F9
Causewayend S Lnrk 260 B2
Causewayhead Cumb 238 G4
Causewayhead Stirl 278 B6
Causewaywood Shrops 131 D10
Causey Durham 242 F6
Causey Park Bridge Northumb 252 E5
Causeyend Aberds 293 B11
Causeyton Aberds 293 B8
Caute Devon 24 E6
Cautley Cumb 222 G3
Cavendish Suff 106 B6
Cavendish Bridge Leics 153 D8
Cavenham Suff 124 D5
Cavers Carre Borders 262 D3
Caversfield Oxon 101 F11
Caversham Reading 65 E8
Caversham Heights Reading 65 D8
Caverswall Staffs 169 G7
Cavil E Yorks 207 G11
Cawdor Highld 301 D8
Cawkeld E Yorks 208 C5
Cawkwell Lincs 190 F3
Cawood N Yorks 207 F7
Cawsand Corn 7 E8
Cawston Norf 160 E2
Cawston Warks 119 C9
Cawthorne N Yorks 216 B5
Cawthorne S Yorks 197 F9
Cawthorpe Lincs 155 E11
Cawton N Yorks 216 D2
Caxton Cambs 122 F6
Caynham Shrops 115 C11
Caythorpe Lincs 172 F6
Caythorpe Notts 171 F11
Cayton N Yorks 217 C11
Ceallan W Isles 296 F4
Ceann a Bhàigh W Isles 305 J4
Ceann a Bhaigh W Isles 296 E3
Ceann a Deas Loch Baghasdail W Isles 297 K3
Ceann Shiphoirt W Isles 305 G4
Ceann Tarabhaigh W Isles 305 G4
Ceannacroc Lodge Highld 290 B4
Cearsiadair W Isles 304 F5
Ceathramh Meadhanach W Isles 296 D4
Cefn Newport 59 B9
Cefn Powys 148 G5
Cefn Berain Conwy 165 B7
Cefn-brith Conwy 164 E6
Cefn-bryn-brain Carms 76 C2
Cefn-bychan Swansea 56 B4
Cefn-bychan Wrex 166 G3
Cefn Canol Powys 148 C4
Cefn-coch Conwy 164 B5
Cefn Coch Powys 129 C10
Cefn Coch Powys 148 D2
Cefn-coed-y-cymmer M Tydf 77 D8
Cefn Cribbwr Bridgend 57 E11
Cefn Cross Bridgend 57 E11
Cefn-ddwysarn Gwyn 147 B9
Cefn Einion Shrops 130 F5
Cefn-eurgain Flint 166 B2
Cefn Fforest Caerph 77 F11
Cefn Glas Bridgend 57 E11
Cefn Golau Bl Gwent 77 D10
Cefn-gorwydd Powys 95 B8
Cefn Hengoed Caerph 77 F10
Cefn-hengoed Swansea 57 B7
Cefn Llwyd Ceredig 128 G2
Cefn-mawr Wrex 166 G3
Cefn Rhigos Rhondda 76 D6
Cefn-y-bedd Flint 166 D4
Cefn-y-Crib Torf 78 F2
Cefn-y-Garth Swansea 76 E2
Cefn-y-pant Carms 92 F3
Cefncaeau Carms 56 B4
Cefneithin Carms 75 C9
Cefnpennar Rhondda 77 E8
Cegidfa = Guilsfield Powys 148 G4
Cei-bach Ceredig 111 F8
Ceinewydd = New Quay Ceredig 111 F7
Ceint Anglesey 179 F7
Ceinws Powys 128 B5
Cellan Ceredig 94 B2
Cellarhead Staffs 169 F7
Cellarhill Kent 70 G3
Celyn-Mali Flint 165 B11
Cemaes Anglesey 178 C5
Cemmaes Powys 128 B6
Cemmaes Road = Glantwymyn Powys 128 C6
Cenarth Carms 92 C5
Cenin Gwyn 163 F7
Central Invclyd 276 F5
Central Milton Keynes M Keynes 102 D6
Ceos W Isles 304 F5
Ceres Fife 287 F8
Ceri = Kerry Powys 130 F2
Cerne Abbas Dorset 29 G11
Cerney Wick Glos 81 F9
Cerrig Llwydion Neath 57 C9
Cerrig-mân Anglesey 179 C7
Cerrigceinwen Anglesey 178 G6
Cerrigydrudion Conwy 165 F7
Cess Norf 161 F8
Cessford Borders 262 E6
Ceunant Gwyn 163 C8
Chaceley Glos 99 E7
Chaceley Hole Glos 98 E6
Chaceley Stock Glos 99 F7
Chacewater Corn 4 G4
Chackmore Bucks 102 D3
Chacombe Northants 101 C9
Chad Valley W Mid 133 F10
Chadbury Worcs 99 B10
Chadderton Gtr Man 196 F2
Chadderton Fold Gtr Man 195 F11
Chaddesden Derby 153 B7
Chaddesley Corbett Worcs 117 C7
Chaddlehanger Devon 12 F5
Chaddlewood Plym 7 D11
Chaddleworth W Berks 64 D2
Chadkirk Gtr Man 184 D6
Chadlington Oxon 100 G6
Chadshunt Warks 118 G6
Chadsmoor Staffs 151 G9
Chadstone Northants 121 F7
Chadwell Leics 154 E5
Chadwell Shrops 150 G5
Chadwell End Beds 121 D11
Chadwell Heath London 68 B3
Chadwell St Mary Thurrock 68 D6
Chadwick Worcs 116 D6
Chadwick End W Mid 118 C4
Chadwick Green Mers 183 B8
Chaffcombe Som 28 E5
Chafford Hundred Thurrock 68 D5
Chagford Devon 13 D10
Chailey E Sus 36 D5
Chain Bridge Lincs 174 G4
Chainbridge Cambs 139 C8
Chainhurst Kent 53 D8
Chalbury Dorset 31 F8
Chalbury Common Dorset 31 F8
Chaldon Sur 51 B10
Chaldon Herring or East Chaldon Dorset 17 E11
Chale I o W 20 F5
Chale Green I o W 20 F5
Chalfont Common Bucks 85 G8
Chalfont Grove Bucks 85 G7
Chalfont St Giles Bucks 85 G7
Chalfont St Peter Bucks 85 G8
Chalford Glos 80 E5
Chalford Oxon 84 E2
Chalford Wilts 45 C11
Chalford Hill Glos 80 E5
Chalgrave C Beds 103 F10
Chalgrove Oxon 83 F10
Chalk Kent 69 E7
Chalk End Essex 87 C10
Chalkfoot Cumb 230 B2
Chalkhill Norf 141 C7
Chalkhouse Green Oxon 65 D8
Chalkshire Bucks 84 D4
Chalksole Kent 55 E9
Chalkway Som 28 F5
Chalkwell Kent 69 G11
Chalkwell Sthend 69 B11
Challaborough Devon 8 G3
Challacombe Devon 41 E7
Challister Shetland 312 G7
Challoch Dumfries 236 C5
Challock Kent 54 C4
Chalmington Dorset 29 G9
Chalton C Beds 103 F10
Chalton Hants 34 D2
Chalvedon Essex 69 B8
Chalvey Slough 66 D3
Chalvington E Sus 23 D8
Chambercombe Devon 40 D4
Chamber's Green Kent 54 E2
Champson Devon 26 B4
Chance Inn Fife 287 F7
Chancery = Rhydgaled Ceredig 111 B11
Chance's Pitch Hereford 98 C4
Chandler's Cross Herts 85 F9
Chandler's Cross Worcs 98 D5
Chandler's Ford Hants 32 C6
Chandlers Green Hants 49 B8
Channel Tunnel Kent 55 F7
Channel's End Beds 122 F2
Channerwick Shetland 313 L6
Chantry Devon 25 C9
Chantry Som 45 D8
Chantry Suff 108 C2
Chapel Corn 4 C6
Chapel Cumb 229 E10
Chapel Fife 280 C5
Chapel Allerton Som 44 C2
Chapel Allerton W Yorks 206 F2
Chapel Amble Corn 10 F5
Chapel Brampton Northants 120 D4
Chapel Chorlton Staffs 150 B6
Chapel Cleeve Som 42 E4
Chapel Cross E Sus 37 C10
Chapel-en-le-Frith Derbys 185 E9
Chapel End Beds 103 B11
Chapel End Beds 122 F2
Chapel End C Beds 103 C11
Chapel End Cambs 138 G2
Chapel End E Ches 167 G11
Chapel End Essex 105 G11
Chapel End Northants 138 F2
Chapel End Warks 134 E6
Chapel Field Gtr Man 195 F9
Chapel Field Norf 161 E7
Chapel Fields W Mid 118 B6
Chapel Fields York 207 C7
Chapel Green Herts 104 D6
Chapel Green Warks 119 E9
Chapel Green Warks 134 F5
Chapel Haddlesey N Yorks 198 B5
Chapel Head Cambs 138 G6
Chapel Hill Aberds 303 F10
Chapel Hill Glos 79 E10
Chapel Hill Lincs 174 E2
Chapel Hill Mon 79 F8
Chapel Hill N Yorks 206 D2
Chapel House Lancs 194 F3
Chapel Knapp Wilts 61 F11
Chapel Lawn Shrops 114 B6
Chapel-le-Dale N Yorks 212 D4
Chapel Leigh Som 27 B10
Chapel Mains Borders 271 G11
Chapel Milton Derbys 185 E9
Chapel of Garioch Aberds 303 G7
Chapel of Stoneywood Aberdeen 293 B10
Chapel on Leader Borders 271 G11
Chapel Outon Dumfries 236 E6
Chapel Plaister Wilts 61 F10
Chapel Row E Sus 23 C10
Chapel Row Essex 88 E3
Chapel Row W Berks 64 F5
Chapel St Leonards Lincs 191 G9
Chapel Stile Cumb 220 D6
Chapel Town Corn 5 D7
Chapelgate Lincs 157 E8
Chapelhall N Lnrk 268 C5
Chapelhill Dumfries 248 E3
Chapelhill Highld 301 B8
Chapelhill N Ayrs 266 G4
Chapelhill Perth 286 D4
Chapelhill Perth 286 E3
Chapelhill Perth 286 E6
Chapelknowe Dumfries 239 C8
Chapels Blkburn 195 C7
Chapels Cumb 210 C4
Chapelthorpe W Yorks 197 D10
Chapelton Angus 287 C10
Chapelton Devon 25 B9
Chapelton Highld 291 B11
Chapelton S Lnrk 268 F3
Chapelton Row Dumfries 237 E8
Chapeltown Blkburn 195 D8
Chapeltown Moray 302 G2
Chapeltown S Yorks 186 B5
Chapeltown W Yorks 206 F2
Chapman's Hill Worcs 117 B9
Chapman's Town E Sus 23 B10
Chapmans Well Devon 12 C3
Chapmanslade Wilts 45 D10
Chapmore End Herts 86 B4
Chappel Essex 107 F7
Charaton Cross Corn 6 B6
Charcott Kent 52 D4
Chard Som 28 F4
Chard Junction Dorset 28 G4
Chardleigh Green Som 28 E4
Chardstock Devon 28 G4
Charfield S Glos 80 G2
Charfield Green S Glos 80 G2
Charfield Hill S Glos 80 G2
Charford Worcs 117 D9
Chargrove Glos 80 B6
Charing Kent 54 D3
Charing Cross Dorset 31 E10
Charing Heath Kent 54 D2
Charing Hill Kent 54 C3
Charingworth Glos 100 D4
Charlbury Oxon 82 B5
Charlcombe Bath 61 F8
Charlcutt Wilts 62 D3
Charlecote Warks 118 F5
Charlemont W Mid 133 E10
Charles Devon 41 G7
Charles Bottom Devon 41 G7
Charles Tye Suff 125 G10
Charlesfield Borders 262 D3
Charlesfield Dumfries 238 D5
Charleshill Sur 49 E11
Charleston Angus 287 C7
Charleston Renfs 267 C9
Charlestown Aberdeen 293 C11
Charlestown Corn 5 E10
Charlestown Derbys 185 C8
Charlestown Dorset 17 F9
Charlestown Fife 279 E11
Charlestown Gtr Man 195 G10
Charlestown Gtr Man 195 G11
Charlestown Highld 299 B8
Charlestown Highld 300 E6
Charlestown W Yorks 196 B3
Charlestown W Yorks 205 F9
Charlestown of Aberlour Moray 302 E2
Charlesworth Derbys 185 C8
Charleton Devon 8 G5
Charlinch Som 43 F8
Charlottetown Fife 286 F6
Charlton Hants 47 D11
Charlton Herts 104 F3
Charlton London 68 D2
Charlton Northants 101 D10
Charlton Northumb 251 F8
Charlton Oxon 64 B2
Charlton Redcar 226 B2
Charlton Som 28 B3
Charlton Som 44 E6
Charlton Som 45 C7
Charlton Sur 66 F5
Charlton Telford 149 G11
Charlton W Sus 34 E5
Charlton Wilts 30 C6
Charlton Wilts 46 B6
Charlton Wilts 62 B3
Charlton Worcs 99 B10
Charlton Worcs 116 C6
Charlton Abbots Glos 99 G10
Charlton Adam Som 29 B8
Charlton-All-Saints Wilts 31 C11
Charlton Down Dorset 17 C9
Charlton Horethorne Som 29 C11
Charlton Kings Glos 99 G9
Charlton Mackrell Som 29 B8
Charlton Marshall Dorset 30 G5
Charlton Musgrove Som 30 B2
Charlton on Otmoor Oxon 83 B9
Charlton on the Hill Dorset 30 G5
Charlton Park Glos 99 G9
Charlton St Peter Wilts 46 B6
Charltonbrook S Yorks 186 B4
Charlwood E Sus 51 G11
Charlwood Hants 49 G7
Charlwood Sur 51 E8
Charlynch Som 43 F8
Charminster Bmouth 19 C8
Charminster Dorset 17 C9
Charmouth Dorset 16 C3
Charnage Wilts 45 G10
Charndon Bucks 102 G3
Charnes Staffs 150 C5
Charney Bassett Oxon 82 G5
Charnock Green Lancs 194 D5
Charnock Hall S Yorks 186 E5
Charnock Richard Lancs 194 D5
Charsfield Suff 126 F5
Chart Corner Kent 53 C9
Chart Hill Kent 53 D9
Chart Sutton Kent 53 D10
Charter Alley Hants 48 B5
Charterhouse Som 44 B3
Chartershall Stirl 278 C6
Charterville Allotments Oxon 82 C4
Chartham Kent 54 C6
Chartham Hatch Kent 54 B6
Chartridge Bucks 84 E6
Charvil Wokingham 65 D9
Charwelton Northants 119 F10
Chase Cross London 87 G8
Chase End Street Worcs 98 D5
Chase Hill S Glos 61 B8
Chase Terrace Staffs 133 B10
Chasetown Staffs 133 B10
Chastleton Oxon 100 F4
Chasty Devon 24 G4
Chat Hill W Yorks 205 G8
Chatburn Lancs 203 E11
Chatcull Staffs 150 C5
Chatford Shrops 131 B9
Chatham Caerph 59 B8
Chatham Medway 69 F9
Chatham Green Essex 88 B2
Chathill Northumb 264 D5
Chatley Worcs 117 E7
Chattenden Medway 69 E9
Chatter End Essex 105 F9
Chatteris Cambs 139 F7
Chatterley Staffs 168 E4
Chattern Hill Sur 66 E5
Chatterton Lancs 195 D9
Chattisham Suff 107 C11
Chattle Hill Warks 134 E3
Chatto Borders 263 F7
Chatton Northumb 264 D3
Chaul End C Beds 103 G11
Chaulden Herts 85 D8
Chavel Shrops 149 G8
Chavenage Green Glos 80 F5
Chavey Down Brack 65 F11
Chawleigh Devon 26 E2
Chawley Oxon 83 E7
Chawson Worcs 117 E7
Chawston Beds 122 F3
Chawton Hants 49 F8
Chaxhill Glos 80 C2
Chazey Heath Oxon 65 D7
Cheadle Gtr Man 184 D5
Cheadle Staffs 169 G8
Cheadle Heath Gtr Man 184 D5
Cheadle Hulme Gtr Man 184 D5
Cheadle Park Staffs 169 G8
Cheam London 67 G8
Cheapside Herts 105 E8
Cheapside Sur 50 B4
Cheapside Windsor 66 F2
Chearsley Bucks 84 C2
Chebsey Staffs 151 D7
Checkendon Oxon 65 C7
Checkley E Ches 168 F2
Checkley Hereford 97 D11
Checkley Staffs 151 B10
Checkley Green E Ches 168 F2
Chedburgh Suff 124 F5
Cheddar Som 44 C3
Cheddington Bucks 84 B6
Cheddleton Staffs 169 E7
Cheddleton Heath Staffs 169 E7
Cheddon Fitzpaine Som 28 B2
Chedglow Wilts 80 G6
Chedgrave Norf 143 D7
Chedington Dorset 29 F7
Chediston Suff 127 B7
Chediston Green Suff 127 B7
Chedworth Glos 81 C9
Chedworth Laines Glos 81 C8
Chedzoy Som 43 F10
Cheeklaw Borders 272 E5
Cheeseman's Green Kent 54 F4
Cheetam Hill Gtr Man 195 G10
Cheglinch Devon 40 E4
Chegworth Kent 53 C10
Cheldon Devon 26 E2
Chelfham Devon 40 F6
Chelford E Ches 184 G4
Chell Heath Stoke 168 E5
Chellaston Derby 153 C7
Chellington Beds 121 F9
Chells Herts 104 F5
Chelmarsh Shrops 132 F4
Chelmer Village Essex 88 D2
Chelmick Shrops 131 E9
Chelmondiston Suff 108 D4
Chelmorton Derbys 169 B10
Chelmsford Essex 88 D2
Chelmsine Som 27 D11
Chelmsley Wood W Mid 134 F3
Chelsea London 67 D9
Chelsfield London 68 G3
Chelsham Sur 51 B11
Chelston Som 27 C11
Chelston Torbay 9 C7
Chelston Heathfield Som 27 C11
Chelsworth Suff 107 B9
Chelsworth Common Suff 107 B9
Cheltenham Glos 99 G8
Chelveston Northants 121 D9
Chelvey N Som 60 F3
Chelvey Batch N Som 60 F3
Chelwood Bath 60 G6
Chelwood Common E Sus 36 B6
Chelwood Gate E Sus 36 B6
Chelworth Wilts 81 G7
Chelworth Lower Green Wilts 81 G9
Chelworth Upper Green Wilts 81 G9
Chelynch Som 45 E7
Chemistry Shrops 167 G8
Cheney Longville Shrops 131 G8
Chenhalls Corn 2 B3
Chenies Bucks 85 F8
Cheny Longville Shrops 131 F8
Chepstow Mon 79 G8
Chequerbent Gtr Man 195 F7
Chequerfield W Yorks 198 C3
Chequers Corner Norf 139 B9
Chequertree Kent 54 F4
Cherhill Wilts 62 E4
Cherington Glos 80 F6
Cherington Warks 100 D5
Cheristow Devon 24 B3
Cheriton Devon 41 D8
Cheriton Hants 33 B9
Cheriton Kent 55 F7
Cheriton Swansea 56 C3
Cheriton Bishop Devon 13 C11
Cheriton Cross Devon 13 C11
Cheriton Fitzpaine Devon 26 F5
Cheriton or Stackpole Elidor Pembs 73 F7
Cherrington Telford 150 E3
Cherry Burton E Yorks 208 E5
Cherry Green Essex 105 F11
Cherry Green Herts 105 F7
Cherry Hinton Cambs 123 F9
Cherry Orchard Shrops 149 G9
Cherry Orchard Worcs 117 G7
Cherry Tree Blkburn 195 B7
Cherry Tree Gtr Man 185 C7
Cherry Willingham Lincs 189 G8
Cherrybank Perth 286 E5
Cherrytree Hill Derby 153 B7
Chertsey Sur 66 F4
Chertsey Meads Sur 66 F5
Cheselbourne Dorset 17 B11
Chesham Bucks 85 E7
Chesham Gtr Man 195 E10
Chesham Bois Bucks 85 F7
Cheshunt Herts 86 E5
Chesley Kent 69 G11
Cheslyn Hay Staffs 133 B9
Chessetts Wood Warks 118 C3
Chessington London 67 G7
Chessmount Bucks 85 E7
Chestall Staffs 151 G11
Chester W Ches 166 B6
Chester-le-Street Durham 243 G7
Chester Moor Durham 233 B11
Chesterblade Som 45 E7
Chesterfield Derbys 186 G5
Chesterfield Staffs 134 B2
Chesterhill Midloth 271 B7
Chesterhope Northumb 251 F9
Chesterknowes Borders 262 D2
Chesters Borders 262 E4
Chesters Borders 262 G4
Chesterton Cambs 123 E9
Chesterton Cambs 138 D2
Chesterton Glos 81 E8
Chesterton Oxon 101 G11
Chesterton Shrops 132 D5
Chesterton Staffs 168 F4
Chesterton Warks 118 F6
Chesterton Green Warks 118 F6
Chesterwood Northumb 241 D8
Chestfield Kent 70 F6
Chestnut Hill Cumb 229 G11
Chestnut Street Kent 69 G11
Cheston Devon 8 D3
Cheswardine Shrops 150 D4
Cheswell Telford 150 F4
Cheswick Northumb 273 F10
Cheswick Buildings Northumb 273 F10
Cheswick Green W Mid 118 B2
Chetnole Dorset 29 F10
Chettiscombe Devon 27 E7
Chettisham Cambs 139 G10
Chettle Dorset 31 E7
Chetton Shrops 132 E3
Chetwode Bucks 102 F2
Chetwynd Aston Telford 150 F5
Cheveley Cambs 124 E3
Chevening Kent 52 B3
Cheverell's Green Herts 85 B9
Chevin End W Yorks 205 E9
Chevington Suff 124 F5
Chevithorne Devon 27 D7
Chew Magna Bath 60 G5
Chew Moor Gtr Man 195 F7
Chew Stoke Bath 60 G5
Chewton Keynsham Bath 61 F7
Chewton Mendip Som 44 C5
Cheylesmore W Mid 118 B6
Chichacott Devon 13 B8
Chicheley M Keynes 103 B8
Chichester W Sus 22 C5
Chickenley W Yorks 197 C9
Chickerell Dorset 17 E8
Chicklade Wilts 46 G2
Chickney Essex 105 F11
Chicksands C Beds 104 D2
Chicksgrove Wilts 46 G3
Chickward Hereford 114 G5
Chidden Hants 33 D11
Chiddingfold Sur 50 F3
Chiddingly E Sus 23 C8
Chiddingstone Kent 52 D3
Chiddingstone Causeway Kent 52 D4
Chiddingstone Hoath Kent 52 E3
Chideock Dorset 16 C4
Chidgley Som 42 F4
Chidham W Sus 22 C3
Chidswell W Yorks 197 C9
Chieveley W Berks 64 E3
Chignall St James Essex 87 D11
Chignall Smealy Essex 87 C11
Chigwell Essex 86 G6
Chigwell Row Essex 87 G7
Chilbolton Hants 47 F11
Chilbolton Down Hants 48 F2
Chilbridge Dorset 31 G7
Chilcomb Hants 33 B8
Chilcombe Dorset 16 C6
Chilcombe Som 42 F6
Chilcompton Som 44 C6
Chilcote Leics 152 G5
Child Okeford Dorset 30 E4
Childer Thornton W Ches 182 F5
Childerditch Essex 68 B6
Childerley Gate Cambs 123 F7
Childrey Oxon 63 B11
Child's Ercall Shrops 150 E3
Child's Hill London 67 B8
Childsbridge Kent 52 B5
Childswickham Worcs 99 D11
Childwall Mers 182 D6
Childwick Bury Herts 85 C10
Childwick Green Herts 85 C10
Chilfrome Dorset 17 B7
Chilgrove W Sus 34 E4
Chilham Kent 54 C5
Chillaton Devon 12 E4
Chillenden Kent 55 C9
Chillerton I o W 20 E5
Chillesford Suff 127 G7
Chillingham Northumb 264 D3
Chillington Devon 8 G5
Chillington Som 28 E5
Chillmill Kent 53 E7
Chilmark Wilts 46 G3
Chilmington Green Kent 54 E3
Chilsham E Sus 23 C10
Chilson Oxon 82 B4
Chilson Som 2
Chilson Common Som 2
Chilsworthy Corn 1
Chilsworthy Devon 2
Chiltern Green Beds 8
Chilthorne Domer Som 2
Chiltington E Sus 3
Chilton Bucks 8
Chilton Durham 23
Chilton Kent 7
Chilton Oxon 6
Chilton Suff 10
Chilton Candover Hants 4
Chilton Cantelo Som 2
Chilton Foliat Wilts 6
Chilton Lane Durham 23
Chilton Moor T & W 23
Chilton Polden Som 4
Chilton Street Suff 10
Chilton Trinity Som 4
Chilvers Coton Warks 13
Chilwell Notts 15
Chilworth Hants 3
Chilworth Sur 5
Chilworth Old Village Hants 3
Chimney Oxon 8
Chimney-end Oxon 8
Chimney Street Suff 10
Chineham Hants 4
Chingford London 8
Chingford Green London 8
Chingford Hatch London 8
Chinley Derbys 18
Chinley Head Derbys 18
Chinnor Oxon 8
Chipley Som 2
Chipmans Platt Glos 8
Chipnall Shrops 15
Chippenhall Green Suff 12
Chippenham Cambs 12
Chippenham Wilts 6
Chipperfield Herts 8
Chipping Herts 10
Chipping Lancs 20
Chipping Barnet London 8
Chipping Campden Glos 10
Chipping Hill Essex 8
Chipping Norton Oxon 10
Chipping Ongar Essex 8
Chipping Sodbury S Glos 6
Chipping Warden Northants 10
Chipstable Som 2
Chipstead Kent 5
Chipstead Sur 5
Chirbury Shrops 13
Chirk = Y Waun Wrex 14
Chirk Bank Shrops 14
Chirk Green Wrex 14
Chirmorrie S Ayrs 23
Chirnside Borders 27
Chirnsidebridge Borders 27
Chirton T & W 24
Chirton Wilts 4
Chisbridge Cross Bucks 6
Chisbury Wilts 6
Chiselborough Som 2
Chiseldon Swindon 6
Chiserley W Yorks 19
Chislehampton Oxon 8
Chislehurst London 6
Chislehurst West London 6
Chislet Kent 7
Chislet Forstal Kent 7
Chiswell Dorset 1
Chiswell Green Herts 8
Chiswick London 6
Chiswick End Cambs 10
Chisworth Derbys 18
Chitcombe E Sus 3
Chithurst W Sus 3
Chittering Cambs 12
Chitterley Devon 2
Chitterne Wilts 4
Chittlehamholt Devon 2
Chittlehampton Devon 2
Chittoe Wilts 6
Chitts Hills Essex 10
Chitty Kent 7
Chivelstone Devon 9
Chivenor Devon 4
Chivery Bucks 8
Chobham Sur 6
Choicelee Borders 27
Cholderton Wilts 4
Cholesbury Bucks 8
Chollerford Northumb 241
Chollerton Northumb 241
Cholmondeston E Ches 167
Cholsey Oxon 6
Cholstrey Hereford 11
Cholwell Bath 4
Chop Gate N Yorks 225
Choppington Northumb 25
Chopwell T & W 24
Chorley E Ches 16
Chorley Lancs 19
Chorley Shrops 13
Chorley Staffs 151
Chorley Common W Sus 3
Chorleywood Herts 8
Chorleywood Bottom Herts 8
Chorleywood West Herts 8
Chorlton E Ches 16
Chorlton-cum-Hardy Gtr Man 18
Chorlton Lane W Ches 16
Choulton Shrops 13
Chowdene T & W 24
Chowley W Ches 16
Chownes Mead W Sus 3
Chreagain Highld 289
Chrishall Essex 10
Christchurch Cambs 13
Christchurch Dorset 1
Christchurch Glos 7
Christchurch Newport 59
Christian Malford Wilts 6
Christleton W Ches 16
Christmas Common Oxon 8
Christon N Som 43
Christon Bank Northumb 26
Christow Devon 1
Chryston N Lnrk 27
Chub Tor Devon 7
Chuck Hatch E Sus 5
Chudleigh Devon 1
Chudleigh Knighton Devon 1
Chulmleigh Devon 25

al Derbys 185 C8
ch Lancs 195 B8
ch Aston Telford 150 F4
ch Brampton
hants 120 D4
ch Brough Cumb 222 C5
ch Broughton
ys 152 C4
ch Charwelton
hants 119 F10
ch Clough Lancs 204 F3
ch Common
s 34 B2
ch Coombe Corn 4 G3
ch Cove Corn 2 G6
ch Crookham
s 49 C10
ch Eaton Staffs 150 F6
ch End Barnet 86 G2
ch End Beds 122 F2
ch End Bucks 84 B6
ch End Bucks 84 D2
ch End Brent 67 C8
ch End C Beds 85 B8
ch End C Beds 103 E9
ch End C Beds 103 G9
ch End C Beds 104 D3
ch End C Beds 122 G3
ch End Cambs 121 C11
ch End Cambs 123 C7
ch End Cambs 123 D7
ch End Cambs 138 G4
ch End Cambs 139 B7
ch End E Yorks 209 C7
ch End Essex 88 B2
ch End Essex 105 C11
ch End Essex 105 F11
ch End Essex 106 F4
ch End Glos 80 D2
ch End Glos 99 D7
ch End Hants 49 B7
ch End Herts 85 C10
ch End Herts 85 F8
ch End Herts 104 E5
ch End Herts 105 G8
ch End Lincs 156 C4
ch End Lincs 190 B6
ch End Norf 157 F10
ch End Oxon 82 D5
ch End Oxon 100 E6
ch End Suff 108 D4
ch End Sur 50 B5
ch End W Mid 119 B7
ch End Warks 134 E4
ch End Warks 134 E5
ch End Wilts 62 D4
ch End Worcs 98 C6
nch Enstone Oxon 101 G7
ch Fenton N Yorks 206 E6
ch Green Devon 15 B9
ch Green Norf 141 E11
ch Gresley Derbys 152 F5
ch Hanborough
n 82 C6
ch Hill Pembs 73 C7
ch Hill Staffs 151 G10
ch Hill W Ches 167 C10
ch Hill W Mid 133 D9
ch Hill Worcs 117 D11
ch Hougham Kent 55 E9
ch Houses N Yorks 226 F3
ch Knowle Dorset 18 E4
ch Laneham
s 188 F4
ch Langton Leics 136 E4
ch Lawford Warks 119 B8
ch Lawton E Ches 168 D4
ch Leigh Staffs 151 B10
ch Lench Worcs 117 G10
ch Mayfield
s 169 G11
ch Minshull
es 167 C11
ch Norton W Sus 22 D5
ch Oakley Hants 48 C5
ch Preen Shrops 131 D10
ch Pulverbatch
ps 131 C8
ch Stowe
hants 120 F2
ch Street Essex 106 C5
ch Street Kent 69 E8
ch Stretton
ps 131 E9
ch Town Corn 4 G3
ch Town Leics 153 F7
ch Town N Lincs 199 F9
ch Town Sur 51 C11
ch Village Rhondda 58 B5
ch Warsop Notts 171 B9
ch Westcote Glos 100 G4
ch Whitfield Kent 55 D10
ch Wilne Derbys 153 C8
cham Glos 80 B3
chbank Shrops 114 B6
chbridge Corn 6 D4
chbridge Staffs 133 B9
chdown Glos 80 B5
chend Essex 89 G8
chend Essex 106 G2
chend Glos 80 D3
chend Reading 65 E7
chend S Glos 80 G3
ches Green E Sus 23 B10
chfield Hereford 98 B4
chfield W Mid 133 E10
chfields Wilts 31 B10
chgate Herts 86 E4
chgate Street
ex 87 C7
chill Devon 28 G4
chill Devon 40 E5
chill N Som 44 B2
chill Oxon 100 G5
chill Worcs 117 B7
chill Worcs 117 G8
chill Green N Som 60 G2
chinford Som 28 E2
chmoor Rough
ps 131 F8
chover Warks 135 G10
chstanton Som 27 E11
chstoke Powys 130 E5
chstow Devon 8 F4
chton Pembs 73 D10
chtown Corn 11 F7
chtown Cumb 230 C3
chtown Derbys 170 C3
chtown Devon 24 G3
chtown Devon 41 E7
chtown I o M 192 C5
chtown Lancs 202 E5
chtown Mers 193 D11
chtown Shrops 130 F5
chtown Som 42 F3
chwood W Sus 35 D8
rnet Grange Staffs 169 E7
rnsike Lodge
thumb 240 B5
rscombe Torbay 9 C7
rston Ferrers Torbay 9 D8
rt Sur 49 F11

Churton W Ches 166 D6
Churwell W Yorks 197 B9
Chute Cadley Wilts 47 C10
Chute Standen Wilts 47 C10
Chwefforrdd Conwy 180 G4
Chwilog Gwyn 145 B8
Chwitffordd = Whitford Flint 181 F10
Chyandour Corn 1 C5
Chyanvounder Corn 2 E5
Chycoose Corn 3 B8
Chynhale Corn 2 C4
Chynoweth Corn 2 C2
Chyvarloe Corn 2 E5
Cicelyford Mon 79 E8
Cil y coed = Caldicot Mon 60 B3
Cilan Uchaf Gwyn 144 E5
Cilau Pembs 91 D8
Cilcain Flint 165 B11
Cilcennin Ceredig 111 E10
Cilcewydd Powys 130 C4
Cilfor Gwyn 146 B2
Cilfrew Neath 76 E3
Cilfynydd Rhondda 77 G9
Cilgerran Pembs 92 C3
Cilgwyn Carms 94 F4
Cilgwyn Ceredig 92 C6
Cilgwyn Gwyn 163 E7
Cilgwyn Pembs 91 D11
Ciliau Aeron Ceredig 111 F9
Cill Amhlaidh W Isles 297 G3
Cill Donnain W Isles 297 J3
Cill Eireabhagh W Isles 297 G4
Cille Bhrighde W Isles 297 K3
Cille Pheadair W Isles 297 K3
Cilmaengwyn Neath 76 D2
Cilmery Powys 113 G10
Cilsan Carms 93 G11
Ciltalgarth Gwyn 164 G5
Ciltwrch Powys 96 C3
Cilybebyll Neath 76 E2
Cilycwm Carms 94 D5
Cimla Neath 57 B9
Cinder Hill Gtr Man 195 F9
Cinder Hill Kent 52 D4
Cinder Hill W Mid 133 E8
Cinder Hill W Sus 36 B5
Cinderford Glos 79 C11
Cinderhill Derbys 170 F5
Cinderhill Nottingham 171 G8
Cinnamon Brow Warr 183 C10
Cippenham Slough 66 C2
Cippyn Pembs 92 B2
Circebost W Isles 304 E3
Cirencester Glos 81 E8
Ciribhig W Isles 304 D3
City London 67 C10
City Powys 130 F4
City V Glam 58 D3
City Dulas Anglesey 179 D7
Clabhach Argyll 288 D3
Clachaig Argyll 276 E2
Clachaig Highld 292 B2
Clachaig N Ayrs 255 E10
Clachan Argyll 255 B8
Clachan Argyll 275 B8
Clachan Argyll 284 F5
Clachan Argyll 289 E10
Clachan Highld 295 B7
Clachan Highld 298 C4
Clachan Highld 307 L6
Clachan W Isles 297 G3
Clachan na Luib W Isles 296 E4
Clachan of Campsie E Dunb 278 F2
Clachan of Glendaruel Argyll 275 E10
Clachan-Seil Argyll 275 B8
Clachan Strachur Argyll 284 G4
Clachaneasy Dumfries 236 B5
Clachanmore Dumfries 236 E2
Clachbreck Argyll 275 F8
Clachnabrain Angus 292 G5
Clachtoll Highld 307 G5
Clackmannan Clack 279 C8
Clackmarras Moray 302 D2
Clacton-on-Sea Essex 89 B11
Cladach N Ayrs 256 B2
Cladach Chairinis W Isles 296 F4
Cladach Chireboist W Isles 296 E3
Claddach Argyll 254 B2
Claddach-knockline W Isles 296 E3
Cladich Argyll 284 E4
Cladich Steading Argyll 284 E4
Cladswell Worcs 117 F10
Claggan Highld 289 E8
Claggan Highld 290 F3
Claggan Perth 285 D11
Claigan Highld 298 D2
Claines Worcs 117 F7
Clandown Bath 45 B7
Clanfield Hants 33 D11
Clanfield Oxon 82 E3
Clanking Bucks 84 D4
Clanville Hants 47 D10
Clanville Som 44 G6
Clanville Wilts 62 D2
Claonaig Argyll 255 B9
Claonel Highld 309 J5
Clap Hill Kent 54 F5
Clapgate Dorset 31 G8
Clapgate Herts 105 G8
Clapham Beds 121 G10
Clapham Devon 14 D3
Clapham London 67 D9
Clapham N Yorks 212 F4
Clapham W Sus 35 F9
Clapham Green Beds 121 G10
Clapham Green N Yorks 205 B10
Clapham Hill Kent 70 G6
Clapham Park London 67 E9
Clapper Corn 10 G6
Clapper Hill Kent 53 F10
Clappers Borders 273 D8
Clappersgate Cumb 221 E7
Clapphoull Shetland 313 L6
Clapton Som 28 F6
Clapton Som 44 C6
Clapton W Berks 63 E11
Clapton in Gordano N Som 60 E3
Clapton-on-the-Hill Glos 81 B11
Clapton Park London 67 B11
Clapworthy Devon 25 C11
Clara Vale T & W 242 E4
Clarach Ceredig 128 G2
Clarack Aberds 292 D6
Clarbeston Pembs 91 G10
Clarbeston Road Pembs 91 G10
Clarborough Notts 188 E2
Clardon Highld 310 C5
Clare Oxon 83 F11
Clare Suff 106 B5

Clarebrand Dumfries 237 C9
Claregate W Mid 133 C7
Claremont Park Sur 66 G6
Claremount W Yorks 196 B5
Clarence Park N Som 59 G10
Clarencefield Dumfries 238 D3
Clarendon Park Leicester 135 C11
Clareston Pembs 73 C7
Clarilaw Borders 262 D3
Clarilaw Borders 262 F2
Clark Green E Ches 184 F6
Clarken Green Hants 48 C5
Clark's Green Sur 51 F7
Clark's Hill Lincs 157 E7
Clarksfield Gtr Man 196 G2
Clarkston E Renf 267 D11
Clarkston N Lnrk 268 B5
Clase Swansea 57 B7
Clashandorran Highld 300 E5
Clashcoig Highld 309 K6
Clasheddy Highld 308 C6
Clashgour Argyll 284 C6
Clashindarroch Aberds 302 F4
Clashmore Highld 306 F5
Clashmore Highld 309 L7
Clashnessie Highld 306 F5
Clashnoir Moray 302 G2
Clate Shetland 313 G7
Clatford Wilts 63 F7
Clatford Oakcuts Hants 47 F10
Clathy Perth 286 F3
Clatt Aberds 302 G5
Clatter Powys 129 E9
Clatterford I o W 20 D5
Clatterford End Essex 87 C10
Clatterford End Essex 87 D9
Clatterford End Essex 87 E8
Clatterin Bridge Aberds 293 F8
Clatto Fife 287 F8
Clatworthy Som 42 G5
Claughton Lancs 202 E6
Claughton Lancs 211 F11
Claughton Mers 182 D4
Clavelshay Som 43 G9
Claverdon Warks 118 E3
Claverham N Som 60 F2
Claverhambury Essex 86 E6
Clavering Essex 105 E9
Claverley Shrops 132 E5
Claverton Bath 61 G9
Claverton Down Bath 61 G9
Clawdd-côch V Glam 58 D5
Clawdd-newydd Denb 165 E9
Clawdd Poncen Denb 165 G9
Clawthorpe Cumb 211 D10
Clawton Devon 12 B3
Claxby Lincs 189 C10
Claxby Lincs 191 G7
Claxby St Andrew Lincs 191 G7
Claxton N Yorks 216 G3
Claxton Norf 142 C6
Clay Common Suff 143 G9
Clay Coton Northants 119 B11
Clay Cross Derbys 170 C5
Clay End Herts 104 F6
Clay Hill Bristol 60 E6
Clay Hill London 86 F4
Clay Hill W Berks 64 E5
Clay Lake Lincs 156 E5
Clay Mills Derbys 152 D5
Claybokie Aberds 292 D2
Claybrooke Magna Leics 135 F9
Claybrooke Parva Leics 135 F9
Claydon Glos 99 E8
Claydon Oxon 119 G9
Claydon Suff 126 G2
Claygate Dumfries 239 B9
Claygate Kent 52 C6
Claygate Kent 53 E8
Claygate Sur 67 G7
Claygate Cross Kent 52 B6
Clayhall Hants 21 B8
Clayhall London 86 G6
Clayhanger Devon 27 C8
Clayhanger Som 28 E4
Clayhanger W Mid 133 C10
Clayhidon Devon 27 D11
Clayhill E Sus 38 C4
Clayhill Hants 32 F4
Clayhithe Cambs 123 E10
Clayholes Angus 287 D9
Clayland Stirl 277 D11
Claylock Highld 310 D5
Claypit Hill Cambs 123 G7
Claypits Devon 27 B7
Claypits Glos 80 D3
Claypits Kent 55 B9
Claypits Suff 140 G4
Claypole Lincs 172 F5
Clays End Bath 61 G8
Claythorpe Lincs 190 F6
Clayton Gtr Man 184 B5
Clayton S Yorks 198 F3
Clayton Staffs 168 G5
Clayton W Sus 36 E3
Clayton W Yorks 205 G8
Clayton Brook Lancs 194 C5
Clayton Green Lancs 194 C5
Clayton Heights W Yorks 205 G8
Clayton-le-Dale Lancs 203 G9
Clayton-le-Moors Lancs 203 G10
Clayton-le-Woods Lancs 194 C5
Clayton West W Yorks 197 E9
Clayworth Notts 188 D2
Cleadale Highld 294 G6
Cleadon T & W 243 E9
Cleadon Park T & W 243 E9
Clearbrook Devon 7 B10
Clearwell Glos 79 D9
Clearwell Newport 59 B9
Clearwood Wilts 45 D10
Cleasby N Yorks 224 C5
Cleat Orkney 314 B4
Cleat Orkney 314 H4
Cleatlam Durham 224 B2
Cleator Cumb 219 C10
Cleator Moor Cumb 219 B10
Cleave Devon 28 G2
Clebrig Highld 308 F5
Cleckheaton W Yorks 197 B7
Cleddon Mon 79 E8
Clee St Margaret Shrops 131 G11
Cleedownton Shrops 131 G11
Cleehill Shrops 115 B11
Cleekhimin N Lnrk 268 D5
Cleemarsh Shrops 131 G11
Cleestanton Shrops 115 B11
Cleethorpes NE Lincs 201 F10
Cleeton St Mary Shrops 116 B2
Cleeve Glos 80 C2
Cleeve N Som 60 F3
Cleeve Oxon 64 C6
Cleeve Hill Glos 99 F9
Cleeve Prior Worcs 99 B11

Cleghorn S Lnrk 269 F8
Clegyrnant Powys 129 B8
Clehonger Hereford 97 D9
Cleirwy = Clyro Powys 96 C4
Cleish Perth 279 B11
Cleland N Lnrk 268 D5
Clement Street Kent 68 E4
Clement's End C Beds 85 B8
Clements End Glos 79 D9
Clench Wilts 63 G7
Clench Common Wilts 63 F7
Clencher's Mill Hereford 98 D4
Clenchwarton Norf 157 E11
Clennell Northumb 251 B10
Clent Worcs 117 B8
Cleobury Mortimer Shrops 116 B3
Cleobury North Shrops 132 F2
Cleongart Argyll 255 D7
Clephanton Highld 301 D8
Clerk Green W Yorks 197 C8
Clerkenwater Corn 5 B11
Clerkenwell London 67 C10
Clerklands Borders 262 E2
Clermiston Edin 280 G3
Clestrain Orkney 314 F3
Cleuch Head Borders 262 G3
Cleughbrae Dumfries 238 C3
Clevancy Wilts 62 D5
Clevans Renfs 267 B7
Clevedon N Som 60 E2
Cleveley Oxon 101 G7
Cleveleys Lancs 202 E2
Cleverton Wilts 62 B3
Clevis Bridgend 57 F10
Clewer Som 44 C2
Clewer Green Windsor 66 D2
Clewer New Town Windsor 66 D3
Clewer Village Windsor 66 D3
Cley next the Sea Norf 177 E8
Cliaid W Isles 297 L2
Cliasmol W Isles 305 H2
Cliburn Cumb 231 G7
Click Mill Orkney 314 D3
Cliddesden Hants 48 D6
Cliff Derbys 185 D8
Cliff Warks 134 D4
Cliff End E Sus 38 E5
Cliff End W Yorks 196 D6
Cliffburn Angus 287 C10
Cliffe Lancs 203 G10
Cliffe Medway 69 D8
Cliffe N Yorks 207 G9
Cliffe N Yorks 224 B4
Cliffe Woods Medway 69 E8
Clifford Devon 24 C4
Clifford Hereford 96 B4
Clifford W Yorks 206 E4
Clifford Chambers Warks 118 G3
Clifford's Mesne Glos 98 G4
Cliffs End Kent 71 G10
Clifftown Sthend 69 B11
Clifton Bristol 60 E5
Clifton C Beds 104 D3
Clifton Cumb 230 F6
Clifton Derbys 169 G11
Clifton Devon 40 E5
Clifton Gtr Man 195 G9
Clifton Lancs 202 G5
Clifton N Yorks 205 D9
Clifton Northumb 252 G6
Clifton Nottingham 153 C11
Clifton Oxon 101 E9
Clifton S Yorks 186 C6
Clifton S Yorks 187 B8
Clifton Stirl 285 D7
Clifton W Ches 183 F8
Clifton W Yorks 197 C7
Clifton Worcs 98 B6
Clifton York 207 C7
Clifton Campville Staffs 152 G5
Clifton Green Gtr Man 195 G9
Clifton Hampden Oxon 83 F8
Clifton Junction Gtr Man 195 G9
Clifton Manor C Beds 104 D3
Clifton Maybank Dorset 29 E9
Clifton Moor York 207 B7
Clifton Reynes M Keynes 121 G8
Clifton upon Dunsmore Warks 119 B10
Clifton upon Teme Worcs 116 E4
Cliftoncote Borders 263 E8
Cliftonville Kent 71 E11
Cliftonville N Lnrk 268 B4
Cliftonville Norf 160 B6
Climping W Sus 35 G8
Climpy S Lnrk 269 D8
Clink Som 45 D9
Clinkham Wood Mers 183 B8
Clint N Yorks 205 B11
Clint Green Norf 159 G10
Clintmains Borders 262 C4
Clints N Yorks 224 E2
Cliobh W Isles 304 E2
Clipiau Gwyn 146 G6
Clippesby Norf 161 G8
Clippings Green Norf 159 G10
Clipsham Rutland 155 F9
Clipston Northants 136 G4
Clipston Notts 154 C2
Clipstone C Beds 103 F8
Clitheroe Lancs 203 E10
Cliuthar W Isles 305 J3
Clive Shrops 149 E10
Clive W Ches 167 B11
Clive Green W Ches 167 C11
Clive Vale E Sus 38 E4
Clivocast Shetland 312 C8
Clixby Lincs 200 G6
Cloatley Wilts 81 G7
Cloatley End Wilts 81 G7
Clocaenog Denb 165 E9
Clochan Aberds 303 E9
Clochan Moray 302 C4
Clock Face Mers 183 C8
Clock House London 67 G9
Clock Mills Hereford 96 B5
Clockmill Borders 272 E5
Cloddiau Powys 130 B4
Cloddymoss Moray 301 D9
Clodock Hereford 96 F6
Cloford Som 45 E8
Cloford Common Som 45 E8
Cloigyn Carms 74 C6
Clola Aberds 303 E10
Clophill C Beds 103 D11
Clopton Northants 137 G11
Clopton Suff 126 G4
Clopton Corner Suff 126 G4
Clopton Green Suff 124 G5
Clopton Green Suff 125 E9
Close Clark I o M 192 E3
Close House Durham 233 F10
Closeburn Dumfries 247 E9
Closworth Som 29 E9
Clothall Herts 104 E5
Clothall Common Herts 104 E5
Clotton W Ches 167 C8

Clotton Common W Ches 167 C8
Cloud Side Staffs 168 C6
Cloudesley Bush Warks 135 F9
Clouds Hereford 97 D11
Clough Gtr Man 196 D2
Clough Gtr Man 196 F2
Clough W Yorks 196 E5
Clough Dene Durham 242 F5
Clough Foot W Yorks 196 C2
Clough Hall Staffs 168 E4
Clough Head W Yorks 196 C5
Cloughfold Lancs 195 C10
Cloughton N Yorks 227 G10
Cloughton Newlands N Yorks 227 F10
Clounlaid Highld 289 D9
Clousta Shetland 313 H5
Clouston Orkney 314 E2
Clova Aberds 302 G4
Clova Angus 292 F5
Clove Lodge Durham 223 B8
Clovelly Devon 24 C4
Clovenfords Borders 261 B10
Clovenstone Aberds 293 B9
Cloves Moray 301 C11
Clovullin Highld 290 G2
Clow Bridge Lancs 195 B10
Clowance Wood Corn 2 C4
Clowne Derbys 187 F7
Clows Top Worcs 116 C4
Cloy Wrex 166 G5
Cluanie Inn Highld 290 B2
Cluanie Lodge Highld 290 B2
Clubmoor Mers 182 C5
Clubworthy Corn 11 C11
Cluddley Telford 150 G2
Clun Shrops 130 G6
Clunbury Shrops 131 G7
Clunderwen Carms 73 B10
Clune Highld 301 D9
Clune Highld 301 G7
Clunes Highld 290 E4
Clungunford Shrops 115 B7
Clunie Aberds 302 D6
Clunie Perth 286 C5
Clunton Shrops 130 G6
Cluny Fife 280 B4
Cluny Castle Aberds 293 B8
Cluny Castle Highld 291 D8
Clutton Bath 44 B6
Clutton W Ches 167 E7
Clutton Hill Bath 44 B6
Clwt-grugoer Conwy 165 C7
Clwt-y-bont Gwyn 163 C9
Clwydyfagwyr M Tydf 77 D8
Clydach Mon 78 C2
Clydach Swansea 75 E11
Clydach Terrace Powys 77 C11
Clydach Vale Rhondda 77 G7
Clydebank W Dunb 277 G9
Clyffe Pypard Wilts 62 D5
Clynder Argyll 276 E4
Clyne Neath 76 E4
Clynelish Highld 311 J2
Clynnog-fawr Gwyn 162 F6
Clyro = Cleirwy Powys 96 C4
Clyst Honiton Devon 14 C5
Clyst Hydon Devon 27 G8
Clyst St George Devon 14 D5
Clyst St Lawrence Devon 27 G8
Clyst St Mary Devon 14 C5
Cnip W Isles 304 E2
Cnoc Amhlaigh W Isles 304 E7
Cnoc an t-Solais W Isles 304 D6
Cnoc Fhionn Highld 295 D10
Cnoc Màiri W Isles 304 E6
Cnoc Rolum W Isles 296 F3
Cnocbreac Argyll 274 F5
Cnwch-coch Ceredig 112 B3
Coachford Aberds 302 E4
Coad's Green Corn 11 F11
Coal Aston Derbys 186 F5
Coal Bank Darl 234 G3
Coal Pool W Mid 133 C10
Coalbrookdale Telford 132 C3
Coalbrookvale Bl Gwent 77 D11
Coalburn S Lnrk 259 C8
Coalburns T & W 242 E4
Coalcleugh Northumb 232 B2
Coaley Glos 80 E3
Coaley Peak Glos 80 E3
Coalford Aberds 293 D10
Coalhall E Ayrs 257 F10
Coalhill Essex 88 F3
Coalmoor Telford 132 B3
Coalpit Field Warks 135 F7
Coalpit Heath S Glos 61 C7
Coalpit Hill Staffs 168 E4
Coalport Telford 132 C3
Coalsnaughton Clack 279 B8
Coaltown of Balgonie Fife 280 B5
Coaltown of Wemyss Fife 280 B6
Coalville Leics 153 G8
Coalway Glos 79 C9
Coanwood Northumb 240 F5
Coarsewell Devon 8 E4
Coat Som 29 C7
Coatbridge N Lnrk 268 C4
Coatdyke N Lnrk 268 C5
Coate Swindon 63 C7
Coate Wilts 62 G4
Coates Cambs 138 D6
Coates Glos 81 E7
Coates Lancs 204 D3
Coates Lincs 188 E6
Coates Midloth 270 C4
Coates Notts 188 E4
Coates W Sus 35 D7
Coatham Redcar 235 F7
Coatham Mundeville Darl 233 G11
Coatsgate Dumfries 248 B3
Cobairdy Aberds 302 E5
Cobbaton Devon 25 B10
Cobbler's Corner Worcs 116 F5
Cobbler's Green Norf 142 E5
Cobbler's Plain Mon 79 E7
Cobbs Warr 183 D10
Cobb's Cross Glos 98 E5
Cobbs Fenn Essex 106 E5
Cobby Syke N Yorks 205 B9
Coberley Glos 81 B7
Cobhall Common Hereford 97 D9
Cobham Kent 69 F7
Cobham Sur 66 G6
Cobleland Stirl 277 B10
Cobler's Green Essex 87 B11
Cobley Dorset 31 C8
Cobley Hill Worcs 117 C10
Cobnash Hereford 115 E9
Cobridge Stoke 168 F5
Cobscot Shrops 150 B3
Coburty Aberds 303 C9

Cock and End Suff 124 G4
Cock Alley Derbys 186 G6
Cock Bank Wrex 166 F5
Cock Bevington Warks 117 G11
Cock Bridge Aberds 292 C4
Cock Clarks Essex 88 E4
Cock Gate Hereford 115 D9
Cock Green Essex 87 B11
Cock Hill N Yorks 206 B6
Cock Marling E Sus 38 D5
Cock Street Kent 53 C9
Cock Street Suff 107 D9
Cockadilly Glos 80 E4
Cockayne N Yorks 226 F2
Cockburnspath Borders 282 G5
Cockden Lancs 204 G3
Cockenzie and Port Seton E Loth 281 F8
Cocker Bar Lancs 194 C4
Cockerham Lancs 202 C5
Cockermouth Cumb 229 E8
Cockernhoe Herts 104 G2
Cockernhoe Green Herts 104 G2
Cockersdale W Yorks 197 B8
Cockerton Darl 224 B5
Cockett Swansea 56 C6
Cocketty Aberds 293 F9
Cockfield Durham 233 G8
Cockfield Suff 125 G8
Cockfosters London 86 F3
Cockhill Som 44 G6
Cocking W Sus 34 D5
Cocking Causeway W Sus 34 D5
Cockington Torbay 9 C7
Cocklake Som 44 D2
Cocklaw Northumb 241 C10
Cockleford Glos 81 C7
Cockley Beck Cumb 220 E4
Cockley Cley Norf 140 C5
Cockley Hill W Yorks 197 D7
Cocknowle Dorset 18 E4
Cockpole Green Wokingham 65 C9
Cocks Corn 4 E5
Cocks Green Suff 125 F7
Cockshead Ceredig 112 F2
Cockshoot Hereford 97 D11
Cockshutford Shrops 131 F11
Cockshutt Shrops 132 G4
Cockshutt Shrops 149 D8
Cockthorpe Norf 177 E7
Cockwells Corn 2 C2
Cockwood Devon 14 E5
Cockwood Som 43 E8
Cockyard Derbys 185 F8
Cockyard Hereford 97 E8
Codda Corn 11 F9
Coddenham Suff 126 G2
Coddenham Green Suff 126 F2
Coddington Hereford 98 C4
Coddington Notts 172 E4
Coddington W Ches 167 D7
Codford St Mary Wilts 46 F3
Codford St Peter Wilts 46 F3
Codicote Herts 86 B2
Codicote Bottom Herts 86 B2
Codmore Bucks 85 E7
Codmore Hill W Sus 35 C9
Codnor Derbys 170 F6
Codnor Breach Derbys 170 F6
Codnor Gate Derbys 170 E6
Codnor Park Derbys 170 E6
Codrington S Glos 61 D8
Codsall Staffs 133 C7
Codsall Wood Staffs 132 B6
Codsend Som 41 F11
Coed Cwnwr Mon 78 F6
Coed Eva Torf 78 G3
Coed Llai = Leeswood Flint 166 D3
Coed Mawr Gwyn 179 G9
Coed Morgan Mon 78 C5
Coed-Talon Flint 166 D3
Coed-y-bryn Ceredig 93 C7
Coed-y-caerau Newport 78 G5
Coed-y-fedw Mon 78 D6
Coed y Garth Ceredig 128 E3
Coed y go Shrops 148 D5
Coed-y-paen Mon 78 F4
Coed-y-parc Gwyn 163 B10
Coed-y-wlad Powys 130 B4
Coed-yr-ynys Powys 96 G3
Coed Ystumgwern Gwyn 145 E11
Coedcae Bl Gwent 77 D11
Coedcae Torf 78 D3
Coedely Rhondda 58 B4
Coedkernew Newport 59 C9
Coedpoeth Wrex 166 E3
Coedway Powys 148 G6
Coelbren Powys 76 C4
Coffee Hall M Keynes 103 D7
Coffinswell Devon 9 B7
Cofton Devon 14 E5
Cofton Common W Mid 117 B10
Cofton Hackett Worcs 117 B10
Cog V Glam 59 F7
Cogan V Glam 59 E7
Cogenhoe Northants 120 E6
Cogges Oxon 82 D5
Coggeshall Essex 106 G6
Coggeshall Hamlet Essex 107 G7
Coggins Mill E Sus 37 B9
Coig Peighinnean W Isles 304 B7
Coig Peighinnean Bhuirgh W Isles 304 C6
Coignafearn Lodge Highld 291 B8
Coignascallan Highld 291 B9
Coilacriech Aberds 292 D5
Coilantogle Stirl 285 G9
Coilessan Argyll 284 G6
Coilleag W Isles 297 K3
Coillemore Highld 300 B6
Coillore Highld 294 B5
Coirea-chrombe Stirl 285 G9
Coisley Hill S Yorks 186 E6
Coity Bridgend 58 C2
Cokenach Herts 105 D7
Cokhay Green Derbys 152 D5
Col W Isles 304 D6
Col Uarach W Isles 304 E6
Colaboll Highld 309 H5
Colan Corn 5 C7
Colaton Raleigh Devon 15 D7
Colbost Highld 298 E2
Colburn N Yorks 224 F3
Colby Cumb 231 G9
Colby I o M 192 E3
Colby Norf 160 C4
Colchester Essex 107 F10
Colchester Green Suff 125 F8
Colcot V Glam 58 F6
Cold Ash W Berks 64 F4
Cold Ash Hill Hants 49 G10
Cold Ashby Northants 120 B3

Cold Ashton S Glos 61 E9
Cold Aston Glos 81 B10
Cold Blow Pembs 73 C10
Cold Brayfield M Keynes 121 G8
Cold Christmas Herts 86 B5
Cold Cotes N Yorks 212 E4
Cold Elm Glos 98 E6
Cold Hanworth Lincs 189 E8
Cold Harbour Dorset 18 D4
Cold Harbour Herts 85 B10
Cold Harbour Kent 69 G11
Cold Harbour Lincs 155 C9
Cold Harbour Oxon 64 D6
Cold Harbour Wilts 45 B11
Cold Harbour Wilts 45 D11
Cold Harbour Windsor 65 D10
Cold Hatton Telford 150 E2
Cold Hatton Heath Telford 150 E2
Cold Hesledon Durham 234 B4
Cold Hiendley W Yorks 197 E11
Cold Higham Northants 120 G3
Cold Inn Pembs 73 D10
Cold Kirby N Yorks 215 C10
Cold Moss Heath E Ches 168 C3
Cold Newton Leics 136 B4
Cold Northcott Corn 11 D10
Cold Norton Essex 88 E4
Cold Overton Leics 154 G6
Cold Row Lancs 202 E3
Cold Well Staffs 151 G11
Coldbackie Highld 308 D6
Coldbeck Cumb 222 E4
Coldblow London 68 E4
Coldbrook Powys 96 D3
Coldean Brighton 36 F4
Coldeast Devon 14 G2
Coldeaton Derbys 169 D10
Colden W Yorks 196 B3
Colden Common Hants 33 C7
Coldfair Green Suff 127 E8
Coldham Cambs 139 C8
Coldham Staffs 133 B7
Coldham's Common Cambs 123 F9
Coldharbour Corn 4 F5
Coldharbour Devon 27 E9
Coldharbour Dorset 17 E9
Coldharbour Glos 79 E9
Coldharbour Kent 52 C5
Coldharbour London 68 D4
Coldharbour Sur 50 E6
Coldingham Borders 273 B8
Coldmeece Staffs 151 C7
Coldoch Stirl 278 B3
Coldra Newport 59 B11
Coldrain Perth 286 G4
Coldred Kent 55 D9
Coldridge Devon 25 F11
Coldstream Angus 287 D7
Coldstream Borders 263 B8
Coldvreath Corn 5 D9
Coldwaltham W Sus 35 D8
Coldwells Aberds 303 E11
Coldwells Croft Aberds 302 G5
Cole Som 45 G7
Cole End Essex 105 D11
Cole End Warks 134 F3
Cole Green Herts 86 C3
Cole Green Herts 105 E8
Cole Henley Hants 48 C3
Cole Park London 67 E7
Colebatch Shrops 130 F6
Colebrook Devon 27 F8
Colebrooke Devon 13 B11
Coleburn Moray 302 D2
Coleby Lincs 173 C7
Coleby N Lincs 199 D11
Coleford Devon 26 G3
Coleford Glos 79 C9
Coleford Som 45 D7
Coleford Water Som 42 G6
Colegate End Norf 142 F3
Colehall W Mid 134 F2
Colehill Dorset 31 G8
Coleman Green Herts 85 C11
Coleman's Hatch E Sus 52 G3
Colemere Shrops 149 C8
Colemore Hants 49 G8
Colemore Green Shrops 132 D4
Coleorton Leics 153 F8
Coleorton Moor Leics 153 F8
Colerne Wilts 61 E10
Cole's Cross Dorset 28 G5
Coles Green Suff 107 C11
Cole's Green Suff 126 E5
Coles Green Worcs 116 G5
Coles Meads Sur 51 C9
Colesbourne Glos 81 C7
Colesbrook Dorset 30 B4
Colesden Beds 122 F2
Coleshill Bucks 85 F7
Coleshill Oxon 82 G2
Coleshill Warks 134 F4
Colestocks Devon 27 G9
Colethrop Glos 80 C4
Coley Bath 44 B5
Coley Reading 65 E8
Coley W Yorks 196 B6
Colfin Dumfries 236 D2
Colgate W Sus 51 G8
Colgrain Argyll 276 E6
Colham Green London 66 C5
Colindale London 67 B8
Colinsburgh Fife 287 G8
Colinton Edin 270 B4
Colintraive Argyll 275 F11
Colkirk Norf 159 D8
Collace Perth 286 D6
Collafield Glos 79 C11
Collafirth Shetland 312 G6
Collam W Isles 305 J3
Collamoor Head Corn 11 C9
Collaton Devon 9 G9
Collaton St Mary Torbay 9 D7
College Milton S Lnrk 268 D2
College of Roseisle Moray 301 C11
College Park London 67 C8
College Town Brack 65 G11
Collennan S Ayrs 257 C8
Collessie Fife 286 F6
Colleton Mills Devon 25 D11
Collett's Br Norf 139 B9
Collett's Green Worcs 116 G6
Collier Row London 87 G8
Collier Street Kent 53 D8
Collier's End Herts 105 G7
Collier's Green E Sus 38 C3
Colliers Green Kent 53 F9
Colliers Hatch Essex 87 E8
Collier's Wood London 67 E9
Colliery Row T & W 234 B2
Collieston Aberds 303 G10
Collin Dumfries 238 B2
Collingbourne Ducis Wilts 47 C8

Collingbourne Kingston Wilts 47 B8
Collingham Notts 172 C4
Collingham W Yorks 206 D3
Collington Hereford 116 E2
Collingtree Northants 120 F5
Collingwood Northumb 243 B7
Collins End Oxon 65 D7
Collins Green Warr 183 C9
Collins Green Worcs 116 F4
Colliprest Devon 27 E7
Colliston Angus 287 C10
Colliton Devon 27 G9
Collycroft Warks 135 F7
Collyhurst Gtr Man 195 G11
Collynie Aberds 303 F8
Collyweston Northants 137 C9
Colmonell S Ayrs 244 F4
Colmslie Borders 262 B2
Colmsliehill Borders 271 G10
Colmworth Beds 122 F2
Coln Rogers Glos 81 D9
Coln St Aldwyns Glos 81 D10
Coln St Dennis Glos 81 C9
Colnabaichin Aberds 292 C4
Colnbrook Slough 66 D4
Colne Cambs 123 B7
Colne Lancs 204 E3
Colne Bridge W Yorks 197 C7
Colne Edge Lancs 204 E3
Colne Engaine Essex 107 E7
Colnefields Cambs 123 B7
Colney Norf 142 B3
Colney Hatch London 86 G3
Colney Heath Herts 86 D2
Colney Street Herts 85 E11
Cologin Argyll 289 G10
Colpitts Grange Northumb 241 F11
Colpy Aberds 302 F6
Colquhar Borders 270 G6
Colscott Devon 24 E5
Colshaw Staffs 169 B8
Colsterdale N Yorks 214 C2
Colsterworth Lincs 155 E8
Colston E Dunb 268 B2
Colston Pembs 91 F9
Colston Bassett Notts 154 C3
Colstrope Bucks 65 B9
Colt Hill Hants 49 C8
Colt Park Cumb 210 E5
Coltfield Moray 301 C11
Colthouse Cumb 221 F7
Colthrop W Berks 64 F4
Coltishall Norf 160 F5
Coltness N Lnrk 268 D6
Colton Cumb 210 B6
Colton N Yorks 206 E6
Colton Norf 142 B2
Colton Staffs 151 E11
Colton Suff 125 D7
Colton W Yorks 206 G3
Colton Hills Staffs 133 D8
Colt's Green S Glos 61 C8
Colt's Hill Kent 52 E6
Columbia T & W 243 F8
Columbjohn Devon 14 B5
Colva Powys 114 G4
Colvend Dumfries 237 D10
Colvister Shetland 312 D7
Colwall Hereford 98 C4
Colwall Green Hereford 98 C4
Colwall Stone Hereford 98 C5
Colwell I o W 20 D2
Colwell Northumb 241 B11
Colwich Staffs 151 E10
Colwick Notts 171 G10
Colwinston = Tregolwyn V Glam 58 D2
Colworth W Sus 22 C6
Colwyn Bay = Bae Colwyn Conwy 180 F4
Colychurch Bridgend 58 D2
Colyford Devon 15 C10
Colyton Devon 15 C10
Colzie Fife 286 F6
Combe Devon 7 E10
Combe Devon 8 B4
Combe Devon 9 G9
Combe E Sus 37 B10
Combe Hereford 114 E6
Combe Oxon 82 B6
Combe Som 28 B6
Combe W Berks 63 G11
Combe Almer Dorset 18 B5
Combe Common Sur 50 F3
Combe Down Bath 61 G9
Combe Fishacre Devon 8 C6
Combe Florey Som 43 G7
Combe Hay Bath 45 B8
Combe Martin Devon 40 D5
Combe Moor Hereford 115 E7
Combe Pafford Torbay 9 B8
Combe Raleigh Devon 27 G11
Combe St Nicholas Som 28 E4
Combe Throop Som 30 C2
Combebow Devon 12 D5
Combeinteignhead Devon 14 G4
Comberbach W Ches 183 F10
Comberford Staffs 134 B3
Comberton Cambs 123 F7
Comberton Hereford 115 D9
Combpyne Devon 15 C11
Combrew Devon 40 G4
Combridge Staffs 151 B11
Combrook Warks 118 G6
Combs Derbys 185 F8
Combs Suff 125 F10
Combs W Yorks 197 D8
Combs Ford Suff 125 F11
Combwich Som 43 E9
Come-to-Good Corn 4 G6
Comers Aberds 293 C8
Comeytrowe Som 28 C2
Comford Corn 2 B6
Comfort Corn 2 D6
Comhampton Worcs 116 D6
Comins Coch Ceredig 128 G2
Comiston Edin 270 B4
Comley Shrops 131 D9
Commercial End Cambs 123 E11
Commins Denb 165 C10
Commins Capel Betws Ceredig 112 F2
Commins Coch Powys 128 C6
Common Cefn-llwyn Mon 78 G4
Common Edge Blkpool 202 G2
Common End Cumb 228 G6
Common End Derbys 170 C6
Common Hill Hereford 97 E11
Common Moor Corn 6 B4
Common Platt Wilts 62 B6
Common Side Derbys 170 F6
Common Side Derbys 186 F4
Common Side W Ches 167 B9
Common-y-coed Mon 60 B2

370 Com – Cro

Commondale N Yorks 226 C3
Commonmoor Corn 6 B4
Commonside Derbys 170 G2
Commonside Notts 171 D7
Commonside W Ches 183 G8
Commonwood Herts 85 E8
Commonwood Shrops 149 D9
Commonwood Wrex 166 E5
Comp Kent 52 B6
Compass Som 43 G9
Compstall Gtr Man 185 C7
Compton Derbys 169 F11
Compton Devon 9 C7
Compton Farnham 49 D11
Compton Hants 32 B4
Compton Hants 33 B7
Compton Plym 7 D9
Compton Staffs 132 G6
Compton Sur 50 D3
Compton W Berks 64 D4
Compton W Mid 133 D7
Compton W Sus 34 E3
Compton W Yorks 206 E3
Compton Wilts 46 C6
Compton Abbas Dorset 30 D5
Compton Abdale Glos 81 B9
Compton Bassett Wilts 62 E4
Compton Beauchamp Oxon 63 B9
Compton Bishop Som 43 B11
Compton Chamberlayne Wilts 31 B8
Compton Common Bath 60 G6
Compton Dando Bath 60 G6
Compton Dundon Som 44 G3
Compton Durville Som 28 D6
Compton End Hants 33 B7
Compton Green Glos 98 F4
Compton Greenfield S Glos 60 C5
Compton Martin Bath 44 B4
Compton Pauncefoot Som 29 B10
Compton Valence Dorset 17 C7
Comrie Fife 279 D10
Comrie Highld 300 D4
Comrie Perth 285 C11
Comrie Perth 285 E11
Conrue Dumfries 248 F3
Conaglen House Highld 290 G2
Conanby S Yorks 187 B7
Conchra Argyll 275 E11
Conchra Highld 295 C10
Concord T & W 243 F8
Concraig Perth 286 F2
Concraigie Perth 286 C5
Conder Green Lancs 202 B5
Conderton Worcs 99 D9
Condicote Glos 100 F3
Condorrat N Lnrk 278 G4
Condover Shrops 131 B9
Coney Hall London 67 G11
Coney Hill Glos 80 B5
Coney Weston Suff 125 B9
Coneyhurst W Sus 35 C10
Coneysthorpe N Yorks 216 E4
Coneythorpe N Yorks 206 B3
Conford Hants 49 G10
Congash Highld 301 G10
Congdon's Shop Corn 11 F11
Congeith Dumfries 237 C10
Congelow Kent 53 D7
Congerstone Leics 135 B7
Congham Norf 158 E4
Congl-y-wal Gwyn 164 G2
Congleton E Ches 168 C5
Congleton Edge E Ches 168 C5
Congresbury N Som 60 G2
Congreve Staffs 151 G8
Conham Bristol 60 E6
Conicavel Moray 301 D9
Coningsby Lincs 174 D2
Conington Cambs 122 D6
Conington Cambs 138 F3
Conisbrough S Yorks 187 B8
Conisby Argyll 274 G3
Conisholme Lincs 190 B6
Coniston Cumb 220 F6
Coniston E Yorks 209 F9
Coniston Cold N Yorks 204 B4
Conistone N Yorks 213 F9
Conkwell Wilts 61 G9
Connage Moray 302 C4
Connah's Quay Flint 166 B3
Connel Argyll 289 F11
Connel Park E Ayrs 258 G4
Conniburrow M Keynes 103 D7
Connista Highld 298 B4
Connon Corn 6 C3
Connor Downs Corn 2 B3
Conock Wilts 46 B5
Conon Bridge Highld 300 D5
Conon House Highld 300 D5
Cononish Stirl 285 E7
Cononley N Yorks 204 D5
Cononley Woodside N Yorks 204 D5
Cononsyth Angus 287 C9
Conordan Highld 295 B7
Conquermoor Heath Telford 150 F3
Consall Staffs 169 F7
Consett Durham 242 G4
Constable Burton N Yorks 224 G3
Constable Lee Lancs 195 C10
Constantine Corn 2 D6
Constantine Bay Corn 10 G3
Contin Highld 300 D4
Contlaw Aberdeen 293 C10
Conwy Conwy 180 F3
Conyer Kent 70 G3
Conyers Green Suff 125 D7
Cooden E Sus 38 F2
Cooil I o M 192 E4
Cookbury Devon 24 F6
Cookbury Wick Devon 24 F5
Cookham Windsor 65 B11
Cookham Dean Windsor 65 C11
Cookham Rise Windsor 65 C11
Cookhill Worcs 117 F11
Cookley Suff 126 B6
Cookley Worcs 132 G6
Cookley Green Oxon 83 G11
Cookney Aberds 293 D10
Cookridge W Yorks 205 E11
Cook's Green Essex 89 B11
Cook's Green Suff 125 G9
Cooksbridge E Sus 36 E6
Cooksey Corner Worcs 117 D8
Cooksey Green Worcs 117 D8
Cookshill Staffs 168 G6
Cooksland Corn 5 B11
Cooksmill Green Essex 87 D10
Cooksongreen W Ches 183 G9
Coolham W Sus 35 C10
Cooling Medway 69 D9
Cooling Street Medway 69 E8
Coolinge Kent 55 F8
Coomb Hill Kent 69 G7
Coombe Bucks 84 D4
Coombe Corn 4 G2
Coombe Corn 4 G5
Coombe Corn 4 G6
Coombe Corn 5 E9
Coombe Corn 6 C4
Coombe Corn 24 E2
Coombe Devon 14 G4
Coombe Devon 27 D8
Coombe Glos 80 G3
Coombe Hants 33 C11
Coombe Kent 55 B9
Coombe London 67 E8
Coombe Som 28 B3
Coombe Som 28 F6
Coombe Wilts 30 C5
Coombe Wilts 47 C7
Coombe Bissett Wilts 31 B10
Coombe Dingle Bristol 60 D5
Coombe Hill Glos 99 F7
Coombe Keynes Dorset 18 E2
Coombes W Sus 35 F11
Coombesdale Staffs 150 B6
Coombeswood W Mid 133 F9
Coombs End S Glos 61 C9
Coombses Som 28 F4
Cooper Street Kent 55 B10
Cooper Turning Gtr Man 194 F6
Cooper's Corner Kent 52 D3
Cooper's Green E Sus 37 C7
Cooper's Green Herts 85 D11
Cooper's Hill C Beds 103 D10
Cooper's Hill Sur 66 E3
Coopersale Common Essex 87 E7
Coopersale Street Essex 87 E7
Cootham W Sus 35 E9
Cop Street Kent 55 B9
Copcut Worcs 117 E7
Copdock Suff 108 C2
Coped Hall Wilts 62 C5
Copenhagen Denb 165 B8
Copford Essex 107 G8
Copford Green Essex 107 G8
Copgrove N Yorks 214 G6
Copister Shetland 312 F6
Cople Beds 104 B2
Copley Durham 233 F7
Copley Gtr Man 185 B7
Copley W Yorks 196 C5
Copley Hill W Yorks 197 B8
Coplow Dale Derbys 185 F11
Copmanthorpe York 207 D7
Copmere End Staffs 150 D6
Copnor Ptsmth 33 G11
Copp Lancs 202 F4
Coppathorne Corn 24 G2
Coppenhall E Ches 168 D2
Coppenhall Staffs 151 F8
Coppenhall Moss E Ches 168 D2
Copperhouse Corn 2 B3
Coppice Gtr Man 196 G2
Coppicegate Shrops 132 G4
Coppingford Cambs 138 G3
Coppins Corner Kent 54 D2
Coppleham Som 42 G2
Copplestone Devon 26 G3
Coppull Lancs 194 E5
Coppull Moor Lancs 194 E5
Copsale W Sus 35 C11
Copse Hill London 67 E8
Copster Green Lancs 203 G9
Copster Hill Gtr Man 196 G2
Copston Magna Warks 135 F9
Copt Green Warks 118 D3
Copt Heath W Mid 118 B3
Copt Hewick N Yorks 214 E6
Copt Oak Leics 153 G9
Copthall Green Essex 86 E6
Copthill Durham 232 C3
Copthorne Corn 11 C11
Copthorne E Ches 167 G11
Copthorne Shrops 149 G9
Copthorne Sur 51 F10
Coptiviney Shrops 149 B8
Copton Kent 54 B4
Copy's Green Norf 159 B8
Copythorne Hants 32 E4
Corbets Tey London 68 B5
Corbridge Northumb 241 E11
Corbriggs Derbys 170 B6
Corby Northants 137 F7
Corby Glen Lincs 155 E9
Corby Hill Cumb 239 F11
Cordon N Ayrs 256 C2
Cordwell Norf 142 E2
Coreley Shrops 116 C2
Cores End Bucks 66 B2
Corfe Som 28 D2
Corfe Castle Dorset 18 E5
Corfe Mullen Dorset 18 B5
Corfton Shrops 131 F9
Corfton Bache Shrops 131 F9
Corgarff Aberds 292 C4
Corgee Corn 5 C10
Corhampton Hants 33 C10
Corlae Dumfries 246 D5
Corlannau Neath 57 C9
Corley Warks 134 F6
Corley Ash Warks 134 F5
Corley Moor Warks 134 F5
Cornaa I o M 192 D5
Cornabus Argyll 254 C4
Cornaigbeg Argyll 288 E1
Cornaigmore Argyll 288 C4
Cornaigmore Argyll 288 E1
Cornard Tye Suff 107 C8
Cornbank Midloth 270 C4
Cornbrook Shrops 116 B2
Corncatterach Aberds 302 F5
Cornel Conwy 164 C2
Corner Row Lancs 202 F4
Cornett Hereford 97 B11
Corney Cumb 220 G2
Cornforth Durham 234 E2
Cornharrow Dumfries 246 E5
Cornhill Aberds 302 D5
Cornhill Powys 96 C2
Cornhill Stoke 168 E5
Cornhill-on-Tweed Northumb 263 B9
Cornholme W Yorks 196 B2
Cornish Hall End Essex 106 D3
Cornquoy Orkney 314 G5
Cornriggs Durham 232 C2
Cornsay Durham 233 C8
Cornsay Colliery Durham 233 C9
Cornton Stirl 278 B5
Corntown Highld 300 D5
Corntown V Glam 58 D2
Cornwell Oxon 100 F5
Cornwood Devon 8 D2
Cornworthy Devon 8 D6
Corpach Highld 290 F2
Corpusty Norf 160 C2
Corran Highld 290 G2
Corran Highld 295 E10
Corran a Chan Uachdaraich Highld 295 C7
Corranbuie Argyll 275 G9
Corrany I o M 192 D5
Corrichoich Highld 311 G4
Corrie N Ayrs 255 C11
Corrie Common Dumfries 248 F6
Corriecravie N Ayrs 255 E10
Corriecravie Moor N Ayrs 255 E10
Corriedoo Dumfries 246 G5
Corriegarth Lodge Highld 291 B7
Corriemoillie Highld 300 C3
Corriemulzie Lodge Highld 309 K3
Corrievarkie Lodge Perth 291 F7
Corrievorrie Highld 301 G7
Corrigall Orkney 314 E3
Corrimony Highld 300 F3
Corringham Lincs 188 C5
Corringham Thurrock 69 C8
Corris Gwyn 128 B5
Corris Uchaf Gwyn 128 B4
Corrour Highld 290 G5
Corrour Shooting Lodge Highld 290 G6
Corrow Argyll 284 G5
Corry Highld 295 C8
Corry of Ardnagrask Highld 300 E5
Corrybrough Highld 301 G8
Corrydon Perth 292 G3
Corryghoil Argyll 284 E5
Corrykinloch Highld 309 G3
Corrylach Argyll 255 D8
Corrymuckloch Perth 286 D2
Corrynachenchy Argyll 289 E8
Cors-y-Gedol Gwyn 145 E11
Corsback Highld 310 B6
Corscombe Dorset 29 F8
Corse Aberds 302 E6
Corse Glos 98 F5
Corse Lawn Worcs 98 E6
Corse of Kinnoir Aberds 302 E5
Corsewall Dumfries 236 C2
Corsham Wilts 61 E11
Corsindae Aberds 293 C8
Corsley Wilts 45 D10
Corsley Heath Wilts 45 D10
Corsock Dumfries 237 B9
Corston Bath 61 F7
Corston Orkney 314 E3
Corston Wilts 62 C2
Corstorphine Edin 280 G3
Cortachy Angus 287 B7
Corton Suff 143 D10
Corton Wilts 46 E2
Corton Denham Som 29 C10
Cortworth S Yorks 186 B6
Coruanan Lodge Highld 290 G2
Corunna W Isles 296 E4
Corvast Highld 309 K5
Corwen Denb 165 G9
Cory Devon 24 D5
Coryates Dorset 17 D8
Coryton Cardiff 58 C6
Coryton Devon 12 E5
Coryton Thurrock 69 C8
Còsag Highld 295 D10
Cosby Leics 135 E10
Coscote Oxon 64 B4
Coseley W Mid 133 E8
Cosford Warks 119 B9
Cosgrove Northants 102 C5
Cosham Ptsmth 33 F11
Cosheston Pembs 73 E8
Cosmeston V Glam 59 F7
Cosmore Dorset 29 F11
Cossall Notts 171 G7
Cossall Marsh Notts 171 G7
Cosses S Ayrs 244 G4
Cossington Leics 154 G2
Cossington Som 43 E11
Costa Orkney 314 D3
Costessey Norf 160 G3
Costessey Park Norf 160 G3
Costhorpe Notts 187 D9
Costislost Corn 10 G6
Costock Notts 153 D11
Coston Leics 154 E6
Coston Norf 141 B11
Coswinsawsin Corn 2 B4
Cote Oxon 82 E4
Cote Som 43 E10
Cote W Sus 35 F10
Cotebrook W Ches 167 B9
Cotehill Cumb 239 G11
Cotes Cumb 211 B9
Cotes Leics 153 E11
Cotes Staffs 150 C6
Cotes Heath Staffs 150 C6
Cotes Park Derbys 170 E6
Cotesbach Leics 135 G10
Cotford St Lukes Som 27 B11
Cotgrave Notts 154 B2
Cothall Aberds 293 B10
Cotham Bristol 60 E5
Cotham Notts 172 F3
Cothelstone Som 43 G7
Cotheridge Worcs 116 G5
Cotherstone Durham 223 B10
Cothill Oxon 83 F7
Cotland Mon 79 E8
Cotleigh Devon 28 G2
Cotmanhay Derbys 171 G7
Cotmarsh Wilts 62 D5
Cotmaton Devon 15 D8
Coton Cambs 123 F8
Coton Northants 120 C3
Coton Shrops 149 C10
Coton Staffs 134 B3
Coton Staffs 150 E6
Coton Staffs 151 C9
Coton Staffs 151 E7
Coton Clanford Staffs 151 E7
Coton Hayes Staffs 151 C9
Coton Hill Shrops 149 G9
Coton Hill Staffs 151 C9
Coton in the Clay Staffs 152 D3
Coton in the Elms Derbys 152 F4
Coton Park Derbys 152 F5
Cotonwood Shrops 149 B10
Cotonwood Staffs 150 E6
Cotswold Community Wilts 81 F8
Cott Devon 8 C5
Cottam E Yorks 217 F9
Cottam Lancs 202 G6
Cottam Notts 188 F4
Cottartown Highld 301 F10
Cottenham Cambs 123 D8
Cottenham Park London 67 F8
Cotterdale N Yorks 222 G6
Cottered Herts 104 F6
Cotterhill Woods S Yorks 187 E9
Cotteridge W Mid 117 B10
Cotterstock Northants 137 E10
Cottesbrooke Northants 120 C4
Cottesmore Rutland 155 G8
Cotteylands Devon 26 E6
Cottingham E Yorks 208 G6
Cottingham Northants 136 E6
Cottingley W Yorks 205 F8
Cottisford Oxon 101 E11
Cotton Staffs 169 F9
Cotton Suff 125 D11
Cotton End Beds 103 B11
Cotton End Northants 120 F5
Cotton Stones W Yorks 196 C4
Cotton Tree Lancs 204 F4
Cottonworth Hants 47 F11
Cottown Aberds 293 B9
Cottown Aberds 302 G5
Cottown Aberds 303 E8
Cotts Devon 7 B8
Cottwood Devon 25 E10
Cotwall Telford 150 F2
Cotwalton Staffs 151 B8
Coubister Orkney 314 E3
Couch Green Hants 48 G4
Couch's Mill Corn 6 D2
Coughton Hereford 97 G11
Coughton Warks 117 E11
Coughton Fields Warks 117 F11
Cougie Highld 300 G2
Coulaghailtro Argyll 275 G8
Coulags Highld 299 E9
Coulby Newham M'bro 225 B10
Coulderton Cumb 219 D9
Couldoran Highld 299 E8
Couligartan Stirl 285 G8
Coulin Highld 299 D10
Coulin Lodge Highld 299 D10
Coull Aberds 293 C7
Coull Argyll 274 G3
Coulmony Ho Highld 301 E9
Coulport Argyll 276 D4
Coulsdon London 51 B9
Coulshill Perth 286 G3
Coulston Wilts 46 C3
Coulter S Lnrk 260 C2
Coultings Som 43 E8
Coulton N Yorks 216 E2
Coultra Fife 287 E7
Cound Shrops 131 C11
Coundlane Shrops 131 B11
Coundmoor Shrops 131 C11
Coundon Durham 233 F10
Coundon W Mid 134 G6
Coundon Grange Durham 233 F10
Coundongate Durham 233 F10
Counters End Herts 85 D8
Countersett N Yorks 213 B8
Countess Wilts 47 E7
Countess Cross Essex 107 E7
Countess Wear Devon 14 D4
Countesthorpe Leics 135 D11
Countisbury Devon 41 D8
County Oak W Sus 51 F9
Coup Green Lancs 194 B5
Coupar Angus Perth 286 C6
Coupland Cumb 222 B4
Coupland Northumb 263 C10
Cour Argyll 255 C9
Courance Dumfries 248 E3
Coursley Som 42 G6
Court-at-Street Kent 54 F5
Court Barton Devon 14 D2
Court Colman Bridgend 57 E11
Court Corner Hants 48 B6
Court Henry Carms 93 G11
Court House Green W Mid 135 G7
Courteenhall Northants 120 G5
Courthill Perth 286 C5
Courtsend Essex 89 G8
Courtway Som 43 G8
Cousland Midloth 271 B7
Cousley Wood E Sus 53 G7
Couston Argyll 275 F11
Cova Shetland 313 J5
Cove Argyll 276 E4
Cove Borders 282 G5
Cove Devon 27 D7
Cove Hants 49 B11
Cove Highld 307 K3
Cove Bay Aberdeen 293 C11
Cove Bottom Suff 127 B9
Covehithe Suff 143 G10
Coven Staffs 133 B8
Coven Heath Staffs 133 C8
Coven Lawn Staffs 133 B8
Covender Hereford 98 C2
Coveney Cambs 139 G9
Covenham St Bartholomew Lincs 190 C4
Covenham St Mary Lincs 190 C4
Coventry W Mid 118 B6
Coverack Corn 3 F7
Coverack Bridges Corn 2 C5
Coverham N Yorks 214 B2
Covesea Moray 301 B11
Covingham Swindon 63 B7
Covington Cambs 121 C11
Covington S Lnrk 259 B11
Cow Ark Lancs 203 D9
Cow Green Suff 125 D11
Cow Hill Lancs 203 G7
Cow Roast Herts 85 C7
Cowan Bridge Lancs 212 D2
Cowbar Redcar 226 B5
Cowbeech E Sus 23 C10
Cowbeech Hill E Sus 23 C10
Cowbit Lincs 156 F5
Cowbog Aberds 303 D8
Cowbridge Lincs 174 F4
Cowbridge Som 42 E3
Cowbridge = Y Bont-Faen V Glam 58 E3
Cowcliffe W Yorks 196 D6
Cowdale Derbys 185 G9
Cowden Kent 52 E3
Cowdenbeath Fife 280 C3
Cowdenburn Borders 270 E4
Cowen Head Cumb 221 F9
Cowers Lane Derbys 170 F4
Cowes I o W 20 B5
Cowesby N Yorks 215 B9
Cowesfield Green Wilts 32 C3
Cowfold W Sus 36 C2
Cowgill Cumb 212 B5
Cowgrove Dorset 18 B5
Cowhill Derbys 170 F5
Cowhill S Glos 79 G10
Cowhorn Hill S Glos 61 E7
Cowie Aberds 293 E10
Cowie Stirl 278 D6
Cowlands Corn 4 G6
Cowleaze Corner Oxon 82 E4
Cowley Derbys 186 F4
Cowley Devon 14 B4
Cowley Glos 81 C7
Cowley London 66 C5
Cowley Oxon 83 E8
Cowley Peachy London 66 C5
Cowleymoor Devon 27 E7
Cowling Lancs 194 D5
Cowling N Yorks 204 E5
Cowling N Yorks 214 B4
Cowlinge Suff 124 G4
Cowlow Derbys 185 G9
Cowmes W Yorks 197 D7
Cowpe Lancs 195 C10
Cowpen Northumb 253 G7
Cowpen Bewley Stockton 234 G5
Cowplain Hants 33 E11
Cowshill Durham 232 C3
Cowslip Green N Som 60 G3
Cowstrandburn Fife 279 C10
Cowthorpe N Yorks 206 C4
Cox Common Suff 143 G8
Cox Green Gtr Man 195 E8
Cox Green Sur 50 G5
Cox Green Windsor 65 D11
Cox Hill Corn 4 G4
Cox Moor Notts 171 D8
Coxall Hereford 115 C7
Coxbank E Ches 167 G11
Coxbench Derbys 170 G5
Coxbridge Som 44 F4
Coxford Corn 11 B9
Coxford Norf 158 D6
Coxford Soton 32 D5
Coxgreen Staffs 132 F6
Coxheath Kent 53 C8
Coxhill Kent 55 D8
Coxhoe Durham 234 D2
Coxley Som 44 E4
Coxley W Yorks 197 D9
Coxley Wick Som 44 E4
Coxlodge T & W 242 D6
Coxpark Corn 12 G4
Coxtie Green Essex 87 F9
Coxwold N Yorks 215 D10
Coychurch Bridgend 58 D2
Coylton S Ayrs 257 E10
Coylumbridge Highld 291 B11
Coynach Aberds 292 C6
Coynachie Aberds 302 F4
Coytrahen Bridgend 57 D11
CoytrahÜn Bridgend 57 D11
Crab Orchard Dorset 31 F9
Crabadon Devon 8 E5
Crabbet Park W Sus 51 F10
Crabble Kent 55 E9
Crabbs Cross Worcs 117 E10
Crabbs Green Herts 105 F9
Crabgate Norf 159 D11
Crabtree Plym 7 D10
Crabtree W Sus 36 B2
Crabtree Green Wrex 166 G4
Crackaig Argyll 274 G6
Crackenedge W Yorks 197 C8
Crackenthorpe Cumb 231 G9
Crackington Haven Corn 11 B8
Crackley Staffs 168 E4
Crackley Warks 118 C5
Crackleybank Shrops 150 G5
Crackpot N Yorks 223 F9
Crackthorn Corner Suff 125 B10
Cracoe N Yorks 213 G9
Cracow Moss E Ches 168 F2
Cracow Moss Staffs 168 F3
Craddock Devon 27 E9
Cradhlastadh W Isles 304 E2
Cradle Edge W Yorks 205 F7
Cradle End Herts 105 G9
Cradley Hereford 98 B4
Cradley W Mid 133 G8
Cradley Heath W Mid 133 F8
Cradoc Powys 95 E10
Crafthole Corn 7 E7
Crafton Bucks 84 B5
Crag Bank Lancs 211 E9
Crag Foot Lancs 211 E9
Cragg Hill W Yorks 205 F10
Cragg Vale W Yorks 196 C4
Craggan Highld 301 G10
Craggan Moray 301 F11
Craggan Stirl 285 E9
Cragganvallie Highld 300 F5
Craggenmore Moray 301 F11
Craggie Highld 301 F7
Craggie Highld 311 H2
Craggiemore Highld 309 J7
Craghead Durham 242 G6
Crahan Corn 2 C5
Crai Powys 95 G7
Craibstone Moray 302 D4
Craichie Angus 287 C9
Craig Dumfries 237 B8
Craig Dumfries 237 C8
Craig Highld 299 E10
Craig Berthlwyd M Tydf 77 F9
Craig Castle Aberds 302 G4
Craig-cefn-parc Swansea 75 E11
Craig Douglas Borders 261 E7
Craig Llangiwg Neath 76 D2
Craig-llwyn Shrops 148 D4
Craig Lodge Argyll 275 G10
Craig-moston Aberds 293 F8
Craig Penllyn V Glam 58 D3
Craig-y-don Conwy 180 E3
Craig-y-Duke Swansea 76 E2
Craig-y-nos Powys 76 B4
Craig-y-penrhyn Ceredig 128 E3
Craig-y-Rhacca Caerph 59 B7
Craiganor Lodge Perth 285 B10
Craigdallie Perth 286 E6
Craigdam Aberds 303 F8
Craigdarroch Dumfries 246 E6
Craigdarroch Highld 300 D4
Craigdhu Highld 300 E4
Craigearn Aberds 293 B9
Craigellachie Moray 302 E2
Craigencallie Ho Dumfries 237 B7
Craigencross Dumfries 236 C2
Craigend Borders 271 F9
Craigend Glasgow 268 B3
Craigend Perth 286 E3
Craigend Perth 286 E5
Craigend Stirl 278 D5
Craigendive Argyll 275 E11
Craigendoran Argyll 276 E6
Craigendowie Angus 293 G7
Craigends Renfs 267 B8
Craigens Argyll 274 G3
Craigens E Ayrs 258 F3
Craigentinny Edin 280 G5
Craigerne Borders 261 B7
Craighall Perth 286 C5
Craighat Stirl 277 E9
Craighead Fife 287 G10
Craighead Highld 301 C7
Craighill Aberds 303 E7
Craighlaw Mains Dumfries 236 C5
Craighouse Argyll 274 G6
Craigie Aberds 293 B11
Craigie Dundee 287 D8
Craigie Perth 286 C5
Craigie Perth 286 E5
Craigie S Ayrs 257 C10
Craigie S Ayrs 257 E8
Craigiefield Orkney 314 E4
Craigiehall Edin 280 F3
Craigielaw E Loth 281 F9
Craigierig Borders 260 E6
Craigleith Edin 280 G4
Craiglockhart Edin 280 G4
Craigmalloch E Ayrs 245 E11
Craigmaud Aberds 303 D8
Craigmill Stirl 278 B6
Craigmillar Edin 280 G5
Craigmore Argyll 266 B2
Craignant Shrops 148 B5
Craignell Dumfries 237 B7
Craigneuk N Lnrk 268 C5
Craigneuk N Lnrk 268 D5
Craignish Castle Argyll 275 C8
Craignure Argyll 289 F9
Craigo Angus 293 G8
Craigow Perth 286 G4
Craigrory Highld 300 E6
Craigrothie Fife 287 F7
Craigroy Moray 301 D11
Craigruie Stirl 285 E8
Craig's End Essex 106 D4
Craigsford Mains Borders 262 B3
Craigshall Dumfries 237 D10
Craigshill W Loth 269 B11
Craigside Durham 233 D8
Craigston Castle Aberds 303 D7
Craigton Aberdeen 293 C10
Craigton Angus 287 B7
Craigton Angus 287 D9
Craigton Glasgow 267 C10
Craigton Highld 300 E6
Craigton Highld 309 H6
Craigton Highld 309 K6
Craigtown Highld 310 D2
Craik Borders 249 B8
Crail Fife 287 G10
Crailing Borders 262 E5
Crailinghall Borders 262 E5
Crakaig Highld 311 H3
Crakehill N Yorks 215 E8
Crakemarsh Staffs 151 B11
Crambe N Yorks 216 G4
Crambeck N Yorks 216 F4
Cramhurst Sur 50 E2
Cramlington Northumb 243 B7
Cramond Edin 280 F3
Cramond Bridge Edin 280 F3
Crampmoor Hants 32 C5
Cranage E Ches 168 B3
Cranberry Staffs 150 B6
Cranborne Dorset 31 E9
Cranbourne Brack 66 E2
Cranbourne Hants 48 C6
Cranbrook Kent 53 F9
Cranbrook London 68 B2
Cranbrook Common Kent 53 F9
Crane Moor S Yorks 197 G10
Crane's Corner Norf 159 G8
Cranfield C Beds 103 C9
Cranford Devon 24 C4
Cranford London 66 D6
Cranford St Andrew Northants 121 B8
Cranford St John Northants 121 B8
Cranham Glos 80 C5
Cranham London 68 B5
Cranhill Glasgow 268 B2
Cranhill Warks 118 G2
Crank Mers 183 B8
Crank Wood Gtr Man 194 G6
Crankwood Gtr Man 194 G6
Cranleigh Sur 50 F5
Cranley Suff 126 C3
Cranley Gardens London 67 B9
Cranmer Green Suff 125 C10
Cranmore I o W 20 D3
Cranmore Som 45 E7
Cranna Aberds 302 D6
Crannich Argyll 289 E7
Crannoch Moray 302 D4
Cranoe Leics 136 D4
Cransford Suff 126 E6
Cranshaws Borders 272 C3
Cranstal I o M 192 B5
Cranswick E Yorks 208 C6
Crantock Corn 4 C5
Cranwell Lincs 173 F8
Cranwich Norf 140 E5
Cranworth Norf 141 C9
Craobh Haven Argyll 275 C8
Crapstone Devon 7 B10
Crarae Argyll 275 D10
Crask Highld 308 C7
Crask Inn Highld 309 G5
Crask of Aigas Highld 300 E4
Craskins Aberds 293 C7
Craster Northumb 265 F7
Craswall Hereford 96 D5
Crateford Shrops 132 F4
Crateford Staffs 133 B8
Cratfield Suff 126 B6
Crathes Aberds 293 D9
Crathie Aberds 292 D4
Crathie Highld 291 D7
Crathorne N Yorks 225 D8
Craven Arms Shrops 131 G8
Crawcrook T & W 242 E4
Crawford Lancs 194 G3
Crawford S Lnrk 259 E11
Crawforddyke S Lnrk 269 F7
Crawfordjohn S Lnrk 259 E9
Crawick Dumfries 259 G7
Crawley Devon 28 F3
Crawley Hants 48 G2
Crawley Oxon 82 C4
Crawley W Sus 51 F9
Crawley Down W Sus 51 F10
Crawley End Essex 105 C8
Crawley Hill Sur 65 G11
Crawleyside Durham 232 C5
Crawshaw W Yorks 197 E8
Crawshawbooth Lancs 195 B10
Crawton Aberds 293 F10
Cray N Yorks 213 D8
Cray Perth 292 G3
Crayford London 68 E4
Crayke N Yorks 215 E11
Crays Hill Essex 88 G2
Cray's Pond Oxon 64 C6
Crazies Hill Wokingham 65 C9
Creacombe Devon 26 D4
Creag Aoil Highld 290 F3
Creag Ghoraidh W Isles 297 G3
Creagan Argyll 289 E11
Creagan Sithe Argyll 284 G6
Creagastrom W Isles 297 G4
Creaguaineach Lodge Highld 290 G5
Creaksea Essex 88 F6
Creamore Bank Shrops 149 C10
Crean Corn 1 E3
Creaton Northants 120 C4
Creca Dumfries 238 C6
Credenhill Hereford 97 C9
Crediton Devon 26 G4
Creebridge Dumfries 236 C6
Creech Dorset 18 E4
Creech Bottom Dorset 18 E4
Creech Heathfield Som 28 B3
Creech St Michael Som 28 B3
Creed Corn 5 F8
Creediknowe Shetland 312 G7
Creegbrawse Corn 4 G4
Creekmoor Poole 18 C6
Creekmouth London 68 C3
Creeksea Essex 88 F6
Creeting Bottoms Suff 126 F2
Creeting St Mary Suff 125 F11
Creeton Lincs 155 E10
Creetown Dumfries 236 D6
Creg-ny-Baa I o M 192 D4
Creggans Argyll 284 G4
Cregneash I o M 192 F2
Cregrina Powys 114 G2
Creich Fife 287 E7
Creigau Mon 79 F7
Creighton Staffs 151 B11
Creigiau Cardiff 58 C5
Crelly Corn 2 C5
Cremyll Corn 7 E9
Crendell Dorset 31 E9
Crepkill Highld 298 E4
Creslow Bucks 102 G6
Cress Green Glos 80 E3
Cressage Shrops 131 C11
Cressbrook Derbys 185 G11
Cresselly Pembs 73 D9
Cressex Bucks 84 G4
Cressing Essex 106 G5
Cresswell Northumb 253 E7
Cresswell Staffs 151 B9
Cresswell Quay Pembs 73 D9
Creswell Derbys 187 G8
Creswell Staffs 151 D7
Creswell Staffs 151 D8
Creswell Green Staffs 151 G11
Cretingham Suff 126 E4
Cretshengan Argyll 275 G8
Creunant = Crynant Neath 76 E3
Crewe E Ches 168 D2
Crewe W Ches 166 E6
Crewe-by-Farndon W Ches 166 E6
Crewgarth Cumb 231 E8
Crewgreen Powys 148 F6
Crewkerne Som 28 F6
Crews Hill London 86 F4
Crew's Hole Bristol 60 E6
Crewton Derby 153 C7
Crianlarich Stirl 285 E7
Cribbs Causeway S Glos 60 C5
Cribden Side Lancs 195 C9
Cribyn Ceredig 111 G10
Criccieth Gwyn 145 B9
Crich Derbys 170 E5
Crich Carr Derbys 170 E4
Crichie Aberds 303 E9
Crichton Midloth 271 C7
Crick Mon 79 G7
Crick Northants 119 C11
Crickadarn Powys 95 C11
Cricket Hill Hants 65 G10
Cricket Malherbie Som 28 E5
Cricket St Thomas Som 28 F5
Crickham Som 44 D2
Crickheath Shrops 148 E5
Crickheath Wharf Shrops 148 E5
Crickhowell Powys 78 B2
Cricklade Wilts 81 G10
Cricklewood London 67 B8
Crickmery Shrops 150 D3
Crick's Green Hereford 116 G2
Criddlestyle Hants 31 E11
Cridling Stubbs N Yorks 198 C4
Cridmore I o W 20 E5
Crieff Perth 286 E2
Criggan Corn 5 C10
Criggion Powys 148 F5
Crigglestone W Yorks 197 D10
Crimble Gtr Man 195 E11
Crimchard Som 28 F4
Crimdon Park Durham 234 D5
Crimond Aberds 303 D10
Crimonmogate Aberds 303 D10
Crimp Corn 24 D3
Crimplesham Norf 140 C3
Crimscote Warks 100 B4
Crinan Argyll 275 D8
Crinan Ferry Argyll 275 D8
Crindau Newport 59 B10
Crindledyke N Lnrk 268 D6
Cringleford Norf 142 B3
Cringles W Yorks 204 D6
Cringletie Borders 270 G4
Crinow Pembs 73 C10
Cripple Corner Essex 107 E7
Cripplesease Corn 2 B2
Cripplestyle Dorset 31 E9
Cripp's Corner E Sus 38 C3
Crispie Argyll 275 F10
Crist Derbys 185 E8
Crit Hall Kent 53 G9
Critchell's Green Hants 32 B3
Critchill Som 45 D9
Critchmere Sur 49 G11
Crizeley Hereford 97 E8
Croanford Corn 10 G6
Croasdale Cumb 219 B11
Crobeag W Isles 304 F5
Crock Street Som 28 E4
Crockenhill Kent 68 F4
Crocker End Oxon 65 B8
Crockerhill Hants 33 F9
Crockerhill W Sus 22 B6
Crockernwell Devon 13 C11
Crockers Devon 40 F5
Crocker's Ash Hereford 79 B8
Crockerton Wilts 45 E11
Crockerton Green Wilts 45 E11
Crocketford or Ninemile Bar Dumfries 237 B10
Crockey Hill York 207 D8
Crockham Heath W Berks 64 G2
Crockham Hill Kent 52 C2
Crockhurst Street Kent 52 E6
Crockleford Heath Essex 107 F10
Crockleford Hill Essex 107 F10
Crockness Orkney 314 G3
Croes-goch Pembs 87 E11
Croes-Hywel Mon 78 C4
Croes-lan Ceredig 93 C7
Croes Llanfair Mon 78 D4
Croes-wian Flint 181 G10
Croes-y-mwyalch Torf 78 G4
Croes y pant Mon 78 E4
Croesau Bach Shrops 148 D4
Croeserw Neath 57 B11
Croesor Gwyn 163 G10
Croespenmaen Caerph 77 F11
Croesyceiliog Carms 74 B6
Croesyceiliog Torf 78 F4
Croesywaun Gwyn 163 D8
Croft Hereford 115 D9
Croft Leics 135 D10
Croft Lincs 1…
Croft Pembs …
Croft Warr 18…
Croft Mitchell Corn …
Croft of Tillymaud Aberds 30…
Croft-on-Tees N Yorks …
Croftamie Stirl 2…
Croftfoot S Lnrk 2…
Crofthandy Corn …
Croftlands Cumb 2…
Croftmalloch W Loth 2…
Croftmoraig Perth 28…
Crofton Cumb 2…
Crofton London …
Crofton W Yorks 19…
Crofton Wilts …
Crofts Dumfries 2…
Crofts Bank Gtr Man 1…
Crofts of Benachielt Highld 3…
Crofts of Haddo Aberds 3…
Crofts of Inverthernie Aberds 3…
Crofts of Meikle Ardo Aberds 3…
Crofty Swansea …
Croggan Argyll 2…
Croglin Cumb 2…
Croich Highld 3…
Croick Highld 3…
Croig Argyll 2…
Cros Dughaill W Isles 2…
Cromarty Highld 3…
Cromasaig Highld 29…
Crombie Fife 27…
Crombie Castle Aberds 3…
Cromblet Aberds 3…
Cromdale Highld 30…
Cromer Herts 1…
Cromer Norf 1…
Cromer-Hyde Herts …
Cromford Derbys 1…
Cromhall S Glos 7…
Cromhall Common S Glos …
Cromor W Isles 3…
Crompton Fold Gtr Man 1…
Cromra Highld 2…
Cromwell Notts 1…
Cromwell Bottom W Yorks 1…
Cronberry E Ayrs 2…
Crondall Hants …
Cronk-y-Voddy I o M 1…
Cronton Mers 1…
Crook Cumb 2…
Crook Devon 2…
Crook Durham 2…
Crook of Devon Perth 2…
Crookdake Cumb 2…
Crooke Gtr Man 1…
Crooked Billet London …
Crooked Soley Wilts …
Crooked Withies Dorset …
Crookedholm E Ayrs 25…
Crookes S Yorks 1…
Crookesmoor S Yorks 1…
Crookfur E Renf 26…
Crookgate Bank Durham 2…
Crookhall Durham 2…
Crookham Northumb 26…
Crookham W Berks …
Crookham Village Hants …
Crookhaugh Borders 2…
Crookhill T & W 2…
Crookhouse Borders 2…
Crooklands Cumb 21…
Crookston Glasgow 26…
Cropredy Oxon 1…
Cropston Leics 15…
Cropthorne Worcs …
Cropton N Yorks 2…
Cropwell Bishop Notts 1…
Cropwell Butler Notts 1…
Cros W Isles 3…
Crosben Highld 2…
Crosbost W Isles 3…
Crosby Cumb 2…
Crosby I o M 1…
Crosby Mers 1…
Crosby N Lincs 19…
Crosby Court N Yorks 2…
Crosby Garrett Cumb 2…
Crosby-on-Eden Cumb 23…
Crosby Ravensworth Cumb 2…
Crosby Villa Cumb 2…
Croscombe Som 4…
Crosemere Shrops 1…
Crosland Edge W Yorks 1…
Crosland Hill W Yorks 1…
Crosland Moor W Yorks 1…
Croslands Park Cumb 2…
Cross Devon 4…
Cross Devon 4…
Cross Shrops 1…
Cross Som 4…
Cross Ash Mon 7…
Cross-at-Hand Kent 5…
Cross Bank Worcs 1…
Cross Coombe Corn …
Cross End Beds 12…
Cross End Essex 1…
Cross End M Keynes 10…
Cross Gate W Sus 3…
Cross Gates W Yorks 2…
Cross Gates W Yorks 2…
Cross Green Devon 1…
Cross Green Staffs 1…
Cross Green Suff 1…
Cross Green Suff 1…
Cross Green Suff 1…
Cross Green Telford 1…
Cross Green W Yorks 2…
Cross Green Warks 1…
Cross Hands Carms …
Cross-hands Carms …
Cross Hands Pembs …
Cross Heath Staffs 1…
Cross Hill Corn …
Cross Hill Derbys 1…
Cross Hill Glos …
Cross Hills N Yorks 2…
Cross Holme N Yorks 22…
Cross Houses Shrops 13…
Cross Houses Shrops 1…
Cross in Hand E Sus …
Cross in Hand Leics 13…
Cross Inn Carms 1…
Cross Inn Ceredig 11…
Cross Inn Ceredig 1…
Cross Inn Rhondda …
Cross Keys Kent …
Cross Keys Wilts …
Cross Lane E Ches 16…
Cross Lane Head Shrops 13…
Cross Lanes Corn …
Cross Lanes Dorset 3…
Cross Lanes N Yorks 21…
Cross Lanes Oxon 6…

ss Lanes Wrex 166 F5
ss Llyde Hereford 97 F8
ss o' th' hands
rbys 170 F3
ss o' th' Hill W Ches 167 F7
ss Oak Powys 96 G2
ss of Jackston
erds 303 F7
ss Roads Devon 12 D5
ss Roads W Yorks 204 F6
ss Stone Aberds 303 G9
ss Street Suff 126 B3
ss Town E Ches 184 F3
ssaig Argyll 255 B9
ssal Highld 294 B6
ssapol Argyll 288 E1
ssbrae Aberds 302 D6
ssburn Falk 279 G7
ssbush W Sus 35 F8
sscanonby Cumb 229 D7
sscrake Cumb 211 B10
ssdale Street Norf 160 B4
ssens Mers 193 D11
ssflatts W Yorks 205 E8
ssford Fife 279 D11
ssford S Lnrk 268 F6
ssgate Lincs 156 D4
ssgate Orkney 314 E4
ssgate Staffs 151 B8
ssgatehall E Loth 271 B7
ssgates Cumb 229 G7
ssgates Fife 280 D2
ssgates N Yorks 217 C10
ssgates Powys 113 E11
ssgill Cumb 231 C10
ssgill Lancs 211 G11
ssgreen Shrops 149 F9
sshands Carms 92 G3
sshill E Ayrs 257 E11
sshill Fife 280 B3
sshill S Ayrs 245 B8
sshouse E Ayrs 257 B9
ssings Cumb 240 B2
sskeys Caerph 78 G2
sskirk Highld 310 B4
sslands Cumb 210 B6
sslanes Shrops 148 F6
sslee Borders 261 F8
sslee Renfs 267 B8
ssley Hall W Yorks 205 G8
ssmichael Dumfries 237 C9
ssmill E Renf 267 D10
ssmoor Lancs 202 F4
ssmount Perth 285 B11
sspost W Sus 36 C3
ssroads Aberds 293 D9
ssroads E Ayrs 257 C11
ssroads Fife 281 B7
sston Angus 287 B9
sstown Corn 24 D2
sstown V Glam 58 F4
sswater Sur 49 F11
ssway Hereford 98 E2
ssway Mon 78 B6
ssway Powys 113 F11
ssway Green Mon 79 G8
ssway Green Worcs 116 D6
ssways Dorset 17 D11
ssways Kent 68 D5
ssways Mon 96 G6
ssways S Glos 79 G11
ssways Sur 49 F11
sswell =
nnongroes Pembs 92 D2
sswood Ceredig 112 C3
sthwaite Cumb 221 G8
ston Lancs 194 D3
stwick Norf 160 F5
stwight Norf 160 D6
thair W Isles 304 E3
ıch Kent 52 B6
ıch Kent 54 B5
ıch End London 67 B9
ıch Hill Dorset 30 E2
ıch House Green
t 52 D2
ıchers W Sus 22 C4
ıcheston Wilts 31 B9
ıghly Moray 301 G11
ıghton Northants 101 E10
ıie Aberds 303 C8
w Hants 31 G11
w Edge S Yorks 197 G7
w Green Essex 87 F9
w Hill Hereford 98 F2
w Nest W Yorks 205 F8
w Wood Halton 183 D8
wan Corn 2 C4
wborough E Sus 52 G4
wborough Staffs 168 D6
wborough Warren
s 52 G4
wcombe Som 42 F6
wcroft Worcs 116 G5
wden Derbys 185 B9
wden Devon 12 B5
wder Park Devon 8 D4
wdhill Hants 33 C7
wdicote Derbys 169 B10
wdleham Kent 52 B5
wdon N Yorks 227 F9
well Oxon 84 F2
well Hill Oxon 84 F3
wfield Northants 102 C2
wfield Suff 126 F2
wgate Street Norf 160 E6
wgreaves Shrops 132 D4
whill Gtr Man 184 B6
whill M Keynes 102 D6
whole Derbys 186 F4
whurst E Sus 38 E3
whurst Sur 51 D11
whurst Lane End
51 D11
wland Lincs 156 G4
wlas Corn 2 C2
wle N Lincs 199 E9
wle Worcs 117 F8
wle Green Worcs 117 F8
wle Hill N Lincs 199 E9
wle Park N Lincs 199 E9
wmarsh Gifford
n 64 B6
wn Corner Suff 126 C5
wn East Worcs 116 G6
wn Hills Leicester 136 C2
wn Wood Brack 65 F11
wnfield Bucks 84 F4
wnhill Plym 7 D9
wnland Suff 125 D10
wnpits Sur 50 E3
wnthorpe Norf 141 C11
wntown Corn 2 C4
ws-an-wra Corn 1 D3
w's Green Essex 106 F3
w's Nest Corn 6 B5
wshill Norf 141 B8
wsley Oxon 65 D8
wsnest Shrops 131 C7
wther's Pool Powys 96 B4
wthorne Brack 65 G10
wton W Ches 183 G9
Croxall Staffs 152 G3
Croxby Lincs 189 B11
Croxby Top Lincs 189 B11
Croxdale Durham 233 D11
Croxden Staffs 151 B11
Croxley Green Herts 85 F9
Croxteth Mers 182 B6
Croxton Cambs 122 E4
Croxton N Lincs 200 E5
Croxton Norf 141 F7
Croxton Norf 159 C9
Croxton Staffs 150 C5
Croxton Green E Ches 167 E8
Croxton Kerrial Leics 154 D6
Croxtonbank Staffs 150 C5
Croy Highld 301 E7
Croy N Lnrk 278 F4
Croyde Devon 40 F2
Croyde Bay Devon 40 F2
Croydon Cambs 104 B6
Croydon London 67 F10
Crozen Hereford 97 B11
Crubenbeg Highld 291 D8
Crubenmore Lodge
Highld 291 D8
Cruckmeole Shrops 131 B8
Cruckton Shrops 149 G8
Cruden Bay Aberds 303 F10
Crudgington Telford 150 F2
Crudie Aberds 303 D7
Crudwell Wilts 81 G7
Crug Powys 114 C3
Crugmeer Corn 10 F4
Crugybar Carms 94 D3
Cruise Hill Worcs 117 E10
Crulabhig W Isles 304 E3
Crumlin Caerph 78 F2
Crumplehorn Corn 6 E4
Crumpsall Gtr Man 195 G10
Crumpsbrook Shrops 116 B2
Crumpton Hill Worcs 98 B5
Crundale Kent 54 D5
Crundale Pembs 73 B7
Cruwys Morchard Devon 26 E5
Crux Easton Hants 48 B2
Cruxton Dorset 17 B8
Crwbin Carms 75 C7
Crya Orkney 314 F3
Cryers Hill Bucks 84 F5
Crymlyn Gwyn 179 G10
Crymych Pembs 92 E3
Crynant = Creunant
Neath 76 E3
Crynfryn Ceredig 111 E11
Cuaich Highld 291 E8
Cuaig Highld 299 D7
Cuan Argyll 275 B8
Cubbington Warks 118 D6
Cubeck N Yorks 213 B9
Cubert Corn 4 D5
Cubitt Town London 67 D11
Cubley S Yorks 197 G8
Cubley Common Derbys 152 B3
Cublington Bucks 102 G6
Cublington Hereford 97 D8
Cuckfield W Sus 36 B4
Cucklington Som 30 B3
Cuckney Notts 187 G9
Cuckold's Green Suff 143 G9
Cuckold's Green Wilts 46 B3
Cuckoo Green Suff 143 D10
Cuckoo Hill Notts 188 C2
Cuckoo Tye Suff 107 C7
Cuckoo's Corner Hants 49 E8
Cuckoo's Corner Wilts 46 B4
Cuckoo's Knob Wilts 63 G7
Cuckron Shetland 313 H6
Cucumber Corner Norf 143 B7
Cuddesdon Oxon 83 E10
Cuddington Bucks 84 C2
Cuddington W Ches 183 G10
Cuddington Heath
W Ches 167 F7
Cuddy Hill Lancs 202 F5
Cudham London 52 B2
Cudliptown Devon 12 F6
Cudliptown Devon 12 F6
Cudworth S Yorks 197 F11
Cudworth Som 28 E5
Cudworth Sur 51 E8
Cudworth Common
S Yorks 197 F11
Cuerden Green Lancs 194 C5
Cuerdley Cross Warr 183 D8
Cufaude Hants 48 B6
Cuffern Pembs 91 G7
Cuffley Herts 86 E4
Cuiashader W Isles 304 C7
Cuidhir W Isles 297 L2
Cuidhtinis W Isles 296 C6
Cuiken Midloth 270 C4
Cuilcheanna Ho Highld 290 G2
Cuin Argyll 288 D6
Cul na h-Aird W Isles 305 H3
Cùl Doirlinn Highld 289 B8
Culbo Highld 300 C6
Culbokie Highld 300 D6
Culburnie Highld 300 E4
Culcabock Highld 300 E6
Culcairn Highld 300 C6
Culcharry Highld 301 D8
Culcheth Warr 183 B11
Culcronchie Dumfries 237 C7
Culdrain Aberds 302 F5
Culduie Highld 299 E7
Culeave Highld 309 K5
Culford Suff 124 D6
Culfordheath Suff 125 C7
Culfosie Aberds 293 C9
Culgaith Cumb 231 F8
Culham Oxon 83 F8
Culkein Highld 306 F5
Culkein Drumbeg Highld 306 F6
Culkerton Glos 80 F6
Cullachie Highld 301 G9
Cullen Moray 302 C5
Cullercoats T & W 243 C9
Cullicudden Highld 300 C6
Cullingworth W Yorks 205 F7
Cullipool Argyll 275 B8
Cullivoe Shetland 312 C7
Culloch Perth 285 F11
Culloden Highld 301 E7
Cullompton Devon 27 F8
Culm Davy Devon 27 D10
Culmaily Highld 311 K2
Culmazie Dumfries 236 D5
Culmer Sur 50 F2
Culmers Kent 70 G5
Culmington Shrops 131 G9
Culmore Stirl 278 B3
Culmstock Devon 27 E10
Culnacraig Highld 307 J5
Culnaightrie Dumfries 237 D9
Culnaknock Highld 298 C5
Culnaneam Highld 294 C6
Culpho Suff 108 B4
Culra Lodge Highld 291 F7
Culrain Highld 309 K5
Culross Fife 279 D9
Culroy S Ayrs 257 G8
Culscadden Dumfries 236 E6
Culsh Aberds 292 D5
Culsh Aberds 303 E8
Culshabbin Dumfries 236 D5
Culswick Shetland 313 J4
Cultercullen Aberds 303 G9
Cults Aberdeen 293 C10
Cults Aberds 302 F5
Cults Dumfries 236 E6
Cults Fife 287 G7
Culverlane Devon 8 C4
Culverstone Green Kent 68 G6
Culverthorpe Lincs 173 G8
Culworth Northants 101 B10
Culzie Lodge Highld 300 B5
Cumberlow Green Herts 104 E6
Cumbernauld N Lnrk 278 G5
Cumbernauld Village
N Lnrk 278 F5
Cumber's Bank Wrex 149 B8
Cumberworth Lincs 191 G8
Cumdivock Cumb 230 B2
Cumeragh Village Lancs 203 F7
Cuminestown Aberds 303 D8
Cumledge Borders 272 D5
Cumlewick Shetland 313 L6
Cumlodden Argyll 275 D11
Cumloden Dumfries 236 C6
Cummersdale Cumb 239 G9
Cummerton Aberds 303 C8
Cummertrees Dumfries 238 D4
Cummingston Moray 301 C11
Cumnock E Ayrs 258 E3
Cumnor Oxon 83 E7
Cumnor Hill Oxon 83 D7
Cumrew Cumb 240 G2
Cumwhinton Cumb 239 G10
Cumwhitton Cumb 240 G2
Cundall N Yorks 215 E8
Cundy Cross S Yorks 197 F11
Cundy Hos S Yorks 186 B4
Cunninghamhead
N Ayrs 267 G7
Cunnister Shetland 312 D7
Cupar Fife 287 F7
Cupar Muir Fife 287 F7
Cupernham Hants 32 C5
Cupid Green Herts 85 D9
Cupid's Hill Mon 97 F8
Curbar Derbys 186 G3
Curborough Staffs 152 G2
Curbridge Hants 33 E8
Curbridge Oxon 82 D4
Curdridge Hants 33 E8
Curdworth Warks 134 E3
Curgurrell Corn 3 B9
Curin Highld 300 D3
Curland Som 28 D3
Curland Common Som 28 D3
Curlew Green Suff 127 D7
Curling Tye Green Essex 88 D4
Curload Som 28 B4
Currarie S Ayrs 244 E5
Currian Vale Corn 5 D9
Curridge W Berks 64 E3
Currie Edin 270 B3
Currock Cumb 239 G10
Curry Lane Corn 11 C11
Curry Mallet Som 28 C4
Curry Rivel Som 28 B5
Cursiter Orkney 314 E3
Curteis' Corner Kent 53 F11
Curtisden Green Kent 53 E8
Curtisknowle Devon 8 E4
Curtismill Green Essex 87 F8
Cury Corn 2 E5
Cusbay Orkney 314 C5
Cusgarne Corn 4 G5
Cushnie Aberds 303 C7
Cushuish Som 43 G7
Cusop Hereford 96 C4
Custards Hants 32 F3
Custom House London 68 C2
Cusveorth Coombe Corn 4 G5
Cusworth S Yorks 198 G4
Cutcloy Dumfries 236 F6
Cutcombe Som 42 F2
Cutgate Gtr Man 195 E11
Cuthill E Loth 281 G7
Cutiau Gwyn 146 F2
Cutlers Green Essex 105 E11
Cutler's Green Som 44 C5
Cutmadoc Corn 5 C11
Cutmere Corn 6 C6
Cutnall Green Worcs 117 D7
Cutsdean Glos 99 E11
Cutsyke W Yorks 198 C2
Cutteslowe Oxon 83 C8
Cutthorpe Derbys 186 G4
Cuttiford's Door Som 28 E4
Cutts Shetland 313 K6
Cuttybridge Pembs 72 B6
Cuttyhill Aberds 303 D10
Cuxham Oxon 83 F11
Cuxton Medway 69 F8
Cuxwold Lincs 201 G7
Cwm Bl Gwent 77 D11
Cwm Denb 181 F9
Cwm Neath 57 C10
Cwm Powys 129 D11
Cwm Powys 130 E5
Cwm Shrops 114 B6
Cwm Swansea 57 B7
Cwm-byr Carms 94 E2
Cwm Capel Carms 75 E7
Cwm-celyn Bl Gwent 78 D2
Cwm-Cewydd Gwyn 147 G7
Cwm-cou Ceredig 92 C5
Cwm Dows Caerph 78 F2
Cwm-Dulais Swansea 75 E10
Cwm felin fach Caerph 77 G11
Cwm Ffrwd-oer Torf 78 E3
Cwm-Fields Torf 78 E3
Cwm Gelli Caerph 77 F11
Cwm Gwyn Swansea 56 C6
Cwm Head Shrops 131 F8
Cwm-hesgen Gwyn 146 D5
Cwm-hwnt Rhondda 76 D6
Cwm Irfon Powys 95 B7
Cwm-Llinau Powys 128 B6
Cwm-mawr Carms 75 C8
Cwm-miles Carms 92 G3
Cwm Nant-gam Bl Gwent 78 C2
Cwm-parc Rhondda 77 F7
Cwm Penmachno Conwy 164 F3
Cwm Plysgog Ceredig 92 C3
Cwm-twrch Isaf Powys 76 C3
Cwm-twrch Uchaf Powys 76 C3
Cwm-y-glo Carms 75 C9
Cwm-y-glo Gwyn 163 C8
Cwmafan Neath 57 C9
Cwmaman Rhondda 77 F8
Cwmann Carms 93 B11
Cwmavon Torf 78 D3
Cwmbach Rhondda 77 E8
Cwmbach Carms 75 E7
Cwmbach Carms 92 F5
Cwmbach Powys 96 D3
Cwmbach Rhondda 77 E8
Cwmbach Llechryd
Powys 113 G10
Cwmbelan Powys 129 G8
Cwmbran Torf 78 G3
Cwmbrwyno Ceredig 128 G4
Cwmcarn Caerph 78 G2
Cwmcarvan Mon 79 D7
Cwmcoednerth Ceredig 92 B6
Cwmcrawnon Powys 77 B10
Cwmcych Carms 92 D5
Cwmdare Rhondda 77 E7
Cwmdu Carms 94 E2
Cwmdu Powys 96 G3
Cwmdu Swansea 56 C6
Cwmduad Carms 93 E7
Cwmdwr Carms 94 E4
Cwmerfyn Ceredig 128 G3
Cwmfelin Bridgend 57 D11
Cwmfelin M Tydf 77 E9
Cwmfelin Boeth Carms 73 B11
Cwmfelin Mynach Carms 92 G4
Cwmffrwd Carms 74 B6
Cwmgiedd Powys 76 C3
Cwmgors Neath 76 C2
Cwmgwili Carms 75 C9
Cwmgwrach Neath 76 E5
Cwmhiraeth Carms 92 D6
Cwmifor Carms 94 F3
Cwmisfael Carms 75 B7
Cwmllynfell Neath 76 C2
Cwmnantyrodyn Caerph 77 F11
Cwmorgan Pembs 92 E5
Cwmparc Rhondda 77 F7
Cwmpengraig Carms 92 D6
Cwmpennar Rhondda 77 E8
Cwmrhos Powys 96 G3
Cwmrhydyceirw Swansea 57 B7
Cwmsychpant Ceredig 93 B9
Cwmsyfiog Caerph 77 E11
Cwmsymlog Ceredig 128 G3
Cwmtillery Bl Gwent 78 D2
Cwmwdig Water Pembs 90 E6
Cwmwysg Powys 95 F7
Cwmynyscoy Torf 78 F3
Cwmyoy Mon 96 G5
Cwmystwyth Ceredig 112 C5
Cwrt Gwyn 128 C3
Cwrt-newydd Ceredig 93 B9
Cwrt-y-cadno Carms 94 C3
Cwrt-y-gollen Powys 78 B2
Cydweli = Kidwelly
Carms 74 D6
Cyffordd Llandudno =
Llandudno Junction
Conwy 180 F3
Cyffylliog Denb 165 D9
Cyfronydd Powys 130 B2
Cymau Flint 166 D3
Cymdda Bridgend 58 C2
Cymer Neath 57 B11
Cymmer Rhondda 77 G8
Cyncoed Cardiff 59 C7
Cynghordy Carms 94 C6
Cynheidre Carms 75 D7
Cynonville Neath 57 B10
Cyntwell Cardiff 58 D6
Cynwyd Denb 165 G9
Cynwyl Elfed Carms 93 F7
Cywarch Gwyn 147 F7

D

Daccombe Devon 9 B8
Dacre Cumb 230 F5
Dacre N Yorks 214 G3
Dacre Banks N Yorks 214 G3
Daddry Shield Durham 232 D3
Dadford Bucks 102 D3
Dadlington Leics 135 D8
Dafarn Faig Gwyn 163 F7
Dafen Carms 75 E8
Daffy Green Norf 141 B9
Dagdale Staffs 151 C11
Dagenham London 68 C3
Daggons Dorset 31 E10
Daglingworth Glos 81 D7
Dagnall Bucks 85 B7
Dagtail End Worcs 117 E10
Dagworth Suff 125 E10
Dail Beag W Isles 304 D4
Dail bho Dheas W Isles 304 B6
Dail bho Thuath W Isles 304 B6
Dail Mor W Isles 304 D4
Daill Argyll 274 G4
Dailly S Ayrs 245 C7
Dainton Devon 9 B7
Dairsie or Osnaburgh
Fife 287 F8
Daisy Green Suff 125 D10
Daisy Green Suff 125 D11
Daisy Hill Gtr Man 195 G7
Daisy Hill W Yorks 197 B9
Daisy Hill W Yorks 205 G8
Daisy Nook Gtr Man 196 G2
Dalabrog W Isles 297 J3
Dalavich Argyll 275 B10
Dalbeattie Dumfries 237 C10
Dalbeg Highld 291 B8
Dalblair E Ayrs 258 F4
Dalbog Angus 293 F7
Dalbrack Stirl 285 G11
Dalbury Derbys 152 C5
Dalby I o M 192 E3
Dalby Lincs 190 G6
Dalby N Yorks 216 E2
Dalchalloch Perth 291 G9
Dalchalm Highld 311 J3
Dalchenna Argyll 284 G4
Dalchirach Moray 301 F11
Dalchonzie Perth 285 E11
Dalchork Highld 309 H5
Dalchreichart Highld 290 B4
Dalchruin Perth 285 F11
Dalderby Lincs 174 B2
Dale Cumb 230 C6
Dale Gtr Man 196 F3
Dale Pembs 72 D4
Dale Shetland 312 G6
Dale Abbey Derbys 153 B8
Dale Bottom Cumb 229 G11
Dale Brow E Ches 184 F6
Dale End Derbys 170 C2
Dale End N Yorks 204 D5
Dale Head Cumb 221 B8
Dale Hill E Sus 53 G7
Dale Hill E Sus 53 G8
Dale Moor Derbys 153 B8
Dale of Walls Shetland 313 H3
Dalebank Derbys 170 C5
Dalelia Highld 289 C9
Dales Brow Gtr Man 195 G9
Dales Green Staffs 168 D5
Daless Highld 301 F8
Dalestie Moray 292 B3
Dalestorth Notts 171 C8
Dalfaber Highld 291 B11
Dalfoil Stirl 277 D11
Dalganachan Highld 310 E4
Dalgarven N Ayrs 266 F5
Dalgety Bay Fife 280 E3
Dalginross Perth 285 E11
Dalguise Perth 286 C3
Dalhalvaig Highld 310 D2
Dalham Suff 124 E4
Dalhastnie Angus 293 F7
Dalhenzean Perth 292 G3
Dalinlongart Argyll 276 E2
Dalkeith Midloth 270 B6
Dallam Warr 183 C9
Dallas Moray 301 D11
Dallas Lodge Moray 301 D11
Dallcharn Highld 308 D6
Dalleagles E Ayrs 258 G3
Dallicott Shrops 132 E5
Dallimores I o W 20 C6
Dallinghoo Suff 126 G5
Dallington E Sus 23 B11
Dallington Northants 120 E4
Dallow N Yorks 214 E3
Dalmadilly Aberds 293 B9
Dalmally Argyll 284 E5
Dalmarnock Glasgow 268 C2
Dalmarnock Perth 286 C3
Dalmary Stirl 277 B10
Dalmellington E Ayrs 245 B11
Dalmeny Edin 280 F2
Dalmigavie Highld 291 B9
Dalmigavie Lodge
Highld 301 G7
Dalmilling S Ayrs 257 E9
Dalmore Highld 300 C6
Dalmuir W Dunb 277 G9
Dalnabreck Highld 289 C8
Dalnacardoch Lodge
Perth 291 F9
Dalnacroich Highld 300 D3
Dalnaglar Castle Perth 292 G3
Dalnahaitnach Highld 301 G8
Dalnamein Lodge Perth 291 G9
Dalnarrow Argyll 289 F9
Dalnaspidal Lodge
Perth 291 F8
Dalnavaid Perth 292 G2
Dalnavie Highld 300 B6
Dalnaw Dumfries 236 B5
Dalnawillan Lodge
Highld 310 E4
Dalness Highld 284 B5
Dalnessie Highld 309 H6
Dalphaid Highld 309 H3
Dalqueich Perth 286 G4
Dalrannoch Argyll 289 E11
Dalreavoch Highld 309 J7
Dalriach Highld 301 F10
Dalrigh Stirl 285 E7
Dalry Edin 280 G4
Dalry N Ayrs 266 F5
Dalrymple E Ayrs 257 G9
Dalscote Northants 120 G3
Dalserf S Lnrk 268 E6
Dalshannon N Lnrk 278 G4
Dalston Cumb 239 G9
Dalston London 67 C10
Dalswinton Dumfries 247 F10
Dalton Cumb 211 D10
Dalton Dumfries 238 C4
Dalton Lancs 194 F3
Dalton N Yorks 215 D8
Dalton N Yorks 224 D2
Dalton Northumb 241 F10
Dalton Northumb 242 C4
Dalton S Lnrk 268 D3
Dalton S Yorks 187 C7
Dalton W Yorks 197 D7
Dalton-in-Furness
Cumb 210 E4
Dalton-le-Dale Durham 234 B4
Dalton Magna S Yorks 187 C7
Dalton-on-Tees N Yorks 224 D5
Dalton Parva S Yorks 187 C7
Dalton Piercy Hrtlpl 234 E5
Dalveallan Highld 300 F6
Dalveich Stirl 285 E10
Dalvina Lo Highld 308 E6
Dalwey Telford 132 B3
Dalwhinnie Highld 291 E8
Dalwood Devon 28 G3
Dalwyne S Ayrs 245 D8
Dam Green Norf 141 F11
Dam Head W Yorks 196 B6
Dam Mill Staffs 133 C7
Dam of Quoiggs Perth 286 G2
Dam Side Lancs 202 D4
Damask Green Herts 104 F5
Damems W Yorks 204 F6
Damerham Hants 31 D10
Damery Glos 80 G2
Damgate Norf 143 B8
Damgate Norf 161 F9
Damhead Moray 301 D10
Damhead Holdings
Midloth 270 B5
Damnaglaur Dumfries 236 F3
Damside Borders 270 F3
Dan Caerlan Rhondda 58 C5
Danaway Kent 69 G11
Danbury Essex 88 E3
Danbury Common Essex 88 E3
Danby N Yorks 226 D4
Danby Wiske N Yorks 224 F6
Dancers Hill Herts 86 F2
Dancing Green Hereford 98 G2
Dandaleith Moray 302 E2
Danderhall Midloth 270 B6
Dandy Corner Suff 125 D11
Dane Bank Gtr Man 184 B6
Dane End Herts 104 G6
Dane in Shaw E Ches 168 C5
Dane Street Kent 54 C5
Danebank E Ches 185 E7
Danebridge E Ches 169 B7
Danegate E Sus 52 G5
Danehill E Sus 36 B6
Danemoor Green Norf 141 B11
Danes Moss E Ches 184 G6
Danesbury Herts 86 B2
Danesfield Bucks 65 C10
Danesford Shrops 132 E4
Daneshill Hants 49 C7
Danesmoor Derbys 170 C6
Daneway Glos 80 E6
Dangerous Corner
Gtr Man 195 G7
Dangerous Corner
Lancs 194 E4
Daniel's Water Kent 54 E3
Danna na Cloiche Argyll 275 F7
Dannonchapel Corn 10 E6
Danskine E Loth 271 B11
Danthorpe E Yorks 209 G10
Danygraig Caerph 78 G2
Danzey Green Warks 118 D2
Dapple Heath Staffs 151 D10
Darby End W Mid 133 F9
Darby Green Hants 65 G10
Darbys Green Worcs 116 F4
Darby's Hill W Mid 133 F9
Darcy Lever Gtr Man 195 F8
Dardy Powys 78 B2
Darenth Kent 68 E5
Daresbury Halton 183 E9
Daresbury Delph Halton 183 E9
Darfield S Yorks 198 G2
Darfoulds Notts 187 F9
Dargate Kent 70 G5
Dargate Common Kent 70 G5
Darite Corn 6 B5
Darkland Moray 302 C2
Darland Wrex 166 D5
Darlaston W Mid 133 D9
Darlaston Green W Mid 133 D9
Darley N Yorks 205 B10
Darley Shrops 132 D3
Darley Abbey Derby 153 B7
Darley Bridge Derbys 170 C3
Darley Dale Derbys 170 C3
Darley Green Warks 118 C3
Darley Head N Yorks 205 B9
Darley Hillside Derbys 170 C3
Darleyford Corn 11 G11
Darleyhall Herts 104 G2
Darlingscott Warks 100 C4
Darlington Darl 224 C5
Darliston Shrops 149 C11
Darlton Notts 188 G3
Darmsden Suff 125 G11
Darn Hill Gtr Man 195 E10
Darnall S Yorks 186 D5
Darnaway Castle Moray 301 D9
Darnford Staffs 134 B2
Darnhall W Ches 167 C10
Darnhall Mains Borders 270 F4
Darnick Borders 262 C2
Darowen Powys 128 C6
Darra Aberds 303 E7
Darracott Devon 24 D2
Darracott Devon 40 F3
Darras Hall Northumb 242 C5
Darrington W Yorks 198 D3
Darrow Green Norf 142 F5
Darsham Suff 127 D8
Darshill Som 44 E6
Dartford Kent 68 E4
Dartford Crossing Kent 68 D5
Dartington Devon 8 C5
Dartmeet Devon 13 G9
Dartmouth Devon 9 E7
Dartmouth Park London 67 B9
Darton S Yorks 197 F10
Darvel E Ayrs 258 B3
Darvillshill Bucks 84 F4
Darwell Hole E Sus 23 B11
Darwen Blkburn 195 C7
Dassels Herts 105 F7
Datchet Windsor 66 D3
Datchet Common
Windsor 66 D3
Datchworth Herts 86 B3
Datchworth Green Herts 86 B3
Daubhill Gtr Man 195 F8
Daugh of Kinermony
Moray 302 E2
Dauntsey Wilts 62 C3
Dauntsey Lock Wilts 62 C3
Dava Moray 301 F10
Davenham W Ches 183 G11
Davenport E Ches 168 B4
Davenport Gtr Man 184 D5
Davenport Green E Ches 184 F4
Davenport Green
Gtr Man 184 D4
Daventry Northants 119 E11
David Street Kent 68 G6
David's Well Powys 113 B11
Davidson's Mains Edin 280 F4
Davidston Highld 301 C7
Davidstow Corn 11 D9
Davington Dumfries 248 C6
Davington Kent 70 G4
Daviot Aberds 303 G7
Daviot Highld 301 F7
Davis's Town E Sus 23 B8
Davo Mains Aberds 293 F9
Davoch of Grange
Moray 302 D4
Davyhulme Gtr Man 184 B3
Daw Cross N Yorks 205 C11
Daw End W Mid 133 C10
Dawdon Durham 234 B4
Dawesgreen Sur 51 D8
Dawker Hill N Yorks 207 F7
Dawley Telford 132 B3
Dawley Bank Telford 132 B3
Dawlish Devon 14 F5
Dawlish Warren Devon 14 F5
Dawn Conwy 180 G5
Daw's Cross Essex 107 E7
Daw's Green Som 27 C11
Daws Heath Essex 69 B10
Daw's House Corn 12 E2
Dawshill Worcs 116 G6
Dawsmere Lincs 157 C8
Day Green E Ches 168 D3
Daybrook Notts 171 F9
Dayhills Staffs 151 C9
Dayhouse Bank Worcs 117 B9
Daylesford Glos 100 F4
Daywall Shrops 148 C5
Ddol Flint 181 G10
Ddôl Cownwy Powys 147 F10
Ddrydwy Anglesey 178 G5
De Beauvoir Town
London 67 C10
Deacons Hill Herts 85 F11
Deadman's Cross
C Beds 104 C2
Deadman's Green
Staffs 151 B10
Deadwater Hants 49 F10
Deadwater Northumb 250 D4
Deaf Hill Durham 234 D3
Deal Kent 55 C11
Deal Hall Essex 89 F8
Dean Cumb 229 F7
Dean Devon 8 C4
Dean Devon 40 D6
Dean Devon 40 E4
Dean Devon 41 D8
Dean Dorset 31 D7
Dean Edin 280 G4
Dean Hants 33 D9
Dean Hants 48 G2
Dean Lancs 195 B11
Dean Oxon 100 G6
Dean Som 45 E7
Dean Bank Durham 233 E11
Dean Court Oxon 83 D7
Dean Cross Devon 40 E4
Dean Head S Yorks 197 G9
Dean Lane Head
W Yorks 205 G7
Dean Park Renfs 267 B10
Dean Prior Devon 8 C4
Dean Row E Ches 184 E5
Dean Street Kent 53 C8
Deanburnhaugh
Borders 261 G9
Deane Gtr Man 195 F7
Deane Hants 48 C4
Deanend Dorset 31 D7
Deanich Lodge Highld 309 L3
Deanland Dorset 31 D7
Deanlane End W Sus 34 E2
Deans W Loth 269 B10
Deans Bottom Kent 69 G11
Dean's Green Warks 118 D2
Deans Hill Kent 69 G11
Deanscales Cumb 229 F7
Deansgreen E Ches 183 D11
Deanshanger Northants 102 D5
Deanston Stirl 285 G11
Dearham Cumb 229 D7
Dearnley Gtr Man 196 D2
Debach Suff 126 G4
Debdale Gtr Man 184 B5
Debden Essex 86 F6
Debden Essex 105 E11
Debden Cross Essex 105 E11
Debden Green Essex 86 F6
Debden Green Essex 105 E11
Debenham Suff 126 E3
Deblin's Green Worcs 98 B6
Dechmont W Loth 279 G10
Deckham T & W 243 E7
Deddington Oxon 101 E9
Dedham Essex 107 E11
Dedham Heath Essex 107 E11
Dedridge W Loth 269 B11
Dedworth Windsor 66 D2
Deebank Aberds 293 D8
Deecastle Aberds 292 D6
Deene Northants 137 E8
Deenethorpe Northants 137 E9
Deepcar S Yorks 186 B3
Deepclough Derbys 185 B8
Deepcut Sur 50 B2
Deepdale C Beds 104 B4
Deepdale Cumb 212 C4
Deepdale N Yorks 213 D7
Deepdene Sur 51 D7
Deepfields W Mid 133 E8
Deeping Gate Lincs 138 B2
Deeping St James Lincs 138 B3
Deeping St Nicholas
Lincs 156 F4
Deepthwaite Cumb 211 C10
Deepweir Mon 60 B3
Deerhill Moray 302 D4
Deerhurst Glos 99 F7
Deerhurst Walton Glos 99 F7
Deerland Pembs 73 C7
Deerness Orkney 314 F5
Deer's Green Essex 105 E9
Deerstones N Yorks 205 C7
Deerton Street Kent 70 G3
Defford Worcs 99 C8
Defynnog Powys 95 F8
Deganwy Conwy 180 F3
Degar V Glam 58 D4
Degibna Corn 2 D5
Deighton N Yorks 225 E7
Deighton W Yorks 197 D7
Deighton York 207 E8
Deiniolen Gwyn 163 C9
Deishar Highld 291 B11
Delabole Corn 11 E7
Delamere W Ches 167 B9
Delfour Highld 291 C10
Delfrigs Aberds 303 G9
Dell Lodge Highld 292 B2
Dell Quay W Sus 22 C4
Delliefure Highld 301 F10
Delly End Oxon 82 C5
Delnabo Moray 292 B3
Delnadamph Aberds 292 C4
Delnamer Angus 292 G3
Delph Gtr Man 196 F3
Delves Durham 233 B8
Delvin End Essex 106 D5
Delvine Perth 286 C5
Dembleby Lincs 155 B10
Demelza Corn 5 C9
Denaby Main S Yorks 187 B7
Denbeath Fife 281 B7
Denbigh Denb 165 B9
Denbury Devon 8 B6
Denby Derbys 170 F5
Denby Bottles Derbys 170 F5
Denby Common Derbys 170 F6
Denby Dale W Yorks 197 F8
Denchworth Oxon 82 G5
Dendron Cumb 210 E4
Dene Park Kent 52 C5
Denel End C Beds 103 D10
Denend Aberds 302 F6
Deneside Durham 234 B4
Denford Northants 121 B9
Denford Staffs 169 E7
Dengie Essex 89 E7
Denham Bucks 66 B4
Denham Bucks 102 G5
Denham Suff 124 E5
Denham Suff 126 C3
Denham Corner Suff 126 C3
Denham End Suff 124 E5
Denham Green Bucks 66 B4
Denham Street Suff 126 C3
Denhead Aberds 303 D9
Denhead Fife 287 F8
Denhead of Arbilot
Angus 287 C9
Denhead of Gray
Dundee 287 D7
Denholm Borders 262 F3
Denholme W Yorks 205 G7
Denholme Clough
W Yorks 205 G7
Denholme Edge
W Yorks 205 G7
Denholme Gate
W Yorks 205 G7
Denholmhill Borders 262 F3
Denio Gwyn 145 B7
Denmead Hants 33 E11
Denmore Aberdeen 293 B11
Denmoss Aberds 302 E6
Dennington Suff 126 D5
Dennington Corner
Suff 126 D5
Dennington Hall Suff 126 D5
Denny Falk 278 E6
Denny Bottom Kent 52 F5
Denny End Cambs 123 D9
Denny Lodge Hants 32 F4
Dennyloanhead Falk 278 E6
Dennystown W Dunb 277 F7
Denshaw Gtr Man 196 E3
Denside Aberds 293 D10
Densole Kent 55 E8
Denston Suff 124 G5
Denstone Staffs 169 G9
Denstroude Kent 70 G6
Dent Cumb 212 B4
Dent Bank Durham 232 F4
Denton Cambs 138 F2
Denton Darl 224 B4
Denton E Sus 23 E7
Denton Gtr Man 184 B6
Denton Kent 55 D8
Denton Kent 69 E7
Denton Lincs 155 C7
Denton N Yorks 205 D8
Denton Norf 142 F5
Denton Northants 120 F6
Denton Oxon 83 E9
Denton Burn T & W 242 D5
Denton Holme Cumb 239 G10
Denton's Green Mers 183 B7
Denver Norf 140 C2
Denvilles Hants 34 F2
Denwick Northumb 264 G6
Deopham Norf 141 C11
Deopham Green Norf 141 D10
Deopham Stalland
Norf 141 D10
Depden Suff 124 F5
Depden Green Suff 124 F5
Deppers Bridge Warks 119 F7
Deptford London 67 D11
Deptford T & W 243 F9
Deptford Wilts 46 F4
Derby Derbys 153 B7
Derby Devon 40 G5
Derbyhaven I o M 192 F3
Derbyshire Hill Mers 183 C8
Dereham Norf 159 G9
Dergoals Dumfries 236 D4
Deri Caerph 77 E10
Derriford Plym 7 D9
Derril Devon 24 G4
Derringstone Kent 55 D8
Derrington Shrops 132 E2
Derrington Staffs 151 E7
Derriton Devon 24 G4
Derry Stirl 285 E10
Derry Downs London 68 F3
Derry Fields Wilts 81 G8
Derry Hill Wilts 62 E3
Derry Lodge Aberds 292 D2
Derrydaroch Stirl 285 E7
Derryguaig Argyll 288 F6
Derrythorpe N Lincs 199 F10
Dersingham Norf 158 C3
Dertfords Wilts 45 D10
Dervaig Argyll 288 D6
Derwen Bridgend 58 C2
Derwen Denb 165 E9
Derwenlas Powys 128 D4
Desborough Northants 136 G6
Desford Leics 135 C9
Deskryshiel Aberds 292 B6
Detchant Northumb 264 B3
Detling Kent 53 B9
Deuchar Angus 292 G6
Deuddwr Powys 148 F4
Deuxhill Shrops 132 F3
Devauden Mon 79 F7
Deveral Corn 2 B3
Devil's Bridge =
Pontarfynach Ceredig 112 B4
Devitts Green Warks 134 E5
Devizes Wilts 62 G4
Devol Invclyd 276 G6
Devon Village Clack 279 B8
Devonport Plym 7 E9
Devonside Clack 279 B8
Devoran Corn 3 B7
Dewar Borders 270 F6
Dewartown Midloth 271 C7
Dewes Green Essex 105 E9
Dewlands Common
Dorset 31 F9
Dewlish Dorset 17 B11
Dewsbury W Yorks 197 C8
Dewsbury Moor W Yorks 197 C8
Dewshall Court Hereford 97 E9
Dhoon I o M 192 D5
Dhoor I o M 192 C5
Dhowin I o M 192 B5
Dhustone Shrops 115 B11
Dial Green W Sus 34 B6
Dial Post W Sus 35 D11
Dibberford Dorset 29 G7
Dibden Hants 32 F6
Dibden Purlieu Hants 32 F6
Dickens Heath W Mid 118 B2
Dickleburgh Norf 142 G3
Dickleburgh Moor Norf 142 G3
Dickon Hills Lincs 174 D6
Didbrook Glos 99 E11
Didcot Oxon 64 B4
Diddington Cambs 122 D3
Diddlebury Shrops 131 F10
Diddywell Devon 25 B7
Didley Hereford 97 E9
Didling W Sus 34 D4
Didlington Norf 140 D5
Didmarton Glos 61 B10
Didsbury Gtr Man 184 C4
Didworthy Devon 8 C3
Diebidale Highld 309 L4
Digbeth W Mid 133 F11
Digby Lincs 173 E9
Digg Highld 298 C4
Diggle Gtr Man 196 F4
Diglis Worcs 116 G6
Digmoor Lancs 194 F3
Digswell Herts 86 B3
Digswell Park Herts 86 C2
Digswell Water Herts 86 C3
Dihewyd Ceredig 111 F9
Dilham Norf 160 D6
Dilhorne Staffs 169 G7
Dill Hall Lancs 195 B8
Dillarburn S Lnrk 268 G6
Dillington Cambs 122 D2
Dillington Som 28 D5
Dilston Northumb 241 E11
Dilton Marsh Wilts 45 D11
Dilwyn Hereford 115 G8
Dimlands V Glam 58 F3
Dimmer Som 44 G6
Dimple Derbys 170 C3
Dimple Gtr Man 195 D8
Dimsdale Staffs 168 F4
Dimson Corn 12 G4
Dinas Carms 92 E5
Dinas Gwyn 144 B5
Dinas Gwyn 163 D7
Dinas Cross Pembs 91 D10
Dinas Dinlle Gwyn 162 D6
Dinas-Mawddwy Gwyn 147 G7
Dinas Mawr Conwy 164 E4
Dinas Powys V Glam 59 E7
Dinbych y Pysgod =
Tenby Pembs 73 E10
Dinckley Lancs 203 F9
Dinder Som 44 E5
Dinedor Hereford 97 D10
Dinedor Cross Hereford 97 D10
Dines Green Worcs 116 F6
Dingestow Mon 79 C7
Dinghurst N Som 44 B2
Dingle Mers 182 D5
Dingleden Kent 53 G10
Dingleton Borders 262 C2
Dingley Northants 136 F4
Dingwall Highld 300 D5
Dinlabyre Borders 250 E2
Dinmael Conwy 165 G8
Dinnet Aberds 292 D6
Dinnington S Yorks 187 D8
Dinnington Som 28 E6
Dinnington T & W 242 C6
Dinorwic Gwyn 163 C9
Dinton Bucks 84 C3
Dinton Wilts 46 G4
Dinwoodie Mains
Dumfries 248 E4

E

Hoathly E Sus 23 B8
Hogaland Shetland 313 K5
Holme Dorset 18 D3
Holton Dorset 18 C5
Holywell Northumb 243 C8
Horndon Essex 68 B6
Horrington Som 44 D5
Horsley Sur 50 C5
Horton Northumb 264 C2
Howdon T & W 243 D8
Howe Bmouth 19 B7
Huntspill Som 43 E10
Hyde C Beds 85 B10
Ilkerton Devon 41 D8
Ilsley W Berks 64 C3
Keal Lincs 174 C5
Kennett Wilts 62 F6
Keswick W Yorks 206 E3
Kilbride S Lnrk 268 E2
Kimber Devon 12 B5
Kingston W Sus 35 G9
Kirkby Lincs 174 C4
Knapton N Yorks 217 D7
Knighton Dorset 18 D2
Knowstone Devon 26 C4
Knoyle Wilts 45 G11
Kyloe Northumb 264 B3
Kyo Durham 242 G5
Lambrook Som 28 D6
Lamington Highld 301 B7
Langdon Kent 55 D10
Langton Leics 136 E4
Langwell Highld 309 J7
Lavant W Sus 22 B5
Lavington W Sus 34 D6
Law Northumb 242 G3
Layton N Yorks 224 D3
Leake Notts 153 D11
Learmouth
thumb 263 B9
Leigh Devon 8 E3
Leigh Devon 25 F11
Lexham Norf 159 F7
Lilburn Northumb 264 E2
Linton E Loth 281 F11
Liss Hants 34 B3
Lockinge Oxon 64 B2
Loftus Redcar 226 B4
Looe Corn 6 E5
Lound N Lincs 188 B3
Lulworth Dorset 18 E3
Lutton N Yorks 217 F8
Lydeard Som 27 B11
Lydford Som 44 G5
Lyng Som 28 B4
Mains Aberds 293 D8
Mains Borders 271 F11
Mains S Lnrk 268 E2
Malling Kent 53 B8
Malling Heath Kent 53 B7
March Angus 287 D8
Marden W Sus 34 E4
Markham Notts 188 G2
Marsh NE Lincs 201 E9
Martin Hants 31 D9
Marton N Yorks 204 C4
Melbury Dorset 30 C5
Meon Hants 33 C11
Mere Devon 27 D7
Mersea Essex 89 C9
Mey Highld 310 B7
Molesey Sur 67 F7
Moor W Yorks 197 C10
Moors Cardiff 59 D8
Morden Dorset 18 B4
Morton W Yorks 205 E7
Moulsecoomb
ghton 36 F4
Ness N Yorks 216 D3
Newton E Yorks 209 F11
Newton N Yorks 216 D2
Norton Leics 136 C5
Nynehead Som 27 C11
Oakley Hants 48 C5
Ogwell Devon 14 G2
Orchard Dorset 30 D4
Ord Northumb 273 E9
Panson Devon 12 C3
Parley Dorset 19 B8
Peckham Kent 53 D7
Pennard Som 44 F5
Perry Cambs 122 D3
Portholland Corn 5 G9
Portlemouth Devon 9 G9
Prawle Devon 9 G10
Preston W Sus 35 G9
Pulham Dorset 30 F2
Putford Devon 24 D5
Quantoxhead Som 42 E6
Rainton T & W 234 B2
Ravendale NE Lincs 190 B2
Raynham Norf 159 D7
Rhidorroch Lodge
hld 307 K7
Rigton W Yorks 206 E3
Rolstone N Som 59 G11
Rounton N Yorks 225 E8
Row N Yorks 227 C7
Rudham Norf 158 D6
Runton Norf 177 E11
Ruston Norf 160 D6
Saltoun E Loth 271 B9
Sheen London 67 D8
Skelston Dumfries 247 F8
Sleekburn
thumb 253 G7
Somerton Norf 161 F9
Stanley Durham 242 G6
Stockwith Lincs 188 C3
Stoke Dorset 18 D3
Stoke Notts 172 F3
Stoke Som 29 D7
Stour Dorset 30 C4
Stour Common
set 30 C4
Stourmouth Kent 71 G9
Stowford Devon 25 B10
Stratton Hants 48 F4
Street Kent 55 B10
Street Som 44 F4
Studdal Kent 55 D10
Suisnish Highld 295 B7
Taphouse Corn 6 C3
-the-Water Devon 25 B7
Third Borders 262 B4
Thirston Northumb 252 D5
Tilbury Thurrock 69 D7
Tisted Hants 49 G8
Torrington Lincs 189 E10
Town Som 42 G6
Town Som 44 E6
Town Wilts 45 B11
Trewent Pembs 73 F8
Tuddenham Norf 159 G11
Tuelmenna Corn 6 B4
Tytherley Hants 32 B3
Tytherton Wilts 62 E3
Village Devon 26 F4
Village V Glam 58 E3
Wall Shrops 131 E10
Walton Norf 158 F4
Water Som 44 C4
East Week Devon 13 C9
East Wellow Hants 32 C4
East Wemyss Fife 280 B6
East Whitburn W Loth 269 B9
East Wickham London 68 D3
East Williamston Pembs 73 E9
East Winch Norf 158 F3
East Winterslow Wilts 47 G8
East Wittering W Sus 21 B11
East Witton N Yorks 214 B2
East Woodburn
Northumb 251 F10
East Woodhay Hants 64 G2
East Woodlands Som 45 E9
East Worldham Hants 49 F8
East Worlington Devon 26 E3
East Worthing W Sus 35 G11
East Wretham Norf 141 E8
East Youlstone Devon 24 D3
Eastacombe Devon 25 B8
Eastacombe Devon 25 C9
Eastacott Devon 25 C10
Eastbourne Darl 224 C6
Eastbourne E Sus 23 F10
Eastbridge Suff 127 D9
Eastbrook Som 28 C2
Eastbrook V Glam 59 E7
Eastburn E Yorks 208 B5
Eastburn W Yorks 204 E6
Eastburn Br W Yorks 204 E6
Eastbury London 85 G9
Eastbury W Berks 63 D10
Eastby N Yorks 204 C6
Eastchurch Kent 70 E3
Eastcombe Glos 80 E5
Eastcote London 66 B6
Eastcote Northants 120 G3
Eastcote W Mid 118 B3
Eastcote Village London 66 B6
Eastcott Corn 24 D3
Eastcott Wilts 46 B4
Eastcotts Beds 103 B11
Eastcourt Wilts 63 G8
Eastcourt Wilts 81 G7
Eastdon Devon 14 F5
Eastdown Devon 8 F6
Eastend Essex 86 C6
Eastend Oxon 100 G6
Easter Aberchalder
Highld 291 B7
Easter Ardross Highld 300 B6
Easter Balgedie Perth 286 G5
Easter Balmoral Aberds 292 D4
Easter Boleskine Highld 300 G5
Easter Brae Highld 300 C6
Easter Cardno Aberds 303 C9
Easter Compton S Glos 60 C5
Easter Cringate Stirl 278 D4
Easter Culfosie Aberds 293 C9
Easter Davoch Aberds 292 C6
Easter Earshaig
Dumfries 248 C2
Easter Ellister Argyll 254 B3
Easter Fearn Highld 309 L6
Easter Galcantray
Highld 301 E8
Easter Housebyres
Borders 262 B2
Easter Howgate Midloth 270 C4
Easter Howlaws
Borders 272 G4
Easter Kinkell Highld 300 D5
Easter Knox Angus 287 D9
Easter Langlee Borders 262 B2
Easter Lednathie Angus 292 G5
Easter Milton Highld 301 D9
Easter Moniack Highld 300 E5
Easter Ord Aberdeen 293 C10
Easter Quarff Shetland 313 K6
Easter Rhynd Perth 286 F5
Easter Row Stirl 278 B5
Easter Silverford
Aberds 303 C7
Easter Skeld Shetland 313 J5
Easter Softlaw Borders 263 C7
Easter Tulloch Highld 291 B11
Easter Whyntie Aberds 302 C6
Eastergate W Sus 22 B6
Easterhouse Glasgow 268 B3
Eastern Green W Mid 134 G5
Easterside M'bro 225 B10
Easterton Wilts 46 C4
Easterton of Lenabo
Aberds 303 E10
Easterton Sands Wilts 46 B4
Eastertown Som 43 C10
Eastertown of
Auchleuchries Aberds 303 F10
Eastfield Borders 262 D2
Eastfield Bristol 60 D5
Eastfield N Lnrk 269 C7
Eastfield N Lnrk 278 G4
Eastfield N Yorks 217 C10
Eastfield Northumb 243 B7
Eastfield P'boro 138 D4
Eastfield S Lnrk 268 C2
Eastfield S Yorks 197 G9
Eastfield Hall Northumb 252 B6
Eastgate Durham 232 D5
Eastgate Norf 160 E2
Eastgate P'boro 138 D4
Easthall Herts 104 G3
Eastham Mers 182 E5
Eastham Worcs 116 D3
Eastham Ferry Mers 182 E5
Easthampstead Brack 65 F11
Easthampton Hereford 115 E8
Easthaugh Norf 159 F11
Eastheath Wokingham 65 F10
Easthope Shrops 131 D11
Easthopewood Shrops 131 D11
Easthorpe Essex 107 G8
Easthorpe Leics 154 B6
Easthorpe Notts 172 E2
Easthouse Shetland 313 J5
Easthouses Midloth 270 B6
Easting Orkney 314 A7
Eastington Devon 26 F2
Eastington Glos 80 D3
Eastington Glos 81 C10
Eastland Gate Hants 33 E11
Eastleach Martin Glos 82 D2
Eastleach Turville Glos 81 D11
Eastleigh Devon 25 B7
Eastleigh Hants 32 D6
Eastling Kent 54 B3
Eastmoor Derbys 186 G4
Eastmoor Norf 140 C4
Eastney Ptsmth 21 B9
Eastnor Hereford 98 D4
Eastoft N Lincs 199 D10
Eastoke Hants 21 B10
Easton Bristol 60 E6
Easton Cambs 122 C2
Easton Cumb 239 C10
Easton Cumb 239 F7
Easton Devon 13 D10
Easton Dorset 17 G9
Easton Hants 48 G4
Easton I o W 20 D2
Easton Lincs 155 D8
Easton Norf 160 G2
Easton Som 44 D4
Easton Suff 126 F5
Easton W Berks 64 E2
Easton Wilts 61 E11
Easton Grey Wilts 61 B11
Easton in Gordano
N Som 60 D4
Easton Maudit Northants 121 F7
Easton on the Hill
Northants 137 C10
Easton Royal Wilts 63 G8
Easton Town Som 44 G5
Easton Town Wilts 61 B11
Eastover Som 43 F10
Eastpark Dumfries 238 D2
Eastrea Cambs 138 D5
Eastriggs Dumfries 238 D6
Eastrington E Yorks 199 B9
Eastrip Wilts 61 E10
Eastrop Hants 48 C6
Eastry Kent 55 C10
Eastville Bristol 60 E6
Eastville Lincs 174 D6
Eastwell Leics 154 D5
Eastwell Park Kent 54 D4
Eastwick Herts 86 C6
Eastwick Shetland 312 F5
Eastwood Hereford 98 C2
Eastwood Notts 171 F7
Eastwood S Yorks 186 C6
Eastwood Sthend 69 B10
Eastwood W Yorks 196 B3
Eastwood End Cambs 139 E8
Eastwood Hall Notts 171 F7
Eathorpe Warks 119 D7
Eaton C Ches 168 B5
Eaton Hereford 115 F10
Eaton Leics 154 D5
Eaton Norf 142 B4
Eaton Notts 188 F2
Eaton Oxon 82 E6
Eaton Shrops 131 F10
Eaton Shrops 131 F7
Eaton W Ches 167 C9
Eaton Bishop Hereford 97 D8
Eaton Bray C Beds 103 G9
Eaton Constantine
Shrops 131 B11
Eaton Ford Cambs 122 E3
Eaton Green C Beds 103 G9
Eaton Hastings Oxon 82 F3
Eaton Mascott Shrops 131 B10
Eaton on Tern Shrops 150 E3
Eaton Socon Cambs 122 F3
Eaton upon Tern Shrops 150 E3
Eau Brink Norf 157 F11
Eau Withington
Hereford 97 C10
Eaves Green W Mid 134 G5
Eavestone N Yorks 214 F4
Ebberly Hill Devon 25 D9
Ebberston N Yorks 217 C7
Ebbesbourne Wake
Wilts 31 C7
Ebblake Hants 31 F10
Ebbw Vale Bl Gwent 77 D11
Ebchester Durham 242 F4
Ebdon N Som 59 G11
Ebernoe W Sus 35 B7
Ebford Devon 14 D5
Ebley Glos 80 D4
Ebnal W Ches 167 F7
Ebnall Hereford 115 F9
Ebreywood Shrops 149 F10
Ebrington Glos 100 C3
Ecchinswell Hants 48 B4
Ecclaw Borders 272 B5
Ecclefechan Dumfries 238 B5
Eccles Borders 272 G5
Eccles Gtr Man 184 B3
Eccles Kent 69 G8
Eccles on Sea Norf 161 D8
Eccles Road Norf 141 E10
Eccleshall S Yorks 186 E4
Ecclesfield S Yorks 186 C5
Ecclesgreig Aberds 293 G9
Eccleshall Staffs 150 D6
Eccleshill W Yorks 205 F9
Ecclesmachan
W Loth 279 G11
Eccleston Lancs 194 D4
Eccleston Mers 183 B7
Eccleston W Ches 166 C6
Eccleston Park Mers 183 C7
Eccliffe Dorset 30 B3
Eccup W Yorks 205 E11
Echt Aberds 293 C9
Eckford Borders 262 D6
Eckfordmoss Borders 262 D6
Eckington Derbys 186 F6
Eckington Worcs 99 C8
Eckington Corner E Sus 23 D8
Ecklands S Yorks 197 G8
Eckworthy Devon 24 D6
Ecton Northants 120 E6
Ecton Staffs 169 D9
Ecton Brook Northants 120 E6
Edale Derbys 185 D10
Edale End Derbys 185 D11
Edbrook Som 43 E8
Edburton W Sus 36 E2
Edderside Cumb 229 B7
Edderton Highld 309 L7
Eddington Kent 71 F7
Eddington W Berks 63 F10
Eddistone Devon 24 C3
Eddleston Borders 270 F4
Eddlewood S Lnrk 268 E4
Eden Mount Cumb 211 D8
Eden Park London 67 F11
Eden Vale Durham 234 D4
Eden Vale Wilts 45 C11
Edenbridge Kent 52 D2
Edenfield Lancs 195 D9
Edenhall Cumb 231 E7
Edenham Lincs 155 E11
Edensor Derbys 170 B2
Edentaggart Argyll 276 C6
Edenthorpe S Yorks 198 F6
Edentown Cumb 239 F9
Ederline Argyll 275 C9
Edern Gwyn 144 B5
Edford Som 45 D7
Edgarley Som 44 F4
Edgbaston W Mid 133 G11
Edgcote Northants 101 B10
Edgcott Bucks 102 G3
Edgcott Som 41 F10
Edgcumbe Corn 2 C6
Edge Glos 80 D4
Edge Shrops 131 B7
Edge End Glos 79 C9
Edge End Lancs 203 G10
Edge Fold Blkburn 195 D8
Edge Fold Gtr Man 195 F8
Edge Green Gtr Man 183 B9
Edge Green Norf 141 F10
Edge Green W Ches 167 E7
Edge Hill Mers 182 C5
Edge Hill Warks 134 D4
Edge Mount S Yorks 186 C3
Edgebolton Shrops 149 E11
Edgefield Norf 159 C11
Edgefield Street Norf 159 C11
Edgehill Warks 101 B7
Edgeley Gtr Man 184 D5
Edgerley Shrops 148 F6
Edgerston Borders 262 G5
Edgerton W Yorks 196 D6
Edgeside Lancs 195 C10
Edgeworth Glos 80 D6
Edginswell Devon 9 B7
Edgiock Worcs 117 E10
Edgmond Telford 150 F4
Edgmond Marsh Telford 150 E4
Edgton Shrops 131 F7
Edgware London 85 G11
Edgwick W Mid 134 G6
Edgworth Blkburn 195 D8
Edham Borders 262 B6
Edial Staffs 133 B11
Edinample Stirl 285 E9
Edinbane Highld 298 D3
Edinburgh Edin 280 G5
Edinchip Stirl 285 E9
Edingale Staffs 152 G4
Edingight Ho Moray 302 D5
Edinglassie Ho Aberds 292 B5
Edingley Notts 171 D11
Edingthorpe Norf 160 C6
Edingthorpe Green
Norf 160 C6
Edington Som 43 E11
Edington Wilts 46 C2
Edingworth Som 43 C11
Edintore Moray 302 E4
Edistone Devon 24 C2
Edith Weston Rutland 137 B8
Edithmead Som 43 D10
Edlaston Derbys 169 G11
Edlesborough Bucks 85 B7
Edlingham Northumb 252 B4
Edlington Lincs 190 G2
Edmondsham Dorset 31 E9
Edmondsley Durham 233 B10
Edmondstown Rhondda 77 G8
Edmondthorpe Leics 155 F7
Edmonston S Lnrk 269 G11
Edmonstone Orkney 314 D5
Edmonton Corn 10 G5
Edmonton London 86 G4
Edmundbyers Durham 242 G2
Ednam Borders 262 B6
Ednaston Derbys 170 G2
Edney Common Essex 87 E11
Edradynate Perth 286 B2
Edrom Borders 272 D6
Edstaston Shrops 149 C10
Edstone Warks 118 E3
Edvin Loach Hereford 116 F3
Edwalton Notts 153 B11
Edwardstone Suff 107 C8
Edwardsville M Tydf 77 F9
Edwinsford Carms 94 E2
Edwinstowe Notts 171 B10
Edworth C Beds 104 C4
Edwyn Ralph Hereford 116 F2
Edzell Angus 293 G7
Efail-fôch Neath 57 B9
Efail Isaf Rhondda 58 C5
Efailnewydd Gwyn 145 B7
Efailwen Carms 92 F2
Efenechtyd Denb 165 D10
Effingham Sur 50 C6
Effirth Shetland 313 H5
Effledge Borders 262 F3
Efflinch Staffs 152 F3
Efford Devon 26 G5
Efford Plym 7 D10
Egbury Hants 48 C2
Egdon Worcs 117 G8
Egerton Gtr Man 195 E8
Egerton Kent 54 D2
Egerton Forstal Kent 53 D11
Egerton Green E Ches 167 E8
Egford Som 45 D9
Eggbeare Corn 12 D2
Eggborough N Yorks 198 C5
Eggbuckland Plym 7 D10
Eggesford Station
Devon 25 E11
Eggington C Beds 103 F9
Egginton Derbys 152 D5
Egginton Common
Derbys 152 D5
Egglesburn Durham 232 G5
Egglescliffe Stockton 225 C8
Eggleston Durham 232 G5
Egham Sur 66 E4
Egham Hythe Sur 66 E4
Egham Wick Sur 66 E3
Egleton Rutland 137 B7
Eglingham Northumb 264 F4
Egloshayle Corn 10 G5
Egloskerry Corn 11 D11
Eglwys-Brewis V Glam 58 F4
Eglwys Cross Wrex 167 G7
Eglwys Fach Ceredig 128 D3
Eglwysbach Conwy 180 G4
Eglwyswen Pembs 92 D3
Eglwyswrw Pembs 92 D2
Egmanton Notts 172 B2
Egmere Norf 159 B8
Egremont Cumb 219 C10
Egremont Mers 182 C4
Egton N Yorks 226 D6
Egton Bridge N Yorks 226 D6
Egypt Bucks 66 B3
Egypt Hants 48 E3
Egypt W Berks 64 D2
Egypt W Yorks 205 G7
Eiden Highld 309 J7
Eight Ash Green Essex 107 F8
Eighton Banks T & W 243 F7
Eign Hill Hereford 97 D10
Eignaig Highld 289 E9
Eil Highld 291 B10
Eilanreach Highld 295 D10
Eildon Borders 262 C3
Eilean Anabaich
W Isles 305 H4
Eilean Darach Highld 307 L6
Eilean Shona Ho Highld 289 B8
Eileanach Lodge Highld 300 C5
Einacleite W Isles 304 F3
Einsiob = Evenjobb
Powys 114 E5
Eisgean W Isles 305 G5
Eisingrug Gwyn 146 C2
Elan Village Powys 113 D8
Eland Green Northumb 242 C5
Elberton S Glos 60 B6
Elborough N Som 43 B11
Elbridge Shrops 149 E7
Elbridge W Sus 22 C6
Elburton Plym 7 E10
Elcho Perth 286 E5
Elcock's Brook Worcs 117 E10
Elcombe Glos 80 F3
Elcombe Swindon 62 C6
Elcot W Berks 63 F11
Eldene Swindon 63 C7
Elder Street Essex 105 E11
Eldernell Cambs 138 D6
Eldersfield Worcs 98 E6
Elderslie Renfs 267 C8
Eldon Durham 233 F10
Eldon Lane Durham 233 F10
Eldrick S Ayrs 245 G7
Eldroth N Yorks 212 F5
Eldwick W Yorks 205 E8
Elemore Vale T & W 234 B3
Elerch = Bont-goch
Ceredig 128 F3
Elfhowe Cumb 221 F9
Elford Northumb 264 C5
Elford Staffs 152 G3
Elford Closes Cambs 123 C10
Elgin Moray 302 C2
Elgol Highld 295 D7
Elham Kent 55 E7
Eliburn W Loth 269 B10
Elie Fife 287 G8
Elim Anglesey 178 D5
Eling Hants 32 E5
Eling W Berks 64 D4
Elishader Highld 298 C5
Elishaw Northumb 251 D9
Elizafield Dumfries 238 C2
Elkesley Notts 187 F11
Elkington Northants 120 B2
Elkins Green Essex 87 E10
Elkstone Glos 81 C7
Ellacombe Torbay 9 C8
Ellan Highld 301 G8
Elland W Yorks 196 C6
Elland Lower Edge
W Yorks 196 C6
Elland Upper Edge
W Yorks 196 C6
Ellary Argyll 275 F8
Ellastone Staffs 169 G10
Ellel Lancs 202 B5
Ellemford Borders 272 C4
Ellenborough Cumb 228 D6
Ellenbrook Herts 86 D2
Ellenbrook I o M 192 E4
Ellenglaze Corn 4 D5
Ellenhall Staffs 150 D6
Ellen's Green Sur 50 F5
Ellerbeck N Yorks 225 F8
Ellerburn N Yorks 216 C6
Ellerby N Yorks 226 C5
Ellerdine Telford 150 E2
Ellerdine Heath Telford 150 E2
Ellerhayes Devon 27 G7
Elleric Argyll 284 C4
Ellerker E Yorks 200 B2
Ellerton E Yorks 207 F10
Ellerton N Yorks 224 F5
Ellerton Shrops 150 D4
Ellesborough Bucks 84 D4
Ellesmere Shrops 149 C8
Ellesmere Park Gtr Man 184 B3
Ellesmere Port W Ches 182 F6
Ellicombe Som 42 E3
Ellingham Hants 31 F10
Ellingham Norf 143 E7
Ellingham Northumb 264 D5
Ellingstring N Yorks 214 C3
Ellington Cambs 122 C3
Ellington Northumb 253 E7
Ellington Thorpe Cambs 122 C3
Elliot Angus 287 D10
Elliots Green Som 45 D9
Elliot's Town Caerph 77 E10
Ellisfield Hants 48 D6
Elliston Borders 262 D3
Elliston Leics 153 G8
Ellon Aberds 303 F9
Ellonby Cumb 230 D4
Ellough Suff 143 F8
Elloughton E Yorks 200 B2
Ellwood Glos 79 D9
Elm Cambs 139 B9
Elm Corner Sur 50 B5
Elm Cross Wilts 62 D6
Elm Hill Dorset 30 B4
Elm Park London 68 B4
Elmbridge Glos 80 B5
Elmbridge Worcs 117 D8
Elmdon Essex 105 D9
Elmdon W Mid 134 G3
Elmdon Heath W Mid 134 G3
Elmer W Sus 35 G7
Elmers End London 67 F11
Elmers Green Lancs 194 F3
Elmers Marsh W Sus 34 B5
Elmesthorpe Leics 135 D9
Elmfield I o W 21 C8
Elmhurst Bucks 84 B4
Elmhurst Staffs 152 G2
Elmley Castle Worcs 99 C9
Elmley Lovett Worcs 117 D7
Elmore Glos 80 B3
Elmore Back Glos 80 B3
Elms Green Hereford 115 F10
Elms Green Worcs 116 D4
Elmscott Devon 24 C2
Elmsett Suff 107 B11
Elmslack Lancs 211 D9
Elmstead Essex 107 F11
Elmstead London 68 E2
Elmstead Heath Essex 107 G11
Elmstead Market
Essex 107 G11
Elmsted Kent 54 E6
Elmsthorpe Leics 135 D9
Elmstone Kent 71 G9
Elmstone Hardwicke
Glos 99 F8
Elmswell E Yorks 208 B5
Elmswell Suff 125 E9
Elmton Derbys 187 G8
Elness Orkney 314 C6
Elphin Highld 307 H7
Elphinstone E Loth 281 G7
Elrick Aberds 293 C10
Elrig Dumfries 236 E5
Elrigbeag Argyll 284 F5
Elrington Northumb 241 E9
Elscar S Yorks 197 G11
Elsdon Hereford 114 G6
Elsdon Northumb 251 E10
Elsecar S Yorks 197 G11
Elsenham Essex 105 F10
Elsenham Sta Essex 105 F10
Elsfield Oxon 83 C8
Elsham N Lincs 200 E4
Elsing Norf 159 F11
Elslack N Yorks 204 D4
Elson Hants 33 G10
Elson Shrops 149 B7
Elsrickle S Lnrk 269 G11
Elstead Sur 50 E2
Elsted W Sus 34 D4
Elsthorpe Lincs 155 E11
Elstob Durham 234 G2
Elston Devon 26 G3
Elston Notts 172 F3
Elston Wilts 46 E5
Elstone Devon 25 D11
Elstow Beds 103 B11
Elstree Herts 85 F11
Elstronwick E Yorks 209 G10
Elswick Lancs 202 F4
Elswick T & W 242 E6
Elswick Leys Lancs 202 F4
Elsworth Cambs 122 E6
Elterwater Cumb 220 E6
Eltham London 68 E2
Eltisley Cambs 122 F5
Elton Cambs 137 E11
Elton Derbys 170 C2
Elton Glos 80 C2
Elton Gtr Man 195 E9
Elton Hereford 115 C9
Elton Notts 154 B5
Elton Stockton 225 B8
Elton W Ches 183 F7
Elton Green W Ches 183 G7
Elton's Marsh Hereford 97 C9
Eltringham Northumb 242 E3
Elvanfoot S Lnrk 259 F11
Elvaston Derbys 153 C8
Elveden Suff 124 B6
Elvet Hill Durham 233 C11
Elvingston E Loth 281 G9
Elvington Kent 55 C9
Elvington York 207 D9
Elwell Devon 41 G7
Elwell Dorset 17 E9
Elwick Hrtlpl 234 E5
Elwick Northumb 264 B4
Elworth E Ches 168 C2
Elworthy Som 42 G5
Ely Cambs 139 G10
Ely Cardiff 58 D6
Emberton M Keynes 103 B7
Embleton Cumb 229 E9
Embleton Durham 234 F4
Embleton Northumb 264 E6
Embo Highld 311 K2
Embo Street Highld 311 K2
Emborough Som 44 C6
Embsay N Yorks 204 C6
Emerson Park London 68 B4
Emerson Valley
M Keynes 102 E6
Emersons Green S Glos 61 D7
Emery Down Hants 32 F3
Emley W Yorks 197 E8
Emmbrook Wokingham 65 F9
Emmer Green Reading 65 D8
Emmett Carr Derbys 187 F7
Emmington Oxon 84 E2
Emneth Norf 139 B9
Emneth Hungate Norf 139 B10
Emorsgate Norf 157 E10
Empingham Rutland 137 B8
Empshott Hants 49 G9
Empshott Green Hants 49 G8
Emscote Warks 118 D5
Emstrey Shrops 149 G10
Emsworth Hants 22 B2
Enborne W Berks 64 F2
Enborne Row W Berks 64 G2
Enchmarsh Shrops 131 D10
Enderby Leics 135 D10
Endmoor Cumb 211 C10
Endon Staffs 168 E6
Endon Bank Staffs 168 E6
Energlyn Caerph 58 B6
Enfield London 86 F4
Enfield Worcs 117 D10
Enfield Highway London 86 F5
Enfield Lock London 86 F5
Enfield Town London 86 F4
Enfield Wash London 86 F5
Enford Wilts 46 C6
Engamoor Shetland 313 H4
Engedi Anglesey 178 F5
Engine Common S Glos 61 C7
Englefield W Berks 64 E6
Englefield Green Sur 66 E3
Englesea-brook E Ches 168 E3
English Bicknor Glos 79 B9
English Frankton
Shrops 149 D9
Englishcombe Bath 61 G8
Engollan Corn 10 G3
Enham Alamein Hants 47 D11
Enis Devon 25 B9
Enisfirth Shetland 312 F5
Enmore Som 43 G8
Enmore Field Hereford 115 E9
Enmore Green Dorset 30 C5
Ennerdale Bridge
Cumb 219 B11
Enniscaven Corn 5 D9
Enoch Dumfries 247 C9
Enochdhu Perth 292 G2
Ensay Argyll 288 E5
Ensbury Bmouth 19 B7
Ensbury Park Bmouth 19 C7
Ensdon Shrops 149 F8
Ensis Devon 25 B9
Enslow Oxon 83 B7
Enstone Oxon 101 G7
Enterkinfoot Dumfries 247 C9
Enterpen N Yorks 225 D9
Enton Green Sur 50 E3
Enville Staffs 132 F6
Eolaigearraidh W Isles 297 L3
Eorabus Argyll 288 G5
Eòropaidh W Isles 304 B7
Epney Glos 80 C3
Epperstone Notts 171 F11
Epping Essex 87 E7
Epping Green Essex 86 D6
Epping Green Herts 86 D3
Epping Upland Essex 86 E6
Eppleby N Yorks 224 C3
Eppleworth E Yorks 208 G6
Epsom Sur 67 G8
Epwell Oxon 101 C7
Epworth N Lincs 199 G9
Epworth Turbary N Lincs 199 G9
Erbistock Wrex 166 G5
Erbusaig Highld 295 C9
Erchless Castle Highld 300 E4
Erdington W Mid 134 E2
Eredine Argyll 275 C10
Eriboll Highld 308 D4
Ericstane Dumfries 260 G3
Eridge Green E Sus 52 F5
Erines Argyll 275 F9
Eriswell Suff 124 B4
Erith London 68 D4
Erlestoke Wilts 46 C3
Ermine Lincs 189 G7
Ermington Devon 8 E2
Ernesettle Plym 7 D8
Erpingham Norf 160 C3
Erriottwood Kent 54 B2
Errogie Highld 300 G5
Errol Perth 286 E6
Errol Station Perth 286 E6
Erskine Renfs 277 G9
Erskine Bridge Renfs 277 G9
Ervie Dumfries 236 C2
Erwarton Suff 108 E4
Erwood Powys 95 C11
Eryholme N Yorks 224 D6
Eryrys Denb 166 D2
Escomb Durham 233 E9
Escott Som 42 F5
Escrick N Yorks 207 E8
Esgairdawe Carms 94 C2
Esgairgeiliog Powys 128 B5
Esgyryn Conwy 180 F4
Esh Durham 233 C9
Esh Winning Durham 233 C9
Esher Sur 66 G6
Eshiels Borders 261 B7
Esholt W Yorks 205 E9
Eshott Northumb 252 D6
Eshton N Yorks 204 B4
Esk Valley N Yorks 226 E6
Eskadale Highld 300 F4
Eskbank Midloth 270 B6
Eskdale Green Cumb 220 E2
Eskdalemuir Dumfries 249 D7
Eske E Yorks 209 E7
Eskham Lincs 190 B5
Eskholme S Yorks 198 D6
Esknish Argyll 274 G4
Eslington Park
Northumb 264 G2
Esperley Lane Ends
Durham 233 G8
Esprick Lancs 202 F4
Essendine Rutland 155 G10
Essendon Herts 86 D3
Essich Highld 300 F6
Essington Staffs 133 C9
Esslemont Aberds 303 G9
Eston Redcar 225 B11
Estover Plym 7 D10
Eswick Shetland 313 H6
Etal Northumb 263 B10
Etchilhampton Wilts 62 G4
Etchingham E Sus 38 B2
Etchinghill Kent 55 F7
Etchinghill Staffs 151 F10
Etchingwood E Sus 37 C8
Etherley Dene Durham 233 F9
Ethie Castle Angus 287 C10
Ethie Mains Angus 287 C10
Etling Green Norf 159 G10
Etloe Glos 79 D11
Eton Windsor 66 D3
Eton Wick Windsor 66 D2
Etruria Stoke 168 F5
Etsell Shrops 131 C7
Etterby Cumb 239 F9
Etteridge Highld 291 D8
Ettersgill Durham 232 F3
Ettiley Heath E Ches 168 C2
Ettingshall W Mid 133 D8
Ettingshall Park W Mid 133 D8
Ettington Warks 100 B5
Etton E Yorks 208 E5
Etton P'boro 138 B2
Ettrick Borders 261 G7
Ettrickbridge Borders 261 E9
Ettrickdale Argyll 275 G11
Ettrickhill Borders 261 G7
Etwall Derbys 152 C5
Etwall Common
Derbys 152 C5
Eudon Burnell Shrops 132 F3
Eudon George Shrops 132 F3
Euston Suff 125 B7
Euximoor Drove Cambs 139 D9
Euxton Lancs 194 D5
Evanstown Bridgend 58 B3
Evanton Highld 300 C6
Eve Hill W Mid 133 E8
Evedon Lincs 173 F9
Evelix Highld 309 K7
Even Pits Hereford 97 D11
Even Swindon Swindon 62 B6
Evendine Hereford 98 C5
Evenjobb = Einsiob
Powys 114 E5
Evenley Northants 101 E11
Evenlode Glos 100 F4
Evenwood Durham 233 G9
Evenwood Gate Durham 233 G9
Everbay Orkney 314 D6
Evercreech Som 44 F6
Everdon Northants 119 F11
Everingham E Yorks 208 E2
Everland Shetland 312 D8
Everleigh Wilts 47 C8
Everley N Yorks 217 B9
Eversholt C Beds 103 E9
Evershot Dorset 29 G9
Eversley Essex 69 B8
Eversley Hants 65 G9
Eversley Centre Hants 65 G9
Eversley Cross Hants 65 G9
Everthorpe E Yorks 208 G4
Everton C Beds 122 G4
Everton Hants 19 C11
Everton Mers 182 C5
Everton Notts 187 C11
Evertown Dumfries 239 B9
Evesbatch Hereford 98 B3
Evesham Worcs 99 C10
Evington Leicester 136 C2
Ewanrigg Cumb 228 D6
Ewden Village S Yorks 186 B3
Ewell Sur 67 G8
Ewell Minnis Kent 55 E9
Ewelme Oxon 83 G10
Ewen Glos 81 F8
Ewenny V Glam 58 D2
Ewerby Lincs 173 F10
Ewerby Thorpe Lincs 173 F10
Ewes Dumfries 249 E9
Ewesley Northumb 252 E3
Ewhurst Sur 50 E5
Ewhurst Green E Sus 38 C3
Ewhurst Green Sur 50 F5
Ewloe Flint 166 B4
Ewloe Green Flint 166 B3
Ewood Blkburn 195 B7
Ewood Bridge Lancs 195 C9
Eworthy Devon 12 C5
Ewshot Hants 49 D10
Ewyas Harold Hereford 97 F7
Exbourne Devon 25 G10
Exbury Hants 20 B4
Exceat E Sus 23 F8
Exebridge Devon 26 C6
Exelby N Yorks 214 B5
Exeter Devon 14 C4
Exford Som 41 F11
Exfords Green Shrops 131 B9
Exhall Warks 118 F2
Exhall Warks 135 F7
Exlade Street Oxon 65 C7
Exley W Yorks 196 C5
Exley Head W Yorks 204 F6
Exminster Devon 14 D4
Exmouth Devon 14 E6
Exnaboe Shetland 313 M5
Exning Suff 124 D2
Exted Kent 55 E7
Exton Devon 14 D5
Exton Hants 33 C10
Exton Rutland 155 G8
Exton Som 42 G2
Exwick Devon 14 C4
Eyam Derbys 186 F2
Eydon Northants 119 G10
Eye Hereford 115 E9
Eye P'boro 138 C4
Eye Suff 126 C2
Eye Green P'boro 138 C4
Eyemouth Borders 273 C8
Eyeworth C Beds 104 B4
Eyhorne Street Kent 53 C10
Eyke Suff 126 G6
Eynesbury Cambs 122 F3
Eynort Highld 294 C5
Eynsford Kent 68 F4
Eynsham Oxon 82 D6
Eype Dorset 16 C5
Eyre Highld 295 B7
Eyre Highld 298 D4
Eyres Monsell Leicester 135 D11
Eythorne Kent 55 D9
Eyton Hereford 115 E9
Eyton Shrops 131 F7
Eyton Shrops 149 G7
Eyton Wrex 166 G4
Eyton on Severn
Shrops 131 B11
Eyton upon the Weald
Moors Telford 150 G3

F

Faberstown Wilts 47 C9
Faccombe Hants 47 B11
Faceby N Yorks 225 E9
Fachell Gwyn 163 B8
Fachwen Gwyn 163 C9
Facit Lancs 195 D11
Fackley Notts 171 C7
Faddiley E Ches 167 E9
Faddonch Highld 295 C11
Fadmoor N Yorks 216 B3
Faerdre Swansea 75 E11
Fagley W Yorks 205 G9
Fagwyr Swansea 75 E11
Faichem Highld 290 C4
Faifley W Dunb 277 G10
Failand N Som 60 E4
Failford S Ayrs 257 D11
Failsworth Gtr Man 195 G11
Fain Highld 299 B11
Faindouran Lodge
Moray 292 C2
Fair Cross London 68 B3
Fair Green Norf 158 F3
Fair Hill Cumb 230 E6
Fair Moor Northumb 252 F5
Fair Oak Hants 33 D7
Fair Oak Hants 64 G5
Fair Oak Lancs 203 D8
Fair Oak Green Hants 65 G7
Fairbourne Gwyn 146 G2
Fairbourne Heath Kent 53 C11
Fairburn N Yorks 198 B3
Fairburn House Highld 300 D4
Fairfield Clack 279 C7
Fairfield Derbys 185 G9
Fairfield Gtr Man 184 B6
Fairfield Gtr Man 195 E10
Fairfield Kent 39 B7
Fairfield Mers 182 C5
Fairfield Stockton 225 B8
Fairfield Worcs 99 C10
Fairfield Worcs 117 B8
Fairfield Park Bath 61 F9
Fairfields Glos 98 E4
Fairford Glos 81 E11
Fairhaven Lancs 193 B10
Fairhaven N Ayrs 255 C10
Fairhill S Lnrk 268 E4
Fairlands Sur 50 C3
Fairlee I o W 20 C6
Fairlie N Ayrs 266 D4
Fairlight E Sus 38 E5
Fairlight Cove E Sus 38 E5
Fairlop London 87 G7
Fairmile Devon 15 B7
Fairmile Dorset 19 C9
Fairmile Sur 66 G6
Fairmilehead Edin 270 B4
Fairoak Caerph 77 F11
Fairoak Staffs 150 B5
Fairseat Kent 68 G6
Fairstead Essex 88 B3
Fairstead Norf 158 F2
Fairview Glos 99 G9
Fairwarp E Sus 37 B7
Fairwater Cardiff 58 D6
Fairwater Torf 78 G3
Fairwood Wilts 45 C10
Fairy Cottage I o M 192 D5
Fairy Cross Devon 24 C6
Fakenham Norf 159 D8
Fakenham Magna Suff 125 B8
Fala Midloth 271 C8
Fala Dam Midloth 271 C8
Falahill Borders 271 D7
Falcon Hereford 98 E2
Falcon Lodge W Mid 134 D2
Falconwood London 68 D3
Falcutt Northants 101 C11
Faldingworth Lincs 189 E9
Faldonside Borders 262 C2
Falfield Fife 287 G8
Falfield S Glos 79 G11
Falkenham Suff 108 D5
Falkenham Sink Suff 108 D5
Falkirk Falk 279 F7
Falkland Fife 286 G6
Falla Borders 262 G6
Fallgate Derbys 170 C5
Fallin Stirl 278 C6
Fallinge Derbys 170 B3
Fallings Heath W Mid 133 D9
Fallowfield Gtr Man 184 C5
Fallside N Lnrk 268 C4
Falmer E Sus 36 F5
Falmouth Corn 3 C8
Falnash Borders 249 B9
Falsgrave N Yorks 217 B10
Falside W Loth 269 B9
Falsidehill Borders 272 G3
Falstone Northumb 250 F6
Fanagmore Highld 306 E6
Fancott C Beds 103 F10
Fangdale Beck N Yorks 225 G11
Fangfoss E Yorks 207 C11
Fanich Highld 311 J2
Fankerton Falk 278 E5
Fanmore Argyll 288 E6
Fanner's Green Essex 87 C11
Fannich Lodge Highld 300 C2
Fans Borders 272 G2
Fanshowe E Ches 184 G5
Fant Kent 53 B8
Faoilean Highld 295 C7
Far Arnside Cumb 211 D8
Far Bank S Yorks 198 E6
Far Banks Lancs 194 C2
Far Bletchley M Keynes 103 E7

ghall Staffs 169 F8
gham Hants 31 E11
gham Kent 55 C9
ghole Kent 52 C2
gholt Kent 55 F7
gland Cross S Glos 60 C6
gmore Devon 8 G5
gmore Hants 33 C11
gmore Hants 49 B10
gmore Herts 85 E11
gnal S Ayrs 257 D8
gnall Lincs 156 G3
gpool Corn 4 G5
gs' Green Essex 105 D11
gshail Norf 160 B5
gwell Corn 6 B6
lesworth Leics 135 E10
me Som 45 D9
me St Quintin Dorset 29 G9
mebridge Glos 80 D3
mefield Som 45 D9
mes Hill Hereford 98 B3
mington Hereford 97 B10
n Denb 165 B9
n Gwyn 145 B7
n Gwyn 163 D8
n Powys 113 D11
n Powys 129 C8
n Powys 130 C4
n Powys 130 D3
n Shrops 148 B5
n-Bache Denb 166 G2
n-dêg Wrex 166 F3
n Isaf Wrex 166 G3
ncysyllte Wrex 166 G3
ngoch Gwyn 147 B8
st Devon 26 F3
st Hill N Som 60 G2
st Row Norf 141 C10
stenden Suff 143 G9
stenden Corner
ff 143 G9
sterley Durham 232 D6
stlane Hants 32 F6
toft Orkney 314 D4
xfield C Beds 103 E9
xfield Wilts 63 F9
xfield Green Hants 34 B2
yle Hants 49 E9
ern Hill Hants 32 C6
erning Essex 87 E10
erns Essex 69 B8
ton N Yorks 216 E3
glestone St Peter
ts 46 G6
beck Lincs 172 E6
beck Northumb 252 F5
bourn Cambs 123 F10
brook Oxon 82 C3
flood Hants 33 B7
ford Som 28 B2
ford Staffs 151 B9
ford York 207 D8
nam London 67 D8
king W Sus 36 E2
Sutton E Yorks 207 B10
abrook Devon 40 E4
arton Glasgow 268 C2
arton N Ayrs 257 B8
er Street Essex 88 B2
er's End Essex 105 F10
er's Moor W Ches 167 E7
ierton Hants 47 F11
etby Lincs 190 G3
shaw S Yorks 197 G8
well Cross London 86 G6
wood E Ayrs 267 E8
wood Gtr Man 196 F2
ner Bucks 66 B3
modestone Norf 159 C9
neck W Yorks 205 G10
netby Lincs 189 F9
ney Lincs 156 E5
ready Warks 100 B5
shaw Park E Ches 184 E4
stone W Yorks 197 F7
stow Lincs 190 B4
thorpe Stockton 234 G4
well Oxon 101 G7
well T & W 243 F9
wood Lancs 202 G6
wood S Yorks 186 D4
wood Som 28 C2
denhall Norf 142 D3
denhall Street Norf 142 D2
tington W Sus 22 B3
tley Hants 33 F9
tullich Perth 285 E11
zie Shetland 312 D8
ley Devon 28 G3
mace Argyll 284 G4
mace Carms 74 E6
mace Carms 75 E8
mace Ceredig 128 D3
mace Highld 299 B9
mace End Warks 134 E4
mace Green W Sus 51 F9
mace Wood W Sus 51 F11
neaux Pelham
rts 105 F8
ner's Green E Sus 36 B6
ness Vale Derbys 185 E8
neux Pelham Herts 105 F8
nham Som 28 F4
ther Ford End Essex 105 E9
ther Quarter Kent 53 F11
ze Northants 102 C5
ze Devon 25 B10
ze Hill Hants 31 E11
ze Platt Windsor 65 C11
zebrook Dorset 18 E4
zedown Hants 32 B5
zedown London 67 E9
zehill Devon 41 D8
zehill Dorset 31 G8
zeley Corner Hants 33 E11
zeley Lodge Hants 32 G5
zley Hants 32 D3
zton M Keynes 102 D6
ett Som 28 E2
eld Essex 87 D9
eld Glos 82 E2
eld Hants 47 C10
eld Oxon 82 F6
eld Wilts 63 F7
eld Wilts 63 G7
ngthorpe N Yorks 227 D8
ing W Sus 34 C4
ie Aberds 303 F7
alfa Cardiff 59 D7
hsann bho Dheas
sles 304 C6
hsann bho Thuath
sles 304 C6
le Head Hants 21 B10
lon Highld 309 K7
roc Hill E Ayrs 267 E9
lbrook Sur 51 D8
Gaddesby Leics 154 G3
Gadebridge Herts 85 D8
Gadfa Anglesey 179 D7
Gadfield Elm Worcs 98 E5
Gadlas Shrops 149 B7
Gadlys Rhondda 77 E7
Gadshill Kent 69 E8
Gaer Newport 59 B9
Gaer Powys 96 G3
Gaer-fawr Mon 78 F6
Gaerllwyd Mon 78 F6
Gaerwen Anglesey 179 G7
Gagingwell Oxon 101 F8
Gaick Lodge Highld 291 E9
Gailey Staffs 151 G8
Gailey Wharf Staffs 151 G8
Gain Hill Kent 53 D8
Gainfield Oxon 82 F4
Gainford Durham 224 B3
Gainsborough Lincs 188 C4
Gainsborough Suff 108 C3
Gainsford End Essex 106 D4
Gairletter Argyll 276 E3
Gairloch Highld 299 B8
Gairlochy Highld 290 E3
Gairney Bank Perth 280 B2
Gairnshiel Lodge
Aberds 292 C4
Gaisgill Cumb 222 D2
Gaitsgill Cumb 230 B3
Galadean Borders 271 G11
Galashiels Borders 261 B11
Galdlys Flint 182 G2
Gale Gtr Man 196 D2
Galgate Lancs 202 B5
Galhampton Som 29 B10
Gallaberry Dumfries 247 G11
Gallachoille Argyll 275 E8
Gallanach Argyll 288 C4
Gallanach Argyll 289 G10
Gallanach Highld 294 G6
Gallantry Bank E Ches 167 E8
Gallatown Fife 280 C5
Galley Common Warks 134 E6
Galley Hill Cambs 122 D6
Galley Hill Lincs 190 F6
Galleyend Essex 88 E2
Galleywood Essex 88 E2
Galligill Cumb 231 B11
Gallin Perth 285 C9
Gallowie Highld 291 E7
Gallowfauld Angus 287 C8
Gallowhill Glasgow 267 D11
Gallowhill Renfs 267 B9
Gallowhills Aberds 303 D10
Gallows Corner London 87 G8
Gallows Green Essex 106 F2
Gallows Green Essex 107 F8
Gallows Green Staffs 169 G9
Gallows Green Worcs 117 E8
Gallows Inn Derbys 171 G7
Gallowsgreen Torf 78 D3
Gallowstree Common
Oxon 65 C7
Gallt Melyd = Meliden
Denb 181 E9
Gallt-y-foel Gwyn 163 C9
Galltair Highld 295 C10
Galltegfa Denb 165 D10
Gallypot Street E Sus 52 F3
Galmington Som 28 C2
Galmisdale Highld 294 G6
Galmpton Devon 8 G3
Galmpton Torbay 9 D7
Galon Uchaf M Tydf 77 D9
Galphay N Yorks 214 E5
Galston E Ayrs 258 B2
Galtrigill Highld 296 F7
Gam Corn 11 F7
Gamble Hill W Yorks 205 G11
Gamble's Green Essex 88 C3
Gamblesby Cumb 231 D8
Gamelsby Cumb 239 G7
Gamesley Derbys 185 C8
Gamlingay Cambs 122 G4
Gamlingay Cinques
Cambs 122 G4
Gamlingay Great
Heath Cambs 122 G4
Gammaton Devon 25 B7
Gammaton Moor Devon 25 C7
Gammersgill N Yorks 213 C11
Gamston Notts 154 B2
Gamston Notts 188 F2
Ganarew Hereford 79 B8
Ganavan Argyll 289 F10
Ganders Green Glos 98 G4
Gang Corn 6 B6
Ganllwyd Gwyn 146 E4
Gannetts Dorset 30 D3
Gannochy Angus 293 F7
Gannochy Perth 286 E5
Gansclet Highld 310 E7
Ganstead E Yorks 209 G9
Ganthorpe N Yorks 216 E3
Ganton N Yorks 217 D9
Gants Hill London 68 B2
Ganwick Corner Herts 86 F3
Gaodhail Argyll 289 F8
Gappah Devon 14 F3
Garafad Highld 298 C4
Garamor Highld 295 F8
Garbat Highld 300 C4
Garbhallt Argyll 275 D11
Garboldisham Norf 141 G10
Garbole Highld 301 G7
Garden City Bl Gwent 77 D11
Garden City Flint 166 B4
Garden Village S Yorks 186 B3
Garden Village Swansea 56 B5
Garden Village W Yorks 206 G4
Garden Village Wrex 166 E4
Gardeners Green
Wokingham 65 F10
Gardenstown Aberds 303 C7
Garderhouse Shetland 313 J5
Gardham E Yorks 208 E5
Gardie Shetland 312 D7
Gardin Shetland 312 G6
Gare Hill Som 45 E9
Garelochhead Argyll 276 C4
Garford Oxon 82 F6
Garforth W Yorks 206 G4
Gargrave N Yorks 204 C4
Gargunnock Stirl 278 C4
Garizim Conwy 179 F11
Garker Corn 5 E10
Garlandhayes Devon 27 D11
Garlands Cumb 239 G10
Garleffin S Ayrs 244 G3
Garlic Street Norf 142 G4
Garlieston Dumfries 236 E6
Garliford Devon 26 B3
Garlinge Kent 71 F10
Garlinge Green Kent 54 C6
Garlogie Aberds 293 C9
Garmelow Staffs 150 D5
Garmond Aberds 303 D8
Garmondsway Durham 234 E2
Garmony Argyll 289 E8
Garmouth Moray 302 C3
Garmston Shrops 132 B2
Garn Powys 130 G2
Garn-swllt Swansea 75 D10
Garn-yr-erw Torf 78 C2
Garnant Carms 75 C11
Garndiffaith Torf 78 E3
Garndolbenmaen Gwyn 163 G7
Garnedd Conwy 164 E2
Garnett Bridge Cumb 221 F10
Garnetts Essex 87 B10
Garnfadryn Gwyn 144 C5
Garnkirk N Lnrk 268 B3
Garnlydan Bl Gwent 77 C11
Garnsgate Lincs 157 E8
Garnswllt Swansea 75 D10
Garra Eallabus Argyll 274 F3
Garrabost W Isles 304 E7
Garrachra Argyll 275 E11
Garralburn Moray 302 D4
Garraron Argyll 275 C9
Garras Corn 2 E6
Garreg Flint 181 F10
Garreg Gwyn 163 G10
Garrets Green W Mid 134 F2
Garrick Perth 286 F2
Garrigill Cumb 231 C10
Garrison Stirl 285 G7
Garriston N Yorks 224 G3
Garroch Dumfries 246 G3
Garrogie Lodge Highld 291 B7
Garros Highld 298 C4
Garrow Perth 286 C2
Garrowhill Glasgow 268 C3
Garrygualach Highld 290 C3
Garryhorn Dumfries 246 E2
Garsdale Cumb 212 B4
Garsdale Head Cumb 222 G5
Garsdon Wilts 62 B3
Garshall Green Staffs 151 C9
Garsington Oxon 83 E9
Garstang Lancs 202 D5
Garston Herts 85 F10
Garston Mers 182 E6
Garswood Mers 183 B9
Gartachoil Stirl 277 C10
Gartbreck Argyll 254 B3
Gartcosh N Lnrk 268 B3
Garth Bridgend 57 C11
Garth Ceredig 128 G2
Garth Flint 181 E10
Garth Gwyn 179 G9
Garth Newport 59 B9
Garth Newport 78 G4
Garth Perth 285 B11
Garth Powys 95 B9
Garth Powys 114 C5
Garth Shetland 313 H4
Garth Shetland 313 H6
Garth Wrex 166 G3
Garth Owen Powys 130 E2
Garth Row Cumb 221 F10
Garth Trevor Wrex 166 G3
Garthamlock Glasgow 268 B3
Garthbeg Highld 291 B7
Garthbrengy Powys 95 E10
Garthdee Aberdeen 293 C11
Gartheli Ceredig 111 F11
Garthmyl Powys 130 D3
Garthorpe Leics 154 E6
Garthorpe N Lincs 199 D11
Gartlea N Lnrk 268 C5
Gartloch Glasgow 268 B3
Gartly Aberds 302 F5
Gartmore Stirl 277 B10
Gartmore Ho Stirl 277 B10
Gartnagrenach Argyll 255 B8
Gartness N Lnrk 268 C5
Gartness Stirl 277 D10
Gartocharn W Dunb 277 D8
Garton E Yorks 209 F11
Garton-on-the-Wolds
E Yorks 208 B5
Gartsherrie N Lnrk 268 B4
Gartur Stirl 277 B11
Gartymore Highld 311 H4
Garvald E Loth 281 G11
Garvamore Highld 291 D8
Garvard Argyll 274 D4
Garvault Hotel Highld 308 F7
Garve Highld 300 C3
Garvestone Norf 141 B10
Garvock Aberds 293 F9
Garvock Invclyd 276 G5
Garvock Hill Fife 280 D2
Garway Hereford 97 G9
Garway Hill Hereford 97 F8
Gaskan Highld 289 B9
Gasper Wilts 45 G9
Gastard Wilts 61 F11
Gasthorpe Norf 141 G9
Gaston Green Essex 87 B7
Gatacre Park Shrops 132 F5
Gatcombe I o W 20 D5
Gate Burton Lincs 188 E4
Gate Helmsley N Yorks 207 B9
Gateacre Mers 182 D6
Gatebeck Cumb 211 B10
Gateford Notts 187 E9
Gateford Common
Notts 187 E9
Gateforth N Yorks 198 B5
Gatehead E Ayrs 257 B9
Gatehouse Northumb 251 F7
Gatehouse of Fleet
Dumfries 237 D8
Gatelawbridge
Dumfries 247 D10
Gateley Norf 159 E9
Gatenby N Yorks 214 B6
Gatesgarth Cumb 220 B3
Gateshead T & W 243 E7
Gatesheath W Ches 167 C7
Gateside Aberds 293 B8
Gateside Angus 287 C8
Gateside Dumfries 248 E4
Gateside E Renf 267 D9
Gateside Fife 286 G5
Gateside N Ayrs 267 E7
Gateside Shetland 312 F4
Gatewen Wrex 166 E4
Gatherley Devon 12 E3
Gathurst Gtr Man 194 F4
Gatlas Newport 78 G4
Gatley Gtr Man 184 D4
Gatley End Cambs 104 C5
Gatton Sur 51 C9
Gattonside Borders 262 B2
Gatwick Glos 80 C2
Gatwick Airport W Sus 51 E9
Gaufron Powys 113 D9
Gaulby Leics 136 C3
Gauldry Fife 287 E7
Gauntons Bank E Ches 167 F9
Gaunt's Common Dorset 31 F8
Gaunt's Earthcott
S Glos 60 C6
Gaunt's End Essex 105 F10
Gautby Lincs 189 G11
Gavinton Borders 272 E5
Gawber S Yorks 197 F10
Gawcott Bucks 102 E3
Gawsworth E Ches 168 B5
Gawthorpe W Yorks 197 C9
Gawthorpe W Yorks 197 D7
Gawthrop Cumb 212 B3
Gawthwaite Cumb 210 C5
Gay Bowers Essex 88 E3
Gay Street W Sus 35 C9
Gaydon Warks 119 G7
Gayfield Orkney 314 A4
Gayhurst M Keynes 103 B7
Gayle N Yorks 213 B7
Gayles N Yorks 224 D3
Gayton Mers 182 E3
Gayton Norf 158 F4
Gayton Northants 120 G4
Gayton Staffs 151 D9
Gayton Engine Lincs 191 D7
Gayton le Marsh Lincs 190 E6
Gayton le Wold Lincs 190 D2
Gayton Thorpe Norf 158 F4
Gaywood Norf 158 E2
Gaza Shetland 312 F5
Gazeley Suff 124 E4
Geàrraidh Sheilidh
W Isles 297 J3
Geanies House Highld 301 B8
Gearraidh Bhailteas
W Isles 297 J3
Gearraidh Bhaird
W Isles 304 F5
Gearraidh Dubh W Isles 296 F4
Gearraidh na h-Aibhne
W Isles 304 E4
Gearraidh na Monadh
W Isles 297 K3
Geary Highld 298 C2
Geat Wolford Warks 100 E4
Geddes House Highld 301 D8
Gedding Suff 125 F9
Geddington Northants 137 G7
Gedgrave Hall Suff 109 B8
Gedintailor Highld 295 B7
Gedling Notts 171 G10
Gedney Lincs 157 E8
Gedney Broadgate Lincs 157 E8
Gedney Drove End Lincs 157 D9
Gedney Dyke Lincs 157 D8
Gedney Hill Lincs 156 G6
Gee Cross Gtr Man 185 C7
Geeston Rutland 137 C9
Gegin Wrex 166 E3
Geilston Argyll 276 F6
Geinas Denb 165 B9
Geirinis W Isles 297 G3
Geise Highld 310 C5
Geisiadar W Isles 304 E3
Geldeston Norf 143 E7
Gell Conwy 164 B5
Gelli Pembs 73 B9
Gelli Rhondda 77 G7
Gelli-gaer Neath 57 C9
Gelli-hôf Caerph 77 F11
Gellideg M Tydf 77 D8
Gellifor Denb 165 C10
Gelligaer Caerph 77 F10
Gelligroes Caerph 77 G11
Gellilydan Gwyn 146 B3
Gellinud Neath 76 E2
Gellinudd Neath 76 E2
Gellyburn Perth 286 D4
Gellygron Neath 76 E2
Gellywen Carms 92 G5
Gelsmoor Leics 153 F8
Gelston Dumfries 237 D9
Gelston Lincs 172 G6
Gembling E Yorks 209 B8
Gemini Warr 183 C9
Gendros Swansea 56 B6
Genesis Green Suff 124 F4
Gentleshaw Staffs 151 G11
Geocrab W Isles 305 J3
George Green Bucks 66 C4
George Nympton Devon 26 C2
Georgefield Dumfries 249 E7
Georgeham Devon 40 F3
Georgetown Bl Gwent 77 D10
Georgia Corn 1 B5
Gergask Highld 291 D8
Gerlan Gwyn 163 B10
Germansweek Devon 12 C4
Germiston Glasgow 268 B2
Germoe Corn 2 D3
Gernon Bushes Essex 87 E7
Gerrans Corn 3 B9
Gerrard's Bromley
Staffs 150 C5
Gerrards Cross Bucks 66 B4
Gerrick Redcar 226 C4
Geseilfa Powys 129 E8
Gestingthorpe Essex 106 D6
Gesto Ho Highld 294 B5
Geuffordd Powys 148 G4
Geufron Denb 166 G2
Gib Heath W Mid 133 F11
Gibb Hill W Ches 183 F10
Gibbet Hill W Mid 118 C6
Gibbet Hill Warks 135 G10
Gibbshill Dumfries 237 B9
Gibraltar Beds 103 B10
Gibraltar Bucks 84 C3
Gibraltar Kent 55 F8
Gibraltar Oxon 83 B7
Gibshill Invclyd 276 G6
Gibsmere Notts 172 F2
Giddeahall Wilts 61 E11
Giddy Green Dorset 18 D2
Gidea Park London 68 B4
Gidleigh Devon 13 D9
Giffard Park M Keynes 103 C7
Giffnock E Renf 267 D11
Gifford E Loth 271 B10
Giffordland N Ayrs 266 F5
Giffordtown Fife 286 F6
Gigg Gtr Man 195 F10
Giggetty Staffs 133 E7
Giggleswick N Yorks 212 G6
Giggshill Sur 67 F7
Gignog Pembs 91 G7
Gilberdyke E Yorks 199 B10
Gilbert Street Hants 49 G7
Gilbert's Coombe Corn 4 G3
Gilbert's End Worcs 98 C6
Gilbert's Green Warks 118 C2
Gilbertstone W Mid 134 G2
Gilchriston E Loth 271 B9
Gilcrux Cumb 229 D8
Gildersome W Yorks 197 B8
Gildersome Street
W Yorks 197 B8
Gildingwells S Yorks 187 D9
Gilesgate Durham 233 C11
Gilesgate Moor
Durham 233 C11
Gileston V Glam 58 F4
Gilfach Caerph 77 F11
Gilfach Hereford 96 E6
Gilfach Goch Rhondda 58 B3
Gilfachrheda Ceredig 111 F8
Gilgarran Cumb 228 G6
Gill N Yorks 204 E5
Gillamoor N Yorks 216 B3
Gillan Corn 3 E7
Gillar's Green Mers 183 B7
Gillbank Cumb 221 F7
Gillbent Gtr Man 184 E5
Gillen Highld 298 D2
Gillesbie Dumfries 248 E5
Gilling East N Yorks 216 D2
Gilling West N Yorks 224 D3
Gillingham Dorset 30 B4
Gillingham Medway 69 F9
Gillingham Norf 143 E8
Gillmoss Mers 182 B6
Gillock Highld 310 D6
Gillow Heath Staffs 168 D5
Gills Highld 310 B7
Gill's Green Kent 53 G9
Gillway Staffs 134 C4
Gilmanscleuch Borders 261 E8
Gilmerton Edin 270 B5
Gilmerton Perth 286 E2
Gilmonby Durham 223 C9
Gilmorton Leics 135 F11
Gilmourton S Lnrk 268 G3
Gilnow Gtr Man 195 F8
Gilroyd S Yorks 197 G10
Gilsland Northumb 240 D4
Gilsland Spa Cumb 240 D4
Gilson Warks 134 E3
Gilstead W Yorks 205 F8
Gilston Borders 271 D8
Gilston Herts 86 C6
Gilston Park Herts 86 C6
Giltbrook Notts 171 F7
Gilver's Lane Worcs 98 C6
Gilwell Park Essex 86 F5
Gilwern Mon 78 C2
Gimingham Norf 160 B5
Ginclough E Ches 185 F7
Ginger's Green E Sus 23 C10
Giosla W Isles 304 F3
Gipping Suff 125 E11
Gipsey Bridge Lincs 174 F3
Gipsy Row Suff 107 D11
Gipsyville Hull 200 B5
Gipton W Yorks 206 F2
Gipton Wood W Yorks 206 F2
Girdle Toll N Ayrs 266 G6
Girlington W Yorks 205 G8
Girlsta Shetland 313 H6
Girsby Lincs 190 D2
Girsby N Yorks 225 D7
Girt Som 29 C10
Girtford C Beds 104 B3
Girtford C Beds 122 G3
Girthon Dumfries 237 D8
Girton Cambs 123 E8
Girton Notts 172 B4
Girvan S Ayrs 244 D5
Gisburn Lancs 204 D2
Gisleham Suff 143 F10
Gislingham Suff 125 C11
Gissing Norf 142 F2
Gittisham Devon 15 B8
Givons Grove Sur 51 C7
Glachavoil Argyll 275 F11
Glack of Midthird
Moray 302 E3
Glackmore Highld 300 D6
Gladestry Powys 114 F4
Gladsmuir E Loth 281 G9
Glaichbea Highld 300 F5
Glais Swansea 76 E2
Glaisdale N Yorks 226 D5
Glame Highld 298 E5
Glamis Angus 287 C7
Glan Adda Gwyn 179 G9
Glan-Conwy Conwy 164 E4
Glan-Duar Carms 93 C10
Glan-Dwyfach Gwyn 163 G7
Glan Gors Anglesey 179 F7
Glan-rhyd Gwyn 163 D7
Glan-rhyd Powys 76 D3
Glan-traeth Anglesey 178 F3
Glan-y-don Flint 181 F11
Glan y Ffer =
Ferryside Carms 74 C5
Glan-y-llyn Rhondda 58 C6
Glan-y-môr Carms 74 C5
Glan-y-nant Caerph 77 F10
Glan-y-nant Powys 129 G8
Glan-y-wern Gwyn 146 C2
Glan-yr-afon Anglesey 179 E10
Glan-yr-afon Flint 181 E10
Glan-yr-afon Gwyn 164 G6
Glan-yr-afon Gwyn 165 G8
Glan-yr-afon Shrops 148 E4
Glanafon Pembs 73 B7
Glanaman Carms 75 C11
Glandford Norf 177 E8
Glandwr Caerph 78 E2
Glandwr Pembs 92 F3
Glandy Cross Carms 92 F2
Glandyfi Ceredig 128 D3
Glangrwyney Powys 78 B2
Glanhanog Powys 129 D8
Glanmule Powys 130 E3
Glanrafon Ceredig 128 G2
Glanrhyd Gwyn 144 B5
Glanrhyd Pembs 92 C2
Glantlees Northumb 252 B4
Glanton Northumb 264 G3
Glanton Pike Northumb 264 G3
Glantwymyn =
Cemmaes Road Powys 128 C6
Glanvilles Wootton
Dorset 29 F11
Glanwern Ceredig 128 F2
Glanwydden Conwy 180 E4
Glapthorn Northants 137 E10
Glapwell Derbys 171 B7
Glas-allt Shiel Aberds 292 E4
Glasbury Powys 96 D3
Glaschoil Highld 301 F10
Glascoed Denb 181 G7
Glascoed Mon 78 E4
Glascoed Powys 129 F11
Glascoed Powys 148 G2
Glascoed Powys 148 F2
Glascoed Wrex 166 E3
Glascorrie Aberds 292 D5
Glascorrie Perth 286 E2
Glascote Staffs 134 C4
Glascwm Powys 114 G3
Glasdir Flint 181 E10
Glasdrum Argyll 284 C4
Glasfryn Conwy 164 E6
Glasgoed Ceredig 92 B6
Glasgoforest Aberds 293 B10
Glasgow Glasgow 267 B11
Glashvin Highld 298 C4
Glasinfryn Gwyn 163 B9
Glasllwch Newport 59 B9
Glasnacardoch Highld 295 F8
Glasnakille Highld 295 D7
Glasphein Highld 297 G7
Glaspwll Powys 128 D4
Glass Houghton W Yorks 198 C2
Glassburn Highld 300 F3
Glassenbury Kent 53 F8
Glasserton Dumfries 236 F6
Glassford S Lnrk 268 F4
Glassgreen Moray 302 C2
Glasshouse Glos 98 G4
Glasshouse Hill Glos 98 G4
Glasshouses N Yorks 214 G3
Glasslie Fife 286 G6
Glasson Cumb 228 D6
Glasson Cumb 239 E7
Glasson Lancs 202 B4
Glassonby Cumb 231 D7
Glasterlaw Angus 287 B9
Glaston Rutland 137 C7
Glastonbury Som 44 F4
Glatton Cambs 138 F3
Glazebrook Warr 183 C11
Glazebury Warr 183 B11
Glazeley Shrops 132 F4
Gleadless S Yorks 186 E5
Gleadless Valley S Yorks 186 E5
Gleadmoss E Ches 168 B4
Gleadsmoss E Ches 168 B4
Gleanhead Dumfries 245 G10
Gleann Tholàstaidh
W Isles 304 D7
Gleaston Cumb 210 E5
Glebe Hants 33 D9
Glebe Shetland 313 J6
Glebe T & W 243 F8
Glecknabae Argyll 275 G11
Gledhow W Yorks 206 F2
Gledrid Shrops 148 B5
Gleiniant Powys 129 E9
Glemsford Suff 106 B6
Glen Dumfries 237 B10
Glen Dumfries 237 D7
Glen Auldyn I o M 192 C5
Glen Bernisdale Highld 298 E4
Glen Ho Borders 261 C7
Glen Mona I o M 192 D5
Glen Mor Highld 295 B10
Glen Nevis House
Highld 290 F3
Glen of Newmill Moray 302 D4
Glen Parva Leics 135 D11
Glen Sluain Argyll 275 D11
Glen Tanar House
Aberds 292 D6
Glen Trool Lodge
Dumfries 245 G10
Glen Vic Askil Highld 298 E3
Glen Village Falk 279 F7
Glen Vine I o M 192 E4
Glenallachie Moray 302 E2
Glenalmond College
Perth 286 E3
Glenalmond Ho Perth 286 E3
Glenamachrie Argyll 289 G11
Glenample Stirl 285 E9
Glenancross Highld 295 F8
Glenapp Castle S Ayrs 244 G3
Glenaros Ho Argyll 289 E7
Glenbarr Argyll 255 D7
Glenbeg Highld 289 C7
Glenbeg Highld 301 G10
Glenbervie Aberds 293 E9
Glenboig N Lnrk 268 B4
Glenborrodale Highld 289 C8
Glenbranter Argyll 276 B2
Glenbreck Borders 260 E3
Glenbrein Lodge
Highld 290 B6
Glenbrittle House
Highld 294 C6
Glenbrook Edin 270 B2
Glenbuchat Castle
Aberds 292 B5
Glenbuchat Lodge
Aberds 292 B5
Glenbuck E Ayrs 259 D7
Glenburn Renfs 267 C9
Glenbyre Argyll 289 G7
Glencalvie Lodge
Highld 309 L4
Glencanisp Lodge
Highld 307 G6
Glencaple Dumfries 237 C11
Glencarron Lodge
Highld 299 D10
Glencarse Perth 286 E5
Glencassley Castle
Highld 309 J4
Glencat Aberds 293 D7
Glenceitlein Highld 284 C5
Glencoe Highld 284 B4
Glencraig Fife 280 B3
Glencripesdale Highld 289 D8
Glencrosh Dumfries 247 F7
Glendavan Ho Aberds 292 C6
Glendearg Borders 262 B2
Glendevon Perth 286 G3
Glendoe Lodge Highld 290 C6
Glendoebeg Highld 290 C6
Glendoick Perth 286 E6
Glendoll Lodge Angus 292 F4
Glendoune S Ayrs 244 D5
Glenduckie Fife 286 F6
Glendye Lodge Aberds 293 E8
Gleneagles Hotel Perth 286 F3
Gleneagles House
Perth 286 G3
Glenearn Perth 286 F5
Glenegedale Argyll 254 B4
Glenelg Highld 295 D10
Glenernie Moray 301 E10
Glenfarg Perth 286 F5
Glenfarquhar Lodge
Aberds 293 E9
Glenferness House
Highld 301 E9
Glenfeshie Lodge
Highld 291 D10
Glenfiddich Lodge
Moray 302 F3
Glenfield Leics 135 B10
Glenfinnan Highld 295 G10
Glenfinnan Lodge
Highld 295 G11
Glenfintaig Ho Highld 290 E4
Glenfoot Perth 286 F5
Glenfyne Lodge Argyll 284 F6
Glengap Dumfries 237 D8
Glengarnock N Ayrs 266 E6
Glengolly Highld 310 C5
Glengorm Castle Argyll 288 D6
Glengoulandie Perth 285 B11
Glengrasco Highld 298 E4
Glenhead Farm Angus 292 G4
Glenholt Plym 7 C10
Glenhoul Dumfries 246 F4
Glenhurich Highld 289 C10
Glenkerry Borders 261 G7
Glenkiln Dumfries 237 B10
Glenkindie Aberds 292 B6
Glenlair Dumfries 237 B9
Glenlatterach Moray 301 D11
Glenlee Dumfries 246 G4
Glenleigh Park E Sus 38 F2
Glenleraig Highld 306 F6
Glenlichorn Perth 285 F11
Glenlicht Ho Highld 290 B2
Glenlivet Moray 301 G11
Glenlochar Dumfries 237 C9
Glenlochsie Perth 292 F2
Glenlocksie Lodge
Perth 292 F2
Glenloig N Ayrs 255 D10
Glenlomond Perth 286 G5
Glenluce Dumfries 236 D4
Glenlussa Ho Argyll 255 E8
Glenmallan Argyll 276 B5
Glenmark Angus 292 E6
Glenmarkie Lodge
Angus 292 G4
Glenmarksie Highld 300 D3
Glenmavis N Lnrk 268 B4
Glenmavis W Loth 269 B9
Glenmaye I o M 192 E3
Glenmayne Borders 261 C11
Glenmeanie Highld 300 D2
Glenmidge Dumfries 247 F9
Glenmoidart Ho Highld 289 B9
Glenmore Argyll 275 B9
Glenmore Argyll 275 G11
Glenmore Highld 298 E4
Glenmore Lodge
Highld 291 C11
Glenmoy Angus 292 G6
Glennoe Argyll 284 D4
Glenogil Angus 292 G6
Glenowen Pembs 73 D7
Glenprosen Lodge
Angus 292 G4
Glenprosen Village
Angus 292 G5
Glenquaich Lodge
Perth 286 D2
Glenquiech Angus 292 G6
Glenquithlie Aberds 303 C8
Glenrath Borders 260 C6
Glenrazie Dumfries 236 C5
Glenreasdell Mains
Argyll 255 B9
Glenree N Ayrs 255 E10
Glenridding Cumb 221 B7
Glenrosa N Ayrs 256 B2
Glenrossal Highld 309 J4
Glenrothes Fife 286 G6
Glensanda Highld 289 E10
Glensaugh Aberds 293 F8
Glensburgh Falk 279 E8
Glenshero Lodge
Highld 291 D7
Glenshoe Lodge Perth 292 G3
Glenstockadale
Dumfries 236 C2
Glenstriven Argyll 275 F11
Glentaggart S Lnrk 259 D8
Glentarkie Perth 286 F5
Glenternie Borders 260 B6
Glentham Lincs 189 C8
Glentirranmuir Stirl 278 C3
Glenton Aberds 302 G6
Glentress Borders 261 B7
Glentromie Lodge
Highld 291 D9
Glentrool Village
Dumfries 236 B5
Glentruan I o M 192 B5
Glentruim House Highld 291 D8
Glentworth Lincs 188 D6
Glenuaig Lodge Highld 299 E11
Glenuig Highld 289 B8
Glenure Argyll 284 C4
Glenurquhart Highld 301 C7
Glenview Argyll 284 E5
Glespin S Lnrk 259 D8
Gletness Shetland 313 H6
Glewstone Hereford 97 G11
Glinton P'boro 138 B3
Globe Town London 67 C11
Glodwick Gtr Man 196 G2
Glogue Pembs 92 E4
Glooston Leics 136 D4
Glororum Northumb 264 C5
Glossop Derbys 185 C8
Gloster Hill Northumb 253 C7
Gloucester Glos 80 B4
Gloup Shetland 312 C7
Gloweth Corn 4 G5
Glusburn N Yorks 204 E6
Glutt Lodge Highld 310 F3
Glutton Bridge Staffs 169 B9
Gluvian Corn 5 C8
Glympton Oxon 101 G8
Glyn Mon 79 F7
Glyn Powys 129 F8
Glyn Castle Neath 76 E4
Glyn-Ceiriog Wrex 148 B4
Glyn-cywarch Gwyn 146 C2
Glyn Etwy Bl Gwent 77 D11
Glyn-neath = Glynedd
Neath 76 D5
Glynarthen Ceredig 92 B6
Glynbrochan Powys 129 G8
Glyncoch Rhondda 77 G9
Glyncoed Bl Gwent 77 C11
Glyncorrwg Neath 57 B11
Glynde E Sus 23 D7
Glyndebourne E Sus 23 C7
Glyndyfrdwy Denb 165 G10
Glyne Gap E Sus 38 F3
Glynedd = Glyn neath
Neath 76 D5
Glynhafren Powys 129 G7
Glynllan Bridgend 58 B2
Glynmorlas Shrops 148 B6
Glynogwr Bridgend 58 B3
Glyntaff Rhondda 58 B5
Glyntawe Powys 76 B4
Gnosall Staffs 150 E6
Gnosall Heath Staffs 150 E6
Goadby Leics 136 D4
Goadby Marwood Leics 154 D5
Goat Lees Kent 54 D4
Goatacre Wilts 62 D4
Goatham Green E Sus 38 C4
Goathill Dorset 29 D11
Goathland N Yorks 226 E6
Goathurst Som 43 G9
Goathurst Common Kent 52 C3
Gobernuisgach Lodge
Highld 308 E4
Gobernuisgeach Highld 310 F3
Gobhaig W Isles 305 H2
Gobowen Shrops 148 C6
Gobley Hole Hants 48 D6
Godalming Sur 50 E3
Goddards Bucks 84 G3
Goddard's Corner Suff 126 D5
Goddard's Green Kent 53 G10
Goddard's Green W Berks 65 F7
Goddards' Green W Sus 36 C3
Godden Green Kent 52 B5
Goddington London 68 F3
Godley Gtr Man 185 B7
Godley Hill Gtr Man 185 C7
Godleybrook Staffs 169 G7
Godleys Green E Sus 36 D5
Godmanchester Cambs 122 C4
Godmanstone Dorset 17 B9
Godmersham Kent 54 C5
Godney Som 44 E3
Godolphin Cross Corn 2 C4
Godre'r-graig Neath 76 D3
God's Blessing Green
Dorset 31 G8
Godshill Hants 31 E11
Godshill I o W 20 E6
Godstone Sur 51 C10
Godswinscroft Hants 19 B9
Godwell Devon 8 D2
Godwick Norf 159 E8
Godwinscroft Hants 19 B9
Goetre Mon 78 D4
Goferydd Anglesey 178 E2
Goff's Oak Herts 86 E4
Gogar Edin 280 G3
Goginan Ceredig 128 G3
Goirtean a'Chladaich
Highld 290 F2
Golan Gwyn 163 G8
Golant Corn 6 E2
Golberdon Corn 12 G2
Golborne Gtr Man 183 B10
Golcar W Yorks 196 D6
Golch Flint 181 F11
Gold Hill Dorset 30 E4
Gold Hill Norf 139 E10
Goldcliff Newport 59 C11
Golden Balls Oxon 83 F9
Golden Cross E Sus 23 C10
Golden Cross E Sus 23 C8
Golden Green Kent 52 D6
Golden Grove Carms 75 B9
Golden Hill Bristol 60 D5
Golden Hill Hants 19 B11
Golden Hill Pembs 73 E7
Golden Hill Pembs 91 G9
Golden Park Devon 24 C2
Golden Pot Hants 49 E8
Golden Valley Derbys 170 E6
Golden Valley Glos 99 G8
Golden Valley Hereford 98 B3
Goldenhill Stoke 168 E5
Golder Field Hereford 115 E11
Golders Green London 67 B9
Goldfinch Bottom
W Berks 64 G4
Goldhanger Essex 88 D6
Golding Shrops 131 C10
Goldington Beds 121 G11
Gold's Cross Bath 60 G5
Golds Green W Mid 133 E9
Goldsborough N Yorks 206 B3
Goldsborough N Yorks 226 C6
Goldsithney Corn 2 C2
Goldstone Shrops 150 D4
Goldthorn Park W Mid 133 D8
Goldthorpe S Yorks 198 G3
Goldworthy Devon 24 C5
Golford Kent 53 F9
Golftyn Flint 182 G3
Golgotha Kent 55 D9
Gollanfield Highld 301 D8
Gollawater Corn 4 E5
Gollinglith Foot N Yorks 214 C3
Golly Wrex 166 D4
Golsoncott Som 42 F4
Golspie Highld 311 J2
Golval Highld 310 C2
Golynos Torf 78 E3
Gomeldon Wilts 47 F7
Gomersal W Yorks 197 B8
Gometra Ho Argyll 288 E5
Gomshall Sur 50 D5
Gonalston Notts 171 F11
Gonamena Corn 11 G11
Gonerby Hill Foot Lincs 155 B8
Gonfirth Shetland 313 G5
Good Easter Essex 87 C10
Gooderstone Norf 140 C5
Goodleigh Devon 40 G6
Goodley Stock Kent 52 C2
Goodmanham E Yorks 208 E3
Goodmayes London 68 B3
Goodnestone Kent 55 C9
Goodnestone Kent 70 G4
Goodrich Hereford 79 B9
Goodrington Torbay 9 D7
Good's Green Worcs 132 G5
Goodshaw Lancs 195 B10
Goodshaw Chapel
Lancs 195 B10
Goodshaw Fold Lancs 195 B10
Goodstone Devon 13 G11
Goodwick = Wdig Pembs 91 D8
Goodworth Clatford
Hants 47 E11
Goodyers End Warks 134 F6
Goodyhills Cumb 229 B8
Goom's Hill Worcs 117 G10
Goon Gumpas Corn 4 G4
Goon Piper Corn 3 B8
Goonabarn Corn 5 E9
Goonbell Corn 4 F4
Goonhavern Corn 4 E5
Goonhusband Corn 2 D5
Goonlaze Corn 2 B6
Goonown Corn 4 E4
Goonvrea Corn 4 F4
Goose Eye W Yorks 204 E6
Goose Green Cumb 211 C10
Goose Green Essex 108 F2
Goose Green Gtr Man 194 G5
Goose Green Hants 32 F4
Goose Green Herts 86 D5
Goose Green Kent 52 C6
Goose Green Kent 53 F10
Goose Green Lancs 194 C3
Goose Green Norf 142 F2
Goose Green S Glos 61 C8
Goose Green W Sus 34 C3
Goose Green W Sus 35 D10
Goose Hill Hants 64 G4
Goose Pool Hereford 97 D9
Gooseberry Green
Essex 87 F11
Gooseford Devon 13 C9
Gooseham Mill Devon 24 D2
Goosehill W Yorks 197 C11
Goosehill Green Worcs 117 E8
Goosemoor Staffs 150 F6
Goosemoor Green
Staffs 151 G11
Goosenford Som 28 B2
Goosewell Devon 40 D5
Goosey Oxon 82 G5
Goosnargh Lancs 203 F7
Goostrey E Ches 184 G3
Gorbals Glasgow 267 C11
Gorcott Hill Warks 117 D11
Gord Shetland 313 L6
Gorddinog Conwy 179 G11
Gordon Borders 272 G2
Gordonbush Highld 311 J2
Gordonsburgh Moray 302 C4
Gordonstoun Moray 301 C11
Gordonstown Aberds 302 D5
Gordonstown Aberds 303 F7
Gore Dorset 29 D9
Gore Kent 55 B10
Gore Cross Wilts 46 C4
Gore End Hants 64 G2
Gore Pit Essex 88 B5
Gore Street Kent 71 F9
Gorebridge Midloth 270 C6
Gorefield Cambs 157 G8
Gorehill W Sus 35 C7
Gorgie Edin 280 G4

376 Gor – Hai

Gorhambury Herts 85 D10
Goring Oxon 64 C6
Goring-by-Sea W Sus 35 G10
Goring Heath Oxon 65 D7
Gorleston-on-Sea Norf 143 C10
Gornalwood W Mid 133 E8
Gorrachie Aberds 303 D7
Gorran Churchtown Corn 5 G9
Gorran Haven Corn 5 G10
Gorran High Lanes Corn 5 G9
Gorrenberry Borders 249 D11
Gorrig Ceredig 93 C8
Gorse Covert Warr 183 C11
Gorse Hill Gtr Man 184 B4
Gorse Hill Swindon 63 B7
Gorsedd Flint 181 F11
Gorseinon Swansea 56 B5
Gorseness Orkney 314 E4
Gorsethorpe Notts 171 B9
Gorseybank Derbys 170 E3
Gorsgoch Ceredig 111 G9
Gorslas Carms 75 C9
Gorsley Glos 98 F3
Gorsley Common Hereford 98 F3
Gorsley Ley Staffs 133 B11
Gorst Hill Worcs 116 C4
Gorstage W Ches 183 G10
Gorstan Highld 300 C3
Gorstanvorran Highld 289 B10
Gorstella W Ches 166 C5
Gorsteyhill E Ches 168 E2
Gorsty Hill Staffs 151 D11
Gorstyhill Staffs 168 E2
Gortan Argyll 274 G3
Gortantaoid Argyll 274 F4
Gortenacullish Highld 295 G8
Gorteneorn Highld 289 C8
Gortenfern Highld 289 C8
Gortinanane Argyll 255 C8
Gorton Gtr Man 184 B5
Gortonallister N Ayrs 256 D2
Gosbeck Suff 126 F3
Gosberton Lincs 156 C4
Gosberton Cheal Lincs 156 D4
Gosberton Clough Lincs 156 D3
Goscote W Mid 133 C10
Goseley Dale Derbys 152 E6
Gosfield Essex 106 F5
Gosford Hereford 115 D10
Gosford Oxon 83 C7
Gosford Green W Mid 118 B6
Gosforth Cumb 219 E11
Gosforth T & W 242 D6
Gosforth Valley Derbys 186 F4
Gosland Green Suff 124 G5
Gosling Green Suff 107 C9
Gosmere Kent 54 B4
Gosmore Herts 104 F3
Gospel Ash Staffs 132 E6
Gospel End Village Staffs 133 E7
Gospel Green W Sus 50 G2
Gospel Oak London 67 B9
Gosport Hants 21 B8
Gosport Hants 32 C5
Gossabrough Shetland 312 E7
Gossard's Green C Beds 103 C9
Gossington Glos 80 E2
Gossops Green W Sus 51 F9
Goswick Northumb 273 F11
Gotham Dorset 31 E9
Gotham E Sus 38 F2
Gotham Notts 153 C10
Gothelney Green Som 43 F9
Gotherington Glos 99 F9
Gothers Corn 5 D9
Gott Argyll 288 E2
Gott Shetland 313 J6
Gotton Som 28 B2
Goudhurst Kent 53 F8
Goukstone Moray 302 D4
Goulceby Lincs 190 F3
Goulton N Yorks 225 E9
Gourdas Aberds 303 E7
Gourdon Aberds 293 F10
Gourock Invclyd 276 F4
Govan Glasgow 267 B11
Govanhill Glasgow 267 C11
Gover Hill Kent 52 C6
Goverton Notts 172 E2
Goveton Devon 8 F5
Govilon Mon 78 C3
Gowanhill Aberds 303 C10
Gowanwell Aberds 303 E8
Gowdall E Yorks 198 C6
Gowerton = Tre-Gwyr Swansea 56 B5
Gowhole Derbys 185 E8
Gowkhall Fife 279 D11
Gowkthrapple N Lnrk 268 E5
Gowthorpe E Yorks 207 C11
Goxhill E Yorks 209 E9
Goxhill N Lincs 200 C6
Goxhill Haven N Lincs 200 B6
Goybre Neath 57 D9
Goytre Neath 57 D9
Gozzard's Ford Oxon 83 F7
Grabhair W Isles 305 G5
Graby Lincs 155 D11
Gracca Corn 5 D10
Gracemount Edin 270 B5
Grade Corn 2 G6
Graffham W Sus 34 D6
Grafham Cambs 122 D3
Grafham Sur 50 E4
Grafton Hereford 97 D9
Grafton N Yorks 215 G8
Grafton Oxon 82 E3
Grafton Shrops 149 F8
Grafton Worcs 99 D9
Grafton Worcs 115 E11
Grafton Flyford Worcs 117 F9
Grafton Regis Northants 102 B5
Grafton Underwood Northants 137 G8
Grafty Green Kent 53 D11
Grahamston Falk 279 E7
Graianrhyd Denb 166 D2
Graig Carms 74 E6
Graig Conwy 180 G4
Graig Denb 181 G9
Graig Rhondda 58 B5
Graig Wrex 148 B4
Graig-Fawr Swansea 75 E10
Graig-fechan Denb 165 E10
Graig Felen Swansea 75 E11
Graig Penllyn V Glam 58 D3
Graig Trewyddfa Swansea 57 B7
Grain Medway 69 D11
Grains Bar Gtr Man 196 F3
Grainsby Lincs 190 B3
Grainthorpe Lincs 190 B5
Grainthorpe Fen Lincs 190 B5
Graiselound N Lincs 188 B3
Grampound Corn 5 F8
Grampound Road Corn 5 E8
Gramsdal W Isles 296 F4
Granborough Bucks 102 F5
Granby Notts 154 B5
Grandborough Warks 119 D9
Grandpont Oxon 83 D8
Grandtully Perth 286 B3
Grange Cumb 220 B5
Grange Dorset 31 G8
Grange E Ayrs 257 B10
Grange Fife 287 G8
Grange Halton 183 E8
Grange Lancs 203 G7
Grange Medway 69 F9
Grange Mers 182 D2
Grange N Yorks 223 G8
Grange NE Lincs 201 F9
Grange Perth 286 E6
Grange Warr 183 C10
Grange Crossroads Moray 302 D4
Grange Estate Dorset 31 G10
Grange Hall Moray 301 C10
Grange Hill Durham 233 F10
Grange Hill Essex 86 G6
Grange Moor W Yorks 197 D8
Grange of Cree Dumfries 236 D6
Grange of Lindores Fife 286 F6
Grange-over-Sands Cumb 211 D8
Grange Park London 86 F4
Grange Park Mers 183 C7
Grange Park Northants 120 F5
Grange Park Swindon 62 C6
Grange Villa Durham 242 G6
Grange Village Glos 79 C11
Grangemill Derbys 170 D2
Grangemouth Falk 279 E8
Grangemuir Fife 287 G9
Grangepans Falk 279 E10
Grangetown Cardiff 59 E7
Grangetown Redcar 235 G7
Grangetown T & W 243 G10
Granish Highld 291 B11
Gransmoor E Yorks 209 B8
Gransmore Green Essex 106 G3
Granston = Treopert Pembs 91 E7
Grant Thorold NE Lincs 201 F9
Grantchester Cambs 123 F8
Grantham Lincs 155 B8
Grantley N Yorks 214 F4
Grantley Hall N Yorks 214 F4
Grantlodge Aberds 293 B9
Granton Dumfries 248 B3
Granton Edin 280 F4
Grantown Aberds 302 D5
Grantown-on-Spey Highld 301 G10
Grantsfield Hereford 115 E10
Grantshouse Borders 272 B6
Graplin Dumfries 237 E8
Grappenhall Warr 183 D10
Grasby Lincs 200 G5
Grasmere Cumb 220 D6
Grass Green Essex 106 D4
Grasscroft Gtr Man 196 G3
Grassendale Mers 182 D5
Grassgarth Cumb 221 F8
Grassgarth Cumb 230 C2
Grassholme Durham 232 G4
Grassington N Yorks 213 G10
Grassmoor Derbys 170 B6
Grassthorpe Notts 172 B3
Grasswell T & W 243 G8
Grateley Hants 47 E9
Gratton Devon 24 E5
Gratwich Staffs 151 C10
Gravel W Ches 167 B11
Gravel Castle Kent 55 D8
Gravel Hill Bucks 85 G8
Gravel Hole Gtr Man 196 F2
Gravel Hole Shrops 149 B7
Graveley Cambs 122 E4
Graveley Herts 104 F4
Gravelhill Shrops 149 G9
Gravelly Hill W Mid 134 E2
Gravels Shrops 130 D6
Gravelsbank Shrops 130 C6
Graven Shetland 312 F6
Graveney Kent 70 G5
Gravenhunger Moss Shrops 168 G2
Gravesend Herts 105 F8
Gravesend Kent 68 E6
Grayingham Lincs 188 B6
Grayrigg Cumb 221 F11
Grays Thurrock 68 D6
Grayshott Hants 49 F11
Grayson Green Cumb 228 F5
Grayswood Sur 50 G2
Graythorp Hrtlpl 234 F6
Grazeley Wokingham 65 F7
Grazeley Green W Berks 65 F7
Greagdhubh Lodge Highld 291 D8
Greamchary Highld 310 F2
Greasbrough S Yorks 186 B6
Greasby Mers 182 D3
Greasley Notts 171 F7
Great Abington Cambs 105 B10
Great Addington Northants 121 B9
Great Alne Warks 118 F2
Great Altcar Lancs 193 F10
Great Amwell Herts 86 C5
Great Asby Cumb 222 C3
Great Ashfield Suff 125 D9
Great Ashley Wilts 61 G10
Great Ayton N Yorks 225 C11
Great Baddow Essex 88 E2
Great Bardfield Essex 106 E3
Great Barford Beds 122 G2
Great Barrington Glos 82 C2
Great Barrow W Ches 167 B7
Great Barton Suff 125 D7
Great Barugh N Yorks 216 D4
Great Bavington Northumb 251 G11
Great Bealings Suff 108 B4
Great Bedwyn Wilts 63 G9
Great Bentley Essex 108 G2
Great Berry Essex 69 B7
Great Billing Northants 120 E6
Great Bircham Norf 158 C5
Great Blakenham Suff 126 G2
Great Blencow Cumb 230 E5
Great Bolas Telford 150 E2
Great Bookham Sur 50 C6
Great Bosullow Corn 1 C4
Great Bourton Oxon 101 B9
Great Bowden Leics 136 F4
Great Bower Kent 54 C4
Great Bradley Suff 124 G3
Great Braxted Essex 88 C5
Great Bricett Suff 125 G10
Great Brickhill Bucks 103 E8
Great Bridge W Mid 133 E9
Great Bridgeford Staffs 151 D7
Great Brington Northants 120 D3
Great Bromley Essex 107 F11
Great Broughton Cumb 229 E7
Great Broughton N Yorks 225 D10
Great Buckland Kent 69 G7
Great Budworth W Ches 183 F11
Great Burdon Darl 224 B6
Great Burgh Sur 51 B8
Great Burstead Essex 87 G11
Great Busby N Yorks 225 D10
Great Canfield Essex 87 B9
Great Carlton Lincs 190 D6
Great Casterton Rutland 137 B10
Great Casterton Rutland 137 B9
Great Cellws Powys 113 E11
Great Chalfield Wilts 61 G11
Great Chart Kent 54 E3
Great Chatwell Staffs 150 G5
Great Chell Stoke 168 E5
Great Chesterford Essex 105 C10
Great Cheverell Wilts 46 C3
Great Chilton Durham 233 E11
Great Chishill Cambs 105 D8
Great Clacton Essex 89 B11
Great Claydons Essex 88 E3
Great Cliff W Yorks 197 D10
Great Clifton Cumb 228 F6
Great Coates NE Lincs 201 F8
Great Comberton Worcs 99 C9
Great Common Suff 143 F7
Great Common W Sus 35 B8
Great Corby Cumb 239 G11
Great Cornard Suff 107 C7
Great Cowden E Yorks 209 E10
Great Coxwell Oxon 82 G3
Great Crakehall N Yorks 224 G4
Great Cransley Northants 120 B6
Great Cressingham Norf 141 C7
Great Crosby Mers 182 B4
Great Crosthwaite Cumb 229 G11
Great Cubley Derbys 152 B3
Great Dalby Leics 154 G4
Great Denham Beds 103 B10
Great Doddington Northants 121 E7
Great Doward Hereford 79 B9
Great Dunham Norf 159 G7
Great Dunmow Essex 106 G2
Great Durnford Wilts 46 F6
Great Easton Essex 106 F2
Great Easton Leics 136 E6
Great Eccleston Lancs 202 E4
Great Edstone N Yorks 216 C4
Great Ellingham Norf 141 D10
Great Elm Som 45 D8
Great Eppleton T & W 234 B3
Great Eversden Cambs 123 G7
Great Fencote N Yorks 224 G5
Great Finborough Suff 125 F10
Great Fransham Norf 159 G7
Great Gaddesden Herts 85 C8
Great Gate Staffs 169 G9
Great Gidding Cambs 138 G2
Great Givendale E Yorks 208 C2
Great Glemham Suff 126 E6
Great Glen Leics 136 D3
Great Gonerby Lincs 155 B7
Great Gransden Cambs 122 F5
Great Green Cambs 104 C5
Great Green Norf 142 F5
Great Green Suff 125 B11
Great Green Suff 125 F8
Great Green Suff 126 B2
Great Habton N Yorks 216 D5
Great Hale Lincs 173 G10
Great Hallingbury Essex 87 B8
Great Hampden Bucks 84 E4
Great Harrowden Northants 121 C7
Great Harwood Lancs 203 G10
Great Haseley Oxon 83 E10
Great Hatfield E Yorks 209 E9
Great Haywood Staffs 151 E10
Great Haywood Staffs 151 E9
Great Heath W Mid 134 G6
Great Heck N Yorks 198 C5
Great Henny Essex 107 D7
Great Hinton Wilts 46 B2
Great Hivings Bucks 85 E7
Great Hockham Norf 141 E9
Great Holcombe Oxon 83 F10
Great Holland Essex 89 B12
Great Hollands Brack 65 F11
Great Holm M Keynes 102 D6
Great Honeyborough Pembs 73 D7
Great Horkesley Essex 107 E9
Great Hormead Herts 105 F7
Great Horton W Yorks 205 G8
Great Horwood Bucks 102 E5
Great Houghton Northants 120 F5
Great Houghton S Yorks 198 F2
Great Howarth Gtr Man 196 D2
Great Hucklow Derbys 185 F11
Great Job's Cross Kent 38 B4
Great Kelk E Yorks 209 B8
Great Kendale E Yorks 217 G10
Great Kimble Bucks 84 D4
Great Kingshill Bucks 84 F5
Great Langton N Yorks 224 F5
Great Lea Common Reading 65 F8
Great Leighs Essex 88 B2
Great Lever Gtr Man 195 F8
Great Limber Lincs 200 F6
Great Linford M Keynes 103 C7
Great Livermere Suff 125 C7
Great Longstone Derbys 186 G2
Great Lumley Durham 233 B11
Great Lyth Shrops 131 B9
Great Malgraves Thurrock 69 C7
Great Malvern Worcs 98 B5
Great Maplestead Essex 106 E6
Great Marton Blkpool 202 F2
Great Marton Moss Blkpool 202 G2
Great Massingham Norf 158 E5
Great Melton Norf 142 B2
Great Milton Oxon 83 E10
Great Missenden Bucks 84 E5
Great Mitton Lancs 203 F10
Great Mongeham Kent 55 C10
Great Moor Gtr Man 184 D6
Great Moor Staffs 132 D6
Great Moulton Norf 142 E3
Great Munden Herts 105 G7
Great Musgrave Cumb 222 C5
Great Ness Shrops 149 F7
Great Notley Essex 106 G4
Great Oak Mon 78 D5
Great Oakley Essex 108 F3
Great Oakley Northants 137 F7
Great Offley Herts 104 F2
Great Ormside Cumb 222 B4
Great Orton Cumb 239 G8
Great Ouseburn N Yorks 215 G8
Great Oxendon Northants 136 G4
Great Oxney Green Essex 87 D11
Great Palgrave Norf 158 G6
Great Parndon Essex 86 D6
Great Pattenden Kent 53 E8
Great Paxton Cambs 122 E4
Great Plumpton Lancs 202 G3
Great Plumstead Norf 160 G6
Great Ponton Lincs 155 C8
Great Preston W Yorks 198 B2
Great Purston Northants 101 D10
Great Raveley Cambs 138 G5
Great Rissington Glos 81 B11
Great Rollright Oxon 100 E6
Great Ryburgh Norf 159 D9
Great Ryle Northumb 264 G2
Great Ryton Shrops 131 C9
Great Saling Essex 106 F4
Great Salkeld Cumb 231 D7
Great Sampford Essex 106 D2
Great Sankey Warr 183 D9
Great Saredon Staffs 133 B9
Great Saxham Suff 124 E5
Great Shefford W Berks 63 E11
Great Shelford Cambs 123 G9
Great Shoddesden Hants 47 D9
Great Smeaton N Yorks 224 E6
Great Snoring Norf 159 C8
Great Somerford Wilts 62 C3
Great Stainton Darl 234 G2
Great Stambridge Essex 88 G5
Great Staughton Cambs 122 E2
Great Steeping Lincs 174 C6
Great Stoke S Glos 60 C6
Great Stonar Kent 55 B10
Great Stretton Leics 136 C3
Great Strickland Cumb 231 G7
Great Stukeley Cambs 122 C4
Great Sturton Lincs 190 F2
Great Sutton Shrops 131 G10
Great Sutton W Ches 182 F5
Great Swinburne Northumb 241 B10
Great Tew Oxon 101 F7
Great Tey Essex 107 F7
Great Thirkleby N Yorks 215 D9
Great Thurlow Suff 124 G3
Great Torrington Devon 25 D7
Great Tosson Northumb 252 C2
Great Totham Essex 88 C5
Great Tows Lincs 190 C2
Great Tree Corn 6 D5
Great Urswick Cumb 210 E5
Great Wakering Essex 70 B2
Great Waldingfield Suff 107 C8
Great Walsingham Norf 159 B8
Great Waltham Essex 87 C11
Great Warley Essex 87 G9
Great Washbourne Glos 99 E9
Great Weeke Devon 13 D10
Great Weldon Northants 137 F8
Great Welnetham Suff 125 F7
Great Wenham Suff 107 D11
Great Whittington Northumb 242 C2
Great Wigborough Essex 89 C7
Great Wilbraham Cambs 123 F10
Great Wilne Derbys 153 C8
Great Wishford Wilts 46 F5
Great Witchingham Norf 160 E2
Great Witcombe Glos 80 C6
Great Witley Worcs 116 D5
Great Wolford Warks 100 E4
Great Wratting Suff 106 B3
Great Wymondley Herts 104 F4
Great Wyrley Staffs 133 B9
Great Wytheford Shrops 149 F11
Great Yarmouth Norf 143 B10
Great Yeldham Essex 106 D5
Greater Doward Hereford 79 B9
Greatfield Wilts 62 B5
Greatford Lincs 155 G11
Greatgap Bucks 84 B6
Greatgate Staffs 169 G9
Greatham Hants 49 G9
Greatham Hrtlpl 234 F5
Greatham W Sus 35 D8
Greatmoor Bucks 102 G4
Greatness Kent 52 B4
Greatstone-on-Sea Kent 39 C9
Greatworth Northants 101 C11
Greave Gtr Man 184 C6
Greave Lancs 195 C11
Grebby Lincs 174 B6
Greeba I o M 192 D4
Green Denb 165 B9
Green Pembs 73 E7
Green Powys 130 E5
Green Bank Cumb 211 C7
Green Bottom Corn 4 F5
Green Bottom Glos 79 B11
Green Close N Yorks 212 F4
Green Clough W Yorks 205 G7
Green Crize Hereford 97 D10
Green Cross Sur 49 F11
Green Down Devon 28 G3
Green End Beds 103 B10
Green End Beds 121 E11
Green End Beds 122 E2
Green End Beds 122 G2
Green End Bucks 84 F4
Green End Bucks 103 E8
Green End C Beds 103 D11
Green End Cambs 122 C4
Green End Cambs 123 F7
Green End Herts 85 D8
Green End Herts 104 E5
Green End Herts 104 E6
Green End Herts 104 G6
Green End Herts 105 F7
Green End Lancs 204 D4
Green End N Yorks 226 E6
Green End Warks 134 F5
Green Gate Devon 27 D8
Green Hailey Bucks 84 E4
Green Hammerton N Yorks 206 B5
Green Haworth Lancs 195 B9
Green Head Cumb 230 B3
Green Heath Staffs 151 G9
Green Hill Kent 53 C9
Green Hill Lincs 155 B8
Green Hill W Yorks 206 F4
Green Hill Wilts 62 B5
Green Lane Devon 13 F11
Green Lane Hereford 98 B2
Green Lane Powys 130 D3
Green Lane Warks 117 E11
Green Lane Warks 118 B6
Green Moor S Yorks 186 B3
Green Ore Som 44 C5
Green Parlour Bath 45 C8
Green Quarter Cumb 221 E9
Green St Green London 68 G3
Green Side W Yorks 197 E7
Green Side W Yorks 205 G11
Green Street E Sus 38 E3
Green Street Essex 87 F10
Green Street Glos 80 B5
Green Street Glos 80 E3
Green Street Herts 85 F11
Green Street Herts 105 G9
Green Street W Sus 35 C10
Green Street Worcs 99 B7
Green Street Worcs 99 C7
Green Street Green Kent 68 E5
Green Street Green London 68 G3
Green Tye Herts 86 B6
Greenacres Gtr Man 196 F2
Greenan Argyll 275 G11
Greenbank Falk 279 F7
Greenbank Shetland 312 C7
Greenbank W Ches 183 G10
Greenburn W Loth 269 C8
Greencroft Durham 242 G5
Greendale E Ches 184 F5
Greendikes Northumb 264 D3
Greendown Som 44 C5
Greendykes Northumb 264 D3
Greenend N Lnrk 268 C4
Greenend Oxon 100 G6
Greenfaulds N Lnrk 278 G5
Greenfield C Beds 103 E11
Greenfield Glasgow 268 C2
Greenfield Gtr Man 196 G3
Greenfield Highld 289 D11
Greenfield Highld 290 C4
Greenfield Oxon 84 G2
Greenfield = Maes-Glas Flint 181 F11
Greenfoot N Lnrk 268 B4
Greenford London 66 C6
Greengairs N Lnrk 278 G5
Greengarth Hall Cumb 219 E11
Greengate Gtr Man 196 D2
Greengate Norf 159 F10
Greengates W Yorks 205 F9
Greengill Cumb 229 D8
Greenhalgh Lancs 202 F4
Greenhall S Lnrk 268 D3
Greenham Dorset 28 G6
Greenham Som 27 C9
Greenham W Berks 64 F3
Greenhaugh Northumb 251 F7
Greenhead Borders 261 D11
Greenhead Dumfries 247 D9
Greenhead N Lnrk 268 E6
Greenhead Northumb 240 D5
Greenhead Staffs 169 F7
Greenheys Gtr Man 195 G8
Greenhill Dumfries 238 B4
Greenhill Durham 234 B3
Greenhill Falk 278 F6
Greenhill Hereford 98 B4
Greenhill Kent 71 F7
Greenhill Leics 153 G8
Greenhill London 67 B7
Greenhill S Yorks 186 E4
Greenhill Worcs 99 B10
Greenhill Worcs 116 B6
Greenhill Bank Shrops 149 B7
Greenhillocks Derbys 170 F6
Greenhills N Ayrs 267 E7
Greenhills S Lnrk 268 E2
Greenhithe Kent 68 E5
Greenholm E Ayrs 258 B2
Greenholme Cumb 221 D11
Greenhouse Borders 262 E3
Greenhow N Yorks 214 G2
Greenhow Hill N Yorks 214 G2
Greenigoe Orkney 314 F4
Greenland Highld 310 C6
Greenland S Yorks 186 D5
Greenland Mains Highld 310 C6
Greenlands Bucks 65 B9
Greenlands Worcs 117 D11
Greenlaw Aberds 302 D6
Greenlaw Borders 272 F4
Greenlaw Mains Midloth 270 C4
Greenlea Dumfries 238 B2
Greenley M Keynes 102 C6
Greenloaning Perth 286 G2
Greenlooms W Ches 167 C7
Greenman's Lane Wilts 62 C3
Greenmeadow Swindon 62 B6
Greenmeadow Torf 78 F3
Greenmount Gtr Man 195 E9
Greenmow Shetland 313 L6
Greenock Invclyd 276 F5
Greenock West Invclyd 276 F5
Greenodd Cumb 210 C6
Greenrigg W Loth 269 C8
Greenrow Cumb 238 G4
Greens Borders 249 F11
Greens Norton Northants 102 B3
Greensforge Staffs 133 F7
Greensgate Norf 160 F2
Greenside Cumb 222 E4
Greenside Derbys 186 F5
Greenside Gtr Man 184 B6
Greenside T & W 242 E4
Greenside W Yorks 197 D7
Greensidehill Northumb 263 F11
Greensplat Corn 5 D9
Greenstead Essex 107 F10
Greenstead Green Essex 106 F6
Greensted Essex 87 E8
Greensted Green Essex 87 E8
Greenstreet Green Suff 107 B10
Greenway Hereford 98 E4
Greenway Pembs 91 E11
Greenway Som 27 B11
Greenway V Glam 58 E5
Greenway Worcs 116 C4
Greenwell Cumb 240 F2
Greenwells Borders 262 C3
Greenwich London 67 D11
Greenwich Suff 108 C3
Greenwich Wilts 46 G2
Greenwith Common Corn 4 G5
Greenwoods Essex 87 F11
Greeny Orkney 314 D2
Greep Highld 298 E2
Greet Glos 99 E10
Greet Kent 54 B2
Greete Shrops 115 C11
Greetham Lincs 190 G4
Greetham Rutland 155 G8
Greetland W Yorks 196 C5
Greetland Wall Nook W Yorks 196 C5
Greetwell N Lincs 200 G2
Gregg Hall Cumb 221 G9
Gregson Lane Lancs 194 B5
Gregynog Powys 129 D11
Greinetobht W Isles 296 D4
Grèin W Isles 297 L2
Greinton Som 44 F2
Gremista Shetland 313 J6
Grenaby I o M 192 E3
Grendon Northants 121 E7
Grendon Warks 134 C5
Grendon Bishop Hereford 115 F11
Grendon Common Warks 134 D5
Grendon Green Hereford 115 F11
Grendon Underwood Bucks 102 G3
Grenofen Devon 12 G5
Grenoside S Yorks 186 C4
Greosabhagh W Isles 305 J3
Gresford Wrex 166 E5
Gresham Norf 160 B3
Greshornish Highld 298 D3
Gressenhall Norf 159 F9
Gressingham Lancs 211 F11
Gresty Green E Ches 168 E2
Greta Bridge Durham 223 C11
Gretna Dumfries 239 D8
Gretna Green Dumfries 239 D8
Gretton Glos 99 E10
Gretton Northants 137 E7
Gretton Shrops 131 D10
Gretton Fields Glos 99 E10
Grewelthorpe N Yorks 214 E4
Grey Green N Lincs 199 F9
Greyfield Bath 44 B6
Greygarth N Yorks 214 E3
Greylake Som 43 G11
Greylake Fosse Som 44 F2
Greynor Carms 75 D9
Greynor-isaf Carms 75 D9
Greyrigg Dumfries 248 F3
Greys Green Oxon 65 C8
Greysouthen Cumb 229 F7
Greystead Northumb 251 F7
Greystoke Cumb 230 E4
Greystoke Gill Cumb 230 F4
Greystone Aberds 292 D6
Greystone Aberds 302 F6
Greystone Angus 287 C9
Greystone Cumb 211 D10
Greystone Dumfries 237 B11
Greystonegill N Yorks 212 F3
Greystones S Yorks 186 D4
Greystones Warks 99 B11
Greytree Hereford 97 F11
Greywell Hants 49 C8
Griais W Isles 304 D6
Grianan W Isles 304 E6
Gribb Dorset 28 G5
Gribthorpe E Yorks 207 F11
Gridley Corner Devon 12 C3
Griff Warks 135 F7
Griffins Hill W Mid 133 G10
Griffithstown Torf 78 F3
Griffydam Leics 153 F8
Grigg Kent 53 E11
Griggs Green Hants 49 G10
Grillis Corn 2 B5
Grilstone Devon 26 C2
Grimbister Orkney 314 E3
Grimblethorpe Lincs 190 D2
Grimeford Village Lancs 194 E6
Grimes Hill Worcs 117 B11
Grimesthorpe S Yorks 186 C5
Grimethorpe S Yorks 198 F2
Griminis W Isles 296 D3
Griminis W Isles 296 F3
Grimister Shetland 312 D6
Grimley Worcs 116 E6
Grimness Orkney 314 G4
Grimoldby Lincs 190 D5
Grimpo Shrops 149 D7
Grimsargh Lancs 203 G7
Grimsbury Oxon 101 C9
Grimsby NE Lincs 201 E9
Grimscote Northants 120 G3
Grimscott Corn 24 F3
Grimshaw Blkburn 195 C8
Grimshaw Green Lancs 194 E3
Grimsthorpe Lincs 155 E10
Grimston E Yorks 209 F11
Grimston Leics 154 E3
Grimston Norf 158 E4
Grimston York 207 C8
Grimstone Dorset 17 C8
Grimstone End Suff 125 D8
Grinacombe Moor Devon 12 C4
Grindale E Yorks 218 E2
Grindigar Orkney 314 F5
Grindiscol Shetland 313 K6
Grindle Shrops 132 C5
Grindleford Derbys 186 F2
Grindleton Lancs 203 D11
Grindley Staffs 151 D10
Grindley Brook Shrops 167 G8
Grindlow Derbys 185 F11
Grindon Northumb 273 G8
Grindon Staffs 169 E9
Grindon Stockton 234 F3
Grindon T & W 243 G9
Grindonmoor Gate Staffs 169 E9
Grindsbrook Booth Derbys 185 D10
Gringley on the Hill Notts 188 C2
Grinsdale Cumb 239 F9
Grinshill Shrops 149 E10
Grinstead Hill Suff 125 G11
Grinton N Yorks 223 F10
Griomasaigh W Isles 297 G4
Griomsidar W Isles 304 F5
Grisdale Cumb 222 G5
Grishipoll Argyll 288 D3
Grisling Common E Sus 36 C6
Gristhorpe N Yorks 217 C11
Griston Norf 141 D8
Gritley Orkney 314 F5
Grittenham Wilts 62 C4
Grittlesend Hereford 98 B4
Grittleton Wilts 61 C11
Grizebeck Cumb 210 C4
Grizedale Cumb 220 G6
Groam Highld 300 E5
Grobister Orkney 314 D6
Grobsness Shetland 313 G5
Groby Leics 135 B10
Groes Conwy 165 C8
Groes Neath 57 D9
Groes Efa Denb 165 B10
Groes-faen Rhondda 58 C5
Groes-fawr Denb 165 B10
Groes-lwyd Mon 96 G6
Groes-lwyd Powys 148 G4
Groes-wen Caerph 58 B6
Groesffordd Gwyn 144 B5
Groesffordd Powys 95 F11
Groesffordd Marli Denb 181 G8
Groeslon Gwyn 163 C8
Groeslon Gwyn 163 D7
Groespluan Powys 130 B4
Grogport Argyll 255 C9
Gromford Suff 127 F7
Gronant Flint 181 E9
Gronwen Shrops 148 D5
Groombridge E Sus 52 F4
Grosmont Mon 97 G8
Grosmont N Yorks 226 D6
Gross Green Warks 119 F7
Grotaig Highld 300 G4
Groton Suff 107 C9
Grotton Gtr Man 196 G3
Grougfoot Falk 279 F10
Grove Bucks 103 G8
Grove Dorset 17 G10
Grove Hereford 98 C2
Grove Kent 71 G8
Grove Notts 188 F2
Grove Oxon 82 G6
Grove Pembs 73 E7
Grove End Kent 69 G11
Grove End Warks 100 D6
Grove End Warks 134 D3
Grove Green Kent 53 B9
Grove Hill E Sus 23 C10
Grove Hill Kent 71 G8
Grove Park London 67 D8
Grove Park London 68 E2
Grove Town W Yorks 198 C3
Grove Vale W Mid 133 E10
Grovehill E Yorks 208 F6
Grovehill Herts 85 D9
Groves Kent 55 B9
Grovesend Swansea 75 E9
Grub Street Staffs 150 D5
Grubb Street Kent 68 F5
Grudie Highld 300 C3
Gruids Highld 309 J5
Gruinard House Highld 307 K4
Gruinards Highld 309 K5
Grula Highld 294 C5
Gruline Argyll 289 E7
Gruline Ho Argyll 289 F7
Grumbeg Highld 308 F6
Grumbla Corn 1 D4
Grunasound Shetland 313 K5
Grundisburgh Suff 126 G4
Grunsagill Lancs 203 C11
Gruting Shetland 313 J4
Grutness Shetland 313 N6
Gryn Goch Gwyn 162 F6
Gualachulain Highld 284 C5
Gualin Ho Highld 308 D3
Guard House W Yorks 204 E6
Guardbridge Fife 287 F8
Guarlford Worcs 98 B6
Guay Perth 286 C4
Gubbion's Green Essex 88 B2
Gubblecote Herts 84 C6
Guesachan Highld 289 B10
Guestling Green E Sus 38 E5
Guestling Thorn E Sus 38 D4
Guestwick Norf 159 D11
Guestwick Green Norf 159 D11
Guide Blkburn 195 B8
Guide Bridge Gtr Man 184 B6
Guide Post Northumb 253 F7
Guilden Morden Cambs 104 C5
Guilden Sutton W Ches 166 B6
Guildford Sur 50 D3
Guildford Park Sur 50 D3
Guildiehaugh W Loth 269 B9
Guildtown Perth 286 D5
Guilford Pembs 73 D7
Guilsborough Northants 120 C3
Guilsfield = Cegidfa Powys 148 G4
Guilthwaite S Yorks 187 D7
Guilton Kent 55 B9
Guineaford Devon 40 F5
Guisachan Highld 300 G3
Guisborough Redcar 226 B2
Guiseley W Yorks 205 E9
Guist Norf 159 D9
Guith Orkney 314 C5
Guiting Power Glos 99 G11
Gulberwick Shetland 313 K6
Gullane E Loth 281 E9
Guller's End Worcs 99 D7
Gulling Green Suff 124 F6
Gullom Holme Cumb 231 F9
Gulval Corn 1 C5
Gulworthy Devon 12 G4
Gumfreston Pembs 73 E10
Gumley Leics 136 E3
Gummow's Shop Corn 5 D7
Gun Green Kent 53 G9
Gun Hill E Sus 23 C9
Gunby E Yorks 207 F10
Gunby Lincs 155 E8
Gunby Lincs 175 B7
Gundenham Som 27 C10
Gundleton Hants 48 G6
Gunn Devon 40 G6
Gunnersbury London 67 D7
Gunnerside N Yorks 223 F9
Gunnerton Northumb 241 C10
Gunness N Lincs 199 E10
Gunnislake Corn 12 G4
Gunnista Shetland 313 J7
Guns Village W Mid 133 E9
Gunstone Staffs 133 C7
Gunter's Bridge W Sus 35 C7
Gunthorpe Lincs 188 B4
Gunthorpe Norf 159 C10
Gunthorpe Notts 171 G11
Gunthorpe P'boro 138 C3
Gunthorpe Rutland 137 B7
Gunton Suff 143 D10
Gunville I o W 20 D5
Gunwalloe Corn 2 E5
Gunwalloe Fishing Cove Corn 2 E5
Gupworthy Som 42 F3
Gurnard I o W 20 B5
Gurnett E Ches 184 G6
Gurney Slade Som 44 D6
Gurnos M Tydf 77 D8
Gurnos Powys 76 D3
Gushmere Kent 54 B4
Gussage All Saints Dorset 31 E8
Gussage St Andrew Dorset 31 E7
Gussage St Michael Dorset 31 E7
Gustard Wood Herts 85 B11
Guston Kent 55 E10
Gutcher Shetland 312 C7
Guthram Gowt Lincs 156 E3
Guthrie Angus 287 B9
Guyhirn Cambs 139 C7
Guyhirn Gull Cambs 139 C7
Guy's Cliffe Warks 118 D5
Guy's Head Lincs 157 D9
Guy's Marsh Dorset 30 C4
Guyzance Northumb 252 C6
Gwaelod-y-garth Cardiff 58 C6
Gwaenysgor Flint 181 E9
Gwalchmai Anglesey 178 F5
Gwalchmai Uchaf Anglesey 178 F5
Gwallon Corn 2 C2
Gwastad Pembs 91 G10
Gwastadgoed Gwyn 145 G11
Gwastadnant Gwyn 163 D10
Gwaun-Cae-Gurwen Neath 76 C2
Gwaun-Leision Neath 76 C2
Gwavas Corn 2 D5
Gwavas Corn 2 G6
Gwbert Ceredig 92 B3
Gwedna Corn 2
Gweek Corn 2
Gwehelog Mon 78
Gwenddwr Powys 95
Gwennap Corn 2
Gwenter Corn 2
Gwern y brenin Shrops 148
Gwern-y-Steeple V Glam 58
Gwernaffield-y-Waun Flint 166
Gwernafon Powys 129
Gwerneirin Powys 129
Gwerneirin Powys 130
Gwernesney Mon 78
Gwernogle Carms 93
Gwernol Denb 166
Gwernydd Powys 129
Gwernymynydd Flint 166
Gwersyllt Wrex 166
Gwespyr Flint 181
Gwills Corn 4
Gwinear Corn 2
Gwinear Downs Corn 2
Gwithian Corn 2
Gwredog Anglesey 178
Gwrhay Caerph 77
Gwyddelwern Denb 165
Gwyddgrug Carms 93
Gwynfryn Wrex 166
Gwystre Powys 113
Gwytherin Conwy 164
Gyfelia Wrex 166
Gyffin Conwy 180
Gylen Park Argyll 289
Gyre Orkney 314
Gyrn Denb 165
Gyrn-goch Gwyn 162

H

Habberley Shrops 131
Habberley Worcs 116
Habergham Lancs 204
Habertoft Lincs 175
Habin W Sus 34
Habrough NE Lincs 200
Haccombe Devon 14
Haceby Lincs 155
Hacheston Suff 126
Hack Green E Ches 167
Hackbridge London 67
Hackenthorpe S Yorks 186
Hackford Norf 141
Hackforth N Yorks 224
Hackland Orkney 314
Hackleton Northants 120
Hacklinge Kent 55
Hackman's Gate Worcs 117
Hackness N Yorks 227
Hackness Orkney 314
Hackness Som 43
Hackney London 67
Hackney Wick London 67
Hackthorn Lincs 189
Hackthorn Wilts 47
Hackthorpe Cumb 230
Haclait W Isles 297
Haconby Lincs 156
Hacton London 68
Haddacott Devon 25
Hadden Borders 263
Haddenham Bucks 84
Haddenham Cambs 123
Haddenham End Field Cambs 123
Haddington E Loth 281
Haddington Lincs 172
Haddiscoe Norf 143
Haddoch Aberds 302
Haddon Cambs 138
Haddon E Ches 169
Hade Edge W Yorks 196
Hademore Staffs 134
Haden Cross W Mid 133
Hadfield Derbys 185
Hadham Cross Herts 86
Hadham Ford Herts 105
Hadleigh Essex 69
Hadleigh Suff 107
Hadleigh Heath Suff 107
Hadley London 86
Hadley Telford 150
Hadley Worcs 117
Hadley Castle Telford 150
Hadley End Staffs 152
Hadley Wood London 86
Hadlow Kent 52
Hadlow Down E Sus 37
Hadlow Stair Kent 52
Hadnall Shrops 149
Hadspen Som 45
Hadstock Essex 105
Hadston Northumb 253
Hady Derbys 186
Hadzor Worcs 117
Haffenden Quarter Kent 53
Hafod Swansea 57
Hafod-Dinbych Conwy 164
Hafod Grove Pembs 92
Hafod-lom Conwy 180
Hafod-y-Green Denb 181
Hafodiwan Ceredig 111
Hafodyrynys Bl Gwent 78
Hag Fold Gtr Man 195
Haggate Gtr Man 196
Haggate Lancs 204
Haggbeck Cumb 239
Haggersta Shetland 313
Haggerston London 67
Haggerston Northumb 273
Hagginton Hill Devon 40
Haggrister Shetland 312
Haggs Falk 278
Haghill Glasgow 268
Hagley Hereford 97
Hagley Worcs 133
Hagloe Glos 79
Hagmore Green Suff 107
Hagnaby Lincs 174
Hagnaby Lincs 191
Hagnaby Lock Lincs 174
Hague Bar Derbys 185
Hagworthingham Lincs 174
Haigh Gtr Man 194
Haigh S Yorks 197
Haigh Moor W Yorks 197
Haighton Green Lancs 203
Haighton Top Lancs 203
Hail Weston Cambs 122
Haile Cumb 219
Hailes Glos 99
Hailey Herts 86
Hailey Oxon 64
Hailey Oxon 82
Hailsham E Sus 23
Hailstone Hill Wilts 81
Haimer Highld 310
Haimwood Powys 148
Hainault London 87
Haine Kent 71
Hainford Norf 160

Heaton Mersey Gtr Man 184 C5
Heaton Moor Gtr Man 184 C5
Heaton Norris Gtr Man 184 C5
Heaton Royds W Yorks 205 F8
Heaton Shay W Yorks 205 F8
Heaton's Bridge Lancs 194 E2
Heaven's Door Som 29 C10
Heaverham Kent 52 B5
Heaviley Gtr Man 184 D6
Heavitree Devon 14 C4
Hebburn T & W 243 E8
Hebburn Colliery T & W 243 D8
Hebburn New Town T & W 243 E8
Hebden N Yorks 213 G10
Hebden Bridge W Yorks 196 B3
Hebden Green W Ches 167 B10
Hebing End Herts 104 G6
Hebron Anglesey 179 E7
Hebron Carms 92 F3
Hebron Northumb 252 F5
Heck Dumfries 248 G3
Heckdyke N Lincs 188 B3
Heckfield Hants 65 G8
Heckfield Green Suff 126 B3
Heckfordbridge Essex 107 G8
Heckingham Norf 143 D7
Heckington Lincs 173 G10
Heckmondwike W Yorks 197 C8
Heddington Wilts 62 F3
Heddington Wick Wilts 62 F3
Heddle Orkney 314 E3
Heddon Devon 25 B11
Heddon-on-the-Wall Northumb 242 D4
Hedenham Norf 142 E6
Hedge End Dorset 30 F4
Hedge End Hants 33 E7
Hedgehog Bridge Lincs 174 F3
Hedgerley Bucks 66 B3
Hedgerley Green Bucks 66 B3
Hedgerley Hill Bucks 66 B3
Hedging Som 28 B4
Hedley Hill Durham 233 C9
Hedley on the Hill Northumb 242 F3
Hednesford Staffs 151 G9
Hedon E Yorks 201 B7
Hedsor Bucks 66 B2
Hedworth T & W 243 E8
Heelands M Keynes 102 D6
Heeley S Yorks 186 E5
Hegdon Hill Hereford 115 G11
Heggerscales Cumb 222 C6
Heggle Lane Cumb 230 D3
Heglibister Shetland 313 H5
Heighington Darl 233 G11
Heighington Lincs 173 B8
Heighley Staffs 168 F3
Height End Lancs 195 C9
Heightington Worcs 116 C5
Heights Gtr Man 196 F3
Heights of Brae Highld 300 C5
Heights of Kinlochewe Highld 299 C10
Heilam Highld 308 C4
Heiton Borders 262 C6
Helbeck Cumb 222 B5
Hele Devon 12 C2
Hele Devon 13 G10
Hele Devon 27 G7
Hele Devon 40 D4
Hele Som 27 C11
Hele Torbay 9 B8
Helebridge Corn 24 G2
Helensburgh Argyll 276 E5
Helford Corn 3 D7
Helford Passage Corn 3 D7
Helham Green Herts 86 B5
Helhoughton Norf 159 D7
Helions Bumpstead Essex 106 C3
Hell Corner W Berks 63 G11
Hellaby S Yorks 187 C8
Helland Corn 11 G7
Helland Som 28 C4
Hellandbridge Corn 11 G7
Hellesdon Norf 160 G4
Hellesveor Corn 2 A2
Hellidon Northants 119 F10
Hellifield N Yorks 204 B3
Hellifield Green N Yorks 204 B3
Hellingly E Sus 23 C9
Hellington Norf 142 C6
Hellister Shetland 313 J5
Hellman's Cross Essex 87 B9
Helm N Yorks 223 G8
Helm Northumb 252 D5
Helmburn Borders 261 E9
Helmdon Northants 101 C11
Helme W Yorks 196 E5
Helmingham Suff 126 F3
Helmington Row Durham 233 D9
Helmsdale Highld 311 H4
Helmshore Lancs 195 C9
Helmside Cumb 212 B3
Helmsley N Yorks 216 C2
Helperby N Yorks 215 F8
Helperthorpe N Yorks 217 E9
Helpringham Lincs 173 G10
Helpston P'boro 138 B2
Helsby W Ches 183 F7
Helscott Corn 24 G2
Helsey Lincs 191 G8
Helston Corn 2 D5
Helston Water Corn 4 G5
Helstone Corn 11 E7
Helton Cumb 230 G6
Helwith Bridge N Yorks 212 F6
Helygain = Halkyn Flint 182 G2
Hem Heath Stoke 168 G5
Hemblington Norf 160 G6
Hemblington Corner Norf 160 G6
Hembridge Som 44 F5
Hemel Hempstead Herts 85 D9
Hemerdon Devon 7 D11
Hemford Shrops 130 C6
Hemingbrough N Yorks 207 G9
Hemingby Lincs 190 G2
Hemingfield S Yorks 197 G11
Hemingford Abbots Cambs 122 C5
Hemingford Grey Cambs 122 C5
Hemingstone Suff 126 G3
Hemington Leics 153 D9
Hemington Northants 137 F11
Hemington Som 45 C8
Hemley Suff 108 C5
Hemlington M'bro 225 C10
Hemp Green Suff 127 D7
Hempholme E Yorks 209 C7
Hempnall Norf 142 E4
Hempnall Green Norf 142 E4
Hempriggs House Highld 310 E7
Hemp's Green Essex 107 F8
Hempshill Vale Notts 171 G8
Hempstead Essex 106 D2
Hempstead Medway 69 G9
Hempstead Norf 160 B2
Hempstead Norf 161 D8
Hempsted Glos 80 B4
Hempton Norf 159 D8
Hempton Oxon 101 E8
Hempton Wainhill Oxon 84 E3
Hemsby Norf 161 F9
Hemsted Kent 54 E6
Hemswell Lincs 188 C6
Hemswell Cliff Lincs 188 D6
Hemsworth Dorset 31 F7
Hemsworth S Yorks 186 E5
Hemsworth W Yorks 198 E2
Hemyock Devon 27 E10
Hen Bentref Llandegfan Anglesey 179 G9
Hên-efail Denb 165 C9
Henaford Devon 24 D2
Henbrook Worcs 117 D8
Henbury Bristol 60 D5
Henbury Dorset 18 B5
Henbury E Ches 184 G5
Hendomen Powys 130 D4
Hendon London 67 B8
Hendon T & W 243 F10
Hendra Corn 2 B6
Hendra Corn 2 C5
Hendra Corn 2 D3
Hendra Corn 2 F6
Hendra Corn 5 C9
Hendra Corn 5 D9
Hendra Corn 11 E7
Hendra Croft Corn 4 D5
Hendrabridge Corn 6 B5
Hendraburnick Corn 11 D8
Hendre Flint 165 B11
Hendre Gwyn 110 B2
Hendre Powys 129 D9
Hendre-ddu Conwy 164 B5
Hendredenny Park Caerph 58 B6
Hendreforgan Rhondda 58 B3
Hendrerwydd Denb 165 C10
Hendrewen Swansea 75 D10
Hendy Carms 75 E9
Hendy-Gwyn Carms 74 B2
Hendy Gwyn = Whitland Carms 73 B11
Heneglwys Anglesey 178 F6
Henfield S Glos 61 D7
Henfield W Sus 36 D2
Henford Devon 12 C3
Henfords Marsh Wilts 45 E11
Henghurst Kent 54 F3
Hengoed Caerph 77 F10
Hengoed Denb 165 D9
Hengoed Powys 114 G4
Hengoed Shrops 148 C5
Hengrave Norf 160 F2
Hengrave Suff 124 D6
Hengrove Bristol 60 F6
Hengrove Park Bristol 60 F5
Henham Essex 105 F10
Heniarth Powys 130 B2
Henlade Som 28 C3
Henleaze Bristol 60 D5
Henley Dorset 29 G11
Henley Glos 80 B6
Henley Shrops 115 B10
Henley Shrops 131 F9
Henley Som 44 G2
Henley Suff 126 G3
Henley W Sus 34 B5
Henley Wilts 47 B10
Henley Wilts 61 F10
Henley Common W Sus 34 B5
Henley Green W Mid 135 G7
Henley-in-Arden Warks 118 D3
Henley-on-Thames Oxon 65 C9
Henley Street Kent 69 F7
Henley's Down E Sus 38 E2
Henllan Ceredig 93 C7
Henllan Denb 165 B8
Henllan Amgoed Carms 92 G3
Henlle Shrops 148 C6
Henllys Torf 78 G3
Henllys Vale Torf 78 G3
Henlow C Beds 104 D3
Hennock Devon 14 E2
Henny Street Essex 107 D7
Henryd Conwy 180 G3
Henry's Moat Pembs 91 F10
Hensall N Yorks 198 C5
Henshaw Northumb 241 E7
Henshaw W Yorks 205 E10
Hensingham Cumb 219 B9
Hensington Oxon 83 B7
Henstead Suff 143 F9
Hensting Hants 33 C7
Henstridge Devon 40 E5
Henstridge Som 30 D2
Henstridge Ash Som 30 C2
Henstridge Bowden Som 29 C11
Henstridge Marsh Som 30 C2
Henton Oxon 84 E3
Henton Som 44 D3
Henwood Corn 11 G11
Henwood Oxon 83 E7
Henwood Green Kent 52 E6
Heogan Shetland 313 J6
Heol-ddu Carms 75 E7
Heol-ddu Swansea 56 B6
Heol-laethog Bridgend 58 C2
Heol-las Bridgend 58 C2
Heol-las Swansea 57 B7
Heol Senni Powys 95 G8
Heol-y-gaer Powys 96 D3
Heol-y-mynydd V Glam 57 G11
Heolgerrig M Tydf 77 D8
Hepburn Northumb 264 E3
Hepple Northumb 251 C11
Hepscott Northumb 252 G6
Hepthorne Lane Derbys 170 C6
Heptonstall W Yorks 196 B3
Hepworth Suff 125 C9
Hepworth W Yorks 197 F7
Herbrandston Pembs 72 D5
Hereford Hereford 97 C10
Heribusta Highld 298 B4
Heriot Borders 271 E7
Hermiston Edin 280 G3
Hermit Hill S Yorks 197 G10
Hermit Hole W Yorks 205 F7
Hermitage Borders 250 D2
Hermitage Dorset 29 F10
Hermitage W Berks 64 E4
Hermitage W Sus 22 B3
Hermitage Green Mers 183 C10
Hermon Anglesey 162 B5
Hermon Carms 93 E7
Hermon Carms 94 F3
Hermon Pembs 92 E4
Herne Kent 71 F7
Herne Bay Kent 71 F7
Herne Common Kent 71 F7
Herne Hill London 67 E10
Herne Pound Kent 53 C7
Herner Devon 25 B9
Hernhill Kent 70 G5
Herniss Corn 2 C6
Herodsfoot Corn 6 C4
Heron Cross Stoke 168 G5
Heronden Kent 55 C9
Herongate Essex 87 G10
Heron's Ghyll E Sus 37 B7
Herons Green Bath 44 B5
Heronsford S Ayrs 244 G4
Heronsgate Herts 85 G8
Heronston Bridgend 58 D2
Herra Shetland 312 D8
Herriard Hants 49 D7
Herringfleet Suff 143 D9
Herring's Green Beds 103 C11
Herringswell Suff 124 C4
Herringthorpe S Yorks 186 C6
Hersden Kent 71 G8
Hersham Corn 24 F3
Hersham Sur 66 G6
Herstmonceux E Sus 23 C10
Herston Dorset 18 F6
Herston Orkney 314 G4
Hertford Herts 86 C4
Hertford Heath Herts 86 C4
Hertingfordbury Herts 86 C4
Hesket Newmarket Cumb 230 D2
Hesketh Bank Lancs 194 C2
Hesketh Lane Lancs 203 E8
Hesketh Moss Lancs 194 C2
Heskin Green Lancs 194 D4
Hesleden Durham 234 D4
Hesleyside Northumb 251 G8
Heslington York 207 C8
Hessay York 206 C6
Hessenford Corn 6 D6
Hessett Suff 125 E8
Hessle E Yorks 200 B4
Hessle W Yorks 198 D2
Hest Bank Lancs 211 F9
Hester's Way Glos 99 G8
Hestinsetter Shetland 313 J4
Heston London 66 D6
Hestwall Orkney 314 E2
Heswall Mers 182 E3
Hethe Oxon 101 F11
Hethel Norf 142 C3
Hethelpit Cross Glos 98 F5
Hethersett Norf 142 C3
Hethersgill Cumb 239 D11
Hetherside Cumb 239 D10
Hetherson Green W Ches 167 F8
Hethpool Northumb 263 D9
Hett Durham 233 D11
Hetton N Yorks 204 B5
Hetton Downs T & W 234 B3
Hetton-le-Hill T & W 234 B3
Hetton-le-Hole T & W 234 B3
Hetton Steads Northumb 264 B2
Heugh Northumb 242 C3
Heugh-head Aberds 292 B5
Heveningham Suff 126 C6
Hever Kent 52 E3
Heversham Cumb 211 C9
Hevingham Norf 160 E3
Hew Green N Yorks 205 B10
Hewas Water Corn 5 F9
Hewelsfield Glos 79 E9
Hewelsfield Common Glos 79 E8
Hewer Hill Cumb 230 D3
Hewish N Som 60 G2
Hewish Som 28 F6
Hewood Dorset 28 G5
Heworth T & W 243 E7
Heworth York 207 C8
Hexham Northumb 241 E10
Hextable Kent 68 E4
Hexthorpe S Yorks 198 G5
Hexton Herts 104 E2
Hexworthy Devon 13 G9
Hey Lancs 204 E3
Hey Green W Yorks 196 E4
Hey Houses Lancs 193 B10
Heybridge Essex 88 D5
Heybridge Essex 87 F10
Heybridge Basin Essex 88 D5
Heybrook Bay Devon 7 F10
Heydon Cambs 105 C8
Heydon Norf 160 D2
Heydour Lincs 155 B10
Heyheads Gtr Man 196 G3
Heylipol Argyll 288 E1
Heylor Shetland 312 E4
Heyope Powys 114 C4
Heyrod Gtr Man 185 B7
Heysham Lancs 211 G8
Heyshaw N Yorks 214 G3
Heyshott W Sus 34 D5
Heyshott Green W Sus 34 D5
Heyside Gtr Man 196 F2
Heytesbury Wilts 46 E2
Heythrop Oxon 101 F7
Heywood Gtr Man 195 E11
Heywood Wilts 45 C11
Hibaldstow N Lincs 200 G3
Hibb's Green Suff 125 G7
Hickford Hill Essex 106 C5
Hickleton S Yorks 198 F3
Hickling Norf 161 E8
Hickling Notts 154 D3
Hickling Green Norf 161 E8
Hickling Heath Norf 161 E8
Hickling Pastures Notts 154 D3
Hickmans Green Kent 54 B5
Hicks Forstal Kent 71 G7
Hicks Gate Bath 60 F6
Hick's Mill Corn 4 G5
Hickstead W Sus 36 C3
Hidcote Bartrim Glos 100 C3
Hidcote Boyce Glos 100 C3
Hifnal Shrops 132 D4
Higginshaw Gtr Man 196 F2
High Ackworth W Yorks 198 D2
High Angerton Northumb 252 F3
High Bankhill Cumb 231 C7
High Banton N Lnrk 278 E4
High Barn Lincs 174 C5
High Barnes T & W 243 F9
High Barnet London 86 F2
High Beach Essex 86 F6
High Bentham N Yorks 212 F3
High Bickington Devon 25 C10
High Biggins Cumb 212 D2
High Birkwith N Yorks 212 D5
High Birstwith N Yorks 205 B10
High Blantyre S Lnrk 268 D3
High Bonnybridge Falk 278 F6
High Bradfield S Yorks 186 C3
High Bradley N Yorks 204 D6
High Bray Devon 41 G7
High Brooms Kent 52 E5
High Brotheridge Glos 80 C5
High Bullen Devon 25 C8
High Buston Northumb 252 B6
High Callerton Northumb 242 C5
High Cark Cumb 211 C7
High Casterton Cumb 212 D2
High Catton E Yorks 207 C10
High Church Northumb 252 F5
High Cogges Oxon 82 D5
High Common Norf 141 B9
High Coniscliffe Darl 224 B4
High Crompton Gtr Man 196 F2
High Cross Cambs 123 F8
High Cross Corn 2 D6
High Cross E Sus 37 B9
High Cross Hants 34 B2
High Cross Herts 85 F10
High Cross Herts 86 B5
High Cross Newport 59 B9
High Cross W Sus 36 D2
High Cross Warks 118 D3
High Crosshill S Lnrk 268 C2
High Cunsey Cumb 221 G7
High Dubmire T & W 234 B2
High Dyke Durham 232 F5
High Easter Essex 87 C10
High Eggborough N Yorks 198 C5
High Eldrig Dumfries 236 C4
High Ellington N Yorks 214 C3
High Ercall Telford 149 F11
High Etherley Durham 233 F9
High Ferry Lincs 174 F5
High Field Lancs 203 C10
High Flatts W Yorks 197 F8
High Forge Durham 242 G6
High Friarside Durham 242 F5
High Gallowhill E Dunb 278 G2
High Garrett Essex 106 F5
High Grange Durham 233 E9
High Grantley N Yorks 214 F4
High Green Cumb 221 E8
High Green Norf 141 B8
High Green Norf 142 B2
High Green Norf 159 G8
High Green S Yorks 186 B4
High Green Shrops 132 G4
High Green Suff 125 E7
High Green W Yorks 197 E7
High Green Worcs 99 B7
High Halden Kent 53 F11
High Halstow Medway 69 D9
High Ham Som 44 G2
High Handenhold Durham 242 G6
High Harrington Cumb 228 F6
High Harrogate N Yorks 206 B2
High Haswell Durham 234 C3
High Hatton Shrops 150 E2
High Hauxley Northumb 253 C7
High Hawsker N Yorks 227 D8
High Heath Shrops 150 D3
High Heath W Mid 133 C10
High Hesket Cumb 230 C5
High Hesleden Durham 234 D5
High Hill Cumb 229 G11
High Houses Essex 87 C11
High Hoyland S Yorks 197 E9
High Hunsley E Yorks 208 F4
High Hurstwood E Sus 37 B7
High Hutton N Yorks 216 F5
High Ireby Cumb 229 D10
High Kelling Norf 177 E10
High Kilburn N Yorks 215 D10
High Lands Durham 233 F8
High Lane Gtr Man 185 D7
High Lane Worcs 116 E3
High Lanes Corn 2 B3
High Laver Essex 87 D8
High Legh E Ches 184 E2
High Leven Stockton 225 C8
High Littleton Bath 44 B6
High Longthwaite Cumb 229 B11
High Lorton Cumb 229 F9
High Marishes N Yorks 216 D6
High Marnham Notts 188 G4
High Melton S Yorks 198 G4
High Mickley Northumb 242 E3
High Mindork Dumfries 236 D5
High Moor Derbys 187 E7
High Moor Lancs 194 E4
High Moorsley T & W 234 B2
High Nash Glos 79 C9
High Newton Cumb 211 C8
High Newton-by-the-Sea Northumb 264 D6
High Nibthwaite Cumb 210 B5
High Oaks Cumb 222 G2
High Offley Staffs 150 D5
High Ongar Essex 87 E9
High Onn Staffs 150 F6
High Onn Wharf Staffs 150 F6
High Park Cumb 221 G10
High Park Mers 193 D11
High Risby N Lincs 200 E2
High Roding Essex 87 B10
High Rougham Suff 125 E8
High Row Cumb 230 D3
High Row Cumb 230 G3
High Salvington W Sus 35 F10
High Scales Cumb 229 B9
High Sellafield Cumb 219 E10
High Shaw N Yorks 223 G7
High Shields T & W 243 D9
High Shincliffe Durham 233 C11
High Side Cumb 229 E10
High Southwick T & W 243 F9
High Spen T & W 242 F4
High Stakesby N Yorks 227 C7
High Stoop Durham 233 C8
High Street Corn 5 E9
High Street Kent 53 G8
High Street Pembs 73 B11
High Street Suff 107 B7
High Street Suff 127 C8
High Street Suff 127 F8
High Street Suff 143 G7
High Street Green Suff 125 F10
High Sunderland Borders 261 C11
High Throston Hrtlpl 234 E5
High Tirfergus Argyll 255 F7
High Town Luton 103 G11
High Town Shrops 132 E4
High Town Staffs 151 G9
High Toynton Lincs 174 B3
High Trewhitt Northumb 252 B2
High Urpeth Durham 242 G6
High Valleyfield Fife 279 D10
High Walton Cumb 219 C9
High Warden Northumb 241 D10
High Water Head Cumb 220 F6
High Westwood Durham 242 F4
High Whinnow Cumb 239 G8
High Woolaston Glos 79 F9
High Worsall N Yorks 225 D7
High Wray Cumb 221 F7
High Wych Herts 87 C7
High Wycombe Bucks 84 G5
Higham Derbys 170 D5
Higham Fife 286 F6
Higham Kent 69 E8
Higham Lancs 204 F2
Higham S Yorks 197 F10
Higham Suff 107 D10
Higham Suff 124 E4
Higham Common S Yorks 197 F10
Higham Dykes Northumb 242 B4
Higham Ferrers Northants 121 D9
Higham Gobion C Beds 104 E2
Higham Hill London 86 G5
Higham on the Hill Leics 135 D7
Higham Wood Kent 52 D5
Highampton Devon 25 G7
Highams Park London 86 G5
Highbridge Cumb 230 C3
Highbridge Hants 33 C7
Highbridge Highld 290 E3
Highbridge Som 43 D10
Highbridge W Mid 133 C10
Highbrook W Sus 51 G11
Highburton W Yorks 197 E7
Highbury London 67 B10
Highbury Ptsmth 33 G11
Highbury Som 45 D7
Highbury Vale Nottingham 171 G8
Highclere Hants 64 G2
Highcliffe Derbys 186 F2
Highcliffe Dorset 19 C10
Higher Alham Som 45 E7
Higher Ansty Dorset 30 G3
Higher Ashton Devon 14 E3
Higher Audley Blkburn 195 B7
Higher Bal Corn 4 E4
Higher Ballam Lancs 202 G3
Higher Bartle Lancs 202 G6
Higher Bebington Mers 182 D4
Higher Berry End C Beds 103 E9
Higher Blackley Gtr Man 195 G10
Higher Boarshaw Gtr Man 195 F11
Higher Bockhampton Dorset 17 C10
Higher Bojewyan Corn 1 C3
Higher Boscaswell Corn 1 C3
Higher Brixham Torbay 9 D8
Higher Broughton Gtr Man 195 G10
Higher Burrow Som 28 C6
Higher Burwardsley W Ches 167 D8
Higher Chalmington Dorset 29 G9
Higher Cheriton Devon 27 G10
Higher Chillington Som 28 E5
Higher Chisworth Derbys 185 C7
Higher Clovelly Devon 24 C4
Higher Condurrow Corn 2 B5
Higher Crackington Corn 11 B9
Higher Cransworth Corn 5 B9
Higher Croft Blkburn 195 B7
Higher Denham Bucks 66 B4
Higher Dinting Derbys 185 C8
Higher Disley E Ches 185 E7
Higher Downs Corn 2 C3
Higher Durston Som 28 B3
Higher End Gtr Man 194 G4
Higher Folds Gtr Man 195 G7
Higher Gabwell Torbay 9 B8
Higher Green Gtr Man 195 G8
Higher Halstock Leigh Dorset 29 F8
Higher Heysham Lancs 211 G8
Higher Hogshead Lancs 195 C11
Higher Holton Som 29 B11
Higher Hurdsfield E Ches 184 G6
Higher Kingcombe Dorset 16 B6
Higher Kinnerton Flint 166 C4
Higher Land Corn 12 G3
Higher Marsh Som 30 C2
Higher Melcombe Dorset 30 G2
Higher Menadew Corn 5 D10
Higher Molland Devon 41 G8
Higher Muddiford Devon 40 F5
Higher Nyland Dorset 30 C2
Higher Penwortham Lancs 194 B4
Higher Pertwood Wilts 45 F11
Higher Porthpean Corn 5 E10
Higher Poynton E Ches 184 E6
Higher Prestacott Devon 12 B3
Higher Rads End C Beds 103 E9
Higher Ridge Shrops 149 C7
Higher Rocombe Barton Devon 9 B8
Higher Row Dorset 31 G8
Higher Runcorn Halton 183 E8
Higher Sandford Dorset 29 C10
Higher Shotton Flint 166 B4
Higher Shurlach W Ches 183 G11
Higher Slade Devon 40 D4
Higher Street Som 42 E6
Higher Tale Devon 27 G9
Higher Tolcarne Corn 5 B7
Higher Totnell Dorset 29 F10
Higher Town Corn 5 C10
Higher Town Scilly 1 F4
Higher Town Som 42 D3
Higher Tremarcoombe Corn 6 B5
Higher Vexford Som 42 F6
Higher Walreddon Devon 12 G5
Higher Walton Lancs 194 B5
Higher Walton Warr 183 D9
Higher Wambrook Som 28 F3
Higher Warcombe Devon 40 D3
Higher Weaver Devon 27 G9
Higher Whatcombe Dorset 30 G4
Higher Wheelton Lancs 194 C6
Higher Whitley W Ches 183 E10
Higher Wincham W Ches 183 F11
Higher Woodsford Dorset 17 D11
Higher Wraxall Dorset 29 G9
Higher Wych W Ches 167 G7
Highercliff Corn 6 D4
Higherford Lancs 204 E3
Highertown Corn 4 G6
Highertown Corn 11 E8
Highfield E Yorks 207 F10
Highfield Glos 79 E10
Highfield Gtr Man 194 G5
Highfield Gtr Man 195 F8
Highfield Herts 85 D9
Highfield N Ayrs 266 E6
Highfield Oxon 101 G11
Highfield S Yorks 186 D5
Highfield Soton 32 E6
Highfield T & W 242 F4
Highfields Cambs 123 F7
Highfields Derbys 170 B6
Highfields Essex 88 B5
Highfields Glos 80 F3
Highfields Leicester 136 C2
Highfields Northumb 273 E9
Highfields S Yorks 198 F4
Highfields Staffs 151 E8
Highgate E Sus 52 G2
Highgate Kent 53 G9
Highgate London 67 B9
Highgate Powys 130 D2
Highgate S Yorks 198 G3
Highgate W Mid 133 F11
Highlane Derbys 186 E6
Highlane E Ches 168 B5
Highlanes Corn 10 G4
Highlanes Staffs 150 C5
Highlaws Cumb 229 B8
Highleadon Glos 98 G5
Highleigh W Sus 22 D4
Highley Shrops 132 G4
Highmoor Cumb 229 B11
Highmoor Oxon 65 B8
Highmoor Cross Oxon 65 C8
Highmoor Hill Mon 60 B3
Highnam Glos 80 B3
Highnam Green Glos 98 G5
Highoak Norf 141 C11
Highridge Bristol 60 F5
Highroad Well Moor W Yorks 196 B5
Highstead Kent 71 F8
Highsted Kent 70 G2
Highstreet Kent 70 G5
Highstreet Green Essex 106 E5
Highstreet Green Sur 50 F3
Hightae Dumfries 238 B3
Highter's Heath W Mid 117 B11
Hightown E Ches 168 C5
Hightown Hants 31 G11
Hightown Mers 193 G10
Hightown Soton 33 E7
Hightown W Yorks 197 C7
Hightown Wrex 166 F4
Hightown Green Suff 125 F9
Hightown Heights W Yorks 197 C7
Highway Corn 4 G4
Highway Hereford 97 B9
Highway Som 29 C7
Highway Wilts 62 E4
Highway Windsor 65 C11
Highweek Devon 14 G2
Highwood Devon 27 F10
Highwood Dorset 18 D3
Highwood Essex 87 E10
Highwood Hants 31 F11
Highwood Worcs 116 D3
Highwood Hill London 86 G2
Highworth Swindon 82 G2
Highworthy Devon 24 F6
Hilborough Norf 140 C6
Hilborough Ho Norf 140 C6
Hilcot Glos 81 B7
Hilcot End Glos 81 E9
Hilcote Derbys 171 D7
Hilcott Wilts 46 B6
Hilden Park Kent 52 D5
Hildenborough Kent 52 D5
Hildersham Cambs 105 B10
Hildersley Hereford 98 G2
Hilderstone Staffs 151 C8
Hilderthorpe E Yorks 218 F3
Hilfield Dorset 29 F10
Hilgay Norf 140 D2
Hill S Glos 79 G10
Hill W Mid 134 D2
Hill Warks 119 D9
Hill Bottom Oxon 64 D6
Hill Brow W Sus 34 B3
Hill Chorlton Staffs 150 B5
Hill Common Norf 161 E8
Hill Corner Som 45 D10
Hill Croome Worcs 99 C7
Hill Dale Lancs 194 E3
Hill Deverill Wilts 45 E11
Hill Dyke Lincs 174 F4
Hill End Durham 232 D6
Hill End Fife 279 B10
Hill End Glos 99 D8
Hill End London 85 G8
Hill End N Yorks 205 C7
Hill End Som 29 E8
Hill End Worcs 117 E8
Hill Furze Worcs 99 B9
Hill Gate Hereford 97 F9
Hill Green Essex 105 E9
Hill Green Kent 69 G10
Hill Head Hants 33 G8
Hill Head Northumb 241 D10
Hill Hoath Kent 52 E3
Hill Hook W Mid 134 C2
Hill Houses Shrops 116 B2
Hill Mountain Pembs 73 D7
Hill of Beath Fife 280 C3
Hill of Drip Stirl 278 B5
Hill of Fearn Highld 301 B8
Hill of Keillor Angus 286 C6
Hill of Mountblairy Aberds 302 D6
Hill of Overbrae Aberds 303 C8
Hill Park Hants 33 F9
Hill Park Kent 52 B2
Hill Ridware Staffs 151 F11
Hill Side Hants 34 B3
Hill Side S Yorks 197 G8
Hill Side W Yorks 197 D7
Hill Side Worcs 116 E5
Hill Somersal Derbys 152 C2
Hill Street Kent 54 D6
Hill Top Derbys 186 F5
Hill Top Durham 232 G5
Hill Top Durham 233 C10
Hill Top Durham 242 G5
Hill Top Gtr Man 195 G8
Hill Top Hants 32 G6
Hill Top N Yorks 214 G3
Hill Top N Yorks 214 G5
Hill Top Notts 171 F7
Hill Top S Yorks 186 C5
Hill Top S Yorks 186 D3
Hill Top S Yorks 187 B7
Hill Top S Yorks 197 F9
Hill Top Staffs 133 B7
Hill Top W Mid 133 E9
Hill Top W Sus 34 C5
Hill Top W Yorks 196 E5
Hill Top W Yorks 197 D10
Hill Top W Yorks 205 G11
Hill Top W Yorks 205 G7
Hill Top Warks 134 E5
Hill Top Warks 135 E7
Hill View Dorset 18 B5
Hill Wood W Mid 134 C2
Hill Wootton Warks 118 D6
Hillam N Yorks 198 B4
Hillbeck Cumb 222 B5
Hillblock Pembs 73 B8
Hillborough Kent 71 F8
Hillbourne Poole 18 C6
Hillbrae Aberds 302 E6
Hillbrae Aberds 303 G7
Hillbutts Dorset 31 G7
Hillcliffe Warr 183 D10
Hillclifflane Derbys 170 F3
Hillcommon Som 27 B11
Hillcross Derbys 152 C6
Hilldyke Lincs 174 F4
Hillend Fife 280 E2
Hillend N Lnrk 268 B6
Hillend N Som 43 B11
Hillend Shrops 132 E6
Hillend Swansea 56 C2
Hillend Green Glos 98 F4
Hillersland Glos 79 C9
Hillerton Devon 13 B10
Hillesden Bucks 102 F3
Hillesden Hamlet Bucks 102 E3
Hillesley Glos 61 B9
Hillfarance Som 27 C11
Hillfarrance Som 27 C11
Hillfield Devon 8 E6
Hillfield W Mid 118 B2
Hillfields S Glos 60 D6
Hillfields W Mid 118 B6
Hillfoot Aberds 303 D9
Hillfoot W Yorks 205 G10
Hillfoot End C Beds 104 E2
Hillgreen W Berks 64 D3
Hillgrove W Sus 34 B6
Hillhampton Hereford 97 B11
Hillhead Aberds 302 F5
Hillhead Aberds 303 G8
Hillhead Corn 5 C11
Hillhead Devon 9 E8
Hillhead E Ayrs 257 B10
Hillhead S Ayrs 257 F10
Hillhead of Auchentumb Aberds 303 D9
Hillhead of Blairy Aberds 302 D6
Hillhead of Cocklaw Aberds 303 E10
Hillhouse Borders 271 D10
Hilliard's Cross Staffs 152 G3
Hilliclay Highld 310 C5
Hillingdon London 66 C5
Hillingdon Heath London 66 C5
Hillington Glasgow 267 C10
Hillington Norf 158 D4
Hillis Corner I o W 20 C5
Hillmoor Devon 27 E10
Hillmorton Warks 119 C10
Hillock Vale Lancs 195 B9
Hillockhead Aberds 292 B6
Hillockhead Aberds 292 C5
Hillpool Worcs 117 B7
Hillpound Hants 33 D9
Hills Town Derbys 171 B7
Hillsborough S Yorks 186 C4
Hillside Aberds 293 D11
Hillside Angus 293 G9
Hillside Devon 8 C4
Hillside Devon 27 F11
Hillside Hants 49 C9
Hillside Mers 193 E10
Hillside Orkney 314 G4
Hillside Orkney 314 D3
Hillside Shetland 313 G6
Hillside Shrops 131 F11
Hillside Wilts 81 G9
Hillstreet Hants 32 D4
Hillswick Shetland 312 F4
Hilltop Bl Gwent 77 D11
Hilltop Bucks 85 E7
Hilltop Derbys 170 C4
Hillview T & W 243 G9
Hillway I o W 21 D8
Hillwell Shetland 313 M5
Hillyfields Hants 32 D5
Hilmarton Wilts 62 D4
Hilperton Wilts 45 B11
Hilperton Marsh Wilts 45 B11
Hilsea Ptsmth 33 G11
Hilston E Yorks 209 G11
Hiltingbury Hants 32 C6
Hilton Aberds 303 F9
Hilton Borders 273 E7
Hilton Cambs 122 D5
Hilton Cumb 231 G10
Hilton Derbys 152 C4
Hilton Dorset 30 G3
Hilton Durham 233 G9
Hilton Highld 309 L7
Hilton Highld 311 L3
Hilton Shrops 132 D5
Hilton Staffs 133 B11
Hilton Stockton 225 C9
Hilton House Gtr Man 194 F6
Hilton Lodge Highld 300 G2
Hilton of Cadboll Highld 301 B8
Hilton Park Gtr Man 195 G10
Himbleton Worcs 117 F8
Himley Staffs 133 E7
Hincaster Cumb 211 C10
Hinchley Wood Sur 67 F7
Hinchliffe Mill W Yorks 196 F6
Hinchwick Glos 100 E2
Hinckley Leics 135 E8
Hinderclay Suff 125 B10
Hinderton W Ches 182 F4
Hinderwell N Yorks 226 B5
Hindford Shrops 148 C6
Hindhead Sur 49 F11
Hindle Fold Lancs 203 G10
Hindley Gtr Man 194 G6
Hindley Northumb 242 F2
Hindley Green Gtr Man 194 G6
Hindlip Worcs 117 F7
Hindolveston Norf 159 D10
Hindon Wilts 46 G2
Hindpool Cumb 210 F3
Hindringham Norf 159 B9
Hindsford Gtr Man 195 G7
Hingham Norf 141 C10
Hinstock Shrops 150 D3
Hintlesham Suff 107 C11
Hinton Glos 79 E11
Hinton Hants 19 B10
Hinton Hereford 96 D6
Hinton Northants 119 G10
Hinton S Glos 61 D8
Hinton Shrops 131 B8
Hinton Som 29 C9
Hinton Ampner Hants 33 B9
Hinton Blewett Bath 44 B5
Hinton Charterhouse Bath 45 B9
Hinton Cross Worcs 99 C10
Hinton-in-the-Hedges Northants 101 D11
Hinton Martell Dorset 31 F8
Hinton on the Green Worcs 99 C10
Hinton Parva Dorset 31 G7
Hinton Parva Swindon 63 C8
Hinton St George Som 28 E6
Hinton St Mary Dorset 30 D3
Hinton Waldrist Oxon 82 F5
Hints Shrops 116 C2
Hints Staffs 134 C3
Hinwick Beds 121 E8
Hinwood Shrops 131 B7
Hinxhill Kent 54 E5
Hinxton Cambs 105 B9
Hinxworth Herts 104 C4
Hipperholme W Yorks 196 B6
Hipplecote Worcs 116 F4
Hipsburn Northumb 264 G6
Hipswell N Yorks 224
Hirael Gwyn 179
Hiraeth Carms 92
Hirn Aberds 293
Hirnant Powys 147
Hirst N Lnrk 269
Hirst Northumb 253
Hirst Courtney N Yorks 198
Hirwaen Denb 165
Hirwaun Rhondda 77
Hirwaun Common Bridgend 58
Hiscott Devon 25
Hislop Borders 249
Hisomley Wilts 45
Histon Cambs 123
Hitcham Suff 125
Hitchill Dumfries 238
Hitchin Herts 104
Hitchin Hill Herts 104
Hitcombe Bottom Wilts 45
Hither Green London 67
Hittisleigh Devon 13
Hittisleigh Barton Devon 13
Hive E Yorks 208
Hixon Staffs 151
Hoaden Kent 55
Hoar Cross Staffs 152
Hoarwithy Hereford 97
Hoath Kent 71
Hoath Corner Kent 52
Hob Hill W Ches 167
Hobarris Shrops 114
Hobbister Orkney 314
Hobble End Staffs 133
Hobbles Green Suff 124
Hobbs Cross Essex 87
Hobbs Cross Essex 87
Hobbs Wall Bath 61
Hobkirk Borders 262
Hobroyd Derbys 185
Hobson Durham 242
Hoby Leics 154
Hoccombe Som 27
Hockenden London 68
Hockerill Herts 105
Hockering Norf 159
Hockering Heath Norf 159
Hockerton Notts 172
Hockholler Som 27
Hockholler Green Som 27
Hockley E Ches 184
Hockley Essex 88
Hockley Kent 54
Hockley Staffs 134
Hockley W Mid 118
Hockley Heath W Mid 118
Hockliffe C Beds 103
Hockwold cum Wilton Norf 140
Hockworthy Devon 27
Hocombe Hants 32
Hoddesdon Herts 86
Hoddlesden Blkburn 195
Hoddom Mains Dumfries 238
Hoddomcross Dumfries 238
Hoden Worcs 99
Hodgefield Staffs 168
Hodgehill E Ches 168
Hodgehill W Mid 134
Hodgeston Pembs 73
Hodley Powys 130
Hodnet Shrops 150
Hodnetheath Shrops 150
Hodsock Notts 187
Hodsoll Street Kent 68
Hodson Swindon 63
Hodthorpe Derbys 187
Hoe Hants 33
Hoe Norf 159
Hoe Sur 50
Hoe Benham W Berks 64
Hoe Gate Hants 33
Hoff Cumb 222
Hoffleet Stow Lincs 156
Hog Hatch Sur 49
Hogaland Shetland 312
Hogben's Hill Kent 54
Hogganfield Glasgow 268
Hoggard's Green Suff 125
Hoggeston Bucks 102
Hoggington Wilts 45
Hoggrill's End Warks 134
Hogha Gearraidh W Isles 296
Hoghton Lancs 194
Hoghton Bottoms Lancs 194
Hogley Green W Yorks 196
Hognaston Derbys 170
Hogpits Bottom Herts 85
Hogsthorpe Lincs 191
Hogstock Dorset 31
Holbeach Lincs 157
Holbeach Bank Lincs 157
Holbeach Clough Lincs 156
Holbeach Drove Lincs 156
Holbeach Hurn Lincs 157
Holbeach St Johns Lincs 156
Holbeach St Marks Lincs 157
Holbeach St Matthew Lincs 157
Holbeache Worcs 116
Holbeck Notts 187
Holbeck W Yorks 205
Holbeck Woodhouse Notts 187
Holberrow Green Worcs 117
Holbeton Devon 8
Holborn London 67
Holborough Kent 69
Holbrook Derbys 170
Holbrook S Yorks 186
Holbrook Suff 108
Holbrook Common S Glos 61
Holbrook Moor Derbys 170
Holbrooks W Mid 134
Holburn Northumb 264
Holbury Hants 32
Holcombe Devon 14
Holcombe Gtr Man 195
Holcombe Som 45
Holcombe Brook Gtr Man 195
Holcombe Rogus Devon 27
Holcot Northants 120
Holdbrook London 86
Holden Lancs 203
Holden Fold Gtr Man 196
Holdenby Northants 120
Holdenhurst Bmouth 19
Holder's Green Essex 106
Holders Hill London 86
Holdfast Worcs 99
Holdgate Shrops 131
Holdingham Lincs 173
Holditch Dorset 28

dsworth W Yorks 196 B5
dworth S Yorks 186 C3
e Devon 24 D4
e W Yorks 204 F6
e Bottom W Yorks 196 C2
e-in-the-Wall
reford 98 F2
e Street W Sus 35 E10
efield Borders 263 C8
ehills N Lnrk 268 B5
ehouse Derbys 185 C8
ehouses E Ches 184 F2
emill Aberdeen 293 C10
emoor Devon 24 F6
e's Hole Devon 7 B8
estane Dumfries 247 D9
estone Derbys 170 C4
ewater Devon 41 F8
ford Som 43 E7
gate York 207 C7
ker Cumb 211 D7
kham Norf 176 E5
lacombe Devon 24 G5
lacombe Devon 26 G4
lacombe Hill Devon 7 E10
land Orkney 314 D6
land Orkney 314 A4
land Sur 52 C2
land Fen Lincs 174 F2
land Lees Lancs 194 F4
land-on-Sea Essex 89 B12
lands Som 29 D9
landstoun Orkney 314 A7
lee Dumfries 239 D7
lesley Suff 109 C7
licombe Torbay 9 C7
lies Common Staffs 150 E6
lin Hall Lancs 204 F4
lin Park W Yorks 206 F2
linfare Warr 183 C11
lingbourne Kent 53 B10
lingbury Brighton 36 F4
lingdean Brighton 36 F4
lingdon Bucks 103 F7
lingrove E Sus 37 C11
lingthorpe W Yorks 197 D10
lington Derbys 152 B4
lington E Sus 38 E3
lington Hants 48 B2
lington Staffs 151 B11
lington Cross Hants 48 B2
lington Grove
rbys 152 B4
lingwood Derbys 186 G6
lingworth Gtr Man 185 B8
lins Cumb 222 G3
lins Derbys 186 G4
lins Gtr Man 195 F10
lins Gtr Man 195 F11
lins Gtr Man 195 F8
lins Staffs 168 D6
lins Staffs 168 E4
lins Staffs 169 F7
lins End S Yorks 186 E5
lins Green Warr 183 C11
lins Lane Lancs 202 C5
lins Lane Shrops 149 B10
linsclough Staffs 169 B9
linsgreen E Ches 168 C2
linswood Telford 132 B4
linthorpe W Yorks 206 G3
linwood Gtr Man 196 G2
linwood Shrops 149 B10
lis Green Devon 27 F9
lis Head Devon 27 G7
locombe Devon 25 E10
locombe Town
von 25 E10
low Brook Bath 60 G5
low Meadows
orks 186 D2
low Oak Dorset 18 C2
low Street Kent 71 G8
loway Derbys 170 D4
loway Wilts 45 G11
loway Windsor 65 C10
loway Hill Sur 50 E3
lowell Northants 120 C3
lowmoor Heath
Ches 167 B7
lows Dumfries 239 B9
ly Bank W Mid 133 C11
ly Brook Som 44 D4
ly Bush Wrex 166 G6
ly Cross Windsor 65 C10
ly End Norf 139 B9
ly Green Bucks 84 E3
ly Green Worcs 99 C7
ly Hill N Yorks 224 E3
lyberry End W Mid 134 G5
lybush Caerph 77 E11
lybush E Ayrs 257 G9
lybush Stoke 168 G5
lybush Torf 78 G3
lybush Worcs 98 D5
lybush Corner Bucks 66 B3
lybush Corner Suff 125 F8
lybush Hill Bucks 66 C3
lybush Hill Essex 89 B10
lybushes Kent 54 B2
lycroft Leics 135 E8
lyhurst Shrops 131 D9
lyhurst Warks 135 F7
lym E Yorks 201 B10
lywaste Shrops 116 B2
lywater Hants 49 G10
lywood Worcs 117 B11
macott Devon 25 B8
man Clavel Som 28 D2
mbridge W Yorks 196 F6
mbury St Mary Sur 50 E6
mbush Corn 5 E10
mbush Dorset 28 G5
mcroft Staffs 151 D8
me C Beds 104 C3
me Cambs 138 F3
me Cumb 211 D10
me N Lincs 200 F2
me N Yorks 215 C7
me Notts 172 D4
me W Yorks 196 F6
me W Yorks 205 G9
me Chapel Lancs 195 B11
me Green C Beds 104 C3
me Green N Yorks 207 E7
me Green Wokingham 65 F10
me Hale Norf 141 B7
me Hill NE Lincs 201 F9
me Lacy Hereford 97 D11
me Lane Notts 154 B2
me Marsh Hereford 114 G6
me Mills Cumb 211 D10
me next the Sea
rf 176 E2
me-on-Spalding-
oor E Yorks 208 F2
me on the Wolds
orks 208 D5
me Pierrepont Notts 154 B2
me St Cuthbert
mb 229 B8
me Slack Lancs 203 G7
Holme Wood W Yorks 205 G9
Holmebridge Dorset 18 D3
Holmer Hereford 97 C10
Holmer Green Bucks 84 F6
Holmes Lancs 194 D2
Holmes Chapel E Ches 168 B3
Holmesdale Derbys 186 F5
Holmesfield Derbys 186 F4
Holmes's Hill E Sus 23 C8
Holmeswood Lancs 194 D2
Holmethorpe Sur 51 C9
Holmewood Derbys 170 B6
Holmfield W Yorks 196 B5
Holmfirth W Yorks 196 F6
Holmhead Angus 293 F7
Holmhead Dumfries 246 F6
Holmhead E Ayrs 258 E3
Holmhill Dumfries 247 D9
Holmisdale Highld 297 G7
Holmley Common
Derbys 186 F5
Holmpton E Yorks 201 C11
Holmrook Cumb 219 F11
Holmsgarth Shetland 313 J6
Holmside Durham 233 B10
Holmsleigh Green Devon 28 G2
Holmston S Ayrs 257 E9
Holmwood Corner Sur 51 E7
Holmwrangle Cumb 230 B6
Holne Devon 8 B4
Holnest Dorset 29 E11
Holnicote Som 42 D2
Holsworthy Devon 24 G4
Holsworthy Beacon
Devon 24 F5
Holt Dorset 31 G8
Holt Hants 49 C8
Holt Mers 183 C7
Holt Norf 159 B11
Holt Wilts 61 G11
Holt Worcs 116 E6
Holt Wrex 166 E6
Holt End Hants 49 F7
Holt End Worcs 117 D11
Holt Fleet Worcs 116 E6
Holt Green Lancs 193 G11
Holt Head W Yorks 196 E5
Holt Heath Dorset 31 G9
Holt Heath Worcs 116 E6
Holt Hill Kent 53 B8
Holt Hill Staffs 152 D2
Holt Park W Yorks 205 E11
Holt Pound Hants 49 E10
Holt Wood Dorset 31 F8
Holtby York 207 C9
Holton Oxon 83 D10
Holton Som 29 B11
Holton Suff 127 B7
Holton cum Beckering
Lincs 189 E10
Holton Heath Dorset 18 C4
Holton le Clay Lincs 201 G9
Holton le Moor Lincs 189 B9
Holton St Mary Suff 107 D11
Holts Gtr Man 196 G3
Holtspur Bucks 84 G6
Holtye E Sus 52 F3
Holway Dorset 28 G5
Holway Dorset 29 C10
Holway Flint 181 F11
Holway Som 28 C2
Holwell Dorset 30 E2
Holwell Herts 104 E3
Holwell Leics 154 E4
Holwell Oxon 82 D2
Holwell Som 45 D8
Holwellbury C Beds 104 E3
Holwick Durham 232 F4
Holworth Dorset 17 E11
Holy City Devon 28 G3
Holy Cross T & W 243 D8
Holy Cross Worcs 117 B8
Holy Island Northumb 273 B11
Holy Vale Scilly 1 G4
Holybourne Hants 49 E8
Holyfield Essex 86 E5
Holyhead = Caergybi
Anglesey 178 E2
Holylee Borders 261 B9
Holymoorside Derbys 170 B4
Holyport Windsor 65 D11
Holystone Northumb 251 C11
Holytown N Lnrk 268 C5
Holywell C Beds 85 B8
Holywell Cambs 122 C6
Holywell Corn 4 D5
Holywell Dorset 29 G9
Holywell E Sus 23 F9
Holywell Glos 80 G3
Holywell Hereford 97 C7
Holywell Herts 85 F9
Holywell Northumb 243 C8
Holywell Som 29 E8
Holywell Warks 118 D3
Holywell = Treffynnon
Flint 181 F11
Holywell Green W Yorks 196 D5
Holywell Lake Som 27 C10
Holywell Row Suff 124 B4
Holywood Dumfries 247 G10
Hom Green Hereford 97 G11
Homedowns Glos 99 E8
Homer Shrops 132 C2
Homer Green Mers 193 G10
Homersfield Suff 142 F5
Homerton London 67 B11
Homington Wilts 31 B10
Honey Hall N Som 60 G2
Honey Hill Kent 70 G6
Honey Street Wilts 62 G6
Honey Tye Suff 107 D9
Honeybourne Worcs 100 C2
Honeychurch Devon 25 G10
Honeydon Beds 122 F2
Honeyhill Wokingham 65 F10
Honeystreet Wilts 62 G6
Honeywick C Beds 103 G9
Honicknowle Plym 7 D9
Honiley Warks 118 C4
Honing Norf 160 D6
Honingham Norf 160 G2
Honington Lincs 172 G6
Honington Suff 125 C8
Honington Warks 100 C5
Honiton Devon 27 G11
Honkley Wrex 166 D4
Honley W Yorks 196 E6
Honley Moor W Yorks 196 E6
Honnington Telford 150 F4
Honor Oak London 67 E11
Honor Oak Park London 67 E11
Honresfeld Gtr Man 196 D2
Hoo Kent 71 G9
Hoo End Herts 85 B11
Hoo Green E Ches 184 E2
Hoo Hole W Yorks 196 B4
Hoo Meavy Devon 7 B10
Hoo St Werburgh
Medway 69 E9
Hoober S Yorks 186 B6
Hoobrook Worcs 116 C6
Hood Green S Yorks 197 G10
Hood Hill S Yorks 186 B5
Hood Manor Warr 183 D9
Hooe E Sus 23 D11
Hooe Plym 7 E10
Hooe Common E Sus 23 C11
Hoofield W Ches 167 C8
Hoohill Blkpool 202 F2
Hook Cambs 139 E8
Hook Devon 28 F4
Hook E Yorks 199 B9
Hook Hants 33 F8
Hook Hants 49 C8
Hook London 67 G7
Hook Pembs 73 C7
Hook Wilts 62 C5
Hook-a-gate Shrops 131 B9
Hook Bank Worcs 98 C6
Hook End Essex 87 F9
Hook End Oxon 65 C7
Hook End W Mid 134 G4
Hook Green Kent 53 F7
Hook Green Kent 68 F6
Hook Heath Sur 50 B3
Hook Norton Oxon 101 E7
Hook Park Hants 33 G7
Hook Street Glos 79 F11
Hook Street Wilts 62 C5
Hooke Dorset 16 B6
Hooker Gate T & W 242 F4
Hookgate Staffs 150 B4
Hook's Cross Herts 104 G5
Hookway Devon 14 B3
Hookwood Sur 51 E9
Hoole W Ches 166 B6
Hoole Bank W Ches 166 B6
Hooley Sur 51 B9
Hooley Bridge Gtr Man 195 E11
Hooley Brow Gtr Man 195 E11
Hooley Hill Gtr Man 184 B6
Hoop Mon 79 D8
Hoopers Pool Wilts 45 C10
Hoops Devon 24 C5
Hooton W Ches 182 F5
Hooton Levitt S Yorks 187 C8
Hooton Pagnell S Yorks 198 F3
Hooton Roberts S Yorks 187 B7
Hop Pole Lincs 156 G3
Hopcroft's Holt Oxon 101 F9
Hope Derbys 185 E11
Hope Devon 9 G8
Hope Highld 308 D4
Hope Powys 130 B5
Hope Shrops 130 C6
Hope Staffs 169 D10
Hope = Yr Hôb Flint 166 D4
Hope Bagot Shrops 115 C11
Hope Bowdler Shrops 131 E9
Hope End Green Essex 105 G11
Hope Green E Ches 184 E6
Hope Mansell Hereford 79 B10
Hope Park Shrops 130 C6
Hope under Dinmore
Hereford 115 G10
Hopebeck Cumb 229 G9
Hopedale Staffs 169 D10
Hopeman Moray 301 C11
Hope's Green Essex 69 B9
Hope's Rough Hereford 98 B2
Hopesay Shrops 131 G7
Hopesgate Shrops 130 C6
Hopetown W Yorks 197 C11
Hopgoods Green W Berks 64 F4
Hopkinstown Rhondda 77 G9
Hopley's Green Hereford 114 G6
Hopperton N Yorks 206 B4
Hopsford Warks 135 G8
Hopstone Shrops 132 E5
Hopton Derbys 170 E3
Hopton Shrops 149 D11
Hopton Shrops 149 E7
Hopton Staffs 151 D8
Hopton Suff 125 B9
Hopton Cangeford
Shrops 131 G10
Hopton Castle Shrops 115 B7
Hopton Heath Staffs 151 D9
Hopton on Sea Norf 143 D10
Hopton Wafers Shrops 116 B2
Hoptonbank Shrops 116 B2
Hoptongate Shrops 131 G10
Hoptonheath Shrops 115 B7
Hopwas Staffs 134 B3
Hopwood Gtr Man 195 F11
Hopwood Worcs 117 B10
Hopworthy Devon 24 G4
Horam E Sus 23 B9
Horbling Lincs 156 B2
Horbury W Yorks 197 D9
Horbury Bridge W Yorks 197 D9
Horbury Junction
W Yorks 197 D10
Horcott Glos 81 E11
Horden Durham 234 C4
Horderley Shrops 131 F8
Hordle Hants 19 B11
Hordley Shrops 149 C7
Horeb Carms 75 D7
Horeb Carms 93 F10
Horeb Ceredig 93 C7
Horeb Flint 166 D3
Horfield Bristol 60 D6
Horgabost W Isles 305 J2
Horham Suff 126 C4
Horkesley Heath Essex 107 F9
Horkstow N Lincs 200 D3
Horkstow Wolds N Lincs 200 D3
Horley Oxon 101 C8
Horley Sur 51 E9
Horn Ash Dorset 28 G5
Horn Hill Som 43 E8
Horn Street Kent 55 F7
Horn Street Kent 69 G7
Hornblotton Som 44 G5
Hornblotton Green Som 44 G5
Hornby Lancs 211 F11
Hornby N Yorks 224 G4
Hornby N Yorks 225 D7
Horncastle Lincs 174 B3
Horncastle Reading 65 E7
Hornchurch London 68 B4
Horncliffe Northumb 273 F8
Horndean Borders 273 F7
Horndean Hants 34 E2
Horndon Devon 12 F6
Horndon on the Hill
Thurrock 69 C7
Horne Sur 51 E10
Horne Row Essex 88 E3
Horner Som 41 D11
Horner's Green Suff 107 C9
Hornestreet Essex 107 E10
Horney Common E Sus 37 B7
Hornick Corn 5 E9
Horniehaugh Angus 292 G6
Horning Norf 160 F6
Horninghold Leics 136 D6
Horninglow Staffs 152 D4
Horningsea Cambs 123 E9
Horningsham Wilts 45 E10
Horningtoft Norf 159 E8
Horningtops Corn 6 C5
Horns Corner Kent 38 B2
Horns Cross Devon 24 C5
Horns Cross E Sus 38 C4
Horns Green Kent 52 B3
Hornsbury Som 28 E4
Hornsby Cumb 240 G2
Hornsea E Yorks 209 D10
Hornsea Bridge
E Yorks 209 D10
Hornsea Burton
E Yorks 209 D10
Hornsey London 67 B10
Hornsey Vale London 67 B10
Hornton Oxon 101 B7
Horpit Swindon 63 C8
Horrabridge Devon 7 B10
Horringer Suff 124 E6
Horringford I o W 20 D6
Horrocks Fold Gtr Man 195 E8
Horrocksford Lancs 203 E10
Horsalls Kent 53 C11
Horse Bridge Staffs 169 E7
Horsebridge Devon 12 G4
Horsebridge Hants 47 G10
Horsebridge Shrops 131 B7
Horsebrook Devon 8 D4
Horsebrook Staffs 151 G7
Horsecastle N Som 60 F2
Horsedown Wilts 61 D10
Horsedowns Corn 2 C4
Horsehay Telford 132 B3
Horseheath Cambs 106 B2
Horseholm Dumfries 238 C2
Horsehouse N Yorks 213 C10
Horseley Heath W Mid 133 E9
Horsell Sur 50 B3
Horsell Birch Sur 50 B3
Horseman Side Essex 87 F8
Horseman's Green
Wrex 166 G6
Horsemere Green W Sus 35 G7
Horsenden Bucks 84 E3
Horsepools Glos 80 C4
Horseway Cambs 139 F8
Horseway Head Hereford 114 E6
Horsey Norf 161 E9
Horsey Som 43 F10
Horsey Corner Norf 161 E9
Horsey Down Wilts 81 G9
Horsford Norf 160 F3
Horsforth W Yorks 205 F10
Horsforth Woodside
W Yorks 205 F10
Horsham W Sus 51 G7
Horsham Worcs 116 F4
Horsham St Faith Norf 160 F4
Horshoe Green Kent 52 E3
Horsington Lincs 173 B11
Horsington Som 30 C2
Horsley Derbys 170 G5
Horsley Glos 80 F4
Horsley Northumb 242 D3
Horsley Northumb 251 D8
Horsley Cross Essex 108 F2
Horsley Hill T & W 243 D9
Horsley Woodhouse
Derbys 170 G5
Horsleycross Street
Essex 108 F2
Horsleyhill Borders 262 F2
Horsleyhope Durham 233 B7
Horsleys Green Bucks 84 F3
Horsmonden Kent 53 E7
Horspath Oxon 83 E9
Horstead Norf 160 F5
Horsted Green E Sus 23 B7
Horsted Keynes W Sus 36 B5
Horton Bucks 84 B6
Horton Dorset 31 F8
Horton Kent 54 B6
Horton Lancs 204 C3
Horton Northants 120 G6
Horton S Glos 61 C9
Horton Shrops 149 D9
Horton Som 28 E4
Horton Staffs 168 D6
Horton Swansea 56 D3
Horton Telford 150 G3
Horton Wilts 62 G5
Horton Windsor 66 D4
Horton Common Dorset 31 F9
Horton Cross Som 28 D4
Horton-cum-Studley
Oxon 83 C9
Horton Green W Ches 167 F7
Horton Heath Dorset 31 F9
Horton Heath Hants 33 D7
Horton in Ribblesdale
N Yorks 212 E6
Horton Kirby Kent 68 F5
Horton Wharf Bucks 84 B6
Hortonlane Shrops 149 G8
Hortonwood Telford 150 G3
Horwich Gtr Man 194 E6
Horwich End Derbys 185 E8
Horwood Devon 25 B8
Horwood Riding S Glos 61 B8
Hoscar Lancs 194 E3
Hose Leics 154 D4
Hoselaw Borders 263 C8
Hoses Cumb 220 G4
Hosey Hill Kent 52 C3
Hosh Perth 286 E2
Hosta W Isles 296 D3
Hoswick Shetland 313 L6
Hotham E Yorks 208 G3
Hothfield Kent 54 D3
Hotley Bottom Bucks 84 E5
Hoton Leics 153 E11
Hotwells Bristol 60 E5
Houbans Shetland 312 F5
Houbie Shetland 312 D8
Houdston S Ayrs 244 D5
Hough Argyll 288 E1
Hough E Ches 168 E2
Hough E Ches 184 F5
Hough Green Halton 183 D7
Hough-on-the-Hill
Lincs 172 F6
Hough Side W Yorks 205 G10
Hougham Lincs 172 G5
Houghton Cambs 122 C5
Houghton Cumb 239 F10
Houghton Hants 47 G10
Houghton Northumb 242 D4
Houghton Pembs 73 D7
Houghton W Sus 35 E8
Houghton Bank Darl 233 G10
Houghton Conquest
C Beds 103 C10
Houghton Green E Sus 38 C6
Houghton Green Warr 183 C10
Houghton-le-Side
Darl 233 G10
Houghton-le-Spring
T & W 234 B2
Houghton on the Hill
Leics 136 C3
Houghton Regis C Beds 103 G10
Houghton St Giles Norf 159 B8
Houghwood Mers 194 G4
Houlland Shetland 312 B7
Houlland Shetland 312 F7
Houlland Shetland 313 H5
Houlland Shetland 313 J6
Houlsyke N Yorks 226 D4
Hound Hants 33 F7
Hound Green Hants 49 B8
Hound Hill Dorset 31 G7
Houndmills Hants 48 C6
Houndscroft Glos 80 E5
Houndslow Borders 272 F2
Houndsmoor Som 27 B10
Houndstone Som 29 D8
Houndwood Borders 272 C6
Hounsdown Hants 32 E5
Hounsley Batch N Som 60 G4
Hounslow London 66 D6
Hounslow Green Essex 87 B11
Hounslow West London 66 D6
Hourston Orkney 314 E2
Housabister Shetland 313 H6
Housay Shetland 312 F8
House of Daviot Highld 301 E7
House of Glenmuick
Aberds 292 D5
Househill Highld 301 D8
Houses Hill W Yorks 197 D7
Housetter Shetland 312 E5
Housham Tye Essex 87 C8
Houss Shetland 313 K5
Houston Renfs 267 B8
Houstry Highld 310 F5
Houton Orkney 314 F3
Hove Brighton 36 G3
Hove Edge W Yorks 196 C6
Hoveringham Notts 171 F11
Hoveton Norf 160 F6
Hovingham N Yorks 216 D3
How Cumb 240 F2
How Caple Hereford 98 E2
How End C Beds 103 C10
How Green Kent 52 D3
How Hill Norf 161 F7
How Wood Herts 85 E10
Howbeck Bank E Ches 167 F11
Howbrook S Yorks 186 B4
Howden Borders 262 E5
Howden E Yorks 199 B8
Howden W Loth 269 B11
Howden Clough W Yorks 197 B8
Howden-le-Wear
Durham 233 E9
Howdon T & W 243 D8
Howdon Pans T & W 243 D8
Howe Highld 310 C7
Howe N Yorks 214 C6
Howe Norf 142 C5
Howe Bridge Gtr Man 195 G7
Howe Green Essex 88 E2
Howe Green Essex 87 B8
Howe Green Warks 134 F6
Howe of Teuchar
Aberds 303 E7
Howe Street Essex 87 C11
Howe Street Essex 106 E3
Howegreen Essex 88 E4
Howell Lincs 173 F10
Howey Powys 113 F11
Howford Borders 261 B8
Howford Borders 261 E9
Howgate Cumb 228 G5
Howgate Midloth 270 D4
Howgill Cumb 222 F2
Howgill Lancs 204 D2
Howgill N Yorks 205 B7
Howick Mon 79 F8
Howick Northumb 265 F7
Howick Cross Lancs 194 B4
Howle Durham 233 F7
Howle Telford 150 E3
Howleigh Som 28 D2
Howlett End Essex 105 E11
Howley Glos 80 G2
Howley Som 28 F3
Howley Warr 183 D10
Hownam Borders 263 F7
Hownam Mains Borders 263 E7
Howpasley Borders 249 B8
Howsen Worcs 116 G5
Howsham N Lincs 200 G4
Howsham N Yorks 216 G4
Howslack Dumfries 248 B3
Howt Green Kent 69 F11
Howtel Northumb 263 C9
Howton Hereford 97 F8
Howtown Cumb 221 B8
Howwood Renfs 267 C7
Hoxne Suff 126 B3
Hoxton London 67 C10
Hoy Orkney 314 F2
Hoylake Mers 182 D2
Hoyland S Yorks 197 G11
Hoyland Common
S Yorks 197 G11
Hoylandswaine S Yorks 197 G9
Hoyle W Sus 34 D6
Hoyle Mill S Yorks 197 F11
Hubbard's Hill Kent 52 C4
Hubberholme N Yorks 213 D8
Hubberston Pembs 72 D5
Hubbersty Head Cumb 221 G8
Hubberton Green
W Yorks 196 C4
Hubbert's Bridge Lincs 174 G3
Huby N Yorks 205 D11
Huby N Yorks 215 F11
Hucclecote Glos 80 B5
Hucking Kent 53 B10
Hucknall Notts 171 F8
Hud Hey Lancs 195 C9
Huddersfield W Yorks 196 D6
Huddington Worcs 117 F8
Huddisford Devon 24 D4
Huddlesford Staffs 134 B3
Hudnall Herts 85 C8
Hudnalls Glos 79 E8
Hudswell N Yorks 224 E3
Hudswell Wilts 61 F11
Huggate E Yorks 208 B3
Hugglepit Devon 24 C4
Hugglescote Leics 153 G8
Hugh Mill Lancs 195 C10
Hugh Town Scilly 1 G4
Hughenden Valley Bucks 84 F5
Hughley Shrops 131 D11
Hugus Corn 4 G5
Huish Devon 25 B7
Huish Devon 25 E8
Huish Wilts 62 G6
Huish Champflower Som 27 B9
Huish Episcopi Som 28 B6
Huisinis W Isles 305 G1
Hulcote C Beds 103 D8
Hulcote Northants 102 B4
Hulcott Bucks 84 B5
Hull End Derbys 185 E9
Hulland Derbys 170 F2
Hulland Moss Derbys 170 F3
Hulland Ward Derbys 170 F3
Hullavington Wilts 61 C11
Hullbridge Essex 88 G4
Hulme Gtr Man 184 B4
Hulme Staffs 168 F6
Hulme Warr 183 C10
Hulme End Staffs 169 D10
Hulme Walfield E Ches 168 B4
Hulseheath E Ches 184 E2
Hulver Street Suff 143 F9
Hulverstone I o W 20 E3
Humber Devon 14 G3
Humber Hereford 115 F10
Humber Bridge N Lincs 200 C4
Humberston NE Lincs 201 F10
Humberston Fitties
NE Lincs 201 F10
Humberstone Leicester 136 B2
Humbie E Loth 271 C9
Humble Green Suff 107 B8
Humbledon T & W 243 F9
Humbleton E Yorks 209 G10
Humbleton Northumb 263 D11
Humby Lincs 155 C10
Hume Borders 272 G4
Hummersknott Darl 224 C5
Humshaugh Northumb 241 C10
Huna Highld 310 B7
Huncoat Lancs 203 G11
Huncote Leics 135 D10
Hundalee Borders 262 F4
Hundall Derbys 186 F5
Hunderthwaite Durham 232 G5
Hunderton Hereford 97 D9
Hundle Houses Lincs 174 E3
Hundleby Lincs 174 B5
Hundleshope Borders 260 B6
Hundleton Pembs 73 E7
Hundon Suff 106 B4
Hundred Acres Hants 33 E9
Hundred End Lancs 194 C2
Hundred House Powys 114 G2
Hungarton Leics 136 B3
Hungate W Yorks 197 B11
Hunger Hill Gtr Man 195 F7
Hunger Hill Lancs 194 E4
Hungerford Hants 31 E11
Hungerford Shrops 131 F10
Hungerford Som 42 E4
Hungerford W Berks 63 F10
Hungerford Windsor 65 E10
Hungerford Green
W Berks 64 D5
Hungerford Newtown
W Berks 63 E11
Hungershall Park Kent 52 F5
Hungerstone Hereford 97 D8
Hungerton Lincs 155 D7
Hungladder Highld 298 B3
Hungreyhatton Shrops 150 D3
Hunmanby N Yorks 217 D11
Hunmanby Moor
N Yorks 218 D2
Hunningham Warks 119 D7
Hunningham Hill Warks 119 D7
Hunnington Worcs 133 G9
Hunny Hill I o W 20 D5
Hunsdon Herts 86 C6
Hunsdonbury Herts 86 C6
Hunsingore N Yorks 206 C4
Hunslet W Yorks 206 G2
Hunslet Carr W Yorks 206 G2
Hunsonby Cumb 231 D7
Hunspow Highld 310 B6
Hunstanton Norf 175 G11
Hunstanworth Durham 232 B5
Hunsterson E Ches 167 F11
Hunston Suff 125 D9
Hunston W Sus 22 C5
Hunston Green Suff 125 D9
Hunstrete Bath 60 G6
Hunsworth W Yorks 197 B7
Hunt End Worcs 117 E10
Huntenhull Green Wilts 45 D10
Huntercombe End Oxon 65 B7
Hunters Forstal Kent 71 F7
Hunter's Quay Argyll 276 F3
Huntham Som 28 B4
Hunthill Lodge Angus 292 F6
Hunting-tower Perth 286 E4
Huntingdon Cambs 122 C4
Huntingfield Suff 126 C6
Huntingford Dorset 45 G10
Huntingford S Glos 80 G2
Huntington E Loth 281 F9
Huntington Hereford 97 C9
Huntington Hereford 114 G5
Huntington Staffs 151 G9
Huntington Telford 132 B3
Huntington W Ches 166 C6
Huntington York 207 B8
Huntley Glos 80 B2
Huntley Staffs 169 G8
Huntly Aberds 302 F5
Huntlywood Borders 272 G2
Hunton Hants 48 F3
Hunton Kent 53 D8
Hunton N Yorks 224 G3
Hunton Bridge Herts 85 E9
Hunt's Corner Norf 141 F11
Hunt's Cross Mers 182 D6
Hunt's Green Bucks 84 E5
Hunt's Green W Berks 64 E2
Hunts Green Warks 134 D3
Hunt's Hill Bucks 84 F4
Hunt's Lane Leics 135 C9
Huntscott Som 42 E2
Huntsham Devon 27 C8
Huntshaw Devon 25 C8
Huntshaw Water Devon 25 C8
Huntspill Som 43 D10
Huntstile Som 43 G9
Huntworth Som 43 G10
Hunwick Durham 233 E9
Hunworth Norf 159 B11
Hurcott Som 28 D5
Hurcott Som 29 B8
Hurcott Worcs 117 B7
Hurdcott Wilts 47 G7
Hurdley Powys 130 E5
Hurdsfield E Ches 184 G6
Hurgill N Yorks 224 E3
Hurlet Glasgow 267 C10
Hurley Warks 134 D4
Hurley Windsor 65 C10
Hurley Bottom Windsor 65 C10
Hurley Common
Warks 134 D4
Hurlford E Ayrs 257 B11
Hurliness Orkney 314 H2
Hurlston Lancs 194 E2
Hurlston Green Lancs 193 E11
Hurn Dorset 19 B8
Hurn E Yorks 208 E6
Hurn's End Lincs 174 F6
Hursey Dorset 28 G6
Hursley Hants 32 B6
Hurst Cumb 230 C4
Hurst Dorset 17 C11
Hurst Gtr Man 196 G2
Hurst N Yorks 223 E10
Hurst Som 29 D7
Hurst Wokingham 65 E9
Hurst Green E Sus 38 B2
Hurst Green Essex 89 B9
Hurst Green Lancs 203 F9
Hurst Green Sur 51 C11
Hurst Green W Mid 133 F9
Hurst Hill W Mid 133 E8
Hurst Park Sur 66 F6
Hurst Wickham W Sus 36 D3
Hurstbourne Priors
Hants 48 D2
Hurstbourne Tarrant
Hants 47 C11
Hurstead Gtr Man 196 D2
Hurstley Hereford 97 B7
Hurstpierpoint W Sus 36 D3
Hurstwood Lancs 204 G3
Hurtmore Sur 50 D3
Hurworth-on-Tees Darl 224 C6
Hurworth Place Darl 224 D5
Hury Durham 223 B9
Husabost Highld 298 D2
Husbands Bosworth
Leics 136 G2
Husbandtown Angus 287 D8
Husborne Crawley
C Beds 103 D9
Husthwaite N Yorks 215 D10
Hut Green N Yorks 198 C5
Hutcherleigh Devon 8 E5
Hutchesontown
Glasgow 267 C11
Hutchwns Bridgend 57 F10
Huthwaite Notts 171 D7
Hutlerburn Borders 261 E10
Huttock Top Lancs 195 C11
Huttoft Lincs 191 F8
Hutton Borders 273 E9
Hutton Cumb 230 F4
Hutton E Yorks 208 C6
Hutton Essex 87 F10
Hutton Lancs 194 B3
Hutton N Som 43 B11
Hutton Bonville N Yorks 224 E6
Hutton Buscel N Yorks 217 C9
Hutton Conyers N Yorks 214 E6
Hutton Cranswick
E Yorks 208 C6
Hutton End Cumb 230 D4
Hutton Gate Redcar 225 B11
Hutton Hang N Yorks 214 B3
Hutton Henry Durham 234 D4
Hutton-le-Hole N Yorks 226 G4
Hutton Magna Durham 224 C2
Hutton Mount Essex 87 G10
Hutton Roof Cumb 211 D11
Hutton Roof Cumb 230 E3
Hutton Rudby N Yorks 225 D9
Hutton Sessay N Yorks 215 D9
Hutton Village Redcar 225 C11
Hutton Wandesley
N Yorks 206 C6
Huttons Ambo N Yorks 216 F5
Huxham Devon 14 B4
Huxham Green Som 44 F5
Huxley W Ches 167 C8
Huxter Shetland 313 G7
Huxter Shetland 313 H3
Huxter Shetland 313 H5
Huxton Borders 273 B7
Huyton Mers 182 C6
Huyton Park Mers 182 C6
Huyton Quarry Mers 183 C7
Hwlffordd =
Haverfordwest Pembs 73 B7
Hycemoor Cumb 210 B1
Hyde Glos 80 E5
Hyde Glos 99 F11
Hyde Gtr Man 184 B6
Hyde Hants 31 E11
Hyde Hants 48 G3
Hyde Hereford 115 F9
Hyde Chase Essex 88 E4
Hyde End W Berks 64 G5
Hyde Heath Bucks 84 E6
Hyde Lea Staffs 151 E8
Hyde Park S Yorks 198 G5
Hydestile Sur 50 E3
Hylton Castle T & W 243 F9
Hylton Red House
T & W 243 F9
Hyltons Crossways
Norf 160 D4
Hyndburn Bridge
Lancs 203 G10
Hyndford Bridge S Lnrk 269 G8
Hyndhope Borders 261 E9
Hynish Argyll 288 F1
Hyssington Powys 130 E6
Hystfield Glos 79 F11
Hythe Hants 32 F6
Hythe Kent 55 G7
Hythe Som 44 C2
Hythe Sur 66 E4
Hythe End Windsor 66 E4
Hythie Aberds 303 D10
Hyton Cumb 210 B1

I

Iarsiadar W Isles 304 E3
Ibberton Dorset 30 F3
Ible Derbys 170 D2
Ibsley Hants 31 F11
Ibstock Leics 153 G8
Ibstone Bucks 84 G3
Ibthorpe Hants 47 C11
Iburndale N Yorks 227 D7
Ibworth Hants 48 C5
Icelton N Som 59 F11
Ichrachan Argyll 284 D4
Ickburgh Norf 140 E6
Ickenham London 66 B5
Ickenthwaite Cumb 210 B6
Ickford Bucks 83 D11
Ickham Kent 55 B8
Ickleford Herts 104 E3
Icklesham E Sus 38 D5
Ickleton Cambs 105 C9
Icklingham Suff 124 C5
Ickornshaw N Yorks 204 E5
Ickwell C Beds 104 B3
Ickwell Green C Beds 104 B3
Icomb Glos 100 G4
Icy Park Devon 8 F3
Idbury Oxon 82 B2
Iddesleigh Devon 25 F9
Ide Devon 14 C3
Ide Hill Kent 52 C3
Ideford Devon 14 F3
Iden E Sus 38 C6
Iden Green Kent 53 F8
Iden Green Kent 53 G10
Idle W Yorks 205 F9
Idle Moor W Yorks 205 F9
Idless Corn 4 F6
Idlicote Warks 100 C5
Idmiston Wilts 47 F7
Idole Carms 74 B6
Idridgehay Derbys 170 F3
Idridgehay Green
Derbys 170 F3
Idrigill Highld 298 C3
Idstone Oxon 63 C9
Idvies Angus 287 C9
Iet-y-bwlch Carms 92 F3
Iffley Oxon 83 E8
Ifield W Sus 51 F8
Ifield Green W Sus 51 F9
Ifieldwood W Sus 51 F8
Ifold W Sus 50 G4
Iford Bmouth 19 C8
Iford E Sus 36 F6
Ifton Heath Shrops 148 B6
Ightfield Shrops 149 B11
Ightfield Heath Shrops 149 B11
Ightham Kent 52 B5
Igtham Common Kent 52 B5
Iken Suff 127 F8
Ilam Staffs 169 E10
Ilchester Som 29 C8
Ilchester Mead Som 29 C8
Ilderton Northumb 264 E2
Ileden Kent 55 C8
Ilford London 68 B2
Ilford Som 28 D5
Ilfracombe Devon 40 D4
Ilkeston Derbys 171 G7
Ilketshall St Andrew
Suff 143 F7
Ilketshall St Lawrence
Suff 143 G7
Ilketshall St Margaret
Suff 142 F6
Ilkley W Yorks 205 D8
Illand Corn 11 F11
Illey W Mid 133 G9
Illidge Green E Ches 168 C3
Illington Norf 141 F8
Illingworth W Yorks 196 B5
Illogan Corn 4 G3
Illogan Highway Corn 4 G3
Illshaw Heath W Mid 118 C2
Illston on the Hill Leics 136 D4
Ilmer Bucks 84 D3
Ilmington Warks 100 C4
Ilminster Som 28 E5
Ilsington Devon 13 F11
Ilston Swansea 56 C5
Ilton N Yorks 214 D3
Ilton Som 28 D5
Imachar N Ayrs 255 C9
Imber Wilts 46 D3
Imeraval Argyll 254 C4
Immervoulin Stirl 285 F9
Immingham NE Lincs 201 E7
Impington Cambs 123 E8
Ince W Ches 183 F7
Ince Blundell Mers 193 G10
Ince in Makerfield
Gtr Man 194 G5
Inch of Arnhall Aberds 293 F8
Inchbae Lodge Highld 300 C4
Inchbare Angus 293 G8
Inchberry Moray 302 D3
Inchbraoch Angus 287 B11
Inchbrook Glos 80 E4
Inchcape Highld 309 J6
Incheril Highld 299 C10
Inchgrundle Angus 292 F6
Inchina Highld 307 K4
Inchinnan Renfs 267 B9
Inchkinloch Highld 308 E5
Inchlaggan Highld 290 C3
Inchlumpie Highld 300 B5
Inchmore Highld 300 E3
Inchmore Highld 300 E5
Inchnacardoch Hotel
Highld 290 B5
Inchnadamph Highld 307 G7
Inchock Angus 287 C10
Inchree Highld 290 G2
Inchrory Moray 292 C3
Inchs Corn 5 C9
Inchture Perth 286 E6
Inchyra Perth 286 E5
Indian Queens Corn 5 D8
Inerval Argyll 254 C4
Ingatestone Essex 87 F11
Ingbirchworth S Yorks 197 F8
Ingerthorpe N Yorks 214 F5
Ingestre Staffs 151 E9
Ingham Lincs 188 E6
Ingham Norf 161 D7
Ingham Suff 125 C7
Ingham Corner Norf 161 D7
Ingleborough Norf 157 F9
Ingleby Derbys 152 D6
Ingleby Lincs 188 F5
Ingleby Arncliffe
N Yorks 225 E8
Ingleby Barwick
Stockton 225 C9
Ingleby Cross N Yorks 225 E9
Ingleby Greenhow
N Yorks 225 D11
Ingleigh Green Devon 25 F10
Inglemire Hull 209 G7
Inglesbatch Bath 61 G8
Inglesham Swindon 82 F2
Ingleton Durham 233 G9
Ingleton N Yorks 212 E3
Inglewhite Lancs 202 E6
Ingmanthorpe N Yorks 206 C4
Ingoe Northumb 242 C2
Ingol Lancs 202 G6
Ingoldisthorpe Norf 158 C3
Ingoldmells Lincs 175 B9
Ingoldsby Lincs 155 C10
Ingon Warks 118 F4
Ingram Northumb 264 F2
Ingrams Green W Sus 34 C4
Ingrave Essex 87 G10
Ingrow W Yorks 205 F7
Ings Cumb 221 F8
Ingst S Glos 60 B5
Ingthorpe Rutland 137 B9
Ingworth Norf 160 D3
Inham's End Cambs 138 D5
Inhurst Hants 64 G5
Inkberrow Worcs 117 F10
Inkerman Durham 233 D8
Inkersall Derbys 186 G6
Inkersall Green
Derbys 186 G6
Inkford Worcs 117 C11
Inkpen W Berks 63 G11
Inkpen Common
W Berks 63 G11
Inkstack Highld 310 B6
Inlands W Sus 22 B3
Inmarsh Wilts 62 G2
Inn Cumb 221 D8
Innellan Argyll 276 G3
Inner Hope Devon 9 G8
Innerleithen Borders 261 B8
Innerleven Fife 287 G7
Innermessan Dumfries 236 C2
Innerwick E Loth 282 G4
Innerwick Perth 285 C9
Innie Argyll 275 B9
Inninbeg Highld 289 E8
Innis Chonain Argyll 284 E5
Innistrynich Argyll 284 E5
Innox Hill Som 45 D9
Innsworth Glos 99 G7

380 Ins – Kip

Insch Aberds 302 G6
Insh Highld 291 C10
Inshegra Highld 306 D7
Inshore Highld 308 C3
Inskip Lancs 202 F5
Inskip Moss Side Lancs 202 F5
Instoneville S Yorks 198 E5
Instow Devon 40 G3
Insworke Corn 7 E8
Intack Blkburn 195 B8
Intake S Yorks 186 E5
Intake S Yorks 198 G5
Intake W Yorks 205 F10
Interfield Worcs 98 B5
Intwood Norf 142 C3
Inver Aberds 292 D4
Inver Highld 311 L2
Inver Perth 286 C4
Inver Mallie Highld 290 E3
Inverailort Highld 295 G9
Inveraldie Angus 287 D8
Inveralivaig Highld 298 E4
Inverallgin Highld 299 D8
Inverallochy Aberds 303 C10
Inveran Highld 299 B8
Inveran Highld 309 K5
Inveraray Argyll 284 G4
Inverarish Highld 295 B7
Inverarity Angus 287 C8
Inverarnan Stirl 285 F7
Inverasdale Highld 307 L3
Inverawe Ho Argyll 284 D4
Inverbeg Argyll 276 B6
Inverbervie Aberds 293 F10
Inverboyndie Aberds 302 C6
Inverbroom Highld 307 L6
Invercarron Mains Highld 309 K5
Invercassley Highld 309 J4
Invercauld House Aberds 292 D3
Inverchaolain Argyll 275 F11
Invercharnan Highld 284 C5
Inverchoran Highld 300 D2
Invercreran Argyll 284 C4
Inverdruie Highld 291 B11
Inverebrie Aberds 303 F9
Invereck Argyll 276 E2
Inverernan Ho Aberds 292 B5
Invereshie House Highld 291 C10
Inveresk E Loth 280 G6
Inverey Aberds 292 E2
Inverfarigaig Highld 300 G5
Invergarry Highld 290 C5
Invergelder Aberds 292 D4
Invergeldie Perth 285 E11
Invergordon Highld 301 C7
Invergowrie Perth 287 D7
Inverguseran Highld 295 E9
Inverhadden Perth 285 B10
Inverhaggernie Stirl 285 E7
Inverharroch Moray 302 F3
Inverherive Stirl 285 E7
Inverie Highld 295 F9
Inverinan Argyll 275 B10
Inverinate Highld 295 C11
Inverkeilor Angus 287 C10
Inverkeithing Fife 280 E2
Inverkeithny Aberds 302 E6
Inverkip Invclyd 276 G4
Inverkirkaig Highld 307 H5
Inverlael Highld 307 L6
Inverleith Edin 280 F4
Inverliever Lodge Argyll 275 C9
Inverliver Argyll 284 D4
Inverlochlarig Stirl 285 F8
Inverlochy Argyll 284 E5
Inverlochy Highld 290 F3
Inverlochy Moray 301 G11
Inverlounin Argyll 276 B4
Inverlussa Argyll 275 E7
Invermark Lodge Angus 292 E6
Invermoidart Highld 289 B8
Invermoriston Highld 290 B6
Invernaver Highld 308 C7
Inverneill Argyll 275 E9
Inverness Highld 300 E6
Invernettie Aberds 303 E11
Invernoaden Argyll 276 B2
Inveronich Argyll 284 G6
Inveroran Hotel Argyll 284 C6
Inverpolly Lodge Highld 307 H5
Inverquharity Angus 287 B8
Inverquhomery Aberds 303 E10
Inverroy Highld 290 E4
Inversanda Highld 289 D11
Invershiel Highld 295 D11
Invershin Highld 309 K5
Invershore Highld 310 F6
Inversnaid Hotel Stirl 285 G7
Invertrossachs Stirl 285 G9
Inverugie Aberds 303 E11
Inveruglas Argyll 285 G7
Inveruglass Highld 291 C10
Inverurie Aberds 303 G7
Invervar Perth 285 C10
Inverythan Aberds 303 E7
Inwardleigh Devon 13 B7
Inwood Shrops 131 D9
Inworth Essex 88 B5
Iochdar W Isles 297 G3
Iping W Sus 34 C5
Ipplepen Devon 8 B6
Ipsden Oxon 64 B6
Ipsley Worcs 117 D11
Ipstones Staffs 169 F8
Ipswich Suff 108 C3
Irby Mers 182 E3
Irby in the Marsh Lincs 175 C7
Irby upon Humber NE Lincs 201 G7
Irchester Northants 121 D8
Ireby Cumb 229 D10
Ireby Lancs 212 D3
Ireland C Beds 104 C2
Ireland Orkney 314 F3
Ireland Shetland 313 L5
Ireland Wilts 45 C10
Ireland Wood W Yorks 205 F11
Ireland's Cross Shrops 168 G2
Ireleth Cumb 210 D4
Ireshopeburn Durham 232 D3
Ireton Wood Derbys 170 F3
Irlam Gtr Man 184 C2
Irlams o' th' Height Gtr Man 195 G9
Irnham Lincs 155 D10
Iron Acton S Glos 61 C7
Iron Bridge Cambs 139 D9
Iron Cross Warks 117 G11
Iron Lo Highld 299 G10
Ironbridge Telford 132 C3
Irongray Dumfries 237 B11
Ironmacannie Dumfries 237 B8
Irons Bottom Sur 51 D9
Ironside Aberds 303 D8
Ironville Derbys 170 E6
Irstead Norf 161 E7
Irstead Street Norf 161 F7
Irthington Cumb 239 E11
Irthlingborough Northants 121 C8
Irton N Yorks 217 C10
Irvine N Ayrs 257 B8
Irwell Vale Lancs 195 C9
Isabella Pit Northumb 253 G8
Isallt Bach Anglesey 178 F3
Isauld Highld 310 C3
Isbister Orkney 314 E3
Isbister Orkney 314 D2
Isbister Shetland 312 D5
Isbister Shetland 313 G7
Isel Cumb 229 E9
Isfield E Sus 36 D6
Isham Northants 121 C7
Ishriff Argyll 289 F8
Isington Hants 49 E9
Island Carr N Lincs 200 F3
Islands Common Cambs 122 E3
Islay Ho Argyll 274 G4
Isle Abbotts Som 28 C5
Isle Brewers Som 28 C5
Isle of Axholme N Lincs 199 F9
Isle of Dogs London 67 D11
Isle of Man Dumfries 238 B2
Isle of Whithorn Dumfries 236 F6
Isleham Cambs 124 C2
Isleornsay Highld 295 D9
Islesburgh Shetland 312 G5
Islesteps Dumfries 237 B11
Isleworth London 67 D7
Isley Walton Leics 153 D8
Islibhig W Isles 304 F1
Islington London 67 C10
Islington Telford 150 E4
Islip Northants 121 B9
Islip Oxon 83 C8
Isombridge Telford 150 G2
Istead Rise Kent 68 F6
Isycoed Wrex 166 E6
Itchen Soton 32 E6
Itchen Abbas Hants 48 G4
Itchen Stoke Hants 48 G5
Itchingfield W Sus 35 B10
Itchington S Glos 61 B7
Itteringham Norf 160 C2
Itteringham Common Norf 160 D3
Itton Devon 13 B9
Itton Mon 79 F7
Itton Common Mon 79 F7
Ivegill Cumb 230 C4
Ivelet N Yorks 223 F8
Iver Bucks 66 C4
Iver Heath Bucks 66 C4
Iverley Staffs 133 G7
Iveston Durham 242 G4
Ivinghoe Bucks 84 B6
Ivinghoe Aston Bucks 85 B7
Ivington Hereford 115 F9
Ivington Green Hereford 115 F9
Ivy Chimneys Essex 86 E6
Ivy Cross Dorset 30 C5
Ivy Hatch Kent 52 C5
Ivy Todd Norf 141 B7
Ivybridge Devon 8 D2
Ivychurch Kent 39 B8
Iwade Kent 69 F11
Iwerne Courtney or Shroton Dorset 30 E5
Iwerne Minster Dorset 30 E5
Iwood N Som 60 G3
Ixworth Suff 125 C8
Ixworth Thorpe Suff 125 C8

J

Jack Green Lancs 194 B5
Jack Hayes Staffs 168 F6
Jack Hill N Yorks 205 C10
Jack in the Green Devon 14 B6
Jackfield Telford 132 C3
Jack's Green Essex 105 G11
Jack's Green Glos 80 D5
Jack's Hatch Essex 86 D6
Jacksdale Notts 170 E6
Jackson Bridge W Yorks 197 F7
Jackstown Aberds 303 F7
Jacobs Well Sur 50 C3
Jacobstow Corn 11 B9
Jacobstowe Devon 25 G9
Jagger Green W Yorks 196 D5
Jameston Pembs 73 F9
Jamestown Dumfries 249 D8
Jamestown Highld 300 D4
Jamestown W Dunb 277 E7
Jamphlars Fife 280 B4
Janetstown Highld 310 C4
Janke's Green Essex 107 F8
Jarrow T & W 243 D8
Jarvis Brook E Sus 37 B8
Jasper's Green Essex 106 F4
Java Argyll 289 F9
Jaw Hill W Yorks 197 C9
Jawcraig Falk 278 F6
Jaywick Essex 89 C11
Jealott's Hill Brack 65 E11
Jeaniefield Borders 271 G10
Jedburgh Borders 262 E5
Jedurgh Borders 262 F5
Jeffreyston Pembs 73 D9
Jellyhill E Dunb 278 G2
Jemimaville Highld 301 C7
Jennetts Hill W Berks 64 E5
Jennyfield N Yorks 205 B11
Jericho Gtr Man 195 E10
Jersey Farm Herts 85 D11
Jersey Marine Neath 57 C8
Jerviswood S Lnrk 269 F7
Jesmond T & W 243 D7
Jevington E Sus 23 E9
Jewell's Cross Corn 24 G3
Jingle Street Mon 79 C7
Jockey End Herts 85 C8
Jodrell Bank E Ches 184 G3
John O'Gaunt Leics 136 B4
John O'Gaunts W Yorks 197 B11
John o'Groats Highld 310 B7
Johnby Cumb 230 E4
John's Cross E Sus 38 C2
Johnshaven Aberds 293 G9
Johnson Fold Gtr Man 195 E7
Johnson Street Norf 161 F7
Johnson's Hillock Lancs 194 C5
Johnston Pembs 72 C6
Johnstone Renfs 267 C8
Johnstone Mains Aberds 293 F9
Johnstonebridge Dumfries 248 E3
Johnstown Carms 74 B6
Johnstown Wrex 166 F4
Jolly's Bottom Corn 4 F5
Joppa Corn 2 B3
Joppa Edin 280 G6
Joppa S Ayrs 257 F10
Jordan Green Norf 159 E11
Jordanhill Glasgow 267 B10
Jordans Bucks 85 G7
Jordanston Pembs 91 E8
Jordanthorpe S Yorks 186 E5
Jordon S Yorks 186 C6
Joyford Glos 79 C9
Joy's Green Glos 79 B10
Jubilee Gtr Man 196 E2
Jubilee Notts 170 E6
Jugbank Staffs 150 B5
Jump S Yorks 197 G11
Jumpers Common Dorset 19 C8
Jumpers Green Dorset 19 C8
Jumper's Town E Sus 52 G3
Junction N Yorks 204 D6
Juniper Northumb 241 F10
Juniper Green Edin 270 B3
Jurby East I o M 192 C4
Jurby West I o M 192 C4
Jurston Devon 13 E9
Jury's Gap E Sus 39 D7

K

Kaber Cumb 222 C5
Kaimend S Lnrk 269 F9
Kaimes Edin 270 B5
Kaimrig End Borders 269 G11
Kalemouth Borders 262 D6
Kame Fife 287 G7
Kames Argyll 275 B9
Kames Argyll 275 F10
Kames E Ayrs 258 D5
Kates Hill W Mid 133 E9
Kea Corn 4 G6
Keadby N Lincs 199 E10
Keal Cotes Lincs 174 C5
Kearby Town End N Yorks 206 D2
Kearnsey Kent 55 E9
Kearsley Gtr Man 195 F9
Kearstwick Cumb 212 C2
Kearton N Yorks 223 F9
Kearvaig Highld 306 B7
Keasden N Yorks 212 F4
Kebroyd W Yorks 196 C4
Keckwick Halton 183 E9
Keddington Lincs 190 D4
Keddington Corner Lincs 190 D5
Kedington Suff 106 B4
Kedleston Derbys 170 G4
Kedslie Borders 271 G11
Keekle Cumb 219 B10
Keelars Tye Essex 107 G11
Keelby Lincs 201 E7
Keele Staffs 168 F4
Keeley Green Beds 103 B10
Keelham W Yorks 205 G7
Keenley Northumb 241 F7
Keenthorne Som 43 F8
Keeres Green Essex 87 C9
Keeston Pembs 72 B6
Keevil Wilts 46 B2
Kegworth Leics 153 D9
Kehelland Corn 4 G2
Keig Aberds 293 B8
Keighley W Yorks 205 E7
Keil Highld 289 D11
Keilarsbrae Clack 279 C7
Keilhill Aberds 303 D7
Keillmore Argyll 275 E7
Keillor Perth 286 C6
Keillour Perth 286 E3
Keills Argyll 274 G5
Keils Argyll 274 G6
Keinton Mandeville Som 44 G4
Keir Mill Dumfries 247 E9
Keisby Lincs 155 D10
Keiss Highld 310 C7
Keistle Highld 298 D4
Keith Moray 302 D4
Keith Hall Aberds 303 G7
Keith Inch Aberds 303 E11
Keithock Angus 293 G8
Kelbrook Lancs 204 E4
Kelby Lincs 173 G8
Kelcliffe W Yorks 205 E9
Keld Cumb 221 C11
Keld N Yorks 223 E7
Keld Houses N Yorks 214 G2
Keldholme N Yorks 216 B4
Kelfield N Lincs 199 G10
Kelfield N Yorks 207 F7
Kelham Notts 172 D3
Kelhurn Argyll 276 F6
Kellacott Devon 12 D4
Kellamergh Lancs 194 B2
Kellan Argyll 289 E7
Kellas Angus 287 D8
Kellas Moray 301 D11
Kellaton Devon 9 G11
Kellaways Wilts 62 D3
Kelleth Cumb 222 D3
Kelleythorpe E Yorks 208 B5
Kelleythorpe E Yorks 208 B6
Kelling Norf 177 E9
Kellingley N Yorks 198 C4
Kellington N Yorks 198 C5
Kelloe Durham 234 D2
Kelloholm Dumfries 258 G6
Kells Cumb 219 B9
Kelly Corn 10 G6
Kelly Devon 12 E3
Kelly Bray Corn 12 G3
Kelmarsh Northants 120 B4
Kelmscott Oxon 82 F3
Kelsale Suff 127 D7
Kelsall W Ches 167 B8
Kelsall Hill W Ches 167 B8
Kelsay Argyll 254 B2
Kelshall Herts 104 D6
Kelsick Cumb 238 G5
Kelso Borders 262 C6
Kelstedge Derbys 170 C4
Kelstern Lincs 190 C3
Kelsterton Flint 182 G3
Kelston Bath 61 F8
Keltneyburn Perth 285 C11
Kelton Dumfries 237 B11
Kelton Durham 232 G4
Kelty Fife 280 C2
Keltybridge Fife 280 B2
Kelvedon Essex 88 B5
Kelvedon Hatch Essex 87 F9
Kelvin S Lnrk 268 E2
Kelvindale Glasgow 267 B11
Kelvinside Glasgow 267 B11
Kelynack Corn 1 D3
Kemacott Devon 41 D7
Kemback Fife 287 F8
Kemberton Shrops 132 C4
Kemble Glos 81 F7
Kemble Wick Glos 81 F7
Kemerton Worcs 99 D8
Kemeys Commander Mon 78 E4
Keminchan E Ches 168 B4
Kemnay Aberds 293 B9
Kemp Town Brighton 36 G4
Kempe's Corner Kent 54 D4
Kempie Highld 308 D4
Kempley Glos 98 F3
Kempley Green Glos 98 F3
Kemps Green Warks 118 C2
Kempsey Worcs 99 B7
Kempsford Glos 81 F11
Kempshott Hants 48 C6
Kempston Beds 103 B10
Kempston Church End Beds 103 B10
Kempston Hardwick Beds 103 C10
Kempston West End Beds 103 B9
Kempton Shrops 131 G7
Kemsing Kent 52 B4
Kemsley Kent 70 F2
Kemsley Street Kent 69 G10
Kenardington Kent 54 G3
Kenchester Hereford 97 C8
Kencot Oxon 82 E3
Kendal Cumb 221 G10
Kendal End Worcs 117 C10
Kendleshire S Glos 61 D7
Kendon Caerph 77 F11
Kendoon Dumfries 246 F4
Kendray S Yorks 197 F11
Kenfig Bridgend 57 E10
Kenfig Hill Bridgend 57 E10
Kengharair Argyll 288 E6
Kenilworth Warks 118 C5
Kenknock Stirl 285 D8
Kenley London 51 B10
Kenley Shrops 131 C11
Kenmore Argyll 284 G4
Kenmore Highld 299 D7
Kenmore Perth 285 C11
Kenmure Dumfries 237 B8
Kenn Devon 14 D4
Kenn N Som 60 F2
Kenn Moor Gate N Som 60 F2
Kennacley W Isles 305 J3
Kennacraig Argyll 275 G9
Kennards House Corn 11 E11
Kenneggy Corn 2 D3
Kenneggy Downs Corn 2 D3
Kennerleigh Devon 26 F4
Kennet Clack 279 C8
Kennet End Suff 124 D3
Kennethmont Aberds 302 G5
Kennett Cambs 124 D3
Kennford Devon 14 D4
Kenninghall Norf 141 F10
Kenninghall Heath Norf 141 G10
Kennington Kent 54 E4
Kennington London 67 D10
Kennington Oxon 83 E8
Kennoway Fife 287 G7
Kenny Som 28 D4
Kenny Hill Suff 124 B3
Kennythorpe N Yorks 216 F5
Kenovay Argyll 288 E1
Kensal Green London 67 C8
Kensal Rise London 67 C8
Kensal Town London 67 C8
Kensaleyre Highld 298 D4
Kensary Highld 310 E6
Kensington London 67 D9
Kensington Mers 182 C5
Kensworth C Beds 85 B8
Kent Street E Sus 38 D3
Kent Street Kent 53 C7
Kent Street W Sus 36 C2
Kentallen Highld 284 B4
Kentchurch Hereford 97 F8
Kentford Suff 124 D4
Kentisbeare Devon 27 F9
Kentisbury Devon 40 E6
Kentisbury Ford Devon 40 E6
Kentish Town London 67 C9
Kentmere Cumb 221 E9
Kenton Devon 14 E5
Kenton London 67 B7
Kenton Suff 126 D3
Kenton T & W 242 D6
Kenton Bankfoot T & W 242 D6
Kenton Bar T & W 242 D6
Kenton Corner Suff 126 D4
Kenton Green Glos 80 C3
Kentra Highld 289 C8
Kentrigg Cumb 221 G10
Kents Corn 11 B9
Kents Bank Cumb 211 D7
Kent's Green Glos 98 G4
Kents Hill M Keynes 103 D7
Kent's Oak Hants 32 C4
Kenwick Shrops 149 C8
Kenwick Park Shrops 149 D8
Kenwyn Corn 4 F6
Kenyon Warr 183 B10
Keoldale Highld 308 C3
Keonchulish Ho Highld 307 K6
Kepdowrie Stirl 277 C11
Kepnal Wilts 63 G7
Keppanach Highld 290 G2
Keppoch Highld 295 C11
Keprigan Argyll 255 F7
Kepwick N Yorks 225 G9
Kerchesters Borders 263 B7
Kerdiston Norf 159 E11
Keresforth Hill S Yorks 197 F10
Keresley W Mid 134 G6
Keresley Newlands Warks 134 G6
Kerfield Borders 270 G5
Kerley Downs Corn 4 G5
Kernborough Devon 8 G5
Kerne Bridge Hereford 79 B9
Kerris Corn 1 D4
Kerry = Ceri Powys 130 F2
Kerry Hill Staffs 168 F6
Kerrycroy Argyll 266 C2
Kerry's Gate Hereford 97 E7
Kerrysdale Highld 299 B8
Kersal Gtr Man 195 G10
Kersall Notts 172 C2
Kersbrook Cross Corn 12 F2
Kerscott Devon 25 B10
Kersey Suff 107 C10
Kersey Tye Suff 107 C9
Kersey Upland Suff 107 C9
Kershopefoot Cumb 249 G11
Kersoe Worcs 99 C9
Kerswell Devon 27 F9
Kerswell Green Worcs 99 B7
Kerthen Wood Corn 2 C3
Kesgrave Suff 108 B4
Kessingland Suff 143 F10
Kessingland Beach Suff 143 F10
Kessington E Dunb 277 G11
Kestle Corn 5 F9
Kestle Mill Corn 5 D7
Keston London 68 G2
Keston Mark London 68 F2
Keswick Cumb 229 G11
Keswick Norf 142 C4
Keswick Norf 161 C7
Kete Pembs 72 E4
Ketford Glos 98 E4
Ketley Telford 150 G3
Ketley Bank Telford 150 G3
Ketsby Lincs 190 F5
Kettering Northants 121 B7
Ketteringham Norf 142 C3
Kettins Perth 286 D6
Kettle Corner Kent 53 C8
Kettle Green Herts 86 B6
Kettlebaston Suff 125 G9
Kettlebridge Fife 287 G7
Kettlebrook Staffs 134 C4
Kettleburgh Suff 126 E5
Kettlehill Fife 287 G7
Kettleholm Dumfries 238 B4
Kettleness N Yorks 226 B6
Kettleshulme E Ches 185 F7
Kettleshume E Ches 185 F7
Kettlesing N Yorks 205 B10
Kettlesing Bottom N Yorks 205 B10
Kettlesing Head N Yorks 205 B10
Kettlestone Norf 159 C9
Kettlethorpe Lincs 188 F4
Kettlethorpe W Yorks 197 D10
Kettletoft Orkney 314 C6
Kettlewell N Yorks 213 E9
Ketton Rutland 137 C9
Kevingtown London 68 F3
Kew London 67 D7
Kew Bridge London 67 D7
Keward Som 44 E4
Kewstoke N Som 59 G10
Kexbrough S Yorks 197 F9
Kexby Lincs 188 D5
Kexby York 207 C10
Key Green E Ches 168 C5
Key Green N Yorks 226 E6
Key Street Kent 69 G11
Keybridge Corn 11 G7
Keycol Kent 69 G11
Keyford Som 45 D9
Keyham Leics 136 B3
Keyhaven Hants 20 C2
Keyingham E Yorks 201 B8
Keymer W Sus 36 D4
Keynsham Bath 61 F7
Key's Green Kent 53 F7
Keysers Estate Essex 86 D5
Keysoe Beds 121 E11
Keysoe Row Beds 121 E11
Keyston Cambs 121 B10
Keyworth Notts 154 C2
Khantore Aberds 292 D4
Kibbear Som 28 C2
Kibblesworth T & W 242 F6
Kibworth Beauchamp Leics 136 E3
Kibworth Harcourt Leics 136 E3
Kidbrooke London 68 D2
Kidburngill Cumb 229 G7
Kiddal Lane End W Yorks 206 F4
Kiddemore Green Staffs 133 B7
Kidderminster Worcs 116 B6
Kiddington Oxon 101 G8
Kidd's Moor Norf 142 C2
Kidlington Oxon 83 C7
Kidmore End Oxon 65 D7
Kidnal W Ches 167 F7
Kidsdale Dumfries 236 F6
Kidsgrove Staffs 168 E4
Kidstones N Yorks 213 C9
Kidwelly = Cydweli Carms 74 D6
Kiel Crofts Argyll 289 F11
Kielder Northumb 250 E4
Kierfiold Ho Orkney 314 E2
Kiff Green W Berks 64 F5
Kilbagie Fife 279 D8
Kilbarchan Renfs 267 C8
Kilbeg Highld 295 E8
Kilberry Argyll 275 G8
Kilbirnie N Ayrs 266 E6
Kilbowie W Dunb 277 G10
Kilbraur Highld 311 H2
Kilbride Argyll 254 C4
Kilbride Argyll 275 D9
Kilbride Argyll 289 G10
Kilbride Argyll 289 G11
Kilbride Highld 295 C7
Kilbridemore Argyll 275 D11
Kilburn Angus 292 G5
Kilburn Derbys 170 F5
Kilburn London 67 C9
Kilburn N Yorks 215 D10
Kilby Leics 136 D2
Kilby Bridge Leics 136 D2
Kilchamaig Argyll 275 G9
Kilchattan Argyll 274 D4
Kilchattan Bay Argyll 266 E2
Kilchenzie Argyll 255 E7
Kilcheran Argyll 289 F10
Kilchiaran Argyll 274 G3
Kilchoan Argyll 275 B8
Kilchoan Highld 288 C6
Kilchoman Argyll 274 G3
Kilchrenan Argyll 284 E4
Kilconquhar Fife 287 G8
Kilcot Glos 98 F3
Kilcoy Highld 300 D5
Kilcreggan Argyll 276 E4
Kildale N Yorks 226 D2
Kildalloig Argyll 255 F8
Kildary Highld 301 B7
Kildaton Ho Argyll 254 C5
Kildavanan Argyll 275 G11
Kildermorie Lodge Highld 300 B5
Kildonan Dumfries 236 D2
Kildonan Highld 298 D3
Kildonan N Ayrs 256 E2
Kildonan Lodge Highld 311 G3
Kildonnan Highld 294 G6
Kildrum N Lnrk 278 F5
Kildrummy Aberds 292 B6
Kildwick N Yorks 204 D6
Kilfinan Argyll 275 F10
Kilfinnan Highld 290 D4
Kilgetty Pembs 73 D10
Kilgour Fife 286 G6
Kilgrammie S Ayrs 245 C7
Kilgwrrwg Common Mon 79 F7
Kilhallon Corn 5 E11
Kilham E Yorks 217 G11
Kilham Northumb 263 C9
Kilkeddan Argyll 255 E8
Kilkenneth Argyll 288 E1
Kilkenny Glos 81 B8
Kilkerran Argyll 255 F8
Kilkhampton Corn 24 E3
Killamarsh Derbys 187 E7
Killaworgey Corn 5 C8
Killay Swansea 56 C6
Killbeg Argyll 289 E8
Killean Argyll 255 C7
Killearn Stirl 277 D10
Killegruer Argyll 255 D7
Killen Highld 300 D6
Killerby Darl 224 B3
Killichonan Perth 285 B9
Killiechoinich Argyll 289 G10
Killiechonate Highld 290 E4
Killiechronan Argyll 289 E7
Killiecrankie Perth 291 G11
Killiemor Argyll 288 F6
Killiemore House Argyll 288 G6
Killilan Highld 295 B11
Killimster Highld 310 D7
Killin Stirl 285 D9
Killin Lodge Highld 291 C7
Killinallan Argyll 274 F4
Killingbeck W Yorks 206 G2
Killinghall N Yorks 205 B11
Killington Cumb 212 B2
Killington Devon 41 D7
Killingworth T & W 243 C7
Killingworth Moor T & W 243 C7
Killingworth Village T & W 243 C7
Killivose Corn 2 B4
Killmahumaig Argyll 275 D8
Killochyett Borders 271 F9
Killocraw Argyll 255 D7
Killundine Highld 289 E7
Killylung Dumfries 247 G11
Kilmacolm Invclyd 267 B7
Kilmaha Argyll 275 C10
Kilmahog Stirl 285 G10
Kilmalieu Highld 289 D10
Kilmaluag Highld 298 B4
Kilmany Fife 287 E7
Kilmarie Highld 295 D7
Kilmarnock E Ayrs 257 B10
Kilmaron Castle Fife 287 F7
Kilmartin Argyll 275 D9
Kilmaurs E Ayrs 267 G8
Kilmelford Argyll 275 B9
Kilmeny Argyll 274 G4
Kilmersdon Som 45 C7
Kilmeston Hants 33 B9
Kilmichael Argyll 255 E7
Kilmichael Argyll 275 F10
Kilmichael Glassary Argyll 275 D9
Kilmichael of Inverlussa Argyll 275 E8
Kilmington Devon 15 B11
Kilmington Wilts 45 F9
Kilmington Common Wilts 45 F9
Kilmoluaig Argyll 288 E1
Kilmonivaig Highld 290 E3
Kilmorack Highld 300 E4
Kilmore Argyll 289 G10
Kilmore Highld 295 E8
Kilmory Argyll 275 F8
Kilmory Highld 289 B7
Kilmory Highld 294 E5
Kilmory N Ayrs 255 E10
Kilmory Lodge Argyll 275 C8
Kilmote Highld 311 H3
Kilmuir Highld 298 B3
Kilmuir Highld 298 E2
Kilmuir Highld 300 E6
Kilmuir Highld 301 B7
Kilmun Argyll 275 B10
Kilmun Argyll 276 E3
Kiln Green Hereford 79 B10
Kiln Green Wokingham 65 D10
Kiln Pit Hill Northumb 242 G2
Kilnave Argyll 274 F3
Kilncadzow S Lnrk 269 F7
Kilndown Kent 53 G8
Kilnhill Cumb 229 E10
Kilnhurst S Yorks 187 B7
Kilninian Argyll 288 E5
Kilninver Argyll 289 G10
Kilnsea E Yorks 201 D12
Kilnsey N Yorks 213 F9
Kilnwick E Yorks 208 D5
Kilnwick Percy E Yorks 208 C2
Kiloran Argyll 274 D4
Kilpatrick N Ayrs 255 E10
Kilpeck Hereford 97 E8
Kilphedir Highld 311 H3
Kilpin E Yorks 199 B9
Kilpin Pike E Yorks 199 B9
Kilrenny Fife 287 G9
Kilsby Northants 119 C11
Kilspindie Perth 286 E6
Kilsyth N Lnrk 278 F4
Kiltarlity Highld 300 E5
Kilton Notts 187 F9
Kilton Redcar 226 B4
Kilton Som 43 E7
Kilton Thorpe Redcar 226 B3
Kiltyrie Perth 285 D10
Kilvaxter Highld 298 C3
Kilve Som 43 E7
Kilvington Notts 172 G3
Kilwinning N Ayrs 266 G6
Kimberley Norf 141 C11
Kimberley Notts 171 G8
Kimberworth S Yorks 186 C6
Kimberworth Park S Yorks 186 C6
Kimble Wick Bucks 84 D4
Kimblesworth Durham 233 B11
Kimbolton Cambs 121 D11
Kimbolton Hereford 115 E10
Kimcote Leics 135 F11
Kimmeridge Dorset 18 F4
Kimmerston Northumb 263 B11
Kimpton Hants 47 D9
Kimpton Herts 85 B11
Kimworthy Devon 24 E4
Kinabus Argyll 254 C3
Kinbeachie Highld 300 C6
Kinbrace Highld 310 F2
Kinbuck Stirl 285 G11
Kincaidston S Ayrs 257 F9
Kincaple Fife 287 F8
Kincardine Fife 279 D8
Kincardine Highld 309 L6
Kincardine Bridge Falk 279 D8
Kincardine O'Neil Aberds 293 D7
Kinclaven Perth 286 D5
Kincorth Aberdeen 293 C11
Kincorth Ho Moray 301 C10
Kincraig Highld 291 C10
Kincraigie Perth 286 C3
Kindallachan Perth 286 C3
Kine Moor S Yorks 197 G9
Kineton Glos 99 F11
Kineton Warks 118 G6
Kineton Green W Mid 134 G2
Kinfauns Perth 286 E5
King Edward Aberds 303 D7
King Sterndale Derbys 185 G9
King Street Essex 87 E9
Kingairloch Highld 289 D10
Kingarth Argyll 255 B11
Kingates I o W 20 F6
Kingbeare Corn 11 G11
Kingcoed Mon 78 D6
Kingdown N Som 60 G4
Kingerby Lincs 189 C9
Kingfield Sur 50 B4
Kingford Devon 24 F3
Kingford Devon 25 D10
Kingham Oxon 100 G5
Kinghay Wilts 30 B5
Kingholm Quay Dumfries 237 B11
Kinghorn Fife 280 D5
Kingie Highld 290 C3
Kinglassie Fife 280 B4
Kingledores Borders 260 D4
Kingoodie Perth 287 E7
King's Acre Hereford 97 C9
King's Bromley Staffs 152 F2
King's Caple Hereford 97 F11
King's Cliffe Northants 137 D10
Kings Clipstone Notts 171 C10
King's Coughton Warks 117 F11
King's Dyke Cambs 138 D4
King's End Oxon 101 G11
King's End Worcs 116 G6
King's Furlong Hants 48 C6
King's Green Glos 98 E5
King's Green Worcs 116 E5
King's Heath Northants 120 E4
King's Heath W Mid 133 G11
Kings Hedges Cambs 123 E9
Kings Hill Glos 81 E8
King's Hill Kent 53 C7
King's Hill W Mid 133 D9
Kings Langley Herts 85 E9
King's Lynn Norf 158 E2
King's Meaburn Cumb 231 G8
King's Mills Derbys 153 D8
King's Mills Wrex 166 F4
Kings Moss Mers 194 G4
Kings Muir Borders 261 B7
King's Newnham Warks 119 B9
King's Newton Derbys 153 D7
King's Norton Leics 136 C3
King's Norton W Mid 117 B11
King's Nympton Devon 25 D11
King's Pyon Hereford 115 G8
Kings Ripton Cambs 122 B5
King's Somborne Hants 47 G11
King's Stag Dorset 30 E2
King's Stanley Glos 80 E4
King's Sutton Northants 101 D9
King's Tamerton Plym 7 D9
King's Thorn Hereford 97 E10
King's Walden Herts 104 G3
Kings Worthy Hants 48 G3
Kingsand Corn 7 E8
Kingsash Bucks 84 D5
Kingsbarns Fife 287 F9
Kingsbridge Devon 8 G4
Kingsbridge Som 42 F3
Kingsburgh Highld 298 D3
Kingsbury London 67 B8
Kingsbury Warks 134 D4
Kingsbury Episcopi Som 28 C6
Kingsbury Regis Som 29 D11
Kingscauseway Highld 301 B7
Kingscavil W Loth 279 F10
Kingsclere Hants 48 B4
Kingsclere Woodlands Hants 64 G4
Kingscote Glos 80 F4
Kingscott Devon 25 D8
Kingscourt Glos 80 E4
Kingscross N Ayrs 256 D2
Kingsditch Glos 99 G8
Kingsdon Som 29 B8
Kingsdown Kent 54 B2
Kingsdown Kent 55 D11
Kingsdown Swindon 63 B7
Kingsdown Wilts 61 F10
Kingseat Fife 280 C2
Kingseathill Fife 280 D2
Kingsett Devon 12 E6
Kingsey Bucks 84 D2
Kingsfield Hereford 97 B10
Kingsfold Lancs 194 B4
Kingsfold W Sus 51 F7
Kingsford Aberds 293 B7
Kingsford E Ayrs 267 F8
Kingsford Worcs 132 G6
Kingsforth N Lincs 200 D4
Kingsgate Kent 71 E11
Kingshall Green Suff 125 E8
Kingshall Street Suff 125 E8
Kingsheanton Devon 40 F5
Kingshill Kent 87 F7
Kingshill Swindon 62 C6
Kingsholm Glos 80 B4
Kingshouse Hotel Highld 284 B6
Kingshurst W Mid 134 F3
Kingside Hill Cumb 238 G5
Kingskerswell Devon 9 B7
Kingskettle Fife 287 G7
Kingsknowe Edin 280 G4
Kingsland Anglesey 178 E2
Kingsland Hereford 115 E8
Kingsland London 67 C10
Kingsland Shrops 149 G9
Kingsley Hants 49 F9
Kingsley Staffs 169 F8
Kingsley W Ches 183 G9
Kingsley Green W Sus 49 G11
Kingsley Holt Staffs 169 F8
Kingsley Moor Staffs 169 F7
Kingsley Park Northants 120 E5
Kingslow Shrops 132 D5
Kingsmead Hants 33 E9
Kingsmoor Essex 86 D6
Kingsmuir Angus 287 C8
Kingsmuir Fife 287 G9
Kingsnordley Shrops 132 F5
Kingsnorth Kent 54 F4
Kingstanding W Mid 133 E11
Kingsteignton Devon 14 G3
Kingsteps Highld 301 D9
Kingsthorpe Northants 120 E5
Kingsthorpe Hollow Northants 120 E5
Kingston Cambs 122 F6
Kingston Devon 8 F2
Kingston Devon 9 E8
Kingston Dorset 18 F5
Kingston Dorset 30 F3
Kingston E Loth 281 E10
Kingston Gtr Man 184 B6
Kingston Hants 31 G11
Kingston I o W 20 E5
Kingston Kent 55 C7
Kingston M Keynes 103
Kingston Moray 30
Kingston Ptsmth 33
Kingston Suff 10
Kingston Bagpuize Oxon 8
Kingston Blount Oxon 8
Kingston by Sea W Sus 3
Kingston Deverill Wilts 45
Kingston Gorse W Sus 3
Kingston Lisle Oxon 63
Kingston Maurward Dorset 17
Kingston near Lewes E Sus 3
Kingston on Soar Notts 153
Kingston Park T & W 24
Kingston Russell Dorset 1
Kingston St Mary Som 2
Kingston Seymour N Som 6
Kingston Stert Oxon 8
Kingston upon Hull Hull 20
Kingston upon Thames London 6
Kingston Vale London 6
Kingstone Hereford 9
Kingstone Hereford 9
Kingstone S Yorks 197
Kingstone Som 2
Kingstone Staffs 151
Kingstone Winslow Oxon 6
Kingstown Cumb 23
Kingsway Bath 6
Kingsway Halton 18
Kingswear Devon
Kingswells Aberdeen 293
Kingswinford W Mid 13
Kingswood Bucks 83
Kingswood Essex 6
Kingswood Glos 8
Kingswood Hereford 11
Kingswood Herts 85
Kingswood Kent 53
Kingswood Powys 13
Kingswood S Glos 6
Kingswood Som 4
Kingswood Sur 5
Kingswood Warks 11
Kingswood Warr 18
Kingswood Brook Warks 11
Kingswood Common Staffs 13
Kingswood Common Worcs 11
Kingthorpe Lincs 189
Kington Hereford 11
Kington S Glos 79
Kington Worcs 11
Kington Langley Wilts 6
Kington Magna Dorset 3
Kington St Michael Wilts 6
Kingussie Highld 29
Kingweston Som 4
Kinhrive Highld 30
Kininvie Ho Moray 30
Kinkell Bridge Perth 28
Kinknockie Aberds 303
Kinknockie Aberds 30
Kinkry Hill Cumb 24
Kinlet Shrops 13
Kinloch Fife 28
Kinloch Highld 28
Kinloch Highld 29
Kinloch Highld 29
Kinloch Highld 30
Kinloch Perth 28
Kinloch Perth 28
Kinloch Damph Highld 29
Kinloch Hourn Highld 295
Kinloch Laggan Highld 29
Kinloch Lodge Highld 30
Kinloch Rannoch Perth 285
Kinlochan Highld 289
Kinlochard Stirl 28
Kinlochbeoraid Highld 295
Kinlochbervie Highld 30
Kinlocheil Highld 289
Kinlochewe Highld 29
Kinlochleven Highld 29
Kinlochmoidart Highld 29
Kinlochmorar Highld 29
Kinlochmore Highld 29
Kinlochspelve Argyll 28
Kinloid Highld 29
Kinloss Moray 301
Kinmel Bay = Bae Cinmel Conwy 18
Kinmuck Aberds 293
Kinmundy Aberds 293
Kinnadie Aberds 30
Kinnaird Perth 28
Kinnaird Perth 28
Kinnaird Castle Angus 287
Kinnauld Highld 30
Kinneff Aberds 293
Kinneil Falk 27
Kinnelhead Dumfries 24
Kinnell Angus 287
Kinnerley Shrops 14
Kinnersley Hereford 9
Kinnersley Worcs 9
Kinnerton Powys 11
Kinnerton Green Flint 16
Kinnesswood Perth 28
Kinninvie Durham 23
Kinnordy Angus 28
Kinoulton Notts 15
Kinross Perth 28
Kinrossie Perth 28
Kinsbourne Green Herts 85
Kinsey Heath E Ches 167
Kinsham Hereford 11
Kinsham Worcs 9
Kinsley W Yorks 19
Kinson Bmouth 1
Kintallan Argyll 27
Kintbury W Berks 63
Kintessack Moray 30
Kintillo Perth 28
Kintocher Aberds 29
Kinton Hereford 11
Kinton Shrops 14
Kintore Aberds 29
Kintour Argyll 25
Kintra Argyll 25
Kintra Argyll 28
Kintradwell Highld 31
Kintraw Argyll 27
Kinuachdrachd Argyll 27
Kinveachy Highld 291
Kinver Staffs 13
Kinwalsey Warks 13
Kip Hill Durham 24
Kiplin N Yorks 22
Kippax W Yorks 20
Kippen Stirl 27
Kippford or Scaur Dumfries 237

pilaw Borders 262 D2
pilaw Mains Borders 262 D2
ping's Cross Kent 52 F6
pington Kent 52 C4
uster Orkney 314 E2
by Bedon Norf 142 B5
by Bellars Leics 154 F4
by Cane Norf 143 E7
by Corner N Mid 118 B5
by Cross Essex 108 G4
by Fields Leics 135 C10
by Green Norf 143 E7
by Grindalythe
  Yorks 217 F8
by Hill N Yorks 215 F7
by Hill N Yorks 224 D2
by Knowle N Yorks 215 B9
by-le-Soken Essex 108 G4
by Misperton N Yorks 216 D5
by Moor Cumb 240 E2
by Muxloe Leics 135 C10
by Row Norf 143 E7
by Sigston N Yorks 225 G8
by Underdale E Yorks 208 B2
by Wiske N Yorks 215 C7
lford W Sus 35 B8
k Highld 310 D6
k Bramwith S Yorks 198 E6
k Deighton N Yorks 206 C3
k Ella E Yorks 200 B4
k Hallam Derbys 171 G7
k Hammerton
  Yorks 206 B5
k Ireton Derbys 170 E3
k Langley Derbys 152 B5
k Merrington
  ham 233 L11
t Michael I o M 192 C4
t of Shotts N Lnrk 268 C6
k Sandall S Yorks 198 F6
k Smeaton N Yorks 198 E4
k Yetholm Borders 263 D8
abister Shetland 312 G6
abister Shetland 313 K6
andrews Dumfries 237 E8
andrews-on-Eden
  239 F9
apol Argyll 288 E2
bampton Cumb 239 F8
bean Dumfries 237 D11
borough Cumb 229 D7
brae Orkney 314 B4
bride Cumb 238 F6
bridge N Yorks 224 G5
buddo Angus 287 C9
burn Borders 261 B7
burn E Yorks 208 B5
burton W Loth 269 C9
by Lincs 189 C7
by Mers 182 B6
by Fenside Lincs 174 C4
by Fleetham N Yorks 224 G5
by Green Lincs 173 D9
by Hill N Yorks 215 F7
by in Ashfield Notts 171 D8
nb—
  210 C4
by la Thorpe Lincs 173 F10
by Lonsdale Cumb 212 D2
by Malham N Yorks 213 G7
by Mallory Leics 135 C9
by Malzeard
  214 E4
by Mills N Yorks 216 B4
by on Bain Lincs 174 C2
by Overblow
  orks 206 D2
by Stephen Cumb 222 D5
by Thore Cumb 231 F8
by Underwood
  155 D11
by Wharfe N Yorks 206 E6
kby Woodhouse
  171 E7
kbymoorside N Yorks 216 B3
kcaldy Fife 280 C5
kcambeck Cumb 240 E2
kcarswell Dumfries 237 E9
kcolm Dumfries 236 C2
kconnel Dumfries 258 G6
kconnell Dumfries 237 C11
kcowan Dumfries 236 C5
kcudbright Dumfries 237 D8
kdale Mers 182 C4
kfieldbank S Lnrk 269 G7
kforthar Feus Fife 286 G6
kgunzeon Dumfries 237 C10
kham Lancs 202 G4
kham N Yorks 216 F4
khamgate N Yorks 197 C9
khams Gtr Man 195 G10
kharle Northumb 252 G2
kheaton Northumb 242 B2
khill Angus 293 G8
khill E Renf 267 D11
khill N Lnrk 300 E5
khill Midloth 270 C4
khill W Loth 279 G11
kholt Gtr Man 195 E11
khope Borders 261 E9
khouse Borders 261 C8
khouse Cumb 240 F3
kiboll Highld 308 D5
kibost Highld 295 D7
kinch Argyll 287 C7
kinner Dumfries 236 D6
kintilloch E Dunb 278 G3
kland Cumb 219 B11
kland Cumb 229 D11
kland Cumb 231 E8
kland Dumfries 237 C8
kland Dumfries 258 G6
kland Dumfries 244 G6
kland Guards Cumb 229 C9
kleatham Redcar 235 G7
klees Gtr Man 195 G9
klevington Stockton 225 C8
kley Suff 143 G10
klington N Yorks 214 C6
klington Notts 171 D11
klinton Cumb 239 D10
kliston Edin 280 G2
kmaiden Dumfries 236 F3
kmichael Perth 286 B4
kmichael S Ayrs 245 B8
kmichael Mains
  mfries 248 F5
kmuirhill S Lnrk 268 G5
knewton Northumb 251 G11
knewton Argyll 275 E8
kntewton Argyll 302 F5
koswald Cumb 231 C7
koswald S Ayrs 244 B6
kpatrick Dumfries 247 C11
kpatrick Durham 237 B9

Kirkpatrick-Fleming
  Dumfries 239 C7
Kirksanton Cumb 210 C3
Kirkshaw N Lnrk 268 C4
Kirkstall W Yorks 205 F11
Kirkstead Borders 261 E7
Kirkstead Lincs 173 C11
Kirkstile Aberds 302 F5
Kirkstyle Highld 310 B7
Kirkthorpe W Yorks 197 C11
Kirkton Aberds 302 G6
Kirkton Aberds 302 G6
Kirkton Angus 286 C6
Kirkton Angus 287 C8
Kirkton Angus 287 C8
Kirkton Argyll 275 C8
Kirkton Borders 262 G2
Kirkton Dumfries 247 G11
Kirkton Fife 280 D4
Kirkton Fife 287 E7
Kirkton Highld 295 C10
Kirkton Highld 299 E9
Kirkton Highld 301 D7
Kirkton Highld 309 K7
Kirkton Perth 286 D4
Kirkton S Lnrk 259 E10
Kirkton Stirl 285 G9
Kirkton W Loth 269 B10
Kirkton Manor Borders 260 B6
Kirkton of Airlie Angus 287 B7
Kirkton of
  Auchterhouse Angus 287 D7
Kirkton of
  Auchterless Aberds 303 E7
Kirkton of Barevan
  Highld 301 E8
Kirkton of Bourtie
  Aberds 303 G9
Kirkton of Collace
  Perth 286 D5
Kirkton of Craig Angus 287 B11
Kirkton of Culsalmond
  Aberds 302 F6
Kirkton of Durris
  Aberds 293 D9
Kirkton of Glenbuchat
  Aberds 292 B5
Kirkton of Glenisla
  Angus 292 G4
Kirkton of Kingoldrum
  Angus 287 B7
Kirkton of Largo Fife 287 G8
Kirkton of Lethendy
  Perth 286 C5
Kirkton of Logie Buchan
  Aberds 303 G9
Kirkton of Maryculter
  Aberds 293 D10
Kirkton of Menmuir
  Angus 293 G7
Kirkton of Monikie
  Angus 287 D9
Kirkton of Oyne Aberds 302 G6
Kirkton of Rayne Aberds 302 G6
Kirkton of Skene
  Aberds 293 C10
Kirkton of Tough
  Aberds 293 B8
Kirktonhill Borders 271 E9
Kirktonhill W Dunb 277 G7
Kirktown E Ayrs 267 G8
Kirktown of Alvah
  Aberds 302 C6
Kirktown of Deskford
  Moray 302 C5
Kirktown of Fetteresso
  Aberds 293 E10
Kirktown of Mortlach
  Moray 302 F3
Kirktown of Slains
  Aberds 303 G10
Kirkurd Borders 270 G2
Kirkwall Orkney 314 E4
Kirkwhelpington
  Northumb 251 G11
Kirmington
  N Lincs 200 E6
Kirmond le Mire Lincs 189 C11
Kirn Argyll 276 F3
Kirriemuir Angus 287 B7
Kirstead Green Norf 142 D5
Kirtlebridge Dumfries 238 C6
Kirtleton Dumfries 249 G7
Kirtling Cambs 124 F3
Kirtling Green Cambs 124 F3
Kirtlington Oxon 83 B7
Kirtomy Highld 308 C7
Kirton Lincs 156 B6
Kirton Notts 171 B11
Kirton Suff 108 D5
Kirton Campus W Loth 269 B10
Kirton End Lincs 174 G3
Kirton Holme Lincs 174 G3
Kirton in Lindsey
  N Lincs 188 B6
Kiskin Cumb 210 B1
Kislingbury Northants 120 F3
Kit Hill Dorset 30 D4
Kitbridge Devon 28 G4
Kitchenroyd W Yorks 197 F8
Kite Green Warks 118 D3
Kitebrook Warks 100 E4
Kites Hardwick Warks 119 C9
Kitlye Glos 80 E5
Kit's Coty Kent 69 G8
Kitt Green Gtr Man 194 F5
Kittisford Som 27 C9
Kittle Swansea 56 D5
Kitt's Green W Mid 134 F3
Kitt's Moss Gtr Man 184 E5
Kittwhistle Dorset 28 G5
Kittybrewster
  Aberdeen 293 C11
Kitwell W Mid 133 G9
Kitwood Hants 49 G7
Kivernoll Hereford 97 E9
Kiveton Park S Yorks 187 E7
Knaith Lincs 188 E4
Knaith Park Lincs 188 E4
Knap Corner Dorset 30 C4
Knaphill Sur 50 B3
Knapp Hants 32 C6
Knapp Perth 286 D6
Knapp Som 28 B4
Knapp Wilts 31 B8
Knapp Hill Wilts 30 B5
Knaptoft Leics 136 F2
Knapton Norf 160 C6
Knapton York 207 C7
Knapton Green Hereford 115 G9
Knapwell Cambs 122 E6
Knaresborough N Yorks 206 B3
Knarsdale Northumb 240 G5
Knatts Valley Kent 68 G5
Knauchland Moray 302 D5
Knaven Aberds 303 E8
Knave's Ash Kent 71 G7

Knaves Green Suff 126 D2
Knavesmire York 207 D7
Knayton N Yorks 215 B8
Knebworth Herts 104 G5
Knedlington E Yorks 199 B8
Kneesall Notts 172 C2
Kneesworth Cambs 104 C6
Kneeton Notts 172 F2
Knelston Swansea 56 D3
Knenhall Staffs 151 B8
Knettishall Suff 141 G9
Knightacott Devon 41 F7
Knightcote Warks 119 G7
Knightcott N Som 43 B11
Knightley Staffs 150 D6
Knightley Dale Staffs 150 E6
Knighton Devon 7 E10
Knighton Dorset 29 E10
Knighton Leicester 135 C11
Knighton Oxon 63 D9
Knighton Poole 18 B6
Knighton Som 43 E7
Knighton Staffs 150 D4
Knighton Staffs 168 G2
Knighton Wilts 63 E9
Knighton Worcs 117 F10
Knighton =
  Tref-y-Clawdd Powys 114 C5
Knighton on Teme
  Worcs 116 C2
Knightor Corn 5 D10
Knight's End Cambs 139 E8
Knights Enham Hants 47 D11
Knight's Hill London 67 E10
Knightsbridge Glos 99 F7
Knightsbridge London 67 D9
Knightsmill Corn 11 E7
Knightsridge W Loth 269 B11
Knightswood Glasgow 267 B10
Knightwick Worcs 116 F4
Knill Hereford 114 E5
Knipe Fold Cumb 220 F6
Knipoch Argyll 289 G10
Knipton Leics 154 C6
Knitsley Durham 233 B8
Kniveton Derbys 170 E2
Knock Argyll 289 F7
Knock Cumb 231 F9
Knock Moray 302 D5
Knockally Highld 311 G5
Knockan Highld 307 H7
Knockandhu Moray 302 G2
Knockando Moray 301 E11
Knockando Ho Moray 302 E2
Knockandoo Highld 301 G7
Knockbain Highld 300 D5
Knockbreck Highld 298 C2
Knockbrex Dumfries 237 E7
Knockcarrach Highld 290 B6
Knockdee Highld 310 C5
Knockdolian S Ayrs 244 F4
Knockdow Argyll 276 G2
Knockdown Glos 61 B10
Knockenbaird Aberds 302 G6
Knockenkelly N Ayrs 256 D2
Knockentiber E Ayrs 257 B9
Knockerdown Derbys 170 E2
Knockfarrel Highld 300 D5
Knockglass Dumfries 236 D2
Knockhall Kent 68 E5
Knockhall Castle
  Aberds 303 G9
Knockholt Kent 52 B3
Knockholt Pound Kent 52 B3
Knockie Lodge Highld 290 B6
Knockin Shrops 148 E6
Knockin Heath Shrops 149 E7
Knockinlaw E Ayrs 257 B10
Knockinnon Highld 310 F5
Knocklaw Northumb 252 C5
Knocklearn Dumfries 237 B9
Knocklearoch Argyll 274 G4
Knockmill Kent 68 G5
Knocknaha Argyll 255 F7
Knocknain Dumfries 236 C1
Knockothie Aberds 303 F9
Knockrome Argyll 274 F6
Knocksharry I o M 192 D3
Knockstapplemore
  Argyll 255 F7
Knockvologan Argyll 274 B4
Knodishall Suff 127 E8
Knokan Argyll 288 G6
Knole Som 29 B7
Knole Green E Ches 184 F4
Knoll Green Som 43 F8
Knoll Top N Yorks 214 F3
Knollbury Mon 60 B2
Knolls Green E Ches 184 F4
Knolton Wrex 149 B7
Knolton Bryn Wrex 149 B7
Knook Wilts 46 E2
Knossington Leics 136 B4
Knotbury Staffs 169 B8
Knott End-on-Sea
  Lancs 202 D3
Knott Lanes Gtr Man 196 G2
Knott Oak Som 28 E4
Knotting Beds 121 E10
Knotting Green Beds 121 E10
Knottingley W Yorks 198 C4
Knotts Cumb 230 G4
Knotts Lancs 203 C11
Knotty Ash Mers 182 C6
Knotty Corner Devon 24 B6
Knotty Green Bucks 84 G6
Knowbury Shrops 115 C11
Knowe Dumfries 236 B6
Knowe Shetland 313 G5
Knowefield Cumb 239 F10
Knowehead Aberds 293 C7
Knowehead Aberds 302 D5
Knowehead Dumfries 246 E4
Knowes E Loth 282 F2
Knowes of Elrick
  Aberds 302 D6
Knowesgate Northumb 251 G11
Knoweton N Lnrk 268 D5
Knowetop N Lnrk 268 D5
Knowhead Aberds 303 D9
Knowl Bank Staffs 168 F3
Knowl Green Essex 106 C5
Knowl Hill Windsor 65 D10
Knowl Wall Staffs 151 B7
Knowl Wood W Yorks 196 C2
Knowle Bristol 60 E6
Knowle Devon 15 E7
Knowle Devon 26 G3
Knowle Devon 40 F3
Knowle Shrops 115 C11
Knowle Som 43 E10
Knowle W Mid 118 B3
Knowle Green Lancs 203 F8
Knowle Green Sur 66 E4
Knowle Grove W Mid 118 B3

Knowle Hill Sur 66 F3
Knowle Park W Yorks 205 E7
Knowle St Giles Som 28 E4
Knowlegate Shrops 115 C11
Knowles Hill Devon 14 G3
Knowlesands Shrops 132 E4
Knowleswood W Yorks 206 G2
Knowlton Devon 26 C4
Knowlton Dorset 31 E8
Knowlton Kent 55 C9
Knowsley Mers 182 B6
Knowsthorpe W Yorks 206 G2
Knowstone Devon 26 C4
Knox Bridge Kent 53 E9
Knucklas Powys 114 C5
Knuston Northants 121 D7
Knutsford E Ches 184 F3
Knutton Staffs 168 F4
Knuzden Brook Lancs 195 B8
Knypersley Staffs 168 D5
Kraiknish Highld 294 C5
Krumlin W Yorks 196 D5
Kuggar Corn 2 F6
Kyle of Lochalsh Highld 295 C10
Kyleakin Highld 295 C10
Kylepark N Lnrk 268 C3
Kylerhea Highld 295 C9
Kyleshnoydart Highld 295 F10
Kylesku Highld 306 F7
Kylesmorar Highld 295 F10
Kylestrome Highld 306 F7
Kyllachy House Highld 301 G7
Kymin Hereford 97 B11
Kymin Mon 79 C8
Kynaston Hereford 97 F10
Kynaston Shrops 149 E7
Kynnersley Telford 150 F3
Kyre Worcs 116 E2
Kyre Green Worcs 116 E2
Kyre Magna Worcs 116 E2
Kyre Park Worcs 116 E2
Kyrewood Worcs 116 D2

L

Labost W Isles 304 D4
Lacasaidh W Isles 304 F5
Lacasdal W Isles 304 E6
Laceby NE Lincs 201 F8
Laceby Acres NE Lincs 201 F8
Lacey Green Bucks 84 F4
Lacey Green E Ches 184 E4
Lach Dennis W Ches 184 G2
Lache W Ches 166 C5
Lackenby Redcar 225 B11
Lackford Suff 124 C5
Lacock Wilts 62 F2
Ladbroke Warks 119 F8
Laddenvean Corn 3 E7
Laddingford Kent 53 D7
Lade Kent 39 C9
Lade Bank Lincs 174 E5
Ladies Riggs N Yorks 214 F2
Ladmanlow Derbys 185 G8
Ladock Corn 5 D7
Ladwell Hants 32 C6
Lady Orkney 314 B6
Lady Green Mers 193 G6
Lady Hall Cumb 210 B3
Lady Halton Shrops 115 B9
Lady House Gtr Man 196 E2
Lady Park T & W 242 F6
Lady Wood W Yorks 206 F2
Ladybank Fife 287 F7
Ladyborough Notts 171 C8
Ladyburn Inverclyd 276 F6
Ladycross Corn 12 D2
Ladyes Hill Warks 118 C5
Ladykirk Borders 273 F7
Ladyoak Shrops 131 C7
Ladyridge Hereford 97 E11
Lady's Green Suff 124 F5
Ladysford Aberds 303 C9
Ladywell London 67 E11
Ladywell Shrops 149 C9
Ladywell W Loth 269 B10
Ladywood Telford 132 C3
Ladywood W Mid 133 F11
Ladywood Worcs 117 E7
Laffak Mers 183 B8
Laga Highld 289 C8
Lagafater Lodge
  Dumfries 236 B3
Lagalochan Argyll 289 G10
Lagavulin Argyll 254 C5
Lagg Argyll 274 F6
Lagg N Ayrs 255 E10
Laggan Argyll 254 B3
Laggan Argyll 289 B9
Laggan Highld 290 D4
Laggan Highld 291 D8
Laggan S Ayrs 245 G7
Laggan Lodge Argyll 289 G8
Lagganlia Highld 291 C10
Lagganmullan
  Dumfries 237 D7
Lagganulva Argyll 288 E6
Lagness W Sus 22 C5
Laide Highld 307 K3
Laig Highld 294 G6
Laigh Carnduff S Lnrk 268 F3
Laigh Fenwick E Ayrs 267 G9
Laigh Glengall S Ayrs 257 F8
Laighmuir E Ayrs 267 F9
Laighstonehall S Lnrk 268 E4
Laindon Essex 69 B7
Lair Highld 299 E10
Lair Perth 292 G3
Laira Plym 7 D10
Lairg Highld 309 J5
Lairg Lodge Highld 309 J5
Lairg Muir Highld 309 J5
Lairgmore Highld 300 F5
Laisterdyke W Yorks 205 G9
Laithes Cumb 230 E5
Laithkirk Durham 232 G5
Laity Moor Corn 2 B6
Lake Devon 12 C6
Lake Devon 24 F6
Lake I o W 21 E7
Lake Poole 18 C5
Lake Wilts 46 F6
Lake End Bucks 66 D2
Lakenham Norf 142 B4
Lakenheath Suff 140 G4
Laker's Green Sur 50 F4
Lakesend Norf 139 D10
Lakeside Cumb 211 B7
Lakeside Thurrock 68 D5
Lakeside Worcs 117 C7
Laleham Sur 66 F5
Laleston = Trelales
  Bridgend 57 F11
Lamanva Corn 3 C7
Lamarsh Essex 107 D7
Lamas Norf 160 E4
Lamb Corner Essex 107 E10
Lambden Borders 272 G5
Lamberden Kent 38 B4
Lamberhead Green
  Gtr Man 194 G4
Lamberhurst Kent 53 E7

Lamberhurst Quarter
  Kent 53 E7
Lamberton Borders 273 D8
Lambert's End W Mid 133 E9
Lambeth London 67 D10
Lambfoot Cumb 229 E9
Lambhill Glasgow 267 B11
Lamborough Aberds 303 G9
Lambourn W Berks 63 D10
Lambourne
  Woodlands
  W Berks 63 D10
Lambourne Corn 4 E5
Lambourne End Essex 87 G7
Lambridge Bath 61 F9
Lambs' Cross Kent 53 D9
Lamesley T & W 243 F7
Laminess Orkney 314 C6
Lamington Highld 301 B7
Lamington S Lnrk 259 C11
Lamlash N Ayrs 256 C2
Lamledra Corn 5 G10
Lamloch Dumfries 246 D2
Lammack Blkburn 195 B7
Lamonby Cumb 230 D4
Lamorick Corn 5 C10
Lamorna Corn 1 E4
Lamorran Corn 5 G7
Lampardbrook Suff 126 E5
Lampeter =
  Llanbedr Pont Steffan
  Ceredig 93 B11
Lampeter Velfrey
  Pembs 73 C11
Lamphey Pembs 73 E8
Lamplugh Cumb 229 F7
Lamport Northants 120 C5
Lampton London 66 D6
Lamyatt Som 45 F7
Lana Devon 12 B2
Lana Devon 24 F4
Lanark S Lnrk 269 G7
Lancaster Lancs 211 G9
Lanchester Durham 233 B9
Lancing W Sus 35 G11
Land Gate Gtr Man 194 G5
Landbeach Cambs 123 D9
Landcross Devon 25 C7
Landerberry Aberds 293 C9
Landewednack Corn 2 G6
Landford Wilts 32 D3
Landford Manor Wilts 32 C3
Landfordwood Wilts 32 C3
Landguard Manor I o W 21 E7
Landhill Devon 12 B4
Landican Mers 182 D3
Landimore Swansea 56 C3
Landkey Devon 40 G5
Landkey Newland Devon 40 G5
Landore Swansea 57 B7
Landport E Sus 36 E6
Landport Ptsmth 33 G10
Landrake Corn 7 C7
Landscove Devon 8 B5
Landshipping Pembs 73 C8
Landshipping Quay
  Pembs 73 C8
Landslow Green
  Gtr Man 185 B7
Landulph Corn 7 C8
Landwade Suff 124 D2
Landywood Staffs 133 B9
Lane Corn 4 C6
Lane Bottom Lancs 204 F3
Lane Bottom W Yorks 205 F7
Lane End Bucks 84 G4
Lane End Cumb 220 G2
Lane End Derbys 170 C6
Lane End Devon 24 G6
Lane End Dorset 18 C3
Lane End Flint 166 C3
Lane End Hants 33 B11
Lane End I o W 21 D9
Lane End Kent 68 E5
Lane End Lancs 204 D3
Lane End S Yorks 186 B5
Lane End Sur 49 G10
Lane Ends Cumb 210 C6
Lane Ends Derbys 152 C4
Lane Ends E Ches 168 D2
Lane Ends Gtr Man 185 C7
Lane Ends Lancs 194 B6
Lane Ends Lancs 203 C11
Lane Ends Lancs 204 E5
Lane Ends N Yorks 204 E6
Lane Ends Stoke 168 G5
Lane Green Staffs 133 C7
Lane Head Derbys 185 F11
Lane Head Durham 224 C2
Lane Head Gtr Man 183 B10
Lane Head Pembs 73 E8
Lane Head W Mid 133 C9
Lane Head W Yorks 197 F7
Lane Heads Lancs 202 F4
Lane Side Lancs 195 C9
Laneast Notts 188 F4
Laneham Notts 188 F4
Lanehead Durham 232 C2
Lanehead Northumb 251 F7
Lanehouse Dorset 17 F8
Lanercost Cumb 240 E3
Lanes End Bucks 84 D6
Lane's End Shrops 132 G2
Lanescot Corn 5 D11
Lanesend Pembs 73 D9
Lanesfield W Mid 133 D8
Laneshaw Bridge Lancs 204 E4
Laney Green Staffs 133 B9
Lanfach Caerph 78 F2
Langaford Devon 12 B4
Langage Devon 7 D11
Langal Highld 289 C9
Langaller Som 28 B2
Langar Notts 154 C4
Langbank Renfs 277 G7
Langbar N Yorks 205 C7
Langbank N Yorks 205 C7
Langburnshiels Borders 250 C2
Langcliffe N Yorks 212 G6
Langdale Ho Highld 308 E6
Langdale End N Yorks 227 G8
Langdon Corn 12 D2
Langdon Beck Durham 232 F3
Langdon Hills Essex 69 B7
Langdown Hants 32 F6
Langdyke Dumfries 238 C2
Langdyke Fife 287 G7

Langenhoe Essex 89 B8
Langford C Beds 104 C3
Langford Devon 14 A4
Langford Devon 27 G8
Langford Essex 88 D4
Langford Notts 172 D4
Langford Oxon 82 E2
Langford Som 28 B2
Langford Budville Som 27 C10
Langford Green N Som 44 B3
Langham Dorset 30 B4
Langham Essex 107 E10
Langham Norf 177 E8
Langham Rutland 154 G6
Langham Som 28 B4
Langham Suff 125 C9
Langhaugh Borders 260 C6
Langho Blkburn 203 G10
Langholm Dumfries 249 G11
Langleeford Northumb 263 D10
Langley Ches 184 G6
Langley Derbys 170 F6
Langley Essex 105 D8
Langley Glos 99 F11
Langley Gtr Man 195 F11
Langley Hants 32 G6
Langley Herts 104 G4
Langley Kent 53 C10
Langley Northumb 241 E8
Langley Oxon 82 A4
Langley Slough 66 D4
Langley Som 27 B9
Langley W Mid 133 F9
Langley W Sus 34 A4
Langley Warks 118 E3
Langley Burrell Wilts 62 D2
Langley Common
  Derbys 152 B5
Langley Corner Bucks 66 C4
Langley Green Derbys 152 B5
Langley Green W Mid 133 F9
Langley Green W Sus 51 F9
Langley Green Warks 118 E3
Langley Heath Kent 53 C10
Langley Marsh Som 27 B9
Langley Mill Derbys 170 F6
Langley Moor Durham 233 C11
Langley Park Durham 233 C10
Langley Street Norf 143 C7
Langley Vale Sur 51 B8
Langleybury Herts 85 E9
Langloan N Lnrk 268 C4
Langney E Sus 23 E10
Langold Notts 187 D9
Langore Corn 12 D2
Langport Som 28 B6
Langrick Lincs 174 F3
Langrick Bridge Lincs 174 F3
Langridge Bath 61 F8
Langridge Ford Devon 25 C8
Langrigg Cumb 229 C9
Langrish Hants 34 C2
Langsett S Yorks 197 G8
Langshaw Borders 262 B2
Langside Glasgow 267 C11
Langside Perth 285 F11
Langskaill Orkney 314 B4
Langstone Devon 13 C10
Langstone Hants 22 C2
Langstone Newport 78 G5
Langthorne N Yorks 224 G5
Langthorpe N Yorks 215 F7
Langthwaite N Yorks 223 E10
Langtoft E Yorks 217 F10
Langtoft Lincs 156 G2
Langton Durham 224 B3
Langton Lincs 174 B2
Langton Lincs 190 G5
Langton by Wragby
  Lincs 189 F11
Langton Green Kent 52 F4
Langton Green Suff 126 C3
Langton Herring Dorset 17 E8
Langton Long Blandford
  Dorset 30 F5
Langton Matravers
  Dorset 18 E6
Langtree Devon 25 D7
Langtree Week Devon 25 D7
Langwathby Cumb 231 E7
Langwell Ho Highld 311 G5
Langwell Lodge Highld 307 J6
Langwith Derbys 171 B8
Langwith Junction
  Derbys 171 B8
Langworth Lincs 189 F9
Langworthy Devon 12 E3
Lanham Green Essex 106 G5
Lanivet Corn 5 C10
Lanjeth Corn 5 E9
Lanjew Corn 5 D9
Lank Corn 11 F7
Lanlivery Corn 5 D11
Lanner Corn 2 B6
Lanreath Corn 6 D2
Lansallos Corn 6 E3
Lansbury Park Caerph 59 B7
Lansdown Bath 61 F8
Lansdown Glos 99 G8
Lanstephan Corn 11 E11
Lanteglos Highway Corn 6 E2
Lanton Borders 262 D4
Lanton Northumb 263 D11
Lantuel Corn 5 B9
Lantyan Corn 6 D2
Lapal W Mid 133 G9
Lapford Devon 26 F2
Lapford Cross Devon 26 F2
Laphroaig Argyll 254 C4
Lapley Staffs 151 F7
Lapworth Warks 118 C3
Larachbeg Highld 289 E8
Larbert Falk 279 E7
Larbreck Lancs 202 E4
Larches Lancs 202 G6
Larden Green E Ches 167 E9
Larg Highld 292 A5
Largie Aberds 302 F6
Largiebaan Argyll 255 G7
Largiemore Argyll 275 E10
Largoward Fife 287 G8
Largs N Ayrs 266 D4
Largue Aberds 302 E6
Largybeg N Ayrs 256 D2
Largymeanoch N Ayrs 256 D2
Largymore N Ayrs 256 D2
Lark Hill Gtr Man 195 G7
Larkfield Inverclyd 276 F4

Larkfield Kent 53 B8
Larkfield W Yorks 205 F10
Larkhall Bath 61 F9
Larkhall S Lnrk 268 E5
Larkhill Wilts 46 E6
Larklands Derbys 171 G7
Larks' Hill Suff 108 B3
Larling Norf 141 F9
Larport Hereford 97 D11
Larrick Corn 12 F2
Larriston Borders 250 E2
Lartington Durham 223 B10
Lary Aberds 292 C5
Lasborough Glos 80 G4
Lasham Hants 49 E7
Lashenden Kent 53 E10
Lask Edge Staffs 168 D6
Lassington Glos 98 G5
Lassodie Fife 280 C2
Lastingham N Yorks 226 G4
Latcham Som 44 D2
Latchbrook Corn 7 D8
Latchford Herts 105 G7
Latchford Oxon 83 E11
Latchford Warr 183 D11
Latchingdon Essex 88 E5
Latchley Corn 12 G4
Latchmere Green Hants 64 G6
Lately Common Warr 183 B11
Lathallan Mill Fife 287 G8
Lathbury M Keynes 103 B7
Latheron Highld 310 F5
Latheronwheel Highld 310 F5
Latheronwheel Ho
  Highld 310 F5
Lathom Lancs 194 E3
Lathones Fife 287 G8
Latimer Bucks 85 F8
Latteridge S Glos 61 C7
Lattiford Som 29 B11
Lattinford Hill Suff 107 D11
Latton Wilts 81 F9
Latton Bush Essex 87 D7
Lauchintilly Aberds 293 B9
Laudale Ho Highld 289 D8
Lauder Borders 271 F10
Lauder Barns Borders 271 F10
Laugharne =
  Talacharn Carms 74 C4
Laughern Hill Worcs 116 F5
Laughterton Lincs 188 F4
Laughton E Sus 23 C8
Laughton Leics 136 F3
Laughton Lincs 155 C11
Laughton Lincs 188 B4
Laughton Common
  S Yorks 187 D8
Laughton en le
  Morthen S Yorks 187 D8
Launcells Corn 24 F2
Launcells Cross Corn 24 F2
Launceston Corn 12 D2
Launcherley Som 44 E4
Laund Lancs 195 C10
Launton Oxon 102 G2
Laurencekirk Aberds 293 F9
Laurieston Dumfries 237 C8
Laurieston Falk 279 F8
Lavender M Keynes 121 G8
Lavendon M Keynes 121 G8
Lavenham Suff 107 B8
Laverackloch Moray 301 C11
Laverhay Dumfries 248 D4
Laverlaw Borders 261 B7
Laverley Som 44 E5
Lavernock V Glam 59 F7
Laversdale Cumb 239 E11
Laverstock Wilts 47 G7
Laverstoke Hants 48 D3
Laverton Glos 99 D11
Laverton N Yorks 214 E4
Laverton Som 45 C9
Lavister Wrex 166 D5
Lavrean Corn 5 D10
Law Hill S Lnrk 268 E6
Lawers Perth 285 D10
Lawers Perth 285 E11
Lawford Essex 107 E11
Lawford Som 42 F6
Lawhill Perth 286 F3
Lawhitton Corn 12 E3
Lawkland N Yorks 212 F5
Lawkland Green N Yorks 212 F5
Lawley Telford 132 B3
Lawnhead Staffs 150 E6
Lawns W Yorks 197 C10
Lawnswood W Yorks 205 F11
Lawnt Denb 165 B8
Lawrenny Pembs 73 D8
Lawrence Weston
  Bristol 60 D4
Lawrenny Quay Pembs 73 D8
Lawshall Suff 125 G7
Lawshall Green Suff 125 G7
Lawton Hereford 115 F9
Lawton Shrops 131 G10
Lawton-gate E Ches 168 D4
Lawton Heath End
  E Ches 168 D4
Laxey I o M 192 D5
Laxfield Suff 126 C5
Laxfirth Shetland 313 H6
Laxfirth Shetland 313 J6
Laxford Bridge Highld 306 E7
Laxo Shetland 313 G6
Laxobigging Shetland 312 F6
Laxton E Yorks 199 B8
Laxton Northants 137 D7
Laxton Notts 172 B2
Laycock N Yorks 204 E6
Layer Breton Essex 88 B6
Layer de la Haye Essex 89 B7
Layer Marney Essex 88 B6
Layerthorpe York 207 C8
Layham Suff 107 C10
Laymore Dorset 28 G4
Layters Green Bucks 85 G7
Laytham E Yorks 207 F10
Layton Blkpool 202 F2
Lazonby Cumb 230 D6
Le Skerne Haughton
  Darl 224 B6
Lea Derbys 170 D4
Lea Hereford 98 G3
Lea Lincs 188 E4
Lea Shrops 131 B8
Lea Shrops 131 F8
Lea Wilts 62 B3
Lea Bridge London 67 B11
Lea by Backford
  W Ches 182 G5
Lea End Worcs 117 B10
Lea Forge E Ches 168 E2
Lea Green Mers 183 C8

Lea Hall W Mid 134 F2
Lea Heath Staffs 151 D10
Lea Line Hereford 98 G3
Lea Marston Warks 134 E4
Lea Town Lancs 202 G5
Lea Valley Herts 85 B11
Lea Yeat Cumb 212 B5
Leabrooks Derbys 170 E6
Leac a' Li W Isles 305 J3
Leacainn W Isles 305 H3
Leachkin Highld 300 E6
Leacnasaide Highld 299 B7
Leadburn Midloth 270 D4
Leaden Roding Essex 87 C9
Leadendale Staffs 151 B8
Leadenham Lincs 173 E7
Leadgate Cumb 231 C10
Leadgate Durham 242 G4
Leadgate T & W 242 F4
Leadhills S Lnrk 259 G9
Leadingcross Green
  Kent 53 C11
Leadmill Derbys 186 E2
Leadmill Flint 166 C2
Leafield Oxon 82 B4
Leafield Wilts 61 F11
Leagrave Luton 103 G10
Leagreen Hants 19 C11
Leake Lincs 174 F6
Leake N Yorks 225 G8
Leake Commonside
  Lincs 174 E5
Leake Fold Hill Lincs 174 E6
Lealham N Yorks 226 D5
Lealham Side N Yorks 226 D5
Lealt Argyll 275 C8
Lealt Highld 298 C5
Leam Derbys 186 F2
Leamington Hastings
  Warks 119 D8
Leamoor Common
  Shrops 131 F8
Leamore W Mid 133 C9
Leamside Durham 234 B2
Leanach Argyll 275 D11
Leanachan Highld 290 F4
Leanaig Highld 300 D5
Leapgate Worcs 116 C6
Leargybreck Argyll 274 F6
Lease Rigg N Yorks 226 E6
Leasey Bridge Herts 85 C11
Leasgill Cumb 211 C9
Leasingham Lincs 173 F9
Leasingthorne Durham 233 F11
Leason Swansea 56 C3
Leasowe Mers 182 C3
Leatherhead Sur 51 B7
Leatherhead
  Common Sur 51 B7
Leathern Bottle Glos 80 E2
Leathley N Yorks 205 D10
Leaths Dumfries 237 C9
Leaton Shrops 149 F9
Leaton Telford 150 G2
Leaton Heath Shrops 149 F9
Leaveland Kent 54 C4
Leavenheath Suff 107 D9
Leavening N Yorks 216 G5
Leaves Green London 68 G2
Leavesden Green Herts 85 E9
Leazes Durham 242 F5
Lebberston N Yorks 217 C11
Leburnick Corn 12 E3
Lechlade-on-Thames
  Glos 82 F2
Leck Lancs 212 D2
Leckford Hants 47 F11
Leckfurin Highld 308 D7
Leckgruinart Argyll 274 G3
Leckhampstead
  W Berks 64 D2
Leckhampstead
  Thicket W Berks 64 D2
Leckhampton Glos 80 B6
Leckie Highld 299 C9
Leckmelm Highld 307 K6
Leckuary Argyll 275 D9
Leckwith V Glam 59 E7
Leconfield E Yorks 208 E6
Ledaig Argyll 289 F11
Ledburn Bucks 103 G8
Ledbury Hereford 98 D4
Ledcharrie Stirl 285 E9
Leddington Glos 98 E3
Ledgemoor Hereford 115 G8
Ledgowan Highld 299 D11
Ledicot Hereford 115 E8
Ledmore Angus 293 G7
Ledmore Highld 307 H7
Lednagullin Highld 308 C7
Ledsham W Ches 182 F5
Ledsham W Yorks 198 B3
Ledston W Yorks 198 B2
Ledston Luck W Yorks 206 G4
Ledstone Devon 8 F4
Ledwell Oxon 101 F8
Lee Argyll 288 G6
Lee Devon 40 D3
Lee Devon 40 D5
Lee Hants 32 D5
Lee Lancs 203 B7
Lee London 67 E11
Lee Northumb 241 F10
Lee Shrops 149 C8
Lee Bank W Mid 133 F11
Lee Brockhurst
  Shrops 149 D10
Lee Chapel Essex 69 B7
Lee Clump Bucks 84 E6
Lee Common Bucks 84 E6
Lee Gate Bucks 84 D5
Lee Ground Hants 33 F8
Lee Head Derbys 185 C8
Lee Mill Devon 7 D11
Lee Moor Devon 7 C11
Lee Moor W Yorks 197 B11
Lee-on-the-Solent
  Hants 33 G9
Lee-over-Sands Essex 89 C10
Leeans Shetland 313 J5
Leebotten Shetland 313 L6
Leebotwood Shrops 131 D9
Leece Cumb 210 F4
Leechpool Mon 60 B4
Leeds Kent 53 C10
Leeds W Yorks 205 G11
Leedstown Corn 2 C5
Leeford Devon 41 D9
Leegomery Telford 150 G3
Leeholme Durham 233 E10
Leek Staffs 169 D7
Leek Wootton Warks 118 D5
Leekbrook Staffs 169 E7
Leeming N Yorks 214 B5
Leeming W Yorks 204 G6
Leeming Bar N Yorks 224 G5
Lees Derbys 152 B5
Lees Gtr Man 196 G3

382 Lee – Lla

Lees W Yorks 204 F6
Leesthorpe Leics 154 G5
Leeswood = Coed-Llai Flint 166 D3
Leetown Perth 286 E6
Leftwich W Ches 183 G11
Legar Powys 78 B2
Legbourne Lincs 190 E5
Legburthwaite Cumb 220 B6
Legerwood Borders 271 G11
Leggatt Hill W Sus 34 C6
Legsby Lincs 189 D10
Leicester Leicester 135 C11
Leicester Forest East Leics 135 C10
Leicester Grange Warks 135 E8
Leigh Devon 26 E2
Leigh Dorset 18 B6
Leigh Dorset 29 F10
Leigh Dorset 30 F3
Leigh Glos 99 F7
Leigh Gtr Man 195 G7
Leigh Kent 52 D4
Leigh Shrops 130 C6
Leigh Sur 51 D8
Leigh Wilts 81 G9
Leigh Worcs 116 G5
Leigh Beck Essex 69 C10
Leigh Common Som 30 B2
Leigh Delamere Wilts 61 D11
Leigh Green Kent 54 G2
Leigh-on-Sea Sthend 69 B10
Leigh Park Hants 22 B2
Leigh Sinton Worcs 116 G5
Leigh upon Mendip Som 45 D7
Leigh Woods N Som 60 E5
Leigham Plym 7 D10
Leighland Chapel Som 42 F4
Leighswood W Mid 133 C11
Leighterton Glos 80 G4
Leighton N Yorks 214 D3
Leighton Shrops 132 B2
Leighton Som 45 E8
Leighton = Tre'r llai Powys 130 B4
Leighton Bromswold Cambs 122 B2
Leighton Buzzard C Beds 103 F8
Leinthall Earls Hereford 115 D8
Leinthall Starkes Hereford 115 D8
Leintwardine Hereford 115 C8
Leire Leics 135 E10
Leirinmore Highld 308 C4
Leiston Suff 127 E8
Leitfie Perth 286 C6
Leith Edin 280 F5
Leithenhall Dumfries 248 D4
Leitholm Borders 272 G5
Lelant Corn 2 B2
Lelant Downs Corn 2 B2
Lelley E Yorks 209 G10
Lem Hill Worcs 116 C4
Lemington T & W 242 E5
Lemmington Hall Northumb 264 G4
Lempitlaw Borders 263 C7
Lemsford Herts 86 C2
Lenacre Cumb 212 B3
Lenborough Bucks 102 E3
Lenchwick Worcs 99 B10
Lendalfoot S Ayrs 244 F4
Lendrick Lodge Stirl 285 G9
Lenham Kent 53 C11
Lenham Forstal Kent 54 C2
Lenham Heath Kent 54 D2
Lennel Borders 273 G7
Lennoxtown E Dunb 278 F2
Lent Bucks 66 C2
Lent Rise Bucks 66 C2
Lenten Pool Denb 165 B8
Lenton Lincs 155 C10
Lenton Nottingham 153 B11
Lenton Abbey Nottingham 153 B10
Lentran Highld 300 E5
Lenwade Norf 159 F11
Leny Ho Stirl 285 G10
Lenzie E Dunb 278 G3
Lenziemill N Lnrk 278 G5
Leoch Angus 287 D7
Leochel-Cushnie Aberds 293 B7
Leominster Hereford 115 F9
Leomonsley Staffs 134 B2
Leonard Stanley Glos 80 E4
Leonardston Pembs 72 D6
Leorin Argyll 254 C4
Lepe Hants 20 B5
Lephin Highld 297 G7
Lephinchapel Argyll 275 D10
Lephinmore Argyll 275 D10
Leppington N Yorks 216 G5
Lepton W Yorks 197 D8
Lepton Edge W Yorks 197 D8
Lerigoligan Argyll 275 C9
Lerrocks Stirl 285 G11
Lerryn Corn 6 D2
Lerwick Shetland 313 J6
Lesbury Northumb 264 G6
Leschangie Aberds 293 B9
Leslie Aberds 302 G5
Leslie Fife 286 G6
Lesmahagow S Lnrk 259 B8
Lesnewth Corn 11 C8
Lessendrum Aberds 302 E5
Lessingham Norf 161 D7
Lessness Heath London 68 D3
Lessonhall Cumb 238 G6
Leswalt Dumfries 236 C2
Letchmore Heath Herts 85 F11
Letchworth Herts 104 E4
Letcombe Bassett Oxon 63 B11
Letcombe Regis Oxon 63 B11
Letham Angus 287 C9
Letham Falk 279 D7
Letham Fife 287 F7
Letham Perth 286 E4
Letham Grange Angus 287 C10
Lethem Borders 250 B5
Lethen Ho Highld 301 D9
Lethenty Aberds 303 E8
Lethenty Aberds 303 G7
Letheringham Suff 126 F5
Letheringsett Norf 159 B11
Lettaford Devon 13 E10
Lettan Orkney 314 B7
Letter Aberds 293 B9
Letterewe Highld 299 B9
Letterfearn Highld 295 C10
Letterfinlay Highld 290 D4
Lettermay Argyll 284 G5
Lettermorar Highld 295 G9
Lettermore Argyll 288 E6
Letters Highld 307 L6
Letterston = Treletert Pembs 91 F8
Lettoch Highld 292 B2
Lettoch Highld 301 F10
Lettoch Moray 302 F3
Lettoch Perth 291 G11
Letton Hereford 96 B6
Letton Hereford 115 C7
Letton Green Norf 141 B9
Lett's Green Kent 52 B3
Letty Brongu Bridgend 57 D11
Letty Green Herts 86 C3
Letwell S Yorks 187 D9
Leuchars Fife 287 E8
Leuchars Ho Moray 302 C2
Leumrabhagh W Isles 305 G5
Levalsa Meor Corn 5 F10
Levan Invclyd 276 F4
Levaneap Shetland 313 G6
Levedale Staffs 151 F7
Level of Mendalgief Newport 59 B10
Level's Green Essex 105 G9
Leven E Yorks 209 D8
Leven Fife 287 G7
Leven Seat W Loth 269 D8
Levencorroch N Ayrs 256 E2
Levenhall E Loth 281 G7
Levens Cumb 211 B9
Levens Green Herts 105 G7
Levenshulme Gtr Man 184 C5
Leventhorpe W Yorks 205 G8
Levenwick Shetland 313 L6
Lever-Edge Gtr Man 195 F8
Leverington Cambs 157 G8
Leverington Common Cambs 157 G8
Leverstock Green Herts 85 D9
Leverton Lincs 174 F6
Leverton W Berks 63 E10
Leverton Highgate Lincs 174 F6
Leverton Lucasgate Lincs 174 F6
Leverton Outgate Lincs 174 F6
Levington Suff 108 D4
Levisham N Yorks 226 G6
Levishie Highld 290 B6
Lew Oxon 82 D4
Lewannick Corn 11 E11
Lewcombe Dorset 29 F9
Lewdown Devon 12 D4
Lewes E Sus 36 E6
Leweston Pembs 91 G8
Lewisham London 67 D11
Lewiston Highld 300 G5
Lewistown Bridgend 58 B2
Lewknor Oxon 84 F2
Leworthy Devon 24 G4
Leworthy Devon 41 F7
Lewson Street Kent 70 G3
Lewth Lancs 202 F5
Lewthorn Cross Devon 13 F11
Lewtrenchard Devon 12 D5
Lexden Essex 107 G9
Ley Aberds 293 B7
Ley Corn 6 B3
Ley Som 41 F10
Ley Green Herts 104 G3
Ley Hey Park Gtr Man 185 D7
Ley Hill W Mid 134 D2
Leybourne Kent 53 B7
Leyburn N Yorks 224 G2
Leycett Staffs 168 F3
Leyfields Staffs 134 B4
Leyhill Bucks 85 E7
Leyhill S Glos 79 G11
Leyland Lancs 194 C4
Leylodge Aberds 293 B9
Leymoor W Yorks 196 D6
Leys Aberds 292 C6
Leys Aberds 303 D10
Leys Cumb 219 B11
Leys Perth 286 D6
Leys Staffs 169 F8
Leys Castle Highld 300 E6
Leys Hill Hereford 79 B9
Leys of Cossans Angus 287 C7
Leysdown-on-Sea Kent 70 E4
Leysmill Angus 287 C10
Leysters Hereford 115 E11
Leysters Pole Hereford 115 E11
Leyton London 67 B11
Leytonstone London 67 B11
Lezant Corn 12 F2
Lezerea Corn 2 C5
Leziate Norf 158 F3
Lhanbryde Moray 302 C2
Liatrie Highld 300 F2
Libanus Powys 95 F9
Libberton S Lnrk 269 G9
Libbery Worcs 117 F9
Liberton Edin 270 B5
Liceasto W Isles 305 J3
Lichfield Staffs 134 B2
Lick Perth 286 B2
Lickey Worcs 117 B9
Lickey End Worcs 117 C9
Lickfold W Sus 34 B6
Lickhill Worcs 116 C6
Lickleyhead Castle Aberds 302 G6
Liddaton Devon 12 E5
Liddel Orkney 314 H4
Liddesdale Highld 289 D9
Liddeston Pembs 72 D5
Liddington Swindon 63 C8
Liden Swindon 63 C7
Lidgate Suff 124 F4
Lidget S Yorks 199 G7
Lidget Green W Yorks 205 G8
Lidgett Notts 171 B10
Lidgett Park W Yorks 206 F2
Lidham Hill E Sus 38 D4
Lidlington C Beds 103 D9
Lidsey W Sus 22 C6
Lidsing Kent 69 G9
Lidstone Oxon 101 G7
Lieurary Highld 310 C4
Liff Angus 287 D7
Lifford W Mid 117 B11
Lifton Devon 12 D3
Liftondown Devon 12 D3
Light Oaks Staffs 168 E6
Lightcliffe W Yorks 196 B6
Lighteach Shrops 149 C10
Lightfoot Green Lancs 202 G6
Lighthorne Warks 118 F6
Lighthorne Heath Warks 119 F7
Lighthorne Rough Warks 118 F6
Lightmoor Telford 132 B3
Lightpill Glos 80 E4
Lightwater Sur 66 G2
Lightwood S Yorks 186 E5
Lightwood Shrops 132 E2
Lightwood Shrops 150 D3
Lightwood Staffs 169 G8
Lightwood Stoke 168 G6
Lightwood Green E Ches 167 G10
Lightwood Green Wrex 166 G5
Lilgartrie S Ayrs 244 F6
Lilbourne Northants 119 B11
Lilburn Tower Northumb 264 E2
Lilford Gtr Man 195 G7
Lillesdon Som 28 C4
Lilleshall Telford 150 F4
Lilley Herts 104 F2
Lilley W Berks 64 D2
Lilliesleaf Borders 262 E2
Lillingstone Dayrell Bucks 102 D4
Lillingstone Lovell Bucks 102 C4
Lillington Dorset 29 E10
Lillington Warks 118 D6
Lilliput Poole 18 C6
Lilstock Som 43 E7
Lilybank Invclyd 276 G6
Lilyhurst Shrops 150 G4
Lilyvale Kent 54 F5
Limbrick Lancs 194 D6
Limbury Luton 103 G11
Lime Side Gtr Man 196 G2
Lime Street Worcs 98 E6
Lime Tree Park W Mid 118 B5
Limebrook Hereford 115 D7
Limefield Gtr Man 195 E10
Limehouse London 67 C11
Limehurst Gtr Man 196 G2
Limekiln Field Derbys 187 G7
Limekilnburn S Lnrk 268 E4
Limekilns Fife 279 E11
Limerigg Falk 279 G7
Limerstone I o W 20 E4
Limestone Brae Northumb 231 B11
Limington Som 29 C8
Limpenhoe Norf 143 C7
Limpenhoe Hill Norf 143 C8
Limpers Hill Wilts 45 G10
Limpley Stoke Wilts 61 G9
Limpsfield Sur 52 C2
Limpsfield Chart Sur 52 C2
Limpsfield Common Sur 52 C2
Linbriggs Northumb 251 B9
Linburn W Loth 270 B2
Linby Notts 171 E8
Linchmere W Sus 49 G11
Lincluden Dumfries 237 B11
Lincoln Lincs 189 G7
Lincomb Worcs 116 D6
Lincombe Devon 8 D4
Lincombe Devon 40 D3
Lindal in Furness Cumb 210 D5
Lindale Cumb 211 C8
Lindean Borders 261 C11
Linden Glos 80 B4
Lindfield W Sus 36 B4
Lindford Hants 49 F10
Lindifferon Fife 287 F7
Lindley N Yorks 205 D10
Lindley W Yorks 196 D6
Lindley Green N Yorks 205 D10
Lindores Fife 286 F6
Lindow End E Ches 184 F4
Lindrick Dale S Yorks 187 E8
Lindridge Worcs 116 D3
Lindsell Essex 106 F2
Lindsey Suff 107 C9
Lindsey Tye Suff 107 B9
Lindwell W Yorks 196 C5
Lineholt Worcs 116 D6
Lineholt Common Worcs 116 D6
Liney Som 43 F11
Linfitts Gtr Man 196 F3
Linford Hants 31 F11
Linford Thurrock 69 D7
Lingague I o M 192 E3
Lingards Wood W Yorks 196 E5
Lingbob W Yorks 205 F7
Lingdale Redcar 226 B3
Lingen Hereford 115 D7
Lingfield Darl 224 C6
Lingfield Sur 51 E11
Lingfield Common Sur 51 E11
Lingley Green Warr 183 D9
Lingley Mere Warr 183 D10
Lingreabhagh W Isles 296 C6
Lingwood Norf 143 B7
Linhope Borders 249 C10
Linhope Northumb 263 F11
Linicro Highld 298 C3
Link N Som 44 B3
Linkend Worcs 98 E6
Linkenholt Hants 47 B11
Linkhill Kent 38 B4
Linkinhorne Corn 12 G2
Linklater Orkney 314 H4
Linklet Orkney 314 A7
Linksness Orkney 314 E5
Linksness Orkney 314 F2
Linktown Fife 280 C5
Linley Shrops 131 E7
Linley Shrops 132 D3
Linley Brook Shrops 132 D3
Linley Green Hereford 116 G3
Linleygreen Shrops 132 D3
Linlithgow W Loth 279 F10
Linlithgow Bridge W Loth 279 F9
Linndhu Ho Argyll 289 D7
Linneraineach Highld 307 J6
Linns Angus 292 F3
Linnyshaw Gtr Man 195 G8
Linshiels Northumb 251 B9
Linsiadar W Isles 304 E4
Linsidemore Highld 309 K5
Linslade C Beds 103 F8
Linstead Parva Suff 126 B6
Linstock Cumb 239 F10
Linthorpe M'bro 225 B9
Linthurst Worcs 117 C9
Linthwaite W Yorks 196 E6
Lintlaw Borders 272 D6
Lintmill Moray 302 C5
Linton Borders 263 D7
Linton Cambs 105 B11
Linton Derbys 152 F5
Linton Hereford 98 F3
Linton Kent 53 D9
Linton N Yorks 213 G9
Linton Northumb 253 E7
Linton W Yorks 206 D3
Linton Heath Derbys 152 F5
Linton Hill Hereford 98 G3
Linton-on-Ouse N Yorks 215 G9
Lintridge Glos 98 E4
Lintz Durham 242 F5
Lintzford T & W 242 F4
Lintzgarth Durham 232 C4
Linwood Hants 31 F11
Linwood Lincs 189 D10
Linwood Renfs 267 C8
Lionacleit W Isles 297 G3
Lional W Isles 304 B7
Lions Green E Sus 23 B9
Liphook Hants 49 G10
Lipley Shrops 150 C4
Lippitts Hill Essex 86 F5
Liquo or Bowhousebog N Lnrk 269 D7
Liscard Mers 182 C4
Liscombe Som 41 G11
Liskeard Corn 6 C5
Liss Hants 34 B3
Liss Forest Hants 34 B3
Lissett E Yorks 209 B8
Lissington Lincs 189 E10
Lisson Grove London 67 C9
Listerdale S Yorks 187 C7
Listock Som 28 C4
Listoft Lincs 191 G8
Liston Essex 107 C7
Liston Garden Essex 106 B6
Lisvane Cardiff 59 C7
Liswerry Newport 59 B10
Litcham Norf 159 F7
Litchard Bridgend 58 C2
Litchborough Northants 120 G2
Litchfield Hants 48 C3
Litchurch Derbys 153 B7
Litherland Mers 182 B4
Litlington Cambs 104 C6
Litlington E Sus 23 E8
Litmarsh Hereford 97 B10
Little Abington Cambs 105 B10
Little Addington Northants 121 C9
Little Airmyn E Yorks 199 B8
Little Almshoe Herts 104 F3
Little Alne Warks 118 E2
Little Altcar Mers 193 F10
Little Ann Hants 47 E10
Little Arowry Wrex 167 G7
Little Asby Cumb 222 D3
Little Ashley Wilts 61 G10
Little Assynt Highld 307 G6
Little Aston Staffs 133 C11
Little Atherfield I o W 20 E5
Little Ayre Orkney 314 G3
Little-ayre Shetland 313 G5
Little Ayton N Yorks 225 C11
Little Baddow Essex 88 D3
Little Badminton S Glos 61 C10
Little Ballinluig Perth 286 B3
Little Bampton Cumb 239 F7
Little Bardfield Essex 106 E3
Little Barford Beds 122 F3
Little Barningham Norf 160 C2
Little Barrington Glos 82 C2
Little Barrow W Ches 183 G7
Little Barugh N Yorks 216 D5
Little Bavington Northumb 241 B11
Little Bayham E Sus 52 F6
Little Bealings Suff 108 B4
Little Beckford Glos 99 E9
Little Bedwyn Wilts 63 F9
Little Bentley Essex 108 F2
Little Berkhamsted Herts 86 D3
Little Billing Northants 120 E6
Little Billington C Beds 103 G8
Little Birch Hereford 97 E10
Little Bispham Blkpool 202 E2
Little Blakenham Suff 108 B2
Little Blencow Cumb 230 E5
Little Bloxwich W Mid 133 C10
Little Bognor W Sus 35 C8
Little Bolehill Derbys 170 E3
Little Bollington E Ches 184 D2
Little Bolton Gtr Man 184 B3
Little Bookham Sur 50 C6
Little Bosullow Corn 1 C4
Little Bourton Oxon 101 C9
Little Bowden Leics 136 F4
Little Boys Heath Bucks 84 F6
Little Bradley Suff 124 G3
Little Braithwaite Cumb 229 G10
Little Brampton Shrops 131 G7
Little Braxted Essex 88 C4
Little Bray Devon 41 F7
Little Brechin Angus 293 G7
Little Brickhill M Keynes 103 E8
Little Bridgeford Staffs 151 D7
Little Brington Northants 120 E3
Little Bristol S Glos 80 G2
Little Britain Warks 118 G2
Little Bromley Essex 107 F11
Little Bromwich W Mid 134 F2
Little Broughton Cumb 229 E7
Little Budworth W Ches 167 B9
Little Burstead Essex 87 G11
Little Bytham Lincs 155 F10
Little Cambridge Essex 106 F2
Little Canfield Essex 105 G11
Little Canford Poole 18 B6
Little Carleton Lancs 202 F2
Little Carlton Lincs 190 D5
Little Carlton Notts 172 D3
Little Casterton Rutland 137 B10
Little Catwick E Yorks 209 E8
Little Catworth Cambs 122 C2
Little Cawthorpe Lincs 190 E5
Little Chalfield Wilts 61 G11
Little Chalfont Bucks 85 F7
Little Chart Kent 54 D2
Little Chart Forstal Kent 54 D3
Little Chell Stoke 168 E5
Little Chester Derby 153 B7
Little Chesterford Essex 105 C10
Little Chesterton Oxon 101 G11
Little Cheverell Wilts 46 C3
Little Chishill Cambs 105 D8
Little Clacton Essex 89 B11
Little Clanfield Oxon 82 E3
Little Clegg Gtr Man 196 E2
Little Clifton Cumb 229 F7
Little Coates NE Lincs 201 F8
Little Colp Aberds 303 E7
Little Comberton Worcs 99 C9
Little Comfort Corn 12 E2
Little Common E Sus 38 F2
Little Common Lincs 156 D6
Little Common Shrops 115 B7
Little Common W Sus 34 C6
Little Compton Warks 100 E5
Little Corby Cumb 239 F11
Little Cornard Suff 107 D7
Little Cowarne Hereford 116 G2
Little Coxwell Oxon 82 G3
Little Crakehall N Yorks 224 G4
Little Cransley Northants 120 B6
Little Crawley M Keynes 103 B8
Little Creaton Northants 120 C4
Little Creich Highld 309 L6
Little Cressingham Norf 141 D7
Little Crosby Mers 193 G10
Little Cubley Derbys 152 B3
Little Dalby Leics 154 G5
Little Dawley Telford 132 B3
Little Dens Aberds 303 E10
Little Dewchurch Hereford 97 E10
Little Ditton Cambs 124 F3
Little Doward Hereford 79 B8
Little Downham Cambs 139 G10
Little Drayton Shrops 150 C3
Little Driffield E Yorks 208 B6
Little Drybrook Glos 79 D9
Little Dunham Norf 159 G7
Little Dunkeld Perth 286 C4
Little Dunmow Essex 106 G3
Little Durnford Wilts 46 G6
Little Eastbury Worcs 116 F6
Little Easton Essex 106 G2
Little Eaton Derbys 170 G5
Little Eccleston Lancs 202 E4
Little Ellingham Norf 141 D10
Little End Cambs 122 F3
Little End E Yorks 208 F2
Little End Essex 87 E8
Little Everdon Northants 119 F11
Little Eversden Cambs 123 G7
Little Faringdon Oxon 82 E2
Little Fencote N Yorks 224 G5
Little Fenton N Yorks 206 F6
Little Finborough Suff 125 G10
Little Fransham Norf 159 G8
Little Frith Kent 54 B2
Little Gaddesden Herts 85 C7
Little Gidding Cambs 138 G2
Little Gight Aberds 303 F8
Little Glemham Suff 126 F6
Little Glenshee Perth 286 D3
Little Gorsley Glos 98 F3
Little Gransden Cambs 122 F5
Little Green Cambs 104 B5
Little Green Notts 172 G2
Little Green Som 45 D8
Little Green Suff 125 C11
Little Green Wrex 167 G7
Little Grimsby Lincs 190 C4
Little Gringley Notts 188 E2
Little Gruinard Highld 307 L4
Little Habton N Yorks 216 D4
Little Hadham Herts 105 G8
Little Hale Lincs 173 G10
Little Hale Norf 141 B8
Little Hallam Derbys 171 G7
Little Hallingbury Essex 87 B7
Little Hampden Bucks 84 E5
Little Haresfield Glos 80 D4
Little Harrowden Northants 121 C7
Little Harwood Blkburn 195 B7
Little Haseley Oxon 83 E10
Little Hatfield E Yorks 209 E9
Little Hautbois Norf 160 E5
Little Haven Pembs 72 C5
Little Haven W Sus 51 G7
Little Hay Staffs 134 C2
Little Hayfield Derbys 185 D8
Little Haywood Staffs 151 E10
Little Heath E Ches 167 G11
Little Heath Herts 85 D8
Little Heath Herts 86 E3
Little Heath London 68 B3
Little Heath Staffs 151 F8
Little Heath Sur 66 G6
Little Heath W Berks 65 E7
Little Heath W Ches 166 B6
Little Heath W Mid 134 G6
Little Heck N Yorks 198 C5
Little Henham Essex 105 E10
Little Henny Essex 107 D7
Little Herbert's Glos 81 B7
Little Hereford Hereford 115 D11
Little Hill Hereford 97 F9
Little Hill Som 28 E3
Little Holbury Hants 32 G6
Little Honeyborough Pembs 73 D7
Little Hoole Moss Houses Lancs 194 C3
Little Horkesley Essex 107 E9
Little Hormead Herts 105 F8
Little Horsted E Sus 23 B7
Little Horton W Yorks 205 G9
Little Horton Wilts 62 G4
Little Horwood Bucks 102 E5
Little Houghton Northants 120 F6
Little Houghton S Yorks 198 G2
Little Hucklow Derbys 185 F11
Little Hulton Gtr Man 195 G8
Little Humber E Yorks 201 C8
Little Hungerford W Berks 64 E4
Little Ilford London 68 B2
Little Ingestre Staffs 151 E9
Little Inkberrow Worcs 117 F10
Little Irchester Northants 121 D8
Little Keyford Som 45 D9
Little Kimble Bucks 84 D4
Little Kineton Warks 118 G6
Little Kingshill Bucks 84 F5
Little Knowles Green Suff 124 F5
Little Langdale Cumb 220 E6
Little Langford Wilts 46 F4
Little Laver Essex 87 D8
Little Lawford Warks 119 B9
Little Layton Blkpool 202 F2
Little Leigh W Ches 183 F10
Little Leighs Essex 88 B2
Little Lepton W Yorks 197 E8
Little Leven E Yorks 209 D8
Little Lever Gtr Man 195 F9
Little Limber Lincs 200 E6
Little Linford M Keynes 102 C6
Little Load Som 29 C7
Little London Bucks 83 C10
Little London Bucks 84 D5
Little London Cambs 139 D8
Little London E Sus 23 B9
Little London Essex 105 F9
Little London Essex 106 D3
Little London Glos 80 B2
Little London Hants 47 D11
Little London Hants 48 B6
Little London Lincs 156 E4
Little London Lincs 157 E8
Little London Lincs 189 D10
Little London Lincs 190 F4
Little London Norf 140 D5
Little London Norf 160 C2
Little London Norf 160 C5
Little London Norf 160 E3
Little London Oxon 83 E8
Little London Powys 129 F10
Little London Shrops 131 F10
Little London Som 44 D6
Little London Suff 125 F10
Little London W Yorks 205 F10
Little London Worcs 116 C2
Little Longstone Derbys 185 G11
Little Lynturk Aberds 293 B7
Little Lyth Shrops 131 B9
Little Madeley Staffs 168 F3
Little Malvern Worcs 98 C5
Little Mancot Flint 166 B4
Little Maplestead Essex 106 E6
Little Marcle Hereford 98 D3
Little Marlow Bucks 65 B11
Little Marsden Lancs 204 F3
Little Marsh Bucks 102 G3
Little Marsh Norf 159 B10
Little Marsh Wilts 45 B11
Little Marton Blkpool 202 G2
Little Mascalls Essex 88 E2
Little Massingham Norf 158 E5
Little Melton Norf 142 B3
Little Merthyr Hereford 96 B5
Little Milford Pembs 73 C7
Little Mill Kent 53 D7
Little Mill Mon 78 E4
Little Milton Newport 59 B11
Little Milton Oxon 83 E10
Little Minster Oxon 82 C4
Little Missenden Bucks 84 F6
Little Mongeham Kent 55 C10
Little Moor Gtr Man 184 D6
Little Moor Lancs 203 E10
Little Moor End Lancs 195 B8
Little Morrell Warks 118 F6
Little Mountain Flint 166 C3
Little Musgrave Cumb 222 C5
Little Ness Shrops 149 F8
Little Neston W Ches 182 F3
Little Newcastle Pembs 91 F9
Little Newsham Durham 224 B2
Little Norlington E Sus 23 C7
Little Norton Som 29 D7
Little Oakley Essex 108 F4
Little Oakley Northants 137 F7
Little Odell Beds 121 F9
Little Offley Herts 104 F2
Little Onn Staffs 150 F6
Little Ormside Cumb 222 B4
Little Orton Cumb 239 F9
Little Orton Leics 134 B6
Little Ouse Norf 140 F2
Little Ouseburn N Yorks 215 G8
Little Overton Wrex 166 G5
Little Oxney Green Essex 87 D11
Little Packington Warks 134 G4
Little Parndon Essex 86 C6
Little Paxton Cambs 122 E3
Little Petherick Corn 10 G4
Little Pitlurg Moray 302 E4
Little Plumpton Lancs 202 G3
Little Plumstead Norf 160 G6
Little Ponton Lincs 155 C8
Little Posbrook Hants 33 G8
Little Poulton Lancs 202 F3
Little Preston Kent 53 B8
Little Preston W Yorks 206 G3
Little Raveley Cambs 122 B5
Little Reedness E Yorks 199 C10
Little Reynoldston Swansea 56 D3
Little Ribston N Yorks 206 C3
Little Rissington Glos 81 B11
Little Rogart Highld 309 J7
Little Rollright Oxon 100 E5
Little Ryburgh Norf 159 D9
Little Ryle Northumb 264 G2
Little Ryton Shrops 131 C9
Little Salisbury Wilts 63 G7
Little Salkeld Cumb 231 D7
Little Sampford Essex 106 E3
Little Sandhurst Brack 65 G10
Little Saredon Staffs 133 B8
Little Saxham Suff 124 E5
Little Scatwell Highld 300 D3
Little Scotland Gtr Man 194 E6
Little Sessay N Yorks 215 E9
Little Shelford Cambs 123 G9
Little Shoddesden Hants 47 D9
Little Shrewley Warks 118 D4
Little Shurdington Glos 80 B6
Little Silver Devon 26 F6
Little Silver Devon 40 E4
Little Singleton Lancs 202 F3
Little Skillymarno Aberds 303 D9
Little Skipwith N Yorks 207 F9
Little Smeaton N Yorks 198 D4
Little Smeaton N Yorks 224 E6
Little Snoring Norf 159 C9
Little Sodbury S Glos 61 C9
Little Sodbury End S Glos 61 C8
Little Somborne Hants 47 G11
Little Somerford Wilts 62 C3
Little Soudley Shrops 150 D4
Little Stainforth N Yorks 212 F6
Little Stainton Darl 234 G2
Little Stanmore London 85 G11
Little Stanney W Ches 182 G6
Little Staughton Beds 122 E2
Little Steeping Lincs 174 C6
Little Stoke S Glos 60 C6
Little Stoke Staffs 151 C8
Little Stonham Suff 126 E2
Little Stretton Leics 136 C3
Little Stretton Shrops 131 E8
Little Strickland Cumb 221 B11
Little Studley N Yorks 214 E5
Little Stukeley Cambs 122 B4
Little Sugnall Staffs 150 C6
Little Sutton Lincs 157 E9
Little Sutton Shrops 131 G10
Little Sutton W Ches 182 F5
Little Swinburne Northumb 241 B10
Little Tarrington Hereford 98 C2
Little Tew Oxon 101 F7
Little Tey Essex 107 G7
Little Thetford Cambs 123 B10
Little Thirkleby N Yorks 215 D9
Little Thornage Norf 159 B11
Little Thornton Lancs 202 E3
Little Thorpe Durham 234 C4
Little Thorpe W Yorks 197 C7
Little Thurlow Suff 124 G3
Little Thurlow Green Suff 124 G3
Little Thurrock Thurrock 68 D6
Little Torboll Highld 309 K7
Little Torrington Devon 25 D7
Little Totham Essex 88 C5
Little Toux Aberds 302 D5
Little Town Cumb 220 B4
Little Town Lancs 203 F9
Little Town Warr 183 C10
Little Tring Herts 84 C6
Little Twycross Leics 134 B6
Little Urswick Cumb 210 E5
Little Vantage W Loth 270 C2
Little Wakering Essex 70 B2
Little Walden Essex 105 C10
Little Waldingfield Suff 107 B8
Little Walsingham Norf 159 B8
Little Waltham Essex 88 C2
Little Walton Warks 135 G9
Little Warley Essex 87 G10
Little Warton Warks 134 C5
Little Washbourne Glos 99 E9
Little Weighton E Yorks 208 G5
Little Weldon Northants 137 F8
Little Welland Worcs 98 D6
Little Welnetham Suff 125 E7
Little Welton Lincs 190 D4
Little Wenham Suff 107 D11
Little Wenlock Telford 132 B2
Little Weston Som 29 B10
Little Whitehouse I o W 20 C5
Little Whittingham Green Suff 126 B5
Little Wigborough Essex 89 B7
Little Wilbraham Cambs 123 F10
Little Wisbeach Lincs 156 C2
Little Wishford Wilts 46 F5
Little Witcombe Glos 80 B6
Little Witley Worcs 116 E5
Little Wittenham Oxon 83 G9
Little Wolford Warks 100 D5
Little Wood Corner Bucks 84 E6
Little Woodcote London 67 G9
Little Woolgarston Dorset 18 E5
Little Worthen Shrops 130 B6
Little Wratting Suff 106 B3
Little Wymington Beds 121 D9
Little Wymondley Herts 104 F4
Little Wyrley Staffs 133 B10
Little Wytheford Shrops 149 F11
Little Yeldham Essex 106 D5
Littlebeck N Yorks 227 D7
Littleborough Devon 26 E4
Littleborough Gtr Man 196 D2
Littleborough Notts 188 E4
Littlebourne Kent 55 B8
Littlebredy Dorset 17 D7
Littlebury Essex 105 D10
Littlebury Green Essex 105 D9
Littlecote Bucks 102 G6
Littlecott Wilts 46 C6
Littledean Glos 79 C11
Littledean Hill Glos 79 C11
Littledown Bmouth 19 C8
Littledown Hants 47 B10
Littleferry Highld 311 K2
Littlefield NE Lincs 201 F9
Littlefield Common Sur 50 C3
Littlefield Green Windsor 65 D11
Littlegain Shrops 132 D5
Littleham Devon 14 E6
Littleham Devon 24 C6
Littlehampton W Sus 35 G8
Littlehempston Devon 8 C6
Littlehoughton Northumb 264 F6
Littlemill Aberds 292 D5
Littlemill E Ayrs 257 F11
Littlemill Highld 301 D9
Littlemill Northumb 264 F6
Littlemoor Derbys 170 C5
Littlemoor Dorset 17 E9
Littlemore Oxon 83 E8
Littlemoss Gtr Man 184 B6
Littleover Derby 152 C6
Littleport Cambs 139 F11
Littler W Ches 167 B10
Littlestead Green Oxon 65 D8
Littlestone-on-Sea Kent 39 C9
Littlethorpe Leics 135 D10
Littlethorpe N Yorks 214 F6
Littleton Bath 60 G5
Littleton Dorset 30 G5
Littleton Guildford 50 D3
Littleton Hants 48 G3
Littleton Perth 286 D6
Littleton Som 44 G3
Littleton Spelthorne 66 F5
Littleton W Ches 166 B6
Littleton Wilts 62 G2
Littleton Common Sur 66 E5
Littleton Drew Wilts 61 C10
Littleton-on-Severn S Glos 60 B5
Littleton Panell Wilts 46 C4
Littleton-upon-Severn S Glos 79 G9
Littletown Durham 234 C2
Littletown I o W 20 C6
Littletown W Yorks 197 C8
Littlewick Green Windsor 65 D10
Littlewindsor Dorset 28 G6
Littlewood Staffs 133 B9
Littlewood Green Warks 117 E11
Littleworth Beds 103 C11
Littleworth Glos 80 E4
Littleworth Glos 100 D2
Littleworth Oxon 82 F4
Littleworth Oxon 83 D9
Littleworth Oxon 83 E10
Littleworth S Yorks 187 B10
Littleworth Staffs 151 E8
Littleworth Staffs 151 G10
Littleworth W Sus 35 C11
Littleworth Warks 118 E4
Littleworth Wilts 63 G7
Littleworth Worcs 117 E9
Littleworth Worcs 117 G7
Littleworth Common Bucks 66 B2
Littleworth End Warks 134 D3
Littley Green Essex 87 B11
Litton Derbys 185 F11
Litton N Yorks 213 E8
Litton Som 44 C5
Litton Cheney Dorset 17 C7
Litton Mill Derbys 185 G11
Liurbost W Isles 304 F5
Livermead Torbay 9 C8
Liverpool Mers 182 C4
Liverpool Airport Mers 182 E6
Liversedge W Yorks 197 C8
Liverton Devon 14 F2
Liverton Redcar 226 B4
Liverton Mines Redcar 226 B4
Liverton Street Kent 53 C11
Livesey Street Kent 53 C8
Livingshayes Devon 27 G7
Livingston W Loth 269 B11
Livingston Village W Loth 269 B10
Lix Toll Stirl 285 D9
Lixwm Flint 181 G11
Lizard Corn 2 G6
Llaingoch Anglesey 178 E2
Llaithddu Powys 129 G11
Llampha V Glam 58 D2
Llan Powys 129 C7
Llan-dafal Bl Gwent 77 E11
Llan eurgain = Northop Flint 166 B2
Llan Ffestiniog Gwyn 164 G2
Llan-mill Pembs 73 C10
Llan-non = Llanon Ceredig 111 D10
Llan-y-pwll Wrex 166 E5
Llanaber Gwyn 146 F2
Llanaelhaearn Gwyn 16
Llanafan Ceredig 112
Llanafan-fawr Powys 11
Llanallgo Anglesey 17
Llananno Powys 113
Llanarmon Gwyn 145
Llanarmon Dyffryn Ceiriog Wrex 148
Llanarmon Mynydd-mawr Powys 148
Llanarmon-yn-Ial Denb 165
Llanarth Ceredig 111
Llanarth Mon 78
Llanarthne Carms 93
Llanasa Flint 181
Llanbabo Anglesey 178
Llanbad Rhondda 58
Llanbadarn Fawr Ceredig 128
Llanbadarn Fynydd Powys 114
Llanbadarn-y-Garreg Powys 96
Llanbadoc Mon 78
Llanbadrig Anglesey 178
Llanbeder Newport 78
Llanbedr Gwyn 145
Llanbedr Powys 96
Llanbedr Powys 96
Llanbedr-Dyffryn-Clwyd Denb 165
Llanbedr Pont Steffan = Lampeter Ceredig 93
Llanbedr-y-cennin Conwy 164
Llanbedrgoch Anglesey 179
Llanbedrog Gwyn 144
Llanberis Gwyn 163
Llanbethery V Glam 58
Llanbister Powys 114
Llanblethian = Llanfleiddan V Glam 58
Llanboidy Carms 92
Llanbradach Caerph 77
Llanbrynmair Powys 129
Llancadle = Llancatal V Glam 58
Llancaiach Caerph 77
Llancarfan V Glam 58
Llancatal = Llancadle V Glam 58
Llancayo Mon 78
Llancloudy Hereford 97
Llancowrid Powys 130
Llancynfelyn Ceredig 128
Llandaff Cardiff 59
Llandaff North Cardiff 59
Llandanwg Gwyn 145
Llandarcy Neath 57
Llandawke Carms 74
Llanddaniel Fab Anglesey 179
Llanddarog Carms 75
Llanddeiniol Ceredig 111
Llanddeiniolen Gwyn 163
Llandderfel Gwyn 147
Llanddeusant Anglesey 178
Llanddeusant Carms 94
Llanddew Powys 95
Llanddewi Swansea 56
Llanddewi-Brefi Ceredig 112
Llanddewi Fach Mon 78
Llanddewi Rhydderch Mon 78
Llanddewi Skirrid Mon 78
Llanddewi Velfrey Pembs 73
Llanddewi Ystradenni Powys 114
Llanddewi'r Cwm Powys 95
Llanddoged Conwy 164
Llanddona Anglesey 179
Llanddowror Carms 74
Llanddulas Conwy 180
Llanddwywe Gwyn 145
Llanddyfnan Anglesey 179
Llandecwyn Gwyn 146
Llandefaelog Powys 95
Llandefaelog Fach Powys 95
Llandefaelog-tre'r-graig Powys 96
Llandefalle Powys 96
Llandegai Gwyn 179
Llandegfan Anglesey 179
Llandegla Denb 165
Llandegley Powys 114
Llandegveth Mon 78
Llandegwning Gwyn 144
Llandeilo Carms 94
Llandeilo Graban Powys 95
Llandeilo'r Fan Powys 95
Llandeloy Pembs 91
Llandenny Mon 78
Llandenny Walks Mon 78
Llandevaud Newport 78
Llandevenny Mon 60
Llandewi Ystradenny Powys 114
Llandilo Pembs 92
Llandilo-yr-ynys Carms 93
Llandinabo Hereford 97
Llandinam Powys 129
Llandissilio Pembs 92
Llandogo Mon 79
Llandough V Glam 58
Llandough V Glam 59
Llandovery = Llanymddyfri Carms 94
Llandow = Llandw V Glam 58
Llandre Carms 94
Llandre Ceredig 128
Llandrillo Denb 147
Llandrillo-yn-Rhôs Conwy 180
Llandrindod Wells Powys 113
Llandrinio Powys 148
Llandruidion Pembs 90
Llandudno Conwy 180
Llandudno Junction = Cyffordd Llandudno Conwy 180
Llandudoch = St Dogmaels Pembs 92
Llandw = Llandow V Glam 58
Llandwrog Gwyn 163
Llandybie Carms 75
Llandyfaelog Carms 74
Llandyfan Carms 75
Llandyfriog Ceredig 92
Llandyfrydog Anglesey 178
Llandygwydd Ceredig 92
Llandynan Denb 165
Llandyrnog Denb 165
Llandysilio Powys 148
Llandyssil Powys 130
Llandysul Ceredig 93

edeyrn Cardiff 59 C8
edi Carms 75 D9
edwen Anglesey 163 B8
eglwys Powys 95 D11
egryn Gwyn 110 B2
egwad Carms 93 G10
ilian Anglesey 179 C7
elian yn-Rhôs
wy 180 F5
elidan Denb 165 E10
elieu Powys 96 E3
ellen Mon 78 C4
elli Carms 56 B4
elltyd Gwyn 146 F4
elly Mon 78 C2
elly Hill Mon 78 C2
elwedd Powys 113 G10
elwy = St Asaph
181 G8
enddwyn Gwyn 145 E11
engan Gwyn 144 D5
erch Powys 130 E6
erch Emrys Powys 148 E4
erchymedd
esey 178 E6
erfyl Powys 129 B10
euddog Anglesey 179 D7
fabon Caerph 77 G10
fachraeth Anglesey 178 E4
fachreth Gwyn 146 E5
faelog Anglesey 178 G4
faelrhys Gwyn 144 D4
faenor Mon 78 B6
faes Anglesey 179 F10
faes Powys 95 F10
faethlu Anglesey 178 D4
faglan Gwyn 163 C7
fair Gwyn 145 D11
fair Caereinion
ys 130 B2
fair Clydogau
dig 112 G2
fair-Dyffryn-
yd Denb 165 D10
fair Kilgeddin Mon 78 D4
fair Kilgheddin Mon 78 D4
fair-Nant-Gwyn
bs 92 D3
fair Talhaiarn
wy 180 G6
fair Waterdine
ps 114 B4
fairfechan Conwy 179 F11
fairpwll-gwyngyll
esey 179 G8
fairyneubwll
178 F3
fairynghornwy
esey 178 C4
fallteg Carms 73 B11
fallteg West Carms 73 B10
faredd Powys 113 G11
farian Ceredig 111 B11
fechain Powys 148 E3
fechan Powys 113 G9
fechell Anglesey 178 C5
ferres Denb 165 C11
flewyn Anglesey 178 D5
figael Anglesey 178 E4
fihangel-ar-arth
ns 93 D9
fihangel-Crucorney
96 G6
fihangel Glyn
yr Conwy 165 F7
fihangel-helygen
ys 113 E10
fihangel Nant Bran
ys 95 E8
fihangel-nant-
an Powys 114 F3
fihangel
dithon Powys 114 D3
fihangel Rogiet
60 B2
fihangel Tal-y-llyn
ys 96 F2
fihangel Tor y
ydd Mon 79 E7
fihangel-uwch-
li Carms 93 G9
fihangel-y-
uddyn Ceredig 112 B3
fihangel-y-
nant Gwyn 128 B3
fihangel-y-pennant
n 163 F8
fihangel-yng-
wynfa Powys 147 F11
fihangel yn
wyn Anglesey 178 F4
filo Powys 96 E2
leiddan =
blethian V Glam 58 E3
oist Mon 78 C3
for Gwyn 147 B8
rechfa Torf 78 G4
rothen Gwyn 163 G10
rynach Powys 95 F11
wrog Anglesey 178 E4
wrog Denb 165 D10
yllin Powys 148 F2
ynydd Carms 93 F11
ynydd Flint 166 D3
yrnach Pembs 92 E4
gadfan Powys 147 G10
gadog Carms 74 D6
gadog Carms 94 F4
gadwaladr
esey 162 B5
gadwaladr Powys 148 C3
gaffo Anglesey 162 B6
gain Carms 74 B5
gammarch Wells
ys 95 B8
gan V Glam 58 D3
garron Hereford 97 G10
gasty Tallyllyn Powys 96 F2
gathen Carms 93 G11
gattock Powys 78 B2
gattock Lingoed
97 G7
gattock nigh Usk
78 D4
gattock-Vibon-
l Mon 79 B7
gedwyn Powys 148 E3
gefni Anglesey 179 F7
geinor Bridgend 58 B2
geitho Ceredig 112 F2
geler Carms 93 D7
gendeirne Carms 75 C7
gennech Carms 75 E9
gennith Swansea 56 C2
genny Powys 78 B2
gernyw Conwy 164 B5
geview Mon 78 E5
gewydd Court
gend 57 E11
gian Gwyn 144 D5
gloffan Pembs 91 E8
glydwen Carms 92 F3
Llangoed Anglesey 179 F10
Llangoedmor Ceredig 92 B3
Llangollen Denb 166 G2
Llangolman Pembs 92 F2
Llangors Powys 96 F2
Llangorwen Ceredig 128 F2
Llangovan Mon 79 D7
Llangower Gwyn 147 C8
Llangrannog Ceredig 110 G6
Llangristiolus Anglesey 178 G6
Llangrove Hereford 79 B8
Llangua Mon 97 F7
Llangunllo Powys 114 C4
Llangunnor Carms 74 B6
Llangurig Powys 113 B8
Llangwm Conwy 165 G7
Llangwm Mon 78 E6
Llangwm Pembs 73 D7
Llangwnnadl Gwyn 144 C4
Llangwyfan Denb 165 B10
Llangwyfan-isaf
Anglesey 162 B4
Llangwyllog Anglesey 178 F6
Llangwyryfon Ceredig 111 C11
Llangybi Ceredig 112 G2
Llangybi Gwyn 162 G6
Llangybi Mon 78 F5
Llangyfelach Swansea 56 B6
Llangyndeyrn Carms 75 C7
Llangynhafal Denb 165 C10
Llangynidr Powys 77 B11
Llangyniew Powys 130 B2
Llangynin Carms 74 B2
Llangynog Carms 74 B4
Llangynog Powys 147 D11
Llangynwyd Bridgend 57 D11
Llanhamlach Powys 95 F11
Llanharan Rhondda 58 C4
Llanharry Rhondda 58 C4
Llanhennock Mon 78 G5
Llanhilleth Bl Gwent 78 E2
Llanhowel Pembs 90 F6
Llanidloes Powys 129 G9
Llaniestyn Gwyn 144 C5
Llanifyny Powys 129 G7
Llanigon Powys 96 D4
Llanilar Ceredig 112 C2
Llanilid Rhondda 58 C3
Llanilltud Fawr =
Llantwit Major V Glam 58 F3
Llanio Ceredig 112 F2
Llanion Pembs 73 E7
Llanishen Cardiff 59 C7
Llanishen Mon 79 E7
Llanllawddog Carms 93 F9
Llanllechid Gwyn 163 B10
Llanllowell Mon 78 F5
Llanllugan Powys 129 C11
Llanllwch Carms 74 B5
Llanllwchaiarn Powys 130 E2
Llanllwni Carms 93 D9
Llanllwyd Shrops 130 G3
Llanllyfni Gwyn 163 E7
Llanmadoc Swansea 56 C2
Llanmaes Cardiff 58 D6
Llanmaes V Glam 58 F3
Llanmartin Newport 59 B11
Llanmerwig Powys 130 E3
Llanmihangel V Glam 58 E3
Llanmiloe Carms 74 D3
Llanmorlais Swansea 56 C4
Llannefydd Conwy 181 G7
Llannerch-y-môr Flint 181 F11
Llannon Carms 75 D8
Llannor Gwyn 145 B7
Llanon Pembs 90 E6
Llanon = Llan-non
Ceredig 111 D10
Llanover Mon 78 D4
Llanpumsaint Carms 93 F8
Llanreath Pembs 73 E7
Llanreithan Pembs 91 F7
Llanrhaeadr Denb 165 C9
Llanrhaeadr-ym-
Mochnant Powys 148 D2
Llanrhian Pembs 90 E6
Llanrhidian Swansea 56 C3
Llanrhos Conwy 180 E3
Llanrhyddlad Anglesey 178 D4
Llanrhystud Ceredig 111 D10
Llanrosser Hereford 96 D5
Llanrothal Hereford 79 B7
Llanrug Gwyn 163 C8
Llanrumney Cardiff 59 C8
Llanrwst Conwy 164 C4
Llansadurnen Carms 74 C3
Llansadwrn Anglesey 179 F9
Llansadwrn Carms 94 E3
Llansaint Carms 74 D5
Llansamlet Swansea 57 B7
Llansanffraid Glan
Conwy Conwy 180 F4
Llansannan Conwy 164 B6
Llansannor V Glam 58 D3
Llansantffraed Ceredig 111 D10
Llansantffraed Powys 96 G2
Llansantffraed
Cwmdeuddwr Powys 113 D9
Llansantffraed-in-
Elwel Powys 113 G11
Llansantffraid-ym-
Mechain Powys 148 E4
Llansawel Carms 94 D2
Llansawel = Briton
Ferry Neath 57 C8
Llansilin Powys 148 D4
Llansoy Mon 78 E6
Llanspyddid Powys 95 F10
Llanstadwell Pembs 72 D6
Llansteffan Carms 74 C5
Llanstephan Powys 96 C2
Llantarnam Torf 78 G4
Llanteems Mon 96 G6
Llanteg Pembs 73 C11
Llanthony Mon 96 F5
Llantilio Crossenny Mon 78 C5
Llantilio Pertholey Mon 78 B4
Llantood Pembs 92 C3
Llantrisant Anglesey 178 E5
Llantrisant Mon 78 F5
Llantrisant Rhondda 58 C4
Llantrithyd V Glam 58 E4
Llantwit Neath 57 B9
Llantwit Fardre Rhondda 58 B5
Llantwit Major =
Llanilltud Fawr V Glam 58 F3
Llanuwchllyn Gwyn 147 C7
Llanvaches Newport 78 G6
Llanvair Discoed Mon 78 G6
Llanvapley Mon 78 C5
Llanvetherine Mon 78 B5
Llanveynoe Hereford 96 E6
Llanvihangel Crucorney
Mon 96 G6
Llanvihangel Gobion
Mon 78 D4
Llanvihangel-Ystern-
Llewern Mon 78 C6
Llanwarne Hereford 97 F10
Llanwddyn Powys 147 F10
Llanwenarth Mon 78 C3
Llanwenog Ceredig 93 B9
Llanwern Newport 59 B11
Llanwinio Carms 92 F5
Llanwnda Gwyn 163 D7
Llanwnda Pembs 91 D8
Llanwnnen Ceredig 93 B10
Llanwnog Powys 129 E10
Llanwrda Carms 94 E4
Llanwrin Powys 128 C5
Llanwrthwl Powys 113 E9
Llanwrtud =
Llanwrtyd Wells Powys 95 B7
Llanwrtyd Powys 95 B7
Llanwrtyd Wells =
Llanwrtud Powys 95 B7
Llanwyddelan Powys 129 C11
Llanyblodwel Shrops 148 E4
Llanybri Carms 74 C4
Llanybydder Carms 93 C10
Llanycefn Pembs 91 G11
Llanychaer Pembs 91 D9
Llanycil Gwyn 147 C8
Llanycrwys Carms 94 B2
Llanymawddwy Gwyn 147 F8
Llanymddyfri =
Llandovery Carms 94 E5
Llanymynech Powys 148 E5
Llanynghenedl Anglesey 178 E4
Llanynys Denb 165 C10
Llanyrafon Torf 78 G4
Llanyre Powys 113 E10
Llanystumdwy Gwyn 145 B9
Llanywern Powys 96 F2
Llawhaden Pembs 73 B9
Llawnt Shrops 148 C5
Llawrdref Bellaf Gwyn 144 D5
Llawr-y-glyn Powys 129 E8
Llay Wrex 166 D4
Llechcynfarwy Anglesey 178 E5
Llecheiddior Gwyn 163 G7
Llechfaen Powys 95 F11
Llechfraith Gwyn 146 F3
Llechryd Caerph 77 D10
Llechryd Ceredig 92 C4
Llechrydau Powys 148 C4
Llechwedd Conwy 180 F3
Lledrod Ceredig 112 C2
Llenmerewig Powys 130 E3
Llethrid Swansea 56 C4
Llettyrychen Carms 75 E7
Llidiad Nenog Carms 93 D10
Llidiardau Gwyn 147 B7
Llidiart-y-parc Denb 165 G10
Llithfaen Gwyn 162 G5
Lloc Flint 181 F10
Llong Flint 166 C3
Llowes Powys 96 C3
Lloyney Powys 114 B4
Llugwy Powys 128 D4
Llundain-fach Ceredig 111 F11
Llwydarth Bridgend 57 C11
Llwydcoed Rhondda 77 E7
Llwyn Denb 165 C9
Llwyn Shrops 130 G5
Llwyn-derw Powys 129 G8
Llwyn-du Mon 78 B3
Llwyn-hendy Carms 56 B4
Llwyn-on Village M Tydf 77 C8
Llwyn-têg Carms 75 D9
Llwyn-y-brain Carms 73 C11
Llwyn-y-go Shrops 148 E6
Llwyn-y-groes Ceredig 111 F11
Llwyn-yr-hwrdd Pembs 92 E4
Llwyncelyn Ceredig 111 F8
Llwyndafydd Ceredig 111 F7
Llwynderw Powys 130 C4
Llwyndyris Ceredig 92 C4
Llwyndyrys Gwyn 162 G5
Llwyngwril Gwyn 110 B2
Llwynhendy Carms 56 B4
Llwynmawr Wrex 148 B4
Llwynygog Powys 129 E7
Llwynypia Rhondda 77 G7
Llynclys Shrops 148 E5
Llynfaes Anglesey 178 F6
Llys-y-frôn Pembs 91 G10
Llysfaen Conwy 180 F5
Llyswen Powys 96 D2
Llysworney V Glam 58 E3
Llywel Powys 95 E7
Llywernog Ceredig 128 G4
Load Brook S Yorks 186 D3
Loan Falk 279 F9
Loandhu Highld 301 B8
Loanend Northumb 273 E8
Loanhead Aberds 302 D6
Loanhead Midloth 270 B5
Loanhead Perth 286 D5
Loanreoch Highld 300 B6
Loans S Ayrs 257 C8
Loans of Tullich Highld 301 B8
Loansdean Northumb 252 G5
Lobb Devon 40 F3
Lobhillcross Devon 12 D5
Lobley Hill T & W 242 E6
Lobthorpe Lincs 155 E9
Loch a Charnain
W Isles 297 G4
Loch a' Ghainmhich
W Isles 304 F4
Loch Baghasdail
W Isles 297 K3
Loch Choire Lodge
Highld 308 F6
Loch Eil Highld 290 F2
Loch Euphoirt W Isles 296 E4
Loch Head Dumfries 236 E5
Loch Head Dumfries 245 E11
Loch Loyal Lodge
Highld 308 E6
Loch nam Madadh
W Isles 296 E5
Loch Sgioport W Isles 297 H4
Lochailort Highld 295 G9
Lochaline Highld 289 E8
Lochanhully Highld 301 G9
Lochans Dumfries 236 D2
Locharbriggs Dumfries 247 G11
Lochassynt Lodge
Highld 307 G6
Lochavich Ho Argyll 275 B10
Lochawe Argyll 284 E5
Lochbuie Argyll 289 G8
Lochbuie Ho Argyll 289 G8
Lochcallater Lodge
Aberds 292 E3
Lochcarron Highld 295 B10
Lochdhu Highld 310 E4
Lochdochart House
Stirl 285 E8
Lochdon Argyll 289 F9
Lochdrum Highld 300 B2
Lochead Argyll 275 E11
Lochead Argyll 275 F8
Lochearnhead Stirl 285 E9
Lochee Dundee 287 D7
Lochend Edin 280 G5
Lochend Highld 300 F5
Lochend Highld 310 C6
Lochend Ho Stirl 277 B11
Locherben Dumfries 247 D11
Lochetive Ho Highld 284 C5
Lochfoot Dumfries 237 B10
Lochgair Argyll 275 D10
Lochgarthside Highld 291 B7
Lochgelly Fife 280 C3
Lochgilphead Argyll 275 E9
Lochgoilhead Argyll 284 G6
Lochhill Moray 302 C2
Lochhussie Highld 300 D4
Lochinch Castle
Dumfries 236 C3
Lochindorb Lodge
Highld 301 F9
Lochinver Highld 307 G5
Lochlane Perth 286 E2
Lochletter Highld 300 G4
Lochluichart Highld 300 C3
Lochmaben Dumfries 248 G3
Lochmore Cottage
Highld 310 E4
Lochmore Lodge Highld 306 F7
Lochnell Ho Argyll 289 F10
Lochore Fife 280 B3
Lochorodale Argyll 255 F7
Lochportain W Isles 296 D5
Lochran Perth 280 B2
Lochranza N Ayrs 255 B10
Lochs Crofts Moray 302 C3
Lochside Aberds 293 G9
Lochside Highld 301 D8
Lochside Highld 308 D4
Lochside Highld 310 F2
Lochside S Ayrs 257 E8
Lochslin Highld 311 L2
Lochstack Lodge Highld 306 E7
Lochton Aberds 293 D9
Lochty Angus 293 G7
Lochty Fife 287 G9
Lochty Perth 286 E4
Lochuisge Highld 289 D9
Lochurr Dumfries 247 F7
Lochwinnoch Renfs 267 D7
Lochwood Dumfries 248 D3
Lochwood Glasgow 268 B3
Lochyside Highld 290 F3
Lockengate Corn 5 C10
Lockerbie Dumfries 248 G4
Lockeridge Wilts 62 F6
Lockeridge Dene Wilts 62 F6
Lockerley Hants 32 B3
Lockhills Cumb 230 B6
Locking N Som 43 B11
Locking Stumps Warr 183 C10
Lockinge Oxon 64 B2
Lockington E Yorks 208 D5
Lockington Leics 153 D9
Lockleaze Bristol 60 D6
Lockleywood Shrops 150 D3
Locks Heath Hants 33 F8
Locksbottom London 68 F2
Locksbrook Bath 61 G8
Locksgreen I o W 20 C4
Lockton N Yorks 226 G6
Lockwood W Yorks 196 D6
Loddington Leics 136 C5
Loddington Northants 120 B6
Loddiswell Devon 8 F4
Loddon Norf 143 D7
Loddon Ingloss Norf 142 D6
Lode Cambs 123 E10
Lode Heath W Mid 134 G3
Loders Dorset 16 C5
Lodge Green N Yorks 223 F9
Lodge Green W Mid 134 G5
Lodge Hill Corn 6 C4
Lodge Hill W Mid 133 G10
Lodge Hill W Yorks 197 C9
Lodge Lees Kent 55 D8
Lodge Moor S Yorks 186 D3
Lodge Park Worcs 117 D10
Lodgebank Shrops 149 D11
Lodsworth W Sus 34 C6
Lodsworth Common
W Sus 34 C6
Lodway Bristol 60 D4
Lofthouse N Yorks 214 E2
Lofthouse W Yorks 197 B10
Lofthouse Gate
W Yorks 197 C10
Loftus Redcar 226 B4
Logan E Ayrs 258 E3
Logan Mains Dumfries 236 E2
Loganlea W Loth 269 C9
Loggerheads Denb 165 C11
Loggerheads Staffs 150 B4
Logie Angus 293 G8
Logie Fife 287 E8
Logie Moray 301 D10
Logie Coldstone Aberds 292 C6
Logie Hill Highld 301 B7
Logie Newton Aberds 302 F6
Logie Pert Angus 293 G8
Logiealmond Lodge
Perth 286 D3
Logierait Perth 286 B3
Login Carms 92 G3
Logmore Green Sur 50 D6
Loidse Mhorsgail
W Isles 304 F3
Lolworth Cambs 123 E7
Lôneshaye Lancs 204 F2
Lon Gwyn 147 C7
Lon-las Swansea 57 B8
Lonbain Highld 298 D6
Londesborough E Yorks 208 D3
London Apprentice
Corn 5 E10
London Beach Kent 53 F11
London Colney Herts 85 E11
London End Cambs 121 D11
London Fields W Mid 133 E8
London Minstead Hants 32 E3
Londonderry N Yorks 214 B6
Londonderry W Mid 133 F10
Londonthorpe Lincs 155 B9
Londubh Highld 307 L3
Lonemore Highld 299 B7
Lonemore Highld 309 L7
Long Ashton N Som 60 E5
Long Bank Worcs 116 C5
Long Bennington Lincs 172 G4
Long Bredy Dorset 17 C7
Long Buckby Northants 120 D2
Long Buckby Wharf
Northants 120 D2
Long Clawson Leics 154 D4
Long Common Hants 33 E8
Long Compton Staffs 151 E7
Long Compton Warks 100 E5
Long Crendon Bucks 83 D11
Long Crichel Dorset 31 E7
Long Cross Wilts 45 G9
Long Dean Wilts 61 D11
Long Ditton Sur 67 F7
Long Drax N Yorks 199 B7
Long Duckmanton
Derbys 186 G6
Long Eaton Derbys 153 C9
Long Gardens Essex 106 D6
Long Green Suff 125 B11
Long Green W Ches 183 G7
Long Green Worcs 98 E6
Long Hanborough Oxon 82 C6
Long Itchington Warks 119 D8
Long John's Hill Norf 142 B4
Long Lane Telford 150 F2
Long Lawford Warks 119 B9
Long Lee W Yorks 205 E7
Long Load Som 29 C7
Long Marston Herts 84 B5
Long Marston N Yorks 206 C6
Long Marston Warks 100 B3
Long Marton Cumb 231 G9
Long Meadow Cambs 123 E10
Long Meadowend
Shrops 131 G8
Long Melford Suff 107 B7
Long Newnton Glos 80 G6
Long Newton E Loth 271 C10
Long Oak Shrops 149 E7
Long Park Hants 48 F2
Long Preston N Yorks 204 B2
Long Riston E Yorks 209 E8
Long Sandall S Yorks 198 F6
Long Sight Gtr Man 196 F2
Long Stratton Norf 142 E3
Long Street M Keynes 102 B5
Long Sutton Hants 49 D8
Long Sutton Lincs 157 E8
Long Sutton Som 29 B7
Long Thurlow Suff 125 D10
Long Whatton Leics 153 E9
Long Wittenham Oxon 83 G8
Longbar N Ayrs 266 E6
Longbarn Warr 183 C10
Longbenton T & W 243 D7
Longborough Glos 100 F3
Longbridge Plym 7 D10
Longbridge W Mid 117 B10
Longbridge Warks 118 E5
Longbridge Deverill
Wilts 45 E11
Longbridge Hayes
Stoke 168 E5
Longbridgemuir
Dumfries 238 D3
Longburgh Cumb 239 F8
Longburton Dorset 29 E11
Longcause Devon 8 C5
Longcliffe Derbys 170 D2
Longcot Oxon 82 G3
Longcroft Cumb 238 F6
Longcroft Falk 278 F5
Longcross Devon 12 F4
Longcross Sur 66 F3
Longdale Cumb 222 D2
Longdales Cumb 230 C6
Longden Shrops 131 B8
Longden Common
Shrops 131 C8
Longdon Staffs 151 G11
Longdon Worcs 98 D6
Longdon Green Staffs 151 G11
Longdon Heath Worcs 98 D6
Longdon Hill End Worcs 98 D6
Longdon on Tern Telford 150 F2
Longdown Devon 14 C3
Longdowns Corn 2 C6
Longdrum Angus 292 G4
Longfield Kent 68 F6
Longfield Shetland 313 M5
Longfield Wilts 45 B11
Longfield Hill Kent 68 F6
Longfleet Poole 18 C6
Longford Derbys 152 B4
Longford Glos 98 G6
Longford Kent 52 B4
Longford London 66 D4
Longford Shrops 150 C2
Longford Telford 150 F4
Longford W Mid 135 G7
Longford Warr 183 C10
Longfordlane Derbys 152 B4
Longforgan Perth 287 E7
Longformacus Borders 272 D3
Longframlington
Northumb 252 C4
Longham Dorset 19 B7
Longham Norf 159 F8
Longhaven Aberds 303 F11
Longhedge Wilts 45 E10
Longhill Aberds 303 D9
Longhirst Northumb 252 F6
Longhope Glos 79 B11
Longhope Orkney 314 G3
Longhorsley Northumb 252 E4
Longhoughton
Northumb 264 G6
Longhouse Bath 61 G8
Longlands Cumb 229 D11
Longlands London 68 E2
Longlane Derbys 152 B5
Longlane W Berks 64 E3
Longlevens Glos 99 G7
Longley W Yorks 196 C5
Longley W Yorks 196 F6
Longley Estate S Yorks 186 C5
Longley Green Worcs 116 G4
Longleys Perth 286 C6
Longmanhill Aberds 303 C7
Longmoor Camp Hants 49 G9
Longmorn Moray 302 D2
Longmoss E Ches 184 G5
Longnewton Borders 262 D3
Longnewton Stockton 225 B7
Longney Glos 80 C3
Longniddry E Loth 281 F8
Longnor Shrops 131 C9
Longnor Staffs 151 G7
Longnor Staffs 169 C9
Longnor Park Shrops 131 C9
Longparish Hants 48 E2
Longpark Cumb 239 E10
Longpark E Ayrs 257 B10
Longport Stoke 168 F5
Longridge Glos 80 D5
Longridge Lancs 203 F8
Longridge Staffs 151 F8
Longridge W Loth 269 C9
Longridge End Glos 98 G6
Longrigg N Lnrk 278 G6
Longriggend N Lnrk 278 G6
Longrock Corn 1 C5
Longscales N Yorks 205 B10
Longsdon Staffs 169 E7
Longshaw Gtr Man 194 G4
Longshaw Staffs 169 F9
Longside Aberds 303 E10
Longsight Gtr Man 184 B5
Longslow Shrops 150 B3
Longsowerby Cumb 239 G9
Longstanton Cambs 123 D7
Longstock Hants 47 F11
Longstone Corn 2 B2
Longstone Corn 11 G7
Longstone Edin 280 G4
Longstone Pembs 73 D10
Longstone Som 28 B5
Longstowe Cambs 122 G6
Longstreet Wilts 46 C6
Longthorpe P'boro 138 D3
Longthwaite Cumb 230 G4
Longton Lancs 194 B3
Longton Stoke 168 G6
Longtown Cumb 239 D9
Longtown Hereford 96 F6
Longtownmail Orkney 314 F4
Longview Mers 182 C6
Longville in the Dale
Shrops 131 E10
Longway Bank Derbys 170 E4
Longwell Green S Glos 61 E7
Longwick Bucks 84 D3
Longwitton Northumb 252 F3
Longwood Shrops 132 B2
Longwood W Yorks 196 D6
Longwood Edge
W Yorks 196 D6
Longworth Oxon 82 F5
Longyester E Loth 271 B10
Lonmay Aberds 303 D10
Lonmore Highld 298 E2
Looe Corn 6 E5
Looe Mills Corn 6 C4
Loose Kent 53 C9
Loose Hill Kent 53 C9
Loosegate Lincs 156 D6
Loosley Row Bucks 84 E4
Lopcombe Corner Wilts 47 F9
Lopen Som 28 E6
Lopen Head Som 28 E6
Loppergarth Cumb 210 D5
Loppington Shrops 149 D9
Lopwell Devon 7 C9
Lorbottle Northumb 252 B2
Lorbottle Hall Northumb 252 B2
Lord's Hill Soton 32 D5
Lords Wood Medway 69 G9
Lordsbridge Norf 157 G11
Lordshill Common Sur 50 E4
Lordswood Soton 32 D6
Lornty Perth 286 C5
Loscoe Derbys 170 F6
Loscoe W Yorks 198 C2
Loscombe Dorset 16 B6
Losgaintir W Isles 305 J2
Lossiemouth Moray 302 B2
Lossit Argyll 254 B2
Lossit Lodge Argyll 274 G5
Lostford Shrops 150 C2
Lostock Gtr Man 195 F7
Lostock Gralam
W Ches 183 F11
Lostock Green W Ches 183 G11
Lostock Hall Lancs 194 B4
Lostock Junction
Gtr Man 195 F7
Lostwithiel Corn 6 D2
Loth Orkney 314 C6
Lothbeg Highld 311 H3
Lothersdale N Yorks 204 D5
Lothianbridge Midloth 270 C6
Lothmore Highld 311 H3
Lottisham Som 44 G5
Loudwater Bucks 84 G6
Loudwater Herts 85 F9
Loughborough Leics 153 F10
Loughor Swansea 56 B5
Loughton Essex 86 F6
Loughton M Keynes 102 D6
Loughton Shrops 132 G2
Lound Lincs 155 F11
Lound Notts 187 D11
Lound Suff 143 D10
Loundsley Green
Derbys 186 G5
Lount Leics 153 F7
Lour Angus 287 C8
Louth Lincs 190 D4
Lovat Highld 300 E5
Lovaton Devon 7 B10
Love Clough Lancs 195 B10
Love Green Bucks 66 C4
Lovedean Hants 33 E11
Lover Wilts 32 C2
Loversall S Yorks 187 B9
Loves Green Essex 87 E10
Lovesome Hill N Yorks 225 F7
Loveston Pembs 73 D9
Lovington Som 44 G5
Low Ackworth W Yorks 198 D3
Low Alwinton Northumb 251 B10
Low Angerton
Northumb 252 G3
Low Barlings Lincs 189 G9
Low Barugh S Yorks 197 F10
Low Bentham N Yorks 212 F2
Low Biggins Cumb 212 D2
Low Blantyre S Lnrk 268 D3
Low Borrowbridge
Cumb 222 E2
Low Bradfield S Yorks 186 C3
Low Bradley N Yorks 204 D6
Low Braithwaite Cumb 230 C4
Low Bridge Wilts 62 E3
Low Brunton Northumb 241 C10
Low Burnham N Lincs 199 G9
Low Burton N Yorks 214 C4
Low Buston Northumb 252 B6
Low Catton E Yorks 207 C10
Low Clanyard Dumfries 236 F3
Low Common Norf 142 E2
Low Compton Gtr Man 196 F2
Low Coniscliffe Darl 224 C5
Low Cotehill Cumb 239 G11
Low Coylton S Ayrs 257 F10
Low Crosby Cumb 239 F10
Low Dalby N Yorks 217 B7
Low Dinsdale Darl 224 C6
Low Eighton T & W 243 F7
Low Ellington N Yorks 214 C4
Low Etherley Durham 233 F9
Low Fell T & W 243 F7
Low Fold W Yorks 205 F10
Low Fulney Lincs 156 E5
Low Garth N Yorks 226 D4
Low Gate N Yorks 214 F5
Low Gate Northumb 241 E10
Low Geltbridge Cumb 240 E2
Low Grantley N Yorks 214 E4
Low Green N Yorks 205 B10
Low Green Suff 125 E7
Low Green W Yorks 205 F10
Low Greenside T & W 242 E4
Low Habberley Worcs 116 B6
Low Ham Som 28 B6
Low Hauxley Northumb 253 C7
Low Hawsker N Yorks 227 D8
Low Hesket Cumb 230 B5
Low Hesleyhurst
Northumb 252 D3
Low Hill W Mid 133 C8
Low Hutton N Yorks 216 F5
Low Knipe Cumb 230 G6
Low Laithe N Yorks 214 G3
Low Laithes S Yorks 197 G11
Low Leighton Derbys 185 D8
Low Lorton Cumb 229 F9
Low Marishes N Yorks 216 D6
Low Marnham Notts 172 B4
Low Mill N Yorks 226 F3
Low Moor Lancs 203 E10
Low Moor W Yorks 197 B7
Low Moorsley T & W 234 B2
Low Moresby Cumb 228 G5
Low Newton Cumb 211 C8
Low Newton-by-the-
Sea Northumb 264 E6
Low Prudhoe Northumb 242 E4
Low Risby N Lincs 200 E2
Low Row Cumb 229 C9
Low Row Cumb 240 E3
Low Row N Yorks 223 F9
Low Salchrie Dumfries 236 C2
Low Smerby Argyll 255 E8
Low Snaygill N Yorks 204 D5
Low Street Norf 141 B10
Low Street Thurrock 69 D7
Low Tharston Norf 142 D3
Low Thornley T & W 242 E5
Low Torry Fife 279 D10
Low Town Shrops 132 E4
Low Toynton Lincs 190 G3
Low Valley S Yorks 198 G2
Low Valleyfield Fife 279 D10
Low Walton Cumb 219 C9
Low Waters S Lnrk 268 E4
Low Westwood Durham 242 F4
Low Whinnow Cumb 239 G8
Low Whita N Yorks 223 F10
Low Wood Cumb 210 C6
Low Worsall N Yorks 225 C7
Low Wray Cumb 221 E7
Lowbands Glos 98 E5
Lowbridge House
Cumb 221 E10
Lowca Cumb 228 G5
Lowcross Hill W Ches 167 E7
Lowdham Notts 171 F11
Lowe Shrops 149 C10
Lowe Hill Staffs 169 D7
Lowedges S Yorks 186 E4
Lower Achachenna
Argyll 284 E4
Lower Aisholt Som 43 F8
Lower Allscot Shrops 132 D4
Lower Altofts W Yorks 197 C11
Lower Amble Corn 10 G5
Lower Ansty Dorset 30 G3
Lower Ardtun Argyll 288 G5
Lower Arncott Oxon 83 B10
Lower Ashtead Sur 51 B7
Lower Ashton Devon 14 E2
Lower Assendon Oxon 65 C8
Lower Badcall Highld 306 E6
Lower Ballam Lancs 202 G3
Lower Bartle Lancs 202 G5
Lower Basildon W Berks 64 D6
Lower Bassingthorpe
Lincs 155 D9
Lower Bearwood
Hereford 115 F7
Lower Bebington Mers 182 E4
Lower Beeding W Sus 36 B2
Lower Benefield
Northants 137 F9
Lower Bentley Worcs 117 D9
Lower Beobridge
Shrops 132 E5
Lower Berry Hill Glos 79 C9
Lower Binton Warks 118 G2
Lower Birchwood
Derbys 170 E6
Lower Bitchet Kent 52 C5
Lower Blandford
St Mary Dorset 30 F5
Lower Blunsdon
Swindon 81 G10
Lower Bobbingworth
Green Essex 87 D8
Lower Bockhampton
Dorset 17 C10
Lower Boddington
Northants 119 G9
Lower Bodham Norf 160 B2
Lower Bodinnar Corn 1 C4
Lower Bois Bucks 85 E7
Lower Bordean Hants 33 C11
Lower Boscaswell Corn 1 C3
Lower Bourne Sur 49 E10
Lower Bradley W Mid 133 D9
Lower Brailes Warks 100 D6
Lower Breakish Highld 295 C8
Lower Bredbury Gtr Man 184 C6
Lower Breinton Hereford 97 D9
Lower Broadheath
Worcs 116 F6
Lower Brook Hants 32 B4
Lower Broughton
Gtr Man 184 B4
Lower Brynmamman
Neath 76 C2
Lower Brynn Corn 5 C9
Lower Buckenhill
Hereford 98 E2
Lower Bullingham
Hereford 97 D10
Lower Bullington Hants 48 E3
Lower Bunbury E Ches 167 D9
Lower Burgate Hants 31 D11
Lower Burrow Som 28 C6
Lower Burton Hereford 115 F8
Lower Bush Medway 69 F7
Lower Cadsden Bucks 84 E4
Lower Caldecote C Beds 104 B3
Lower Cam Glos 80 E2
Lower Canada N Som 43 B11
Lower Carden W Ches 167 E7
Lower Catesby
Northants 119 F10
Lower Cator Devon 13 F9
Lower Caversham
Reading 65 E8
Lower Chapel Powys 95 D10
Lower Chedworth Glos 81 C9
Lower Cheriton Devon 27 G10
Lower Chicksgrove Wilts 46 G3
Lower Chute Wilts 47 C10
Lower Clapton London 67 B11
Lower Clent Worcs 117 B8
Lower Clicker Corn 6 C5
Lower Clopton Warks 118 F3
Lower Common Hants 48 E6
Lower Common Hants 65 G9
Lower Common Mon 78 B2
Lower Common Mon 78 E4
Lower Common Shrops 131 B9
Lower Copthurst Lancs 194 C5
Lower Cotburn Aberds 303 D7
Lower Cousley Wood
E Sus 53 G7
Lower Cox Street Kent 69 G10
Lower Cragabus Argyll 254 C4
Lower Creedy Devon 26 G4
Lower Croan Corn 10 G6
Lower Crossings Derbys 185 E8
Lower Cumberworth
W Yorks 197 F8
Lower Cwm-twrch
Powys 76 C3
Lower Daggons Hants 31 E9
Lower Darwen Blkburn 195 B7
Lower Dean Beds 121 D11
Lower Dean Devon 8 C4
Lower Dell Highld 292 B2
Lower Denby W Yorks 197 F8
Lower Denzell Corn 5 B7
Lower Deuchries
Aberds 302 D6
Lower Diabaig Highld 299 C7
Lower Dicker E Sus 23 C9
Lower Dinchope Shrops 131 G9
Lower Dowdeswell Glos 81 B8
Lower Down Shrops 130 G6
Lower Drift Corn 1 D4
Lower Dunsforth
N Yorks 215 G8
Lower Durston Som 28 B3
Lower Earley Wokingham 65 E9
Lower East Carleton
Norf 142 C3
Lower Eastern Green
W Mid 118 B5
Lower Edmonton
London 86 G4
Lower Egleton Hereford 98 B2
Lower Elkstone Staffs 169 D9
Lower Ellastone Staffs 169 G10
Lower End Bucks 83 D11
Lower End Bucks 102 E4
Lower End C Beds 103 D8
Lower End C Beds 103 G9
Lower End Glos 81 E7
Lower End Northants 120 F6
Lower End Northants 120 G5
Lower End Northants 121 E7
Lower End Oxon 82 B4
Lower Everleigh Wilts 47 C7
Lower Eythorne Kent 55 D9
Lower Failand N Som 60 E4
Lower Faintree Shrops 132 F3
Lower Falkenham Suff 108 D5
Lower Farringdon Hants 49 F8
Lower Feltham London 66 E5
Lower Fittleworth
W Sus 35 D8
Lower Forge Shrops 132 F4
Lower Foxdale I o M 192 E3
Lower Frankton Shrops 149 C7
Lower Freystrop Pembs 73 C7
Lower Froyle Hants 49 E9
Lower Gabwell Devon 9 B8
Lower Gledfield Highld 309 K5
Lower Godney Som 44 E3
Lower Goldstone Kent 71 G9
Lower Gornal W Mid 133 E8
Lower Grange W Yorks 205 G8
Lower Gravenhurst
C Beds 104 D2
Lower Green Essex 88 E2
Lower Green Essex 105 E8
Lower Green Essex 106 E4
Lower Green Gtr Man 184 B2
Lower Green Herts 104 E3
Lower Green Kent 52 E5
Lower Green Kent 52 E6
Lower Green Norf 159 B9
Lower Green Staffs 133 B8
Lower Green Suff 124 D4
Lower Green Sur 66 F6
Lower Green W Berks 63 G11
Lower Green Warks 119 D10
Lower Grove Common
Hereford 97 F11
Lower Hacheston Suff 126 F6
Lower Halistra Highld 298 D2
Lower Halliford Sur 66 F5
Lower Halstock Leigh
Dorset 29 F8
Lower Halstow Kent 69 F11
Lower Hamswell S Glos 61 E8
Lower Hamworthy Poole 18 C6
Lower Hardres Kent 55 C7
Lower Hardwick
Hereford 115 F8
Lower Harpton Powys 114 E5
Lower Hartlip Kent 69 G10
Lower Hartshay Derbys 170 E5
Lower Hartwell Bucks 84 C3
Lower Hatton Staffs 150 B6
Lower Hawthwaite
Cumb 210 B4
Lower Haysden Kent 52 D5
Lower Hayton Shrops 131 G10
Lower Hazel S Glos 60 B6
Lower Heath E Ches 168 C5
Lower Hempriggs
Moray 301 C11
Lower Heppington Kent 54 C6
Lower Hergest Hereford 114 F5
Lower Herne Kent 71 F7
Lower Heyford Oxon 101 G9
Lower Heysham Lancs 211 G8
Lower Higham Kent 69 E8
Lower Highmoor Oxon 65 B8
Lower Holbrook Suff 108 E3
Lower Holditch Dorset 28 G4
Lower Holloway London 67 B10
Lower Holwell Dorset 31 E9
Lower Hook Worcs 98 C6
Lower Hookner Devon 13 E10
Lower Hopton Shrops 149 E7
Lower Hopton W Yorks 197 D7
Lower Hordley Shrops 149 D7
Lower Horncroft W Sus 35 D8
Lower Horsebridge
E Sus 23 C9
Lower House Halton 183 D8
Lower Houses W Yorks 197 D7
Lower Howsell Worcs 98 B5
Lower Illey Worcs 133 G9
Lower Island Kent 70 F6
Lower Kersal Gtr Man 195 G10
Lower Kilburn Derbys 170 F5
Lower Kilcott Glos 61 B9
Lower Killeyan Argyll 254 C3
Lower Kingcombe
Dorset 17 B7
Lower Kingswood Sur 51 C8
Lower Kinnerton
W Ches 166 C4
Lower Kinsham
Hereford 115 E7
Lower Knapp Som 28 B4
Lower Knightley Staffs 150 E6
Lower Knowle Bristol 60 E5
Lower Langford N Som 60 G3
Lower Largo Fife 287 G8
Lower Layham Suff 107 C10
Lower Ledwyche
Shrops 115 C10
Lower Leigh Staffs 151 B10
Lower Lemington Glos 100 E4
Lower Lenie Highld 300 G5
Lower Lode Glos 99 E7
Lower Lovacott Devon 25 B8
Lower Loxhore Devon 40 F6
Lower Lydbrook Glos 79 B9
Lower Lye Hereford 115 D8
Lower Machen Newport 59 B8
Lower Maes-coed
Hereford 96 E6
Lower Mains Clack 279 B9
Lower Mannington
Dorset 31 F9
Lower Marsh Som 30 C2
Lower Marston Som 45 E9
Lower Meend Glos 79 E9

Lower Menadue Corn 5 D10
Lower Merridge Som 43 G8
Lower Mickletown W Yorks 198 B2
Lower Middleton Cheney Northants 101 C10
Lower Midway Derbys 152 E6
Lower Mill Corn 3 B10
Lower Milovaig Highld 296 F7
Lower Milton Som 44 D4
Lower Moor Wilts 81 G8
Lower Moor Worcs 99 B9
Lower Morton S Glos 79 G10
Lower Mountain Flint 166 D4
Lower Nazeing Essex 86 D5
Lower Netchwood Shrops 132 E2
Lower Netherton Devon 14 G3
Lower New Inn Torf 78 F4
Lower Ninnes Corn 1 C5
Lower Nobut Staffs 151 C10
Lower North Dean Bucks 84 F5
Lower Norton Warks 118 E4
Lower Nyland Dorset 30 C2
Lower Ochrwyth Caerph 59 B8
Lower Odcombe Som 29 D8
Lower Oddington Glos 100 F4
Lower Ollach Highld 295 B7
Lower Padworth W Berks 64 F6
Lower Penarth V Glam 59 F7
Lower Penn Staffs 133 D7
Lower Pennington Hants 20 C2
Lower Penwortham Lancs 194 B4
Lower Peover W Ches 184 G2
Lower Pexhill E Ches 184 G5
Lower Pilsley Derbys 170 C6
Lower Pitkerrie Highld 311 L2
Lower Place Gtr Man 196 E2
Lower Place London 67 C8
Lower Pollicot Bucks 84 C2
Lower Porthkerry V Glam 58 F5
Lower Porthpean Corn 5 E10
Lower Quinton Warks 100 B3
Lower Rabber Hereford 114 G5
Lower Race Torf 78 E3
Lower Radley Oxon 83 F8
Lower Rainham Medway 69 F10
Lower Ratley Hants 32 C4
Lower Raydon Suff 107 D10
Lower Rea Glos 80 B4
Lower Ridge Devon 28 G2
Lower Ridge Shrops 148 C6
Lower Roadwater Som 42 F4
Lower Rochford Worcs 116 D2
Lower Rose Corn 4 E5
Lower Row Dorset 31 G8
Lower Sapey Worcs 116 E3
Lower Seagry Wilts 62 C3
Lower Sheering Essex 87 C7
Lower Shelton C Beds 103 C9
Lower Shiplake Oxon 65 D9
Lower Shuckburgh Warks 119 E9
Lower Skelty Swansea 56 C6
Lower Slackstead Hants 32 B5
Lower Slade Devon 40 D4
Lower Slaughter Glos 100 G3
Lower Solva Pembs 87 G11
Lower Soothill W Yorks 197 C9
Lower Soudley Glos 79 D11
Lower Southfield Hereford 98 C3
Lower Stanton St Quintin Wilts 62 C2
Lower Stoke Medway 69 D10
Lower Stoke W Mid 119 B7
Lower Stondon C Beds 104 D3
Lower Stone Glos 79 G11
Lower Stonnall Staffs 133 C11
Lower Stow Bedon Norf 141 E9
Lower Stratton Som 28 D6
Lower Stratton Swindon 63 B7
Lower Street E Sus 38 E2
Lower Street Norf 160 B5
Lower Street Norf 160 C3
Lower Street Norf 160 F6
Lower Street Suff 108 E3
Lower Street Suff 124 G5
Lower Strensham Worcs 99 C8
Lower Stretton Warr 183 E10
Lower Studley Wilts 45 B11
Lower Sundon C Beds 103 F10
Lower Swainswick Bath 61 F9
Lower Swanwick Hants 33 F7
Lower Swell Glos 100 F3
Lower Sydenham London 67 E11
Lower Tadmarton Oxon 101 D8
Lower Tale Devon 27 G9
Lower Tasburgh Norf 142 D3
Lower Tean Staffs 151 B10
Lower Thorpe Northants 101 B10
Lower Threapwood Wrex 166 G6
Lower Thurlton Norf 143 D8
Lower Thurnham Lancs 202 C5
Lower Thurvaston Derbys 152 B4
Lower Todding Hereford 115 B8
Lower Tote Highld 298 C5
Lower Town Devon 27 E8
Lower Town Hereford 98 C2
Lower Town Pembs 91 D9
Lower Town W Yorks 204 G6
Lower Town Worcs 117 F7
Lower Trebullett Corn 12 F2
Lower Tregunnon Corn 11 E10
Lower Treworrick Corn 6 B4
Lower Tuffley Glos 80 C4
Lower Turmer Hants 31 F10
Lower Twitchen Devon 24 D5
Lower Twydall Medway 69 F10
Lower Tysoe Warks 100 B6
Lower Upham Hants 33 D8
Lower Upnor Medway 69 E9
Lower Vexford Som 42 F6
Lower Wainhill Oxon 84 E3
Lower Walton Warr 183 D10
Lower Wanborough Swindon 63 C8
Lower Weacombe Som 42 E6
Lower Weald M Keynes 102 D5
Lower Wear Devon 14 D4
Lower Weare Som 44 C2
Lower Weedon Northants 120 F2
Lower Welson Hereford 114 G5
Lower Westholme Som 44 E5
Lower Westhouse N Yorks 212 E3
Lower Westmancote Worcs 99 D8
Lower Weston Bath 61 F8
Lower Whatcombe Dorset 30 G4
Lower Whatley Som 45 D8
Lower Whitley W Ches 183 F10
Lower Wick Glos 80 F2
Lower Wick Worcs 116 G6
Lower Wield Hants 48 E6
Lower Willingdon E Sus 23 E9
Lower Winchendon or Nether Winchendon Bucks 84 C2
Lower Withington E Ches 168 B4
Lower Wolverton Worcs 117 G8
Lower Woodend Aberds 293 B8
Lower Woodend Bucks 65 B10
Lower Woodford Wilts 46 G6
Lower Woodley Corn 5 B10
Lower Woodside Herts 86 D2
Lower Woolston Som 29 B11
Lower Woon Corn 5 C10
Lower Wraxall Dorset 29 G9
Lower Wraxall Som 44 F6
Lower Wraxall Wilts 61 G10
Lower Wych W Ches 167 G7
Lower Wyche Worcs 98 C5
Lower Wyke W Yorks 197 B7
Lower Yelland Devon 40 G3
Lower Zeals Wilts 45 G9
Lowerford Lancs 204 F3
Lowerhouse E Ches 184 F6
Lowerhouse Lancs 204 G2
Lowertown Corn 2 D5
Lowertown Corn 5 C11
Lowertown Devon 12 E5
Lowes Barn Durham 233 C11
Lowesby Leics 136 B4
Lowestoft Suff 143 E10
Loweswater Cumb 229 G8
Lowfield S Yorks 186 D5
Lowfield Heath W Sus 51 E9
Lowford Hants 33 E7
Lowgill Cumb 222 F2
Lowgill Lancs 212 G3
Lowick Cumb 210 B5
Lowick Northants 137 G9
Lowick Northumb 264 B2
Lowick Bridge Cumb 210 B5
Lowick Green Cumb 210 B5
Lowlands Torf 78 F3
Lowmoor Row Cumb 231 F8
Lowna N Yorks 226 G3
Lownie Moor Angus 287 C8
Lowood Borders 262 B2
Lowsonford Warks 118 D3
Lowther Cumb 230 G6
Lowthertown Dumfries 238 D6
Lowtherville I o W 21 F7
Lowthorpe E Yorks 217 G11
Lowton Gtr Man 183 B10
Lowton Som 27 D11
Lowton Common Gtr Man 183 B10
Lowton Heath Gtr Man 183 B10
Lowton St Mary's Gtr Man 183 B10
Loxbeare Devon 26 D6
Loxford London 68 B2
Loxhill Sur 50 F4
Loxhore Devon 40 F6
Loxhore Cott Devon 40 F6
Loxley S Yorks 186 D4
Loxley Warks 118 G5
Loxley Green Staffs 151 C11
Loxter Hereford 98 C4
Loxton N Som 43 B11
Loxwood W Sus 50 G4
Loyter's Green Essex 87 C8
Loyterton Kent 70 G3
Lozells W Mid 133 F11
Lubachlaggan Highld 300 B3
Lubachoinnich Highld 309 K4
Lubberland Shrops 116 B2
Lubcroy Highld 309 J3
Lubenham Leics 136 F4
Lubinvullin Highld 308 C5
Lucas End Herts 86 E4
Lucas Green Lancs 194 C5
Lucas Green Sur 50 B2
Luccombe Som 42 E2
Luccombe Village I o W 21 F7
Lucker Northumb 264 C5
Luckett Corn 12 G3
Lucking Street Essex 106 E6
Luckington Wilts 61 C10
Lucklawhill Fife 287 E8
Luckwell Bridge Som 42 F2
Lucton Hereford 115 E8
Ludag W Isles 297 K3
Ludborough Lincs 190 B3
Ludbrook Devon 8 E3
Ludchurch Pembs 73 C10
Luddenden W Yorks 196 B4
Luddenden Foot W Yorks 196 C4
Ludderburn Cumb 221 G8
Luddesdown Kent 69 F7
Luddington N Lincs 199 D10
Luddington Warks 118 G3
Luddington in the Brook Northants 138 G2
Lude House Perth 291 G10
Ludford Lincs 190 D2
Ludford Shrops 115 C10
Ludgershall Bucks 83 B11
Ludgershall Wilts 47 C9
Ludgvan Corn 2 C2
Ludham Norf 161 F7
Ludlow Shrops 115 C10
Ludney Lincs 190 B5
Ludney Som 28 E5
Ludstock Hereford 98 D3
Ludstone Shrops 132 E6
Ludwell Wilts 30 C6
Ludworth Durham 234 C3
Luffenhall Herts 104 F5
Luffincott Devon 12 C2
Lufton Som 29 D8
Lugar E Ayrs 258 E3
Lugate Borders 271 G8
Lugg Green Hereford 115 E9
Luggate Burn E Loth 282 G2
Luggiebank N Lnrk 278 G5
Lugsdale Halton 183 D8
Lugton E Ayrs 267 E8
Lugwardine Hereford 97 C11
Luib Highld 295 C7
Luibeilt Highld 290 G4
Lulham Hereford 97 C8
Lullenden Sur 52 E2
Lullington Derbys 152 G5
Lullington Som 45 C9
Lulsgate Bottom N Som 60 F4
Lulsley Worcs 116 F4
Lulworth Camp Dorset 18 E2
Lumb Lancs 195 C10
Lumb Lancs 195 D9
Lumb W Yorks 196 C4
Lumb W Yorks 197 E7
Lumb Foot W Yorks 204 F6
Lumburn Devon 12 G5
Lumbutts W Yorks 196 C3
Lumby N Yorks 206 G5
Lumley W Sus 22 B3
Lumley Thicks Durham 243 G8
Lumloch E Dunb 268 B2
Lumphanan Aberds 293 C7
Lumphinnans Fife 280 C3
Lumsdaine Borders 273 B7
Lumsden Aberds 302 G4
Lunan Angus 287 B10
Lunanhead Angus 287 B8
Luncarty Perth 286 E4
Lund E Yorks 208 D5
Lund N Yorks 207 G9
Lund Shetland 312 C7
Lundal W Isles 304 E3
Lundavra Highld 290 G2
Lunderton Aberds 303 E11
Lundie Angus 286 D6
Lundie Highld 290 B3
Lundin Links Fife 287 G8
Lundwood S Yorks 197 F11
Lundy Green Norf 142 E4
Lunga Argyll 275 C8
Lunna Shetland 312 G6
Lunning Shetland 312 G7
Lunnister Shetland 312 F5
Lunnon Swansea 56 D4
Lunsford Kent 53 B7
Lunsford's Cross E Sus 38 E2
Lunt Mers 193 G10
Luntley Hereford 115 F7
Lunts Heath Halton 183 D8
Lupin Staffs 152 F2
Luppitt Devon 27 F11
Lupridge Devon 8 E4
Lupset W Yorks 197 D10
Lupton Cumb 211 C2
Lurg Aberds 293 C8
Lurgashall W Sus 34 B6
Lurignich Argyll 289 D11
Lurley Devon 26 E6
Lusby Lincs 174 B4
Luscombe Devon 8 D5
Luson Devon 8 F2
Luss Argyll 277 C7
Lussagiven Argyll 275 E7
Lusta Highld 298 D2
Lustleigh Devon 13 E11
Lustleigh Cleave Devon 13 E11
Luston Hereford 115 E9
Lusty Som 45 G7
Luthermuir Aberds 293 G8
Luthrie Fife 287 F7
Lutley W Mid 133 G8
Luton Devon 14 F4
Luton Devon 27 G9
Luton Luton 103 G11
Luton Medway 69 F9
Lutsford Devon 24 D3
Lutterworth Leics 135 G10
Lutton Devon 7 D11
Lutton Devon 8 C3
Lutton Lincs 157 D8
Lutton Northants 138 F2
Lutton Gowts Lincs 157 E8
Lutworthy Devon 26 D3
Luxborough Som 42 F3
Luxley Glos 98 G3
Luxted London 68 G2
Luxton Devon 28 E2
Luxulyan Corn 5 D11
Luzley Gtr Man 196 G3
Luzley Brook Gtr Man 196 F2
Lyatts Som 29 E8
Lybster Highld 310 F6
Lydbury North Shrops 131 F7
Lydcott Devon 41 F7
Lydd Kent 39 C8
Lydd on Sea Kent 39 C9
Lydden Kent 55 D9
Lydden Kent 71 F11
Lyddington Rutland 137 D7
Lyde Orkney 314 E3
Lyde Shrops 130 C6
Lyde Cross Hereford 97 C10
Lyde Green Hants 49 B8
Lyde Green S Glos 61 D7
Lydeard St Lawrence Som 42 G6
Lydford Devon 12 E6
Lydford Fair Place Som 44 G5
Lydford-on-Fosse Som 44 G5
Lydgate Derbys 186 F4
Lydgate Gtr Man 196 G3
Lydgate W Yorks 196 B2
Lydham Shrops 130 E6
Lydiard Green Wilts 62 B5
Lydiard Millicent Wilts 62 B5
Lydiard Plain Wilts 62 B5
Lydiard Tregoze Swindon 62 C6
Lydiate Mers 193 G11
Lydiate Ash Worcs 117 B9
Lydlinch Dorset 30 E2
Lydmarsh Som 28 F5
Lydney Glos 79 E10
Lydstep Pembs 73 F9
Lye W Mid 133 G8
Lye Cross N Som 60 G3
Lye Green Bucks 85 E7
Lye Green E Sus 52 G4
Lye Green Warks 118 D3
Lye Green Wilts 45 B10
Lye Head Worcs 116 C5
Lye Hole N Som 60 G4
Lyewood Common E Sus 52 F4
Lyford Oxon 82 G5
Lymbridge Green Kent 54 E6
Lyme Green E Ches 184 G6
Lyme Regis Dorset 16 C2
Lymiecleuch Borders 249 C9
Lyminge Kent 55 E7
Lymington Hants 20 B2
Lyminster W Sus 35 G8
Lymm Warr 183 D11
Lymore Hants 19 C11
Lympne Kent 54 F6
Lympsham Som 43 C10
Lympstone Devon 14 E5
Lynbridge Devon 41 D8
Lynch Hants 48 D4
Lynch Som 42 D2
Lynch Hill Hants 48 D3
Lynch Hill Slough 66 C2
Lynchat Highld 291 C9
Lynchgate Shrops 131 F7
Lyndale Ho Highld 298 D3
Lyndhurst Hants 32 F4
Lyndon Rutland 137 C8
Lyndon Green W Mid 134 F2
Lyne Borders 270 G4
Lyne Sur 66 F4
Lyne Down Hereford 98 E2
Lyne of Gorthleck Highld 300 G5
Lyne of Skene Aberds 293 B9
Lyne Station Borders 260 B6
Lyneal Shrops 149 C8
Lyneal Mill Shrops 149 C9
Lyneal Wood Shrops 149 C9
Lyneham Oxon 100 G5
Lyneham Wilts 62 D4
Lynemore Highld 301 G10
Lynemouth Northumb 253 E7
Lyness Orkney 314 G3
Lynford Norf 140 E6
Lyng Norf 159 F11
Lyng Som 28 B4
Lyngate Norf 160 C5
Lyngford Som 28 B2
Lynmore Highld 301 F10
Lynmouth Devon 41 D8
Lynn Staffs 133 C11
Lynn Telford 150 F5
Lynnwood Borders 261 G11
Lynsore Bottom Kent 55 D7
Lynsted Kent 70 G2
Lynstone Corn 24 F2
Lynton Devon 41 D8
Lynwilg Highld 291 B10
Lynworth Glos 99 G9
Lyons T & W 234 B3
Lyon's Gate Dorset 29 F11
Lyon's Green Norf 159 G8
Lyons Hall Essex 88 B2
Lyonshall Hereford 114 F6
Lypiatt Glos 80 D6
Lyrabus Argyll 274 G3
Lytchett Matravers Dorset 18 B4
Lytchett Minster Dorset 18 C5
Lyth Highld 310 C6
Lytham Lancs 193 B11
Lytham St Anne's Lancs 193 B10
Lythbank Shrops 131 B9
Lythe N Yorks 226 C6
Lythes Orkney 314 H4
Lythmore Highld 310 C4

M

Maam Argyll 284 F5
Mabe Burnthouse Corn 3 C7
Mabie Dumfries 237 B11
Mabledon Kent 52 E5
Mablethorpe Lincs 191 D8
Macclesfield E Ches 184 G6
Macclesfield Forest E Ches 185 G7
Macduff Aberds 303 C7
Mace Green Suff 108 C2
Machan S Lnrk 268 E5
Macharioch Argyll 255 G8
Machen Caerph 59 B8
Machrie N Ayrs 255 D9
Machrie Hotel Argyll 254 C4
Machrihanish Argyll 255 E7
Machroes Gwyn 144 D6
Machynlleth Powys 128 C4
Machynys Carms 56 B4
Mackerel's Common W Sus 35 B8
Mackerye End Herts 85 B11
Mackham Devon 27 F11
Mackney Oxon 64 B5
Mackside Borders 262 G4
Mackworth Derbys 152 B6
Macmerry E Loth 281 G8
Madderty Perth 286 E3
Maddington Wilts 46 E5
Maddiston Falk 279 F8
Maddox Moor Pembs 73 C7
Madehurst W Sus 35 E7
Madeley Staffs 168 G3
Madeley Telford 132 C3
Madeley Heath Staffs 168 F3
Madeley Heath Worcs 117 B9
Madeley Park Staffs 168 G3
Madeleywood Telford 132 C3
Maders Corn 12 G2
Madford Devon 27 E10
Madingley Cambs 123 E7
Madjeston Dorset 30 B4
Madley Hereford 97 D8
Madresfield Worcs 98 B6
Madron Corn 1 C5
Maen-y-groes Ceredig 111 F7
Maenaddwyn Anglesey 179 E7
Maenclochog Pembs 91 F11
Maendy V Glam 58 D4
Maenporth Corn 3 D7
Maentwrog Gwyn 163 G11
Maer Corn 24 F2
Maer Staffs 150 B5
Maerdy Carms 94 G2
Maerdy Conwy 165 G8
Maerdy Rhondda 77 F7
Maes-bangor Ceredig 128 G3
Maes-glas Newport 59 B9
Maes Glas = Greenfield Flint 181 F11
Maes llyn Ceredig 93 C7
Maes Pennant Flint 181 F11
Maes-Treylow Powys 114 D5
Maes-y-dre Flint 166 C2
Maesbrook Shrops 148 E5
Maesbury Shrops 148 D6
Maesbury Marsh Shrops 148 D6
Maesgeirchen Gwyn 179 G9
Maesgwyn-Isaf Powys 148 G3
Maeshafn Denb 166 C2
Maesllyn Ceredig 93 C7
Maesmynis Powys 95 B10
Maesteg Bridgend 57 C10
Maesybont Carms 75 B9
Maesycoed Rhondda 58 B5
Maesycrugiau Carms 93 C9
Maesycwmmer Caerph 77 G11
Maesygwartha Mon 78 C2
Maesymeillion Ceredig 93 B8
Maesypandy Powys 129 D9
Maesyrhandir Powys 129 E11
Magdalen Laver Essex 87 D8
Maggieknockater Moray 302 E3
Maggots End Essex 105 F9
Magham Down E Sus 23 C10
Maghull Mers 193 G11
Magor Mon 60 B2
Magpie Green Suff 125 B11
Mahaar Dumfries 236 B2
Maida Vale London 67 C9
Maiden Bradley Wilts 45 F10
Maiden Head N Som 60 F5
Maiden Law Durham 233 B9
Maiden Newton Dorset 17 B7
Maiden Wells Pembs 73 F7
Maidenbower W Sus 51 F9
Maidencombe Torbay 9 B8
Maidenhall Suff 108 C3
Maidenhead Windsor 65 C11
Maidenhead Court Windsor 66 C2
Maidenpark Falk 279 E9
Maidens S Ayrs 244 B6
Maiden's Green Brack 65 E11
Maiden's Hall Northumb 252 D6
Maidensgrave Suff 108 B5
Maidensgrove Oxon 65 B8
Maidenwell Corn 11 G8
Maidenwell Lincs 190 F4
Maidford Northants 120 G2
Maids Moreton Bucks 102 D4
Maidstone Kent 53 B9
Maidwell Northants 120 B4
Mail Shetland 313 L6
Mailand Shetland 312 C8
Mailingsland Borders 270 G4
Main Powys 148 F3
Maindee Newport 59 B10
Maindy Cardiff 59 D7
Mainholm S Ayrs 257 E9
Mains Cumb 229 G7
Mains of Airies Dumfries 236 C1
Mains of Allardice Aberds 293 F10
Mains of Annochie Aberds 303 E9
Mains of Ardestie Angus 287 D9
Mains of Arnage Aberds 303 F9
Mains of Auchoynanie Moray 302 E4
Mains of Baldoon Dumfries 236 D6
Mains of Balhall Angus 293 G7
Mains of Ballindarg Angus 287 B8
Mains of Balnakettle Aberds 293 F8
Mains of Birness Aberds 303 F9
Mains of Blackhall Aberds 303 G7
Mains of Burgie Moray 301 D10
Mains of Cairnbrogie Aberds 303 G8
Mains of Cairnty Moray 302 D3
Mains of Clunas Highld 301 E8
Mains of Crichie Aberds 303 E9
Mains of Daltulich Highld 301 E7
Mains of Dalvey Highld 301 F11
Mains of Dellavaird Aberds 293 E9
Mains of Drum Aberds 293 D10
Mains of Edingight Moray 302 D5
Mains of Fedderate Aberds 303 E8
Mains of Flichity Highld 300 G6
Mains of Hatton Aberds 303 D9
Mains of Hatton Aberds 303 E7
Mains of Inkhorn Aberds 303 F9
Mains of Innerpeffray Perth 286 F3
Mains of Kirktonhill Aberds 293 G8
Mains of Laithers Aberds 302 E6
Mains of Mayen Moray 302 E5
Mains of Melgund Angus 287 B9
Mains of Taymouth Perth 285 C11
Mains of Thornton Aberds 293 F8
Mains of Towie Aberds 303 E7
Mains of Ulbster Highld 310 E7
Mains of Watten Highld 310 D6
Mainsforth Durham 234 E2
Mainsriddle Dumfries 237 D11
Mainstone Shrops 130 F5
Maisemore Glos 98 G6
Maitland Park London 67 C9
Major's Green W Mid 118 B2
Makeney Derbys 170 G5
Malacleit W Isles 296 D3
Malborough Devon 9 G9
Malcoff Derbys 185 E9
Malden Rushett London 67 G7
Maldon Essex 88 D4
Malehurst Shrops 131 B7
Malham N Yorks 213 G8
Maligar Highld 298 C4
Malinbridge S Yorks 186 D4
Malinslee Telford 132 B3
Malkin's Bank E Ches 168 D3
Mallaig Highld 295 F8
Mallaig Bheag Highld 295 F8
Malleny Mills Edin 270 B3
Malling Stirl 285 G9
Mallows Green Essex 105 F9
Malltraeth Anglesey 162 B6
Mallwyd Gwyn 147 G7
Malmesbury Wilts 62 B2
Malmsmead Devon 41 D9
Malpas Corn 4 G6
Malpas Newport 78 G4
Malpas W Berks 64 E6
Malpas W Ches 167 F7
Malswick Glos 98 F4
Maltby Lincs 190 E4
Maltby S Yorks 187 C8
Maltby Stockton 225 C9
Maltby le Marsh Lincs 191 E7
Malting End Suff 124 G4
Malting Green Essex 107 G9
Maltings Angus 293 G9
Maltman's Hill Kent 54 E2
Malton N Yorks 216 E5
Malvern Common Worcs 98 C5
Malvern Link Worcs 98 B5
Malvern Wells Worcs 98 C5
Mambeg Argyll 276 D4
Mamble Worcs 116 C3
Mamhilad Mon 78 E4
Man-moel Caerph 77 E11
Manaccan Corn 3 E7
Manadon Plym 7 D9
Manafon Powys 130 C2
Manais W Isles 296 C7
Manar Ho Aberds 303 G7
Manaton Devon 13 E11
Manby Lincs 190 D5
Mancetter Warks 134 D6
Manchester Gtr Man 184 B4
Manchester Airport Gtr Man 184 D4
Mancot Flint 166 B4
Mancot Royal Flint 166 B4
Mandally Highld 290 C4
Manea Cambs 139 F9
Maney W Mid 134 D2
Manfield N Yorks 224 C4
Mangaster Shetland 312 F5
Mangotsfield S Glos 61 D7
Mangrove Green Herts 104 G2
Mangurstadh W Isles 304 E2
Manhay Corn 2 C5
Manian-fawr Pembs 92 B3
Mankinholes W Yorks 196 C3
Manley Devon 27 E7
Manley W Ches 183 G8
Manley Common W Ches 183 G8
Manmoel Caerph 77 E11
Mannal Argyll 288 E1
Mannamead Plym 7 D9
Mannerston W Loth 279 F10
Manningford Abbots Wilts 46 B6
Manningford Bohune Wilts 46 B6
Manningford Bruce Wilts 46 B6
Manningham W Yorks 205 G9
Mannings Heath W Sus 36 B2
Mannington Dorset 31 F9
Manningtree Essex 107 E11
Mannofield Aberdeen 293 C11
Manor London 68 B2
Manor Bourne Devon 7 F9
Manor Estate S Yorks 186 D5
Manor Hill Corner Lincs 157 F8
Manor House W Mid 135 G7
Manor Park Bucks 84 C4
Manor Park E Sus 37 C7
Manor Park London 68 B2
Manor Park Notts 153 C11
Manor Park S Yorks 186 D5
Manor Park Slough 66 C3
Manor Park W Ches 167 B11
Manor Park W Yorks 205 D9
Manor Parsley Corn 4 F4
Manor Royal W Sus 51 F9
Manorbier Pembs 73 F9
Manorbier Newton Pembs 73 F8
Manordeilo Carms 94 F3
Manorhill Borders 262 C5
Manorowen Pembs 91 D8
Man's Cross Essex 106 D5
Mansegate Dumfries 247 G9
Mansel Lacy Hereford 97 B8
Manselfield Swansea 56 D5
Mansell Gamage Hereford 97 C7
Manselton Swansea 57 B7
Mansergh Cumb 212 C2
Mansewood Glasgow 267 C11
Mansfield E Ayrs 258 G4
Mansfield Notts 171 C8
Mansfield Woodhouse Notts 171 C8
Manson Green Norf 141 C10
Mansriggs Cumb 210 C5
Manston Dorset 30 D4
Manston Kent 71 F10
Manston W Yorks 206 F3
Manswood Dorset 31 F7
Manthorpe Lincs 155 B8
Manthorpe Lincs 155 F11
Mantles Green Bucks 85 F7
Manton N Lincs 200 G2
Manton Notts 187 F9
Manton Rutland 137 C7
Manton Wilts 63 F7
Manton Warren N Lincs 200 F2
Manuden Essex 105 F9
Manwood Green Essex 87 C8
Manywells Height W Yorks 205 F7
Maperton Som 29 B11
Maple Cross Herts 85 G8
Maple End Essex 105 D11
Maplebeck Notts 172 C2
Mapledurham Oxon 65 D7
Mapledurwell Hants 49 C7
Maplehurst W Sus 35 C11
Maplescombe Kent 68 G5
Mapleton Derbys 169 F11
Mapperley Derbys 170 G6
Mapperley Nottingham 171 G9
Mapperley Park Nottingham 171 G9
Mapperton Dorset 16 B6
Mapperton Dorset 18 B4
Mappleborough Green Warks 117 D11
Mappleton E Yorks 209 E10
Mapplewell S Yorks 197 F10
Mappowder Dorset 30 F2
Mar Lodge Aberds 292 D2
Maraig W Isles 305 H3
Marazanvose Corn 4 E6
Marazion Corn 2 C2
Marbhig W Isles 305 G6
Marbrack Dumfries 246 E3
Marbury E Ches 167 F9
March Cambs 139 D8
March S Lnrk 259 G11
Marcham Oxon 83 F7
Marchamley Shrops 149 D11
Marchamley Wood Shrops 149 C11
Marchington Staffs 152 C2
Marchington Woodlands Staffs 152 D2
Marchroes Gwyn 144 D6
Marchwiel Wrex 166 F5
Marchwood Hants 32 E5
Marcross V Glam 58 F2
Marden Hereford 97 B10
Marden Kent 53 E8
Marden T & W 243 C9
Marden Wilts 46 B5
Marden Ash Essex 87 E9
Marden Beech Kent 53 E8
Marden Thorn Kent 53 E9
Marden's Hill E Sus 52 G3
Mardleybury Herts 86 B3
Mardu Shrops 130 G5
Mardy Mon 78 B4
Mardy Shrops 148 C5
Marefield Leics 136 B4
Mareham le Fen Lincs 174 C3
Mareham on the Hill Lincs 174 B3
Marehay Derbys 170 F5
Marehill W Sus 35 D9
Maresfield E Sus 37 C7
Maresfield Park E Sus 37 C7
Marfleet Hull 200 B6
Marford Wrex 166 D5
Margam Neath 57 D9
Margaret Marsh Dorset 30 D4
Margaret Roding Essex 87 C9
Margaretting Essex 87 E11
Margaretting Tye Essex 87 E11
Margate Kent 71 E11
Margery Sur 51 C9
Margnaheglish N Ayrs 256 C2
Margreig Dumfries 237 B10
Margrove Park Redcar 226 B3
Marham Norf 158 G4
Marhamchurch Corn 24 G2
Marholm P'boro 138 C2
Marian Flint 181 F9
Marian Cwm Denb 181 F9
Marian-glas Anglesey 179 E8
Marian y de = South Beach Gwyn 145 C7
Marian y mor = West End Gwyn 145 C7
Mariandyrys Anglesey 179 E10
Marianglas Anglesey 179 E8
Mariansleigh Devon 26 C2
Marine Town Kent 70 E2
Marionburgh Aberds 293 C9
Marishader Highld 298 C4
Marjoriebanks Dumfries 248 G3
Mark Dumfries 236 D3
Mark Dumfries 237 C7
Mark S Ayrs 236 B2
Mark Som 43 D11
Mark Causeway Som 43 D11
Mark Cross E Sus 23 C7
Mark Cross E Sus 52 G5
Mark Hall North Essex 87 C7
Mark Hall South Essex 87 C7
Markbeech Kent 52 E3
Markby Lincs 191 F7
Markeaton Derbys 152 B6
Market Bosworth Leics 135 C8
Market Deeping Lincs 138 B2
Market Drayton Shrops 150 C3
Market Harborough Leics 136 F4
Market Lavington Wilts 46 C4
Market Overton Rutland 155 F7
Market Rasen Lincs 189 D10
Market Stainton Lincs 190 F2
Market Warsop Notts 171 B9
Market Weighton E Yorks 208 E3
Market Weston Suff 125 B9
Markethill Perth 286 D6
Markfield Leics 153 G9
Markham Caerph 77 E11
Markham Moor Notts 188 G2
Markinch Fife 286 G6
Markington N Yorks 214 F5
Markland Hill Gtr Man 195 F7
Markle E Loth 281 F11
Mark's Corner I o W 20 C5
Marks Gate London 87 G7
Marks Tey Essex 107 G8
Marksbury Bath 61 G7
Markyate Herts 85 B9
Marl Bank Worcs 98 C5
Marland Gtr Man 195 E11
Marlas Hereford 97 F8
Marlborough Wilts 63 F7
Marlbrook Hereford 115 G10
Marlbrook Worcs 117 C9
Marlcliff Warks 117 G11
Marldon Devon 9 C7
Marle Green E Sus 23 B9
Marle Hill Glos 99 G9
Marlesford Suff 126 F6
Marley Kent 55 C10
Marley Kent 55 C7
Marley Green E Ches 167 F9
Marley Heights W Sus 49 G11
Marley Hill T & W 242 F6
Marley Pots T & W 243 F9
Marlingford Norf 142 B2
Marloes Pembs 72 D3
Marlow Bucks 65 B10
Marlow Hereford 115 B8
Marlow Bottom Bucks 65 B11
Marlow Common Bucks 65 B10
Marlpit Hill Kent 52 D2
Marlpits E Sus 38 E2
Marlpool Derbys 170 F6
Marnhull Dorset 30 D3
Marnoch Aberds 302 D5
Marnock N Lnrk 268 B4
Marple Gtr Man 185 D7
Marple Bridge Gtr Man 185 D7
Marpleridge Gtr Man 185 D7
Marr S Yorks 198 F4
Marr Green Wilts 63 G8
Marrel Highld 311 H4
Marrick N Yorks 223 F11
Marrister Shetland 313 G7
Marros Carms 74 D2
Marsden T & W 243 E9
Marsden W Yorks 196 E4
Marsden Height Lancs 204 F3
Marsett N Yorks 213 B8
Marsh Bucks 84 D4
Marsh Devon 28 E3
Marsh W Yorks 196 D6
Marsh W Yorks 204 F6
Marsh Baldon Oxon 83 F9
Marsh Benham W Berks 64 F2
Marsh Common S Glos 60 C5
Marsh End Worcs 98 D6
Marsh Gate W Berks 63 F10
Marsh Gibbon Bucks 102 G2
Marsh Green Devon 14 C6
Marsh Green Gtr Man 194 F5
Marsh Green Kent 52 E2
Marsh Green Staffs 168 D5
Marsh Green Telford 150 G2
Marsh Green W Ches 183 F8
Marsh Houses Lancs 202 C5
Marsh Lane Derbys 186 F6
Marsh Lane Glos 79 D9
Marsh Mills Som 43 F7
Marsh Side Norf 176 E3
Marsh Street Som 42 E3
Marshall Meadows Northumb 273 D9
Marshall's Cross Mers 183 C8
Marshall's Elm Som 44 G3
Marshall's Heath Herts 85 B11
Marshalsea Dorset 28 G5
Marshalswick Herts 85 D11
Marsham Norf 160 E3
Marshaw Lancs 203 C7
Marshborough Kent 55 B10
Marshbrook Shrops 131 F8
Marshchapel Lincs 190 B5
Marshfield Newport 59 C9
Marshfield S Glos 61 E9
Marshfield Bank E Ches 167 D11
Marshgate Corn 11 C9
Marshland St James Norf 139 B10
Marshmoor Herts 86 D2
Marshside Kent 71 F8
Marshside Mers 193 D11
Marshwood Dorset 16 B3
Marske N Yorks 224 E2
Marske-by-the-Sea Redcar 235 G8
Marston Hereford 115 F7
Marston Lincs 172 G5
Marston Oxon 83 D8
Marston Staffs 150 G6
Marston Staffs 151 D8
Marston W Ches 183 F11
Marston Warks 119 B8
Marston Warks 134 E4
Marston Wilts 46 B3
Marston Bigot Som 45 E9
Marston Doles Warks 119 F9
Marston Gate Som 45 D9
Marston Green W Mid 134 F3
Marston Hill Glos 81 F11
Marston Jabbett Warks 135 F7
Marston Magna Som 29 C9
Marston Meysey Wilts 81 F10
Marston Montgomery Derbys 152 B2
Marston Moretaine C Beds 10
Marston on Dove Derbys 15
Marston St Lawrence Northants 101
Marston Stannett Hereford 11
Marston Trussell Northants 13
Marstow Hereford 7
Marsworth Bucks 8
Marten Wilts 4
Marthall E Ches 18
Martham Norf 16
Marthwaite Cumb 22
Martin Hants 3
Martin Kent 5
Martin Lincs 17
Martin Lincs 17
Martin Dales Lincs 17
Martin Drove End Hants 3
Martin Hussingtree Worcs 11
Martin Mill Kent 5
Martin Moor Lincs 17
Martindale Cumb 22
Martinhoe Devon 4
Martinhoe Cross Devon 4
Martin's Moss E Ches 16
Martinscroft Warr 18
Martinstown Dorset 1
Martinstown or Winterbourne St Martin Dorset 1
Martlesham Suff 10
Martlesham Heath Suff 10
Martletwy Pembs 7
Martley Worcs 11
Martock Som 2
Marton Cumb 2
Marton E Ches 1
Marton E Yorks 2
Marton Lincs 1
Marton M'bro 22
Marton N Yorks 2
Marton N Yorks 2
Marton Shrops 1
Marton Shrops 1
Marton W Ches 16
Marton Warks 1
Marton Green W Ches 16
Marton Grove M'bro 2
Marton-in-the-Forest N Yorks 21
Marton-le-Moor N Yorks 2
Marton Moor Warks 1
Marton Moss Side Blkpool 2
Martyr Worthy Hants 4
Martyr's Green Sur 5
Marwick Orkney 3
Marwood Devon
Mary Tavy Devon
Marybank Highld 30
Marybank Highld 3
Maryburgh Highld 30
Maryfield Aberds 2
Maryfield Corn
Maryhill Glasgow 26
Marykirk Aberds 2
Maryland Mon 7
Marylebone Gtr Man 1
Marypark Moray 30
Maryport Cumb 2
Maryport Dumfries 2
Maryton Angus 28
Maryton Angus 28
Marywell Aberds 29
Marywell Aberds 2
Marywell Angus 28
Masbrough S Yorks 1
Mascle Bridge Pembs 7
Masham N Yorks 2
Mashbury Essex 8
Masongill N Yorks 2
Masonhill S Ayrs 2
Mastin Moor Derbys 1
Mastrick Aberdeen 29
Matchborough Worcs 11
Matching Essex
Matching Green Essex
Matching Tye Essex
Matfen Northumb 2
Matfield Kent
Mathern Mon 7
Mathon Hereford
Mathry Pembs
Matlaske Norf 1
Matley Gtr Man 1
Matlock Derbys 17
Matlock Bank Derbys 17
Matlock Bath Derbys 17
Matlock Bridge Derbys 17
Matlock Cliff Derbys 17
Matlock Dale Derbys 17
Matshead Lancs 2
Matson Glos 8
Matterdale End Cumb 2
Mattersey Notts 18
Mattersey Thorpe Notts 18
Matthewsgreen Wokingham 6
Mattingley Hants 4
Mattishall Norf 15
Mattishall Burgh Norf 15
Mauchline E Ayrs 25
Maud Aberds 3
Maudlin Corn
Maudlin Dorset
Maudlin W Sus
Maudlin Cross Dorset
Maugersbury Glos 1
Maughold I o M 1
Mauld Highld 3
Maulden C Beds 10
Maulds Meaburn Cumb 22
Maunby N Yorks 2
Maund Bryan Hereford 11
Maundown Som
Mauricewood Midloth 2
Mautby Norf 16
Mavesyn Ridware Staffs 15
Mavis Enderby Lincs 1
Maviston Highld 30
Maw Green E Ches 16
Mawbray Cumb 22
Mawdesley Lancs 1
Mawdlam Bridgend 5
Mawgan Corn
Mawgan Porth Corn
Mawla Corn
Mawnan Corn
Mawnan Smith Corn
Mawsley Northants 1
Mawson Green S Yorks 1
Mawthorpe Lincs 1
Maxey P'boro 1
Maxstoke Warks 1

Moor of Balvack Aberds 293 B8
Moor of Granary Moray 301 D10
Moor of Ravenstone Dumfries 236 E5
Moor Park Cumb 229 D7
Moor Park Hereford 97 C9
Moor Park Herts 85 G9
Moor Park Sur 49 D11
Moor Row Cumb 219 C10
Moor Row Cumb 229 B10
Moor Side Lancs 202 F5
Moor Side Lancs 202 G4
Moor Side Lincs 174 D2
Moor Side W Yorks 197 B7
Moor Side W Yorks 204 F6
Moor Street Kent 69 F10
Moor Top W Yorks 197 C7
Mooradale Shetland 312 F6
Mooray Wilts 46 G3
Moorby Lincs 174 C3
Moorclose Cumb 228 F5
Moorclose Gtr Man 195 F11
Moorcot Hereford 115 F7
Moordown Bmouth 19 C7
Moore Halton 183 E9
Moorend Cumb 239 G8
Moorend Derbys 170 F2
Moorend Dumfries 239 C7
Moorend Glos 80 C5
Moorend Glos 80 E2
Moorend Gtr Man 185 D7
Moorend S Glos 61 D7
Moorend Cross Hereford 98 B4
Moorends S Yorks 199 D7
Moorfield Derbys 185 C8
Moorgate Norf 160 C3
Moorgate S Yorks 186 C6
Moorgreen Hants 33 D7
Moorgreen Notts 171 F7
Moorhaigh Notts 171 C8
Moorhall Derbys 186 G4
Moorhampton Hereford 97 B7
Moorhaven Village Devon 8 D3
Moorhayne Devon 28 F2
Moorhead W Yorks 205 F8
Moorhey Gtr Man 196 G2
Moorhole S Yorks 186 E6
Moorhouse Cumb 239 F8
Moorhouse Cumb 239 G7
Moorhouse Notts 172 B3
Moorhouse S Yorks 198 E3
Moorhouse Bank Sur 52 C2
Moorhouses Lincs 174 D3
Moorland or Northmoor Green Som 43 G10
Moorledge Bath 60 G5
Moorlinch Som 43 F11
Moorsholm Redcar 226 C3
Moorside Dorset 30 D3
Moorside Durham 233 B7
Moorside Gtr Man 195 G9
Moorside Gtr Man 196 F3
Moorside W Ches 182 F3
Moorside W Yorks 197 B8
Moorside W Yorks 205 F10
Moorstock Kent 54 F6
Moorswater Corn 6 C4
Moorthorpe W Yorks 198 E3
Moortown Devon 12 B2
Moortown Devon 12 G6
Moortown Devon 25 C8
Moortown Hants 31 G11
Moortown I o W 20 E4
Moortown Lincs 189 B9
Moortown Telford 150 F2
Moortown W Yorks 206 F2
Morangie Highld 309 L7
Morar Highld 295 F8
Moravian Settlement Derbys 153 B8
Mōrawelon Anglesey 178 E3
Morayhill Highld 301 E7
Morborne Cambs 138 E2
Morchard Bishop Devon 26 F3
Morchard Road Devon 26 G3
Morcombelake Dorset 16 C4
Morcott Rutland 137 C8
Morda Shrops 148 D5
Morden Dorset 18 B4
Morden London 67 F9
Morden Green Cambs 104 C5
Morden Park London 67 F8
Mordiford Hereford 97 D11
Mordington Holdings Borders 273 D8
Mordon Durham 234 F2
More Shrops 130 E6
More Crichel Dorset 31 F7
Morebath Devon 27 C7
Morebattle Borders 263 E7
Morecambe Lancs 211 G8
Moredon Swindon 62 B6
Moredun Edin 270 B5
Morefield Highld 307 K6
Morehall Kent 55 F8
Moreleaggan Argyll 284 G6
Moreleigh Devon 8 E5
Morenish Perth 285 D9
Moresby Cumb 228 G5
Moresby Parks Cumb 219 B9
Morestead Hants 33 B8
Moreton Dorset 18 D2
Moreton Essex 87 D8
Moreton Hereford 115 E10
Moreton Mers 182 C3
Moreton Oxon 82 E6
Moreton Oxon 83 E11
Moreton Staffs 150 F5
Moreton Staffs 152 D2
Moreton Corbet Shrops 149 E11
Moreton-in-Marsh Glos 100 E4
Moreton Jeffries Hereford 98 B2
Moreton Morrell Warks 118 F6
Moreton on Lugg Hereford 97 B10
Moreton Paddox Warks 118 G6
Moreton Pinkney Northants 101 B11
Moreton Say Shrops 150 C2
Moreton Valence Glos 80 D3
Moretonhampstead Devon 13 D11
Moretonwood Shrops 150 C2
Morfa Carms 56 B4
Morfa Carms 75 C9
Morfa Ceredig 110 G6
Morfa Gwyn 144 C3
Morfa Bach Carms 74 C5
Morfa Bychan Gwyn 145 B10
Morfa Dinlle Gwyn 162 D6
Morfa Glas Neath 76 D5
Morfa Nefyn Gwyn 162 G3
Morfydd Denb 165 F10
Morgan's Vale Wilts 31 C11
Morganstown Cardiff 58 C6
Moriah Ceredig 112 B2
Mork Glos 79 D9
Morland Cumb 231 G7
Morley Derbys 170 G5
Morley Durham 233 F8
Morley E Ches 184 E4
Morley W Yorks 197 B9
Morley Green E Ches 184 E4
Morley Park Derbys 170 F5
Morley St Botolph Norf 141 D11
Morley Smithy Derbys 170 G5
Morleymoor Derbys 170 G5
Mornick Corn 12 G2
Morningside Edin 280 G3
Morningside N Lnrk 268 D6
Morningthorpe Norf 142 E4
Morpeth Northumb 252 F6
Morphie Aberds 293 G9
Morrey Staffs 152 F2
Morridge Side Staffs 169 E8
Morrilow Heath Staffs 151 B9
Morris Green Essex 106 E4
Morriston = Treforys Swansea 57 B7
Morristown V Glam 59 E7
Morston Norf 177 E8
Mortehoe Devon 40 D3
Morthen S Yorks 187 D7
Mortimer W Berks 65 G7
Mortimer West End Hants 64 G6
Mortimer's Cross Hereford 115 E8
Mortlake London 67 D8
Mortomley S Yorks 186 B4
Morton Cumb 230 D4
Morton Cumb 239 G9
Morton Derbys 170 C6
Morton I o W 21 D8
Morton Lincs 155 E11
Morton Lincs 172 C5
Morton Lincs 188 C4
Morton Norf 160 F2
Morton Notts 172 E2
Morton S Glos 79 G10
Morton Shrops 148 E5
Morton Bagot Warks 118 E2
Morton Common Shrops 148 E5
Morton Mains Dumfries 247 D9
Morton Mill Shrops 149 E11
Morton-on-Swale N Yorks 224 G6
Morton Spirt Warks 117 G10
Morton Tinmouth Durham 233 G9
Morton Underhill Worcs 117 F10
Morvah Corn 1 B4
Morval Corn 6 D5
Morven Lodge Aberds 292 C5
Morvich Highld 295 C11
Morvich Highld 309 J7
Morville Shrops 132 E3
Morville Heath Shrops 132 E3
Morwellham Quay Devon 7 B8
Morwenstow Corn 24 E2
Mosborough S Yorks 186 E6
Moscow E Ayrs 267 G9
Mose Shrops 132 E5
Mosedale Cumb 230 E3
Moseley W Mid 133 D8
Moseley W Mid 133 G11
Moseley Worcs 116 F6
Moses Gate Gtr Man 195 F8
Mosley Common Gtr Man 195 G8
Moss Argyll 288 E1
Moss Highld 289 C8
Moss S Yorks 198 E5
Moss Wrex 166 E4
Moss Bank Halton 183 D8
Moss Bank Mers 183 B8
Moss Edge Lancs 202 D4
Moss Edge Lancs 202 E4
Moss End Brack 65 E11
Moss End E Ches 183 F11
Moss Houses E Ches 184 G5
Moss Lane E Ches 184 G6
Moss Nook Gtr Man 184 D4
Moss Nook Mers 183 C8
Moss of Barmuckity Moray 302 C2
Moss of Meft Moray 302 C2
Moss Pit Staffs 151 E8
Moss Side Cumb 238 G5
Moss Side Gtr Man 184 B4
Moss-side Highld 301 D8
Moss Side Lancs 193 G11
Moss Side Lancs 194 C4
Moss Side Lancs 202 G3
Moss Side Mers 182 B6
Moss-side Moray 302 D5
Mossat Aberds 292 B6
Mossbank Shetland 312 F6
Mossbay Cumb 228 F5
Mossblown S Ayrs 257 E10
Mossbrow Gtr Man 184 D2
Mossburnford Borders 262 F5
Mossdale Dumfries 237 B8
Mossedge Cumb 239 D11
Mossend N Lnrk 268 C4
Mosser Mains Cumb 229 F8
Mossfield Highld 300 B6
Mossgate Staffs 151 B8
Mossgiel E Ayrs 257 D11
Mosshouses Borders 262 B2
Mosside Angus 287 B8
Mossley E Ches 168 C5
Mossley Gtr Man 196 G3
Mossley Brow Gtr Man 196 G3
Mossley Hill Mers 182 D5
Mosspark Glasgow 267 C10
Mosstodloch Moray 302 D3
Mosston Angus 287 C9
Mosstown Aberds 303 C10
Mossy Lea Lancs 194 E4
Mosterton Dorset 29 F7
Moston E Ches 168 C2
Moston Gtr Man 195 G11
Moston Shrops 149 D11
Moston W Ches 182 G6
Moston Green E Ches 168 C2
Mostyn Flint 181 E11
Mostyn Quay Flint 181 E11
Motcombe Dorset 30 B5
Mothecombe Devon 8 F2
Motherby Cumb 230 F4
Motherwell N Lnrk 268 D5
Motspur Park London 67 F8
Mottingham London 68 E2
Mottisfont Hants 32 B4
Mottistone I o W 20 E4
Mottram in Longdendale Gtr Man 185 B7
Mottram Rise Gtr Man 185 B7
Mottram St Andrew E Ches 184 F5
Mott's Green Essex 87 B8
Mott's Mill E Sus 52 F4
Mouldsworth W Ches 183 G8
Moulin Perth 286 B3
Moulsecoomb Brighton 36 F4
Moulsford Oxon 64 C5
Moulsham Essex 88 D2
Moulsoe M Keynes 103 C8
Moultavie Highld 300 B6
Moulton Lincs 156 E6
Moulton N Yorks 224 E4
Moulton Northants 120 D5
Moulton Suff 124 E3
Moulton V Glam 58 E5
Moulton W Ches 167 B11
Moulton Chapel Lincs 156 F5
Moulton Eaugate Lincs 156 F6
Moulton Park Northants 120 E5
Moulton St Mary Norf 143 B7
Moulton Seas End Lincs 156 D6
Moulzie Angus 292 F4
Mounie Castle Aberds 303 G7
Mount Corn 4 D5
Mount Corn 6 B2
Mount Highld 301 E9
Mount W Yorks 196 D5
Mount Ambrose Corn 4 G4
Mount Ballan Mon 60 B3
Mount Batten Plym 7 E9
Mount Bovers Essex 88 G4
Mount Bures Essex 107 E8
Mount Canisp Highld 301 B7
Mount Charles Corn 5 B10
Mount Charles Corn 5 E10
Mount Cowdown Wilts 47 C9
Mount End Essex 87 E7
Mount Ephraim E Sus 23 B7
Mount Gould Plym 7 D9
Mount Hawke Corn 4 F4
Mount Hermon Corn 2 F6
Mount Hermon Sur 50 B4
Mount Hill S Glos 61 E7
Mount Lane Devon 12 B3
Mount Pleasant Bucks 102 E3
Mount Pleasant Corn 5 C10
Mount Pleasant Derbys 152 D6
Mount Pleasant Derbys 152 F5
Mount Pleasant Derbys 170 F4
Mount Pleasant Devon 27 G11
Mount Pleasant Durham 233 E11
Mount Pleasant E Ches 168 D4
Mount Pleasant E Sus 23 E7
Mount Pleasant E Sus 36 D6
Mount Pleasant Flint 182 G2
Mount Pleasant Hants 19 B11
Mount Pleasant Kent 71 F10
Mount Pleasant London 85 G8
Mount Pleasant M Tydf 77 E9
Mount Pleasant Neath 57 B9
Mount Pleasant Norf 141 E9
Mount Pleasant Pembs 73 D8
Mount Pleasant Shrops 149 G9
Mount Pleasant Stockton 234 G4
Mount Pleasant Stoke 168 G5
Mount Pleasant Suff 106 B4
Mount Pleasant T & W 243 E7
Mount Pleasant W Yorks 197 C8
Mount Pleasant Warks 135 F7
Mount Pleasant Worcs 99 D10
Mount Pleasant Worcs 117 E10
Mount Sion Wrex 166 E3
Mount Skippett Oxon 82 B5
Mount Sorrel Wilts 31 C8
Mount Tabor W Yorks 196 B5
Mount Vernon Glasgow 268 C3
Mount Wise Corn 7 E9
Mountain Anglesey 178 E2
Mountain W Yorks 205 G7
Mountain Air Bl Gwent 77 D11
Mountain Ash = Aberpennar Rhondda 77 F8
Mountain Bower Wilts 61 D10
Mountain Cross Borders 270 F2
Mountain Street Kent 54 C5
Mountain Water Pembs 91 G8
Mountbenger Borders 261 D8
Mountbengerburn Borders 261 D8
Mountblow W Dunb 277 G9
Mounters Dorset 30 D3
Mountfield E Sus 38 C2
Mountgerald Highld 300 C5
Mountjoy Corn 5 C7
Mountnessing Essex 87 F10
Mounton Mon 79 G8
Mountsolie Aberds 303 D9
Mountsorrel Leics 153 F11
Mousehill Sur 50 E2
Mousehole Corn 1 D5
Mousen Northumb 264 C4
Mousley End Warks 118 D4
Mouswald Dumfries 238 C3
Mouth Mill Devon 24 B3
Mow Cop E Ches 168 D5
Mowbreck Lancs 202 G4
Mowden Darl 224 B5
Mowden Essex 88 C3
Mowhaugh Borders 263 E8
Mowmacre Hill Leicester 135 B11
Mowshurst Kent 52 D3
Mowsley Leics 136 F2
Moxby N Yorks 215 F11
Moxley W Mid 133 D9
Moy Argyll 255 E8
Moy Highld 290 E6
Moy Highld 301 F7
Moy Hall Highld 301 F7
Moy Ho Moray 301 C10
Moy Lodge Highld 290 E6
Moyles Court Hants 31 F11
Moylgrove = Trewyddel Pembs 92 C2
Muasdale Argyll 255 C7
Much Birch Hereford 97 E10
Much Cowardne Hereford 98 B2
Much Cowarne Hereford 98 B2
Much Dewchurch Hereford 97 E9
Much Hadham Herts 86 B5
Much Hoole Lancs 194 C3
Much Hoole Moss Houses Lancs 194 C3
Much Hoole Town Lancs 194 C3
Much Marcle Hereford 98 E3
Much Wenlock Shrops 132 C2
Muchalls Aberds 293 D11
Muchelney Som 28 C6
Muchelney Ham Som 28 C6
Muchlarnick Corn 6 D4
Muchrachd Highld 300 F2
Muckairn Argyll 289 F11
Muckernich Highld 300 D5
Mucking Thurrock 69 C7
Muckle Breck Shetland 312 G7
Muckleford Dorset 17 C8
Mucklestone Staffs 150 B4
Muckleton Norf 158 B6
Muckleton Shrops 149 E11
Muckletown Aberds 302 G5
Muckley Shrops 132 D2
Muckley Corner Staffs 133 B11
Muckley Cross Shrops 132 D2
Muckton Lincs 190 E5
Muckton Bottom Lincs 190 E5
Mudale Highld 308 F5
Mudd Gtr Man 185 C7
Muddiford Devon 40 F5
Muddlebridge Devon 40 G4
Muddles Green E Sus 23 C8
Mudeford Dorset 19 C9
Mudford Som 29 D9
Mudford Sock Som 29 D9
Mudgley Som 44 D2
Mugdock Stirl 277 F11
Mugeary Highld 294 B6
Mugginton Derbys 170 G3
Muggintonlane End Derbys 170 G3
Muggleswick Durham 232 B6
Mugswell Sur 51 C9
Muie Highld 309 J6
Muir Aberds 292 E2
Muir of Alford Aberds 293 B7
Muir of Fairburn Highld 300 D4
Muir of Fowlis Aberds 293 B7
Muir of Kinellar Aberds 293 B10
Muir of Miltonduff Moray 301 D11
Muir of Ord Highld 300 D5
Muir of Pert Angus 287 D8
Muircleugh Borders 271 F10
Muirden Aberds 303 D7
Muirdrum Angus 287 D9
Muiredge Fife 281 B7
Muirend Glasgow 267 C11
Muirhead Angus 287 D7
Muirhead Fife 286 G6
Muirhead Fife 287 F8
Muirhead N Lnrk 268 B3
Muirhead S Ayrs 257 C8
Muirhouse Edin 280 F4
Muirhouse N Lnrk 268 D5
Muirhouselaw Borders 262 D4
Muirhouses Falk 279 E10
Muirkirk E Ayrs 258 D5
Muirmill Stirl 278 E4
Muirshearlich Highld 290 E3
Muirskie Aberds 293 D10
Muirtack Aberds 303 F9
Muirton Aberds 303 D7
Muirton Highld 301 C7
Muirton Perth 286 E5
Muirton Perth 286 F3
Muirton Mains Highld 300 D4
Muirton of Ardblair Perth 286 C5
Muirton of Ballochy Angus 293 G8
Muiryfold Aberds 303 D7
Muker N Yorks 223 F8
Mulbarton Norf 142 C3
Mulben Moray 302 D3
Mulberry Corn 5 B10
Mulfra Corn 1 C5
Mulindry Argyll 254 B4
Mulla Shetland 313 G6
Mullardoch House Highld 300 F2
Mullenspond Hants 47 D9
Mullion Corn 2 F5
Mullion Cove Corn 2 F5
Mumbles Hill Swansea 56 D6
Mumby Lincs 191 G8
Mumps Gtr Man 196 F2
Mundale Moray 301 D10
Munderfield Row Hereford 116 G2
Munderfield Stocks Hereford 116 G2
Mundesley Norf 160 B6
Mundford Norf 140 E6
Mundham Norf 142 D6
Mundon Essex 88 E5
Mundurno Aberdeen 293 B11
Mundy Bois Kent 54 D2
Munerigie Highld 290 C4
Muness Shetland 312 C8
Mungasdale Highld 307 K4
Mungrisdale Cumb 230 E3
Munlochy Highld 300 D6
Munsary Cottage Highld 310 E6
Munsley Hereford 98 C3
Munslow Shrops 131 F10
Munstone Hereford 97 C10
Murch V Glam 59 E7
Murchington Devon 13 D9
Murcot Worcs 99 C11
Murcott Oxon 83 B9
Murcott Wilts 81 G7
Murdieston Stirl 278 B3
Murdishaw Halton 183 E9
Murieston W Loth 269 C11
Murkle Highld 310 C5
Murlaggan Highld 290 D2
Murlaggan Highld 290 E5
Murra Orkney 314 F2
Murrayfield Edin 280 G4
Murrayshall Perth 286 E5
Murraythwaite Dumfries 238 C4
Murrell Green Hants 49 B8
Murrell's End Glos 98 E4
Murrell's End Glos 98 G5
Murrion Shetland 312 F4
Murrow Cambs 139 B7
Mursley Bucks 102 F6
Murston Kent 70 G2
Murthill Angus 287 B8
Murthly Perth 286 D4
Murton Cumb 231 G10
Murton Durham 234 B3
Murton Northumb 273 F9
Murton Swansea 56 D5
Murton T & W 243 C8
Murton York 207 C8
Murton Grange N Yorks 215 B10
Murtwell Devon 8 D5
Musbury Devon 15 C11
Muscliff Bmouth 19 B7
Muscoates N Yorks 216 C3
Muscott Northants 120 E2
Musdale Argyll 289 G11
Mushroom Green W Mid 133 F8
Musselburgh E Loth 280 G6
Musselwick Pembs 72 D4
Mustard Hyrn Norf 161 F8
Muston Leics 154 B6
Muston N Yorks 217 D11
Mustow Green Worcs 117 C7
Muswell Hill London 86 G3
Mutehill Dumfries 237 E8
Mutford Suff 143 F9
Muthill Perth 286 F2
Mutley Plym 7 D9
Mutterton Devon 27 G8
Mutton Hall E Sus 37 C9
Muxton Telford 150 G4
Mwdwl-eithin Flint 181 F11
Mwynbwll Flint 165 B11
Mybster Highld 310 D5
Myddfai Carms 94 F5
Myddle Shrops 149 E9
Myddlewood Shrops 149 E9
Myddyn-fych Carms 75 C10
Mydroilyn Ceredig 111 F9
Myerscough Lancs 202 F5
Myerscough Smithy Lancs 203 G8
Mylor Bridge Corn 3 B8
Mylor Churchtown Corn 3 B8
Mynachdy Cardiff 59 D7
Mynachdy Rhondda 77 F8
Mynachlog-ddu Pembs 92 E2
Mynd Shrops 115 C7
Myndd Llandegai Gwyn 163 B10
Myndtown Shrops 131 F7
Mynydd Bach Ceredig 112 B4
Mynydd-bach Mon 79 G7
Mynydd-Bach Swansea 57 B7
Mynydd-bach-y-glo Swansea 56 B6
Mynydd Bodafon Anglesey 179 D7
Mynydd Fflint = Flint Mountain Flint 182 G2
Mynydd Gilan Gwyn 144 E5
Mynydd-isa Flint 166 C3
Mynydd-llan Flint 181 G11
Mynydd Marian Conwy 180 F5
Mynydd Mechell Anglesey 178 D5
Mynyddislwyn Caerph 77 G11
Mynyddygarreg Carms 74 D6
Mynytho Gwyn 144 C6
Myrebird Aberds 293 D9
Myrelandhorn Highld 310 D6
Myreside Perth 286 E6
Myrtle Hill Carms 94 E5
Mytchett Sur 49 B11
Mytchett Place Sur 49 C11
Mytholm W Yorks 196 B3
Mytholmes W Yorks 204 F6
Mytholmroyd W Yorks 196 B4
Mythop Lancs 202 G3
Mytice Aberds 302 F4
Myton Warks 118 E6
Myton Hall N Yorks 215 F8
Myton-on-Swale N Yorks 215 F8
Mytton Shrops 149 F8

N

Na Gearrannan W Isles 304 D3
Naast Highld 307 L3
Nab Hill W Yorks 197 D7
Nab Wood W Yorks 205 F8
Nab's Head Lancs 194 B6
Naburn York 207 D7
Naccolt Kent 54 E4
Nackington Kent 55 C7
Nacton Suff 108 C4
Nadderwater Devon 14 C3
Nafferton E Yorks 209 B7
Nag's Head Glos 80 F5
Naid-y-march Flint 181 F11
Nailbridge Glos 79 B10
Nailsbourne Som 28 B2
Nailsea N Som 60 D3
Nailstone Leics 135 B8
Nailsworth Glos 80 F5
Nailwell Bath 61 G8
Nairn Highld 301 D8
Nalderswood Sur 51 D8
Nance Corn 4 G3
Nanceddan Corn 2 C2
Nancegollan Corn 2 C4
Nancemellin Corn 4 G2
Nancenoy Corn 2 D6
Nancledra Corn 1 B5
Nangreaves Lancs 195 D10
Nanhoron Gwyn 144 C5
Nanhyfer = Nevern Pembs 91 D11
Nannau Gwyn 146 E4
Nannerch Flint 165 B11
Nanpantan Leics 153 F10
Nanpean Corn 5 D9
Nanquidno Corn 1 D3
Nanstallon Corn 5 B10
Nant Carms 74 B6
Nant Denb 165 D11
Nant Alyn Flint 165 B11
Nant-ddu Powys 77 B8
Nant-glas Powys 113 E9
Nant Mawr Flint 166 C3
Nant Peris = Old Llanberis Gwyn 163 D10
Nant Uchaf Denb 165 D8
Nant-y-Bai Carms 94 C5
Nant-y-Bwch Bl Gwent 77 C10
Nant-y-cafn Neath 76 D4
Nant y Caws Shrops 148 D5
Nant-y-ceisiad Caerph 59 B8
Nant-y-derry Mon 78 D4
Nant-y-felin Conwy 179 G11
Nant-y-ffin Carms 93 E11
Nant-y-gollen Shrops 148 D4
Nant-y-moel Bridgend 76 G6
Nant-y-pandy Conwy 179 G11
Nant-y-Rhiw Conwy 164 D4
Nanternis Ceredig 111 F7
Nantgaredig Carms 93 G9
Nantgarw Rhondda 58 B6
Nantglyn Denb 165 C8
Nantgwyn Powys 113 B9
Nantithet Corn 2 E5
Nantlle Gwyn 163 E8
Nantmawr Shrops 148 E5
Nantmel Powys 113 D10
Nantmor Gwyn 163 F10
Nantserth Powys 113 C9
Nantwich E Ches 167 E11
Nantycaws Carms 75 B7
Nantyffyllon Bridgend 57 C11
Nantyglo Bl Gwent 77 C11
Nantyronen Station Ceredig 112 B3
Napchester Kent 55 D10
Naphill Bucks 84 F4
Napleton Worcs 99 B7
Napley Staffs 150 B4
Napley Heath Staffs 150 B4
Nappa N Yorks 204 C3
Nappa Scar N Yorks 223 G9
Napton on the Hill Warks 119 E9
Narberth = Arberth Pembs 73 C10
Narberth Bridge Pembs 73 C10
Narborough Leics 135 D10
Narborough Norf 158 G4
Narfords Som 28 F3
Narkurs Corn 6 D6
Narracott Devon 24 D5
Narrowgate Corner Norf 161 F8
Nasareth Gwyn 163 E7
Naseby Northants 120 B3
Nash Bucks 102 E5
Nash Hereford 114 E6
Nash Kent 55 B9
Nash London 68 G2
Nash Newport 59 C10
Nash Shrops 116 C2
Nash Som 29 E8
Nash End Worcs 132 G5
Nash Lee Bucks 84 D4
Nash Mills Herts 85 E9
Nash Street E Sus 23 C8
Nash Street Kent 68 F6
Nashend Glos 80 D5
Nashes Green Hants 49 D7
Nassington Northants 137 D11
Nast Hyde Herts 86 D2
Nastend Glos 80 D3
Nasty Herts 105 G7
Natcott Devon 24 C3
Nateby Cumb 222 D5
Nateby Lancs 202 E5
Nately Scures Hants 49 C8
Natland Cumb 211 B10
Natton Glos 99 E8
Naughton Suff 107 B10
Naunton Glos 100 G2
Naunton Worcs 99 D7
Naunton Beauchamp Worcs 117 G9
Navant Hill W Sus 34 B6
Navenby Lincs 173 D7
Navestock Heath Essex 87 F8
Navestock Side Essex 87 F9
Navidale Highld 311 H4
Navity Highld 301 C7
Nawton N Yorks 216 C3
Nayland Suff 107 E9
Nazeing Essex 86 D6
Nazeing Gate Essex 86 D6
Nazeing Long Green Essex 86 E6
Nazeing Mead Essex 86 D5
Neacroft Hants 19 B9
Nealhouse Cumb 239 G8
Neal's Green Warks 134 G6
Neames Forstal Kent 54 B5
Neap Shetland 313 H7
Near Hardcastle N Yorks 214 F2
Near Sawrey Cumb 221 F7
Nearton End Bucks 102 F6
Neasden London 67 B8
Neasham Darl 224 C6
Neat Enstone Oxon 101 G7
Neat Marsh E Yorks 209 G9
Neath = Castell-nedd Neath 57 B8
Neath Abbey Neath 57 B8
Neath Hill M Keynes 103 C7
Neatham Hants 49 E8
Neatishead Norf 160 E6
Neaton Norf 141 C8
Nebo Anglesey 179 C7
Nebo Ceredig 111 D10
Nebo Conwy 164 D4
Nebo Gwyn 163 E7
Nebsworth Warks 100 C3
Nechells W Mid 133 F11
Necton Norf 141 B7
Nedd Highld 306 F6
Nedderton Northumb 252 G6
Nedge Hill Som 44 C5
Nedge Hill Telford 132 B4
Nedging Suff 107 B9
Nedging Tye Suff 107 B10
Needham Norf 142 G4
Needham Green Essex 87 B9
Needham Market Suff 125 G11
Needham Street Suff 124 D4
Needingworth Cambs 122 C6
Needwood Staffs 152 E3
Neen Savage Shrops 116 B3
Neen Sollars Shrops 116 C3
Neenton Shrops 132 F2
Nefod Shrops 148 B6
Nefyn Gwyn 162 G4
Neighbourne Som 44 D6
Neight Hill Worcs 117 F8
Neilston E Renf 267 D9
Neinthirion Powys 129 B9
Neithrop Oxon 101 C8
Nelly Andrews Green Powys 130 B5
Nelson Caerph 77 F10
Nelson Lancs 204 F3
Nelson Village Northumb 243 B7
Nemphlar S Lnrk 269 G7
Nempnett Thrubwell N Som 60 G4
Nene Terrace Lincs 138 B5
Nenthall Cumb 231 B11
Nenthead Cumb 231 C11
Nenthorn Borders 262 B5
Neopardy Devon 13 B11
Nep Town W Sus 36 D2
Nepcote W Sus 35 F10
Nepgill Cumb 229 F7
Nerabus Argyll 254 B3
Nercwys Flint 166 C2
Nerston S Lnrk 268 D2
Nesbit Northumb 263 C11
Ness Orkney 314 C4
Ness W Ches 182 F4
Nesscliffe Shrops 149 F7
Nessholt W Ches 182 F4
Nesstoun Orkney 314 A7
Neston W Ches 182 F3
Neston Wilts 61 F11
Netchells Green W Mid 133 F11
Netham Bristol 60 E6
Nethanfoot S Lnrk 268 F6
Nether Alderley E Ches 184 F4
Nether Blainslie Borders 271 G10
Nether Booth Derbys 185 D10
Nether Broughton Leics 154 D3
Nether Burrow Lancs 212 D2
Nether Burrows Derbys 152 B5
Nether Cassock Dumfries 248 C6
Nether Cerne Dorset 17 B9
Nether Chanderhill Derbys 186 G4
Nether Compton Dorset 29 D9
Nether Crimond Aberds 303 G8
Nether Dalgliesh Borders 249 B7
Nether Dallachy Moray 302 C3
Nether Edge S Yorks 186 E4
Nether End Derbys 186 G3
Nether End Leics 154 G4
Nether End W Yorks 197 F8
Nether Exe Devon 26 G6
Nether Glasslaw Aberds 303 D8
Nether Hall Leicester 136 B2
Nether Handley Derbys 186 F6
Nether Handwick Angus 287 C7
Nether Haugh S Yorks 186 B6
Nether Headon Notts 188 F2
Nether Heage Derbys 170 E5
Nether Heyford Northants 120 F3
Nether Hindhope Borders 263 G7
Nether Horsburgh Borders 261 B8
Nether Howecleuch S Lnrk 260 G2
Nether Kellet Lancs 211 F10
Nether Kidston Borders 270 G4
Nether Kinmundy Aberds 303 E10
Nether Kirton E Renf 267 D9
Nether Langwith Notts 187 G8
Nether Leask Aberds 303 F10
Nether Lenshie Aberds 302 E6
Nether Loads Derbys 170 B4
Nether Monynut Borders 272 C4
Nether Moor Derbys 170 B5
Nether Padley Derbys 186 F3
Nether Park Aberds 303 D10
Nether Poppleton York 207 B7
Nether Row Cumb 230 D2
Nether Savock Aberds 303 E10
Nether Shiels Borders 271 F8
Nether Silton N Yorks 225 G9
Nether Skyborry Shrops 114 C5
Nether St Suff 125 E8
Nether Stowe Staffs 152 G2
Nether Stowey Som 43 F7
Nether Street Essex 87 C9
Nether Street Herts 86 B6
Nether Urquhart Fife 286 G5
Nether Wallop Hants 47 F10
Nether Warden Northumb 241 D10
Nether Wasdale Cumb 220 E2
Nether Welton Cumb 230 B3
Nether Westcote Glos 100 G4
Nether Whitacre Warks 134 E4
Nether Winchendon or Lower Winchendon Bucks 84 C2
Nether Worton Oxon 101 E8
Nether Yeadon W Yorks 205 E10
Netheravon Wilts 46 D6
Netherbrae Aberds 303 D7
Netherbrough Orkney 314 E3
Netherburn S Lnrk 268 F6
Netherbury Dorset 16 B5
Netherby Cumb 239 C9
Netherby N Yorks 206 D2
Netherclay Som 28 C3
Nethercote Oxon 101 C9
Nethercote Warks 119 E10
Nethercott Devon 12 B3
Nethercott Devon 40 F3
Nethercott Oxon 101 G9
Nethercott Som 42 G6
Netherdale Shetland 313 H3
Netherend Glos 79 E9
Netherfield E Sus 38 D2
Netherfield M Keynes 103 D7
Netherfield Notts 171 G10
Nethergate Norf 159 D11
Netherhampton Wilts 31 B10
Netherland Green Staffs 152 C2
Netherlaw Dumfries 237 E9
Netherley Aberds 293 D10
Netherley Mers 182 D6
Netherley W Yorks 196 E4
Nethermill Dumfries 248 F2
Nethermills Moray 302 D5
Nethermuir Aberds 303 E9
Netherne on-the-Hill Sur 51 B9
Netheroyd Hill W Yorks 196 D6
Netherplace E Renf 267 D10
Netherraw Borders 262 E3
Netherseal Derbys 152 G5
Netherstoke Dorset 29 F8
Netherthird E Ayrs 258 F3
Netherthong W Yorks 196 F6
Netherthorpe Derbys 186 G6
Netherthorpe S Yorks 187 E8
Netherton Aberds 303 E8
Netherton Angus 287 B9
Netherton Corn 11 G11
Netherton Cumb 228 D6
Netherton Devon 14 G3
Netherton Glos 81 E11
Netherton Hants 47 B11
Netherton Hereford 97 F10
Netherton Mers 193 G11
Netherton N Lnrk 268 E5
Netherton Northumb 251 B11
Netherton Oxon 82 F6
Netherton Perth 286 B5
Netherton Shrops 132 G4
Netherton Stirl 277 F11
Netherton W Ches 183 F8
Netherton W Mid 133 F8
Netherton W Yorks 196 E6
Netherton W Yorks 197 D9
Netherton Worcs 99 C9
Netherton of Lonmay Aberds 303 C10
Nethertown Cumb 219 D9
Nethertown Highld 310 B7
Nethertown Lancs 203 F10
Nethertown Staffs 152 F2
Netherwitton Northumb 252 E4
Netherwood E Ayrs 258 D5
Nethy Bridge Highld 301 G10
Netley Hants 33 F7
Netley Hill Soton 33 E7
Netley Marsh Hants 32 E4
Nettacott Devon 14 B4
Netteswell Essex 87 C7
Nettlebed Oxon 65 B8
Nettlebridge Som 44 D6
Nettlecombe Dorset 16 B6
Nettlecombe I o W 20 F6
Nettleden Herts 85 C8
Nettleham Lincs 189 F8
Nettlestead Kent 53 C7
Nettlestead Suff 107 B11
Nettlestead Green Kent 53 C7
Nettlestone I o W 21 C8
Nettlesworth Durham 233 B11
Nettleton Glos 80 C6
Nettleton Lincs 200 G6
Nettleton Wilts 61 D10
Nettleton Green Wilts 61 D10
Nettleton Hill W Yorks 196 D5
Nettleton Shrub Wilts 61 D10
Nettleton Top Lincs 189 B10
Netton Wilts 46 F6
Neuadd Carms 94 G3
Nevendon Essex 88 G2
Nevern = Nanhyfer Pembs 91 D11
Nevilles Cross Durham 233 C11
New Abbey Dumfries 237 C11
New Aberdour Aberds 303 C8
New Addington London 67 G11
New Alresford Hants 48 G5
New Alyth Perth 286 C6
New Arley Warks 134 F5
New Arram E Yorks 208 E6
New Ash Green Kent 68 F6
New Balderton Notts 172 E4
New Barn Kent 68 F6
New Barnet London 8
New Barnetby N Lincs 20
New Barton Northants 12
New Basford Nottingham 17
New Beaupre V Glam 5
New Beckenham London 67
New Bewick Northumb 26
New-bigging Angus 28
New Bilton Warks 11
New Bolingbroke Lincs 17
New Bolsover Derbys 18
New Boston Mers 18
New Botley Oxon 8
New Boultham Lincs 18
New Bradwell M Keynes 10
New Brancepeth Durham 233
New Bridge Wrex 16
New Brighton Flint 16
New Brighton Mers 18
New Brighton W Sus 2
New Brighton W Yorks 19
New Brighton W Yorks 20
New Brighton Wrex 16
New Brimington Derbys 18
New Brinsley Notts 17
New Brotton Redcar 23
New Broughton Wrex 16
New Buckenham Norf 141
New Buildings Bath 4
New Buildings Dorset 1
New Bury Gtr Man 19
New Byth Aberds 30
New Catton Norf 16
New Charlton London 6
New Cheltenham S Glos 6
New Cheriton Hants 3
New Clipstone Notts 17
New Costessey Norf 16
New Coundon Durham 233
New Cowper Cumb 22
New Crofton W Yorks 197
New Cross Ceredig 11
New Cross London 67
New Cross Oxon 6
New Cross Som 2
New Cross Gate London 67
New Cumnock E Ayrs 25
New Deer Aberds 30
New Delaval Northumb 24
New Delph Gtr Man 19
New Denham Bucks 6
New Downs Corn
New Downs Corn
New Duston Northants 12
New Earswick York 20
New Eastwood Notts 17
New Edlington S Yorks 18
New Elgin Moray 30
New Ellerby E Yorks 20
New Eltham London 6
New End Lincs 19
New End Warks 11
New End Worcs 117
New England Essex 10
New England Lincs 17
New England P'boro 13
New England Som 2
New Farnley W Yorks 205
New Ferry Mers 18
New Fletton P'boro 13
New Fryston W Yorks 19
New Galloway Dumfries 23
New Gilston Fife 28
New Greens Herts 85
New Grimsby Scilly
New Ground Herts 8
New Hainford Norf 16
New Hall Hey Lancs 195
New Hartley Northumb 24
New Haw Sur 6
New Headington Oxon 8
New Heaton Northumb 27
New Hedges Pembs 73
New Herrington T & W 24
New Hinksey Oxon 8
New Ho Durham 23
New Holkham Norf 15
New Holland N Lincs 20
New Holland W Yorks 20
New Horwich Derbys 18
New Houghton Derbys 17
New Houghton Norf 15
New House Kent 6
New Houses Gtr Man 19
New Houses N Yorks 21
New Humberstone Leicester 13
New Hunwick Durham 23
New Hutton Cumb 221
New Hythe Kent 5
New Inn Carms 9
New Inn Devon 2
New Inn Mon 7
New Inn Pembs 91
New Inn Torf 7
New Invention Shrops 11
New Invention W Mid 13
New Kelso Highld 29
New Kingston Notts 153
New Kyo Durham 24
New Ladykirk Borders 27
New Lanark S Lnrk 26
New Lane Lancs 19
New Lane End Warr 183
New Langholm Dumfries 24
New Leake Lincs 17
New Leeds Aberds 30
New Lodge S Yorks 197
New Longton Lancs 19
New Luce Dumfries 23
New Malden London 6
New Marske Redcar 23
New Marston Oxon 8
New Marton Shrops 14
New Micklefield W Yorks 20
New Mill Aberds 29
New Mill Borders 262
New Mill Corn
New Mill Corn
New Mill Cumb 219
New Mill Herts 8
New Mill W Yorks 19
New Mill Wilts 63
New Mills Borders 271
New Mills Corn
New Mills Derbys 18
New Mills E Ches 18
New Mills Glos 79
New Mills Hereford 98
New Mills = Felin Newydd Powys 129
New Milton Hants 19
New Mistley Essex 10
New Moat Pembs 91
New Moston Gtr Man 195
New Ollerton Notts 171
New Oscott W Mid 133
New Pale W Ches 183
New Park N Yorks 205

Parks Leicester 135 B11
Passage S Glos 60 B4
Pitsligo Aberds 303 D8
Polzeath Corn 10 F4
Quay =
newydd Ceredig 111 F7
Rackheath Norf 160 G5
Radnor Powys 114 E4
Rent Cumb 230 D5
Ridley Northumb 242 F3
Road Side N Yorks 204 E5
Road Side W Yorks 197 B7
Romney Kent 39 C9
Rossington
rks 187 B10
Row Ceredig 112 C4
Row Lancs 203 F8
Row N Yorks 226 C2
Sarum Wilts 46 G6
Sawley Derbys 153 C9
Scarbro W Yorks 205 G10
Sharlston W Yorks 197 C11
Silksworth T & W 243 G9
Skelton Redcar 226 B3
Smithy Derbys 185 E9
Southgate London 86 G3
Springs Gtr Man 194 F6
Sprowston Norf 160 G4
Stanton Derbys 153 B9
Stevenston N Lnrk 268 D5
Street Kent 68 G6
Street Staffs 169 E9
Swanage Dorset 18 E6
Swannington Leics 153 F8
Thirsk N Yorks 215 C8
Thundersley Essex 69 B9
Totley S Yorks 186 F4
Town Bath 45 B9
Town Bath 60 G5
Town Dartford 68 E4
Town Dorset 30 C3
Town Dorset 30 D6
Town Dorset 31 D7
Town Dorset 31 F7
Town E Loth 281 G8
Town E Sus 37 C7
Town Edin 280 G4
Town Edin 280 G5
Town Glos 99 E10
Town Lancs 203 E8
Town Luton 103 G11
Town Maidstone 53 B7
Town Medway 69 G8
Town Oxon 100 F5
Town Reading 65 E8
Town Shetland 312 E6
Town Som 29 D11
Town Som 29 D9
Town Som 44 D3
Town Soton 33 E7
Town Swindon 63 C7
Town T & W 234 B2
Town T & W 243 E8
Town W Berks 64 D6
Town W Mid 133 B11
Town W Mid 133 E9
Town W Sus 35 B11
Town W Yorks 198 C3
Town Wilts 46 C6
Town Wilts 47 B7
Tredegar Caerph 77 E10
Trows S Lnrk 259 B8
Ulva Argyll 275 E8
Village E Yorks 209 G7
Village S Yorks 198 F5
Walsoken Cambs 139 B9
Waltham NE Lincs 201 G9
Well Powys 113 B11
Wells Powys 130 D3
Whittington Derbys 186 F5
Wimpole
bs 104 B6
Winton E Loth 281 G8
Woodhouses
ps 167 G9
Works Telford 132 B3
Wortley W Yorks 205 G11
Yatt Oxon 82 C5
York Lincs 174 D2
York N Yorks 214 G3
York T & W 243 C8
Zealand Wilts 62 D4
all W Yorks 205 D10
all Green Gtr Man 184 D4
ark Orkney 314 B7
ark P'boro 138 C4
ark-on-Trent Notts 172 E3
arthill N Lnrk 268 D5
ball Lincs 189 F9
barn Kent 55 F7
barns Cumb 210 E4
battle Midloth 270 B6
bie Dumfries 238 D5
biggin Cumb 210 F5
biggin Cumb 211 D11
biggin Cumb 219 G11
biggin Cumb 230 F5
biggin Cumb 231 B7
biggin Cumb 231 F8
biggin Durham 232 B5
biggin Durham 232 F4
biggin Durham 233 D8
biggin N Yorks 213 B9
biggin N Yorks 223 G9
biggin-by-the-Sea
humb 253 F8
biggin Hall Estate
y 242 D6
biggin-on-Lune
b 222 D4
bigging Aberds 303 G7
bigging Angus 287 D8
bigging Borders 262 F6
bigging Edin 280 F2
bigging S Lnrk 269 F10
biggings Orkney 314 B6
bold Derbys 186 G5
bold Gtr Man 196 E2
bold Leics 136 B5
bold Leics 153 F8
bold Heath Leics 135 B8
bold on Avon Warks 119 B9
bold on Stour
ks 100 B4
bold Pacey Warks 118 F5
bold Verdon Leics 135 C8
bold W Mid 133 C8
borough P'boro 138 B4
borough Staffs 152 D2
bottle Northants 101 D10
bottle T & W 243 G8
bourne Suff 108 C5
bridge Bath 61 F8
bridge Caerph 78 F2
bridge Ceredig 111 F10
bridge Corn 1 C4
bridge Corn 4 G5
bridge Corn 7 B7
bridge Dumfries 237 B11
bridge E Sus 52 G3
bridge Edin 280 G2
bridge Hants 32 D3
Newbridge I o W 20 D4
Newbridge Lancs 204 F3
Newbridge N Yorks 216 B6
Newbridge Oxon 82 E6
Newbridge Pembs 91 E8
Newbridge Shrops 148 D6
Newbridge W Mid 133 D7
Newbridge Wrex 166 G3
Newbridge Green Worcs 98 D6
Newbridge-on-Usk Mon 78 G5
Newbridge-on-Wye
Powys 113 F10
Newbrough Northumb 241 D9
Newbuildings Devon 26 G3
Newburgh Aberds 303 D9
Newburgh Aberds 303 G9
Newburgh Borders 261 F8
Newburgh Fife 286 F6
Newburgh Lancs 194 E3
Newburn T & W 242 D5
Newbury Kent 54 B2
Newbury W Berks 64 F3
Newbury Wilts 45 E10
Newbury Park London 68 B2
Newby Cumb 231 G7
Newby Lancs 204 D2
Newby N Yorks 205 D11
Newby N Yorks 212 E4
Newby N Yorks 215 F7
Newby N Yorks 225 C10
Newby N Yorks 227 G10
Newby Bridge Cumb 211 B7
Newby Cote N Yorks 212 E4
Newby East Cumb 239 F11
Newby Head Cumb 231 G7
Newby West Cumb 239 G9
Newby Wiske N Yorks 215 B7
Newcastle Bridgend 58 D2
Newcastle Mon 78 B6
Newcastle Shrops 130 G4
Newcastle Emlyn =
Castell Newydd Emlyn
Carms 92 C6
Newcastle-under-Lyme
Staffs 168 F4
Newcastle upon Tyne
T & W 242 E6
Newcastleton or
Copshaw Holm
Borders 249 F11
Newchapel Powys 129 G9
Newchapel Staffs 168 E5
Newchapel Sur 51 E11
Newchapel =
Capel Newydd Pembs 92 D4
Newchurch Bl Gwent 77 C11
Newchurch Carms 93 G7
Newchurch Hereford 115 G7
Newchurch I o W 21 D7
Newchurch Kent 54 G5
Newchurch Lancs 195 C10
Newchurch Mon 79 F7
Newchurch Powys 114 G4
Newchurch Staffs 152 E2
Newchurch in Pendle
Lancs 204 F2
Newcott Devon 28 F2
Newcraighall Edin 280 G6
Newdigate Sur 51 E7
Newell Green Brack 65 E11
Newenden Kent 38 B4
Newent Glos 98 F4
Newerne Glos 79 E10
Newfield Durham 233 E10
Newfield Durham 242 G6
Newfield Highld 301 B7
Newfield Stoke 168 E6
Newford Scilly 1 G4
Newfound Hants 48 C5
Newgale Pembs 90 G6
Newgarth Orkney 314 E2
Newgate Lancs 194 F4
Newgate Norf 177 E9
Newgate Corner Norf 161 G8
Newgate Street Herts 86 D4
Newgrounds Hants 31 E11
Newhailes Edin 280 G6
Newhall Derbys 152 E5
Newhall E Ches 167 F10
Newhall Green Warks 134 F5
Newhall House Highld 300 C6
Newhall Point Highld 301 C7
Newham Lincs 174 E3
Newham Northumb 264 D5
Newhaven Derbys 169 C11
Newhaven Devon 24 C5
Newhaven E Sus 36 G6
Newhaven Edin 280 F5
Newhay N Yorks 207 G9
Newhey Gtr Man 196 E2
Newhill Fife 286 F6
Newhill Perth 286 G5
Newhill S Yorks 186 B6
Newhills Aberdeen 293 C10
Newholm N Yorks 227 C7
Newhouse Borders 262 E2
Newhouse N Lnrk 268 C5
Newhouse Shetland 313 G6
Newhouses Borders 271 G10
Newick E Sus 36 C6
Newingreen Kent 54 F6
Newington Edin 280 G5
Newington Kent 55 F7
Newington Kent 69 G11
Newington Kent 71 F11
Newington London 67 D10
Newington Notts 187 C11
Newington Oxon 83 F10
Newington Shrops 131 G8
Newington Bagpath
Glos 80 G4
Newland Cumb 210 D6
Newland E Yorks 199 B10
Newland Glos 79 D9
Newland Hull 209 G7
Newland N Yorks 199 C7
Newland Oxon 82 C5
Newland Worcs 98 B5
Newland Bottom Cumb 210 C5
Newland Common
Worcs 117 E8
Newland Green Kent 54 D2
Newlandrig Midloth 271 C7
Newlands Borders 250 E2
Newlands Borders 262 E2
Newlands Cumb 229 G10
Newlands Cumb 230 D2
Newlands Derbys 170 F6
Newlands Dumfries 247 F11
Newlands Glasgow 267 C11
Newlands Highld 301 E7
Newlands Moray 302 D3
Newlands Northumb 242 F3
Newlands Notts 171 C9
Newlands Staffs 151 E11
Newlands Corner Sur 50 D4
Newlands of Geise
Highld 310 C4
Newlands of Tynet
Moray 302 C3
Newlands Park Anglesey 178 E3
Newlandsmuir S Lnrk 268 E2
Newliston Edin 280 G2
Newliston Fife 280 C5
Newlot Orkney 314 E5
Newlyn Corn 1 D5
Newmachar Aberds 293 B10
Newmains N Lnrk 268 D6
Newman's End Essex 87 C8
Newman's Green Suff 107 C7
Newman's Place
Hereford 96 B5
Newmarket Glos 80 F4
Newmarket Suff 124 E2
Newmarket W Isles 304 E6
Newmill Borders 261 G11
Newmill Corn 1 C5
Newmill Moray 302 D4
Newmill of Inshewan
Angus 292 G6
Newmillerdam W Yorks 197 D10
Newmills Corn 11 D11
Newmills Fife 279 D10
Newmills Highld 300 C6
Newmills of Boyne
Aberds 302 D5
Newmiln Perth 286 D5
Newmilns E Ayrs 258 B2
Newmore Highld 300 B6
Newmore Highld 300 D5
Newnes Shrops 149 C7
Newney Green Essex 87 D11
Newnham Cambs 123 F8
Newnham Glos 79 C11
Newnham Hants 49 C8
Newnham Herts 104 D4
Newnham Kent 54 B3
Newnham Northants 119 F11
Newnham Warks 118 E3
Newnham Bridge
Worcs 116 D2
Newpark Fife 287 F8
Newpool Staffs 168 D5
Newport Corn 12 D2
Newport Devon 40 G5
Newport Dorset 18 C3
Newport E Yorks 208 G3
Newport Essex 105 E10
Newport Glos 79 F11
Newport Highld 311 G5
Newport I o W 20 D6
Newport Newport 59 B10
Newport Norf 161 F10
Newport Som 28 C4
Newport Telford 150 F4
Newport = Trefdraeth
Pembs 91 D11
Newport-on-Tay Fife 287 E8
Newport Pagnell
M Keynes 103 C7
Newpound Common
W Sus 35 B9
Newquay Corn 4 C6
Newsam Green W Yorks 206 G3
Newsbank E Ches 168 B4
Newseat Aberds 303 E10
Newseat Aberds 303 F7
Newsells Herts 105 D7
Newsham Lancs 202 F6
Newsham N Yorks 215 C7
Newsham N Yorks 224 C2
Newsham Northumb 243 B8
Newsholme E Yorks 199 B8
Newsholme Lancs 204 C2
Newsholme W Yorks 204 F6
Newsome W Yorks 196 E6
Newstead Borders 262 C3
Newstead Northumb 264 D5
Newstead Notts 171 E8
Newstead Staffs 168 G5
Newstead W Yorks 197 E11
Newstreet Lane Shrops 150 B2
Newtake Devon 14 G3
Newthorpe N Yorks 206 G5
Newthorpe Notts 171 F7
Newthorpe Common
Notts 171 F7
Newtoft Lincs 189 D8
Newton Argyll 275 D11
Newton Borders 262 E3
Newton Borders 262 F2
Newton Bridgend 57 F10
Newton C Beds 104 C4
Newton Cambs 105 B8
Newton Cambs 157 G8
Newton Cardiff 59 D8
Newton Corn 5 C11
Newton Cumb 210 E4
Newton Derbys 170 D6
Newton Dorset 30 E3
Newton Dumfries 239 C7
Newton Dumfries 248 E4
Newton Gtr Man 185 B7
Newton Hereford 96 C5
Newton Hereford 96 E6
Newton Hereford 115 D7
Newton Hereford 115 G10
Newton Highld 301 C7
Newton Highld 301 E7
Newton Highld 306 F7
Newton Highld 310 E7
Newton Lancs 202 F2
Newton Lancs 202 G4
Newton Lancs 203 C8
Newton Lancs 211 E11
Newton Lincs 155 B10
Newton Mers 182 D2
Newton Moray 301 C11
Newton Norf 158 F6
Newton Northants 137 G7
Newton Northumb 242 E2
Newton Notts 171 G11
Newton Perth 286 D2
Newton S Glos 79 G10
Newton S Lnrk 259 C10
Newton S Lnrk 268 C3
Newton S Yorks 198 G5
Newton Shetland 312 E5
Newton Shetland 313 K5
Newton Shrops 132 D4
Newton Shrops 149 C8
Newton Som 42 F6
Newton Staffs 151 D10
Newton Suff 107 C8
Newton Swansea 56 D6
Newton W Ches 166 B6
Newton W Ches 167 D8
Newton W Ches 183 F8
Newton W Loth 279 F11
Newton W Mid 133 E10
Newton Warks 119 B10
Newton Wilts 32 C2
Newton Abbot Devon 14 G3
Newton Arlosh Cumb 238 F5
Newton Aycliffe
Durham 233 G11
Newton Bewley Hrtlpl 234 F5
Newton Blossomville
M Keynes 121 G8
Newton Bromswold
Northants 121 D9
Newton Burgoland
Leics 135 B7
Newton by Toft Lincs 189 D9
Newton Cross Pembs 91 F7
Newton Ferrers Devon 7 F10
Newton Flotman Norf 142 D4
Newton Green Mon 79 G8
Newton Hall Durham 233 B11
Newton Hall Northumb 242 D2
Newton Harcourt Leics 136 D2
Newton Heath Gtr Man 195 G11
Newton Hill W Yorks 197 C10
Newton Ho Aberds 302 G6
Newton Hurst Staffs 151 D11
Newton Ketton Darl 234 G2
Newton Kyme N Yorks 206 E5
Newton-le-Willows
Mers 183 B9
Newton-le-Willows
N Yorks 214 B4
Newton Longville Bucks 102 E6
Newton Mearns E Renf 267 D10
Newton Morrell N Yorks 224 D4
Newton Morrell Oxon 102 F2
Newton Mulgrave
N Yorks 226 B5
Newton of Ardtoe
Highld 289 B8
Newton of Balcanquhal
Perth 286 F5
Newton of Balcormo
Fife 287 G9
Newton of Falkland
Fife 286 G6
Newton of Mountblairy
Aberds 302 D6
Newton of Pitcairns
Perth 286 F4
Newton on Ayr S Ayrs 257 E8
Newton on Ouse N Yorks 206 B6
Newton-on-Rawcliffe
N Yorks 226 G6
Newton on the Hill
Shrops 149 E9
Newton on the Moor
Northumb 252 B5
Newton on Trent Lincs 188 G4
Newton Park Argyll 266 B2
Newton Park Mers 183 C9
Newton Peveril Dorset 18 B4
Newton Poppleford
Devon 15 D7
Newton Purcell Oxon 102 E2
Newton Regis Warks 134 B5
Newton Reigny Cumb 230 E5
Newton Rigg Cumb 230 E5
Newton St Boswells
Borders 262 C3
Newton St Cyres Devon 14 B3
Newton St Faith Norf 160 F4
Newton St Loe Bath 61 G8
Newton St Petrock Devon 24 E6
Newton Solney Derbys 152 D5
Newton Stacey Hants 48 E2
Newton Stewart
Dumfries 236 C6
Newton Tony Wilts 47 E8
Newton Tracey Devon 25 B8
Newton under
Roseberry Redcar 225 C11
Newton Underwood
Northumb 252 F4
Newton upon
Derwent E Yorks 207 D10
Newton Valence Hants 49 G8
Newton with Scales
Lancs 202 G4
Newton Wood Gtr Man 184 B6
Newtonairds Dumfries 247 G9
Newtongrange Midloth 270 C6
Newtonhill Aberds 293 D11
Newtonhill Highld 300 E5
Newtonia E Ches 167 B11
Newtonmill Angus 293 G8
Newtonmore Highld 291 D9
Newtown Argyll 284 G4
Newtown Bl Gwent 77 C11
Newtown Bucks 85 E7
Newtown Caerph 78 G2
Newtown Cambs 121 D11
Newtown Corn 2 D3
Newtown Corn 11 F11
Newtown Cumb 229 B7
Newtown Cumb 239 F9
Newtown Cumb 240 E2
Newtown Derbys 185 E7
Newtown Devon 26 B3
Newtown Dorset 29 G7
Newtown E Ches 184 E6
Newtown Falk 279 E9
Newtown Glos 79 E11
Newtown Glos 80 D3
Newtown Glos 99 E8
Newtown Gtr Man 194 F5
Newtown Gtr Man 195 G9
Newtown Hants 21 B8
Newtown Hants 32 C4
Newtown Hants 32 E3
Newtown Hants 33 D8
Newtown Hants 33 E10
Newtown Hants 33 F7
Newtown Hants 49 F8
Newtown Hants 49 G10
Newtown Hants 64 G3
Newtown Hereford 97 E10
Newtown Hereford 98 C2
Newtown Hereford 98 C3
Newtown Highld 290 C5
Newtown I o M 192 E4
Newtown I o W 20 C4
Newtown Mers 183 B7
Newtown Norf 143 B10
Newtown Northumb 252 C2
Newtown Northumb 263 C11
Newtown Northumb 264 D2
Newtown Oxon 65 C9
Newtown Poole 18 C6
Newtown Powys 130 E2
Newtown Rhondda 77 F9
Newtown Shrops 132 C2
Newtown Shrops 149 C9
Newtown Shrops 149 E8
Newtown Som 28 E3
Newtown Som 43 F9
Newtown Staffs 133 C9
Newtown Staffs 168 C6
Newtown Staffs 169 C9
Newtown W Ches 183 F8
Newtown W Mid 133 F11
Newtown Wilts 30 B6
Newtown Wilts 63 G10
Newtown Worcs 116 F5
Newtown Worcs 117 E7
Newtown-in-St Martin
Corn 2 E6
Newtown Linford Leics 135 B10
Newtown St Boswells
Borders 262 C3
Newtown Unthank Leics 135 C9
Newtyle Angus 286 C6
Newyears Green London 66 B5
Nextend Hereford 114 F6
Neyland Pembs 73 D7
Niarbyl I o M 192 E3
Nib Heath Shrops 149 F8
Nibley Glos 79 D11
Nibley S Glos 61 C7
Nibley Green Glos 80 F2
Nibon Shetland 312 F5
Nicholashayne Devon 27 D10
Nicholaston Swansea 56 D4
Nidd N Yorks 214 G6
Niddrie Edin 280 G5
Nigg Aberdeen 293 C11
Nigg Highld 301 B8
Nigg Ferry Highld 301 C7
Nightcott Som 26 B5
Nilig Denb 165 D8
Nimble Nook Gtr Man 196 G2
Nimlet S Glos 61 E8
Nimmer Som 28 E4
Nine Ashes Essex 87 E9
Nine Elms London 67 D9
Nine Elms Swindon 62 B6
Nine Maidens Downs Corn 2 B5
Nine Mile Burn Midloth 270 D3
Nine Wells Pembs 90 G5
Ninebanks Northumb 241 G7
Nineveh Worcs 116 C3
Nineveh Worcs 116 E2
Ninewells Glos 79 C9
Ninfield E Sus 38 E2
Ningwood I o W 20 D3
Ningwood Common
I o W 20 D3
Ninnes Bridge Corn 2 B2
Nisbet Borders 262 D5
Nisthouse Orkney 314 E3
Nisthouse Shetland 313 G7
Nithbank Dumfries 247 D9
Nitshill Glasgow 267 C10
Niton I o W 20 F6
No Man's Heath W Ches 167 F8
No Man's Heath Warks 134 B5
No Man's Land Corn 6 D5
No Man's Land Hants 33 B8
Noah's Arks Kent 52 B5
Noah's Green Worcs 117 E10
Noak Bridge Essex 87 G11
Noak Hill Essex 87 G11
Noak Hill London 87 G8
Nob End Gtr Man 195 F9
Nobland Green Herts 86 B5
Noblethorpe S Yorks 197 F9
Nobold Shrops 149 G9
Nobottle Northants 120 E3
Nob's Crook Hants 33 C7
Nocton Lincs 173 C9
Noctorum Mers 182 D3
Nodmore W Berks 64 D2
Noel Park London 86 G4
Nog Tow Lancs 202 G6
Nogdam End Norf 143 C7
Noke Oxon 83 C8
Noke Street Medway 69 E8
Nolton Pembs 72 B5
Nolton Haven Pembs 72 B5
Nomansland Devon 26 E4
Nomansland Herts 85 C11
Nomansland Wilts 32 D3
Noneley Shrops 149 D9
Noness Shetland 313 L6
Nonikiln Highld 300 B6
Nonington Kent 55 C9
Nook Cumb 211 C10
Noon Nick W Yorks 205 F8
Noonsbrough Shetland 313 H4
Noonsun E Ches 184 F4
Noonvares Corn 2 C3
Noranside Angus 292 G6
Norbiton London 67 F7
Norbreck Blkpool 202 E2
Norbridge Hereford 98 C4
Norbury Derbys 169 G10
Norbury E Ches 167 F9
Norbury London 67 F10
Norbury Shrops 131 E7
Norbury Staffs 150 E5
Norbury Common
E Ches 167 F9
Norbury Junction
Staffs 150 E5
Norbury Moor Gtr Man 184 D6
Norby N Yorks 215 C8
Norby Shetland 313 H3
Norchard Worcs 116 D6
Norcote Glos 81 E8
Norcott Brook W Ches 183 E10
Norcross Blkpool 202 E2
Nordelph Norf 139 C11
Nordelph Corner Norf 141 C10
Norden Dorset 18 E4
Norden Gtr Man 195 E11
Norden Heath Dorset 18 E4
Nordley Shrops 132 D3
Norham Northumb 273 F8
Norham West Mains
Northumb 273 F8
Nork Sur 51 B8
Norland Town W Yorks 196 C5
Norleaze Wilts 45 C11
Norley Devon 25 G8
Norley W Ches 183 G9
Norley Common Sur 50 E4
Norleywood Hants 20 B3
Norlington E Sus 36 E6
Normacot Stoke 168 G6
Norman Cross Cambs 138 E3
Norman Hill Glos 80 F3
Normanby N Lincs 199 D11
Normanby N Yorks 216 C4
Normanby Redcar 225 B10
Normanby-by-Spital
Lincs 189 D7
Normanby by Stow
Lincs 188 E5
Normanby le Wold
Lincs 189 B10
Norman's Bay E Sus 23 D11
Norman's Green Devon 27 G9
Normanston Suff 143 E10
Normanton Derby 152 C6
Normanton Leics 172 G4
Normanton Lincs 172 F6
Normanton Notts 172 E2
Normanton Rutland 137 B8
Normanton W Yorks 197 C11
Normanton Wilts 46 E6
Normanton le Heath
Leics 153 G7
Normanton on Soar
Notts 153 E10
Normanton-on-the-
Wolds Notts 154 C2
Normanton on Trent
Notts 172 B3
Normoss Lancs 202 F2
Norney Sur 50 E2
Norr W Yorks 205 F7
Norrington Common
Wilts 61 G11
Norris Green Corn 7 B8
Norris Green Mers 182 C5
Norris Hill Leics 152 F6
Norristhorpe W Yorks 197 C8
Norseman Orkney 314 E3
Norsey Green Essex 87 F11
North Acton London 67 C8
North Anston S Yorks 187 E8
North Ascot Brack 66 F2
North Aston Oxon 101 F9
North Ayre Shetland 312 F6
North Baddesley Hants 32 D5
North Ballachulish
Highld 290 G2
North Barrow Som 29 B10
North Barsham Norf 159 C8
North Batsom Som 41 G10
North Beer Corn 12 C2
North Benfleet Essex 69 B9
North Bersted W Sus 22 C6
North Berwick E Loth 281 D11
North Bitchburn
Durham 233 E9
North Blyth Northumb 253 G8
North Boarhunt Hants 33 E10
North Bockhampton
Dorset 19 B9
North Bovey Devon 13 E10
North Bradley Wilts 45 C11
North Brentor Devon 12 E5
North Brewham Som 45 F8
North Brook End
Cambs 104 C5
North Broomage Falk 279 E7
North Buckland Devon 40 E3
North Burlingham Norf 161 G7
North Cadbury Som 29 B10
North Cairn Dumfries 236 B1
North Camp Hants 49 C11
North Carlton Lincs 188 F6
North Carlton Notts 187 E9
North Carrine Argyll 255 G7
North Cave E Yorks 208 G3
North Cerney Glos 81 D8
North Chailey E Sus 36 C5
North Charford Wilts 31 D11
North Charlton
Northumb 264 E5
North Cheam London 67 F8
North Cheriton Som 29 B11
North Cliff E Yorks 209 D10
North Cliffe E Yorks 208 F3
North Clifton Notts 188 G4
North Close Durham 233 E11
North Cockerington
Lincs 190 C5
North Coker Som 29 E8
North Collafirth
Shetland 312 E5
North Common S Glos 61 E7
North Common Suff 125 B9
North Connel Argyll 289 F11
North Cornelly Bridgend 57 E10
North Corner Corn 3 F7
North Corner S Glos 61 C7
North Corriegills N Ayrs 256 C2
North Corry Highld 289 D10
North Cotes Lincs 201 G11
North Country Corn 4 G3
North Court Som 41 F11
North Cove Suff 143 F9
North Cowton N Yorks 224 E5
North Craigo Angus 293 G8
North Crawley M Keynes 103 C8
North Cray London 68 E3
North Creake Norf 159 B7
North Curry Som 28 B4
North Dalton E Yorks 208 C4
North Darley Corn 11 G11
North Dawn Orkney 314 F4
North Deighton N Yorks 206 C3
North Denes Norf 161 G10
North Dronley Angus 287 D7
North Drumachter
Lodge Highld 291 F8
North Duffield N Yorks 207 F9
North Dykes Cumb 230 D6
North Eastling Kent 54 B3
North Elham Kent 55 E7
North Elkington Lincs 190 C3
North Elmham Norf 159 E9
North Elmsall W Yorks 198 E3
North Elmshall W Yorks 198 E3
North Elphinestone
E Loth 281 G7
North End Bath 60 G6
North End Beds 103 B9
North End Beds 121 F10
North End Bexley 68 D4
North End Bucks 102 F4
North End Bucks 102 F6
North End Camden 67 B9
North End Cumb 239 F8
North End Devon 27 D10
North End Dorset 30 B4
North End Durham 233 C11
North End E Yorks 209 C9
North End E Yorks 209 E9
North End E Yorks 209 G11
North End Essex 87 B11
North End Essex 106 D5
North End Hants 31 D10
North End Hants 33 B9
North End Hants 64 G2
North End Leics 153 F11
North End Lincs 174 G2
North End Lincs 189 B8
North End Lincs 190 C5
North End Lincs 190 D6
North End Lincs 191 D7
North End Lincs 201 G10
North End N Lincs 200 C6
North End N Som 60 F2
North End Norf 141 E10
North End Northumb 252 C4
North End Ptsmth 33 G11
North End Som 28 B3
North End W Sus 35 F10
North End W Sus 35 G7
North End W Sus 51 F11
North End Wilts 81 G8
North Erradale Highld 307 L2
North Evington
Leicester 136 C2
North Ewster N Lincs 199 G10
North Fambridge Essex 88 F5
North Fearns Highld 295 B7
North Featherstone
W Yorks 198 C2
North Feltham London 66 E6
North Feorline N Ayrs 255 E10
North Ferriby E Yorks 200 B3
North Finchley London 86 G3
North Flobbets Aberds 303 F7
North Frodingham
E Yorks 209 C8
North Gluss Shetland 312 F5
North Gorley Hants 31 E11
North Green Norf 141 B10
North Green Norf 142 F4
North Green Suff 126 B6
North Green Suff 126 E6
North Green Suff 127 D7
North Greetwell Lincs 189 G8
North Grimston N Yorks 216 F6
North Halley Orkney 314 F5
North Halling Medway 69 F8
North Harrow London 66 B6
North Hayling Hants 22 C2
North Hazelrigg
Northumb 264 C3
North Heasley Devon 41 G8
North Heath W Berks 64 E3
North Heath W Sus 35 C9
North Hill Corn 11 F11
North Hillingdon London 66 C5
North Hinksey Oxon 83 D7
North Hinksey Village
Oxon 83 D7
North Ho Shetland 313 J5
North Holmwood Sur 51 D7
North Houghton Hants 47 G10
North Howden E Yorks 207 G11
North Huish Devon 8 D4
North Hyde London 66 D6
North Hykeham Lincs 172 B6
North Hylton T & W 243 F8
North Kelsey Lincs 200 G4
North Kelsey Moor
Lincs 200 G5
North Kensington London 67 C8
North Kessock Highld 300 E6
North Killingholme
N Lincs 200 D6
North Kilvington
N Yorks 215 B8
North Kilworth Leics 136 G2
North Kingston Hants 31 G11
North Kirkton Aberds 303 D11
North Kiscadale N Ayrs 256 D2
North Kyme Lincs 173 E11
North Laggan Highld 290 D4
North Lancing W Sus 35 F11
North Landing E Yorks 218 E4
North Lee Bucks 84 D4
North Lees N Yorks 214 E6
North Leigh Kent 54 D6
North Leigh Oxon 82 C5
North Leverton with
Habblesthorpe Notts 188 E3
North Littleton Worcs 99 B11
North Looe Sur 67 G8
North Lopham Norf 141 G10
North Luffenham
Rutland 137 C8
North Marden W Sus 34 D4
North Marston Bucks 102 G5
North Middleton
Midloth 271 D7
North Middleton
Northumb 264 E2
North Millbrex Aberds 303 E8
North Molton Devon 26 B2
North Moreton Oxon 64 B5
North Mosstown
Aberds 303 D10
North Motherwell
N Lnrk 268 D4
North Moulsecoomb
Brighton 36 F4
North Mundham W Sus 22 C5
North Muskham Notts 172 D3
North Newbald E Yorks 208 F4
North Newington Oxon 101 D8
North Newnton Wilts 46 B6
North Newton Som 43 G9
North Nibley Glos 80 F2
North Oakley Hants 48 C4
North Ockendon London 68 C5
North Ormesby M'bro 234 G6
North Ormsby Lincs 190 C3
North Otterington
N Yorks 215 B7
North Owersby Lincs 189 C9
North Perrott Som 29 F7
North Petherton Som 43 G9
North Petherwin Corn 11 D11
North Pickenham Norf 141 B7
North Piddle Worcs 117 G9
North Poorton Dorset 16 B6
North Port Argyll 284 E4
North Poulner Hants 31 F11
North Queensferry Fife 280 E2
North Radworthy Devon 41 G9
North Rauceby Lincs 173 F8
North Reddish Gtr Man 184 C5
North Reston Lincs 190 E5
North Rigton N Yorks 205 D11
North Ripley Hants 19 B9
North Rode E Ches 168 B5
North Roe Shetland 312 E5
North Row Cumb 229 E10
North Runcton Norf 158 F2
North Sandwick
Shetland 312 D7
North Scale Cumb 210 F3
North Scarle Lincs 172 B5
North Seaton Northumb 253 F7
North Seaton Colliery
Northumb 253 F7
North Sheen London 67 D7
North Shian Argyll 289 E11
North Shields T & W 243 D9
North Shoebury Shend 70 B2
North Shore Blkpool 202 F2
North Side Cumb 228 F6
North Side P'boro 138 D5
North Skelmanae
Aberds 303 D9
North Skelton Redcar 226 B3
North Somercotes
Lincs 190 B6
North Stainley N Yorks 214 D5
North Stainmore Cumb 222 B6
North Stifford Thurrock 68 C6
North Stoke Bath 61 F8
North Stoke Oxon 64 B6
North Stoke W Sus 35 E8
North Stoneham Hants 32 D6
North Street Hants 31 D11
North Street Hants 48 G6
North Street Kent 54 B4
North Street Medway 69 E10
North Street W Berks 64 E6
North Sunderland
Northumb 264 C6
North Synton Borders 261 E11
North Tamerton Corn 12 B2
North Tawton Devon 25 G11
North Thoresby Lincs 190 B3
North Tidworth Wilts 47 D8
North Togston Northumb 252 C6
North Town Devon 25 F8
North Town Hants 49 C11
North Town Som 29 B10
North Town Som 44 E5
North Town Windsor 65 C11
North Tuddenham
Norf 159 G10
North Walbottle T & W 242 D5
North Walney Cumb 210 F3
North Walsham Norf 160 C5
North Waltham Hants 48 D5
North Warnborough
Hants 49 C8
North Water Bridge
Angus 293 G8
North Waterhayne
Devon 28 F3
North Watford Herts 85 F10
North Watten Highld 310 D6
North Weald Bassett
Essex 87 E7
North Weirs Hants 32 G3
North Wembley London 67 B7
North Weston N Som 60 D3
North Weston Oxon 83 D11
North Wheatley Notts 188 D3
North Whilborough
Devon 9 B7
North Whiteley Moray 302 E4
North Wick Bath 60 F5
North Widcombe Bath 44 B5
North Willingham
Lincs 189 D11
North Wingfield Derbys 170 B6
North Witham Lincs 155 E8
North Woolwich London 68 D2
North Wootton Dorset 29 E11
North Wootton Norf 158 E2
North Wootton Som 44 E5
North Wraxall Wilts 61 D10
North Wroughton
Swindon 63 C7
Northacre Norf 141 D9
Northall Bucks 103 G9
Northall Green Norf 159 G9
Northallerton N Yorks 225 G7
Northam Devon 24 B6
Northam Soton 32 E6
Northampton Northants 120 E5
Northaw Herts 86 E3
Northay Devon 28 G5
Northay Som 28 E3
Northbeck Lincs 173 G9
Northborough P'boro 138 B3
Northbourne Bmouth 19 B7
Northbourne Kent 55 C10
Northbridge Street E Sus 38 C2
Northbrook Dorset 17 C11
Northbrook Hants 33 D9
Northbrook Hants 48 F4
Northbrook Oxon 101 G9
Northbrook Wilts 46 C4
Northchapel W Sus 35 B7
Northchurch Herts 85 D7
Northcote Devon 27 G11
Northcott Corn 24 F2
Northcott Devon 12 C2
Northcott Devon 27 E9
Northcott Devon 27 F10
Northcourt Oxon 83 F8
Northdown Kent 71 E11
Northdyke Orkney 314 D2
Northedge Derbys 170 B5
Northend Bath 61 F9
Northend Bucks 84 G2
Northend Essex 89 E7
Northend Essex 105 D10
Northend Warks 119 G7
Northenden Gtr Man 184 C4
Northern Moor Gtr Man 184 C4
Northfield Aberdeen 293 C11
Northfield Borders 262 D3
Northfield Borders 273 B8
Northfield E Yorks 200 B4
Northfield Edin 280 G5
Northfield Highld 301 B7
Northfield M Keynes 103 C7
Northfield Northants 137 E7
Northfield Som 43 F9
Northfield W Mid 117 B10
Northfields Hants 33 B7
Northfields Lincs 137 B10
Northfleet Kent 68 E6
Northfleet Green Kent 68 E6
Northgate Lincs 156 D3
Northgate Som 27 B9
Northgate W Sus 51 F9
Northhouse Borders 249 B10
Northiam E Sus 38 B4
Northill C Beds 104 B2
Northington Glos 80 D2
Northington Hants 48 F5
Northlands Lincs 174 E4
Northlea Durham 243 G10
Northleach Glos 81 C10
Northleigh Devon 15 B9
Northleigh Devon 40 G6
Northlew Devon 12 B6
Northmoor Devon 24 D4
Northmoor Oxon 82 E6
Northmoor Corner Som 43 G10
Northmoor Green or
Moorland Som 43 G10
Northmuir Angus 287 B7
Northney Hants 22 C2
Northolt London 66 C6
Northop =
Llan-eurgain Flint 166 B2
Northop Hall Flint 166 B3
Northorpe Lincs 155 F11
Northorpe Lincs 156 B4
Northorpe Lincs 188 B5
Northorpe W Yorks 197 C8
Northover Som 29 C8
Northover Som 44 F3
Northowram W Yorks 196 B6
Northpark Argyll 275 G11
Northport Dorset 18 D4
Northpunds Shetland 313 L6
Northrepps Norf 160 B4
Northside Aberds 303 D8
Northside Orkney 314 D2
Northton Aberds 293 C9
Northtown Orkney 314 G4
Northtown Shetland 313 M5
Northumberland Heath
London 68 D4
Northville Torf 78 F3
Northway Devon 24 C5
Northway Glos 99 E8
Northway Som 27 B10
Northway Swansea 56 D5
Northwich W Ches 183 G11
Northwick S Glos 60 B5
Northwick Som 43 D11
Northwick Worcs 116 F6
Northwold Norf 140 D5
Northwood Derbys 170 C3
Northwood I o W 20 C5
Northwood Kent 71 F11
Northwood London 85 G9
Northwood Mers 182 B6
Northwood Shrops 149 C9
Northwood Staffs 168 G5
Northwood Stoke 168 F5
Northwood Green Glos 80 B2
Northwood Hills London 85 G9
Norton Devon 9 E7
Norton Devon 24 B3
Norton E Sus 23 E7
Norton Glos 99 G7
Norton Halton 183 E9
Norton Herts 104 E4
Norton I o W 20 D2

388 Nor – Par

Norton Mon 78 B6
Norton N Som 59 G10
Norton Northants 120 E2
Norton Notts 187 G9
Norton Powys 114 D6
Norton S Yorks 186 E5
Norton S Yorks 198 D4
Norton Shrops 131 B11
Norton Shrops 131 G9
Norton Shrops 132 C4
Norton Stockton 234 G4
Norton Suff 125 D9
Norton Swansea 56 D3
Norton Swansea 56 D6
Norton W Mid 133 G7
Norton W Sus 22 B6
Norton W Sus 22 D5
Norton Wilts 61 C11
Norton Worcs 99 B10
Norton Worcs 117 G7
Norton Ash Kent 70 G3
Norton Bavant Wilts 46 E2
Norton Bridge Staffs 151 C7
Norton Canes Staffs 133 B10
Norton Canon Hereford 97 B7
Norton Corner Norf 159 D11
Norton Disney Lincs 172 D5
Norton East Staffs 133 B10
Norton Ferris Wilts 45 F9
Norton Fitzwarren Som 27 B11
Norton Green Herts 104 G4
Norton Green I o W 20 D2
Norton Green Staffs 168 E6
Norton Green W Mid 118 C3
Norton Hawkfield Bath 60 G5
Norton Heath Essex 87 E10
Norton in Hales Shrops 150 B4
Norton-in-the-Moors Stoke 168 E5
Norton-Juxta-Twycross Leics 134 B6
Norton-le-Clay N Yorks 215 E8
Norton Lindsey Warks 118 E4
Norton Little Green Suff 125 D9
Norton Malreward Bath 60 F6
Norton Mandeville Essex 87 E9
Norton-on-Derwent N Yorks 216 E5
Norton St Philip Som 45 B9
Norton sub Hamdon Som 29 D7
Norton Subcourse Norf 143 D8
Norton Woodseats S Yorks 186 E5
Norton's Wood N Som 60 E2
Norwell Notts 172 C3
Norwell Woodhouse Notts 172 C2
Norwich Norf 142 B4
Norwick Shetland 312 B8
Norwood Derbys 187 E7
Norwood Dorset 29 F8
Norwood End Essex 87 D9
Norwood Green London 66 D6
Norwood Green W Yorks 196 B6
Norwood Hill Sur 51 E8
Norwood New Town London 67 E10
Norwoodside Cambs 139 D8
Noseley Leics 136 D4
Noss Highld 310 D7
Noss Shetland 313 M5
Noss Mayo Devon 7 F11
Nosterfield N Yorks 214 C5
Nosterfield End Cambs 106 C2
Nostie Highld 295 C10
Notgrove Glos 100 G2
Nottage Bridgend 57 F10
Notter Corn 7 C7
Notting Hill London 67 C8
Nottingham Nottingham 153 B11
Nottington Dorset 17 E9
Notton W Yorks 197 E10
Notton Wilts 62 F2
Nounsley Essex 88 C3
Noutard's Green Worcs 116 D5
Nova Scotia W Ches 167 B10
Novar House Highld 300 C6
Novers Park Bristol 60 F5
Noverton Glos 99 G9
Nowton Suff 125 E7
Nox Shrops 149 G8
Noyadd Trefawr Ceredig 92 B5
Noyadd Wilym Ceredig 92 C4
Nuffield Oxon 65 B7
Nun Appleton N Yorks 207 F7
Nun Hills Lancs 195 C11
Nun Monkton N Yorks 206 B6
Nunburnholme E Yorks 208 D2
Nuncargate Notts 171 E8
Nunclose Cumb 230 B5
Nuneaton Warks 135 E7
Nuneham Courtenay Oxon 83 F9
Nuney Green Oxon 65 D7
Nunhead London 67 D11
Nunney Som 45 D8
Nunney Catch Som 45 E8
Nunnington N Yorks 216 D3
Nunnykirk Northumb 252 E3
Nunsthorpe NE Lincs 201 F9
Nunthorpe M'bro 225 C10
Nunthorpe York 207 C8
Nunton Wilts 31 B11
Nunwick N Yorks 214 E6
Nup End Bucks 84 B5
Nup End Herts 86 B2
Nupdown S Glos 79 F10
Nupend Glos 80 D3
Nupend Glos 80 F4
Nuper's Hatch Essex 87 G8
Nuppend Glos 79 E10
Nuptown Brack 65 E11
Nursling Hants 32 D5
Nursted Hants 34 C3
Nursteed Wilts 62 G4
Nurston V Glam 58 F5
Nurton Staffs 132 D6
Nurton Hill Staffs 132 D6
Nut Grove Mers 183 C7
Nutbourne W Sus 22 B3
Nutbourne W Sus 35 D9
Nutbourne Common W Sus 35 D9
Nutburn Hants 32 C5
Nutcombe Sur 49 G11
Nutfield Sur 51 C10
Nuthall Notts 171 G8
Nuthampstead Herts 105 E8
Nuthurst W Sus 35 B11
Nuthurst Warks 118 C3
Nutley E Sus 36 B6
Nutley Hants 48 E6
Nuttall Gtr Man 195 D9
Nutwell S Yorks 198 G6
Nybster Highld 310 C7
Nye N Som 60 G2
Nyetimber W Sus 22 D5
Nyewood W Sus 34 C4
Nyland Som 44 C3
Nymet Rowland Devon 26 F2
Nymet Tracey Devon 26 G2
Nympsfield Glos 80 E4
Nynehead Som 27 C10
Nythe Som 44 G2
Nythe Swindon 63 B7
Nyton W Sus 22 B6

O

Oad Street Kent 69 G11
Oadby Leics 136 C2
Oak Bank Gtr Man 195 F10
Oak Cross Devon 12 B6
Oak Hill Stoke 168 G5
Oak Hill Suff 109 B7
Oak Tree Darl 225 C7
Oakall Green Worcs 116 E6
Oakamoor Staffs 169 G9
Oakbank W Loth 269 B11
Oakdale Caerph 77 F11
Oakdale N Yorks 205 B11
Oakdale Poole 18 C6
Oake Som 27 B11
Oake Green Som 27 B11
Oaken Staffs 133 C7
Oakenclough Lancs 202 D6
Oakengates Telford 150 G4
Oakenholt Flint 182 G3
Oakenshaw Durham 233 D10
Oakenshaw Lancs 203 G10
Oakenshaw W Yorks 197 B7
Oakerthorpe Derbys 170 E5
Oakes W Yorks 196 D6
Oakfield Herts 104 F3
Oakfield I o W 21 C7
Oakfield Torf 78 G4
Oakford Ceredig 111 F9
Oakford Devon 26 C6
Oakfordbridge Devon 26 C6
Oakgrove E Ches 168 B6
Oakgrove M Keynes 103 D7
Oakham Rutland 137 B7
Oakham W Mid 133 F9
Oakhanger E Ches 168 E3
Oakhanger Hants 49 F9
Oakhill Som 44 D6
Oakhill W Sus 51 G7
Oakhurst Kent 52 C4
Oakington Cambs 123 E8
Oaklands Carms 74 B6
Oaklands Herts 86 B2
Oaklands Powys 113 G10
Oakle Street Glos 80 B3
Oakleigh Park London 86 G3
Oakley Beds 121 G10
Oakley Bucks 83 C10
Oakley Fife 279 D10
Oakley Glos 99 G9
Oakley Hants 48 C5
Oakley Oxon 84 E3
Oakley Poole 18 B6
Oakley Staffs 150 B4
Oakley Suff 126 B3
Oakley Court Oxon 64 B6
Oakley Green Windsor 66 D2
Oakley Park Powys 129 F9
Oakley Park Suff 126 B3
Oakley Wood Oxon 64 B6
Oakmere W Ches 167 B9
Oakridge Glos 80 E6
Oakridge Hants 48 C6
Oakridge Lynch Glos 80 E6
Oaks Shrops 131 C8
Oaks Green Derbys 152 C3
Oaks in Charnwood Leics 153 F9
Oaksey Wilts 81 G7
Oakshaw Ford Cumb 240 B2
Oakshott Hants 34 B2
Oakthorpe Leics 152 G6
Oakwell W Yorks 197 B8
Oakwood Derby 153 B7
Oakwood London 86 F3
Oakwood Northumb 241 D10
Oakwood W Yorks 206 F2
Oakwood Warr 183 C11
Oakwoodhill Sur 50 F6
Oakworth W Yorks 204 F6
Oape Highld 309 J4
Oare Kent 70 G4
Oare Som 41 D10
Oare W Berks 64 E4
Oare Wilts 63 G7
Oareford Som 41 D10
Oasby Lincs 155 B10
Oath Som 28 B5
Oathill Dorset 28 F6
Oathlaw Angus 287 B8
Oatlands Glasgow 267 C11
Oatlands N Yorks 205 C11
Oatlands Park Sur 66 G5
Oban Argyll 289 G10
Oban Highld 295 G10
Oban W Isles 305 H3
Obley Shrops 114 B6
Oborne Dorset 29 D11
Obthorpe Lincs 155 F11
Obthorpe Lodge Lincs 156 F2
Occlestone Green W Ches 167 C11
Occold Suff 126 C3
Ocean Village Soton 32 E6
Ochiltree E Ayrs 258 E2
Ochr-y-foel Denb 181 F9
Ochtermuthill Perth 286 F2
Ochtertyre Perth 286 E2
Ochtow Highld 309 J4
Ockbrook Derbys 153 B8
Ocker Hill W Mid 133 E9
Ockeridge Worcs 116 E5
Ockford Ridge Sur 50 E3
Ockham Sur 50 B5
Ockle Highld 289 B7
Ockley Sur 50 F6
Ocle Pychard Hereford 97 B11
Octon E Yorks 217 F10
Octon Cross Roads E Yorks 217 F10
Odam Barton Devon 26 D2
Odcombe Som 29 D8
Odd Down Bath 61 G8
Oddendale Cumb 221 C11
Odder Lincs 188 G6
Oddingley Worcs 117 F8
Oddington Glos 100 F4
Oddington Oxon 83 C9
Odell Beds 121 F9
Odham Devon 25 G7
Odie Orkney 314 D6
Odiham Hants 49 C8
Odsal W Yorks 197 B7
Odsey Cambs 104 D5
Odstock Wilts 31 B10
Odstone Leics 135 B7
Offchurch Warks 119 D7
Offenham Worcs 99 B11
Offenham Cross Worcs 99 B11
Offerton Gtr Man 184 D6
Offerton T & W 243 F8
Offerton Green Gtr Man 184 D6
Offham E Sus 36 E5
Offham Kent 53 B7
Offham W Sus 35 F8
Offleyhay Staffs 150 D5
Offleymarsh Staffs 150 D5
Offleyrock Staffs 150 D5
Offord Cluny Cambs 122 D4
Offord D'Arcy Cambs 122 D4
Offton Suff 107 B11
Offwell Devon 15 B9
Ogbourne Maizey Wilts 63 E7
Ogbourne St Andrew Wilts 63 E7
Ogbourne St George Wilts 63 E8
Ogden W Yorks 205 G7
Ogdens Hants 31 E11
Ogil Angus 292 G6
Ogle Northumb 242 B4
Ogmore V Glam 57 F11
Ogmore-by-Sea = Aberogwr V Glam 57 F11
Ogmore Vale Bridgend 76 G6
Okeford Fitzpaine Dorset 30 E4
Okehampton Devon 13 B7
Okehampton Camp Devon 13 C7
Oker Derbys 170 C3
Okewood Hill Sur 50 F6
Okle Green Glos 98 F5
Okraquoy Shetland 313 K6
Okus Swindon 62 C6
Olchard Devon 14 F3
Old Northants 120 C5
Old Aberdeen Aberdeen 293 C11
Old Alresford Hants 48 G5
Old Arley Warks 134 E5
Old Balornock Glasgow 268 B2
Old Basford Nottingham 171 G8
Old Basing Hants 49 C7
Old Belses Borders 262 E3
Old Bewick Northumb 264 E3
Old Bexley London 68 E3
Old Blair Perth 291 G10
Old Bolingbroke Lincs 174 B4
Old Boston Mers 183 B9
Old Bramhope W Yorks 205 E10
Old Brampton Derbys 186 G4
Old Bridge of Tilt Perth 291 G10
Old Bridge of Urr Dumfries 237 C9
Old Buckenham Norf 141 E11
Old Burdon T & W 243 G9
Old Burghclere Hants 48 B3
Old Byland N Yorks 215 B11
Old Cambus Borders 272 B6
Old Cardinham Castle Corn 6 B2
Old Carlisle Cumb 229 B11
Old Cassop Durham 234 D2
Old Castleton Borders 250 E2
Old Catton Norf 160 G4
Old Chalford Oxon 100 F6
Old Church Stoke Powys 130 E5
Old Clee NE Lincs 201 F9
Old Cleeve Som 42 E4
Old Colwyn Conwy 180 F5
Old Coppice Shrops 131 B9
Old Corry Highld 295 C8
Old Coulsdon London 51 B10
Old Country Hereford 98 C4
Old Craig Aberds 303 G9
Old Craig Angus 292 G4
Old Crombie Aberds 302 D5
Old Cryals Kent 53 E7
Old Cullen Moray 302 C5
Old Dailly S Ayrs 244 D6
Old Dalby Leics 154 E3
Old Dam Derbys 185 F10
Old Deer Aberds 303 E9
Old Denaby S Yorks 187 B7
Old Ditch Som 44 D4
Old Dolphin W Yorks 205 G8
Old Down S Glos 60 B6
Old Duffus Moray 301 C11
Old Edlington S Yorks 187 B8
Old Eldon Durham 233 F10
Old Ellerby E Yorks 209 F9
Old Fallings W Mid 133 C8
Old Farm Park M Keynes 103 D8
Old Felixstowe Suff 108 D6
Old Field Shrops 115 B9
Old Fletton P'boro 138 D3
Old Fold T & W 243 E7
Old Ford London 67 C11
Old Forge Hereford 79 B9
Old Furnace Torf 78 E3
Old Gate Lincs 157 E8
Old Glossop Derbys 185 C8
Old Goginan Ceredig 128 G3
Old Goole E Yorks 199 C8
Old Gore Hereford 98 F2
Old Graitney Dumfries 239 D8
Old Grimsby Scilly 1 F3
Old Hall Powys 129 G8
Old Hall Green Herts 105 G7
Old Hall Street Norf 160 C6
Old Harlow Essex 87 C7
Old Hatfield Herts 86 D2
Old Heath Essex 107 G10
Old Heathfield E Sus 37 C9
Old Hill W Mid 133 F9
Old Hills Worcs 98 B6
Old Hunstanton Norf 175 G11
Old Hurst Cambs 122 B5
Old Hutton Cumb 211 B11
Old Johnstone Dumfries 248 D6
Old Kea Corn 4 G6
Old Kilpatrick W Dunb 277 G9
Old Kinnernie Aberds 293 C9
Old Knebworth Herts 104 G4
Old Langho Lancs 203 F10
Old Laxey I o M 192 D5
Old Leake Lincs 174 E6
Old Leckie Stirl 278 C3
Old Lindley W Yorks 196 D5
Old Linslade C Beds 103 F8
Old Llanberis = Nant Peris Gwyn 163 D10
Old Malden London 67 F8
Old Malton N Yorks 216 E5
Old Marton Shrops 148 C6
Old Mead Essex 105 F10
Old Micklefield W Yorks 206 G4
Old Mill Corn 12 G3
Old Milton Hants 19 C10
Old Milverton Warks 118 D5
Old Monkland N Lnrk 268 C4
Old Nenthorn Borders 262 B5
Old Netley Hants 33 F7
Old Neuadd Powys 129 F11
Old Newton Suff 125 E11
Old Oak Common London 67 C8
Old Park Corn 6 B4
Old Park Telford 132 B3
Old Passage S Glos 60 B5
Old Perton Staffs 133 D7
Old Philpstoun W Loth 279 F11
Old Polmont Falk 279 F8
Old Portsmouth Ptsmth 21 B8
Old Quarrington Durham 234 D2
Old Radnor Powys 114 F5
Old Rattray Aberds 303 D10
Old Rayne Aberds 302 G6
Old Romney Kent 39 B8
Old Shirley Soton 32 E5
Old Shoreham W Sus 36 F2
Old Snydale W Yorks 198 C2
Old Sodbury S Glos 61 C9
Old Somerby Lincs 155 C9
Old Stillington Stockton 234 G3
Old Stratford Common Worcs 116 G4
Old Stratford Northants 102 C5
Old Struan Perth 291 G10
Old Swan Mers 182 C5
Old Swarland Northumb 252 C5
Old Swinford W Mid 133 G8
Old Tame Gtr Man 196 F3
Old Tebay Cumb 222 D2
Old Thirsk N Yorks 215 C8
Old Tinnis Borders 261 D9
Old Toll S Ayrs 257 E9
Old Town Cumb 211 C11
Old Town Cumb 230 C5
Old Town E Sus 23 F9
Old Town E Sus 38 F2
Old Town E Sus 38 F4
Old Town E Yorks 218 F3
Old Town Edin 280 G5
Old Town Herts 104 F4
Old Town Scilly 1 G4
Old Town Swindon 63 C7
Old Town W Yorks 196 B3
Old Trafford Gtr Man 184 B4
Old Tree Kent 71 G8
Old Tupton Derbys 170 B5
Old Warden C Beds 104 C2
Old Warren Flint 166 C4
Old Way Som 28 D5
Old Weston Cambs 121 B11
Old Wharf Hereford 98 D4
Old Whittington Derbys 186 G5
Old Wick Highld 310 D7
Old Wimpole Cambs 122 G6
Old Windsor Windsor 66 E3
Old Wingate Durham 234 D3
Old Wives Lees Kent 54 C5
Old Woking Sur 50 B4
Old Wolverton M Keynes 102 C6
Old Woodhall Lincs 174 B2
Old Woodhouses Shrops 167 G9
Old Woodstock Oxon 82 B6
Oldany Highld 306 F6
Oldberrow Warks 118 D2
Oldborough Devon 26 F3
Oldbrook M Keynes 103 D7
Oldbury Kent 52 B5
Oldbury Shrops 132 E4
Oldbury W Mid 133 F9
Oldbury Warks 134 E6
Oldbury Naite S Glos 79 G10
Oldbury-on-Severn S Glos 79 G10
Oldbury on the Hill Glos 61 B10
Oldcastle Mon 96 G6
Oldcastle Heath W Ches 167 F7
Oldcotes Notts 187 D9
Oldcroft Glos 79 D10
Oldend Glos 80 D3
Oldfallow Staffs 151 G9
Oldfield Cumb 229 F7
Oldfield Shrops 132 F3
Oldfield W Yorks 196 E6
Oldfield W Yorks 204 F6
Oldfield Worcs 116 E6
Oldfield Brow Gtr Man 184 D3
Oldfield Park Bath 61 G8
Oldford Som 45 C9
Oldfurnace Staffs 169 G8
Oldhall Renfs 267 C10
Oldhall Green Suff 125 F7
Oldhall Ho Highld 310 D6
Oldham Gtr Man 196 F2
Oldham Edge Gtr Man 196 F2
Oldhamstocks E Loth 282 G4
Oldhurst Cambs 122 B6
Oldington Shrops 132 D4
Oldland S Glos 61 E7
Oldland Common S Glos 61 E7
Oldmeldrum Aberds 303 G8
Oldmixon N Som 43 B10
Oldshore Beg Highld 306 D6
Oldshoremore Highld 306 D7
Oldstead N Yorks 215 C10
Oldtown Aberds 293 C7
Oldtown Aberds 302 G5
Oldtown Highld 309 L5
Oldtown of Ord Aberds 302 D6
Oldwalls Swansea 56 C3
Oldway Swansea 56 D5
Oldway Torbay 9 C7
Oldways End Devon 26 B5
Oldwhat Aberds 303 D8
Oldwich Lane W Mid 118 C4
Oldwood Worcs 115 D11
Olgrinmore Highld 310 D4
Olive Green Staffs 152 F2
Oliver's Battery Hants 33 B7
Ollaberry Shetland 312 E5
Ollag W Isles 297 G3
Ollerbrook Booth Derbys 185 D10
Ollerton E Ches 184 F3
Ollerton Notts 171 B11
Ollerton Shrops 150 D2
Ollerton Fold Lancs 194 C6
Ollerton Lane Shrops 150 D3
Olmarch Ceredig 112 F2
Olmstead Green Essex 106 C2
Olney M Keynes 121 G7
Olrig Ho Highld 310 C5
Olton W Mid 134 G2
Olveston S Glos 60 B6
Olwen Ceredig 93 B11
Ombersley Worcs 116 E6
Ompton Notts 171 B11
Omunsgarth Shetland 313 J5
Onchan I o M 192 E4
Onecote Staffs 169 D9
Onehouse Suff 125 F10
Onen Mon 78 C6
Onesacre S Yorks 186 C3
Ongar Hill Norf 157 E11
Ongar Street Hereford 115 D7
Onibury Shrops 115 B9
Onich Highld 290 G2
Onllwyn Neath 76 C4
Onneley Staffs 168 G3
Onslow Village Sur 50 D3
Onthank E Ayrs 267 G8
Onziebust Orkney 314 D4
Openshaw Gtr Man 184 B5
Openwoodgate Derbys 170 F5
Opinan Highld 299 B7
Opinan Highld 307 K3
Orange Lane Borders 272 G5
Orange Row Norf 157 E10
Orasaigh W Isles 305 G5
Orbiston N Lnrk 268 D4
Orbliston Moray 302 D3
Orbost Highld 298 E2
Orby Lincs 175 B7
Orchard Hill Devon 24 B6
Orchard Leigh Bucks 85 E7
Orchard Portman Som 28 C2
Orcheston Wilts 46 D5
Orcop Hereford 97 F9
Orcop Hill Hereford 97 F9
Ord Highld 295 D8
Ordale Shetland 312 C8
Ordhead Aberds 293 B8
Ordie Aberds 292 C6
Ordiequish Moray 302 D3
Ordiqhill Aberds 302 D5
Ordley Northumb 241 F10
Ordsall Gtr Man 184 B4
Ordsall Notts 187 E11
Ore E Sus 38 E4
Oreston Plym 7 E10
Oreton Shrops 132 G3
Orford Suff 109 B8
Orford Warr 183 C10
Organford Dorset 18 C4
Orgreave S Yorks 186 D6
Orgreave Staffs 152 F3
Oridge Street Glos 98 F5
Orlandon Pembs 72 D4
Orlestone Kent 54 G3
Orleton Hereford 115 D9
Orleton Worcs 116 D3
Orleton Common Hereford 115 D9
Orlingbury Northants 121 C7
Ormacleit W Isles 297 H3
Ormathwaite Cumb 229 F11
Ormesby Redcar 225 B10
Ormesby St Margaret Norf 161 G9
Ormesby St Michael Norf 161 G9
Ormiclate Castle W Isles 297 H3
Ormidale Lodge Argyll 275 F11
Ormiscaig Highld 307 K3
Ormiston Borders 262 G2
Ormiston E Loth 271 B8
Ormsaigbeg Highld 288 C6
Ormsaigmore Highld 288 C6
Ormsary Argyll 275 F8
Ormsgill Cumb 210 E3
Ormskirk Lancs 194 F2
Ornsby Hill Durham 233 B9
Orpington London 68 F3
Orrell Gtr Man 194 F5
Orrell Mers 182 B4
Orrell Post Gtr Man 194 G4
Orrisdale I o M 192 C4
Orrock Fife 280 D4
Orroland Dumfries 237 E9
Orsett Thurrock 68 C6
Orsett Heath Thurrock 68 D6
Orslow Staffs 150 F6
Orston Notts 172 G3
Orthwaite Cumb 229 E11
Ortner Lancs 202 C6
Orton Cumb 222 D2
Orton Northants 120 B6
Orton Staffs 133 D7
Orton Brimbles P'boro 138 D3
Orton Goldhay P'boro 138 D3
Orton Longueville P'boro 138 D3
Orton Malborne P'boro 138 D3
Orton-on-the-Hill Leics 134 C6
Orton Rigg Cumb 239 G8
Orton Southgate P'boro 138 E2
Orton Waterville P'boro 138 D3
Orton Wistow P'boro 138 D2
Orwell Cambs 123 G7
Osbaldeston Lancs 203 G8
Osbaldeston Green Lancs 203 G8
Osbaldwick York 207 C8
Osbaston Leics 135 C8
Osbaston Shrops 148 E6
Osbaston Telford 149 F11
Osbaston Hollow Leics 135 B8
Osbournby Lincs 155 B11
Oscroft W Ches 167 B8
Ose Highld 298 E3
Osea Island Essex 88 D6
Osehill Green Dorset 29 F11
Osgathorpe Leics 153 F8
Osgodby Lincs 189 C9
Osgodby N Yorks 207 F8
Osgodby N Yorks 217 C11
Osgodby Common N Yorks 207 F8
Osidge London 86 G3
Oskaig Highld 295 B7
Oskamull Argyll 288 E6
Osleston Derbys 152 B4
Osmaston Derby 153 C7
Osmaston Derbys 170 G2
Osmington Dorset 17 E10
Osmington Mills Dorset 17 E10
Osmondthorpe W Yorks 206 G2
Osmotherley N Yorks 225 F9
Osney Oxon 83 D8
Ospisdale Highld 309 L7
Ospringe Kent 70 G4
Ossaborough Devon 40 E3
Ossemsley Hants 19 B10
Ossett W Yorks 197 C9
Ossett Street Side W Yorks 197 C9
Ossington Notts 172 C3
Ostend Essex 88 F6
Ostend Norf 161 C7
Osterley London 66 D6
Oswaldkirk N Yorks 216 D2
Oswaldtwistle Lancs 195 B8
Oswestry Shrops 148 D5
Otby Lincs 189 C10
Oteley Shrops 149 C8
Otford Kent 52 B4
Otham Kent 53 C9
Otham Hole Kent 53 C10
Otherton Staffs 151 G8
Othery Som 43 G11
Otley Suff 126 F4
Otley W Yorks 205 D10
Otter Ferry Argyll 275 E10
Otter Ho Argyll 275 F10
Otterbourne Hants 33 C7
Otterburn N Yorks 204 B3
Otterburn Northumb 251 E9
Otterburn Camp Northumb 251 D9
Otterden Place Kent 54 C2
Otterford Som 28 E2
Otterham Corn 11 C9
Otterham Quay Kent 69 F10
Otterham Station Corn 11 D9
Otterhampton Som 43 E8
Ottershaw Sur 66 G4
Otterspool Mers 182 D5
Otterswick Shetland 312 E7
Otterton Devon 15 D7
Otterwood Hants 32 G6
Ottery St Mary Devon 15 B8
Ottinge Kent 55 E7
Ottringham E Yorks 201 C9
Oughterby Cumb 239 F7
Oughtershaw N Yorks 213 C7
Oughterside Cumb 229 C8
Oughtibridge S Yorks 186 C4
Oughtrington Warr 183 D11
Oulston N Yorks 215 E10
Oulton Cumb 238 G6
Oulton Norf 160 D2
Oulton Staffs 150 E5
Oulton Staffs 151 B8
Oulton Suff 143 D10
Oulton W Yorks 197 B11
Oulton Broad Suff 143 E10
Oulton Grange Staffs 151 B8
Oulton Heath Staffs 151 B8
Oulton Street Norf 160 D3
Oultoncross Staffs 151 C8
Oundle Northants 137 F10
Ounsdale Staffs 133 E7
Ousby Cumb 231 E8
Ousdale Highld 311 G4
Ousden Suff 124 F4
Ousefleet E Yorks 199 C10
Ousel Hole W Yorks 205 E8
Ouston Durham 243 G7
Ouston Northumb 241 G7
Ouston Northumb 242 C3
Out Elmstead Kent 55 C8
Out Newton E Yorks 201 C11
Out Rawcliffe Lancs 202 E4
Outcast Cumb 210 D6
Outer Hope Devon 8 G3
Outertown Orkney 314 E2
Outgate Cumb 221 F7
Outhgill Cumb 222 E5
Outhill Warks 118 D2
Outhills Aberds 303 D10
Outlands Staffs 150 C5
Outlane W Yorks 196 D5
Outlane Moor W Yorks 196 D5
Outlet Village W Ches 182 G6
Outmarsh Wilts 61 G11
Outwell Norf 139 C10
Outwick Hants 31 D10
Outwood Gtr Man 195 F9
Outwood Som 28 B4
Outwood Sur 51 D10
Outwood W Yorks 197 C10
Outwoods Leics 153 F8
Outwoods Staffs 150 F5
Outwoods Staffs 152 E4
Outwoods Warks 134 G4
Ouzlewell Green W Yorks 197 B10
Ovenden W Yorks 196 B5
Ovenscloss Borders 261 C11
Over Cambs 123 C7
Over Glos 80 B4
Over S Glos 60 C5
Over W Ches 167 B10
Over Burrow Lancs 212 D2
Over Burrows Derbys 152 B5
Over Compton Dorset 29 D9
Over End Cambs 137 E11
Over End Derbys 186 G3
Over Green W Mid 134 E3
Over Haddon Derbys 170 B2
Over Hulton Gtr Man 195 F7
Over Kellet Lancs 211 E10
Over Kiddington Oxon 101 G8
Over Knutsford E Ches 184 F3
Over Langshaw Borders 271 G10
Over Monnow Mon 79 C8
Over Norton Oxon 100 F6
Over Peover E Ches 184 G3
Over Silton N Yorks 225 G9
Over Stowey Som 43 F7
Over Stratton Som 28 D6
Over Tabley E Ches 184 E2
Over Town Lancs 195 B11
Over Wallop Hants 47 F9
Over Whitacre Warks 134 E5
Over Worton Oxon 101 F8
Overa Farm Stud Norf 141 F9
Overbister Orkney 314 B6
Overbury Worcs 99 D9
Overcombe Dorset 17 E9
Overend W Mid 133 G9
Overgreen Derbys 186 G4
Overleigh Som 44 F3
Overley Staffs 152 F3
Overley Green Warks 117 F11
Overmoor Staffs 169 F7
Overpool W Ches 182 F5
Overs Shrops 131 D7
Overscaig Hotel Highld 309 G4
Overseal Derbys 152 F5
Overslade Warks 119 C9
Oversland Kent 54 B5
Oversley Green Warks 117 F11
Overstone Northants 120 D6
Overstrand Norf 160 A4
Overthorpe Northants 101 C9
Overthorpe W Yorks 197 D8
Overton Aberdeen 293 B10
Overton Aberds 293 B9
Overton Dumfries 237 C11
Overton Glos 80 C2
Overton Hants 48 D4
Overton Invclyd 276 G5
Overton Lancs 202 B4
Overton N Yorks 207 B7
Overton Shrops 115 C10
Overton Shrops 131 B10
Overton Staffs 151 B10
Overton Swansea 56 D3
Overton W Ches 183 F8
Overton W Yorks 197 D9
Overton = Owrtyn Wrex 166 G5
Overton Bridge Wrex 166 G5
Overtown Lancs 212 D2
Overtown N Lnrk 268 E6
Overtown Swindon 63 D7
Overtown W Yorks 197 D11
Oving Bucks 102 G5
Oving W Sus 22 C6
Ovingdean Brighton 36 G5
Ovingham Northumb 242 E3
Ovington Durham 224 C2
Ovington Essex 106 C5
Ovington Hants 48 G5
Ovington Norf 141 C8
Ovington Northumb 242 E3
Owen's Bank Staffs 152 D4
Ower Hants 32 D4
Ower Hants 32 E6
Owermoigne Dorset 17 D11
Owl End Cambs 122 B4
Owlbury Shrops 130 E6
Owlcotes Derbys 170 B6
Owler Bar Derbys 186 F3
Owlerton S Yorks 186 D4
Owlet W Yorks 205 F9
Owlpen Glos 80 F4
Owl's Green Suff 126 D5
Owlsmoor Brack 65 G11
Owlswick Bucks 84 D3
Owlthorpe S Yorks 186 E6
Owmby Lincs 200 G5
Owmby-by-Spital Lincs 189 D8
Ownham W Berks 64 E2
Owrtyn = Overton Wrex 166 G5
Owslebury Hants 33 C8
Owston Leics 136 B5
Owston S Yorks 198 E5
Owston Ferry N Lincs 199 G10
Owstwick E Yorks 209 G11
Owthorne E Yorks 201 B10
Owthorpe Notts 154 C3
Owton Manor Hrtlpl 234 F5
Oxborough Norf 140 C4
Oxclose S Yorks 186 E6
Oxclose T & W 243 F7
Oxcombe Lincs 190 F4
Oxcroft Derbys 187 G7
Oxcroft Estate Derbys 187 G7
Oxen End Essex 106 F3
Oxen Park Cumb 210 B6
Oxenhall Glos 98 F4
Oxenholme Cumb 211 B10
Oxenhope W Yorks 204 F6
Oxenpill Som 44 E2
Oxenton Glos 99 E9
Oxenwood Wilts 47 B10
Oxford Oxon 83 D8
Oxford Stoke 168 E5
Oxgang E Dunb 278 G3
Oxgangs Edin 270 B4
Oxhey Herts 85 F10
Oxhill Durham 242 G5
Oxhill Warks 100 B6
Oxlease Herts 86 D2
Oxley W Mid 133 C8
Oxley Green Essex 88 C6
Oxley's Green E Sus 37 C11
Oxlode Cambs 139 F9
Oxnam Borders 262 F5
Oxnead Norf 160 E4
Oxshott Sur 66 G6
Oxspring S Yorks 197 G9
Oxted Sur 51 C11
Oxton Borders 271 E9
Oxton Mers 182 D3
Oxton N Yorks 206 E6
Oxton Notts 171 E10
Oxton Rakes Derbys 186 G4
Oxwich Swansea 56 D3
Oxwich Green Swansea 56 D3
Oxwick Norf 159 D8
Oykel Bridge Highld 309 J3
Oyne Aberds 302 G6
Oystermouth Swansea 56 D6
Ozleworth Glos 80 G3

P

Pabail Iarach W Isles 304 E7
Pabail Uarach W Isles 304 E7
Pabo Conwy 180 F4
Pace Gate N Yorks 205 C8
Pachesham Park Sur 51 B7
Packers Hill Dorset 30 E2
Packington Leics 153 G7
Packmoor Staffs 168 E5
Packmores Warks 118 D5
Packwood W Mid 118 C3
Packwood Gullet W Mid 118 C3
Padanaram Angus 287 B8
Padbury Bucks 102 E4
Paddington London 67 C9
Paddington Warr 183 D10
Paddlesworth Kent 55 F7
Paddlesworth Kent 69 G7
Paddock Kent 54 C3
Paddock W Yorks 196 D6
Paddock Wood Kent 53 E7
Paddockhaugh Moray 302 D2
Paddockhill E Ches 184 F4
Paddockhole Dumfries 248 G6
Paddolgreen Shrops 149 C10
Padfield Derbys 185 B8
Padgate Warr 183 D10
Padham's Green Essex 87 F10
Padiham Lancs 203 G11
Padney Cambs 123 C10
Padog Conwy 164 E4
Padside N Yorks 205 B9
Padside Green N Yorks 205 B9
Padson Devon 13 B7
Padstow Corn 10 F4
Padworth W Berks 64 F6
Padworth Common Hants 64 G6
Paganhill Glos 80 D4
Page Bank Durham 233 D10
Page Moss Mers 182 C6
Page's Green Suff 126 D2
Pagham W Sus 22 D5
Paglesham Churchend Essex 88 G6
Paglesham Eastend Essex 88 G6
Paibeil W Isles 296 E3
Paible W Isles 305 J2
Paignton Torbay 9 C7
Pailton Warks 135 G9
Painleyhill Staffs 151 C10
Pains Hill Sur 52 C2
Painscastle Powys 96 B3
Painshawfield Northumb 242 E3
Painsthorpe E Yorks 208 B2
Painswick Glos 80 D5
Painter's Forstal Kent 54 B3
Painter's Green Herts 86 B3
Painters Green Wrex 167 G8
Painthorpe W Yorks 197 D10
Paintmoor Som 28 F4
Pairc Shiaboist W Isles 304 D4
Paisley Renfs 267 C9
Pakefield Suff 143 E10
Pakenham Suff 125 D8
Pale Gwyn 147 B9
Pale Green Essex 106 C3
Palehouse Common E Sus 23 B7
Palestine Hants 47 E9
Paley Street Windsor 65 D11
Palfrey W Mid 133 D10
Palgowan Dumfries 245 G9
Palgrave Suff 126 B2
Pallaflat Cumb 219 C9
Pallington Dorset 17 C11
Pallion T & W 243 F9
Pallister M'bro 225 B10
Palmarsh Kent 54 G6
Palmer Moor Derbys 152 C2
Palmers Cross Staffs 133 C7
Palmers Cross Sur 50 E4
Palmer's Flat Glos 79 D9
Palmer's Green Kent 53 E7
Palmers Green London 86 G4
Palmersbridge Corn 11 F9
Palmerstown V Glam 5
Palmersville T & W 24
Palmstead Kent 5
Palnackie Dumfries 23
Palnure Dumfries 23
Palterton Derbys 17
Pamber End Hants 4
Pamber Green Hants 4
Pamber Heath Hants 6
Pamington Glos 9
Pamphill Dorset 3
Pampisford Cambs 10
Pan I o W 2
Pan Orkney 31
Panborough Som 4
Panbride Angus 28
Pancakehill Glos 8
Pancrasweek Devon 2
Pancross V Glam 5
Pandy Gwyn 12
Pandy Gwyn 14
Pandy Gwyn 14
Pandy Mon 9
Pandy Powys 12
Pandy Wrex 14
Pandy Wrex 16
Pandy Tudur Conwy 16
Pandy'r Capel Denb 16
Panfield Essex 10
Pangbourne W Berks 6
Panhall Fife 28
Panks Bridge Hereford 9
Pannal N Yorks 20
Pannal Ash N Yorks 20
Pannel's Ash Essex 10
Panpunton Powys 11
Panshanger Herts 8
Pant Denb 16
Pant Flint 18
Pant Gwyn 14
Pant M Tydf 7
Pant Powys 12
Pant Shrops 14
Pant Wrex 16
Pant Wrex 16
Pant-glâs Powys 12
Pant-glas Gwyn 16
Pant-glas Shrops 14
Pant-lasau Swansea 5
Pant Mawr Powys 12
Pant-pastynog Denb 16
Pant-teg Carms 9
Pant-y-Caws Carms 9
Pant-y-crûg Ceredig 11
Pant-y-dwr Powys 11
Pant-y-dwr Powys 11
Pant-y-ffridd Powys 13
Pant-y-pyllau Bridgend 5
Pant-y-Wacco Flint 18
Pant-yr-awel Bridgend 5
Pantasaph Flint 18
Pantdu Neath 5
Panteg Ceredig 1
Panteg Torf 7
Pantersbridge Corn
Pantgwyn Carms 9
Pantgwyn Ceredig 9
Pantmawr Cardiff 5
Panton Lincs 18
Pantperthog Gwyn 12
Pantside Caerph 7
Pantyffynnon Carms 7
Pantygasseg Torf 7
Pantymwyn Flint 16
Panxworth Norf 16
Papcastle Cumb 22
Papermill Bank Shrops 14
Papigoe Highld 31
Papil Shetland 31
Papley Northants 1
Papley Orkney 31
Papple E Loth 28
Papplewick Notts 17
Papworth Everard Cambs 12
Papworth St Agnes Cambs 12
Papworth Village Settlement Cambs 12
Par Corn
Paradise Glos 8
Paradise Green Hereford 9
Paramoor Corn
Paramour Street Kent 7
Parbold Lancs 1
Parbrook Som 4
Parbrook W Sus 3
Parc Gwyn 14
Parc Erissey Corn
Parc-hendy Swansea 5
Parc Mawr Caerph 7
Parc-Seymour Newport 7
Parc-y-rhôs Carms 9
Parchey Som 4
Parciau Anglesey 1
Parcllyn Ceredig 1
Pardown Hants 4
Pardshaw Cumb 2
Pardshaw Hall Cumb 2
Parham Suff 1
Park Corn
Park Devon 1
Park Dumfries 24
Park Som 4
Park Swindon 6
Park Barn Sur 5
Park Bottom Corn
Park Bridge Gtr Man 19
Park Broom Cumb 23
Park Close Lancs 20
Park Corner Bath 4
Park Corner E Sus 3
Park Corner E Sus 5
Park Corner Oxon 6
Park Corner Windsor 6
Park End Beds 12
Park End Cambs 12
Park End M'bro 22
Park End Northumb 24
Park End Som 4
Park End Staffs 16
Park End Worcs 11
Park Gate Dorset 3
Park Gate Hants 3
Park Gate Kent 5
Park Gate Suff 12
Park Gate W Yorks 19
Park Gate Worcs 11
Park Green Essex 10
Park Hall Shrops 14
Park Head Cumb 23
Park Head Derbys 17
Park Head W Yorks 19
Park Hill Glos 7
Park Hill Kent 5
Park Hill Mers 19
Park Hill N Yorks 21
Park Hill Notts 17
Park Hill S Yorks 18
Park Lane Staffs 13
Park Lane Wrex 14
Park Langley London 6

Mains Renfs 277 G9
Mill W Yorks 197 E9
Royal London 67 C7
Street Herts 85 E10
Street W Sus 50 G6
Town Luton 103 G11
Town Oxon 83 D8
Village Northumb 240 E5
Village W Mid 133 C8
Villas W Yorks 206 F2
Wood Kent 53 C9
Wood Medway 69 G10
end Glos 79 D10
end Glos 80 C3
engear Corn 5 F8
er's Corner W Berks 64 E6
er's Green Herts 104 F6
er's Green Kent 52 D6
eston Essex 108 E4
field Corn 6 B6
field S Glos 61 D7
field W Mid 133 D8
foot Falk 278 F6
gate Cumb 229 B10
gate Durham 248 F2
gate E Ches 184 G3
gate Essex 87 B11
gate Kent 53 G11
gate N Yorks 186 B6
gate Sur 51 E8
gate W Ches 182 F3
hall W Dunb 277 G9
ham Devon 24 C5
ham Ash Devon 24 C5
head Cumb 230 C2
head Glasgow 268 C2
head S Yorks 186 E4
hill Aberds 303 E10
hill Invclyd 277 G7
hill Ho Aberds 293 B10
house Mon 79 E7
house Green
ys 170 C6
hurst I o W 20 C5
lands W Yorks 206 F3
mill Swansea 56 D4
neuk Aberds 293 F9
neuk Fife 279 D11
side C Beds 103 G10
side Cumb 219 B10
side Durham 234 B4
side N Lnrk 268 D6
side Staffs 151 D8
side Wrex 166 D5
stone Poole 18 C6
way Hereford 98 D4
way Som 29 C9
wood Springs
ks 186 D4
ey Cross Dorset 19 B7
ey Green Dorset 19 B7
ament Heath Suff 107 C9
ngton W Yorks 206 F4
oor Bucks 65 B9
acott Devon 24 F4
ey Heath Essex 107 E10
Mers 183 C8
Brow Gtr Man 195 G8
acombe Devon 41 E7
og Pembs 91 D10
ey Hay Derbys 169 C10
ow's Hillock Bucks 84 E4
on Cross S Yorks 186 C5
on Drove Cambs 139 B7
onage Green Essex 88 D2
onby Cumb 229 D8
ons Green London 67 D9
on's Heath Essex 107 F10
ck Glasgow 267 B11
ngton Gtr Man 184 C2
ney Lincs 174 B6
on Cumb 228 G5
on Cumb 239 G7
on Dumfries 237 B8
on Glos 99 G7
on Hereford 96 B6
idge Green W Sus 35 D11
ishow Powys 96 G5
ich Derbys 169 E11
ord Staffs 132 D6
enham Northants 102 D5
field Hants 49 G10
ngford Bridge
x 87 F8
mores Essex 86 D6
on Norf 160 C6
on P'boro 138 C3
on Green Norf 160 C6
urefields Staffs 151 D9
nacott Devon 12 B5
ham Brighton 36 F4
netts Green Herts 85 F10
hing W Sus 35 F9
hole Devon 40 E6
nway S Glos 60 C6
gill Cumb 230 F6
ey Bridge N Yorks 214 F3
noster Heath
x 88 C6
Head T & W 242 E5
of Condie Perth 286 F4
e Som 43 G11
er N Lnrk 268 E5
finder Village Devon 14 C2
head Aberds 293 G9
head E Ayrs 258 G4
head Fife 280 C5
head Midloth 271 C7
low Warks 118 F3
struie Perth 286 F4
ent End Herts 105 F8
ore Heath Herts 105 F8
a E Ayrs 257 G10
ey Wilts 46 B5
ck I o M 192 D3
ck Brompton
rks 224 G4
croft Gtr Man 184 B3
ngton E Yorks 201 C10
ngton Haven
rks 201 C10
xbourne Kent 55 B7
ford Devon 40 F4
erdale Cumb 221 B7
esmuir Fife 279 E11
ngham Staffs 132 D6
shall Northants 120 G3
swick Essex 106 G6
on Shrops 131 E11
on Bridge Cumb 221 F11
Corn 1 D5
erspury Northants 102 B4
E Yorks 201 B7
's Green Corn 2 C4
sgrove Ptsmth 33 F10
ton Bath 45 B7
ville W Loth 269 B9
Lane Telford 150 F5
nham Beds 121 F9
ett Som 43 E10
ett Hill Som 43 E9
ston Northumb 263 C9
Paxford Glos 100 D3
Paxton Borders 273 E8
Payden Street Kent 54 C2
Payhembury Devon 27 G9
Paynes Green Sur 50 F6
Paynter's Cross Corn 7 C7
Paynter's Lane End Corn 4 G3
Paythorne Lancs 204 C2
Payton Som 27 C10
Peacehaven E Sus 36 G6
Peacehaven Heights
E Sus 36 G6
Peacemarsh Dorset 30 B4
Peak Dale Derbys 185 F9
Peak Forest Derbys 185 F10
Peak Hill Lincs 156 F5
Peakirk P'boro 138 B3
Pean Hill Kent 70 G6
Pear Ash Som 45 G9
Pear Tree Derby 153 C7
Pearsie Angus 287 B7
Pearson's Green Kent 53 E7
Peartree Herts 86 C2
Peartree Green Essex 87 F9
Peartree Green
Hereford 97 E11
Peartree Green Soton 32 E6
Peartree Green Sur 50 F3
Peas Acre W Yorks 205 E8
Peas Hill Cambs 139 D8
Pease Pottage W Sus 51 G9
Peasedown St John Bath 45 B8
Peasehill Derbys 170 F6
Peaseland Green Norf 159 F11
Peasemore W Berks 64 D3
Peasenhall Suff 127 D7
Peaslake Sur 50 E5
Peasley Cross Mers 183 C8
Peasmarsh E Sus 38 C5
Peasmarsh Som 28 E4
Peasmarsh Sur 50 D3
Peaston E Loth 271 B8
Peastonbank E Loth 271 B8
Peat Inn Fife 287 G8
Peathill Aberds 303 C9
Peatling Magna Leics 135 E11
Peatling Parva Leics 135 F11
Peaton Shrops 131 G10
Peatonstrand Shrops 131 G10
Peats Corner Suff 126 E3
Pebmarsh Essex 107 E7
Pebsham E Sus 38 F3
Pebworth Worcs 100 B2
Pecket Well W Yorks 196 B3
Peckforton E Ches 167 D8
Peckham London 67 D10
Peckham Bush Kent 53 D7
Pecking Mill Som 44 F6
Peckingell Wilts 62 E2
Peckleton Leics 135 C9
Pedair-ffordd Powys 148 E2
Pedham Norf 160 G6
Pedlars End Essex 87 D8
Pedlar's Rest Shrops 131 G9
Pedlinge Kent 54 F6
Pedmore W Mid 133 G8
Pednor Bottom Bucks 84 E6
Pednormead End Bucks 85 E7
Pedwell Som 44 F2
Peebles Borders 270 G5
Peel Borders 261 B10
Peel I o M 192 D3
Peel Lancs 202 G3
Peel Common Hants 33 G9
Peel Green Gtr Man 184 B2
Peel Hall Gtr Man 184 D4
Peel Hill Lancs 202 G3
Peel Park S Lnrk 268 E2
Peene Kent 55 F7
Peening Quarter Kent 38 B5
Peggs Green Leics 153 F8
Pegsdon C Beds 104 E2
Pegswood Northumb 252 F6
Pegwell Kent 71 G11
Peinaha Highld 298 D4
Peinchorran Highld 295 B7
Peingown Highld 298 B4
Peinlich Highld 298 D4
Peinmore Highld 298 E4
Pelaw T & W 243 E7
Pelcomb Pembs 72 B6
Pelcomb Bridge Pembs 72 B6
Pelcomb Cross Pembs 72 B6
Peldon Essex 89 B7
Pelhamfield I o W 21 C7
Pell Green E Sus 52 G6
Pellon W Yorks 196 B5
Pelsall W Mid 133 C10
Pelsall Wood W Mid 133 C10
Pelton Durham 243 G7
Pelton Fell Durham 243 G7
Pelutho Cumb 229 B8
Pelynt Corn 6 D4
Pemberton Carms 75 E8
Pemberton Gtr Man 194 G5
Pembles Cross Kent 53 D11
Pembre = Pembrey
Carms 74 E6
Pembrey = Pembre
Carms 74 E6
Pembridge Hereford 115 F7
Pembroke Pembs 73 E7
Pembroke Dock =
Doc Penfro Pembs 73 E7
Pembroke Ferry Pembs 73 E7
Pembury Kent 52 E6
Pempwell Corn 12 F3
Pen-allt Hereford 97 F11
Pen-bedw Pembs 92 D4
Pen-bont
Rhydybeddau Ceredig 128 G3
Pen-caer-fenny Swansea 56 B4
Pen-clawdd Swansea 56 B4
Pen-common Powys 76 D6
Pen-gilfach Gwyn 163 C9
Pen-groes-oped Mon 78 D4
Pen-lan Swansea 56 B6
Pen-Lan-mabws Pembs 91 F7
Pen-llyn Anglesey 178 E4
Pen-lon Anglesey 162 B6
Pen Mill Som 29 D9
Pen-onn V Glam 58 F5
Pen-Rhiw-fawr Neath 76 C2
Pen-rhos Wrex 166 E3
Pen-sarn Gwyn 145 D11
Pen-sarn Gwyn 162 G6
Pen-twyn Caerph 78 E2
Pen-twyn Carms 75 C9
Pen-twyn Mon 79 D8
Pen-twyn Torf 78 E3
Pen-Uchar Plwyf Flint 181 G11
Pen-y-Ball Top Flint 181 F11
Pen-y-banc Carms 93 G8
Pen-y-banc Carms 94 G2
Pen-y-bank Caerph 77 E10
Pen-y-Bont Bl Gwent 78 D2
Pen-y-bont Carms 92 F6
Pen-y-bont Gwyn 128 C4
Pen-y-bont Gwyn 146 D2
Pen-y-bont Powys 148 E4
Pen y Bont ar ogwr =
Bridgend Bridgend 58 C2
Pen-y-Bryn Gwyn 145 B9
Pen-y-bryn Gwyn 146 F3
Pen-y-bryn Pembs 92 C3
Pen-y-bryn Powys 130 C3
Pen-y-Bryn Shrops 148 B6
Pen-y-bryn Wrex 166 G3
Pen-y-cae Bridgend 58 C2
Pen-y-cae Neath 57 D9
Pen-y-cae Powys 76 C4
Pen-y-cae-mawr Mon 78 F6
Pen-y-cefn Flint 181 F10
Pen-y-clawdd Mon 79 D7
Pen-y-coed Shrops 148 E5
Pen-y-coedcae Rhondda 58 B5
Pen-y-Darren M Tydf 77 D9
Pen-y-fai Bridgend 57 E11
Pen-y-fai Carms 75 E7
Pen-y-fan Carms 56 B4
Pen-y-fan Mon 79 D8
Pen-y-felin Flint 165 B11
Pen-y-ffordd Denb 181 F8
Pen-y-ffordd Flint 181 E10
Pen y Foel Shrops 148 E5
Pen-y-garn Carms 93 E11
Pen-y-garn Ceredig 128 F2
Pen-y-garnedd
Anglesey 179 F8
Pen-y-gop Conwy 164 G6
Pen-y-graig Gwyn 144 C3
Pen-y-groes Carms 75 C9
Pen-y-groeslon Gwyn 144 C4
Pen-y-Gwryd Hotel
Gwyn 163 D11
Pen-y-lan Cardiff 59 D7
Pen-y-lan Newport 59 B9
Pen-y-lan V Glam 58 D3
Pen-y-maes Flint 181 F11
Pen-y-Myndd Carms 75 E7
Pen-y-Park Hereford 96 C5
Pen-y-rhiw Rhondda 58 B5
Pen-y-stryt Denb 165 E11
Pen-y-wern Shrops 114 B6
Pen-yr-englyn Rhondda 76 F6
Pen-yr-heol Bridgend 58 C2
Pen-yr-heol Mon 78 C6
Pen-yr-Heolgerrig
M Tydf 77 D8
Penallt Mon 79 C8
Penally = Penalun
Pembs 73 F10
Penalt Hereford 97 F11
Penalun = Penally
Pembs 73 F10
Penare Corn 5 G9
Penarlâg = Hawarden
Flint 166 B4
Penarron Powys 130 F2
Penarth V Glam 59 E7
Penarth Moors Cardiff 59 E7
Penbeagle Corn 2 B2
Penbedw Flint 165 B11
Penbidwal Mon 96 G6
Penbodlas Gwyn 144 C5
Penboyr Carms 93 D7
Penbryn Ceredig 110 G5
Pencader Carms 93 D8
Pencaenewydd Gwyn 162 G6
Pencaerau Neath 57 B8
Pencaitland E Loth 271 B8
Pencarnisiog Anglesey 178 G5
Pencarreg Carms 93 B10
Pencarrow Corn 11 E8
Penceiliogi Carms 75 E8
Pencelli Powys 95 F11
Pencoed Bridgend 58 C3
Pencombe Hereford 115 G11
Pencoyd Hereford 97 F10
Pencoys Corn 2 B5
Pencraig Anglesey 179 F7
Pencraig Hereford 97 G11
Pencraig Powys 147 D10
Pencroesoped Mon 78 D4
Pencuke Corn 11 C9
Pendas Fields W Yorks 206 F3
Pendeen Corn 1 C3
Pendeford W Mid 133 C7
Penderyn Rhondda 77 D7
Pendine = Pentywyn
Carms 74 D2
Pendlebury Gtr Man 195 G9
Pendleton Gtr Man 184 B4
Pendleton Lancs 203 F11
Pendock Worcs 98 E5
Pendoggett Corn 10 F6
Pendomer Som 29 E8
Pendoylan V Glam 58 D5
Pendre Bridgend 58 C2
Pendre Gwyn 110 C2
Pendre Powys 95 F10
Pendrift Corn 11 G8
Penegoes Powys 128 C5
Penelewey Corn 4 G6
Penenden Heath Kent 53 B9
Penffordd Pembs 91 G11
Penffordd Lâs =
Staylittle Powys 129 E7
Pengam Caerph 77 F11
Pengam Cardiff 59 D8
Penge London 67 E11
Pengegon Corn 2 B5
Pengelly Corn 11 E7
Pengenffordd Powys 96 E3
Pengersick Corn 2 D3
Pengold Corn 11 C8
Pengorffwysfa Anglesey 179 C7
Pengover Green Corn 6 B5
Penguithal Hereford 97 G10
Pengwern Denb 181 F8
Penhale Corn 2 F5
Penhale Corn 5 D8
Penhale Jakes Corn 2 D4
Penhallick Corn 3 F7
Penhallick Corn 4 G3
Penhallow Corn 4 E5
Penhalurick Corn 2 B6
Penhalvean Corn 2 B6
Penhelig Gwyn 128 D2
Penhill Devon 40 G4
Penhill Swindon 63 B7
Penhow Newport 78 G6
Penhurst E Sus 23 B11
Peniarth Gwyn 128 B2
Penicuik Midloth 270 C4
Peniel Carms 93 G8
Peniel Denb 165 C8
Penifiler Highld 298 E4
Peninver Argyll 255 E8
Penisa'r Waun Gwyn 163 C9
Penistone S Yorks 197 G8
Penjerrick Corn 3 C7
Penketh Warr 183 D9
Penkhull Stoke 168 G5
Penkill S Ayrs 244 D6
Penknap Wilts 45 D11
Penkridge Staffs 151 G8
Penleigh Wilts 45 C11
Penley Wrex 149 B8
Penllech Gwyn 144 C4
Penllergaer Swansea 56 B6
Penllwyn Caerph 77 F11
Penllwyn Ceredig 128 G3
Penllyn V Glam 58 D3
Penmachno Conwy 164 E3
Penmaen Caerph 77 F11
Penmaen Swansea 56 D4
Penmaen Rhôs Conwy 180 F5
Penmaenan Conwy 180 F2
Penmaenmawr Conwy 180 F2
Penmaenpool Gwyn 146 F3
Penmark V Glam 58 F5
Penmarth Corn 2 B6
Penmayne Corn 10 F4
Penmon Anglesey 179 E10
Penmore Mill Argyll 288 D6
Penmorfa Ceredig 110 G6
Penmorfa Gwyn 163 G8
Penmynydd Anglesey 179 G8
Penn Bucks 84 G6
Penn W Mid 133 D7
Penn Bottom Bucks 84 G6
Penn Street Bucks 84 F6
Pennal Gwyn 128 C4
Pennan Aberds 303 C8
Pennance Corn 4 G4
Pennant Ceredig 111 E10
Pennant Conwy 164 D5
Pennant Denb 147 C10
Pennant Denb 165 E8
Pennant Powys 129 D7
Pennant Melangell
Powys 147 D10
Pennar Pembs 73 E7
Pennar Park Pembs 72 E6
Pennard Swansea 56 D5
Pennerley Shrops 131 D7
Pennington Cumb 210 D5
Pennington Gtr Man 183 B11
Pennington Hants 20 C2
Pennington Green
Gtr Man 194 F6
Pennorth Powys 96 F2
Pennsylvania Devon 14 C4
Pennsylvania S Glos 61 E8
Penny Bridge Cumb 210 C6
Penny Green Derbys 187 F8
Penny Hill Lincs 157 D7
Penny Hill W Yorks 196 D5
Pennycross Argyll 289 G7
Pennycross Plym 7 D9
Pennygate Norf 160 E6
Pennygown Argyll 289 E7
Pennylands Lancs 194 F3
Pennymoor Devon 26 E5
Pennypot Kent 54 G6
Penny's Green Norf 142 D3
Pennytinney Corn 10 F6
Pennywell T & W 243 F9
Penparc Ceredig 92 B4
Penparc Pembs 91 E7
Penparcau Ceredig 111 B11
Penpedairheol Caerph 77 F10
Penpedairheol Mon 78 E4
Penpergym Mon 78 C4
Penperlleni Mon 78 E4
Penpethy Corn 11 D7
Penpillick Corn 5 D11
Penplas Carms 74 B5
Penpol Corn 3 B8
Penpoll Corn 6 E2
Penponds Corn 2 B4
Penpont Corn 11 G7
Penpont Dumfries 247 E8
Penpont Powys 95 F9
Penprysg Bridgend 58 C3
Penquit Devon 8 E2
Penrallt Gwyn 145 B7
Penrallt Powys 129 F9
Penrhôs Mon 78 C6
Penrherber Carms 92 D5
Penrhiw Caerph 78 G2
Penrhiw-llan Ceredig 93 C7
Penrhiw-pal Ceredig 92 B6
Penrhiwceiber Rhondda 77 F8
Penrhiwgarreg Bl Gwent 78 E2
Penrhiwtyn Neath 57 B8
Penrhos Anglesey 178 E3
Penrhos Gwyn 144 C6
Penrhos Hereford 114 F6
Penrhos Mon 78 C6
Penrhos Powys 76 C3
Penrhos-garnedd Gwyn 179 G9
Penrhosfeilw Anglesey 178 E2
Penrhyd Lastra Anglesey 178 C6
Penrhyn Bay =
Bae-Penrhyn Conwy 180 E4
Penrhyn Castle Pembs 92 B2
Penrhyn-coch Ceredig 128 G2
Penrhyn side Conwy 180 E4
Penrhyndeudraeth
Gwyn 146 B2
Penrhynside Conwy 180 E4
Penrhys Rhondda 77 F8
Penrice Swansea 56 D3
Penrith Cumb 230 E6
Penrose Corn 10 G3
Penrose Corn 11 F7
Penrose Hill Corn 2 D4
Penruddock Cumb 230 F4
Penryn Corn 3 C7
Pensarn Carms 74 B6
Pensarn Conwy 181 F7
Pensax Worcs 116 D4
Pensby Mers 182 E3
Penselwood Som 45 G9
Pensford Bath 60 G6
Pensham Worcs 99 C8
Penshaw T & W 243 G8
Penshurst Kent 52 E4
Pensilva Corn 6 B5
Pensnett W Mid 133 F8
Penston E Loth 281 G8
Penstone Devon 26 G3
Penstraze Corn 4 F5
Pentewan Corn 5 F10
Pentiken Shrops 130 G4
Pentir Gwyn 163 B9
Pentire Corn 4 C5
Pentirvin Shrops 130 C6
Pentlepoir Pembs 73 D10
Pentlow Essex 106 B6
Pentlow Street Essex 106 B6
Pentney Norf 158 G4
Penton Corner Hants 47 D10
Penton Grafton Hants 47 D10
Penton Mewsey Hants 47 D10
Pentonville London 67 C10
Pentowin Carms 74 B3
Pentraeth Anglesey 179 F8
Pentrapeod Caerph 77 E11
Pentre Carms 75 C8
Pentre Denb 165 D10
Pentre Flint 165 C11
Pentre Flint 166 B4
Pentre Flint 166 D2
Pentre Flint 182 G2
Pentre Powys 129 F11
Pentre Powys 130 B4
Pentre Powys 130 E5
Pentre Powys 147 D11
Pentre Powys 148 G3
Pentre Rhondda 77 F7
Pentre Shrops 148 D4
Pentre Shrops 149 F7
Pentre Wrex 148 B2
Pentre Wrex 166 G3
Pentre-bâch Ceredig 93 B11
Pentre-bach Powys 95 E8
Pentre Berw Anglesey 179 G7
Pentre-bont Conwy 164 E2
Pentre Broughton Wrex 166 E4
Pentre Bychan Wrex 166 F4
Pentre-cefn Shrops 148 D4
Pentre-celyn Denb 165 E11
Pentre-Celyn Powys 129 B7
Pentre-chwyth Swansea 57 B7
Pentre Cilgwyn Wrex 148 B4
Pentre-clawdd Shrops 148 C5
Pentre-coed Shrops 149 B7
Pentre-cwrt Carms 93 D7
Pentre Dolau-Honddu
Powys 95 C9
Pentre-dwr Swansea 57 B7
Pentre-Ffwrndan Flint 182 G3
Pentre-galar Pembs 92 E3
Pentre-Gwenlais Carms 75 B10
Pentre Gwynfryn Gwyn 145 D11
Pentre Halkyn Flint 182 G2
Pentre Hodre Shrops 114 B6
Pentre Isaf Conwy 164 B5
Pentre Llanrhaeadr
Denb 165 C9
Pentre Llifior Powys 130 D2
Pentre-llwyn-llwyd
Powys 113 G9
Pentre-llyn Ceredig 112 C2
Pentre-llyn cymmer
Conwy 165 E7
Pentre Maelor Wrex 166 F5
Pentre Meyrick V Glam 58 D3
Pentre-newydd Shrops 148 B5
Pentre-Piod Torf 78 E3
Pentre-Poeth Carms 75 E8
Pentre-poeth Newport 59 B9
Pentre-rhew Ceredig 112 G3
Pentre-tafarn-y-fedw
Conwy 164 C4
Pentre-ty-gwyn Carms 94 D6
Pentre-uchaf Conwy 180 F5
Pentrebach Carms 94 E6
Pentrebach M Tydf 77 E9
Pentrebach Rhondda 58 B5
Pentrebach Swansea 75 D10
Pentrebane Cardiff 58 D6
Pentrebeirdd Powys 148 G3
Pentrecagal Carms 92 C6
Pentredwr Denb 165 F11
Pentref-y-groes
Caerph 77 F11
Pentrefelin Anglesey 178 C6
Pentrefelin Carms 93 G11
Pentrefelin Ceredig 94 B2
Pentrefelin Conwy 180 G4
Pentrefelin Denb 166 G2
Pentrefelin Gwyn 145 B10
Pentrefoelas Conwy 164 E5
Pentregat Ceredig 111 G7
Pentreheyling Shrops 130 E5
Pentrellwyn Ceredig 93 C8
Pentre'r beirdd Powys 148 G3
Pentre'r Felin Conwy 164 B4
Pentre'r-felin Denb 165 B10
Pentre'r-felin Powys 95 E8
Pentreuchaf Gwyn 145 B7
Pentrich Derbys 170 E5
Pentridge Dorset 31 D8
Pentrisil Pembs 91 E11
Pentwyn Caerph 77 E10
Pentwyn Cardiff 59 C8
Pentwyn = Pendine
Carms 74 D2
Pentwyn Berthlwyd
Caerph 77 F10
Pentwyn-mawr Caerph 77 F11
Pentyrch Cardiff 58 C6
Penuchadre V Glam 57 G11
Penuwch Ceredig 111 E11
Penwartha Corn 4 E5
Penwartha Coombe Corn 4 E5
Penweathers Corn 4 G6
Penwithick Corn 5 D10
Penwood Hants 64 G2
Penwortham Lane
Lancs 194 B4
Penwyllt Powys 76 B5
Penybanc Carms 75 C10
Penybedd Carms 74 E6
Penybont Ceredig 128 F2
Penybont Powys 114 E2
Penybontfawr Powys 147 E11
Penybryn Caerph 77 F10
Penycae Wrex 166 F3
Penycaerau Gwyn 144 D3
Penycwm Pembs 90 G6
Penydre Swansea 75 E11
Penyfeidr Pembs 91 F7
Penyffordd Flint 166 C4
Penyffridd Gwyn 163 D8
Penygarn Torf 78 E3
Penygarnedd Powys 148 E2
Penygelli Powys 130 E2
Penygraig Rhondda 77 G7
Penygraigwen Anglesey 178 D6
Penygroes Gwyn 163 E7
Penygroes Pembs 92 D3
Penymynydd Flint 166 C4
Penyraber Pembs 91 D9
Penyrheol Caerph 58 B6
Penyrheol Swansea 56 B5
Penyrheol Torf 78 F3
Penysarn Anglesey 179 C7
Penywaun Rhondda 77 E7
Penzance Corn 1 C5
Peopleton Worcs 117 G8
Peover Heath E Ches 184 G3
Peper Harow Sur 50 E2
Pepper Hill Som 43 F7
Pepper Hill W Yorks 196 B6
Peppercombe Devon 24 C5
Peppermoor Northumb 264 F6
Pepper's Green Essex 87 C10
Pepperstock C Beds 85 B9
Per-ffordd-llan Flint 181 F10
Perceton N Ayrs 267 G7
Percie Aberds 293 D7
Percuil Corn 3 C9
Percy Main T & W 243 D8
Percyhorner Aberds 303 C9
Perham Down Wilts 47 D9
Periton Som 42 D3
Perivale London 67 C7
Perkhill Aberds 293 C7
Perkinsville Durham 243 G7
Perlethorpe Notts 187 G11
Perran Downs Corn 2 C3
Perran Wharf Corn 3 B7
Perranarworthal Corn 3 B7
Perrancoombe Corn 4 E5
Perranporth Corn 4 E5
Perranuthnoe Corn 2 D2
Perranwell Corn 3 B7
Perranwell Corn 4 E5
Perranwell Station Corn 3 B7
Perranzabuloe Corn 4 E5
Perrott's Brook Glos 81 D8
Perry Devon 26 F5
Perry Kent 55 B9
Perry W Mid 133 E11
Perry Barr W Mid 133 E11
Perry Beeches W Mid 133 E11
Perry Common W Mid 133 E11
Perry Crofts Staffs 134 C4
Perry Green Essex 106 G6
Perry Green Herts 86 B6
Perry Green Som 43 F9
Perry Green Wilts 62 B3
Perry Street Kent 68 E6
Perry Street Som 28 F4
Perryfields Worcs 117 C8
Perryfoot Derbys 185 E10
Perrymead Bath 61 G9
Perrystone Hill Hereford 98 F2
Perrywood Kent 54 B4
Pershall Staffs 150 C6
Pershore Worcs 99 B8
Pert Angus 293 G8
Pertenhall Beds 121 D11
Perth Perth 286 E5
Perthcelyn Rhondda 77 F9
Perthy Shrops 149 C7
Perton Hereford 97 C11
Perton Staffs 133 D7
Pertwood Wilts 45 F11
Pested Kent 54 C4
Peter Tavy Devon 12 F6
Peterborough P'boro 138 D3
Peterburn Highld 307 L2
Peterchurch Hereford 96 D6
Peterculter Aberdeen 293 C10
Peterhead Aberds 303 E11
Peterlee Durham 234 C4
Peter's Finger Devon 12 D3
Peter's Green Herts 85 B10
Peters Marland Devon 25 E7
Petersburn N Lnrk 268 C5
Petersfield Hants 34 C2
Petersham London 67 E7
Peterston-super-Ely
V Glam 58 D5
Peterstone Wentlooge
Newport 59 C9
Peterstow Hereford 97 G11
Petertown Orkney 314 F3
Peterville Corn 4 E4
Petham Kent 54 C6
Petherwin Gate Corn 11 D11
Petrockstow Devon 25 F8
Petsoe End M Keynes 103 B7
Pett E Sus 38 E5
Pett Bottom Kent 54 E6
Pett Bottom Kent 55 C7
Pett Level E Sus 38 E5
Pettaugh Suff 126 F3
Petteridge Kent 53 E7
Pettinain S Lnrk 269 G9
Pettings Kent 68 G6
Pettistree Suff 126 G5
Petton Devon 27 C8
Petton Shrops 149 D8
Petts Wood London 68 F2
Petty Aberds 303 F7
Petty France S Glos 61 B9
Pettycur Fife 280 D5
Pettymuick Aberds 303 G9
Pettywell Norf 159 E11
Petworth W Sus 35 C7
Pevensey E Sus 23 E10
Pevensey Bay E Sus 23 E11
Peverell Plym 7 D9
Pewsey Wilts 63 G7
Pewsey Wharf Wilts 63 G7
Pewterspear Warr 183 E10
Phantassie E Loth 281 F11
Pharisee Green Essex 106 G2
Pheasants Bucks 65 B9
Pheasant's Hill Bucks 65 B9
Pheasey W Mid 133 D11
Pheonix Green Hants 49 B9
Phepson Worcs 117 F8
Philadelphia T & W 243 G8
Philham Devon 24 C3
Philiphaugh Borders 261 D10
Phillack Corn 2 B3
Philleigh Corn 3 B9
Phillip's Town Caerph 77 E10
Philpot End Essex 87 B10
Philpstoun W Loth 279 F10
Phocle Green Hereford 98 F2
Phoenix Green Hants 49 B9
Phoenix Row Durham 233 F9
Phorp Moray 301 D10
Pibsbury Som 28 B6
Pibwrlwyd Carms 74 B6
Pica Cumb 228 G6
Piccadilly S Yorks 187 B7
Piccadilly Warks 134 D4
Piccadilly Corner Norf 142 F5
Piccotts End Herts 85 D9
Pickburn S Yorks 198 F4
Picken End Worcs 98 C6
Pickering N Yorks 216 C5
Pickering Nook Durham 242 F5
Picket Hill Hants 31 F11
Picket Piece Hants 47 D11
Picket Post Hants 31 F11
Pickford W Mid 134 G5
Pickford Green W Mid 134 G5
Pickhill N Yorks 214 C6
Picklenash Glos 98 F4
Pickles Hill W Yorks 204 F6
Picklescott Shrops 131 D8
Pickletillem Fife 287 E8
Pickley Green Gtr Man 195 G7
Pickmere E Ches 183 F11
Pickney Som 27 B11
Pickstock Telford 150 E4
Pickup Bank Blkburn 195 C8
Pickwell Devon 40 E3
Pickwell Leics 154 G5
Pickwick Wilts 61 E11
Pickwood Scar W
Yorks 196 C5
Pickworth Lincs 155 C10
Pickworth Rutland 155 G9
Picton Flint 181 E10
Picton N Yorks 225 D8
Picton W Ches 182 G6
Pict's Hill Som 28 B6
Piddinghoe E Sus 36 G6
Piddington Bucks 84 G4
Piddington Northants 120 G6
Piddington Oxon 83 B10
Piddlehinton Dorset 17 B10
Piddletrenthide
Dorset 17 B10
Pidley Cambs 122 B6
Pidney Dorset 30 F2
Piece Corn 2 B5
Piercebridge Darl 224 B4
Piercing Hill Essex 86 F6
Pierowall Orkney 314 B4
Piff's Elm Glos 99 F8
Pig Oak Dorset 31 G8
Pigdon Northumb 252 F5
Pightley Som 43 F8
Pigstye Green Essex 87 D10
Pike End W Yorks 196 D4
Pike Hill Lancs 204 G3
Pike Law W Yorks 196 D4
Pikehall Derbys 169 D11
Pikeshill Hants 32 F3
Pikestye Hereford 97 B10
Pilford Dorset 31 G8
Pilgrims Hatch Essex 87 F9
Pilham Lincs 188 C5
Pilhough Derbys 170 C3
Pill N Som 60 D4
Pill Pembs 72 D6
Pillaton Corn 7 C7
Pillaton Staffs 151 G8
Pillerton Hersey Warks 100 B6
Pillerton Priors Warks 100 B5
Pilleth Powys 114 D5
Pilley Glos 81 B7
Pilley Hants 20 B2
Pilley S Yorks 197 G10
Pilley Bailey Hants 20 B2
Pillgwenlly Newport 59 B10
Pilling Lancs 202 D4
Pilling Lane Lancs 202 D3
Pillmouth Devon 25 C7
Pillowell Glos 79 D10
Pillows Green Glos 98 F5
Pillwell Dorset 30 D3
Pilmuir Borders 261 G11
Pilning S Glos 60 B5
Pilrig Edin 280 F5
Pilsbury Derbys 169 C10
Pilsdon Dorset 16 B4
Pilsgate P'boro 137 B11
Pilsley Derbys 170 C6
Pilsley Derbys 186 G2
Pilsley Green Derbys 170 C6
Pilson Green Norf 161 G7
Piltdown E Sus 36 C6
Pilton Devon 40 G5
Pilton Edin 280 F4
Pilton Northants 137 G10
Pilton Rutland 137 C8
Pilton Som 44 E5
Pilton Green Swansea 56 D2
Piltown Som 44 F5
Pimhole Gtr Man 195 E10
Pimlico Herts 85 D9
Pimlico Lancs 203 E10
Pimlico London 67 D9
Pimlico Northants 102 C2
Pimperne Dorset 29 F9
Pimperne Dorset 30 F6
Pin Green Herts 104 F4
Pin Mill Suff 108 D4
Pinchbeck Lincs 156 D4
Pinchbeck Bars Lincs 156 D3
Pinchbeck West Lincs 156 E4
Pincheon Green S Yorks 199 D7
Pinckney Green Wilts 61 G10
Pincock Lancs 194 D5
Pineham Kent 55 D10
Pineham M Keynes 103 C7
Pinehurst Swindon 63 B7
Pinfarthings Glos 80 E5
Pinfold Lancs 193 E11
Pinfold Hill S Yorks 197 G9
Pinfoldpond C Beds 103 E8
Pinford End Suff 124 F6
Pinged Carms 74 E6
Pingewood W Berks 65 F7
Pinhoe Devon 14 C5
Pink Green Worcs 117 D11
Pinkett's Booth W Mid 134 G5
Pinkie Braes E Loth 281 G7
Pinkney Wilts 61 B11
Pinkneys Green
Windsor 65 C11
Pinksmoor Som 27 D10
Pinley W Mid 119 B7
Pinley Green Warks 118 D4
Pinminnoch Dumfries 236 D2
Pinminnoch S Ayrs 244 E5
Pinmore S Ayrs 244 E6
Pinmore Mains S Ayrs 244 E6
Pinnacles Essex 86 D6
Pinner London 66 B6
Pinner Green London 85 G10
Pinnerwood Park
London 85 G10
Pin's Green Worcs 98 B6
Pinsley Green E Ches 167 F9
Pinstones Shrops 131 F9
Pinvin Worcs 99 B9
Pinwall Leics 134 C6
Pinwherry S Ayrs 244 F5
Pinxton Derbys 171 E7
Pipe and Lyde Hereford 97 C10
Pipe Aston Hereford 115 C9
Pipe Gate Shrops 168 G2
Pipe Ridware Staffs 151 F11
Pipehill Staffs 133 B11
Pipehouse Bath 45 B9
Piperhall Argyll 266 D2
Piperhill Highld 301 D8
Piper's Ash W Ches 166 B6
Piper's End Worcs 98 E6
Piper's Hill Worcs 117 D9
Piper's Pool Corn 11 E11
Pipewell Northants 136 F6
Pippacott Devon 40 F4
Pippin Street Lancs 194 C5
Pipps Hill Essex 69 B7
Pipsden Kent 53 G9
Pipton Powys 96 D3
Pirbright Sur 50 B2
Pirbright Camp Sur 50 B2
Pirnmill N Ayrs 255 C9
Pirton Herts 104 E2
Pirton Worcs 99 B7
Pisgah Ceredig 112 B3
Pisgah Stirl 285 G11
Pishill Oxon 65 B8
Pishill Bank Oxon 84 G2
Pismire Hill S Yorks 186 C5
Pistyll Gwyn 162 G4
Pit Mon 78 D5
Pitagowan Perth 291 G10
Pitblae Aberds 303 C9
Pitcairngreen Perth 286 E4
Pitcalnie Highld 301 B8
Pitcaple Aberds 303 G7
Pitch Green Bucks 84 E3
Pitch Place Sur 49 F11
Pitch Place Sur 50 C3
Pitchcombe Glos 80 D5
Pitchcott Bucks 102 G5
Pitcher's Green Suff 125 F8
Pitchford Shrops 131 C10
Pitcombe Som 45 G7
Pitcorthie Fife 280 D2
Pitcorthie Fife 287 G9
Pitcot Som 45 D7
Pitcot V Glam 57 G11
Pitcox E Loth 282 F2
Pitcur Perth 286 D6
Pitfancy Aberds 302 E5
Pitfichie Aberds 293 B8
Pitforthie Aberds 293 F10
Pitgair Aberds 303 D7
Pitgrudy Highld 309 K7
Pithmaduthy Highld 301 B7
Pitkennedy Angus 287 B9
Pitkevy Fife 286 G6
Pitkierie Fife 287 G9
Pitlessie Fife 287 G7
Pitlochry Perth 286 B3
Pitmachie Aberds 302 G6
Pitmain Highld 291 C9
Pitmedden Aberds 303 G8
Pitminster Som 28 D2
Pitmuies Angus 287 C9
Pitmunie Aberds 293 B8
Pitney Som 29 B7
Pitrocknie Perth 286 C6
Pitscottie Fife 287 F8
Pitsea Essex 69 B8
Pitses Gtr Man 196 G2
Pitsford Northants 120 D5
Pitsford Hill Som 42 G6
Pitsmoor S Yorks 186 D5
Pitstone Bucks 84 B6
Pitstone Green Bucks 84 B6
Pitstone Hill Bucks 85 C7
Pitt Hants 33 B7
Pitt Court Glos 80 F3
Pittachar Perth 286 E2
Pittendreich Moray 301 C11
Pittentrail Highld 309 J7
Pittenweem Fife 287 G9
Pitteuchar Fife 280 B5
Pittington Durham 234 C2
Pittodrie Aberds 302 G6
Pitton Swansea 56 D2
Pitton Wilts 47 G8
Pitts Hill Stoke 168 E5
Pittswood Kent 52 D6
Pittulie Aberds 303 C9
Pittville Glos 99 G9
Pity Me Durham 233 B11
Pityme Corn 10 F5
Pityoulish Highld 291 B11
Pixey Green Suff 126 B4
Pixham Sur 51 C7
Pixham Worcs 98 B6
Pixley Hereford 98 D3
Pixley Shrops 150 D3
Pizien Well Kent 53 C7
Place Newton N Yorks 217 E7
Plaidy Aberds 303 D7
Plaidy Corn 6 E5
Plain-an-Gwarry Corn 4 G3
Plain Dealings Pembs 73 B9
Plain Spot Notts 171 E7
Plain Street Corn 10 F5
Plains N Lnrk 268 B5
Plainsfield Som 43 F7
Plaish Shrops 131 D10
Plaistow Bromley 68 E2
Plaistow Newham 68 C2
Plaistow W Sus 50 G4
Plaistow Green Essex 106 F6
Plaitford Wilts 32 D3
Plaitford Green Hants 32 C3
Plank Lane Gtr Man 194 G6
Plans Dumfries 238 D3
Plantation Bridge Cumb 221 F9
Plantationfoot Dumfries 248 E4
Plardiwick Staffs 150 E6
Plas-canol Gwyn 145 F11
Plas Coch Wrex 166 E4
Plas Dinam Powys 129 F10
Plas Gogerddan Ceredig 128 G2
Plas Llwyngwern Powys 128 C5
Plas Meredydd Powys 130 D3
Plas Nantyr Wrex 148 B3
Plas-yn-Cefn Denb 181 G8
Plasau Shrops 149 E7
Plashet London 68 C2
Plashett Carms 74 D3
Plasiolyn Powys 129 C11
Plasnewydd Powys 129 D9
Plaster's Green Bath 60 G4
Platt Kent 52 B6
Platt Bridge Gtr Man 194 G6
Platt Lane Shrops 149 B10
Platts Common S Yorks 197 G11
Platt's Heath Kent 53 C11
Plawsworth Durham 233 B11
Plaxtol Kent 52 C6
Play Hatch Oxon 65 D8
Playden E Sus 38 C6
Playford Suff 108 B4
Playing Place Corn 4 G6
Playley Green Glos 98 E5
Plealey Shrops 131 B8
Pleamore Cross Som 27 D10
Plean Stirl 278 D6
Pleasant Valley Pembs 73 D10
Pleasington Blkburn 194 B6
Pleasley Derbys 171 C8
Pleasleyhill Notts 171 C8
Pleck Dorset 30 D3
Pleck Dorset 30 E2
Pleck W Mid 133 D9
Pleck or Little Ansty
Dorset 30 G3
Pleckgate Blkburn 203 G9
Pledgdon Green Essex 105 F11
Pledwick W Yorks 197 D10
Plemstall W Ches 183 G7
Plenmeller Northumb 240 E6
Plâs Berwyn Denb 165 G11
Plesheys Essex 87 C11
Plockton Highld 295 B10
Plocrapol W Isles 305 J3
Plot Gate Som 44 G4
Plot Street Som 44 F5
Plough Hill Warks 134 E6
Ploughfield Hereford 97 C7
Plowden Shrops 131 F7
Ploxgreen Shrops 131 C7
Pluckley Kent 54 D2
Pluckley Thorne Kent 54 E2
Plucks Gutter Kent 71 G9
Plumbland Cumb 229 D9
Plumbley S Yorks 186 E6
Plumford Kent 54 B4
Plumley E Ches 184 F2
Plump Hill Glos 79 B11
Plumpton Cumb 230 D5
Plumpton E Sus 36 E5
Plumpton Northants 101 B11
Plumpton End
Northants 102 B4
Plumpton Foot Cumb 230 D5
Plumpton Green E Sus 36 D5
Plumpton Head Cumb 230 E6
Plumstead London 68 D3
Plumstead Norf 160 C2
Plumstead Common
London 68 D3
Plumstead Green Norf 160 C2
Plumtree Notts 154 C2
Plumtree Green Kent 53 D10
Plumtree Park Notts 154 C2
Plungar Leics 154 C5
Plush Dorset 30 G2
Plusha Corn 11 E11
Plushabridge Corn 12 G2
Plusterwine Glos 79 F9
Plwmp Ceredig 111 G7
Plymouth Plym 7 E9

cliffe E Yorks 199 C7
cliffe York 207 C7
cliffe Bridge
rks 199 C7
don W Yorks 205 F10
don Carrs W Yorks 205 F10
folds W Yorks 197 C7
green Northumb 241 F10
marsh S Yorks 186 B6
nsley Staffs 151 G10
eth Essex 88 G3
eth Shot Essex 88 G3
ridge Devon 28 F5
son Green Derbys 170 F5
enstall Lancs 195 C10
thorpe W Yorks 197 D7
yards N Lnrk 268 B5
on Aberds 303 F8
on Suff 107 D11
ill N Yorks 204 D4
ees Northumb 251 E10
eigh Essex 88 G4
e Essex 106 G4
ers Lane London 66 B6
es Park London 67 F8
brook Shrops 131 C7
h Cambs 123 D11
Lancs 203 G11
er's Corner Essex 88 E2
ing Reading 65 E8
ing Street Kent 54 G2
ing Street Kent 71 F11
ings Glos 79 B10
y Token Glos 81 E10
ymoney Corn 6 E2
ill Cumb 222 B2
quhar Highld 309 K7
sby Leics 154 G3
by Lincs 189 F9
e Heath E Ches 167 E10
ter Highld 310 C6
lay Highld 299 D7
wick Shetland 313 J5
la Corn 2 B4
Highld 310 C3
ullin Highld 299 D8
lver Kent 71 F8
Ball Devon 27 D9
Bridge Lancs 211 D9
Bull E Ches 168 D4
Bull Staffs 150 B4
Dial Cumb 229 B11
Hill Bmouth 19 B7
Hill Hants 34 E2
Hill Hereford 97 D10
Hill Kent 53 C7
Hill Leics 135 D10
Hill Pembs 72 B6
Hill W Yorks 198 B2
Hill Warks 118 F2
Hill Worcs 117 G7
House Common
s 36 C5
Lake Telford 150 G3
Lodge Suff 124 C3
Lumb Gtr Man 195 D10
Pits Norf 159 D11
Post Corn 24 F3
Rail Hereford 97 F10
Rice Hants 47 E10
Rock Gtr Man 194 F5
Roses Carms 74 C2
Row Northumb 253 D7
Scar Lancs 203 G7
Street Staffs 168 E4
Wharf Bay Anglesey 179 E8
erth Pembs 73 E9
ourn Herts 85 C10
ournbury Herts 85 C10
ourne N Lincs 189 B7
ourne N Lincs 200 G3
ridge Dorset 17 D11
ridge London 68 B2
ridge Soton 32 E5
rook Mon 79 C8
rook Wrex 167 G8
urn Highld 300 C5
urn Highld 301 E9
urn Northumb 241 E7
car Redcar 235 G8
castle Angus 287 B10
astle Highld 300 E5
liff Bay N Som 60 D2
croft Dumfries 237 B9
cross Worcs 117 C7
licap Heath W Mid 134 D2
ling Falk 279 F8
lingmuirhead Falk 279 F8
lish Gtr Man 184 C5
lish Warr 183 D11
litch Worcs 117 D10
Suff 124 F6
enhall Norf 142 G5
enham Hants 47 D10
esdale Camp
humb 251 D8
esmouth Northumb 251 G9
ord Aberds 293 E9
ord Angus 287 C9
ord Dorset 29 F10
ord Durham 233 E7
ord W Sus 34 B5
ordgreen Borders 261 F9
gorton Perth 286 E4
grave Suff 125 B10
heugh Angus 292 G6
hill Aberds 293 C9
hill Aberds 302 F6
hill Herts 104 E6
hill N Som 60 G4
hill Notts 171 F9
hill Shrops 131 B9
hill Shrops 150 G3
hill Staffs 150 D6
hill Sur 51 C9
hill Telford 150 G4
hills Cumb 230 F6
hills Devon 14 C4
house Argyll 275 G9
houses Argyll 274 G4
sham Suff 143 G8
and Bristol 60 D5
and Orkney 314 D3
and End Bucks 84 E4
ands Dorset 17 E9
ands Som 44 G3
ands Swindon 81 G11
ane Som 28 E2
ingfield Suff 126 C3
ynch Som 45 G8
ynch Wilts 32 C2
main Cumb 229 E8
marley D'Abitot Glos 98 E5
marshall Stockton 234 G3
mile Leics 154 E5
mire N Yorks 223 G10
monsford Devon 24 D4
moor Corn 5 C11
moss Aberds 303 F8
nal Shrops 149 D7
nal W Mid 117 B10
path Borders 262 B3
Redpoint Highld 299 C7
Redruth Corn 4 G3
Redscarhead Borders 270 G4
Redstocks Wilts 62 G2
Redtye Corn 5 C10
Redvales Gtr Man 195 F10
Redwick Newport 60 C2
Redwick S Glos 60 B4
Redwith Shrops 148 E6
Redworth Darl 233 G10
Reed Herts 105 D7
Reed End Herts 104 D6
Reed Point Lincs 174 E2
Reedham Lincs 174 D2
Reedham Norf 143 C8
Reedley Lancs 204 F2
Reedness E Yorks 199 C9
Reeds Beck Lincs 174 B2
Reeds Holme Lancs 195 C10
Reedsford Northumb 263 C9
Reedy Devon 14 D2
Reen Manor Corn 4 E5
Reepham Lincs 189 G8
Reepham Norf 159 E11
Reeth N Yorks 223 F10
Reeves Green W Mid 118 B5
Refail Powys 130 C3
Regaby I o M 192 C5
Regil Bath 60 G4
Regoul Highld 301 D8
Reiff Highld 307 H4
Reigate Sur 51 C9
Reigate Heath Sur 51 C8
Reighton N Yorks 218 D2
Reighton Gap N Yorks 218 D2
Reinigeadal W Isles 305 H4
Reisque Aberds 293 B10
Reiss Highld 310 D7
Rejerrah Corn 4 D5
Releath Corn 2 C5
Relubbus Corn 2 C3
Relugas Moray 301 E9
Remenham Wokingham 65 C9
Remenham Hill
Wokingham 65 C9
Remony Perth 285 C11
Rempstone Notts 153 E11
Remusaig Highld 309 J7
Rendcomb Glos 81 D8
Rendham Suff 126 E6
Rendlesham Suff 126 G6
Renfrew Renfs 267 B10
Renhold Beds 121 G11
Renishaw Derbys 186 F6
Renmure Angus 287 B10
Rennington Northumb 264 F6
Renshaw Wood Shrops 132 B6
Renton W Dunb 277 F7
Renwick Cumb 231 C7
Repps Norf 161 F8
Repton Derbys 152 D6
Reraig Highld 295 C10
Reraig Cot Highld 295 B10
Rerwick Shetland 313 M5
Rescassa Corn 5 G9
Rescobie Angus 287 B9
Rescorla Corn 5 D10
Resipole Highld 289 C9
Reskadinnick Corn 4 G2
Resolfen = Resolven
Neath 76 E4
Resolis Highld 300 C6
Resolven = Resolfen
Neath 76 E4
Restalrig Edin 280 G5
Reston Borders 273 C7
Reston Cumb 221 F9
Restronguet Passage Corn 3 B8
Restrop Wilts 62 B5
Resugga Green Corn 5 D10
Reswallie Angus 287 B9
Retallack Corn 5 B8
Retew Corn 5 D8
Retford Notts 188 E2
Retire Corn 5 C10
Rettendon Essex 88 F3
Rettendon Place Essex 88 F3
Revesby Lincs 174 C3
Revesby Bridge Lincs 174 C4
Revidge Blkburn 195 B7
Rew Devon 9 G9
Rew Devon 13 G11
Rew Dorset 29 F11
Rew Street I o W 20 C5
Rewe Devon 14 B4
Rexon Devon 12 D4
Rexon Cross Devon 12 D4
Reybridge Wilts 62 F2
Reydon Suff 127 B9
Reydon Smear Suff 127 B9
Reymerston Norf 141 B10
Reynalton Pembs 73 D9
Reynoldston Swansea 56 C3
Rezare Corn 12 F3
Rhadyr Mon 78 E5
Rhaeadr Gwy =
Rhayader Powys 113 D9
Rhandir Conwy 180 G4
Rhandirmwyn Carms 94 C5
Rhayader =
Rhaeadr Gwy Powys 113 D9
Rhedyn Gwyn 144 C5
Rhegreanoch Highld 307 H5
Rhemore Highld 289 D7
Rhencullen I o M 192 C4
Rhenetra Highld 298 D4
Rhes-y-cae Flint 181 G11
Rhewl Denb 165 C10
Rhewl Denb 165 F11
Rhewl Shrops 148 C6
Rhewl Wrex 149 B7
Rhewl-fawr Flint 181 E10
Rhewl-Mostyn Flint 181 E11
Rhian Highld 309 H5
Rhicarn Highld 307 G5
Rhiconich Highld 306 D7
Rhicullen Highld 300 B6
Rhidorroch Ho Highld 307 K6
Rhiews Shrops 150 B2
Rhifail Highld 308 E7
Rhigolter Highld 308 D3
Rhigos Rhondda 76 D6
Rhilochan Highld 309 J7
Rhippinllwyd Ceredig 92 C5
Rhippinllwyd Ceredig 92 B4
Rhiroy Highld 307 L6
Rhitongue Highld 308 D6
Rhivichie Highld 306 D7
Rhiw Gwyn 144 D4
Rhiwabon = Ruabon
Wrex 166 G4
Rhiwbebyll Denb 165 B10
Rhiwbina Cardiff 59 C7
Rhiwbryfdir Gwyn 163 F11
Rhiwceiliog Bridgend 58 C3
Rhiwderin Newport 59 B9
Rhiwen Gwyn 163 C9
Rhiwfawr Neath 76 C2
Rhiwinder Rhondda 58 B4
Rhiwlas Gwyn 147 B8
Rhiwlas Gwyn 163 B9
Rhiwlas Powys 148 C3
Rhode Som 43 G9
Rhode Common Kent 54 B5
Rhodes Gtr Man 195 F11
Rhodes Minnis Kent 55 E7
Rhodesia Notts 187 F9
Rhodiad Pembs 90 F5
Rhonadale Argyll 255 D8
Rhondda Rhondda 77 F7
Rhonehouse or
Kelton Hill Dumfries 237 D9
Rhoose V Glam 58 F5
Rhos Carms 93 D7
Rhos Neath 76 E2
Rhôs Denb 165 C10
Rhos Powys 148 F5
Rhôs Common Powys 148 F5
Rhos-ddû Gwyn 144 B5
Rhos-fawr Gwyn 145 B7
Rhos-goch Powys 96 B3
Rhos Haminiog
Ceredig 111 E10
Rhos-hill Pembs 92 C3
Rhos Isaf Gwyn 163 D7
Rhôs Lligwy Anglesey 179 D7
Rhôs-on-Sea Conwy 180 E4
Rhos-y-brithdir Powys 148 E2
Rhos-y-garth Ceredig 112 C2
Rhos-y-gwaliau Gwyn 147 C8
Rhos-y-llan Gwyn 144 B4
Rhos-y-Madoc Wrex 166 G4
Rhos-y-meirch Powys 114 D5
Rhosaman Carms 76 C2
Rhosbeirio Anglesey 178 C5
Rhoscefnhir Anglesey 179 F8
Rhoscolyn Anglesey 178 F3
Rhoscrowther Pembs 72 E6
Rhosddu Wrex 166 E4
Rhosdylluan Gwyn 147 D7
Rhosesmor Flint 166 B2
Rhosfach Pembs 92 F2
Rhosgadfan Gwyn 163 D8
Rhosgoch Anglesey 178 D6
Rhosgoch Powys 96 B3
Rhosgyll Gwyn 163 G7
Rhoshirwaun Gwyn 144 D3
Rhoslan Gwyn 163 G7
Rhoslefain Gwyn 110 B2
Rhosllanerchrugog
Wrex 166 F3
Rhosmaen Carms 94 G2
Rhosmeirch Anglesey 179 F7
Rhosneigr Anglesey 178 G4
Rhosnesni Wrex 166 E5
Rhosrobin Wrex 166 E4
Rhossili Swansea 56 D2
Rhosson Pembs 90 F4
Rhostrehwfa Anglesey 178 G6
Rhostryfan Gwyn 163 D7
Rhostyllen Wrex 166 F4
Rhoswiel Shrops 148 B5
Rhosybol Anglesey 178 D6
Rhosycaerau Pembs 91 D8
Rhosygadair Newydd
Ceredig 92 B4
Rhosygadfa Shrops 148 C6
Rhosygilwen Pembs 92 C4
Rhosymedre Wrex 166 G3
Rhosyn-coch Carms 92 G5
Rhu Argyll 275 G9
Rhu Argyll 276 E5
Rhualt Denb 181 F9
Rhubodach Argyll 275 F11
Rhuddall Heath W Ches 167 C9
Rhuddlan Ceredig 93 C9
Rhuddlan Denb 181 F8
Rhue Highld 307 K5
Rhulen Powys 96 B2
Rhunahaorine Argyll 255 C8
Rhyd Ceredig 92 C5
Rhyd Gwyn 163 G10
Rhyd Powys 129 C9
Rhyd-Ddu Gwyn 163 E9
Rhyd-Rosser Ceredig 111 D11
Rhyd-uchaf Gwyn 147 B8
Rhyd-y-Brown Pembs 91 G11
Rhyd-y-clafdy Gwyn 144 B6
Rhyd-y-cwm Shrops 130 G3
Rhyd-y-foel Conwy 180 F6
Rhyd-y-fro Neath 76 D2
Rhyd-y-gwin Swansea 75 E11
Rhyd-y-gwystl Gwyn 145 B8
Rhyd-y-meirch Mon 78 D4
Rhyd-y-meudwy Denb 165 E10
Rhyd-y-pandy Swansea 75 E11
Rhyd-y-sarn Gwyn 163 G11
Rhyd-yr-onen Gwyn 128 C2
Rhydaman =
Ammanford Carms 75 C10
Rhydargaeau Carms 93 F8
Rhydcymerau Carms 93 D11
Rhydd Worcs 98 B6
Rhydd Green Worcs 98 B6
Rhydding Neath 57 B8
Rhydfudr Ceredig 111 D11
Rhydgaled Conwy 165 C7
Rhydgaled =
Chancery Ceredig 111 B11
Rhydlewis Ceredig 92 B6
Rhydlios Gwyn 144 C3
Rhydlydan Conwy 164 E5
Rhydlydan Powys 129 E11
Rhydmoelddu Powys 113 B11
Rhydness Powys 96 C2
Rhydowen Carms 92 F3
Rhydowen Ceredig 93 B8
Rhydspence Hereford 96 B4
Rhydtalog Flint 166 D2
Rhydwyn Anglesey 178 D4
Rhydycroesau Powys 148 C4
Rhydyfelin Carms 92 D5
Rhydyfelin Ceredig 111 B11
Rhydyfelin Powys 129 E11
Rhydyfelin Rhondda 58 B5
Rhydygele Pembs 91 G7
Rhydymain Gwyn 146 E6
Rhydymwyn Flint 166 B2
Rhydywrach Carms 73 B11
Rhyl Denb 181 E8
Rhymney Caerph 77 D10
Rhyn Wrex 148 B6
Rhynd Fife 287 E8
Rhynd Perth 286 E5
Rhynie Aberds 302 G4
Rhynie Highld 301 B8
Ribbesford Worcs 116 C5
Ribble Head N Yorks 212 D5
Ribblehead N Yorks 212 D5
Ribbleton Lancs 203 G7
Ribby Lancs 202 G4
Ribchester Lancs 203 F8
Riber Derbys 170 D4
Ribigill Highld 308 D5
Riby Lincs 201 F7
Riby Cross Roads Lincs 201 F7
Riccall N Yorks 207 F8
Riccarton E Ayrs 257 B10
Richards Castle
Hereford 115 D9
Richborough Port Kent 71 G10
Richings Park Bucks 66 D4
Richmond London 67 E7
Richmond N Yorks 224 E3
Richmond S Yorks 186 D6
Richmond Hill W Yorks 206 G2
Richmond's Green
Essex 106 F2
Rich's Holford Som 42 G6
Rickard's Down Devon 24 B6
Rickarton Aberds 293 E10
Rickerby Cumb 239 F10
Rickerscote Staffs 151 E8
Rickford N Som 44 B3
Rickinghall Suff 125 B10
Rickleton T & W 243 G7
Rickling Essex 105 E9
Rickling Green Essex 105 F10
Rickmansworth Herts 85 G9
Rickney E Sus 23 D10
Riddell Borders 262 E2
Riddings Derbys 170 E6
Riddlecombe Devon 25 E10
Riddlesden W Yorks 205 E7
Riddrie Glasgow 268 B2
Ridgacre W Mid 133 G10
Ridge Bath 44 B5
Ridge Dorset 18 D4
Ridge Hants 32 D4
Ridge Herts 86 E2
Ridge Lancs 211 G9
Ridge Som 28 F3
Ridge Wilts 46 G3
Ridge Common Hants 34 C2
Ridge Green Sur 51 D10
Ridge Hill Gtr Man 185 B7
Ridge Lane Warks 134 E5
Ridge Row Kent 55 E8
Ridgebourne Powys 113 E11
Ridgehill N Som 60 G4
Ridgemarsh Herts 85 G8
Ridgeway Bristol 60 D6
Ridgeway Derbys 170 E5
Ridgeway Derbys 186 E6
Ridgeway Kent 54 E5
Ridgeway Newport 59 B9
Ridgeway Pembs 73 D10
Ridgeway Som 45 D8
Ridgeway Staffs 168 E5
Ridgeway Cross Hereford 98 B4
Ridgeway Moor Derbys 186 E6
Ridgewell Essex 106 C4
Ridgewood E Sus 23 B7
Ridgmont C Beds 103 D9
Ridgway Shrops 131 F7
Ridgway Sur 50 B4
Riding Gate Som 30 B2
Riding Mill Northumb 242 E2
Ridley Kent 68 G6
Ridley Northumb 241 E7
Ridley Stokoe Northumb 250 F6
Ridleywood Wrex 166 E6
Ridlington Norf 160 C6
Ridlington Rutland 136 C6
Ridlington Street Norf 160 C6
Ridsdale Northumb 251 G10
Riechip Perth 286 C4
Riemore Perth 286 C4
Rienachait Highld 306 F5
Rievaulx N Yorks 215 B11
Riff Orkney 314 E4
Riffin Aberds 303 E7
Rifle Green Torf 78 D3
Rift House Hrtlpl 234 E5
Rigg Dumfries 239 D7
Riggend N Lnrk 278 G5
Rigsby Lincs 190 F6
Rigside S Lnrk 259 B9
Riley Green Lancs 194 B6
Rileyhill Staffs 152 F2
Rilla Mill Corn 11 G11
Rillaton Corn 11 G11
Rillington N Yorks 217 E7
Rimac Lincs 191 C7
Rimington Lancs 204 D2
Rimpton Som 29 C10
Rimswell E Yorks 201 B10
Rimswell Valley E Yorks 201 B10
Rinaston Pembs 91 F9
Rindleford Shrops 132 D4
Ring o' Bells Lancs 194 E3
Ringasta Shetland 313 M5
Ringford Dumfries 237 D8
Ringing Hill Leics 153 F9
Ringinglow S Yorks 186 E3
Ringland Newport 59 B11
Ringland Norf 160 G2
Ringles Cross E Sus 37 C7
Ringlestone Kent 53 B11
Ringlestone Kent 53 B9
Ringley Gtr Man 195 F9
Ringmer E Sus 36 E6
Ringmore Devon 8 F3
Ringorm Moray 302 E2
Ring's End Cambs 139 C7
Ringsfield Suff 143 F8
Ringsfield Corner Suff 143 F8
Ringshall Herts 85 C7
Ringshall Suff 125 G10
Ringshall Stocks Suff 125 G10
Ringstead Norf 176 E2
Ringstead Northants 121 B9
Ringtail Green Essex 87 B11
Ringwood Hants 31 F11
Ringwould Kent 55 D11
Rinmore Aberds 292 B6
Rinnigill Orkney 314 G3
Rinsey Corn 2 D3
Rinsey Croft Corn 2 D4
Riof W Isles 304 E3
Ripe E Sus 23 C8
Ripley Derbys 170 E5
Ripley Hants 19 B9
Ripley N Yorks 214 G5
Ripley Sur 50 B5
Riplingham E Yorks 208 G5
Ripon N Yorks 214 E6
Ripper's Cross Kent 54 E3
Rippingale Lincs 155 D11
Ripple Kent 55 D10
Ripple Worcs 99 D7
Ripponden W Yorks 196 D4
Rireavach Highld 307 K5
Risabus Argyll 254 C4
Risbury Hereford 115 G10
Risby E Yorks 208 G6
Risby Lincs 189 C10
Risby Suff 124 D5
Risca Caerph 78 G2
Rise E Yorks 209 E9
Rise Carr Darl 224 B5
Rise End Derbys 170 D3
Rise Park London 87 G8
Rise Park Nottingham 171 F9
Riseden E Sus 52 G6
Riseden Kent 53 F8
Risegate Lincs 156 D4
Riseholme Lincs 189 F7
Risehow Cumb 228 E6
Riseley Beds 121 E10
Riseley Wokingham 65 G8
Rishangles Suff 126 D3
Rishton Lancs 203 G10
Rishworth W Yorks 196 D4
Rising Bridge Lancs 195 B9
Rising Sun Corn 12 G3
Risingbrook Staffs 151 E8
Risinghurst Oxon 83 D9
Risley Derbys 153 B9
Risley Warr 183 C10
Risplith N Yorks 214 F4
Rispond Highld 308 C4
Rivar Wilts 63 G10
Rivenhall Essex 88 B4
Rivenhall End Essex 88 B4
River Kent 55 E9
River W Sus 34 C6
River Bank Cambs 123 D10
Riverhead Kent 52 B4
Rivers' Corner Dorset 30 E3
Riverside Cardiff 59 D7
Riverside Plym 7 D8
Riverside Stirl 278 C6
Riverside Worcs 117 D10
Riverside Docklands
Lancs 194 B4
Riverton Devon 40 G6
Riverview Park Kent 69 E7
Rivington Lancs 194 E6
Rixon Dorset 30 E3
Rixton Warr 183 C11
Roa Island Cumb 210 G4
Roach Bridge Lancs 194 B5
Roaches Gtr Man 196 G3
Roachill Devon 26 C4
Road Green Norf 142 E5
Road Weedon Northants 120 F2
Roade Northants 120 G5
Roadhead Cumb 240 C2
Roadmeetings S Lnrk 269 F7
Roadside Highld 310 C5
Roadside of Catterline
Aberds 293 F10
Roadside of Kinneff
Aberds 293 F10
Roadwater Som 42 F4
Roag Highld 298 E2
Roast Green Essex 105 E9
Roath Cardiff 59 D7
Roath Park Cardiff 59 D7
Rob Roy's House Argyll 284 F5
Roberton Borders 261 G10
Roberton S Lnrk 259 D10
Robertsbridge E Sus 38 C2
Robertstown Moray 302 E2
Robertstown Rhondda 77 E8
Roberttown W Yorks 197 C7
Robeston Back Pembs 73 B9
Robeston Cross Pembs 72 D5
Robeston Wathen Pembs 73 B9
Robeston West Pembs 72 D5
Robhurst Kent 54 G2
Robin Hill Staffs 168 D6
Robin Hood Derbys 186 G3
Robin Hood Lancs 194 E4
Robin Hood W Yorks 197 B10
Robin Hood's Bay
N Yorks 227 D9
Robinhood End Essex 106 D4
Robins W Sus 34 B4
Robinson's End Warks 134 E6
Roborough Devon 7 C10
Roborough Devon 25 D9
Robroyston Glasgow 268 B2
Roby Mers 182 C6
Roby Mill Lancs 194 F4
Rocester Staffs 152 B2
Roch Pembs 91 G7
Roch Gate Pembs 91 G7
Rochdale Gtr Man 195 E11
Roche Corn 5 C9
Roche Grange Staffs 169 C7
Rochester Medway 69 F8
Rochester Northumb 251 D8
Rochford Essex 88 G5
Rochford Worcs 116 D2
Rock Caerph 77 F11
Rock Corn 10 F4
Rock Devon 28 G3
Rock Neath 57 C9
Rock Northumb 264 E6
Rock Som 28 C4
Rock W Sus 35 E10
Rock Worcs 116 C4
Rock End Staffs 168 D5
Rock Ferry Mers 182 D4
Rockbeare Devon 14 C6
Rockbourne Hants 31 D10
Rockcliffe Cumb 239 E9
Rockcliffe Dumfries 237 D10
Rockcliffe Flint 182 G3
Rockcliffe Lancs 195 C11
Rockcliffe Cross Cumb 239 E8
Rockfield Highld 311 L3
Rockfield Mon 79 C7
Rockford Devon 41 D9
Rockford Hants 31 F11
Rockgreen Shrops 115 B10
Rockhampton S Glos 79 G11
Rockhead Corn 11 E7
Rockhill Shrops 114 B5
Rockingham Northants 137 E7
Rockland All Saints
Norf 141 D9
Rockland St Mary Norf 142 C6
Rockland St Peter Norf 141 D9
Rockley Notts 188 G2
Rockley Wilts 63 E7
Rockley Ford Som 45 C8
Rockness Glos 80 F4
Rockrobin E Sus 52 G6
Rocks Park E Sus 37 C7
Rocksavage Halton 183 E8
Rockstowes Glos 80 F3
Rockville Argyll 276 C4
Rockwell End Bucks 65 B9
Rockwell Green Som 27 C10
Rocky Hill Scilly 1 G4
Rodbaston Staffs 151 G8
Rodborough Glos 80 E4
Rodbourne Swindon 62 C6
Rodbourne Wilts 62 C2
Rodbourne Bottom Wilts 62 C2
Rodbourne Cheney
Swindon 62 B6
Rodbridge Corner
Essex 107 C7
Rodd Hereford 114 E6
Rodd Hurst Hereford 114 E6
Roddam Northumb 264 E2
Rodden Dorset 17 E8
Roddymoor Durham 233 D9
Rode Som 45 C10
Rode Heath E Ches 168 D3
Rode Hill Som 45 C10
Rodeheath E Ches 168 B5
Roden Telford 149 F11
Rodford S Glos 61 C7
Rodgrove Som 30 C2
Rodhuish Som 42 F4
Rodington Telford 149 G11
Rodington Heath
Telford 149 G11
Rodley Glos 80 C2
Rodley W Yorks 205 F10
Rodmarton Glos 80 F6
Rodmell E Sus 36 F6
Rodmer Clough W Yorks 196 B3
Rodmersham Kent 70 G2
Rodmersham Green
Kent 70 G2
Rodney Stoke Som 44 C3
Rodsley Derbys 170 G2
Rodway Som 43 F9
Rodway Telford 150 F3
Rodwell Dorset 17 F9
Roe Cross Gtr Man 185 B7
Roe End Herts 85 B8
Roe Green Gtr Man 195 G9
Roe Green Herts 86 D2
Roe Green Herts 104 E6
Roe Lee Blkburn 203 G9
Roebuck Low Gtr Man 196 F3
Roecliffe N Yorks 215 F7
Roedean Brighton 36 G4
Roehampton London 67 E8
Roesound Shetland 312 G5
Roestock Herts 86 D2
Roffey W Sus 51 G7
Rogart Highld 309 J7
Rogart Station Highld 309 J7
Rogate W Sus 34 C4
Roger Ground Cumb 221 F7
Rogerstone Newport 59 B9
Rogerton S Lnrk 268 D2
Roghadal W Isles 296 C6
Rogiet Mon 60 B3
Rogue's Alley Cambs 139 B7
Roke Oxon 83 G10
Rokemarsh Oxon 83 G10
Roker T & W 243 F10
Rollesby Norf 161 F8
Rolleston Leics 136 C4
Rolleston Notts 172 E2
Rolleston-on-Dove
Staffs 152 D4
Rollestone S Yorks 186 E5
Rollestone Wilts 46 E5
Rollestone Camp Wilts 46 E5
Rolls Mill Dorset 30 E3
Rolston E Yorks 209 D10
Rolstone N Som 59 G11
Rolvenden Kent 53 G10
Rolvenden Layne Kent 53 G11
Romaldkirk Durham 232 G5
Roman Hill Suff 143 E10
Romanby N Yorks 225 G7
Romannobridge Borders 270 F3
Romansleigh Devon 26 C2
Rome Angus 293 G7
Romesdal Highld 298 D4
Romford Dorset 31 F9
Romford Kent 52 E6
Romford London 68 B4
Romiley Gtr Man 184 C6
Romney Street Kent 68 G4
Rompa Shetland 313 L6
Romsey Hants 32 C5
Romsey Town Cambs 123 F9
Romsley Shrops 132 G5
Romsley Worcs 117 B9
Romsley Hill Worcs 117 B9
Ronachan Ho Argyll 255 B8
Ronague I o M 192 E3
Rondlay Telford 132 B4
Ronkswood Worcs 117 G7
Rood End W Mid 133 F10
Rook End Essex 105 E11
Rookby Cumb 222 C6
Rookhope Durham 232 C4
Rooking Cumb 221 B8
Rookley I o W 20 E6
Rookley Green I o W 20 E6
Rooks Bridge Som 43 C11
Rooks Hill Kent 52 C5
Rook's Nest Som 42 G5
Rooksey Green Suff 125 G8
Rooksmoor Glos 80 E4
Rookwith N Yorks 214 B4
Rookwood W Sus 21 B11
Roos E Yorks 209 G11
Roose Cumb 210 F4
Roosebeck Cumb 210 F5
Roosecote Cumb 210 F4
Roost End Essex 106 C4
Rootham's Green Beds 122 F2
Rooting Street Kent 54 D3
Rootpark S Lnrk 269 E9
Ropley Hants 48 G6
Ropley Dean Hants 48 G6
Ropley Soke Hants 49 G7
Ropsley Lincs 155 C9
Rora Aberds 303 D10
Rorandle Aberds 293 B8
Rorrington Shrops 130 C5
Rosarie Moray 302 E3
Roscroggan Corn 4 G3
Rose Corn 4 E5
Rose-an-Grouse Corn 2 B2
Rose Ash Devon 26 C3
Rose Green Essex 107 F8
Rose Green Suff 107 C9
Rose Green Suff 107 D8
Rose Green W Sus 22 D6
Rose Grove Lancs 204 G2
Rose Hill Bucks 66 C2
Rose Hill Derbys 153 B7
Rose Hill E Sus 23 B7
Rose Hill Gtr Man 195 F8
Rose Hill Lancs 204 G2
Rose Hill Oxon 83 E8
Rose Hill Suff 108 C3
Rose Hill Sur 51 D7
Rose Valley Pembs 73 E8
Roseacre Kent 53 B9
Roseacre Lancs 202 F4
Rosebank E Dunb 278 G3
Rosebank S Lnrk 268 F6
Rosebery Midloth 270 D6
Rosebrae Moray 301 C11
Rosebrough Northumb 264 D4
Rosebush Pembs 91 F11
Rosecare Corn 11 B9
Rosedale Herts 86 E4
Rosedale Abbey N Yorks 226 F4
Roseden Northumb 264 E2
Rosedinnick Corn 5 B8
Rosedown Devon 24 C3
Rosefield Highld 301 D8
Rosehall Highld 309 J4
Rosehall N Lnrk 268 C4
Rosehaugh Mains
Highld 300 D6
Rosehearty Aberds 303 C9
Rosehill Blkburn 195 C8
Rosehill Corn 4 E5
Rosehill Corn 5 C10
Rosehill Gtr Man 184 D3
Rosehill London 67 F9
Rosehill Pembs 72 B5
Rosehill Shrops 150 C3
Rosehill T & W 243 D8
Roseisle Moray 301 C11
Roseland Corn 6 C5
Roselands E Sus 23 E10
Rosemarket Pembs 73 D7
Rosemarkie Highld 301 D7
Rosemary Lane Devon 27 E11
Rosemelling Corn 5 D10
Rosemergy Corn 1 B4
Rosemount Perth 286 C5
Rosenannon Corn 5 B9
Rosenithon Corn 3 E8
Roser's Cross E Sus 37 C9
Rosevean Corn 5 D10
Rosevear Corn 2 E5
Roseville W Mid 133 E8
Rosevine Corn 3 B9
Rosewarne Corn 2 B4
Rosewarne Corn 4 G2
Rosewell Midloth 270 C5
Roseworth Stockton 234 G4
Roseworthy Corn 2 B4
Roseworthy Corn 4 F5
Roseworthy Barton Corn 2 B4
Rosgill Cumb 221 B10
Roshven Highld 289 B9
Roskear Croft Corn 4 G3
Roskhill Highld 298 E2
Roskill House Highld 300 D6
Roskorwell Corn 3 E7
Rosley Cumb 230 B2
Roslin Midloth 270 C5
Rosliston Derbys 152 F4
Rosneath Argyll 276 E5
Ross Borders 273 C9
Ross Dumfries 237 E8
Ross Northumb 264 B4
Ross Perth 285 E11
Ross Green Worcs 116 E5
Ross-on-Wye Hereford 98 F2
Rossett Wrex 166 D5
Rossett Green N Yorks 206 C2
Rossie Ochill Perth 286 F4
Rossie Priory Perth 286 D6
Rossington S Yorks 187 B10
Rosskeen Highld 300 C6
Rossland Renfs 277 G8
Rossmore Poole 19 C7
Roster Highld 310 F6
Rostherne E Ches 184 E2
Rostholme S Yorks 198 F5
Rosthwaite Cumb 220 C5
Rosthwaite Cumb 220 G4
Roston Derbys 169 G10
Rosudgeon Corn 2 D3
Rosyth Fife 280 E2
Rotchfords Essex 107 E8
Rotcombe Bath 44 B6
Rothbury Northumb 252 C3
Rotherbridge W Sus 35 C7
Rotherby Leics 154 F3
Rotherfield E Sus 37 B9
Rotherfield Greys Oxon 65 C8
Rotherfield Peppard
Oxon 65 C8
Rotherham S Yorks 186 C6
Rotherhithe London 67 D11
Rothersthorpe Northants 120 F4
Rotherwas Hereford 97 D10
Rotherwick Hants 49 B8
Rothes Moray 302 E2
Rothesay Argyll 275 G11
Rothiebrisbane Aberds 303 F7
Rothiemay Crossroads
Moray 302 E5
Rothiemurchus Lodge
Highld 291 C11
Rothienorman Aberds 303 F7
Rothiesholm Orkney 314 D6
Rothley Leics 153 G11
Rothley Northumb 252 F2
Rothley Plain Leics 153 G11
Rothley Shield East
Northumb 252 E2
Rothmaise Aberds 302 F6
Rothwell Lincs 189 B11
Rothwell Northants 136 G6
Rothwell W Yorks 197 B10
Rothwell Haigh
W Yorks 197 B10
Rotsea E Yorks 209 C7
Rottal Angus 292 G5
Rotten End Essex 106 F4
Rotten End Suff 127 D7
Rotten Green Hants 49 B9
Rotten Row W Berks 64 E5
Rotten Row W Mid 118 B3
Rottingdean Brighton 36 G5
Rottington Cumb 219 C9
Rotton Park W Mid 133 F10
Roud I o W 20 E6
Rough Bank Gtr Man 196 E2
Rough Close Staffs 151 B8
Rough Common Kent 54 B6
Rough Haugh Highld 308 E7
Rough Hay Staffs 152 E4
Rougham Norf 158 E6
Rougham Suff 125 E8
Roughbirchworth
S Yorks 197 G9
Roughburn Highld 290 E5
Roughcote Staffs 168 G6
Roughlee Lancs 204 E2
Roughley W Mid 134 D2
Roughmoor Som 28 B2
Roughmoor Swindon 62 B6
Roughrigg N Lnrk 278 G6
Roughsike Cumb 240 B2
Roughton Lincs 174 C2
Roughton Norf 160 B4
Roughton Shrops 132 E5
Roughton Moor Lincs 174 C2
Roughway Kent 52 C6
Round Bush Herts 85 F10
Round Green Luton 103 G11
Round Maple Suff 107 C9
Round Oak Shrops 131 G7
Round Oak W Mid 133 F8
Round Spinney
Northants 120 D5
Round Street Kent 69 F7
Roundbush Essex 88 E5
Roundbush Green Essex 87 C9
Roundham Som 28 F6
Roundhay W Yorks 206 F2
Round's Green W Mid 133 F9
Roundshaw London 67 G10
Roundstonefoot
Dumfries 248 B4
Roundstreet Common
W Sus 35 B9
Roundswell Devon 40 G4
Roundthorn Gtr Man 184 D4
Roundthwaite Cumb 222 E2
Roundway Wilts 62 G4
Roundyhill Angus 287 B7
Rous Lench Worcs 117 G10
Rousdon Devon 15 C11
Rousham Oxon 101 G9
Routenburn N Ayrs 266 C3
Routh E Yorks 209 E7
Rout's Green Bucks 84 F3
Row Corn 11 F7
Row Cumb 211 B8
Row Cumb 231 E8
Row Ash Hants 33 E8
Row Brow Cumb 229 D7
Row Green Essex 106 G4
Row Heath Essex 89 B10
Row-of-trees E Ches 184 F4
Row Town Sur 66 G4
Rowanburn Dumfries 239 B10
Rowanfield Glos 99 G8
Rowardennan Stirl 277 B7
Rowarth Derbys 185 D8
Rowbarton Som 28 B2
Rowberrow Som 44 B3
Rowde Wilts 62 G3
Rowden Devon 13 B8
Rowden N Yorks 205 B11
Rowe Head Cumb 210 D5
Rowen Conwy 180 G3
Rowfoot Northumb 240 E5
Rowford Som 28 B2
Rowhedge Essex 107 G10
Rowhill Sur 66 G4
Rowhook W Sus 50 G6
Rowington Warks 118 D4
Rowington Green Warks 118 D4
Rowland Derbys 186 G2
Rowlands Castle Hants 34 E2
Rowlands Gill T & W 242 F5
Rowland's Green
Hereford 98 D3
Rowledge Sur 49 E10
Rowlestone Hereford 97 F7
Rowley E Yorks 208 G5
Rowley Shrops 130 B6
Rowley Green London 86 F2
Rowley Hill W Yorks 197 E7
Rowley Park Staffs 151 E8
Rowley Regis W Mid 133 F9
Rowley's Green W Mid 134 G6
Rowling Kent 55 C9
Rowly Sur 50 E4
Rownall Staffs 169 F7
Rowner Hants 33 G9
Rowney Green Worcs 117 C10
Rownhams Hants 32 D5
Rowrah Cumb 219 B11
Rowsham Bucks 84 B4
Rowsley Derbys 170 B3
Rowstock Oxon 64 B3
Rowston Lincs 173 D9
Rowthorne Derbys 171 C7
Rowton Shrops 149 G7
Rowton Telford 150 F2
Rowton W Ches 166 C6
Rowton Moor W Ches 166 C6
Roxburgh Borders 262 C5
Roxburgh Mains
Borders 262 D5
Roxby N Lincs 200 D2
Roxby N Yorks 226 B5
Roxeth London 66 B6
Roxton Beds 122 G3
Roxwell Essex 87 D10
Royal British Legion
Village Kent 53 B8
Royal Leamington Spa
Warks 118 D6
Royal Oak Darl 233 G10
Royal Oak Lancs 194 G2
Royal Oak N Yorks 218 D2
Royal Tunbridge Wells =
Tunbridge Wells Kent 52 F5
Royal Wootton Bassett
Wilts 62 C5
Royal's Green E Ches 167 G10
Roybridge Highld 290 E4
Royd S Yorks 197 G8
Royd Moor S Yorks 197 G8
Royd Moor W Yorks 198 E2
Roydhouse W Yorks 197 E8
Roydon Essex 86 D6
Roydon Norf 141 G11
Roydon Norf 158 E4
Roydon Hamlet Essex 86 D6
Royds Green W Yorks 197 B11
Royston Glasgow 268 B2
Royston Herts 105 C7
Royston S Yorks 197 E11
Royston Water Som 28 E2
Royton Gtr Man 196 F2
Ruabon = Rhiwabon
Wrex 166 G4
Ruaig Argyll 288 E2
Ruan High Lanes Corn 3 B10
Ruan Lanihorne Corn 5 G7
Ruan Major Corn 2 F6
Ruan Minor Corn 2 F6
Ruarach Highld 295 C11
Ruardean Glos 79 B10
Ruardean Hill Glos 79 B10
Ruardean Woodside
Glos 79 B10
Rubery Worcs 117 B9
Rubha Ghaisinis W Isles 297 G4
Rubha Stoer Highld 306 F5
Ruchazie Glasgow 268 B3
Ruchill Glasgow 267 B11
Ruckcroft Cumb 230 C6
Ruckhall Hereford 97 D9
Ruckinge Kent 54 G4
Ruckland Lincs 190 F4
Rucklers Lane Herts 85 E9
Ruckley Shrops 131 C10
Rudbaxton Pembs 91 G9
Rudby N Yorks 225 D9
Ruddington Notts 153 C11
Ruddle Glos 79 C11
Rudford Glos 98 G5
Rudge Shrops 132 D6
Rudge Som 45 C10
Rudge Heath Shrops 132 D5
Rudgeway S Glos 60 B6
Rudgwick W Sus 50 G5
Rudhall Hereford 98 F2
Rudheath W Ches 183 G11
Rudheath Woods
W Ches 184 G2
Rudhja Garbh Argyll 289 E11
Rudley Green Essex 88 E4
Rudloe Wilts 61 E10
Rudry Caerph 59 B7
Rudston E Yorks 217 F11
Rudyard Staffs 169 D7
Ruewood Shrops 149 D9
Rufford Lancs 194 D3
Rufforth York 206 C6
Ruffs Notts 171 F8
Rugby Warks 119 B10
Rugeley Staffs 151 F10
Ruggin Som 27 D11
Ruglen S Ayrs 245 C7
Rugley Northumb 264 G5
Ruilick Highld 300 E5
Ruishton Som 28 C3
Ruisigearraidh W Isles 296 C5
Ruislip London 66 B5
Ruislip Common London 66 B5
Ruislip Gardens London 66 B5
Ruislip Manor London 66 B6
Ruiton W Mid 133 E8
Ruloe W Ches 183 G9
Rumach Highld 295 G8

Rumbling Bridge Perth 279 B10
Rumbow Cottages Worcs 117 B8
Rumburgh Suff 142 G6
Rumbush W Mid 118 B2
Rumer Hill Staffs 133 B9
Rumford Corn 10 G3
Rumford Falk 279 F8
Rumney Cardiff 59 D8
Rumsam Devon 40 G5
Rumwell Som 27 C11
Runcorn Halton 183 E8
Runcton W Sus 22 C5
Runcton Holme Norf 140 B2
Rundlestone Devon 13 G7
Runfold Sur 49 D11
Runhall Norf 141 B11
Runham Norf 143 B10
Runham Norf 161 G9
Runham Vauxhall Norf 143 B10
Running Hill Head Gtr Man 196 F4
Running Waters Durham 234 C2
Runnington Som 27 C10
Runsell Green Essex 88 D3
Runshaw Moor Lancs 194 D4
Runswick Bay N Yorks 226 B6
Runwell Essex 88 G2
Ruscombe Glos 80 D4
Ruscombe Wokingham 65 D9
Ruscote Oxon 101 C8
Rush Green Essex 89 B11
Rush Green Herts 86 C5
Rush Green Herts 104 G4
Rush Green London 68 B4
Rush Green Norf 141 B11
Rush-head Aberds 303 E8
Rush Hill Bath 61 G8
Rushall Hereford 98 E2
Rushall Norf 142 G3
Rushall W Mid 133 C10
Rushall Wilts 46 B6
Rushbrooke Suff 125 E7
Rushbury Shrops 131 E10
Rushcombe Bottom Poole 18 B5
Rushden Herts 104 E6
Rushden Northants 121 D9
Rushenden Kent 70 E2
Rusher's Cross E Sus 37 B10
Rushey Mead Leicester 136 B2
Rushford Devon 12 F4
Rushford Norf 141 G8
Rushgreen Warr 183 D11
Rushington Hants 32 E5
Rushlake Green E Sus 23 B10
Rushland Cross Cumb 210 B6
Rushley Green Essex 106 D5
Rushmere C Beds 103 F8
Rushmere Suff 143 F9
Rushmere St Andrew Suff 108 B4
Rushmere Street Suff 108 B4
Rushmoor Sur 49 E11
Rushmoor Telford 150 G2
Rushmore Hants 33 E11
Rushmore Hill London 68 G3
Rushock Hereford 114 F6
Rushock Worcs 117 C7
Rusholme Gtr Man 184 B5
Rushton Dorset 18 D3
Rushton N Yorks 217 C9
Rushton Northants 136 G6
Rushton Shrops 132 B2
Rushton W Ches 167 C9
Rushton Spencer Staffs 168 C6
Rushwick Worcs 116 G6
Rushy Green E Sus 23 C7
Rushyford Durham 233 F11
Ruskie Stirl 285 G10
Ruskington Lincs 173 E9
Rusland Cumb 210 B6
Rusling End Herts 104 G4
Rusper W Sus 51 F8
Ruspidge Glos 79 C11
Russ Hill Sur 51 E8
Russel Highld 299 E8
Russell Hill London 67 G10
Russell's Green E Sus 38 E2
Russell's Hall W Mid 133 F8
Russell's Water Oxon 65 B8
Russel's Green Suff 126 C5
Rusthall Kent 52 F5
Rustington W Sus 35 G9
Ruston N Yorks 217 C9
Ruston Parva E Yorks 217 G11
Ruswarp N Yorks 227 D7
Ruthall Shrops 131 F11
Rutherford Borders 262 C4
Rutherglen S Lnrk 268 C2
Ruthernbridge Corn 5 B10
Ruthin Denb 165 D10
Ruthin V Glam 58 D3
Ruthrieston Aberdeen 293 C11
Ruthven Aberds 302 E5
Ruthven Angus 286 C6
Ruthven Highld 291 D9
Ruthven Highld 301 F8
Ruthven House Angus 287 C7
Ruthvoes Corn 5 C8
Ruthwaite Cumb 229 D10
Ruthwell Dumfries 238 D3
Ruxley London 68 E3
Ruxton Hereford 97 F11
Ruxton Green Hereford 79 B8
Ruyton-XI-Towns Shrops 149 E7
Ryal Northumb 242 C2
Ryal Fold Blkburn 195 C7
Ryall Dorset 16 C4
Ryall Worcs 99 C7
Ryarsh Kent 53 B7
Rychraggan Highld 300 F4
Rydal Cumb 221 D7
Ryde I o W 21 C7
Rydens Sur 66 F6
Rydeshill Sur 50 C3
Rydon Devon 14 G3
Rye E Sus 38 C6
Rye Common Hants 49 C9
Rye Foreign E Sus 38 C5
Rye Harbour E Sus 38 D6
Rye Park Herts 86 C5
Rye Street Worcs 98 D5
Ryebank Shrops 149 C10
Ryecroft S Yorks 186 B6
Ryecroft W Yorks 205 F7
Ryecroft Gate Staffs 168 C6
Ryeford Glos 80 E4
Ryehill E Yorks 201 B8
Ryeish Green Wokingham 65 F8
Ryelands Hereford 115 F9
Ryeworth Glos 99 G9
Ryhall Rutland 155 G10
Ryhill W Yorks 197 E11
Ryhope T & W 243 G10
Rylah Derbys 171 B7
Rylands Notts 153 B10
Rylstone N Yorks 204 B5
Ryme Intrinseca Dorset 29 E9
Ryther N Yorks 207 F7
Ryton Glos 98 E4
Ryton N Yorks 216 D5
Ryton Shrops 132 C5
Ryton T & W 242 E5
Ryton Warks 135 F7
Ryton-on-Dunsmore Warks 119 C7
Ryton Woodside T & W 242 E4

S

Sabden Lancs 203 F11
Sabine's Green Essex 87 F8
Sackers Green Suff 107 D8
Sacombe Herts 86 B4
Sacombe Green Herts 86 B4
Sacriston Durham 233 B10
Sadberge Darl 224 B6
Saddell Argyll 255 D8
Saddell Ho Argyll 255 D8
Saddington Leics 136 E3
Saddle Bow Norf 158 F2
Saddle Street Dorset 28 G5
Saddlescombe W Sus 36 E3
Sadgill Cumb 221 D9
Saffron Walden Essex 105 D10
Saffron's Cross Hereford 115 G10
Sageston Pembs 73 E9
Saham Hills Norf 141 C8
Saham Toney Norf 141 C8
Saighdinis W Isles 296 E4
Saighton W Ches 166 C6
Sain Dunwyd = St Donats V Glam 58 F2
Sain Tathon = St Athan V Glam 58 F4
St Abbs Borders 273 B8
St Abb's Haven Borders 273 B8
St Agnes Corn 4 E4
St Agnes Scilly 1 H3
St Albans Herts 85 D10
St Allen Corn 4 E6
St Andrews Fife 287 F9
St Andrew's Major V Glam 58 E6
St Andrew's Wood Devon 27 F9
St Annes Lancs 193 B10
St Anne's Park Bristol 60 E6
St Ann's Dumfries 248 E3
St Ann's Nottingham 171 G9
St Ann's Chapel Corn 12 G4
St Ann's Chapel Devon 8 F3
St Anthony Corn 3 C9
St Anthony-in-Meneage Corn 3 D7
St Anthony's T & W 243 E7
St Anthony's Hill E Sus 23 E10
St Arvans Mon 79 F8
St Asaph = Llanelwy Denb 181 G8
St Athan = Sain Tathon V Glam 58 F4
St Augustine's Kent 54 C6
St Austell Corn 5 E10
St Austins Hants 20 B2
St Bees Cumb 219 C9
St Blazey Corn 5 E11
St Blazey Gate Corn 5 E11
St Boswells Borders 262 C3
St Breock Corn 10 G5
St Breward Corn 11 F7
St Briavels Glos 79 E9
St Briavels Common Glos 79 E8
St Bride's Pembs 72 C4
St Brides Major = Saint-y-Brid V Glam 57 G11
St Bride's Netherwent Mon 60 B2
St Brides-super-Ely V Glam 58 D5
St Brides Wentlooge Newport 59 C9
St Budeaux Plym 7 D8
St Buryan Corn 1 D4
St Catherine Bath 61 E9
St Catherine's Argyll 284 G5
St Catherine's Hill Dorset 19 B8
St Chloe Glos 80 E4
St Clears = Sanclêr Carms 74 B3
St Cleer Corn 6 B5
St Clement Corn 4 G6
St Clether Corn 11 E10
St Colmac Argyll 275 G11
St Columb Major Corn 5 C8
St Columb Minor Corn 4 C6
St Columb Road Corn 5 D8
St Combs Aberds 303 C10
St Cross Hants 33 B7
St Cross South Elmham Suff 142 G5
St Cyrus Aberds 293 G9
St David's Perth 286 E3
St David's = Tyddewi Pembs 90 F5
St Day Corn 4 G4
St Decumans Som 42 E5
St Dennis Corn 5 D9
St Denys Soton 32 E6
St Devereux Hereford 97 E8
St Dials Torf 78 G3
St Dogmaels = Llandudoch Pembs 92 B3
St Dominick Corn 7 B8
St Donat's = Sain Dunwyd V Glam 58 F2
St Edith's Wilts 62 G3
St Endellion Corn 10 F5
St Enoder Corn 5 D7
St Erme Corn 4 E6
St Erney Corn 7 D7
St Erth Corn 2 B3
St Erth Praze Corn 2 B3
St Ervan Corn 10 G3
St Eval Corn 5 B7
St Ewe Corn 5 F9
St Fagans Cardiff 58 D6
St Fergus Aberds 303 D10
St Fillans Perth 285 E10
St Florence Pembs 73 E9
St Gennys Corn 11 B8
St George Bristol 60 E6
St George Conwy 181 F7
St George in the East London 67 C10
St George's Gtr Man 184 B4
St Georges N Som 59 G11
St George's Telford 150 G4
St George's V Glam 58 D5
St George's Hill Sur 66 G5
St George's Well Devon 27 F8
St Germans Corn 7 D7
St Giles Lincs 189 G7
St Giles London 67 C10
St Giles in the Wood Devon 25 D8
St Giles on the Heath Devon 12 C3
St Giles's Hill Hants 33 B7
St Gluvias Corn 3 C7
St Godwalds Worcs 117 D9
St Harmon Powys 113 C9
St Helen Auckland Durham 233 F9
St Helena Warks 134 C5
St Helens Cumb 228 E6
St Helen's E Sus 38 E4
St Helens I o W 21 D8
St Helens Mers 183 B8
St Helen's S Yorks 197 F11
St Helen's Wood E Sus 38 E4
St Helier London 67 F9
St Hilary Corn 2 C3
St Hilary V Glam 58 E4
St Ibbs Herts 104 F3
St Illtyd Bl Gwent 78 E2
St Ippollytts Herts 104 F3
St Ishmael's Pembs 72 D4
St Issey Corn 10 G4
St Ive Corn 6 B6
St Ive Cross Corn 6 B6
St Ives Cambs 122 C6
St Ives Corn 2 A2
St Ives Dorset 31 G10
St James Dorset 30 C5
St James London 67 C9
St James Norf 160 E5
St James South Elmham Suff 142 G6
St James's End Northants 120 E4
St Jidgey Corn 5 B8
St John Corn 7 E8
St John's E Sus 52 G4
St John's I o M 192 D3
St John's Sevenoaks 52 B4
St Johns London 67 D11
St John's Sevenoaks 52 B4
St John's Southborough 52 E5
St John's Sur 50 B3
St John's W Yorks 206 F4
St Johns Warks 118 C5
St John's Worcs 116 G6
St John's Chapel Devon 25 B8
St John's Chapel Durham 232 D3
St John's Fen End Norf 157 G10
St John's Highway Norf 157 G10
St John's Park I o W 21 C8
St John's Town of Dalry Dumfries 246 G4
St John's Wells Aberds 303 F7
St John's Wood London 67 C9
St Judes I o M 192 C4
St Julians Herts 85 D10
St Julians Newport 59 B10
St Just in Roseland Corn 3 B9
St Just Corn 1 C3
St Justinian Pembs 90 F4
St Katharines Wilts 63 G9
St Katherine's Aberds 303 F7
St Keverne Corn 3 E7
St Kew Corn 10 F6
St Kew Highway Corn 10 F6
St Keyne Corn 6 C4
St Lawrence Corn 5 B10
St Lawrence Essex 89 E7
St Lawrence I o W 20 F6
St Lawrence Kent 71 F11
St Leonards Bucks 84 D6
St Leonards Dorset 31 G10
St Leonards E Sus 38 F3
St Leonards S Lnrk 268 E2
St Leonard's Street Kent 53 B7
St Levan Corn 1 E3
St Luke's Derby 152 B6
St Luke's London 67 C10
St Lythans V Glam 58 E6
St Mabyn Corn 10 G6
St Madoes Perth 286 E5
St Margaret South Elmham Suff 142 G6
St Margaret's Hereford 97 E7
St Margarets Herts 86 C5
St Margarets London 67 E7
St Margaret's at Cliffe Kent 55 E11
St Margaret's Hope Orkney 314 G4
St Mark's Glos 99 G8
St Mark's I o M 192 E3
St Martin Corn 2 E6
St Martin Corn 6 E5
St Martins Perth 286 D5
St Martin's Shrops 148 B6
St Martin's Moor Shrops 148 B6
St Mary Bourne Hants 48 C2
St Mary Church V Glam 58 E4
St Mary Cray London 68 F3
St Mary Hill V Glam 58 D3
St Mary Hoo Medway 69 D10
St Mary in the Marsh Kent 39 B9
St Marychurch Torbay 9 B8
St Mary's Orkney 314 F4
St Mary's Bay Kent 39 B9
St Maughans Mon 79 B7
St Maughans Green Mon 79 B7
St Mawes Corn 3 C8
St Mawgan Corn 5 B7
St Mellion Corn 7 B7
St Mellons Cardiff 59 C8
St Merryn Corn 10 G3
St Mewan Corn 5 E9
St Michael Caerhays Corn 5 G9
St Michael Church Som 43 G10
St Michael Penkevil Corn 5 G7
St Michael South Elmham Suff 142 G6
St Michaels Kent 53 F11
St Michaels Torbay 9 C7
St Michaels Worcs 115 D11
St Michael's Hamlet Mers 182 D5
St Michael's on Wyre Lancs 202 E5
St Minver Corn 10 F5
St Monans Fife 287 G9
St Neot Corn 6 B3
St Neots Cambs 122 E3
St Newlyn East Corn 4 D6
St Nicholas Herts 104 F5
St Nicholas Pembs 91 D7
St Nicholas V Glam 58 E5
St Nicholas at Wade Kent 71 F9
St Nicholas South Elmham Suff 142 G6
St Nicolas Park Warks 135 E7
St Ninians Stirl 278 C5
St Olaves Norf 143 D9
St Osyth Essex 89 B10
St Osyth Heath Essex 89 B10
St Owens Cross Hereford 97 G10
St Pancras London 67 C10
St Paul's Glos 80 B4
St Paul's Cray London 68 F3
St Paul's Walden Herts 104 G3
St Peter South Elmham Suff 142 G6
St Peter The Great Worcs 117 G7
St Peter's Glos 99 G8
St Peters Kent 71 F11
St Peter's T & W 243 E7
St Petrox Pembs 73 F7
St Pinnock Corn 6 C4
St Quivox S Ayrs 257 E9
St Ruan Corn 2 F6
St Stephen Corn 5 E8
St Stephens Corn 7 D8
St Stephens Corn 12 D2
St Stephen's Herts 85 D10
St Teath Corn 11 E7
St Thomas Devon 14 C4
St Thomas Swansea 57 C7
St Tudy Corn 11 F7
St Twynnells Pembs 73 F7
St Veep Corn 6 E2
St Vigeans Angus 287 C10
St Vincent's Hamlet Essex 87 G9
St Wenn Corn 5 C9
St Weonards Hereford 97 G9
St Winnow Corn 6 D2
St y-Nyll V Glam 58 D5
Saint Hill Devon 27 F9
Saint Hill W Sus 51 F11
Saint y Brid = St Brides Major V Glam 57 G11
Saintbridge Glos 80 B5
Saintbury Glos 100 D2
Saint's Hill Kent 52 E4
Saith ffynnon Flint 181 F11
Salcombe Devon 9 G9
Salcombe Regis Devon 15 D9
Salcott-cum-Virley Essex 88 C6
Salden Bucks 102 F6
Sale Gtr Man 184 C3
Sale Green Worcs 117 F8
Saleby Lincs 191 F7
Salehurst E Sus 38 C2
Salem Carms 94 F2
Salem Ceredig 128 G3
Salem Corn 4 G4
Salen Argyll 289 E7
Salen Highld 289 C8
Salendine Nook W Yorks 196 D6
Salenside Borders 261 E11
Salesbury Lancs 203 G9
Saleway Worcs 117 F8
Salford C Beds 103 D8
Salford Gtr Man 184 B4
Salford Oxon 100 F5
Salford Ford C Beds 103 D8
Salford Priors Warks 117 G11
Salfords Sur 51 D9
Salhouse Norf 160 G6
Saligo Argyll 274 G3
Salisbury Wilts 31 B10
Salkeld Dykes Cumb 230 D6
Sallachan Highld 289 C11
Sallachy Highld 295 B11
Sallachy Highld 309 J5
Salle Norf 160 E2
Salmans Kent 52 E4
Salmonby Lincs 190 G4
Salmond's Muir Angus 287 D9
Salmonhutch Devon 14 B2
Salperton Glos 99 G11
Salperton Park Glos 81 B9
Salph End Beds 121 G11
Salsburgh N Lnrk 268 C6
Salt Staffs 151 D9
Salt Coates Cumb 238 G5
Salt End E Yorks 201 B7
Salt Hill Slough 66 C3
Salta Cumb 229 B7
Saltaire W Yorks 205 F8
Saltash Corn 7 D8
Saltburn Highld 301 C7
Saltburn-by-the-Sea Redcar 235 G9
Saltby Leics 155 D7
Saltcoats Cumb 219 F11
Saltcoats E Loth 281 E9
Saltcoats N Ayrs 266 G4
Saltcotes Lancs 193 B11
Saltdean Brighton 36 G5
Salter Lancs 212 G2
Salter Street W Mid 118 C2
Salterbeck Cumb 228 F5
Salterforth Lancs 204 D3
Salters Heath Hants 48 B6
Salters Lode Norf 139 C11
Saltershill Shrops 150 D2
Salterswall W Ches 167 B10
Salterton Wilts 46 F6
Saltfleet Lincs 191 C7
Saltfleetby All Saints Lincs 191 C7
Saltfleetby St Clement Lincs 191 C7
Saltfleetby St Peter Lincs 190 D6
Saltford Bath 61 F7
Salthouse Cumb 210 F4
Salthouse Norf 177 E9
Saltley W Mid 133 F11
Saltmarsh Newport 59 C11
Saltmarshe E Yorks 199 C9
Saltness Orkney 314 G2
Saltness Shetland 313 J4
Saltney Flint 166 B5
Salton N Yorks 216 D4
Saltrens Devon 25 C7
Saltwell T & W 243 E7
Saltwick Northumb 242 B5
Saltwood Kent 55 F7
Salum Argyll 288 E2
Salvington W Sus 35 F10
Salwarpe Worcs 117 E7
Salwayash Dorset 16 B5
Sambourne Warks 117 E11
Sambourne Wilts 45 E11
Sambrook Telford 150 E4
Samhla W Isles 296 E3
Samlesbury Lancs 203 G7
Samlesbury Bottoms Lancs 194 B6
Sampford Arundel Som 27 D10
Sampford Brett Som 42 E5
Sampford Chapple Devon 25 G10
Sampford Courtenay Devon 25 G10
Sampford Moor Som 27 D10
Sampford Peverell Devon 27 E8
Sampford Spiney Devon 12 G6
Sampool Bridge Cumb 211 B9
Samuel's Corner Essex 70 B3
Samuelston E Loth 281 G9
Sanachan Highld 299 E8
Sanaigmore Argyll 274 F3
Sanclêr = St Clears Carms 74 B3
Sancreed Corn 1 D4
Sancton E Yorks 208 F4
Sand Highld 307 K4
Sand Shetland 313 J5
Sand Som 44 D2
Sand Gate Cumb 211 D7
Sand Hole E Yorks 208 F2
Sand Hutton N Yorks 207 B9
Sand Side Cumb 210 C4
Sand Side Lancs 202 C4
Sandaig Highld 295 E9
Sandal W Yorks 197 D10
Sandal Magna W Yorks 197 D10
Sandale Cumb 229 C10
Sandavore Highld 294 G6
Sandbach E Ches 168 C3
Sandbach Heath E Ches 168 C3
Sandbank Argyll 276 E3
Sandbanks Kent 70 G4
Sandbanks Poole 18 D6
Sandborough Staffs 152 F2
Sandbraes Lincs 200 G6
Sandend Aberds 302 C5
Sanderstead London 67 G10
Sandfields Glos 99 G8
Sandfields Neath 57 C8
Sandfields Staffs 134 B2
Sandford Cumb 222 B4
Sandford Devon 26 G4
Sandford Dorset 18 D4
Sandford Hants 31 G11
Sandford I o W 20 E6
Sandford N Som 44 B2
Sandford S Lnrk 268 G4
Sandford Shrops 148 E6
Sandford Shrops 149 C11
Sandford W Yorks 205 F11
Sandford Worcs 99 B7
Sandford Batch N Som 44 B2
Sandford Hill Stoke 168 G6
Sandford on Thames Oxon 83 E8
Sandford Orcas Dorset 29 C10
Sandford St Martin Oxon 101 F8
Sandfordhill Aberds 303 E11
Sandgate Kent 55 G7
Sandgreen Dumfries 237 D7
Sandhaven Aberds 303 C9
Sandhaven Argyll 276 E3
Sandhead Dumfries 236 E2
Sandhill Bucks 102 F4
Sandhill Cambs 139 F11
Sandhill S Yorks 198 F2
Sandhills Dorset 29 E11
Sandhills Dorset 29 G9
Sandhills Mers 182 C4
Sandhills Oxon 83 D9
Sandhills Sur 50 F2
Sandhills W Yorks 206 F3
Sandhoe Northumb 241 D11
Sandhole Argyll 275 D11
Sandholme E Yorks 208 G2
Sandholme Lincs 156 B6
Sandhurst Brack 65 G10
Sandhurst Glos 98 G6
Sandhurst Kent 38 B3
Sandhurst Cross Kent 38 B3
Sandhutton N Yorks 215 C7
Sandiacre Derbys 153 B9
Sandilands Lincs 191 E8
Sandilands S Lnrk 259 B9
Sandiway W Ches 183 G10
Sandleheath Hants 31 E10
Sandling Kent 53 B9
Sandlow Green E Ches 168 B3
Sandness Shetland 313 H3
Sandon Essex 88 E2
Sandon Herts 104 E6
Sandon Staffs 151 C8
Sandonbank Staffs 151 D8
Sandown I o W 21 E7
Sandown Park Kent 52 E6
Sandpit Dorset 28 G6
Sandpits Glos 98 F6
Sandplace Corn 6 D5
Sandridge Herts 85 C11
Sandridge Wilts 62 F2
Sandringham Norf 158 D3
Sands Bucks 84 G4
Sands End London 67 D9
Sandsend N Yorks 227 C7
Sandside Cumb 210 D6
Sandside Cumb 211 C9
Sandside Orkney 314 F2
Sandside Ho Highld 310 C3
Sandsound Shetland 313 J5
Sandtoft N Lincs 199 F8
Sandvoe Shetland 312 D5
Sandway Kent 53 C11
Sandwell W Mid 133 F10
Sandwich Kent 55 B10
Sandwich Bay Estate Kent 55 B11
Sandwick Cumb 221 B8
Sandwick Orkney 314 H4
Sandwick Shetland 313 L6
Sandwith Cumb 219 C9
Sandwith Newtown Cumb 219 C9
Sandy C Beds 104 B3
Sandy Carms 75 E7
Sandy Bank Lincs 174 E3
Sandy Carrs Durham 234 C3
Sandy Cross E Sus 37 C9
Sandy Cross Sur 49 D11
Sandy Down Hants 20 B2
Sandy Gate Devon 14 C5
Sandy Haven Pembs 72 D5
Sandy Lane W Yorks 205 F8
Sandy Lane Wilts 62 F3
Sandy Lane Wrex 166 G5
Sandy Way I o W 20 E5
Sandybank Orkney 314 C5
Sandycroft Flint 166 B4
Sandyford Dumfries 248 E6
Sandyford Stoke 168 E5
Sandygate Devon 14 G3
Sandygate I o M 192 C4
Sandygate S Yorks 186 D4
Sandyhills Dumfries 237 D10
Sandylake Corn 6 C2
Sandylands Lancs 211 G8
Sandylands Som 27 C10
Sandylane Swansea 56 D5
Sandypark Devon 13 D10
Sandysike Cumb 239 D9
Sangobeg Highld 308 C4
Sangomore Highld 308 C4
Sanham Green W Berks 63 F10
Sankey Bridges Warr 183 D9
Sankyns Green Worcs 116 E5
Sanna Highld 288 C6
Sannadhbaig W Isles 297 G4
Sannadhbaig W Isles 304 E6
Sannox N Ayrs 255 C11
Sanquhar Dumfries 247 B7
Sansaw Heath Shrops 149 E10
Santon Cumb 220 E2
Santon N Lincs 200 E2
Santon Bridge Cumb 220 E2
Santon Downham Suff 140 F6
Sapcote Leics 135 E9
Sapey Bridge Worcs 116 F4
Sapey Common Hereford 116 E4
Sapiston Suff 125 B8
Sapley Cambs 122 C4
Sapperton Derbys 152 C3
Sapperton Glos 80 E6
Sapperton Lincs 155 C10
Saracen's Head Lincs 156 D6
Sarclet Highld 310 E7
Sardis Carms 75 D9
Sardis Pembs 73 D10
Sarisbury Hants 33 F8
Sarn Bridgend 58 C2
Sarn Flint 181 F10
Sarn Powys 130 E4
Sarn Bach Gwyn 144 D6
Sarn Meyllteyrn Gwyn 144 C4
Sarnau Carms 74 B4
Sarnau Ceredig 110 G6
Sarnau Gwyn 147 B9
Sarnau Powys 95 E10
Sarnau Powys 148 F4
Sarnesfield Hereford 115 G7
Saron Carms 75 C10
Saron Carms 93 D7
Saron Denb 165 C8
Saron Gwyn 163 B8
Saron Gwyn 163 D7
Sarratt Herts 85 F8
Sarratt Bottom Herts 85 F8
Sarre Kent 71 G9
Sarsden Oxon 100 G5
Sarsden Halt Oxon 100 G5
Sarsgrum Highld 308 C3
Sasaig Highld 295 E8
Sascott Shrops 149 G8
Satley Durham 233 C8
Satmar Kent 55 F9
Satran Highld 294 B6
Satron N Yorks 223 F8
Satterleigh Devon 25 C11
Satterthwaite Cumb 220 G6
Satwell Oxon 65 C8
Sauchen Aberds 293 B8
Saucher Perth 286 D5
Sauchie Clack 279 C7
Sauchieburn Aberds 293 G8
Saughall W Ches 182 G5
Saughall Massie Mers 182 D3
Saughton Edin 280 G4
Saughtree Borders 250 D3
Saul Glos 80 D2
Saundby Notts 188 D3
Saundersfoot Pembs 73 E10
Saunderton Bucks 84 E3
Saunderton Lee Bucks 84 F4
Saunton Devon 40 F3
Sausthorpe Lincs 174 B5
Saval Highld 309 J5
Savary Highld 289 E8
Saveock Corn 4 F5
Saverley Green Staffs 151 B9
Savile Park W Yorks 196 C5
Savile Town W Yorks 197 C8
Sawbridge Warks 119 D10
Sawbridgeworth Herts 87 B7
Sawdon N Yorks 217 B8
Sawley Derbys 153 C9
Sawley Lancs 203 D11
Sawley N Yorks 214 F4
Sawood W Yorks 204 G6
Sawston Cambs 105 B9
Sawtry Cambs 138 G3
Sawyer's Hill Som 27 C11
Sawyers Hill Wilts 81 G8
Saxby Leics 154 F6
Saxby Lincs 189 D8
Saxby W Sus 35 G7
Saxby All Saints N Lincs 200 D3
Saxelbye Leics 154 E4
Saxham Street Suff 125 E11
Saxilby Lincs 188 F5
Saxlingham Norf 159 B10
Saxlingham Green Norf 142 D4
Saxlingham Nethergate Norf 142 D4
Saxlingham Thorpe Norf 142 D4
Saxmundham Suff 127 E7
Saxon Street Cambs 124 F3
Saxondale Notts 154 B3
Saxtead Suff 126 D5
Saxtead Green Suff 126 E5
Saxtead Little Green Suff 126 D5
Saxthorpe Norf 160 C2
Saxton N Yorks 206 F5
Sayers Common W Sus 36 D3
Scackleton N Yorks 216 E2
Scadabhagh W Isles 305 J3
Scaftworth Notts 187 C11
Scagglethorpe N Yorks 216 E6
Scaitcliffe Lancs 195 B9
Scalan Moray 292 B4
Scalasaig Argyll 274 D4
Scalby E Yorks 199 B10
Scalby N Yorks 227 G10
Scald End Beds 121 F10
Scaldwell Northants 120 C5
Scale Hall Lancs 211 G9
Scale Houses Cumb 231 B7
Scaleby Cumb 239 E11
Scalebyhill Cumb 239 E10
Scales Cumb 210 E5
Scales Cumb 230 F2
Scales Cumb 231 C7
Scales Lancs 202 G5
Scalford Leics 154 E5
Scaling Redcar 226 C4
Scaliscro W Isles 304 F3
Scallasaig Highld 295 D10
Scallastle Argyll 289 F8
Scalloway Shetland 313 K6
Scalpay W Isles 305 J4
Scalpay Ho Highld 295 C8
Scalpsie Argyll 255 B11
Scamadale Highld 295 F9
Scamblesby Lincs 190 F3
Scamland E Yorks 207 E11
Scammadale Argyll 289 G10
Scamodale Highld 289 B10
Scampston N Yorks 217 D7
Scampton Lincs 189 F7
Scaniport Highld 300 F6
Scapa Orkney 314 F4
Scapegoat Hill W Yorks 196 D5
Scar Orkney 314 B6
Scar Head Cumb 220 G5
Scarborough N Yorks 217 B10
Scarcewater Corn 5 E8
Scarcliffe Derbys 171 B7
Scarcroft W Yorks 206 E3
Scarcroft Hill W Yorks 206 E3
Scardroy Highld 300 D2
Scarff Shetland 312 E4
Scarfskerry Highld 310 B6
Scargill Durham 223 C11
Scarinish Argyll 288 E2
Scarisbrick Lancs 193 E11
Scarness Cumb 229 E10
Scarning Norf 159 G9
Scarrington Notts 172 G2
Scarth Hill Lancs 194 F2
Scarthingwell N Yorks 206 F5
Scartho NE Lincs 201 F9
Scarvister Shetland 313 J5
Scarwell Orkney 314 D2
Scatness Shetland 313 M5
Scatraig Highld 301 F7
Scatwell Ho Highld 300 D3
Scawby N Lincs 200 F3
Scawsby S Yorks 198 G5
Scawthorpe S Yorks 198 F5
Scawton N Yorks 215 C10
Scayne's Hill W Sus 36 C5
Scethrog Powys 96 F2
Scholar Green E Ches 168 D4
Scholemoor W Yorks 205 G8
Scholes Gtr Man 194 F5
Scholes S Yorks 186 B5
Scholes W Yorks 197 B7
Scholes W Yorks 197 F7
Scholes W Yorks 204 F6
Scholes W Yorks 206 F3
Scholey Hill W Yorks 197 B11
School Aycliffe Durham 233 G11
School Green Essex 106 E4
School Green I o W 20 D2
School Green W Ches 167 C10
School Green W Yorks 205 G8
School House Dorset 28 G5
Schoolgreen Wokingham 65 F8
Schoolhill Aberds 293 D11
Sciberscross Highld 309 H7
Scilly Bank Cumb 219 B9
Scissett W Yorks 197 E8
Scleddau Pembs 91 E8
Sco Ruston Norf 160 E5
Scofton Notts 187 E10
Scole Norf 126 B2
Scole Common Norf 142 G2
Scolpaig W Isles 296 D3
Scone Perth 286 E5
Sconser Highld 295 B7
Scoonie Fife 287 G7
Scoor Argyll 274 B5
Scopwick Lincs 173 D9
Scoraig Highld 307 K5
Scorborough E Yorks 208 D6
Scorrier Corn 4 G4
Scorriton Devon 8 B4
Scorton Lancs 202 D6
Scorton N Yorks 224 E5
Scot Hay Staffs 168 F4
Scot Lane End Gtr Man 194 F6
Scotbheinn W Isles 296 F4
Scotby Cumb 239 G10
Scotch Corner N Yorks 224 E4
Scotches Derbys 170 F4
Scotforth Lancs 202 B5
Scotgate W Yorks 196 E6
Scothern Lincs 189 F8
Scotland Leics 136 D3
Scotland Leics 153 E7
Scotland Lincs 155 C10
Scotland W Berks 64 F5
Scotland End Oxon 100 E6
Scotland Gate Northumb 253 G7
Scotland Street Suff 107 D9
Scotlands W Mid 133 C8
Scotlandwell Perth 286 G5
Scots' Gap Northumb 252 F2
Scotsburn Highld 301 B7
Scotscalder Station Highld 310 D4
Scotscraig Fife 287 E8
Scotston Aberds 293 F9
Scotston Perth 286 C3
Scotstoun Glasgow 267 B10
Scotstown Highld 289 C10
Scotswood T & W 242 E5
Scotswood Windsor 66 F2
Scott Willoughby Lincs 155 B11
Scottas Highld 295 E9
Scotter Lincs 199 G11
Scotterthorpe Lincs 199 G11
Scottlethorpe Lincs 155 E11
Scotton Lincs 188 B5
Scotton N Yorks 206 B2
Scotton N Yorks 224 F3
Scottow Norf 160 E5
Scoughall E Loth 282 E2
Scoulag Argyll 266 D2
Scoulton Norf 141 C9
Scounslow Green Staffs 151 D11
Scourie Highld 306 E6
Scourie More Highld 306 E6
Scousburgh Shetland 313 M5
Scout Dike S Yorks 197 G8
Scout Green Cumb 221 D11
Scouthead Gtr Man 196 F3
Scowles Glos 79 C9
Scrabster Highld 310 B4
Scraesburgh Borders 262 F5
Scrafield Lincs 174 B4
Scragged Oak Kent 69 G10
Scrainwood Northumb 251 B11
Scrane End Lincs 174 G5
Scrapsgate Kent 70 E2
Scraptoft Leics 136 B2
Scrapton Som 28 E3
Scratby Norf 161 F10
Scrayingham N Yorks 216 G4
Scredda Corn 5 E10
Scredington Lincs 173 G9
Screedy Som 27 B9
Scremby Lincs 174 B6
Scremerston Northumb 273 F10
Screveton Notts 172 G2
Scrivelsby Lincs 174 B3
Scriven N Yorks 206 B2
Scronkey Lancs 202 D4
Scrooby Notts 187 C11
Scropton Derbys 152 C3
Scrub Hill Lincs 174 D2
Scruton N Yorks 224 G5
Scrwgan Powys 148 E3
Scuddaborg Highld 298 C3
Scuggate Cumb 239 C10
Sculcoates Hull 209 G7
Sculthorpe Norf 159 C7
Scunthorpe N Lincs 199 E11
Scurlage Swansea 56 D3
Sea Som 28 E4
Sea Mill Cumb 210 F5
Sea Mills Bristol 6
Sea Mills Corn 1
Sea Palling Norf 16
Seaborough Dorset 2
Seabridge Staffs 16
Seabrook Kent 5
Seaburn T & W 243
Seacombe Mers 18
Seacox Heath Kent 5
Seacroft Lincs 17
Seacroft W Yorks 20
Seadyke Lincs 15
Seafar N Lnrk 27
Seafield Highld 31
Seafield Midloth 27
Seafield S Ayrs 25
Seafield W Loth 269
Seaford E Sus 2
Seaforth Mers 18
Seagrave Leics 15
Seagry Heath Wilts 6
Seaham Durham 23
Seahouses Northumb 26
Seal Kent 5
Sealand Flint 16
Seale Sur 49
Seamer N Yorks 217
Seamer N Yorks 22
Seamill N Ayrs 26
Searby Lincs 20
Seasalter Kent 7
Seascale Cumb 219
Seathorne Lincs 17
Seathwaite Cumb 22
Seathwaite Cumb 22
Seatle Cumb 21
Seatoller Cumb 22
Seaton Corn 6
Seaton Cumb 22
Seaton Devon 15
Seaton Durham 23
Seaton E Yorks 20
Seaton Kent 5
Seaton Northumb 24
Seaton Rutland 13
Seaton Burn T & W 24
Seaton Carew Hrtlpl 23
Seaton Delaval Northumb 24
Seaton Ross E Yorks 207
Seaton Sluice Northumb 24
Seatown Aberds 30
Seatown Aberds 303
Seatown Dorset 1
Seaureaugh Moor Corn
Seave Green N Yorks 225
Seaview I o W 2
Seaville Cumb 23
Seavington St Mary Som 2
Seavington St Michael Som 2
Seawick Essex 89
Sebastopol Torf 7
Sebay Orkney 31
Sebergham Cumb 23
Sebiston Velzian Orkney 31
Seckington Warks 13
Second Coast Highld 30
Second Drove Cambs 139
Sedbergh Cumb 22
Sedbury Glos 7
Sedbusk N Yorks 22
Seddington C Beds 10
Sedgeberrow Worcs 99
Sedgebrook Lincs 15
Sedgefield Durham 23
Sedgeford Norf 15
Sedgehill Wilts 3
Sedgemere W Mid 11
Sedgley W Mid 13
Sedgley Park Gtr Man 195
Sedgwick Cumb 211
Sedlescombe E Sus 3
Sedlescombe Street E Sus 3
Sedrup Bucks 8
Seed Kent 5
Seed Lee Lancs 19
Seedley Gtr Man 18
Seend Wilts 6
Seend Cleeve Wilts 6
Seend Head Wilts 6
Seer Green Bucks 8
Seething Norf 14
Seething Wells London 6
Sefton Mers 193
Segensworth Hants 3
Seggat Aberds 30
Seghill Northumb 24
Seifton Shrops 13
Seighford Staffs 15
Seilebost W Isles 30
Seion Gwyn 16
Seisdon Staffs 13
Seisiadar W Isles 30
Selattyn Shrops 14
Selborne Hants 4
Selby N Yorks 20
Selgrove Kent 5
Selham W Sus 3
Selhurst London 6
Selkirk Borders 26
Sellack Hereford 9
Sellack Boat Hereford 9
Sellafirth Shetland 31
Sellan Corn
Sellibister Orkney 31
Sellick's Green Som 2
Sellindge Kent 5
Selling Kent 5
Sells Green Wilts 6
Selly Hill N Yorks 22
Selly Oak W Mid 13
Selly Park W Mid 13
Selmeston E Sus 2
Selsdon London 6
Selsey W Sus 2
Selsfield Common W Sus 5
Selside Cumb 22
Selside N Yorks 21
Selsley Glos 8
Selsmore Hants 2
Selson Kent 5
Selsted Kent 5
Selston Notts 17
Selston Common Notts 17
Selston Green Notts 17
Selwick Orkney 31
Selworthy Som 4
Sem Hill Wilts 3
Semblister Shetland 31
Semer Suff 10
Semington Wilts 6
Semley Wilts 3
Sempringham Lincs 15
Send Sur 5
Send Grove Sur 5
Send Marsh Sur 5
Senghenydd Caerph 7
Sennen Corn 1

Column 1 (left edge cut off)

nen Cove Corn 1 D3
nybridge =
en Senni Powys 95 F8
by Notts 187 D10
rington Wilts 46 F5
say N Yorks 215 D9
hey Norf 158 G2
er Hants 32 G4
er Mains E Loth 281 E8
er Shetland 312 G6
er Shetland 313 H5
er Shetland 313 L6
iscarth Orkney 314 E3
en N Yorks 212 G6
rington N Lnrk 216 E6
en Kings London 68 B3
en Sisters =
endulais Neath 76 D4
en Springs Glos 81 B7
en Star Green Essex 107 F8
enhampton Glos 99 G10
nhampton Swindon 82 G2
enoaks Kent 52 C4
enoaks Common 52 C4
enoaks Weald Kent 52 C4
ern Beach S Glos 60 B4
ern Stoke Worcs 99 C7
ernhampton Swindon 82 G2
ck End Beds 121 G11
ngton Kent 54 E4
ards End Essex 105 C11
ardstone Beds 86 F5
ardstonebury Essex 86 F5
ell C Beds 103 G9
erby E Yorks 218 F3
organ Corn 2 C6
stern Leics 155 E7
ow N Yorks 225 D9
ncote Glos 100 E3
rasta Mhor W Isles 305 J2
garstaigh W Isles 304 B7
ven = Skewen Neath 57 B8
o Hill Glos 80 B6
kerley Shrops 132 B6
kerstone Leics 135 B7
klecross Derbys 153 C8
kleford Sur 50 D2
kleton N Yorks 196 B3
klewell London 67 B10
klford Sur 50 D2
le W Yorks 196 C2
loxhurst Kent 234 C2
lingfield Suff 143 G8
loxhurst Kent 54 F3
lsworth Blkburn 195 B8
lwell Glos 80 F3
lwell Norf 141 G8
lwell W Yorks 206 F2
don Devon 14 G4
fleet I o W 20 D4
ford Essex 106 F4
ford Som 45 G8
ford Sur 50 D4
ford Green Essex 106 F4
loch Shrops 302 G3
lowford Devon 25 B11
lowford Devon 41 E8
lowford Staffs 151 D7
msford West Kent 102 D7
stone Bucks 102 D7
inley Green Sur 50 E4
don Argyll 276 D5
dwick Highld 301 B8
combe I o W 20 D6
den Hants 49 E7
den Green Hants 49 E7
khouse Northumb 243 B7
franklin I o W 21 E7
nochie S Ayrs 255 E10
nnochill Stirl 277 B10
nquhar Aberds 302 F5
nwell Fife 287 E8
nzie Perth 286 B6
o Cumb 221 B11
bridge Glos 79 B11
wick Dorset 30 G6
wick Som 44 F2
cott Wilts 45 D9
t End W Mid 134 F3
dlow Derbys 153 C8
reshill Staffs 133 B8
lston N Yorks 197 D11
lston Common 197 D11
mans Cross W Mid 118 B2
ral Street Medway 69 E9
nbrook Beds 121 B11
nheyford Lancs 195 C11
nford Leics 135 E9
nhill Green Dorset 30 F2
roe Green Lancs 202 G6
row N Yorks 214 E6
p Street Norf 161 E7
npenhoe C Beds 103 C11
nperton Staffs 251 C11
ngs Gtr Man 195 E8
pley Heath Staffs 151 B11
press Glos 79 E11
rp's Corner E Sus 23 B9
rpsbridge E Sus 36 C6
rpstone Bath 45 B9
rpthorpe W Sus 51 G11
rptor Corn 11 G11
rpway Gate Worcs 117 D9
rrington S Yorks 197 B10
rrow S Yorks 186 B4
rterling Kent 55 B9
tterford Worcs 132 G5
ugh Prior Devon 7 C10
vington I o W ...
n Gtr Man 196 F2
n Swindon 62 B6
n W Berks 64 F3
n Wilts 61 E11
n Common Glos 98 F3
n Green Herts 104 C5
n Green Lancs 194 D4
n Green S Lnrk 205 C11
n Heath E Ches 184 F3
n Heath Gtr Man 184 B6
w'Lands S Yorks 197 F10

Column 2

Shaw Mills N Yorks 214 G5
Shaw Side Gtr Man 196 F2
Shawbank Shrops 131 G9
Shawbirch Telford 150 G2
Shawbury Shrops 149 E11
Shawclough Gtr Man 195 E11
Shawdon Hall Northumb 264 G3
Shawell Leics 135 G10
Shawfield Gtr Man 195 E11
Shawfield Staffs 169 C9
Shawfield Head N Yorks 205 C11
Shawford Hants 33 C7
Shawford Som 45 C9
Shawforth Lancs 195 C11
Shawhead Dumfries 237 B10
Shawhead S Lnrk 268 C4
Shawlands Glasgow 267 C11
Shawsburn S Lnrk 268 E5
Shawton S Lnrk 268 F3
Shawtonhill S Lnrk 268 F3
Shay Gate W Yorks 205 F8
Sheandow Moray 302 F2
Shear Cross Wilts 45 E11
Shearington Dumfries 238 D2
Shearsby Leics 136 E2
Shearston Som 43 G9
Shebbear Devon 24 F6
Shebdon Staffs 150 D5
Shebster Highld 310 C4
Sheddens E Renf 267 D11
Shedfield Hants 33 E8
Sheen Staffs 169 C10
Sheepbridge Derbys 186 G5
Sheepdrove W Berks 63 D10
Sheeplane C Beds 103 E8
Sheepridge Kent 65 B11
Sheepridge W Yorks 197 D7
Sheepscar Leeds 206 G2
Sheepscombe Glos 80 C5
Sheepstor Devon 7 B11
Sheepwash Devon 25 F7
Sheepwash Northumb 253 F7
Sheepway N Som 60 D3
Sheepy Magna Leics 134 C6
Sheepy Parva Leics 134 C6
Sheering Essex 87 C8
Sheerness Kent 70 E2
Sheerwater Sur 66 G4
Sheet Hants 34 C3
Sheet Shrops 115 C10
Sheffield Corn 1 D5
Sheffield S Yorks 186 D5
Sheffield Bottom W Berks 64 F6
Sheffield Green E Sus 36 C6
Sheffield Park S Yorks 186 D5
Shefford C Beds 104 D2
Shefford Woodlands W Berks 63 E11
Sheigra Highld 306 C6
Sheildmuir N Lnrk 268 D5
Sheinton Shrops 132 C2
Shelderton Shrops 115 B8
Sheldon Derbys 169 B11
Sheldon Devon 27 F10
Sheldon W Mid 134 G3
Sheldwich Kent 54 B4
Sheldwich Lees Kent 54 B4
Shelf Bridgend 58 C2
Shelf W Yorks 197 B8
Shelfanger Norf 142 G2
Shelfield W Mid 133 C10
Shelfield Warks 118 E2
Shelfield Green Warks 118 E2
Shelfleys Northants 120 F4
Shelford Notts 171 G11
Shelford Warks 135 F8
Shelland Suff 125 E10
Shellbrook Leics 152 F6
Shelley Essex 87 E9
Shelley Suff 107 D10
Shelley W Yorks 197 E8
Shelley Woodhouse W Yorks 197 E8
Shellingford Oxon 82 G4
Shellow Bowells Essex 87 D10
Shellwood Cross Sur 51 D8
Shelsley Beauchamp Worcs 116 E4
Shelsley Walsh Worcs 116 E4
Shelthorpe Leics 153 F10
Shelton Beds 121 D10
Shelton Norf 142 E4
Shelton Notts 172 G3
Shelton Shrops 149 G9
Shelton Stoke 168 F5
Shelton Green Norf 142 E4
Shelton Lock Derby 153 C7
Shelton under Harley Staffs 150 B6
Shelve Shrops 130 D6
Shelvin Devon 27 G11
Shelvingford Kent 71 F8
Shelwick Hereford 97 C10
Shelwick Green Hereford 97 C10
Shenfield Essex 87 G10
Shenington Oxon 101 C7
Shenley Herts 85 E11
Shenley Brook End M Keynes 103 D7
Shenley Church End M Keynes 103 D7
Shenley Fields W Mid 133 G10
Shenley Lodge M Keynes 103 D7
Shenley Wood M Keynes 102 D6
Shenmore Hereford 97 D7
Shennanton Dumfries 236 C5
Shenstone Staffs 134 C2
Shenstone Worcs 117 C7
Shenstone Woodend Staffs 134 C2
Shenton Leics 135 C7
Shenval Highld 300 G4
Shenval Moray 302 G2
Shenvault Moray 301 E10
Shepeau Stow Lincs 156 G6
Shephall Herts 104 G5
Shepherd Hill W Yorks 197 C9
Shepherd's Bush London 67 D8
Shepherd's Gate Norf 157 F11
Shepherd's Green Oxon 65 D8
Shepherd's Hill Sur 50 G2
Shepherd's Patch Glos 80 D2
Shepherd's Port Norf 158 C3
Shepherdswell or Sibertswold Kent 55 D9
Shepley W Yorks 197 F7
Shepperdine S Glos 79 G10
Shepperton Sur 66 F5
Shepperton Green Sur 66 F5
Shepreth Cambs 105 B7

Column 3

Shepshed Leics 153 F9
Shepton Beauchamp Som 28 D6
Shepton Mallet Som 44 E6
Shepton Montague Som 45 G7
Shepway Kent 53 C9
Sheraton Durham 234 D4
Sherborne Dorset 13 G8
Sherborne Bath 44 B5
Sherborne Glos 81 C11
Sherborne St John Hants 48 B6
Sherbourne Warks 118 E5
Sherburn Street Suff 107 C9
Sherburn Durham 234 C2
Sherburn N Yorks 217 D9
Sherburn Grange Durham 234 C2
Sherburn Hill Durham 234 C2
Sherburn in Elmet N Yorks 206 G5
Shere Sur 50 D5
Shereford Norf 159 D7
Sherfield English Hants 32 C4
Sherfield on Loddon Hants 49 B7
Sherfin Lancs 195 B9
Sherford Devon 8 G5
Sherford Dorset 18 C4
Sherford Som 28 C2
Sheriff Hill T & W 243 E7
Sheriff Hutton N Yorks 216 F3
Sheriffhales Shrops 150 G5
Sheringham Norf 160 A3
Sherington M Keynes 103 B7
Shermanbury W Sus 36 D2
Shernal Green Worcs 117 E8
Shernborne Norf 158 C4
Sherrard's Green Worcs 98 B5
Sherrardspark Herts 86 C2
Sherrington Wilts 46 F3
Sherston Wilts 61 B11
Sherwood Nottingham 171 G9
Sherwood Green Devon 25 C9
Sherwood Park Kent 52 E6
Shettleston Glasgow 268 C2
Shevington Gtr Man 194 F4
Shevington Moor Gtr Man 194 E5
Shevington Vale Gtr Man 194 F4
Sheviock Corn 7 D7
Shewalton N Ayrs 257 B8
Shibden Head W Yorks 196 B5
Shide I o W 20 D5
Shiel Aberds 292 B4
Shiel Bridge Highld 295 D11
Shield Row Durham 242 G6
Shieldaig Highld 299 B8
Shieldaig Highld 299 D8
Shieldhall Glasgow 267 B10
Shieldhill Dumfries 248 F2
Shieldhill Falk 279 F7
Shieldhill S Lnrk 269 G10
Shielfoot Highld 289 C8
Shielhill Angus 287 B8
Shielhill Invclyd 276 G4
Shifford Oxon 82 E5
Shifnal Shrops 132 B4
Shilbottle Northumb 252 B5
Shilbottle Grange Northumb 252 B6
Shildon Durham 233 F10
Shillford E Renf 267 D8
Shillingford Devon 27 C7
Shillingford Oxon 83 G9
Shillingford Abbot Devon 14 D4
Shillingford St George Devon 14 D4
Shillingstone Dorset 30 E4
Shillington C Beds 104 E2
Shillmoor Northumb 251 B9
Shilton Oxon 82 D3
Shilton Warks 135 G8
Shilvington Northumb 252 G5
Shimpling Norf 142 G3
Shimpling Suff 125 G7
Shimpling Street Suff 125 G7
Shincliffe Durham 233 C11
Shiney Row T & W 243 G8
Shinfield Wokingham 65 F8
Shingay Cambs 104 B6
Shingham Norf 140 C5
Shingle Street Suff 109 C7
Shinner's Bridge Devon 8 C5
Shinness Highld 309 H5
Shipbourne Kent 52 C5
Shipdham Norf 141 B9
Shipdham Airfield Norf 141 B9
Shipham Som 44 B3
Shiphay Torbay 9 B7
Shiplake Oxon 65 D9
Shiplake Bottom Oxon 65 D8
Shiplake Row Oxon 65 D9
Shiplate N Som 43 B11
Shiplaw Borders 270 F4
Shipley Derbys 170 G6
Shipley Northumb 264 F5
Shipley Shrops 132 D6
Shipley W Sus 35 C10
Shipley W Yorks 205 F8
Shipley Bridge Sur 51 E10
Shipley Common Derbys 171 G7
Shipley Shiels Northumb 251 E7
Shipmeadow Suff 143 F7
Shippea Hill Cambs 140 G2
Shippon Oxon 83 F7
Shipston-on-Stour Warks 100 C5
Shipton Bucks 102 F5
Shipton Glos 81 B8
Shipton N Yorks 207 B7
Shipton Shrops 131 E11
Shipton Bellinger Hants 47 D8
Shipton Gorge Dorset 16 C5
Shipton Green W Sus 22 C4
Shipton Lee Bucks 102 G5
Shipton Moyne Glos 61 B11
Shipton Oliffe Glos 81 B8
Shipton on Cherwell Oxon 83 B7
Shipton Solers Glos 81 B8
Shipton-under-Wychwood Oxon 82 B3
Shirburn Oxon 83 F11
Shirdley Hill Lancs 193 E11
Shire Oak W Mid 133 C11
Shirecliffe S Yorks 186 C4
Shiregreen S Yorks 186 C5
Shirehampton Bristol 60 D4
Shiremoor T & W 243 C8
Shirenewton Mon 79 G7
Shireoaks Derbys 185 E9
Shireoaks Notts 187 E9
Shires Mill Fife 279 D10

Column 4

Shirkoak Kent 54 F2
Shirl Heath Hereford 115 F8
Shirland Derbys 170 D6
Shirlett Shrops 132 D3
Shirley Derbys 170 G2
Shirley Hants 19 B9
Shirley London 67 F11
Shirley W Mid 118 B2
Shirley Heath W Mid 118 B2
Shirley holms Hants 19 B11
Shirley Warren Soton 32 E5
Shirrell Heath Hants 33 E9
Shirwell Devon 40 F5
Shirwell Cross Devon 40 F5
Shiskine N Ayrs 255 E10
Shitterton Dorset 18 C2
Shobdon Hereford 115 E8
Shobley Hants 31 F11
Shobnall Staffs 152 E4
Shobrooke Devon 26 G5
Shoby Leics 154 F3
Shocklach W Ches 166 F6
Shocklach Green W Ches 166 F6
Shoeburyness Sthend 70 C2
Sholden Kent 55 C11
Sholing Soton 32 E6
Sholing Common Soton 33 E7
Sholver Gtr Man 196 F3
Shoot Hill Shrops 149 G8
Shootash Hants 32 C4
Shooters Hill London 68 D2
Shooterswood Herts 85 D7
Shop Corn 10 G3
Shop Corn 24 E2
Shop Devon 24 E5
Shop Corner Suff 108 E4
Shopford Cumb 240 C3
Shopnoller Som 43 G7
Shopp Hill W Sus 34 B6
Shopwyke W Sus 22 B5
Shore Gtr Man 196 D2
Shore W Yorks 196 B2
Shore Bottom Devon 28 G2
Shore Mill Highld 301 C7
Shoreditch London 67 C10
Shoreditch Som 28 C2
Shoregill Cumb 222 E5
Shoreham Kent 68 G4
Shoreham Beach W Sus 36 G2
Shoreham-by-Sea W Sus 36 G2
Shores Green Oxon 82 D5
Shoresdean Northumb 273 F9
Shoreside Shetland 313 J4
Shoreswood Northumb 273 F8
Shoreton Highld 300 C6
Shorley Hants 33 B9
Shorncliffe Camp Kent 55 F7
Shorncote Glos 81 F8
Shorne Kent 69 E7
Shorne Ridgeway Kent 69 E7
Shorne West Kent 69 E7
Short Cross W Mid 133 G9
Short Green Norf 141 F11
Short Heath Derbys 152 F6
Short Heath W Mid 133 C9
Short Heath W Mid 133 E11
Short Street Wilts 45 D10
Shortacombe Devon 12 D6
Shortacross Corn 6 D5
Shortbridge E Sus 37 C7
Shortfield Common Sur 49 E10
Shortgate E Sus 23 B7
Shortheath Hants 49 F9
Shortheath Sur 49 E10
Shorthill Shrops 131 B8
Shortlands London 67 F11
Shortlanesend Corn 4 F6
Shortlees E Ayrs 257 B10
Shortmoor Dorset 28 G2
Shortmoor Dorset 29 G7
Shorton Torbay 9 C7
Shortroods Renfs 267 B9
Shortstanding Glos 79 C9
Shortstown Beds 103 B11
Shortwood Glos 80 F4
Shortwood S Glos 61 D7
Shorwell I o W 20 D5
Shoscombe Bath 45 B8
Shoscombe Vale Bath 45 B8
Shotatton Shrops 149 E7
Shotesham Norf 142 D4
Shotgate Essex 88 G3
Shotley Northants 137 D8
Shotley Suff 108 E4
Shotley Bridge Durham 242 G4
Shotley Gate Suff 108 E4
Shotleyfield Northumb 242 G4
Shottenden Kent 54 C4
Shottermill Sur 49 G11
Shottery Warks 118 G3
Shotteswell Warks 101 C8
Shottisham Suff 108 C6
Shottle Derbys 170 F4
Shottlegate Derbys 170 F4
Shotton Durham 234 C4
Shotton Durham 234 F3
Shotton Flint 166 B4
Shotton Northumb 242 B6
Shotton Northumb 263 B11
Shotton Colliery Durham 234 C4
Shotts N Lnrk 269 C7
Shotwick W Ches 182 G4
Shouldham Norf 140 B3
Shouldham Thorpe Norf 140 B3
Shoulton Worcs 116 F6
Shover's Green E Sus 53 G7
Shraleybrook Staffs 168 F3
Shrawardine Shrops 149 F8
Shrawley Worcs 116 E6
Shreding Green Bucks 66 C4
Shrewley Warks 118 D4
Shrewsbury Shrops 149 G9
Shrewton Wilts 46 E5
Shripney W Sus 22 C6
Shrivenham Oxon 63 D9
Shropham Norf 141 E9
Shroton or Iwerne Courtney Dorset 30 E5
Shrub End Essex 107 G9
Shrubs Hill Sur 66 F3
Shrutherhill S Lnrk 268 F5
Shucknall Hereford 97 C11
Shudy Camps Cambs 106 C2
Shulishadermor Highld 298 E4
Shulista Highld 298 B4
Shuna Ho Argyll 275 C8
Shurdington Glos 81 C7
Shurlock Row Windsor 65 E11
Shurnock Worcs 117 E10
Shurrery Highld 310 D4
Shurrery Lodge Highld 310 D4
Shurton Som 43 E8
Shustoke Warks 134 E4
Shut Heath Staffs 151 E7
Shute Heath Staffs 151 E11

Column 5

Shute Devon 26 G5
Shute End Wilts 31 B11
Shutford Oxon 101 C7
Shuthonger Glos 99 D7
Shutlanger Northants 120 G4
Shutt Green Staffs 133 B7
Shutta Corn 6 E5
Shuttington Warks 134 C5
Shuttlesfield Kent 55 E7
Shuttlewood Derbys 187 G7
Shuttleworth Gtr Man 195 D10
Shutton Hereford 98 F3
Shwt Bridgend 57 D11
Siabost bho Dheas W Isles 304 D4
Siabost bho Thuath W Isles 304 D4
Siadar W Isles 304 C5
Siadar Iarach W Isles 304 C5
Siadar Uarach W Isles 304 C5
Sibbaldbie Dumfries 248 F4
Sibbertoft Northants 136 G3
Sibdon Carwood Shrops 131 F8
Sibford Ferris Oxon 101 D7
Sibford Gower Oxon 101 D7
Sible Hedingham Essex 106 F5
Sibley's Green Essex 106 F2
Sibsey Lincs 174 E4
Sibsey Fen Side Lincs 174 E4
Sibson Cambs 137 D11
Sibson Leics 135 C7
Sibster Highld 310 D7
Sibthorpe Notts 172 F3
Sibthorpe Notts 188 G2
Sibton Suff 127 D7
Sibton Green Suff 127 C7
Sicklesmere Suff 125 E7
Sicklinghall N Yorks 206 D3
Sid Devon 15 D8
Sidbrook Som 28 B3
Sidbury Devon 15 C8
Sidbury Shrops 132 F3
Sidcot N Som 44 B3
Sidcup London 68 E3
Siddal W Yorks 196 C6
Siddick Cumb 228 E6
Siddington E Ches 184 G4
Siddington Glos 81 F8
Siddington Heath E Ches 184 G4
Side of the Moor Gtr Man 195 E8
Sidemoor Worcs 117 C9
Sidestrand Norf 160 B5
Sideway Stoke 168 G5
Sidford Devon 15 C8
Sidlesham W Sus 22 D5
Sidlesham Common W Sus 22 C5
Sidley E Sus 38 E2
Sidlow Sur 51 D9
Sidmouth Devon 15 D8
Sidway Staffs 150 B5
Sigglesthorne E Yorks 209 D9
Sighthill Edin 280 G3
Sighthill Glasgow 268 B2
Sigingstone = Tresigin V Glam 58 E3
Signet Oxon 82 C2
Sigwells Som 29 C10
Silchester Hants 64 G6
Sildinis W Isles 305 G4
Sileby Leics 153 F11
Silecroft Cumb 210 C2
Silfield Norf 142 D2
Silford Devon 24 B6
Silian Ceredig 111 G11
Silk Willoughby Lincs 173 G9
Silkstead Hants 32 C6
Silkstone S Yorks 197 F9
Silkstone Common S Yorks 197 G9
Silloth Cumb 238 G4
Sills Northumb 251 C8
Sillyearn Moray 302 D5
Siloh Carms 94 D4
Silpho N Yorks 227 G9
Silsden W Yorks 204 D6
Silsoe C Beds 103 D11
Silton Dorset 30 B3
Silver End Essex 88 B4
Silver End W Mid 133 F8
Silver Green Norf 142 E5
Silver Hill E Sus 38 B2
Silver Knap Som 29 C11
Silver Street Glos 80 E3
Silver Street Kent 69 G11
Silver Street Som 27 C11
Silver Street Som 44 A4
Silver Street Worcs 117 B11
Silverburn Midloth 270 C4
Silverdale Lancs 211 E9
Silverdale Staffs 168 F4
Silverdale Green Lancs 211 E9
Silvergate Norf 160 D3
Silverhill E Sus 38 E3
Silverhill Park E Sus 38 E4
Silverknowes Edin 280 F4
Silverley's Green Suff 126 B5
Silvermuir S Lnrk 269 F8
Silverstone Northants 102 C3
Silverton Devon 27 G7
Silverton W Dunb 277 E8
Silvertonhill S Lnrk 268 E4
Silvertown London 68 D2
Silverwell Corn 4 F4
Silvington Shrops 116 B2
Silwick Shetland 313 J4
Sim Hill S Yorks 197 G9
Simister Gtr Man 195 F10
Simmondley Derbys 185 C8
Simm's Cross Halton 183 D8
Simm's Lane End Mers 194 G4
Simonburn Northumb 241 C9
Simonsbath Som 41 F8
Simonside T & W 243 E8
Simonstone Lancs 203 G11
Simonstone N Yorks 223 G8
Simprim Borders 272 F6
Simpson M Keynes 103 D7
Simpson Pembs 72 B5
Simpson Cross Pembs 72 B5
Simpson Green W Yorks 205 F8
Sinclair's Hill Borders 272 E6
Sinclairston E Ayrs 257 F11
Sinclairtown Fife 280 C5
Sinderby N Yorks 214 C6
Sinderhope Northumb 241 G8
Sinderland Green Gtr Man 184 C2
Sindlesham Wokingham 65 F9
Sinfin Derby 152 C6
Sinfin Moor Derby 153 C7
Singdean Borders 250 C4
Single Hill Bath 45 B8
Singleborough Bucks 102 E5
Singleton Lancs 202 F3
Singleton W Sus 34 D4
Singlewell Kent 69 E7
Singret Wrex 166 D4

Column 6

Sinkhurst Green Kent 53 E10
Sinnahard Aberds 292 B6
Sinnington N Yorks 216 B4
Sinton Worcs 116 E6
Sinton Green Worcs 116 E6
Sion Hill Bath 61 E8
Sipson London 66 D5
Sirhowy Bl Gwent 77 C11
Sisland Norf 142 D6
Sissinghurst Kent 53 F9
Sisterpath Borders 272 F5
Siston S Glos 61 D7
Sithney Corn 2 D5
Sithney Common Corn 2 D5
Sittingbourne Kent 70 G2
Six Ashes Staffs 132 F5
Six Bells Bl Gwent 78 E2
Six Hills Leics 154 E2
Six Mile Bottom Cambs 123 F11
Sixhills Lincs 189 D11
Sixmile Kent 54 E6
Sixpenny Handley Dorset 31 D7
Sizewell Suff 127 E9
Skaigh Devon 13 B8
Skail Highld 308 E7
Skaill Orkney 314 F5
Skaill Orkney 314 E2
Skaill Orkney 314 G4
Skares E Ayrs 258 F2
Skateraw E Loth 282 F4
Skaw Shetland 312 B8
Skaw Shetland 312 G7
Skeabost Highld 298 E4
Skeabrae Orkney 314 D2
Skeeby N Yorks 224 E4
Skeete Kent 54 E6
Skeffington Leics 136 C4
Skeffling E Yorks 201 D11
Skegby Notts 171 C7
Skegby Notts 188 G3
Skegness Lincs 175 C9
Skelberry Shetland 313 G6
Skelberry Shetland 313 M5
Skelbo Highld 309 K7
Skelbo Street Highld 309 K7
Skelbrooke S Yorks 198 E4
Skeldyke Lincs 156 B6
Skelfhill Borders 249 C11
Skellingthorpe Lincs 188 G6
Skellister Shetland 313 H6
Skellorn Green E Ches 184 E6
Skellow S Yorks 198 E4
Skelmanthorpe W Yorks 197 E8
Skelmersdale Lancs 194 G3
Skelmonae Aberds 303 F8
Skelmorlie N Ayrs 266 B3
Skelmuir Aberds 303 E9
Skelpick Highld 308 D7
Skelton Cumb 230 D4
Skelton E Yorks 199 B9
Skelton N Yorks 223 E11
Skelton Redcar 226 B3
Skelton York 207 B7
Skelton Green Redcar 226 B3
Skelton-on-Ure N Yorks 215 F7
Skelwick Orkney 314 B4
Skelwith Bridge Cumb 220 E6
Skendleby Lincs 174 B6
Skendleby Psalter Lincs 190 G6
Skene Ho Aberds 293 C9
Skenfrith Mon 97 G9
Skerne Darl 224 B5
Skerne Park Darl 224 C5
Skeroblingarry Argyll 255 E8
Skerray Highld 308 C6
Skerricha Highld 306 D7
Skerryford Pembs 72 C5
Skerton Lancs 211 G9
Sketchley Leics 135 E8
Sketty Swansea 56 C6
Skewen = Sgiwen Neath 57 B8
Skewes Corn 5 B9
Skewsby N Yorks 216 E3
Skeyton Norf 160 D4
Skeyton Corner Norf 160 D5
Skiag Bridge Highld 307 G7
Skibo Castle Highld 309 L7
Skidbrooke Lincs 190 B6
Skidbrooke North End Lincs 190 B6
Skidby E Yorks 208 G6
Skilgate Som 27 C7
Skillington Lincs 155 D7
Skinburness Cumb 238 F4
Skinflats Falk 279 E8
Skinidin Highld 298 E2
Skinner's Bottom Corn 4 F4
Skinners Green W Berks 64 F3
Skinnet Highld 308 C5
Skinningrove Redcar 226 B4
Skipness Argyll 255 B9
Skippool Lancs 202 E3
Skiprigg Cumb 230 B3
Skipsea E Yorks 209 C9
Skipsea Brough E Yorks 209 C9
Skipton N Yorks 204 C5
Skipton-on-Swale N Yorks 215 D7
Skipwith N Yorks 207 F8
Skirbeck Lincs 174 G4
Skirbeck Quarter Lincs 174 G4
Skirethorns N Yorks 213 G9
Skirlaugh E Yorks 209 F8
Skirling Borders 260 B3
Skirmett Bucks 65 B9
Skirpenbeck E Yorks 207 B10
Skirwith Cumb 231 D8
Skirza Highld 310 C7
Skitby Cumb 239 D10
Skitham Lancs 202 E4
Skittle Green Bucks 84 E3
Skulamus Highld 295 C8
Skullomie Highld 308 C6
Skyborry Green Shrops 114 C5
Skye Green Essex 107 G7
Skye of Curr Highld 301 G9
Skyreholme N Yorks 213 G11
Slack Derbys 170 C5
Slack Derbys 170 D4
Slack W Yorks 196 B3
Slack Head Cumb 211 E9
Slackcote Gtr Man 196 F3
Slackhall Derbys 185 E9
Slackhead Moray 302 C4
Slackholme End Lincs 191 G8
Slacks of Cairnbanno Aberds 303 E8
Slad Glos 80 D5
Sladbrook Glos 98 E5
Slade Devon 27 D10
Slade Devon 40 D4
Slade Pembs 72 C6
Slade Swansea 56 E3
Slade End Oxon 83 G9
Slade Green London 68 D4
Slade Heath Staffs 133 B8
Slade Hooton S Yorks 187 D7
Sladen Green Hants 48 B4
Slades Green Worcs 99 E7
Sladesbridge Corn 10 G6

Column 7

Slaggyford Northumb 240 G5
Slaithwaite W Yorks 196 E5
Slaley Derbys 170 D3
Slaley Northumb 241 F11
Slamannan Falk 279 G7
Slape Cross Som 43 F10
Slapewath Redcar 226 B2
Slapton Bucks 103 G8
Slapton Devon 8 G6
Slapton Northants 102 B2
Slate Haugh Moray 302 C4
Slateford Edin 280 G4
Slatepit Dale Derbys 170 B4
Slattocks Gtr Man 195 F11
Slaugham W Sus 36 B3
Slaughterbridge Corn 11 D8
Slaughterford Wilts 61 E10
Slawston Leics 136 E5
Slay Pits S Yorks 199 F7
Sleaford Hants 49 F10
Sleaford Lincs 173 F9
Sleagill Cumb 221 B11
Sleap Shrops 149 D9
Sleapford Telford 150 F2
Sleapshyde Herts 85 D11
Sleastary Highld 309 K6
Slebech Pembs 73 B8
Sledge Green Worcs 98 E6
Sledmere E Yorks 217 G8
Sleetbeck Cumb 240 B2
Sleight Dorset 18 B5
Sleights N Yorks 227 D7
Slepe Dorset 18 C4
Sliabhna h-Airde W Isles 296 F3
Slickly Highld 310 C6
Sliddery N Ayrs 255 E10
Slideslow Worcs 117 C9
Sligachan Hotel Highld 294 C6
Slimbridge Glos 80 E2
Slindon Staffs 150 C6
Slindon W Sus 35 F7
Slinfold W Sus 50 G6
Sling Glos 79 D9
Sling Gwyn 163 B10
Slingsby N Yorks 216 E3
Slioch Aberds 302 F5
Slip End Beds 85 B9
Slip End Herts 104 D5
Slipper Ford W Yorks 204 E6
Slipton Northants 121 B9
Slitting Mill Staffs 151 F10
Slochd Highld 301 G8
Slockavullin Argyll 275 D9
Slogan Moray 302 E3
Sloley Norf 160 E5
Sloncombe Devon 13 D10
Sloothby Lincs 191 G7
Slough Slough 66 D3
Slough Green Som 28 C3
Slough Green W Sus 36 B3
Slough Hill Suff 125 G9
Soake Hants 33 E11
Soar Anglesey 178 G5
Soar Carms 94 F2
Soar Devon 9 G9
Soar Gwyn 146 B2
Soar Powys 95 E9
Soar-y-Mynydd Ceredig 112 G5
Soberton Hants 33 D10
Soberton Heath Hants 33 E10
Sockbridge Cumb 230 F6
Sockburn Darl 224 D6
Sockety Dorset 29 F7
Sodom Denb 181 G9
Sodom Shetland 313 G7
Sodom Wilts 62 C4
Sodylt Bank Shrops 148 B6
Soham Cambs 123 C11
Soham Cotes Cambs 123 B11
Soho London 67 C9
Soho Som 45 D7
Soho W Mid 133 F10
Solas W Isles 296 D4
Soldon Cross Devon 24 E4
Soldridge Hants 49 G7
Sole Street Kent 54 D5
Sole Street Kent 69 F7
Solfach = Solva Pembs 90 F5
Solihull W Mid 118 B2
Solihull Lodge W Mid 117 C11
Sollers Dilwyn Hereford 115 F8
Sollers Hope Hereford 98 E2
Sollom Lancs 194 D3
Solva = Solfach Pembs 90 F5
Somerby Leics 154 G5
Somerby Lincs 200 G5
Somercotes Derbys 170 E6
Somerdale Bath 61 F7
Somerford Dorset 19 C9
Somerford Staffs 133 B8
Somerford Keynes Glos 81 F8
Somerley W Sus 22 D4
Somerleyton Suff 143 D9
Somers Town London 67 C9
Somers Town Ptsmth 21 B8
Somersal Herbert Derbys 152 B2
Somersby Lincs 190 G4
Somersham Cambs 123 B8
Somersham Suff 107 B11
Somerton Newport 59 B10
Somerton Oxon 101 F9
Somerton Som 29 B7
Somerton Suff 124 G6
Somerton Hill Som 29 B7
Somerwood Shrops 149 G11
Sompting W Sus 35 F11
Sompting Abbotts W Sus 35 F11
Sonning Wokingham 65 D8
Sonning Common Oxon 65 D8
Sonning Eye Oxon 65 D8
Sontley Wrex 166 F4
Sookholme Notts 171 B8
Sopley Hants 19 B9
Sopwell Herts 85 D11
Sopworth Wilts 61 B10
Sorbie Dumfries 236 E6
Sordale Highld 310 C5
Sorisdale Argyll 288 C4
Sorley Devon 8 F4
Sorn E Ayrs 258 C2
Sornhill E Ayrs 258 C2
Sortat Highld 310 C6
Sotby Lincs 190 F2
Sothall S Yorks 186 E6
Sots Hole Lincs 173 C10
Sotterley Suff 143 G9
Soudley Shrops 131 F11
Soudley Shrops 150 E4
Soughley S Yorks 197 G8
Soughton = Sychdyn Flint 166 B2
Soulbury Bucks 103 F7

394 Sou – Sto

Soulby Cumb 222 C4
Soulby Cumb 230 F5
Souldern Oxon 101 E10
Souldrop Beds 121 E9
Sound E Ches 167 F10
Sound Shetland 313 H5
Sound Shetland 313 J6
Sound Heath E Ches 167 F10
Soundwell S Glos 60 D6
Sour Nook Cumb 230 C3
Sourhope Borders 263 E8
Sourin Orkney 314 C4
Sourlie N Ayrs 266 G6
Sourton Devon 12 C6
Soutergate Cumb 210 C4
South Acre Norf 158 G6
South Acton London 67 D7
South Alkham Kent 55 E8
South Allington Devon 9 G10
South Alloa Falk 279 C7
South Ambersham W Sus 34 C6
South Anston S Yorks 187 E8
South Ascot Windsor 66 F2
South Ashford Kent 54 E4
South Auchmachar Aberds 303 E9
South Baddesley Hants 20 B3
South Ballachulish Highld 284 B4
South Balloch S Ayrs 245 D8
South Bank Redcar 234 G6
South Bank York 207 C7
South Barrow Som 29 B10
South Beach Northumb 243 B8
South Beach = Marian-y-de Gwyn 145 C7
South Beddington London 67 G9
South Benfleet Essex 69 B9
South Bents T & W 243 E10
South Bersted W Sus 22 C6
South Blainslie Borders 271 G10
South Bockhampton Dorset 19 B9
South Bramwith S Yorks 198 E6
South Brent Devon 8 D3
South Brewham Som 45 F8
South Bromley London 67 C11
South Broomage Falk 279 E7
South Broomhill Northumb 252 D6
South Burlingham Norf 143 B7
South Cadbury Som 29 B10
South Cairn Dumfries 236 C1
South Carlton Lincs 189 F7
South Carlton Notts 187 E9
South Carne Corn 11 E10
South Cave E Yorks 208 G4
South Cerney Glos 81 F8
South Chailey E Sus 36 D5
South Chard Som 28 F4
South Charlton Northumb 264 E5
South Cheriton Som 29 C11
South Church Durham 233 F10
South Cliffe E Yorks 208 F3
South Clifton Notts 188 G4
South Clunes Highld 300 E5
South Cockerington Lincs 190 D5
South Common Devon 28 G4
South Cornelly Bridgend 57 E10
South Corriegills N Ayrs 256 C2
South Corrielaw Dumfries 248 G5
South Cove Suff 143 G9
South Creagan Argyll 289 E11
South Creake Norf 159 B7
South Crosland W Yorks 196 E6
South Croxton Leics 154 G3
South Croydon London 67 G10
South Cuil Highld 298 C3
South Dalton E Yorks 208 D5
South Darenth Kent 68 F5
South Denes Norf 143 C10
South Down Hants 33 C7
South Down Som 28 E2
South Duffield N Yorks 207 G9
South Dunn Highld 310 D5
South Earlswood Sur 51 D9
South Elkington Lincs 190 D3
South Elmsall W Yorks 198 E3
South Elphinstone E Loth 281 G7
South End Beds 103 B10
South End Bucks 103 F7
South End Cumb 210 G4
South End E Yorks 209 E9
South End Hants 31 D10
South-end Herts 86 B6
South End N Lincs 200 C6
South End Norf 141 E9
South Erradale Highld 299 B7
South Fambridge Essex 88 F5
South Farnborough Hants 49 C11
South Fawley W Berks 63 C11
South Ferriby N Lincs 200 C3
South Field E Yorks 200 B4
South Field Windsor 66 D3
South Flobbets Aberds 303 F7
South Garth Shetland 312 D7
South Garvan Highld 289 B11
South Glendale W Isles 297 K3
South Gluss Shetland 312 F5
South Godstone Sur 51 D11
South Gorley Hants 31 E11
South Gosforth T & W 242 D6
South Green Essex 89 B8
South Green Essex 87 G11
South Green Kent 69 G11
South Green Norf 157 F10
South Green Norf 159 G11
South Green Suff 126 B3
South Gyle Edin 280 G3
South-haa Shetland 312 E5
South Hackney London 67 C11
South Ham Hants 48 C6
South Hampstead London 67 C9
South Hanningfield Essex 88 F2
South Harefield London 66 B5
South Harrow London 66 B6
South Harting W Sus 34 D3
South Hatfield Herts 86 D2
South Hayling Hants 21 B10
South Hazelrigg Northumb 264 C3
South Heath Bucks 84 E6
South Heath Essex 89 B10
South Heighton E Sus 23 E7
South-heog Shetland 312 E5
South Hetton Durham 234 B3
South Hiendley W Yorks 197 E11
South Hill Corn 12 G2
South Hill N Som 43 B10
South Hill Pembs 72 C4
South Hinksey Oxon 83 E8
South Hole Devon 24 C2
South Holme N Yorks 216 D3
South Holmwood Sur 51 D7
South Hornchurch London 68 C4
South Huish Devon 8 G3
South Hykeham Lincs 172 C6
South Hylton T & W 243 F9
South Kelsey Lincs 189 B8
South Kensington London 67 D9
South Kessock Highld 300 E6
South Killingholme N Lincs 201 D7
South Kilvington N Yorks 215 C8
South Kilworth Leics 136 G2
South Kirkby W Yorks 198 E2
South Kirkton Aberds 293 C9
South Kiscadale N Ayrs 256 D2
South Knighton Devon 14 G2
South Knighton Leicester 136 C2
South Kyme Lincs 173 F11
South Lambeth London 67 D10
South Lancing W Sus 35 G11
South Lane S Yorks 197 F9
South Leigh Oxon 82 D5
South Leverton Notts 188 E3
South Littleton Worcs 99 B11
South Lopham Norf 141 G10
South Luffenham Rutland 137 C8
South Malling E Sus 36 E6
South Marston Swindon 63 B7
South Merstham Sur 51 C9
South Middleton Northumb 263 E11
South Milford N Yorks 206 G5
South Millbrex Aberds 303 E8
South Milton Devon 8 G4
South Mimms Herts 86 E2
South Molton Devon 26 B2
South Moor Durham 242 G5
South Moreton Oxon 64 B5
South Mundham W Sus 22 C5
South Muskham Notts 172 D3
South Newbald E Yorks 208 F4
South Newbarns Cumb 210 F4
South Newington Oxon 101 E8
South Newsham Northumb 243 B8
South Newton Wilts 46 G5
South Normanton Derbys 170 D6
South Norwood London 67 F10
South Nutfield Sur 51 D10
South Ockendon Thurrock 68 C5
South Ormsby Lincs 190 F5
South Ossett W Yorks 197 D9
South Otterington N Yorks 215 B7
South Owersby Lincs 189 C9
South Oxhey Herts 85 G10
South Park Sur 51 D8
South Pelaw Durham 243 G7
South Perrott Dorset 29 F7
South Petherton Som 28 D6
South Petherwin Corn 12 E2
South Pickenham Norf 141 C7
South Pill Corn 7 D8
South Pool Devon 8 G5
South Poorton Dorset 16 B6
South Port Argyll 284 E4
South Quilquox Aberds 303 F8
South Radworthy Devon 41 G9
South Rauceby Lincs 173 F8
South Raynham Norf 159 E7
South Reddish Gtr Man 184 C5
South Reston Lincs 190 E6
South Ruislip London 66 B6
South Runcton Norf 140 B2
South Scarle Notts 172 C4
South Shian Argyll 289 E11
South Shields T & W 243 D9
South Shore Blkpool 202 G2
South Side Durham 233 F8
South Side Orkney 314 D5
South Somercotes Lincs 190 C6
South Stainley N Yorks 214 G6
South Stainmore Cumb 222 C6
South Stanley Durham 242 G5
South Stifford Thurrock 68 D6
South Stoke Oxon 64 C6
South Stoke W Sus 35 F8
South Stour Kent 54 F4
South Street E Sus 36 D5
South Street Kent 54 B5
South Street Kent 68 G6
South Street Kent 69 G10
South Street Kent 70 F6
South Street London 52 B2
South Tawton Devon 13 C9
South Tehidy Corn 4 G3
South Thoresby Lincs 190 F6
South Tidworth Wilts 47 D8
South Tottenham London 67 B10
South Town Devon 14 E5
South Town Hants 49 F7
South Twerton Bath 61 G8
South Ulverston Cumb 210 D6
South View Hants 48 C6
South Voxter Shetland 313 G5
South Walsham Norf 161 G7
South Warnborough Hants 49 D8
South Weald Essex 87 G9
South Weirs Hants 32 G3
South Weston Oxon 84 F2
South Wheatley Corn 11 C10
South Wheatley Notts 188 D3
South Whiteness Shetland 313 J5
South Widcombe Bath 44 B5
South Wigston Leics 135 D11
South Willesborough Kent 54 E4
South Willingham Lincs 189 E11
South Wimbledon London 67 E9
South Wingate Durham 234 E4
South Wingfield Derbys 170 D5
South Witham Lincs 155 F8
South Wonford Devon 24 F5
South Wonston Hants 48 F3
South Woodford London 86 G6
South Woodham Ferrers Essex 88 F4
South Wootton Norf 158 E2
South Wraxall Wilts 61 G10
South Yardley W Mid 134 G2
South Yarrows Highld 310 E7
South Yeo Devon 25 G8
South Zeal Devon 13 C9
Southall London 66 C6
Southam Cumb 219 C9
Southam Glos 99 F9
Southam Warks 119 E8
Southampton Soton 32 E6
Southay Som 28 D6
Southborough Kent 52 E5
Southborough Bromley 68 F2
Southborough Kingston-u-Thames 67 F7
Southbourne Bmouth 19 C8
Southbourne W Sus 22 B3
Southbrook Wilts 45 G10
Southburgh Norf 141 C9
Southburn E Yorks 208 C5
Southchurch Sthend 70 B2
Southcoombe Oxon 100 F6
Southcote Reading 65 E7
Southcott Corn 11 B9
Southcott Devon 24 D6
Southcott Wilts 47 B7
Southcourt Bucks 84 C4
Southcrest Worcs 117 D10
Southdean Borders 250 B4
Southdene Mers 182 B6
Southdown Bath 61 G8
Southdown Corn 7 E8
Southease E Sus 36 F6
Southend Argyll 255 G7
Southend Bucks 65 B9
Southend Glos 80 F2
Southend London 67 E11
Southend Oxon 83 E9
Southend W Berks 64 D2
Southend W Berks 64 E5
Southend Wilts 63 E7
Southend-on-Sea Sthend 69 B11
Southerhouse Shetland 313 K5
Southerly Devon 12 D6
Southern Cross Brighton 36 F3
Southern Green Herts 104 E6
Southernby Cumb 230 D3
Southernden Kent 53 D11
Southerndown V Glam 57 G11
Southerness Dumfries 237 D11
Southery Norf 140 E2
Southey Green Essex 106 E5
Southfield Northumb 243 B7
Southfields London 67 E9
Southfields Thurrock 69 C7
Southfleet Kent 68 E6
Southford I o W 20 F6
Southgate Ceredig 111 A11
Southgate London 86 G3
Southgate Norf 159 C7
Southgate Norf 160 E2
Southgate Swansea 56 D5
Southgate W Sus 51 F9
Southill C Beds 104 C3
Southill Dorset 17 E9
Southington Hants 48 D4
Southlands Dorset 17 F9
Southleigh Devon 15 C10
Southmarsh Som 45 G8
Southmead Bristol 60 D5
Southminster Essex 89 F7
Southmoor Oxon 82 F5
Southoe Cambs 122 E3
Southolt Suff 126 D3
Southorpe P'boro 137 C11
Southover Dorset 17 C8
Southover E Sus 36 F6
Southover E Sus 37 B11
Southowram W Yorks 196 C6
Southport Mers 193 D10
Southpunds Shetland 313 L6
Southrepps Norf 160 B5
Southrey Lincs 173 B10
Southrop Glos 81 E11
Southrop Oxon 101 E7
Southrope Hants 49 E7
Southsea Ptsmth 21 B8
Southsea Wrex 166 E4
Southstoke Bath 61 G8
Southtown Norf 143 B10
Southtown Orkney 314 G4
Southtown Som 28 D4
Southtown Som 44 F5
Southville Devon 8 G4
Southville Torf 78 F3
Southwaite Cumb 230 C4
Southwark London 67 D10
Southwater W Sus 35 B11
Southwater Street W Sus 35 B11
Southway Plym 7 C9
Southway Som 44 E4
Southwell Dorset 17 G9
Southwell Notts 172 E2
Southwick Hants 33 F10
Southwick Northants 137 E10
Southwick Som 43 D11
Southwick T & W 243 F9
Southwick W Sus 36 F2
Southwick Wilts 45 B10
Southwold Suff 127 B10
Southwood Derbys 153 E7
Southwood Hants 49 B10
Southwood Norf 143 B7
Southwood Som 44 G5
Southwood Worcs 116 E4
Soval Lodge W Isles 304 F5
Sowber Gate N Yorks 215 B7
Sower Carr Lancs 202 E3
Sowerby N Yorks 215 C8
Sowerby W Yorks 196 C4
Sowerby Bridge W Yorks 196 C5
Sowerby Row Cumb 230 D3
Sowley Green Suff 124 G4
Sowood W Yorks 196 D5
Sowood Green W Yorks 196 D5
Sowton Devon 14 C5
Sowton Barton Devon 14 D2
Soyal Highld 309 K5
Soyland Town W Yorks 196 C4
Spa Common Norf 160 C5
Spacey Houses N Yorks 206 C2
Spalding Lincs 156 E4
Spaldington E Yorks 207 G11
Spaldwick Cambs 122 C2
Spalford Notts 172 B4
Spanby Lincs 155 B11
Spango Invclyd 276 G4
Spanish Green Hants 49 B7
Sparham Norf 159 F11
Sparhamhill Norf 159 F11
Spark Bridge Cumb 210 C6
Sparkbrook W Mid 133 G11
Sparkford Som 29 B10
Sparkhill W Mid 133 G11
Sparkwell Devon 7 D11
Sparl Shetland 312 G5
Sparnon Corn 1 E3
Sparnon Gate Corn 4 G3
Sparrow Green Norf 159 G9
Sparrow Hill Som 44 C2
Sparrowpit Derbys 185 E9
Sparrow's Green E Sus 52 G6
Sparsholt Hants 48 G2
Sparsholt Oxon 63 B10
Spartylea Northumb 232 B3
Spath Staffs 151 B11
Spaunton N Yorks 226 G4
Spaxton Som 43 F8
Spean Bridge Highld 290 E4
Spear Hill W Sus 35 D10
Spearywell Hants 32 B4
Speckington Som 29 C9
Speed Gate Kent 68 F5
Speedwell Bristol 60 E6
Speen Bucks 84 F4
Speen W Berks 64 F3
Speeton N Yorks 218 E2
Speke Mers 182 E6
Speldhurst Kent 52 E5
Spellbrook Herts 87 B7
Spelsbury Oxon 101 G7
Spelter Bridgend 57 C11
Spen W Yorks 197 B7
Spen Green E Ches 168 C4
Spencers Wood Wokingham 65 F8
Spennells Worcs 116 C6
Spennithorne N Yorks 214 B2
Spennymoor Durham 233 E11
Spernall Warks 117 E11
Spetchley Worcs 117 G7
Spetisbury Dorset 30 G6
Spexhall Suff 143 G7
Spey Bay Moray 302 C3
Speybank Highld 291 C10
Speybridge Highld 301 G10
Speyview Moray 302 E2
Spillardsford Aberds 303 D10
Spilsby Lincs 174 B6
Spindlestone Northumb 264 C5
Spinkhill Derbys 187 F7
Spinney Hill Northants 120 E5
Spinney Hills Leicester 136 C2
Spinningdale Highld 309 L6
Spion Kop Notts 171 B9
Spirthill Wilts 62 D3
Spital Mers 182 E4
Spital Windsor 66 D3
Spital Hill S Yorks 187 C10
Spital in the Street Lincs 189 D7
Spital Tongues T & W 242 D6
Spitalbrook Herts 86 D5
Spitalfields London 67 C10
Spitalhill Derbys 169 F11
Spithurst E Sus 36 D6
Spittal Dumfries 236 D5
Spittal E Loth 281 F9
Spittal E Yorks 207 C11
Spittal Highld 310 D5
Spittal Northumb 273 E10
Spittal Pembs 91 G9
Spittal Stirl 277 D10
Spittal Houses S Yorks 186 B5
Spittal of Glenmuick Aberds 292 E5
Spittal of Glenshee Perth 292 F3
Spittalfield Perth 286 C5
Spittlegate Lincs 155 C8
Spixworth Norf 160 F4
Splatt Corn 10 F4
Splatt Corn 11 D10
Splatt Devon 25 F10
Splatt Som 43 F8
Splayne's Green E Sus 36 C6
Splott Cardiff 59 D7
Spofforth N Yorks 206 C3
Spon End W Mid 118 B6
Spon Green Flint 166 C3
Spondon Derby 153 B8
Spooner Row Norf 141 D11
Spooneygate Shrops 132 D6
Sporle Norf 158 G6
Spotland Bridge Gtr Man 195 E11
Spott E Loth 282 F3
Spratton Northants 120 C4
Spreakley Sur 49 E10
Spreyton Devon 13 B9
Spriddlestone Devon 7 E10
Spridlington Lincs 189 E8
Sprig's Alley Oxon 84 F3
Spring Bank Cumb 229 G10
Spring Cottage Leics 152 F6
Spring End N Yorks 223 F9
Spring Gardens Som 45 D9
Spring Green Lancs 204 E4
Spring Grove London 67 D7
Spring Hill Gtr Man 196 F2
Spring Hill Lancs 195 B8
Spring Hill W Mid 133 D7
Spring Park London 67 F11
Spring Vale S Yorks 197 G9
Spring Valley I o M 192 E4
Springbank Glos 99 G8
Springboig Glasgow 268 C3
Springbourne Bmouth 19 C8
Springburn Glasgow 268 B2
Springfield Argyll 275 F11
Springfield Caerph 77 F11
Springfield Dumfries 239 D8
Springfield Essex 88 D2
Springfield Fife 287 F7
Springfield Gtr Man 194 F5
Springfield Highld 300 C6
Springfield M Keynes 103 D7
Springfield Moray 301 D10
Springfield W Mid 133 D8
Springfield W Mid 133 F9
Springfield W Mid 133 G11
Springfields Stoke 168 G5
Springhead Gtr Man 196 G3
Springhill E Renf 267 D10
Springhill I o W 20 B6
Springhill N Lnrk 269 D7
Springhill Staffs 133 B11
Springhill Staffs 133 C9
Springholm Dumfries 237 C10
Springkell Dumfries 239 B7
Springside N Ayrs 257 B9
Springthorpe Lincs 188 D5
Springwell Essex 105 C10
Springwell T & W 243 F7
Springwell T & W 243 F9
Springwells Dumfries 248 E3
Sproatley E Yorks 209 G9
Sproston Green W Ches 168 B2
Sprotbrough S Yorks 198 G4
Sproughton Suff 108 C2
Sprouston Borders 263 B7
Sprowston Norf 160 G4
Sproxton Leics 155 E7
Sproxton N Yorks 216 C2
Sprunston Cumb 230 B3
Spunhill Shrops 149 C8
Spurlands End Bucks 84 F5
Spurstow E Ches 167 D9
Spurtree Shrops 116 D2
Spynie Moray 302 C2
Spyway Dorset 16 C6
Square and Compass Pembs 91 E7
Squires Gate Blkpool 202 G2
Sraid Ruadh Argyll 288 E1
Srannda W Isles 296 C6
Sronphadruig Lodge Perth 291 F9
Stableford Shrops 132 D5
Stableford Staffs 150 B6
Stacey Bank S Yorks 186 C3
Stackhouse N Yorks 212 F6
Stackpole Pembs 73 F7
Stackpole Quay Pembs 73 F7
Stacksford Norf 141 E11
Stacksteads Lancs 195 C10
Stackyard Green Suff 107 B9
Staddiscombe Plym 7 E10
Staddlethorpe E Yorks 199 B10
Staddon Devon 24 C3
Staddon Devon 24 G5
Staden Derbys 185 G9
Stadhampton Oxon 83 F10
Stadhlaigearraidh W Isles 297 H3
Stadmorslow Staffs 168 D5
Staffield Cumb 230 C6
Staffin Highld 298 C4
Stafford Staffs 151 E8
Stafford Park Telford 132 B4
Stafford's Corner Essex 89 B7
Stafford's Green Dorset 29 C10
Stagbatch Hereford 115 F9
Stagden Cross Essex 87 C10
Stagehall Borders 271 G9
Stag's Head Devon 25 B11
Stagsden Beds 103 B9
Stagsden West End Beds 103 B9
Stain Highld 310 C7
Stainburn Cumb 228 F6
Stainburn N Yorks 205 D10
Stainby Lincs 155 E8
Staincliffe W Yorks 197 C8
Staincross S Yorks 197 E10
Staindrop Durham 233 G8
Staines Green Herts 86 C3
Staines-upon-Thames Sur 66 E4
Stainfield Lincs 155 D11
Stainfield Lincs 189 G10
Stainforth N Yorks 212 F6
Stainforth S Yorks 198 E6
Staining Lancs 202 F3
Stainland W Yorks 196 D5
Stainsacre N Yorks 227 D8
Stainsby Derbys 170 B6
Stainsby Lincs 190 G4
Stainton Cumb 211 B10
Stainton Cumb 230 F5
Stainton Cumb 239 F9
Stainton Durham 223 B11
Stainton M'bro 225 C9
Stainton N Yorks 224 F2
Stainton S Yorks 187 C9
Stainton by Langworth Lincs 189 F9
Stainton le Vale Lincs 189 C11
Stainton with Adgarley Cumb 210 E5
Staintondale N Yorks 227 F9
Stair Cumb 229 G10
Stair E Ayrs 257 E10
Stairfoot S Yorks 197 F11
Stairhaven Dumfries 236 D4
Staithes N Yorks 226 B5
Stake Hill Gtr Man 195 F11
Stake Pool Lancs 202 D4
Stakeford Northumb 253 F7
Stakenbridge Worcs 117 B7
Stalbridge Dorset 30 D2
Stalbridge Weston Dorset 30 D2
Stalham Norf 161 D7
Stalham Green Norf 161 E7
Stalisfield Green Kent 54 C3
Stallen Dorset 29 D10
Stalling Busk N Yorks 213 B8
Stallingborough NE Lincs 201 E7
Stallington Staffs 151 B8
Stalmine Lancs 202 D3
Stalmine Moss Side Lancs 202 D3
Stalybridge Gtr Man 185 B7
Stambermill W Mid 133 G8
Stamborough Som 42 F4
Stambourne Essex 106 D4
Stambourne Green Essex 106 C4
Stamford Lincs 137 B10
Stamford Bridge E Yorks 207 B10
Stamford Bridge W Ches 167 B7
Stamford Hill London 67 B10
Stamfordham Northumb 242 C3
Stamperland E Renf 267 D11
Stamshaw Ptsmth 33 G10
Stanah Cumb 220 B6
Stanah Lancs 202 E3
Stanborough Herts 86 C2
Stanbridge C Beds 103 G9
Stanbridge Dorset 31 G8
Stanbridgeford C Beds 103 G9
Stanbrook Essex 106 F2
Stanbrook Worcs 98 B6
Stanbury W Yorks 204 F6
Stand Gtr Man 195 F9
Stand N Lnrk 268 B5
Standburn Falk 279 G8
Standeford Staffs 133 B8
Standen Kent 53 E11
Standen Hall Lancs 203 E10
Standen Street Kent 53 G10
Standerwick Som 45 C10
Standford Hants 49 G10
Standford Bridge Telford 150 E4
Standingstone Cumb 229 B11
Standingstone Cumb 229 E7
Standish Glos 80 D4
Standish Gtr Man 194 E5
Standish Lower Ground Gtr Man 194 F5
Standlake Oxon 82 E5
Standon Hants 32 B6
Standon Herts 105 G7
Standon Staffs 150 B6
Standon Green End Herts 86 B5
Stane N Lnrk 269 D7
Stanecastle N Ayrs 257 B8
Stanfield Norf 159 E8
Stanfield Stoke 168 E5
Stanford C Beds 104 C3
Stanford Kent 54 F6
Stanford Norf 141 E7
Stanford Shrops 148 G6
Stanford Bishop Hereford 116 G3
Stanford Bridge Worcs 116 D4
Stanford Dingley W Berks 64 E5
Stanford End Wokingham 65 G8
Stanford Hills Notts 153 E10
Stanford in the Vale Oxon 82 G4
Stanford-le-Hope Thurrock 69 C7
Stanford on Avon Northants 119 B11
Stanford on Soar Notts 153 E10
Stanford on Teme Worcs 116 D4
Stanford Rivers Essex 87 E8
Stanfree Derbys 187 G7
Stanground P'boro 138 D4
Stanhill Lancs 195 B8
Stanhoe Norf 158 B6
Stanhope Borders 260 D4
Stanhope Durham 232 D5
Stanhope Kent 54 E3
Stanion Northants 137 F8
Stank Cumb 210 E4
Stanklyn Worcs 117 C7
Stanks W Yorks 206 F3
Stanley Derbys 170 G6
Stanley Durham 242 G5
Stanley Lancs 194 F3
Stanley Notts 171 C7
Stanley Perth 286 D5
Stanley Shrops 132 G3
Stanley Shrops 132 G5
Stanley Staffs 168 E6
Stanley W Yorks 197 C10
Stanley Wilts 62 E3
Stanley Common Derbys 170 G6
Stanley Crook Durham 233 D9
Stanley Downton Glos 80 E4
Stanley Ferry W Yorks 197 C11
Stanley Gate Lancs 194 G2
Stanley Green E Ches 184 E5
Stanley Green Poole 18 C6
Stanley Green Shrops 149 B10
Stanley Hill Hereford 98 C3
Stanley Moor Staffs 168 E6
Stanley Pontlarge Glos 99 E9
Stanleytown Rhondda 77 G8
Stanlow Staffs 132 D5
Stanlow W Ches 182 F6
Stanmer Brighton 36 F4
Stanmore Hants 33 B7
Stanmore London 85 G11
Stanmore Shrops 132 E4
Stanmore W Berks 64 D3
Stanner Powys 114 F5
Stannergate Dundee 287 D8
Stanners Hill Sur 66 G3
Stannersburn Northumb 250 F6
Stanningfield Suff 125 F7
Stanningley W Yorks 205 G10
Stannington Northumb 242 B6
Stannington S Yorks 186 D4
Stanpit Dorset 19 C9
Stansbatch Hereford 114 E6
Stansfield Suff 124 G5
Stanshope Staffs 169 E10
Stanstead Suff 106 B6
Stanstead Abbotts Herts 86 C5
Stansted Kent 68 G6
Stansted Airport Essex 105 G11
Stansted Mountfitchet Essex 105 G10
Stanthorne W Ches 167 B11
Stanton Glos 99 E11
Stanton Mon 96 G6
Stanton Northumb 252 F4
Stanton Staffs 169 F10
Stanton Suff 125 C9
Stanton by Bridge Derbys 153 D7
Stanton-by-Dale Derbys 153 B9
Stanton Chare Suff 125 C9
Stanton Drew Bath 60 G5
Stanton Fitzwarren Swindon 81 G11
Stanton Gate Notts 153 B9
Stanton Harcourt Oxon 82 D6
Stanton Hill Notts 171 C7
Stanton in Peak Derbys 170 C2
Stanton Lacy Shrops 115 B9
Stanton Lees Derbys 170 C3
Stanton Long Shrops 131 E11
Stanton-on-the-Wolds Notts 154 C2
Stanton Prior Bath 61 G7
Stanton St Bernard Wilts 62 G5
Stanton St John Oxon 83 D9
Stanton St Quintin Wilts 62 D2
Stanton Street Suff 125 D9
Stanton under Bardon Leics 153 G9
Stanton upon Hine Heath Shrops 149 E11
Stanton Wick Bath 60 G6
Stantonbury M Keynes 102 C6
Stantway Glos 80 C2
Stanwardine in the Fields Shrops 149 E8
Stanwardine in the Wood Shrops 149 D8
Stanway Essex 107 G8
Stanway Glos 99 E11
Stanway Green Essex 107 G9
Stanway Green Suff 126 C4
Stanwell Sur 66 E5
Stanwell Moor Sur 66 E4
Stanwick Northants 121 C9
Stanwick-St-John N Yorks 224 C3
Stanwix Cumb 239 F10
Stanycliffe Gtr Man 195 F11
Stanydale Shetland 313 H4
Staoinebrig W Isles 297 H3
Stape N Yorks 226 G5
Stapehill Dorset 31 G9
Stapeley E Ches 167 F11
Stapenhill Staffs 152 E5
Staple Kent 55 B9
Staple Som 42 E6
Staple Cross Devon 27 C8
Staple Fitzpaine Som 28 D3
Staple Hill S Glos 61 D7
Staple Hill Worcs 117 C9
Staple Lawns Som 28 D3
Staplecross E Sus 38 C3
Staplefield W Sus 36 B3
Stapleford Cambs 123 G9
Stapleford Herts 86 B4
Stapleford Leics 154 F6
Stapleford Lincs 172 D5
Stapleford Notts 153 B9
Stapleford Wilts 46 F5
Stapleford Abbotts Essex 87 G8
Stapleford Tawney Essex 87 F8
Staplegrove Som 28 B2
Staplehay Som 28 C2
Staplehurst Kent 53 E9
Staplers I o W 20 D6
Staples Hill W Sus 35 B8
Staplestreet Kent 70 G5
Stapleton Bristol 60 D6
Stapleton Cumb 240 C2
Stapleton Hereford 114 D6
Stapleton Leics 135 D8
Stapleton N Yorks 198 D4
Stapleton N Yorks 224 C5
Stapleton Shrops 131 C9
Stapleton Som 29 C7
Stapley Som 27 E11
Staploe Beds 122 E2
Staplow Hereford 98 C3
Stapness Shetland 313 J4
Star Fife 287 G7
Star Pembs 92 E4
Star Som 44 B2
Star Hill Mon 79 E7
Stara Orkney 314 D2
Starbeck N Yorks 206 B2
Starbotton N Yorks 213 E9
Starcross Devon 14 E5
Stareton Warks 118 C6
Stargate T & W 242 E5
Starkholmes Derbys 170 D4
Starling Gtr Man 195 E9
Starlings Green Essex 105 E9
Starr's Green E Sus 38 D3
Starston Norf 142 G4
Start Devon 8 G6
Start Hill Essex 105 G10
Startforth Durham 223 B10
Startley Wilts 62 C2
Startop's End Bucks 84 C6
Starveall S Glos 61 B9
Starvecrow Kent 52 D5
Statenborough Kent 55 B10
Statford St Andrew Suff 127 E7
Statham Warr 183 D11
Stathe Som 28 B5
Stathern Leics 154 C5
Station Hill Cumb 229 B11
Station Town Durham 234 D4
Statland Common Norf 141 D10
Staughton Green Cambs 122 D2
Staughton Highway Cambs 122 E2
Staughton Moor Beds 122 E2
Staunton Glos 79 C8
Staunton Glos 98 F5
Staunton in the Vale Notts 172 G4
Staunton on Arrow Hereford 115 E7
Staunton on Wye Hereford 97 B7
Staupes N Yorks 205 B10
Staveley Cumb 211 B7
Staveley Cumb 221 F9
Staveley Derbys 186 G6
Staveley N Yorks 215 G7
Staveley-in-Cartmel Cumb 211 B7
Staverton Devon 8 C5
Staverton Glos 99 G7
Staverton Northants 119 E10
Staverton Wilts 61 G11
Staverton Bridge Glos 99 G7
Stawell Som 43 F11
Stawley Som 27 C9
Staxigoe Highld 310 D7
Staxton N Yorks 217 D10
Staylittle Ceredig 128 F2
Staylittle = Penffordd-Lâs Powys 129 E7
Staynall Lancs 202 E3
Staythorpe Notts 172 E3
Stead W Yorks 205 D8
Steam Mills Glos 79 B10
Stean N Yorks 213 E11
Steanbow Som 44 F5
Stearsby N Yorks 216 E2
Steart Som 29 B9
Steart Som 43 D9
Stebbing Essex 106 G3
Stebbing Green Essex 106 G3
Stechford W Mid 134 F2
Stede Quarter Kent 53 F11
Stedham W Sus 34 C5
Steel Northumb 241 F10
Steel Northumb 251 G9
Steel Bank S Yorks 186 D4
Steel Cross E Sus 52 G4
Steel Green Cumb 210 D3
Steel Heath Shrops 149 B10
Steele Road Borders 250 E2
Steelend Fife 279 C10
Steeleroad-end Borders 250 E2
Steen's Bridge Hereford 115 F10
Steep Hants 34 B2
Steep Lane W Yorks 196 C4
Steep Marsh Hants 34 B3
Steephill I o W 21 F7
Steeple Dorset 18 E4
Steeple Essex 88 E6
Steeple Ashton Wilts 46 B2
Steeple Aston Oxon 101 F9
Steeple Barton Oxon 101 G8
Steeple Bumpstead Essex 106 C3
Steeple Claydon Bucks 102 F3
Steeple Gidding Cambs 138 G2
Steeple Langford Wilts 46 F4
Steeple Morden Cambs 104 C5
Steeraway Telford 132 B3
Steeton W Yorks 204 E6
Stein Highld 298 D2
Steinmanhill Aberds 303 E7
Stella T & W 242 E5
Stelling Minnis Kent 54 D6
Stelvio Newport 59 B9
Stembridge Som 28 C6
Stembridge Swansea 56 C3
Stemster Highld 310 C5
Stemster Ho Highld 310 C5
Stenalees Corn 5 D10
Stenaquoy Orkney 314 C5
Stencoose Corn 4 F4
Stenhill Devon 27 E9
Stenhouse Dumfries 247 E8
Stenhouse Edin 280 G4
Stenhousemuir Falk 279 E7
Stenigot Lincs 190 E3
Stennack Corn 2 B5
Stenness Shetland 312 F4
Stenscholl Highld 298 C4
Stenso Orkney 314 D3
Stenson Derbys 152 D6
Stenton E Loth 282 G2
Stenton Fife 280 B5
Stentwood Devon 27 F10
Stenwith Lincs 154 B6
Stepaside Corn 5 F9
Stepaside Pembs 73 D10
Stepaside Powys 129 F11
Stepney London 67 C11
Stepping Hill Gtr Man 184 D6
Steppingley C Beds 103 D10
Stepps N Lnrk 268 B3
Sterndale Moor Derbys 169 B10
Sternfield Suff 127 E7
Sterridge Devon 4
Stert Wilts 4
Sterte Poole 1
Stetchworth Cambs 12
Stevenage Herts 10
Steven's Crouch E Sus 3
Stevenston N Ayrs 26
Stevenstone Devon 2
Steventon Hants 4
Steventon Oxon 8
Steventon Shrops 115
Steventon End Essex 105
Stevington Beds 12
Stewards Essex 8
Steward's Green Essex 8
Stewartby Beds 103
Stewarton Argyll 25
Stewarton E Ayrs 26
Stewkley Bucks 10
Stewkley Dean Bucks 10
Stewley Som 2
Stewton Lincs 19
Steyne Cross I o W 2
Steyning W Sus 35
Steynton Pembs 7
Stibb Corn 2
Stibb Cross Devon 2
Stibb Green Wilts 6
Stibbard Norf 15
Stibbington Cambs 137
Stichill Borders 26
Stick Hill Kent 5
Sticker Corn
Stickford Lincs 17
Sticklepath Devon 1
Sticklepath Devon 4
Sticklepath Som 2
Sticklepath Som 4
Sticklinch Som 4
Stickling Green Essex 10
Stickney Lincs 17
Stiff Street Kent 69
Stiffkey Norf 17
Stifford's Bridge Hereford 9
Stileway Som 4
Stillingfleet N Yorks 20
Stillington N Yorks 215
Stillington Stockton 23
Stilton Cambs 13
Stinchcombe Glos 8
Stinsford Dorset 17
Stiperstones Shrops 13
Stirchley Telford 13
Stirchley W Mid 133
Stirkoke Ho Highld 31
Stirling Aberds 303
Stirling Stirl 27
Stirtloe Cambs 12
Stirton N Yorks 20
Stisted Essex 10
Stitchcombe Wilts 6
Stitchin's Hill Worcs 11
Stithians Corn
Stittenham Highld 30
Stivichall W Mid 11
Stixwould Lincs 173
Stoak W Ches 18
Stobhill Northumb 25
Stobhillgate Northumb 25
Stobieside S Lnrk 25
Stobo Borders 26
Stoborough Dorset 1
Stoborough Green Dorset 1
Stobs Castle Borders 25
Stobshiel E Loth 27
Stobswood Northumb 25
Stock Essex 87
Stock Lancs 20
Stock N Som 6
Stock Green Worcs 11
Stock Hill Suff 12
Stock Wood Worcs 117
Stockbridge Hants 47
Stockbridge S Yorks 19
Stockbridge W Sus 2
Stockbridge W Yorks 20
Stockbridge Village Mers 18
Stockbury Kent 69
Stockcross W Berks 6
Stockend Glos 8
Stocker's Head Kent 5
Stockerston Leics 13
Stockfield W Mid 13
Stockheath Hants 2
Stockholes Turbary N Lincs 19
Stockiemuir Stirl 277
Stocking Hereford 9
Stocking Green Essex 105
Stocking Pelham Herts 10
Stockingford Warks 13
Stockland Devon 2
Stockland Bristol Som 4
Stockland Green Kent 5
Stockland Green W Mid 133
Stockleigh English Devon 2
Stockleigh Pomeroy Devon 2
Stockley Wilts 6
Stocklinch Som 2
Stockport Gtr Man 18
Stocks Green Kent 5
Stocksbridge S Yorks 18
Stocksfield Northumb 24
Stockstreet Essex 10
Stockton Hereford 115
Stockton Norf 14
Stockton Shrops 13
Stockton Shrops 13
Stockton Telford 15
Stockton Warks 11
Stockton Wilts 4
Stockton Brook Staffs 16
Stockton Heath Warr 183
Stockton-on-Tees Stockton 22
Stockton on Teme Worcs 11
Stockton on the Forest York 20
Stocktonwood Shrops 13
Stockwell Devon 2
Stockwell Glos 8
Stockwell London 67
Stockwell End W Mid 13
Stockwell Heath Staffs 151
Stockwitch Cross Som 2
Stockwood Bristol 6
Stockwood Dorset 2
Stockwood Vale Bath 6
Stodday Lancs 20
Stodmarsh Kent 7
Stody Norf 159
Stoer Highld 30
Stoford Som 2
Stoford Wilts 4

ord Water Devon 27 F9
umber Som 42 F5
ursey Som 43 E8
e Devon 24 C2
e Hants 22 C2
e Hants 48 C2
e Medway 69 D10
e Plym 7 D9
e Suff 108 C3
e W Mid 119 B7
e Abbott Dorset 29 G7
e Albany Northants 136 F6
e Aldermoor W Mid 119 B7
e Ash Suff 126 C2
e Bardolph Notts 171 G10
e Bishop Bristol 60 D5
e Bliss Worcs 116 E3
e Bruerne
hants 102 B4
e by Clare Suff 106 C4
e-by-Nayland Suff 107 D9
e Canon Devon 14 B4
e Charity Hants 48 F3
e Climsland Corn 12 G3
e Common Hants 33 C7
e Cross Hereford 116 G2
e D'Abernon Sur 50 B6
e Doyle Northants 137 D10
e Dry Rutland 137 D7
e Edith Hereford 98 C2
e End Warks 134 D3
e Farthing Wilts 31 B9
e Ferry Norf 140 D4
e Fleming Devon 9 F7
e Gabriel Devon 8 D6
e Gifford S Glos 60 D6
e Golding Leics 135 D7
e Goldington
eynes 102 B6
e Green Bucks 66 C3
e Hammond Bucks 103 F7
e Heath Shrops 150 D3
e Heath W Mid 135 G7
e Heath Worcs 117 D8
e Hill Devon 14 C4
e Hill Hereford 98 B2
e Holy Cross Norf 142 C4
e Lacy Hereford 98 B2
e Lane Hereford 116 G2
e Lyne Oxon 101 F11
e Mandeville Bucks 84 C4
e Newington
on 67 B10
e on Tern Shrops 150 E2
e-on-Trent Stoke 168 F5
e Orchard Glos 99 F8
e Park Suff 108 C3
e Poges Bucks 66 C3
e Pound Worcs 117 D9
e Prior Hereford 115 F10
e Prior Worcs 117 D8
e Rivers Devon 40 F6
e Rochford Lincs 155 D8
e Row Oxon 65 B8
e St Gregory Som 28 B4
e St Mary Som 28 C3
e St Michael Som 45 D7
e St Milborough
ps 131 G11
e sub Hamdon Som 29 D7
e Talmage Oxon 83 F11
e Trister Som 30 B2
e Wake Dorset 30 F3
e Water Dorset 29 G7
e Wharf Worcs 117 D9
eford Dorset 18 D3
egorse Shrops 131 G11
eham Notts 188 F3
eininghead Devon 14 G4
enchurch Bucks 84 F3
enham Devon 8 G6
escay Shrops 131 G8
esby Norf 161 G8
esley N Yorks 225 D10
e Northumb 250 F6
ord Som 43 D8
Easton Som 44 C6
on Madessey Essex 87 E9
e Bucks 84 C3
e Glos 79 F11
e Kent 38 B6
e Kent 68 E5
e S Yorks 187 D9
e Som 44 G5
e Staffs 151 C8
e Worcs 117 B7
e Allerton Som 44 C2
e Bridge Corner
o 138 C5
e Chair W Yorks 196 B6
e Cross E Sus 23 E10
e Cross E Sus 37 B8
e Cross E Sus 52 G6
e Cross Kent 52 F4
e Cross Kent 54 F4
e Cross Kent 55 B10
e Cross W Mid 133 E10
e-edge Batch
m 60 E3
e Head N Yorks 204 E4
e Heath Staffs 151 B9
e Hill Kent 54 D2
e Hill Kent 54 F5
e Hill S Glos 60 E6
e Hill S Yorks 199 F7
e House Cumb 212 B5
e in Oxney Kent 38 B6
e Raise Cumb 230 B4
e Street Kent 52 C5
e Street Suff 107 D9
e Street Suff 143 G7
ea Cambs 139 E9
eacton Shrops 131 E10
ebow Worcs 99 B8
ebridge Essex 70 B2
ebridge London 67 C8
ebridge N Som 43 B11
ebridge Norf 141 E8
ebridge Sur 51 D7
ebridge W Mid 134 G4
ebridge Green Kent 54 D2
ebroom Derbys 170 D6
ebyres Holdings
k 268 G6
eclough Gtr Man 195 F9
ecombe Devon 40 E6
ecrouch Kent 53 G7
edge Borders 250 B3
eferry Hull 209 G8
efield Argyll 289 F11
efield S Lnrk 268 D3
efield Staffs 151 C7
efield Castle Hotel
275 F9
egate E Sus 37 B11
egate N Yorks 226 D5
egrave N Yorks 216 D3
egravels Derbys 186 G5
ehall Kent 55 D9
ehall Worcs 99 B7
ehaugh Northumb 241 B7
ehaven Aberds 293 E10
Stonehill Sur 66 G4
Stonehills Hants 33 G7
Stonehouse Aberds 303 F8
Stonehouse Glos 80 D4
Stonehouse Northumb 240 F5
Stonehouse Plym 7 E9
Stonehouse S Lnrk 268 F5
Stonehouses Staffs 169 G7
Stoneleigh London 67 G8
Stoneleigh Warks 118 C6
Stoneley Green E Ches 167 E10
Stonely Cambs 122 D2
Stonepits Worcs 117 F10
Stonequarry W Sus 52 F2
Stoner Hill Hants 34 B2
Stones Green Essex 108 F3
Stonesby Leics 154 E6
Stonesfield Oxon 82 B5
Stonestreet Green Kent 54 F5
Stonethwaite Cumb 220 C5
Stoneton Warks 119 G9
Stonewells Moray 302 C2
Stonewood Kent 68 E5
Stoney Cross Hants 32 E3
Stoney Hill Worcs 117 C9
Stoney Middleton
Derbys 186 F2
Stoney Royd W Yorks 196 C5
Stoney Stanton Leics 135 E9
Stoney Stoke Som 45 G8
Stoney Stratton Som 45 F7
Stoney Stretton Shrops 131 B7
Stoneyard Green
Hereford 98 C4
Stoneybank E Loth 280 G6
Stoneybreck Shetland 313 N2
Stoneyburn W Loth 269 C9
Stoneycombe Devon 9 B7
Stoneycroft Mers 182 C5
Stoneyfield Gtr Man 195 E11
Stoneyfield Moray 301 D11
Stoneyford Derbys 170 F6
Stoneyford Devon 27 F8
Stoneygate Aberds 303 F10
Stoneygate Leicester 136 C2
Stoneyhills Essex 88 F6
Stoneykirk Dumfries 236 D2
Stoneylane Shrops 115 B11
Stoneywood Aberdeen 293 B10
Stoneywood Falk 278 E5
Stonganess Shetland 312 C7
Stonham Aspal Suff 126 F2
Stonnall Staffs 133 C11
Stonor Oxon 65 B8
Stonton Wyville Leics 136 D4
Stony Batter Hants 32 B3
Stony Cross Devon 25 B8
Stony Cross Hereford 98 B4
Stony Cross Hereford 115 D10
Stony Dale Notts 172 G2
Stony Gate T & W 243 G9
Stony Green Bucks 84 F5
Stony Heap Durham 242 G4
Stony Heath Hants 48 B5
Stony Houghton Derbys 171 B7
Stony Knaps Dorset 28 G5
Stony Littleton Bath 45 B8
Stony Stratford
M Keynes 102 C5
Stonyfield Highld 300 B6
Stonyford Hants 32 D4
Stonyland Devon 25 B8
Stonymarsh Hants 32 B4
Stoodleigh Devon 26 D6
Stop-and-Call Pembs 91 D8
Stopes S Yorks 186 D3
Stopgate Devon 28 F2
Stopham W Sus 35 D8
Stopper Lane Lancs 204 D2
Stopsley Luton 104 G2
Stoptide Corn 10 F4
Stores Corner Suff 109 B7
Storeton Mers 182 E4
Storiths N Yorks 205 C7
Stormontfield Perth 286 E5
Stormore Wilts 45 D10
Stornoway W Isles 304 E6
Storridge Hereford 98 B4
Storrington W Sus 35 E9
Storrs Cumb 221 G7
Storrs S Yorks 186 D3
Storth Cumb 211 C9
Storwood E Yorks 207 E10
Stotfield Moray 302 B2
Stotfold C Beds 104 D4
Stottesdon Shrops 132 G3
Stoughton Leics 136 C2
Stoughton Sur 50 C3
Stoughton W Sus 34 E4
Stoughton Cross Som 44 D2
Stoul Highld 295 F9
Stoulton Worcs 99 B8
Stour Provost Dorset 30 C3
Stour Row Dorset 30 C4
Stourbridge W Mid 133 G8
Stourpaine Dorset 30 F5
Stourport on Severn
Worcs 116 C6
Stourton Staffs 133 F7
Stourton W Yorks 206 G2
Stourton Warks 100 D5
Stourton Wilts 45 G9
Stourton Caundle
Dorset 30 D2
Stourton Hill Warks 100 D6
Stout Som 44 G2
Stove Orkney 314 C6
Stove Shetland 313 L6
Stoven Suff 143 G8
Stow Borders 271 G9
Stow Lincs 155 B11
Stow Lincs 188 E5
Stow Bardolph Norf 140 B2
Stow Bedon Norf 141 D9
Stow cum Quy Cambs 123 E10
Stow Lawn W Mid 133 D8
Stow Longa Cambs 122 C2
Stow Maries Essex 88 F4
Stow-on-the-Wold
Glos 100 F3
Stow Park Newport 59 B10
Stowbridge Norf 140 B2
Stowe Glos 79 D9
Stowe Hereford 96 B5
Stowe Lincs 156 G2
Stowe Shrops 114 C6
Stowe Staffs 152 G2
Stowe-by-Chartley
Staffs 151 D10
Stowe Green Glos 79 D9
Stowell Glos 81 C9
Stowell Som 29 C11
Stowey Bath 44 B5
Stowfield Hereford 79 B9
Stowford Devon 12 B4
Stowford Devon 12 D4
Stowford Devon 24 E3
Stowford Devon 25 B10
Stowford Devon 41 E7
Stowgate Lincs 156 G3
Stowlangtoft Suff 125 D9
Stowmarket Suff 125 F10
Stowting Kent 54 E6
Stowting Common Kent 54 E6
Stowting Court Kent 54 E6
Stowupland Suff 125 F11
Straad Argyll 275 G11
Strachan Aberds 293 D8
Strachurmore Argyll 284 G5
Stradbroke Suff 126 C4
Stradishall Suff 124 G4
Stradsett Norf 140 C3
Stragglethorpe Lincs 172 E6
Straid S Ayrs 244 E4
Straight Soley Wilts 63 E10
Straith Dumfries 247 F8
Straiton Edin 270 B5
Straiton S Ayrs 245 C9
Straloch Aberds 303 G8
Straloch Perth 292 G2
Stramshall Staffs 151 B11
Strand Glos 80 C2
Strand London 67 C10
Strands Cumb 210 C3
Strang I o M 192 E4
Strangeways Gtr Man 184 B4
Strangford Hereford 97 F11
Stranghow Redcar 226 B3
Strangways Wilts 46 E6
Stranog Aberds 293 D10
Stranraer Dumfries 236 C2
Strata Florida Ceredig 112 D4
Stratfield Mortimer
W Berks 65 G7
Stratfield Saye Hants 65 G7
Stratfield Turgis Hants 49 B7
Stratford C Beds 104 B3
Stratford Glos 99 D7
Stratford London 67 C11
Stratford Marsh London 67 C11
Stratford New Town
London 67 C11
Stratford St Andrew
Suff 127 E7
Stratford St Mary Suff 107 E10
Stratford Sub Castle
Wilts 46 G6
Stratford Tony Wilts 31 B9
Stratford-upon-Avon
Warks 118 F3
Strath Highld 299 B7
Strath Highld 310 D6
Strathallan Castle
Perth 286 F3
Strathan Highld 295 F11
Strathan Highld 307 G5
Strathan Highld 308 C5
Strathan Skerray Highld 308 C6
Strathaven S Lnrk 268 G4
Strathavon Lo Moray 301 G11
Strathblane Stirl 277 F11
Strathcanaird Highld 307 J6
Strathcarron Highld 299 E9
Strathcoil Argyll 289 F8
Strathcoul Highld 310 D5
Strathdon Aberds 292 B5
Strathellie Aberds 303 C10
Strathgarve Lodge
Highld 300 C4
Strathkinness Fife 287 F8
Strathmashie House
Highld 291 D7
Strathmiglo Fife 286 F6
Strathmore Lodge
Highld 310 E5
Strathpeffer Highld 300 D4
Strathrannoch Highld 300 B3
Strathtay Perth 286 B3
Strathvaich Lodge
Highld 300 B3
Strathwhillan N Ayrs 256 B2
Strathy Highld 300 B6
Strathy Highld 310 C2
Strathyre Stirl 285 F9
Stratton Corn 24 F2
Stratton Dorset 17 C9
Stratton Glos 81 E8
Stratton Audley Oxon 102 F2
Stratton Chase Bucks 85 G7
Stratton-on-the-Fosse
Som 45 C7
Stratton St Margaret
Swindon 63 B7
Stratton St Michael
Norf 142 E4
Stratton Strawless Norf 160 E4
Stravithie Fife 287 F9
Strawberry Bank Cumb 211 B8
Strawberry Hill E Sus 52 F5
Strawberry Hill London 67 E7
Strawberry Hill W Yorks 198 C2
Streat E Sus 36 D5
Streatham London 67 E10
Streatham Hill London 67 E10
Streatham Park London 67 E9
Streatham Vale London 67 E9
Streatley C Beds 103 F11
Streatley W Berks 64 C5
Street Cumb 222 D2
Street Lancs 202 C6
Street N Yorks 226 E4
Street Som 28 F5
Street Som 44 F3
Street Ash Som 28 E3
Street Ashton Warks 135 G9
Street Dinas Shrops 148 B6
Street End E Sus 37 C9
Street End Hants 33 D9
Street End Kent 54 C6
Street End W Sus 22 D5
Street Gate T & W 242 F6
Street Houses N Yorks 206 D6
Street Lane Derbys 170 F5
Street Lydan Wrex 149 B8
Street of Kincardine
Highld 291 B11
Street on the Fosse
Som 44 F6
Streethay Staffs 152 G2
Streethouse W Yorks 197 C11
Streetlam N Yorks 224 F6
Streetly W Mid 133 D11
Streetly End Cambs 106 B2
Strefford Shrops 131 F8
Strelley Notts 171 G8
Strensall York 216 G2
Strensham Worcs 99 C8
Stretch Down Devon 26 E4
Stretcholt Som 43 E9
Strete Devon 8 F6
Stretford Gtr Man 184 C4
Stretford Hereford 115 F10
Stretford Court
Hereford 115 F8
Strethall Essex 105 D9
Stretham Cambs 123 C10
Strettington W Sus 22 B5
Stretton Derbys 170 C5
Stretton Rutland 155 F8
Stretton Staffs 151 G7
Stretton Staffs 152 D5
Stretton W Ches 166 E6
Stretton Warr 183 E10
Stretton en le Field
Leics 152 G6
Stretton Grandison
Hereford 98 C2
Stretton-on-Dunsmore
Warks 119 C8
Stretton-on-Fosse
Warks 100 D4
Stretton Sugwas
Hereford 97 C9
Stretton under Fosse
Warks 135 G8
Stretton Westwood
Shrops 131 D11
Strichen Aberds 303 D9
Strines Gtr Man 185 D7
Stringston Som 43 E7
Strixton Northants 121 E8
Stroat Glos 79 F9
Strode N Som 60 G4
Strom Shetland 313 J5
Stromeferry Highld 295 B10
Stromemore Highld 295 B10
Stromness Orkney 314 F2
Stronaba Highld 290 E4
Stronachlachar Stirl 285 F8
Stronachullin Lodge
Argyll 275 F9
Stronchreggan Highld 290 F2
Stronchrubie Highld 307 H7
Strone Argyll 255 F7
Strone Argyll 274 G6
Strone Argyll 276 E3
Strone Highld 290 E3
Strone Highld 291 D9
Strone Highld 300 G5
Strone Invclyd 276 G5
Stronelairg Lodge
Highld 291 C7
Stroneskar Argyll 275 C9
Stronmachair Stirl 285 G8
Stronmilchan Argyll 284 E5
Stronord Dumfries 236 C6
Stronsaul Argyll 276 F2
Strontian Highld 289 C10
Stronvar Stirl 285 E9
Strood Kent 53 G11
Strood Medway 69 F8
Strood Green Sur 51 D8
Strood Green W Sus 35 C8
Strood Green W Sus 50 G6
Strothers Dale
Northumb 241 F11
Stroud Glos 80 D4
Stroud Hants 34 C2
Stroud Sur 50 F2
Stroud Green Essex 88 G5
Stroud Green Glos 80 D4
Stroud Green London 67 B10
Stroude Sur 66 F4
Strouden Bmouth 19 C8
Stroul Argyll 276 E4
Stroupster Highld 310 C7
Stroxton Lincs 155 C8
Stroxworthy Devon 24 D4
Struan Highld 294 B5
Struan Perth 291 G10
Strubby Lincs 191 E7
Structon's Heath Worcs 116 D5
Strugg's Hill Lincs 156 B5
Strumpshaw Norf 142 B6
Strutherhill S Lnrk 268 F5
Struthers Fife 287 G7
Struy Highld 300 F3
Stryd Anglesey 178 E2
Stryd y Facsen Anglesey 178 E4
Stryt-issa Wrex 166 F3
Stuartfield Aberds 303 E9
Stub Place Cumb 219 G11
Stubb Norf 161 E8
Stubbermere W Sus 22 B3
Stubber's Green W Mid 133 C10
Stubbings Windsor 65 C10
Stubbing's Green Suff 125 C11
Stubbington Hants 33 G9
Stubbins Lancs 195 D9
Stubbins Lancs 202 E6
Stubble Green Cumb 219 F11
Stubbles W Berks 64 D5
Stubbs Cross Kent 54 F3
Stubb's Green Norf 142 D5
Stubbs Green Norf 143 D7
Stubhampton Dorset 30 E6
Stubshaw Cross
Gtr Man 194 G5
Stubton Lincs 172 F5
Stubwood Staffs 151 B11
Stuckgowan Argyll 285 G7
Stuckton Hants 31 E11
Stud Green E Ches 168 C2
Stud Green Windsor 65 D11
Studd Hill Kent 71 F7
Studdal Kent 55 D10
Studfold N Yorks 212 E6
Studham C Beds 85 B8
Studland Dorset 18 E6
Studley Warks 117 E11
Studley Wilts 62 E3
Studley Green Bucks 84 F3
Studley Green Wilts 45 B10
Studley Roger N Yorks 214 E5
Studley Royal N Yorks 214 E5
Stump Cross Essex 105 C10
Stumps Cross Glos 99 E11
Stuntney Cambs 123 B11
Stunts Green E Sus 23 C10
Sturbridge Staffs 150 C6
Sturford Wilts 45 E10
Sturgate Lincs 188 D5
Sturmer Essex 106 C3
Sturminster Common
Dorset 30 E3
Sturminster Marshall
Dorset 31 G7
Sturminster Newton
Dorset 30 E3
Sturry Kent 71 G7
Stursdon Corn 24 E2
Sturton N Lincs 200 G3
Sturton by Stow Lincs 188 E5
Sturton le Steeple Notts 188 E3
Stuston Suff 126 B2
Stutton N Yorks 206 E5
Stutton Suff 108 E3
Styal E Ches 184 E4
Styants Bottom Kent 52 B5
Stydd Lancs 203 F9
Styrrup Notts 187 C10
Suainebost W Isles 304 B7
Suardail W Isles 304 E6
Succoth Aberds 302 F4
Succoth Argyll 284 G6
Suckley Worcs 116 G4
Suckley Green Worcs 116 G4
Suckley Knowl Worcs 116 G4
Sucksted Green Essex 105 F11
Suckquoy Orkney 314 H4
Sudborough Northants 137 G9
Sudbourne Suff 127 G8
Sudbrook Lincs 173 G7
Sudbrook Mon 60 B4
Sudbrooke Lincs 189 F8
Sudbury Derbys 152 C3
Sudbury London 67 C7
Sudbury Suff 107 C7
Sudden Gtr Man 195 E11
Suddie Highld 300 D6
Sudgrove Glos 80 D6
Suffield N Yorks 227 G9
Suffield Norf 160 C4
Sugnall Staffs 150 C5
Sugwas Pool Hereford 97 C9
Suisnish Highld 295 D7
Suladale Highld 298 D3
Sulaisiadar W Isles 304 E7
Sulby I o M 192 C4
Sulgrave Northants 101 B11
Sulgrave T & W 243 F8
Sulham W Berks 64 E6
Sulhampstead W Berks 64 F6
Sulhampstead Abbots
W Berks 64 F6
Sulhampstead Bannister
Upper End W Berks 64 F6
Sulhamstead W Berks 64 F6
Sulland Orkney 314 B5
Sullington W Sus 35 E9
Sullington Warren
W Sus 35 E9
Sullom Shetland 312 F5
Sullom Voe Oil
Terminal Shetland 312 F5
Sully V Glam 59 F7
Sumburgh Shetland 313 N6
Summer Bridge N Yorks 214 G4
Summer Heath Bucks 84 G2
Summer Hill E Sus 23 D9
Summer Hill W Mid 133 E8
Summerbridge N Yorks 214 G4
Summercourt Corn 5 D7
Summerfield Kent 55 B9
Summerfield Norf 158 B5
Summerfield Worcs 116 C6
Summerfield Park
W Mid 133 F10
Summergangs Hull 209 G8
Summerhill Newport 59 B10
Summerhill Pembs 73 D11
Summerhill Staffs 133 B11
Summerhill Telford 150 F4
Summerhill Worcs 116 B6
Summerhill Wrex 166 E4
Summerhouse Darl 224 B4
Summerlands Cumb 211 B10
Summerlands Som 29 D8
Summerleaze Mon 60 B2
Summerley Derbys 186 F5
Summersdales N Yorks 205 C8
Summersdale W Sus 22 B5
Summerseat Gtr Man 195 E9
Summerston Glasgow 277 G11
Summerstown Bucks 102 G3
Summerstown London 67 E9
Summertown Oxon 83 D8
Summit Gtr Man 195 E10
Summit Gtr Man 196 D2
Summit Gtr Man 196 F2
Summit Gtr Man 185 B7
Sun Green Gtr Man 210 E5
Sunbrick Cumb 66 E5
Sunbury Common Sur
Sunbury-on-Thames
Sur 66 F6
Sundayshill S Glos 79 G11
Sundaywell Dumfries 247 G8
Sunderland Argyll 274 G3
Sunderland Cumb 229 D9
Sunderland Lancs 202 B4
Sunderland T & W 243 F9
Sunderland Bridge
Durham 233 D11
Sundhope Borders 261 D8
Sundon Park Luton 103 F11
Sundridge Kent 52 B3
Sundridge London 68 E2
Sunhill Glos 81 E10
Sunipol Argyll 288 D5
Sunk Island E Yorks 201 D9
Sunken Marsh Essex 69 C10
Sunningdale Windsor 66 F3
Sunninghill Windsor 66 F2
Sunningwell Oxon 83 E7
Sunniside Durham 233 D8
Sunniside T & W 242 F6
Sunniside T & W 243 G8
Sunny Bank Gtr Man 195 F10
Sunny Bower Lancs 203 G10
Sunny Hill Derby 152 C6
Sunnybrow Durham 233 E9
Sunnyfields S Yorks 198 F4
Sunnyhurst Blkburn 195 C7
Sunnylaw Stirl 278 B5
Sunnymead Oxon 83 D8
Sunnymeads Windsor 66 D4
Sunnymede Essex 87 G11
Sunnyside S Yorks 187 C7
Sunnyside W Sus 51 F11
Sunset Hereford 114 F6
Sunton Wilts 47 C8
Surbiton London 67 F7
Surby I o M 192 E3
Surfleet Lincs 156 D5
Surfleet Seas End Lincs 156 D5
Surlingham Norf 142 B6
Surrex Essex 107 G7
Suspension Bridge
Norf 139 E10
Sustead Norf 160 B3
Susworth Lincs 199 G10
Sutcombe Devon 24 E4
Sutcombemill Devon 24 E4
Sutherland Grove
Argyll 289 E11
Suton Norf 141 D11
Sutors of Cromarty
Highld 301 C8
Sutterby Lincs 190 G5
Sutterton Lincs 156 B5
Sutterton Dowdyke
Lincs 156 C5
Sutton Bucks 66 D4
Sutton C Beds 104 B4
Sutton Cambs 123 B8
Sutton Devon 8 G4
Sutton E Sus 23 F7
Sutton Kent 55 D10
Sutton Lincs 172 E5
Sutton London 67 G9
Sutton Mers 183 C8
Sutton N Yorks 198 B3
Sutton Norf 161 E7
Sutton Notts 154 B5
Sutton Notts 187 E11
Sutton Oxon 82 D6
Sutton P'boro 137 D11
Sutton Pembs 72 B6
Sutton S Yorks 198 E5
Sutton Shrops 132 F4
Sutton Shrops 149 D7
Sutton Shrops 149 G10
Sutton Shrops 150 C3
Sutton Som 44 G6
Sutton Staffs 150 E5
Sutton Suff 108 B6
Sutton Sur 50 D5
Sutton W Sus 35 D7
Sutton Abinger Sur 50 D6
Sutton at Hone Kent 68 E5
Sutton Bassett
Northants 136 E5
Sutton Benger Wilts 62 D2
Sutton Bingham Som 29 E8
Sutton Bonington
Notts 153 E10
Sutton Bridge Lincs 157 E9
Sutton Cheney Leics 135 C8
Sutton Coldfield W Mid 134 D2
Sutton Corner Lincs 157 D8
Sutton Courtenay Oxon 83 G8
Sutton Crosses Lincs 157 E8
Sutton Cum Lound
Notts 187 E11
Sutton End W Sus 35 D7
Sutton Forest Side
Notts 171 D8
Sutton Gault Cambs 123 B8
Sutton Green Sur 50 C4
Sutton Green W Ches 182 F5
Sutton Green Wrex 166 F6
Sutton Hall Shrops 132 C4
Sutton Heath Mers 183 C8
Sutton Hill Telford 132 C4
Sutton Holms Dorset 31 F9
Sutton Howgrave
N Yorks 214 D6
Sutton in Ashfield
Notts 171 D7
Sutton-in-Craven
N Yorks 204 E6
Sutton in the Elms
Leics 135 E10
Sutton Ings Hull 209 G8
Sutton Lakes Hereford 97 B10
Sutton Lane Ends
E Ches 184 G6
Sutton Leach Mers 183 C8
Sutton Maddock Shrops 132 C4
Sutton Mallet Som 43 F11
Sutton Mandeville
Wilts 31 B7
Sutton Manor Mers 183 C8
Sutton Marsh Hereford 97 C10
Sutton Mill N Yorks 204 E6
Sutton Montis Som 29 C10
Sutton on Hull Hull 209 G8
Sutton on Sea Lincs 191 E8
Sutton-on-the-
Forest N Yorks 215 G11
Sutton on the Hill
Derbys 152 C4
Sutton on Trent Notts 172 B3
Sutton Poyntz Dorset 17 E10
Sutton Row Wilts 31 B7
Sutton St Edmund
Lincs 157 G7
Sutton St James Lincs 157 F7
Sutton St Michael
Hereford 97 B10
Sutton St Nicholas
Hereford 97 B10
Sutton Scarsdale
Derbys 170 B6
Sutton Scotney Hants 48 F3
Sutton Street Suff 108 C6
Sutton under Brailes
Warks 100 D6
Sutton-under-
Whitestonecliffe
N Yorks 215 C9
Sutton upon Derwent
E Yorks 207 D10
Sutton Valence Kent 53 D10
Sutton Veny Wilts 45 E11
Sutton Waldron Dorset 30 D5
Sutton Weaver W Ches 183 F8
Sutton Wick Bath 44 B5
Sutton Wick Oxon 83 G7
Swaby Lincs 190 F5
Swadlincote Derbys 152 F6
Swaffham Norf 140 B6
Swaffham Bulbeck
Cambs 123 E11
Swaffham Prior Cambs 123 E11
Swafield Norf 160 C5
Swaile's Green E Sus 38 C3
Swain House W Yorks 205 F9
Swainby N Yorks 225 E9
Swainshill Hereford 97 C9
Swainsthorpe Norf 142 C4
Swainswick Bath 61 F9
Swaithe S Yorks 197 G11
Swalcliffe Oxon 101 D7
Swalecliffe Kent 70 F6
Swallow Lincs 201 G7
Swallow Beck Lincs 173 B7
Swallowcliffe Wilts 31 B7
Swallowfield Wokingham 65 G8
Swallowfields Devon 8 C5
Swallowhurst Cumb 220 G2
Swallownest S Yorks 187 E7
Swallows Cross Essex 87 F10
Swalwell T & W 242 E6
Swampton Hants 48 C2
Swan Bottom Bucks 84 D6
Swan Green Suff 126 C5
Swan Green W Ches 184 G2
Swan Street Essex 107 F7
Swan Village W Mid 133 E9
Swanage Dorset 18 F6
Swanbach E Ches 167 G11
Swanbister Orkney 314 F3
Swanborough Swindon 81 G11
Swanbourne Bucks 102 F6
Swanbridge V Glam 59 F7
Swanland E Yorks 200 B3
Swanley Glos 80 F2
Swanley Kent 68 F4
Swanley Bar Herts 86 E3
Swanley Village Kent 68 F4
Swanmore Hants 33 D9
Swanmore I o W 21 C7
Swannay Orkney 314 D2
Swannington Leics 153 F8
Swannington Norf 160 F2
Swanpool Lincs 189 G7
Swanscombe Kent 68 E6
Swansea = Abertawe
Swansea 56 C6
Swanside Mers 182 C6
Swanston Edin 270 B4
Swanton Abbott Norf 160 D5
Swanton Hill Norf 160 D5
Swanton Morley Norf 159 F10
Swanton Novers Norf 159 C10
Swanton Street Kent 53 B11
Swanwick Derbys 170 E6
Swanwick Hants 33 F8
Swanwick Green E Ches 167 F9
Swarby Lincs 173 G8
Swarcliffe W Yorks 206 F3
Swardeston Norf 142 C4
Swarister Shetland 312 E7
Swarkestone Derbys 153 D7
Swarland Northumb 252 C5
Swarraton Hants 48 F5
Swartha W Yorks 205 D7
Swarthmoor Cumb 210 D5
Swartland Orkney 314 D2
Swathwick Derbys 170 B5
Swaton Lincs 156 B2
Swavesey Cambs 123 D7
Sway Hants 19 B11
Swayfield Lincs 155 E9
Swaythling Soton 32 D6
Sweet Green Worcs 116 E2
Sweetham Devon 14 B3
Sweethaws E Sus 37 B8
Sweethay Som 28 C2
Sweetholme Cumb 221 B11
Sweethouse Corn 5 C11
Sweets Corn 11 B9
Sweetshouse Corn 5 C11
Sweffling Suff 126 E6
Swell Som 28 C5
Swelling Hill Hants 49 G7
Swepstone Leics 153 G7
Swerford Oxon 101 E7
Swettenham E Ches 168 B4
Swetton N Yorks 214 E3
Swffryd Caerph 78 F2
Swift's Green Kent 53 E11
Swiftsden E Sus 38 B2
Swilland Suff 126 G3
Swillbrook Lancs 202 G5
Swillington W Yorks 206 G3
Swillington Common
W Yorks 206 G3
Swimbridge Devon 25 B10
Swimbridge Newland
Devon 40 G6
Swinbrook Oxon 82 C3
Swincliffe N Yorks 205 B10
Swincliffe W Yorks 197 B8
Swincombe Devon 41 E7
Swinden N Yorks 204 C3
Swinderby Lincs 172 C5
Swindon Glos 99 G8
Swindon Staffs 133 E7
Swindon Swindon 63 C7
Swine E Yorks 209 F8
Swinefleet E Yorks 199 C9
Swineford S Glos 61 F7
Swineshead Beds 121 D11
Swineshead Lincs 174 G2
Swineshead Bridge
Lincs 174 G2
Swinethorpe Lincs 172 B5
Swiney Highld 310 F6
Swinford Leics 119 B11
Swinford Oxon 82 D6
Swingate Notts 171 G8
Swingbrow Cambs 139 F7
Swingfield Minnis Kent 55 E8
Swingfield Street Kent 55 E8
Swingleton Green Suff 107 B9
Swinhoe Northumb 264 D6
Swinhope Lincs 190 B2
Swining Shetland 312 G6
Swinister Shetland 312 E5
Swinister Shetland 313 L6
Swinithwaite N Yorks 213 B10
Swinmore Common
Hereford 98 C3
Swinnie Borders 262 F4
Swinnow Moor
W Yorks 205 G10
Swinscoe Staffs 169 F10
Swinside Cumb 229 G10
Swinside Townfoot
Borders 262 F6
Swinstead Lincs 155 E10
Swinton Borders 272 F6
Swinton Glasgow 268 C3
Swinton Gtr Man 195 G9
Swinton N Yorks 214 D4
Swinton N Yorks 216 E5
Swinton S Yorks 186 B6
Swinton Bridge S Yorks 187 B7
Swinton Hill Borders 272 F6
Swinton Park Gtr Man 195 G9
Swintonmill Borders 272 F6
Swiss Valley Carms 75 E8
Swithland Leics 153 G10
Swordale Highld 300 C5
Swordale Highld 309 K6
Swordland Highld 295 F9
Swordly Highld 308 C7
Sworton Heath E Ches 183 E11
Swyddffynnon Ceredig 112 D3
Swynnerton Staffs 151 B7
Swyre Dorset 16 D6
Sycamore Devon 28 F3
Sychdyn = Soughton
Flint 166 B2
Sychtyn Powys 129 B9
Sydallt Wrex 166 D4
Syde Glos 81 C7
Sydenham London 67 E11
Sydenham Oxon 84 E2
Sydenham Som 43 F10
Sydenham Damerel
Devon 12 F4
Syderstone Norf 158 C6
Sydling St Nicholas
Dorset 17 B8
Sydmonton Hants 48 B3
Sydney E Ches 168 D2
Syerston Notts 172 F2
Syke Gtr Man 195 D11
Sykehouse S Yorks 198 D6
Sykes Lancs 203 C8
Syleham Suff 126 B4
Sylen Carms 75 D8
Symbister Shetland 313 G7
Symington Borders 271 F8
Symington S Ayrs 257 C9
Symington S Lnrk 259 B11
Symonds Green Herts 104 F4
Symonds Yat Hereford 79 B9
Symondsbury Dorset 16 C4
Synderford Dorset 28 G5
Synod Inn = Post Mawr
Ceredig 111 G8
Synton Borders 261 E11
Synton Mains Borders 261 E11
Synwell Glos 80 G3
Syre Highld 308 E6
Syreford Glos 99 G10
Syresham Northants 102 C2
Syster Highld 310 C6
Syston Leics 154 G2
Syston Lincs 172 G6
Sytch Ho Green Shrops 132 E5
Sytch Lane Telford 150 E2
Sytchampton Worcs 116 D6
Sywell Northants 120 D6

T

Taagan Highld 299 C10
Tabley Hill E Ches 184 F2
Tabor Gwyn 146 F5
Tabost W Isles 305 G5
Tabost W Isles 304 B7
Tachbrook Mallory
Warks 118 E6
Tacker Street Som 42 F4
Tackley Oxon 101 G9
Tacleit W Isles 304 E3
Tacolneston Norf 142 D2
Tadcaster N Yorks 206 E5
Tadden Dorset 31 G7
Taddington Derbys 185 G10
Taddington Glos 99 E11
Taddiport Devon 25 D7
Tadhill Som 45 D7
Tadley Hants 64 G6
Tadley Oxon 64 B4
Tadlow Beds 104 B5
Tadlow C Beds 104 B5
Tadmarton Oxon 101 D7
Tadnoll Dorset 17 D11
Tadwick Bath 61 E8
Tadworth Sur 51 B8
Tafarn-y-bwlch Pembs 91 E11
Tafarn-y-gelyn Denb 165 C11
Tafarnau-bach
Bl Gwent 77 C10
Taff Merthyr Garden
Village M Tydf 77 F10
Taff's Well Rhondda 58 C6
Tafolwern Powys 129 C7
Tai Conwy 164 C3
Tai-bach Powys 148 D3
Tai-mawr Conwy 165 G7
Tai-morfa Gwyn 144 D5
Tai-nant Wrex 166 F3
Tai-Ucha Denb 165 D8
Taibach Neath 57 D9
Taigh a Ghearraidh
W Isles 296 D3
Taigh Bhalaigh W Isles 296 D3
Tain Highld 309 L7
Tain Highld 310 C6
Tainlon Gwyn 162 E6
Tai'r-Bull Powys 95 F9
Tai'r-heol Caerph 77 G10
Tai'r-ysgol Swansea 57 B7
Tairbeart W Isles 305 H3
Tairgwaith Neath 76 C2
Takeley Essex 105 G11
Takeley Street Essex 105 G10
Tal-sarn Ceredig 111 F10
Tal-y-bont Ceredig 128 F3
Tal-y-Bont Conwy 164 B3
Tal-y-bont Gwyn 145 E11
Tal-y-bont Gwyn 179 G10
Tal-y-bont Gwyn 180 G3
Tal-y-cafn Conwy 180 G3
Tal-y-coed Mon 78 B6
Tal-y-llyn Gwyn 128 B4
Tal-y-waenydd Gwyn 163 F11
Tal-y-wern Powys 128 C6
Talacharn = Laugharne
Carms 74 C4
Talachddu Powys 95 E11
Talacre Flint 181 E10
Talardd Gwyn 147 D7
Talaton Devon 15 B7
Talbenny Pembs 72 C4
Talbot Green Rhondda 58 C4
Talbot Heath Poole 19 C7
Talbot Village Poole 19 C7
Talbot Woods Bmouth 19 C7
Talbot's End S Glos 80 G2
Tale Devon 27 G9
Talerddig Powys 129 C8
Talgarreg Ceredig 111 G8
Talgarth Powys 96 E3
Talgarth's Well Swansea 56 D2
Talisker Highld 294 B5
Talke Staffs 168 E4
Talke Pits Staffs 168 E4
Talkin Cumb 240 F3
Talla Linnfoots Borders 260 E4
Talladale Highld 299 B9
Tallaminnoch S Ayrs 245 D10
Talland Corn 6 E4
Tallarn Green Wrex 166 G6
Tallentire Cumb 229 D8
Talley Carms 94 E2
Tallington Lincs 137 B11
Talmine Highld 308 C5
Talog Carms 92 F6
Talsarn Carms 94 F5
Talsarnau Gwyn 146 B2
Talskiddy Corn 5 B8
Talwrn Anglesey 179 F7
Talwrn Wrex 166 F3
Talybont-on-Usk Powys 96 G2
Talygarn Rhondda 58 C4
Talyllyn Powys 96 F2
Talysarn Gwyn 163 E7
Talywain Torf 78 E3
Tamanabhagh W Isles 304 F2
Tame Bridge N Yorks 225 D10
Tame Water Gtr Man 196 F3
Tamer Lane End
Gtr Man 194 G6
Tamerton Foliot Plym 7 C9
Tamfourhill Falk 279 E7
Tamworth Staffs 134 C4
Tamworth Green Lincs 174 G5
Tan Hills Durham 233 B11
Tan Hinon Powys 129 F7
Tan-lan Conwy 164 C3
Tan-lan Gwyn 163 G10
Tan Office Suff 126 E2
Tan Office Green Suff 124 F5
Tan-y-bwlch Gwyn 163 G11
Tan-y-fron Conwy 165 C7
Tan-y-graig Anglesey 179 F8
Tan-y-graig Gwyn 144 B6
Tan-y-groes Ceredig 92 B5
Tan-y-mynydd Gwyn 144 C6
Tan-y-pistyll Powys 147 D11
Tan-yr-allt Denb 181 E9
Tan-yr-allt Gwyn 163 E7
Tancred N Yorks 206 B5
Tandem W Yorks 197 D7
Tanden Kent 54 F2
Tandlehill Renfs 267 C8
Tandridge Sur 51 C11
Tanerdy Carms 93 G8
Tanfield Durham 242 F5
Tanfield Lea Durham 242 G5
Tang N Yorks 205 B10
Tang Hall York 207 C8
Tangasdal W Isles 297 M2
Tangiers Pembs 73 B7
Tangley Hants 47 C10
Tanglwst Carms 92 E6
Tangmere W Sus 22 B6
Tangwick Shetland 312 F4
Tangy Argyll 255 E7
Tanhouse Lancs 194 F3
Tanis Wilts 62 G3
Tankersley S Yorks 197 G10
Tankerton Kent 70 F6
Tanlan Flint 181 F10
Tanlan Banks Flint 181 E10
Tannach Highld 310 E7
Tannachie Aberds 293 E9
Tannadice Angus 287 B8
Tanner's Green Worcs 117 C11
Tannington Suff 126 D4
Tannington Place Suff 126 D4
Tannochside N Lnrk 268 C4
Tansley Derbys 170 D4
Tansley Hill W Mid 133 F9

396 Tan – Tix

Tansley Knoll Derbys 170 C4
Tansor Northants 137 E11
Tanterton Lancs 202 G6
Tantobie Durham 242 G5
Tanton N Yorks 225 C10
Tanwood Worcs 117 C8
Tanworth-in-Arden Warks 118 C2
Tanyfron Wrex 166 E3
Tanygrisiau Gwyn 163 F11
Tanyrhydiau Ceredig 112 D4
Tanysgafell Gwyn 163 B10
Taobh a Chaolais W Isles 297 K3
Taobh a' Ghlinne W Isles 305 G5
Taobh a Thuath Loch Aineort W Isles 297 J3
Taobh a Tuath Loch Baghasdail W Isles 297 J3
Taobh Siar W Isles 305 H3
Taobh Tuath W Isles 296 C5
Taplow Bucks 66 C2
Tapnage Hants 33 E9
Tapton Derbys 186 G5
Tapton Hill S Yorks 186 D4
Tarbat Ho Highld 301 B7
Tarbert Argyll 255 B7
Tarbert Argyll 275 E7
Tarbert Argyll 275 G9
Tarbet Argyll 285 G7
Tarbet Highld 295 F9
Tarbet Highld 306 E6
Tarbock Green Mers 183 D7
Tarbolton S Ayrs 257 D10
Tarbrax S Lnrk 269 D10
Tardebigge Worcs 117 D10
Tardy Gate Lancs 194 B4
Tarfside Angus 292 F6
Tarland Aberds 292 C6
Tarleton Lancs 194 C3
Tarleton Moss Lancs 194 C2
Tarlogie Highld 309 L7
Tarlscough Lancs 194 E2
Tarlton Glos 81 F7
Tarn W Yorks 205 F9
Tarnbrook Lancs 203 B7
Tarnock Som 43 C11
Tarns Cumb 229 B8
Tarnside Cumb 221 G8
Tarporley W Ches 167 C9
Tarpots Essex 69 B9
Tarr Som 42 G6
Tarraby Cumb 239 F10
Tarrant Crawford Dorset 30 G6
Tarrant Gunville Dorset 30 E6
Tarrant Hinton Dorset 30 E6
Tarrant Keyneston Dorset 30 G6
Tarrant Launceston Dorset 30 F6
Tarrant Monkton Dorset 30 F6
Tarrant Rawston Dorset 30 F6
Tarrant Rushton Dorset 30 F6
Tarrel Highld 311 L2
Tarring Neville E Sus 36 G6
Tarrington Hereford 98 C2
Tarrington Common Hereford 98 D2
Tarryblake Ho Moray 302 E5
Tarsappie Perth 286 E5
Tarskavaig Highld 295 E7
Tarts Hill Shrops 149 B8
Tarves Aberds 303 F8
Tarvie Highld 300 D4
Tarvie Perth 292 G2
Tarvin W Ches 167 B7
Tarvin Sands W Ches 167 B7
Tasburgh Norf 142 D4
Tasley Shrops 132 E3
Taston Oxon 101 G7
Tat Bank W Mid 133 F9
Tatenhill Staffs 152 E4
Tatenhill Common Staffs 152 E3
Tathall End M Keynes 102 B6
Tatham Lancs 212 F2
Tathwell Lincs 190 E4
Tatling End Bucks 66 B4
Tatsfield Sur 52 B2
Tattenhall W Ches 167 D7
Tattenhoe M Keynes 102 E6
Tatterford Norf 159 D7
Tattersett Norf 158 C6
Tattershall Lincs 174 D2
Tattershall Bridge Lincs 173 D11
Tattershall Thorpe Lincs 174 D2
Tattingstone Suff 108 D2
Tattingstone White Horse Suff 108 D2
Tattle Bank Warks 118 E3
Tatton Dale E Ches 184 E2
Tatworth Som 28 F4
Taunton Gtr Man 196 G2
Taunton Som 28 C2
Taverham Norf 160 G3
Taverners Green Essex 87 B9
Tavernspite Pembs 73 C11
Tavistock Devon 12 G5
Taw Green Devon 13 B9
Tawstock Devon 25 B9
Taxal Derbys 185 F8
Tay Bridge Dundee 287 E8
Tayinloan Argyll 255 C7
Taymouth Castle Perth 285 C11
Taynish Argyll 275 E8
Taynton Glos 98 G4
Taynton Oxon 82 C2
Taynuilt Argyll 284 D4
Tayport Fife 287 E8
Tayvallich Argyll 275 E8
Tea Green Herts 104 G2
Tealby Lincs 189 C11
Tealing Angus 287 D8
Team Valley T & W 242 E6
Teams T & W 242 E6
Teanford Staffs 169 G8
Teangue Highld 295 E8
Teanna Mhachair W Isles 296 E3
Teasley Mead E Sus 52 F4
Tebay Cumb 222 E2
Tebworth C Beds 103 F9
Tedburn St Mary Devon 14 C2
Teddington Glos 99 E9
Teddington London 67 E7
Teddington Hands Worcs 99 E9
Tedsmore Shrops 149 D7
Tedstone Delamere Hereford 116 F3
Tedstone Wafer Hereford 116 F3
Teesville Redcar 225 B10
Teeton Northants 120 C3
Teffont Evias Wilts 46 G3
Teffont Magna Wilts 46 G3
Tegryn Pembs 92 E4
Teigh Rutland 155 F7
Teign Village Devon 14 E2
Teigncombe Devon 13 D9
Teigngrace Devon 14 G2
Teignmouth Devon 14 G4
Telford Telford 132 B3
Telham E Sus 38 E3
Tellisford Som 45 B10
Telscombe E Sus 36 G6
Telscombe Cliffs E Sus 36 G5
Templand Dumfries 248 F3
Temple Corn 11 G8
Temple Glasgow 267 B10
Temple Midloth 270 D6
Temple Wilts 45 E10
Temple Windsor 65 C10
Temple Balsall W Mid 118 B4
Temple Bar Carms 75 B9
Temple Bar Ceredig 111 G10
Temple Bar W Sus 22 B5
Temple Cloud Bath 44 B6
Temple Cowley Oxon 83 E8
Temple End Essex 106 C6
Temple End Suff 124 G3
Temple Ewell Kent 55 E9
Temple Fields Essex 87 C7
Temple Grafton Warks 118 G2
Temple Guiting Glos 99 F11
Temple Herdewyke Warks 119 G7
Temple Hill Kent 68 D5
Temple Hirst N Yorks 198 C6
Temple Normanton Derbys 170 B6
Temple Sowerby Cumb 231 F8
Templeborough S Yorks 186 C6
Templecombe Som 30 C2
Templehall Fife 280 C5
Templeman's Ash Dorset 28 G6
Templeton Devon 26 E5
Templeton Pembs 73 C10
Templeton W Berks 63 F11
Templeton Bridge Devon 26 E5
Templetown Durham 242 G4
Tempsford C Beds 122 G3
Ten Acres W Mid 133 G11
Ten Mile Bank Norf 140 D2
Tenandry Perth 291 G11
Tenbury Wells Worcs 115 D11
Tenby = Dinbych-y-Pysgod Pembs 73 E10
Tencreek Corn 6 E4
Tendring Essex 108 G2
Tendring Green Essex 108 F2
Tendring Heath Essex 108 F2
Tenston Orkney 314 E2
Tenterden Kent 53 G11
Terfyn Conwy 180 F6
Terfyn Gwyn 163 C9
Terhill Som 43 G7
Terling Essex 88 B3
Ternhill Shrops 150 C2
Terpersie Castle Aberds 302 G5
Terras Corn 5 E8
Terregles Banks Dumfries 237 B11
Terrible Down E Sus 23 B7
Terrick Bucks 84 D4
Terriers Bucks 84 G5
Terrington N Yorks 216 E3
Terrington St Clement Norf 157 E10
Terrington St John Norf 157 G10
Terryhorn Aberds 302 F4
Terry's Green Warks 118 C2
Terwick Common W Sus 34 C4
Teston Kent 53 C8
Testwood Hants 32 E5
Tetbury Glos 80 G5
Tetbury Upton Glos 80 F5
Tetchill Shrops 149 C7
Tetchwick Bucks 83 B11
Tetcott Devon 12 B2
Tetford Lincs 190 G4
Tetley N Lincs 199 E9
Tetney Lincs 201 G10
Tetney Lock Lincs 201 G10
Tetsworth Oxon 83 E11
Tettenhall W Mid 133 D7
Tettenhall Wood W Mid 133 D7
Tetworth Cambs 122 G4
Teuchan Aberds 303 F10
Teversal Notts 171 C7
Teversham Cambs 123 F9
Teviothead Borders 249 B10
Tewel Aberds 293 E10
Tewin Herts 86 C3
Tewin Wood Herts 86 B3
Tewitfield Lancs 211 E10
Tewkesbury Glos 99 E7
Teynham Kent 70 G3
Teynham Street Kent 70 G3
Thackley W Yorks 205 F9
Thackley End W Yorks 205 F9
Thackthwaite Cumb 229 G8
Thainston Aberds 293 F8
Thakeham W Sus 35 D10
Thame Oxon 84 D2
Thames Ditton Sur 67 F7
Thames Haven Thurrock 69 C8
Thames Head Glos 81 F7
Thamesmead London 68 C3
Thanington Kent 54 B6
Thankerton S Lnrk 259 B11
Tharston Norf 142 E3
Thatcham W Berks 64 F4
Thatto Heath Mers 183 C8
Thaxted Essex 106 E2
The Aird Highld 298 D4
The Alders Staffs 134 C3
The Arms Norf 141 D7
The Bage Hereford 96 C5
The Balloch Perth 286 F2
The Bank E Ches 168 D4
The Banks Gtr Man 185 D7
The Banks Wilts 62 D4
The Barony E Ches 167 E11
The Barony Orkney 314 D2
The Barton Wilts 62 D5
The Batch S Glos 61 E7
The Beeches Glos 81 E8
The Bell Gtr Man 194 F4
The Bents Staffs 151 C10
The Blythe Staffs 151 D10
The Bog Shrops 131 D7
The Borough Dorset 30 E2
The Borough London 67 D10
The Bourne Sur 49 E10
The Bourne Worcs 117 F9
The Bows Stirl 285 G11
The Braes Highld 295 B7
The Brampton Staffs 168 F4
The Brand Leics 153 G10
The Bratch Staffs 133 E7
The Breck Orkney 314 F3
The Brents Kent 70 G4
The Bridge Dorset 30 E3
The Broad Hereford 115 E9
The Brook Suff 125 B11
The Brushes Derbys 186 F5
The Bryn Mon 78 D4
The Burf Worcs 116 D6
The Butts Hants 49 F8
The Butts Som 45 D9
The Camp Glos 80 D6
The Camp Herts 85 D11
The Cape Warks 118 D5
The Chart Kent 52 C3
The Chequer Wrex 167 G7
The Chuckery W Mid 133 D10
The City Bucks 84 F3
The Cleaver Hereford 97 F10
The Close W Sus 22 C5
The Colony Oxon 100 D6
The Common Bath 60 G6
The Common Bucks 102 E5
The Common Dorset 30 E3
The Common Shrops 150 D3
The Common Suff 108 B2
The Common Swansea 56 C4
The Common W Sus 51 G7
The Common Wilts 47 G8
The Common Wilts 61 G11
The Common Wilts 62 C4
The Corner Kent 53 E8
The Corner Shrops 131 F8
The Cot Mon 79 F8
The Craigs Highld 309 K4
The Crofts E Yorks 218 E4
The Cronk I o M 192 C4
The Cross Hands Leics 134 C6
The Cwm Mon 79 G7
The Dell Suff 143 D9
The Delves W Mid 133 D10
The Den N Ayrs 266 E6
The Dene Durham 242 G4
The Dene Hants 47 C11
The Down Kent 53 F7
The Down Shrops 132 E3
The Downs Sur 50 F3
The Dunks Wrex 166 E4
The Eals Northumb 251 F7
The Eaves Glos 79 D10
The Fall W Yorks 197 B10
The Fence Glos 79 D8
The Flat Glos 80 B3
The Flatt Cumb 240 B3
The Flourish Derbys 153 B8
The Folly Herts 85 C11
The Folly S Glos 61 E8
The Fording Hereford 98 F3
The Forge Hereford 114 F6
The Forstal Kent 54 F4
The Forties Derbys 152 F6
The Four Alls Shrops 150 C3
The Fox Wilts 62 B6
The Foxholes Shrops 132 G2
The Frenches Hants 32 C4
The Frythe Herts 86 C2
The Garths Shetland 312 B8
The Gibb Wilts 61 D10
The Glack Borders 260 B6
The Gore Shrops 131 G11
The Grange N Yorks 225 F11
The Grange Norf 160 E2
The Green C Beds 85 B8
The Green Cambs 122 D5
The Green Cumb 210 C3
The Green Cumb 211 D7
The Green Essex 88 B3
The Green Hants 32 B3
The Green M Keynes 103 C7
The Green Norf 141 C11
The Green Norf 159 B11
The Green Northants 102 C5
The Green Oxon 101 F9
The Green S Yorks 197 G8
The Green Shrops 130 G6
The Green Warks 118 F4
The Green Wilts 45 G11
The Grove Dumfries 237 B11
The Grove Durham 242 G3
The Grove Herts 85 F9
The Grove Shrops 131 B7
The Grove Shrops 131 G8
The Grove Worcs 99 C7
The Gutter Derbys 170 F5
The Gutter Worcs 117 B9
The Hacket S Glos 61 B7
The Hague Derbys 185 C8
The Hall Shetland 312 D8
The Hallands N Lincs 200 C5
The Ham Wilts 45 C11
The Handfords Staffs 151 E7
The Harbour Kent 53 D10
The Haven W Sus 50 G5
The Headland Hrtlpl 234 E6
The Heath Norf 159 D8
The Heath Norf 160 E3
The Heath Norf 160 E4
The Heath Staffs 151 C11
The Heath Suff 108 D2
The Hem Shrops 132 B4
The Hendre Mon 79 C7
The Herberts V Glam 58 E3
The Hermitage Cambs 123 C7
The High Essex 86 C6
The Highlands E Sus 38 F2
The Hill Cumb 210 C3
The Hobbins Shrops 132 E4
The Hollands Staffs 168 D6
The Hollies Notts 172 E4
The Holmes Derbys 153 B7
The Holt Wokingham 65 D10
The Hook Worcs 98 C6
The Hope Shrops 115 B10
The Howe Cumb 211 B9
The Howe I o M 192 F2
The Humbers Telford 150 G3
The Hundred Hereford 115 E10
The Hyde London 67 B8
The Hyde Worcs 98 C6
The Hythe Essex 107 G10
The Inch Edin 280 G5
The Knab Swansea 56 D6
The Knap V Glam 58 F5
The Knapp Hereford 116 G3
The Knapp S Glos 79 G11
The Knowle W Mid 133 F9
The Laches Staffs 133 B8
The Lake Dumfries 237 E8
The Lakes Worcs 116 B5
The Lawe T & W 243 D9
The Lawns E Yorks 208 G6
The Leacon Kent 54 G3
The Leath Shrops 131 F11
The Lee Bucks 84 E6
The Lees Kent 54 C4
The Leigh Glos 99 F7
The Leys Staffs 134 C4
The Lhen I o M 192 B4
The Ling Norf 142 D6
The Lings Norf 141 B10
The Lings S Yorks 199 F7
The Linleys Wilts 61 F11
The Lunt W Mid 133 D9
The Manor W Sus 22 C4
The Marsh E Ches 168 C4
The Marsh Hereford 115 F9
The Marsh Powys 130 D6
The Marsh Shrops 150 D3
The Marsh Staffs 150 D6
The Marsh Suff 125 B11
The Marsh Suff 126 B2
The Marsh Wilts 62 C5
The Middles Durham 242 G6
The Mint Hants 34 B3
The Moor Flint 166 B4
The Moor Kent 38 B3
The Moors Hereford 97 E10
The Mount Hants 64 G2
The Mount Reading 65 E8
The Mumbles = Y Mwmbwls Swansea 56 D6
The Murray S Lnrk 268 E2
The Mythe Glos 99 E7
The Nant Wrex 166 E3
The Narth Mon 79 D8
The Neuk Aberds 293 D9
The Node Herts 104 G4
The Nook Shrops 149 C11
The Nook Shrops 150 E3
The North Mon 79 D8
The Oval Bath 61 G8
The Park Glos 99 G8
The Parks S Yorks 198 F6
The Pitts Wilts 31 B9
The Platt Oxon 83 E9
The Pludds Glos 79 B10
The Point Devon 14 E5
The Pole of Itlaw Aberds 302 D6
The Port of Felixstowe Suff 108 E5
The Potteries Stoke 168 F5
The Pound Glos 98 E4
The Quarry Glos 80 F2
The Quarry Shrops 149 G9
The Quarter Kent 53 E11
The Quarter Kent 53 G11
The Rampings Worcs 99 E7
The Rectory Lincs 156 G2
The Reddings Glos 99 G8
The Rhos Pembs 73 C8
The Rhydd Hereford 97 E9
The Riddle Hereford 115 E9
The Ridge Wilts 61 F11
The Ridges Wokingham 65 G10
The Ridgeway Herts 86 E3
The Riding Northumb 241 D10
The Riggs Borders 261 C8
The Rink Borders 261 C11
The Rise Windsor 66 F2
The Rock Telford 132 B3
The Rocks Kent 53 B8
The Rocks S Glos 61 C8
The Roe Denb 181 G8
The Rookery Herts 85 G10
The Rookery Staffs 168 D5
The Row Lancs 211 D9
The Rowe Staffs 150 B6
The Ryde Herts 86 D2
The Sands Sur 49 D11
The Scarr Glos 98 F4
The Shoe Wilts 61 E10
The Shruggs Staffs 151 C8
The Slack Durham 233 F8
The Slade W Berks 64 F4
The Smeeth Norf 157 G10
The Smithies Shrops 132 D3
The Spa Wilts 62 G2
The Spring Warks 118 C5
The Square Torf 78 F3
The Stocks Kent 38 B6
The Stocks Wilts 62 G2
The Straits Hants 49 F9
The Straits W Mid 133 E8
The Strand Wilts 46 B2
The Swillett Herts 85 F8
The Sydnall Shrops 150 C3
The Thrift Cambs 104 D6
The Throat Wokingham 65 F10
The Toft Staffs 151 F8
The Towans Corn 2 B3
The Town Scilly 1 F3
The Twittocks Glos 99 D7
The Tynings Glos 80 B6
The Vale W Mid 133 G11
The Valley E Ches 167 D11
The Valley Kent 54 C3
The Valley Leics 154 F4
The Valley Pembs 73 D10
The Vauld Hereford 97 B10
The Village Newport 78 G4
The Village W Mid 133 F7
The Village Windsor 66 E3
The Walshes Worcs 116 C6
The Warren Kent 54 E3
The Warren Wilts 63 F8
The Waterwheel Shrops 131 C7
The Weaven Hereford 97 E10
The Wells Sur 67 G7
The Wern Wrex 166 E3
The Willows NE Lincs 201 F8
The Wood Shrops 148 E6
The Wood Shrops 149 D9
The Woodlands Leics 136 D3
The Woodlands Suff 107 C11
The Woodlands Suff 108 D3
The Woods W Mid 133 D10
The Wrangle Bath 44 B4
The Wrythe London 67 F9
The Wyke Shrops 132 B4
The Wymm Hereford 97 B10
The Yeld Shrops 131 G11
Theakston N Yorks 214 B6
Thealby N Lincs 199 D11
Theale Som 44 D3
Theale W Berks 64 E6
Thearne E Yorks 209 F7
Theberton Suff 127 D8
Theddingworth Leics 136 F3
Theddlethorpe All Saints Lincs 191 D7
Theddlethorpe St Helen Lincs 191 D7
Thelbridge Barton Devon 26 E3
Thelnetham Suff 125 B10
Thelveton Norf 142 G3
Thelwall Warr 183 D10
Themelthorpe Norf 159 E11
Thenford Northants 101 C10
Theobald's Green Wilts 62 F4
Therfield Herts 104 D6
Thetford Lincs 156 F2
Thetford Norf 141 G7
Theydon Bois Essex 86 F6
Theydon Garnon Essex 87 F7
Theydon Mount Essex 87 F7
Thick Hollins W Yorks 196 E6
Thicket Mead Bath 45 B7
Thickthorn Hall Norf 142 B3
Thickwood Wilts 61 E10
Thimble End W Mid 134 E2
Thimbleby Lincs 190 G2
Thimbleby N Yorks 225 F9
Thinford Durham 233 E11
Thingley Wilts 61 E11
Thingwall Mers 182 E3
Thirdpart N Ayrs 266 F3
Thirlby N Yorks 215 C9
Thirlestane Borders 271 F11
Thirn N Yorks 214 B4
Thirsk N Yorks 215 C8
Thirtleby E Yorks 209 G9
Thistleton Lancs 202 F4
Thistleton Rutland 155 F8
Thistley Green Essex 88 B2
Thistley Green Suff 124 B3
Thixendale N Yorks 216 G6
Thockrington Northumb 241 B11
Tholomas Drove Cambs 139 B7
Tholthorpe N Yorks 215 F9
Thomas Chapel Pembs 73 D10
Thomas Close Cumb 230 C4
Thomastown Aberds 302 F5
Thomastown Rhondda 58 B4
Thompson Norf 141 D8
Thomshill Moray 302 D2
Thong Kent 69 E7
Thongsbridge W Yorks 196 F6
Thoralby N Yorks 213 B10
Thoresby Notts 187 G10
Thoresthorpe Lincs 191 F7
Thoresway Lincs 189 B11
Thorganby Lincs 190 B2
Thorganby N Yorks 207 E9
Thorgill N Yorks 226 F4
Thorington Suff 127 C8
Thorington Street Suff 107 D10
Thorlby N Yorks 204 C5
Thorley Herts 87 B7
Thorley I o W 20 D3
Thorley Houses Herts 105 G9
Thorley Street Herts 87 B7
Thorley Street I o W 20 D3
Thormanby N Yorks 215 E9
Thorn Devon 13 D9
Thorn Powys 114 E5
Thorn Hill S Yorks 186 C6
Thornaby on Tees Stockton 225 B9
Thornage Norf 159 B11
Thornborough Bucks 102 E4
Thornborough N Yorks 214 D5
Thornbury Devon 24 F6
Thornbury Hereford 116 F2
Thornbury S Glos 79 G10
Thornbury W Yorks 205 G9
Thornby Cumb 239 G7
Thornby Northants 120 B3
Thorncliff W Yorks 197 E8
Thorncliffe Staffs 169 D8
Thorncombe Dorset 28 G5
Thorncombe Dorset 30 G5
Thorncombe Street Sur 50 E4
Thorncote Green C Beds 104 B3
Thorncross I o W 20 E4
Thorndon Suff 126 D2
Thorndon Cross Devon 12 C6
Thorne Corn 24 G2
Thorne S Yorks 199 E7
Thorne Coffin Som 29 D8
Thorne Moor Devon 12 D3
Thorne St Margaret Som 27 C9
Thornehillhead Devon 24 D6
Thornend Wilts 62 D3
Thorner W Yorks 206 E3
Thornes Staffs 133 C11
Thornes W Yorks 197 D10
Thorney Bucks 66 D4
Thorney Notts 188 G5
Thorney P'boro 138 C4
Thorney Som 28 C6
Thorney Close T & W 243 G9
Thorney Crofts E Yorks 201 C8
Thorney Green Suff 125 E11
Thorney Hill Hants 19 B9
Thorney Island W Sus 22 C3
Thorney Toll P'boro 138 C6
Thorneywood Notts 171 G9
Thornfalcon Som 28 C3
Thornford Dorset 29 E10
Thorngrafton Northumb 241 D7
Thorngrove Som 43 G11
Thorngumbald E Yorks 201 B8
Thornham Norf 176 E2
Thornham Fold Gtr Man 195 F11
Thornham Magna Suff 126 C2
Thornham Parva Suff 126 C2
Thornhaugh P'boro 137 C11
Thornhill Cardiff 59 C7
Thornhill Cumb 219 D10
Thornhill Derbys 185 E11
Thornhill Dumfries 247 D9
Thornhill Soton 33 E7
Thornhill Stirl 278 B3
Thornhill Torf 78 F3
Thornhill W Yorks 197 D9
Thornhill Wilts 62 D5
Thornhill Edge W Yorks 197 D8
Thornhill Lees W Yorks 197 D8
Thornhill Park Hants 33 E7
Thornhills W Yorks 197 C7
Thornholme E Yorks 218 G2
Thornicombe Dorset 30 G5
Thornielee Borders 261 B10
Thornley Durham 233 D8
Thornley Durham 234 D3
Thornliebank E Renf 267 D10
Thorns N Yorks 223 E7
Thorns Suff 124 F4
Thorns Green Ches 184 E3
Thornseat S Yorks 186 C2
Thornsett Derbys 185 D8
Thornthwaite Cumb 229 F10
Thornthwaite N Yorks 205 B9
Thornton Angus 287 C7
Thornton Bucks 102 D5
Thornton E Yorks 207 D11
Thornton Fife 280 B5
Thornton Lancs 202 E2
Thornton Leics 135 B9
Thornton Lincs 174 B2
Thornton M'bro 225 C9
Thornton Mers 193 G10
Thornton Northumb 273 F9
Thornton Pembs 72 D6
Thornton W Yorks 205 G8
Thornton Curtis N Lincs 200 D5
Thornton Heath London 67 F10
Thornton Hough Mers 182 E4
Thornton in Craven N Yorks 204 D4
Thornton in Lonsdale N Yorks 212 E3
Thornton-le-Beans N Yorks 225 G7
Thornton-le-Clay N Yorks 216 F3
Thornton-le-Dale N Yorks 216 C6
Thornton le Moor Lincs 189 B9
Thornton-le-Moor N Yorks 215 B7
Thornton-le-Moors W Ches 182 G6
Thornton-le-Street N Yorks 215 B8
Thornton Rust N Yorks 213 B9
Thornton Steward N Yorks 214 B3
Thornton Watlass N Yorks 214 B4
Thorntonhall S Lnrk 267 D11
Thorntonloch E Loth 282 G4
Thornton Park Northumb 273 F8
Thornwood Common Essex 87 D7
Thornydykes Borders 272 F2
Thoroton Notts 172 G3
Thorp Gtr Man 196 F2
Thorp Arch W Yorks 206 D4
Thorpe Cumb 230 F5
Thorpe Derbys 169 E11
Thorpe E Yorks 208 D5
Thorpe Lincs 191 E7
Thorpe N Yorks 213 G10
Thorpe Norf 143 D8
Thorpe Notts 172 F3
Thorpe Sur 66 F4
Thorpe Abbotts Norf 126 B3
Thorpe Acre Leics 153 E10
Thorpe Arnold Leics 154 E5
Thorpe Audlin W Yorks 198 D3
Thorpe Bassett N Yorks 217 E7
Thorpe Bay Sthend 70 B2
Thorpe by Water Rutland 137 D7
Thorpe Common Suff 108 D5
Thorpe Constantine Staffs 134 B5
Thorpe Culvert Lincs 175 C7
Thorpe Edge W Yorks 205 F9
Thorpe End Norf 160 G5
Thorpe Fendykes Lincs 175 C7
Thorpe Green Essex 108 G3
Thorpe Green Lancs 194 C5
Thorpe Green Suff 125 G8
Thorpe Green Sur 66 F4
Thorpe Hamlet Norf 142 B4
Thorpe Hesley S Yorks 186 B5
Thorpe in Balne S Yorks 198 E5
Thorpe in the Fallows Lincs 188 E6
Thorpe Langton Leics 136 E4
Thorpe Larches Durham 234 F3
Thorpe Latimer Lincs 156 B2
Thorpe-le-Soken Essex 108 G3
Thorpe le Street E Yorks 208 E2
Thorpe le Vale Lincs 190 C2
Thorpe Lea Sur 66 E4
Thorpe Malsor Northants 120 B6
Thorpe Mandeville Northants 101 B10
Thorpe Market Norf 160 B4
Thorpe Marriot Norf 160 F3
Thorpe Morieux Suff 125 G8
Thorpe on the Hill Lincs 172 B6
Thorpe on The Hill W Yorks 197 B10
Thorpe Row Norf 141 B9
Thorpe St Andrew Norf 142 B5
Thorpe St Peter Lincs 175 C7
Thorpe Salvin S Yorks 187 E8
Thorpe Satchville Leics 154 G4
Thorpe Street Suff 125 B10
Thorpe Thewles Stockton 234 G4
Thorpe Tilney Lincs 173 D10
Thorpe Underwood N Yorks 206 B5
Thorpe Underwood Northants 136 G5
Thorpe Waterville Northants 137 G10
Thorpe Willoughby N Yorks 207 G7
Thorpe Wood N Yorks 207 G7
Thorpeness Suff 127 F9
Thorpland Norf 140 B2
Thorrington Essex 89 B9
Thorverton Devon 26 G6
Thoulstone Wilts 45 D10
Thrandeston Suff 126 B2
Thrapston Northants 121 B9
Thrashbush N Lnrk 268 B5
Threapland Cumb 229 D9
Threapland N Yorks 213 G9
Threapwood Staffs 169 G8
Threapwood W Ches 166 F6
Three Ashes Hants 64 G6
Three Ashes Hereford 97 G10
Three Ashes Shrops 115 B7
Three Ashes Som 45 D7
Three Bridges Argyll 284 F4
Three Bridges Lincs 190 D6
Three Bridges W Sus 51 F9
Three Burrows Corn 4 F4
Three Chimneys Kent 53 F10
Three Cocked Hat Norf 143 D8
Three Cocks = Aberllynfi Powys 96 D3
Three Crosses Swansea 56 C5
Three Cups Corner E Sus 37 C10
Three Fingers Wrex 167 G7
Three Gates Dorset 29 F10
Three Hammers Corn 11 D10
Three Holes Norf 139 C10
Three Holes Cross Corn 10 G6
Three Leg Cross E Sus 53 G7
Three Legged Cross Dorset 31 F9
Three Maypoles W Mid 118 B2
Three Mile Cross Wokingham 65 F8
Three Oaks E Sus 38 E4
Three Sisters Denb 165 C9
Threehammer Common Norf 160 E6
Threekingham Lincs 155 B11
Threelows Staffs 169 F9
Threemile Cross Wokingham 65 F8
Threemilestone Corn 4 G5
Threemiletown W Loth 279 F11
Threepwood Borders 271 G10
Threewaters Corn 5 B10
Threlkeld Cumb 230 F2
Threshers Bush Essex 87 D7
Threshfield N Yorks 213 G9
Thrigby Norf 161 G9
Thringarth Durham 232 G4
Thringstone Leics 153 F8
Thrintoft N Yorks 224 G6
Thriplow Cambs 105 B8
Throapham S Yorks 187 D8
Throckenholt Lincs 139 B7
Throcking Herts 104 E6
Throckley T & W 242 D5
Throckmorton Worcs 99 B9
Throop Dorset 18 C2
Throphill Northumb 252 F4
Thropton Northumb 252 C2
Throsk Stirl 279 C7
Througham Glos 80 D6
Throughgate Dumfries 247 G9
Throwleigh Devon 13 C9
Throwley Kent 54 B3
Throwley Forstal Kent 54 C3
Throxenby N Yorks 217 B10
Thrumpton Notts 153 C10
Thrumpton Notts 188 E2
Thrumster Highld 310 E7
Thrunton Northumb 264 G3
Thrupe Som 44 D6
Thrupp Glos 80 E5
Thrupp Oxon 82 F3
Thrupp Oxon 83 B7
Thruscross N Yorks 205 B9
Thrushelton Devon 12 D4
Thrussington Leics 154 F2
Thruxton Hants 47 D9
Thruxton Hereford 97 E8
Thrybergh S Yorks 187 B7
Thulston Derbys 153 C8
Thunder Bridge W Yorks 197 E7
Thunder Hill Norf 161 F8
Thundergay N Ayrs 255 C9
Thunder's Hill E Sus 23 C9
Thundersley Essex 69 B9
Thundridge Herts 86 B5
Thurcaston Leics 153 G11
Thurcroft S Yorks 187 D7
Thurdon Corn 24 E3
Thurgarton Norf 160 C3
Thurgarton Notts 171 F11
Thurgoland S Yorks 197 G9
Thurlaston Leics 135 D10
Thurlaston Warks 119 C9
Thurlbear Som 28 C3
Thurlby Lincs 156 F2
Thurlby Lincs 172 C6
Thurlby Lincs 191 F7
Thurleigh Beds 121 F11
Thurlestone Devon 8 G3
Thurloxton Som 43 G9
Thurlstone S Yorks 197 G8
Thurlton Norf 143 D8
Thurlton Links Norf 143 D8
Thurlwood E Ches 168 D4
Thurmaston Leics 136 B2
Thurnby Leics 136 C2
Thurne Norf 161 F8
Thurnham Kent 53 B10
Thurnham Lancs 202 C5
Thurning Norf 159 D11
Thurning Northants 137 G11
Thurnscoe S Yorks 198 F3
Thurnscoe East S Yorks 198 F3
Thursby Cumb 239 G8
Thursford Norf 159 C9
Thursford Green Norf 159 C9
Thursley Sur 50 F2
Thurso Highld 310 C5
Thurso East Highld 310 C5
Thurstaston Mers 182 E2
Thurston Suff 125 D8
Thurston Clough Gtr Man 196 F3
Thurston End Suff 124 G5
Thurstonfield Cumb 239 F8
Thurstonland W Yorks 197 E7
Thurton Norf 142 C6
Thurvaston Derbys 152 B2
Thurvaston Derbys 152 B4
Thuxton Norf 141 B10
Thwaite N Yorks 223 F7
Thwaite Suff 126 D2
Thwaite Flat Cumb 210 E4
Thwaite Head Cumb 220 G6
Thwaite St Mary Norf 142 E6
Thwaites W Yorks 205 E7
Thwaites Brow W Yorks 205 E7
Thwing E Yorks 217 E11
Tibbermore Perth 286 E4
Tibberton Glos 98 G5
Tibberton Telford 150 E3
Tibberton Worcs 117 F8
Tibenham Norf 142 F2
Tibshelf Derbys 170 C6
Tibshelf Wharf Notts 171 C7
Tibthorpe E Yorks 208 B5
Ticehurst E Sus 53 G7
Tichborne Hants 48 G5
Tickencote Rutland 137 B9
Tickenham N Som 60 E3
Ticket Wood Devon 8 G4
Tickford End M Keynes 103 C7
Tickhill S Yorks 187 C9
Tickleback Row Brack 65 E11
Ticklerton Shrops 131 E9
Tickmorend Glos 80 F4
Ticknall Derbys 153 E7
Tickton E Yorks 209 E7
Tidbury Green W Mid 117 B11
Tidcombe Wilts 47 B9
Tiddington Oxon 83 E11
Tiddington Warks 118 F4
Tidebrook E Sus 37 B10
Tideford Corn 6 D6
Tideford Cross Corn 6 C6
Tidenham Glos 79 F9
Tidenham Chase Glos 79 F9
Tideswell Derbys 185 F11
Tidmarsh W Berks 64 E6
Tidmington Warks 100 D5
Tidnor Hereford 97 D11
Tidpit Hants 31 D9
Tidworth Wilts 47 D8
Tiers Cross Pembs 72 C6
Tiffield Northants 120 G3
Tifty Aberds 303 E7
Tigerton Angus 293 G7
Tigh-na-Blair Perth 285 F11
Tighnabruaich Argyll 275 F10
Tighnacachla Argyll 274 G3
Tighnafiline Highld 307 L3
Tighness Argyll 284 G6
Tigley Devon 8 C5
Tilbrook Cambs 121 D11
Tilbury Thurrock 68 D6
Tilbury Green Essex 106 C4
Tilbury Juxta Clare Essex 106 C5
Tile Cross W Mid 134 F3
Tile Hill W Mid 118 B5
Tilegate Green Essex 87 D8
Tilehouse Green W Mid 118 B3
Tilehurst Reading 65 E7
Tilekiln Green Essex 105 G10
Tiley Dorset 29 F11
Tilford Sur 49 E11
Tilford Common Sur 49 E11
Tilford Reeds Sur 49 E11
Tilgate W Sus 51 G9
Tilgate Forest Row W Sus 5
Tilkey Essex 10
Tilland Corn
Tillathrowie Aberds 30
Tillers' Green Glos
Tilley Shrops 149
Tilley Green Shrops 149
Tillicoultry Clack 27
Tillietudlem S Lnrk 26
Tillingham Essex 8
Tillington Hereford 9
Tillington Staffs 15
Tillington W Sus 3
Tillington Common Hereford 9
Tillislow Devon 1
Tillworth Devon 2
Tilly Down Hants 47
Tilly Lo Aberds 29
Tillyarblet Angus 29
Tillybirloch Aberds 29
Tillycorthie Aberds 30
Tillydrine Aberds 29
Tillyfour Aberds 29
Tillyfourie Aberds 29
Tillygarmond Aberds 29
Tillygreig Aberds 30
Tillykerrie Aberds 30
Tillynaught Aberds 30
Tilmanstone Kent 55
Tilney All Saints Norf 157
Tilney cum Islington Norf 157
Tilney Fen End Norf 157
Tilney High End Norf 157
Tilney St Lawrence Norf 157
Tilsdown Glos 8
Tilshead Wilts 4
Tilsmore E Sus 3
Tilsop Shrops 11
Tilstock Shrops 149
Tilston W Ches 16
Tilstone Bank W Ches 16
Tilstone Fearnall W Ches 16
Tilsworth C Beds 10
Tilton on the Hill Leics 13
Tilts S Yorks 19
Tiltups End Glos 8
Tilty Essex 10
Timberden Bottom Kent 6
Timberhonger Worcs 11
Timberland Lincs 173
Timbersbrook E Ches 16
Timberscombe Som 4
Timble N Yorks 20
Timbold Hill Kent 5
Timbrelham Corn 1
Timperley Gtr Man 18
Timsbury Bath 4
Timsbury Hants 3
Timsgearraidh W Isles 30
Timworth Suff 12
Timworth Green Suff 12
Tincleton Dorset 1
Tindale Cumb 24
Tindale Crescent Durham 23
Tindon End Essex 10
Tingewick Bucks 10
Tingley W Yorks 19
Tingon Shetland 31
Tingrith C Beds 10
Tingwall Orkney 31
Tinhay Devon 1
Tinkers End Bucks 10
Tinshill W Yorks 20
Tinsley S Yorks 18
Tinsley Green W Sus 5
Tintagel Corn 1
Tintern Parva Mon 7
Tintinhull Som 2
Tintwistle Derbys 18
Tinwald Dumfries 24
Tinwell Rutland 13
Tipner Ptsmth 3
Tippacott Devon 4
Tipper's Hill Warks 13
Tipperty Aberds 30
Tipperty Aberds 30
Tipps End Norf 13
Tip's Cross Essex 8
Tiptoe Hants 1
Tipton W Mid 13
Tipton Green W Mid 13
Tipton St John Devon 1
Tiptree Essex 8
Tiptree Heath Essex 8
Tir-y-berth Caerph 7
Tir-y-dail Carms 7
Tirabad Powys 9
Tiraghoil Argyll 28
Tircanol Swansea 5
Tirdeunaw Swansea 5
Tirinie Perth 29
Tirley Glos 9
Tirley Knowle Glos 9
Tirphil Caerph 7
Tirril Cumb 23
Tirryside Highld 30
Tisbury Wilts 3
Tisman's Common W Sus 5
Tissington Derbys 16
Titchberry Devon 2
Titchfield Hants 3
Titchfield Common Hants 3
Titchfield Park Hants 3
Titchmarsh Northants 12
Titchwell Norf 17
Titcomb W Berks 6
Tithby Notts 15
Tithe Barn Hillock Mers 18
Tithebarn Staffs 16
Titley Hereford 11
Titlington Northumb 26
Titmore Green Herts 10
Titsey Sur 5
Titson Corn 2
Tittenhurst Windsor 6
Tittensor Staffs 15
Titterhill Shrops 13
Tittle Row Windsor 6
Tittleshall Norf 15
Titton Worcs 11
Titty Hill W Sus 3
Tiverton Devon 2
Tiverton W Ches 16
Tivetshall St Margaret Norf 14
Tivetshall St Mary Norf 14
Tividale W Mid 13
Tivington Som 4
Tivington Knowle Som 4
Tivoli Cumb 22
Tivy Dale S Yorks 19
Tixall Staffs 15

ver Rutland 137 C9
Orkney 314 F5
Shetland 313 M5
Row Suff 143 F10
moor Derbys 170 E4
ermory Argyll 289 D7
ronochy Argyll 275 C8
a Beag W Isles 296 D5
a Mor W Isles 297 H3
tarol W Isles 304 E3
on W Isles 304 E3
's Hill Lincs 191 C7
er Aberds 302 F6
enham Wilts 62 D4
enham Wick Wilts 62 C4
holes Blkburn 195 C7
ngton S Glos 60 B6
with N Yorks 206 C5
er Dorset 30 C4
ing Hereford 115 B8
ington C Beds 103 F10
ington Glos 99 E10
ington W Sus 35 G8
lehills Aberds 303 E10
's Green Herts 104 F4
nham Glos 100 D4
ill Angus 287 D8
ills Cumb 239 E9
ills Durham 233 E10
achie Aberds 293 B8
orden W Yorks 196 C2
ool Corn 4 G4
g Borders 261 F10
ick S Yorks 187 E7
Cambs 123 F7
incs 155 F11
Shetland 312 F6
Warks 119 C9
Hill Durham 233 F9
Hill Lincs 174 C2
Monks Norf 143 E8
Next Newton Lincs 189 D8
ees Norf 159 D7
Highld 310 C7
haw W Yorks 197 B7
wood Norf 159 G9
ton Northumb 252 C6
waig Highld 295 D8
rs Green Oxon 65 D8
ngton London 67 C7
tadh a Chaolais
es 304 E3
tadh bho Thuath
es 304 D7
rough Corn 11 F9
rne Corn 2 B5
rne Corn 2 C5
rne Wartha Corn 2 B5
sh Corn 5 D8
s Mount Corn 8 C4
rst E Sus 53 G7
ar Mers 183 C7
ar Rutland 137 B10
ar S Yorks 198 F5
ar W Mid 133 E9
f Birness Aberds 303 F10
dine Worcs 117 F7
nd Som 42 G6
rd Farnham Dorset 30 D6
rd Royal Wilts 30 D6
ar End W Mid 119 B7
Fratrum Dorset 17 B7
Porcorum Dorset 17 B7
Whelme Dorset 29 G8
ford Dorset 17 C9
ton N Yorks 215 G10
ton Notts 154 C2
sbury Essex 89 C7
bury M'bro 225 B10
shunt D'Arcy Essex 88 C6
shunt Knights
x 88 C6
shunt Major Essex 88 C5
Highld 300 D5
W Isles 304 E6
ers Herts 86 E4
ddle Dorset 17 C11
thy Corn 4 G3
ddon Downs Corn 4 G3
h Highld 291 D10
rth London 67 F7
an Fhuadain
es 305 G5
knock Perth 286 E2
tin Highld 301 G8
reck Highld 300 F6
ui Perth 286 B2
hrasky Highld 290 B4
oun Highld 290 C3
ch Highld 300 B6
ch Highld 300 G3
ch House Highld 300 E5
ntoul Aberds 292 D3
ntoul Moray 292 B3
ow Warks 119 F9
aven Moray 302 F4
avoulin Moray 302 G2
errow Corn 4 G5
kin Staffs 168 E6
set's Bank E Sus 52 G2
leibhe Argyll 289 F8
horn Derbys 185 F9
on 78 F5
reigam V Glam 58 D3
Pentre Rhondda 77 F7
eg Rhondda 58 B5
-pistyll Caerph 77 F11
ridge Kent 52 D5
erghie Dumfries 236 F6
Bridgend 57 E11
Som 27 C10
Green Som 27 C11
Hale Som 27 C10
Kent 53 D10
Shrops 132 B5
W Yorks 205 G10
Forge Shrops 132 B5
Green Kent 54 C3
Norton Shrops 132 B5
Park W Yorks 205 F9
Street W Yorks 205 G9
Leics 153 E8
Corner Kent 70 F2
Fold Gtr Man 195 F8
Moor Gtr Man 195 E8
am Sur 49 D11
and Dumfries 237 D8
e Highld 308 D5
e End Lincs 156 F3
vell M Keynes 103 C7
vynlais Cardiff 58 C6
awr Neath 57 B10
= Tonnau Neath 57 B9
au = Tonna Neath 57 B9
ne Lincs 194 G4
ell Herts 86 B4
andy Rhondda 77 G7
efail Rhondda 58 B4
aldon Oxon 83 E9
ill Essex 87 E8
ill Staffs 169 G9
ill Hants 32 D5
Toothill Swindon 62 C6
Toothill W Yorks 196 C6
Tooting Graveney London 67 E9
Top End Beds 121 E10
Top Green Notts 172 F3
Top Lock Gtr Man 194 F6
Top o' th' Lane Lancs 194 C5
Top o' th' Meadows Gtr Man 196 F3
Top of Hebers Gtr Man 195 F11
Top Valley Nottingham 171 F9
Topcliffe N Yorks 215 D8
Topcliffe W Yorks 197 B9
Topcroft Norf 142 E5
Topcroft Street Norf 142 E5
Topham S Yorks 198 D6
Topleigh W Sus 34 D6
Toppesfield Essex 106 D4
Toppings Gtr Man 195 E8
Toprow Norf 142 D3
Topsham Devon 14 D5
Torbeg N Ayrs 255 E10
Torboll Farm Highld 309 K7
Torbothie N Lnrk 269 D7
Torbreck Highld 309 J7
Torbrex Stirl 278 C5
Torbryan Devon 8 B6
Torbush N Lnrk 268 D6
Torcross Devon 8 G6
Torcroy Highld 291 D9
Tore Highld 300 D6
Torfrey Corn 6 E2
Torgyle Highld 290 B5
Torinturk Argyll 275 G9
Torkington Gtr Man 184 D6
Torksey Lincs 188 F4
Torlum W Isles 296 F3
Torlundy Highld 290 F3
Tormarton S Glos 61 D9
Tormisdale Argyll 254 B2
Tormitchell S Ayrs 244 E6
Tormore Highld 295 E8
Tormore N Ayrs 255 D9
Tornagrain Highld 301 E7
Tornahaish Aberds 292 C4
Tornapress Highld 299 E8
Tornaveen Aberds 293 C8
Torness Highld 300 G5
Toronto Durham 233 E9
Torpenhow Cumb 229 D10
Torphichen W Loth 279 G9
Torphin Edin 270 B4
Torphins Aberds 293 C8
Torpoint Corn 7 E8
Torquay Torbay 9 C8
Torquhan Borders 271 F8
Torr Devon 7 E11
Torr Devon 8 C2
Torra Argyll 254 B4
Torran Argyll 275 C9
Torran Highld 298 E5
Torran Highld 301 B7
Torrance E Dunb 278 G2
Torrans Argyll 288 G6
Torranyard N Ayrs 267 G7
Torre Som 42 E4
Torre Torbay 9 C8
Torridon Highld 299 D9
Torridon Ho Highld 299 D8
Torries Aberds 293 B8
Torrin Highld 295 C7
Torrisdale Highld 308 C6
Torrisdale Castle Argyll 255 D8
Torrisdale-Square Argyll 255 D8
Torrish Highld 311 H3
Torrisholme Lancs 211 G9
Torroble Highld 309 J5
Torroy Highld 309 K5
Torrpark Corn 11 D10
Torry Aberdeen 293 C11
Torry Aberds 302 F4
Torryburn Fife 279 D10
Torsonce Borders 271 G9
Torsonce Mains Borders 271 G9
Torterston Aberds 303 E10
Torthorwald Dumfries 238 B2
Tortington W Sus 35 F8
Torton Worcs 116 C6
Tortworth S Glos 80 G2
Torvaig Highld 298 E4
Torver Cumb 220 G5
Torwood Falk 278 E6
Torwoodlee Mains Borders 261 B11
Torworth Notts 187 D11
Tosberry Devon 24 C3
Toscaig Highld 295 B9
Toseland Cambs 122 E4
Tosside N Yorks 203 B11
Tostock Suff 125 E9
Tot Hill Hants 64 G3
Totaig Highld 295 C10
Totaig Highld 298 D2
Totardor Highld 294 B5
Tote Highld 298 E4
Tote Hill Hants 32 C4
Tote Hill W Sus 34 C5
Totegan Highld 310 C2
Totford Hants 48 F5
Totham Hill Essex 88 C5
Totham Plains Essex 88 C5
Tothill Lincs 190 E6
Totland I o W 20 D2
Totley S Yorks 186 F4
Totley Brook S Yorks 186 E4
Totley Rise S Yorks 186 E4
Totmonslow Staffs 151 B9
Totnell Dorset 29 F10
Totnes Devon 8 C6
Totnor Hereford 97 E11
Toton Notts 153 C10
Totronald Argyll 288 D3
Totscore Highld 298 C3
Tottenham London 86 G4
Tottenham Hale London 67 B10
Tottenhill Norf 158 G2
Tottenhill Row Norf 158 G2
Totteridge Bucks 84 G5
Totteridge London 86 G2
Totternhoe C Beds 103 G9
Totteroak S Glos 61 C8
Totterton Shrops 131 F7
Totties W Yorks 197 F7
Tottington Gtr Man 195 E9
Tottington Norf 141 D7
Tottlebank Cumb 210 C6
Tottleworth Lancs 203 G10
Totton Hants 32 E5
Touchen End Windsor 65 D11
Toulston N Yorks 206 E5
Toulton Som 43 G7
Toulvaddie Highld 311 L2
Tournaig Highld 307 L3
Toux Aberds 303 D9
Tovil Kent 53 C9
Tow House Northumb 241 E7
Tow Law Durham 233 D8
Towan Corn 10 G3
Towan Cross Corn 4 F4
Toward Argyll 266 B2
Towcester Northants 102 B3
Towednack Corn 1 B5
Tower End Norf 158 F3
Tower Hamlets Kent 55 E10
Tower Hill Devon 12 C3
Tower Hill E Ches 184 F6
Tower Hill Essex 108 E5
Tower Hill Herts 85 E8
Tower Hill Mers 194 G2
Tower Hill Sur 51 D7
Tower Hill W Mid 133 E11
Tower Hill W Sus 35 B11
Towerage Bucks 84 G4
Towerhead N Som 44 B2
Towersey Oxon 84 D2
Towie Aberds 292 B6
Towie Aberds 302 G5
Towie Aberds 303 C8
Towiemore Moray 302 E3
Town Barton Devon 14 C2
Town End Bucks 84 F3
Town End Cambs 139 D8
Town End Cumb 211 B7
Town End Cumb 211 C8
Town End Cumb 212 C2
Town End Cumb 220 D6
Town End Cumb 221 E8
Town End Cumb 221 F7
Town End Cumb 231 F8
Town End Derbys 185 F11
Town End E Yorks 207 C10
Town End Mers 183 D7
Town End W Yorks 196 D5
Town Fields W Ches 167 B10
Town Green Gtr Man 183 B9
Town Green Lancs 194 F2
Town Green Norf 161 G7
Town Head Cumb 220 D6
Town Head Cumb 221 E8
Town Head Cumb 222 B3
Town Head Cumb 222 C3
Town Head Cumb 231 F7
Town Head Cumb 231 F8
Town Head Cumb 231 G8
Town Head Cumb 231 G9
Town Head Derbys 185 F11
Town Head N Yorks 204 B2
Town Head N Yorks 212 F5
Town Head Staffs 169 F8
Town Head W Yorks 204 D6
Town Kelloe Durham 234 D3
Town Lane Gtr Man 183 B11
Town Littleworth E Sus 36 D6
Town of Lowton Mers 183 B10
Town Park Telford 132 B3
Town Row E Sus 52 G5
Town Street Glos 98 F6
Town Yetholm Borders 263 D8
Townend Derbys 185 E9
Townend Staffs 151 B9
Townend W Dunb 277 F8
Townfield Durham 232 B5
Towngate Cumb 230 B6
Towngate Lincs 156 G2
Townhead Argyll 275 G11
Townhead Cumb 229 D7
Townhead Cumb 230 D6
Townhead Cumb 231 E8
Townhead Dumfries 237 E8
Townhead N Lnrk 268 B4
Townhead Northumb 251 E9
Townhead S Ayrs 244 C6
Townhead S Yorks 186 E4
Townhead S Yorks 197 G7
Townhead of Greenlaw Dumfries 237 C9
Townhill Fife 280 D2
Townhill Swansea 56 C6
Townhill Park Hants 33 E7
Townlake Devon 12 G4
Townland Green Kent 54 G2
Town's End Bucks 102 G2
Town's End Dorset 18 B3
Town's End Dorset 18 E5
Town's End Dorset 29 F9
Towns End Hants 48 B5
Town's End Som 30 D2
Towns End Som 45 D7
Townsend Bath 44 B5
Townsend Bucks 84 D2
Townsend Devon 25 B10
Townsend Herts 85 D10
Townsend Oxon 63 B11
Townsend Pembs 72 D4
Townsend Som 44 C4
Townsend Stoke 168 F6
Townsend Wilts 46 B3
Townsend Wilts 46 B4
Townsend Fold Lancs 195 C10
Townshend Corn 2 C3
Townwell S Glos 79 G11
Towthorpe E Yorks 217 G8
Towthorpe York 207 B8
Towton N Yorks 206 F5
Towyn Conwy 181 F7
Toxteth Mers 182 D5
Toynton All Saints Lincs 174 C5
Toynton Fen Side Lincs 174 C5
Toynton St Peter Lincs 174 C6
Toy's Hill Kent 52 C3
Trabboch E Ayrs 257 E10
Traboe Corn 2 E6
Trabrown Borders 271 F10
Tracebridge Som 27 C9
Tradespark Highld 301 D8
Tradespark Orkney 314 F4
Trafford Park Gtr Man 184 B3
Tragh Ho Highld 295 F8
Trallong Powys 95 F9
Trallwn Rhondda 77 G9
Trallwn Swansea 57 B7
Tram Inn Hereford 97 E9
Tramagenna Corn 11 E7
Tranch Torf 78 E3
Tranent E Loth 281 G8
Tranmere Mers 182 D4
Trantlebeg Highld 310 D2
Trantlemore Highld 310 D2
Tranwell Northumb 252 G5
Trapp Carms 75 B11
Traprain E Loth 281 F11
Trap's Green Warks 118 D2
Trapshill W Berks 63 G11
Traquair Borders 261 C8
Trash Green W Berks 65 F7
Travellers' Rest Carms 74 B5
Trawden Lancs 204 F4
Trawscoed Powys 95 E11
Trawsfynydd Gwyn 146 B4
Trawsnant Ceredig 111 D11
Tre-Aubrey V Glam 58 E4
Tre-Beferad V Glam 58 F3
Tre-boeth Swansea 57 B7
Tre-derwen Powys 148 F4
Tre-Forgan Neath 76 D3
Tre-gagle Mon 79 D8
Tre-Gibbon Rhondda 77 E7
Tre Gwyr = Gowerton Swansea 56 B5
Tre-gynwr Carms 74 B6
Tre-hill V Glam 58 E5
Tre-Ifor Rhondda 77 D7
Tre-lan Flint 165 B11
Tre-Mostyn Flint 181 F10
Tre-pit V Glam 58 E2
Tre-Taliesin Ceredig 128 E3
Tre-vaughan Carms 93 G8
Tre-wyn Mon 96 G6
Treadam Mon 78 B5
Treaddow Hereford 97 G10
Treal Corn 2 F6
Trealaw Rhondda 77 G8
Treales Lancs 202 G4
Trearddur Anglesey 178 F3
Treaslane Highld 298 D3
Treath Corn 3 D7
Treator Corn 10 F4
Trebanog Rhondda 77 G8
Trebanos Neath 76 E2
Trebarber Corn 5 C7
Trebartha Corn 11 F11
Trebarwith Corn 11 D7
Trebarwith Strand Corn 10 D6
Trebeath Corn 11 D11
Trebell Green Corn 5 C11
Treberfydd Powys 96 F2
Trebetherick Corn 10 F4
Trebilcock Corn 5 C9
Treble's Holford Som 43 G7
Treborough Som 42 F4
Trebudannon Corn 5 C7
Trebullett Corn 12 F2
Treburgett Corn 11 F7
Treburgie Corn 6 C4
Treburley Corn 12 F3
Treburrick Corn 10 G3
Trebyan Corn 5 C11
Trecastle Powys 95 F7
Trecenydd Caerph 58 B6
Trecott Devon 25 G10
Trecwn Pembs 91 E9
Trecynon Rhondda 77 E7
Tredannick Corn 10 G6
Tredaule Corn 11 E10
Tredavoe Corn 1 D5
Treddiog Pembs 91 F7
Tredegar Bl Gwent 77 D10
Trederwen Powys 148 F5
Tredethy Corn 11 G7
Tredington Glos 99 F8
Tredington Warks 100 C5
Tredinnick Corn 1 C4
Tredinnick Corn 5 D10
Tredinnick Corn 6 B3
Tredinnick Corn 6 D4
Tredinnick Corn 10 G4
Tredogan V Glam 58 F5
Tredomen Caerph 77 G10
Tredomen Powys 96 E2
Tredown Devon 24 D2
Tredrizzick Corn 10 F5
Tredunnock Mon 78 G5
Tredustan Powys 96 E2
Tredworth Glos 80 B4
Treen Corn 1 B4
Treen Corn 1 E3
Treesmill Corn 5 D11
Treeton S Yorks 186 D6
Tref y Clawdd = Knighton Powys 114 C5
Trefaes Gwyn 144 C5
Trefanny Hill Corn 6 D4
Trefasser Pembs 91 D7
Trefdraeth Anglesey 178 G6
Trefdraeth = Newport Pembs 91 D11
Trefecca Powys 96 E2
Trefechan Ceredig 111 A11
Trefechan M Tydf 77 D8
Trefechan Wrex 166 F3
Trefeglwys Powys 129 E9
Trefeitha Powys 96 E2
Trefenter Ceredig 112 D2
Treffgarne Pembs 91 G9
Treffynnon Pembs 90 F6
Treffynnon = Holywell Flint 181 F11
Trefgarn Owen Pembs 91 F7
Trefil Bl Gwent 77 C10
Trefilan Ceredig 111 F11
Trefin = Trevine Pembs 90 E6
Treflach Shrops 148 D5
Trefnanney Powys 148 F4
Trefnant Denb 181 G9
Trefonen Shrops 148 D5
Trefor Anglesey 178 E5
Trefor Gwyn 162 F5
Treforda Corn 11 E7
Treforest Rhondda 58 B5
Treforgan Ceredig 92 B4
Treforys = Morriston Swansea 57 B7
Trefriw Conwy 164 C3
Trefrize Corn 12 F2
Trefynwy = Monmouth Mon 79 C8
Tregada Corn 12 E2
Tregadgwith Corn 1 D4
Tregadillett Corn 12 E2
Tregaian Anglesey 178 F6
Tregajorran Corn 4 G3
Tregamere Corn 5 C8
Tregardock Corn 10 E6
Tregare Mon 78 C6
Tregarland Corn 6 D5
Tregarlandbridge Corn 6 D4
Tregarne Corn 3 E7
Tregaron Ceredig 112 F3
Tregarrick Mill Corn 6 D4
Tregarth Gwyn 163 B10
Tregath Gwyn 163 B10
Tregatillian Corn 5 C8
Tregatta Corn 11 D7
Tregavarah Corn 1 D4
Tregear Corn 2 E5
Tregeare Corn 11 D10
Tregeiriog Wrex 148 C3
Tregele Anglesey 178 C5
Tregellist Corn 10 F6
Tregeseal Corn 1 C3
Tregew Corn 3 C8
Tregidden Corn 3 E7
Treginnis Pembs 90 G4
Treglemais Pembs 90 F6
Tregole Corn 11 B9
Tregolls Corn 2 B6
Tregolwyn = Colwinston V Glam 58 D2
Tregona Corn 5 B7
Tregonce Corn 10 G4
Tregonetha Corn 5 C9
Tregonna Corn 10 G4
Tregonning Corn 5 D7
Tregony Corn 5 G8
Tregoodwell Corn 11 E8
Tregorden Corn 10 G6
Tregorrick Corn 5 E10
Tregoss Corn 5 C9
Tregoyd Powys 96 D4
Tregoyd Mill Powys 96 D3
Tregreenwell Corn 11 E7
Tregrehan Mills Corn 5 E10
Tregroes Ceredig 93 C8
Tregullon Corn 5 C11
Tregunna Corn 10 G5
Tregurrian Corn 5 B7
Tregurtha Downs Corn 2 C2
Tregyddulan Pembs 91 D7
Tregynon Powys 129 D11
Trehafod Rhondda 77 G8
Trehafren Powys 129 E11
Trehan Corn 7 D8
Treharris M Tydf 77 F9
Trehemborne Corn 10 G3
Treherbert Rhondda 76 F6
Trehunist Corn 6 C6
Trekeivesteps Corn 11 G10
Trekenner Corn 12 F2
Trekenning Corn 5 C8
Treknow Corn 11 D7
Trelales = Laleston Bridgend 57 F11
Trelan Corn 2 F6
Trelash Corn 11 C9
Trelassick Corn 5 E7
Trelawnyd Flint 181 F9
Trelech Carms 92 E5
Treleddyd-fawr Pembs 90 F5
Treleigh Corn 4 G4
Treletert = Letterston Pembs 91 F8
Trelew Corn 3 B8
Trelewis M Tydf 77 F10
Treligga Corn 11 E7
Trelights Corn 10 F5
Trelill Corn 10 F6
Trelion Corn 5 E8
Treliske Corn 4 F6
Trelissick Corn 3 B8
Trellech Mon 79 D8
Trelleck Grange Mon 79 E7
Trelogan Flint 181 E10
Treloquithack Corn 2 D5
Trelowia Corn 6 D5
Trelowth Corn 5 E9
Trelystan Powys 130 C5
Tremadog Gwyn 163 G9
Tremail Corn 11 D9
Tremain Ceredig 92 B4
Tremaine Corn 11 D10
Tremains Bridgend 58 D2
Tremar Corn 6 B5
Trematon Corn 7 D7
Trematon Castle Corn 7 D8
Tremayne Corn 2 B4
Trembraze Corn 6 B5
Tremedda Corn 1 B5
Tremeirchion Denb 181 G9
Tremethick Cross Corn 1 C4
Tremore Corn 5 C10
Tremorebridge Corn 5 C10
Tremorfa Cardiff 59 D8
Trenance Corn 4 C6
Trenance Corn 5 B7
Trenance Corn 5 C9
Trenance Corn 10 G4
Trenant Corn 6 B4
Trenant Corn 10 G5
Trenarren Corn 5 F10
Trenay Corn 6 B3
Trench Telford 150 G3
Trench Green Oxon 65 D7
Trench Wood Kent 52 D5
Trencreek Corn 4 C6
Trencrom Corn 2 B2
Trendeal Corn 5 E7
Trenear Corn 2 C5
Treneglos Corn 11 D10
Trenerth Corn 2 B4
Trenewan Corn 6 E3
Trengune Corn 11 C9
Trenhorne Corn 11 F11
Treningle Corn 5 B10
Treninnick Corn 4 C6
Trenoon Corn 2 F6
Trenoweth Corn 3 C7
Trent Dorset 29 D9
Trent Vale Stoke 168 G5
Trentham Stoke 168 G5
Trentishoe Devon 40 D6
Trentlock Derbys 153 C9
Trenwheal Corn 2 C4
Treoes V Glam 58 D2
Treopert = Granston Pembs 91 E7
Treorchy = Treorci Rhondda 77 F7
Treorci = Treorchy Rhondda 77 F7
Treowen Caerph 78 F2
Treowen Powys 130 E2
Trequite Corn 10 F6
Tre'r-ddôl Ceredig 128 E3
Trer llai = Leighton Powys 130 B4
Trerhyngyll V Glam 58 D4
Trerise Corn 2 F6
Trerose Corn 3 D7
Trerulefoot Corn 6 D6
Tresaith Ceredig 110 G5
Tresamble Corn 3 B7
Tresarrett Corn 11 G7
Tresavean Corn 2 B6
Tresawle Corn 5 F7
Tresawsen Corn 4 F5
Trescoll Corn 5 C10
Trescott Staffs 132 D6
Trescowe Corn 2 C3
Tresean Corn 4 D5
Tresevern Croft Corn 2 B6
Tresham Glos 80 G3
Tresigin = Sigingstone V Glam 58 E3
Tresillian Corn 5 F7
Tresimwn = Bonvilston V Glam 58 E5
Tresinney Corn 11 E8
Tresinwen Pembs 91 C7
Treskerby Corn 4 G4
Treskillard Corn 2 B5
Treskilling Corn 5 D10
Treskinnick Cross Corn 11 B10
Treslothan Corn 2 B5
Tresmeer Corn 11 D10
Tresowes Green Corn 2 D3
Tresoweshill Corn 2 D4
Tresparrett Corn 11 C8
Tresparrett Posts Corn 11 C8
Tressady Highld 309 J7
Tressait Perth 291 G10
Tresta Shetland 312 D8
Tresta Shetland 313 H5
Treswell Notts 188 F3
Treswithian Corn 4 G2
Treswithian Downs Corn 4 G2
Trethellan Water Corn 2 B6
Trethevy Corn 11 D7
Trethewell Corn 3 B9
Trethewey Corn 1 E3
Trethillick Corn 10 F4
Trethomas Caerph 59 B7
Trethosa Corn 5 E8
Trethowel Corn 5 E10
Trethurgy Corn 5 D10
Tretio Pembs 90 F5
Tretire Hereford 97 G10
Tretower Powys 96 G3
Treuddyn Flint 166 D3
Trevadlock Corn 11 F11
Trevail Corn 4 D5
Trevalga Corn 11 D7
Trevalgan Corn 1 A5
Trevalyn Wrex 166 D5
Trevance Corn 10 G4
Trevanger Corn 10 F5
Trevanson Corn 10 G5
Trevarrack Corn 1 C5
Trevarren Corn 5 C8
Trevarrian Corn 4 B6
Trevarrick Corn 5 G9
Trevarth Corn 4 G4
Trevaughan Carms 73 B11
Trevaughan Carms 93 G7
Treveal Corn 1 A5
Trevegean Corn 1 D3
Treveighan Corn 11 F7
Trevellas Corn 4 E4
Trevelmond Corn 6 C4
Trevelver Corn 10 G5
Trevemper Corn 4 D6
Treven Corn 11 D7
Trevena Corn 2 D4
Trevenen Corn 2 D5
Trevenen Bal Corn 2 D5
Trevenning Corn 11 F7
Treveor Corn 5 G9
Treverbyn Corn 5 D10
Treverbyn Corn 6 B4
Treverva Corn 3 C7
Trevescan Corn 1 E3
Trevethin Torf 78 E3
Trevia Corn 11 E7
Trevigro Corn 6 B6
Trevilder Corn 10 G6
Trevilla Corn 3 B8
Trevilson Corn 4 D6
Trevine Corn 10 F5
Trevine = Trefin Pembs 90 E6
Treviscoe Corn 5 D8
Treviskey Corn 2 B6
Trevithal Corn 1 D5
Trevoll Corn 4 D6
Trevone Corn 10 F3
Trevor Wrex 166 G3
Trevor Uchaf Denb 166 G2
Trevorrick Corn 10 G4
Trevowah Corn 4 D5
Trevowhan Corn 1 B4
Trew Corn 2 D4
Trewalder Corn 11 E7
Trewarmett Corn 11 D7
Trewartha Corn 2 B2
Trewartha Corn 3 B10
Trewassa Corn 11 D8
Treween Corn 11 E10
Trewellard Corn 1 C3
Trewen Corn 11 E11
Trewen Corn 11 E7
Trewen Mon 79 G7
Trewennack Corn 2 D5
Trewennan Corn 11 E7
Trewern Powys 148 G5
Trewetha Corn 10 E6
Trewethen Corn 10 F6
Trewethern Corn 10 F6
Trewey Corn 1 B5
Trewidland Corn 6 D5
Trewindle Corn 6 C2
Trewint Corn 6 C5
Trewint Corn 11 B9
Trewint Corn 11 E10
Trewithian Corn 3 B9
Trewithick Corn 11 D11
Trewollock Corn 5 G10
Trewoodloe Corn 12 G2
Trewoofe Corn 1 D4
Trewoon Corn 2 F5
Trewoon Corn 5 E9
Treworga Corn 5 G7
Treworgan Common Mon 78 D6
Treworlas Corn 3 B9
Treworld Corn 11 C8
Trewornan Corn 10 F5
Treworrick Corn 6 B4
Treworthal Corn 3 B9
Trewyddel = Moylgrove Pembs 92 C2
Trewyn Devon 24 G4
Treyarnon Corn 10 G3
Treyford W Sus 34 D4
Trezaise Corn 5 D9
Trezelah Corn 1 C5
Triangle Glos 79 E8
Triangle Staffs 133 B11
Triangle W Yorks 196 C4
Trickett's Cross Dorset 31 G9
Triffleton Pembs 91 G9
Trillacott Corn 11 D11
Trimdon Durham 234 E3
Trimdon Colliery Durham 234 D3
Trimdon Grange Durham 234 D3
Trimingham Norf 160 B5
Trimley Lower Street Suff 108 D5
Trimley St Martin Suff 108 D5
Trimley St Mary Suff 108 D5
Trimpley Worcs 116 B5
Trims Green Herts 87 B7
Trimsaran Carms 75 E7
Trimstone Devon 40 E3
Trinafour Perth 291 G9
Trinant Caerph 78 E2
Tring Herts 84 C6
Tring Wharf Herts 84 C6
Tringford Herts 84 C6
Trinity Angus 293 G8
Trinity Devon 27 F7
Trinity Edin 280 F4
Trinity Fields Staffs 151 D8
Trisant Ceredig 112 B4
Triscombe Som 43 F7
Trislaig Highld 290 F2
Trispen Corn 4 E6
Tritlington Northumb 252 E6
Troan Corn 5 D7
Trochry Perth 286 C3
Trodigal Argyll 255 E7
Troearhiwgwair Bl Gwent 77 D11
Troedrhiwdalar Powys 113 G9
Troedrhiwffenyd Ceredig 93 C8
Troedrhiwfuwch Caerph 77 E10
Troedyraur Ceredig 92 B6
Troedyrhiw M Tydf 77 E9
Trofarth Conwy 180 G5
Trolliloes E Sus 23 C10
Tromode I o M 192 E4
Trondavoe Shetland 312 F5
Troon Corn 2 B5
Troon S Ayrs 257 C8
Trooper's Inn Pembs 73 C7
Trosaraidh W Isles 297 K3
Trossachs Hotel Stirl 285 G9
Troston Suff 125 C7
Trostre Carms 56 B4
Trostrey Common Mon 78 E5
Troswell Corn 11 C11
Trotshill Worcs 117 F7
Trotten Marsh W Sus 34 B4
Trottiscliffe Kent 68 G6
Trotton W Sus 34 C4
Trough Gate Lancs 195 C11
Troutbeck Cumb 221 E8
Troutbeck Cumb 230 F3
Troutbeck Bridge Cumb 221 F8
Trow Green Glos 79 D9
Troway Derbys 186 F5
Trowbridge Cardiff 59 C8
Trowbridge Wilts 45 B11
Trowell Notts 153 B9
Trowle Common Wilts 45 B10
Trowley Bottom Herts 85 C9
Trows Borders 262 C5
Trowse Newton Norf 142 B4
Troy Town Kent 52 D2
Troy Town Kent 54 E5
Troy Town Medway 69 F8
Troydale W Yorks 205 G10
Truas Corn 11 D7
Trub Gtr Man 195 F11
Trudoxhill Som 45 E8
True Street Devon 8 C6
Trueman's Heath Worcs 117 B11
Trull Som 28 C2
Trumaisgearraidh W Isles 296 D4
Trumfleet S Yorks 198 E6
Trumpan Highld 298 C2
Trumpet Hereford 98 D3
Trumpington Cambs 123 F8
Trumpsgreen Sur 66 F3
Trunch Norf 160 C5
Trunnah Lancs 202 E2
Truro Corn 4 G6
Truscott Corn 12 D2
Trusham Devon 14 E3
Trusley Derbys 152 B5
Trussall Corn 2 D5
Trussell Corn 11 D10
Trusthorpe Lincs 191 E8
Truthan Corn 4 E6
Truthwall Corn 2 C2
Trwstllewelyn Powys 130 D3
Tryfil Anglesey 178 E6
Trysull Staffs 133 E7
Trythogga Corn 1 C5
Tubbs Mill Corn 5 G9
Tubney Oxon 82 F6
Tubslake Kent 53 G9
Tuckenhay Devon 8 D6
Tuckermarsh Devon 7 B8
Tuckerton Som 28 B3
Tuckhill Shrops 132 F5
Tucking Mill Bath 61 G9
Tuckingmill Corn 4 G3
Tuckingmill Corn 11 F7
Tuckingmill Wilts 30 B6
Tuckton Bmouth 19 C8
Tuddenham Suff 108 B3
Tuddenham Suff 124 C4
Tuddenham St Martin Suff 108 B3
Tudeley Kent 52 D6
Tudeley Hale Kent 52 D6
Tudhay Devon 28 G4
Tudhoe Durham 233 D11
Tudhoe Grange Durham 233 E11
Tudor Hill W Mid 134 D2
Tudorville Hereford 97 G11
Tudweiliog Gwyn 144 B4
Tuebrook Mers 182 C5
Tuesley Sur 50 E3
Tuesnoad Kent 54 E2
Tuffley Glos 80 C4
Tufnell Park London 67 B9
Tufton Hants 48 D3
Tufton Pembs 91 F10
Tugby Leics 136 C5
Tugford Shrops 131 F11
Tughall Northumb 264 D6
Tulchan Lodge Angus 292 F3
Tullecombe W Sus 34 B4
Tullibardine Perth 286 F3
Tullibody Clack 279 B7
Tullich Argyll 284 F4
Tullich Highld 299 E9
Tullich Highld 300 G6
Tullich Muir Highld 301 B7
Tulliemet Perth 286 B3
Tulloch Aberds 293 F9
Tulloch Aberds 303 F8
Tulloch Highld 290 E5
Tulloch Perth 286 E4
Tulloch Castle Highld 300 C5
Tulloch-gribban Highld 301 G9
Tullochgorm Argyll 275 D10
Tullochroisk Perth 285 B11
Tullochvenus Aberds 293 C7
Tulloes Angus 287 C9
Tullybannocher Perth 285 E11
Tullybelton Perth 286 D4
Tullycross Stirl 277 D9
Tullyfergus Perth 286 C6
Tullymurdoch Perth 286 B5
Tullynessle Aberds 293 B7
Tulse Hill London 67 E10
Tumble = Y Tymbl Carms 75 C8
Tumbler's Green Essex 106 F6
Tumby Lincs 174 D2
Tumby Woodside Lincs 174 D3
Tummel Bridge Perth 285 B11
Tumpy Green Glos 80 E2
Tumpy Lakes Hereford 97 B10
Tunbridge Hill Medway 69 E10
Tunbridge Wells = Royal Tunbridge Wells Kent 52 F5
Tunga W Isles 304 E6
Tungate Norf 160 D5
Tunley Bath 45 B7
Tunley Glos 80 E6
Tunnel Hill Worcs 98 C6
Tunnel Pits N Lincs 199 G8
Tunshill Gtr Man 196 E2
Tunstall E Yorks 209 G12
Tunstall Kent 69 G11
Tunstall Lancs 212 E2
Tunstall N Yorks 224 F4
Tunstall Norf 143 B8
Tunstall Staffs 150 D5
Tunstall Stoke 168 E5
Tunstall Suff 127 G7
Tunstall T & W 243 G9
Tunstead Derbys 185 G10
Tunstead Gtr Man 196 G4
Tunstead Norf 160 E5
Tunworth Hants 49 D7
Tupsley Hereford 97 C10
Tupton Derbys 170 B5
Tur Langton Leics 136 E4
Turbary Common Poole 19 C7
Turf Hill Gtr Man 196 E2
Turfdown Corn 5 B11
Turfholm S Lnrk 259 B8
Turfmoor Devon 28 G3
Turfmoor Shrops 149 F7
Turgis Green Hants 49 B7
Turin Angus 287 B9
Turkdean Glos 81 B10
Turkey Island Hants 33 E9
Turkey Island W Sus 34 D3
Turkey Tump Hereford 97 F10
Turleigh Wilts 61 G10
Turleygreen Shrops 132 F5
Turlin Moor Poole 18 C5
Turmer Hants 31 F10
Turn Lancs 195 D10
Turnalt Argyll 275 C9
Turnastone Hereford 97 D7
Turnberry S Ayrs 244 B6
Turnchapel Plym 7 E9
Turnditch Derbys 170 F3
Turner Green Lancs 203 G8
Turner's Green E Sus 23 B10
Turner's Green E Sus 52 G6
Turner's Green W Berks 64 F4
Turner's Green Warks 118 D3
Turners Hill W Sus 51 F10
Turners Puddle Dorset 18 C2
Turnerwood S Yorks 187 E8
Turnford Herts 86 E5
Turnhouse Edin 280 G3
Turnhurst Stoke 168 E5
Turnstead Milton Derbys 185 E8
Turnworth Dorset 30 F4
Turrerich Perth 286 D2
Turriff Aberds 303 D7
Tursdale Durham 234 D2
Turton Bottoms Blkburn 195 D8
Turves Cambs 138 D6
Turves Green W Mid 117 B10
Turvey Beds 121 G8
Turville Bucks 84 G3
Turville Heath Bucks 84 G2
Turweston Bucks 102 D2
Tushielaw Borders 261 F8
Tutbury Staffs 152 D4
Tutnall Worcs 117 C9
Tutnalls Glos 79 E10
Tutshill Glos 79 G8
Tutt Hill Kent 54 D3
Tuttington Norf 160 D4
Tutts Clump W Berks 64 E5
Tutwell Corn 12 F3
Tuxford Notts 188 G2
Twatt Orkney 314 D2
Twatt Shetland 313 H5
Twechar E Dunb 278 F4
Tweedale Telford 132 C4
Tweeddaleburn Borders 270 E5
Tweedmouth Northumb 273 E9
Tweedsmuir Borders 260 E3
Twelve Heads Corn 4 G5
Twelve Oaks E Sus 37 C11
Twelvewoods Corn 6 B4
Twemlow Green E Ches 168 B3
Twenties Kent 71 F10
Twenty Lincs 156 E3
Twerton Bath 61 G8
Twickenham London 67 E7
Twigworth Glos 98 G6
Twineham W Sus 36 D3
Twineham Green W Sus 36 C3
Twinhoe Bath 45 B8
Twinstead Essex 107 D7
Twinstead Green Essex 106 D6
Twiss Green Warr 183 B11
Twist Devon 28 G3
Twiston Lancs 204 E2
Twitchen Devon 41 G9
Twitchen Shrops 115 B7
Twitchen Mill Devon 41 G9
Twitham Kent 55 B9
Twitton Kent 52 B4
Two Bridges Devon 13 G8
Two Bridges Glos 79 E11
Two Burrows Corn 4 F4
Two Dales Derbys 170 C3
Two Gates Staffs 134 C4
Two Mile Ash M Keynes 102 D6
Two Mile Ash W Sus 35 B10
Two Mile Hill Bristol 60 E6
Two Mile Oak Cross Devon 8 B6
Two Mills W Ches 182 G5
Two Pots Devon 40 E4
Two Waters Herts 85 D9
Twr Anglesey 178 E2
Twycross Leics 134 C6
Twydall Medway 69 F9
Twyford Bucks 102 F3
Twyford Derbys 152 D6
Twyford Dorset 30 D5
Twyford Hants 33 C7
Twyford Leics 154 G4
Twyford Lincs 155 E8
Twyford Norf 159 E10
Twyford Oxon 101 D9
Twyford Shrops 148 D6
Twyford Wokingham 65 D9
Twyford Worcs 99 B10
Twyford Common Hereford 97 D10
Twyn-Allws Mon 78 C3
Twyn Shôn-Ifan Caerph 77 G11
Twyn-y-Sheriff Mon 78 D6
Twyn-yr-odyn V Glam 58 E6
Twynholm Dumfries 237 D8
Twyning Glos 99 D7
Twyning Green Glos 99 D8
Twynllanan Carms 94 G5
Twynmynydd Carms 75 C11
Twynyrodyn M Tydf 77 D9
Twywell Northants 121 B9
Ty-coch Swansea 56 C6
Ty-draw Conwy 164 D5
Ty-draw Swansea 57 C7
Ty-fry Mon 78 F6
Ty-hen Carms 92 G6
Ty-hen Gwyn 144 C3
Ty-isaf Carms 56 B4
Ty Llwyn Bl Gwent 77 D11
Ty-mawr Anglesey 179 D7
Ty Mawr Carms 93 C10
Ty-mawr Conwy 181 F7
Ty Mawr Cwm Conwy 164 F6
Ty-nant Conwy 165 G7
Ty-nant Gwyn 147 D8
Ty-newydd Ceredig 111 D10
Ty Rhiw Rhondda 58 C6
Ty-Sign Caerph 78 G2
Ty-uchaf Powys 147 E10
Tyberton Hereford 97 D7
Tyburn W Mid 134 E2

le Gtr Man 196 D2
le Bank E Ches 167 D10
ley Gtr Man 195 G9
ley Rutland 136 C6
ley T & W 243 E7
ley W Sus 34 B4
ow Derbys 185 G11
our Wilts 30 B6
park N Lnrk 278 F5
robes Bucks 84 E4
send E Ches 184 E6
y Hill Cambs 139 G9
Herts 86 C5
Kent 71 G9
Street Kent 53 B9
nam Dorset 18 D4
norne Kent 54 G3
n Mill Northumb 264 C4
nford Northumb 264 D4
nton Northumb 264 C4
side Herts 86 B5
sley Cambs 122 G4
sley Worcs 116 C6
eld Brack 65 E11
eet Devon 9 E7
ate Lincs 156 C4
rave Mers 183 C9
rave Wokingham 65 D9
am Hereford 97 D9
am Norf 176 E6
ll Gtr Man 185 B7
g's Green W Mid 118 C3
Northumb 241 B9
Northumb 263 B8
Common
umb 263 B8
eigh Devon 25 C10
on Northants 121 B7
worth Northants 101 C9
worth Northumb 252 B6
by N Yorks 224 G6
nd W Yorks 196 C2
ggan Corn 6 B3
igh Bath 61 G9
y Essex 87 G9
y Town W Yorks 196 B5
y Woods W Mid 133 F10
ngham Sur 51 B11
brook Derbys 170 E3
field W Yorks 197 C11
ingham E Ches 168 C2
inghurst W Sus 35 D10
ington Northants 137 E11
ington Warks 101 B8
inster Wilts 45 D11
inster Common
45 E11
lake Kent 53 C10
ley S Glos 61 E7
ley Hill S Glos 61 E7
ley Tower S Glos 61 E7
onds Hill
ants 121 D9
sworth S Yorks 198 G4
well Dorset 17 D11
borough Green
49 C8
don Worcs 117 F7
ers End Herts 85 D8
ford Hants 33 C10
nam W Sus 51 G7
ngcamp W Sus 35 F8
nglid W Sus 36 B2
sgrove Oxon 83 F10
en Dorset 18 C3
en E Ches 184 G5
en Pembs 72 F6
en S Yorks 186 B5
en Corner Hants 34 B2
en Corner Hants 49 C10
en Heath Suff 108 C4
en Row Windsor 65 C10
en Street Kent 54 C2
enby Redcar 235 F7
en's Green Herts 104 F5
ngton M Keynes 121 G7
ngton Warr 183 D10
ston Edin 280 F5
ish Hants 33 F7
ll N Yorks 214 F4
ow Staffs 169 D9
op Vale Notts 171 B8
ock W Mid 117 B11
one Staffs 133 B9
r E Yorks 208 C3
ermarske
s 214 D4
ill N Yorks 207 B9
e Aberds 293 C7
ing E Sus 23 D11
aby Leics 154 E4
en Lancs 194 B2
en Lancs 211 E9
en Northumb 252 C2
en Warks 134 C5
n Bank Lancs 194 B2
ick Warks 118 E5
ick Bridge Cumb 239 F11
ick on Eden
239 F11
ick Wold Sur 51 C10
icksland Cumb 239 B10
ister Orkney 314 C3
ale Head Cumb 220 D3
Derbys 185 E9
Common W Berks 64 G3
Dyke Norf 157 F10
Water W Berks 64 G3
all Green Herts 105 E8
away Corn 5 B10
bourne Devon 8 E5
brook Som 44 C2
brook Suff 108 C2
brook Street Suff 108 C2
erwall Staffs 168 F6
field Devon 26 D6
fold N Yorks 223 E11
ford Som 42 E5
ford Worcs 117 D11
ford Pyne Devon 26 F4
ingborough Lincs 189 G8
ingley Cambs 138 F2
ington T & W 243 F8
ington W Sus 35 E10
ington Village
243 F8
mere Green Suff 107 B8
pit W Yorks 196 F6
wood Heath
134 F2
ng W Berks 64 G5
erley Durham 233 B7
Green Sur 51 D10
erton Warks 118 F5
less Lincs 173 C9
N Yorks 215 D11
Green Warks 118 D4
or Devon 8 F2
n House Green
106 G3
net Som 42 E5
nfield Oxon 63 B8
Watchfield Som 43 D10
Watchgate Cumb 221 F10
Watchhill Cumb 229 C9
Watchill Dumfries 238 D6
Watchill Dumfries 248 G3
Watcombe Torbay 9 B8
Watendlath Cumb 220 B5
Water Devon 13 E11
Water Lancs 195 B10
Water Eaton M Keynes 103 E7
Water Eaton Oxon 83 C8
Water End Beds 104 B2
Water End C Beds 103 D11
Water End C Beds 104 B5
Water End E Yorks 207 F11
Water End Essex 105 C11
Water End Hants 49 C7
Water End Herts 85 C8
Water End Herts 86 E2
Water Fryston W Yorks 198 B3
Water Garth Nook
Cumb 210 F3
Water Houses N Yorks 213 F7
Water Newton Cambs 138 D2
Water Orton Warks 134 E3
Water Stratford Bucks 102 E3
Water Yeat Cumb 210 B5
Waterbeach Cambs 123 D9
Waterbeach W Sus 22 B5
Waterbeck Dumfries 238 B6
Waterdale Herts 85 E10
Waterden Norf 159 B7
Waterditch Hants 19 B9
Waterend Bucks 84 F3
Waterend Cumb 229 G8
Waterend Glos 80 C3
Waterend Herts 86 C2
Waterfall Staffs 169 E9
Waterfoot Argyll 255 D9
Waterfoot Cumb 230 G5
Waterfoot E Renf 267 D11
Waterfoot Lancs 195 C10
Waterford Hants 20 B2
Waterford Herts 86 C4
Watergate Corn 6 E4
Watergate Corn 11 E8
Watergore Som 28 D6
Waterhales Essex 87 F8
Waterham Kent 70 G5
Waterhay Wilts 81 G9
Waterhead Angus 292 F6
Waterhead Cumb 221 E7
Waterhead Devon 8 F3
Waterhead Dumfries 248 E5
Waterhead on
Minnoch S Ayrs 245 E9
Waterheads Borders 270 E4
Waterheath Norf 143 E8
Waterhouses Durham 233 C9
Waterhouses Staffs 169 E9
Wateringbury Kent 53 C7
Waterlane Glos 80 E6
Waterlip Som 45 E7
Waterloo Blkburn 195 B7
Waterloo Corn 11 G8
Waterloo Derbys 170 C6
Waterloo Gtr Man 196 G2
Waterloo Highld 295 C8
Waterloo Mers 182 B4
Waterloo N Lnrk 268 E6
Waterloo Norf 126 B2
Waterloo Norf 143 E8
Waterloo Norf 160 F4
Waterloo Pembs 73 E7
Waterloo Perth 286 D4
Waterloo Poole 18 C6
Waterloo Shrops 149 C9
Waterloo Park Mers 182 B4
Waterloo Port Gwyn 163 C7
Waterlooville Hants 33 F11
Waterman Quarter
Kent 53 E10
Watermead Glos 80 B5
Watermeetings S Lnrk 259 G11
Watermill E Sus 38 E2
Watermillock Cumb 230 G4
Watermoor Glos 81 E8
Waterperry Oxon 83 D10
Waterrow Som 27 B9
Water's Nook Gtr Man 195 F7
Waters Upton Telford 150 F2
Watersfield W Sus 35 D8
Watersheddings
Gtr Man 196 F2
Waterside Aberds 292 B5
Waterside Aberds 303 G10
Waterside Blkburn 195 C8
Waterside Bucks 85 E7
Waterside Cumb 229 B10
Waterside Derbys 185 E8
Waterside E Ayrs 245 B10
Waterside E Ayrs 267 G9
Waterside E Dunb 278 G3
Waterside E Renf 267 D10
Waterside S Yorks 199 E7
Waterside Sur 51 D11
Waterside Telford 150 F2
Waterslack Lancs 211 D9
Waterstein Highld 297 G7
Waterstock Oxon 83 D10
Waterston Pembs 72 D6
Waterthorpe S Yorks 186 E6
Waterton Aberds 303 F9
Waterton Bridgend 58 D2
Watford Herts 85 F10
Watford Northants 120 D2
Watford Gap Staffs 134 C2
Watford Heath Herts 85 G10
Watford Park Caerph 58 B6
Wath Cumb 222 D3
Wath N Yorks 214 D6
Wath N Yorks 214 F2
Wath N Yorks 216 D3
Wath Brow Cumb 219 C10
Wath upon Dearne
S Yorks 198 G2
Watherston Borders 271 F8
Watledge Glos 80 E4
Watley's End S Glos 61 C7
Watlington Norf 158 G2
Watlington Oxon 83 G11
Watnall Notts 171 F8
Watsness Shetland 313 H3
Watten Highld 310 D6
Wattisfield Suff 125 C10
Wattisham Suff 125 G10
Wattisham Stone Suff 125 G10
Wattlefield Norf 142 D2
Wattlesborough Heath
Shrops 149 G7
Watton E Yorks 208 C6
Watton Norf 141 C8
Watton at Stone Herts 86 B4
Watton Green Norf 141 C8
Watton's Green Essex 87 F8
Wattston N Lnrk 268 B5
Wattstown Rhondda 77 G8
Wattsville Caerph 78 G2
Wauchan Highld 295 G11
Waulkmill Lodge
Orkney 314 F3
Waun Gwyn 163 C9
Waun Powys 148 F4
Waun Beddau Pembs 90 F5
Waun Fawr Ceredig 128 G2
Waun-Lwyd Bl Gwent 77 D11
Waun-y-clyn Carms 75 E7
Waun y Gilfach Bridgend 57 D11
Waunarlwydd Swansea 56 B6
Waunclunda Carms 94 E3
Waunfawr Gwyn 163 D8
Waungilwen Carms 92 D6
Waungron Swansea 75 E9
Waunlwyd Bl Gwent 77 D11
Wavendon M Keynes 103 D8
Wavendon Gate
M Keynes 103 D8
Waverbridge Cumb 229 B10
Waverton Cumb 229 B10
Waverton W Ches 167 C7
Wavertree Mers 182 D5
Wawcott W Berks 63 F11
Wawne E Yorks 209 F7
Waxham Norf 161 D8
Waxholme E Yorks 201 B10
Way Kent 71 F10
Way Village Devon 26 E5
Way Wick N Som 59 G11
Waye Devon 13 G11
Wayend Street Hereford 98 D4
Wayfield Medway 69 F9
Wayford Som 28 F6
Waymills Shrops 167 G9
Wayne Green Mon 78 B6
Way's Green W Ches 167 B10
Waytown Devon 24 C5
Waytown Devon 40 G5
Wdig = Goodwick
Pembs 91 D8
Weachyburn Aberds 302 D6
Weacombe Som 42 E6
Weald Oxon 82 E4
Wealdstone London 67 B7
Wearde Corn 7 D8
Weardley W Yorks 205 E11
Weare Som 44 C2
Weare Giffard Devon 25 C7
Wearhead Durham 232 D3
Wearne Som 28 B6
Weasdale Cumb 222 E3
Weasenham All Saints
Norf 158 E6
Weasenham St Peter
Norf 159 E7
Weaste Gtr Man 184 B4
Weatherhill Sur 51 E10
Weatheroak Hill
Worcs 117 C11
Weaverham W Ches 183 G10
Weavering Street Kent 53 B9
Weaverslake Staffs 152 F2
Weaverthorpe N Yorks 217 E9
Webbington Som 43 B11
Webheath Worcs 117 D10
Webscott Shrops 149 E9
Wecock Hants 33 E11
Wedderlairs Aberds 303 F8
Wedderlie Borders 272 E2
Weddington Kent 55 B9
Weddington Warks 135 E7
Wedhampton Wilts 46 B5
Wedmore Som 44 D2
Wednesbury W Mid 133 D9
Wednesbury Oak
W Mid 133 E9
Wednesfield W Mid 133 C8
Weecar Notts 172 B4
Weedon Bucks 84 B4
Weedon Bec Northants 120 F2
Weedon Lois Northants 102 B2
Weeford Staffs 134 C2
Week Devon 8 C5
Week Devon 12 E5
Week Devon 25 B9
Week Devon 26 D2
Week Green Corn 11 B10
Week St Mary Corn 11 B10
Weeke Devon 26 F3
Weeke Hants 48 G3
Weekley Northants 137 G7
Weekmoor Som 27 B10
Weeks I o W 21 C7
Weel E Yorks 209 F7
Weeley Essex 108 G2
Weeley Heath Essex 108 G3
Weelsby NE Lincs 201 F9
Weem Perth 286 C2
Weeping Cross Staffs 151 E8
Weethley Warks 117 F11
Weethley Bank Warks 117 G11
Weethley Gate Warks 117 G11
Weeting Norf 140 F5
Weeton E Yorks 201 C11
Weeton Lancs 202 G3
Weeton N Yorks 205 D11
Weetwood W Yorks 205 F11
Weetwood Common
W Ches 167 B8
Weetwood Hall
Northumb 264 D2
Weir Essex 69 B10
Weir Lancs 195 B11
Weir Quay Devon 7 C8
Weirbrook Shrops 148 E6
Welborne Norf 159 G11
Welborne Common
Norf 141 B11
Welbourn Lincs 173 E7
Welburn N Yorks 216 C3
Welburn N Yorks 216 F4
Welbury N Yorks 225 E7
Welby Lincs 155 B9
Welches Dam Cambs 139 F9
Welcombe Devon 24 D2
Weld Bank Lancs 194 D5
Weldon Northants 137 F8
Weldon Northumb 252 D4
Welford Northants 136 G2
Welford W Berks 64 E2
Welford-on-Avon
Warks 118 G3
Welham Leics 136 E5
Welham Notts 188 E2
Welham Som 45 G7
Welham Green Herts 86 D2
Welhambridge E Yorks 207 G11
Well Hants 49 D9
Well Lincs 190 G6
Well N Yorks 214 C5
Well Bottom Dorset 30 D6
Well End Bucks 65 B11
Well End Herts 86 F2
Well Green Gtr Man 184 D3
Well Heads W Yorks 205 G7
Well Hill Kent 68 G3
Well Place Oxon 65 B7
Well Street Kent 53 B7
Well Town Devon 26 F6
Welland Worcs 98 C5
Welland Stone Worcs 98 D6
Wellbank Angus 287 D8
Wellbrook E Sus 37 B9
Welldale Dumfries 238 D5
Weller's Town Kent 52 E4
Wellesbourne Warks 118 F5
Wellheads Aberds 302 F4
Wellhouse W Berks 64 E4
Wellhouse W Yorks 196 E5
Welling London 68 D3
Wellingborough
Northants 121 D7
Wellingham Norf 159 E7
Wellingore Lincs 173 D7
Wellington Cumb 219 E11
Wellington Hereford 97 B9
Wellington Som 27 C10
Wellington Telford 150 G3
Wellington Heath
Hereford 98 C4
Wellington Hill W Yorks 206 F2
Wellisford Som 27 C9
Wellow Bath 45 B8
Wellow I o W 20 D3
Wellow NE Lincs 201 F9
Wellow Notts 171 B11
Wellow Wood Hants 32 C3
Wellpond Green Herts 105 G8
Wellroyd W Yorks 205 F10
Wells Som 44 D5
Wells Green E Ches 167 E11
Wells-Next-The-Sea
Norf 176 E6
Wellsborough Leics 135 C7
Wellsprings Som 28 B2
Wellstye Green Essex 87 B10
Wellswood Torbay 9 C8
Welltown Corn 6 B2
Wellwood Fife 279 D11
Welney Norf 139 E10
Welsford Devon 24 C3
Welsh Bicknor Hereford 79 B9
Welsh End Shrops 149 B10
Welsh Frankton Shrops 149 C7
Welsh Harp London 67 B8
Welsh Hook Pembs 91 F8
Welsh Newton Hereford 79 B7
Welsh Newton
Common Hereford 79 B8
Welsh St Donats V Glam 58 D4
Welshampton Shrops 149 B8
Welshpool Powys 130 B4
Welshwood Park Essex 107 F10
Welstor Devon 13 G10
Welton Bath 45 C7
Welton Cumb 230 C3
Welton E Ayrs 258 D2
Welton E Yorks 200 B3
Welton Lincs 189 F8
Welton Northants 119 D11
Welton Hill Lincs 189 E8
Welton le Marsh Lincs 175 B7
Welton le Wold Lincs 190 D3
Welwick E Yorks 201 C10
Welwyn Herts 86 B2
Welwyn Garden City
Herts 86 C2
Wem Shrops 149 D10
Wembdon Som 43 F9
Wembley London 67 B7
Wembley Park London 67 B7
Wembury Devon 7 F10
Wembworthy Devon 25 F11
Wemyss Bay Invclyd 266 B3
Wenallt Ceredig 112 C3
Wenallt Gwyn 146 F4
Wenallt Gwyn 165 G7
Wendens Ambo Essex 105 D10
Wendlebury Oxon 83 B9
Wendling Norf 159 G8
Wendover Bucks 84 D5
Wendover Dean Bucks 84 E5
Wendron Corn 2 C5
Wendy Cambs 104 B6
Wenfordbridge Corn 11 F7
Wenhaston Suff 127 B8
Wenhaston Black
Heath Suff 127 C8
Wennington Cambs 122 B4
Wennington Lancs 212 E2
Wennington London 68 C4
Wensley Derbys 170 C3
Wensley N Yorks 213 B11
Wentbridge W Yorks 198 D3
Wentnor Shrops 131 E7
Wentworth Cambs 123 B9
Wentworth S Yorks 186 B5
Wenvoe V Glam 58 E6
Weobley Hereford 115 G8
Weobley Marsh
Hereford 115 G8
Weoley Castle W Mid 133 G10
Wepham W Sus 35 F8
Wepre Flint 166 B3
Wereham Norf 140 C3
Wereham Row Norf 140 C3
Wereton Staffs 168 E3
Wergs W Mid 133 C7
Wern Gwyn 145 B10
Wern Powys 77 B10
Wern Powys 147 G9
Wern Powys 148 E5
Wern Powys 148 G5
Wern Shrops 148 C5
Wern Swansea 56 C4
Wern ddu Shrops 148 D4
Wern-Gifford Mon 96 G6
Wern-olau Swansea 56 B5
Wern Tarw Bridgend 58 C3
Wern-y-cwrt Mon 78 D5
Wern-y-gaer Flint 166 B2
Werneth Gtr Man 196 G2
Werneth Low Gtr Man 185 C7
Wernffrwd Swansea 56 C4
Wernlas Shrops 148 E6
Wernrheolydd Mon 78 C5
Wernyrheolydd Mon 78 C5
Werrington Corn 12 D2
Werrington P'boro 138 C3
Werrington Staffs 168 F6
Wervin W Ches 182 G6
Wescoe Hill N Yorks 205 D11
Wesham Lancs 202 G4
Wessington Derbys 170 D5
West Aberthaw V Glam 58 F4
West Acre Norf 158 F5
West Acton London 67 C7
West Adderbury Oxon 101 D9
West Allerdean
Northumb 273 F9
West Allotment T & W 243 C8
West Alvington Devon 8 G4
West Amesbury Wilts 46 E6
West Anstey Devon 26 B5
West Appleton N Yorks 224 G4
West Ardhu Argyll 288 D6
West Ardsley W Yorks 197 B9
West Ardwell Dumfries 236 E2
West Arthurlie E Renf 267 D9
West Ashby Lincs 190 G3
West Ashford Devon 40 F4
West Ashling W Sus 22 B4
West Ashton Wilts 45 B11
West Auckland Durham 233 F9
West Ayton N Yorks 217 C9
West Bagborough Som 43 G7
West Bank Bl Gwent 78 D2
West Bank Halton 183 E8
West Barkwith Lincs 189 E11
West Barnby N Yorks 226 C6
West Barnes London 67 F8
West Barns E Loth 282 F3
West Barsham Norf 159 C8
West Bay Dorset 16 C5
West Beckham Norf 160 B2
West Bedfont Sur 66 E5
West Benhar N Lnrk 269 C7
West Bergholt Essex 107 F9
West Bexington Dorset 16 D6
West Bilney Norf 158 F4
West Blackdene
Durham 232 D3
West Blackdown Devon 12 E5
West Blatchington
Brighton 36 F3
West Bold Borders 261 B9
West Boldon T & W 243 E9
West Bourton Dorset 30 B3
West Bowling W Yorks 205 G9
West Bradford Lancs 203 E10
West Bradley Som 44 F5
West Bretton W Yorks 197 E9
West Bridgford Notts 153 B11
West Brompton London 67 D9
West Bromwich
W Mid 133 E10
West Broughton
Derbys 152 C2
West Buckland Devon 41 G7
West Buckland Som 27 C11
West Burnside Aberds 293 F8
West Burrafirth
Shetland 313 H4
West Burton N Yorks 213 B10
West Burton W Sus 35 E7
West Butsfield Durham 233 C8
West Butterwick
N Lincs 199 F10
West Byfleet Sur 66 G4
West Caister Norf 161 G10
West Calder W Loth 269 C10
West Camel Som 29 C9
West Carlton W Yorks 205 E10
West Carr Hull 209 G7
West Carr N Lincs 199 F8
West Chadsmoor Staffs 151 G9
West Challow Oxon 63 B11
West Charleton Devon 8 G5
West Chelborough
Dorset 29 F8
West Chevington
Northumb 252 D6
West Chiltington W Sus 35 D9
West Chiltington
Common W Sus 35 D9
West Chinnock Som 29 E7
West Chirton T & W 243 D8
West Chisenbury Wilts 46 C6
West Clandon Sur 50 C4
West Cliff Bmouth 19 C7
West Cliff N Yorks 227 C7
West Cliffe Kent 55 E10
West Clyne Highld 311 J2
West Clyth Highld 310 F6
West Coker Som 29 E8
West Common Hants 32 G6
West Compton Dorset 17 C7
West Compton Som 44 E5
West Cornforth
Durham 234 E2
West Cowick E Yorks 199 C7
West Cranmore Som 45 E7
West Cross Kent 53 G10
West Cross Swansea 56 D6
West Crudwell Wilts 80 G6
West Curry Corn 11 C11
West Curthwaite Cumb 230 B2
West Darlochan Argyll 255 E7
West Dean W Sus 34 E5
West Dean Wilts 32 B3
West Deeping Lincs 138 B2
West Denant Pembs 72 C6
West Denton T & W 242 D5
West Derby Mers 182 C5
West Dereham Norf 140 C3
West Didsbury Gtr Man 184 C4
West Down Devon 40 E4
West Down Hants 47 F11
West Downs Corn 5 C10
West Drayton London 66 D5
West Drayton Notts 188 G2
West Ealing London 67 C7
West Edge Derbys 170 C4
West Ella E Yorks 200 B4
West End Beds 121 E11
West End Beds 121 G9
West End Brack 65 E11
West End Bracknell 66 G2
West End Caerph 78 F2
West End Cumb 239 F8
West End Dorset 30 G6
West End Esher 66 G6
West End E Yorks 201 B9
West End E Yorks 208 G4
West End E Yorks 209 B9
West End E Yorks 209 G9
West End E Yorks 217 G11
West End Glos 80 F5
West End Hants 33 E7
West End Hants 33 F9
West End Hants 48 F6
West End Herts 86 D3
West End Kent 54 B2
West End Kent 71 F7
West End Lancs 195 B8
West End Lancs 211 G8
West End Leics 153 F8
West End Lincs 174 F5
West End Lincs 190 B5
West End Mon 78 F6
West End N Som 60 F3
West End N Yorks 205 B8
West End N Yorks 206 E6
West End N Yorks 207 F7
West End Norf 141 B8
West End Norf 161 G10
West End Oxon 64 B5
West End Oxon 82 E6
West End S Glos 61 B8
West End S Lnrk 269 F9
West End S Yorks 199 F7
West End Som 44 C5
West End Som 45 G7
West End Suff 143 G9
West End Surrey Heath 49 E10
West End W Sus 36 D2
West End W Yorks 197 B7
West End W Yorks 205 F10
West End Wilts 30 C6
West End Wilts 31 C7
West End Wilts 62 D3
West End Windsor 65 D10
West End Worcs 99 D11
West End = Marian-y-
mor Gwyn 145 C7
West End Green Hants 65 G7
West-end Town V Glam 58 F3
West Ewell Sur 67 G8
West Farleigh Kent 53 C8
West Farndon
Northants 119 G10
West Felton Shrops 148 D6
West Fenton E Loth 281 E9
West Ferry Dundee 287 D8
West Field N Lincs 200 D6
West Field York 207 C7
West Fields W Berks 64 F3
West Firle E Sus 23 D7
West Fleetham
Northumb 264 D5
West Flodden
Northumb 263 C10
West Garforth W Yorks 206 G3
West Ginge Oxon 64 B2
West Gorton Gtr Man 184 B5
West Grafton Wilts 63 G8
West Green Hants 49 B8
West Green London 67 B10
West Green S Yorks 197 F11
West Green W Sus 51 F9
West Greenskares
Aberds 303 C7
West Grimstead Wilts 32 B2
West Grinstead W Sus 35 C11
West Haddlesey
N Yorks 198 B5
West Haddon Northants 120 C2
West Hagbourne Oxon 64 B4
West Hagley Worcs 133 G8
West Hall Cumb 240 D3
West Hallam Derbys 170 G6
West Halton N Lincs 200 C2
West Ham Hants 48 C6
West Ham London 68 C2
West Hampstead London 67 B9
West Handley Derbys 186 F5
West Hanney Oxon 82 G6
West Hanningfield
Essex 88 F2
West Hardwick W Yorks 198 D2
West Harling Norf 141 G9
West Harlsey N Yorks 225 F8
West Harnham Wilts 31 B10
West Harptree Bath 44 B5
West Harrow London 66 B6
West Harting W Sus 34 C3
West Harton T & W 243 E9
West Hatch Som 28 C3
West Hatch Wilts 30 B6
West Head Norf 139 B11
West Heath E Ches 168 C4
West Heath Hants 48 B5
West Heath Hants 49 B11
West Heath London 68 D3
West Heath W Mid 117 B10
West Helmsdale Highld 311 H4
West Hendon London 67 B8
West Hendred Oxon 64 B2
West Herrington
T & W 243 G8
West Heslerton N Yorks 217 D8
West Hewish N Som 59 G11
West Hill Devon 15 C7
West Hill E Sus 38 E4
West Hill E Yorks 218 F3
West Hill London 67 E8
West Hill N Som 60 D3
West Hill Som 30 B2
West Hill Staffs 151 G9
West Hill W Sus 51 G10
West Hill Wilts 61 F11
West Hoathly W Sus 51 G11
West Holme Dorset 18 D3
West Holywell T & W 243 C8
West Horndon Essex 68 B6
West Horrington Som 44 D5
West Horsley Sur 50 C5
West Horton Northumb 264 C2
West Hougham Kent 55 E9
West Houlland
Shetland 313 H4
West Houses Lincs 174 E4
West Howe Bmouth 19 B7
West Howetown Som 42 G2
West Huntington York 207 B8
West Huntspill Som 43 E10
West Hurn Dorset 19 B8
West Hyde Herts 85 G8
West Hynish Argyll 288 F1
West Hythe Kent 54 G6
West Ilkerton Devon 41 D8
West Ilsley W Berks 64 C3
West Itchenor W Sus 22 C3
West Jesmond T & W 243 D7
West Keal Lincs 174 C5
West Kennett Wilts 62 F6
West Kensington
London 67 D8
West Kilbride N Ayrs 266 F4
West Kilburn London 67 C8
West Kingsdown Kent 68 G5
West Kingston W Sus 35 G9
West Kington Wilts 61 D10
West Kington Wick
Wilts 61 D10
West Kinharrachie
Aberds 303 F9
West Kirby Mers 182 D2
West Kirkby Mers 182 D2
West Knapton N Yorks 217 D7
West Knighton Dorset 17 D10
West Knoyle Wilts 45 G11
West Kyloe Northumb 273 G11
West Kyo Durham 242 G5
West Lambrook Som 28 D6
West Langdon Kent 55 D10
West Langwell Highld 309 J6
West Lavington W Sus 34 C5
West Lavington Wilts 46 C4
West Layton N Yorks 224 D2
West Lea Durham 234 B4
West Leake Notts 153 D10
West Learmouth
Northumb 263 B9
West Leigh Devon 25 F11
West Leigh Hants 22 B2
West Leigh Som 42 G6
West Lexham Norf 158 F6
West Lilling N Yorks 216 F2
West Linton Borders 270 E2
West Liss Hants 34 B3
West Littleton S Glos 61 D9
West Lockinge Oxon 64 B2
West Looe Corn 6 E5
West Luccombe Som 41 D11
West Lulworth Dorset 18 E2
West Lutton N Yorks 217 F8
West Lydford Som 44 G5
West Lydiatt Hereford 97 C11
West Lyn Devon 41 D8
West Lyng Som 28 B4
West Lynn Norf 158 E2
West Mains Borders 271 F11
West Mains S Lnrk 268 E2
West Malling Kent 53 B7
West Malvern Worcs 98 B5
West Marden W Sus 34 E3
West Marina E Sus 38 F3
West Markham Notts 188 G2
West Marsh NE Lincs 201 E9
West Marton N Yorks 204 C3
West Mathers Aberds 293 G9
West Melbury Dorset 30 C5
West Melton S Yorks 198 G2
West Meon Hants 33 C10
West Meon
Woodlands Hants 33 B10
West Merkland Highld 308 F3
West Mersea Essex 89 C8
West Milton Dorset 16 B6
West Minster Kent 70 E2
West Molesey Sur 66 F6
West Monkseaton
T & W 243 C8
West Monkton Som 28 B3
West Moor T & W 243 C7
West Moors Dorset 31 G9
West Morden Dorset 18 B4
West Morriston
Borders 272 G2
West Morton W Yorks 205 E7
West Mudford Som 29 C9
West Muir Angus 293 G7
West Myreriggs Perth 286 C6
West Ness N Yorks 216 D3
West Newham
Northumb 242 B3
West Newton E Yorks 209 F9
West Newton Norf 158 D3
West Newton Som 28 B3
West Norwood London 67 E10
West Ogwell Devon 14 G2
West Orchard Dorset 30 D4
West Overton Wilts 62 F6
West Panson Devon 12 C2
West Park Hrtlpl 234 E5
West Park Hull 200 B5
West Park Mers 183 B7
West Park T & W 243 D9
West Park W Yorks 205 F11
West Parley Dorset 19 B7
West Pasture Durham 232 G4
West Peckham Kent 52 C6
West Pelton Durham 242 G6
West Pennard Som 44 F4
West Pentire Corn 4 C5
West Perry Cambs 122 D2
West Pontnewydd Torf 78 F3
West Poringland Norf 142 C5
West Porlock Som 41 D11
West Portholland Corn 5 G9
West Porton Renfs 277 G8
West Pulham Dorset 30 F2
West Putford Devon 24 D5
West Quantoxhead Som 42 E6
West Rainton Durham 234 B2
West Rasen Lincs 189 D9
West Ravendale
NE Lincs 190 B2
West Raynham Norf 159 D7
West Retford Notts 187 E11
West Rounton N Yorks 225 E8
West Row Suff 124 B3
West Royd W Yorks 205 F9
West Rudham Norf 158 D6
West Ruislip London 66 B5
West Runton Norf 177 E11
West Saltoun E Loth 271 B9
West Sandford Devon 26 G4
West Sandwick
Shetland 312 E6
West Scholes W Yorks 205 G7
West Scrafton N Yorks 213 C11
West Shepton Som 44 E6
West Side Bl Gwent 77 D11
West Side Orkney 314 C5
West Skelston
Dumfries 247 F8
West Sleekburn
Northumb 253 G7
West Somerton Norf 161 F9
West Southbourne
Bmouth 19 C8
West Stafford Dorset 17 D10
West Stockwith Notts 188 C3
West Stoke Devon 13 G9
West Stoke Som 29 D7
West Stoke W Sus 22 B4
West Stonesdale
N Yorks 223 E7
West Stoughton Som 44 D2
West Stour Dorset 30 C3
West Stourmouth Kent 71 G9
West Stow Suff 124 C6
West Stowell Wilts 62 G6
West Strathan Highld 308 C5
West Stratton Hants 48 E4
West Street Kent 54 C2
West Street Kent 55 C10
West Street Medway 69 D8
West Street Suff 125 C9
West Tanfield N Yorks 214 D5
West Taphouse Corn 6 C3
West Tarbert Argyll 275 G9
West Tarring W Sus 35 G10
West Third Borders 262 B4
West Thirston
Northumb 252 D5
West Thorney W Sus 22 C3
West Thurrock Thurrock 68 D5
West Tilbury Thurrock 69 D7
West Tisted Hants 33 B11
West Tofts Norf 140 E6
West Tofts Perth 286 D5
West Tolgus Corn 4 G3
West Torrington Lincs 189 E10
West Town Bath 60 G4
West Town Devon 14 B3
West Town Devon 24 C4
West Town Hants 21 B10
West Town Hereford 115 E8
West Town N Som 60 F3
West Town Som 44 F4
West Town W Sus 36 D3
West Tytherley Hants 32 B3
West Tytherton Wilts 62 E2
West Vale W Yorks 196 C5
West View Hrtlpl 234 D5
West Village V Glam 58 E3
West Walton Norf 157 G9
West Walton Highway
Norf 157 G9
West Watergate Corn 6 E4
West Watford Herts 85 F10
West Wellow Hants 32 D3
West Wemyss Fife 280 C6
West Wick N Som 59 G11
West Wickham Cambs 106 B2
West Wickham London 67 F11
West Williamston
Pembs 73 D8
West Willoughby Lincs 173 G7
West Winch Norf 158 F2
West Winterslow Wilts 47 G8
West Wittering W Sus 21 B11
West Witton N Yorks 213 B11
West Woodburn
Northumb 251 F9
West Woodhay W Berks 63 G11
West Woodlands Som 45 E9
West Worldham Hants 49 F8
West Worlington Devon 26 E3
West Worthing W Sus 35 G10
West Wratting Cambs 124 G2
West Wycombe Bucks 84 G4
West Wylam Northumb 242 E4
West Yatton Wilts 61 E11
West Yell Shetland 312 E6
West Yeo Som 43 G10
West Yoke Kent 68 F5
West Youlstone Corn 24 D3
Westacott Devon 40 G5
Westbere Kent 71 G7
Westborough Lincs 172 G5
Westbourne Bmouth 19 C7
Westbourne Suff 108 B2
Westbourne W Sus 22 B3
Westbourne Green
London 67 C9
Westbrook Hereford 96 C5
Westbrook Kent 71 E10
Westbrook Sur 50 E3
Westbrook W Berks 64 E2
Westbrook Warr 183 C9
Westbrook Wilts 62 F3
Westbrook Green Norf 142 G2
Westbrook Hay Herts 85 D8
Westburn S Lnrk 268 C3
Westbury Bucks 102 D2
Westbury Shrops 131 B7
Westbury Wilts 45 C11
Westbury Leigh Wilts 45 C11
Westbury-on-Severn
Glos 80 C2
Westbury on Trym Bristol 60 D5
Westbury Park Bristol 60 D5
Westbury-sub-Mendip
Som 44 D4
Westby Lancs 202 G3
Westby Lincs 155 D9
Westcliff-on-Sea
Sthend 69 B11
Westcombe Som 29 B7
Westcombe Som 45 F7
Westcot Oxon 63 B10
Westcote Glos 100 G4
Westcotes Leicester 135 C11
Westcott Bucks 84 B2
Westcott Devon 27 G8
Westcott Shrops 131 C8
Westcott Sur 50 D6
Westcott Barton Oxon 101 F8
Westcourt Wilts 63 G8
Westcroft M Keynes 102 E6
Westcroft W Mid 133 C8
Westdean E Sus 23 F8
Westdene Brighton 36 F3
Westdown Camp Wilts 46 D4
Westdowns Corn 11 E7
Westend Oxon 100 G6
Westend S Glos 79 G10
Westend Town
Northumb 241 D7
Westenhanger Kent 54 F6
Wester Aberchalder
Highld 300 G5
Wester Arboll Highld 311 L2
Wester Auchinloch
N Lnrk 278 G3
Wester Auchnagallin
Highld 301 F10
Wester Balgedie Perth 286 G5
Wester Brae Highld 300 C6
Wester Broomhouse
E Loth 282 F3
Wester Craiglands
Highld 301 D7
Wester Culbeuchly
Aberds 302 C6
Wester Dalvoult
Highld 291 B11
Wester Dechmont
W Loth 269 B10
Wester Deloraine
Borders 261 E8
Wester Denoon Angus 287 C7
Wester Ellister Argyll 254 B2
Wester Essendy Perth 286 C5
Wester Essenside
Borders 261 E10
Wester Feddal Perth 286 G2
Wester Fintray
Aberds 293 B10
Wester Galgantray
Highld 301 E8
Wester Gospetry Fife 286 G5
Wester Gruinards
Highld 309 K5
Wester Hailes Edin 270 B4
Wester Housebyres
Borders 262 B2
Wester Kershope
Borders 261 D9
Wester Lealty Highld 300 B6
Wester Lix Stirl 285 E9
Wester Milton Highld 301 D9
Wester Mosshead
Aberds 302 F5
Wester Newburn Fife 287 G8
Wester Ord Aberds 293 C10
Wester Parkgate
Dumfries 248 F2
Wester Quarff Shetland 313 K6
Wester Skeld Shetland 313 J4
Wester Strath Highld 300 D6
Wester Watten Highld 310 D6
Westerdale Highld 310 D5
Westerdale N Yorks 226 D3
Westerfield Shetland 313 H5
Westerfield Suff 108 B3
Westerfolds Moray 301 C11
Westergate W Sus 22 C6
Westerham Kent 52 C2
Westerhope T & W 242 D5
Westerleigh S Glos 61 D8
Westerleigh Hill S Glos 61 D8
Western Bank Cumb 229 B10
Western Downs Staffs 151 E8
Western Heights Kent 55 E10
Western Hill Durham 233 C11
Western Park
Leicester 135 C11
Westerton Aberds 293 B9
Westerton Aberds 302 E5
Westerton Angus 287 B10
Westerton Durham 233 E10
Westerton Moray 302 D3
Westerton W Sus 22 B5
Westertown Aberds 303 F7
Westerwick Shetland 313 J4
Westfield Bath 45 C7
Westfield Cumb 228 F5
Westfield E Sus 38 D4
Westfield Hants 21 B10
Westfield Hereford 98 B4
Westfield Highld 310 C4
Westfield N Lnrk 278 G4
Westfield Norf 141 B9

400 Wes – Win

Westfield Redcar 235 G7
Westfield S Yorks 186 E6
Westfield Sur 50 B4
Westfield W Loth 279 G8
Westfield W Yorks 197 C8
Westfield W Yorks 205 E9
Westfield Sole Kent 69 G9
Westfields Dorset 30 F2
Westfields Hereford 97 C9
Westfields of Rattray Perth 286 C5
Westford Som 27 C10
Westgate Durham 232 D4
Westgate N Lincs 199 F9
Westgate Norf 176 E4
Westgate Norf 177 E7
Westgate Hill W Yorks 197 B8
Westgate on Sea Kent 71 E10
Westgate Street Norf 160 E3
Westhall Aberds 302 G6
Westhall Suff 143 G8
Westhall Hill Oxon 82 C3
Westham Dorset 17 F9
Westham E Sus 23 E10
Westham Som 44 D2
Westhampnett W Sus 22 B5
Westhay Som 44 E2
Westhead Lancs 194 F2
Westhide Hereford 97 C11
Westhill Aberds 293 C10
Westhill E Yorks 209 F10
Westhill Highld 301 E7
Westhope Hereford 115 G9
Westhope Shrops 131 F9
Westhorp Northants 119 G10
Westhorpe Lincs 156 C4
Westhorpe Notts 171 E11
Westhorpe Suff 125 D10
Westhoughton Gtr Man 195 F7
Westhouse N Yorks 212 E3
Westhouses Derbys 170 D6
Westhumble Sur 51 C7
Westing Shetland 312 C7
Westington Glos 100 D2
Westlake Devon 8 E2
Westland Argyll 275 G11
Westland Green Herts 105 G8
Westlands Staffs 168 G4
Westlands Worcs 117 E7
Westlea Northumb 252 G6
Westlea Swindon 62 C6
Westleigh Devon 25 B7
Westleigh Devon 27 D9
Westleigh Gtr Man 194 G6
Westleton Suff 127 D8
Westley Shrops 131 B7
Westley Suff 124 E6
Westley Heights Essex 69 B7
Westley Waterless Cambs 124 F2
Westlington Bucks 84 C3
Westlinton Cumb 239 E9
Westmancote Worcs 99 D8
Westmarsh Kent 71 G9
Westmeston E Sus 36 E4
Westmill Herts 104 E3
Westmill Herts 105 F7
Westminster London 67 D10
Westmoor End Cumb 229 D8
Westmuir Angus 287 B7
Westness Orkney 314 D3
Westnewton Cumb 229 C8
Westnewton Northumb 263 C10
Westoe T & W 243 D9
Weston Bath 61 F8
Weston Devon 15 D9
Weston Devon 27 G10
Weston Dorset 17 G9
Weston Dorset 29 F8
Weston E Ches 168 E2
Weston E Ches 184 G5
Weston Halton 183 E8
Weston Hants 34 C2
Weston Hereford 115 F7
Weston Herts 104 E5
Weston Lincs 156 D5
Weston N Yorks 205 D9
Weston Northants 101 B11
Weston Notts 172 B3
Weston Pembs 73 C8
Weston S Lnrk 269 F10
Weston Shrops 114 C6
Weston Shrops 131 E11
Weston Shrops 148 D5
Weston Shrops 149 D11
Weston Soton 32 E6
Weston Staffs 151 D9
Weston Suff 143 F8
Weston W Berks 63 E11
Weston Bampfylde Som 29 C10
Weston Beggard Hereford 97 C11
Weston by Welland Northants 136 E5
Weston Colley Hants 48 F4
Weston Colville Cambs 124 G2
Weston Common Soton 33 E7
Weston Corbett Hants 49 D7
Weston Coyney Stoke 168 G6
Weston Ditch Suff 124 B3
Weston Favell Northants 120 E5
Weston Green Cambs 124 G2
Weston Green Norf 160 G2
Weston Green Sur 67 F7
Weston Heath Shrops 150 G5
Weston Hills Lincs 156 E5
Weston in Arden Warks 135 F7
Weston-in-Gordano N Som 60 E2
Weston Jones Staffs 150 E5
Weston Longville Norf 160 F2
Weston Lullingfields Shrops 149 E8
Weston Manor I o W 20 D2
Weston Mill Plym 7 D9
Weston-on-Avon Warks 118 G3
Weston-on-the-Green Oxon 83 B8
Weston-on-Trent Derbys 153 D8
Weston Park Bath 61 F8
Weston Patrick Hants 49 D7
Weston Point Halton 183 E7
Weston Rhyn Shrops 148 B5
Weston-sub-Edge Glos 100 C2
Weston-super-Mare N Som 59 G10
Weston Town Som 45 E8
Weston Turville Bucks 84 C5
Weston under Lizard Staffs 150 G6
Weston under Penyard Hereford 98 G2
Weston under Wetherley Warks 119 D7
Weston Underwood Derbys 170 G3
Weston Underwood M Keynes 121 G7
Westonbirt Glos 61 B11
Westoncommon Shrops 149 D8
Westoning C Beds 103 E10
Westonwharf Shrops 149 D8
Westonzoyland Som 43 G11
Westow N Yorks 216 F5
Westowe Som 42 G6
Westown Devon 27 E10
Westown Perth 286 E6
Westport Argyll 255 E7
Westport Som 28 D5
Westquarter Falk 279 F8
Westra V Glam 58 E6
Westridge Green W Berks 64 D5
Westrigg W Loth 269 B8
Westrip Glos 80 D4
Westrop Wilts 61 E11
Westrop Green W Berks 64 E4
Westrum N Lincs 200 F4
Westruther Borders 272 F2
Westry Cambs 139 D7
Westthorpe Derbys 187 F7
Westvale Mers 182 B6
Westville Devon 8 G4
Westville Notts 171 F8
Westward Cumb 229 C11
Westward Ho! Devon 24 B6
Westweekmoor Devon 12 C4
Westwell Kent 54 D3
Westwell Oxon 82 D2
Westwell Leacon Kent 54 D3
Westwells Wilts 61 F11
Westwick Cambs 123 D8
Westwick Durham 223 B11
Westwick Norf 160 D5
Westwick Row Herts 85 D9
Westwood Devon 14 B6
Westwood Devon 14 E5
Westwood Kent 55 D7
Westwood Kent 71 F11
Westwood Notts 171 E7
Westwood P'boro 138 D3
Westwood S Lnrk 268 E2
Westwood Wilts 45 B10
Westwood Wilts 46 G6
Westwood Heath W Mid 118 B5
Westwood Park Essex 107 E9
Westwood Park Gtr Man 184 B3
Westwoodside N Lincs 188 B3
Westy Warr 183 D10
Wetham Green Kent 69 F10
Wetheral Cumb 239 G11
Wetheral Plain Cumb 239 F11
Wetherby W Yorks 206 D4
Wetherden Suff 125 E10
Wetherden Upper Town Suff 125 D10
Wetheringsett Suff 126 D2
Wethersfield Essex 106 E4
Wethersta Shetland 312 G5
Wetherup Street Suff 126 E2
Wetley Rocks Staffs 169 F7
Wetmore Staffs 152 E5
Wettenhall E Ches 167 C10
Wettenhall Green E Ches 167 C10
Wettles Shrops 131 F8
Wetton Staffs 169 D10
Wetwang E Yorks 208 B4
Wetwood Staffs 150 C5
Wexcombe Wilts 47 B9
Wexham Street Bucks 66 C3
Weybourne Norf 177 E10
Weybourne Sur 49 D11
Weybread Suff 142 G4
Weybridge Sur 66 G5
Weycroft Devon 16 B2
Weydale Highld 310 C5
Weyhill Hants 47 D10
Weymouth Dorset 17 F9
Weythel Powys 114 F4
Whaddon Bucks 102 E6
Whaddon Cambs 104 B6
Whaddon Glos 80 C4
Whaddon Glos 99 G9
Whaddon Wilts 31 B11
Whaddon Wilts 61 G11
Whaddon Gap Cambs 104 B6
Whale Cumb 230 G6
Whaley Derbys 187 G8
Whaley Bridge Derbys 185 E8
Whaley Thorns Derbys 187 G8
Whaligoe Highld 310 E7
Whalley Lancs 203 F10
Whalley Banks Lancs 203 F10
Whalley Range Gtr Man 184 C4
Whalleys Lancs 194 F3
Whalton Northumb 252 G4
Wham N Yorks 212 G5
Whaplode Lincs 156 E6
Whaplode Drove Lincs 156 G6
Whaplode St Catherine Lincs 156 E6
Wharf Warks 119 G8
Wharfe N Yorks 212 F5
Wharles Lancs 202 F4
Wharley End C Beds 103 C8
Wharmley Northumb 241 D9
Wharncliffe Side S Yorks 186 C3
Wharram le Street N Yorks 217 F7
Wharram Percy N Yorks 217 G7
Wharton Hereford 115 F10
Wharton Lincs 188 C4
Wharton W Ches 167 B11
Wharton Green W Ches 167 B11
Whashton N Yorks 224 D3
Whasset Cumb 211 C10
Whatcombe Dorset 30 G4
Whatcote Warks 100 C6
Whatcroft W Ches 167 B11
Whateley Staffs 134 D4
Whatfield Suff 107 B10
Whatley Som 28 F5
Whatley Som 45 D8
Whatlington E Sus 38 D3
Whatmore Shrops 116 C2
Whatsole Street Kent 54 E6
Whatstandwell Derbys 170 E4
Whatton Notts 154 B4
Whauphill Dumfries 236 E6
Whaw N Yorks 223 E9
Wheal Alfred Corn 2 B3
Wheal Baddon Corn 4 G5
Wheal Busy Corn 4 G4
Wheal Frances Corn 4 E5
Wheal Kitty Corn 4 E4
Wheal Rose Corn 4 G4
Wheat Hold Hants 64 G5
Wheatacre Norf 143 E9
Wheatcroft Derbys 170 D5
Wheatenhurst Glos 80 D3
Wheathall Shrops 131 C9
Wheathampstead Herts 85 C11
Wheathill Shrops 132 G2
Wheathill Som 44 G5
Wheatley Devon 14 C4
Wheatley Hants 49 E9
Wheatley Oxon 83 D9
Wheatley S Yorks 198 G5
Wheatley W Yorks 196 B5
Wheatley Hill Durham 234 D3
Wheatley Hills S Yorks 198 G6
Wheatley Lane Lancs 204 F2
Wheatley Park S Yorks 198 F5
Wheaton Aston Staffs 151 G7
Wheddon Cross Som 42 F2
Wheedlemont Aberds 302 G4
Wheelbarrow Town Kent 55 D7
Wheeler End Bucks 84 G4
Wheelerstreet Sur 50 E2
Wheelock E Ches 168 D3
Wheelock Heath E Ches 168 D2
Wheelton Lancs 194 C5
Wheelton Lancs 194 C6
Wheelton Lancs 194 D5
Wheelton Lancs 194 D6
Wheen Angus 292 F5
Wheldale W Yorks 198 B3
Wheldrake York 207 D9
Whelford Glos 81 F11
Whelley Gtr Man 194 F5
Whelp Street Suff 107 B8
Whelpley Hill Herts 85 E7
Whelpo Cumb 230 D2
Whelston Flint 182 F2
Whempstead Herts 104 G6
Whenby N Yorks 216 F2
Whepstead Suff 124 F6
Wherry Town Corn 1 D5
Wherstead Suff 108 C3
Wherwell Hants 47 E11
Wheston Derbys 185 F10
Whetley Cross Dorset 29 G7
Whetsted Kent 53 D7
Whetstone Leics 135 D11
Whetstone London 86 G3
Whettleton Shrops 131 G8
Whicham Cumb 210 C2
Whichford Warks 100 E6
Whickham T & W 242 E6
Whickham Fell T & W 242 F6
Whiddon Devon 40 F5
Whiddon Down Devon 13 C9
Whifflet N Lnrk 268 C4
Whigstreet Angus 287 C8
Whilton Northants 120 E2
Whilton Locks Northants 120 E2
Whim Farm Borders 270 E4
Whimble Devon 24 G5
Whimple Devon 14 B6
Whimpwell Green Norf 161 D7
Whinburgh Norf 141 B10
Whin Lane End Lancs 202 E3
Whinfield Darl 224 B6
Whinhall N Lnrk 268 B5
Whinmoor W Yorks 206 F3
Whinney Hill S Yorks 187 C7
Whinney Hill Stockton 225 B7
Whinnieliggate Dumfries 237 D9
Whinny Heights Blkburn 195 B7
Whinnyfold Aberds 303 F10
Whins of Milton Stirl 278 C5
Whins Wood W Yorks 205 F7
Whipcott Devon 27 D9
Whippendell Botton Herts 85 E9
Whippingham I o W 20 C6
Whipsiderry Corn 4 C6
Whipsnade C Beds 85 B8
Whipton Devon 14 C5
Whirley Grove E Ches 184 F6
Whirlow S Yorks 186 E4
Whisby Lincs 172 B6
Whissendine Rutland 154 G6
Whissonsett Norf 159 E8
Whisterfield E Ches 184 G4
Whistlefield Argyll 276 C2
Whistlefield Argyll 276 C4
Whistley Green Wokingham 65 E9
Whistlow Oxon 101 F9
Whiston Mers 183 C7
Whiston Northants 120 E6
Whiston S Yorks 186 D6
Whiston Staffs 151 G7
Whiston Staffs 169 F8
Whiston Cross Mers 183 C7
Whiston Cross Shrops 132 C5
Whitacre Heath Warks 134 E4
Whitbarrow Village Cumb 230 F4
Whitbeck Cumb 210 C2
Whitbourne Hereford 116 F4
Whitbourne Moor Wilts 45 D10
Whitburn T & W 243 E10
Whitburn W Loth 269 C8
Whitburn Colliery T & W 243 E10
Whitby N Yorks 227 C7
Whitby W Ches 182 F5
Whitbyheath W Ches 182 F5
Whitchurch Bath 60 F6
Whitchurch Bucks 102 G5
Whitchurch Cardiff 59 C7
Whitchurch Devon 12 G5
Whitchurch Hants 48 D3
Whitchurch Hereford 79 B9
Whitchurch Pembs 90 F5
Whitchurch Shrops 167 G8
Whitchurch Som 30 C2
Whitchurch Canonicorum Dorset 16 B3
Whitchurch Hill Oxon 64 D6
Whitchurch-on-Thames Oxon 64 D6
Whitcombe Dorset 17 D10
Whitcombe Som 29 C10
Whitcot Shrops 131 E7
Whitcott Keysett Shrops 130 G5
White Ball Som 27 D9
White Colne Essex 107 F7
White Coppice Lancs 194 D6
White Cross Bath 44 B5
White Cross Bath 44 B6
White Cross Corn 2 E5
White Cross Corn 5 D7
White Cross Hereford 97 C9
White Cross Som 43 D10
White Cross Wilts 45 G9
White Cross Hill Cambs 123 B9
White End Worcs 98 E5
White Gate Gtr Man 195 G11
White Gate Som 28 F4
White Grit Shrops 130 D6
White Hall Herts 104 G5
White Hill Bath 45 B8
White Hill W Yorks 204 E6
White Hill Wilts 45 G10
White Hills Northants 120 E4
White House Suff 108 B2
White Houses Notts 188 F2
White Lackington Dorset 17 B10
White Ladies Aston Worcs 117 G8
White-le-Head Durham 242 G5
White Lee W Yorks 197 B8
White Lund Lancs 211 G8
White Mill Carms 93 G9
White Moor Derbys 170 F5
White Ness Shetland 313 J5
White Notley Essex 88 B3
White Oak Kent 68 F4
White Ox Mead Bath 45 B8
White Pit Lincs 190 F5
White Post Kent 52 E4
White Post Notts 171 D10
White Rocks Hereford 97 G8
White Roding or **White Roothing** Essex 87 C9
White Stake Lancs 194 B4
White Stone Hereford 97 C11
White Waltham Windsor 65 D10
Whiteacen Moray 302 E2
Whiteacre Kent 54 D6
Whiteacre Heath Warks 134 E4
Whiteash Green Essex 106 E5
Whitebirk Blkburn 195 B8
Whitebog Highld 301 C7
Whitebridge Highld 290 B6
Whitebrook Mon 79 D8
Whiteburn Borders 271 F11
Whitebushes Sur 51 D9
Whitecairn Dumfries 236 D4
Whitecairns Aberds 293 B11
Whitecastle S Lnrk 269 G10
Whitechapel Lancs 203 E7
Whitechapel London 67 C10
Whitechurch Maund Hereford 97 B11
Whitecleat Orkney 314 F5
Whitecliff Glos 79 C9
Whiteclosegate Cumb 239 F10
Whitecote W Yorks 205 F10
Whitecraig E Loth 281 G7
Whitecraigs E Renf 267 D11
Whitecroft Glos 79 D10
Whitecrook W Dunb 267 B10
Whitecross Corn 2 C2
Whitecross Corn 6 E2
Whitecross Corn 10 G5
Whitecross Falk 279 F9
Whitecross Som 28 C6
Whitecross Staffs 151 E7
Whiteface Highld 309 L7
Whitefarland N Ayrs 255 C9
Whitefaulds S Ayrs 245 B7
Whitefield Aberds 303 G7
Whitefield Dorset 18 C4
Whitefield Gtr Man 195 F10
Whitefield Perth 286 D5
Whitefield Som 27 B9
Whitefield Lane End Mers 183 D7
Whiteflat E Ayrs 258 D2
Whiteford Aberds 303 G7
Whitegate W Ches 167 B10
Whitehall Blkburn 195 C7
Whitehall Bristol 60 E6
Whitehall Devon 27 E10
Whitehall Devon 40 F4
Whitehall Hants 49 C8
Whitehall Herts 104 E6
Whitehall W Sus 35 C10
Whitehall Village Orkney 314 D6
Whitehaven Cumb 219 B9
Whitehaven Shrops 148 E5
Whitehawk Brighton 36 G4
Whiteheath Gate W Mid 133 F9
Whitehill E Sus 37 B8
Whitehill Hants 49 G9
Whitehill Kent 54 B4
Whitehill Midloth 271 B7
Whitehill Moray 302 D5
Whitehill S Lnrk 268 D4
Whitehill Staffs 168 E3
Whitehills Aberds 302 C6
Whitehills S Lnrk 268 E2
Whitehills T & W 243 E7
Whiteholme Blkpool 202 E2
Whitehough Derbys 185 E8
Whitehouse Aberds 293 B8
Whitehouse Argyll 275 G9
Whitehouse Common W Mid 134 D2
Whitehouse Green W Berks 65 F7
Whiteinch Glasgow 267 B10
Whitekirk E Loth 281 E10
Whiteknights Reading 65 E8
Whiteknowes Aberds 293 C7
Whitelackington Som 28 D5
Whitelaw S Lnrk 268 G2
Whiteleaf Bucks 84 E4
Whiteleas T & W 243 E9
Whiteleaved Oak Glos 98 D5
Whitelee Borders 262 C3
Whitelee Northumb 250 B6
Whitelees S Ayrs 257 C9
Whiteley Bank I o W 21 E7
Whiteley Green E Ches 184 F6
Whiteley Village Sur 66 G5
Whitelye Mon 79 E8
Whitemans Green W Sus 36 B4
Whitemire Moray 301 D9
Whitemoor Corn 5 D9
Whitemoor Nottingham 171 G8
Whitemoor Warks 118 C5
Whitemore Staffs 168 C5
Whitenap Hants 32 C5
Whiteoak Green Oxon 82 C4
Whiteparish Wilts 32 C2
Whitepits Wilts 45 F10
Whiterashes Aberds 303 G8
Whiterigg Borders 262 C3
Whiterock Bridgend 58 D2
Whiterow Highld 310 E7
White's Green W Sus 34 B6
Whiteshill Glos 80 D4
Whiteshill S Glos 60 D6
Whiteside Northumb 240 D6
Whiteside W Loth 269 B9
Whitesmith E Sus 23 C8
Whitespots Dumfries 247 F10
Whitestaunton Som 28 E3
Whitestone Aberds 293 D8
Whitestone Devon 14 C3
Whitestone Devon 40 D3
Whitestone Warks 135 F7
Whitestones Aberds 303 D8
Whitestreet Green Suff 107 D9
Whitewall Common Mon 60 B2
Whitewall Corner N Yorks 216 E5
Whiteway Bath 61 G8
Whiteway Dorset 18 E3
Whiteway Glos 80 C6
Whiteway Glos 80 F4
Whitewell Aberds 303 C9
Whitewell Corn 11 E7
Whitewell Highld 291 C11
Whitewell Lancs 203 D9
Whitewell Wrex 167 G7
Whitewell Bottom Lancs 195 C10
Whiteworks Devon 13 G8
Whitfield Kent 55 D10
Whitfield Northants 102 D2
Whitfield Northumb 241 F7
Whitfield S Glos 79 G11
Whitfield Court Sur 50 B3
Whitfield Hall Northumb 241 F7
Whitford Devon 15 B11
Whitford = Chwitffordd Flint 181 F10
Whitgift E Yorks 199 C10
Whitgreave Staffs 151 D7
Whithaugh Borders 249 F11
Whithebeir Orkney 314 C5
Whithorn Dumfries 236 E6
Whiting Bay N Ayrs 256 D2
Whitington Norf 140 D4
Whitkirk W Yorks 206 G3
Whitland = Hendy-Gwyn Carms 73 B11
Whitlaw Borders 271 F9
Whitleigh Plym 7 C9
Whitletts S Ayrs 257 E9
Whitley Gtr Man 194 F5
Whitley N Yorks 198 C5
Whitley Reading 65 E8
Whitley S Yorks 186 C4
Whitley W Mid 119 B7
Whitley Wilts 61 F11
Whitley Bay T & W 243 C9
Whitley Bridge N Yorks 198 C5
Whitley Chapel Northumb 241 F10
Whitley Head W Yorks 204 E6
Whitley Heath Staffs 150 D6
Whitley Lower W Yorks 197 D8
Whitley Reed W Ches 183 E10
Whitley Row Kent 52 C3
Whitley Sands T & W 243 C9
Whitley Thorpe N Yorks 198 C5
Whitley Wood Reading 65 F8
Whitlock's End W Mid 118 B2
Whitminster Glos 80 D3
Whitmoor Devon 27 E9
Whitmore Dorset 31 F9
Whitmore Staffs 168 G4
Whitmore Park W Mid 134 G6
Whitnage Devon 27 D8
Whitnash Warks 118 E6
Whitnell Som 43 F8
Whitney Bottom Som 28 E4
Whitney-on-Wye Hereford 96 B5
Whitrigg Cumb 229 D10
Whitrigg Cumb 238 F6
Whitriggs Borders 262 F3
Whitsbury Hants 31 D10
Whitslaid Borders 271 G11
Whitsome Borders 273 E7
Whitsomehill Borders 273 F7
Whitson Newport 59 C11
Whitstable Kent 70 F6
Whitstone Corn 11 B11
Whittingham Northumb 264 G3
Whittingslow Shrops 131 F8
Whittington Glos 99 G10
Whittington Lancs 212 D2
Whittington Norf 140 D4
Whittington Shrops 148 C6
Whittington Staffs 133 G7
Whittington Staffs 134 B3
Whittington Staffs 150 C5
Whittington Worcs 117 G7
Whittington Moor Derbys 186 G5
Whittlebury Northants 102 C3
Whittlesey Cambs 138 D5
Whittlesford Cambs 105 B9
Whittlestone Head Blkburn 195 D8
Whitton Borders 263 E7
Whitton Hereford 115 C8
Whitton London 66 E6
Whitton N Lincs 200 C2
Whitton Northumb 252 C3
Whitton Powys 114 D5
Whitton Shrops 115 C11
Whitton Stockton 234 G3
Whitton Suff 108 B2
Whittonditch Wilts 63 E9
Whittonstall Northumb 242 F3
Whittytree Shrops 115 B8
Whitway Hants 48 B3
Whitwell Derbys 187 F8
Whitwell Herts 104 G3
Whitwell I o W 20 F6
Whitwell N Yorks 224 F5
Whitwell Rutland 137 B8
Whitwell-on-the-Hill N Yorks 216 F4
Whitwell Street Norf 160 E2
Whitwick Leics 153 F8
Whitwood W Yorks 198 C2
Whitworth Lancs 195 D11
Whixall Shrops 149 C10
Whixley N Yorks 206 B4
Whoberley W Mid 118 B6
Wholeflats Falk 279 E8
Whome Orkney 314 G3
Whorlton Durham 224 C2
Whorlton N Yorks 225 E9
Whydown E Sus 38 F2
Whygate Northumb 241 B7
Whyke W Sus 22 C5
Whyle Hereford 115 E11
Whyteleafe Sur 51 B10
Wibdon Glos 79 F9
Wibsey W Yorks 205 G8
Wibtoft Leics 135 F9
Wichenford Worcs 116 E5
Wichling Kent 54 B2
Wick Bmouth 19 C8
Wick Devon 27 G11
Wick Highld 310 D7
Wick S Glos 61 E8
Wick Shetland 313 K6
Wick Som 28 B6
Wick Som 43 C10
Wick Som 43 E8
Wick V Glam 58 E2
Wick W Sus 35 G8
Wick Wilts 31 C11
Wick Worcs 99 B9
Wick Episcopi Worcs 116 G6
Wick Hill Brack 65 E11
Wick Hill Kent 53 E10
Wick Hill Wokingham 65 G9
Wick Rocks S Glos 61 E8
Wick St Lawrence N Som 59 F11
Wick Street Glos 80 D5
Wicken Cambs 123 C11
Wicken Northants 102 D4
Wicken Bonhunt Essex 105 E9
Wicken Green Village Norf 158 C6
Wickenby Lincs 189 E9
Wicker Street Green Suff 107 C9
Wickersley S Yorks 187 C7
Wickford Essex 88 G3
Wickham Hants 33 E9
Wickham W Berks 63 E11
Wickham Bishops Essex 88 C4
Wickham Green Suff 125 D11
Wickham Green W Berks 63 E11
Wickham Heath W Berks 64 F2
Wickham Market Suff 126 F6
Wickham St Paul Essex 106 D6
Wickham Skeith Suff 125 D11
Wickham Street Suff 124 G5
Wickham Street Suff 125 D11
Wickhambreaux Kent 55 B8
Wickhambrook Suff 124 G4
Wickhamford Worcs 99 C11
Wickhampton Norf 143 B8
Wickham's Cross Som 44 G4
Wickhurst Kent 52 D4
Wicklane Bath 45 B7
Wicklewood Norf 141 C11
Wickmere Norf 160 C3
Wickridge Street Glos 98 F6
Wickstreet E Sus 23 D8
Wickwar S Glos 61 B8
Widbrook Wilts 45 B10
Widcombe Bath 61 G9
Widdington Essex 105 E10
Widdrington Northumb 253 D7
Widdrington Station Northumb 252 E6
Widecombe in the Moor Devon 13 F10
Widegates Corn 6 D5
Widemarsh Hereford 97 C10
Widemouth Bay Corn 24 G2
Wideopen T & W 242 C6
Widewall Orkney 314 G4
Widewell Plym 7 C9
Widford Essex 87 D11
Widford Herts 86 B6
Widgham Green Cambs 124 F3
Widham Wilts 62 B5
Widley Hants 33 F11
Widmer End Bucks 84 F5
Widmerpool Notts 154 D2
Widmoor Bucks 66 B2
Widmore London 68 F2
Widnes Halton 183 D8
Wierton Kent 53 D9
Wig Powys 130 F2
Wig Fach Bridgend 57 F10
Wigan Gtr Man 194 F5
Wiganthorpe N Yorks 216 E3
Wigbeth Dorset 31 F8
Wigborough Som 28 D6
Wiggaton Devon 15 C8
Wiggenhall St Germans Norf 157 G11
Wiggenhall St Mary Magdalen Norf 157 G11
Wiggenhall St Mary the Virgin Norf 157 G11
Wiggenhall St Peter Norf 158 G2
Wiggens Green Essex 106 C3
Wiggington Staffs 134 B4
Wigginstall Staffs 169 C9
Wiggington Herts 84 C6
Wigginton Oxon 101 E7
Wigginton Shrops 148 B6
Wigginton Staffs 134 B4
Wigginton York 207 B7
Wigginton Bottom Herts 84 D6
Wigginton Heath Oxon 101 D7
Wigglesworth N Yorks 204 B2
Wiggonby Cumb 239 G7
Wiggonholt W Sus 35 D9
Wighill N Yorks 206 D5
Wighton Norf 159 B8
Wightwick Manor Staffs 133 D7
Wigley Derbys 186 G4
Wigley Hants 32 D4
Wigmarsh Shrops 149 D7
Wigmore Hereford 115 D8
Wigmore Medway 69 G10
Wigsley Notts 188 G5
Wigsthorpe Northants 137 G10
Wigston Leics 136 D2
Wigston Magna Leics 136 D2
Wigston Parva Leics 135 F9
Wigthorpe Notts 187 E9
Wigtoft Lincs 156 B5
Wigton Cumb 229 B11
Wigtown Dumfries 236 D6
Wigtwizzle S Yorks 186 B2
Wike W Yorks 206 E2
Wike Well End S Yorks 199 E7
Wilbarston Northants 136 F6
Wilberfoss E Yorks 207 C10
Wilberlee W Yorks 196 E5
Wilburton Cambs 123 C9
Wilby Norf 141 F10
Wilby Northants 121 D7
Wilby Suff 126 C4
Wilcot Wilts 62 G6
Wilcott Shrops 149 F7
Wilcott Marsh Shrops 149 F7
Wilcove Corn 7 D8
Wilcrick Newport 60 B2
Wild Mill Bridgend 58 C2
Wildboarclough E Ches 169 B7
Wilde Street Suff 124 B4
Wilden Beds 121 F11
Wilden Worcs 116 C6
Wildern Hants 33 E7
Wildernesse Kent 52 B4
Wilderspool Warr 183 D10
Wilderswood Gtr Man 194 E6
Wildhern Hants 47 C11
Wildhill Herts 86 D3
Wildmanbridge S Lnrk 268 E6
Wildmoor Hants 49 B7
Wildmoor Oxon 83 F7
Wildmoor Worcs 117 B9
Wildridings Brack 65 F11
Wildsworth Lincs 188 B4
Wildwood Staffs 151 E8
Wilford Nottingham 153 B11
Wilgate Green Kent 54 B3
Wilkesley E Ches 167 G10
Wilkhaven Highld 311 L3
Wilkieston W Loth 270 B2
Wilkin Throop Som 29 C11
Wilkinthroop Som 29 C11
Wilksby Lincs 174 C3
Will Row Lincs 191 D7
Willacy Lane End Lancs 202 F5
Willand Devon 27 E8
Willand Som 27 E11
Willand Moor Devon 27 E8
Willard's Hill E Sus 38 C2
Willaston E Ches 167 E11
Willaston Shrops 149 B11
Willaston W Ches 182 F4
Willen M Keynes 103 C7
Willenhall W Mid 119 B7
Willenhall W Mid 133 D9
Willerby E Yorks 208 G6
Willerby N Yorks 217 D10
Willersey Glos 100 D2
Willersley Hereford 96 B6
Willesborough Kent 54 E4
Willesborough Lees Kent 54 E4
Willesden London 67 C8
Willesden Green London 67 C8
Willesley Leics 152 G6
Willesley Wilts 61 B11
Willett Som 42 G6
Willey Shrops 132 D3
Willey Warks 135 G9
Willey Green Sur 50 C2
Willhayne Som 28 E4
Williamhope Borders 261 C10
William's Green Suff 107 C9
Williamscott Oxon 101 B9
Williamslee Borders 270 G6
Williamstown Rhondda 77 G8
Williamthorpe Derbys 170 B6
Willian Herts 104 E4
Willicote Pastures Worcs 100 B3
Willingale Essex 87 D9
Willingcott Devon 40 E3
Willingdon E Sus 23 E9
Willingham Cambs 123 C8
Willingham Suff 143 G8
Willingham by Stow Lincs 188 E5
Willingham Green Cambs 124 G2
Willington Beds 104 B2
Willington Derbys 152 D5
Willington Durham 233 D9
Willington Kent 53 C9
Willington T & W 243 D8
Willington Warks 100 D5
Willington Corner W Ches 167 B8
Willington Quay T & W 243 D8
Willisham Suff 125 G11
Willisham Tye Suff 125 G11
Willitoft E Yorks 207 F10
Williton Som 42 E5
Willoughbridge Staffs 168 G3
Willoughby Lincs 191 G7
Willoughby Warks 119 D10
Willoughby Hills Lincs 174 F4
Willoughby-on-the-Wolds Notts 154 D2
Willoughby Waterleys Leics 135 E11
Willoughton Lincs 188 C6
Willow Green W Ches 183 F10
Willow Green Worcs 116 F5
Willow Holme Cumb 239 F9
Willowbank Bucks 66 B5
Willows Gtr Man 195 F8
Willows Green Essex 88 B2
Willowtown Bl Gwent 77 C11
Willsbridge S Glos 61 E7
Willslock Staffs 151 C11
Willstone Shrops 131 D9
Willsworthy Devon 12 E6
Willtown Som 28 B5
Wilmcote Warks 118 F3
Wilmington Bath 61 G7
Wilmington Devon 15 B10
Wilmington E Sus 23 E8
Wilmington Kent 68 E4
Wilmington Green E Sus 23 D8
Wilminstone Devon 12 F5
Wilmslow E Ches 184 E4
Wilmslow Park E Ches 184 E5
Wilnecote Staffs 134 C4
Wilney Green Norf 141 G11
Wilpshire Lancs 203 G9
Wilsden W Yorks 205 F7
Wilsden Hill W Yorks 205 F7
Wilsford Lincs 173 G8
Wilsford Wilts 46 B6
Wilsford Wilts 46 F6
Wilsham Devon 41 D9
Wilshaw W Yorks 196 F6
Wilsic S Yorks 187 B9
Wilsill N Yorks 214 G3
Wilsley Green Kent 53 F9
Wilsley Pound Kent 53 F9
Wilsom Hants 49 F8
Wilson Hereford 97 G11
Wilson Leics 153 E8
Wilsontown S Lnrk 269 D9
Wilstead Beds 103 C11
Wilsthorpe Derbys 153 C9
Wilsthorpe Lincs 155 G11
Wilstone Herts 84 C6
Wilstone Green Herts 84 C6
Wilthorpe S Yorks 197 F10
Wilton Borders 261 G11
Wilton Cumb 219 C10
Wilton Hereford 97 G11
Wilton N Yorks 217 C7
Wilton Redcar 225 B11
Wilton Som 28 C2
Wilton Wilts 46 G5
Wilton Wilts 63 G9
Wilton Park Bucks 85 G7
Wiltown Devon 27 D11
Wiltown Som 28 C5
Wimbish Essex 105 D11
Wimbish Green Essex 106 D2
Wimble Hill Hants 49 D10
Wimblebury Staffs 151 G10
Wimbledon London 67 E8
Wimblington Cambs 139 E8
Wimbolds Trafford W Ches 182 G6
Wimboldsley W Ches 167 C11
Wimborne Minster Dorset 18 B6
Wimborne St Giles Dorset 31 E8
Wimbotsham Norf 140 B2
Wimpole Cambs 104 B6
Wimpson Soton 32 E5
Wimpstone Warks 100 B4
Wincanton Som 30 B2
Winceby Lincs 174 B4
Wincham W Ches 183 F11
Winchburgh W Loth 279 G11
Winchcombe Glos 99 F10
Winchelsea E Sus 38 D6
Winchelsea Beach E Sus
Winchester Hants
Winchestown Bl Gwent 7
Winchet Hill Kent
Winchfield Hants
Winchfield Hurst Hants
Winchmore Hill Bucks
Winchmore Hill London
Wincle E Ches 1
Wincobank S Yorks 1
Wind Hill Cumb 2
Wind Hill Pembs
Winder Cumb 21
Windermere Cumb 2
Winderton Warks 1
Windhill Highld 3
Windhill S Yorks 1
Windhill W Yorks 2
Windhouse Shetland 3
Winding Wood W Berks 6
Windle Hill W Ches 1
Windlehurst Gtr Man 1
Windlesham Sur
Windley Derbys 1
Windmill Corn
Windmill Flint 18
Windmill Flint 1
Windmill Hill Bristol
Windmill Hill E Sus 2
Windmill Hill Halton 1
Windmill Hill Kent 6
Windmill Hill Som
Windmill Hill W Yorks 19
Windmill Hill Worcs
Windrush Glos 8
Windsor N Lincs 1
Windsor Windsor
Windsor Green Suff 1
Windsoredge Glos
Windwhistle Som
Windy Arbor Mers 1
Windy Arbour Warks 1
Windy Hill Wrex 1
Windy Nook T & W 2
Windy-Yett E Ayrs 2
Windydoors Borders 2
Windygates Fife 2
Windyharbour E Ches 1
Windyknowe W Loth 2
Windywalls Borders 2
Wineham W Sus
Winestead E Yorks 2
Winewall Lancs 2
Winfarthing Norf 1
Winford I o W
Winford N Som
Winforton Hereford
Winfrith Newburgh Dorset
Wing Bucks 1
Wing Rutland 1
Wingate Durham 2
Wingates Gtr Man 1
Wingates Northumb 2
Wingerworth Derbys 1
Wingfield C Beds 1
Wingfield S Yorks 1
Wingfield Suff 1
Wingfield Wilts 4
Wingfield Green Suff 1
Wingfield Park Derbys 1
Wingham Kent
Wingham Green Kent
Wingham Well Kent
Wingmore Kent
Wingrave Bucks
Winkburn Notts 1
Winkfield Brack
Winkfield Place Brack
Winkfield Row Brack 6
Winkhill Staffs 1
Winkhurst Green Kent
Winklebury Hants
Winkleigh Devon 2
Winksley N Yorks 2
Winkton Dorset
Winlaton T & W 2
Winlaton Mill T & W 2
Winless Highld 3
Winllan Powys 1
Winmarleigh Lancs 2
Winmarleigh Moss Lancs 2
Winnal Hereford
Winnal Common Hereford
Winnall Hants
Winnall Worcs 1
Winnard's Perch Corn
Winnersh Wokingham
Winnington Staffs 1
Winnington W Ches 18
Winnington Green Shrops 1
Winnothdale Staffs 1
Winscales Cumb 2
Winscombe N Som
Winsdon Hill Luton 10
Winsford Som
Winsford W Ches 16
Winsh-wen Swansea
Winsham Devon
Winsham Som
Winshill Staffs 1
Winsick Derbys 1
Winskill Cumb 2
Winslade Devon
Winslade Hants
Winsley N Yorks 2
Winsley Wilts 6
Winslow Bucks 1
Winslow Mill Hereford
Winson Glos
Winson Green W Mid 13
Winsor Hants
Winstanley Gtr Man 1
Winstanleys Gtr Man 1
Winster Cumb 2
Winster Derbys 1
Winston Durham 2
Winston Suff 1
Winston Green Suff 1
Winstone Glos
Winswell Devon
Winter Gardens Essex
Winter Well Som
Winterborne Bassett Wilts
Winterborne Came Dorset 1
Winterborne Clenston Dorset
Winterborne Herringston Dorset
Winterborne Houghton Dorset
Winterborne Kingston Dorset
Winterborne Monkton Dorset

County and unitary authority boundaries

Ordnance Survey National Grid

The blue lines which divide the Navigator map pages into squares for indexing match the Ordnance Survey National Grid and correspond to the small squares on the boundary map below. Each side of a grid square measures 10km on the ground.

The National Grid 100-km square letters and kilometre values are indicated for the grid intersection at the outer corners of each page. For example, the intersection SE6090 at the upper right corner of page 215 is 60km East and 90km North of the south-west corner of National Grid square SE.

Using GPS with Navigator mapping

Since Navigator Britain is based on Ordnance Survey mapping, and rectified to the National Grid, it can be used with in-car or handheld GPS for locating identifiable waypoints such as road junctions, bridges, railways and farms, or assessing your position in relation to any of the features shown on the map.

On your receiver, choose British Grid as the location format and for map datum select Ordnance Survey (this may be described as Ord Srvy GB or similar, or more specifically as OSGB36). Your receiver will automatically convert the latitude/longitude co-ordinates transmitted by GPS into compatible National Grid data.

Positional accuracy of any particular feature is limited to 50–100m, due to the limitations of the original survey and the scale of Navigator mapping.

For further information see www.gps.gov.uk

Greater London

1 City and County of the City of London
2 Hackney
3 Tower Hamlets
4 Southwark
5 Lambeth
6 Wandsworth
7 Hammersmith and Fulham
8 Royal Borough of Kensington and Chelsea
9 City of Westminster
10 Camden
11 Islington
12 Haringey
13 Waltham Forest
14 Newham
15 Greenwich
16 Lewisham
17 Merton
18 Richmond upon Thames
19 Hounslow
20 Ealing
21 Brent
22 Barnet
23 Enfield
24 Redbridge
25 Barking and Dagenham
26 Havering
27 Bexley
28 Bromley
29 Croydon
30 Sutton
31 Kingston upon Thames
32 Hillingdon
33 Harrow

1 Central Scotland

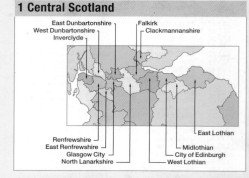

2 Northern England

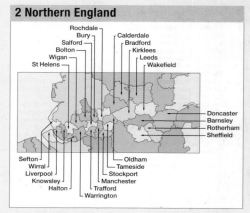

3 West Midlands

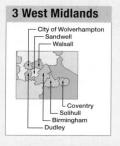

4 South Wales and Bristol area

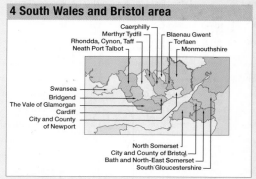

5 Thames Valley

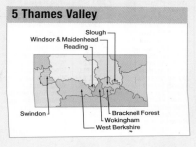

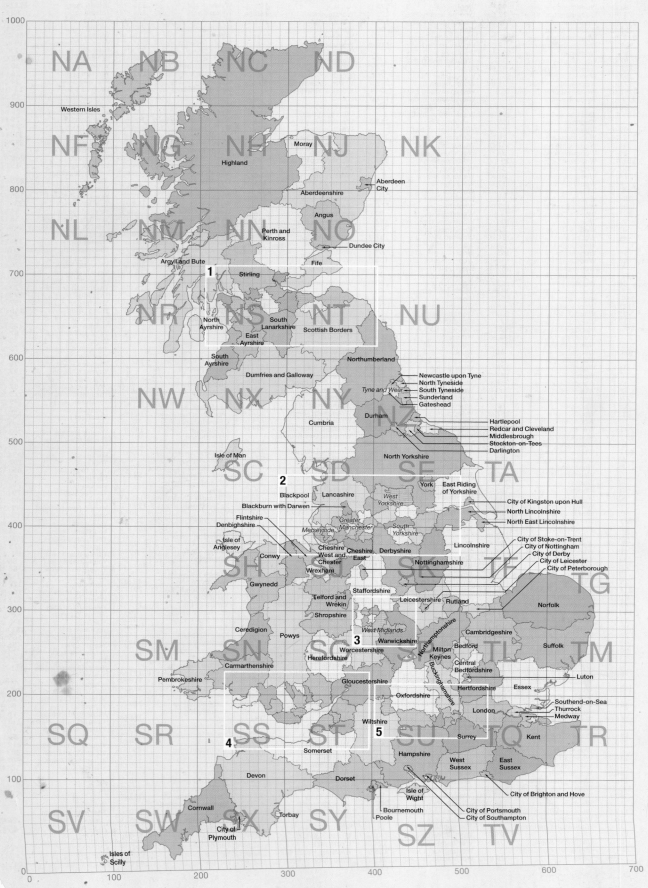